A SELECT LIBRARY

OF

NICENE AND POST-NICENE FATHERS

OF

THE CHRISTIAN CHURCH

Second Series

TRANSLATED INTO ENGLISH WITH PROLEGOMENA AND EXPLANATORY NOTES.

UNDER THE EDITORIAL SUPERVISION OF

PHILIP SCHAFF, D.D., LL.D.,
Professor of Church History in the Union Theological Seminary, New York.

AND

HENRY WACE, D.D.,
Principal of King's College, London.

IN CONNECTION WITH A NUMBER OF PATRISTIC SCHOLARS OF EUROPE AND AMERICA.

VOLUME XII

LEO THE GREAT

GREGORY THE GREAT

T&T CLARK
EDINBURGH

WM. B. EERDMANS PUBLISHING COMPANY
GRAND RAPIDS, MICHIGAN

British Library Cataloguing in Publication Data

Nicene & Post-Nicene Fathers. — 2nd series
1. Fathers of the church
I. Schaff, Philip II. Mace, Henry
230'.11 BR60.A62

T&T Clark ISBN 0 567 09421 9

Eerdmans ISBN 0-8028-8126-2

Reprinted, March 1989

PHOTOLITHOPRINTED BY EERDMANS PRINTING COMPANY
GRAND RAPIDS, MICHIGAN, UNITED STATES OF AMERICA

THE LETTERS AND SERMONS OF LEO THE GREAT

BISHOP OF ROME,

TRANSLATED, WITH INTRODUCTION, NOTES, AND INDICES,

BY THE

REV. CHARLES LETT FELTOE, M.A.,

LATE FELLOW OF CLARE COLLEGE, CAMBRIDGE.

PREFATORY NOTE

Except for such valuable help—chiefly however in the way of comment and explanation—as Canon Bright's volume (S. Leo on the Incarnation) has supplied, both the selection and the translation of the Letters and Sermons of Leo Magnus are practically original. It is even more difficult to feel satisfied oneself, than to satisfy others either with a selection from a great man's works or with a translation of them. The powers of Leo as a preacher both of doctrine and of practice are very remarkable, and in my anxiety to keep within the limits imposed by the publishers, I have erred in presenting too few rather than too many of the Sermons to the English reader. Only those that are generally held genuine are represented, though several of the doubtful ones are fine sermons, and those translated are in most cases no better than those omitted. Even when the same thought is repeated again and again (as is often the case), it is almost always clothed in such different language, and surrounded with so many other thoughts of value, that every sermon has an almost equal claim to be selected.

With regard to the Letters, the series connected with the Eutychian controversy—the chief occupation of Leo's episcopate—is given nearly complete, whereas only specimens of his mode of dealing with other matters have been selected for presentation. With one or two exceptions, however, I feel more confident about the Letters than about the Sermons that the omitted are less important than the included. I wish I could make even a similar boast about the merits of the translation.

The text rendered is for the most part that of the Ballerinii as given by Migne (Patrologie, Vol. LIV.), though a more critical edition is much to be desired.

CHARLES LETT FELTOE.

Fornham All Saints',
Eastertide, 1894.

CONTENTS OF LEO THE GREAT

SELECT LETTERS AND SERMONS.

INTRODUCTION

Life.

The details of Leo's early life are extremely scanty and uncertain. Is is probable that he was born between 390 and 400 A.D. There is a tradition that his father was a Tuscan named Quintian, and that Volaterræ[1], a town in the north of Etruria, was his birthplace. Of his youth we know nothing: his writings contain no allusions to that or to any other part of his personal history. One may reasonably infer from the essentially Roman character of his literary style, from the absence of quotations out of pagan literature, and from his self-confessed gnorance of Greek, that his education was, though thorough after its kind, limited to Christian and Latin culture. A reference to the pages of any secular history of the Roman empire will give the reader an idea of the scenes amidst which, and no doubt by the aid of which, Leo the boy was formed and moulded into Leo Magnus, the first great Latin-speaking pope and bishop of Rome, the first great Italian theologian, "the final defender of the truth of our Lord's Person against both its assailants[2]" (i.e. Nestorius and Eutyches), whom it pleased God in His providence to raise up in the Western (and not as oftenest hitherto in the Eastern) portion of His Church. Politically, intellectually, and theologically the period in which this great character grew up, lived and worked, was one of transition: the Roman Empire, learning and thought, paganism were each alike at the last gasp, and neither in Church nor State was there any other at all of Leo's calibre. This consideration will account for the wonderful influence, partly for good and partly for bad, which his master-mind and will was permitted to exercise on the after-ages of Christendom.

During his early manhood the Pelagian controversy was raging, and it is thought that the acolyte named Leo, whom Augustine mentions in his letters on this subject as employed by pope Zosimus to carry communications between Rome and the African church, is the future pope. Under Celestine, who was pope from 422 to 432, he was archdeacon of Rome, and he seems already to have made a name for himself: for Cassian, the Gallican writer whom he had urged to write a work on the Incarnation, in yielding to his suggestion, calls him "the ornament of the Roman church and of the Divine ministry," and S. Cyril (in 431, the date of the Council of Ephesus) appeals to Leo (as Leo has himself recorded in Letter CXIX., chap. 4) to procure the pope's support in stopping the ambitious designs of Juvenal, bishop of Jerusalem. Under the next pope, Sixtus (432—440), we hear of him in Prosper's *Chronicon* (under the year 439) again in connexion with Pelagianism[3]: he seems to have stirred up the vigilance of the pope against the crafty designs of one Julius of Eclanum, who, having been deprived of his bishopric for holding that heresy, was attempting to be restored without full proof of orthodoxy.

---

[1] The objection that Prosper and Leo himself both speak of Rome as his *patria* does not seem of sufficient weight to overthrow a tradition, which it is somewhat hard to account for the existence of. To a native of central Italy under the Empire, who had spent all his public life in Rome, the Eternal city was equally *patria*, whether it was his actual birthplace or not. At the same time there is no evidence that Volaterræ any more than Rome or any other Italian city can claim the honour with certainty.

[2] Wilberforce on *Doctrine of the Holy Eucharist*, p. 246, quoted by Bright.

[3] The chief error of *Pelagius* (= Morgan), who is commonly thought to have been of British origin, was, as is well-known, the denial of original or birth-sin: see Article ix

Next year (440) was a momentous one in the life of Leo, and in the history of the papacy. Leo was away on one of those political missions, which bear out our estimate of him as perhaps the most conspicuous and popular figure of his times [4]. The powerful general Aetius Placidia, the queen-regent's chief adviser and *aide-de-camp*, was quarrelling (a not unusual occurrence at this stage of the empire) with Albinus, a rival general in Gaul. Leo was sent to bring about a reconciliation, and apparently with success. In his absence Sixtus died, and it is not surprising that without any hesitation clergy and people should have elected Leo into his place. A deputation was sent after him to hasten his return, and after an interval of forty days he arrived. The whole church received him with acclamation, and on Sept. 29 he was ordained both priest and 47th bishop of Rome. His brief sermon on the occasion is the earliest in the collection, and will be found translated on p. 115 of our selection. His earliest extant letter belongs likewise to the first year of his episcopate, which we have also included in our selection: it is addressed to the bishop of Aquileia in reproof of his and his fellow-bishops' remissness in dealing with Pelagianism in that province. Thus early did he give proof of his conception of his office, as investing him with an authority which extended over the whole of Christendom as the successor of S. Peter. Still clearer proofs were soon forthcoming. Not to speak of a letter in a similarly dictatorial strain to the bishops of the home provinces of Campania, Picenum, and Etruria, which belongs to the year 443, we find him in 444 interfering, though more guardedly, with the province of Illyricum, which was then debatable ground between the East and West; in 445 dictating church regulations to S. Cyril's new successor at Alexandria, Dioscorus, his future adversary; and in 446 and 447 asserting his authority on various pretexts, now in Africa, now in Spain, now in Sicily; while in 444 also occurred his famous and not very creditable encounter with Hilary, bishop of Arles in Gaul. The incidents in this quarrel are briefly these: Hilary in a provincial synod had deposed a bishop, Celidonius, for technical irregularities in accordance with the Gallican canons. Celidonius appealed to Rome. Thereupon Hilary set out in the depth of winter on foot to Rome, but, after an ineffectual statement of his case and some rough treatment from Leo, returned to Gaul. Leo gave orders that Celidonius was to be restored, and Hilary deprived of all his metropolitical rights in the province of Vienne. How far the sentence was carried out is not clear. In a later letter he desires that the bishop of Vienne should be regarded as metropolitan, and yet he seems to recognize Hilary's successor, Ravennius, as still metropolitan in Letter XL., while in 450 the bishops of the one district addressed a formal petition for the restoration of Arles to its old rank, and the bishops of the other a counter-petition in favour of Vienne; whereupon Leo effected a temporary *modus vivendi* by dividing the jurisdiction between the two sees.

Returning to the year 444, besides consulting S. Cyril and Paschasinus, bishop of Lilybæum, on the right day for keeping Easter that year (a moot point which recurred in other years) we find Leo still taking active measures against heresy, this time that of the Manichæans [5]. The followers of this sect had since 439 greatly increased at Rome, owing to the number of refugees who came over from Carthage after its capture by Genseric and his Vandal hosts (see Sermon XVI. 5). They were an universally abhorred body, and deservedly so, if all we read about them be really true. In 444, therefore, it was determined, if possible, to stamp them out. By Leo's order a strict search was instituted throughout the city, and the large number of those who were discovered, were brought up for trial before a combined bench of civil and ecclesiastical judges. The most heinous crimes were revealed. Those

4 This is seen still more clearly when we remember how completely he held the Western, if not always the Eastern, Emperors in his power, and made them support and carry out his wishes.

5 The essential point in the Manichæan heresy (which took its rise in the far East) was the existence of two independent and conflicting principles: *good*, whose kingdom was light and the spiritual world, and *evil*, whose kingdom was over the elements of matter.

who refused to recant were banished for life and suffered various other penalties by the emperor Valentinian's decree, while Leo used all his influence to obtain similar treatment for them in other parts of Christendom. Three years later the spread of Priscillianism, a heresy which in some points was akin to Manichæism among other heresies, and a long account of which will be found in Letter XV., was the occasion to which we have referred as giving a pretext for his interference in the affairs of the Spanish church.

We now reach the famous Eutychian controversy, on which Leo's chief claim to our thanks and praise rests: for to his action in it the Church owes the final and complete definition of the cardinal doctrine of the Incarnation. The heresy of Eutyches, as was the case with so many other heresies, sprang from the reaction against a counter heresy. Most of the controversies which have again and again imperilled the cause of Christianity, have been due to human frailty, which has been unable to keep the proportion of the Faith. Over-statement on the one side leads to over-statement on the other, and thus the golden mean is lost sight of. Eutyches, an archimandrite (or head of a monastery) at Constantinople, had distinguished himself for zeal during the years 428 to 431 in combating the heresy of Nestorius, who had denied the perfect union of the Godhead and the Manhood in the one Person, Christ Jesus. He had objected to the Virgin being called *Theotokos* (God-bearing), and said that *Christotokos* (Christ-bearing) would be more correct. This position, as involving two persons as well as two natures in our LORD, was condemned by the 3rd General Council, which met at Ephesus in 431, S. Cyril being its chief opponent. But Eutyches in his eagerness to proclaim the Unity of the Person of Christ fell into the opposite extreme, and asserted that though the two natures of Christ were originally distinct, yet after the union they became but one nature, the human being changed into the Divine. Eutyches appears to have been a highly virtuous person, but possessed of a dull, narrow mind, unfit for the subtleties of theological discussion, and therefore unable to grasp the conception of two Natures in one Person: and nothing worse than stupidity and obstinacy is brought against him by his stern but clear-headed opponent Leo.

The person, however, who first brought the poor recluse's heretical statements prominently into notice was much more reckless and intemperate in his language. This was Eusebius, bishop of Dorylæum, who took the opportunity of a local synod held in Constantinople under the presidency of the gentle Flavian, in November, 448, for other business, to petition against his former friend and ally as a blasphemer and a madman. The synod, after expostulating with the accuser for his violence, at last reluctantly consented to summon Eutyches to an account. The summons was at least twice repeated and disobeyed under the pretext first that he might not leave the monastery, then that he was ill. At last Eutyches yielded, and appeared accompanied by a crowd of monks and soldiers and by Florentius, a patrician for whom the weak Emperor (Theodosius II.) had been influenced by the eunuch Chrysaphius, Eutyches' godson, to demand a seat at the council. After a long conversation, in which Eutyches tried to evade a definite statement, he was at last forced to confess that our Lord was of two natures before the union, but that after the union there was but one nature (see Letter XXVIII. (Tome), chap vi.). As he persisted in maintaining this position, he was condemned and thrust out of the priesthood and Church-communion. During the reading of the condemnation and the breaking up of the conclave, Eutyches is alleged to have told Florentius that he appealed to the bishops of Rome, Alexandria, and Jerusalem. Flavian, as president of the council, thought it his duty to acquaint the bishops of Rome and other Sees of the first rank with what had taken place. For some unknown reason his letter to Leo was delayed, and the appeal of Eutyches and a letter from the Emperor was the first information that he received. As might be expected from Leo's conception of his office, he was much incensed at this apparent neglect, and wrote to the Emperor explaining his ignorance of the facts, and to

Flavian, complaining of being kept in ignorance, and *prima facie* of Eutyches' treatment. Meanwhile the delayed epistle arrived from Flavian, and the account given was enough to satisfy Leo, who thereupon (May, 449) replied briefly expressing his approval and promising a fuller treatment of the question. This promise was fulfilled next month in the shape of the world-famous "Tome," which forms Letter XXVIII. in the Leonine collection. The proper significance of this document is well expressed by Mr. Gore [6]: it is, he says, "still more remarkable for its contents than for the circumstances which produced it," though "in itself it is a sign of the times: for here we have a Latin bishop, ignorant of Greek, defining the faith for Greek-speaking bishops, in view of certain false opinions of Oriental origin." Without reviewing in detail the further correspondence that Leo carried on with the various civil and ecclesiastical authorities at Constantinople (among them being the influential and orthodox Pulcheria the Emperor's sister), we pass on to the events connected with the second council of Ephesus. Through the influence of Chrysaphius, as we have already seen, the Emperor was all along on the side of Eutyches, and it was apparently at his instigation and in spite of Leo's guarded dissuasion that the council was now convened and met in August, 449. The bishop of Rome excused himself from personal attendance on the score of pressing business at home, and sent three legates with instructions to represent his views, viz. Julius, bishop of Puteoli, Renatus, a presbyter, and Hilary, a deacon, together with Dulcitius, a notary [7]. They started about the middle of June, and the Synod opened on the 8th of August, in the church of the B.V.M. By the Emperor's order Dioscorus, patriarch of Alexandria, was president, Leo's chief representative sat next him, and Flavian was placed only 5th, the bishop of Antioch and Jerusalem being set above him: 130 bishops in all were admitted, those who had condemned Eutyches being excluded. Owing partly to the presence of the soldiery and a number of turbulent monks under the Syrian archimandrite Barsubas, the proceedings soon became riotous and disorderly. The "Tome" was not read at all, though that was the purpose of its composition. Eutyches was admitted to make his defence, which was received as completely satisfactory. The acts of the Synod of Constantinople on being read excited great indignation. Amid tremendous uproar Eutyches was formally restored to communion and his former position, and the president pronounced deposition upon Flavian and Eusebius. Flavian appealed, and Hilary [8], after uttering a monosyllabic protest, "*contradicitur*," managed to make good his escape and carry the lamentable tidings to his anxiously-expectant chief at Rome. The other bishops all more or less reluctantly subscribed the restoration of Eutyches and the deposition of Flavian and Eusebius. The end of Flavian is variously recorded, but the most accurate version appears to be that amid many blows and rough usage he was cast into prison, then driven into exile, and that within a few days he died of the bodily and mental injuries he had received at Epypa, a village in Lydia. These calamitous proceedings Leo afterwards stigmatized as *Latrocinium* (brigandage), and the council is generally known as the Robber council of Ephesus.

At the time when the disastrous news arrived at Rome, Leo was presiding over a council which he had convened; in violent indignation he immediately dispatched letters right and left in his own and his colleagues' name. There is a letter to Flavian, of whose death of course he was not yet aware; there are others to the archimandrites and the whole church of Constantinople, to Julian, bishop of Cos, and to Anastasius, bishop of Thessalonica. He used all his influence to prevail on the Emperor to summon a fresh council, this time in Italy,

6 Leo the Great, p. 53 (S.P.C.K.): this writer should also be consulted (pp. 53 to 70), on the merits and importance of the Eutychian controversy generally.

7 Of these Renatus is said to have died at Delos on the way, and Hilary is the future pope of that name. Julius of Puteoli must be carefully distinguished from Julian of Cos, who was also a confidant of Leo's.

8 What happened to Julius and Dulcitius is not known, though Leo does not express any disapproval of their action.

writing to him himself, and getting Pulcheria on the spot, and Valentinian, his mother Placidia and his wife Eudoxia, by letters from Rome, to assist his cause. As yet, however, the very stars in their courses seemed to fight against him, and the outlook grew yet darker. In the spring of 450 Dioscorus' predominance in the East had become so great that ten bishops were found to join with him in actually excommunicating the bishop of Rome. At the Court, though Pulcheria remained true to the Faith, Chrysaphius still seems to have swayed the Emperor, and to have obtained from him the edict which was issued confirming the acts of the Ephesine council. The fact, too, that Flavian's successor, Anatolius, had in the past been associated with Dioscorus caused him not unnatural anxiety, and this feeling turned to one of actual offence on receiving a letter from Anatolius, in which he simply announces his consecration without asking his consent. Thereupon Leo demanded of the Emperor that Anatolius should make some public proof and profession of his orthodoxy on the lines of the Tome and other catholic statements, and in the month of July sent legates to support this demand.

At this moment the horizon suddenly brightened. Before the arrival of the legates, Theodosius was killed by a fall from his horse, and to the triumph of the orthodox cause, his sister, Pulcheria (the first Roman Empress), succeeded him. The whole aspect of things was soon changed. Chrysaphius was almost at once executed, and shortly afterwards Pulcheria married and shared the Eastern empire with Marcian, who was for bravery, wisdom and orthodoxy an altogether suitable partner of her throne.

Leo's petition for a new Synod was now granted, but the place of meeting was to be in the East, not in the West, as more convenient for the Emperor. In the interval S. Flavian's body was brought by reverent hands to Constantinople and buried in the church of the Apostles, and a still more hopeful sign of the times—Anatolius and many other bishops signed the Tome. Hitherto Leo had asked that both councils (that which had condemned and that which had acquitted Eutyches of heresy) should be treated as null and void, and that the matter should be discussed *de novo*. Now, however, he shows a significant change of front: the Faith, he maintains, is decided: nothing needs now to be done but to reject the heretics and to use proper caution in re-admitting the penitents: there is no occasion for a general council. And consequently he sends bishop Lucentius and Basil a presbyter as legates to assist Anatolius in this matter of rejection and re-admission. But, as the Emperor adhered to his determination, Leo was obliged to give way, and though still declining to attend in person, sent bishop Paschasinus of Sicily and Boniface a presbyter with written instructions to act with the former two as his representatives; Julian of Cos, who from his knowledge of Greek and Eastern affairs was a most useful addition, was also asked to be of the number. Nicæa in Bithynia had been fixed upon as the rendezvous, and there on Sept. 1, 451, 520 bishops assembled[9]. The Emperor, however, was too busy and too anxious over his military operations against Attila and the Huns to meet them there, and therefore invites them to Chalcedon, which being on the Bosporus was much nearer to Constantinople. There accordingly on Oct. 8, in the church of S. Euphemia the Martyr, the council was at last opened. The Emperor himself was still absent, but he was well represented by a goodly number of state officials. In accordance with Leo's request, Paschasinus, with his brother legates, presided: next sat Anatolius, Dioscorus, Maximus of Antioch and Juvenal of Jerusalem, with a copy of the Gospels in the midst. Leo's representatives began by trying to have Dioscorus ejected: they only succeeded in getting him deposed from his seat of honour and placed in the middle of the room together with Eusebius of Dorylæum, his accuser, and Theodoret of Cyrus, the eminent theologian, who was suspected of Nestorian-

9 110 others voted by proxy in absence through their metropolitans (Gore).

izing language. The remainder of the first day was spent in reading the acts of the Ephesine council, which in the midst of much uproar were provisionally condemned.

At the second session (Oct. 10), the Tome was read by the Imperial secretary, Veronician, and enthusiastically received: "Peter has spoken by Leo," they said. But objections being raised by the bishops of Palestine and Illyria that the twofold Nature was over-stated, its final acceptance was postponed for a few days, that a committee which was nominated might reason with the dissentients.

At the third Session (Oct. 13), Dioscorus, who refused to appear, was accused by Eusebius and by general consent condemned, being deprived of his rank and office as bishop, and the Emperor having confirmed the sentence, he was banished to Gangra in Paphlagonia, and there three years later (in 454) died. His successor at Alexandria was the orthodox Proterius, who was however never recognized by a large portion of the Egyptian Church: even in the Synod of Chalcedon many of the Egyptian bishops refused to sign the "Tome" at the fourth session, on the plea that the custom of their church forbade them to act without the consent of the archbishop, who was not yet appointed, and the still surviving "Jacobite" schism originated with the deposition of Dioscorus.

The fourth session was held on the 17th, and the misgivings of the Palestinian and Illyrian bishops having been quieted in the interval, the Tome was adopted.

In the fifth session (Oct. 24), a difficulty arose over a definition of the Faith which had been composed, but did not satisfy the Roman legates with regard to Eutychianism. However a committee, which was appointed, took it in hand again, and the result of their labours was accepted as fully guarding against the errors both of Nestorius and Eutyches. The remaining sessions were occupied with less important matters, and with drawing up the canons of the Council, of which one—the 28th—was designed to settle the precedence of the patriarch of Constantinople ("New Rome" as it was called), and to give him a place second to the bishop of old Rome. Against this audacious innovation the Roman legates in vain protested; the bitter pill, enwrapped in much sugar, was conveyed to Leo in the synodal letter, and produced the most lamentable results.

The last meeting of the Council on Nov. 1 was graced by the attendance in full state of Marcian and Pulcheria. The Emperor delivered an address, and at its conclusion he and the Empress were vociferously applauded, Marcian being styled the "second Constantine."

To return to Leo, we have letters from Marcian, Anatolius, and Julian, all trying to carry off the difficulty of the 28th Canon under the triumph of the Roman views in other respects. But Leo refused to be conciliated. The canon, he maintains, is in direct violation of the decrees of Nicæa (in which statement he makes an unpardonable[1] confusion between the Nicene canons and those of Sardica, which were often appended to them). With Anatolius he was especially displeased, considering that his doubtful precedents ought to have made him extremely careful not to offend. He therefore ceased all communication with him, eagerly seizing at pretexts of complaint against him, and appointing Julian his *apocrisiarius* or resident representative and correspondent. All this time Marcian continued pleading and Leo inflexible, until Anatolius at last yielded, and the matter for the time is satisfactorily settled, though it must not be imagined that the disputed canon was ever annulled.

Eutychianism still lingered on and caused disturbances in various parts of the East, especially among the monks. In Palestine, Juvenal, the bishop of Jerusalem, was deposed, and the Empress Eudocia, Theodosius II.'s widow, who was living in retirement in that city, was suspected of favouring the rioters. Leo therefore wrote letters to her and to others,

[1] Unpardonable in any case from one in his position, but especially so, if he was really connected with the church of Rome, as we have suggested, under Zosimus, in whose time the confusion, already existing then, was completely cleared up: see Gore's Life, pp. 113 and 114. The Canon itself professed only to confirm one already passed in 381.

in which he re-states the doctrine of the Incarnation, endeavouring to clear up any misconceptions which the inaccuracy of the Greek version of the Tome may possibly have caused. Eventually he was able to congratulate the Emperor on the restoration of peace and order in that quarter of their empire.

Similar riots were reported in Cappadocia, where the monks were led by one of their number named George, in Constantinople itself, where the ringleaders were Carosus and Dorotheus, and in Egypt.

But before we narrate the final victory of the orthodox cause throughout Christendom against the Eutychians, there are two events in the political world, belonging one to the year 452 and the other to 455, to which reference must be made, as showing the remarkable prestige which Leo's character had gained for him among all classes of society. When he was made pope we found him absent in Gaul mediating between rival generals. We now find him employed on still harder missions. Leo himself makes none but the slightest indirect allusion to either of these later incidents, but this silence is only characteristic of the man, in whom there is no trace of vain-boasting, and who consistently sank the personality of himself as well as of others in the principles and causes which absorbed him. There seems no reason, however, to doubt the substantial truth of what Prosper and others have related. In 452 Attila and the Huns, notwithstanding the defeat they had sustained from Aetius at Chalons, continued their devastating inroad into Italy. The whole city of Rome was paralysed with terror, and at last sent Leo with the Consular Avienus and the Prefect Tregetius to intercede with them. The meeting took place on lake Benacus, and Leo's arguments, aided, it is thought, by rumours of threatened invasion at home, persuaded Attila to retire beyond the Danube, on condition of receiving Honoria with a rich dowry as his wife. This was the last time that Attila troubled the Romans: for he died the next year.

Less than three years after this successful encounter with the barbarian, in 455 Leo's powerful services were again brought into requisition by the State. That year the licentious Valentinian was murdered at the instigation of an enraged husband, Maximus, who subsequently compelled the widow, Eudoxia, to marry him. Eudoxia, however, discovering the part Maximus had taken in Valentinian's death, invited the Vandals under Genseric to invade Italy. Maximus himself was put to death before the invaders reached Rome: but, when they did arrive, the panic-stricken citizens again threw themselves into the hands of Leo, who at the head of the clergy went forth to meet the foe outside the city. Once more his intercessions in some measure prevailed, but not sufficiently to prevent the city being pillaged fourteen days.

We now return to more purely religious matters. In 457 Marcian died (his wife having pre-deceased him four years), and was succeeded by a Thracian, named Leo [2]. Fresh outbreaks immediately took place both at Constantinople and at Alexandria: at the former place they were soon stopped, but at Alexandria they were more serious and prolonged. The disaffected monks set up one of their number, Timothy Ælurus (or the Cat) in opposition to Proterius, who was soon after foully murdered in the baptistery, to which he had fled. This flagrant outrage at once aroused the bishop of Rome to fresh energy in every direction: by his promptitude the new Emperor was stirred to action, among the other means employed being a re-statement of the Faith in a long epistle with a catena of patristic authority, sometimes called "the Second Tome." Ælurus was deposed and banished, and another Timothy, surnamed Solophaciolus, of well-approved orthodoxy, elected into his place. This satisfactory consummation was effected in 460, while a no less orthodox successor, named Gennadius, had been found two years before, when Anatolius died, for the See of Constantinople. Thus

[2] Styled "Magnus," like his great namesake, though with infinitely less good reason.

Leo's joy was full at last, as his latest letters testify. Late in the year 461 he died, after a rule of twenty-one years, during which he had won at least one great victory for the Faith, and had given the See of Rome a prestige, which may be said to have lasted even to the present day.

His body was buried in the church of S. Peter's, since which time it has been thrice moved to different positions, once towards the end of the 7th century by Pope Sergius, again in 1607, after the re-building of the church in its present form, and lastly in 1715. As "saint" and "confessor" from the earliest times, as "doctor of the church" since 1754, he is commemorated in the East on Feb. 18, in the West on April 11.

"It will not be wholly out of place," says Mr. Gore[3], "to mention that tradition looks "back to Leo as the benefactor of many of the Roman churches: he is said to have "restored their silver ornaments after the ravages of the Vandals, and to have repaired the "basilicas of S. Peter and S. Paul, placing a mosaic in the latter, which represented the "adoration of the four and twenty elders: we are told also that he built a church of S. Cor-"nelius, established some monks at S. Peter's, instituted guardians for the tombs of the "Apostles, and erected a fountain before S. Paul's, where the people might wash before "entering the church."

The only writings of Leo which are usually accepted as authentic are his numerous Sermons and Letters. Certain anti-Pelagian treatises and a long tract upon Humility in the form of a letter to Demetrias, a virgin, have been ascribed to him; but the most important work of all the doubtful ones is a "Sacramentary," which is one of the earliest extant of the Roman church, and is sometimes held to be Leo's composition or compilation. Many of the collects and prayers which it contains bear a remarkable resemblance to his teaching, and may well have come from his pen: there is indeed good reason for the opinion that the Collect proper, which is a distinct feature of the Western Church, owes its origin to Leo.

As a theologian Leo is thoroughly Western in type, being not speculative but dogmatic: no one was better suited in God's Providence to give the final completeness to the Church's Doctrine of the Incarnation than this clear-sighted, unimaginative, and persistent bishop of Rome. His theological position on the cardinal doctrines of the Faith is identical with that of the Athanasian symbol, to the language of which his own language often bears a close resemblance. With his theory of the Pope as universal Ruler of the Church in virtue of his being the successor of S. Peter, the vast majority of English-speaking people will have but little sympathy: and yet it can but be admired from an objective standpoint as a bold, grand, and almost original[4] conception. And there are no doubt many smaller points of detail in his writings connected more with discipline than with doctrine, which will now be reckoned if not as actually objectionable, at least as arising from forgotten needs or belonging to a byegone system: among these may be instanced his objection to slaves as clergy and to the celebration of the Eucharist more than once in one day except on festivals, where the church is too small to hold all the worshippers at once: his advocacy of the innovation of private instead of public confession for ordinary penitents, and on the other hand his insisting on the old rule that baptism should be administered only twice a year (at Easter and at Whitsuntide): and again the somewhat undue prominence that he gives to fasting and almsgiving as being on a level with prayer for Lenten or Ember exercises, and to the intercessions of the saints—particularly of the patron saints of Rome, SS. Peter, Paul, and Lawrence. And yet at the same time there is very much more to

3 Life, p. 165.

4 Milman attributes the real initiation of the Papal theory to the imperious Innocent I., who held the See of Rome at the beginning of the fifth century (402—417).

be thankful for as instructive than to object to as obsolete or dangerous. For on the negative side we have no trace after all of the later direct invocation of the Saints, nor of the modern *cultus* of the B. V. M. and of relics, while among the many positive good points in his teaching must be reckoned his most proper theory of a bishop as not only the channel of divine grace in virtue of ordination (*sacerdos*) but also the overseer of the flock (*episcopus*), in virtue of the people's choice and approval, which is essential to his office; his strong condemnation of the practice of usury in laity as well as clergy; his high appreciation of corporate even more than individual action among the faithful; the thoroughly practical view he always puts before us of the Christian life; and above all the "singularly Christian" character of all his sermons, in which Christ is the Alpha and Omega of all his thoughts and of all his exhortations. These are some of the benefits which Leo has conferred upon the Church, and which have rightfully earned for him the title "Great."

Manuscripts.

I. At the *Vatican*. (α) *Of the Sermons.* (1) Codd. 3835 and 6 are two volumes in Roman Character of a Lectionary of about the 8th century; the second volume contains the "Tome" (which in the 8th and 9th centuries used to be read in the Church offices before Christmas): (2) 3828, a parchment (10th century), also a lectionary: (3) 1195, a parchment folio (11th century), a lectionary containing *inter alia* some of Leo's homilies: (4) 1267, 8 and 9 of the same character (11th century): (5) 1270 contains the Sermon *de Festo Petri cathedræ* (now xiv. in Migne's Appendix), from which Cacciari restored Quesnel's imperfect edition of it to its present state: (6) 1271 and 2 are also lectionaries: (7) 4222 in Lombardic characters (9th century), a lectionary: (8) 5451 in Roman characters (12th century), a lectionary: (9) 6450 parchment (12th century): a lectionary containing the sermon *de Festo Petri cathedræ* in the form found and printed by Quesnel; (10) 6451 similar: it contains sermons *de Quadragesima* and others: (11) 6454 similar.

(β) Of the *Letters:* these are mostly rather later (i.e. about 12th or 13th century): but (1) 1322 is of an older date, and contains besides the epistles, all the acts of the Council of Chalcedon: (2) 5759 is earlier than the 9th century; it used to belong to the monastery of S. Columban at Bobbio, and contains 31 letters: (3) 5845 is very ancient, and according to Cacciari, Lombardic: it contains 24 letters.

(γ) *Letters and Sermons together:* of these there are nine collections in the Vatican, of which 548 and 9 contain the sermon *de Absalom* which is condemned by Cacciari. The *Regio-Vaticanus codex* 139 is a fine collection of Leo's works (12th century).

II. *At other places:* (1) The codex *Urbinas* 65 is thought to be a copy of the Regio-Vaticanus 139 made in the 14th century.

(2) Codex *Grimanicus* [5] is a MS. on which Quesnel lays great stress: Quesnel assigns it to the ninth century; it contains 107 letters, of which 28 had never been printed before Quesnel.

(3) The *Thuanei;* (α) 129 contains 123 letters: (β) 780 contains the Tome: (γ) 729 contains the spurious *de vocatione gentium* and some epistles.

(4) The *Corbeienses* are old.

(5) The *Taurinensis* 29 D. iv. is a fine 13th-century MS. containing 52 letters.

(6) The *Florentinus codex* belongs to the 13th century also.

(7) *Ratisbonensis* 113 DD. AA., in the monastery of S. Emeramus, contains 72 letters: it is said to date from about 750 A.D.

(8) The two *Bergonenses* are of 12th century, and contain 12 sermons.

[5] *Grimanus*, from whom this Codex is named, was Cardinal of S. Mark, &c., in the 16th century.

(9) Two *Chigiani* also of 12th century contain 4 sermons.

(10) The *Padilironenses* contain 9 sermons and the Tome.

(11) There are three *Patavini*, of which two contain the Tome.

(12) *Vallicellani:* these are a number of 11th or 12th-century codices.

There are also the *Veneti*, the *Vercellenses*, the *Veronenses*, *&c.*

N.B. The foregoing account is taken from Schönemann's *Notitia Historico-Literaria* (1794), and the translator has no means of knowing whether it is still correct (1890).

Editions.

1. The earliest important edition is *P. Quesnel's* (*prêtre de l'oratoire*), Paris, 1675, Lyons, 1700, of which Migne's *Dict. de Bibliogr. catholique* says, '*on reproche aux éditions du P. Quesnel un grand nombre de falsifications, par lesquelles le P. Quesnel se proposait notamment d'affaiblir l'autorité pontificale*[6]. . . . *L'édition que l'on doit aujourd'hui préférer, est* (naturally enough!) *celle qui a été publiée par M. l'abbé Migne sous le titre d'*

2. *Œuvres très complètes de Saint Leon le Grand publiées d'après l'édition des frères Ballerinii et celle de Paschase Quesnel enrichées de préfaces, d'avertissements et de commentaires, suivies des exercices de Cacciari sur toutes les œuvres du saint docteur. Paris* 1846.

3. *P. Cacciari* (a carmelite) brought out editions at Rome, 1751 and 1753-5, the latter with dissertations.

4. The edition of the brothers P. and H. Ballerinii (Jesuists), Venice, 1753-7, was a recension of Quesnel's second edition with copious dissertations and notes.

5. *H. Hurter*, S. J., has published selections of Sermons and Letters in vols. xiv., xxv. and xxvi. of his *SS. PP. opuscula selecta*, 1871-4.

Translations.

1 *Bright's Leo on the Incarnation*, London, 1862 (2nd edn. enlarged, 1886, in which the Tome is translated), consists of xviii. sermons translated and the Tome in Latin, with many valuable notes.

2. *Reithmayr's Bibliothek* (1869) contains a German translation.

3. *Dr. Neale's History of the Alexandrian Patriarchate* embodies a translation of the Tome.

4. Dr. Heurtley published a version of the Tome in 1886.

Authorities and Materials.

The chief ancient and mediæval authorities for the life and times of Leo the Great are such works as *Prosper's*, and *Idatius' Chronicles*, *Iornandes de rebus Geticis*, *Anastasius Bibliothecarius Historia de vitis Romanorum Pontificum* (9th cent.), the *Historia Miscella* (10th cent.), &c.

Among *lives* may be mentioned the following:—(1) *La vie et religion de deux bons papes Léon premier et Gregoire premier par* Pierre du Moulin (the younger: a protestant theologian), *Sedan*, 1650. 12mo. (2) Quesnel's valuable *Dissertatio de vita et rebus gestis S. Leonis Magni*, originally included in his edition of Leo and re-printed by Migne in Vol. ii. of his edition with the Ballerinii's annotations and critical remarks, *Paris*, 1675, *Lyons*, 1700. (3) *Histoire du Pontificat de Saint Léon le Grand par Monsr. L. Maimbourg La Haye*, 1687. (4) *The Bollandists' Life by Canisius* (*Acta Sanctorum*), *April*, vol. ii. pp. 14-22. (5) Alphonsi Ciaconii *Vitæ Pontificum* (*Tom* 1, pp. 303-314), *Rome*, 1677, *4to.* (6) Le Nain de Tillemont, *Memoires pour servir à l'histoire Ecclesiastique* (vol. xv. pp. 414—832, 885—934), *Paris*, 1711. (7)

[6] That is to say, it upheld the Gallican opinions; and so it was condemned and put on the Index in 1632. But being too valuable a work to be altogether suppressed, Benedict XIV. enjoined the issue of (4), which rebutted and rectified Quesnel's false deductions in its notes and excursuses.

Breve Descrizione della vita di S. Leone Primo di GABRIELLE BERTAZZOLO: *Mantova*, 1727. (8) *Memoire istoriche di Sa. Leone Papa da* TEOFILO PACIFICO: *Brescia*, 1791, 8*vo*. (9) DU PIN, L. E., *History of Ecc. writers* (Eng. Edn. vol. 1, pp. 464—480), *Dublin*, 1722. (10) C. OUDINUS, *de Scriptoribus Ecclesiæ* (vol. 1, pp. 1271-5), *Leipzig*, 1722. (11) WILHELM AMADEUS ARENDT (*Roman Catholic*), *Leo der Grosse und seine Zeit*, *Mainz*, 1835, 8*vo*. (12) EDUARD PERTHEL, *Papst Leo's I. Leben und Lehren*, *Jena*, 1843, 8vo. (a counterblast to No. 11, and no less exaggerated and prejudiced in statement). (13) A. DE SAINT-CHRON, *Histoire du pontificat de Saint Léon le Grand*, *Paris*, 1846. (14) F. BÖHRINGER, *die Kirche Xti und ihre Zeugen* (vol. 1 part 4, pp. 170—309), *Zürich*, 1845. (15) CHARLES GORE'S *Life of Leo the Great* (S.P.C.K.); also his article in Smith's *Dict. of Christian Biogr.* (16) The article in HERZOG'S *Real-Encyklopädie* of which a condensed English edition was edited by Dr. Philip Schaff at New York in 1883. Other more general accounts of his times will be found in (1) *l'abbé* FLEURY, *Histoire du Xtianisme* (vol. ii. pp. 384—480), *Paris*, 1836. (2) BRIGHT'S *History of the Church from* 313—451 (chaps. xiv., xv.), *Oxford and London*, 1860. (3) MILMAN'S *Latin Christianity* (Book ii. chap. 4), *London*, 1864. (4) R. J. ROHRBACHER'S *Histoire Universelle de l'Eglise catholique* (15th edn., vol. 4, pp. 461—575), *Paris*, 1868. A short account of Leo's writings is given in ALZOG'S *Grundriss der Patrologie*, § 78, pp. 368—375: a most exhaustive one in CEILLIER'S *Histoire génèrale des Auteurs sacrés* (new edition) (vol. x., pp. 169—276), 1858—1869. BÄHR'S *Geschichte der Römischer Literatur-Supplement Band. II. Abtheilung* (pp. 354—362), *im Abendland*, vol. 1, p. 448, may also be consulted; and EBERT'S *Allgemeine Geschichte der Literatur des Mittelalters*.

LETTERS

LETTER I.

To the Bishop of Aquileia.

I. *Through the negligence of the authorities the Pelagian heresy has been spreading in his province.*

From the account of our holy brother and fellow-bishop Septimus which is contained in the subjoined letter[1], we have understood that certain priests and deacons and clergy of various orders[2] in your province who have been drawn in by the Pelagian or Cælestian heresy, have attained to catholic communion without any recantation of their peculiar error being required of them; and that, whilst the shepherds set to watch were fast asleep, wolves clothed in sheep-skins but without laying aside their bestial minds have entered into the Lord's sheep-fold: and that they make a practice of what is not allowed even to non-offenders by the injunctions of our canons and decrees[3]: to wit that they should leave the churches in which they received or regained their office and carry their uncertainty in all directions, loving to continue wandering and never to remain on the foundations of the Apostles. For without being sifted by any test or bound by any previous confession of faith, they make a great point of their right to the privilege of going to one house after another under cover of their being in communion with the Church, and corrupting the hearts of many through men's ignorance[4] of their false name. And yet I am sure they could not do this, if the rulers of the churches had exercised their rightful diligence in the matter of receiving such, and had not allowed any of them to wander from place to place.

II. *He orders a provincial synod to be convened to receive the recantation of the heretics in express terms.*

Accordingly, lest this should be attempted any further, and lest this pernicious habit, which owes its introduction to certain persons' negligence, should result in the overthrow of many souls, by this our authoritative injunction we charge you, brother, to give diligence that a synod of the clergy[5] of your province be convened, and all, whether priests or deacons or clerics of any rank who have been re-admitted from their alliance with the Pelagians and the Cælestians into catholic communion with such precipitation that they were not first constrained to recant their error, be now at least forced to a true correction, which can advantage themselves and hurt no one, since their deceitfulness has in part been disclosed. Let them by their public confession condemn the authors of this presumptuous[6] error and renounce all that the universal Church has repudiated in their doctrine: and let them announce by full and open statements, signed by their own hand, that they embrace and entirely approve of all the synodal decrees which the authority of the Apostolic See has ratified to the rooting out of this heresy. Let nothing obscure, nothing ambiguous be found in their words. For we know that their cunning is such that they reckon that the meaning of any particular clause of their execrable doctrine can be defended if they only keep it distinct from the main body of their damnable views[7].

---

1 It is to be supposed that the letter of Septimus, bp. of Altinum, was sent with this letter. See Lett. XVIII. n. 3.

2 Viz. members of the "minor orders" as they are now called, subdeacons, exorcists, &c.

3 It had been the rule at least since the council of Nicæa (325) that the clergy should stay in the church (or diocese as we should call it) of their ordination, cf. Canons of Nicæa xxi. *de his qui Ecclesias deserunt et ad alias transeunt*, and xxii. *de non suscipiendis alterius Ecclesiæ clericis*. And we often find Leo insisting on the observance of the rule.

4 *Inscientiam*: the general reading being *scientiam*, the sense of which is not clear.

5 *Sacerdotum*: I am in doubt as to what this term here includes, but think it probable that all ranks of the clergy were to be summoned. The words *sacerdos* and *antistes* in early ecclesiastical Latin very often mean the bishop (*episcopus*) specifically rather than the presbyter (*sacerdos secundi ordinis*), because it was the bishop who offered the "sacrifice of praise and thanksgiving" (i.e. the Eucharist), and the presbyter only in his default; but the term *sacerdos* does certainly often include the presbyters and also the deacons (*sacerdotes tertii ordinis*) when in connexion with the priests and bishops, and it seems likely that the whole body of the clergy of the province would be summoned to the synod: see Bright's note 110: also Bingham, Antiq., Bk. II., chap. xix., §§ 14, 15.

6 *Superbi* (proud): the epithet is well chosen and not a random one: for pride and presumption are at the root of the Pelagian views as birth-sin and baptismal grace: perfectionism is little in accordance with Christian humility.

7 For the same sentiment cf. Prosper, *de ingratis*, v. 188.

III. *The Pelagian view of God's grace is unscriptural.*

And when they pretend to disapprove of and give up all their definitions to facilitate evasion through their complete art of deception, unless their meaning is detected, they make exception of the dogma that the grace of God is given according to the merits of the recipient. And yet surely, unless it is given freely, it is not a gift[8], but a price and compensation for merits: for the blessed Apostle says, "by grace ye have been saved through faith, and that not of yourselves but it is the gift of God; not of works lest any should perchance be exalted. For we are His workmanship created in Christ Jesus in good works, which God prepared that we should walk in them[9]." Thus every bestowal of good works is of God's preparing: because a man is justified by grace rather than by his own excellence: for grace is to every one the source of righteousness, the source of good and the fountain of merit. But these heretics say it is anticipated by men's natural goodness for this reason, that that nature which (in their view) is before grace conspicuous for good desires of its own, may not seem marred by any stain of original sin, and that what the Truth says may be falsified: "For the Son of Man came to seek and to save that which was lost[1]."

IV. *Prompt measures are essential.*

You must take heed, therefore, beloved, and with great diligence make provision that offences which have long been removed be not set up again through such men and that no seed of the same evil spring up in your province from a doctrine which has once been uprooted: for not only will it take root and grow, but also will taint the future generations of the Church with its poisonous exhalations. Those who wish to appear corrected must purge themselves of all suspicion: and by obeying us, prove themselves ours. And if any of them decline to satisfy our wholesome injunctions, be he cleric or layman, he must be driven from the society of the Church lest he deal treacherously by others' safety as well as forfeit his own soul.

V. *The canons must be enforced against clerics who wander from one church to another.*

We admonish you also to restore to full working that part of the discipline of the Church whereby the holy Fathers and we have often in former times decreed that neither in the grade of the priesthood nor in the order of the diaconate nor in the lower ranks of the clergy, is any one at liberty to migrate from church to church: to the end that each one may persevere where he was ordained without being enticed by ambition, or led astray by greed, or corrupted by men's evil beliefs: and thus that if any one, seeking his own interests, not those of Jesus Christ[2], neglect to return to his own people[3] and church, he may be reckoned out of the pale both in respect of promotion and of the bond of communion. But do not doubt, beloved, that we must be somewhat sorely moved if, as we think not, our decrees for the maintenance of the canons and the integrity of the faith be neglected: because the short-comings of the lower orders[4] are to be laid at the door of none so much as of those slothful and remiss rulers who often foster much pestilence by shrinking from the application of a stringent remedy.

LETTER II.

To Septimus, Bishop of Altinum.

(Caution must be observed in receiving Pelagians back, and clergy must stay in the church of their ordination.)

LETTER III.

From Paschasinus, Bishop of Lilybæum.

(About the keeping of Easter in 444; recommending the Alexandrine calculation.)

LETTER IV.

To the Bishops appointed in Campania, Picenum, Etruria, and all the Provinces.

Leo, bishop of the city of Rome, to all the bishops appointed in Campania, Picenum, Etruria, and all the provinces, greeting in the Lord.

I. *Introduction.*

As the peaceful settlement of the churches causes us satisfaction, so are we saddened with no slight sorrow whenever we learn that anything has been taken for granted or done contrary to the ordinances of the canons and the discipline of the Church: and if we do not repress such things with the vigilance we ought, we cannot excuse ourselves to Him

8 The reader need hardly be reminded that in the New Testament "grace" (Lat. *gratia*, Gk. χάρις) signifies "a free gift."

9 Eph. ii. 8-10.

1 S. Luke ix. 10. Between this and the next chapter some of the MSS. and the earlier editions insert a passage from Augustine's Enchiridion, which thus formed chapter iv.

2 A reminiscence of Phil. ii. 21.

3 *Plebem*: this being the regular term for the "laity" in early Christian Latin.

4 Sc. of the clergy.

who intended us to be watchmen[5], for permitting the pure body of the Church, which we ought to keep clean from every stain, to be defiled by contact with wicked schemers, since the framework of the members loses its harmony by such dissimulation.

II. *Slaves and serfs* (*coloni*) *are not to be ordained.*

Men are admitted commonly to the Sacred Order who are not qualified by any dignity of birth or character: even some who have failed to obtain their liberty from their masters are raised to the rank of the priesthood[6], as if sorry slaves were fit for that honour; and it is believed that a man can be approved of GOD who has not yet been able to approve himself to his master. And so the cause for complaint is twofold in this matter, because both the sacred ministry is polluted by such poor partners in it, and the rights of masters are infringed so far as unlawful possession is rashly taken of them[7]. From these men, therefore, beloved brethren, let all the priests of your province keep aloof; and not only from them, but from others also, we wish you to keep, who are under the bond of origin or other condition of service[8]: unless perchance the request or consent be intimated of those who claim some authority over them. For he who is to be enrolled on the divine service ought to be exempt from others, that he be not drawn away from the LORD's camp in which his name is entered, by any other bonds of duty.

III. *A man who has married twice or a widow is not eligible as a priest.*

Again, when each man's respectability of birth and conduct has been established, what sort of person should be associated with the ministry of the Sacred Altar we have learnt both from the teaching of the Apostle and the Divine precepts and the regulations of the canons, from which we find very many of the brethren have turned aside and quite gone out of the way. For it is well known that the husbands of widows have attained to the priesthood: certain, too, who have had several wives, and have led a life given up to all licentiousness, have had all facilities put in their way, and been admitted to the Sacred Order, contrary to that utterance of the blessed Apostle, in which he proclaims and says to such, "the husband of one wife[9]," and contrary to that precept of the ancient law which says by way of caution: "Let the priest take a virgin to wife, not a widow, not a divorced woman[1]." All such persons, therefore, who have been admitted we order to be put out of their offices in the church and from the title of priest by the authority of the Apostolic See: for they will have no claim[2] to that for which they were not eligible, on account of the obstacle in question: and we specially claim for ourselves the duty of settling this, that if any of these irregularities have been committed, they may be corrected and may not be allowed to occur again, and that no excuse may arise from ignorance: although it has never been allowed a priest to be ignorant of what has been laid down by the rules of the canons. These writings, therefore, we have addressed to your provinces by the hand of Innocent, Legitimus and Segetius, our brothers and fellow-bishops: that the evil shoots which are known to have sprung up may be torn out by the roots, and no tares may spoil the LORD's harvest. For thus all that is genuine will bear much fruit, if that which has been wont to kill the growing crop be carefully cleared away.

IV. *Usurious practices forbidden for clergy and for laity*[3].

This point, too, we have thought must not be passed over, that certain possessed with the love of base gain lay out their money at in-

5 Cf. Ezek. iii. 17.

6 *Sacerdotii*, see note 5 on Letter 1.

7 Though no doubt S. Leo's language is here harsh and offensive to modern ears, it is not, I think, substantially out of agreement with S. Paul's own teaching (cf. Philemon; 1 Cor. vii. 21; Ephes. vi. 5; Col. iii. 22; Tit. ii. 9), and certainly not with the spirit of the age. The 73rd Apost. Canon forbids any slave to be ordained without his master's consent, and without previously obtaining his freedom. However, in the times of S. Jerome, S. Basil and S. Greg. Nazianzen, we find cases of slaves being ordained. However much we in the latter half of the nineteenth century regret to hear a great father of the Church speak in this way, we must not forget that in the first half of this self-same century the very same opinion would have been held on the subject in many parts of the civilized world.

8 *Qui originali* (*al. origini*) *aut alicui condicioni obligati sunt.* The class of people here alluded to were the *coloni* (serfs): such of them as were so by birth were called *originarii*: and there were other classes of them also (*alicui condicioni obligati*). The essential difference between all *coloni* and the ordinary *servi* was that the latter's service was *personal*, the former were *servi terræ, adscripti glæbæ*. Thus there is a strong resemblance between them and the villeins (*villani*) of mediæval and modern Europe. For the order concerning them here given, cf. 2nd Council of Orleans (538), which ordains "*ut nullus servilibus colonariisque condicionibus obligatus iuxta statuta sedis Apostolicæ ad honores ecclesiasticos admittatur nisi prius aut testamento aut per tabulas legitime constiterit absolutum.*

9 1 Tim. iii. 2, *unius uxoris virum* with the Vulgate, cf. Letter xii. 3.

1 Lev. xxi. 13, 14, cf. a letter of Innocent I. to Victricius, bishop of Rothomagus (Rouen), chap. v., *ut mulierem* (*viduam*) *clericus non ducat uxorem: quia scriptum est: sacerdos virginem uxorem accipiat non viduam non eiectam*," and for the former quotation, cf. ibid. chap. vii. *ne is qui secundam duxerit uxorem, clericus fiat: quia scriptum est unius uxoris virum.* The 18th Apostolic Canon gives a similar order. All these rules would seem to refer to marriage *before*, not after, ordination. The latter was against the spirit of the early Church.

2 The older editions here add *pro arbitrio* (by dispensation). which Quesnel considers a gloss added later when dispensation was sometimes granted to digamous clerks.

3 The practice of usury and trading generally is often forbidden in the Canons, &c., for the clergy, but its prohibition for the laity is much more unusual: cf., however, Canon V. of the Council of Carthage (419), *quod* (*sc. fenus accipere*) *in laicis, reprehenditur id multo magis debet et in clericis prædamnari.* Scripture

terest, and wish to enrich themselves as usurers. For we are grieved that this is practised not only by those who belong to the clergy, but also by laymen who desire to be called Christians. And we decree that those who have been convicted be punished sharply, that all occasion of sinning be removed.

V. *A cleric may not make money in another's name any more than in his own.*

The following warning, also, we have thought fit to give, that no cleric should attempt to make money in another's name any more than in his own: for it is unbecoming to shield one's crime under another man's gains [4]. Nay, we ought to look at and aim at only that usury whereby what we bestow in mercy here we may recover from the LORD, who will restore a thousand fold what will last for ever.

VI. *Any bishop who refuses consent to these rules must be deposed.*

This admonition of ours, therefore, proclaims that if any of our brethren endeavour to contravene these rules and dare to do what is forbidden by them, he may know that he is liable to deposition from his office, and that he will not be a sharer in our communion who refuses to be a sharer of our discipline. But lest there be anything which may possibly be thought to be omitted by us, we bid you, beloved, to keep all the decretal rules of Innocent of blessed memory [5], and also of all our predecessors, which have been promulgated about the orders of the Church and the discipline of the canons, and to keep them in such wise that if any have transgressed them he may know at once that all indulgence is denied him.

Dated 10th of October, in the consulship of the illustrious Maximus (a second time) and Paterius (A.D. 443).

LETTER V.

TO THE METROPOLITAN BISHOPS OF ILLYRICUM.

(Appointing Anastasius of Thessalonica his Vicar in the province, and expressing his wishes about its government, for which see Letter VI.)

LETTER VI.

TO ANASTASIUS, BISHOP OF THESSALONICA.

Leo to his beloved brother Anastasius.

I. *He is pleased to have been consulted by the bishops [6] of Illyricum on important questions.*

The brotherly love of our colleagues makes us read with grateful mind the letters of all priests [7]; for in them we embrace one another in the spirit as if we were face to face, and by the intercourse of such epistles we are associated in mutual converse [8]. But in this present letter the affection displayed seems to us greater than usual: for it informs us of the state of the churches [9], and urges us to a vigilant exercise of care by a consideration of our office, so that being placed, as it were, on a watch-tower, according to the will of the LORD, we should both lend our approval to things when they run in accordance with our wishes, and correct, by applying the remedies of compulsion, what we observe gone wrong through any aggression: hoping that abundant fruit will be the result of our sowing the seed, if we do not allow those things to increase which have begun to spring up to the spoiling of the harvest.

II. *Following the examples of his predecessors he nominates Anastasius Metropolitan of Illyricum.*

Now therefore, dear brother, that your request has been made known to us through our son Nicolaus the priest, that you, too, like your predecessors, might receive from us in our turn authority over Illyricum for the observance of the rules, we give our consent and earnestly exhort that no concealment and no negligence may be allowed in the management of the churches situated throughout Illyricum, which we commit to you in our stead, following the precedent of Siricius of blessed remembrance, who then, for the first time, acting on a fixed method, entrusted them to your last predecessor but one [1], Anysius of holy memory, who had at the time well deserved of the Apostolic See, and was approved by after events: that he might render assistance to the churches situated in that province whom he wished kept up to discipline. Noble precedents must be followed with eagerness that

certainly is against the clergy participating in lucrative employments, though it was not easy always to prevent them: it had become, for instance, a common practice in S. Cyprian's day in the North African Church (cf. *de laps.* 6). But the secular laws certainly countenanced it in the laity (as Aug. Ep. 154 acknowledges). Leo the Emperor is said by Grotius to have been the first who '*existimans omne fenus Christiano interdictum, lege id ipsum communi sanxit*' (Quesnel).

4 *Crimen suum commodis alienis impendere.* I am not sure that this can mean what I say.

5 This was S. Innocent I., who was Pope from 402 to 417. One of his decretal letters was quoted from in note 1 to chap. iii. of this Letter.

6 The letter to the college of bishops was written the same day, and forms No. 5 in the Leonine series (in Migne).

7 *Sacerdotum* here obviously = *episcoporum*, see Letter I. note 5.

8 *quibus sermone epistolis mutuo commeantibus sociamur*: notice the interlaced order of the words in the sentence which is not, I think, without design as quaintly expressing his meaning.

9 Sc. in your province.

1 Siricius was Bishop of Rome 384-398. Damasus, 366-384, is said by Innocent I. to have been the first to do this, but not like Siricius, "acting on a fixed method," *certa quadam ratione*.

we may show ourselves in all things like those whose privileges we wish to enjoy. We wish you to imitate your last predecessor[2] but one as well as of your immediate predecessor who is known equally with the former to have both deserved and employed this privilege: so that we may rejoice in the progress of the churches which we commit to you in our stead. For as the conduct of matters progresses creditably when committed to one who acts well and carries out skilfully the duties of the priestly position, so it is found to be only a burden to him who, when power is entrusted to him, uses not the moderation that is due.

III. *Ordinees must be carefully selected with especial reference to the Canons of the Church.*

And so, dear brother, hold with vigilance the helm entrusted to you, and direct your mind's gaze around on all which you see put in your charge, guarding what will conduce to your reward and resisting those who strive to upset the discipline of the canons. The sanction of GOD's law must be respected, and the decrees of the canons should be more especially kept. Throughout the provinces committed to thee let such priests be consecrated to the LORD as are commended only by their deserving life and position among the clergy. Permit no licence to personal favour, nor to canvassing, nor to purchased votes. Let the cases of those who are to be ordained be investigated carefully and let them be trained in the discipline of the Church through a considerable period of their life. But if all the requirements of the holy Fathers are found in them, and if they have observed all that we read the blessed Apostle Paul to have enjoined on such, viz., that he be the husband of one wife, and that she was a virgin when he married her, as the authority of GOD's law requires, [then ordain them[3]]. And this we are extremely anxious should be observed, so as to do away with all place for excuses, lest any one should believe himself able to attain to the priesthood who has taken a wife before he obtained the grace of Christ, and on her decease joined himself to another after baptism. Seeing that the former wife cannot be ignored, nor the previous marriage put out of the reckoning, and that he is as much the father of the children whom he begat by that wife before baptism as he is of those whom he is known to have begotten by the second after baptism. For as sins and things which are known to be unlawful are washed away in the font of baptism, so what are allowed or lawful are not done away.

IV. *The Metropolitans must not ordain hastily nor without consulting their Primate.*

Let none be ordained a priest[4] throughout these churches inconsiderately; for by this means ripe judgments will be formed about those to be elected, if your scrutiny, brother, is dreaded. But let any bishop who, contrary to our command, is ordained by his metropolitan without your knowledge, know that he has no assured position with us, and that those who have taken on themselves so to do must render an account of their presumption[5]. But as to each metropolitan is committed such power that he has the right of ordaining in his province, so we wish those metropolitans to be ordained, but not without ripe and well-considered judgment. For although it is seemly that all who are consecrated priests should be approved and well-pleasing to GOD, yet we wish those to have peculiar excellence whom we know are going to preside over the fellow-priests who are assigned to them. And we admonish you, beloved, to see to this the more diligently and carefully, that you may be proved to keep that precept of the Apostles which runs, "lay hands suddenly on no man[6]."

V. *Points which cannot be settled at the provincial synod are to be referred to Rome.*

Any of the brethren who has been summoned to a synod should attend and not deny himself to the holy congregation: for there especially he should know that what will conduce to the good discipline of the Church must be settled. For all faults will be better avoided if more frequent conferences take place between the priests of the LORD, and intimate association is the greatest help alike to improvement and to brotherly love. There, if any questions arise, under the LORD's guidance they will be able to be determined, so that no bad feeling remains, and only a firmer love exists among the brethren. But if any more important question spring up, such as cannot be settled there under your presidency, brother, send your report and consult us, so that we may write back under the revelation of the LORD, of whose mercy it is that we can do ought, because He has breathed favourably upon us[7]: that by our decision we may vindicate

[2] *Prædecessoris tui.* Anysius is said to have lived on into the time of Innocent. Anastasius' immediate predecessor, selected by Innocent (*decessoris tui* in the next line), was named Rufus.

[3] These words are not found in the MSS. apparently, but are necessary to the sense. For the requirement cf. Letter IV. chapter iii.

[4] Here the word is *antistes*, and no doubt it signifies "bishop," as the next sentence clearly shows.

[5] The organization of the province then included (1) the bishops under (2) metropolitans of districts, under (3) one supreme primate of the province, who was in his turn responsible to the Bishop of Rome.

[6] 1 Tim. v. 22.

[7] The word is a*spiraverit* (the notion of which is to favour), not in*spiraverit* (to inspire), as we might have expected.

our right of cognizance in accordance with old-established tradition and the respect that is due to the Apostolic See: for as we wish you to exercise your authority in our stead, so we reserve to ourselves points which cannot be decided on the spot and persons who have made appeal to us.

VI. *Priests and deacons may not be ordained on weekdays any more than bishops.*

You shall take order that this letter reach the knowledge of all the brethren, so that no one hereafter find an opportunity to excuse himself through ignorance in observing these things which we command. We have directed our letter of admonition [8] to the metropolitans themselves also of the several provinces, that they may know that they must obey the Apostolic injunctions, and that they obey us in beginning to obey you, brother, our delegate according to what we have written. We hear, indeed, and we cannot pass it over in silence, that only bishops are ordained by certain brethren on Sundays only; but presbyters and deacons, whose consecration should be equally solemn [9], receive the dignity of the priestly office indiscriminately on any day, which is a reprehensible practice contrary to the canons and tradition of the Fathers [1], since the custom ought by all means to be kept by those who have received it with respect to all the sacred orders: so that after a proper lapse of time he who is to be ordained a priest or deacon [2] may be advanced through all the ranks of the clerical office, and thus a man may have time to learn that of which he himself also is one day to be a teacher. Dated the 12th of January, in the consulship of Theodosius (18th time) and Albinus (444).

LETTER VII.

To the Bishops throughout Italy.

Leo to all the bishops set over the provinces of Italy greeting.

I. *Many Manichæans have been discovered in Rome.*

We call you to a share in our anxiety, that with the diligence of shepherds you may take more careful heed to your flocks entrusted to you that no craft of the devil's be permitted: lest that plague, which by the revealing mercy of the Lord is driven off from our flocks through our care, should spread among your churches before you are forewarned, and are still ignorant of what is happening, and should find means of stealthily burrowing into your midst, and thus what we are checking in the City should take hidden root among you and grow up. Our search has discovered in the City a great many followers and teachers of the Manichæan impiety, our watchfulness has proclaimed them, and our authority and censure has checked them: those whom we could reform we have corrected and driven to condemn Manichæus with his preachings and teachings by public confession in church, and by the subscription of their own hand, and thus we have lifted those who have acknowledged their fault from the pit of their iniquity by granting them room for repentance [3]. A good many, however, who had so deeply involved themselves that no remedy could assist them, have been subjected to the laws in accordance with the constitutions of our Christian princes, and lest they should pollute the holy flock by their contagion, have been banished into perpetual exile by public judges. And all the profane and disgraceful things which are found as well in their writings as in their secret traditions, we have disclosed and clearly proved to the eyes of the Christian laity [4] that the people might know what to shrink from or avoid: so that he that was called their bishop was himself tried by us, and betrayed the criminal views which he held in his mystic religion, as the record of our proceedings can show you. For this, too, we have sent you for instruction: and after reading them you will be in a position to understand all the discoveries we have made.

II. *The bishops of Italy must not allow those Manichæans who have quitted the city to escape or lie concealed.*

And because we know that a good many of those who are involved here in too close an accusation for them to clear themselves have escaped, we have sent this letter to you, beloved, by our acolyth: that your holiness, dear brothers, may be informed of this, and see fit to act with diligence and caution, lest the men of the Manichæan error be able to find opportunity of hurting your people and of teaching their impious doctrines. For we cannot otherwise rule those entrusted to us unless

8 Viz., Letter V.

9 *Circa quos par consecratio fieri debet.* I take this as a valuable statement in the mouth of Leo, who so seldom refers specifically to the lower orders of the ministry.

1 There seems to be no canon on the point before Leo's time: but he alludes to the tradition again in Letter IX. chap. 1 and CXI. chap. 2 (q.v.).

2 *Qui sacerdos* (? *secundi ordinis* here) *vel levita* (= *diaconus*) *ordinandus est.*

3 *Pœnitentiam concedendo*, i.e. we have not finally excommunicated them, but, dealing leniently, we have given them opportunity of reinstating themselves in the peace of the Church, by going through a due course of penance (*satisfactio*). It is important to explain this clearly to those who, in the present day, are ignorant of the strict discipline of the early Church, and are liable to forget that penance was then a valuable means to repentance.

4 *Plebei.*

we pursue with the zeal of faith in the LORD those who are destroyers and destroyed: and with what severity we can bring to bear, cut them off from intercourse with sound minds, lest this pestilence spread much wider. Wherefore I exhort you, beloved, I beseech and warn you to use such watchful diligence as you ought and can employ in tracking them out, lest they find opportunity of concealment anywhere. For as he will have a due recompense of reward from GOD, who carries out what conduces to the health of the people committed to him; so before the LORD's judgment-seat no one will be able to excuse himself from a charge of carelessness who has not been willing to guard his people against the propagators of an impious misbelief. Dated 30 January, in the consulship of the illustrious Theodosius Augustus (18th time) and Albinus (444).

LETTER VIII.

THE ORDINANCE OF VALENTINIAN III. CONCERNING THE MANICHÆANS.

(The Manichæans are to be turned out of the army and the City, and to lose all their rights as citizens.)

LETTER IX.

TO DIOSCORUS, BISHOP OF ALEXANDRIA.

Leo, the bishop, to Dioscorus, bishop of Alexandria, greeting.

I. *The churches of Rome and Alexandria should be at one in everything.*

How much of the divine love we feel for you, beloved, you will be able to estimate from this, that we are anxious to establish your beginnings on a surer basis, lest anything should seem lacking to the perfection of your love, since your meritorious acts of spiritual grace, as we have proved, are already in your favour. Fatherly and brotherly conference, therefore, ought to be most grateful to you, holy brother, and received by you in the same spirit as you know it is offered by us. For you and we ought to be at one in thought and act, so that as we read[5], in us also there may be proved to be one heart and one mind. For since the most blessed Peter received the headship of the Apostles from the LORD, and the church of Rome still abides by His institutions, it is wicked to believe that His holy disciple Mark, who was the first to govern the church of Alexandria[6], formed his decrees on a different line of tradition: seeing that without doubt both disciple and master drew but one Spirit from the same fount of grace, and the ordained could not hand on aught else than what he had received from his ordainer. We do not therefore allow it that we should differ in anything, since we confess ourselves to be of one body and faith, nor that the institutions of the teacher should seem different to those of the taught.

II. *Fixed days should be observed for ordaining priests and deacons.*

That therefore which we know to have been very carefully observed by our fathers, we wish kept by you also, viz. that the ordination of priests or deacons should not be performed at random on any day: but after Saturday, the commencement of that night which precedes the dawn of the first day of the week should be chosen on which the sacred benediction should be bestowed on those who are to be consecrated, ordainer and ordained alike fasting. This observance will not be violated, if actually on the morning of the LORD's day it be celebrated without breaking the Saturday fast: for the beginning of the preceding night forms part of that period, and undoubtedly belongs to the day of resurrection as is clearly laid down with regard to the feast of Easter[7]. For besides the weight of custom which we know rests upon the Apostles' teaching, Holy Writ also makes this clear, because when the Apostles sent Paul and Barnabas at the bidding of the Holy Ghost to preach the gospel to the nations, they laid hands on them fasting and praying: that we may know with what devoutness both giver and receiver must be on their guard lest so blessed a sacrament should seem to be carelessly performed. And therefore you will piously and laudably follow Apostolic precedents if you yourself also maintain this form of ordaining priests throughout the churches over which the Lord has called you to preside: viz. that those who are to be consecrated should never receive the blessing except on the day of the Lord's resurrection, which is commonly held to begin on the evening of Saturday, and which has been so often hallowed in the mysterious dispensations of GOD that all the more notable institutions of the LORD were accomplished on that high day. On it the world took its beginning. On it through the resurrection of Christ death received its destruction, and life its commencement. On it the apostles take from the LORD's hands the trumpet of the gospel

5 Sc. in Acts iv. 32.

6 S. Mark, the evangelist and disciple of S. Peter, is the traditional founder of the church of Alexandria.

7 That is to say, the weekly resurrection festival (Sunday) begins with the vespers of the preceding evening: this is notably the case in the yearly festival of Easter at least in Western use.

which is to be preached to all nations, and receive the sacrament of regeneration[8] which they are to bear to the whole world. On it, as blessed John the Evangelist bears witness when all the disciples were gathered together in one place, and when, the doors being shut, the LORD entered to them, He breathed on them and said: "Receive the Holy Ghost: whose sins ye have remitted they are remitted to them: and whose ye have retained, they shall be retained[9]." On it lastly the Holy Spirit that had been promised to the Apostles by the LORD came: and so we know it to have been suggested and handed down by a kind of heavenly rule, that on that day we ought to celebrate the mysteries of the blessing of priests on which all these gracious gifts were conferred.

III. *The repetition of the Holy Eucharist on the great festivals is not undesirable.*

Again, that our usage may coincide at all points, we wish this thing also to be observed, viz. that when any of the greater festivals has brought together a larger congregation than usual, and too great a crowd of the faithful has assembled for one church[1] to hold them all at once, there should be no hesitation about repeating the oblation of the sacrifice: lest, if those only are admitted to this service who come first, those who flock in afterwards, should seem to be rejected: for it is fully in accordance with piety and reason, that as often as a fresh congregation has filled the church where service is going on, the sacrifice should be offered as a matter of course. Whereas a certain portion of the people must be deprived of their worship, if the custom of only one celebration[2] be kept, and only those who come early in the day can offer the sacrifice[3]. We admonish you, therefore, beloved, earnestly and affectionately that your carefulness also should not neglect what has become a part of our own usage on the pattern of our fathers' tradition, so that in all things we may agree together in our beliefs and in our performances. Consequently, we have given this letter to our son Possidonius, a presbyter, on his return, that he may bear it to you, brother; he has so often taken part in our ceremonials and ordinations, and has been sent to us so many times that he knows quite well what Apostolic authority we possess in all things. Dated 21 June (? 445).

LETTER X.

TO THE BISHOPS OF THE PROVINCE OF VIENNE. IN THE MATTER OF HILARY, BISHOP OF ARLES[4].

To the beloved brothers, the whole body of bishops of the province of Vienne, Leo, bishop of Rome.

I. *The solidarity of the Church built upon the rock of S. Peter must be everywhere maintained.*

Our LORD Jesus Christ, Saviour of mankind, instituted the observance of the Divine religion which He wished by the grace of GOD to shed its brightness upon all nations and all peoples in such a way that the Truth, which before was confined to the announcements of the Law and the Prophets, might through the Apostles' trumpet blast go out for the salvation of all men[5], as it is written: "Their sound has gone out into every land, and their words into the ends of the world[6]." But this mysterious function[7] the LORD wished to be indeed the concern of all the apostles, but in such a way that He has placed the principal charge on the blessed Peter, chief of all the Apostles[8]: and from him as from the Head wishes His gifts to flow to all the body: so that any one who dares to secede from Peter's solid rock may understand that he has no part or lot in the divine mystery. For He wished him who had been received into partnership in His undivided unity to be named what He Himself was, when He said: "Thou art Peter, and upon this rock I will build My Church[9]:" that the building of the eternal temple by the wondrous gift of GOD's grace might rest on Peter's solid rock: strengthening His Church so surely that neither could human rashness assail it nor the gates of hell prevail against it. But this most holy firmness of the rock, reared, as we have said, by the building hand of GOD, a man must wish to destroy in over-weaning

8 *Sacramentum regenerationis:* the reference in the first part of the sentence seems to be S. Mark xvi. 15, and here in the latter part to S. Matt. xxviii. 19, and both these records seem to refer to the same manifestation. S. Matthew says it was to "the eleven disciples" in Galilee, in "the mountain where Jesus had appointed them," that He gave the command, if indeed vv. 16-20 of the xxviiith chapter form one continuous narrative. The author of S. Mark xvi. 9-20 says it was to the eleven "as they sat at meat." Is it possible that Leo took ἀνακειμένοις to mean as they were partaking of the Holy Eucharist? if not, what countenance is there for his assertion of its being on the first day of the week?

9 S. John xx. 22, 23.

1 *Basilica*, q.v. in Smith's *Dict. of Christian Antiquities.*

2 *Missæ.*

3 It can hardly escape notice that the people here are distinctly said "to offer the sacrifice" in the person of their representative and mouthpiece, the priest. And this is the language and intention of all Liturgies (ancient and modern) of the Church.

4 Cf. Introduction, p. vi.

5 *Per Apostolicam tubam in salutem universitatis* (Gk. τῆς οἰκουμένης) *exiret*, cf. Letter IX. chap. ii. *apostoli a Domino prædicandi omnibus gentibus evangelii tubam sumunt.*

6 Ps. xix. 4.

7 *Huius muneris sacramentum*, his mind is running forward to his favourite *sacramentum*, that of Peter as the rock-man of the Church.

8 Cf. Letter XXVIII. chap. v. *a principali petra* (*B. Petrus*), *soliditatem et virtutis traxit et nominis, etc.:* also Cyprian *de unit. eccl.* chap. iv.

9 S. Matt. xvi. 18.

wickedness when he tries to break down its power, by favouring his own desires, and not following what he received from men of old: for he believes himself subject to no law, and held in check by no rules of GOD's ordinances, and breaks away, in his eagerness for novelty, from your use and ours, by adopting illegal practices, and letting what he ought to keep fall into abeyance.

II. *Hilary is disturbing the peace of the Church by his insubordination.*

But with the approval, as we believe, of GOD, and retaining towards you the fulness of our love which the Apostolic See always, as you remember, expends upon you, holy brethren, we are striving to correct these things by mature counsel, and to share with you the task of setting your churches in order, not by innovations but by restoration of the old; that we may persevere in the accustomed state which our fathers handed down to us, and please our GOD through the ministry of a good work by removing the scandals of disturbances. And so we would have you recollect, brethren, as we do, that the Apostolic See, such is the reverence in which it is held, has times out of number been referred to and consulted by the priests of your province as well as others, and in the various matters of appeal, as the old usage demanded, it has reversed or confirmed decisions: and in this way "the unity of the spirit in the bond of peace [1]" has been kept, and by the interchange of letters, our honourable proceedings have promoted a lasting affection: for "seeking not our own but the things of Christ [2]," we have been careful not to do despite to the dignity which GOD has given both to the churches and their priests. But this path which with our fathers has been always so well kept to and wisely maintained, Hilary has quitted, and is likely to disturb the position and agreement of the priests by his novel arrogance: desiring to subject you to his power in such a way as not to suffer himself to be subject to the blessed Apostle Peter, claiming for himself the ordinations of all the churches throughout the provinces of Gaul, and transferring to himself the dignity which is due to metropolitan priests; he diminishes even the reverence that is paid to the blessed Peter himself with his proud words: for not only was the power of loosing and binding given to Peter before the others, but also to Peter more especially was entrusted the care of feeding the sheep [3]. Yet any one who holds that the headship must be denied to Peter, cannot really diminish his dignity: but is puffed up with the breath of his pride, and plunges himself into the lowest depth.

III. *Celidonius has been restored to his bishopric, the charges against him having been found false.*

Accordingly the written record of our proceedings shows what action we have taken in the matter of Celidonius [4], the bishop, and what Hilary said in the presence and hearing of the aforesaid bishop. For when Hilary had no reasonable answer to give in the council of the holy priests, "the secrets of his heart [5]" gave vent to utterances such as no layman could make and no priest listen to. We were grieved, I acknowledge, brothers, and endeavoured to appease the tumult of his mind by patient treatment. For we did not wish to exasperate those wounds which he was inflicting on his soul by his insolent retorts, and strove rather to pacify him whom we had taken up as a brother, although it was he who was entangling himself by his replies, than to cause him pain by our remarks. Celidonius, the bishop, was therefore acquitted, for he had proved himself wrongfully deposed from the priesthood, by the clear replies of his witnesses made in his own presence: so that Hilary, who remained with us, had no opposition to offer. The judgment, therefore, was rescinded, which was brought forward and read to the effect that, as the husband of a widow [6], he could not hold the priesthood. Now this rule we, maintaining the legal constitutions [7], have wished scrupulously adhered to, not only in respect of priests but also of clergy of the lower ranks: that those who have contracted such a marriage, or those who are proved not to be the husbands of only one wife contrary to the apostle's discipline, should not be suffered to enter the sacred service [8]. But though we decree that those, whom their own acts condemn, must either not be admitted at all, or, if they have, must be removed, so those who are falsely so accused we are bound to clear after examination held, and not allow to lose their office. For the sentence pronounced would have remained against him, if the truth of the charge had been proved. And so Celidonius, our fellow-bishop, was restored to his church and to that dignity which he ought not to have

1 Eph. iv. 3.
2 Phil. ii. 21.
3 *Cui cum præ* (Quesnel conj. *pro*) *cæteris solvendi et ligandi tradita sit potestas, pascendarum tamen ovium cura specialius mandata est.* Cf. S. John xxi. 15—17.

4 Celidonius was probably either bishop of Vienne or of Vesontis (Besançon): see Perthel, p. 25.
5 Quesnel well refers this phrase to 1 Cor. xiv. 25.
6 Cf. Letter IV. chap. iii.
7 *Servantes legalia constituta*, these are taken to be not so much the canons of the Church as the provisions of the Mosaic Law, e.g. Lev. xxi. 14; Ezek. xliv. 22.
8 *Militiam* (lit. military service).

lost, as the course of our proceedings, and the sentence which was pronounced by us after holding the inquiry testifies.

IV. *Hilary's treatment of Projectus does not redound to his credit.*

When this business was so concluded, the complaint of our brother and fellow-bishop, Projectus[9], next came before us: who addressed us in a tearful and piteous letter, about the ordaining of a bishop over his head. A letter was also brought to us from his own fellow-citizens, corroborated by a great many individual signatures, and full of the most unpleasant complaints against Hilary: to the effect that Projectus, their bishop, was not allowed to be ill, but his priesthood had been transferred to another without their knowledge, and the heir brought into possession by Hilary, the intruder, as if to fill up a vacancy, though the possessor was still alive[1]. We should like to hear what you, brothers, think on the point: although we ought not to entertain any doubt about your feelings, when you picture to yourselves a brother lying on a sick-bed and tortured, not so much by his bodily weakness as by pains of another kind. What hope in life is left a man who is visited with despair about his priesthood, whilst another is set up in his place? Hilary gives a clear proof of his gentle heart when he believed that the tardiness of a brother's death is but a hindrance to his own ambitious designs. For, as far as in him lay, he quenched the light for him; he robbed him of life by setting up another in his room, and thus causing him such pain as to hinder his recovery. And supposing that his brother's passage from this world was brief, but after the common course of men, what does Hilary seek for himself in another's province, and why does he claim that which none of his predecessors before Patroclus possessed? whereas that very position which seemed to have been temporarily granted to Patroclus by the Apostolic See was afterwards withdrawn by a wiser decision[2]. At least the wishes of the citizens should have been waited for, and the testimony of the people[3]: the opinion of those held in honour should have been asked, and the choice of the clergy—things which those who know the rules of the fathers are wont to observe in the ordination of priests: that the rule of the Apostle's authority might in all things be kept, which enjoins that one who is to be the priest of a church should be fortified, not only by the attestation of the faithful but also by the testimony of "those who are without[4]," and that no occasion for offence be left, when, in peace and in God-pleasing harmony with the full approval of all, one who will be a teacher of peace is ordained.

V. *Hilary's action was very reprehensible throughout, and we have restored Projectus.*

But Hilary came upon them unawares and departed no less suddenly, accomplishing many journeys with great speed, as we have ascertained, and traversing distant provinces with such haste that he seems to have coveted a reputation for the swiftness of a courier rather than for the sobriety of a priest[5]. For these are the words of the citizens in the letter that has been addressed to us:—"He departed before we knew he had come." This is not to return but to flee, not to exercise a shepherd's wholesome care, but to employ the violence of a thief and a robber, as saith the Lord: "he that entereth not by the door into the sheepfold[6], but climbeth up some other way, is a thief and a robber." Hilary, therefore, was anxious not so much to consecrate a bishop as to kill him who was sick, and to mislead the man whom he set over his head by wrongful ordination. We, however, have done what, as God is our Judge, we believe you will approve: after holding counsel with all the brethren we have decreed that the wrongfully ordained man should be deposed and the Bishop Projectus abide in his priesthood: with the further provision that when any of our brethren in whatsoever province shall decease, he who has been agreed upon to be metropolitan of that province shall claim for himself the ordination of his successor.

These two matters, as we see, have been settled, though there are many other points in them which seem to have violated the principles of the Church, and ought to be visited with just censure and judgment. But we cannot linger on them any further, for we are called off to other matters on which we must carefully confer with you, holy brethren.

---

9 *Projectus* was perhaps a bishop of the province of Gallia Narbonensis I.: Perthel, p. 27.

1 *Quod Projecto episcopo suo ægrotare liberum non fuisset, eiusque sacerdotium in alium præter suam notitiam esse translatum, et tamquam in vacuam possessionem ab Hilario pervasore hæredem viventis inductum.* The construction is changed from *quod . . . . fuisset*, to the ordinary accus. and infin.

2 Patroclus had been Bishop of Arles *circ.* 416, and the then Bishop of Rome, Zosimus, had granted him metropolitan rights over the provinces of S.E. Gaul, which did not gain the acceptance of the other chief bishops in the district, and Boniface I. (Ep. 12), in 422, seems to have withdrawn the rights granted by Zosimus (Schaff, 1, p. 297).

3 *Civium: populorum.* The former are apparently called lower down *fidelium*, and the latter *qui foris sunt.*

4 1 Tim. iii. 17.

5 *Gloriam de scurrili velocitate potius quam de sacerdotali moderatione captasse.*

6 *In* cortem *ovium*: the low Latin word (*cors*) is in the Vulgate changed to *ovile.*

VI. *Hilary's practice of using armed violence must be suppressed.*

A band of soldiers, as we have learnt, follows the priest through the provinces and helps him who relies upon their armed support in turbulently invading churches, which have lost their own priests. Before this court[7] are dragged for ordination men who are quite unknown to the cities over which they are to be set. For as one who is well known and approved is sought out in peace, so must one who is unknown, when brought forward, be established by violence. I beg and entreat and beseech you in God's name prevent such things, brethren, and remove all occasion for discord from your provinces. At all events we acquit ourselves before God in beseeching you not to allow this to proceed further. In peace and quietness should they be asked for who are to be priests. The consent of the clergy, the testimony of those held in honour, the approval of the orders and the laity should be required[8]. He who is to govern all, should be chosen by all[9]. As we said before, each metropolitan should keep in his own hands the ordinations that occur in his own province, acting in concert with those who precede the rest in seniority of priesthood, a privilege restored to him through us. No man should claim for himself another's rights. Each should keep within his own limits and boundaries, and should understand that he cannot pass on to another a privilege that belongs to himself. But if any one neglecting the Apostle's prohibitions and paying too much heed to personal favour, wishes to give up his precedence, thinking he can pass his rights on to another, not he to whom he has yielded, but he who ranks before the rest of the priests within the province in episcopal seniority, should claim to himself the power of ordaining. The ordination should be performed not at random but on the proper day: and it should be known that any one who has not been ordained on the evening of Saturday, which precedes the dawn of the first day of the week[1], or actually on the Lord's day cannot be sure of his status. For our forefathers judged the day of the Lord's resurrection[2] as alone worthy of the honour of being the occasion on which those who are to be made priests are given to God.

VII. *Hilary is deposed not only from his usurped jurisdiction, but also from what of right belongs to him, and is restricted to his own single bishopric.*

Let each province be content with its own councils, and let not Hilary dare to summon synodal meetings besides, and by his interference disturb the judgments of the Lord's priests. And let him know that he is not only deposed from another's rights, but also deprived of his power over the province of Vienne which he had wrongfully assumed. For it is but fair, brethren, that the ordinances of antiquity should be restored, seeing that he who claimed for himself the ordinations of a province for which he was not responsible, has been shown in a similar way in the present case also to have acted so that, as he has on more than one occasion brought on himself sentence of condemnation by his rash and insolent words, he may now be kept by our command in accordance with the clemency of the Apostolic See[3] to the priesthood of his own city alone. He is not to be present then at any ordination: he is not to ordain because, conscious of his deserts, when he was required to answer for his action, he trusted to make good his escape by disgraceful flight, and has put himself out of Apostolic communion, of which he did not deserve to be a partaker[4]: and we believe this was by God's providence, who brought him to our court, though we did not expect him, and caused him to retire by stealth in the midst of holding the inquiry, that he should not be a partner in our communion[5].

VIII. *Excommunication should be inflicted only on those who are guilty of some great crime, and even then not hastily.*

No Christian should lightly be denied communion[6], nor should that be done at the will of an angry priest which the judge's mind ought to a certain extent unwillingly and regretfully to carry out for the punishment of a great crime. For we have ascertained that some have been cut off from the grace of communion for trivial deeds and words, and that the soul for which Christ's blood was shed has been exposed to the devil's attacks and wounded, disarmed, so to say, and stript of all

7 *Ante hoc officium.*

8 Cf. Cypr. Ep. lv. cap. vii., *factus est Cornelius episcopus de Dei et Christi eius iudicio, de clericorum pæne omnium testimonio, de plebis, quæ tunc adfuit, suffragio et sacerdotum antiquorum et bonorum virorum collegio.*

9 Quesnel appositely quotes Pliny (Paneg. Traiani) *imperaturus omnibus eligi debet ex omnibus.*

1 *Quod lucescit in prima sabbati*; the phrase is repeated from Letter IX., chap. ii., to which refer for the whole passage.

2 Viz., Sunday.

3 *Pro apostolicæ sedis pietate*, or "as loyalty to the Apostolic See demands."

4 This does not mean that Hilary is excommunicated, but that he is to have no share in episcopal privileges, as a successor of the apostles.

5 These words of course refer to Hilary's journey on foot to Rome, and his subsequent escape from something very much like prison: see Introduction, p. vi.: for his degradation, cf. Letter XII., chap. ix., where a similar punishment is enacted.

6 Here, no doubt, excommunication pure and simple is meant. Cf. note 4, *supr.*

defence by the infliction of so savage a punishment as to fall an easy prey to him. Of course if ever a case has arisen of such a kind as in due proportion to the nature of the crime committed to deprive a man of communion, he only who is involved in the accusation must be subjected to punishment: and he who is not shown to be a partner in its commission ought not to share in the penalty. But what wonder that one who is wont to exult over the condemnation of priests, should show himself in the same light towards laymen.

IX. *Leontius is appointed in Hilary's room.*

Wherefore, because our desire seems very different to this (for we are anxious that the settled state of all the Churches and the harmony of the priests should be maintained,) exhorting you to unity in the bond of love, we both entreat, and consistently with our affection admonish you, in the interests of your peace and dignity, to keep what has been decreed by us at the inspiration of God and the most blessed Apostle Peter, after sifting and testing all the matters at issue, being assured that what we are known to have decided in this way is not so much to our own advantage as to yours. For we are not keeping in our own hands the ordinations of your provinces, as perhaps Hilary, with his usual untruthfulness, may suggest in order to mislead your minds, holy brethren: but in our anxiety we are claiming for you that no further innovations should be allowed, and that for the future no opportunity should be given for the usurper to infringe your privileges. For we acknowledge that it can only redound to our credit, if the diligence of the Apostolic See be kept unimpaired among you, and if in our maintenance of Apostolic discipline we do not allow what belongs to your position to fall to the ground through unscrupulous aggressions. And since seniority is always to be respected, we wish Leontius[7], our brother and fellow-bishop, a priest well approved among you, to be promoted to this dignity, if it please you that without his consent no further council be summoned by you, holy brethren, and that he may be honoured by you all as his age and good fame demands, the metropolitans being secured in their own dignity and rights. For it is but fair, and no injury seems to accrue to any of the brethren, if those who come first in seniority of the priesthood should, as their age deserves, have deference paid to them by the rest of the priests in their own provinces. God keep you safe, beloved brethren.

LETTER XI.

An Ordinance of Valentinianus III.

(Confirming Leo's sentence upon Hilary.)

LETTER XII.

Leo, bishop of the city of Rome, to all the bishops of Mauritania Cæsariensis in Africa greeting in the Lord.

I. *The disorderly appointments of bishops which have been made in the province are reprehensible.*

Inasmuch as the frequent accounts of those who visited us made mention of certain unlawful practices among you with regard to the ordination of priests, the demands of religion required that we should strive to arrive at the exact state of the case in accordance with that solicitude which by the Divine command we bestow on the whole Church: and so we delegated the charge of this to our brother and fellow-priest, Potentius. who was setting out from us: and who, according to what we wrote and addressed to you by him, was to make inquiry as to the facts about the bishops whose election was said to be faulty, and to report everything faithfully to us. Wherefore, because the same Potentius has most fully disclosed all to our knowledge, and has by his truthful account made clear to us, under what and what manner of governors some of Christ's congregations are placed in certain parts of the province of (Mauritania) Cæsariensis, we have found it necessary to open out the grief wherewith our hearts are vexed for the dangers of the Lord's flocks, by sending this letter also to you beloved: for we are surprised that either the over-bearing conduct of intriguers or the rioting of the people had so much weight with you in a time of disorder, that the chief pastorate and governance of the Church was handed over to the unworthiest persons, and such as were farthest removed from the priestly standard. This is not to consult but harm the peoples' interests: and not to enforce discipline but to increase differences. For the integrity of the rulers is the safeguard of those who are under them: and where there is complete obedience, there the form of doctrine is sound. But an appointment which has either been made by sedition or seized by intrigue, even though it offend not in morals or in practice, is nevertheless pernicious from the mere example of its beginning: and it is hard for

7 Leontius seems to have had little but his age to recommend him for this promotion: the name of his bishopric is unknown: and the weakness of the appointment may, I think, be gathered from Leo's insisting so strongly on the principle of seniority both here and in chap. vi. above.

things to be carried to a good issue which were started with a bad beginning.

II. *In no case ought bishops to be ordained hastily.*

But if in every grade of the Church great forethought and knowledge has to be employed, lest there be any thing disorderly or out of place[8] in the house of the LORD: how much more carefully must we strive to prevent mistakes in the election of him who is set over all the grades? For the peace and order of the LORD's whole household will be shaken, if what is required in the body be not found in the head. Where is that precept of the blessed Apostle Paul uttered through the Spirit of GOD, whereby in the person of Timothy the whole number of Christ's priests are instructed, and to each one of us is said: "Lay hands hastily on no one, and do not share in other men's sins[9]?" What is to lay on hands hastily but to confer the priestly dignity on unproved men before the proper age[1], before there has been time to test them, before they have deserved it by their obedience, before they have been tried by discipline? And what is to share in other men's sins but for the ordainer to become such as is he who ought not to have been ordained by him? For just as a man stores up for himself the fruit of his good work, if he maintains a right judgment in choosing a priest: so one who receives an unworthy priest into the number of his colleagues, inflicts grievous loss upon himself. We must not then pass over in the case of any one that which is laid down in the general ordinances: nor is that advancement to be reckoned lawful which has been made contrary to the precepts of GOD's law.

III. *The Apostolic precept about the marriage of the clergy based upon the marriage of Christ with the Church of which it is a figure.*

For as the Apostle says that among other rules for election he shall be ordained bishop who is known to have been or to be "the husband of one wife," this command was always held so sacred that the same condition was understood as necessary to be observed even in the wife[2] of the priest-elect: lest she should happen to have been married to another man before she entered into wedlock with him, even though he himself had had no other wife. Who then would dare to allow this injury to be perpetrated upon so great a sacrament[3], seeing that this great and venerable mystery is not without the support of the statutes of GOD's law as well, whereby it is clearly laid down that a priest is to marry a virgin, and that she who is to be the wife of a priest[4] is not to know another husband? For even then in the priests was prefigured the Spiritual marriage of Christ and His Church: so that since "the man is the head of the woman[5]," the spouse of the Word may learn to know no other man but Christ, who did rightly choose her only, loves her only, and takes none but her into His alliance. If then even in the Old Testament this kind of marriage among priests is adhered to, how much more ought we who are placed under the grace of the Gospel to conform to the Apostle's precepts: so that though a man be found endowed with good character, and furnished with holy works, he may nevertheless in no wise ascend either to the grade of deacon, or the dignity of the presbytery, or to the highest rank of the bishopric, if it has been spread abroad either that he himself is not the husband of one wife, or that his wife is not the wife of one husband.

IV. *Premature promotions are to be avoided.*

But when the Apostle warns and says: "and let these also first be proved, and so let them minister[6]," what else do we think must be understood but that in these promotions we should consider not only the chastity of their marriages, but also the deserts of their labours, lest the pastoral office be entrusted to men who are either fresh from baptism, or suddenly diverted from worldly pursuits? for through all the ranks of the Christian army in the matter of promotions it ought to be considered whether a man can manage a greater charge. Rightly did the venerable opinions of the blessed Fathers in speaking of the election of priests reckon those men fit for the administration of sacred things who had been slowly advanced through the various grades of office, and had given such good proof of themselves therein that in each one of them the character of their practices bore witness to their lives[7]. For

---

8 *Nihil sit inordinatum nihilque præposterum*: the two words are well chosen (as usual), and bearing a distinct meaning: the former expressing "disorder" in the sense of want of the divine commission, the latter, "disorder" in the sense of choosing the younger over the old, the inferior over the superior, &c.; the same two epithets occur in Lett. XIX., chap. i.

9 1 Tim. v. 22.

1 *Ante ætatem maturitatis.* The Council of Carthage (A.D. 397), c. 4, fixed the downward limit for deacons at 25, and for priests at 30: and we may presume that that was the general rule in Leo's time, for we find the same ages ordained afterwards in the *Novellæ* of Justinian (535-565) and elsewhere.

2 Cf. Letter IV., chap. ii., and elsewhere.

3 No one will by this time be surprised to find Leo calling Sacred Orders either a *sacramentum*, as here, or a *mysterium*, as in the next sentence: the two terms are indeed in his usage almost equivalents.

4 Lev. xxi. 13.

5 Eph. v. 23.

6 1 Tim. iii. 10.

7 The shorter edition of this letter, which is extant, gives this

if it is improper to attain to the world's dignities without the help of time and without the merit of having toiled, and if the seeking of office is branded unless it be supported by proofs of uprightness, how diligently and how carefully ought the dispensing of divine duties and heavenly dignities to be carried out, lest in aught the apostolic and canonical decrees be violated, and the ruling of the LORD's Church be committed to men who being ignorant of the lawful constitutions and devoid of all humility wish not to rise from the lowest grade, but to begin with the highest: for it is extremely unfair and preposterous that the inexpert should be preferred to the expert, the young to the old, the raw recruits to those who have seen much service. In a great house, indeed, as the Apostle explains[8], there must needs be divers vessels, some of gold and of silver, and some of wood and of earth: but their purpose varies with the quality of their material, and the use of the precious and of the cheap kinds is not the same. For everything will be in disorder if the earthen ware be preferred to the golden, or the wooden to the silver. And as the wooden or earthen vessels are a figure of those men who are hitherto conspicuous for no virtues; so in the golden or silver vessels they no doubt are represented who, having passed through the fire of long experience, and through the furnace of protracted toil, have deserved to be tried gold and pure silver. And if such men get no reward for their devotion, all the discipline of the Church is loosened, all order is disturbed, while men who have undergone no service obtain undeserved preferment by the wrongful choice of the electing body.

V. *He distinguishes between laymen who have been raised to the bishoprics and digamous clerks, forgiving the former and not the latter.*

Since then either the eager wishes of the people or the intrigues of the ambitious have had so much weight among you that we understand not only laymen, but even husbands of second wives or widows have been promoted to the pastoral office, are there not the clearest reasons for requiring that the churches in which such things have been done should be cleansed by a severer judgment than usual, and that not only the rulers themselves, but also those who ordained them should receive condign punishment? But there stand on our one hand the gentleness of mercy, on our other the strictness of justice. And because "all the paths of the LORD are loving-kindness and truth[9]," we are forced according to our loyalty to the Apostolic See so to moderate our opinion as to weigh men's misdeeds in the balance (for of course they are not all of one measure), and to reckon some as to a certain extent[1] pardonable, but others as altogether to be repressed. For they who have either entered into second marriages or joined themselves in wedlock with widows are not allowed to hold the priesthood, either by the apostolic or legal authority: and much more is this the case with him who, as it was reported to us, is the husband of two wives at once, or him who being divorced by his wife is said to have married another, that is, supposing these charges are in your judgment proved. But the rest, whose preferment only so far incurs blame that they have been chosen to the episcopal function from among the laity, and are not culpable in the matter of their wives, we allow to retain the priesthood upon which they have entered, without prejudice to the statutes of the Apostolic See, and without breaking the rules of the blessed Fathers, whose wholesome ordinance it is that no layman, whatever amount of support he may receive, shall ascend to the first, second, or third rank in the Church until he reach that position by the legitimate steps[2]. For what we now suffer to be to a certain extent[3] venial, cannot hereafter pass unpunished, if any one perpetrates what we altogether forbid: because the forgiveness of a sin does not grant a licence to do wrong, nor will it be right to repeat an offence with impunity which has partly[4] been condoned.

VI. *Donatus, a converted Novatian, and Maximus, an ex-Donatist, are retained in their episcopal office.*

Donatus of Salacia, who, as we learn, has been converted from the Novatians[5] with his people, we wish to preside over the LORD's flock, on condition that he remembers he must send a certificate of his faith to us, in which

sentence in a very different form: the qualifications are much more exactly defined, e.g., bishops are to have spent their lives in orders *a puerilibus exordiis usque ad provectiores annos*. I think Quesnel is right in considering this a later version and alteration the better to inculcate the usage of the Church. For although no doubt persons were often mere boys [Readers (*lectores*) for instance: see Bright's note 46] when they entered minor orders, yet the fact that one was an adult layman before taking orders could not *ipso facto* have precluded a man from becoming bishop, however desirable the rule and general principle might be: in fact Cyprian at least is evidence to the contrary.

8 Sc. 2 Tim. ii. 20.

9 Ps. xxv. 10.

1 *Utcumque.*

2 *Per legitima augmenta*, cf. n. 7 above. This passage makes it clear what is there required is not the *puerilia exordia* of the shorter edition of this letter, but the *multum tempus* of this longer edition.

3 *Utcumque* again.

4 *Aliqua ratione.*

5 In the case of these two noted African schisms it is hardly necessary to do more than refer the reader to Smith's or any other standard dictionary

he not only condemns the error of the Novatian dogma, but also unreservedly confesses the catholic truth. Maximus, also, although he was culpably ordained when a layman, yet if he is now no longer a Donatist, and has abjured the spirit of schismatic depravity, we do not depose from his episcopal dignity, which he has obtained irregularly, on condition that he declare himself a catholic by drawing up a certificate for us.

VII. *The case of Aggarus and Tyberianus (ordained with tumult) is referred to the bishops.*

But concerning Aggarus and Tyberianus, whose case is different from the others who were ordained from among the laity, in this that their ordination is reported to have been accompanied by fierce riots and savage disturbances, we have entrusted the whole matter to your judgment, that relying upon your investigation of the case, we may know what to decide about them.

VIII. *Maidens who have suffered violence are not to compare themselves with others.*

Those handmaids of God who have lost their chastity by the violence of barbarians, will be more praiseworthy in their humility and shame-fastness, if they do not venture to compare themselves to undefiled virgins. For although every sin springs from the desire, and the will may have remained unconquered and unpolluted by the fall of the flesh, still this will be less to their detriment, if they grieve over losing even in the body what they did not lose in spirit.

IX. *These injunctions to be carried out without contentiousness.*

And so now that you see yourselves, beloved, fully instructed through David, our brother and fellow-bishop, who is approved to us both by his personal character and his priestly worth, on [nearly][6] all the points which our brother Potentius' account contained, it remains, brothers, that you receive our healthful exhortations harmoniously, and that doing nothing in rivalry, but acting unanimously with entire devotion and zeal, you obey the constitution of God and His Apostles, and in nothing suffer the well-considered decrees of the canons to be violated. For what we from the consideration of certain reasons have now relaxed must henceforward be guarded by the ancient rules, lest, what we have on this occasion with merciful lenity conceded, we may hereafter have to visit with condign punishment[7], acting with special and direct vigour against those who in ordaining bishops have neglected the statutes of the holy fathers, and have consecrated men whom they ought to have rejected. Wherefore if any bishops have consecrated such an one priest as ought not to be, even though in some measure they have escaped any loss of their personal dignity, yet they shall have no further right of ordination, nor shall ever be present at that sacrament which, neglecting the judgment of God, they have improperly conferred.

X. *The appointment of bishops over too small places is inexpedient and must be discontinued.*

That of course which pertains to the priestly dignity we wish to be observed in common with all the statutes of the canons, viz., that bishops be not consecrated in any place nor in any hamlet[8], nor where they have not been consecrated before; for where the flocks are small and the congregations small, the care of the presbyters may suffice, whereas the episcopal authority ought to preside only over larger flocks and more crowded cities, lest contrary to the divinely-inspired decrees of the holy Fathers the priestly office be assigned over villages and rural estates[9] or obscure and thinly-populated townships, and the position of honour, to which only the more important charges should be given, be held cheap from the very number of those that hold it. And this bishop Restitutus has reported to have been done in his own diocese, and he has with good reason requested that when the bishops of those places where they ought not to have been ordained die in the natural course, the places themselves should revert to the jurisdiction of the same prelate to whom they formerly belonged and were attached. It is indeed useless for the priestly dignity to be diminished by the superfluous multiplications of the office through the inconsiderate complaisance of the ordainer.

XI. *Virgins violated against their will are to be treated as somewhat different to the others, but not to be denied Communion.*

Now concerning those who, having made a holy vow of virginity [as we said above, chap. viii.], have suffered the violence of barbarians, and have lost their spotless purity not in spirit but in body, we consider such mode-

6 *Fere* here added probably to account for the long tail of extraneous or repeated matter tacked on to the letter.

7 Here the shorter edition of the letter breaks off, and there are certainly difficulties in considering that the long coda of repetitions and fresh matter here attached formed part of the original draft of the letter. Is it possible that two letters (the one later than the other) have been welded into one?

8 *Castellis*. Cf. Liv. xxi. chaps. 33, 34, where the word is used of the Alpine villages. In the Vulgate it represents the Gk. κώμη (e.g. S. Mark vi. 6: S. Luke v. 17.)

9 *Possessionibus*.

ration ought to be observed that they should be neither degraded to the rank of widows[1] nor yet reckoned in the number of holy and undefiled virgins: yet, if they persevere in the virgin life, and in heart and mind guard the reality of chastity, participation in the sacraments is not to be denied them, because it is unfair that they should be accused or branded for what their wishes did not surrender, but was stolen by the violence of foes.

XII. *The case of Lupicinus is in part dealt with and in part referred to them.*

The case also of bishop Lupicinus[2] we order to be heard there, but at his urgent and frequent entreaties we have restored him to communion for this reason, that, as he had appealed to our judgment, we saw that while the matter was pending he had been undeservedly suspended from communion. Moreover there is this also in addition, that it was clearly rash to ordain one over his head who ought not to have been ordained until Lupicinus, having been placed before you or convicted, or having at least confessed, had opportunity to submit to a just sentence, so that, according to the requirements of ecclesiastical discipline, he who was consecrated might receive his vacant place.

XIII. *All disputes to be dealt with on the spot first and then referred to the Apostolic See.*

But whenever other cases arise which concern the state of the Church and the harmony of priests, we wish them to be first sifted by yourselves in the fear of the LORD, and a full account of all matters settled or needing settlement sent to us, that those things which have been properly and reasonably decided, according to the usage of the Church, may receive our corroborative sanction also. Dated 10th August.

LETTER XIII.

TO THE METROPOLITAN BISHOPS IN THE PROVINCES OF ILLYRICUM.

Leo congratulates them on accepting the authority of Anastasius over them (given in Lett. IV.).

[1] Cyprian (*de hab. Virg.*) speaks of women who have lost their virginity by their own fault as *viduæ antequam nuptæ*, and S. Jerome, using the same expression (Lett. to Eustochius on the preservation of Virginity), implies that they very often dressed like widows (*plerasque viduas antequam nuptas infelicem conscientiam mentita tantum veste protegere*): this will account for Leo's here providing that these unhappy women are not *deiici in viduarum gradum*. Ball.

[2] The case of Lupicinus seems somewhat similar to that of Projectus in Lett. X., chap. iv., and was similarly referred to local experts.

LETTER XIV.

TO ANASTASIUS, BISHOP OF THESSALONICA.

Leo, bishop of the City of Rome, to Anastasius, bishop of Thessalonica.

I. *Prefatory.*

If with true reasoning you perceived all that has been committed to you, brother, by the blessed apostle Peter's authority, and what has also been entrusted to you by our favour, and would weigh it fairly, we should be able greatly to rejoice at your zealous discharge of the responsibility imposed on you[3].

II. *Anastasius is taxed with exceeding the limits of his vicariate, especially in his violent and unworthy treatment of Atticus.*

Seeing that, as my predecessors acted towards yours, so too I, following their example, have delegated my authority to you[4], beloved: so that you, imitating our gentleness, might assist us in the care which we owe primarily to all the churches by Divine institution, and might to a certain extent make up for our personal presence in visiting those provinces which are far off from us: for it would be easy for you by regular and well-timed inspection to tell what and in what cases you could either, by your own influence, settle or reserve for our judgment. For as it was free for you to suspend the more important matters and the harder issues while you awaited our opinion, there was no reason nor necessity for you to go out of your way to decide what was beyond your powers. For you have numerous written warnings of ours in which we have often instructed you to be temperate in all your actions: that with loving exhortations you might provoke the churches of Christ committed to you to healthy obedience. Because, although as a rule there exist among careless or slothful brethren things which demand a strong hand in rectifying them; yet the correction ought to be so applied as ever to keep love inviolate. Wherefore also it is that the blessed Apostle Paul, in instructing Timothy upon the ruling of the Church, says: "an elder rebuke not, but intreat him as a father: the young men as brethren: old women as mothers: young women as sisters in all purity[5]." And if this moderation is due by the Apostle's precept to all and any of the lower members, how much more is it to be paid without offence to our brethren and

[3] *De iniunctæ tibi sollicitudinis devotione* (an obscure expression).

[4] See Letter IV., where it will be remembered the appointment of Anastasius, as Vicar of Illyricum, was made.

[5] 1 Tim. v. 1, 2.

fellow-bishops? in order that although things sometimes happen which have to be reprimanded in the persons of priests, yet kindness may have more effect on those who are to be corrected than severity: exhortation than perturbation: love than power. But they who "seek their own, not the things which are Jesus Christ's[6]," easily depart from this law, and finding pleasure rather in domineering over their subjects than in consulting their interests, are swoln with the pride of their position, and thus what was provided to secure harmony ministers to mischief. That we are obliged to speak thus causes us no small grief. For I feel myself in a certain measure drawn into blame, on discovering you to have so immoderately departed from the rules handed down to you. If you were careless of your own reputation, you ought at least to have spared my good name: lest what only your own mind prompted should seem done with our approval. Do but read, brother, our pages with care, and peruse all the letters sent by holders of the Apostolic See to your predecessors, and you will find injunctions either from me or from my predecessors on that in which we learn you have presumed.

For there has come to us our brother Atticus, the metropolitan[7] bishop of Old Epirus, with the bishops of his province, and with tearful pleading has complained of the undeserved contumely he has suffered, in the presence of your own deacons who, by giving no contradiction to these woeful complaints, showed that what was impressed upon us did not want for truth. We read also in your letter, which those same deacons of yours brought, that brother Atticus had come to Thessalonica, and that he had also sealed his agreement in a written profession, so that we could not but understand concerning him that it was of his own will and free devotion that he had come, and that he had composed the statement of his promise of obedience, although in the very mention of this statement a sign of injury was betrayed. For it was not necessary that he should be bound in writing, who was already proving his obedience by the very dutifulness of his voluntary coming. Wherefore these words in your letter bore witness to the bewailings of the aforesaid, and through his outspoken account that which had been passed over in silence is laid bare, namely that the Præfecture of Illyricum had been approached, and the most exalted functionary among the potentates of the world[8] had been set in motion to expose an innocent prelate: so that a company was sent to carry out the aweful deed who were to enlist all the public servants in giving effect to their orders, and from the church's holy sanctuary charged with no crime, or at best a false one, was dragged a priest, to whom no truce was granted in consideration of his grievous ill-health or the cruel winter weather: but he was forced to take a journey full of hardships and dangers through the pathless snows. And this was a task of such toil and peril that some of those who accompanied the bishop are said to have succumbed[9].

I am quite dumb-founded, beloved brother, yea and I am also sore grieved that you brought yourself to be so savagely and violently moved against one about whom you had laid no further information than that when summoned to appear he put off and excused himself on the grounds of illness; especially when, even if he deserved any such treatment, you should have waited till I had replied to your consulting letter. But, as I perceive, you thought too well of my habits, and most truly foresaw how fair-minded[1] an answer I was likely to make to preserve harmony among priests: and therefore you made haste to carry out your movements without concealment, lest when you had received the letter of our forbearance dictating another course, you should have no licence to do that which is done. Or perhaps some crime had reached your ears, and metropolitan[2] bishop that you are, the weight of some new charge pressed you hard? But that this is not consistent with the fact, you yourself make certain by laying nothing against him. Yet even if he had committed some grave and intolerable misdemeanour, you should have waited for our opinion: so as to arrive at no decision by yourself until you knew our pleasure. For we made you our deputy, beloved, on the understanding that you were engaged to share our responsibility, not to take plenary powers on yourself. Wherefore as what you bestow a pious care on delights us much, so your wrongful acts grieve us sorely. And after experience in many cases we must show greater foresight, and use more diligent precaution: to the end that through the spirit of love and peace all matter of offence may be removed from the LORD's churches,

6 Phil. ii. 21.

7 Some for *metropolitanus* here read *Nicopolitanus*, Bishop of Nicopolis, the metropolitan see of old Epirus. Quesnel.

8 The language is, I think, intentionally exaggerated and high-flown: *parturiunt montes nascetur ridiculus mus.*

9 Anastasius seems to have arraigned Atticus before the civil court of the Prefect of Illyricum: he sent his apparitors, who violently dragged him out of the church, and brought him in mid-winter across country to be tried.

1 The word is *civilia*, in which Brissonius thinks he sees an allusion either to the opposition between *civil* law and *prætor's* law (to which Anastasius had appealed), or else to the technical meaning of the word in jurisprudence as equivalent to 'legitimate' or 'fair.' The latter is more likely.

2 Quesnel here accepts *Nicopolitanum* instead of *metropolitanum* (see n. 7 above), but with little reason.

which we have commended to you: the pre-eminence of your bishopric being retained in the provinces, but all your usurping excesses being shorn off.

III. *The rights of the metropolitans under the vicariate of Anastasius are to be observed.*

Therefore according to the canons of the holy Fathers, which are framed by the spirit of GOD and hallowed by the whole world's reverence, we decree that the metropolitan bishops of each province over which your care, brother, extends by our delegacy, shall keep untouched the rights of their position which have been handed down to them from olden times: but on condition that they do not depart from the existing regulations by any carelessness or arrogance.

IV. *The negative qualifications of a bishop determined.*

In cities whose governors[3] have died let this form be observed in filling up their place: he, who is to be ordained, even though his good life be not attested, shall be not a layman, not a neophyte, nor yet the husband of a second wife, or one who, though he has or has had but one, married a widow. For the choosing of priests is of such surpassing importance that things which in other members of the Church are not blame-worthy, are yet held unlawful in them.

V. *Continence is required even in sub deacons.*

For although they who are not within the ranks of the clergy are free to take pleasure in the companionship of wedlock and the procreation of children, yet for the exhibiting of the purity of complete continence, even subdeacons are not allowed carnal marriage: that "both those that have, may be as though they had not[4]," and those who have not, may remain single. But if in this order, which is the fourth from the Head[5], this is worthy to be observed, how much more is it to be kept in the first, or second, or third, lest any one be reckoned fit for either the deacon's duties or the presbyter's honourable position, or the bishop's pre-eminence, who is discovered not yet to have bridled his uxorious desires.

VI. *The election of a bishop must proceed by the wishes of the clergy and people.*

When therefore the choice of the chief priest is taken in hand, let him be preferred before all whom the unanimous consent of clergy and people demands, but if the votes chance to be divided between two persons, the judgment of the metropolitan should prefer him who is supported by the preponderance of votes and merits: only let no one be ordained against the express wishes of the place: lest a city should either despise or hate a bishop whom they did not choose, and lamentably fall away from religion because they have not been allowed to have whom they wished.

VII. *Metropolitans are to refer to their Vicar: the mode of electing metropolitans is laid down.*

However the metropolitan bishop should refer to you, brother, about the person to be consecrated bishop, and about the consent of the clergy and people: and he should acquaint you with the wishes of the province: that the due celebration of the ordination may be strengthened by your authority also. But to right selections it will be your duty to cause no delay or hindrance, lest the LORD's flocks should remain too long with their shepherd's care.

Moreover when a metropolitan is defunct and another has to be elected in to his place, the bishops of the province must meet together in the metropolitical city: that after the wishes of all the clerics and all the citizens have been sifted, the best man may be chosen from the presbyters of that same church or from the deacons, and you are to be informed of his name by the priests of the province, who will carry out the wishes of his supporters on ascertaining that you agree with their choice[6]. For whilst we desire proper elections to be hampered by no delays, we yet allow nothing to be done presumptuously without your knowledge.

VIII. *Bishops are to hold provincial councils twice a year.*

Concerning councils of bishops we give no other instructions than those laid down for the Church's health by the holy Fathers[7]: to wit that two meetings should be held a year, in which judgment should be passed upon all the complaints which are wont to arise between the various ranks of the Church. But if perchance among the rulers themselves a

3 *Rectores.*

4 1 Cor. vii. 29. A reference to this passage will show that S. Paul does not limit himself to the clergy in what he says: for an interesting note on the text (written, of course, from the Roman standpoint), the reader is referred to Hurter's edition *in loc.*, who adduces some valuable illustrations from Epiphanius, Jerome, &c.

5 *Quartus a Capite*, i.e. from Jesus Christ, the Head of the Church, or perhaps from the Bishop of Rome, His *soi-disant* representative on earth (cf. chap. xii., below).

6 This method of electing the metropolitan will at once strike the reader: the electors apparently are (1) the bishops of the province (who are not eligible for the office); (2) the clergy of the diocese (who alone are eligible); and (3) the laity of the diocese. Only if one remembers how limited each diocese was in extent, can one realize the working of the method.

7 The Council of Nicæa (325) fixed two councils a year, one *ante quadragesimam Paschæ* (i.e. before Eastertide), the other *circa tempus autumni.*

cause arise (which God forbid) concerning one of the greater sins, such as cannot be decided by a provincial trial, the metropolitan shall take care to inform you, brother, concerning the nature of the whole matter, and if, after both parties have come before you, the thing be not set at rest even by your judgment, whatever it be, let it be transferred to our jurisdiction.

IX. *Translation from one see to another is to be prohibited.*

If any bishop, despising the insignificance of his city, shall intrigue for the government of a more populous place, and transfer himself by whatever means to a larger flock, he shall first be driven from the chair he has usurped, and also shall be deprived of his own: so shall he preside neither over those whom in his greed he coveted, nor over those whom in his arrogance he spurned. Therefore let each be content with his own bounds, and not seek to be raised above the limits of his present post.

X. *Bishops are not to entice or receive the clergy of another diocese.*

A cleric from another diocese let no (bishop) accept or invite against the wishes of his own bishop: but only when giver and receiver agree together thereupon by friendly compact. For a man is guilty of a serious injury who ventures either to entice or withhold from a brother's church that which is of great use or high value. And so, if such a thing happen within the province, the metropolitan shall force the deserting cleric to return to his church: but if he has withdrawn himself still further off, he shall be recalled by your authoritative command: so that no occasion be left for either desire of gain or intrigue.

XI. *When the Vicar shall require a meeting of bishops, two from each province will be sufficient.*

In summoning bishops to your presence, we wish you to show great forbearance: lest under a show of much diligence you seem to exult in your brethren's injuries. Wherefore if any greater case arise for which it is reasonable and necessary to convene a meeting of brethren, it may suffice, brother, that two bishops should attend from each province, whom the metropolitans shall think proper to be sent, on the understanding that those who answer the summons be not detained longer than fifteen days from the time fixed.

XII. *In case of difference of opinion between the Vicar and the bishops, the bishop of Rome must be consulted. The subordination of authorities in the Church expounded.*

But if in that which you believed necessary to be discussed and settled with the brethren, their opinion differs from your own wishes, let all be referred to us, with the minutes of your proceedings attested, that all ambiguities may be removed, and what is pleasing to God decided. For to this end we direct all our desires and pains, that what conduces to our harmonious unity and to the protection of discipline may be marred by no dissension and neglected by no slothfulness. Therefore, dearly beloved brother, you and those our brethren who are offended at your extravagant conduct (though the matter of complaint is not the same with all), we exhort and warn not to disturb by any wrangling what has been rightfully ordained and wisely settled. Let none "seek what is his own, but what is another's," as the Apostle says: "Let each one of you please his neighbour for his good unto edifying[8]." For the cementing of our unity cannot be firm unless we be bound by the bond of love into an inseparable solidity: because "as in one body we have many members, but all the members have not the same office; so we being many are one body in Christ, and all of us members one of another[9]." The connexion of the whole body makes all alike healthy, all alike beautiful: and this connexion requires the unanimity indeed of the whole body, but it especially demands harmony among the priests. And though they have a common dignity, yet they have not uniform rank; inasmuch as even among the blessed Apostles, notwithstanding the similarity of their honourable estate, there was a certain distinction of power, and while the election of them all was equal, yet it was given to one[1] to take the lead of the rest. From which model has arisen a distinction between bishops also, and by an important ordinance it has been provided[2] that every one should not claim everything for himself: but that there should be in each province one whose opinion should have the priority among the brethren: and again that certain whose appointment is in the greater cities should undertake a fuller responsibility, through whom the care of the universal Church should converge towards Peter's one seat, and nothing anywhere should be separated from its Head. Let not him then who knows he has been set over certain others

8 Phil. ii. 4, and Rom. xv. 2.

9 1 Cor. xii. 12, &c.: the quotation is loose, cf. Rom. xii. 5.

1 Viz., S. Peter.

2 *Magna ordinatione provisum est.*

take it ill that some one has been set over him, but let him himself render the obedience which he demands of them: and as he does not wish to bear a heavy load of baggage, so let him not dare to place on another's shoulders a weight that is insupportable. For we are disciples of the humble and gentle Master who says: "Learn of Me, for I am gentle and humble of heart, and ye shall find rest for your souls. For My yoke is easy and My burden light[3]." And how shall we experience this, unless this too comes to our remembrance which the same LORD says: "He that is greater among you, shall be your servant. But he that exalteth himself, shall be humbled: and he that humbleth himself, shall be exalted[4]."

LETTER XV.

TO TURRIBIUS, BISHOP OF ASTURIA[5], UPON THE ERRORS OF THE PRISCILLIANISTS.

Leo, bishop, to Turribius, bishop, greeting.

I. *Introductory.*

Your laudable zeal for the truth of the catholic Faith, and the painstaking devotion you expend in the exercise of your pastoral office upon the LORD's flock is proved by your letter, brother, which your deacon has handed to us, in which you have taken care to bring to our knowledge the nature of the disease which has burst forth in your district from the remnants of an ancient plague. For the language of your letter, and your detailed statement, and the text of your pamphlet[6], explains clearly that the filthy puddle of the Priscillianists again teems with life amongst you[7]. For there is no dirt which has not flowed into this dogma from the notions of all sorts of heretics: since they have scraped together the motley dregs from the mire of earthly opinions and made for themselves a mixture[8] which they alone may swallow whole, though others have tasted little portions of it.

In fact, if all the heresies which have arisen before the time of Priscillian were to be studied carefully, hardly any mistake will be discovered with which this impiety has not been infected: for not satisfied with accepting the falsehoods of those who have departed from the Gospel under the name of Christ, it has plunged itself also in the shades of heathendom, so as to rest their religious faith and their moral conduct upon the power of demons and the influences of the stars through the blasphemous secrets of the magic arts and the empty lies of astrologers. But if this may be believed and taught, no reward will be due for virtues, no punishment for faults, and all the injunctions not only of human laws but also of the Divine constitutions will be broken down: because there will be no criterion of good or bad actions possible, if a fatal necessity drives the impulses of the mind to either side, and all that men do is through the agency not of men but of stars. To this madness belongs that monstrous division of the whole human body among the twelve signs of the zodiac, so that each part is ruled by a different power: and the creature, whom GOD made in His own image, is as much under the domination of the stars as his limbs are connected one with the other. Rightly then our fathers, in whose times this abominable heresy sprung up, promptly pursued it throughout the world, that the blasphemous error might everywhere be driven from the Church: for even the leaders of the world so abhorred this profane folly that they laid low its originator, with most of his disciples, by the sword of the public laws. For they saw that all desire for honourable conduct was removed, all marriage-ties undone, and the Divine and the human law simultaneously undermined, if it were allowed for men of this kind to live anywhere under such a creed. And this rigourous treatment was for long a help to the Church's law of gentleness which, although it relies upon the priestly judgment, and shuns blood-stained vengeance, yet is assisted by the stern decrees of Christian princes at times when men, who dread bodily punishment, have recourse to merely spiritual correction. But since many provinces have been taken up with the invasions of the enemy[9], the carrying out of the laws also has been suspended by these stormy wars. And since intercourse came to be difficult among GOD's priests and meetings rare, secret treachery was free to act through the general disorder, and was roused to the upsetting of many minds by those very ills which ought to have counteracted it. But which of the peoples and how many of them are free from the contagion of this plague in a district where, as you point out, dear brother, the

3 S. Matt. xi. 29, 30.

4 Ibid. xxiii. 11. 12.

5 This Turribius was a man of learning and zeal, Bishop of Asturia (Astorga) in Spain (province of Gallicia): canonized by the Roman Church and commemorated on April 16 (Hurter). The date of the letter is given as 21 Jul., 447.

6 Hurter distinguishes these three documents thus: (1) *epistola*, the private letter of Turribius to Leo; (2) *commonitorium*, the detailed statement (under 16 heads) of the Priscillianist errors; and (3) *libellus*, Turribius' refutation of each head. This heresy was of Spanish origin, having been broached by Priscillian about 380. Their views will be seen in the sequel.

7 *Priscillianistarum fœtidissimam apud vos recaluisse sentinam.*

8 *Multiplicem sibi fæculentiam miscuerunt.*

9 He alludes to the invasion of Spain by the German tribes (Perthel, p. 38).

minds even of certain priests have sickened of this deadly disease: and they who were believed the necessary quellers of falsehood and champions of the Truth are the very ones through whom the Gospel of God is enthralled to the teaching of Priscillian: so that the fidelity of the holy volumes being distorted to profane meanings, under the names of prophets and apostles, is proclaimed not that which the Holy Spirit has taught, but what the devil's servant has inserted. Therefore as you, beloved, with all the faithful diligence in your power, have dealt under 16 heads with these already condemned opinions[1], we also subject them once more to a strict examination; lest any of these blasphemies should be thought either bearable or doubtful.

II. (1) *The Priscillianists' denial of the Trinity refuted.*

And so under the first head is shown what unholy views they hold about the Divine Trinity: they affirm that the person of the Father, the Son, and the Holy Ghost is one and the same, as if the same GOD were named now Father, now Son, and now Holy Ghost: and as if He who begat were not one, He who was begotten, another, and He who proceeded from both, yet another; but an undivided unity must be understood, spoken of under three names, indeed, but not consisting of three persons. This species of blasphemy they borrowed from Sabellius, whose followers were rightly called Patripassians also: because if the Son is identical with the Father, the Son's cross is the Father's passion (*patris-passio*): and the Father took on Himself all that the Son took in the form of a slave, and in obedience to the Father. Which without doubt is contrary to the catholic faith, which acknowledges the Trinity of the Godhead to be of one essence (ὁμοούσιον) in such a way that it believes the Father, the Son, and the Holy Ghost indivisible without confusion, eternal without time, equal without difference: because it is not the same person but the same essence which fills the Unity in Trinity

III. (2) *Their fancy about virtues proceeding from GOD refuted.*

Under the second head is displayed their foolish and empty fancy about the issue of certain virtues from GOD which he began to possess, and which were posterior to GOD Himself in His own essence. In this again they support the Arians' mistake, who say that the Father is prior to the Son, because there was a time when He was without the Son: and became the Father then when He begat the Son. But as the catholic Church abhors them, so also does it abhor these who think that what is of the same essence was ever wanting to GOD. For it is as wicked to speak of Him as progressing as it is to call Him changeable. For increase implies change as much as does decrease.

IV. (3) *Their account of the epithet "Only begotten" refuted.*

Again the third head is concerned with these same folk's impious assertion that the Son of GOD is called "only-begotten" for this reason that He alone was born of a virgin. To be sure they would not have dared to say this, had they not drunk the poison of Paul of Samosata and Photinus: who said that our LORD Jesus Christ did not exist till He was born of the virgin Mary. But if they wish something else to be understood by their tenet, and do not date Christ's beginning from His mother's womb, they must necessarily assert that there is not one Son of GOD, but others also were begotten of the most High Father, of whom this one is born of a woman, and therefore called only-begotten, because no other of GOD's sons underwent this condition of being born. Therefore, whithersoever they betake themselves, they fall into an abyss of great impiety, if they either maintain that Christ the LORD took His beginning from His mother, or do not believe Him to be the only-begotten of GOD the Father: since He who was GOD was born of a mother, and no one was born of the Father except the Word.

V. (4) *Their fasting on the Nativity and Sunday disapproved of.*

The fourth head deals with the fact that the Birth-day of Christ, which the catholic Church thinks highly of as the occasion of His taking on Him true man, because "the Word became flesh and dwelt in us[2]," is not truly honoured by these men, though they make a show of honouring it, for they fast on that day, as they do also on the LORD's day, which is the day of Christ's resurrection. No doubt they do this, because they do not believe that Christ the LORD was born in true man's nature, but maintain that by a sort of illusion there was an appearance of what was not a reality, following the views of Cerdo and Marcion, and being in complete agreement with their kinsfolk, the

[1] See above, n. 6. Quesnel draws attention to the fact that Leo's refutation of the Priscillianist heresy, which here follows, was adopted (almost) word for word by the first council of Bracara (Braga, in Portugal), held in 563, as a sufficient exposition of their own position.

[2] S. John i. 14.

Manichæans. For as our examination has disclosed and brought home to them, they[3] drag out in mournful fasting the LORD's day which for us is hallowed by the resurrection of our Saviour: devoting this abstinence, as the explanation goes, to the worship of the sun: so that they are throughout out of harmony with the unity of our faith, and the day which by us is spent in gladness is past in self-affliction by them. Whence it is fitting that these enemies of Christ's cross and resurrection should accept an opinion (like this) which tallies with the doctrine they have selected.

VI. (5) *Their view that the soul is part of the Divine being refuted.*

The fifth head refers to their assertion that man's soul is part of the Divine being[4], and that the nature of our human state does not differ from its Creator's nature. This impious view has its source in the opinions of certain philosophers, and the Manichæans and the catholic Faith condemns it: knowing that nothing that is made is so sublime and so supreme as that its nature should be itself GOD. For that which is part of Himself is Himself, and none other than the Son and Holy Spirit. And besides this one consubstantial, eternal, and unchangeable Godhead of the most high Trinity there is nothing in all creation which, in its origin, is not created out of nothing. Besides anything that surpasses its fellow-creatures is not *ipso facto* GOD, nor, if a thing is great and wonderful, is it identical with Him "who alone doeth great wonders[5]." No *man* is truth, wisdom, justice; but many are partakers of truth, wisdom, and justice. But GOD alone is exempt from any participating: and anything which is in any degree worthily predicated of Him is not an attribute, but His very essence. For in the Unchangeable there is nothing added, there is nothing lost: because "to be[6]" is ever His peculiar property, and that is eternity. Whence abiding in Himself He renews all things[7], and receives nothing which He did not Himself give. Accordingly they are over-proud and stone-blind who, when they say the soul is part of the Divine Being, do not understand that they merely assert that GOD is changeable, and Himself suffers anything that may be inflicted upon His nature.

VII. (6) *Their view that the devil was never good, and is therefore not GOD'S creation, refuted.*

The sixth notice points out that they say the devil never was good, and that his nature is not GOD's handiwork, but he came forth out of chaos and darkness: because I suppose he has no instigator, but is himself the source and substance of all evil: whereas the true Faith, which is the catholic, acknowledges that the substance of all creatures spiritual or corporeal is good, and that evil has no positive existence[8]; because GOD, who is the Maker of the Universe, made nothing that was not good. Whence the devil also would be good, if he had remained as he was made. But because he made a bad use of his natural excellence, and "stood not in the truth[9]," he did not pass into the opposite substance, but revolted from the highest good to which he owed adherence: just as they themselves who make such assertions run headlong from truth into falsehood, and accuse nature of their own spontaneous delinquencies, and are condemned for their voluntary perversity: though of course this evil is in them, but is itself not a substance but a penalty inflicted on substance.

VIII. (7) *Their rejection of marriage condemned.*

In the seventh place follows their condemnation of marriages and their horror of begetting children: in which, as in almost all points, they agree with the Manichæans' impiety. But it is for this reason, as their own practices prove, that they detest the marriage tie, because there is no liberty for lewdness where the chastity of wedlock and of offspring is preserved.

IX. (8) *Their disbelief in the resurrection of the body has been already condemned by the Church.*

Their eighth point is that the formation[1] of men's bodies is the device of the devil, and that the seed of conception is shaped by the aid of demons in the wombs of women: and that for this reason the resurrection of the flesh is not to be believed because the stuff of which the body is made is not consistent with

3 Viz. the Manichæans.

4 This Pantheistic view was not, of course, a new one, nor pseudo-Christian in its origin, as Leo himself shows. Cf. Virg., Georg. IV. 219—227, and Aen. vi. 724—727.
The *philosophi quidam* to which he makes reference are the Pythagoreans, and following them with modifications the Platonists and the Stoics.

5 Ps. cxxxvi. 4.

6 The reader need hardly be reminded of the recorded revelation of the great "I am" (Jehovah) to Moses (Ex. iii.).

7 Cf. Rev. xxi. 5.

8 i.e. that evil is not anything positive, but only the negation or absence of good which *is* positive, just as black is not itself a colour, but only the absence of colour, whereas white is the presence (in due proportion) of all the colours of the spectrum.

9 S. John viii. 24.

1 *Plasmationem*, a vile hybrid, being the Greek πλάσμα with a Latin ending (*-atio*); for which apparently the Low Latin of the Vulgate is responsible. Cf. Ps. cxix. 73, "et plasmaverunt me" (quoted below, chap. x.).

the dignity of the soul. This falsehood is without doubt the devil's work, and such monstrous opinions are the devices of demons who do not mould men in women's bellies, but concoct such errors in heretics' hearts. This unclean poison which flows especially from the fount of the Manichæan wickedness has been already[2] arraigned and condemned by the catholic Faith.

X. (9) *Their notion that "the children of promise" are conceived by the Holy Ghost is utterly unscriptural and uncatholic.*

The ninth notice declares that they say the sons of promise are born indeed of women, but conceived by the Holy Spirit: lest that offspring which is born of carnal seed should seem to share in God's estate. This is repugnant and contrary to the catholic Faith, which acknowledges every man to be formed by the Maker of the Universe in the substance of his body and soul, and to receive the breath of life within his mother's womb: though that taint of sin and liability to die remains which passed from the first parent into his descendants; until the sacrament of Regeneration comes to succour him, whereby through the Holy Spirit we are re-born the sons of promise, not in the fleshly womb, but in the power of baptism. Whence David also, who certainly was a son of promise, says to God: "Thy hands have made me and fashioned me[3]." And to Jeremiah says the Lord, "Before I formed thee in the womb I knew thee, and in thy mother's belly I sanctified thee[4]."

XI. (10) *Their theory that souls have a previous existence before entering man refuted.*

Under the tenth head they are reported as asserting that the souls which are placed in men's bodies have previously been without body and have sinned in their heavenly habitation, and for this reason having fallen from their high estate to a lower one alight upon ruling spirits[5] of divers qualities, and after passing through a succession of powers of the air and stars, some fiercer, some milder, are enclosed in bodies of different sorts and conditions, so that whatever variety and inequality is meted out to us in this life, seems the result of previous causes. This blasphemous fable they have woven for themselves out of many persons' errors[6]: but all of them the catholic Faith cuts off from union with its body, persistently and truthfully proclaiming that men's souls did not exist until they were breathed into their bodies, and that they were not there implanted by any other than God, who is the creator both of the souls and of the bodies. And because through the transgression of the first man the whole stock of the human race was tainted, no one can be set free from the state of the old Adam save through Christ's sacrament of baptism, in which there are no distinctions between the re-born, as says the Apostle: "For as many of you as were baptized in Christ did put on Christ: there is neither Jew nor Greek: there is neither bond nor free: there is neither male nor female: for ye are all one in Christ Jesus[7]." What then have the course of the stars to do with it, or the devices of destiny? what the changing state of mundane things and their restless diversity? Behold how the grace of God makes all these unequals equal, who, whatever their labours in this life, if they abide faithful, cannot be wretched, for they can say with the Apostle in every trial: "who shall separate us from the love of Christ? shall tribulation, or distress, or persecution, or famine, or nakedness, or peril, or sword? As it is written, 'For thy sake we are killed all the day long, we are accounted as sheep for the slaughter.' (Ps. xliv. 22.) But in all these things we overcome through Him that loved us[8]." And therefore the Church, which is the body of Christ, has no fear about the inequalities of the world, because she has no desire for temporal goods: nor does she dread being overwhelmed by the empty threats of destiny, for she knows she is strengthened by patience in tribulations.

XII. (11) *Their astrological notions condemned.*

Their eleventh blasphemy is that in which they suppose that both the souls and bodies of men are under the influence of fatal stars: this folly compels them to become entangled in all the errors of the heathen, and to strive to attract stars that are as they think favourable to them, and to soften those that are against them. But for those who follow such pursuits there is no place in the catholic Church; a man who gives himself up to such convictions separates himself from the body of Christ altogether.

---

2 *Olim.* Perhaps Leo refers to his own action mentioned in Lett. vii. 1.

3 Ps. cxix. 73.

4 Jer. i. 5.

5 *In diversæ qualitatis principes incidisse*, cf. Rom. viii. 38; Eph. iii. 10; Col. ii. 10, &c.

6 The Pythagorean doctrine of μετεμψύχωσις (transmigration of souls) which was in a modified form accepted by Plato (*Phædr. et alibi*), would seem to have been the original source of this view of the soul's origin. It would naturally be palatable doctrine to the Gnostics and other philosophizing sects. In Lett. XXXV., chap. iii., it is attributed to Origen. For a modern exposition the reader cannot do better than refer to Wordsworth's ode on the intimations of Immortality in childhood.

7 Gal. iii. 27, 28.

8 Rom. viii. 35—37.

XIII. (12) *Their belief that certain powers rule the soul and the stars the body, is unscriptural and preposterous.*

The twelfth of these points is this. that they map out the parts of the soul under certain powers, and the limbs of the body under others: and they suggest the characters of the inner powers that rule the soul by giving them the names of the patriarchs, and on the contrary they attribute the signs of the stars to those under which they put the body. And in all these things they entangle themselves in an inextricable maze, not listening to the Apostle when he says, "See that no one deceive you through philosophy and vain deceit after the tradition of men, after the rudiments of the world, and not after Christ; for in Him dwells all the fulness of the Godhead bodily, and in Him ye are made full, who is the head of every principality and power[9]." And again: "let no man beguile you by a voluntary humility and worshipping of angels, treading on things which he hath not seen, vainly puffed up by the senses of his flesh, not holding fast the Head from whom all the body, being supplied and knit together through the joints and bands, increaseth with the increase of God[1]." What then is the use of admitting into the heart what the law has not taught, prophecy has not sung, the truth of the Gospel has not proclaimed, the Apostles' teaching has not handed down? But these things are suited to the minds of those of whom the Apostle speaks, "For the time will come when they will not endure sound doctrine, but having itching ears, will heap to themselves teachers after their own lusts: and will turn away indeed their hearing from the truth, and turn aside unto fables[2]." And so we can have nothing in common with men who dare to teach or believe such things, and strive by any means in their power to persuade men that the substance of flesh is foreign to the hope of resurrection, and so break down the whole mystery of Christ's incarnation: because it was wrong for Christ to take upon Him complete manhood if it was wrong for Him to emancipate complete manhood.

XIV. (13) *Their fanciful division of the Scriptures rejected.*

In the thirteenth place comes their assertion that the whole body of the canonical Scriptures is to be accepted, under the names of the patriarchs[3]: because those twelve virtues which work the reformation of the inner man are pointed out in their names, and without this knowledge no soul can effect its reformation, and return to that substance from which it came forth. But this wicked delusion the Christian wisdom holds in disdain, for it knows that the nature of the true Godhead is inviolable and immutable: but the soul, whether living in the body or separated from the body, is subject to many passions: whereas, of course, if it were part of the divine essence, no adversity could happen to it. And therefore there is no comparison between them: One is the Creator, the other is the creature. For He is always the same, and suffers no change: but the soul is changeable, even if not changed, because its power of not changing is a gift, and not a property.

XV. (14) *Their idea that the Scriptures countenance their subjecting of the body to the starry influences denied.*

Under the fourteenth heading their sentiments upon the state of the body are stated, viz., that it is, on account of its earthly properties, held under the power of stars and constellations, and that many things are found in the holy books which have reference to the outer man with this object, that in the Scriptures themselves a certain opposition may be seen at work between the divine and the earthly nature: and that that which the powers that rule the soul claim for themselves may be distinguished from that which the fashioners of the body claim. These stories are invented that the soul may be maintained to be part of the divine substance, and the flesh believed to belong to the bad nature: since the world itself, with its elements, they hold to be not the work of the good God, but the outcome of an evil author: and that they might disguise these sacrilegious lies under a fair cloak, they have polluted almost all the divine utterances with the colouring of their unholy notions.

XVI. (15) *Their falsified copies of the Scriptures, and their apocryphal books prohibited.*

And on this subject your remarks under the fifteenth head make a complaint, and express a well-deserved abhorrence of their devilish presumption, for we too have ascertained this from the accounts of trustworthy witnesses, and have found many of their copies most corrupt, though they are entitled canonical. For how could they deceive the simple-

9 Col. ii. 8–10. 1 Ibid. 18, 19. 2 2 Tim. iv. 3, 4.

3 Leo's commentary on this obscure fancy of the Priscillianists is disappointing, as it is merely a repetition or continuation of his remarks on the 12th head. They seem to have divided the scriptures in some mystic fashion into portions corresponding to the *qualitates interiorum præsulum in patriarcharum nominibus* (*statutæ*) of chap. xiii., and to have insisted on knowledge of the Scriptures as necessary to the proper action of those "ruling principles" on the soul. Cf. S. Aug. Letter CCXXXVII., chap. iii (Hurter.)

minded unless they sweetened their poisoned cups with a little honey, lest what was meant to be deadly should be detected by its over-nastiness? Therefore care must be taken, and the priestly diligence exercised to the uttermost, to prevent falsified copies that are out of harmony with the pure Truth being used in reading. And the apocryphal scriptures, which, under the names of Apostles[4], form a nursery-ground for many falsehoods, are not only to be proscribed, but also taken away altogether and burnt to ashes in the fire. For although there are certain things in them which seem to have a show of piety, yet they are never free from poison, and through the allurements of their stories they have the secret effect of first beguiling men with miraculous narratives, and then catching them in the noose of some error. Wherefore if any bishop has either not forbidden the possession of apocryphal writings in men's houses, or under the name of being canonical has suffered those copies to be read in church which are vitiated with the spurious alterations of Priscillian, let him know that he is to be accounted heretic, since he who does not reclaim others from error shows that he himself has gone astray.

XVII. (16) *About the writings of Dictinius*[5].

Under the last head a just complaint was made that the treatises of Dictinius which he wrote in agreement with Priscillian's tenets were read by many with veneration: for if they think any respect is due to Dictinius' memory, they ought to admire his restoration rather than his fall. Accordingly it is not Dictinius but Priscillian that they read: and they approve of what he wrote in error, not what he preferred after recantation. But let no one venture to do this with impunity, nor let any one be reckoned among catholics who makes use of writings that have been condemned not by the catholic Church alone, but by the author himself as well. Let not those who have gone astray be allowed to make a fictitious show, and under the veil of the Christian name shirk the provisions of the imperial decrees. For they attach themselves to the catholic Church with all this difference of opinion in their heart, with the object of both making such converts as they can, and escaping the rigour of the law by passing themselves off as ours. This is done by Priscillianists and Manichæans alike; for there is such a close bond of union between the two that they are distinct only in name, but in their blasphemies are found at one: because although the Manichæans reject the Old Testament which the others pretend to accept, yet the purpose of both tends to the same end, seeing that the one side corrupts while receiving what the other assails and rejects.

But in their abominable mysteries, which the more unclean they are, are so much the more carefully concealed, their crime is but one, their filthy-mindedness one, and their foul conduct similar. And although we blush to speak so plainly, yet we have tracked it out with the most painful searches, and exposed it by the confession of Manichæans who have been arrested, and thus brought it to the public knowledge: lest by any means it might seem matter of doubt, although it has been disclosed by the mouth of the men themselves, who had performed the crime, in our court, which was attended not only by a large gathering of priests, but also by men of repute and dignity, and a certain number of the senate and the people, even as the missive which we have addressed to you, beloved, shows to have been done. And there has been found out and widely published about the immoral practices of the Priscillianists just what was also found out about the foul wickedness of the Manichæans. For they who are throughout on a level of depravity in their ideas, cannot be unlike in their religious matters.

So having run through all that the detailed refutation contains, with which the contents of the memorial of their views does not disagree, we have, I think, satisfactorily shown what our opinion on the matters which you, brother, have referred to us, and how unbearable it is if such blasphemous errors find acceptance in the hearts even of some priests, or to put it more mildly, are not actively opposed by them. With what conscience can they maintain the honourable position which has been given them, who do not labour for the souls entrusted to them? Beasts rush in, and they do not close the fold. Robbers lay wait, and they set no watch. Diseases multiply, and they seek out no remedies. But when in addition they refuse assent to those who act more warily, and shrink from anathematizing by their written confession blasphemies which the whole world has already condemned, what do they wish men to understand except that they are not of the number of the brethren, but on the enemy's side?

---

4 Viz., such writings as the *Actus* of Thomas, Andrew and John, and the *Memoria apostolorum, qui totam destruit legem veteris Testamenti*, according to Turribius' letter to Idacius and Ceponius, chap. v., subjoined to this letter in the Leonine series.

5 Dictinius was a bishop who had turned Priscillianist, and afterwards, at the synod of Toledo (400), had returned to the fold of the Church (Perthel, p. 41)

XVIII. *The body of Christ really rested in the tomb, and really rose again.*

Furthermore in the matter which you placed last in your confidential letter, I am surprised that any intelligent Christian should be in difficulty as to whether when Christ descended to the realms below, his flesh rested in the tomb: for as it truly died and was buried, so it was truly raised the third day. For this the LORD Himself also had announced, saying to the Jews, "destroy this temple, and in three days I will raise it up[6]." Where the evangelist adds this comment: "but this He spake of the temple of His body." The truth of which the prophet David also had predicted, speaking in the person of the LORD and Saviour, and saying: "Moreover my flesh also shall rest in hope; because Thou will not leave my soul in Hades, nor give Thy Holy One to see corruption[7]." From these words surely it is clear that the LORD's flesh being buried, both truly rested and did not undergo corruption: because it was quickly revived by the return of the soul, and rose again. Not to believe this is blasphemous enough, and is undoubtedly of a piece with the doctrine of Manichæus and Priscillian, who with their blasphemous conceptions pretend to confess Christ, but only in such a way as to destroy the reality of His incarnation, and death, and resurrection.

Therefore let a council of bishops be held among you, and let the priests of neighbouring provinces meet at a place suitable to all: that, on the lines of our reply to your request for advice, a full inquiry may be made as to whether here are any of the bishops who are tainted with the contagion of this heresy: for they must without doubt be cut off from communion, if they refuse to condemn this most unrighteous sect with all its wrongful conceptions. For it can nohow be permitted that one who has undertaken the duty of preaching the Faith should dare to maintain opinions contrary to Christ's gospel and the creed of the universal Church. What kind of disciples will there be in a place where such masters teach? What will the people's religion, or the salvation of the laity be, where against the interests of human society the holiness of chastity is uprooted, the marriage-bond overthrown, the propagation of children forbidden, the nature of the flesh condemned, and, in opposition to the true worship of the true GOD, the Trinity of the Godhead is denied, the individuality of the persons confounded, man's soul declared to be the Divine essence, and enclosed in flesh at the Devil's will, the Son of GOD proclaimed only-begotten in right of being born of a Virgin, not begotten of the Father, and at the same time maintained to be neither true offspring of GOD, nor true child of the virgin: so that after a false passion and an unreal death, even the resurrection of the flesh re-assumed out of the tomb should be considered fictitious? But it is vain for them to adopt the name of catholic, as they do not oppose these blasphemies: they must believe them, if they can listen so patiently to such words. And so we have sent a letter to our brethren and fellow-bishops of the provinces of Tarraco, Carthago, Lusitania and Gallicia, enjoining a meeting of the general synod. It will be yours, beloved, to take order that our authoritative instuctions be conveyed to the bishops of the aforesaid provinces. But should anything, which GOD forbid, hinder the coming together of a general council of Gallicia[8], at least let the priests come together, the assembling of whom our brothers Idacius and Ceponius shall look to, assisted by your own strenuous efforts to hasten the applying of remedies to these serious wounds by a provincial synod also. Dated July 21, in the consulship of the illustrious Calipius and Ardaburis (447).

LETTER XVI.

To the Bishops of Sicily.

Leo the bishop to all the bishops throughout Sicily greeting in the LORD.

I. *Introductory.*

By GOD'S precepts and the Apostle's admonitions we are incited to keep a careful watch over the state of all the churches: and, if anywhere ought is found that needs rebuke, to recall men with speedy care either from the stupidity of ignorance or from forwardness and presumption. For inasmuch as we are warned by the LORD's own command whereby the blessed Apostle Peter had the thrice repeated mystical injunction pressed upon him, that he who loves Christ should feed Christ's sheep, we are compelled by reverence for that see which, by the abundance of the Divine Grace, we hold, to shun the danger of sloth as much as possible: lest the confession of the chief Apostle whereby he testified that he loved GOD be not found in us: because if he (through us) carelessly

[6] S. John ii. 19.

[7] Ps. xvi. 10.

[8] The whole district over which Turribius was Vicar is here called *Gallicia*, though, as just above, we find it included the provinces of *Tarraco*, *Carthago*, and *Lusitania* a well as *Gallicia*.

feed the flock so often commended to him he is proved not to love the chief Shepherd.

II. *Baptism is to be administered at Easter-tide and not on the Epiphany.*

Accordingly when it reached my ears on reliable testimony (and I already felt a brother's affectionate anxiety about your acts, beloved) that in what is one of the chief sacraments of the Church you depart from the practice of the Apostles' constitution[9] by administering the sacrament of baptism to greater numbers on the feast of the Epiphany than at Eastertide, I was surprised that you or your predecessors could have introduced so unreasonable an innovation as to confound the mysteries of the two festivals and believe there was no difference between the day on which Christ was worshipped by the wise men and that on which He rose again from the dead. You could never have fallen into this fault, if you had taken the whole of your observances from the source whence you derive your consecration to the episcopate; and if the see of the blessed Apostle Peter, which is the mother of your priestly dignity, were the recognized teacher of church-method. We could indeed have endured your departure from its rules with less equanimity, if you had received any previous rebuke by way of warning from us. But now as we do not despair of correcting you, we must show gentleness. And although an excuse which affects ignorance is scarce tolerable in priests, yet we prefer to moderate our needful rebuke and to instruct you plainly in the true method of the Church.

III. *One must distinguish one festival from another in respect of dignity and occasion.*

The restoration of mankind has indeed ever remained immutably fore-ordained in GOD's eternal counsel: but the series of events which had to be accomplished in time through Jesus Christ our LORD was begun at the Incarnation of the Word. Hence there is one time when at the angel's announcement the blessed Virgin Mary believed she was to be with child through the Holy Ghost and conceived: another, when without loss of her virgin purity the Boy was born and shown to the shepherds by the exulting joy of the heavenly attendants: another, when the Babe was circumcised: another, when the victim required by the Law is offered for him: another, when the three wise men attracted by the brightness of the new star[1] arrive at Bethlehem from the East and worship the Infant with the mystic offering of Gifts.

And again the days are not the same on which by the divinely appointed pasage into Egypt He was withdrawn from wicked Herod, and on which He was recalled from Egypt into Galilee on His pursuer's death. Among these varieties of circumstance must be included His growth of body: the LORD increases, as the evangelist bears witness, with the progress of age and grace: at the time of the Passover He comes to the temple at Jerusalem with His parents, and when He was absent from the returning company, He is found sitting with the elders and disputing among the wondering masters and rendering an account of His remaining behind: "why is it," He says, "that ye sought Me? did ye not know that I must be in that which is My Father's[2]," signifying that He was the Son of Him whose temple He was in. Once more when in later years He was to be declared more openly and sought out the baptism of His forerunner John, was there any doubt of His being GOD remaining when after the baptism of the LORD Jesus the Holy Spirit in form of a dove descended and rested upon Him, and the Father's voice was heard from the skies, "Thou art My beloved Son: in Thee I am well pleased[3]?" All these things we have alluded to with as much brevity as possible for this reason, that you may know, beloved, that though all the days of Christ's life were hallowed by many mighty works of His[4], and though in all His actions mysterious sacraments[5] shone forth, yet at one time intimations of events were given by signs, and at one time fulfilment realized: and that all the Saviour's works that are recorded are not suitable to the time of baptism. For if we were to commemorate with indiscriminate honour these things also which we know to have been done by the LORD after His baptism by the blessed John, His whole life-

9 From this letter it might be gathered that it was a universal practice of the early Church, based on the precepts of the apostles, to restrict Baptism to the feasts of Easter and Whitsuntide, and exclude Epiphany. Whereas as a matter of fact the restriction was almost exclusively Roman; all the Eastern Churches and a good many of the Western recognizing the Epiphany as a suitable occasion for the rite. Leo is too fond of claiming Apostolic authority for his dictates, and none such exists here, as far as we know.

1 It will be noticed that Leo's order of events, though probably correct, is not that of the modern Kalendar, which places the Epiphany (Jan. 6) soon after the Circumcision (Jan. 1), and not after the Purification (Feb. 2): unless it was some little time after, Herod's cruelty was unnecessarily great in including children of *two years* old in his massacre (S. Matt. ii. 16).

2 S. Luke ii. 49, *in his quæ Patris mei sunt* (Vulgate): this version leaves the expression ἐν τοῖς τοῦ Πατρός μου in its original ambiguity, but Leo's commentary immediately following gives his decision in favour of "in My Father's house."

3 S. Matt. iii. 17.

4 *Innumeris consecratos fuisse virtutibus*, where *virtutes*, as often, corresponds to the Gk. δυνάμεις.

5 *Sacramentorum mysteria coruscasse*: it is instructive to find the two words here conjoined, Leo so often using them apparently as equivalents. No one, moreover, after reading this sentence, can doubt what in early times Western Christians meant by *sacramentum*, see Letter XII. chap. 3, &c.

time would have to be observed in a continuous succession of festivals, because all His acts were full of miracles. But because the Spirit of wisdom and knowledge so instructed the Apostles and teachers of the whole Church as to allow nothing disordered or confused to exist in our Christian observances, we must discern the relative importance of the various solemnities and observe a reasonable distinction in all the institutions of our fathers and rulers: for we cannot otherwise "be one flock and one shepherd[6]," except as the Apostle teaches us, "that we all speak the same thing: and that we be perfected in the same mind and in the same judgment[7]."

IV. *The reason explained why Easter and Whitsuntide are the proper seasons for Baptism.*

Although, therefore, both these things which are connected with Christ's humiliation and those which are connected with His exaltation meet in one and the same Person, and all that is in Him of Divine power and human weakness conduces to the accomplishment of our restoration: yet it is appropriate that the power of baptism should change the old into the new creature on the death-day of the Crucified and the Resurrection-day of the Dead: that Christ's death and His resurrection may operate in the re-born[8], as the blessed Apostle says: "Are ye ignorant that all we who were baptized in Christ Jesus, were baptized in His death? We were buried with Him through baptism into death; that as Christ rose from the dead through the glory of the Father, so we also should walk in newness of life. For if we have become united with the likeness of His death, we shall be also (with the likeness) of His resurrection[9]," and the rest which the Teacher of the Gentiles discusses further in recommending the sacrament of baptism: that it might be seen from the spirit of this doctrine that that is the day, and that the time chosen for regenerating the sons of men and adopting them among the sons of GOD, on which by a mystical symbolism and form[1], what is done in the limbs coincides with what was done in the Head Himself, for in the baptismal office death ensues through the slaying of sin, and threefold immersion imitates the lying in the tomb three days, and the raising out of the water is like Him that rose again from the tomb[2]. The very nature, therefore of the act teaches us that that is the recognized day for the general reception of the grace[3], on which the power of the gift and the character of the action originated. And this is strongly corroborated by the consideration that the LORD Jesus Christ Himself, after He rose from the dead, handed on both the form and power of baptizing to His disciples, in whose persons all the chiefs of the churches received their instructions with these words, "Go ye and teach all nations, baptizing them in the name of the Father and of the Son and of the Holy Ghost[4]." On which of course He might have instructed them even before His passion, had He not especially wished it to be understood that the grace of regeneration began with His resurrection. It must be added, indeed, that the solemn season of Pentecost, hallowed by the coming of the Holy Ghost is also allowed, being, as it were, the sequel and completion of the Paschal feast. And while other festivals are held on other days of the week, this festival (of Pentecost) always occurs on that day, which is marked by the LORD's resurrection: holding out, so to say, the hand of assisting grace and inviting those, who have been cut off from the Easter feast by disabling sickness or length of journey or difficulties of sailing, to gain the purpose that they long for through the gift of the Holy Spirit. For the Only-begotten of GOD Himself wished no difference to be felt between Himself and the Holy Spirit in the Faith of believers and in the efficacy of His works: because there is no diversity in their nature, as He says, "I will ask the Father and He shall give you another Comforter that He may be with you for ever, even the Spirit of Truth[5];" and again: "But the Comforter which is the Holy Ghost, whom the Father will send in My name, He shall teach you all things and bring to your remembrance all that I said unto you[6];" and again: "When He, the Spirit of Truth, is come, He shall guide you into all the Truth[7]." And thus, since Christ is the Truth, and the Holy Spirit the Spirit of Truth, and the name of "Comforter" appropriate to both, the two festivals are not dissimilar, where the sacrament is the same[8].

6 S. John x. 17. 7 1 Cor. i. 10.

8 *Renascentibus* (pres. part.) here, not *renatis* (past).

9 Rom vi. 3-5. Notice the support here given to the marginal alternative of the R.V., "united with," instead of "united in" (Lat. *complantati similitudini*, &c.).

1 *Per similitudinem et formam mysterii.*

2 This was a favourite interpretation of the symbolism with the fathers. Cf. Serm. LXX., chap. 4, and Bright's n. 97 thereon.

3 *Celebrandæ generaliter gratiæ*, where *generaliter* has much the same sense as the Eng. "generally" has in the definition of a sacrament in the Eng. Ch. Catechism as "*generally* necessary to salvation."

4 S. Matt. xxviii. 19. 5 S. John xiv. 16.

6 Ibid. 26. 7 Ibid. xvi. 13.

8 It need hardly be pointed out that these words, "where the sacrament is the same," refer to the *sacramentum* (in its Leonine sense), that has just been explained, viz., that *Christus est veritas et spiritus sanctus est spiritus veritatis.*

V. *S. Peter's example as an authority for Whitsuntide baptisms.*

And that we do not contend for this on our own conviction but retain it on Apostolic authority, we prove by a sufficiently apt example, following the blessed Apostle Peter, who, on the very day on which the promised coming of the Holy Ghost filled up the number of those that believed, dedicated to God in the baptismal font three thousand of the people who had been converted by his preaching. The Holy Scripture, which contains the Acts of Apostles[9], teaches this in its faithful narrative, saying, "Now when they heard this, they were pricked in the heart, and said unto Peter and to the rest of the Apostles, what shall we do, brethren? But Peter said unto them, Repent ye and be baptized every one of you in the name of Jesus Christ, unto the remission of your sins, and ye shall receive the gift of the Holy Ghost. For to you is the promise, and to your children and to all that are afar off, even as many as the LORD our GOD shall call unto Him. With many other words also he testified and exhorted them saying, Save yourselves from this crooked generation. They then that received his word were baptized, and there were added in that day about three thousand[1]."

VI. *In cases of urgency other times are allowable for baptism.*

Wherefore, as it is quite clear that these two seasons of which we have been speaking are the rightful ones for baptizing the chosen in Church, we admonish you, beloved, not to add other days to this observance. Because, although there are other festivals also to which much reverence is due in GOD's honour, yet we must rationally guard this principal and greatest sacrament as a deep mystery and not part of the ordinary routine[2]: not, however, prohibiting the licence to succour those who are in danger by administering baptism to them at any time. For whilst we put off the vows of those who are not pressed by ill health and live in peaceful security to those two closely connected and cognate festivals, we do not at any time refuse this which is the only safeguard of true salvation to any one in peril of death, in the crisis of a siege, in the distress of persecution, in the terror of shipwreck.

VII. *Our LORD'S baptism by John very different to the baptism of believers.*

But if any one thinks the feast of the Epiphany, which in proper degree is certainly to be held in due honour, claims the privilege of baptism because, according to some the LORD came to St. John's baptism on the same day, let him know that the grace of that baptism and the reason of it were quite different, and is not on an equal footing with the power by which they are re-born of the Holy Ghost, of whom it is said, "which were born not of blood, nor of the will of the flesh, nor of the will of man, but of GOD[3]." For the LORD who needed no remission of sin and sought not the remedy of being born again, desired to be baptized just as He desired to be circumcised, and to have a victim offered for His purification: that He, who had been "made of a woman[3a]," as the Apostle says, might become also "under the law" which He had come, "not to destroy but to fulfil[3b]," and by fulfilling to end, as the blessed Apostle proclaims, saying: "but Christ is the end of the law unto righteousness to every one that believeth[4]." But the sacrament of baptism He founded in His own person[5], because "in all things having the pre-eminence[6]," He taught that He Himself was the Beginning. And He ratified the power of re-birth on that occasion, when from His side flowed out the blood of ransom and the water of baptism[7]. As, therefore, the Old Testament was the witness to the new, and "the law was given by Moses: but grace and truth came through Jesus Christ[8];" as the divers sacrifices prefigured the one Victim, and the slaughter of many lambs was ended by the offering up of Him, of whom it is said, "Behold the Lamb of God; behold Him that taketh away the sin of the world[9];" so too John, not Christ, but Christ's forerunner, not the bridegroom, but the friend of the bridegroom, was so faithful in seeking, "not His own, but the things which are Jesus Christ's[9a]," as to profess himself unworthy to undo the shoes of His feet: seeing that He Himself indeed baptized "in water unto repentance," but He who with twofold power should both restore life and destroy sins, was about to "baptize in the Holy Ghost and fire[9b]." As

9 Leo does not often quote from the Acts, and here he expressly includes it in the Canon, and alludes to its authenticity (*fideli historia docet*).

1 Acts ii. 37-41.

2 *Principalis et maximi sacramenti custodienda nobis est mystica et rationalis exceptio* (another reading being *exemplatio* (symbolism), which Quesnel prefers, thinking that the words have reference to the appropriateness of this symbolical rite of Baptism being performed at Easter-tide).

3 S. John i. 13. 3a Gal. iv. 4. 3b S. Matt. v. 17.

4 Rom. x. 4.

5 *Baptismi sui in se condidit sacramentum*: the baptism of Christ has very generally been associated with the Epiphany: the record of it, for instance, in S. Luke iii. 15—23, is the 2nd morning lesson for the Festival in the English Church. It is, however, not clear who the "some" were whom Leo mentions above as putting Christ's baptism on the same day as the Epiphany; perhaps he means the Eastern Church."

6 1 Col. i. 18.

7 Cf. Lett. XXVIII. (The Tome), chap. vi., where the same explanation of the sacred incident in the Lord's passion is given.

8 S. John i. 17. Cf. Rev. xix. 20, "for the testimony of Jesus is the spirit of prophecy."

9 S. John i. 29.

9a Phil. ii. 21. 9b S. Matt. iii. 11; S. Luke iii. 16.

then, beloved brethren, all these distinct proofs come before you, whereby to the removal of all doubt you recognize that in baptizing the elect who, according to the Apostolic rule have to be purged by exorcisms, sanctified by fastings and instructed by frequent sermons, two seasons only are to be observed, viz. Easter and Whitsuntide: we charge you, brother, to make no further departure from the Apostolic institutions. Because hereafter no one who thinks the Apostolic rules can be set at defiance will go unpunished.

VIII. *The Sicilian bishops are to send three of their number to each of the half-yearly meetings of bishops at Rome.*

Wherefore we require this first and foremost for the keeping of perfect harmony, that, according to the wholesome rule of the holy Fathers that there should be two meetings of bishops every year[1], three of you should appear without fail each time, on the 29th of September, to join in the council of the brethren: for thus, by the aid of GOD's grace, we shall the easier guard against the rise of offences and errors in Christ's Church: and this council must always meet and deliberate in the presence of the blessed Apostle Peter, that all his constitutions and canonical decrees may remain inviolate with all the LORD's priests.

These matters, upon which we thought it necessary to instruct you by the inspiration of the LORD, we wish brought to your knowledge by our brothers and fellow-bishops, Bacillus and Paschasinus. May we learn by their report that the institutions of the Apostolic See are reverently observed by you. Dated 21 Oct., in the consulship of the illustrious Alipius and Ardaburis (447).

LETTER XVII[2].

To all the bishops of Sicily (*forbidding the sale of church property except for the advantage of the church*).

Leo, the pope[2a], to all the bishops of Sicily.

The occasion of specific complaints claims our attention as having "the care of all the churches," that we should make a perpetual decree precluding all bishops from adopting as a practice what in two churches of your province has been unscrupulously suggested and wrongfully carried out. Upon the clergy of the church in Tauromenium deploring the destitution they were in from the bishop having squandered all its estates by selling, giving away, and otherwise disposing of them, the clergy of Panormus, who have lately had a new bishop, raised a similar complaint about the misgovernment of the former bishop in the holy synod, at which we were presiding. Although, therefore, we have already given instructions as to what is for the advantage of both Churches, yet lest this vicious example of abominable plundering should hereafter be taken as a precedent, we wish to make this our formal command binding on you, beloved, for ever. We decree, therefore, that no bishop without exception shall dare to give away, or to exchange, or to sell any of the property of his church: unless he foresees an advantage likely to accrue from so doing, and after consultation with the whole of the clergy, and with their consent, he decides upon what will undoubtedly profit that church. For presbyters, or deacons, or clerics of any rank who have connived at the church's losses, must know that they will be deprived of both rank and communion: because it is absolutely fair, beloved brethren, that not only the bishop, but also the whole of the clergy should advance the interests of their church and keep the gifts unimpaired of those who have contributed their own substance to the churches for the salvation of their souls. Dated 20 Oct., in the consulship of the illustrious Calepius (447).

LETTER XVIII.

To JANUARIUS, BISHOP OF AQUILEIA[3].

Leo, bishop of the city of Rome, to Januarius, bishop of Aquileia.

Those who renounce heresy and schism and return to the Church must make their recantation very clear: those who are clerics may retain their rank but not be promoted.

On reading your letter, brother, we recognized the vigour of your faith, which we already were aware of, and congratulate you on the watchful care you bestow as pastor on the keeping of Christ's flock: lest the wolves, that enter in under guise of sheep, should tear the simple ones to pieces in their bestial fierce-

[1] Cf. Lett. XIV., chap. 8, where the same rule is laid down.

[2] This letter is suspected by Quesnel as being, if not spurious, at least the production of some later Leo than our own: but he would seem to have hardly sufficient ground for his conjecture and the document is interesting as showing the existence of Church endowments at the time, and alas! of their mismanagement. Two centuries before indeed we have Cyprian in Africa uttering a somewhat similar complaint: e.g. *de laps.* vi., *de unit. eccl.* xxvi., Lett. XV. 3. It does not appear, however, there that the clergy actually misappropriated Church funds, only that they were greedy and intent on worldly gain.

[2a] *Papa.* This title, which in later times came throughout the West to denote exclusively the Bishop of Rome, was originally in the West no less than it is still in the East, the common appellation of all priests and spiritual fathers of the Church.

[3] The Ballerinii's conjecture is at least very plausible, that this Januarius was the successor of that Bishop of Aquileia to whom Letter I. was written 5 years previously upon the same subject of the Pelagian error. The text of this letter is almost word for word identical with Letter II., written to Septimus, Bishop of Altinum, on the same occasion as Lett. I.

ness, and not only themselves run riot without restraint, but also spoil those which are sound. And lest the vipery deceit should effect this, we have thought it meet to warn you, beloved, reminding you that it is at the peril of his soul, for any one of them who has fallen away from us into a sect of heretics and schismatics[4], and stained himself to whatever extent with the pollution of heretical communion, to be received into catholic communion on coming to his senses without making legitimate and express satisfaction. For it is most wholesome and full of all the benefits of spiritual healing that presbyters or deacons, or sub-deacons or clerics of any rank, who wish to appear reformed, and entreat to return once more to the catholic Faith which they had long ago lost, should first confess without ambiguity that their errors and the authors of the errors themselves are condemned by them, that their base opinions may be utterly destroyed, and no hope survive of their recurrence, and that no member may be harmed by contact with them, every point having been met with its proper recantation. With regard to them we also order the observance of this regulation of the canons[5], that they consider it a great indulgence, if they be allowed to remain undisturbed in their present rank without any hope of further advancement: but only on consideration of their not being defiled with second baptism[6]. No slight penalty does he incur from the LORD, who judges any such person fit to be advanced to Holy Orders. If advancement is granted to those who are without blame, only after full examination, how much more ought it to be refused to those who are under suspicion. Accordingly, beloved brother, in whose devotion we rejoice, bestow your care on our directions, and take order for the circumspect and speedy carrying out of these laudable suggestions and wholesome injunctions, which affect the welfare of the whole Church. But do not doubt, beloved, that, if what we decree for the observance of the canons, and the integrity of the Faith be neglected (which we do not anticipate), we shall be strongly moved: because the faults of the lower orders are to be referred to none more than to slothful and careless governors, who often foster much disease by refusing to apply the needful remedy. Dated 30 Dec., in the consulship of the illustrious Calepius and Ardaburis (447).

LETTER XIX.

To Dorus, Bishop of Beneventum.

Leo, bishop, to Dorus his well-beloved brother.

I. *He rebukes Dorus for allowing a junior presbyter to be promoted over the heads of the seniors, and the first and second in seniority for acquiescing.*

We grieve that the judgment, which we hoped to entertain of you, has been frustrated by our ascertaining that you have done things which by their blame-worthy novelty infringe the whole system of Church discipline: although you know full well with what care we wish the provisions of the canons to be kept through all the churches of the LORD, and the priests of all the peoples to consider it their especial duty to prevent the violation of the rules of the holy constitutions by any extravagances. We are surprised, therefore, that you who ought to have been a strict observer of the injunctions of the Apostolic See have acted so carelessly, or rather so contumaciously, as to show yourself not a guardian, but a breaker of the laws handed on to you. For from the report of your presbyter, Paul, which is subjoined, we have learnt that the order of the presbyterate has been thrown into confusion with you by strange intrigues and vile collusion; in such a way that one man has been hastily and prematurely promoted, and others passed over whose advancement was recommended by their age, and who were charged with no fault. But if the eagerness of an intriguer or the ignorant zeal of his supporters demanded that which custom never allowed, viz., that a beginner should be preferred to veterans, and a mere boy to men of years, it was your duty by diligence and teaching to check the improper desires of the petitioners with all reasonable authority: lest he whom you advanced hastily to the priestly rank should enter on his office to the detriment of those with whom he associated and become demoralized by the growth within him, not of the virtue of humility, but of the vice of conceit[7]. For you were not unaware that the LORD had said that "he that humbleth himself shall be exalted: but he that exalteth

4 *Schismaticorum*, considering how easily heresy leads to schism and schism to heresy, there is no need with Quesnel to consider that Novatians or Donatists are being here attacked. The Ballerinii say with justice:—*generalis regula hic indicatur omnibus tum hæreticis tum schismaticis ad ecclesiam redeuntibus communis*.

5 What canon is here alluded to is uncertain: the Ballerinii think perhaps the 8th Nicene canon, extending its application from the Cathari or Novatians to all heresies and schism.

6 *Si tamen iterata tinctione non fuerint maculati*. Cf. Can. Afric., 27, *neque permittendum ut rebaptizati ad clericatus gradum promoveantur*.

7 *Ne quem sacerdotali propere provehebas honore, ad iniuriam eorum quibus sociabatur, inciperet minorque se fieret*: the text no doubt corrupt, though the general sense is clear: the emendation *minorque se* for *miror quis* is made almost certain by the quotations that follow, especially the second.

himself shall be humbled[8]," and also had said, "but ye seek from little to increase, and from the greater to be less[9]." For both actions are out of order and out of place[1]: and all the fruit of men's labours is lost, all the measure of their deserts is rendered void, if the gaining of dignity is proportioned to the amount of flattery used: so that the eagerness to be eminent belittles not only the aspirer himself, but also him that connives at him. But if, as is asserted, the first and second presbyter were so agreeable to Epicarpius being put over their heads as to demand his being honoured to their own disgrace, that which they wished ought not to have been granted them when they were voluntarily degrading themselves: because it would have been worthier of you to oppose than to yield to such a pitiable wish. But their base and cowardly submission could not be to the prejudice of others whose consciences were good, and who had not done despite to God's grace; so that, whatever the transaction was whereby they gave up their precedence to another, they could not lower the dignity of those that came next to them, nor because they had placed the last above themselves, could he take precedence of the rest.

II. *The presbyters, who gave way, to be degraded with the usurper to the bottom: the rest to keep their places.*

The aforesaid presbyters, therefore, who have declared themselves unworthy of their proper rank, though they even deserved to be deprived of their priesthood; yet, that we may show the gentleness of the Apostolic See in sparing them, are to be put last of all the presbyters of the Church: and that they may bear their own sentence, they shall be below him also whom they preferred to themselves by their own judgment: all the other presbyters remaining in the order which the time of his ordination assigns to each. And let none except the two aforesaid suffer any loss of dignity, but let this disgrace attach to those only who chose to put themselves below a junior who had only lately been ordained: that they may feel that that sentence of the gospels applies to themselves when it is said: "with what judgment ye judge, ye shall be judged: and with what measure ye mete, the same shall be measured unto you[2]." But let Paul the presbyter retain his place from which with praiseworthy firmness he did not budge: and let no further encroachments be made to any one's harm: so that you, beloved, who not undeservedly get the discredit of the whole matter, may with all speed take measures to cure it at least by putting these our injunctions into effect; lest, if a second time a just complaint be lodged with us, we be forced into stronger displeasure: for we would rather restore discipline by correcting what is done wrong, than increase the punishment. Know that we have entrusted the carrying out of our commands to our brother and fellow-bishop Julius, that all things may straightway be established, as we have ordained. Dated 8th March, in the consulship of the illustrious Postumianus (448).

LETTER XX.

To Eutyches, an Abbot of Constantinople.

Leo, the bishop, to his dearly-beloved son, Eutyches, presbyter.

He thanks him for his information about the revival of Nestorianism and commends his zeal.

You have brought to our knowledge, beloved, by your letter that through the activity of some[3] the heresy of Nestorius has been again reviving. We reply that your solicitude in this matter has pleased us, since the remarks we have received are an indication of your mind. Wherefore do not doubt that the Lord, the Founder of the catholic Faith, will befriend you in all things. And when we have been able to ascertain more fully by whose wickedness this happens, we must make provision with the help of God for the complete uprooting of this poisonous growth which has long ago been condemned. God keep thee safe, my beloved son. Dated 1st June, in the consulship of the illustrious Postumianus and Zeno (448).

LETTER XXI.

From Eutyches to Leo[4].

I. *He states his account of the proceedings at the Synod.*

God the Word is before all else my witness,

---

8 S. Luke xiv. 11 and xviii. 14.

9 *Vos autem quæritis de pusillo crescere et de maiore minores esse.* This remarkable addition to S. Matt. xx. 28 is found in Cod. D, in some Syriac and many Latin copies: read Westcott's note in Appendix C 3 to *Introduction to Study, &c.*

1 *Inordinatum, præposterum.* Cf. Lett. XII., chap. 2, n. 8.

2 S. Matt. vii. 2; S. Mark iv. 24; S. Luke vi. 36

3 Quesnel is of opinion that Eutyches' letter had accused Domnus, Bishop of Antioch, and Theodoret, Bishop of Cyrus (cf. Lett. CXX., chapters iv. and v.), of Nestorianizing, and that he thus had gained the approbation of Leo before his own unsoundness had been made known.

4 Contrary to my general plan, I have thought it wiser, in the matter of the Eutychian controversy, to include other than Leo's own writings, that the reader may fulfil the precept *audi alteram partem* in what was the most important doctrinal discussion of Leo's term of office. This Letter (XXI.) bears the stamp of genuineness upon it, though the Gk. original is not found. It is from a collection of documents bearing on Nestorianism published *ex MS. Casinensi*, first by Christianus Lupus (?), and afterwards by Stephanus Baluzius (1630—1718).

being confident of my hope and faith in Christ the LORD and GOD of all, and discerning the proof of my holding the truth in these matters: but I call on your holiness, too, to bear witness to my heart and to the reasonableness of my opinions and words. But the wicked devil has exercised his evil influence upon my zeal and determination, whereby his power ought to have been destroyed. Whereupon he has exerted all his proper power and aroused Eusebius, bishop of the town of Dorylæum, against me, who presented an allegation [5] to the holy bishop of the church in Constantinople, Flavian, and to certain others whom he found in the same city assembled on various matters of their own: in this he called me heretic, not raising any true accusation but contriving destruction for me and disturbance for the churches of GOD.

Their holinesses summoned me to reply to his accusation: but though I was delayed by a serious illness besides my advanced age, I came to clear myself, knowing well that a faction had been formed against my safety. And, indeed, together with a writ of appeal [6] to which my signature was appended, I offered them a statement showing my confession upon the holy Faith. But when the holy Flavian did not receive the document, nor order it to be read, yet heard me in reply utter word for word that Faith which was put forth at Nicæa by the holy Synod, and confirmed at Ephesus, I was required to acknowledge two natures, and to anathematize those who denied this. But I, fearing the decision of the synod, and not wishing either to take away or to add one word contrary to the Faith put forth by the holy Synod of Nicæa, knowing, too, that our holy and blessed fathers and bishops Julius, Felix, Athanasius, and Gregorius [7] rejected the phrase "two natures," and not daring to discuss the nature of GOD the Word, who came into flesh in the last days entering the womb of the holy virgin Mary unchangeably as he willed and knew, becoming man in reality, not in fancy, nor yet venturing to anathematize our aforesaid Fathers, I asked them to let your holiness know these things, that you might judge what seemed right to you, undertaking by all means to follow your ruling.

II. *His explanations were allowed no hearing.*

But without listening to any thing which I said, they broke up the Synod and published the sentence of my degradation, which they were getting ready against me before the inquiry. So much slander were they factiously making up against me that even my safety would have been endangered had not the help of GOD at the intercession of your holiness quickly snatched me from the assault of military force. Then they began to force the heads of other monasteries [8] to subscribe to my degradation (a thing which was never done either towards those who have professed themselves heretics, nor even against Nestorius himself), insomuch that when to reassure the people I tried to set forth [9] statements of my faith, not only did they, who were plotting the aforesaid faction against me, prevent them being heard, but also seized them that straightway I might be held a heretic before all.

III. *He appeals to Leo for protection.*

I take refuge, therefore, with you the defender of religion and abhorrer of such factions, bringing in even still nothing strange against the faith as it was originally handed down to us, but anathematizing Apollinaris, Valentinus, Manes, and Nestorius, and those who say that the flesh of our Lord Jesus Christ, the Saviour, descended from heaven and not from the Holy Ghost and from the holy Virgin, along with all heresies down to Simon Magus. Yet nevertheless I stand in jeopardy of my life as a heretic. I beseech you not to be prejudiced against me by their insidious designs about me, but to pronounce the sentence which shall seem to you right upon the Faith, and in future not to allow any slander to be uttered against me by this faction, nor let one be expelled and banished from the number of the orthodox who has spent his seventy years of life in continence and all chastity, so that at the very end of life he should suffer shipwreck. I have subjoined to this my letter both documents, that which was presented by my accuser at the Synod, and that which was brought by me but not received, as well as the statement of my faith and those things which have been decreed upon the two natures by our holy Fathers [1].

---

5 See Introduction, p. vii.

6 *Libelli* sc. (*appellationis ad Leonem*): this is referred to by Flavian (Lett. XXVI., chap. iii.) and denied.

7 Of these four worthies, *Athanasius* is too well known to need further notice: *Gregorius* is either Greg. Nazianzen, Bishop of Constantinople (circ. 380), or Greg. of Nyssa, both great champions of the Church against Arianism (*not*, as the Ball., Greg. Thaumaturgus, Bishop of Neo-Cæsarea, 244-70): *Julius* was a Bishop of Rome (337-52): an excerpt from one of his letters is printed by the Ball. at the end of this letter as the passage on which Eutyches based his error, though they suspect it (not unnaturally) as being an Apollinarian imposition: *Felix* is probably no other than the Arian Bishop of Rome, Felix II. (355-8) whose appointment is characterized by Athanasius as effected "by antichristian wickedness," but who is yet a canonized saint and martyr of the Roman Church (see Schaff's Hist., vol. ii. p. 371; iii. 635, 6).

8 Abbots' signatures are found attached to the condemnation of Eutyches by the synod of Constantinople.

9 Cf. Letter XXVI., chap. ii., *propositiones iniuriarum publice ponens et maledictionibus plenas* Gk. προθεμετα ὕβρεως καὶ λοιδορίας ἀνάμεστα), which is Flavian's account of the matter.

1 Of these four documents (1) Eusebius' *libellus* is preserved in

EUTYCHES' CONFESSION OF FAITH.

I call upon you before GOD, who gives life to all things, and Christ Jesus, who witnessed that good confession under Pontius Pilate, that you do nothing by favour. For I have held the same as my forefathers and from my boyhood have been illuminated by the same Faith as that which was laid down by the holy Synod of 318 most blessed bishops who were gathered at Nicæa from the whole world, and which was confirmed and ratified afresh for sole acceptance by the holy Synod assembled at Ephesus: and I have never thought otherwise than as the right and only true orthodox Faith has enjoined. And I agree to everything that was laid down about the same Faith by the same holy Synod: of which Synod the leader and chief was Cyril of blessed memory bishop of the Alexandrians, the partner and sharer in the preaching and in the Faith of those saints and elect of GOD, Gregory the greater, and the other Gregory [2], Basil, Athanasius, Atticus and Proclus. Him and all of them I have held orthodox and faithful, and have honoured as saints, and have esteemed my masters. But I utter an anathema on Nestorius, Apollinaris, and all heretics down to Simon, and those who say that the flesh of our LORD Jesus Christ came down from heaven. For He who is the Word of GOD came down from heaven without flesh and was made flesh in the holy Virgin's womb unchangeably and unalterably as He Himself knew and willed. And He who was always perfect GOD before the ages, was also made perfect man in the end of the days for us and for our salvation. This my full profession may your holiness consider.

I, Eutyches, presbyter and archimandrite, have subscribed to this statement with my own hand.

LETTER XXII [3].

THE FIRST FROM FLAVIAN, BP. OF CONSTANTINOPLE TO POPE LEO.

To the most holy and God-loving father and fellow-bishop, Leo, Flavian greeting in the LORD.

I. *The designs of the devil have led Eutyches astray.*

There is nothing which can stay the devil's wickedness, that "restless evil, full of deadly poison [4]." Above and below it "goes about," seeking "whom it may" strike, dismay, and "devour [5]." Whence to watch, to be sober unto prayer, to draw near to GOD, to eschew foolish questionings, to follow the fathers and not to go beyond the eternal bounds, this we have learnt from Holy Writ. And so I give up the excess of grief and abundant tears over the capture of one of the clergy who are under me, and whom I could not save nor snatch from the wolf, although I was ready to lay down my life for him. How was he caught, how did he leap away, hating the voice of the caller and turning aside also from the memory of the Fathers and thoroughly detesting their paths. And thus I proceed with my account.

II. *The seductions of heretics capture the unwary.*

There are some "in sheep's clothing, but inwardly they are ravening wolves [6]:" whom we know by their fruit. These men seem indeed at first to be of us, but they are not of us: "for if they had been of us, they would no doubt have continued with us [7]." But when they have spewed out their impiety, throwing out the guile that is in them, and seizing the weaker ones, and those who have their senses unpractised in the divine utterances, they carry them along with themselves to destruction, wresting and doing despite to the Fathers' doctrines, just as they do the Holy Scriptures also to their own destruction: whom we must be forewarned of and take heed lest some should be misled by their wickedness and shaken in their firmness. "For they have sharpened their tongues like serpents: adder's poison is under their lips [8]," as the prophet has cried out about them.

III. *Eutyches' heresy stated.*

Such a one, therefore, has now shown himself amongst us, Eutyches, for many years a presbyter and archimandrite [9], pretending to hold the same belief as ours, and to have the right Faith in him: indeed he resists the blasphemy of Nestorius, and feigns a controversy with him, but the exposition of the Faith composed by the 318 holy fathers, and the letter that Cyril of holy memory wrote to Nestorius, and one by the same author on the same subject to the Easterns, these writings, to which

Act 1 Chalcedon; (2) is not forthcoming; (3) is appended below; and (4) a fragment of the testimony of Julius, which is given, does not seem important enough to be added in this edition, especially as its genuineness is denied.

2 Here we have the two Gregorys mentioned: cf. n. 7, above.

3 There are two Latin versions of the original Gk. of this letter, an older and a later: the later, as being more accurate, is here translated, though Canon Bright would seem to be right (n. 139) in saying that we must think of Leo as writing the Tome (Lett. XXVIII.) with the older Latin version of Flavian's letter before him.'

4 S. Jam. iii. 8.

5 1 S. Pet. v. 8.

6 S. Matt. vii. 15.

7 1 John ii. 19.

8 Ps. cxl. 3.

9 Viz., head of a monastery (Gk. μάνδρα) or abbot.

all have given their assent, he has tried to upset, and revive the old evil dogmas of the blasphemous Valentinus and Apollinaris. He has not feared the warning of the True King: "Whoso shall cause one of the least of these little ones to stumble, it was better that a millstone should be hanged about his neck, and that he should be sunk in the depth of the sea[1]." But casting away all shame, and shaking off the cloak which covered his error[2], he openly in our holy synod persisted in saying that our LORD Jesus Christ ought not to be understood by us as having two natures after His incarnation in one substance and in one person: nor yet that the LORD's flesh was of the same substance with us, as if assumed from us and united to GOD the Word hypostatically: but he said that the Virgin who bare him was indeed of the same substance with us according to the flesh, but the LORD Himself did not assume from her flesh of the same substance with us: but the LORD's body was not a man's body, although that which issued from the Virgin was a human body, resisting all the expositions of the holy Fathers.

IV. *He has sent Leo the minutes of their proceedings that he may see all the details.*

But not to make my letter too long by detailing everything, we have sent your holiness the proceedings which some time since we took in the matter: therein we deprived him as convicted on these charges, of his priesthood, of the management of his monastery and of our communion: in order that your holiness also knowing the facts of his case may make his wickedness manifest to all the GOD-loving bishops who are under your reverence; lest perchance if they do not know the views which he holds, and of which he has been openly convicted, they may be found to be in correspondence with him as a fellow-believer by letter or by other means. I and those who are with me give much greeting to you and to all the brotherhood in Christ. The LORD keep you in safety and prayer for us, O most GOD-loving father[3]

LETTER XXIII.

To Flavian, Bishop of Constantinople.

To his well-beloved brother Flavian the bishop, Leo the bishop.

I. *He complains that Flavian has not sent him a full account of Eutyches' case.*

Seeing that our most Christian and merciful Emperor, in his holy and praiseworthy faith and anxiety for the peace of the Catholic Church, has sent us a letter[4] upon the matters which have roused the din of disturbance among you, we wonder, brother, that you have been able to keep silence to us upon the scandal that has been caused, and that you did not rather take measures for our being at once informed by your own report, that we might not have any doubt about the truth of the case. For we have received a document from the presbyter Eutyches[5], who complains that on the accusation of bishop Eusebius he has been wrongfully deprived of communion, notwithstanding that he says he attended your summons and did not refuse his presence: and moreover asserts that he presented a deed of appeal in the very court, which was however not accepted: whereupon he was forced to put forth letters of defence[6] in the city of Constantinople. Pending which matter we do not yet know with what justice he has been separated from the communion of the Church. But having regard to the importance of the matter, we wish to know the reason of your action and to have the whole thing brought to our knowledge: for we, who desire the judgments of the LORD's priests to be deliberate, cannot without information decide one way or another, until we have all the proceedings accurately before us.

II. *And now demands it.*

And therefore, brother, signify to us in a full account by the hand of the most fit and competent person, what innovation has arisen against the ancient faith, which needed to be corrected by so severe a sentence. For both the moderation of the Church and the devout faith of our most godly prince insist upon our showing much anxiety for the peace of Christendom: that dissensions may be cleared away and the Catholic Faith kept unimpaired, and that those whose faith has been proved may be fortified by our authority, when those who

---

1 S. Matt. xviii. 6, but it will be noticed that the quotation is confused with xxv. 40, *minimis* being substituted for *qui in me credunt*.

2 *Pudorem* (instead of the *impudenter* of the MSS.) *omnem abiciens et pellem quæ eum circumdabat excutiens*, the Gk. version of this somewhat obscure passage running αἰδῶ πᾶσαν ἀποβαλὼν καὶ ἣν περιέκειτο τῆς πλάνης δορὰν ἀποτιναξάμενος.

3 This was the letter "which was somewhat unaccountably delayed in its transit to Rome" (Bright), which reached Leo after XXIII. was written, and to which Leo refers in the Tome, chap. i., *litteris, quas miramur fuisse tam seras*. Bright's note 139 should be read throughout as a clear exposition of the preliminary steps in the controversy.

4 This letter from Theodosius II. came soon after Eutyches, letter (XXI), and "apparently gave Leo the impression, that Eutyches had been badly treated." Bright.

5 See Letter XXI., above.

6 *Contestatorios libellos*. See Lett. XXI., chap. ii.

maintain what is wrong have been recalled from their error. And no difficulty can arise on this side, since the said presbyter has professed himself, by his own statement, ready to be corrected if anything be found in him worthy of rebuke. For it beseems us in such matters to take every precaution that charity be kept and the Truth defended without the din of strife. And therefore because you see, beloved, that we are anxious about so great a matter, hasten to inform us of everything in as full and clear a manner as possible (for this ought to have been done before), lest in the cross-statements of both sides we be misled by some uncertainty, and the dissension, which ought to be stifled in its infancy, be fostered: for our heart is impressed by God's inspiration with the need of saving from violation by anyone's misinterpretation those constitutions of the venerable fathers which have received Divine ratification and belong to the groundwork of the Faith. God keep thee safe, dear brother. Dated 18 February (449), in the consulship of the illustrious Asturius and Protogenes.

LETTER XXIV.

To Theodosius Augustus II.

Leo the bishop, to Theodosius Augustus.

I. *He praises the Emperor's piety and mentions Eutyches' appeal.*

How much protection the Lord has vouchsafed His Church through your clemency and faith, is shown again by this letter which you have sent me: so that we rejoice at there being not only a kingly, but also a priestly mind within you. Seeing that, besides your imperial and public cares, you have a most devout anxiety for the Christian religion, lest schisms or heresies or other offences should grow up among God's people. For your realm is then in its best state when men serve the eternal and unchangeable Trinity by the confession of one Godhead [7]. What the disturbance was which occurred in the Church of Constantinople, and which could have so moved my brother and fellow-bishop Flavian, that he deprived Eutyches, the presbyter, of communion, I have not yet been able to understand clearly. For although the aforesaid presbyter sent in writing a complaint concerning his trouble to the Apostolic See, yet he only briefly touched on some points, asserting that he kept the constitutions of the Nicene synod and had been vainly blamed for difference of faith.

II. *He finds fault with Flavian's silence.*

But the statement of bishop Eusebius, his accuser, copies of which the said presbyter has sent us, contained nothing clear about his objections, and though he charged a presbyter with heresy, he did not say expressly what opinion he disapproved of in him: although the bishop himself also professed that he adhered to the decrees of the Nicene synod: for which reason we had no means of learning anything more fully. And because the method of our Faith and the laudable anxiety shown by your piety requires the merits of the case to be known, there must now be no place allowed for deception, but we must be informed of the points on which he considers him unsound, that the right judgment may be passed after full information. I have sent a letter to the aforesaid bishop, from which he may gather that I am displeased at his still keeping silence upon what has been done in so grave a matter, when he ought to have been forward in disclosing all to us at the outset: and we believe that even after the reminder he will acquaint us with the whole, in order that, when what now seems obscure, has been brought into the light, judgment may be passed agreeably to the teaching of the Gospels and the Apostles. Dated the 18th of February [8], in the consulship of the illustrious Asturius and Protogenes (449).

LETTER XXV.

From Peter Chrysologus, Bishop of Ravenna, to Eutyches, the Presbyter.

[In answer to a letter from Eutyches, he urges him to accept the decisions of the Church on the Faith in fear and without too close inquiry, and to abide by the ruling of the bishop of Rome.]

LETTER XXVI [9].

A second one from Flavian to Leo.

To the most holy and blessed father and fellow-minister Leo, Flavian greeting in the Lord.

7 Is it fanciful to trace an analogy between these words and the language of the Collect for Trinity Sunday (out of the Sacramentary of Gregory), "grace by the confession of a true faith to acknowledge the glory of the Eternal Trinity, and in the power of the Divine Majesty to worship the Unity?"

8 Quesnel reads the 1st of March as the date.

9 In reading the Tome (Lett. XXVIII.) the reader is warned to remember that he must take no account of this letter, which did not reach Leo until later, and which is acknowledged in Lett. XXXVI. dated a week after the Tome. Bright (n. 139). There are two versions of this letter also, the ancient one and a modern one by Joannes Cotelerius, which latter, as being a more exact reproduction of the Gk. original, we have taken as the basis of our English translation.

I. *Eutyches' heresy restated.*

Nothing, as you know, most beloved of God, is more precious to priests than piety and the right dividing of the word of truth. For all our hope and safety, and the recompense of promised good depend thereon. For this reason we must take all pains about the true Faith, and those things which have been set forth and decreed by the holy Fathers, that always, and in all circumstances, they may be kept and guarded whole and uninjured. And so it was necessary on the present occasion for us, who see the orthodox Faith suffering harm, and the heresy of Apollinaris and Valentinus being revived by the wicked monk Eutyches, not to overlook it, but publicly to disclose it for the people's safety. For this man, this Eutyches, keeping his diseased and sickly opinion hid within him, has dared to attack our gentleness, and unblushingly and shamelessly to instil his own blasphemy into many minds: saying that before the Incarnation, indeed, our Saviour Jesus Christ had two natures, Godhead and manhood: but that after the union they became one nature; not knowing[1] what he says, or on what he is speaking so decidedly. For even the union of the two natures that came together in Christ did not, as your piety knows, confuse their properties in the process: but the properties of the two natures remain entire even in the union. And he added another blasphemy also, saying that the Lord's body which sprang from Mary was not of our substance, nor of human matter: but, though he calls it human, he refuses to say it was consubstantial with us or with her who bare him, according to the flesh[2].

II. *The means Eutyches has taken to circumvent the Synod.*

And this notwithstanding that the acts of Ephesus[3], in the letter written by the holy and ecumenical synod to the wicked and deposed Nestorius, contain these express words: "the natures which came together to form true unity are indeed different: and yet from them both there is but one Christ and Son. Not as if the difference between the two natures was done away with through the union, but rather that these same natures, His Godhead and His Manhood perfected for us one Lord Jesus Christ, through an ineffable and incomprehensible meeting which resulted in unity." And this does not escape your holiness, who have no doubt read the record of what was done at Ephesus. Yet this same Eutyches attaching no weight to these words, thinks he is not liable to the penalties fixed by that holy and ecumenical synod. For this reason, finding that many of the simpler-minded folk were injured in their faith by his contention, upon his being accused by the devout Bishop Eusebius, and upon his attending at the holy council, and with his own mouth declaring what he thought to the members of the synod, we have deposed him for his estrangement from the true Faith, as your holiness will learn from the resolutions passed about him: which we have sent with this our letter. Moreover, it is fair in my opinion that you should be told this also that this same Eutyches, after suffering just and canonical deposition, instead of making amends for his earlier by his later conduct[4], and appeasing God by careful penitence and many tears, and by a true repentance, comforting our heart which was greatly saddened at his fall: not only did not do so, but even made every effort to throw the most holy church of this place into confusion: setting up in public placards full of insults and maledictions, and beyond this addressing his entreaties to our most religious and Christ-loving Emperor, and these too over-flowing with arrogance and sauciness, whereby he tried to override the divine canons in everything.

III. *He acknowledges the receipt of Leo's letter.*

But after all this had occurred, your holiness' letter was conveyed to us by the most honourable count Pansophius: and from it we learnt that the same Eutyches had sent you a letter full of falsehood and cunning, saying that at the time of trial he had presented letters of appeal to us, and to the holy synod of bishops who were then present, and had appealed to your holiness: this he certainly never did, but in this matter, too, he has been guilty of deceit, like the father of lies, thinking to gain your ear. Therefore, most holy father, being stirred by all that he has ventured, and by what has been done, and is being done against us and the most holy Church, use your accustomed promptitude as becomes the priesthood, and in defending the commonweal and peace of the holy churches, consent by your own letter[5] to endorse the resolution that has been

---

1 *Ignarus:* it will be remembered that in the Tome (chap. i.) this is the chief fault which Leo also has to find with Eutyches, calling him *multum imprudens et nimis imperitus*, &c.

2 So in Lett. XXII., chap. iii., *Domini corpus non esse quidem corpus hominis, humanum autem corpus esse quod ex Virgine est.*

3 The date of this Council is 431 B.C.

4 *Saltem secundis curare priora* (Gk. κἂν τοῖς δευτέροις ἰάσασθαι τὰ πρότερα).

5 Cf. Lett. XXVII., n. 7, where the difference between Flavian's request here and in Lett. XXII., chap iv., is pointed out.

canonically passed against him, and to confirm the faith of our most religious and Christ-loving Emperor. For the matter only requires your weight and support, which through your wisdom will at once bring about general peace and quietness. For thus both the heresy which has arisen, and the disorder it has excited, will easily be appeased by GOD's assistance through a letter from you: and the rumoured synod will also be prevented, and so the most holy churches throughout the world need not be disturbed. I and all that are with me salute all the brethren that are with you. May you be granted to us safe in the LORD, and still praying for us, O most GOD-loving and holy father.

LETTER XXVII.

TO FLAVIAN, BISHOP OF CONSTANTINOPLE.

Leo to Flavian, bishop of Constantinople.

An acknowledgment of Flavian's first letter and a promise of a fuller reply.

On the first opportunity we could find, which was the coming of our honourable son Rodanus, we acknowledge, beloved, the arrival of your packet[6], which was to give us information about the case which has been stirred up to our grief among you by misguided error. Since this man, who has long seemed to be religiously disposed, has expressed himself in the Faith otherwise than is right, though he never ought to have departed from the catholic tradition, but to have persevered in the same belief as is held by all. But on this matter we are replying more fully[7] by him who brought your letter to us, beloved: that we may give you all necessary instructions, beloved, on the whole matter. For we do not allow either him to persist in his perverse conviction; or you, beloved, who with such faithful zeal are resisting his wrong and foolish error to be long disturbed by the adversary's opposition. Our aforesaid son, by whom we are sending this letter, we desire you to receive with the affection he deserves, and to reply when he returns to us. Dated 21st May in the consulship of Asturius and Protogenes (449).

6 *Epistolas.* This refers to Lett. XXII., and includes the *gesta* (or minutes of the synod's proceedings) which accompanied it.

7 This is the Tome (Letter XXVIII.): it will be noticed that Flavian (in Lett. XXII.) had not asked for any instructions, but only that Leo should inform the bishops under his jurisdiction of Eutyches' deposition (chap. iv.). Flavian's second letter (XXVI.), however, does mention *vestras sacras litteras*, which he hopes will avoid the necessity of a council (chap. iii.). Leo himself seems to be conscious of this: for in Letter XXXIII., chap. 2, he twice pointedly puts in the word "seems," as if Flavian had not expressed himself quite clearly: "the points which he seems to have referred to us," and "this error which seems to have arisen."

LETTER XXVIII.

TO FLAVIAN COMMONLY CALLED "THE TOME."

I. *Eutyches has been driven into his error by presumption and ignorance*[8].

Having read your letter, beloved, at the late arrival of which we are surprised[9], and having perused the detailed account of the bishops' acts[1], we have at last found out what the scandal was which had arisen among you against the purity of the Faith: and what before seemed concealed has now been unlocked and laid open to our view: from which it is shown that Eutyches, who used to seem worthy of all respect in virtue of his priestly office, is very unwary and exceedingly ignorant, so that it is even of him that the prophet has said: "he refused to understand so as to do well: he thought upon iniquity in his bed[2]." But what more iniquitous than to hold blasphemous opinions[3], and not to give way to those who are wiser and more learned than ourself. Now into this unwisdom fall they who, finding themselves hindered from knowing the truth by some obscurity, have recourse not to the prophets' utterances, not to the Apostles' letters, nor to the injunctions of the Gospel but to their own selves: and thus they stand out as masters of error because they were never disciples of truth. For what learning has he acquired about the pages of the New and Old Testament, who has not even grasped the rudiments of the Creed? And that which, throughout the world, is professed by the mouth of every one who is to be born again[4], is not yet taken in by the heart of this old man.

II. *Concerning the twofold nativity and nature of Christ.*

Not knowing, therefore, what he was bound to think concerning the incarnation of the Word of GOD, and not wishing to gain the light of knowledge by researches through the length

8 The original word (*imperitia*) implies that a recluse like Eutyches (an archimandrite of a convent) ought never to have entered into a nice controversy like the present: he has not enough *savoir faire*, and his knowledge is not quite up to date, is a little old-fashioned.

9 The exact reason of the delay is not altogether certain: we know Flavian had written much earlier than the date of arrival warranted: it is No. XXII. in the series.

1 Viz., the proceedings of the σύνοδος ἐνδημοῦσα summoned by Flavian at Constantinople.

2 Ps. xxxvi. 4.

3 *Impia sapere*, to think disloyal things against God: cf. the *recta sapere*, "to have a right judgment" of the Collect for Whitsunday.

4 Knowledge of and belief in the principles of the Faith as contained in the Creed (*symbolum*) have of course always been required before Baptism from very early times. Leo here calls catechumens *regenerandi*, just as those who are being baptized are spoken of as *renascentes* (e.g. Lett. XVII. 8), those who have been baptized as *renati* (*passim*), and the rite itself as *sacramentum regenerationis* (e.g. Lett. IX. 2)

and breadth of the Holy Scriptures, he might at least have listened attentively to that general and uniform confession, whereby the whole body of the faithful confess that they *believe in* GOD *the Father Almighty, and in Jesus Christ, His only Son*[5], *our Lord, who was born of the Holy Spirit and*[6] *the Virgin Mary*. By which three statements the devices of almost all heretics are overthrown. For not only is GOD believed to be both Almighty and the Father, but the Son is shown to be co-eternal with Him, differing in nothing from the Father because He is *God from. God*[7], Almighty from Almighty, and being born from the Eternal one is co-eternal with Him; not later in point of time, not lower in power, not unlike in glory, not divided in essence: but at the same time the only begotten of the eternal Father was born eternal of the Holy Spirit and the Virgin Mary. And this nativity which took place in time took nothing from, and added nothing to that divine and eternal birth, but expended itself wholly on the restoration of man who had been deceived[8]: in order that he might both vanquish death and overthrow by his strength[9], the Devil who possessed the power of death. For we should not now be able to overcome the author of sin and death unless He took our nature on Him and made it His own, whom neither sin could pollute nor death retain. Doubtless then, He was conceived of the Holy Spirit within the womb of His Virgin Mother, who brought Him forth without the loss of her virginity, even as she conceived Him without its loss.

But if He could not draw a rightful understanding (of the matter) from this pure source of the Christian belief, because He had darkened the brightness of the clear truth by a veil of blindness peculiar to Himself, He might have submitted Himself to the teaching of the Gospels. And when Matthew speaks of "the Book of the Generation of Jesus Christ, the Son of David, the Son of Abraham[1]," He might have also sought out the instruction afforded by the statements of the Apostles. And reading in the Epistle to the Romans, "Paul, a servant of Jesus Christ, called an Apostle, separated unto the Gospel of GOD, which He had promised before by His prophets in the Holy Scripture concerning His son, who was made unto Him[2] of the seed of David after the flesh[3]," he might have bestowed a loyal carefulness upon the pages of the prophets. And finding the promise of God who says to Abraham, "In thy seed shall all nations be blest[4]," to avoid all doubt as to the reference of this seed, he might have followed the Apostle when He says, "To Abraham were the promises made and to his seed. He saith not and to seeds, as if in many, but as in one, and to thy seed which is Christ[5]." Isaiah's prophecy also he might have grasped by a closer attention to what he says, "Behold, a virgin shall conceive and bear a Son and they shall call His name Immanuel," which is interpreted "GOD with us[6]." And the same prophet's words he might have read faithfully. "A child is born to us, a Son is given to us, whose power is upon His shoulder, and they shall call His name the Angel of the Great Counsel, Wonderful, Counsellor, the Mighty GOD, the Prince of Peace, the Father of the age to come[7]." And then he would not speak so erroneously as to say that the Word became flesh in such a way that Christ, born of the Virgin's womb, had the form of man, but had not the reality of His mother's body[8]. Or is it possible that he thought our LORD Jesus Christ was not of our nature for this reason, that the angel, who was sent to the blessed Mary ever Virgin, says, "The Holy Ghost shall come upon thee and the power of the Most High shall overshadow thee: and therefore that Holy Thing also that shall be born of thee shall be called the Son of GOD[9]," on the supposition that as the conception of the Virgin was a Divine act, the flesh of the conceived did not partake of the conceiver's nature? But that birth so uniquely wondrous and so wondrously unique, is not to be understood in such wise that the properties of His kind were removed through the novelty of His creation. For though the Holy Spirit imparted fertility to the Virgin, yet a real body was received from her body; and, "Wisdom building her a house[1]," "the Word became flesh and dwelt in us[2]," that is, in that flesh which he took from man and which he quickened with the breath of a higher life[3].

5 The Latin *unicus* is not so exact as the Greek original *μονογενής*: elsewhere, however, *unigenitus* is used.

6 N.B. *et* (and) not *ex* (out of).

7 The language of the Nicene Creed.

8 I.e. by the Devil: the allusion is to Adam's fall in Paradise.

9 *Sua virtute*: in patristic Latin *virtus* is, as is well known, usually the translation of the Greek *δύναμις* and has a much wider meaning than moral excellence, our virtue.

1 S. Matt. i. 1.

2 *ei*. So the Vulgate.

3 Rom. i. 1-3.

4 Gen. xii. 3.

5 Gal. iii. 16.

6 Is. vii. 14. and S. Matt. i. 23.

7 Is. ix. 6. "The angel of the great counsel" (*magni consilii angelus*) is a translation of the LXX. (which in the rest of the verse either represents a very different original text, or contents itself with a loose paraphrase), and is again repeated in the "Counsellor" (*Consiliarius*), two words farther on (which is also the Vulgate reading).

8 This was the third dogma of Apollinaris (more fully stated in Lett. CXXIV. 2 and CLXV. 2), that our Lord's acts and sufferings as man belonged entirely to His Divine nature, and were not really human at all.

9 S. Luke i. 35.

1 Prov. ix. 1.

2 *In nobis*, which he seems from the immediately following words to interpret as meaning "in our flesh," and not "amongst us," as the R.V. and others.

3 *Quam spiritu vitæ rationalis* (λογικοῦ) *animavit*.

III. *The Faith and counsel of God in regard to the incarnation of the Word are set forth.*

Without detriment therefore to the properties of either nature and substance which then came together in one person[4], majesty took on humility, strength weakness, eternity mortality: and for the paying off of the debt belonging to our condition inviolable nature was united with passible nature, so that, as suited the needs of our case[5], one and the same Mediator between God and men, the Man Christ Jesus, could both die with the one and not die with the other. [6] Thus in the whole and perfect nature of true man was true God born, complete in what was His own, complete in what was ours. And by "ours" we mean what the Creator formed in us from the beginning and what He undertook to repair. For what the Deceiver brought in and man deceived committed, had no trace in the Saviour. Nor, because He partook of man's weaknesses, did He therefore share our faults. He took the form of a slave[7] without stain of sin, increasing the human and not diminishing the divine: because that emptying of Himself whereby the Invisible made Himself visible and, Creator and Lord of all things though He be, wished to be a mortal, was the bending down[8] of pity, not the failing of power. Accordingly He who while remaining in the form of God made man, was also made man in the form of a slave. For both natures retain their own proper character without loss: and as the form of God did not do away with the form of a slave, so the form of a slave did not impair the form of God. For inasmuch as the Devil used to boast that man had been cheated by his guile into losing the divine gifts, and bereft of the boon of immortality had undergone sentence of death, and that he had found some solace in his troubles from having a partner in delinquency[9], and that God also at the demand of the principle of justice had changed His own purpose towards man whom He had created in such honour: there was need for the issue of a secret counsel, that the unchangeable God whose will cannot be robbed of its own kindness, might carry out the first design of His Fatherly care[1] towards us by a more hidden mystery[2]; and that man who had been driven into his fault by the treacherous cunning of the devil might not perish contrary to the purpose of God[3].

IV. *The properties of the twofold nativity and nature of Christ are weighed one against another.*

There enters then these lower parts of the world the Son of God, descending from His heavenly home and yet not quitting His Father's glory, begotten in a new order by a new nativity. In a new order, because being invisible in His own nature, He became visible in ours, and He whom nothing could contain was content to be contained[4]: abiding before all time He began to be in time: the Lord of all things, He obscured His immeasurable majesty and took on Him the form of a servant: being God that cannot suffer, He did not disdain to be man that can, and, immortal as He is, to subject Himself to the laws of death. The Lord assumed His mother's nature without her faultiness: nor in the Lord Jesus Christ, born of the Virgin's womb, does the wonderfulness of His birth make His nature unlike ours. For He who is true God is also true man: and in this union there is no lie[5], since the humility of manhood and the loftiness of the Godhead both meet there. For as God is not changed by the showing of pity, so man is not swallowed up by the dignity. For each form does what is proper to it with the co-operation of the other[6]; that is the Word performing what appertains to the Word, and the flesh carrying out what appertains to the flesh. One of

---

4 A famous passage quoted by Hooker, Eccl. Pol. v. 53, 2, and Liddon Bampt. Lect., p. 267. Compare Serm. lxii. 1, *quod . . . in unam personam concurrat proprietas utriusque substantiæ* (Bright), also xxii. 2, xxiii. 2.

5 *Quod nostris remediis congruebat*, where *remedia* must mean the disease which needs remedies (a sort of passive use).

6 This passage from "Thus in the whole" to "not the failing of power" is repeated again in Sermon xxiii. 2, almost word for word.

7 The reference, of course, is to Phil. ii. 6: no passage is a greater favourite with the Fathers than this.

8 Compare S. Aug. ad Catech. § 6, *humilitas Christi quid est? manum Deus homini iacenti porrexit: nos cecidimus, ille descendit: nos iacebamus, ille se inclinavit. Prendamus et surgamus ut non in pœnam cadamus.*

9 *De prævaricatoris consortio: prævaricator* originally is a legal term, signifying "a shuffler" in a suit, an advocate who plays into the hands of the other side.

1 *Pietas*, as in the collect for xvi. S. aft. Trin., where the English "pity" represents the Latin "pietas" philologically as well as in meaning. Cf. n. 2 in chap. vi.

2 *Sacramento*, (μυστηρίῳ): what the "mystery" was is finely set forth by Canon Bright's hymn, No. 172, H. A. and M. (new edition).

3 The whole of the end of this chapter from "For inasmuch as," and the beginning of the next down to "laws of death," is repeated word for word in Sermon XXII., chaps. i. and ii.

4 *Incomprehensibilis voluit comprehendi.* Canon Bright's references are most apposite: "compare Serm. lxviii., *idem est qui impiorum manibus comprehenditur et qui nullo fine concluditur:* and Serm. xxxvii. 1, *genetricis gremio continetur qui nullo fine concluditor.* This 'antithesis' has been grandly expressed in Milman's 'Martyr of Antioch.'

"'And Thou wast laid within the tomb . . .
Whom heaven could not contain,
Nor the immeasurable plain
Of vast infinity enclose or circle round.'"

5 I.e., there is no fancy, no pretending: each nature is in equal reality present, the human as well as the Divine, thus opposing all Docetic and Monophysite heresies.

6 This passage (which is repeated in Serm. liv., chap. 2, down to "injuries"), was objected to by the Illyrian and Palestinian bishops as savouring of the heresy of Nestorius who "divided the substance:" but it is obvious that the same words might have an orthodox meaning in the mouth of one who was orthodox and to the unorthodox would bear an unorthodox construction.

them sparkles with miracles, the other succumbs to injuries. And as the Word does not cease to be on an equality with His Father's glory, so the flesh does not forego the nature of our race. For it must again and again be repeated that one and the same is truly Son of GOD and truly son of man. GOD in that "in the beginning was the Word, and the Word was with GOD, and the Word was GOD[7];" man in that "the Word became flesh and dwelt in us[8]." GOD in that "all things were made by Him[9], and without Him was nothing made:" man in that "He was made of a woman, made under law[1]." The nativity of the flesh was the manifestation of human nature: the childbearing of a virgin is the proof of Divine power. The infancy of a babe is shown in the humbleness of its cradle[2]: the greatness of the Most High is proclaimed by the angels' voices[3]. He whom Herod treacherously endeavours to destroy is like ourselves in our earliest stage[4]: but He whom the Magi delight to worship on their knees is the LORD of all. So too when He came to the baptism of John, His forerunner, lest He should not be known through the veil of flesh which covered His Divinity, the Father's voice, thundering from the sky, said, "This is My beloved Son, in whom I am well pleased[5]." And thus Him whom the devil's craftiness attacks as man, the ministries of angels serve as GOD. To be hungry and thirsty, to be weary, and to sleep, is clearly human: but to satisfy 5,000 men with five loaves, and to bestow on the woman of Samaria living water, draughts of which can secure the drinker from thirsting any more, to walk upon the surface of the sea with feet that do not sink, and to quell the risings of the waves by rebuking the winds, is, without any doubt, Divine. Just as therefore, to pass over many other instances, it is not part of the same nature to be moved to tears of pity for a dead friend, and when the stone that closed the four-days' grave was removed, to raise that same friend to life with a voice of command: or, to hang on the cross, and turning day to night, to make all the elements tremble: or, to be pierced with nails, and yet open the gates of paradise to the robber's faith: so it is not part of the same nature to say, "I and the Father are one," and to say, "the Father is greater than I[6]." For although in the LORD Jesus Christ GOD and man is one person, yet the source of the degradation, which is shared by both, is one, and the source of the glory, which is shared by both, is another. For His manhood, which is less than the Father, comes from our side: His Godhead, which is equal to the Father, comes from the Father.

V. *Christ's flesh is proved real from Scripture.*

Therefore in consequence of this unity of person which is to be understood in both natures[7], we read of the Son of Man also descending from heaven, when the Son of GOD took flesh from the Virgin who bore Him. And again the Son of GOD is said to have been crucified and buried, although it was not actually in His Divinity whereby the Only-begotten is co-eternal and con-substantial with the Father, but in His weak human nature that He suffered these things. And so it is that in the Creed also we all confess that the Only-begotten Son of GOD was crucified and buried, according to that saying of the Apostle: "for if they had known, they would never have crucified the LORD of glory[8]." But when our LORD and Saviour Himself would instruct His disciples' faith by His questionings, He said, "Whom do men say that I, the Son of Man, am?" And when they had put on record the various opinions of other people, He said, "But *ye*, whom do ye say that I am?" Me, that is, who am the Son of Man, and whom ye see in the form of a slave, and in true flesh, whom do ye say that I am? Whereupon blessed Peter, whose divinely inspired confession was destined to profit all nations, said, "Thou art Christ, the Son of the living GOD[9]." And not undeservedly was he pronounced blessed by the LORD, drawing from the chief corner-stone[1] the solidity of power which his name also expresses, he, who, through the revelation of the Father, confessed Him to be at once Christ

7 S. John i. 1. 8 Ibid. 14.

9 Ibid. 3, the Latin is *per ipsum* (Gk. δι' αὐτοῦ) (through Him).

1 Gal. iv. 4.

2 Viz., that it was laid "in a manger:" the Gk. version has σπαργάνων, "swaddling clothes," to represent *cunarum*, and this meaning is adopted by Bright [and Heurtley], S. Luke ii. 7.

3 Ibid. 13.

4 *Similis est rudimentis hominum.*

5 S. Matt. iii. 17.

6 S. John xiv. 28; x. 30: the reconciliation of this class of apparently contradictory statements is often undertaken by Leo [e.g. Sermon xxiii. 2 and lxxvii. 5; Ep. xxviii. 4 and lix. 3], and by other fathers (e.g. by Augustine *de Fide et Symbolo*, 18).

7 This is what theologians call *communicatio idiomatum*, or in Gk. ἀντίδοσις, the interchange of the properties of the two natures in Christ. The passage from the beginning of the chapter to "the Lord of glory" is somewhat freely adapted from S. Aug., c. Serm. Arian., cap. 8. 8 1 Cor. ii. 8.

9 S. Matt. xvi. 13—16.

1 *A principali petra*. the Gk. version giving ἀπὸ τῆς πρωτοτύπου πέτρας: others translate it "from the original (or archetypal) rock," but it seems better to link the passage more closely with Eph. ii. 20; 1 Pet. ii. 6, &c., although the Greek rendering is against this: see Serm. iv. chap. 2, where Leo is expounding the same favourite text. Bright's note 64 is most useful in explaining the Leonine exposition. "Three elements," he says, combine in the idea; (1) Christ Himself; (2) the faith in Christ; and (3) Peter considered as the chief o the Apostles and under Christ, the head of the Church." Hence *petra* is applied to each of these at different times.

and Son of God: because the receiving of the one of these without the other was of no avail to salvation, and it was equally perilous to have believed the Lord Jesus Christ to be either only God without man, or only man without God. But after the Lord's resurrection (which, of course, was of His true body, because He was raised the same as He had died and been buried), what else was effected by the forty days' delay than the cleansing of our faith's purity from all darkness? For to that end He talked with His disciples, and dwelt and ate with them, He allowed Himself to be handled with diligent and curious touch by those who were affected by doubt, He entered when the doors were shut upon the Apostles, and by His breathing upon them gave them the Holy Spirit[2], and bestowing on them the light of understanding, opened the secrets of the Holy Scriptures[3]. So again He showed the wound in His side, the marks of the nails, and all the signs of His quite recent suffering, saying, "See My hands and feet, that it is I. Handle Me and see that a spirit hath not flesh and bones, as ye see Me have[4];" in order that the properties of His Divine and human nature might be acknowledged to remain still inseparable: and that we might know the Word not to be different from the flesh, in such a sense as also to confess that the one Son of God is both the Word and flesh[5]. Of this mystery of the faith[6] your opponent Eutyches must be reckoned to have but little sense if he has recognized our nature in the Only-begotten of God neither through the humiliation of His having to die, nor through the glory of His rising again. Nor has he any fear of the blessed apostle and evangelist John's declaration when he says, "every spirit which confesses Jesus Christ to have come in the flesh, is of God: and every spirit which destroys Jesus is not of God, and this is Antichrist[7]." But what is "to destroy Jesus," except to take away the human nature from Him, and to render void the mystery, by which alone we were saved, by the most barefaced fictions. The truth is that being in darkness about the nature of Christ's body, he must also be befooled by the same blindness in the matter of His sufferings. For if he does not think the cross of the Lord fictitious, and does not doubt that the punishment He underwent to save the world is likewise true, let him acknowledge the flesh of Him whose death he already believes: and let him not disbelieve Him man with a body like ours, since he acknowledges Him to have been able to suffer: seeing that the denial of His true flesh is also the denial of His bodily suffering. If therefore he receives the Christian faith, and does not turn away his ears from the preaching of the Gospel: let him see what was the nature that hung pierced with nails on the wooden cross, and, when the side of the Crucified was opened by the soldier's spear, let him understand whence it was that blood and water flowed, that the Church of God might be watered from the font and from the cup[8]. Let him hear also the blessed Apostle Peter, proclaiming that the sanctification of the Spirit takes place through the sprinkling of Christ's blood[9]. And let him not read cursorily the same Apostle's words when he says, "Knowing that not with corruptible things, such as silver and gold, have ye been redeemed from your vain manner of life which is part of your fathers' tradition, but with the precious blood of Jesus Christ as of a lamb without spot and blemish[1]." Let him not resist too the witness of the blessed Apostle John, who says: "and the blood of Jesus the Son of God cleanseth us from all sin[2]." And again: "this is the victory which overcometh the world, our faith." And "who is He that overcometh the world save He that believeth that Jesus is the Son of God. This is He that came by water and blood, Jesus Christ: not by water only, but by water and blood. And it is the Spirit that testifieth, because the Spirit is the truth[3], because there are three that bear witness, the Spirit, the water and the blood, and the three are one[4]." The Spirit, that is, of sanctification, and the blood of redemption, and the water of baptism: because the three are one, and remain undivided, and none of them is separated from this connection; because the catholic Church lives and progresses by this faith, so that in Christ Jesus neither the manhood without the true Godhead nor

2 S. John xx. 22. 3 S. Luke xxiv. 27. 4 Ibid. 39.

5 i.e. not to fall into the Charybdis of Nestorianism in avoiding the Scylla of Eutychianism.

6 *Fidei sacramento.*

7 1 John iv. 2, 3: the Lat. for "destroys" (or "dissolves," Bright) is *solvit* (so also in Lett. CXLIV. 3), which appears to be an exclusively Western reading: for Socrates, "the only Greek authority for λύει" (the Gk. equivalent), according to Dr. Westcott, quotes no Gk. MSS. as giving it, though he unhesitatingly makes use of that reading. The Gk. version here, however, gives διαιρεῖν, which simply begs the question (in Leo's favour) as to the original meaning of the phrase *solvere Jesum*, though on the face of it that is not at all necessarily obvious.

8 *Et lavacro rigaretur et poculo:* that is by the two great "generally necessary" sacraments of which he takes the water and the blood "from His riven side which flowed," to be a symbol. 9 This refers to 1 Pet. i. 2 (*q.v.*).

1 1 Pet. i. 18. 2 1 S. John i. 7.

3 Some of the MSS. here give *Christus* for *Spiritus* (the reading adopted also by the Vulgate): in this case you must translate *that Christ* is the Truth instead of *because the Spirit, &c.*: but see Westcott's note *in loc.*

4 1 S. John v. 4-8. The absence of the verse on the "Heavenly witnesses" (distinctly a western insertion) is to be noticed. On Leo's interpretation of this mysterious passage Canon Bright's note 168 should be consulted.

the Godhead without the true manhood is believed in.

VI. *The wrong and mischievous concession of Eutyches. The terms on which he may be restored to communion. The sending of deputies to the East.*

But when during your cross-examination Eutyches replied and said, "I confess that our LORD had two natures before the union: but after the union I confess but one[5]," I am surprised that so absurd and mistaken a statement of his should not have been criticised and rebuked by his judges, and that an utterance which reaches the height of stupidity and blasphemy should be allowed to pass as if nothing offensive had been heard: for the impiety of saying that the Son of GOD was of two natures before His incarnation is only equalled by the iniquity of asserting that there was but one nature in Him after "the Word became flesh." And to the end that Eutyches may not think this a right or defensible opinion because it was not contradicted by any expression of yourselves, we warn you beloved brother, to take anxious care that if ever through the inspiration of GOD's mercy the case is brought to a satisfactory conclusion, his ignorant mind be purged from this pernicious idea as well as others. He was, indeed, just beginning to beat a retreat from his erroneous conviction, as the order of proceedings shows[6], in so far as when hemmed in by your remonstrances he agreed to say what he had not said before and to acquiesce in that belief to which before he had been opposed. However, when he refused to give his consent to the anathematizing of his blasphemous dogma, you understood, brother[7], that he abode by his treachery and deserved to receive a verdict of condemnation. And yet, if he grieves over it faithfully and to good purpose, and, late though it be, acknowledges how rightly the bishops' authority has been set in motion; or if with his own mouth and hand in your presence he recants his wrong opinions, no mercy that is shown to him when penitent can be found fault with[8]: because our LORD, that true and "good shepherd" who laid down His life for His sheep[9] and who came to save not lose men's souls[1], wishes us to imitate His kindness[2]; in order that while justice constrains us when we sin, mercy may prevent our rejection when we have returned. For then at last is the true Faith most profitably defended when a false belief is condemned even by the supporters of it.

Now for the loyal and faithful execution of the whole matter, we have appointed to represent us our brothers Julius[3] Bishop and Renatus[4] priest [of the Title of S. Clement], as well as my son Hilary[5], deacon. And with them we have associated Dulcitius our notary, whose faith is well approved: being sure that the Divine help will be given us, so that he who had erred may be saved when the wrongness of his view has been condemned. GOD keep you safe, beloved brother.

The 13 June, 449, in the consulship of the most illustrious Asturius and Protogenes.

LETTER XXIX.

TO THEODOSIUS AUGUSTUS.

To Cæsar Theodosius, the most religious and devout Augustus Leo pope of the Catholic Church of the city of Rome[6].

He notifies the appointment of his representatives at the Council of Ephesus.

How much GOD's providence vouchsafes to consult for the interests of men is shown by your merciful care which, incited by GOD's Spirit, is unwilling that there should be any disturbance or difference: since the Faith, which is absolutely one, cannot be different from itself in any thing. Hence although Eutyches, as the minutes of the bishops' proceeds reveals, has been detected in an ignorant and unwise error, and ought to have withdrawn from his conviction which is rightly condemned, yet since your piety which loves the Catholic Truth with great jealousy for GOD's honour, has determined on a synodal judgment at Ephesus, that that Truth on

5 This was the only compromise of his views which Eutyches could be brought to make at the synod of Constantinople. Though it was rejected, and did not hinder his condemnation, it was never met with a direct, categorical refutation.

6 *Gestorum ordo*, as before, in chap. 1. A report of the proceedings had accompanied Flavian's letter.

7 *Fraternitas vestra:* or, as the Gk. version apparently took it, "you and the rest of the brethren" (ἡ ὑμῶν ἀδελφότης).

8 It will be remembered that he had been degraded from the priesthood and deprived of his monastery, as well as excommunicated: he might be reinstated in all these privileges, the mercifulness of Leo hints, if he recant his errors.

9 S. John x. 11 and 15.

1 S. Luke ix. 50.

2 *Pietatis*, a beautiful word, expressing now the Father's pitying protection, now the children's loyal affection, and here the Elder Brother's love for the younger and weaker. Cf. n. 1. on chap. iii.

3 Bishop of Puteoli.

4 Died at Delos on the way. The words "of the title of S. Clement" are of doubtful authenticity, and not found in the Gk. version. The parish churches of Rome seem to have been called *tituli* at their first founding about the beginning of the 4th cent. A.D. Cf. our Eng. term "title," and refer to Bingham, Bk. viii. § 1.

5 Afterwards Leo's successor in the see of Rome, 461-8.

6 This is the title retained by Quesnel and the Ballerinii, though many MSS. exhibit the simpler *gloriosissimo et clementissimo Theodosio Augusto Leo episcopus*, which is favoured by the Gk. version τῷ ἐνδοξοτάτῳ καὶ φιλανθρωποτάτῳ κ.τ.λ. Quesnel takes occasion to warn us to distinguish between this use of the title *papa* and that adopted later when it was equivalent to *œcumenicus et universalis episcopus*.

which he is blind may be brought home to the ignorant old man; I have sent my brothers Julius the Bishop, Renatus the presbyter, and my son Hilary the deacon to act as my representatives as the matter requires, and they shall bring with them such a spirit of justice and kindness that while the whole misguided error is condemned (for there can be no doubt as to what is the integrity of the Christian Faith), yet if he who has gone astray repents and entreats for pardon, he may receive the succour of priestly indulgence: seeing that in his appeal[7] which he sent us, he reserved to himself the right of earning our forgiveness by promising to correct whatever our opinion disapproved of in his opinion. But what the catholic Church universally believes and teaches on the mystery of the LORD's Incarnation is contained more fully in the letter which I have sent to my brother and fellow-bishop Flavian. Dated 13th June in the consulship of the illustrious Asturius and Protogenes (449).

LETTER XXX.

To Pulcheria Augusta.

Much shorter than, but to nearly the same effect as, xxxi., which was written on the same day as this. As xxx. has a Greek translation accompanying it and is duly dated, whereas xxxi. has neither, the Ballerinii would seem to be correct in thinking that xxx. was despatched but did not reach Pulcheria (cf. Lett. xlv. i.) and that xxxi. was for some reason never used. Of the two we have printed xxxi. by preference, as being the fuller discussion of the subject.

LETTER XXXI.

To Pulcheria Augusta[8].

Leo to Pulcheria Augusta.

I. *He reminds Pulcheria of her former services to the Church, and suggests her interference in the Eutychian controversy.*

How much protection the LORD has extended to His Church through your clemency, we have often tested by many signs. And whatever stand the strenuousness of the priesthood has made in our times against the assailers of the catholic Truth, has redounded chiefly to your glory: seeing that, as you have learnt from the teaching of the Holy Spirit, you submit your authority in all things to Him, by whose favour and under whose protection you reign. Wherefore, because I have ascertained from my brother and fellow-bishop Flavian's report, that a certain dispute has been raised through the agency of Eutyches in the church of Constantinople against the integrity of the Christian faith (and the text of the synod's minutes has shown me the exact nature of the whole matter), it is worthy of your great name that the error which in my opinion proceeds rather from ignorance than ingenuity, should be dispelled before, with the pertinacity of wrong-headedness, it gains any strength from the support of the unwise. Because even ignorance sometimes falls into serious mistakes, and very frequently the simple-minded rush through unwariness into the devil's pit: and it is thus, I believe, that the spirit of falsehood has crept over Eutyches: so that, whilst he imagines himself to appreciate the majesty of the Son of GOD more devoutly, by denying in Him the real presence of our nature, he came to the conclusion that the whole of that Word which "became flesh" was of one and the same essence. And greatly as Nestorius fell away from the Truth, in asserting that Christ was only born man of His mother, this man also departs no less far from the catholic path, who does not believe that our substance was brought forth from the same Virgin: wishing it of course to be understood as belonging to His Godhead only; so that that which took the form of a slave, and was like us and of the same form[9], was a kind of image, not the reality of our nature.

II. *Man's salvation required the union of the two natures in Christ.*

But it is of no avail to say that our LORD, the Son of the blessed Virgin Mary, was true and perfect man, if He is not believed to be Man of that stock which is attributed to Him in the Gospel. For Matthew says, "The book of the generation of Jesus Christ, the son of David, the son of Abraham[1]:" and follows the order of His human origin, so as to bring the lines of His ancestry down to Joseph to whom the LORD's mother was espoused. Whereas Luke going backwards step by step traces His succession to the first of the human race himself, to show that the first Adam and the last Adam were of the same nature. No doubt the Almighty Son of GOD could have appeared for the purpose

[7] Viz., Lett. XXI., chaps. i. and iii.

[8] This was the Emperor Theodosius the younger's sister, a woman of noted zeal in the cause of the Church: for many years she had practically ruled the empire owing to her brother's youthfulness. When the intrigues of Chrysaphius had brought about a quarrel between brother and sister, she retired for a time from public life. But becoming the virgin wife of Marcian, she, through him, helped to effect the victory of the Catholic cause at the Council of Chalcedon 451).

[9] *Quod nostri similis fuit atque conformis.*

[1] S. Matt. i. 1.

of teaching, and justifying men in exactly the same way that He appeared both to patriarchs and prophets in the semblance of flesh[2]; for instance, when He engaged in a struggle, and entered into conversation (with Jacob), or when He refused not hospitable entertainment, and even partook of the food set before Him. But these appearances were indications of that Man whose reality it was announced by mystic predictions would be assumed from the stock of preceding patriarchs. And the fulfilment of the mystery of our atonement, which was ordained from all eternity, was not assisted by any figures because the Holy Spirit had not yet come upon the Virgin, and the power of the Most High had not over-shadowed her: so that "Wisdom building herself a house[3]" within her undefiled body, "the Word became flesh;" and the form of GOD and the form of a slave coming together into one person, the Creator of times was born in time; and He Himself through whom all things were made, was brought forth in the midst of all things. For if the New Man had not been made in the likeness of sinful flesh, and taken on Him our old nature, and being consubstantial with the Father, had deigned to be consubstantial with His mother also, and being alone free from sin, had united our nature to Him, the whole human race would be held in bondage beneath the Devil's yoke[4], and we should not be able to make use of the Conqueror's victory, if it had been won outside our nature.

III. *From the union of the two natures flows the grace of baptism. He makes a direct appeal to Pulcheria for her help.*

But from Christ's marvellous sharing of the two natures, the mystery of regeneration shone upon us that through the self-same spirit, through whom Christ was conceived and born, we too, who were born through the desire of the flesh, might be born again from a spiritual source: and consequently, the Evangelist speaks of believers as those "who were born not of bloods, nor of the will of the flesh, nor of the will of man, but of GOD[5]." And of this unutterable grace no one is a partaker, nor can be reckoned among the adopted sons of GOD, who excludes from his faith that which is the chief means of our salvation. Wherefore, I am much vexed and saddened that this man, who seemed before so laudably disposed towards humility, dares to make these empty and stupid attacks on the one Faith of ourselves and of our fathers. When he saw that his ignorant notion offended the ears of catholics, he ought to have withdrawn from his opinion, and not to have so disturbed the Church's rulers, as to deserve a sentence of condemnation: which, of course, no one will be able to remit, if he is determined to abide by his notion. For the moderation of the Apostolic See uses its leniency in such a way as to deal severely with the contumacious, while desiring to offer pardon to those who accept correction. Seeing then that I possess great confidence in your lofty faith and piety, I entreat your illustrious clemency, that, as the preaching of the catholic Faith has always been aided by your holy zeal, so now, also, you will maintain its free action. Perchance the LORD allowed it to be thus assailed for this reason that we might discover what sort of persons lurked within the Church. And clearly, we must not neglect to look after such, lest we be afflicted with their actual loss.

IV. *His personal presence at the council must be excused. The question at issue is a very grave one.*

But the most august and Christian Emperor, being anxious that the disturbances may be set at rest with all speed, has appointed too short and early a date for the council of bishops, which he wishes held at Ephesus, in fixing the first of August for the meeting: for from the fifth of May, on which we received His Majesty's letter, most of the time remaining has to be spent in making complete arrangements for the journey of such priests as are competent to represent me. For as to the necessity of my attending the council also, which his piety suggested, even if there were any precedent for the request, it could by no means be managed now: for the very uncertain state of things at present would not permit my absence from the people of this great city: and the minds of the riotously-disposed might be driven to desperate deeds, if they were to think that I took occasion of ecclesiastical business to desert my country[6] and the Apostolic See. As then you recognize that it concerns the public weal that with your merciful indulgence I should not deny myself to the affectionate prayers of my

[2] Gen. xxxii. 24 and xviii. 1. It will be noticed that Leo unhesitatingly pronounces these and similar appearances to be manifestations of the Second Person in the Trinity.

[3] Prov. ix. 1. Cf. Letter XXVIII. (The Tome), chap. ii., towards the end.

[4] *Sub iugo diaboli generaliter teneretur humana captivitas*: for the word *generaliter*, cf. Letter XVI., chap. iv., no. 3.

[5] S. John i. 13.

[6] *Patriam.* I can see very little ground for pressing this quite general expression to mean that he was a native of Rome, or even a native of Italy. The most that can be said is that it does not forbid the supposition.

people, consider that in these my brethren, whom I have sent in my stead, I also am present with the rest who appear: to them I have clearly and fully explained what is to be maintained in view of the satisfactory exposition of the case which has been given me by the detailed report, and by the defendant's own statement to me. For the question is not about some small portion of our Faith, on which no very distinct declaration has been made: but the foolish opposition that is raised ventures to impugn that which our LORD desired no one of either sex in the Church to be ignorant of. For the short but complete confession of the catholic creed which contains the twelve sentences of the twelve apostles[7] is so well furnished with the heavenly panoply, that all the opinions of heretics can receive their death-blow from that one weapon. And if Eutyches had been content to receive that creed in its entirety with a pure and simple heart, he would at no point go astray from the decrees of the most sacred council of Nicæa, and he would understand that the holy Fathers laid this down, to the end that no mental or rhetorical ingenuity should lift itself up against the Apostolic Faith which is absolutely one. Deign then, with your accustomed piety to do your best endeavour, that this blasphemous and foolish attack upon the one and only sacrament of man's salvation may be driven from all men's minds. And if the man himself, who has fallen into this temptation, recover his senses, so as to condemn his own error by a written recantation, let him not be denied communion with his order[8]. Your clemency is to know that I have written in the same strain to the holy bishop Flavian also: that loving-kindness be not lost sight of, if the error be dispelled. Dated 13 June in the consulship of the illustrious Asturius and Protogenes (449).

LETTER XXXII.

To the Archimandrites of Constantinople [9].

To his well-beloved sons Faustus, Martinus, and the rest of the archimandrites, Leo the bishop.

He acknowledges their zeal and refers them to the Tome.

As on behalf of the faith which Eutyches has tried to disturb, I was sending legates *de latere*[9a] to assist the defence of the Truth, I thought it fitting that I should address a letter to you also, beloved: whom I know for certain to be so zealous in the cause of religion that you can by no means listen calmly to such blasphemous and profane utterances: for the Apostle's command lingers in your hearts, in which it is said, "If any man hath preached unto you any gospel other than that which he received, let him be anathema[1]." And we also decide that the opinion of the said Eutyches is to be rejected, which, as we have learnt from perusing the proceedings, has been deservedly condemned: so that, if its foolish maintainer will abide by his perverseness, he may have fellowship with those whose error he has followed. For one who says that Christ had not a human, that is our, nature, is deservedly put out of Christ's Church. But, if he be corrected through the pity of GOD's Spirit and acknowledge his wicked error, so as to condemn unreservedly what catholics reject, we wish him not to be denied mercy, that the LORD's Church may suffer no loss: for the repentant can always be readmitted, it is only error that must be shut out. Upon the mystery of great godliness[2], whereby through the Incarnation of the Word of GOD comes our justification and redemption, what is our opinion, drawn from the tradition of the fathers, is now sufficiently explained according to my judgment in the letter which I have sent to our brother Flavian the bishop[3]: so that through the declaration of your chief you may know what, according to the gospel of our LORD Jesus Christ, we desire to be fixed in the hearts of all the faithful. Dated 13th June, in the consulship of the illustrious Asturius and Protogenes (449).

LETTER XXXIII.

To the Synod of Ephesus [4].

Leo, bishop, to the holy Synod which is assembled at Ephesus.

I. *He commends the Emperor's appeal to the chair of Peter.*

The devout faith of our most clement prince,

---

7 Let the reader beware of accepting the plausible account here suggested of the formation of the Apostles' Creed, and still more so of accepting the popular derivation of the word *symbolum* (σύμβολον) as the twelve Apostles' twelve "contributions" (one each) to the Church's rule of faith.

8 *Communio sui ordinis.*

9 It will be remembered that 23 abbots signed the condemnation of Eutyches: cf. Lett. XXI. chap. 2.

9a *De latere meo.* This is interesting as an early instance of the use of this expression for the legates of the pope (now so familiar): even though Quesnel is incorrect in saying for certain that Leo is the first Bishop of Rome who employed them. He himself quotes Concil. Sardic., canon 7, where the fathers ask the Roman bishop to send some one *e latere suo* (A.D. 347).

1 Gal. i. 9.

2 I cannot doubt he has 1 Tim. iii. 27, μέγα ἐστὶ τὸ τῆς ἐυσεβείας μυστήριον (here *sacramentum*, as usual) in his mind, though the Gk. translator apparently did not see it, his version being utterly inaccurate (περὶ δὲ τῆς ἁγιότητος τῆς μεγάλης πίστεως).

3 Viz., Letter XXVIII. (The Tome).

4 This letter has a note prefixed to it in some Gk. and Latin MSS., to the effect that it was produced but suppressed, and not allowed to be read through Dioscorus, Bishop of Alexandria

knowing that it especially concerns his glory to prevent any seed of error from springing up within the catholic Church, has paid such deference to the Divine institutions as to apply to the authority of the Apostolic See for a proper settlement: as if he wished it to be declared by the most blessed Peter himself what was praised in his confession, when the LORD said, "whom do men say that I, the Son of man, am[5]?" and the disciples mentioned various people's opinion: but, when He asked what they themselves believed, the chief of the apostles, embracing the fulness of the Faith in one short sentence, said, "Thou art the Christ, the son of the living GOD[5]:" that is, Thou who truly art Son of man art also truly Son of the living GOD: Thou, I say, true in Godhead, true in flesh and one altogether[6], the properties of the two natures being kept intact. And if Eutyches had believed this intelligently and thoroughly, he would never have retreated from the path of this Faith. For Peter received this answer from the LORD for his confession. "Blessed art thou, Simon Barjona; for flesh and blood hath not revealed it unto thee, but My Father which is in heaven. And I say unto thee, that thou art Peter, and upon this rock I will build My Church: and the gates of Hades shall not prevail against it[7]." But he who both rejects the blessed Peter's confession, and gainsays Christ's Gospel, is far removed from union with this building; for he shows himself never to have had any zeal for understanding the Truth, and to have only the empty appearance of high esteem, who did not adorn the hoary hairs of old age with any ripe judgment of the heart.

II. *The heresy of Eutyches is to be condemned, though his full repentance may lead to his restitution.*

But because the healing even of such men must not be neglected, and the most Christian Emperor has piously and devoutly desired a council of bishops to be held, that all error may be destroyed by a fuller judgment, I have sent our brothers Julius the bishop, Renatus the presbyter, and my son Hilary the deacon, and with them Dulcitius the notary, whose faith we have proved, to be present in my stead at your holy assembly, brethren, and settle in common with you what is in accordance with the LORD's will. To wit, that the pestilential error may be first condemned, and then the restitution of him, who has so unwisely erred, discussed, but only if embracing the true doctrine he fully and openly with his own voice and signature condemns those heretical opinions in which his ignorance has been ensnared: for this he has promised in the appeal which he sent to us, pledging himself to follow our judgment in all things[8]. On receiving our brother and fellow-bishop Flavian's letter, we have replied to him at some length on the points which he seems to have referred to us[9]: that when this error which seems to have arisen, has been destroyed, there may be one Faith and one and the same confession throughout the whole world to the praise and glory of GOD, and that "in the name of Jesus every knee should bow, of things in heaven, and things on earth, and things under the earth, and that every tongue should confess that the LORD Jesus Christ is in the glory of GOD the Father[1]." Dated 13th June in the consulship of the illustrious Asturius and Protogenes (449).

LETTER XXXIV.

To JULIAN, BISHOP OF COS.

Leo, the bishop, to Julian, the bishop, his well-beloved brother.

I. *Eutyches is now clearly seen to have deviated from the Faith.*

Your letter, beloved, which has just reached me, shows with what spiritual love of the Catholic Faith you are inspired: and it makes me very glad that devout hearts all agree in the same opinion, so that according to the teaching of the Holy Ghost there may be fulfilled in us what the Apostle says: "Now I beseech you, brethren, through the name of our LORD Jesus Christ, that ye all speak the same things, and there be no divisions among you: but that ye be perfect in the same mind and in the same judgment[2]." But Eutyches has put himself quite outside this unity, if he perseveres in his perversity, and still does not understand the bonds with which the devil has bound him, and thinks any one is to be reckoned among the LORD's priests, who is a party to his ignorance and madness. For some time we were uncertain in what he was displeasing to catholics: and when we received no letter from our brother Flavian, and Eutyches himself complained in his letter[3] that the Nestorian heresy was being revived, we could not fully learn the source or the motive of so crafty an accusation. But as soon as the minutes of the bishops' proceedings reached us, all those things which were hidden beneath

5 S. Matt. xvi. 13 and 16
6 *Utrumque* (Gk. ἑκάτερον) *unus.*
7 S. Matt. xvi. 17, 18.
[8] Cf. Lett. XXI., chaps. i. and ii.
9 See Lett. XXVII., n. 7.
1 Phil. ii. 10.
2 1 Cor. i. 10.
3 See Lett. XX., above.

the veil of his deceitful complaints were revealed in their abomination.

II. *He announces the appointment of legates a latere.*

And because our most clement Emperor in the loving-kindness and godliness of his mind, wished a more careful judgment to be passed about the position of one who hitherto has seemed to be in high esteem, and for this purpose has thought fit to convene a council of bishops, by the hands of our brothers Julius the bishop, and Renatus the presbyter, and also my son Hilary, the deacon whom I have sent *ex latere* [4] in my stead, I have addressed a letter suited to the needs of the case to our brother Flavian, from which you also, beloved, and the whole Church may know about the ancient and unique Faith, which this unlearned opponent has assailed, what we hold as handed down from God and what we preach without alteration. Yet, because we must not forget the duty of mercy, we have considered it consonant with our moderation as priests, that, if the condemned presbyter corrects himself unreservedly, the sentence by which he is bound should be remitted: if, however, he chooses to lie in the mire of his foolishness, let the decree remain, and let him have his lot with those whose error he has followed. Dated 13th June in the consulship of the illustrious Asturius and Protogenes (449) [5].

LETTER XXXV.

To Julian, Bishop of Cos [6].

Leo, bishop of the city of Rome to his well-beloved brother, Julian the bishop.

I. *Eutyches' heresy involves many other heresies.*

Although by the hands of our brothers, whom we have despatched from the city on behalf of the Faith, we have sent a most full refutation of Eutyches' excessive heresy to our brother Flavian, yet because we have received, through our son Basil, your letter, beloved, which has given us much pleasure from the fervour of its catholic spirit, we have added this page also which agrees with the other document, that you may offer a united and strenuous resistance to those who seek to corrupt the gospel of Christ, since the wisdom and the teaching of the Holy Spirit is one and the same in you as in us: and whosoever does not receive it, is not a member of Christ's body and cannot glory in that Head in which he denies the presence of his own nature. What advantage is it to that most unwise old man under the name of the Nestorian heresy to mangle the belief of those, whose most devout faith he cannot tear to pieces: when in declaring the only-begotten Son of God to have been so born of the blessed Virgin's womb that He wore the appearance of a human body without the reality of human flesh being united to the Word, he departs as far from the right path as did Nestorius in separating the Godhead of the Word from the substance of His assumed Manhood [7]? From which prodigious falsehood who does not see what monstrous opinions spring? for he who denies the true Manhood of Jesus Christ, must needs be filled with many blasphemies, being claimed by Apollinaris as his own, seized upon by Valentinus, or held fast by Manichæus: none of whom believed that there was true human flesh in Christ. But, surely, if that is not accepted, not only is it denied that He, who was in the form of God, but yet abode in the form of a slave, was born Man according to the flesh and reasonable soul: but also that He was crucified, dead, and buried, and that on the third day He rose again, and that, sitting at the right hand of the Father, he will come to judge the quick and the dead [8] in that body in which He Himself was judged.: because these pledges [9] of our redemption are rendered void if Christ is not believed to have the true and whole nature of true Manhood.

II. *The two natures are to be found in Christ.*

Or because the signs of His Godhead were undoubted, shall the proof of his having a human body be assumed false, and thus the indications of both natures be accepted to prove Him Creator, but not be accepted for the salvation of the creature [1]? No, for the

4 See Lett. XXXII., n. 9, above.

5 This letter (XXXIV.) is written on the same day and subject and to the same person as the next letter (XXXV.): the differences between them being (1) the greater length and fuller treatment of the second; and (2) that the one is entrusted to Leo's legates, the other to Julius' own messenger, Basil the deacon; and (3) that the shorter has no Gk. version as the longer has. I think the Ballerinii are undoubtedly right in facing the difficulty boldly, the evidence of the MSS. being invariable, except that XXXIV. is only found in a few collections: and I would suggest that XXXIV. is a formal, official communication, and XXXV. a private, confidential one. This will account for the difference of messengers, and the identity of date, subject and person addressed, and is justifiable as a piece of necessary diplomatic secrecy. In XXX. and XXXI. we have another instance of two letters to the same person on the same day, one of these (XXXI.) being also without a Gk. version, this time the longer one: but here we have adopted the Ballerinii's suggestion that only the first was sent. It should further be noticed that out of the very large batch of letters that are dated the 13th of June, which includes the Tome (8 in all, XXVIII.—XXXV.), it may well have been convenient to delay one and send it by another hand.

6 See Lett. XXXIV., chap. ii. n. 5.

7 The Gk. version here adds and "from the very conception of the Virgin," but this is probably only a repetition of the words "of the Virgin's womb," just above.

8 It can escape no one that he is here, and frequently throughout this letter, quoting from the Creed.

9 *Sacramenta.*

1 i.e. shall the signs of His being God. which are undoubted, and the signs that He had a body of some sort be allowed to prove Him one with the Creator of the world, but not go so far as to show that that body which He had was a fully human one?

flesh did not lessen what belongs to His Godhead, nor the Godhead destroy what belongs to His flesh. For He is at once both eternal from His Father and temporal from His mother, inviolable in His strength, passible in our weakness: in the Triune Godhead, of one and the same substance with the Father and the Holy Spirit, but in taking Manhood on Himself, not of one substance but of one and the same person [so that He was at once rich in poverty, almighty in submission, impassible in punishment, immortal in death [2]]. For the Word was not in any part of It turned either into flesh or into soul, seeing that the absolute and unchangeable nature of the Godhead is ever entire in its Essence, receiving no loss nor increase, and so beatifying the nature that It had assumed that that nature remained for ever glorified in the person of the Glorifier. [But why should it seem unsuitable or impossible that the Word and flesh and soul should be one Jesus Christ, and that the Son of God and the Son of Man should be one, if flesh and soul which are of different natures make one person even without the Incarnation of the Word: since it is much easier for the power of the Godhead to produce this union of Himself and man than for the weakness of manhood by itself to effect it in its own substance.] Therefore neither was the Word changed into flesh nor flesh into the Word: but both remains in one and one is in both, not divided by the diversity and not confounded by intermixture: He is not one by His Father and another by His mother, but the same, in one way by His Father before every beginning, and in another by His mother at the end of the ages: so that He was "mediator between God and men, the man Christ Jesus [3]," in whom dwelt "the fulness of the Godhead bodily [4]:" because it was the assumed (nature) not the Assuming (nature) which was raised, because GOD "exalted Him and gave Him the Name which is above every name: that in the name of Jesus every knee should bow, of things in heaven and things on earth and things under the earth, and that every tongue should confess that Jesus Christ the LORD is in the glory of GOD the Father [5]."

III. *The soul of Christ and the body of Christ were real in the full human sense, though the circumstances of His birth were unique.*

[But as to that which Eutyches dared to say in the court of bishops "that before the Incarnation there were two natures in Christ, but after the Incarnation one [6]," he ought to have been pressed by the frequent and anxious questions of the judges to render an account of his acknowledgment, lest it should be passed over as something trivial, though it was seen to have issued from the same fount as his other poisonous opinions. For I think that in saying this he was convinced that the soul, which the Saviour assumed, had had its abode in the heavens before He was born of the Virgin Mary, and that the Word joined it to Himself in the womb. But this is intolerable to catholic minds and ears: because the LORD who came down from heaven brought with Him nothing that belonged to our state: for He did not receive either a soul which had existed before nor a flesh which was not of his mother's body. Undoubtedly our nature was not assumed in such a way that it was created first and then assumed, but it was created by the very assumption. And hence that which was deservedly condemned in Origen must be punished in Eutyches also, unless he prefers to give up his opinion, viz. the assertion that souls have had not only a life but also different actions before they were inserted in men's bodies [7]]. For although the LORD's nativity according to the flesh has certain characteristics wherein it transcends the ordinary beginnings of man's being, both because He alone was conceived and born without concupiscence of a pure Virgin, and because He was so brought forth of His mother's womb that her fecundity bare Him without loss of virginity: yet His flesh was not of another nature to ours: nor was the soul breathed into Him from another source to that of all other men, and it excelled others not in difference of kind but in superiority of power. For He had no opposition in His flesh [nor did the strife of desires give rise to a conflict of wishes [8]]. His bodily senses were active without the law of sin, and the reality of His emotions being under the control of His Godhead and His mind, was neither assaulted by temptations nor yielded to injurious influences. But true Man was united to GOD and was not brought down from heaven as regards a pre-existing soul, nor created out of nothing as regards the flesh: it wore the same person in the Godhead of the Word and possessed a nature in common with us in its body and soul. For He would not be "the mediator between GOD

2 *So that—in death*, bracketed by the editors as not being translated in the Gk. version, and perhaps here we have a gloss to explain the somewhat obscure words that precede it: but throughout this letter large portions are so bracketed, in each case the Gk. version omitting them.

3 1 Tim. ii. 5. 4 Col. ii. 9. 5 Phil. ii. 9-11.

6 Cf. the Tome, Lett. XXVIII., chap. vi., n. 5.

7 Cf. Lett. XV., chap. xi., n. 6.

8 Here again the second clause (in brackets) seems a gloss on the first, see n. 2, above: what is meant will be seen by comparing S. Paul's famous disquisition (Rom. vii.)

and man," unless GOD and man had co-existed in both natures forming one true Person. The magnitude of the subject urges us to a lengthy discussion: but with one of your learning there is no need for such copious dissertations, especially as we have already sent a sufficient letter to our brother Flavian by our delegates for the confirmation of the minds, not only of priests but also of the laity. The mercy of GOD will, we believe, provide that without the loss of one soul the sound may be defended against the devil's wiles, and the wounded healed. Dated 13th June in the consulship of the illustrious Asturius and Protogenes (449).

LETTER XXXVI.

To FLAVIAN, BISHOP OF CONSTANTINOPLE.

(He acknowledges the receipt of Flavian's second letter (xxvi) and protests against the necessity for a general council, though at the same time he acquiesces in it. Dated 21 June, a week after the Tome).

LETTER XXXVII[1].

To THEODOSIUS AUGUSTUS.

Leo to Theodosius Augustus.

Unity of Faith is essential but the point at issue hardly required a general council, it is so clear.

On receiving your clemency's letter, I perceived that the universal Church has much cause for joy, that you will have the Christian Faith, whereby the Divine Trinity is honoured and worshipped, to be different or out of harmony with itself in nothing. For what more effectual support can be given to human affairs in calling upon GOD's mercy than when one thanksgiving, and the sacrifice of one confession is offered to His majesty by all. Wherein the devotions of the priests and all the faithful will reach at last their completeness, if in what was done for our redemption by GOD the Word, the only Son of GOD, nothing else be believed than what He Himself ordered to be preached and believed. Wherefore although every consideration prevents my attendance on the day which your piety has fixed for the councils of bishops[2]: for there are no precedents for such a thing, and the needs of the times do not allow me to leave the city, especially as the point of Faith at issue is so clear, that it would have been more reasonable to abstain from proclaiming a synod: yet as far as the LORD vouchsafes to help me, I have bestowed my zeal upon obeying your clemency's commands, by appointing my brethren who are competent to act as the case requires in removing offences, and who can represent me: because no question has arisen on which there can or ought to be any doubt. Dated 21st of June, in the consulship of the illustrious Asturius and Protogenes, (449).

LETTER XXXVIII[3].

To FLAVIAN, BISHOP OF CONSTANTINOPLE.

Leo to Flavian, bishop of Constantinople.

He acknowledges the receipt of a letter and advises mercy if Eutyches will recant.

When our brethren had already started whom we despatched to you in the cause of the Faith, we received your letter, beloved, by our son Basil the deacon, in which you rightly said very little on the subject of our common anxiety, both because the accounts which had already arrived had given us full information on every thing, and because for purposes of private inquiry it was easy to converse with the aforesaid Basil, by whom now through the grace of GOD, in whom we trust, we exhort you, beloved, in reply, using the Apostle's words, and saying: "Be ye in nothing affrighted by the adversaries; which is for them a cause of perdition, but to you of salvation[4]." For what is so calamitous as to wish to destroy all hope of man's salvation by denying the reality of Christ's Incarnation, and to contradict the Apostle who says distinctly: "great is the mystery of godliness which was manifest in the flesh[5]?" What so glorious as to fight for the Faith of the gospel against the enemies of Christ's nativity and cross? About whose most pure light and unconquered power we have already disclosed what was in our heart, in the letter which has been sent to you beloved[6]: lest anything might seem doubtful between us on those things which we have learnt, and teach in accordance with the catholic doctrine. But seeing that the testimonies to the Truth are so clear

[1] This letter is on the same subject as Lett. XXIX. above, but as the wording of it contains some interesting matter, it is here given in full. There is no Gk. version extant, and how there some to be two letters within a week of one another on the same topic is not clear.

[2] Cf. Lett. XXIX. above, and especially XXXI., chap. iv., where the reasons are given rather more fully.

[3] If we are right in thinking that Lett. XXXVI. is Leo's acknowledgment of Flavian's second letter (XXVI.), this (which again has no Gk. version) must be an acknowledgment of yet a third, not extant, sent by the hand of one Basil, the deacon, who is probably the same as Julian's messenger (XXXV., chap. i.).

[4] Phil. i. 28.

[5] 1 Tim. iii. 16: the reading here is *quod manifestum est in carne*, in agreement with the general Western usage.

[6] Sc. the Tome (XXVIII.).

and strong that a man must be reckoned thoroughly blind and stubborn, who does not at once shake himself free from the mists of falsehood in the bright light of reason; we desire you to use the remedy of long-suffering in curing the madness of ignorance that through your fatherly admonitions they who though old in years are infants in mind, may learn to obey their elders. And if they give up the vain conceits of their ignorance and come to their senses, and if they condemn all their errors and receive the one true Faith, do not deny them the mercifulness of a bishop's kind heart: although your judgment must remain, if their impiety which you have deservedly condemned persists in its depravity. Dated 23 July in the consulship of the illustrious Asturius and Protogenes (449).

LETTER XXXIX.

To Flavian, Bishop of Constantinople.

Leo, the bishop, to Flavian, the bishop.

He rebukes Flavian for not answering his repeated letters.

Our anxiety is increased by your silence, for it is long now since we received a letter from you, beloved: while we who bear a chief share in your cares[7], through our anxiety for the defence of the Faith, have several times[8], as occasion served, sent letters to you: that we might aid you with the comfort of our exhortations not to yield to the assaults of your adversaries in defence of the Faith, but to feel that we were the sharers in your labour. Some time since we believe our messengers have reached you, brother, through whom you find yourself fully instructed by our writings and injunctions, and we have ourselves sent back Basil to you as you desired[9]. Now, lest you should think we had omitted any opportunity of communicating with you, we have sent this note by our son Eupsychius, a man whom we hold in great honour and affection, asking you to reply to our letter with all speed, and inform us at once about your own actions and those of our representatives, and about the completion of the whole matter: so that we may allay the anxiety which we now feel in defence of the Faith, by happier tidings. Dated 11th August in the consulship of the illustrious Asturius and Protogenes (449).

LETTER XL.

To the Bishops of the Province of Arles in Gaul.

To his well-beloved brethren Constantinus Audentius, Rusticus, Auspicius, Nicetas, Nectarius, Florus, Asclepius, Justus, Augustalis, Ynantius, and Chrysaphius[1], Leo the pope.

He approves of their having unanimously elected Ravennius, Bishop of Arles.

We have just and reasonable reason for rejoicing, when we learn that the Lord's priests have done what is agreeable both to the rules of the Father's canons and to the Apostles' institutions. For the whole body of the Church must needs increase with a healthy growth, if the governing members excel in the strength of their authority, and in peaceful management. Accordingly, we ratify with our sanction your good deed, brethren, in unanimously, on the death of Hilary[2] of holy memory, consecrating our brother Ravennius, a man well approved by us, in the city of Arles, in accordance with the wishes of the clergy, the leading citizens, and the laity. Because a peace-making and harmonious election, where neither personal merits nor the good will of the congregation are wanting, is we believe the expression not only of man's choice, but of God's inspiration. So dearly beloved brethren, let the said priest use God's gift, and understand what self-devotion is expected of him, that by diligently and prudently carrying out the office entrusted to him, he may prove himself equal to your testimony, and fully worthy of our favour. God keep you safe, beloved brethren. Dated 22 August in the consulship of Asturius and Protogenes (449).

LETTER XLI.

To Ravennius, Bishop of Arles.

(He congratulates him on his appointment, exhorts him to firm but gentle government, and advises him frequently to consult the Apostolic See. Undated, but no doubt sent about the same time as XL.)

LETTER XLII.

To Ravennius, Bishop of Arles.

Leo the Pope to his well-beloved brother Ravennius.

7 *Curarum tuarum principes.*

8 *Frequenter*, four times in all (Letters XXVII., XXVIII., XXXVI. and XXXVIII.).

9 This must be in the third lost letter to which we have assumed Lett. XXXVIII. to be an answer.

1 These twelve bishops do not include the Bishop of Vienne, according to Perthel (p. 29). following apparently Quesnel, whose wish-fathered thought, though possibly right, has little evidence to go upon. Cf. Letters LXV. and LXVI. below.

2 It will be noticed that Leo speaks of Hilary not only with respect, but as if he acquiesced in his sentence (passed against Hilary in Lett. X. above) not having been carried out.

He asks him to deal with the imposture of a certain Petronianus.

We wish you to be circumspect and careful lest any blameworthy presumption should put forth undue claims: for, when it once finds an entrance by crafty stealth, it spreads itself into greater rashness in the name of the dignity it has assumed. We have learnt, on the trustworthy evidence of your clergy, that a certain wandering and vagabond Petronianus has boasted himself throughout the provinces of Gaul as our deacon, and under cover of this office is going about the various churches of that country. We desire you, beloved brother, so to check his abominable effrontery, as to disclose his imposture, by warning the bishops of the whole district. and to expel him from communion with all the Churches, lest he continue his claim. The LORD keep you safe, dearly beloved brother. Dated 26th August, in the consulship of the illustrious Asturius and Protogenes (449).

LETTER XLIII[3].

To Theodosius Augustus.

To the most glorious and serene Emperor Theodosius.

Leo the bishop.

I. *He complains of the conduct of Dioscorus at the Council of Ephesus.*

Already and from the beginning, in the synods which have been held, we have received such freedom of speech from the most holy Peter, chief of the Apostles, as to have the power both to maintain the Truth in the cause of peace, and to allow no one to disturb it in its firm position, but at once to repel the mischief. Since then the council of bishops which you ordered to be held in the city of Ephesus on account of Flavian, does mischief to the Faith itself and inflicts wounds on all the churches ——[4]; and this has been brought to our knowledge not by some untrustworthy messenger, but by the most reverend bishops[5] themselves who were sent by us and by the most trusty Hilarus our deacon, who have narrated to us what took place. And the occurrences are to be put down to the fault of those who met, not having, as is customary, with a pure conscience and right judgment made a definite statement about the faith and those who erred therefrom. For we have learnt that all did not come together in the conference who ought, some being ejected and others received: who were ensnared into an ungodly act of subscription by the designs of the aforesaid priest[6]. For the declaration effected by him is of such a nature as to injure all the churches. For when those who were sent by us saw how exceedingly impious and hostile to the Faith it was, they notified it to us.

II. *He asks him to restore the ancient catholic doctrine.*

Wherefore, most peace-loving prince, vouchsafe for the Faith's sake to avert this danger from your godly conscience, and let not man's presumption use violence upon Christ's Gospel In my sincere desire, which is shared by the bishops that are with me, that you, most Christian and revered prince, should before all things please GOD, to whom the prayers of the whole Church are poured with one accord for your empire, I give you counsel, for fear lest, if we keep silence on so great a matter, we incur punishment before the tribunal of Christ. I entreat you therefore before the undivided Trinity of the one Godhead, which is injured by these evil doings, and which is the guardian of your kingdom, and before Christ's holy angels that all things remain intact as they were before the judgment, and that they await the weightier decision of the Synod at which the whole number of the bishops in the whole world is gathered together: and do not allow yourselves to bear the weight of others' misdoing. We are constrained to say this plainly by the fear of a constraining necessity[7]. But keep before your eyes the blessed Peter's glory, and the crowns which all the Apostles have in common with him, and the joys of the martyrs who had no other incentive to suffering but the confession of the true Godhead and the perfect continuance in Christ[8].

III. *And asks for another Synod to be summoned.*

And now that this confession is being god-

3 No satisfactory conclusion can be reached about this letter as it has come down to us, the Ballerinii not thinking that the Latin version extant is the original on which the Gk. version is based. On the whole I have thought it safer to make my translation chiefly from the Gk., though I am not at all sure that there is sufficient ground for the Ballerinii s suspicion oi the Latin.

4 A *lacuna* is here visible in the sense though not in the MSS.

5 The Gk. and the Lat. both read the plural here ἐπισκόπων (*episcopis*) which the Ballerinii alter to the singular. As far as we know, Julius was the only bishop in the party, but the greater ncludes the less.

6 Viz., Dioscorus, who must have been mentioned in the *lacuna* above, if anywhere.

7 The old Lat. version has here something very different *quia quod necesse est nos dicere, veremur ne cuius religio dissipatur, indignatio provocetur* (for we are bound to say we fear lest He whose religion is being undermined, should have His wrath aroused).

8 ἡ ἐν Χριστῷ τελεία διαμονή: here again the Latin version diverges, reading *veræ humanitatis* (sc. *confessio*) *in Christo*. So too the next sentence begins with *cui sacramento*, instead of the Gk. ἧς τινος ὁμολογίας, and elsewhere.

lessly impugned by some few men, all the churches of our parts and all the priests implore your clemency with tears in accordance with the request which Flavian makes in his appeal, to command the assembling together of a special Synod in Italy, in order that all opposition may be expelled or pacified, and that there may be no deviation from or ambiguity in the Faith: and to it should also come the bishops of all the Eastern provinces, that, if any have wandered out of the way of Truth, they may be recalled to their allegiance by wholesome remedies, and they who are under a more grievous charge may either be reduced to submission by counsel or cut off from the one Church. So that we are bound to preserve both what the Nicene canon enjoins and what the definitions of the bishops of the whole world enjoin according to the custom of the catholic Church, and also (to maintain) the freedom of our fathers' Faith, on which your tranquillity rests. For we pray that when those who harm the Church are driven out, and your provinces enjoy the possession of justice, and vengeance has been executed on these heretics, your royal power also may be defended by Christ's right hand.

LETTER XLIV.

To Theodosius Augustus.

Leo, the bishop, and the holy Synod which is assembled at Rome to Theodosius Augustus.

I. *He exposes the unscrupulous nature of the proceedings at Ephesus.*

From your clemency's letter, which in your love of the catholic Faith you sent sometime ago to the see of the blessed Apostle Peter, we drew such confidence in your defence of truth and peace that we thought nothing harmful could happen in so plain and well-ordered a matter; especially when those who were sent to the episcopal council, which you ordered to be held at Ephesus, were so fully instructed that, if the bishop of Alexandria had allowed the letters, which they brought either to the holy synod or to Flavian the bishop, to be read in the ears of the bishops, by the declaration of the most pure Faith, which being Divinely inspired we both have received and hold, all noise of disputings would have been so completely hushed that neither ignorance could any longer disport itself, nor jealousy find occasion to do mischief. But because private interests are consulted under cover of religion, the disloyalty of a few has wrought that which must wound the whole Church. For not from some untrustworthy messenger, but from a most faithful narrator of the things which have been done, Hilary, our deacon, who, lest he should be compelled by force to subscribe to their proceedings, with great difficulty made his escape, we have learnt that a great many priests came together at the synod, whose numbers would doubtless have assisted the debate and decision, if he who claimed for himself the chief place had consented to maintain priestly moderation, in order that, according to custom, when all had freely expressed their opinion, after quiet and fair deliberation, that might be ordained which was both agreeable to the Faith and helpful to those in error. But we have been told that all who had come were not present at the actual decision: for we have learnt that some were rejected while others were admitted, who at the aforesaid priest's requisition surrendered themselves to an unrighteous subscription, knowing they would suffer harm unless they obeyed his commands, and that such a resolution was brought forward by him that in attacking one man he might wreak his fury of the whole Church. Which our delegates from the Apostolic See saw to be so blasphemous and opposed to the catholic Faith that no pressure could force them to assent; for in the same synod they stoutly protested, as they ought, that the Apostolic See would never receive what was being passed: since the whole mystery of the Christian Faith is absolutely destroyed (which Heaven forfend in your Grace's reign), unless this abominable wickedness, which exceeds all former blasphemies, be abolished.

II. *And entreats the Emperor to help in reversing their decision.*

But because the devil with wicked subtlety deceives the unwary, and so mocks the imprudence of some by a show of piety as to persuade them to things harmful instead of profitable, we pray your Grace, renounce all complicity in this endangering of religion and Faith, and afford in the treatment of Divine things that which is granted in worldly matters by the equity of your laws, that human presumption may not do violence to Christ's Gospel. Behold, I, O most Christian and honoured Emperor, with my fellow-priests[9] fulfilling towards your revered clemency the offices of sincere love, and desiring you in all things to please God, to whom prayers are offered for you by the Church, lest before

9 *Cum consacerdotibus meis.* The Gk. version here reads the singular (μετὰ τοῦ συλλειτουργοῦ μου). This, if intentional and not a slip, is, I suppose, Flavian, of whose death Leo was not yet apprized.

the LORD Christ's tribunal we be judged guilty for our silence,—we beseech you in the presence of the Undivided Trinity of the One Godhead, Whom such an act wrongs (for He is Himself the Guardian and the Author of your empire), and in the presence of Christ's holy angels, order everything to be in the position in which they were before the decision until a larger number of priests be assembled from the whole world. Suffer not yourself to be weighted with another's sin because (and we must say it) we are afraid lest He, Whose religion is being destroyed, be provoked to wrath. Keep before your eyes, and with all your mental vision gaze reverently upon the blessed Peter's glory, and the crowns which all the Apostles have in common with him and the palms of all the martyrs, who had no other reason for suffering than the confession of the true Godhead and the true Manhood in Christ.

III. *He asks for a Council in Italy.*

And because this mystery is now being impiously opposed by a few ignorant persons, all the churches of our parts, and all the priests entreat your clemency, with groans and tears, seeing that our delegates faithfully protested, and bishop Flavian gave them an appeal in writing, to order a general synod to be held in Italy, which shall either dismiss or appease all disputes in such a way that there be nothing any longer either doubtful in the Faith or divided in love, and to it, of course, the bishops of the Eastern provinces must come, and if any of them were overcome by threats and injury, and deviated from the path of truth, they may be fully restored by health-giving measures, and they themselves, whose case is harder, if they acquiesce in wiser counsels, may not fall from the unity of the Church. And how necessary this request is after the lodging of an appeal is witnessed by the canonical decrees passed at Nicæa by the bishops of the whole world, which are added below [9a]. Show favour to the catholics after your own and your parents' custom. Give us such liberty to defend the catholic Faith as no violence, no fear of the world, while your revered clemency is safe, shall be able to take away. For it is the cause not only of the Church but of your Kingdom and prosperity that we plead, that you may enjoy the peaceful sway of your provinces. Defend the Church in unshaken peace against the heretics, that your empire also may be defended by Christ's right hand. Dated the 13th of October, in the consulship of the illustrious Asturius and Protogenes (449).

LETTER XLV.

(TO PULCHERIA AUGUSTA.)

Leo, the bishop, and the holy Synod which is assembled in the City of Rome to Pulcheria Augusta.

I. *He sends a copy of the former letter which failed to reach her.*

If the letters respecting the Faith which were despatched to your Grace by the hands of our clergy had reached you, it is certain you would have been able, the LORD helping you, to provide a remedy for these things which have been done against the Faith. For when have you failed either the priests or the religion or the Faith of Christ? But when those who were sent were so completely hindered from reaching your clemency that only one of them, namely Hilary our deacon, with difficulty fled and returned, we thought it necessary to re-write our letter: and that our prayers may deserve to receive more weight, we have subjoined a copy of the very document which did not reach your clemency, entreating you even more earnestly than before to take under protection that religion in which you excel which will win you the greater glory in proportion to the heinousness of the crimes against which your royal faith requires you to proceed, lest the integrity of the Christian Faith be violated by any plot of man's devising. For the things which were believed to require setting at rest and healing by the meeting of a Synod at Ephesus, have not only resulted in still greater disturbances of peace but, which is the more to be regretted, even in the overthrow of the very Faith whereby we are Christians.

II. *He also sends a copy of his letter to the Emperor and explains its contents.*

And they indeed, who were sent, and one of whom, escaping the violence of the bishop of Alexandria who claims everything for himself, faithfully reported to us what took place in the Synod, opposed, as it became them, what I will call the frenzy not the judgment of one man, protesting that those things which

---

[9a] Both Quesnel and the Ball. agree that the Canon here quoted by Leo really belongs not to the Nicene collection, but to that of Sardica (about 344), in which it stands as no. 4. (Exactly the same mistake is made in Letter LVI., where Galla Placidia Augusta quotes Canon 5 of Sardica to Theodosius as *secundum definitiones Nicæni concilii*). Cf. Gore's Leo, pp. 113, 114. The wording of this fourth Canon is as follows: "Gaudentius, the bishop, said, If it please you to add to this admirable declaration which you have passed, I propose that whensoever one bishop has been deposed by the judgment of other bishops, and appeals for his case to be heard in *Civitas Novorum*, the other bishop cannot by any means be considered confirmed in the same See after the appeal of the one who appears to be deposed, until he receive the decision of the judges there." In applying this to the present case, Leo no doubt proposed to substitute *Urbs Roma* for *Civitas Novorum*, though this was hardly the same thing.

were being carried through by violence and fear could not reverse the mysteries of the Church and the Creed itself composed by the Apostles, and that no injuries could sever them from that Faith which they had brought fully set forth and expounded from the See of the blessed Apostle Peter to the holy synod. And since this statement was not allowed to be read out at the bishop's request, in order forsooth that by the rejection of that Faith which has crowned patriarchs, prophets, apostles and martyrs, the birth according to the flesh of Jesus Christ our LORD and the confession of His true Death and Resurrection (we shudder to say it) might be overthrown, we have written[1] on this matter according to our ability, to our most glorious and (what is far greater) our Christian Prince, and at the same time have subjoined a copy of the letter to you to the end that he may not allow the Faith, in which he was re-born and reigns through GOD's grace, to be corrupted by any innovation, since Bishop Flavian continues in communion with us all, and that which has been done without regard to justice and contrary to all the teaching of the canons can, under no consideration, be held valid. And because the Synod of Ephesus has not removed but increased the scandal of disagreement (I have asked him) to appoint a place and time for holding a council within Italy, all quarrels and prejudices on both sides being suspended, that everything which has engendered offence may be the more diligently reconsidered and without wounding the Faith, without injuring religion those priests may return into the peace of Christ, who through irresolution were forced to subscribe, and only their errors be removed.

III. *He asks her to assist his petition with the Emperor.*

And that we may be worthy to obtain this, let your well-tried faith and protection, which has always helped the Church in her labours, deign to advance our petition with our most clement Prince, under a special commission so to act from the blessed Apostle Peter; so that before this civil and destructive war gains strength within the Church, he may grant opportunity of restoring unity by GOD's aid, knowing that the strength of his empire will be increased by every extension of catholic freedom that his kindly will affects.

Dated 13th of October in the consulship of the illustrious Asturius and Protogenes (449).

[1] This is, of course, Letter XLIV.

LETTER XLVI.

FROM HILARY, THEN DEACON (AFTERWARDS BISHOP OF ROME), TO PULCHERIA AUGUSTA.

(Describing his ill-treatment, as Leo's delegate, by Dioscorus.)

LETTER XLVII.

TO ANASTASIUS, BISHOP OF THESSALONICA.

(Congratulating him on being present at the synod of Ephesus)

LETTER XLVIII.

TO JULIAN, BISHOP OF COS.

(Consoling him after the riots at Ephesus and exhorting him to stand firm.)

LETTER XLIX.

TO FLAVIAN, BISHOP OF CONSTANTINOPLE.

(Whose death he is unaware of, promising him all the support in his power.)

LETTER L.

TO THE PEOPLE OF CONSTANTINOPLE, BY THE HAND OF EPIPHANIUS AND DIONYSIUS, NOTARY OF THE CHURCH OF ROME.

(Exhorting them to stand firm and consoling them for Flavian's deposition.)

LETTER LI.

TO FAUSTUS AND OTHER PRESBYTERS AND ARCHIMANDRITES IN CONSTANTINOPLE.

(With the same purport as the last.)

LETTER LII.

FROM THEODORET, BISHOP OF CYRUS, TO LEO. (See vol. iii. of this Series, p. 293.)

To Leo, bishop of Rome.

I. *If Paul appealed to Peter how much more must ordinary folk have recourse to his successor.*

If Paul, the herald of the Truth, the trumpet of the Holy Ghost, had recourse to the great Peter, in order to obtain a decision from him for those at Antioch who were disputing about living by the Law, much more do we small and humble folk run to the Apostolic See to get healing from you for the sores of the churches. For it is fitting that you should in all things have the pre-eminence, seeing that your See possesses many peculiar privileges. For other cities get a name for size or beauty or population, and some that are devoid of these advantages are compensated by certain spiritual gifts: but your city has the fullest abundance of good things from the Giver of all good. For she is of all cities the greatest and most famous, the mistress of the world and teeming with population. And besides this she has created an empire which is still predominant and has imposed her own name upon her subjects. But her chief decoration is her Faith, to which the Divine Apostle is a sure witness when he exclaims "your faith is proclaimed in all the world [1a];" and if immediately after receiving the seeds of the saving Gospel she bore such a weight of wondrous fruit, what words are sufficient to express the piety which is now found in her? She has, too, the tombs of our common fathers and teachers of the Truth, Peter and Paul [2], to illumine the souls of the faithful. And this blessed and divine pair arose indeed in the East, and shed its rays in all directions, but voluntarily underwent the sunset of life in the West, from whence now it illumines the whole world. These have rendered your See so glorious: this is the chief of all your goods. And their See is still blest by the light of their GOD's presence, seeing that therein He has placed your Holiness to shed abroad the rays of the one true Faith.

II. *He commends Leo's zeal against the Manichees, and latterly against Eutychianism, as evidenced especially in the Tome.*

Of which thing indeed, though there are many other proofs to be found, your zeal against the ill-famed Manichæans is proof enough, that zeal which your holiness has of late years displayed [3], thereby revealing the intensity of your devotion to GOD in things Divine. Proof enough, too, of your Apostolic character is what you have now written. For we have met with what your holiness has written about the Incarnation of our GOD and Saviour, and have admired the careful diligence of the work [4]. For it has proved both points equally well, viz., the Eternal Godhead of the Only-begotten of the Eternal Father, and at the same time His manhood of the seed of Abraham and David, and His assumption of a nature in all things like ours, except in this one thing, that He remained free from all sin: for sin is engendered not of nature, but of free will [5]. This also was contained in your letter, that the only-begotten Son of GOD is One and His Godhead impassible, irreversible, unchangeable even as the Father who begat Him and the All-holy Spirit. And since the Divine nature could not suffer, He took the nature that could suffer to this end, that by the suffering of His own Flesh He might give exemption from suffering to those that believed on Him. These points, and all that is akin thereto, the letter contained. And we, admiring your spiritual wisdom, extolled the grace of the Holy Ghost which spake through you, and ask and pray, and beg and beseech your holiness to come to the rescue of the churches of GOD that are now tempest tossed.

III. *He complains of Dioscorus' ill-treatment of himself.*

For when we expected a stilling of the waves through those who were sent to Ephesus from your holiness, we have fallen into yet worse storm. For the most righteous [5a] prelate of Alexandria was not satisfied with the illegal and most unrighteous deposition of the LORD's most holy and GOD-loving bishop of Constantinople, Flavian, nor was his wrath appeased by the slaughter of the other bishops likewise. But me, too, he murdered with his pen in my absence, without calling me to judgment, without passing judgment on me in person, without questioning me on what I hold about the Incarnation of our GOD and Saviour. But even murderers, tomb-breakers, and ravishers of other men's beds, those who sit in judgment do not condemn until they either themselves corroborate the accusations by their confessions, or are clearly convicted by others. But us, when five and thirty days' journey distant, he, though brought up on Divine laws, has condemned at his will. And not now only has he done this, but also last year, after that two persons infected with the Apollinarian disorder had come hither and laid false information against us, he rose up in church and anathematized us, and that when I had written to him and expressed what I hold in a letter.

IV. *This ill-treatment has come after 20 years' good work in his diocese of Cyrus.*

I bemoan the distress of the Church and yearn after its peace. For having ruled through your prayers the church committed to me by the GOD of the universe for 20 years, neither in the time of the blessed Theodotus, president of the East, nor in the time of those

[1a] Rom. i. 8.

[2] It is sufficient here to quote Eusebius (*Hist. Eccl.* ii. 25) as one of the earliest (before 340) maintainers of this tradition. In this passage he again quotes Gaius of Rome (3rd cent.) and Dionysius of Corinth (2nd cent.) as corroborative authorities. Eusebius' own words are these; "Paul is recorded to have been beheaded in Rome itself, and Peter likewise to have been impaled. And this statement is supported by their names, which remain to this day inscribed in the cemeteries there."

[3] Viz., in 444: cf. Letter VII. *supra*, together with the Emperor's decree (Lett. VIII.).

[4] This is, of course, the Tome (Lett. XXVIII.).

[5] Here 'nature' must mean 'man's original nature before the Fall,' when it was still in the image of Him who so created it, to which nature Christ's manhood was a triumphant return. Otherwise it is hard to see how Theodoret escapes the pitfall of Pelagianism.

[5a] The epithet is shown by the context to be bitterly sarcastic.

who have succeeded him in the See of Antioch, have I received the slightest blame, but, the Divine Grace working with me, have freed more than 1,000 souls from the disease of Marcion, and have won over many others from the company of Arius and Eunomius to the Master, Christ. And 800 churches have I had to shepherd: for that is the number of parishes in Cyrus, in which not a single tare through your prayers has lingered. But our flock has been freed from every heretical error. He that sees all things knows how I have been stoned by the ill-famed heretics that have been sent against me, and what struggles I have had in many cities of the East against Greeks, Jews, and every heretical error. And after all these toils and troubles, I have been condemned without a hearing.

V. *He appeals to the Apostolic See with confidence.*

I however await the verdict of your Apostolic See, and beg and pray your Holiness to succour me when I appeal to your upright and just tribunal, and bid me come to you and show that my teaching follows in the track of the Apostles. For there are writings of mine some 20 years ago, some 18, some 15, and some 12, some again against the Arians and Eunomians, some against the Jews and Greeks, some against the Magi in Persia, some also about the universal Providence, others about the nature of God and about the Divine Incarnation. I have interpreted, through the Divine grace, both the Apostolic writings and the prophetic utterances, and it is easy therefrom to gather whether I have kept unswervingly the standard of the Faith, or have turned aside from its straight path. And I beg you not to spurn my petition, nor to overlook the insults heaped on my poor white hairs.

VI. *Ought he to acquiesce in his deposition?*

First of all, I beg you to tell me, whether I ought to acquiesce in this unrighteous deposition or not. For I await your verdict: and, if you bid me abide by my condemnation, I will abide by it, and will trouble no one hereafter, but await the unerring verdict of our God and Saviour. I indeed, the Master God is my witness, care nought for honour and glory, but only for the stumbling-block that is put in men's way: because many of the simpler folk, and especially those who have been rescued by us from divers heresies, will give credence to those who have condemned us, and perchance reckon us heretics, not being able to discern the exact truth of the dogma, and because, after my long episcopate, I have acquired neither house, nor land, nor obol, nor tomb, only a voluntary poverty, having straightway distributed even what came to me from my fathers after their death, as all know who live in the East.

VII. *Being prevented himself, he has sent delegates to plead his cause.*

And before all things I entreat you, holy and God-loved brother, render assistance to my prayers. These things I have brought to your Holiness' knowledge, by the most religious and God-beloved presbyters, Hypatius and Abramius the chorepiscopi[6], and Alypius, superintendent[7] of the monks in our district: seeing that I was hindered from coming to you myself by the Emperor's restraining letter, and likewise the others. And I entreat your holiness both to look on them with fatherly regard, and to lend them your ears in sincere kindness, and also to deem my slandered and falsely attacked position worthy of your protection, and above all to defend with all your might the Faith that is now plotted against, and to keep the heritage of the fathers intact for the churches, so shall your holiness receive from the Bountiful Master a full reward. (Date about the end of 449.)

LETTER LIII.

A fragment of a letter from Anatolius, bishop of Constantinople, to Leo (about his consecration).

LETTER LIV.

To Theodosius Augustus (asking for a synod in Italy).

LETTERS LV. to LVIII.

A series of Letters.

(1) From Valentinian the Emperor to Theodosius Augustus.

(2) From Galla Placidia Augusta to Theodosius Augustus.

(3) From Licinia Eudoxia Augusta to Theodosius Augustus.

(4) From Galla Placidia Augusta to Pulcheria Augusta, all graphically describing how Leo had appealed to them in public to press his suit with Theodosius. Of these, LVI. is subjoined as perhaps the most interesting specimen.

LETTER LVI.

(From Galla Placidia Augusta to Theodosius).

To the Lord Theodosius, Conqueror and

6 *Chorepiscopi* (country bishops) were a kind of suffragan bishop to assist the town bishops in the remoter parts of their diocese. They continued in use from the end of the 3rd till the 9th century, when they were abolished. 7 *Exarchus.*

Emperor, her ever august son, Galla Placidia, most pious and prosperous, perpetual Augusta and mother.

When on our very arrival in the ancient city, we were engaged in paying our devotion to the most blessed Apostle Peter, at the martyr's very altar, the most reverend Bishop Leo waiting behind awhile after the service, uttered laments over the catholic Faith to us, and taking to witness the chief of the Apostles himself likewise, whom we had just approached, and surrounded by a number of bishops whom he had brought together from numerous cities in Italy by the authority and dignity of his position, adding also tears to his words, called upon us to join our moans to his own. For no slight harm has arisen from those occurrences, whereby the standard of the catholic Faith so long guarded since the days of our most Divine father Constantine, who was the first in the palace to stand out as a Christian, has been recently disturbed by the assumption of one man, who in the synod held at Ephesus is alleged to have rather stirred up hatred and contention, intimidating by the presence of soldiers, Flavianus, the bishop of Constantinople, because he had sent an appeal to the Apostolic See, and to all the bishops of these parts by the hands of those who had been deputed to attend the Synod by the most reverend Bishop of Rome, who have been always wont so to attend, most sacred Lord and Son and adored King, in accordance with the provisions of the Nicene Synod [8]. For this cause we pray your clemency to oppose such disturbances with the Truth, and to order the Faith of the catholic religion to be preserved without spot, in order that according to the standard and decision of the Apostolic See, which we likewise revere as pre-eminent, Flavianus may remain altogether uninjured in his priestly office, and the matter be referred to the Synod of the Apostolic See, wherein assuredly he first adorned the primacy, who was deemed worthy to receive the keys of heaven: for it becomes us in all things to maintain the respect due to this great city, which is the mistress of all the earth; and this too we must most carefully provide that what in former times our house guarded seem not in our day to be infringed, and that by the present example schisms be not advanced either between the bishops or the most holy churches.

LETTER LIX.

To the Clergy and People of the City of Constantinople.

Leo the bishop to the clergy, dignitaries, and people, residing at Constantinople.

I. *He congratulates them on their outspoken resistance to error.*

Though we are greatly grieved at the things reported to have been done recently in the council of priests at Ephesus, because, as is consistently rumoured, and also demonstrated by results, neither due moderation nor the strictness of the Faith was there observed, yet we rejoice in your devoted piety and in the acclamations of the holy people [9], instances of which have been brought to our notice, we have approved of the right feeling of you all; because there lives and abides in good sons due affection for their excellent Father, and because you suffer the fulness of catholic teaching to be in no part corrupted. For undoubtedly, as the Holy Spirit has unfolded to you, they are leagued with the Manichæans' error, who deny that the only-begotten Son of God took our nature's true Manhood, and maintain that all His bodily actions were the actions of a false apparition. And lest you should in aught give your assent to this blasphemy, we have now sent you, beloved, by my son Epiphanius and Dionysius, notary of the Roman Church, letters of exhortation wherein we have of our own accord rendered you the assistance which you sought, that you may not doubt of our bestowing all a father's care on you, and labouring in every way, by the help of God's mercy, to destroy all the stumbling-blocks which ignorant and foolish men have raised. And let no one venture to parade his priestly dignity who can be convicted of holding such detestably blasphemous opinions. For if ignorance seems hardly tolerable in laymen, how much less excusable or pardonable is it in those who govern; especially when they dare even to defend their mendacious and perverse views, and persuade the unsteadfast to agree with them either by intimidation or by cajoling.

II. *They are to be rejected who deny the truth of Christ's flesh, a truth repeated by every recipient at the Holy Eucharist.*

Let such men be rejected by the holy members of Christ's Body, and let not catholic

[8] See no. 9a to Lett. XLIV., 3, where it is shown that this is a mistake, wilful or otherwise, on Leo's part.

[9] *Sanctæ plebis acclamationibus.* It seems that the people had openly expressed their disapproval of the maltreatment to which Flavian had been subjected.

liberty suffer the yoke of the unfaithful to be laid upon it. For they are to be reckoned outside the Divine grace, and outside the mystery of man's salvation, who, denying the nature of our flesh in Christ, gainsay the Gospel and oppose the Creed. Nor do they perceive that their blindness leads them into such an abyss that they have no sure footing in the reality either of the LORD's Passion or His Resurrection: because both are discredited in the Saviour, if our fleshly nature is not believed in Him. In what density of ignorance, in what utter sloth must they hitherto have lain, not to have learnt from hearing, nor understood from reading, that which in GOD's Church is so constantly in men's mouths, that even the tongues of infants do not keep silence upon the truth of Christ's Body and Blood at the rite of Holy Communion [1]? For in that mystic distribution of spiritual nourishment, that which is given and taken is of such a kind that receiving the virtue of the celestial food we pass into the flesh of Him, Who became our flesh [2]. Hence to confirm you, beloved, in your laudably faithful resistance to the foes of Truth, I shall fitly and opportunely use the language and sentiments of the Apostle, and say: "Therefore I also hearing of your faith, which is in the LORD Jesus, and love towards all saints, do not cease to give thanks for you, making mention of you in my prayers that the GOD of our LORD Jesus Christ, the Father of glory, may give you the spirit of wisdom and revelation in the knowledge of Him, the eyes of your hearts being enlightened that you may know what is the hope of His calling, and what the riches of the glory of His inheritance among the saints, and what is the exceeding greatness of His power in us, who believed according to the working of His mighty power which he has wrought in Christ, raising Him from the dead, and setting Him at His right hand in heavenly places above every principality, and power, and strength, and dominion, and every name which is named not only in this age, but also in that which is to come: and hath put all things under His feet, and given Him to be the head over all the Church which is His body, and the fulness of Him Who filleth all in all [3]."

[1] Two things are here to be noticed: (1) that the allusion appears to be to the formula of reception then in use at the Eucharist, the priest saying *Corpus Christi*, and the recipient answering *Amen*. Cf. Serm. xci. 3, *sic sacræ mensæ communicare debetis ut nihil prorsus de veritate corporis Christi et sanguinis ambigatis. Hoc enim ore sumitur quod fide creditur: et frustra ab illis Amen respondetur a quibus contra id quod accipitur disputatur*; (2) that infant communion is implied as regular: this we know to have been the case in much earlier days. Cf. *Apost. Const.* viii. 13, Cyprian *de Lapsis*, ix. and xxv. &c., also Bingham's Antiq. xv. chap. iv. § 7.

[2] Cf. Sermon LXIII. 7, where much the same language is used.

[3] Ephes. i. 15—23.

III. *Perfect God and perfect Man were united in Christ.*

In this passage let the adversaries of the Truth say when or according to what nature did the Almighty Father exalt His Son above all things, or to what substance did He subject all things. For the Godhead of the Word is equal in all things, and consubstantial with the Father, and the power of the Begetter and the Begotten is one and the same always and eternally. Certainly, the Creator of all natures, since "through Him all things were made, and without Him was nothing made [4]," is above all things which He created, nor were the things which He made ever not subject to their Creator, Whose eternal property it is, to be from none other than the Father, and in no way different to the Father. If greater power, grander dignity, more exalted loftiness was granted Him, then was He that was so increased less than He that promoted Him, and possessed not the full riches of His nature from Whose fulness He received. But one who thinks thus is hurried off into the society of Arius, whose heresy is much assisted by this blasphemy which denies the existence of human nature in the Word of GOD, so that, in rejecting the combination of humility with majesty in GOD, it either asserts a false phantom-body in Christ, or says that all His bodily actions and passions belonged to the Godhead rather than to the flesh. But everything he ventures to uphold is absolutely foolish: because neither our religious belief nor the scope of the mystery admits either of the Godhead suffering anything or of the Truth belying Itself in anything. The impassible Son of GOD, therefore, whose perpetually it is with the Father and with the Holy Spirit to be what He is in the one essence of the Unchangeable Trinity, when the fulness of time had come which had been fore-ordained by an eternal purpose, and promised by the prophetic significance of words and deeds, became man not by conversion of His substance but by assumption of our nature, and "came to seek and to save that which was lost [5]." But He came not by local approach nor by bodily motion, as if to be present where He had been absent, or to depart where He had come: but He came to be manifested to onlookers by that which was visible and common to others, receiving, that is to say, human flesh and soul in the Virgin mother's womb, so that, abiding in the form of GOD, He united to Himself the form of a slave, and

[4] S. John i. 3.

[5] S. Luke xix. 10.

the likeness of sinful flesh, whereby He did not lessen the Divine by the human, but increased the human by the Divine.

IV. *The Sacrament of Baptism typifies and realizes this union to each individual believer.*

For such was the state of all mortals resulting from our first ancestors that, after the transmission of original sin to their descendants, no one would have escaped the punishment of condemnation, had not the Word become flesh and dwelt in us, that is to say, in that nature which belonged to our blood and race. And accordingly, the Apostle says: "As by one man's sin (judgment passed) upon all to condemnation, so also by one man's righteousness (it) passed upon all to justification of life. For as by one man's disobedience many were made sinners, so also by one man's obedience shall many be made righteous[6];" and again, "For because by man (came) death, by man also (came) the resurrection of the dead. And as in Adam all die, so also in Christ shall all be made alive[7]." All they to wit who though they be born in Adam, yet are found reborn in Christ, having a sure testimony both to their justification by grace, and to Christ's sharing in their nature[8]; for he who does not believe that God's only-begotten Son did assume our nature in the womb of the Virgin-daughter of David, is without share in the Mystery of the Christian religion, and, as he neither recognizes the Bridegroom nor knows the Bride, can have no place at the wedding-banquet. For the flesh of Christ is the veil of the Word, wherewith every one is clothed who confesses Him unreservedly. But he that is ashamed of it and rejects it as unworthy, shall have no adornment from Him, and though he present himself at the Royal feast, and unseasonably join in the sacred banquet, yet the intruder will not be able to escape the King's discernment, but, as the Lord Himself asserted, will be taken, and with hands and feet bound, be cast into outer darkness; where will be weeping and gnashing of teeth[9]. Hence whosoever confesses not the human body in Christ, must know that he is unworthy of the mystery of the Incarnation, and has no share in that sacred union of which the Apostle speaks, saying, "For we are His members, of His flesh and of His bones. For this cause a man shall leave father and mother and shall cleave to his wife, and there shall be two in one flesh[1]." And explaining what was meant by this, he added, "This mystery is great, but I speak in respect of Christ and the Church." Therefore, from the very commencement of the human race, Christ is announced to all men as coming in the flesh. In which, as was said, "there shall be two in one flesh," there are undoubtedly two, God and man, Christ and the Church, which issued from the Bridegroom's flesh, when it received the mystery of redemption and regeneration, water and blood flowing from the side of the Crucified. For the very condition of a new creature which at baptism puts off not the covering of true flesh but the taint of the old condemnation, is this, that a man is made the body of Christ, because Christ also is the body of a man[2].

V. *The true doctrine of the Incarnation restated and commended to their keeping.*

Wherefore we call Christ not God only, as the Manichæan heretics, nor Man only, as the Photinian[3] heretics, nor man in such a way that anything should be wanting in Him which certainly belongs to human nature, whether soul or reasonable mind or flesh which was not derived from woman, but made from the Word turned and changed into flesh; which three false and empty propositions have been variously advanced by the three sections of the Apollinarian heretics[4]. Nor do we say that the blessed Virgin Mary conceived a Man without Godhead, Who was created by the Holy Ghost and afterwards assumed by the Word, which we deservedly and properly condemned Nestorius for preaching: but we call Christ the Son of God, true God, born of God the Father without any beginning in time, and likewise true Man, born of a human Mother, at the ordained fulness of time, and we say that His Manhood, whereby the Father is the greater, does not in anything lessen that nature whereby He is equal with the Father. But these two natures form one Christ, Who has said most truly both according to His Godhead: "I and the Father are one[5]," and according to His manhood "the Father is greater than I[5]." This true and indestruct-

6 Rom. v. 18. 19. 7 1 Cor. xv. 21, 22.

8 *Habentes fidei testimonium et de justificatione gratiæ et de communione naturæ.*

9 The reference is to S. Matt. xxii. 11—13.

1 Eph. v. 30, 31, 32.

2 *Ipsa est enim novæ conditio creaturæ quæ in baptismate non indumento veræ carnis sed contagio damnatæ vetustatis exuitur ut efficiatur homo corpus Christi, quia et Christus corpus est hominis.* The most crabbed of the several crabbed passages in this letter. The mystical transmutation of the believer's body into the body of Christ is here referred to the sacrament of Baptism, while earlier in the letter (chap. ii.) it is described as one of the effects of Holy Communion.

3 The followers of Photinus, Bishop of Sirmium (*circ.* 410 A.D.): for an account of his heretical opinions see Schaff's History of the Christian Church. *in loc.* Cf. Letter XV. 4.

4 *Apollinaristarum tres partes*; see Sermon xxviii. chap. 4 (end) with Bright's n. 32 on Apollinarianism generally.

5 S. John x. 30; xiv. 28.

ible Faith, dearly-beloved, which alone makes us true Christians, and which, as we hear with approval, you are defending with loyal zeal and praiseworthy affection, hold fast and maintain boldly. And since, besides GOD'S aid, you must win the favour of catholic Princes also, humbly and wisely make request that the most clement Emperor be pleased to grant our petition, wherein we have asked for a plenary synod to be convened; that by the aid of GOD'S mercy the sound may be increased in courage, and the sick, if they consent to be treated, have the remedy applied. (Dated October 15, in the consulship of the illustrious Asturius and Protogenes, 449.)

LETTER LX.

TO PULCHERIA AUGUSTA.

(He hopes for her intercession to procure the condemnation of Eutyches.)

LETTER LXI.

TO MARTINUS AND FAUSTUS, PRESBYTERS.

(Reminding them of a former letter he has written to them, viz. Lett. LI.)

(Letters LXII., LXIII., LXIV., are the Emperor Theodosius' answers (*a*) to Valentinian, (*b*) to Galla Placidia, and (*c*) to Licinia Eudoxia (assuring them of his orthodoxy and care for the Faith.)

LETTER LXV.

FROM THE BISHOPS OF THE PROVINCE OF ARLES.

(Asking Leo to confirm the privileges of that city, which they allege date from the mission of Trophimus, by S. Peter, and more recently ratified by the Emperor Constantine.)

LETTER LXVI.

LEO'S REPLY TO LETTER LXV.

Leo, the pope, to the dearly-beloved brethren Constantinus, Armentarius, Audientius, Severianus, Valerianus, Ursus, Stephanus, Nectarius, Constantius, Maximus, Asclepius, Theodorus, Justus Ingenuus, Augustalis, Superventor, Ynantius, Fonteius, and Palladius.

I. *The bishop of Vienne has anticipated their appeal. He proposes to arbitrate with impartiality.*

When we read your letter, beloved, which was brought to us by our sons Petronius the presbyter and Regulus the deacon, we recognized how affectionate is the regard in which you hold our brother and fellow-bishop, Ravennius: for your request is that what his predecessor[6] deservedly lost for his excessive presumption may be restored to him. But your petition, brothers, was forestalled by the bishop of Vienne, who sent a letter and legates with the complaint that the bishop of Arles had unlawfully claimed the ordination of the bishop of Vasa. Accordingly, as we had to show such respect both for the canons of the fathers and for your good opinion of us, that in the matter of the churches' privileges we should allow no infringement or deprivation, it were incumbent on us to preserve the peace within the province of Vienne by employing such righteous moderation as should disregard neither ancient usage nor your desires.

II. *The bishop of Vienne is to retain jurisdiction over four neighbouring cities: the rest to belong to Arles.*

For after considering the arguments advanced by the clergy present on either side, we find that the cities of Vienne and Arles within your province have always been so famous, that in certain matters of ecclesiastical privilege, now one, now the other, has alternately taken precedence, though the national tradition is that formerly they had community of rights. And hence we suffer not the city of Vienne to be altogether without honour, so far as concerns ecclesiastical jurisdiction, especially as it already possesses the authority of our decree for the enjoyment of its privilege: to wit the power which, when taken away from Hilary, we thought proper to confer on the bishop of Vienne. And that he seem not suddenly and unduly lowered, he shall hold rule over the four neighbouring towns, that is, Valentia, Tarantasia, Genava and Gratianopolis, with Vienne herself for the fifth, to the bishop of which shall belong the care of all the said churches. But the other churches of the same province shall be placed under the authority and management of the bishop of Arles, who from his temperate moderation we believe will be so anxious for love and peace as by no means to consider himself deprived of that which he sees conceded to his brother. Dated 5th of May, in the consulship of Valentinianus Augustus (7th time), and the most famous Avienus (450.)

LETTER LXVII[7].

TO RAVENNIUS, BISHOP OF ARLES.

To his dearly-beloved brother Ravennius, Leo the pope.

---

[6] This, it will be remembered, was Hilary: see Letter X. above.

[7] This letter, together with Letters XL., LXV. and LXVI.,

We have kept our sons Petronius the presbyter, and Regulus the deacon, long in the City, both because they deserved this from their favour in our eyes, and because the needs of the Faith, which is now being assailed by the error of some, demanded it. For we wished them to be present when we discussed the matter, and to ascertain everything which we desire through you, beloved, should reach the knowledge of all our brethren and fellow-bishops, specially deputing this to you, dear brother, that through your watchful diligence our letter, which we have issued to the East in defence of the Faith, or else [8] that of Cyril of blessed memory, which agrees throughout with our views, may become known to all the brethren; in order that being furnished with arguments they may fortify themselves with spiritual strength against those who think fit to insult the LORD's Incarnation with their misbeliefs. You have a favourable opportunity, beloved brother, of recommending the commencement of your episcopacy to all the churches and to our GOD, if you will carry out these things in the way we have charged and enjoined you. But the matters which were not to be committed to paper, in reliance on GOD's aid, you shall carry out effectually, as we have said, and laudably, when you have learnt about them from the mouths of our aforesaid sons. GOD keep you safe, dearest brother. Dated 5th of May, in the consulship of the most glorious Valentinianus (for the 7th time) and of the famous Avienus (450).

LETTER LXVIII.

FROM THREE GALLIC BISHOPS TO ST. LEO.

Ceretius, Salonius and Veranus to the holy Lord, most blessed father, and pope most worthy of the Apostolic See, Leo.

I. *They congratulate and thank Leo for the Tome.*

Having perused your Excellency's letter, which you composed for instruction in the Faith, and sent to the bishop of Constantinople, we thought it our duty, being enriched with so great a wealth of doctrine, to pay our debt of thanks by at least inditing you a letter. For we appreciate your fatherly solicitude on our behalf, and confess that we are the more indebted to your preventing care because we now have the benefit of the remedy before experiencing the evils. For knowing that those remedies are well-nigh too late which are applied after the infliction of the wounds, you admonish us with the voice of loving forethought to arm ourselves with those Apostolic means of defence. We acknowledge frankly, most blessed pope [8a], with what singular loving-kindness you have imparted to us the innermost thoughts of your breast, by the efficacy of which you secure the safety of others: and while you extract the old Serpent's infused poison from the hearts of others, standing as it were on the watch-tower of Love, with Apostolic care and watchfulness you cry aloud, lest the enemy come on us unawares and off our guard, lest careless security expose us to attack, O holy Lord, most blessed father and pope, most worthy of the Apostolic See. Moreover we, who specially belong to you [9], are filled with a great and unspeakable delight, because this special statement of your teaching is so highly regarded wherever the Churches meet together, that the unanimous opinion is expressed that the primacy of the Apostolic See is rightfully there assigned, from whence the oracles of the Apostolic Spirit still receive their interpretations.

II. *They ask him to correct or add to their copy of the Tome.*

Therefore, if you deem it worth while, we entreat your holiness to run through and correct any mistake of the copyist in this work, so valuable both now and in the future, which we have had committed to parchment [10], in our desire to preserve it, or if you have devised anything further in your zeal, which will profit all who read, give orders in your loving care that it be added to this copy, so that not only many holy bishops our brethren throughout the provinces of Gaul, but also many of your sons among the laity, who greatly desire to see this letter for the revelation of the Truth, may be permitted, when it is sent back to us, corrected by your holy hand, to transcribe, read and keep it. If you think fit, we are anxious that our messengers should return soon, in order that we may the speedier have an account of your good health over which to rejoice: for your well-being is our joy and health.

May Christ the Lord long keep your eminence mindful of our humility, O holy Lord, most blessed father and pope most worthy of the Apostolic See.

---

are found only in the Collection of Arles (numbered XV. by the Ballerinii).

8 *Vel* can hardly equal *et* as the Ball. would wish. So that here Leo recommends *either* his own Tome *or* Cyril's second letter to Nestorius. Cf. Letter LXIX., chap. i. below; also Letter LXX.

8a Cf. Lett. XVII. n. 2a.

9 *Peculiares tui.* So in each one's autograph subscription at the end of the letter Ceretius calls himself *susceptus vester*, Salonius *venerator vester*, and Veranus *cultor vestri apostolatus*.

10 *Foliis.*

I, Ceretius, your adopted (son ?), salute your apostleship, commending me to your prayers.

I, Salonius, your adorer, salute your apostleship, entreating the aid of your prayers.

I, Veranus, the worshipper of your apostleship, salute your blessedness, and beseech you to pray for me.

LETTER LXIX.

(To Theodosius Augustus.)

Leo, the bishop, to Theodosius ever Augustus.

I. *He suspends his opinion on the appointment of Anatolius till he has made open confession of the catholic Faith.*

In all your piously expressed letters amid the anxieties, which we suffer for the Faith, you have afforded us hope of security by supporting the Council of Nicæa so loyally as not to allow the priests of the Lord to budge from it, as you have often written us already. But lest I should seem to have done anything prejudicial to the catholic defence, I thought nothing rash on either side ought meanwhile to be written back on the ordination of him who has begun to preside over the church of Constantinople, and this not through want of loving interest, but waiting for the catholic Truth to be made clear. And I beg your clemency to bear this with equanimity that when he has proved himself such as we desire towards the catholic Faith, we may the more fully and safely rejoice over his sincerity. But that no evil suspicion may assail him about our disposition towards him, I remove all occasion of difficulty, and demand nothing which may seem either hard or controvertible but make an invitation which no catholic would decline. For they are well known and renowned throughout the world, who before our time have shone in preaching the catholic Truth whether in the Greek or the Latin tongue, to whose learning and teaching some even of our own day have recourse, and from whose writings a uniform and manifold statement of doctrine is produced: which, as it has pulled down the heresy of Nestorius, so has it cut off this error too which is now sprouting out again. Let him then read again what is the belief on the Lord's Incarnation which the holy fathers guarded and has always been similarly preached, and when he has perceived that the letter of Cyril of holy memory, bishop of Alexandria, agrees with the view of those who preceded him [wherein he wished to correct and cure Nestorius, refuting his wrong statements and setting out more clearly the Faith as defined at Nicæa, and which was sent by him and placed in the library of the Apostolic See [1]], let him further reconsider the proceedings of the Ephesian Synod [2] wherein the testimonies of catholic priests on the Lord's Incarnation are inserted and maintained by Cyril of holy memory. Let him not scorn also to read my letter [3] over, which he will find to agree throughout with the pious belief of the fathers. And when he has realized that that is required and desired from him which shall serve the same good end, let him give his hearty assent to the judgment of the catholics, so that in the presence of all the clergy and the whole people he may without any reservation declare his sincere acknowledgment of the common Faith, to be communicated to the Apostolic See and all the Lord's priests and churches, and thus the world being at peace through the one Faith, we may all be able to say what the angels sang at the Saviour's birth of the Virgin Mary, "Glory in the highest to God and on earth peace to men of good will [4]."

II. *He promises to accept Anatolius on making this confession, and asks for a council in Italy to finally define the Faith.*

But because both we and our blessed fathers, whose teaching we revere and follow, are in concord on the one Faith, as the bishops of all the provinces attest, let your clemency's most devout faith see to it that such a document as is due may reach us as soon as may be from the bishop of Constantinople, as from an approved and catholic priest, that is, openly and distinctly affirming that he will separate from his communion any one who believes or maintains any other view about the Incarnation of the Word of God than my statement and that of all catholics lays down, that we may fairly be able to bestow on him brotherly love in Christ. And that swifter and fuller effect, God aiding us, may be given through your clemency's faith to our wholesome desires, I have sent to your piety my brethren and fellow-bishops Abundius and Asterius, together with Basilius and Senator presbyters, whose devotion is well proved to me, through whom, when they have displayed the instructions which we have sent, you may be able properly to apprehend what is the standard of our faith, so that, if the bishop of Constantinople gives his hearty assent to the same confession, we may securely, as is due, rejoice over the peace of the Church and no

1 *Wherein—see*, probably a gloss by way of identifying the letter: it is the 2nd letter to Nestorius. See Letter LXVII above.

2 Viz., the third Ecumenical Council held at Ephesus 431, in which Nestorius was condemned.

3 Viz., XXVIII (The Tome).

4 S. Luke ii. 14.

ambiguity may seem to lurk behind which may trouble us with perhaps ungrounded suspicions. But if any dissent from the purity of our Faith and from the authority of the Fathers, the Synod which has met at Rome for that purpose joins with me in asking your clemency to permit a universal council within the limits of Italy; so that, if all those come together in one place who have fallen either through ignorance or through fear, measures may be taken to correct and cure them, and no one any longer may be allowed to quote the Synod of Nicæa in a way which shall prove him opposed to its Faith; since it will be of advantage both to the whole Church and to your rule, if one God, one Faith and one mystery of man's Salvation, be held by the one confession of the whole world.

Dated 17th July in the consulship of the illustrious Valentinianus (for the seventh time) and Avienus (450).

LETTER LXX.

To Pulcheria Augusta.

(In which he again says he is waiting for Anatolius' acceptance of Cyril's and his own statement of the Faith, and looks forward to a Synod in Italy.)

LETTER LXXI.

To the Archimandrites of Constantinople.

(Complaining of Anatolius' silence.)

LETTER LXXII.

To Faustus, one of the Archimandrites at Constantinople.

(Commending his faith and exhorting him to steadfastness.)

LETTER LXXIII.

From Valentinian and Marcian.

(Announcing their election as Emperors[5] (A.D. 450), and asking his prayers that (*per celebrandam synodum, te auctore*), peace may be restored to the Church.)

LETTER LXXIV.

To Martinus, another of the Archimandrites at Constantinople.

(Commending his steadfastness in the Faith.)

LETTER LXXV.

To Faustus and Martinus together.

(Condemning the Latrocinium and maintaining that Eutyches equally with Nestorius promotes the cause of Antichrist.)

LETTER LXXVI.

From Marcianus Augustus to Leo.

(Proposing that he should either attend a Synod at Constantinople or help in arranging some other more convenient place of meeting.)

LETTER LXXVII.

From Pulcheria Augusta to Leo.

(In which she expresses her assurance that Anatolius is orthodox, and begs him to assist her husband in arranging for the Synod, and announces that Flavian's body has been buried in the Basilica of the Apostles at Constantinople and the exiled bishops restored.)

LETTER LXXVIII.

Leo's answer to Marcianus.

(Briefly thanking him.)

LETTER LXXIX.

To Pulcheria Augusta.

Leo, bishop of the city of Rome to Pulcheria Augusta.

I. *He rejoices at Pulcheria's zeal both against Nestorius and Eutyches.*

That which we have always anticipated concerning your Grace's holy purposes, we have now proved fully true, viz. that, however varied may be the attacks of wicked men upon the Christian Faith, yet when you are present and prepared by the Lord for its defence, it cannot be disturbed. For God will not forsake either the mystery of His mercy or the deserts of your labours, whereby you long ago repelled the crafty foe of our holy religion from the very vitals of the Church: when the impiety of Nestorius failed to maintain his heresy because it did not escape you the handmaid and pupil of the Truth, how much poison was instilled into simple folk by the coloured falsehoods of that glib fellow. And the sequel to that mighty struggle was that through your vigilance the things which the devil contrived by means of Eutyches, did not escape detection, and they who had chosen to themselves one side in the twofold heresy, were overthrown by the one and undivided power of the catholic Faith.

5 Valentinian III. had been nominally Emperor of the West since 425, but his mother's (Galla Placidia) death this year compelled him to rule as well as have the name of ruler: almost simultaneously in the East the death of Theodosius II. brought to the front his sister Pulcheria and her soldier husband Marcian.

This then is your second victory over the destruction of Eutyches' error: and, if he had had any soundness of mind, that error having been once and long ago routed and put to confusion in the person of his instigators, he would easily have been able to avoid the attempt to rekindle into life the smouldering ashes, and thus only share the lot of those, whose example he had followed, most glorious Augusta. We desire, therefore, to leap for joy and to pay due vows for your clemency's prosperity to God, who has already bestowed on you a double palm and crown through all the parts of the world, in which the Lord's Gospel is proclaimed.

II. *He thanks her for her aid to the catholic cause, and explains his wishes about the restoration of the lapsed bishops.*

Your clemency must know, therefore, that the whole church of Rome is highly grateful for all your faithful deeds, whether that you have with pious zeal helped our representatives throughout and brought back the catholic priests, who had been expelled from their churches by an unjust sentence, or that you have procured the restoration with due honour of the remains of that innocent and holy priest, Flavian, of holy memory, to the church, which he ruled so well. In all which things assuredly your glory is increased manifold, so long as you venerate the saints according to their deserts, and are anxious that the thorns and weeds should be removed from the Lord's field. But we learn as well from the account of our deputies as from that of my brother and fellow-bishop, Anatolius, whom you graciously recommend to me, that certain bishops crave reconciliation for those who seem to have given their consent to matters of heresy, and desire catholic communion for them: to whose request we grant effect on condition that the boon of peace should not be vouchsafed them till, our deputies acting in concert with the aforesaid bishop, they are corrected, and with their own hand condemn their evil doings; because our Christian religion requires both that true justice should constrain the obstinate, and love not reject the penitent.

III. *He commends certain bishops and churches to her care.*

And because we know how much pious care your Grace deigns to bestow on catholic priests, we have ordered that you should be informed that my brother and fellow-bishop, Eusebius, is living with us, and sharing our communion, whose church we commend to you; for he that is improperly asserted to have been elected in his place, is said to be ravaging it. And this too we ask of your Grace, which we doubt not you will do of your own free will, to extend the favour which is due as well to my brother and fellow-bishop, Julian, as to the clergy of Constantinople, who clung to the holy Flavian with faithful loyalty. On all things we have instructed your Grace by our deputies as to what ought to be done or arranged. Dated April 13, in the consulship of the illustrious Adelfius (451).

LETTER LXXX.

(To Anatolius, Bishop of Constantinople.)

Leo, the bishop, to Anatolius, the bishop.

I. *He rejoices at Anatolius having proved himself orthodox.*

We rejoice in the Lord and glory in the gift of His Grace, Who has shown you a follower of Gospel-teaching as we have found from your letter, beloved, and our brothers' account whom we sent to Constantinople: for now through the approved faith of the priest, we are justifying in presuming that the whole church committed to him will have no wrinkle nor spot of error, as says the Apostle, "for I have espoused you to one husband to present you a pure virgin to Christ[6]." For that virgin is the Church, the spouse of one husband Christ, who suffers herself to be corrupted by no error, so that through the whole world we have one entire and pure communion in which we now welcome you as a fellow, beloved, and give our approval to the order of proceedings which we have received, ratified, as was proper, with the necessary signatures. In order, therefore, that your spirit in turn, beloved, might be strengthened by words of ours, we sent back after the Easter festival with our letters, our sons, Casterius, the Presbyter, and Patricius and Asclepias, the Deacons, who brought your writings to us, informing you, as we said above, that we rejoice at the peace of the church of Constantinople, on which we have ever spent such care that we wish it to be polluted by no heretical deceit.

II. *The penitents among the backsliding bishops are to be received back into full communion upon some plan to be settled by Anatolius and Leo's delegates.*

But concerning the brethren whom we learn from your letters, and from our delegates' account, to be desirous of communion with us, on the ground of their sorrow that they did

6 2 Cor. xi. 2.

not remain constant against violence and intimidation, but gave their assent to another's crime when terror had so bewildered them, that with hasty acquiescence they ministered to the condemnation of the catholic and guiltless bishop (Flavian), and to the acceptance of the detestable heresy (of Eutyches), we approve of that which was determined upon in the presence and with the co operation of our delegates, viz., that they should be content meanwhile with the communion of their own churches, but we wish our delegates whom we have sent to consult with you, and come to some arrangement whereby those who condemn their ill-doings with full assurances of penitence, and choose rather to accuse than to defend themselves, may be gladdened by being at peace and in communion with us; on condition that what has been received against the catholic Faith is first condemned with complete anathema. For otherwise in the Church of GOD, which is Christ's Body, there are neither valid priesthoods nor true sacrifices, unless in the reality of our nature the true High Priest makes atonement for us, and the true Blood of the spotless Lamb makes us clean. For although He be set on the Father's right hand, yet in the same flesh which He took from the Virgin, he carries on the mystery of propitiation, as says the Apostle, "Christ Jesus Who died, yea, Who also rose, Who is on the right hand of GOD, Who also maketh intercession for us[7]." For our kindness cannot be blamed in any case where we receive those who give assurance of penitence, and at whose deception we were grieved. The boon of communion with us, therefore, must neither harshly be withheld nor rashly granted, because as it is fully consistent with our religion to treat the oppressed with a Christlike charity, so it is fair to lay the full blame upon the authors of the disturbance.

III. *The names of Dioscorus, Juvenal, and Eustathius are not to be read aloud at the holy altar.*

Concerning the reading out of the names of Dioscorus, Juvenal, and Eustathius[8] at the holy altar, it beseems you, beloved, to observe that which our friends who were there present said ought to be done, and which is consistent with the honourable memory of S. Flavian, and will not turn the minds of the laity away from you. For it is very wrong and unbecoming that those who have harassed innocent catholics with their attacks, should be mingled indiscriminately with the names of the saints, seeing that by not forsaking their condemned heresy, they condemn themselves by their perversity: such men should either be chastised for their unfaithfulness, or strive hard after forgiveness.

IV. *One or two instructions about individuals.*

But our brother and fellow-bishop, Julian, and the clergy who adhered to Flavian of holy memory, rendering him faithful service, we wish to adhere to you also beloved, that they may know him who we are sure lives by the merits of his faith with our GOD to be present with them in you. We wish you to know this too, beloved, that our brother and fellow-bishop Eusebius[9], who for the Faith's sake endured many dangers and toils, is at present staying with us and continuing in our communion; whose church we would that your care should protect, that nothing may be destroyed in his absence, and no one may venture to injure him in anything until he come to you bearing a letter from us. And that our or rather all Christian people's affection for you may be stirred up in greater measure, we wish this that we have written to you, beloved, to come to all men's knowledge, that they who serve our GOD may give thanks for the consummation of the peace of the Apostolic See with you. But on other matters and persons you will be more fully instructed, beloved, by the letter you will have received through our delegates. Dated 13 April, in the consulship of the illustrious Adelfius (451).

LETTER LXXXI.

To BISHOP JULIAN.

(Warning him to be circumspect in receiving the lapsed.)

LETTER LXXXII.

To MARCIAN AUGUSTUS.

I. *After congratulating the Emperor on his noble conduct, he deprecates random inquiries into the tenets of the Faith.*

Although I have replied[1] already to your Grace by the hand of the Constantinopolitan clergy, yet on receiving your clemency's mercy through the illustrious prefect of the

7 Rom. viii. 34.

8 Juvenal (Bishop of Jerusalem), and Eustathius (Bishop of Berytus), had been two of the principal abettors of Dioscorus in the *Latrocinium*. The "reading out of their names at the altar" alludes to the practice in the early Church of keeping registers (called "diptychs') of the members (alive and dead) of the Church, from which one or two of the more prominent names (clerical and lay) were read out at the celebration of the Holy mysteries: cf. the modern "Bidding" prayer, &

9 This is the Bishop of Dorylæum in Phrygia, Eutyches former friend, but more recently his relentless accuser of heresy.

1 i.e. Lett. LXXVIII. of the series.

city, my son Tatian, I found still greater cause for congratulation, because I have learnt your strong eagerness for the Church's peace. And this holy desire as in fairness it deserves, secures for your empire the same happy condition as you seek for religion. For when the Spirit of God establishes harmony among Christian princes, a twofold confidence is produced throughout the world, because the progress of love and faith makes the power of their arms in both directions unconquerable, so that God being propitiated by one confession, the falseness of heretics and the enmity of barbarians are simultaneously overthrown, most glorious Emperor. The hope, therefore, of heavenly aid being increased through the Emperor's friendship, I venture with the greater confidence to appeal to your Grace on behalf of the mystery of man's salvation, not to allow any one in vain and presumptuous craftiness to inquire what must be held, as if it were uncertain. And although we may not in a single word dissent from the teaching of the Gospels and Apostles, nor entertain any opinion on the Divine Scriptures different to what the blessed Apostles and our Fathers learnt and taught, now in these latter days unlearned and blasphemous inquiries are set on foot, which of old the Holy Spirit crushed by the disciples of the Truth, so soon as the devil aroused them in hearts which were suited to his purpose.

II. *The points to be settled are only which of the lapsed shall be restored, and on what terms.*

But it is most inopportune that through the foolishness of a few we should be brought once more into hazardous opinions, and to the warfare of carnal disputes, as if the wrangle was to be revived, and we had to settle whether Eutyches held blasphemous views, and whether Dioscorus gave wrong judgment, who in condemning Flavian of holy memory struck his own death-blow, and involved the simpler folk in the same destruction. And now that many, as we have ascertained, have betaken themselves to the means of amendment, and entreat forgiveness for their weak hastiness, we have to determine not the character of the Faith, but whose prayers we shall receive, and on what terms. And hence that most religious anxiety which you deign to feel for the proclamation of a Synod, shall have fully and timely put before it all that I judge pertinent to the needs of the case, by means of the deputies who will with all speed, if God permit, reach your Grace. Dated the 23rd of April in the consulship of the illustrious Adelfius (451).

LETTER LXXXIII.

To the same Marcian.

(Congratulating him on his benefits to the Church, and deprecating a Synod as inopportune.)

LETTER LXXXIV.

To Pulcheria Augusta.

(Announcing the despatch of his legates to deal with the lapsed, and asking that Eutyches should be superseded in his monastery by a catholic, and dismissed from Constantinople.)

LETTER LXXXV.

To Anatolius, Bishop of Constantinople.

Leo, the bishop, to the bishop Anatolius.

I. *Anatolius with Leo's delegates is to settle the question of the receiving back of those who had temporarily gone astray after Eutyches.*

Although I hope, beloved, you are devoted to every good work, yet that your activity may be rendered the more effective, it was needful and fitting to despatch my brothers Lucentius the bishop and Basil the presbyter, as we[2] promised, to ally themselves with you, beloved, that nothing may be done either indecisively or lazily in matters, which concern the welfare of the universal Church; for as long as you are on the spot, to whom we have entrusted the carrying out of our will, all things can be conducted with such moderation that the claims of neither kindness nor justice may be neglected, but without the accepting of persons, the Divine judgment may be considered in everything. But that this may be properly observed and guarded, the integrity of the catholic Faith must first of all be preserved, and, because in all cases "narrow" and steep "is the way that leadeth unto life[3]," there must be no deviation from its track, either to the right hand or to the left. And because the evangelical and Apostolic Faith has to combat all errors, on the one side casting down Nestorius, on the other crushing Eutyches and his accomplices, remember the need of observing this rule, that all those who in that synod[4], which cannot, and does not deserve to have the name of Synod, and in which Dioscorus displayed his bad feeling, and Juvenal[5] his ignorance, grieve as we learn from your account, beloved, that they were

[2] Viz., in Letter LXXX., chap. iv. : see also chap. iii.
[3] S. Matt. vii. 14.
[4] Sc. the so-called *Latrocinium*.
[5] See n. 8 to Letter LXXX., chap. iii.

conquered by fear, and being overcome with terror, were able to be forced to assent to that iniquitous judgment, and who now desire to obtain catholic communion, are to receive the peace of the brethren after due assurance of repentance, on condition that in no doubtful terms they anathematize, execrate and condemn Eutyches and his dogma and his adherents.

II. *The case of the more serious offenders must be reserved for the present.*

But concerning those who have sinned more gravely in this matter, and claimed for themselves a higher place in the same unhappy synod, in order to irritate the simple minds of their lowlier brethren by their pernicious arrogance, if they return to their right mind, and ceasing to defend their action, turn themselves to the condemnation of their particular error, if these men give such assurance of penitence as shall seem indisputable, let their case be reserved for the maturer deliberations of the Apostolic See, that when all things have been sifted and weighed, the right conclusion may be arrived at about their real actions. And in the Church over which the LORD has willed you to rule, let none such as we have already written [6] have their names read at the altar until the course of events shows what ought to be determined concerning them.

III. *Anatolius is requested to co-operate loyally with Leo's delegates.*

But concerning the address [7] presented to us by your clergy, beloved, there is no need to put my sentiments into a letter: it is sufficient to entrust all to my delegates, whose words shall carefully instruct you on every point. And so, dearest brother, do your endeavour with these brethren whom we have chosen as suitable agents in so great a matter faithfully and effectually to carry out what is agreeable to the Church of GOD: especially as the very nature of the case, and the promise of Divine aid incite you, and our most gracious princes show such holy faith, such religious devotion, that we find in them not only the general sympathy of Christians, but even that of the priesthood. Who assuredly in accordance with that piety, whereby they boast themselves to be servants of GOD, will receive all your suggestions for the benefit of the catholic Faith in a worthy spirit, so that by their aid also the peace of Christendom can be restored and wicked error destroyed. And if on any points more advice is needed, let word be quickly sent to us, that after investigating the nature of the case, we may carefully prescribe the rightful measures. Dated 9th of June in the consulship of the illustrious Adelfius (451).

6 Viz., in Letter LXXX., chap. iii., where see note.

7 *Commonitorium.* Nothing further seems known of this.

LETTER LXXXVI.

TO JULIAN, BISHOP OF COS.

(Begging him for friendship's and the Church's sake to assist his legates in quelling the remnants of heresy.)

LETTER LXXXVII.

TO ANATOLIUS, BISHOP OF CONSTANTINOPLE.

(Commending to him two presbyters, Basil and John, who being accused of heresy had come to Rome, and quite convinced Leo of their orthodoxy.)

LETTER LXXXVIII.

TO PASCHASINUS, BISHOP OF LILYBÆUM.

Leo, the bishop, to Paschasinus, bishop of Lilybæum.

I. *He sends a copy of the Tome and still further explains the heterodoxy of Eutyches.*

Although I doubt not all the sources of scandal are fully known to you, brother, which have arisen in the churches of the East about the Incarnation of our LORD Jesus Christ, yet, lest anything might have chanced to escape your care, I have despatched for your attentive perusal and study our letter [8], which deals with this matter in the fullest way, which we sent to Flavian of holy memory, and which the universal Church has accepted; in order that, understanding how completely this whole blasphemous error has with GOD's aid been destroyed, you yourself also in your love towards GOD may show the same spirit, and know that they are utterly to be abhorred, who, following the blasphemy and madness of Eutyches, have dared to say there are not two natures, i.e. perfect Godhead and perfect manhood, in our LORD, the only-begotten Son of GOD, who took upon Himself to restore mankind; and think they can deceive our wariness by saying they believe the one nature of the Word to be Incarnate, whereas the Word of GOD in the Godhead of the Father, and of Himself, and of the Holy Spirit has indeed one nature; but when He took on Him the reality of our flesh, our nature also was united to His unchangeable substance: for even Incarnation could not be spoken of, unless the Word took on Him the flesh. And this taking on of

8 Sc. Letter XXVIII. (Tome).

flesh forms so complete a union, that not only in the blessed Virgin's child-bearing, but also in her conception, no division must be imagined between the Godhead and the life-endowed flesh [9], since in the unity of person the Godhead and the manhood came together both in the conception and in the child-bearing of the Virgin.

II. *Eutyches might have been warned by the fate of former heretics.*

A like blasphemy, therefore, is to be abhorred in Eutyches, as was once condemned and overthrown by the Fathers in former heretics: and their example ought to have benefited this foolish fellow, in putting him on his guard against that which he could not grasp by his own sense, lest he should render void the peerless mystery of our salvation by denying the reality of human flesh in our LORD Jesus Christ. For, if there is not in Him true and perfect human nature, there is no taking of us upon Him, and the whole of our belief and teaching according to his heresy is emptiness and lying. But because the Truth does not lie and the Godhead is not passible, there abides in GOD the Word both substances in one Person, and the Church confesses her Saviour in such a way as to acknowledge Him both impassible in Godhead and passible in flesh, as says the Apostle, "although He was crucified through (our) weakness, yet He lives by the power of GOD [1]."

III. *He sends quotations from the Fathers, and announces that the churches of the East have accepted the Tome.*

And in order that you may be the fuller instructed in all things, beloved, I have sent you certain quotations from our holy Fathers, that you may clearly gather what they felt and what they preached to the churches about the mystery of the LORD's Incarnation, which quotations our deputies produced at Constantinople also together with our epistle. And you must understand that the whole church of Constantinople, with all the monasteries and many bishops, have given their assent to it, and by their subscription have anathematized Nestorius and Eutyches with their dogmas. You must also understand that I have recently received the bishop of Constantinople's letter, which states that the bishop of Antioch has sent instructions to all the bishops throughout his provinces, and gained their assent to my epistle, and their condemnation of Nestorius and Eutyches in like manner.

IV. *He asks him to settle the discrepancy between the Alexandrine and the Roman calculation of Easter for 455, by consulting the proper authority.*

This also we think necessary to enjoin upon your care that you should diligently inquire in those quarters where you are sure of information concerning that point in the reckoning of Easter, which we have found in the table [2] of Theophilus, and which greatly exercises us, and that you should discuss with those who are learned in such calculations, as to the date, when the day of the LORD's resurrection should be held four years hence. For, whereas the next Easter is to be held by GOD's goodness on March 23rd, the year after on April 12th, the year after that on April 4th, Theophilus of holy memory has fixed April 24th to be observed in 455, which we find to be quite contrary to the rule of the Church; but in our Easter cycles [3] as you know very well, Easter that year is set down to be kept on April 17th. And therefore, that all our doubts may be removed, we beg you carefully to discuss this point with the best authorities, that for the future we may avoid this kind of mistake. Dated June 24th in the consulship of the illustrious Adelfius (451).

LETTER LXXXIX.

To MARCIAN AUGUSTUS.

(Appointing Paschasinus the bishop and Boniface a presbyter, and Julian the bishop, his representatives at the Synod, as the Emperor is determined it should be held at once.)

LETTER XC.

To MARCIAN AUGUSTUS.

(Assenting perforce to the meeting of the Synod, but begging him to see that the Faith be not discussed as doubtful.)

LETTER XCI.

To ANATOLIUS, BISHOP OF CONSTANTINOPLE.

(Telling him that he has appointed Paschasinus, Boniface, and Julian, bishop of Cos, to represent him at the Synod.)

LETTER XCII.

To JULIAN, BISHOP OF COS.

(Asking him to act as one of his representatives at the Synod.)

---

9 *Caro animata.*

1 2 Cor. xiii. 4.

2 His *Laterculum Paschale* is meant, in which he calculated Easter for 100 years from 375. A similar dispute had occurred in 444, in which we have S. Cyril's and Paschasinus' Letters (II. and III. of the series) to Leo, but not Leo's answers.

3 The Latin Easter cycles were calculated for 84 years.

LETTER XCIII.

To the Synod of Chalcedon.

Leo, the bishop of the city of Rome, to the holy Synod, assembled at Nicæa[4].

I. *He excuses his absence from the Synod, and introduces his representatives.*

I had indeed prayed, dearly beloved, on behalf of my dear colleagues that all the Lord's priests would persist in united devotion to the catholic Faith, and that no one would be misled by favour or fear of secular powers into departure from the way of Truth; but because many things often occur to produce penitence and God's mercy transcends the faults of delinquents, and vengeance is postponed in order that reformation may have place, we must make much of our most merciful prince's piously intentioned Council, in which he has desired your holy brotherhood to assemble for the purpose of destroying the snares of the devil and restoring the peace of the Church, so far respecting the rights and dignity of the most blessed Apostle Peter as to invite us too by letter to vouchsafe our presence at your venerable Synod. That indeed is not permitted either by the needs of the times or by any precedent. Yet in these brethren, that is Paschasinus and Lucentius, bishops, Boniface and Basil, presbyters, who have been deputed by the Apostolic See, let your brotherhood reckon that I am presiding[5] at the Synod; for my presence is not withdrawn from you, who am now represented by my vicars, and have this long time been really with you in the proclaiming of the catholic Faith: so that you who cannot help knowing what we believe in accordance with ancient tradition, cannot doubt what we desire.

II. *He entreats them to re-state the Faith as laid down in the Tome.*

Wherefore, brethren most dear, let all attempts at impugning the Divinely-inspired Faith be entirely put down, and the vain unbelief of heretics be laid to rest: and let not that be defended which may not be believed: since in accordance with the authoritative statements of the Gospel, in accordance with the utterances of the prophets, and the teaching of the Apostles, with the greatest fulness and clearness in the letter which we sent to bishop Flavian of happy memory, it has been laid down what is the loyal and pure confession upon the mystery of our Lord Jesus Christ's Incarnation.

III. *The ejected bishops must be restored, and the Nestorian canons retain their force.*

But because we know full well that through evil jealousies the state of many churches has been disturbed, and a large number of bishops have been driven from their sees for not receiving the heresy and conveyed into exile, while others have been put into their places though yet alive, to these wounds first of all must the healing of justice be applied, nor must any one be deprived of his own possession that some one else may enjoy it: for if, as we desire, all forsake their error, no one need lose his present rank, and those who have laboured for the Faith ought to have their rights restored with every privilege. Let the decrees specially directed against Nestorius of the former Synod of Ephesus, at which bishop Cyril of holy memory presided, still retain their force, lest the heresy then condemned flatter itself in aught because Eutyches is visited with condign execration. For the purity of the Faith and doctrine which we proclaim in the same spirit as our holy Fathers, equally condemns and impugns the Nestorian and the Eutychian misbelief with its supporters. Farewell in the Lord, brethren most dear. Dated 26th[5a] of June, in the consulship of the illustrious Adelfius (451).

LETTER XCIV.

To Marcian Augustus.

(Commending his legates to him and praying for the full success of the Synod, if it adhere to the Faith once delivered to the saints.)

LETTER XCV.

To Pulcheria Augusta by the hand of Theoctistus the Magistrian[6].

Leo, the bishop to Pulcheria Augusta.

I. *He informs the Empress that he has loyally recognized the Council ordered by her, and sent representatives with letters to it.*

Your clemency's religious care which you unceasingly bestow on the catholic Faith, I recognize in everything, and give God thanks at seeing you take such interest in the universal Church, that I can confidently suggest what I think agreeable to justice and kindness,

[4] In accordance with instructions, the bishops, to the number of 529, first met at Nicæa, in Bithynia, the scene of the famous First General Council: but the Emperor Marcian was afraid to go so far from Constantinople, and so they were summoned to Chalcedon, which was much nearer, on the eastern shore of the Bosporus. There the Council opened on Oct. 8, 451.

[5] The right of presiding, which he here virtually claims for his delegates, seems actually to have been accorded to them by the Council.

[5a] The Ball. think the date should be the 27th.

[6] The *Magistriani* were what would now be called King's Messengers: another name for them was *agentes in rebus*, and they were under the direction of the Imperial *Magister Officiorum*.

and so what thus far your pious zeal through the mercy of Christ has irreproachably accomplished, may the more speedily be brought to an issue which we shall be thankful for, O most noble Augusta. Your clemency's command, therefore, that a Synod should be held at Nicæa[7], and your gently expressed refusal of my request that it should be held in Italy, so that all the bishops in our parts might be summoned and assemble, if the state of affairs had permitted them, I have received in a spirit so far removed from scorn as to nominate two of my fellow-bishops and fellow-presbyters respectively to represent me, sending also to the venerable synod an appropriate missive from which the brotherhood therein assembled might learn the standard necessary to be maintained in their decision, lest any rashness should do detriment either to the rules of the Faith, or to the provisions of the canons, or to the remedies required by the spirit of loving kindness.

II. *In the settlement of this matter that moderation must be observed which was entirely absent at Ephesus.*

For, as I have very often stated in letters from the beginning of this matter, I have desired that such moderation should be observed in the midst of discordant views and carnal jealousies that, whilst nothing should be allowed to be wrested from or added to the purity of the Faith, yet the remedy of pardon should be granted to those who return to unity and peace. Because the works of the devil are then more effectually destroyed when men's hearts are recalled to the love of God and their neighbours. But how contrary to my warnings and entreaties were their actions then, it is a long story to explain, nor is their need to put down in the pages of a letter all that was allowed to be perpetrated in that meeting, not of judges but of robbers, at Ephesus; where the chief men of the synod spared neither those brethren who opposed them nor those who assented to them, seeing that for the breaking down of the catholic Faith and the strengthening of execrable heresy, they stripped some of their rightful rank and tainted others with complicity in guilt; and surely their cruelty was worse to those whom by persuasion they divorced from innocence, than to those whom by persecution they made blessed confessors.

III. *Those who recant their error must be treated with forbearance.*

And yet because such men have harmed themselves most by their wrong-doing, and because the greater the wounds, the more careful must be the application of the remedy, I have never in any letter maintained that pardon must be withheld even from them if they came to their right mind. And although we unchangeably abhor their heresy, which is the greatest enemy of Christian religion, yet the men themselves, if they without any doubt amend their ways and clear themselves by full assurances of repentance, we do not judge to be outcasts from the unspeakable mercy of God: but rather we lament with those that lament, "we weep with those that weep[7a]," and obey the requirements of justice in deposing without neglecting the remedies of loving-kindness: and this, as your piety knows, is not a mere word-promise, but is also borne out by our actions, inasmuch as nearly all who had been either misled or forced into assenting to the presiding bishops, by rescinding what they had decreed and by condemning what they had written, have obtained complete acquittal from guilt and the boon of Apostolic peace.

IV. *Even the authors of the mischief may find room for forgiveness by repentance.*

If, therefore, your clemency deigns to reflect upon my motives, it will be satisfied that I have acted throughout with the design of bringing about the abolition of the heresy without the loss of one soul; and that in the case of the authors of these cruel disturbances I have modified my practice somewhat in order that their slow minds might be aroused by some feelings of compunction to ask for lenient treatment. For although since their decision, which is no less blasphemous than unjust, they cannot be held in such honour by the catholic brotherhood as they once were, yet they still retain their sees and their rank as bishops, with the prospect either of receiving the peace of the whole Church, after true and necessary signs of repentance or, if (which God forbid) they persist in their heresy, of reaping the reward of their misbelief. Dated 20th of July, in the consulship of the illustrious Adelfius (451).

LETTER XCVI.

To Ravennius, Bishop of Arles.

(Requesting him to keep Easter on March 23 in 452.)

LETTER XCVII.

From Eusebius, Bishop of Milan, to Leo.

(Informing him that the Tome has been

7 See n. 4 on Letter XCIII., 1.

7a Rom. xii. 15.

approved by the Synod of Milan, and containing the subscriptions of the bishops there assembled.)

LETTER XCVIII.

From the Synod of Chalcedon to Leo.

The great and holy and universal Synod, which by the grace of God and the sanction of our most pious and Christ-loving Emperors has been gathered together in the metropolis of Chalcedon in the province of Bithynia, to the most holy and blessed archbishop of Rome, Leo.

I. *They congratulate Leo on taking the foremost part in maintaining the Faith.*

"Our mouth was filled with joy and our tongue with exultation[8]." This prophecy grace has fitly appropriated to us for whom the security of religion is ensured. For what is a greater incentive to cheerfulness than the Faith? what better inducement to exultation than the Divine knowledge which the Saviour Himself gave us from above for salvation, saying, "go ye and make disciples of all the nations, baptizing them into the name of the Father, and of the Son, and of the Holy Ghost, teaching them to observe all things that I have enjoined you[9]." And this golden chain leading down from the Author of the command to us, you yourself have stedfastly preserved, being set as the mouthpiece unto all of the blessed Peter, and imparting the blessedness of his Faith unto all. Whence we too, wisely taking you as our guide in all that is good, have shown to the sons of the Church their inheritance of Truth, not giving our instruction each singly and in secret, but making known our confession of the Faith in concert, with one consent and agreement And we were all delighted, revelling, as at an imperial banquet, in the spiritual food, which Christ supplied to us through your letter: and we seemed to see the Heavenly Bridegroom actually present with us. For if "where two or three are gathered together in His name," He has said that "there He is in the midst of them[1]," must He not have been much more particularly present with 520 priests, who preferred the spread of knowledge concerning Him to their country and their ease? Of whom you were chief, as the head to the members, showing your goodwill[2] in the person of those who represented you; whilst our religious Emperors presided to the furtherance of due order, inviting us to restore the doctrinal fabric of the Church, even as Zerubbabel invited Joshua to rebuild Jerusalem[2a].

II. *They detail Dioscorus' wicked acts.*

And the adversary would have been like a wild beast outside the fold, roaring to himself and unable to seize any one, had not the late bishop of Alexandria thrown himself for a prey to him, who, though he had done many terrible things before, eclipsed the former by the latter deeds; for contrary to all the injunctions of the canons, he deposed that blessed shepherd of the saints at Constantinople, Flavian, who displayed such Apostolic faith, and the most pious bishop Eusebius, and acquitted by his terror-won votes Eutyches, who had been condemned for heresy, and restored to him the dignity which your holiness had taken away from him as unworthy of it, and like the strangest of wild beasts, falling upon the vine which he found in the finest condition, He uprooted it and brought in that which had been cast away as unfruitful, and those who acted like true shepherds he cut off, and set over the flocks those who had shown themselves wolves: and besides all this he stretched forth his fury even against him who had been charged with the custody of the vine by the Saviour, we mean of course your holiness, and purposed excommunication against one who had at heart the unifying of the Church. And instead of showing penitence for this, instead of begging mercy with tears, he exulted as if over virtuous actions, rejecting your holiness' letter and resisting all the dogmas of the Truth.

III. *We have deposed Eutyches, treating him as mercifully as we could.*

And we ought to have left him in the position where he had placed himself: but, since we profess the teaching of the Saviour "who wishes all men to be saved and to come to a knowledge of the Truth[3]," as a fact we took pains to carry out this merciful policy towards him, and called him in brotherly fashion to judgment, not as if trying to cut him off but affording him room for defence and healing; and we prayed that he might be victorious over the many charges they had brought against him, in order that we might conclude our meeting in peace and happiness and Satan might gain no advantage over us. But he, being absolutely convicted by his own conscience[4], by shirking the trial gave countenance to the accusations and rejected the three lawful

---

8 Ps. cxxvi. 2.

9 S. Matt. xxviii. 19, 20.

1 Ibid. xviii. 20.

2 εὔνοιαν: others read εὐβουλίαν (good advice).

2a The reference is to Ezra iii. 2.

3 1 Tim. ii. 4.

4 ἐν ἑαυτῷ ἄκρατον τοῦ συνειδότος ἔχων τὸν ἔλεγχον. There seems, however, some grounds, but no actual necessity for the reading ἔγγραφον = written (instead of ἄκρατον) adopted by the Ball.

summonses he received. In consequence of which, we ratified with such moderation as we could the vote which he had passed against himself by his blunders, stripping the wolf of his shepherd's skin, which he had long been convicted of wearing for a pretence. Thereupon our troubles ceased and straightway a time of welcome happiness set in: and having pulled up one tare, we filled the whole world to our delight with pure grain: and having received, as it were, full power to root up and to plant, we limited the up-rooting to one and carefully plant a crop of good fruit. For it was GOD who worked, and the triumphant Euphemia who crowned the meeting as for a bridal[4a], and who, taking our definition of the Faith as her own confession, presented it to her Bridegroom by our most religious Emperor and Christ-loving Empress, appeasing all the tumult of opponents and establishing our confession of the Truth as acceptable to Him, and with hand and tongue setting her seal[5] to the votes of us all in proclamation thereof. These are the things we have done, with you present in the spirit and known to approve of us as brethren, and all but visible to us through the wisdom of your representatives.

IV. *They announce their decision that Constantinople should take precedence next to Rome, and ask Leo's consent to it.*

And we further inform you that we have decided on other things also for the good management and stability of church matters, being persuaded that your holiness will accept and ratify them, when you are told. The long prevailing custom, which the holy Church of GOD at Constantinople had of ordaining metropolitans for the provinces of Asia, Pontus and Thrace, we have now ratified by the votes of the Synod, not so much by way of conferring a privilege on the See of Constantinople as to provide for the good government of those cities, because of the frequent disorders that arise on the death of their bishops, both clergy and laity being then without a leader and disturbing church order. And this has not escaped your holiness, particularly in the case of Ephesus, which has often caused you annoyance[6]. We have ratified also the canon of the 150 holy Fathers who met at Constantinople in the time of the great Theodosius of holy memory, which ordains that after your most holy and Apostolic See, the See of Constantinople shall take precedence, being placed second: for we are persuaded that with your usual care for others you have often extended that Apostolic prestige which belongs to you, to the church in Constantinople also, by virtue of your great disinterestedness in sharing all your own good things with your spiritual kinsfolk. Accordingly vouchsafe most holy and blessed father to accept as your own wish, and as conducing to good government the things which we have resolved on for the removal of al confusion and the confirmation of church order. For your holiness' delegates, the most pious bishops Paschasinus and Lucentius, and with them the right godly presbyter Boniface, attempted vehemently to resist these decisions, from a strong desire that this good work also should start from your foresight, in order that the establishment of good order as well as of the Faith should be put to your account. For we duly regarding our most devout and Christ loving Emperors, who delight therein, and the illustrious senate and, so to say, the whole imperial city, considered it opportune to use the meeting of this ecumenical Synod for the ratification of your honour, and confidently corroborated this decision as if it were initiated by you with your customary fostering zeal, knowing that every success of the children rebounds to the parent's glory. Accordingly, we entreat you, honour our decision by your assent, and as we have yielded to the head our agreement on things honourable, so may the head also fulfil for the children what is fitting. For thus will our pious Emperors be treated with due regard, who have ratified your holiness' judgment as law, and the See of Constantinople will receive its recompense for having always displayed such loyalty on matters of religion towards you, and for having so zealously linked itself to you in full agreement. But that you may know that we have done nothing for favour or in hatred, but as being guided by the Divine Will, we have made known to you the whole scope of our proceedings to strengthen our position and to ratify and establish what we have done[7].

LETTER XCIX.

FROM RAVENNIUS AND OTHER GALLIC BISHOPS.

(Announcing that the Tome has been accepted in Gaul also as a definitive statement of the Faith, with the bishops' subscriptions.)

[4a] ἡ τὸν σύλλογον τῷ νυμφῶνι (lit. bride-chamber) στεφανοῦσα καλλίνικος Εὐφημια; this obscure passage is to a certain extent elucidated by Letter CI., chap. iii. (*q.v.*). The martyr, Euphemia, seems to have been a sort of patron saint of Chalcedon.

[5] ἐπισφραγίσασα; others ἐπιψηφίσασα, which seems meaningless here.

[6] The reference (acc. to Ball.) is to the dispute about the bishopric between Bassian and Stephen, in which Leo interfered, though the letter is not extant.

[7] One of the Latin versions adds the names and titles of the subscribing bishops here. For the subiect matter of Chap. iv., see Introduction, p. viii.

LETTER C.

From the Emperor Marcian.

(Dealing much more briefly with the same subjects as Letter XCVIII. above.)

LETTER CI.

From Anatolius, Bishop of Constantinople, to Leo.

(Dealing with much the same subjects as Letter XCVIII. from Anatolius' own standpoint: Chap. iii. is translated *in extenso* as illustrating XCVIII., chap. iii.)

III. *He describes the circumstances under which the doctrine of the Incarnation had been formulated by the Synod.*

But since after passing judgment upon him we had to come to an agreement with prayers and tears upon a definition of the right Faith; for that was the chief reason for the Emperor's summoning the holy Synod, at which your holiness was present in the spirit with us, and wrought with us by the God-fearing men who were sent from you; we, having the protection of the most holy and beautiful martyr Euphemia, have all given ourselves to this important matter with all deliberateness. And as the occasion demanded that all the assembled holy bishops should publish a unanimous decision for clearness and for an explicit statement of the Faith in our Lord Jesus Christ, the Lord God who is found and revealed even to those who seek Him not, yes, even to those who ask not for Him[8], in spite of some attempts to resist at first, nevertheless showed us His Truth, and ordained that it should be written down and proclaimed by all unanimously and without gainsaying, which thus confirmed the souls of the strong, and invited into the way of Truth all who were swerving therefrom. And, indeed, after unanimously setting our names to this document, we who have assembled in this ecumenical Synod in the name of the Faith of the same most holy and triumphant martyr, Euphemia, and of our most religious and Christ-loving Emperor Marcian, and our most religious and in all things most faithful daughter the Empress Pulcheria Augusta, with prayer and joy and happiness, having laid on the holy altar the definition written in accordance with your holy epistle for the confirmation of our Fathers' Faith, presented it to their pious care; for thus they had asked to receive it, and, having received it, they glorified with us their Master Christ, who had driven away all the mist of heresy and had graciously made clear the word of Truth. And in this way was simultaneously established the peace of the Church and the agreement of the priests concerning the pure Faith by the Saviour's mercy.

[8] Cf. Is. lxv. 1.

LETTER CII.

To the Gallic Bishops.

(Thanking them for their letter (viz. XCIX.) to him, and announcing the result of the Synod of Chalcedon.)

LETTER CIII.

To the Gallic Bishops.

(Written later: enclosing a copy of the sentence against Eutyches and Dioscorus.)

LETTER CIV.

(To Marcian Augustus, about the presumption of Anatolius, by the hand of Lucian the bishop and Basil the deacon.)

Leo, the bishop, to Marcian Augustus.

I. *He congratulates the Emperor on his share in the triumph of the catholic Faith.*

By the great bounty of God's mercy the joys of the whole catholic Church were multiplied when through your clemency's holy and glorious zeal the most pestilential error was abolished among us; so that our labours the more speedily reached their desired end, because your God-serving Majesty had so faithfully and powerfully assisted them. For although the liberty of the Gospel had to be defended against certain dissentients in the power of the Holy Ghost, and through the instrumentality of the Apostolic See, yet God's grace has shown itself more manifestly (than we could have hoped) by vouchsafing to the world that in the victory of the Truth only the authors of the violation of the Faith should perish[9] and the Church restored to her soundness. Accordingly the war which the enemy of our peace had stirred up, was so happily ended, the Lord's right hand fighting for us, that when Christ triumphed all His priests shared in the one victory, and when the light of Truth shone forth, only the shades of error, with its champions, were dispelled. For as in believing the Lord's own resurrection, with a view to strengthen the beginnings of Faith, confidence was much increased by the fact that certain Apostles doubted of the bodily reality of our Lord Jesus Christ, and by examining the prints of the nails and the wound of the

[9] Perish *spiritually* he means, as the sequel shows, for at least one great and good man on the catholic side, Flavian perished corporeally.

spear with sight and touch removed the doubts of all by doubting; so now, too, while the misbelief of some is refuted, the hearts of all hesitaters are strengthened, and that which caused blindness to some few avails for the enlightenment of the whole body. In which work your clemency duly and rightly rejoices, having faithfully and properly provided that the devil's snares should do no hurt to the Eastern churches, but that to propitiate GOD everywhere more acceptable holocausts should be offered; seeing that through the mediator between GOD and man, the Man Christ Jesus, one and the self-same creed is held by people, priests, and princes, O most glorious son and most clement Augustus.

II. *Considering all the circumstances Anatolius might have been expected to show more modesty.*

But now that these things, about which so great a concourse of priests assembled, have been brought to a good and desirable conclusion, I am surprised and grieved that the peace of the universal Church which had been divinely restored is again being disturbed by a spirit of self-seeking. For although my brother Anatolius seems necessarily to have consulted his own interest in forsaking the error of those who ordained him, and with salutary change of mind accepting the catholic Faith, yet he ought to have taken care not to mar by any depravity of desire that which he is known to have obtained through your means [1]. For we, having regard to your faith and intervention, though his antecedents were suspicious on account of those who consecrated him [2], wished to be kind rather than just towards him, that by the use of healing measures we might assuage all disturbances which through the operations of the devil had been excited; and this ought to have made him modest rather than the opposite. For even if he had been lawfully and regularly ordained for conspicuous merit, and by the wisest selection yet without respect to the canons of the Fathers, the ordinances of the Holy Ghost, and the precedents of antiquity, no votes could have availed in his favour. I speak before a Christian and a truly religious, truly orthodox prince (when I say that) Anatolius the bishop detracts greatly from his proper merits in desiring undue aggrandizement.

III. *The City of Constantinople, royal though it be, can never be raised to Apostolic rank.*

Let the city of Constantinople have, as we desire, its high rank, and under the protection of GOD's right hand, long enjoy your clemency's rule. Yet things secular stand on a different basis from things divine: and there can be no sure building save on that rock which the LORD has laid for a foundation. He that covets what is not his due, loses what is his own. Let it be enough for Anatolius that by the aid of your piety and by my favour and approval he has obtained the bishopric of so great a city. Let him not disdain a city which is royal, though he cannot make it an Apostolic See [3]; and let him on no account hope that he can rise by doing injury to others. For the privileges of the churches determined by the canons of the holy Fathers, and fixed by the decrees of the Nicene Synod, cannot be overthrown by any unscrupulous act, nor disturbed by any innovation. And in the faithful execution of this task by the aid of Christ I am bound to display an unflinching devotion; for it is a charge entrusted to me, and it tends to my condemnation if the rules sanctioned by the Fathers and drawn up under the guidance of GOD's Spirit at the Synod of Nicæa for the government of the whole Church are violated with my connivance (which GOD forbid), and if the wishes of a single brother have more weight with me than the common good of the LORD's whole house.

IV. *He asks the Emperor to express his disapproval of Anatolius' self-seeking spirit.*

And therefore knowing that your glorious clemency is anxious for the peace of the Church and extends its protection and approval to those measures which conduce to pacific unity, I pray and beseech you with earnest entreaty to refuse all sanction and protection to these unscrupulous attempts against Christian unity and peace, and put a salutary check upon my brother Anatolius' desires, which will only injure himself, if he persists: that he may not desire things which are opposed to your glory and the needs of the times, and wish to be greater than his predecessors, and that it may be free for him to be as pre-eminent as he can in virtues, in which he will be partaker only if he prefer to be adorned with love rather than puffed up with ambition. The conception of this unwarrantable wish he ought indeed never to have received within the secret of his heart, but when my brothers and fellow-bishops who were there to represent me withstood him, he might at least have desisted from his unlawful

[1] Viz., the See of Constantinople.
[2] Dioscorus in particular.

[3] The chief *Apostolicæ sedes* were Rome and Antioch, according to tradition founded by S. Peter, and Alexandria founded by his disciple S. Mark, and the See of Constantinople could not exercise jurisdiction over them.

self-seeking at their wholesome opposition. For both your gracious Majesty and his own letter affirm that the legates of the Apostolic See opposed him as they ought with the most justifiable resistance, so that his presumption was the less excusable in that not even when rebuked did it restrain itself.

V. *And to try to bring him to a right mind.*

And hence, because it becomes your glorious faith that, as heresy was overthrown, God acting through you, so now all self-seeking should be defeated, do that which beseems both your Christian and your kingly goodness, so that the said bishop may obey the Fathers, further the cause of peace, and not think he had any right to ordain a bishop[4] for the Church of Antioch, as he presumed to do without any precedent and contrary to the provisions of the canons: an act which from a longing to re-establish the Faith and in the interests of peace we have determined not to cancel. Let him abstain therefore from doing despite to the rules of the Church and shun unlawful excesses, lest in attempting things unfavourable to peace he cut himself off from the universal Church. I had much liefer love him for acting blamelessly than find him persist in this presumptuous frame of mind which may separate him from us all. My brother and fellow-bishop, Lucian, who with my son, Basil the deacon, brought your clemency's letter to me, has fulfilled the duties he undertook as legate with all devotion: for he must not be reckoned to have failed in his mission, the course of events having rather failed him. Dated the 22nd of May in the consulship of the illustrious Herculanus (452).

LETTER CV.

(To Pulcheria Augusta about the self-seeking of Anatolius.)

Leo the bishop to Pulcheria Augusta.

I. *He congratulates the Empress on the triumph of the Faith, but regrets the introduction of a new controversy into the Church.*

We rejoice ineffably with your Grace that the catholic Faith has been defended against heretics and peace restored to the whole Church through your clemency's holy and God-pleasing zeal: giving thanks to the Merciful and Almighty God that He has suffered none save those who loved darkness rather than light to be defrauded of the gospel-truth: so that by the removal of the mists of error the purest light might arise in the hearts of all, and that darkness-loving foe might not triumph over certain weak souls, whom not only those who stood unhurt but also those whom he had made to totter have overcome, and that by the abolition of error the true Faith might reign throughout the world, and "every tongue might confess that the Lord Jesus Christ is in the glory of God the Father[5]." But when the whole world had been confirmed in the unity of the Gospel, and the hearts of all priests had been guided into the same belief, it had been better that besides those matters for which the holy Synod was assembled, and which were brought to a satisfactory agreement through your Grace's zeal, nothing should be introduced to counteract so great an advantage, and that a council of bishops should not be made an occasion for the inopportune advancing of an illegitimate desire.

II. *The Nicene canons are unalterable and binding universally.*

For my brother and fellow-bishop Anatolius not sufficiently considering your Grace's kindness and the favour of my assent, whereby he gained the priesthood of the church of Constantinople, instead of rejoicing at what he has gained, has been inflamed with undue desires beyond the measure of his rank, believing that his intemperate self-seeking could be advanced by the assertion that certain persons had signified their assent thereto by an extorted signature: notwithstanding that my brethren and fellow-bishops, who represented me, faithfully and laudably expressed their dissent from these attempts which are doomed to speedy failure. For no one may venture upon anything in opposition to the enactments of the Fathers' canons which many long years ago in the city of Nicæa were founded upon the decrees of the Spirit, so that any one who wishes to pass any different decree injures himself rather than impairs them. And if all pontiffs will but keep them inviolate as they should, there will be perfect peace and complete harmony through all the churches: there will be no disagreements about rank, no disputes about ordinations, no controversies about privileges, no strifes about taking that which is another's; but by the fair law of love a reasonable order will be kept both in conduct and in office, and he will be truly great who is found free from all self-seeking, as the Lord says, "Whosoever will become greater among you, let him be your minister, and whosoever will be first among you shall be your slave; even as the Son of Man came not to be ministered unto but to minister[6]." And yet these precepts were at the time given to men who

[4] One Maximus by name.

[5] Phil. ii. 11.

[6] S. Matt. xx. 26—28.

wished to rise from a mean estate and to pass from the lowest to the highest things; but what more does the ruler of the church of Constantinople covet than he has gained? or what will satisfy him, if the magnificence and renown of so great a city is not enough? It is too arrogant and intemperate thus to step beyond all proper bounds and trampling on ancient custom to wish to seize another's right: to increase one man's dignity at the expense of so many metropolitans' primacy, and to carry a new war of confusion into peaceful provinces which were long ago set at rest by the enactments of the holy Nicene Synod: to break through the venerable Fathers' decrees by alleging the consent of certain bishops, which even the course of so many years has not rendered effective. For it is boasted that this has been winked at for almost 60 years now, and the said bishop thinks that he is assisted thereby; but it is vain for him to look for assistance from that which, even if a man dared to wish for it, yet he could never obtain.

III. *Only by imitating his predecessor will he regain Leo's confidence: the assent of the bishops is declared null and void.*

Let him realize what a man he has succeeded, and expelling all the spirit of pride let him imitate Flavian's faith, Flavian's modesty, Flavian's humility, which has raised him right to a confessor's glory. If he will shine with his virtues, he will merit all praise, and in all quarters he will win an abundance of love not by seeking human advancement but by deserving Divine favour. And by this careful course I promise he will bind my heart also to him, and the love of the Apostolic See, which we have ever bestowed on the church of Constantinople, shall never be violated by any change. Because if sometimes rulers fall into errors through want of moderation, yet the churches of Christ do not lose their purity. But the bishops' assents, which are opposed to the regulations of the holy canons composed at Nicæa in conjunction with your faithful Grace, we do not recognize, and by the blessed Apostle Peter's authority we absolutely disannul in comprehensive terms, in all ecclesiastical cases obeying those laws which the Holy Ghost set forth by the 318 bishops for the pacific observance of all priests in such sort that even if a much greater number were to pass a different decree to theirs, whatever was opposed to their constitution would have to be held in no respect.

IV. *He requests the Empress to give his letter her favourable consideration.*

And so I request your Grace to receive in a worthy spirit this lengthy letter, in which I had to explain my views, at the hands of my brother and fellow-bishop Lucianus, who, as far as in him lies, has faithfully executed the anxious duties of his undertaking as my delegate, and of my son Basil, the deacon. And because it is your habit to labour for the peace and unity of the Church, for his soul's health keep my brother Anatolius the bishop, to whom I have extended my love by your advice, within those limits which shall be profitable to him, that as your clemency's glory is magnified already for the restoration of the Faith, so it may be published abroad for the restraint of self-seeking. Dated the 22nd of May, in the consulship of the illustrious Herculanus (452).

LETTER CVI.

To Anatolius, Bishop of Constantinople, in rebuke of his Self-seeking.

Leo, the bishop, to Anatolius, the bishop.

I. *He commends Anatolius for his orthodoxy, but condemns him for his presumption.*

Now that the light of Gospel Truth has been manifested, as we wished, through God's grace, and the night of most pestilential error has been dispelled from the universal Church, we are unspeakably glad in the Lord, because the difficult charge entrusted to us has been brought to the desired conclusion, even as the text of your letter announces, so that, according to the Apostle's teaching, "we all speak the same thing, and that there be no schisms among us: but that we be perfect in the same mind and in the same knowledge[7]." In devotion to which work we commend you, beloved, for taking part: for thus you benefited those who needed correction by your activity, and purged yourself from all complicity with the transgressors. For when your predecessor Flavian, of happy memory, was deposed for his defence of catholic Truth, not unjustly it was believed that your ordainers seemed to have consecrated one like themselves, contrary to the provision of the holy canons. But God's mercy was present in this, directing and confirming you, that you might make good use of bad beginnings, and show that you were promoted not by men's judgment, but by God's loving-kindness: and this may be accepted as true, on condition that you lose not the grace of this Divine gift by another cause of offence. For the catholic, and especially the Lord's priest, must not only be entangled in no error, but also be corrupted by no covetousness; for, as says the Holy Scripture,

[7] 1 Cor. i. 10.

"Go not after thy lusts, and decline from thy desire[8]." Many enticements of this world, many vanities must be resisted, that the perfection of true self-discipline may be attained: the first blemish of which is pride, the beginning of transgression and the origin of sin. For the mind greedy of power knows not either how to abstain from things forbidden nor to enjoy things permitted, so long as transgressions go unpunished and run into undisciplined and wicked excesses, and wrong doings are multiplied, which were only endured in our zeal for the restoration of the Faith and love of harmony[9].

II. *Nothing can cancel or modify the Nicene canons.*

And so after the not irreproachable beginning of your ordination, after the consecration of the bishop of Antioch, which you claimed for yourself contrary to the regulations of the canons, I grieve, beloved, that you have fallen into this too, that you should try to break down the most sacred constitutions of the Nicene canons[1]: as if this opportunity had expressly offered itself to you for the See of Alexandria to lose its privilege of second place, and the church of Antioch to forego its right to being third in dignity, in order that when these places had been subjected to your jurisdiction, all metropolitan bishops might be deprived of their proper honour. By which unheard of and never before attempted excesses you went so far beyond yourself as to drag into an occasion of self-seeking, and force connivance from that holy Synod which the zeal of our most Christian prince had convened, solely to extinguish heresy and to confirm the catholic Faith: as if the unlawful wishes of a multitude could not be rejected, and that state of things which was truly ordained by the Holy Spirit in the canon of Nicæa could in any part be overruled by any one. Let no synodal councils flatter themselves upon the size of their assemblies, and let not any number of priests, however much larger, dare either to compare or to prefer themselves to those 318 bishops, seeing that the Synod of Nicæa is hallowed by GOD with such privilege, that whether by fewer or by more ecclesiastical judgments are supported, whatever is opposed to their authority is utterly destitute of all authority.

III. *The Synod of Chalcedon, which met for one purpose, ought never to have been used for another.*

Accordingly these things which are found to be contrary to those most holy canons are exceedingly unprincipled and misguided. This haughty arrogance tends to the disturbance of the whole Church, which has purposed so to misuse a synodal council, as by wicked arguments to over-persuade, or by intimidation to compel, the brethren to agree with it, when they had been summoned simply on a matter of Faith, and had come to a decision on the subject which was to engage their care. For it was on this ground that our brothers sent by the Apostolic see, who presided in our stead at the synod with commendable firmness, withstood their illegal attempts, openly protesting against the introduction of any reprehensible innovation contrary to the enactments of the Council of Nicæa. And there can be no doubt about their opposition, seeing that you yourself in your epistle complain of their wish to contravene your attempts. And therein indeed you greatly commend them to me by thus writing, whereas you accuse yourself in refusing to obey them concerning your unlawful designs, vainly seeking what cannot be granted, and craving what is bad for your soul's health, and can never win our consent. For may I never be guilty of assisting so wrong a desire, which ought rather to be subverted by my aid, and that of all who think not high things, but agree with the lowly.

IV. *The Nicene canons are for universal application and not to be wrested to private interpretations.*

These holy and venerable fathers who in the city of Nicæa, after condemning the blasphemous Arius with his impiety, laid down a code of canons for the Church to last till the end of the world, survive not only with us but with the whole of mankind in their constitutions; and, if anywhere men venture upon what is contrary to their decrees, it is *ipso facto* null and void; so that what is universally laid down for our perpetual advantage can never be modified by any change, nor can the things which were destined for the common good be perverted to private interests; and thus so long as the limits remain, which the Fathers fixed, no one may invade another's right but each must exercise himself within the proper and lawful bounds, to the extent of his power, in the breadth of love; of which the bishop of Constantinople may reap the fruits

8 Ecclesiasticus xviii. 30. The application of the description "Holy Scripture" to an Apocryphal book will not escape notice.

9 Cf. Letter CIV., chap. v.

1 The wording of Canon 6 is as follows: *mos antiquus perduret, in Aegypto vel Libya et Pentapoli, ut Alexandrinus episcopus horum omnium habeat potestatem, quoniam quidem et episcopo Romano parilis mos est. Similiter autem et apud Antiochiam ceterasque provincias* (ἐπαρχίας) *honor suus unicuique servetur ecclesiæ*: where, it will be noticed, no mention is made of Constantinople at all, so that its position is not explicitly defined either way.

richly enough, if he rather relies on the virtue of humility than is puffed up with the spirit of self-seeking.

V. *The sanction alleged to have been accorded 60 years ago to the supremacy of Constantinople over Alexandria and Antioch is worthless.*

"Be not highminded," brother, "but fear[2]," and cease to disquiet with unwarrantable demands the pious ears of Christian princes, who I am sure will be better pleased by your modesty than by your pride. For your purpose is in no way whatever supported by the written assent of certain bishops given, as you allege, 60 years ago[3], and never brought to the knowledge of the Apostolic See by your predecessors; and this transaction, which from its outset was doomed to fall through and has now long done so, you now wish to bolster up by means that are too late and useless, viz., by extracting from the brethren an appearance of consent which their modesty from very weariness yielded to their own injury. Remember what the LORD threatens him with, who shall have caused one of the little ones to stumble, and get wisdom to understand what a judgment of GOD he will have to endure who has not feared to give occasion of stumbling to so many churches and so many priests. For I confess I am so fast bound by love of the whole brotherhood that I will not agree with any one in demands which are against his own interests, and thus you may clearly perceive that my opposition to you, beloved, proceeds from the kindly intention to restrain you from disturbing the universal Church by sounder counsel. The rights of provincial primates may not be overthrown nor metropolitan bishops be defrauded of privileges based on antiquity. The See of Alexandria may not lose any of that dignity which it merited through S. Mark, the evangelist and disciple of the blessed Peter, nor may the splendour of so great a church be obscured by another's clouds, Dioscorus having fallen through his persistence in impiety. The church of Antioch too, in which first at the preaching of the blessed Apostle Peter the Christian name arose[4], must continue in the position assigned it by the Fathers, and being set in the third place must never be lowered therefrom. For the See is on a different footing to the holders of it; and each individual's chief honour is his own integrity. And since that does not lose its proper worth in any place, how much more glorious must it be when placed in the magnificence of the city of Constantinople, where many priests may find both a defence of the Fathers' canons and an example of uprightness in observing you?

VI. *Christian love demands self-denial not self-seeking.*

In thus writing to you, brother, I exhort and admonish you in the LORD, laying aside all ambitious desires to cherish rather a spirit of love and to adorn yourself to your profit with the virtues of love, according to the Apostle's teaching. For love "is patient and kind, and envies not, acts not iniquitously, is not puffed up, is not ambitious, seeks not its own[5]." Hence if love seeks not its own, how greatly does he sin who covets another's? From which I desire you to keep yourself altogether, and to remember that sentence which says, "Hold what thou hast, that no other take thy crown[6]." For if you seek what is not permitted, you will deprive yourself by your own action and judgment of the peace of the universal Church. Our brother and fellow-bishop Lucian and our son Basil the deacon, attended to your injunctions with all the zeal they possessed, but justice refused to give effect to their pleadings. Dated the 22nd of May in the consulship of the illustrious Herculanus (452).

LETTER CVII.

TO JULIAN, BISHOP OF COS.

(Expostulating with him for putting personal considerations before the good of the Church in the matter of the precedence of the See of Constantinople.)

LETTER CVIII.

TO THEODORE, BISHOP OF FORUM JULII.

Leo, the bishop, to Theodore, bishop of Forum Julii.

I. *Theodorus should not have approached him except through his metropolitan.*

Your first proceeding, when anxious, should have been to have consulted your metropolitan on the point which seemed to need inquiry, and if he too was unable to help you, beloved, you should both have asked to be instructed (by us); for in matters, which concern all the LORD's priests as a whole, no inquiry ought to be made without the primates. But in order that the consulter's doubts may in any case be set at rest, I will not keep back the Church's rules about the state of penitents.

2 Rom. xi. 20.
3 Cf. Letter CV., chap. ii. end).
4 Acts xi. 26.
5 1 Cor. xiii. 4.
6 Revel. iii. 11.

II. *The grace of penitence is for those who fall after baptism.*

The manifold mercy of God so assists men when they fall, that not only by the grace of baptism but also by the remedy of penitence is the hope of eternal life revived, in order that they who have violated the gifts of the second birth, condemning themselves by their own judgment, may attain to remission of their crimes, the provisions of the Divine Goodness having so ordained that God's indulgence cannot be obtained without the supplications of priests. For the Mediator between God and men, the Man Christ Jesus, has transmitted this power to those that are set over the Church that they should both grant a course of penitence[7] to those who confess, and, when they are cleansed by wholesome correction admit them through the door of reconciliation to communion in the sacraments. In which work assuredly the Saviour Himself unceasingly takes part and is never absent from those things, the carrying out of which He has committed to His ministers, saying: "Lo, I am with you all the days even to the completion of the age[8]:" so that whatever is accomplished through our service in due order and with satisfactory results we doubt not to have been vouchsafed through the Holy Spirit.

III. *Penitence is sure only in this life.*

But if any one of those for whom we entreat God be hindered by some obstacle and lose the benefit of immediate absolution, and before he attain to the remedies appointed, end his days in the course of nature, he will not be able when stripped of the flesh to gain that which when yet in the body he did not receive. And there will be no need for us to weigh the merits and acts of those who have thus died, seeing that the Lord our God, whose judgments cannot be found out, has reserved for His own decision that which our priestly ministry could not complete: for He wishes His power to be so feared that this fear may benefit all, and every one may dread that which happens to the lukewarm or careless. For it is most expedient and essential that the guilt of sins should be loosed by priestly supplication before the last day of life.

IV. *And yet penitence and reconciliation must not be refused to men in extremis.*

But to those who in time of need and in urgent danger implore the aid first of penitence, then of reconciliation, must neither means of amendment nor reconciliation be forbidden: because we cannot place limits to God's mercy nor fix times for Him with whom true conversion suffers no delay of forgiveness, as says God's Spirit by the prophet, "when thou hast turned and lamented, then shalt thou be saved[9];" and elsewhere, "Declare thou thy iniquities beforehand, that thou may'st be justified[1];" and again, "For with the Lord there is mercy, and with Him is plenteous redemption[2]." And so in dispensing God's gifts we must not be hard, nor neglect the tears and groans of self-accusers, seeing that we believe the very feeling of penitence springs from the inspiration of God, as says the Apostle, "lest perchance God will give them repentance that they may recover themselves from the snares of the devil, by whom they are held captive at his will[3]."

V. *Hazardous as deathbed repentance is, the grace of absolution must not be refused even when it can be asked for only by signs.*

Hence it behoves each individual Christian to listen to the judgment of his own conscience, lest he put off the turning to God from day to day and fix the time of his amendment at the end of his life; for it is most perilous for human frailty and ignorance to confine itself to such conditions as to be reduced to the uncertainty of a few hours, and instead of winning indulgence by fuller amendment, to choose the narrow limits of that time when space is scarcely found even for the penitent's confession or the priest's absolution. But, as I have said, even such men's needs must be so assisted that the free action of penitence and the grace of communion be not denied them, if they demand it even when their voice is gone, by the signs of a still clear intellect. And if they be so overcome by the stress of their malady that they cannot signify in the priest's presence what just before they were asking for, the testimony of believers standing by must prevail for them, that they may obtain the benefit of penitence and reconciliation simultaneously, so long as the regulations of the Fathers' canons be observed in reference to those persons who have sinned against God by forsaking the Faith.

VI. *He is to bring this letter to the notice of the metropolitan.*

These answers, brother, which I have given to your questions in order that nothing different be done under the excuse of ignorance, you shall bring to the notice of your

7 *Actionem* (others not so well *sanctionem*) *pœnitentiæ.*
8 S. Matt. xxviii. 20.

9 Is. xxx. 15 (LXX.).
1 Is. xliii. 26 (LXX).
2 Ps. cxxx. 7.
3 2 Tim. ii. 25, 26.

metropolitan; that if there chance to be any of the brethren who before now have thought there was any doubt about these points, they may be instructed by him concerning what I have written to you. Dated June 11th in the consulship of the illustrious Herculanus (452).

LETTER CIX.

To Julian, Bishop of Cos.

Leo, the pope, to Julian, the bishop.

I. *He laments over the recent rioting in Palestine.*

The information which you give, brother, about the riotous doings of the false monks[4] is serious and to no slight degree lamentable; for they are due to the war which the wicked Eutyches by the madness of deceivers is waging against the preaching of the Gospel and the Apostles, though it will end in his own destruction and that of his followers: but this is delayed by the long-suffering of God, in order that it may appear how greatly the enemies of the cross of Christ are enslaved to the devil; because heretical depravity, breaking through its ancient veil of pretence can no longer restrain itself within the limits of its hypocrisy, and has poured forth all its long-concealed poison, raging against the disciples of the Truth not only with pen but also with deeds of violence[5], in order to wrest consent from unlearned simplicity or from panic-stricken faith. But the sons of light ought not to be so afraid of the sons of darkness, as being sane to acquiesce in the ideas of madmen or to think that any respect should be shown to men of this kind; for, if they would rather perish than recover their senses, provision must be made lest their escape from punishment should do wider harm, and long toleration of them should lead to the destruction of many.

II. *The ringleaders must be removed to a distance.*

I am not unaware what love and favour is due to our sons, those holy and true monks, who forsake not the moderation of their profession, and carry into practice what they promised by their vows. But these insolent disturbers, who boast of their insults and injuries to priests[6], are to be held not the slaves of Christ, but the soldiers of Antichrist, and must be chiefly humiliated in the person of their leaders, who incite the ignorant mob to uphold their insubordination. And hence, seeing that our most merciful Prince loves the catholic Faith with all the devotion of a religious heart, and is greatly offended at the effrontery of these rebel heretics, as is everywhere reported, we must appeal to his clemency that the instigators of these seditions be removed from their mad congregations; and not only Eutyches and Dioscorus but also any who have been forward in aiding their wrongheaded madness, be placed where they can hold no intercourse with their partners in blasphemy: for the simpleness of some may chance to be healed by this method, and men will be more easily recalled to soundness of mind, if they be set free from the incitements of pestilential teachers.

III. *He sends a letter of S. Athanasius to show that the present heresy is only a revival of former exploded heresies.*

But lest the instruction necessary for the confirmation of faithful spirits or the refutation of heretics should be wanting or not expressed, I have sent the letter of bishop Athanasius of holy memory addressed to bishop Epictetus[7], whose testimony Cyril of holy memory made use of at the Synod of Ephesus against Nestorius, because it has so clearly and carefully set forth the Incarnation of the Word, as to overthrow both Nestorius and Eutyches by anticipation in the heresies of those times. Let the followers of Eutyches and Dioscorus dare to accuse such an authority as this of ignorance or of heresy, who assert that our preaching goes astray from the teaching and the knowledge of the Fathers. But it ought to avail for the confirmation of the minds of all the Lord's priests, who, having been already detected and condemned of heresy in respect of the authorities they followed, now begin more openly to set forth their blasphemous dogma, lest, if their meaning were hid beneath the cloke of silence it might still be doubtful whether the triple error of Apollinaris[8], and the mad notion of the Manichees was really revived in them. And as they no longer seek to hide themselves but rise boldly against the churches of Christ, must we not take care to destroy all the strength of their attempts,

4 These were the monks of Palestine who immediately on Theodosius' return from the Synod stirred up great riots first in Jerusalem and then throughout Palestine.

5 Letters of the Emperor Marcian (quoted by the Ball.) speak (1) of a letter written by Theodosius *quas solus poterat fingere diabolus;* and (2) of cruelties, tortures, and insults committed particularly *in mulieres honestas et nobiles,* whereby the rioters had not hesitated to force many to acquiesce in their wicked teaching.

6 They had slain Severian, Bishop of Scythopolis, and would also have slain Juvenal, Bishop of Jerusalem, if he had not taken refuge in flight (Ball.).

7 A portion of this letter is among the quotations added at the end of Letter CLXV. See also Vol. IV. p. 570.

8 What this triple error was will be found in Lett. LIX., chap. v. (*q.v.*): cf. also Lett. CXXIV. and CLXVII.

observing, as I have said, such discrimination as to separate the incorrigible from the more docile spirits: for "evil conversations corrupt good manners[9]," and "the wise man will be sharper than the pestilent person who is chastised[1];" in order that in whatever way the society of the wicked is broken up, some vessels may be snatched from the devil's hand? For we ought not to be so offended at scurrilous and empty words as to have no care for their correction.

IV. *He expresses a hope that Juvenal's timely acknowledgment of error will be imitated by the rest.*

But bishop Juvenal, whose injuries are to be lamented, joined himself too rashly to those blasphemous heretics, and by embracing Eutyches and Dioscorus, drove many ignorant folk headlong by his example, albeit he afterwards corrected himself by wiser counsels. These men, however, who drank in more greedily the wicked poison, have become the enemies of him, whose disciples they had been before, so that the very food he had supplied them was turned to his own ruin: and yet it is to be hoped they will imitate him in amending his ways, if only the holy associations of the neighbourhood in which they dwell will help them to recover their senses. But the character of him[2] who has usurped the place of a bishop still living cannot be doubted from the character of his actions, nor is it to be disputed that he who is loved by the assailants of the Faith must be a misbeliever. Meanwhile, brother, do not hesitate to continue with anxious care to keep me acquainted with the course of events by more frequent letters. Dated November 25th in the consulship of Herculanus (452).

LETTER CX.

From Marcian Augustus.

(Expressing surprise that Leo has not by now confirmed the acts of the Synod, and asking for a speedy confirmation.)

LETTER CXI.

To Marcian Augustus.

(About Anatolius' mistake in deposing Aetius from the office of archdeacon and putting in Andrew instead.)

LETTER CXII.

To Pulcheria Augusta.

(On the same subject more briefly.)

[9] 1 Cor. xv. 33. [1] Prov. xxi. 11, LXX. [2] Sc. Theodosius.

LETTER CXIII.

To Julian, Bishop of Cos.

Leo, bishop of Rome, to Julian, bishop of Cos.

I. *After thanks for Julian's sympathy he complains of the deposition of Aetius from the archdeaconry.*

I acknowledge in your letter, beloved, the feelings of brotherly love, in that you sympathize with us in true grief at the many grievous evils we have borne. But we pray that these things which the Lord has either allowed or wished us to suffer, may avail to the correction of those who live through them[3], and that adversities may cease through the cessation of offences. Both which results will follow through the mercy of God, if only He remove the scourge and turn the hearts of His people to Himself. But as you, brother, are saddened by the hostilities which have raged around us, so I am made anxious because, as your letter indicates, the treacherous attacks of heretics are not set at rest in the church of Constantinople, and men seek occasion to persecute those who have been the defenders of the catholic Faith. For so long as Aetius is removed from his office of archdeacon under pretence of promotion[4] and Andrew is taken into his place, who had been cast off for associating with heretics; so long as respect is shown to the accusers of Flavian of holy memory, and the partners or disciples of that most pious confessor are put down, it is only too clearly shown what pleases the bishop of the church itself. Towards whom I put off taking action till I hear the merits of the case and await his own dealing with me in the letter our son Aetius tells me he will send, giving opportunity for voluntary correction, whereby I desire my vexation to be appeased. Nevertheless, I have written to our most clement Prince and the most pious Augusta about these things which concern the peace of the Church; and I do not doubt they will in the devoutness of their faith take heed lest a heresy already condemned should succeed in springing up again to the detriment of their own glorious work.

II. *He asks Julian to act for him as Anatolius is deficient in vigour.*

See then, beloved brother, that you bestow

[3] *Servatorum.* I am not sure whether this is the right sense; others read *multorum*.

[4] In Lett. CXI., chap. ii., he is said to have been *cœmeterio deputatus*, and, according to Quesnel, when the cemeteries (or catacombs) had no longer to be used as refuges for the persecuted Christians, the custom had grown up of putting priests in charge to perpetuate the memory of the martyrs therein buried; in process of time, when love grew cold, this was looked upon as a sort of exile, and an onerous duty in consequence.

the necessary thought on the cares of the Apostolic See, which by her rights as your mother commends to you, who were nourished at her breast, the defence of the catholic Truth against Nestorians and Eutychians, in order that, supported by the Divine help, you may not cease to watch the interests of the city of Constantinople, lest at any time the storms of error arise within her. And because the faith of our glorious Princes is so great that you may confidently suggest what is necessary to them, use their piety for the benefit of the universal Church. But if ever you consult me, beloved, on things which you think doubtful, my reply shall not fail to supply instruction, so that, apart from cases which ought to be decided by the inquiries of the bishops of each particular church, you may act as my legate and undertake the special charge of preventing the Nestorian or Eutychian heresy reviving in any quarter; because the bishop of Constantinople does not possess catholic vigour, and is not very jealous either for the mystery of man's salvation or for his own reputation: whereas, if he had any spiritual activity, he ought to have considered by whom he was ordained, and whom he succeeded in such a way as to follow the blessed Flavian rather than the instruments of his promotion. And, therefore, when our most religious Princes deign in accordance with my entreaties to reprimand our brother Anatolius on those matters, which deservedly come under blame, join your diligence to theirs, beloved, that all causes of offences may be removed by the application of the fullest correction and he cease from injuring our son Aetius. For with a catholic-minded bishop even though there was something which seemed calculated to annoy in his archdeacon, it ought to have been passed over from regard for the Faith, rather than that the most worthless heretic should take the place of a catholic. And so when I have learnt the rest of the story, I shall then more clearly gather what ought to be done. For, meanwhile, I have thought better to restrain my vexation and to exercise patience that there might be room for forgiveness.

III. *He asks for further information about the rioting in Palestine and in Egypt.*

But with regard to the monks of Palestine, who are said this long time to be in a state of mutiny, I know not by what spirit they are at present moved. Nor has any one yet explained to me what reasons they seem to bring forward for their discontent: whether for instance, they wish to serve the Eutychian heresy by such madness, or whether they are irreconcilably vexed that their bishop could have been misled into that blasphemy, whereby, in spite of the very associations of the holy spots, from which issued instruction for the whole world, he has alienated himself from the Truth of the LORD's Incarnation, and in their opinion that cannot be venial in him which in others had to be wiped out by absolution. And therefore I desire to be more fully informed about these things that proper means may be taken for their correction; because it is one thing to arm oneself wickedly against the Faith, and another thing to be immoderately disturbed on behalf of it. You must know, too, that the documents which Aetius the presbyter told me before had been dispatched, and the epitome of the Faith which you say you have sent, have not yet arrived. Hence, if an opportunity offers itself of a more expeditious messenger, I shall be glad for any information that may seem expedient to be sent me as soon as possible. I am anxious to know about the monks of Egypt [5], whether they have regained their peacefulness and their faith, and about the church of Alexandria, what trustworthy tidings reaches you: I wish you to know what I wrote to its bishop or his ordainers, or the clergy, and have therefore sent you a copy of the letter. You will learn also what I have said to our most clement Prince and our most religious Empress from the copies sent.

IV. *He asks for a Latin translation of the acts of Chalcedon.*

I wish to know whether my letter [6] has been delivered to you, brother, which I sent you by Basil the deacon, upon the Faith of the LORD's Incarnation, while Flavian of holy memory was still alive; for I fancy you have never made any comment on its contents. We have no very clear information about the acts of the Synod, which were drawn up at the time of the council at Chalcedon, on account of the difference of language [7]. And therefore I specially enjoin upon you, brother, that you have the whole collected into one volume, accurately translated of course into Latin, that we may not be in doubt on any portion of the proceedings, and that there may be no manner of uncertainty after you have taken pains to bring it fully within my understanding. Dated March 11th, in the consulship of the illustrious Opilio (453).

5 There had been riots among the monks of Egypt about the appointment of Proterius as bishop, instead of Dioscorus, deposed.

6 This is Letter XXXV. (*q.v.*).

7 It is, of course, well known that Leo knew no Greek whatever.

LETTER CXIV.

To the Bishops assembled in Synod at Chalcedon.

(In answer to their Letter (XCVIII.), approving of their acts in the general so long as nothing is contrary to the canons of Nicæa.)

LETTER CXV.

To Marcian Augustus.

(Congratulating him upon the restoration of peace to the Church, and the suppression of the riotous monks; giving his consent also, as a liege subject of the Emperor's, to the acts of Chalcedon, and asking him to make this known to the Synod.)

LETTER CXVI.

To Pulcheria Augusta.

(Commending her pious zeal and informing her of his assent to the acts of Chalcedon.)

LETTER CXVII.

To Julian, Bishop of Cos.

Leo to Julian the bishop.

I. *He wishes his assent to the Acts of Chalcedon to be widely known.*

How watchfully and how devotedly you guard the catholic Faith, brother, the tenor of your letter shows, and my anxiety is greatly relieved by the information it contains; supplemented as it is by the most religious piety of our religious Emperor, which is clearly shown to be prepared by the Lord for the confirmation of the whole Church; so that, whilst Christian princes act for the Faith with holy zeal, the priests of the Lord may confidently pray for their realm.

What therefore our most clement Emperor deemed needful I have willingly complied with, by sending letters to all the brethren, who were present at the Synod of Chalcedon, in which to show that I approved of what was resolved upon by our holy brethren about the Rule of Faith; on their account to wit, who, in order to cloke their own treachery, pretend to consider invalid or doubtful such conciliar ordinances as are not ratified by my assent: albeit, after the return of the brethren whom I had sent in my stead, I dispatched a letter to the bishop of Constantinople; so that, if he had been minded to publish it, abundant proof might have been furnished thereby how gladly I approved of what the synod had passed concerning the Faith. But, because it contained such an answer as would have run counter to his self-seeking, he preferred my acceptance of the brethren's resolutions to remain unknown, lest at the same time my reply should become known on the absolute authority of the Nicene canons. Wherefore take heed, beloved, that you warn our most gracious prince by frequent reminders that he add his words to ours and order the letter of the Apostolic See to be sent round to the priests of each single province, that hereafter no enemy of the Truth may venture to excuse himself under cover of my silence.

II. *He expresses his thanks for the zeal shown by the Emperor and the Empress.*

And as to the edict of the most Christian Emperor, in which he has shown what the ignorant folly of certain monks deserved and as to the reply of the most gracious Augusta, in which she rebuked the heads of the monasteries, I wish my great rejoicing to be known, being assured that this fervour of faith is bestowed upon them by Divine inspiration, in order that all men may acknowledge their superiority to rest not only on their royal state but also on their priestly holiness: whom both now and formerly I have asked to treat you with full confidence, being assured of their good will, and that they will not refuse to give ear to necessary suggestions.

III. *He wishes to know the effect of his letter to the Empress Eudocia.*

And, because the most clement Emperor has been pleased to charge me secretly by our son Paulus with the task of admonishing our daughter the most clement Augusta Eudocia[8], I have done what he wished, in order that from my letter she may learn how profitable it will be to her if she espouses the cause of the catholic Faith, and have managed that she should further be admonished by a letter from that most clement prince her son; nothing doubting that she herself, too, will set to work with pious zeal to bring the leaders of sedition to a knowledge of the consequences of their action, and, if they understand not the utterances of those who teach them, to make them at least afraid of the powers of those who will punish them. And so what effect this care of ours produces, I wish to know at once by a letter from you, beloved, and whether their ignorant contumacy has at length subsided: as to which if they think there is any doubt about our teaching, let them at least not reject the writings of such holy priests as

---

8 This is Eudocia, the widow of Theodosius II., and the Prince, her son, mentioned below, is Valentinianus III., who had married her daughter Eudoxia. The letter of Leo here mentioned is probably not Letter CXXIII. below. For a graphic sketch of the elder lady see Gore's Life of Leo, pp. 131, 2.

Athanasius, Theophilus and Cyril of Alexandria, with whom our statement of the Faith so completely harmonizes that any one who professes consent to them disagrees in nothing with us.

IV. *Aetius must be content at present with the Emperor's favour.*

With our son Aetius[9] the presbyter we sympathize in his sorrow; and, as one has been put into his place who had previously been judged worthy of censure, there is no doubt that this change tends to the injury of catholics. But these things must be borne patiently meanwhile, lest we should be thought to exceed the measure of our usual moderation, and for the present Aetius must be content with the encouragement of our most clement prince's favour, to whom I have but lately so commended him by letter that I doubt not his good repute has been increased in their most religious minds.

V. *Anatolius shows no contrition in his subsequent acts.*

This too we would have you know, that bishop Anatolius after our prohibition so persisted in his rash presumption as to call upon the bishops of Illyricum to subscribe their names: this news was brought us by the bishop who was sent by the bishop of Thessalonica[1] to announce his consecration. We have declined to write to Anatolius about this, although you might have expected us to do so, because we perceived he did not wish to be reformed. I have made two versions of my letter to the Synod, one with a copy of my letter to Anatolius subjoined, one without it; leaving it to your judgment to deliver the one which you think ought to be given to our most clement prince and to keep the other. Dated 21st March, in the consulship of the illustrious Opilio (453).

LETTER CXVIII.

To the same Julian, Bishop of Cos.

(In which, after speaking of his own efforts for the Faith, he objects to monks being permitted to preach, especially if heretically inclined, and asks Julian to stir up the Emperor's zeal for the Faith.)

LETTER CXIX.

To Maximus, Bishop of Antioch, by the hand of Marian the Presbyter, and Olympius the Deacon.

Leo to Maximus of Antioch.

I. *The Faith is the mean between the two extremes of Eutyches and Nestorius.*

How much, beloved, you have at heart the most sacred unity of our common Faith and the tranquil harmony of the Church's peace, the substance of your letter shows, which was brought me by our sons, Marian the presbyter and Olympius the deacon, and which was the more welcome to us because thereby we can join as it were in conversation, and thus the grace of God becomes more and more known and greater joy is felt through the whole world over the revelation of catholic Truth. And yet we are sore grieved at some who still (so your messengers indicate) love their darkness; and though the brightness of day has arisen everywhere, even still delight in the obscurity of their blindness, and abandoning the Faith, remain Christians in only the empty name, without knowledge to discern one error from another, and to distinguish the blasphemy of Nestorius from the impiety of Eutyches. For no delusion of theirs can appear excusable, because they contradict themselves in their perverseness. For, though Eutyches' disciples abhor Nestorius, and the followers of Nestorius anathematize Eutyches, yet in the judgment of catholics both sides are condemned and both heresies alike are cut away from the body of the Church: because neither falsehood can be in unison with us. Nor does it matter in which direction of blasphemy they disagree with the truth of the Lord's Incarnation, since their erroneous opinions hold neither with the authority of the Gospel nor with the significance of the mystery[2].

II. *Maximus is to keep the churches of the East free from these two opposite heresies.*

And therefore, beloved brother, you must with all your heart consider over which church the Lord has set you to preside, and remember that system of doctrine of which the chief of all the Apostles, the blessed Peter, laid the foundation, not only by his uniform preaching throughout the world, but especially by his teaching in the cities of Antioch and Rome: so that you may understand that he demands of him who is set over the home of his own renown those institutions which he handed down, as he received them from the Truth Itself, which he confessed. And in the churches of the East, and especially in those which the canons of the most holy Fathers at Nicæa[3] assigned to the See of Antioch, you must not by any means allow unscrupulous heretics to make assaults on the Gospel, and

9 Cf. Letter CXIII. above.

1 This is Euxitheus, the successor of Anastasius: Letter CL. is addressed to him.

2 *Ratio sacramenti.*

3 These were apparently twenty in number, but include no very important towns except Seleucia the seaport of Antioch.

the dogmas of either Nestorius or Eutyches to be maintained by any one. Since, as I have said, the rock (*petra*) of the catholic Faith, from which the blessed Apostle Peter took his name at the LORD's hands, rejects every trace of either heresy; for it openly and clearly anathematizes Nestorius for separating the nature of the Word and of the flesh in the blessed Virgin's conception, for dividing the one Christ into two, and for wishing to distinguish between the person of the Godhead and the person of the Manhood: because He is altogether one and the same who in His eternal Deity was born of the Father without time, and in His true flesh was born of His mother in time; and similarly it eschews Eutyches for ignoring the reality of the human flesh in the LORD Jesus Christ, and asserting the transformation of the Word Himself into flesh, so that His birth, nurture, growth, suffering, death and burial, and resurrection on the third day, all belonged to His Deity only, which put on not the reality but the semblance of the form of a slave.

III. *Antioch as the third See in Christendom is to retain her privileges.*

And so it behoves you to use the utmost vigilance, lest these depraved heretics dare to assert themselves; for you must resist them with all the authority of priests, and frequently inform us by your reports what is being done for the progress of the churches. For it is right that you should share this responsibility with the Apostolic See, and realize that the privileges of the third See in Christendom[4] give you every confidence in action, privileges which no intrigues shall in any way impair: because my respect for the Nicene canons is such that I never have allowed nor ever will the institutions of the holy Fathers to be violated by any innovation. For different sometimes as are the deserts of individual prelates, yet the rights of their Sees are permanent: and although rivalry may perchance cause some disturbance about them, yet it cannot impair their dignity. Wherefore, brother, if ever you consider any action ought to be taken to uphold the privileges of the church of Antioch, be sure to explain it in a letter of your own, that we may be able to reply to your application completely and appropriately.

IV. *Anatolius' attempts to subvert the decisions of Nicæa are futile.*

But at the present time let it be enough to make a general proclamation on all points, that if in any synod any one makes any attempt upon or seems to take occasion of wresting an advantage against the provisions of the Nicene canons, he can inflict no discredit upon their inviolable decrees: and it will be easier for the compacts of any conspiracy to be broken through than for the regulations of the aforesaid canons to be in any particular invalidated. For intrigue loses no opportunity of stealing an advantage, and whenever the course of things brings about a general assembly of priests, it is difficult for the greediness of the unscrupulous not to try to gain some unfair point: just as in the Synod of Ephesus which overthrew the blasphemous Nestorius with his dogma, bishop Juvenal believed that he was capable of holding the presidency of the province of Palestine, and ventured to rally the insubordinate by a lying letter[5]. At which Cyril of blessed memory, bishop of Alexandria, being properly dismayed, pointed out in his letter to me[6] to what audacity the other's cupidity had led him: and with anxious entreaty begged me hard that no assent should be given his unlawful attempts. For be it known to you that we found the original document of Cyril's letter which was sought for in our book-case, and of which you sent us copies. On this, however, my judgment lays especial stress that, although a majority of priests through the wiliness of some came to a decision which is found opposed to those constitutions of the 318 fathers, it must be considered void on principles of justice: since the peace of the whole Church cannot otherwise be preserved, except due respect be invariably shown to the canons.

V. *If Leo's legates in any way exceeded their instructions, they did so ineffectually.*

Of course, if anything is alleged to have been done by those brethren whom I sent in my stead to the holy Synod, beyond that which was germane to the Faith, it shall be of no weight at all: because they were sent by the Apostolic See only for the purpose of

4 *Privilegia tertiæ sedis.* Leo here still assigns to Antioch the third place in order of precedence, Rome and Alexandria being first and second respectively; but since 381, as we have seen e.g. in Lett. XCVIII., chap. iv., it had been lowered to the 4th place by the insertion of Constantinople between Rome and Alexandria: see Schaff's Hist., Vol. II. § 56, pp. 277 and following, and Gore's Leo, pp. 119 and foll.

5 It is a curious fact in the history of Church government that the bishopric of Jerusalem for the first centuries never had the first place in Palestine: this was assigned to the metropolitan of Cæsarea, although on great occasions the Bishop of Jerusalem sat next to the patriarch of Antioch: cf. Schaff's Hist., Vol. II. § 56, p. 283, and the viith. Nicene canon: *mos antiquus obtineat ut Aeliæ, id est Ierosolymæ, episcopus honoretur salva metropolis propria dignitate.*

6 The Ballerinii point out that the 1st Council of Ephesus was held in 431, at which Cyril presided for Celestinus I. of Rome, and that Leo was not bishop till 441; this letter was probably addressed to him when archdeacon of Rome, in which case the authority which he had already gained is remarkably illustrated.

extirpating heresy and upholding the catholic Faith. For whatever is laid before bishops for inquiry beyond the particular subjects which come before synodal councils may admit of a certain amount of free discussion, if the holy Fathers have laid down nothing thereon at Nicæa. For anything that is not in agreement with their rules and constitutions can never obtain the assent of the Apostolic See. But how great must be the diligence with which this rule is kept, you will gather from the copies of the letter which we sent to the bishop of Constantinople, restraining his cupidity; and you shall take order that it reach the knowledge of all our brethren and fellow-priests.

VI. *No one but priests are allowed to preach.*

This too it behoves you, beloved, to guard against, that no one except those who are the LORD'S priests dare to claim the right of teaching or preaching, be he monk or layman [7], who boasts himself of some knowledge. Because although it is desirable that all the Church's sons should understand the things which are right and sound, yet it is permitted to none outside the priestly rank to assume the office of preacher, since in the Church of GOD all things ought to be orderly, that in Christ's one body the more excellent members should fulfil their own duties, and the lower not resist the higher. Dated the 11th of June, in the consulship of the illustrious Opilio (453).

LETTER CXX.

TO THEODORET, BISHOP OF CYRUS, ON PERSEVERANCE IN THE FAITH.

Leo, the bishop, to his beloved brother Theodoret, the bishop.

I. *He congratulates Theodoret on their joint victory, and expresses his approval of an honest inquiry which leads to good results.*

On the return of our brothers and fellow-priests, whom the See of the blessed Peter sent to the holy council, we ascertained, beloved, the victory you and we together had won by assistance from on high over the blasphemy of Nestorius, as well as over the madness of Eutyches. Wherefore we make our boast in the LORD, singing with the prophet: "our help is in the name of the LORD, who hath made heaven and earth [8]:" who has suffered us to sustain no harm in the person of our brethren, but has corroborated by the irrevocable assent of the whole brotherhood what He had already laid down through our ministry: to show that, what had been first formulated by the foremost See of Christendom, and then received by the judgment of the whole Christian world, had truly proceeded from Himself: that in this, too, the members may be at one with the Head. And herein our cause for rejoicing grows greater when we see that the more fiercely the foe assailed Christ's servants, the more did he afflict himself. For lest the assent of other Sees to that which the LORD of all has appointed to take precedence of the rest might seem mere complaisance, or lest any other evil suspicion might creep in, some were found to dispute our decisions before they were finally accepted [9]. And while some, instigated by the author of the disagreement, rush forward into a warfare of contradictions, a greater good results through his fall under the guiding hand of the Author of all goodness. For the gifts of GOD'S grace are sweeter to us when they are gained with mighty efforts: and uninterrupted peace is wont to seem a lesser good than one that is restored by labours. Moreover, the Truth itself shines more brightly, and is more bravely maintained when what the Faith had already taught is afterwards confirmed by further inquiry. And still further, the good name of the priestly office gains much in lustre where the authority of the highest is preserved without it being thought that the liberty of the lower ranks has been at all infringed. And the result of a discussion contributes to the greater glory of GOD when the debaters exert themselves with confidence in overcoming the gainsayers: that what of itself is shown wrong may not seem to be passed over in prejudicial silence.

II. *Christ's victory has won back many to the Faith.*

Exult therefore, beloved brother, yes, exult triumphantly in the only-begotten Son of GOD. Through us He has conquered for Himself the reality of Whose flesh was denied. Through us and for us He has conquered, in whose cause we have conquered. This happy day ranks next to the LORD'S Advent for the world. The robber is laid low, and there is restored to our age the mystery of the Divine Incarnation which the enemy of mankind was obscuring with his chicaneries, because the facts would not let him actually destroy it. Nay, the immortal mystery had

7 See Lett. CXX., chap. vi., note 7

8 Ps. cxxiii. 8.

9 These were, of course, the bishops of Illyricum and Palestine, who raised objections at various points in the reading of Leo's Tome at Chalcedon. They were allowed five days to reconsider the matter, and ultimately yielded their consent. See Introduction, p. x., and Bright's notes to the Tome, who gives their objections and the answers in detail, esp. nn. 148, 156, 160, and 173.

perished from the hearts of unbelievers, because so great salvation is of no avail to unbelievers, as the Very Truth said to His disciples: "he that believeth and is baptized shall be saved; but he that believeth not shall be condemned [1]." The rays of the Sun of Righteousness which were obscured throughout the East by the clouds of Nestorius and Eutyches, have shone out brightly from the West, where it has reached its zenith in the Apostles and teachers of the Church. And yet not even in the East is it to be believed that it was ever eclipsed where noble confessors [2] have been found among your ranks: so that, when the old enemy was trying afresh, through the impenitent heart of a modern Pharaoh [3], to blot out the seed of faithful Abraham and the sons of promise, he grew weary, through God's mercy, and could harm no one save himself. And in regard to him the Almighty has worked this wonder also, in that He has not overwhelmed with the founder of the tyranny those who were associated with him in the slaughter of the people of Israel, but has gathered them into His own people; and as the Source of all mercy knew to be worthy of Himself and possible for Himself alone, He has made them conquerors with us who were conquered by us. For whilst the spirit of falsehood is the only true enemy of the human race, it is undoubted that all whom the Truth has won over to His side share in His triumph over that enemy. Assuredly it now is clear how divinely authorized are these words of our Redeemer, which are so applicable to the enemies of the Faith that one may not doubt they were said of them: "You," He says, "are of your father the devil, and the lusts of your father it is your will to fulfil. He was a murderer from the beginning and stood not in the truth, because the truth is not in him. When he speaketh a lie, he speaketh of his own: for he is a liar and the father thereof [4]."

III. *Dioscorus, who in his madness has attacked even the bishop of Rome, has shown himself the instrument of Satan.*

It is not to be wondered, then, that they who have accepted a delusion as to our nature in the true God agree with their father on these points also, maintaining that what was seen, heard, and in fact, by the witness of the gospel, touched and handled in the only Son of God, belonged not to that to which it was proved to belong [5], but to an essence co-eternal and consubstantial with the Father: as if the nature of the Godhead could have been pierced on the Cross, as if the Unchangeable could grow from infancy to manhood, or the eternal Wisdom could progress in wisdom, or God, who is a Spirit, could thereafter be filled with the Spirit. In this, too, their sheer madness betrayed its origin, because, as far as it could, it attempted to injure everybody. For he, who afflicted you with his persecutions, led others wrong by driving them to consent to his wickedness. Yea, even us too, although he had wounded us in each one of the brethren (for they are our members), even us he did not exempt from special vexation in attempting to inflict an injury upon his Head with strange and unheard of and incredible effrontery [6]. But would that he had recovered his senses even after all these enormities, and had not saddened us by his death and eternal damnation. There was no measure of wickedness that he did not reach: it was not enough for him that, sparing neither living nor dead, and forswearing truth and allying himself with falsehood, he imbrued his hands, that had been already long polluted, in the blood of a guiltless, catholic priest [7]. And since it is written: "he that hateth his brother is a murderer [8]:" he has actually carried out what he was said already to have done in hate, as if he had never heard of this nor of that which the Lord says, "learn of Me; for I am meek and lowly in heart, and ye shall find rest unto your souls: for My yoke is easy and My burden is light [9]." A worthy preacher of the devil's errors has been found in this Egyptian plunderer, who, like the cruellest tyrant the Church has had, forced his villainous blasphemies on the reverend brethren through the violence of riotous mobs and the blood-stained hands of soldiers. And when our Redeemer's voice assures us that the author of murder and of lying is one and the same, He has carried out both equally: as if these things were written not to be avoided but to be perpetrated: and thus does he apply to the completion of his destruction the salutary warnings of the Son of God, and turns a deaf ear to what the same Lord has said, "I speak that which I have

1 S. Mark xvi. 16.
2 He is thinking especially of the martyred Flavian.
3 Dioscorus of Alexandria is meant.
4 S. John viii. 44.

5 Viz. to human nature.
6 A reference to Letter XCVIII. (from the Synod of Chalcedon to Leo), chap. ii. shows that Dioscorus had threatened Leo with excommunication; *excommunicationem meditatus est contra te qui corpus ecclesiæ unire festinas.*
7 This was of course Flavian. Quesnel quotes Liberatus the deacon (chap. x. of the Breviary) as asserting that no sooner was Dioscorus made bishop of Alexandria than *oppressit Cyrilli heredes et per calumnias multas ab eis abstulit pecunias.* His accusers at Chalcedon charge him with being an Origenist, an Arian, a murderer, an incendiary, and an evil liver generally
8 1 S. John iii. 15. 9 S. Matt. xi. 29, 30.

seen with My Father; and ye do that which ye have seen with your father[1]."

IV. *Those who undertake to speak authoritatively on doctrine, must preserve the balance between the extremes.*

Accordingly while he strove to cut short Flavian of blessed memory's life in the present world, he has deprived himself of the light of true life. While he tried to drive you out of your churches, he has cut off himself from fellowship with Christians. While he drags and drives many into agreement with error, he has stabbed his own soul with many a wound, a solitary convicted offender beyond all, and through all and for all, for he was the cause of all men's being accused. But, although, brother, you who are nurtured on solid food, have little need of such reminders, yet that we may fulfil what belongs to our position according to that utterance of the Apostle who says, "Besides these things that are without, that which presseth on me daily, anxiety for all the churches. Who is weakened and I am not weak? Who is made to stumble and I burn not[2]?" we believe this admonition ought to be given especially on the present occasion, that whenever by the ministration of the Divine grace we either overwhelm or cleanse those who are without, in the pool of doctrine, we go not away in aught from those rules of Faith which the Godhead of the Holy Ghost brought forward at the Council of Chalcedon, and weigh our words with every caution so as to avoid the two extremes of new false doctrine[3]: not any longer (GOD forbid it) as if debating what is doubtful, but with full authority laying down conclusions already arrived at; for in the letter which we issued from the Apostolic See, and which has been ratified by the assent of the entire holy Synod, we know that so many divinely authorised witnesses are brought together, that no one can entertain any further doubt, except one who prefers to enwrap himself in the clouds of error, and the proceedings of the Synod whether those in which we read the formulating of the definition of Faith, or those in which the aforesaid letter of the Apostolic See was zealously supported by you, brother, and especially the address of the whole Council to our most religious Princes, are corroborated by the testimonies of so many fathers in the past that they must persuade any one, however unwise and stubborn his heart, so long as he be not already joined with the devil in damnation for his wickedness.

[1] S. John viii. 38. [2] 2 Cor. xi. 28, 29.

[3] *Inter utrumque hostem novellæ perfidiæ*, sc. Nestorianism and Eutychianism.

V. *Theodoret's orthodoxy has been happily and thoroughly vindicated.*

Wherefore this, too, it is our duty to provide against the Church's enemies, that, as far as in us lies, we leave them no occasion for slandering us, nor yet, in acting against the Nestorians or Eutychians, ever seem to have retreated before the other side, but that we shun and condemn both the enemies of Christ in equal measure, so that whenever the interests of the hearers in any way require it, we may with all promptitude and clearness strike down them and their doctrines with the anathema that they deserve, lest if we seem to do this doubtfully or tardily, we be thought to act against our will[4]. And although the facts themselves are sufficient to remind your wisdom of this, yet now actual experience has brought the lesson home. But blessed be our GOD, whose invincible Truth has shown you free from all taint of heresy in the judgment of the Apostolic See[5]. To whom you will repay due thanks for all these labours, if you keep yourself such a defender of the universal Church as we have proved and do still prove you. For that GOD has dispelled all calumnious fallacies, we attribute to the blessed Peter's wondrous care of us all, for after sanctioning the judgment of his See in defining the Faith, he allowed no sinister imputation to rest on any of you, who have laboured with us for the catholic Faith: because the Holy Spirit adjudged that no one could fail to come out conqueror of those whose Faith had now conquered.

VI. *He asks Theodoret for his continued co-operation, and refers him to a letter which he has written to the bishop of Antioch.*

It remains that we exhort you to continue your co-operation with the Apostolic See, because we have learnt that some remnants of the Eutychian and Nestorian error still linger amongst you. For the victory which Christ our LORD has vouchsafed to His Church, although it increases our confidence, does not yet entirely destroy our anxiety, nor is it granted us to sleep but to work on more calmly. Hence it is we wish to be assisted in this too by your watchful care, that you

[4] The Ballerinii remind us that all these allusions to keeping the balance of Truth in this and the last chapter, and here to acting *promptissime et evidentissime* were intended for Theodoret's especial benefit, who from his former defence of Nestorius and attacks on Cyril had been suspected of the Nestorian taint, but had expressly cleared himself at the Council of Chalcedon. This explains the *res ipsæ* and *experimenta* of the next sentence, and the solemn adjuration of the sentence next but one.

[5] See the Acts of Chalcedon 1, *ingrediatur et reverendissimus episcopus Theodoretus ut sit particeps synodi, quia et restituit ei episcopatum sanctissimus archiepiscopus Leo*, and 8, where the judges ask for a verdict, "*sicut et sanctissimus Leo archiepiscopus iudicavit*," to which the whole council replied *Post Deum Leo iudicavit.*

hasten to inform the Apostolic See by your periodic reports what progress the LORD's teaching makes in those regions; to the end that we may assist the priests of that district in whatever way experience suggests.

On those matters which were mooted in the often-quoted council, in unlawful opposition to the venerable canons of Nicæa, we have written to our brother and fellow-bishop, the occupant of the See of Antioch [6], adding that too which you had given us verbal information about by your delegates with reference to the unscrupulousness of certain monks, and laying down strict injunctions that no one, be he monk [7] or layman, that boasts himself of some knowledge, should presume to preach except the LORD's priests. That letter, however, we wish to reach all men's knowledge for the benefit of the universal Church through our aforesaid brother and fellow-bishop Maximus; and for that reason we have not thought fit to add a copy of it to this; because we have no doubt of the due carrying out of our injunctions to our aforesaid brother and fellow-bishop. (In another hand.) GOD keep thee safe, beloved brother. Dated 11 June in the consulship of the illustrious Opilio (453).

LETTERS CXXI. AND CXXII.

THE FORMER TO MARCIAN AUGUSTUS, AND THE OTHER TO JULIAN THE BISHOP.

Asking him for further inquiries and information about the proper date for Easter in 455; cf. Letter LXXXVIII. chap. 4, above.

LETTER CXXIII.

TO EUDOCIA AUGUSTA [8], ABOUT THE MONKS OF PALESTINE [9].

Leo, the bishop, to Eudocia Augusta.

I. *A request that she should use her influence with the monks of Palestine in reducing them to order.*

I do not doubt that your piety is aware how great is my devotion to the catholic Faith, and with what care I am bound, GOD helping me, to guard against the Gospel of truth being withstood at any time by ignorant or disloyal men. And, therefore, after expressing to you my dutiful greetings which your clemency is ever bound to receive at my hands, I entreat the LORD to gladden me with the news of your safety, and to bring aid evermore and more by your means to the maintenance of that article of the Faith over which the minds of certain monks within the province of Palestine have been much disturbed; so that to the best of your pious zeal all confidence in such heretical perversity may be destroyed. For what but sheer destruction was to be feared by men who were not moved either by the principles of GOD's mysteries [1], or by the authority of the Scriptures, or by the evidence of the sacred places themselves [2]. May it advantage then the Churches, as by GOD's favour it does advantage them, and may it advantage the human race itself which the Word of GOD adopted at the Incarnation, that you have conceived the wish to take up your abode in that country [3] where the proofs of His wondrous acts and the signs of His sufferings speak to you of our LORD Jesus Christ as not only true GOD but also true Man.

II. *They are to be told that the catholic Faith rejects both the Eutychian and the Nestorian extremes. He wishes to be informed how far she succeeds.*

If then the aforesaid revere and love the name of "catholic," and wish to be numbered among the members of the LORD's body, let them reject the crooked errors which in their rashness they have committed, and let them show penitence [4] for their wicked blasphemies and deeds of bloodshed [5]. For the salvation of their souls let them yield to the synodal decrees which have been confirmed in the city of Chalcedon. And because nothing but true faith and quiet humility attains to the understanding of the mystery of man's salvation, let them believe what they read in the Gospel, what they confess in the Creed, and not mix themselves up with unsound doctrines. For as the catholic Faith condemns Nestorius, who dared to maintain two persons in our one LORD Jesus Christ, so does it also condemn Eutyches and Dioscorus [6] who deny that the

---

6 This is Letter CXIX. to Maximus, bishop of Antioch (*q.v.*).

7 It must be remembered that *monachus esse* in those days meant complete withdrawal from all active life in the world, the preaching orders being a much later institution. The Ballerinii suggest that it may have been a certain abbot Barsumas, who with his followers is said (Act. Chalc. 4) *totam Syriam commovisse*. See also Lett. CXIX., chap. vi.

8 See Letter CXVII., chap. iii., n. 8.

9 See Letter CIX. above.

1 *Ratio sacramentorum*, it cannot be too often repeated that to Leo and other early Fathers, all nature, and all its phenomena, and all God's dealings with mankind are *sacramenta*, and capable of a sacramental (i.e. higher, inner) interpretation: the particular *sacramentum* he is thinking of here is the Incarnation, which he speaks of just below, as often elsewhere, as the *sacramentum salutis humanæ* (the sacrament or mystery whereby man is saved).

2 Viz., the places in Palestine where these monks themselves lived, which trustworthy history or tradition connects with the various incidents in our Lord's life.

3 Eudocia had just made a pilgrimage to the Holy Land.

4 *Agant pœnitentiam*: this is the regular and very expressive translation in the Latin Versions and among the Fathers of the Greek μετανοεῖν.

5 They had seized Jerusalem, and deposed Juvenal, the Bishop, setting up a partisan of their own in his stead.

6 Leo not infrequently joins these two together as equally responsible (e.g. Lett. CIX. 3).

true human flesh was assumed in the Virgin Mother's womb by the only-begotten Word of God.

If your exhortations have any success in convincing these persons, which will win for you eternal glory, I beseech your clemency to inform me of it by letter; that I may have the joy of knowing that you have reaped the fruit of your good work, and that they through the Lord's mercy have not perished. Dated the 15th of June, in the consulship of the illustrious Opilio (453).

LETTER CXXIV.

To the Monks of Palestine.

Leo, the bishop, to the whole body of monks settled throughout Palestine.

I. *They have possibly been misled by a wrong translation of his letter on the Incarnation to Flavian.*

The anxious care, which I owe to the whole Church and to all its sons, has ascertained from many sources that some offence has been given to your minds, beloved, through my interpreters[7], who being either ignorant, as it appears, or malicious, have made you take some of my statements in a different sense to what I meant, not being capable of turning the Latin into Greek with proper accuracy, although in the explanation of subtle and difficult matters, one who undertakes to discuss them can scarcely satisfy himself even in his own tongue. And yet this has so far been of advantage to me, that by your disapproving of what the catholic Faith rejects, we know you are greater friends to the true than to the false: and that you quite properly refuse to believe what I myself also abhor, in accordance with ancient doctrine[8]. For although my letter addressed to bishop Flavian, of holy memory, is of itself sufficiently explicit, and stands in no need either of correction or explanation, yet other of my writings harmonize with that letter, and in them my position will be found similarly set forth. For necessity was laid upon me to argue against the heretics who have thrown many of Christ's peoples into confusion, both before our most merciful princes and the holy synodal Council, and the church of Constantinople, and thus I have laid down what we ought to think and feel on the Incarnation of the Word according to the teaching of the Gospel and Apostles, and in nothing have I departed from the creed of the holy Fathers: because the Faith is one, true, unique, catholic, and to it nothing can be added, nothing taken away: though Nestorius first, and now Eutyches, have endeavoured to assail it from an opposite standpoint, but with similar disloyalty, and have tried to impose on the Church of God two contradictory heresies, which has led to their both being deservedly condemned by the disciples of the Truth; because the false view which they both held in different ways was exceedingly mad and sacrilegious.

II. *Eutyches, who confounds the persons, is as much to be rejected as Nestorius, who separates them*[9].

Nestorius, therefore, must be anathematized for believing the Blessed Virgin Mary to be mother of His manhood only, whereby he made the person of His flesh one thing, and that of His Godhead another, and did not recognize the one Christ in the Word of God and in the flesh, but spoke of the Son of God as separate and distinct from the son of man: although, without losing that unchangeable essence which belongs to Him together with the Father and the Holy Spirit from all eternity and without respect of time, the "Word became flesh" within the Virgin's womb in such wise that by that one conception and one parturition she was at the same time, in virtue of the union of the two substances, both handmaid and mother of the Lord. This Elizabeth also knew, as Luke the evangelist declares, when she said: "Whence is this to me that the mother of my Lord should come to me[1]?" But Eutyches also must be stricken with the same anathema, who, becoming entangled in the treacherous errors of the old heretics, has chosen the third dogma of Apollinaris[2]: so that he denies the reality of his human flesh and soul, and maintains the whole of our Lord Jesus Christ to be of one nature, as if the Godhead of the Word had turned itself into flesh and soul: and as if to be conceived and born, to be nursed and grow, to be crucified and die, to be buried and rise again, and to ascend into heaven and to sit on the Father's right hand, from whence He shall come to judge the living and the dead—as if all those things belonged to that essence only which admits of none of them

---

7 It will be remembered that Leo himself knew not a word of the language, which will account for his uncertainty, consequent helplessness, and uneasiness in this and other cases where a knowledge of the language would have served him in excellent stead.

8 I.e. so much good at all events has come from your objection that we know you are strongly opposed to Eutyches, at present my own special abhorrence.

9 The whole of chap. ii. will be found repeated in Ep. clxv. chap. ii.

1 Luke i. 43.

2 Cf. Ep. xxii. chap. 3 "*conatus—antiqua impii Valentini*" (the adherent of Apollinaris and head of one of the sections of Apollinarians after his death) "*et Apollinaris mala dogmata renovare.*" The third dogma of Apollinaris was that "Christ's manhood was formed out of a divine substance." Bright, 147.

without the reality of the flesh: seeing that the nature of the Only-begotten is the nature of the Father, the nature of the Holy Spirit, and that the undivided unity and consubstantial equality of the eternal Trinity is at once impassible and unchangeable. But if[3] this heretic withdraws from the perverse views of Apollinaris, lest he be proved to hold that the Godhead is passible[4] and mortal: and yet dares to pronounce the nature of the Incarnate Word that is of the Word made Flesh one, he undoubtedly crosses over into the mad view of Manichæus[5] and Marcion[6], and believes that the man Jesus Christ, the mediator between God and men, did all things in an unreal way, and had not a human body, but that a phantom-like apparition presented itself to the beholders' eyes.

III. *The acknowledgment of our nature in Christ is necessary to orthodoxy.*

As these iniquitous lies were once rejected by the catholic Faith, and such men's blasphemies condemned by the unanimous votes of the blessed Fathers throughout the world, whoever these are that are so blinded and strange to the light of truth as to deny the presence of human, that is our, nature in the Word of God from the time of the Incarnation, they must show on what ground they claim the name of Christian, and in what way they harmonize with the true Gospel, if the child-bearing of the blessed Virgin produced either the flesh without the Godhead or the Godhead without the flesh. For as it cannot be denied that "the Word became flesh and dwelt in us[7]," so it cannot be denied that "God was in Christ, reconciling the world to Himself[8]." But what reconciliation can there be, whereby God might be propitiated for the human race, unless the mediator between God and man took up the cause of all?

3 Eutyches had expressly tried to guard himself against this imputation: Ep. xxi. chap. 3, "*anathematizans Apollinarium Valentinum, Manem et Nestorium, &c.*" See Bright's valuable notes 32, 33, 34, and esp. 35, where he shows that "it was polemical rhetoric to say that he was reviving Apollinarian or Valentinian theories."

4 It must be clearly understood that this ugly word is here and elsewhere employed to translate *passibilis* (παθητός) for no reason except the necessity of the case: *pati* and πάσχειν are both of far wider and broader signification than "suffer" or its synonyms: they are simply the passive of *facere* and ποιεῖν (πράσσειν), and there is no proper equivalent in ordinary English parlance. This tendency of terms to become more and more narrow and of particular application is constantly meeting and baffling one in translating the Latin and Greek languages.

5 Leo elsewhere also makes this hardly justifiable inference that Eutychianism is a new form of Docetism as this view was called; chap. vi. below, and Serm. lxv. c. 4 "*isti phantasmatici Christiani*," also xxviii. 4, and lxiv. 1, 2. That the Manichæans naturally held Docetic views on the Incarnation is obvious when we remember that their fundamental misconception was that matter is identical with evil.

6 Marcion was the founder of one of the most formidable Gnostic sects towards the close of the second century: Tertullian wrote a famous treatise (still extant) against him. Like other Gnostics, his views involved him in Docetism.

7 S. John i. 14.

8 2 Cor. v. 19.

And in what way could He properly fulfil His mediation, unless He who in the form of God was equal to the Father, were a sharer of our nature also in the form of a slave: so that the one new Man might effect a renewal of the old: and the bond of death fastened on us by one man's wrong-doing[9] might be loosened by the death of the one Man who alone owed nothing to death. For the pouring out of the blood of the righteous on behalf of the unrighteous was so powerful in its effect[1], so rich a ransom that, if the whole body of us prisoners only believed in their Redeemer, not one would be held in the tyrant's bonds: since as the Apostle says, "where sin abounded, grace also did much more abound[2]." And since we, who were born under the imputation[3] of sin, have received the power of a new birth unto righteousness, the gift of liberty has become stronger than the debt of slavery.

IV. *They only benefit by the blood of Christ who truly share in His death and resurrection.*

What hope then do they, who deny the reality of the human person in our Saviour's body, leave for themselves in the efficacy of this mystery? Let them say by what sacrifice they have been reconciled, by what blood-shedding brought back. Who is He "who gave Himself for us an offering and a victim to God for a sweet smell[4]:" or what sacrifice was ever more hallowed than that which the true High priest placed upon the altar of the cross by the immolation of His own flesh? For although in the sight of the Lord the death of many of His saints has been precious[5], yet no innocent's death was the propitiation of the world. The righteous have received, not given, crowns: and from the endurance of the faithful have arisen examples of patience, not the gift of justification. For their deaths affected themselves alone, and no one has paid off another's debt by his own death[6]: one alone among the sons of

9 *Prævaricatio:* this is a legal term which is often used of sin (esp. in connexion with Adam's transgression). Its original technical meaning is the action of an advocate who plays into the enemy's hand. In theology the devil (διάβολος) is man's adversary, and man himself is befooled into collusion with him by breaking God's law.

1 *Potens ad privilegium: privilegium* is another legal term signifying technically a bill framed to meet an individual case generally in a detrimental way, such bills being against the spirit of the Roman law: here Leo uses it in a sense more nearly approaching our English idea of "privilege."

2 Rom. v. 20.

3 *Sub peccati præiudicio:* yet a third legal term: *præiudicium* in Roman law was a semi-formal and anticipatory verdict by the judge before the case came on for final decision in court; in chapter vi. we have the verb *præiudicare*.

4 Eph. v. 2.

5 Cf. Ps. cxv. 5.

6 The idea of vicarious death was not unfamiliar to the Greeks and Romans: e.g. Alkestis dying for her husband Admetos, and the fairly numerous examples of "devotion" of Roman Generals on the battlefield.

men, our LORD Jesus Christ, stands out as One in whom all are crucified, all dead, all buried, all raised again. Of them He Himself said: "when I am lifted from the earth, I will draw all (things) unto Me[7]." True faith also, that justifies the transgressors and makes them just, is drawn to Him who shared their human nature, and wins salvation in Him, in whom alone man finds himself not guilty; and thus is free to glory in the power of Him who in the humiliation of our flesh engaged in conflict with the haughty foe, and shared His victory with those in whose body He had triumphed.

V. *The actions of Christ's two natures must be kept distinct.*

Although therefore in our one LORD Jesus Christ, the true Son of GOD and man, the person of the Word and of the flesh is one, and both beings have their actions in common[8]: yet we must understand the character of the acts themselves, and by the contemplation of sincere faith distinguish those to which the humility of His weakness is brought from those to which His sublime power is inclined: what it is that the flesh without the Word or the Word without the flesh does not do. For instance, without the power of the Word the Virgin would not have conceived nor brought forth: and without the reality of the flesh His infancy would not have laid wrapt in swaddling clothes. Without the power of the Word the Magi would not have adored the Child that a new star had pointed out to them: and without the reality of the flesh that Child would not have been ordered to be carried away into Egypt and withdrawn from Herod's persecution. Without the power of the Word the Father's voice uttered from the sky would not have said, "This is My beloved Son, in whom I am well pleased[9]:" and without the reality of the flesh John would not have been able to point to Him and say: "Behold the Lamb of GOD, behold Him that beareth away the sins of the world[1]." Without the power of the Word there would have been no restoring of the sick to health, no raising of the dead to life: and without the reality of the flesh He would not have hungered and needed food, nor grown weary and needed rest. Lastly, without the power of the Word, the LORD would not have professed Himself equal to the Father, and without the reality of the flesh He would not also have said that the Father was greater than He: for the catholic Faith upholds and defends both positions, believing the only Son of GOD to be both Man and the Word according to the distinctive properties of His divine and human substance.

VI. *There is no confusion of the two natures in Christ[2].*

Although therefore from that beginning whereby in the Virgin's womb "the Word became flesh," no sort of division ever arose between the Divine and the human substance, and through all the growth and changes of His body, the actions were of one Person the whole time, yet we do not by any mixing of them up confound those very acts which were done inseparably: and from the character of the acts we perceive what belonged to either form. For neither do His Divine acts affect[3] His human, nor His human acts His Divine, since both concur in this way and to this very end that in their operation His twofold qualities be not absorbed the one by the other, nor His individuality doubled. Therefore let those Christian phantom-mongers[4] tell us, what nature of the Saviour's it was that was fastened to the wood of the Cross, that lay in the tomb, and that on the third day rose in the flesh when the stone was rolled away from the grave: or what kind of body Jesus presented to His disciples' eyes entering when the doors were shut upon them: seeing that to drive away the beholders' disbelief, He required them to inspect with their eyes and to handle with their hands the still open prints of the nails and the flesh wound of His pierced side. But if in spite of the truth being so clear, their persistence in heresy will not abandon their position in the darkness, let them show whence they promise themselves the hope of eternal life, which no one can attain to, save through the mediator between GOD and man, the man Jesus Christ. For "there is not another name given to men under heaven, in which they must be saved[5]." Neither is there any ransoming of men from captivity, save in His blood, "who gave Himself a ransom for all[6]:" who, as the blessed apostle proclaims, "when He was in the form of GOD, thought it not robbery that He was equal with GOD; but emptied Himself, receiving the form of a slave, being made in the likeness of men, and being found in fashion as a man He humbled Himself, being made obedient even unto death, the death of the cross. For which reason GOD

7 S. John xii. 32, *omnia:* with the Vulgate.
8 It is scarcely necessary to point out that the old story of the '*communicatio idiomatum*' is here again discussed: cf. the Tome, chapters iv. and v.
9 S. Matt. iii. 17, and Bright's note 5.
1 S. John i. 29: the repetition of the *Ecce* (behold) is in accordance with the old Latin versions: cf. Westcott *in loc.*

2 Considerable portions of this chapter are found repeated word for word in Sermon LXIV. chap. i. and iv.
3 Lat. *præiudicant*, see note 3 to chap. iii., above.
4 *Isti phantasmatici Christiani*, cf. note 5, above.
5 Acts iv. 12. 6 1 Tim. ii. 6.

also exalted Him, and gave Him a name which is above every name: that in the name of Jesus every knee may bow of things in heaven, of things on the earth, and of things under the earth, and that every tongue may confess that the Lord Jesus Christ is in the glory of GOD the Father[7]."

VII. *It was as being "in form of a slave," not as Son of God that He was exalted.*

[8] Although therefore the LORD Jesus Christ is one, and the true Godhead and true Manhood in Him forms absolutely one and the same person, and the entirety of this union cannot be separated by any division, yet the exaltation wherewith "GOD exalted Him," and "gave Him a name which excels every name," we understand to belong to that form which needed to be enriched by this increase of glory[9]. Of course "in the form of GOD" the Son was equal to the Father, and between the Father and the Only-begotten there was no distinction in point of essence, no diversity in point of majesty: nor through the mystery[1] of the Incarnation had the Word been deprived of anything which should be restored Him by the Father's gift. But "the form of a slave" by which the impassible Godhead fulfilled a pledge of mighty loving-kindness[2], is human weakness which was lifted up into the glory of the divine power, the Godhead and the manhood being right from the Virgin's conception so completely united that without the manhood the divine acts, and without the Godhead the human acts were not performed. For which reason as the LORD of majesty is said to have been crucified, so He who from eternity is equal with GOD is said to have been exalted. Nor does it matter by which substance Christ is spoken of, since the unity of His person inseparably remaining He is at once both wholly Son of man according to the flesh and wholly Son of GOD according to His Godhead, which is one with the Father. Whatever therefore Christ received in time, He received in virtue of His manhood, on which are conferred whatsoever it had not. For according to the power of the Word, "all things that the Father hath" the Son also hath indiscriminately, and what "in the form of a slave" He received from the Father, He also Himself gave in the form of the Father. He is in Himself at once both rich and poor; rich, because "in the beginning was the Word, and the Word was with GOD, and GOD was the Word. This was in the beginning with GOD. All things were made through Him, and without Him was made nothing:" and poor because "the Word became flesh and dwelt in us[3]." But what is that emptying of Himself, or that poverty except the receiving of the form of a slave by which the majesty of the Word was veiled, and the scheme for man's redemption carried out? For as the original chains of our captivity could not be loosed, unless a man of our race and of our nature appeared who was not under the prejudice of the old debt, and who with his untainted blood might blot out the bond of death[4], as it had from the beginning been divinely fore-ordained, so it came to pass in the fulness of the appointed time that the promise which had been proclaimed in many ways might reach its long expected fulfilment, and that thus, what had been frequently announced by one testimony after another, might have all doubtfulness removed.

VIII. *A protest against their faithlessness and inconsistency in this matter.*

And so, as all these heresies have been destroyed, which through the holy devotion of the presiding Fathers have been cut off from the body of the catholic unity, and which deserved to be exiles from Christ, because they have made the Incarnation of the Word, which is the one salvation of those who believe aright, a stone of offence and a stumbling-block to themselves, I am surprised that you, beloved, have any difficulty in discerning the light of the Truth. And since it has been made clear by numerous explanations that the Christian Faith was right in condemning both Nestorius and Eutyches with Dioscorus, and that a man cannot be called a Christian who gives his assent to the blasphemous opinion of either the one or the other, I am grieved that you are, as I hear, doing despite to the teaching of the Gospel and the Apostles by stirring up the various bodies of citizens with seditions, by disturbing the churches, and by inflicting not only insults, but even death, upon priests and bishops, so that you lose sight of your resolves and profession[5] through your fury and cruelty. Where is your rule of meekness and quietness? where is the long-suffering of patience? where the tranquillity of peace? where the firm foundation of love and courage of endurance? what evil persuasion has carried you off, what persecution has

[7] Phil. ii. 6—11.
[8] The whole of this chapter is repeated with slight variations in his letter (CLXV.) to Leo the Emperor (chaps. 8 and 9).
[9] *Quæ ditanda erat tantæ glorificationis augmento* acc. to Leo's use of the gerundive, see Tome, chap. i. *quod . . . omnium regenerandorum voce depromitur.*
[1] Here the word is actually *mysterium*, not, as usual, *sacramentum.*
[2] *Sacramentum magnæ pietatis*, 1 Tim. iii. 16: cf. Bright's note 8.
[3] S. John i. 1—3, 14.
[4] The reference is to Col. ii. 14.
[5] Viz. as monks as well as baptized members of the church.

separated you from the gospel of Christ? or what strange craftiness of the Deceiver has shown itself that, forgetting the prophets and apostles, forgetting the health-giving creed and confession which you pronounced before many witnesses when you received the sacrament of baptism you should give yourselves up to the the Devil's deceits? what effect would "the Claws [6]" and other cruel tortures have had on you if the empty comments of heretics have had so much weight in taking the purity of your faith by storm? you think you are acting for the Faith and yet you go against the Faith. You arm yourselves in the name of the Church and yet fight against the Church. Is this what you have learnt from prophets, evangelists, and apostles? to deny the true flesh of Christ, to subject the very essence of the Word to suffering and death, to make our nature different from His who repaired it, and to reckon all that the cross uplifted, that the spear pierced, that the stone on the tomb received and gave back, to be only the work of Divine power, and not also of human humility? It is in reference to this humility that the Apostle says, "For I do not blush for the Gospel [7]," inasmuch as he knew what a slur was cast upon Christians by their enemies. And, therefore, the LORD also made proclamation, saying: "he that shall confess Me before men him will I also confess before My Father [8]." For these will not be worthy of the Son and the Father's acknowledgment in whom the flesh of Christ awakens no respect: and they will prove themselves to have gained no virtue from the sign of the cross [9] who blush to avow with their lips what they have consented to bear upon their brows.

IX. *An exhortation to accept the catholic view of the Incarnation.*

Give up, my sons, give up these suggestions of the devil. GOD's Truth nothing can impair, but the Truth does not save us except in our flesh. For, as the prophet says, "truth is sprung out of the earth [1]," and the Virgin Mary conceived the Word in such wise that she ministered flesh of her substance to be united to Him without the addition of a second person, and without the disappearance of her nature: seeing that He who was in the form of GOD took the form of a slave in such wise that Christ is one and the same in both forms: GOD bending Himself to the weak things of man, and man rising up to the high things of the Godhead, as the Apostle says, "whose are the fathers, and from whom, according to the flesh is Christ, who is above all things GOD blessed for ever. Amen [2]."

LETTER CXXV.

TO JULIAN, THE BISHOP, BY COUNT RODANUS.

(Asking him to write quickly, and not keep him in suspense.)

LETTER CXXVI.

TO MARCIAN AUGUSTUS.

(Congratulating him on the restoration of peace in Palestine.)

LETTER CXXVII.

TO JULIAN, BISHOP OF COS.

(About (1) affairs in Palestine, (2) a letter from Proterius, (3) the date of Easter, (4) his reply to the Synod of Chalcedon, (5) the deposition of Aetius.)

LETTER CXXVII.

TO MARCIAN AUGUSTUS.

(Professing readiness to be reconciled to Anatolius if he will abide by the canons and not infringe the prerogatives of others.)

LETTER CXXIX.

TO PROTERIUS, BISHOP OF ALEXANDRIA.

Leo to Proterius, bishop of Alexandria.

I. *He commends his persistent loyalty to the Faith.*

Your letter, beloved, which our brother and fellow-bishop Nestorius duly brought us, has caused me great joy. For it was seemly that such an epistle should be sent by the head of the church of Alexandria to the Apostolic See, as showed that the Egyptians had from the first learnt from the teaching of the most blessed Apostle Peter through his blessed disciple Mark [3], that which it is agreed the Romans have believed, that beside the LORD Jesus Christ "there is no other name given to men under heaven, in which they must be saved [4]." But because "all men have not faith [5]" and the crafty Tempter never delights so much in wounding the hearts of men as when he can poison their unwary minds with errors that are opposed to Gospel Truth, we must strive by the mighty teaching of the Holy Ghost to prevent Christian know-

6 The *Ungulæ* (Claws) were among the numerous instruments with which Christians were tortured: cf. Tert. Apol. xii. 57, *ungulis deraditis latera christianorum*; Cypr. *de lapsis* chap. xiii. (*cum*) *ungula effoderet, caro me in colluctatione deseruit.*

7 Rom. i. 16. 8 S. Matt. x. 32. 9 Viz. in Baptism.

1 Ps. lxxxv. 12.

2 Rom. ix. 5.

3 S. Mark was the reputed founder of the church of Alexandria. Cf. Letter IX. chap. 1.

4 Acts iv. 12. 5 2 Thess. iii. 2.

ledge from being perverted by the devil's falsehoods. And against this danger it behoves the rulers of the churches especially to guard and to avert from the minds of simple folk lies which are coloured by a certain show of truth [6]. "For narrow and steep is the way which leads to life [7]." And they seek to entrap men not so much b· watching their actions as by nice distinctions of meaning, corrupting the force of sentences by some very slight addition or alteration, whereby sometimes a statement, which made for salvation, by a subtle change is turned to destruction. But since the Apostle says, "there must be heresies, that they which are approved may be made manifest among you [8]," it tends to the progress of the whole Church, that, whenever wickedness reveals itself in setting forth wrong opinions, the things which are harmful be not concealed, and that what will inevitably end in ruin may not injure the innocence of others. Wherefore they must put down their blind wanderings and downfalls to themselves, who with rash obstinacy prefer to glory in their shame than to accept the offered remedy. You do right, brother, to be displeased at their stubbornness, and we commend you for holding fast that teaching which has come down to us from the blessed Apostles and the holy Fathers.

II. *Let him fortify the faithful by the public reading aloud of quotations from the Fathers bearing on the question and of the Tome.*

For there is no new preaching in the letter, which I wrote in reply to Flavian of holy memory, when he consulted me about the Incarnation of our LORD Jesus Christ; for in nothing did I depart from that rule of Faith which was outspokenly maintained by your ancestors and ours. And if Dioscorus had been willing to follow and imitate them, he would have abided in the Body of Christ, having in the works of Athanasius [9] of blessed memory the materials for instruction, and in the discourses of Theophilus [9] and Cyril [9] of holy remembrance the means rather of praiseworthily opposing the already condemned dogma than of choosing to consort with Eutyches in his blasphemy. This therefore, beloved brother, I advise in my anxiety for our common Faith that, because the enemies of Christ's cross lie in watch for all our words and syllables, we give them not the slightest occasion for falsely asserting that we agree with the Nestorian doctrine. And you must so diligently exhort the laity and clergy and all the brotherhood to advance in the Faith as to show that you teach nothing new but instil into all men's breasts those things, which the Fathers of revered memory have with harmony of statement taught, and with which in all things our epistle agrees. And this must be shown not only by your words but also by the actually reading aloud of previous statements, that GOD's people may know that what the Fathers received from their predecessors and handed on to their descendants, is still instilled into them in the present day. And to this end, when the statements of the aforesaid priests have first been read, then lastly let my writings also be recited, that the ears of the faithful may attest that we preach nothing else than what we received from our forefathers. And because their understandings are but little practised in discerning these things, let them at least learn from the letters of the Fathers, how ancient this evil is, which is now condemned by us in Nestorius as well as in Eutyches, who have both been ashamed to preach the gospel of Christ according to the LORD's own teaching.

III. *The ancient precedents are to be maintained throughout.*

Accordingly, both in the rule of Faith and in the observance of discipline, let the standard of antiquity be maintained throughout, and do thou, beloved, display the firmness of a prudent ruler, that the church of Alexandria may get the benefit of my earnest resistance to the unprincipled ambition of certain people in maintaining its ancient privileges, and of my determination that all metropolitans should retain their dignity undiminished, as you will ascertain from the tenor of my letters, which I have addressed, whether to the holy Synod or to the most Christian Emperor, or to the Bishop of Constantinople; for you will perceive that I have made it my special care to allow no deviation from the rule of Faith in the LORD's churches, nor any diminution of their privileges through any individual's unscrupulousness. And as this is so, hold fast, brother, to the custom of your predecessors, and keep due authority over your comprovincial bishops, who by ancient constitution are subject to the See of Alexandria; so that they resist not ecclesiastical usage, and refuse not to meet together under your presidency, either at fixed times or when any reasonable cause demands it: and that if anything has to be discussed in a general meeting which will be to the benefit of the Church, when the brethren have thus met together, they may unanimously come to

[6] See chap. ii. and more particularly Lett. CXXX. chap. 3 from which it is evident that the Eutychians had sought to foist upon certain passages in the Tome a Nestorian interpretation.

[7] S. Matt. vii. 14.

[8] 1 Cor. xi. 19.

[9] Who as he himself says in the next letter, *eidem ecclesiæ præfuerunt* (CXXX. ii.).

some resolution thereupon. For there is nothing which ought to recall them from this obedience, seeing that both for faith and conduct we have such good knowledge of you, brother, that we will not allow you to lose any of your predecessor's authority, nor to be slighted with impunity. Dated March 10th, in the consulship of the illustrious Aetius and Studius (454).

LETTER CXXX.

To Marcian Augustus.

(Praising the orthodoxy of Proterius, advocating the public recital by him of passages bearing on the present controversy from the writings of Athanasius and others, and also of the Tome itself in a new Greek translation.)

LETTER CXXXI.

To Julian, Bishop of Cos.

(Telling him he has received Proterius' letter, and asking for (1) a new Greek translation of the Tome; (2) a report on the Easter difficulty of the next year (455)).

LETTER CXXXII.

From Anatolius, Bishop of Constantinople, to Leo.

(In which he complains of the intermission in their correspondence, maintains his allegiance to Rome, announces the restitution of Aetius, deprecates the charge of personal ambition, and remits the proceedings of Chalcedon for his approval.)

LETTER CXXXIII.

From Proterius, Bishop of Alexandria, to Leo.

(Upon the Easter difficulty of 455.)

LETTER CXXXIV.

To Marcian Augustus.

(Suggesting that Eutyches should be banished to a still remoter place, where he cannot do so much harm by his false teaching.)

LETTER CXXXV.

To Anatolius.

(In answer to CXXXII.)

LETTER CXXXVI.

To Marcian Augustus.

(Simultaneously with CXXXV., on the subject of his reconciliation with Anatolius.)

LETTER CXXXVII.

To the same, and on the same day.

(On the subject of Easter, acknowledging the trouble Proterius has taken,—to which is joined a request that the accounts of the *œconomi*[1] should be audited by priests, not lay persons.)

LETTER CXXXVIII.

To the Bishops of Gaul and Spain.

(On Easter.)

LETTER CXXXIX.

To Juvenal, Bishop of Jerusalem.

Leo, bishop of the city of Rome, to Juvenal, bishop of Jerusalem.

I. *He rejoices over Juvenal's return to orthodoxy, though chiding him for having gone astray.*

When I received your letter, beloved, which our sons Andrew the presbyter and Peter the deacon brought me, I rejoiced indeed that you had been allowed to return to the seat of your bishopric; but when all the reasons came to my remembrance, which brought you into such excessive troubles, I grieved to think you had been yourself the source of your adversities by failing in persistency of opposition to the heretics: for men can but think you were not bold enough to refute those with whom when in error you professed yourself satisfied. For the condemnation of Flavian of blessed memory, and the acceptance of the most unholy Eutyches, what was it but the denial of our Lord Jesus Christ according to the flesh? which He Himself of His great mercy caused to be overthrown, when by the authority of the holy Council of Chalcedon He brought to nought that accursed judgment of the Synod of Ephesus without debarring any of the attainted from being healed by correction. And therefore, because in the time of long-suffering, you have chosen return to wisdom rather than persistency in folly, I rejoice that you have so sought the heavenly remedies as at last to have become a defender of the Faith which is assailed by heretics. For, though no priest ought to be ignorant of that which he preaches[2], yet any Christian living at Jerusalem is more inexcusable than all the

[1] *Œconomi* (stewards) were officers appointed to manage the revenues of each diocese under the bishops' direction, when the bishops and their archdeacons had enough to do otherwise: cf. Bingham, *Antiq.*, Bk. III. chap. xii.

[2] *Quod prædicat*, some MSS. *quid prædicat* (what to preach): some also add *quoniam qui ignorat, ignorabitur* (from 1 Cor. xiv. 38).

ignorant, seeing that he is taught to understand the power of the Gospel, not only by the written word but by the witness of the places themselves, and what elsewhere may not be disbelieved, cannot there remain unseen. Why is the understanding in difficulty, where the eyes are its instructors? And why are things read or heard doubtful, where all the mysteries of man's salvation obtrude themselves upon the sight and touch? As if to each individual doubter the LORD still used His human voice and said, why are "ye disturbed and why do thoughts arise into your hearts? see My hands and My feet that it is I myself. Handle Me and see because (*or* that) a spirit hath not bones and flesh, as ye see Me have [3]."

II. *Let him be strengthened in his faith by the holy associations of the place where he lives.*

Make use, therefore, beloved brother, of these incontrovertible proofs of the catholic Faith and support the preaching of the Evangelists by the testimony of the holy places in which you live. In your country is Bethlehem, in which the Light of Salvation sprang from the womb of the Virgin of the house of David [4], whom wrapped in swaddling clothes the manger of the crowded inn received. In your country was the Saviour's infancy announced by angels, adored by magi, sought by Herod through the death of many infants. In your country was it that His boyhood grew, His youth ripened, and His true man's nature reached to perfect manhood by the increase of the body, not without food for hunger, not without sleep for rest, not without tears of pity, not without fear and dread: for He is one and the same Person, who in the form of GOD wrought great miracles of power, and in the form of a slave underwent the cruelty of the passion. This the very cross unceasingly says to you: this the stone of the sepulchre cries out, under which the LORD in human condition lay, and from which by Divine power He rose. And when you approach the mount of Olivet, to venerate the place of the Ascension, does not the angel's voice ring in your ears, which says to those who were dumbfounded at the LORD's uplifting, "ye men of Galilee, why stand ye gazing into heaven? this Jesus, Who was taken up from you into heaven, shall so come, as ye saw Him going into heaven [5]."

III. *The facts of the Gospel attest the Incarnation.*

The true birth of Christ, therefore, is confirmed by the true cross; since He is Himself born in our flesh, Who is crucified in our flesh, which, as no sin entered into it, could not have been mortal, unless it had been that of our race. But in order that He might restore life to all, He undertook the cause of all and rendered void the force of the old bond, by paying it for all, because He alone of us all did not owe it: that, as by one man's guilt all had become sinners, so by one man's innocence all might become innocent, righteousness being bestowed upon men by Him Who had undertaken man's nature. For in no way is He outside our true bodily nature, of Whom the Evangelist in beginning his story says, "the book of the generation of Jesus Christ, the son of David, the son of Abraham [6]," with which the blessed Apostle Paul's teaching agrees, when he says "whose are the fathers and of whom is Christ according to the flesh, Who is above all GOD blessed for ever [7]," and so to Timothy "remember," he says, "that Jesus Christ has risen from the dead, of the seed of David [8]."

IV. *Those who are still in error must be thoroughly instructed in the historic Faith.*

But how many are the authorities, both in the New and Old Testaments, by which this truth is declared, as befits the antiquity of your See, you clearly understand, seeing that the belief of the Fathers and my letter written to Flavian, of holy memory, of which you yourself made mention, confirmed, as they have been, by the universal synod, are sufficient for you. And therefore it behoves you, beloved, to take heed that no one raise a murmur against the unspeakable mystery of our Redemption and Hope. But if there are any who are still in the darkness of ignorance or the discord of perversity, let them be instructed by the authority of those whose doctrine in GOD's Church was apostolical and clear, that they may recognize that on the Incarnation of GOD's Word we believe what they did, and may not by their obstinacy place themselves outside the Body of Christ, in which we died and rose with Him: because neither loyalty to the Faith nor the plan of the mystery admits that either the Godhead should be passible in its own essence, or the reality be falsified in His taking on Him of our flesh. Dated 4th September, in the consulship of the illustrious Aetius and Studius (454).

3 S. Luke xxiv. 38, 39.
4 *Salutifer Davidicæ Virginis partus illuxit.*
5 Acts i. 11.
6 S. Matt. i. 1.
7 Rom. ix. 5.
8 2 Tim. ii. 8.

LETTER CXL.

To Julian, Bishop of Cos.

(Now that Dioscorus is dead, the peace of the Church will be more easily restored.)

LETTER CXLI.

To the same.

(On several minor points of detail.)

LETTER CXLII.

To Marcian Augustus.

(*Inter alia* thanking him for the trouble he has taken about the Easter of 455.)

LETTER CXLIII.

To Anatolius, Bishop of Constantinople.

(Briefly asking him to extirpate all remains of heresy.)

LETTER CXLIV.

To Julian, Bishop of Cos.

(Speaking of rumours which have reached him of disturbances at Alexandria, and begging of him to be on the alert.)

LETTER CXLV.

To Leo Augustus[9].

(Asking him to help the church of Alexandria in appointing a good bishop in place of the murdered Proterius[1].)

LETTER CXLVI.

To Anatolius, Bishop of Constantinople.

(Begging him to take precautions lest the change of Emperor should be made the occasion for fresh outbreaks of heresy.)

LETTER CXLVII.

To Julian, Bishop of Cos, and Aetius, the Presbyter.

(Charging him to uphold the acts of Chalcedon, and to help in choosing a good successor to Proterius.)

LETTER CXLVIII.

To Leo Augustus.

(Thanking him for assurances made that he would guard the interests of the Church.)

LETTER CXLIX.

To Basil, Bishop of Antioch.

(Asking him to give no countenance to the demand for a new Synod.)

LETTER CL.

To Euxitheus, Bishop of Thessalonica (and others).

(To the same effect.)

LETTER CLI.

To Anatolius, Bishop of Constantinople.

(He is to keep the church of Constantinople free from all heresy.)

LETTER CLII.

To Julian, Bishop of Cos.

(Charging him to see that the preceding letters reach their destination.)

LETTER CLIII.

To Aetius, Presbyter of Constantinople.

(Asking him to assist in the distribution of these letters.)

LETTER CLIV.

To the Egyptian Bishops.

(See Letter CLVIII.)

LETTER CLV.

To Anatolius, Bishop of Constantinople.

(In which he incites him to watchfulness, and complains that certain of the clergy in Constantinople are in collusion with the adversary.)

LETTER CLVI.

To Leo Augustus.

Leo, the bishop, to Leo Augustus.

I. *There is no need to open the question of doctrine again now.*

Your clemency's letter, which was full of vigorous faith and of the light of truth, I have respectfully received, which I wish I could obey, even in the matter of my personal attendance, which your Majesty thinks necessary; for then I should gain the greater advantage from the sight of your splendour. But I believe you will approve of my view when reason has shown it preferable. For since with holy and spiritual zeal you consistently maintain the Church's peace, and nothing is more conducive to the defence of the Faith than to adhere to those things which have been incontrovertibly defined under the unceasing guidance of the Holy Spirit, we shall seem[2] to be doing our best to upset

9 Marcian died in 457, and was succeeded by Leo of Thrace.
1 On Marcian's death, there had been a rising, in which Proterius had been brutally murdered, and a monk named Timothy Ælurus set up in his stead.

2 i.e. by carrying out your plan. The appeal to the Emperor's orthodoxy must be regarded as diplomatic rather than accurate: for Leo was the nominee of Arianism, if not himself an Arian.

the decrees, and at the bidding of a heretic's petition to overthrow the authorities which the universal Church has adopted, and thus to remove all limits from the conflicts of Churches, and giving full rein to rebellion, to extend rather than appease contentions. And hence because after the disgraceful scenes at the synod of Ephesus, whereat through the wickedness of Dioscorus the catholic Faith was rejected, and Eutyches' heresy accepted, nothing more useful could be devised for the preservation of the Christian Faith than that the holy Synod of Chalcedon should rescind his wicked acts, and that such care should be bestowed thereat on heavenly doctrine, that nothing should linger in any one's mind in disagreement with the utterances of either the Prophets or the Apostles, such moderation of course being observed that only the persistent rebels should be cast off from the unity of the Church, and no one who was penitent should be denied pardon, what more in accordance with men's expectations or with religion will your Majesty be able to decree, than that no one henceforth be permitted to attack what has been determined by decrees which are Divine rather than human, lest they be truly worthy but to lose GOD's gift, who have dared to doubt concerning His Truth?

II. *The proposal to reconsider the question proceeds from antichrist or the devil himself.*

Since, therefore, the universal Church has become a rock (*petra*) through the building up of that original Rock [3], and the first of the Apostles, the most blessed Peter, heard the voice of the LORD saying, "Thou art Peter, and upon this rock (*petra*) I will build My Church [4]," who is there who dare assail such impregnable strength, unless he be either antichrist or the devil, who, abiding unconverted in his wickedness, is anxious to sow lies by the vessels of wrath which are suited to his treachery, whilst under the false name of diligence he pretends to be in search of the Truth. And his unrestrained madness and blind wickedness has deservedly brought contempt and disrepute on himself, so that while he rages against the holy church of Alexandria with diabolical purpose, men may learn the character of those who desire to reconsider the Synod of Chalcedon. For it cannot possibly have been that an opinion was there expressed contrary to the holy Synod of Nicæa, as the heretics falsely maintain, who pretend that they hold the faith of the Nicene Council, in which our holy and venerable fathers, being assembled against Arius, affirmed not that the LORD's Flesh, but that the Son's Godhead was *homoousion* with the Father, whereas in the Council of Chalcedon against the blasphemy of Eutyches, it was defined that the LORD Jesus Christ took the reality of our body from the substance of the Virgin-mother.

III. *All the bishops of Christendom agree with him in this.*

Therefore in addressing our most Christian Emperor, who is worthy to be classed among the champions of Christ, I use the freedom of the catholic Faith and fearlessly exhort you to throw in your lot with Apostles and Prophets; firmly to despise and reject those who have deprived themselves of their Christian name, and not to let blasphemous parricides, who, it is agreed, wish to annul the Faith, discuss that Faith under treacherous pretexts. For since the LORD has enriched your clemency with such insight into His mystery, you ought unhesitatingly to consider that the kingly power has been conferred on you not for the governance of the world alone but more especially for the guardianship of the Church: that by quelling wicked attempts you may both defend that which has been rightly decreed, and restore true peace where there has been disturbance, that is to say by deposing usurpers [5] of the rights of others and reinstating the ancient Faith in the See of Alexandria, that by your reforms GOD's wrath may be appeased, and so He take not vengeance for their doings on a people hitherto religious, but forgive them. Set before the eyes of your heart, venerable Emperor, the fact that all the LORD's priests which are in all the world, are beseeching you on behalf of that Faith, wherein is Redemption for the whole world. In which those maintainers of the Apostolic Faith more particularly appeal to you who have presided over the Church of Alexandria, entreating your Majesty not to allow heretics who have rightfully been condemned for their perversity, to continue in their usurpation [6]; for, whether you look at the wickedness of their error or consider the deed which their madness has perpetrated, not only are they unable to be admitted to the dignity of the priesthood, but they even deserve to be cut off from the name of Christian. For—and I entreat your Majesty's forgiveness for saying so—they to some extent dim your own splendour, most glorious Emperor, when such treacherous parricides dare to ask for

3 *Per illius principalis petræ ædificationem:* here *petra* is apparently Christ Himself, cf. Letter XXVIII. chap. 5, and Bright's n. 64.

4 S. Matt. xvi. 18.

5 Sc. Timothy Ælurus.

6 *Pervasione*, others read *persuasione* (false opinion).

that which even the guiltless could not lawfully obtain.

IV. *The difference between the two petitions which have been presented to the Emperor.*

Petitions have been presented to your Majesty[7], copies of which you subjoined to your letter. But in that which comes in deprecation from the catholics, a list of signatures is contained: and because their case had good reason in it, the names of individuals, and even their dignified rank is confidently disclosed. But in that, which heretical intrusion has not feared to offer to our orthodox Emperor under the vague sanction of a motley body, all particular names are withheld for this reason, lest not only the paucity of members but also their worth might be discovered. For they think it expedient to conceal their number, though their quality is indicated, and not improperly they are afraid to proclaim their position, seeing that they deserve to be condemned. In the one document therefore is contained the petition of catholics, in the other the fictions of heretics are set forth. Here the overthrow of the LORD's priests, of the whole Christian people, and of the monasteries is bemoaned: there is displayed the continuance of gigantic wrongs, so that what ought never to have been heard of[8] is allowed to be widely extended.

V. *It is a great opportunity for the Emperor to show his faith.*

Is it not clear which side you ought to support and which to oppose, if the Church of Alexandria, which has always been the "house of prayer," is not now to be "a den of robbers[8a]?" For surely it is manifest that through the cruellest and maddest savagery all the light of the heavenly mysteries is extinguished. The offering of the sacrifice is cut off, the hallowing of the chrism has failed[9], and from the murderous hands of wicked men all the mysteries have withdrawn themselves. Nor can there be any manner of doubt what decree ought to be passed on these men, who after unutterable acts of sacrilege, after shedding the blood of a most highly reputed priest, and scattering the ashes of his burnt body to be the sport of the winds of heaven, dare to demand for themselves the rights of a usurped dignity and to arraign before councils the inviolable Faith of the Apostolic teaching. Great, therefore, is the opportunity for you to add to your diadem from the LORD's hand the crown of faith also, and to triumph over the Church's foes: for, if it be matter of praise to you to vanquish the armies of opposing nations, how great will be the glory of freeing from its mad tyrant the church of Alexandria, the affliction of which is an injury to all Christians?

VI. *He promises more detailed statements on the Faith subsequently, and begs him to correct certain things in which Anatolius is remiss.*

But in order that my correspondence may have the effect on your Majesty of a mouth to mouth colloquy, I have seen that whatever suggestions I would make about our common Faith, must be conveyed in subsequent communications[1]. And lest the pages of this epistle reach too great a length, I have comprised in another letter what is agreeable to the maintenance of the catholic Faith, in order that, though the published statements of the Apostolic See were sufficient, yet these additional statements might also break down the snares of the heretics. For your Majesty's priestly and Apostolic mind ought to be still further kindled to righteous vengeance by this pestilential evil, which mars the purity of the church of Constantinople, in which are found certain clerics, who agree with the interpretations of the heretics and within the very heart of the Church assist them by their support[2]. In removing whom if my brother Anatolius is found remiss through too good-natured leniency, vouchsafe to show your faith by administering this remedy also to the Church, that such men be driven not only from the ranks of the clergy, but also from dwelling in the city. I commend to you your Majesty's loyal subjects, bishop Julian and presbyter Aetius, with a request that you will deign to listen quietly to their suggestions in defence of the catholic Faith, because they are in good truth men who may be found helpful to your faith in all things. Dated the 1st of Dec. in the consulship of the illustrious Constantine and Rufus (457).

7 These had come, one from either side, as the sequel shows: that of the catholics was signed by fourteen bishops, four presbyters, and two deacons (Ball.).

8 *Audiri*: others *auderi* (to have been ventured on).

8a S. Luke xix. 46.

9 Cf. Serm. LXVI. chap. 2, *nobiscum est signaculum circumcisionis, sanctificatio chrismatum, consecratio sacerdotum*: see Bright's n. 90, from which we learn that "this chrism was that which, from the second century, had been administered in connection with Confirmation." This rite, which had at first been part of the Baptism itself, was now apparently performed at a shorter or longer interval after Baptism according to the convenience of the Bishop: cf. Serm. LXXVII. 1.

1 Viz. Letters CLXII., CLXIV., and esp. CLXV. (which last is in a large measure a rescription of Letter CXXIV. q.v.).

2 Two of these are mentioned by name subsequently, e.g. in Lett. CLVII. (to Anatolius), chap. 4, viz. Atticus a presbyter, and Andrew, in which chapter he blames Anatolius severely for his double-dealing (*cogor vehementius de tua dissimulatione causari, etc.*).

LETTER CLVII.

To Anatolius, Bishop of Constantinople.

(Urging him to active measures in certain specified matters.)

LETTER CLVIII[3].

To the Catholic Bishops of Egypt sojourning in Constantinople.

Leo to the catholic Egyptian bishops sojourning in Constantinople.

He encourages them in their sufferings for the Faith, and in their entreaties for redress to the Emperor.

I have before now been so saddened by tidings of the crimes committed in Alexandria, and my spirit has been so wounded by the atrocity of the deed itself, that I know not what tears to show and what lamentation to utter over it, and am fain to use the prophet's language, "who will give waters to my head and a fountain of tears to my eyes[4]?" Yet anticipating your complaint, beloved, I have entreated our most clement and Christian Emperor for a remedy of these great evils, and by our sons and assistants Gerontius and Olympius have at a different time demanded that he should make haste to purge of a heresy already condemned the church of that city, in which so many Catholic teachers have flourished, and not allow murderous spirits whom no reverence for place or time[5] could deter from shedding their ruler's blood, to gain anything from his clemency, more particularly when they desire to reconsider the council of Chalcedon to the overthrow of the Faith. Accordingly the same reason, beloved, which drove you from your own Sees, ought to console you for your sufferings; for it is certain that afflicted souls, that suffer adversity for His name, are in no wise deprived of the Lord's protection. Bear it therefore bravely, and mindful of that country which is yours, rejoice over your present sojourn in a strange land. Abstain from grieving over your exile and indulge not in sorrow for your present weariness, ye who know that the Apostle glories even in his many perils on behalf of the Lord's Faith. You have One who knows your conflicts and has prepared the rewards of recompense. Let no one shrink from this labour, whose guerdon is to reign and[6] live for ever. Let the feet of all who fight be fixed in the halls of Jerusalem; for in the hope of that retribution they will have no cause to fear the camp nor the onsets of the enemy. Victory is never hard nor triumph difficult over the remnants of an abject foe who has been routed by the whole world alike, especially over those whose ringleaders you see already prostrate. With unceasing prayers, therefore (even as I also have not failed to do), entreat the favour of the most Christian Emperor, who in God's mercy is ready to hear: that in accordance with the letter I have sent[7], he may strengthen the cause of the common Faith with that devotion of mind, which we are well assured he possesses, and in his piety may remove all the harmful charges which the madness of heretics has invented, and arrange for your return, beloved, and so may cause each several province and all the churches with their priests to rejoice in the unshaken peace of Christ. Dated the 1st of Dec. in the consulship of Constantine and Rufus (457).

3 One of three Letters, the other two being CLIV. and CLX., first printed by Quesnel on the authority apparently of a single MS. (Codex Grimanicus), and addressed to the bishops (and clergy) who had fled out of Egypt to Constantinople in consequence of the recent disturbances. Letter CLX. mentions fifteen of them by name but is not otherwise so interesting as CLVIII., the one selected for translation.

4 Jer. ix. 1 (Vulg.)

5 Proterius had been slain in the baptistery *die Cœnæ Domini* (? Thursday in Holy Week)

6 The MS. reads *vel* here, but I think the Ball. are right in maintaining that Leo does at times use *vel* for *et*.

7 Viz. Lett. CLVI. q.v.

LETTER CLIX.

To Nicætas, Bishop of Aquileia.

(Leo, the bishop, to Nicætas, bishop of Aquileia, greeting.)

I. *Prefatory.*

My son Adeodatus, deacon of our See, on returning to us has delivered your request, beloved, to receive from us the authority of the Apostolic See upon matters which seem indeed to be hard to decide, but which we must make provision for with a view to the necessities of the times that the wounds which have been inflicted by the attacks of the enemy may be healed chiefly by the agency of religion.

II. *About the women who married again when their husbands were taken prisoners.*

As then you say that through the disasters of war and through the grievous inroads of the enemy families have in certain cases been so broken up that the husbands have been carried off into captivity and their wives remain forsaken, and these latter thinking their own husbands either dead or never likely to be freed from their masters, have contracted another marriage under stress of loneliness, and as, now that the state of things has improved through the LORD's help, some of those who were thought to have perished have returned, you seem, dear brother, naturally to be in doubt what ought to be settled by us about women thus joined to other husbands. But because we know it is written that "a woman is joined to a man by GOD[8]," and again, we are aware of the precept that "what GOD hath joined, man may not put asunder[9]," we are bound to hold that the compact of the lawful marriage must be renewed, and after the removal of the evils inflicted by the enemy, what each lawfully had must be restored to him; and we must take every pains that each should recover what is his own.

III. *Whether he is blameable who has taken the prisoner's wife?*

But notwithstanding let him not be held blameable and treated as the invader of another's right, who took the place of the husband, who was thought no longer alive. For thus many things which belonged to those led into captivity happened to pass into the possession of others, and yet it is altogether fair that on their return their property should be restored. And if this is duly observed in the case of slaves or of lands, or even of houses and personal goods, how much more ought it to be done in the restoration of wives, that what has been disturbed by the necessities of war may be restored by the remedy of peace?

IV. *The wife must be restored to her first husband.*

And, therefore, if husbands who have returned after a long captivity still feel such affection for their wives as to desire them to return to partnership[1], that, which necessity brought about, must be passed over and judged blameless and the demands of fidelity satisfied.

V. *Women must be excommunicated who refuse to return.*

And if any women are so possessed by love of their later husbands as to prefer to remain with them than to return to their lawful partners, they are deservedly to be branded: so that they be even deprived of the Church's communion; for in a pardonable matter they have chosen to taint themselves with crime, showing that they have sought their own pleasure in their incontinence, when a rightful restitution could have obtained their forgiveness. Let them return then to their former state and make voluntary reparation, nor let that which a condition of necessity extorted from them be by any means turned into disgrace through evil desires; because, as those women who refuse to return to their husbands are to be held unholy, so they who return to an affection entered on with GOD's sanction are deservedly to be praised.

VI. *About captives, who were compelled to eat of sacrificial food.*

Concerning those Christians who are asserted to have been polluted with sacrificial food, while among those by whom they were taken prisoners, we have thought it right to make this reply to your enquiry, dear brother, that they be purged by a satisfactory penitence which is to be measured not so much by the duration of the process as by the intensity of the feeling. And whether their compliance was wrung from them by terror or hunger, there need be no hesitation at acquitting them, since the food was taken from fear or want, not from superstitious reverence.

VII. *About those who in fear or by mistake were re-baptized*

But as to those about whom you thought, beloved, we ought likewise to be consulted who were either forced by fear or led by mistake to repeat their baptism, and now understand that they acted contrary to the ordinances of the catholic Faith, such moderation must be observed towards them that they be received into full communion with us, but not without the healing of penitence and the imposition of the bishop's hands, the length of the penance (with due regard to moderation) being left to your judgment, as you shall perceive the minds of the penitents to be disposed: in which you must not forget to consider old age, illness, and other risks. For if a man be in so dangerous a case that his life is despaired of, while he is still under penance, he should receive the gracious aid of communion by the priest's tender care.

VIII. *About baptism by heretics.*

For they who have received baptism from heretics, not having been previously baptized, are to be confirmed by imposition of hands with only the invocation of the Holy Ghost, because they have received the bare form of baptism without the power of sanctification[2]. And this regulation, as you know, we

---

[8] Prov. xix 14 (LXX.). [9] Matt. xix. 6.

[1] There is little doubt, I think, that the return of the wife was at the husband's option in Leo's opinion, and could not be forced upon him.

[2] Leo repeats this injunction in Letter CLXVI. chap. 2. and Lett. CLXVII., inquiry 18. Quesnel identifies this ceremony with the right of Confirmation, but the Ballerinii are probably

require to be kept in all the churches, that the font once entered may not be defiled by repetition, as the LORD says, "One LORD, one faith, one baptism." And that washing may not be polluted by repetition, but, as we have said, only the sanctification of the Holy Ghost invoked, that what no one can receive from heretics may be obtained from catholic priests. This letter of ours, which we have sent in reply to the inquiries of the brotherhood, you shall bring to the knowledge of all your brethren and fellow-bishops of the province, that our authority, now that it is given, may avail for the general observance. Dated 21st March, in the consulship of Majorian Augustus (458).

LETTER CLX.

(See Letter CLVIII.)

LETTER CLXI.

TO THE PRESBYTERS, DEACONS AND CLERGY OF THE CHURCH OF CONSTANTINOPLE.

(Exhorting them to remain stedfast in the Faith as fixed at Chalcedon, and to have no dealings with Atticus and Andrew unless they recant.)

LETTER CLXII.

TO LEO AUGUSTUS.

By the hand of Philoxenus *agens in rebus* [2a].

Leo the Bishop to Leo Augustus.

I. *The decrees of Chalcedon and Nicæa are identical and final.*

With much joy my mind exults in the LORD, and great is my cause for thankfulness, now that I perceive your clemency's most excellent faith to be in all things enlarged by the gifts of heavenly grace, and I experience by increased diligence the devotion of a priestly mind in you. For in your Majesty's communications it is beyond doubt revealed what the Holy Spirit is working through you for the good of the whole Church, and how greatly it is to be desired by the prayers of all the faithful that your empire may be everywhere extended with glory, seeing that besides your care for things temporal you so perseveringly exercise a religious foresight in the service of what is divine and eternal: to wit that the catholic Faith, which alone gives life to and alone hallows mankind, may abide in the one confession, and the dissensions which spring from the variety of earthly opinions may be driven away, most glorious Emperor, from that solid Rock, on which the city of GOD is built. And these gifts of GOD will at last be granted us from Him, if we be not found ungrateful for what has been vouchsafed, and as though what we have gained were naught, we seek not rather the very opposite. For to seek what has been discovered, to reconsider what has been completed, and to demolish what has been defined, what else is it but to return no thanks for things gained and to indulge the unholy longings of deadly lust on the food of the forbidden tree? And hence by deigning to show a more careful regard for the peace of the universal Church, you manifestly recognize what is the design of the heretics' mighty intrigues that a more careful discussion should take place between the disciples of Eutyches and Dioscorus and the emissary of the Apostolic See, as if nothing had already been defined, and that what with the glad approval of the catholic priests of the whole world was determined at the holy Synod of Chalcedon should be rendered invalid to the detriment also of the most sacred Council of Nicæa. For what in our own days at Chalcedon was determined concerning our LORD Jesus Christ's Incarnation, was also so defined at Nicæa by that mystic number of Fathers [3], lest the confession of catholics should believe that GOD's Only-begotten Son was in aught unequal to the Father, or that when He was made Son of man He had not the true nature of our flesh and soul.

II. *The wicked designs of heretics must be stedfastly resisted.*

Therefore we must abhor and persistently avoid what heretical deceit is striving to obtain, nor must what has been well and fully defined be brought again under discussion, lest we ourselves should seem at the will of condemned men to have doubts concerning things which it is clear agree throughout with the authority of Prophets, Evangelists, and Apostles. And hence, if there are any who disagree with these heaven-inspired decisions, let them be left to their own opinions and depart from the unity of the Church with that perverse sect which they have chosen. For it can in no wise be that men who dare to speak against divine mysteries are associated in any communion with us. Let them pride themselves on the emptiness of their talk and boast of the cleverness of their arguments against the Faith: we

---

right in thinking this a mistake, and in identifying it with the *manuum impositio in pœnitentiam* mentioned by Cyprian and other fathers. See Lett. CLXVI. chap. 2 n. 5b.

[2a] Cf. Lett. XCV. n. 6.

[3] The number was 318: cf. Lett. CVI. 2, where the exact number is quoted and the explanation perhaps given of Leo's epithet "mystic" here applied to it.

are pleased to obey the Apostle's precepts, where he says, "See that no one deceive you with philosophy and vain seductions of men[4]." For according to the same Apostle, "if I build up those things which I destroyed, I prove myself a transgressor[5]," and subject myself to those conditions of punishment which not only the authority of Prince Marcian of blessed memory, but I myself also by my consent have accepted. Because as you have justly and truthfully maintained perfection admits of no increase nor fulness of addition. And hence, since I know you, venerable Prince, imbued as you are with the purest light of truth, waver in no part of the Faith, but with just and perfect judgment distinguish right from wrong, and separate what is to be embraced from what is to be rejected, I beseech you not to think that my humility is to be blamed for want of confidence, since my cautiousness is not only in the interests of the universal Church but also for the furtherance of your own glory, that under your reign the unscrupulousness of heretics may not seem to be advanced and the security of catholics disturbed.

III. *He promises to send envoys not to discuss with the Eutychians, but to explain the Faith to the Emperor.*

Although, therefore, I am very confident of the piety of your heart in all things, and perceive that through the Spirit of God dwelling in you, you are sufficiently instructed, nor can any error delude your faith, yet I will endeavour to follow your bidding so far as to send certain of my brothers to represent my person before you, and to set forth what the Apostolic rule of Faith is, although, as I have said, it is well known to you, in all things making it clear and certain that they are not in any way to be reckoned among catholics, who do not accept the definitions of the venerable Synod of Nicæa or the ordinances of the holy Council of Chalcedon, inasmuch as it is evident the holy decrees of both proceed from the Evangelical and Apostolical source, and whatever is not of Christ's watering is like a snake-poisoned draught[6]. Your Majesty should understand beforehand, most venerable Emperor, that those whom I undertake to send will come from the Apostolic See, not to fight with the enemies of the Faith nor to strive against any, because of matters already settled as it has pleased God both at Nicæa and at Chalcedon we dare not enter upon any discussion, as if what so great an authority has fixed by the Holy Spirit were doubtful or weak.

4 Col. ii. 8. 5 Gal. ii. 18. 6 *Poculi esse viperei.*

IV. *The heretics must be forced to give up their usurpations and left to the judgment of God.*

But we do not refuse the assistance of our ministry for the instruction of our little ones, who after being fed with milk desire to be satisfied with more solid food: and as we do not scorn the simple folk, so we will have no dealings with rebel heretics, remembering the Lord's command, who says, "Give not that which is holy to the dogs, nor cast your pearls before swine[7]." Surely it is altogether unworthy and unjust to admit to freedom of discussion men whom the Holy Spirit describes in the words of the prophet, "the sons of the stranger have lied unto me[8]." For even though they resist not the Gospel, yet they have shown themselves to be of those of whom it is written "they profess that they know God but by their deeds they deny Him[9]," while the blood of just Abel[1] still cries against wicked Cain[1], who being rebuked by the Lord did not set quietly about his repentance but burst forth into murder. Whose punishment we wish to be reserved for the Lord's judgment in such a way that, unprincipled plunderer and blood-thirsty murderer as he is, he may be thrown back upon himself and relinquish what is ours. We pray you also not to suffer the lamentable captivity of the holy church of Alexandria to be any further prolonged, which by the help of your faith and justice ought to be restored to its liberty, that through all the cities of Egypt the dignity of the Fathers and their priestly rights may be restored. Dated 21st of March in the consulship of Leo and Majorian Augusti (458).

LETTER CLXIII.

To Anatolius, Bishop of Constantinople.

By Patritius the deacon.

(Glorying over the harshness of his former letter, to which Anatolius had objected, but persisting that he is not satisfied with the explanation Atticus had furnished of his orthodoxy.)

LETTER CLXIV[2].

To Leo Augustus.

Leo, the bishop, to Leo Augustus.

I. *He sends envoys but deprecates any fresh discussion of the Faith.*

Rejoicing that it has been proved to me by

7 S. Matt. vii. 6. 8 Ps. xviii. 44 (Vulg.). 9 Tit. i. 16.

1 Sc. in the persons of Proterius and Timothy Ælurus.

2 Portions of this letter are found quoted by various ancient Fathers, e.g. by Popes Vigilius and Pelagius II. in the sixth cent.; by Facundus, bishop of Hermiæ, in the same century, and about one half of the whole by Prudentius, bishop of Troyes (ninth cent.) in his famous treatise on Predestination against John Scotus

many clear proofs with what earnestness you consult the interests of the universal Church, I have not delayed to obey your Majesty's commands on the first opportunity, by despatching Domitian and Geminian my brothers and fellow-bishops, who in furtherance of my earnest prayers, shall entreat you for the peaceful acceptance of the gospel-teaching and obtain the liberty of the Faith in which through the instruction of the Holy Spirit you yourself are so conspicuously eminent, now that the enemies of Christ are driven far away, who even if they had wished to conceal their madness, could not lie hid, because the holy simplicity of the LORD's flock is very different from the pretences of beasts who hide themselves in sheeps' clothing, nor can they creep in by hypocrisy now that their exceeding madness has revealed them. Recognize, therefore, august and venerable Emperor, how that you are called by Divine providence to the guardianship of the whole world, and understand what aid you owe to your Mother, the Church, who makes especial boast of you. Disputes that are ended must not be allowed to rise with renewed vigour against the triumphs of the Almighty's right hand, especially when this can in no wise be allowed to heretics, whose attempts have long ago been condemned and the labours of the faithful have a just claim to this result, that all the fulness of the Church shall remain secure in the completeness of her unity, and that nothing whatever of what has been well laid down shall be reconsidered, because, after constitutions have been legitimately framed under Divine guidance, to wish still to wrangle is the sign not of a peace-making but of a rebellious spirit, as says the Apostle, "for to strive with words is profitable for nothing, but for the subverting of them that hear[2]."

II. *In matters of Faith human rhetoric is out of place.*

For if it be always free for human fancies to assert themselves in dispute, there never will be wanting men who will dare to oppose the Truth, and to put their trust in the glib utterances of this world's wisdom, whereas the Christian Faith and wisdom knows from the teaching of our LORD Jesus Christ Himself how strictly it ought to shun this most harmful vanity. For when Christ was about to summon all nations to the illumination of the Faith, He chose those who were to devote themselves to the preaching of the Gospel not from among philosophers or orators, but took humble fishermen as the instruments by which He would reveal Himself, lest the heavenly teaching, which was of itself full of mighty power, should seem to need the aid of words. And hence the Apostle protests and says, "For Christ sent me not to baptize but to preach the Gospel, not in wisdom of words lest the cross of Christ should be made void; for the word of the cross is to them indeed that perish foolishness, but to those which are being saved it is the power of GOD. For it is written, I will destroy the wisdom of the wise and the prudence of the prudent will I reject. Where is the wise? where is the scribe? where is the inquirer of this age? has not GOD made foolish the wisdom of this world[3]?" For rhetorical arguments and clever debates of man's device make their chief boast in this, that in doubtful matters which are obscured by the variety of opinions they can induce their hearers to accept that view which each has chosen for his own genius and eloquence to bring forward; and thus it happens that what is maintained with the greatest eloquence is reckoned the truest. But Christ's Gospel needs not this art; for in it the true teaching stands revealed by its own light: nor is there any seeking for that which shall please the ear, when to know Who is the Teacher is sufficient for true faith.

III. *Eutyches' dogma is condemned by the testimony of Scripture and cannot further be entertained.*

But nothing severs those who are deceived by their own inventions, from the light of the Gospel so much as their not thinking that the LORD's Incarnation appertains in a true sense to man's, that is, our, nature: as if it were unworthy of GOD's glory that the majesty of the impassible Word should have taken the reality of human flesh, whereas men's salvation could not otherwise have been restored had not He Who is in the form of GOD deigned also to take the form of a slave. And hence since the holy Synod of Chalcedon, which was attended by all the provinces of the Roman world and obtained universal acceptance for its decisions, and is in complete harmony therein with the most sacred council of Nicæa, has cut off all the wicked followers of the Eutychian dogma from the body of the catholic communion, how shall any of the lapsed regain the peace of the church, without purging himself by a full course of penitence? For what licence can be granted them for discussing, when they have deserved to be condemned by a just and holy

Erigena. Quesnel, however, appears to have been the first to print it as a whole *ex codice Grimanico;* after which the Ball. also discovered it in the Ratisbon MS.

[2] Loosely quoted from 2 Tim. ii. 14.

[3] 1 Cor. i. 17—20.

judgment, so that they might most truly fall under that sentence of the blessed Apostle, wherewith at the very outset of the infant Church he overthrew the enemies of Christ's cross, saying: "every spirit which confesses Jesus Christ to have come in the flesh is of God, and every spirit which dissolves Jesus is not of God, but this is antichrist [4]." And this pre-existent teaching of the Holy Ghost we must faithfully and stedfastly make use of, lest, by admitting the discussions of such men the authority of the divinely-inspired decrees be diminished, when in all parts of your kingdom and in all borders of the earth that Faith which was confirmed at Chalcedon is being established on the surest basis of peace, nor is any one worthy of the name of Christian who cuts himself off from communion with us. Of whom the Apostle says, "a man that is heretical after a first and a second admonition, avoid, knowing that such a one is perverse and condemned by his own judgment [4a]."

IV. *If the Divine mercy is to be exercised, the heretics must cease entirely from the error of their ways.*

What therefore the unholy parricide has perpetrated by seizing on the holy Church and cruelly murdering its very ruler, cannot be expiated by man's forgiveness, unless He Who alone can rightly punish such things, and alone can of His unspeakable mercy remit them, be propitiated. But though we are not anxious for vengeance, we cannot in any way be allied with the devil's servants. Yet if we learn they are quitting the ranks of heresy, repenting them of their error and turning from the weapons of discord to the lamentations of sorrow, we also can intercede for them, lest they perish for ever, thus following the example of the Lord's loving-kindness, who, when nailed to the wood of the cross prayed for His persecutors, "Father, forgive them; for they know not what they do [5]." And that Christian love may do this profitably for its enemies, wicked heretics must cease to harass God's ever religious and ever devout Church; they must not dare to disturb the souls of the simple by their falsehoods, to the end that, where in all former times the purest faith has flourished, the teaching of the Gospel and of the Apostles may now also have free course; because we also imitating, so far as we can, the Divine mercy desire no one to be punished by justice, but all to be released by mercy.

V. *Let him restore the refugee clergy and laity and utterly reject those who persist in heresy.*

I entreat your clemency, listen to the suggestions of my brethren already mentioned, whom, as I some time ago have said in a former letter [5a], I have sent not to wrangle with the condemned, but merely to intercede with you for the stability of the catholic Faith. And in accordance with your faith in and regard for the Divine Majesty this especially you should grant, that completely setting aside the contentions of heretics you should deign to bestow a merciful attention on those who have fallen upon such evil days, and, after restoring the liberty of the church of Alexandria to its pristine state, should set up there a bishop who, upholding the decrees of the Synod of Chalcedon and agreeing with the ordinances of the Gospel, shall be able to restore peace among that greatly disturbed people. Those bishops and clergy also whom the unholy parricide has driven out of their churches, should be recalled at your Majesty's command, all others also, whom a like maliciousness has banished from their dwellings, being restored to their former estate, to the end that we may have due cause fully and perfectly to rejoice in the grace of God and your faith without any further noise of strife. For if any one is so forgetful of the Christian hope and his own salvation as to venture by any dispute to assail the Evangelical and Apostolical decrees of the holy Synod of Chalcedon, thus overthrowing the most sacred Council of Nicæa also, him with all heretics who have held blasphemous and abominable views on the Incarnation of our Lord Jesus Christ we condemn by a like anathema and equal curse, so that, without refusing the remedy of repentance to those who make full and legitimate atonement, the sentence of the Synod, which is based on truth, may rest upon those who still resist. Dated 17th of August, in the consulship of Leo and Majorian Augusti (458).

LETTER CLXV.

To Leo Augustus.

[This letter, which is sometimes called the Second Tome, contains the detailed statement of the catholic doctrine of the Incarnation, which Leo had promised the Emperor in Letter CLVI. It consists of 9 chapters, but, as chaps. iii. to viii. and parts of ii. and ix. are almost identical in language with Letter CXXIV., already given in full, I have not thought it necessary to reproduce the letter here. At the end a long series of quotations

---

4 1 John iv. 2, 3. For the reading *solvit* (dissolves), cf. Lett. XXVIII. (Tome), chap. 5 and note.

4a Tit. iii. 10, 11.

5 S. Luke xxiii. 34.

5a Viz. Lett. CLXII. chap. iii.

from Hilary, Ambrose and other Fathers bearing upon the doctrine are also added, but these also are dispensed with in accordance with our general practice, as we are now presenting Leo and no one else to the reader.]

LETTER CLXVI.

To Neo, Bishop of Ravenna.

Leo, the bishop, to Neo, bishop of Ravenna, greeting.

I. *Those, who being taken captives in infancy cannot remember or bring witnesses of their baptism, must not be denied this sacrament.*

We have indeed frequently, God's Spirit instructing us, steadied the brethren's hearts, when they were tottering on the slippery places of doubtful questions, by formulating an answer either out of the teaching of the Holy Scriptures or from the rules of the Fathers: but lately in Synod a new and hitherto unheard-of subject of debate has arisen. For at the instance of certain brethren we have discovered that some of the prisoners of war, on their free return to their own homes, such to wit as went into captivity at an age when they could have no sure knowledge of anything, crave the healing waters of baptism, but in the ignorance of infancy cannot remember whether they have received the mystery and rites of baptism, and that therefore in this uncertainty of defective recollection their souls are brought into jeopardy, so long as under a show of caution they are denied a grace, which is withheld, because it is thought to have been bestowed. And so, since certain brethren in a not unjustifiable fear have hesitated to perform the rites of the Lord's mystery, at a synodal meeting, as we have said, we have received a formal request for advice on this matter, and in carefully discussing it, we have desired to weigh each member s opinion, and to handle it in so cautious a manner as to arrive with certainty at the truth by making use of the knowledge of many. Consequently the same things, which have come into our mind by the Divine inspiration, have received the assent and confirmation of a large number of the brethren. And so we are bound before all things to take heed lest, while we hold fast to a certain show of caution, we incur a loss of souls who are to be regenerated. For who is so given over to suspicions as to decide that to be true which without any evidence he suspects by mere guesswork? And so wherever the man himself who is anxious for the new birth does not recollect his baptism, and no one can bear witness about him being unaware of his consecration to God, there is no possibility for sin to creep in, seeing that, so far as their knowledge goes, neither the bestower or receiver of the consecration is guilty. We know indeed that an unpardonable offence is committed, whenever in accordance with the institutions of heretics which the holy Fathers have condemned, any one is forced twice to enter the font, which is but once available for those who are to be re-born, in opposition to the Apostle's teaching[5b], which speaks to us of One Godhead in Trinity, one confession in Faith, one sacrament in Baptism. But in this nothing similar is to be apprehended, since, what is not known to have been done at all, cannot come under the charge of repetition. And so, whenever such a case occurs, first sift it by careful investigation, and spend a considerable time, unless his last end is near, in inquiring whether there be absolutely no one who by his testimony can assist the other's ignorance. And when it is established that the man who requires the sacrament of baptism is prevented by a mere baseless suspicion, let him come boldly to obtain the grace, of which he is conscious of no trace in himself. Nor need we fear thus to open the door of salvation which has not been shown to have been entered before.

II. *Baptism by heretics must not be invalidated by second baptism.*

But if it is established that a man has been baptized by heretics, on him the mystery of regeneration must in no wise be repeated, but only that conferred which was wanting before, so that he may obtain the power of the Holy Ghost by the laying on of the Bishop's hands[6]. This decision, beloved brother, we wish to be brought to the knowledge of you all generally, to the end that God's mercy may not be refused to those who desire to be saved through undue timidity. Dated the 24th of Oct., in the consulship of Majorian Augustus (458).

LETTER CLXVII[7].

To Rusticus, Bishop of Gallia Narbonensis, with the replies to his Questions on various points.

Leo, the bishop, to Rusticus, bishop of Gallia Narbonensis.

5b Viz. Eph. iv. 5. It will be remembered that the practice of re-baptism was very definitely condemned in the times of S. Cyprian (3rd cent.), who himself went wrong in advocating it in the case of heretics.

6 See n. 2 to Lett. CLIX. chap. 8.

7 The date of this important letter has been variously conjectured, Quesnel assigning it to the years 442-4, Sirmond and Baluze to 452, and the Ball. preferring 458 or 9.

I. *He exhorts him to act with moderation towards two bishops who have offended him.*

Your letter, brother, which Hermes your archdeacon[8] brought, I have gladly received; the number of different matters it contains makes it indeed lengthy, but not so tedious to me on a patient perusal that any point should be passed over, amid the cares that press upon me from all sides. And hence having grasped the gist of your allegation and reviewed what took place at the inquiry of the bishops and leading men[9], we gather that Sabinian and Leo, presbyters, lacked confidence in your[1] action, and that they have no longer any just cause for complaint, seeing that of their own accord they withdrew from the discussion that had been begun. What form or what measure of justice you ought to mete out to them I leave to your own discretion, advising you, however, with the exhortation of love that to the healing of the sick you ought to apply spiritual medicine, and that remembering the Scripture which says "be not over just[2]," you should act with mildness towards these who in zeal for chastity seem to have exceeded the limits of vengeance, lest the devil, who deceived the adulterers, should triumph over the avengers of the adultery.

II. *He expostulates with him for wishing to give up his office, which would imply distrust of* GOD'S *promises.*

But I am surprised, beloved, that you are so disturbed by opposition in consequence of offences, from whatever cause arising, as to say you would rather be relieved of the labours of your bishopric, and live in quietness and ease than continue in the office committed to you. But since the LORD says, "blessed is he who shall persevere unto the end[3]," whence shall come this blessed perseverance, except from the strength of patience? For as the Apostle proclaims, "All who would live godly in Christ shall suffer persecution[4]." And it is not only to be reckoned persecution, when sword or fire or other active means are used against the Christian religion; for the direst persecution is often inflicted by nonconformity of practice and persistent disobedience and the barbs of ill-natured tongues: and since all the members of the Church are always liable to these attacks, and no portion of the faithful are free from temptation, so that a life neither of ease nor of labour is devoid of danger, who shall guide the ship amidst the waves of the sea, if the helmsman quit his post? Who shall guard the sheep from the treachery of wolves, if the shepherd himself be not on the watch? Who, in fine, shall resist the thieves and robbers, if love of quietude draw away the watchman that is set to keep the outlook from the strictness of his watch? One must abide, therefore, in the office committed to him and in the task undertaken. Justice must be stedfastly upheld and mercy lovingly extended. Not men, but their sins must be hated[5]. The proud must be rebuked, the weak must be borne with; and those sins which require severer chastisement must be dealt with in the spirit not of vindictiveness but of desire to heal. And if a fiercer storm of tribulation fall upon us, let us not be terror-stricken as if we had to overcome the disaster in our own strength, since both our Counsel and our Strength is Christ, and through Him we can do all things, without Him nothing, Who, to confirm the preachers of the Gospel and the ministers of the mysteries, says, "Lo, I am with you all the days even to the consummation of the age[6]." And again He says, "these things I have spoken unto you that in me ye may have peace. In this world ye shall have tribulation, but be of good cheer, because I have overcome the world[7]." The promises, which are as plain as they can be, we ought not to let any causes of offence to weaken, lest we should seem ungrateful to GOD for making us His chosen vessels, since His assistance is powerful as His promises are true.

III. *Many of the questions raised could be more easily settled in a personal interview than on paper.*

On those points of inquiry, beloved, which your archdeacon has brought me separately written out, it would be easier to arrive at conclusions on each point face to face, if you could grant us the advantage of your presence. For since some questions seem to exceed the limits of ordinary diligence, I perceive that they are better suited to conversation than to writing: for as there are certain things which can in no wise be controverted, so there are many things which require to be modified either by considerations of age or by the necessities of the case; always provided that we remember in things which are doubtful or obscure, that

---

[8] In an inscription quoted from Gruter and Baluze by Quesnel, Hermes is mentioned as *diaconus* to *Rusticus episcopus*. He was afterwards made bp of Biterra, but being unfairly expelled by that city, he succeeded Rusticus in Narbonensis.

[9] *Honorati.*

[1] *Tuæ*, others *suæ* (the bishops).

[2] Eccl. vii. 17 (A.V. over *wicked*).

[3] S. Matt. xxiv. 13.

[4] 2 Tim. iii. 12.

[5] The thought of this fine passage is more fully worked out in Sermon XLVIII., chaps. 2 and 3. Cf. esp. the remark, *bellum vitiis potius quam hominibus indicunt, "nulli malum pro malo reddentes" sed correctionem peccantium semper optantes.*

[6] S. Matt. xxviii. 20.

[7] S. John xvi. 33.

must be followed which is found to be neither contrary to the commands of the Gospel nor opposed to the decrees of the holy Fathers.

QUESTION I. *Concerning a presbyter or deacon, who falsely claims to be a bishop, and those whom they have ordained.*

REPLY. No consideration permits men to be reckoned among bishops who have not been elected by the clergy, demanded by the laity, and consecrated by the bishops of the province with the assent of the metropolitan [8]. And hence, since the question often arises concerning advancement unduly obtained, who need doubt that that can in no wise be which is not shown to have been conferred on them. And if any clerics have been ordained by such false bishops in those churches which have bishops of their own, and their ordination took place with the consent and approval of the proper bishops, it may be held valid on condition that they continue in the same churches. Otherwise it must be held void, not being connected with any place nor resting on any authority.

QUESTION II. *Concerning a presbyter or deacon, who on his crime being known asks for public penance, whether it is to be granted him by laying on of hands?*

REPLY. It is contrary to the custom of the Church that they who have been dedicated to the dignity of the presbyterate or the rank of the diaconate, should receive the remedy of penitence by laying on of hands for any crime; which doubtless descends from the Apostles' tradition, according to what is written, "If a priest shall have sinned, who shall pray for him [9]?" And hence such men when they have lapsed in order to obtain GOD's mercy must seek private retirement, where their atonement may be profitable as well as adequate.

QUESTION III. *Concerning those who minister at the altar and have wives, whether they may lawfully cohabit with them?*

REPLY. The law of continence is the same for the ministers [1] of the altar as for bishops and priests, who when they were laymen or readers, could lawfully marry and have offspring. But when they reached to the said ranks, what was before lawful ceased to be so. And hence, in order that their wedlock may become spiritual instead of carnal, it behoves them not to put away their wives but to "have them as though they had them not [2]," whereby both the affection of their wives may be retained and the marriage functions cease.

QUESTION IV. *Concerning a presbyter or deacon who has given his unmarried daughter in marriage to a man who already had a woman joined to him, by whom he had also had children.*

REPLY. Not every woman that is joined to a man is his wife, even as every son is not his father's heir. But the marriage bond is legitimate between the freeborn and between equals: this was laid down by the LORD long before the Roman law had its beginning. And so a wife is different from a concubine, even as a bondwoman from a freewoman. For which reason also the Apostle in order to show the difference of these persons quotes from Genesis, where it is said to Abraham, "Cast out the bondwoman and her son: for the son of the bondwoman shall not be heir with my son Isaac [3]." And hence, since the marriage tie was from the beginning so constituted as apart from the joining of the sexes to symbolize the mystic union of Christ and His Church, it is undoubted that that woman has no part in matrimony, in whose case it is shown that the mystery of marriage has not taken place. Accordingly a clergyman of any rank who has given his daughter in marriage to a man that has a concubine, must not be considered to have given her to a married man, unless perchance the other woman should appear to have become free, to have been legitimately dowered and to have been honoured by public nuptials.

QUESTION V. *Concerning young women who have married men that have concubines.*

REPLY. Those who are joined to husbands by their fathers' will are free from blame, if the women whom their husbands had were not in wedlock.

QUESTION VI. *Concerning those who leave the women by whom they have children and take wives.*

REPLY. Seeing that the wife is different from the concubine, to turn a bondwoman from one's couch and take a wife whose free birth is assured, is not bigamy but an honourable proceeding.

---

8 The same requisites of ordination of bishops are laid down in Lett. X. chap. 6.

9 1 Sam. ii. 25.

1 The order of sub-deacons (acc. to Quesnel) is here particularly meant: cf. Lett. XIV. chap. 4. The readers (*lectores*) mentioned below were of course one of the Minor Orders of clergy: cf. Bingham, *Antiq.* Bk.V. chap. iii.

2 1 Cor. vii. 29. This was also provided by the Apostolic Canons (quoted by Quesnel), *episcopus aut presbyter uxorem propriam nequaquam sub obtentu religionis abiciat.*

3 Gal. iv. 30, from Gen. xxi. 10.

Question VII. *Concerning those who in sickness accept terms of penitence, and when they have recovered, refuse to keep them.*

Reply. Such men's neglect is to be blamed but not finally to be abandoned, in order that they may be incited by frequent exhortations to carry out faithfully what under stress of need they asked for. For no one is to be despaired of so long as he remain in this body, because sometimes what the diffidence of age puts off is accomplished by maturer counsels.

Question VIII. *Concerning those who on their deathbed promise repentance and die before receiving communion.*

Reply. Their cause is reserved for the judgment of God, in Whose hand it was that their death was put off until the very time of communion. But we cannot be in communion with those, when dead, with whom when alive we were not in communion.

Question IX. *Concerning those who under pressure of great pain ask for penance to be granted them, and when the presbyter has come to give what they seek, if the pain has abated somewhat, make excuses and refuse to accept what is offered.*

Reply. This tergiversation cannot proceed from contempt of the remedy but from fear of falling into worse sin. Hence the penance which is put off, when it is more earnestly sought must not be denied in order that the wounded soul may in whatever way attain to the healing of absolution.

Question X. *Concerning those who have professed repentance, if they begin to go to law in the forum.*

Reply. To demand just debts is indeed one thing and to think nothing of one's own property from the perfection of love is another. But one who craves pardon for unlawful doings ought to abstain even from many things that are lawful, as says the Apostle, "all things are lawful for me, but all things are not expedient[4]." Hence, if the penitent has a matter which perchance he ought not to neglect, it is better for him to have recourse to the judgment of the Church than of the forum.

Question XI. *Concerning those who during or after penance transact business.*

Reply. The nature of their gains either excuses or condemns the trafficker, because there is an honourable and a base kind of profit. Notwithstanding it is more expedient for the penitent to suffer loss than to be involved in the risks of trafficking, because it is hard for sin not to come into transactions between buyer and seller.

Question XII. *Concerning those who return to military service after doing penance.*

Reply. It is altogether contrary to the rules of the Church to return to military service in the world after doing penance, as the Apostle says, "No soldier in God's service entangles himself in the affairs of the world[5]." Hence he is not free from the snares of the devil who wishes to entangle himself in the military service of the world.

Question XIII. *Concerning those who after penance take wives or join themselves to concubines.*

Reply. If a young man under fear of death or the dangers of captivity has done penance, and afterwards fearing to fall into youthful incontinence has chosen to marry a wife lest he should be guilty of fornication, he seems to have comitted a pardonable act, so long as he has known no woman whatever save his wife. Yet herein we lay down no rule, but express an opinion as to what is less objectionable. For according to a true view of the matter nothing better suits him who has done penance than continued chastity both of mind and body.

Question XIV. *Concerning monks who take to military service or to marriage.*

Reply. The monk's vow being undertaken of his own will or wish cannot be given up without sin. For that which a man has vowed to God, he ought also to pay. Hence he who abandons his profession of a single life and betakes himself to military service or to marriage, must make atonement and clear himself publicly, because although such service may be innocent and the married state honourable, it is transgression to have forsaken the higher choice.

Question XV. *Concerning young women who have worn the religious habit for some time but have not been dedicated, if they afterwards marry.*

Reply. Young women, who without being forced by their parents' command but of their own free-will have taken the vow and habit of virginity, if afterwards they choose wedlock, act wrongly, even though they have not re-

4 1 Cor. vi. 12.

5 2 Tim. ii. 4.

ceived dedication: of which they would doubtless not have been defrauded, if they had abided by their vow.

QUESTION XVI. *Concerning those who have been left as infants by Christian parents, if no proof of their baptism can be found whether they ought to be baptized?*

REPLY. If no proof exist among their kinsfolk and relations, nor among the clergy or neighbours whereby those, about whom the question is raised, may be proved to have been baptized, steps must be taken for their regeneration: lest they evidently perish; for in their case reason does not allow that what is not shown to have been done should seem to be repeated.

QUESTION XVII. *Concerning those who have been captured by the enemy and are not aware whether they have been baptized but know they were several times taken to church by their parents, whether they can or ought to be baptized when they come back to Roman territory*[6]*?*

REPLY. Those who can remember that they used to go to church with their parents can remember whether they received what used to be given to their parents[7]. But if this also has escaped their memory, it seems that that must be bestowed on them which is not known to have been bestowed because there can be no presumptuous rashness where the most loyal carefulness has been exercised.

QUESTION XVIII. *Concerning those who have come from Africa or Mauretania and know not in what sect they were baptized, what ought to be done in their case*[6]*?*

REPLY. These persons are not doubtful of their baptism, but profess ignorance as to the faith of those who baptized them: and hence since they have received the form of baptism in some way or other, they are not to be baptized but are to be united to the catholics by imposition of hands, after the invocation of the Holy Spirit's power, which they could not receive from heretics.

QUESTION XIX. *Concerning those who after being baptized in infancy were captured by the Gentiles, and lived with them after the manner of the Gentiles, when they come back to Roman territory as still young men, if they seek communion, what shall be done?*

REPLY. If they have only lived with Gentiles and eaten sacrificial food, they can be purged by fasting and laying on of hands, in order that for the future abstaining from things offered to idols, they may be partakers of Christ's mysteries. But if they have either worshipped idols or been polluted with manslaughter or fornication, they must not be admitted to communion, except by public penance.

LETTER CLXVIII.

TO ALL THE BISHOPS OF CAMPANIA, SAMNIUM AND PICENUM.

(Rebuking them first for performing baptisms without due preparation or sufficient cause on ordinary saints'-days (Easter and Whitsuntide being the only recognized times), and secondly for requiring from penitents that a list of their offences should be read out publicly, a practice which is in many ways objectionable.)

LETTER CLXIX.

TO LEO AUGUSTUS.

Leo, the bishop, to Leo Augustus.

I. *He heartily thanks the Emperor for what he has done, and asks him to complete the work in any way he can.*

If we should seek to reward your Majesty's glorious resolution in defence of the Faith with all the praise that the greatness of the issue demands, we should be found unequal to the task of giving thanks and celebrating the joy of the universal Church with our feeble tongue. But His worthier recompense awaits your acts and deserts, in whose cause you have shown so excellent a zeal, and are now triumphing gloriously over the attainment of the wished-for end. Your clemency must know therefore that all the churches of GOD join in praising you and rejoicing that the unholy parricide has been cast off from the neck of the Alexandrine church, and that GOD's people, on whom the abominable robber has been so great a burden, restored to the ancient liberty of the Faith, can now be recalled into the way of salvation by the preaching of faithful priests, when it sees the whole hotbed of pestilence done away with in the person of the originator himself. Now therefore, because you have accomplished this by firm resolution and stedfast will, complete your tale of work for the Faith by passing such decrees as shall be well-pleasing to GOD in favour of this city's catholic ruler[8], who is tainted by no trace of the heresy

[6] On these points, cf. Letter CLXVI., to Neo, bp. of Ravenna.
[7] Viz. the sacred elements of the Eucharist.

[8] This is another Timothy surnamed Solophaciolus, supposed to be the same as that *Timotheus presbyter et œconomus Ecclesiæ*, mentioned among the Egyptian refugees who petitioned the Emperor against Ælurus

now so often condemned: lest, perchance, the wound apparently healed but still lurking beneath the scar should grow, and the Christian laity, which by your public action has been freed from the perversity of heretics, should again fall a prey to deadly poison.

II. *Good works as well as integrity of faith is required in a priest.*

But you see, venerable Emperor, and clearly understand, that in the person, whose excommunication is contemplated, it is not only the integrity of his faith that must be considered; for even, if that could be purged by any punishments and confessions, and completely restored by any conditions, yet the wicked and bloody deeds that have been committed can never be done away by the protestations of plausible words: because in God's pontiff, and particularly in the priest of so great a church, the sound of the tongue and the utterance of the lips is not enough, and nothing is of avail, if God makes proclamation with His voice and the mind is convicted of blasphemy. For of such the Holy Ghost speaks by the Apostle, "having an appearance of godliness, but denying the power thereof," and again elsewhere, "they profess that they know God, but in deeds they deny Him[9]." And hence, since in every member of the Church both the integrity of the true Faith and abundance of good works is looked for, how much more ought both these things to predominate in the chief pontiff, because the one without the other cannot be in union with the Body of Christ.

III. *Timothy's request for indulgence on the score of orthodoxy must not be allowed.*

Nor need we now state all that makes Timothy accursed, since what has been done through him and on his account, has abundantly and conspicuously come to the knowledge of the whole world, and whatever has been perpetrated by an unruly mob against justice, all rests on his head, whose wishes were served by its mad hands. And hence, even if in his profession of faith he neglects nothing, and deceives us in nothing, it best consorts with your glory absolutely to exclude him from this design of his[1], because in the bishop of so great a city the universal Church ought to rejoice with holy exultation, so that the true peace of the Lord may be glorified not only by the preaching of the Faith, but also by the example of men's conduct. Dated 17th of June, in the consulship of Magnus and Apollonius (460). (By the hand of Philoxenus *agens in rebus*[1a].)

LETTER CLXX.

To Gennadius, Bishop of Constantinople[2].

(Complaining of Timothy Ælurus having been allowed to come to Constantinople, and saying that there is no hope of his restitution.)

LETTER CLXXI.

To Timothy, Bishop of Alexandria.

Leo, the bishop, to Timothy, catholic bishop of the church of Alexandria.

I. *He congratulates him on his election, and bids him win back wanderers to the fold.*

It is clearly apparent from the brightness of the sentiment quoted by the Apostle, that "all things work together for good to them that love God[3]," and by the dispensation of God's pity, where adversities are received, there also prosperity is given. This the experience of the Alexandrine church shows, in which the moderation and long suffering of the humble has laid up for themselves great store in return for their patience: because "the Lord is nigh them that are of a contrite heart, and shall save those that are humble in spirit[4]," our noble Prince's faith being glorified in all things, through whom "the right-hand of the Lord hath done great acts[4]," in preventing the abomination of antichrist any longer occupying the throne of the blessed Fathers; whose blasphemy has hurt no one more than himself, because although he has induced some to be partners of his guilt, yet he has inexpiably stained himself with blood. And hence concerning that which under the direction of Faith your election, brother, by the clergy, and the laity, and all the faithful, has brought about, I assure you that the whole of the Lord's Church rejoices with me, and it is my strong desire that the Divine pity will in its loving-kindness confirm this joy with manifold signs of grace, your own devotion ministering thereto in all things, so that you may sedulously win over, through the Church's prayers, those also who have hitherto resisted the Truth, to reconciliation with God, and, as a zealous ruler, bring them into union with the mystic body of the catholic Faith, whose entirety admits of no division, imitating that true and gentle Shepherd, who laid down His

9 2 Tim. iii. 5, and Tit. i. 16.
1 Apparently to be allowed to reside in Constantinople (or perhaps at this stage to remain in Alexandria).

1a See Lett. CLXII. n. 2a.
2 He had succeeded to the see on the death of Anatolius in 458.
3 Rom. viii. 28.
4 Ps. xxxiv. 18, and cxviii. 16.

life for His sheep, and, when one sheep wandered, drove it not back with the lash, but carried it back to the fold on His own shoulders.

II. *Let him be watchful against heresy and send frequent reports to Rome.*

Take heed, then, dearly beloved brother, lest any trace of either Nestorius' or Eutyches' error be found in God's people: because "no one can lay any foundation except that which is laid, which is Christ Jesus[5];" who would not have reconciled the whole world to God the Father, had He not by the regeneration of Faith adopted us all in the reality of our flesh[6]. Whenever, therefore, opportunities arise which you can use for writing, brother, even as you necessarily and in accordance with custom have done in sending a report of your ordination to us by our sons, Daniel the presbyter and Timothy the deacon, so continue to act at all times and send us, who will be anxious for them, as frequent accounts as possible of the progress of peace, in order that by regular intercourse we may feel that "the love of God is shed abroad in our hearts through the Holy Ghost, which is given unto us[7]." Dated the 18th of August, in the consulship of Magnus and Apollonius (460).

5 1 Cor. iii. 11.

6 *Per fidei regenerationem omnes in nostræ carnis veritate susciperet.* The doctrine of the Atonement in the light of the Incarnation is here expressed in a rather unusual way, and I have therefore translated the expression as literally as possible.

LETTER CLXXII.

To the Presbyters and Deacons of the Church of Alexandria.

(Inviting them to aid in confirming the peace of the Church, and in winning those who had given way to heresy.)

LETTER CLXXIII.

To certain Egyptian Bishops.

(Congratulating them on the election of Timothy, and begging them to assist in maintaining unity and bringing back wanderers to the fold.)

7 Rom. v. 5.

SERMONS.

SERMON I.

Preached on his Birthday[1], or day of Ordination.

Having been elected in absence[2] he returns thanks for the kindness and earnestly demands the prayers of his church.

"Let my mouth speak the praise of the Lord[3]," and my breath and spirit, my flesh and tongue bless His holy Name. For it is a sign, not of a modest, but an ungrateful mind, to keep silence on the kindnesses of God: and it is very meet to begin our duty as consecrated pontiff with the sacrifices of the Lord's praise[4]. Because "in our humility" the Lord "has been mindful of us[5]" and has blessed us: because "He alone has done great wonders for me[5]," so that your holy affection for me reckoned me present, though my long journey had forced me to be absent. Therefore I give and always shall give thanks to our God for all the things with which He has recompensed me. Your favourable opinion also I acknowledge publicly, paying you the thanks I owe, and thus showing that I understand how much respect, love and fidelity your affectionate zeal could expend on me who long with a shepherd's anxiety for the safety of your souls, who have passed so conscientious a judgment on me, with absolutely no deserts of mine to guide you. I entreat you, therefore, by the mercies of the Lord, aid with your prayers him whom you have sought out by your solicitations that both the Spirit of grace may abide in me and that your judgment may not change. May He who inspired you with such unanimity of purpose, vouchsafe to us all in common the blessing of peace: so that all the days of my life being ready for the service of Almighty God, and for my duties towards you, I may with confidence entreat the Lord: "Holy Father, keep in Thy name those whom Thou hast given me[6]:" and while you ever go on unto salvation, may "my soul magnify the Lord[7]," and in the retribution of the judgment to come may the account of my priesthood so be rendered to the just Judge[8] that through your good deeds you may be my joy and my crown, who by your good will have given an earnest testimony to me in this present life.

1 *Natalis* seems to have been applied to the day or anniversary of a Bishop's consecration as well as to the festivals of Martyrs in the Calendar. Cf. Serm. IV. chap. 4, *illi ergo hunc servitutis nostræ natalitium diem ascribamus*. One reason for the shortness of this sermon, which used to be joined with Sermon II. (a few necessary alterations in the text of the latter being made) is, I think, rightly given by the Ballerinii: "perhaps," they say, "the unusual length of the ceremonies that day did not allow of a longer sermon."

2 Viz. on his mission of reconciling Ætius and Albinus the Roman generals in Gaul: see Introduction.

3 Ps. cxliv. 21.

4 Especially of course in the Holy Eucharist.

5 Ps. cxxxv. 23, 24.

6 1 S. John xvii. 11.

7 S. Luke i. 46.

8 The words of S. Paul to the Thessalonians (1 Thess. ii. 19) are clearly in his mind.

SERMON II.

On his Birthday, II.: delivered on the Anniversary[9] of his Consecration.)

I. *The Lord raises up the weak and gives him grace according to his need.*

The Divine condescension has made this an honourable day for me, for it has shown by raising[1] my humbleness to the highest rank, that He despised not any of His own. And hence, although one must be diffident of merit, yet it is one's bounden duty to rejoice over the gift, since He who is the Imposer of the burden[2] is Himself[3] the Aider in its execution: and lest the weak recipient should fall beneath the greatness of the grace, He who conferred the dignity will also give the power. As the day therefore returns in due course on which the Lord purposed that I should begin my episcopal office, there is true cause for me to rejoice to the glory of God, Who that I might love Him much, has forgiven me much, and that I might make His Grace wonderful, has conferred His gifts upon me in whom He found no recommendations of merit. And by this His work what does the Lord suggest and commend to our hearts but that no one should presume upon his own righteousness nor distrust God's mercy which shines out more pre-eminently then, when the sinner is made holy and the downcast lifted

9 This sermon, which in the older editions used to be joined in one with the first was separated by the Ballerinii and assigned to the (1st?) anniversary of his pontifical consecration. Quesnel, who did not go so far as to separate the two parts, saw that there were certain expressions in the first portion which did not suit the common title given to the whole *in anniversario die assumptionis eius*, proposed to alter it to *in octava consecrationis eius* (on the octave, &c.). I have adhered to the Ball.'s division, though I am not entirely convinced by their arguments,

1 *Provexit* unwillingly altered by the Ball. from *provehit*, against all the MSS., to suit their view.

2 *Oneris*, others *honoris* (advancement).

3 *Ipse est*, others (including Quesnel) *ipse mihi fiet* (future).

up. For the measure of heavenly gifts does not rest upon the quality of our deeds, nor in this world, in which "all life is temptation [4]," is each one rewarded according to his deserving, for if the LORD were to take count of a man's iniquities, no one could stand before His judgment.

II. *The mighty assemblage of prelates testifies to men's loyal acceptance of Peter in Peter's unworthy successor.*

Therefore, dearly-beloved, "magnify the LORD with me and let us exalt His name together [5]," that the whole reason of to-day's concourse may be referred to the praise of Him Who brought it to pass. For so far as my own feelings are concerned, I confess that I rejoice most over the devotion of you all; and when I look upon this splendid assemblage of my venerable brother-priests [6], I feel that, where so many saints are gathered, the very angels are amongst us. Nor do I doubt that we are to-day visited by a more abundant outpouring of the Divine Presence, when so many fair tabernacles of GOD, so many excellent members of the Body of Christ are in one place and shine with one light. Nor yet I feel sure, is the fostering condescension and true love of the most blessed Apostle Peter absent from this congregation: he has not deserted your devotion, in whose honour you are met together. And so he too rejoices over your good feeling and welcomes your respect for the LORD's own institution as shown towards the partners of His honour, commending the well ordered love of the whole Church, which ever finds Peter in Peter's See, and from affection for so great a shepherd grows not lukewarm even over so inferior a successor as myself. In order therefore, dearly beloved, that this loyalty which you unanimously display towards my humbleness may obtain the fruit of its zeal, on bended knee entreat the merciful goodness of our GOD that in our days He will drive out those who assail us, strengthen faith, increase love, increase peace and deign to render me His poor slave, whom to show the riches of His grace He has willed to stand at the helm of the Church, sufficient for so great a work and useful in building you up, and to this end to lengthen our time for service that the years He may grant us may be used to His glory through Christ our LORD. Amen.

SERMON III.

ON HIS BIRTHDAY, III: DELIVERED ON THE ANNIVERSARY OF HIS ELEVATION TO THE PONTIFICATE.

I. *The honour of being raised to the episcopate must be referred solely to the Divine Head of the Church.*

As often as GOD's mercy deigns to bring round the day of His gifts to us, there is, dearly-beloved, just and reasonable cause for rejoicing, if only our appointment to the office be referred to the praise of Him who gave it. For though this recognition of GOD may well be found in all His priests, yet I take it to be peculiarly binding on me, who, regarding my own utter insignificance and the greatness of the office undertaken, ought myself also to utter that exclamation of the Prophet, "LORD, I heard Thy speech and was afraid: I considered Thy works and was dismayed [7]." For what is so unwonted and so dismaying as labour to the frail, exaltation to the humble, dignity to the undeserving? And yet we do not despair nor lose heart, because we put our trust not in ourselves but in Him who works in us. And hence also we have sung with harmonious voice the psalm of David, dearly beloved, not in our own praise, but to the glory of Christ the LORD. For it is He of whom it is prophetically written, "Thou art a priest for ever after the order of Melchizedeck [8]," that is, not after the order of Aaron, whose priesthood descending along his own line of offspring was a temporal ministry, and ceased with the law of the Old Testament, but after the order of Melchizedeck, in whom was prefigured the eternal High Priest. And no reference is made to his parentage because in him it is understood that He was portrayed, whose generation cannot be declared. And finally, now that the mystery of this Divine priesthood has descended to human agency, it runs not by the line of birth, nor is that which flesh and blood created, chosen, but without regard to the privilege of paternity and succession by inheritance, those men are received by the Church as its rulers whom the Holy Ghost prepares: so that in the people of GOD's adoption, the whole body of which is priestly and royal, it is not the prerogative of earthly origin which obtains the unction [9], but the condescension of Divine grace which creates the bishop.

4 Job. vii. 1 (LXX.). 5 Ps. xxxiv. 3.

6 The Ball. quote from several more or less contemporary authorities to prove that this concourse is more likely to have been on the anniversary than on the day of consecration itself, and they say that such a celebration of the octave as Quesnel suggests is unknown to all antiquity.

7 Hab. iii. 2 (LXX.). 8 Ps. cx. 4.

9 Quesnel is no doubt correct in taking this literally as alluding to the anointing of bishops at consecration: cf. Serm. IV. chap. 1. *Sancti Spiritus unctio consecrat sacerdotes*, and lower down he speaks of the *effusum benedictionis unguentum*: so also in Serm. LIX. chap. 7, *sacratior est unctio sacerdotum*.

II. *From Christ and through S. Peter the priesthood is handed on in perpetuity.*

Although, therefore, dearly beloved, we be found both weak and slothful in fulfilling the duties of our office, because, whatever devoted and vigorous action we desire to do, we are hindered by the frailty of our very condition; yet having the unceasing propitiation of the Almighty and perpetual Priest, who being like us and yet equal with the Father, brought down His Godhead even to things human, and raised His Manhood even to things Divine, we worthily and piously rejoice over His dispensation, whereby, though He has delegated the care of His sheep to many shepherds, yet He has not Himself abandoned the guardianship of His beloved flock. And from His overruling and eternal protection we have received the support of the Apostles' aid also, which assuredly does not cease from its operation: and the strength of the foundation, on which the whole superstructure of the Church is reared, is not weakened [1] by the weight of the temple that rests upon it. For the solidity of that faith which was praised in the chief of the Apostles is perpetual: and as that remains which Peter believed in Christ, so that remains which Christ instituted in Peter. For when, as has been read in the Gospel lesson [2], the LORD had asked the disciples whom they believed Him to be amid the various opinions that were held, and the blessed Peter had replied, saying, "Thou art the Christ, the Son of the living GOD," the LORD says, "Blessed art thou, Simon Bar-Jona, because flesh and flood hath not revealed it to thee, but My Father, which is in heaven. And I say to thee, that thou art Peter, and upon this rock will I build My church, and the gates of Hades shall not prevail against it. And I will give unto thee the keys of the kingdom of heaven. And whatsoever thou shalt bind on earth, shall be bound in heaven; and whatsoever thou shalt loose on earth, shall be loosed also in heaven [3]."

III. *S. Peter's work is still carried out by his successors.*

The dispensation of Truth therefore abides, and the blessed Peter persevering in the strength of the Rock, which he has received, has not abandoned the helm of the Church, which he undertook. For he was ordained before the rest in such a way that from his being called the Rock, from his being pronounced the Foundation, from his being constituted the Doorkeeper of the kingdom of heaven, from his being set as the Umpire to bind and to loose, whose judgments shall retain their validity in heaven, from all these mystical titles we might know the nature of his association with Christ. And still to-day he more fully and effectually performs what is entrusted to him, and carries out every part of his duty and charge in Him and with Him, through Whom he has been glorified. And so if anything is rightly done and rightly decreed by us, if anything is won from the mercy of GOD by our daily supplications, it is of his work and merits whose power lives and whose authority prevails in his See. For this, dearly-beloved, was gained by that confession, which, inspired in the Apostle's heart by GOD the Father, transcended all the uncertainty of human opinions, and was endued with the firmness of a rock, which no assaults could shake. For throughout the Church Peter daily says, "Thou art the Christ, the Son of the living GOD," and every tongue which confesses the LORD, accepts the instruction his voice conveys. This Faith conquers the devil, and breaks the bonds of his prisoners. It uproots us from this earth and plants us in heaven, and the gates of Hades cannot prevail against it. For with such solidity is it endued by GOD that the depravity of heretics cannot mar it nor the unbelief of the heathen overcome it.

IV. *This festival then is in S. Peter's honour, and the progress of his flock redounds to his glory.*

And so, dearly beloved, with reasonable obedience we celebrate to-day's festival by such methods, that in my humble person he may be recognized and honoured, in whom abides the care of all the shepherds, together with the charge of the sheep commended to him, and whose dignity is not abated even in so unworthy an heir. And hence the presence of my venerable brothers and fellow-priests, so much desired and valued by me, will be the more sacred and precious, if they will transfer the chief honour of this service in which they have deigned to take part to him whom they know to be not only the patron of this see, but also the primate of all bishops. When therefore we utter our exhortations in your ears, holy brethren, believe that he is speaking whose representative we are: because it is his warning that we give, nothing else but his teaching that we preach, beseeching you to "gird up the loins of your

[1] We read *lassescit* with Hurter, instead of the unintelligible *lacessit* of the MSS.

[2] By the *evangelica lectio* is meant the Gospel for the day, just as, for instance, in Sermon XXXIII. chap. 1, &c.

[3] S. Matt. xvi. 16—19.

mind[4]," and lead a chaste and sober life in the fear of GOD, and not to let your mind forget his supremacy and consent to the lusts of the flesh. Short and fleeting are the joys of this world's pleasures which endeavour to turn aside from the path of life those who are called to eternity. The faithful and religious spirit, therefore, must desire the things which are heavenly, and being eager for the Divine promises, lift itself to the love of the incorruptible GOOD and the hope of the true Light. But be sure, dearly-beloved, that your labour, whereby you resist vices and fight against carnal desires, is pleasing and precious in GOD's sight, and in GOD's mercy will profit not only yourselves but me also, because the zealous pastor makes his boast of the progress of the LORD's flock. "For ye are my crown and joy[5]," as the Apostle says; if your faith, which from the beginning of the Gospel has been preached in all the world, has continued in love and holiness. For though the whole Church, which is in all the world, ought to abound in all virtues, yet you especially, above all people, it becomes to excel in deeds of piety, because founded as you are on the very citadel of the Apostolic Rock, not only has our LORD Jesus Christ redeemed you in common with all men, but the blessed Apostle Peter has instructed you far beyond all men. Through the same Christ our LORD.

SERMON IX.

UPON THE COLLECTIONS[6], IV.

I. *The devil's wickedness in leading men astray is now counteracted by the work of Redemption in restoring them to the Truth.*

GOD's mercy and justice, dearly-beloved, has in loving-kindness disclosed to us through our LORD Jesus Christ's teaching, the manner of His retributions, as they have been ordained from the foundation of the world, that accepting the significance of facts we might take what we believe will happen, to have, as it were, already come to pass. For our Redeemer and Saviour knew what great errors the devil's deceit had dispersed throughout the world and by how many superstitions he had subjected the chief part of mankind to himself. But that the creature formed in GOD's image might not any longer through ignorance of the Truth be driven on to the precipice of perpetual death, He inserted in the Gospel-pages the nature of His judgment that it might recover every man from the snares of the crafty foe; for now all would know what rewards the good might hope for and what punishments the evil must fear. For the instigator and author of sin in order first to fall through pride and then to injure us through envy, because "he stood not in the Truth[7]" put all his strength in lying and produced every kind of deceit from this poisoned source of his cunning, that he might cut off man's devout hopes from that happiness which he had lost by his own uplifting, and drag them into partnership with his condemnation, to whose reconciliation he himself could not attain. Whoever therefore among men has wronged GOD by his wickednesses, has been led astray by his guile, and depraved by his villainy. For he easily drives into all evil doings those whom he has deceived in the matter of religion. But knowing that GOD is denied not only by words but also by deeds, many whom he could not rob of their faith, he has robbed of their love, and by choking the ground of their heart with the weeds of avarice, has spoiled them of the fruit of good works, when he could not spoil them of the confession of their lips.

II. *GOD'S just judgment against sin is denounced that we may avoid it by deeds of mercy and love.*

On account therefore, dearly-beloved, of these crafty designs of our ancient foe, the unspeakable goodness of Christ has wished us to know, what was to be decreed about all mankind in the day of retribution, that, while in this life healing remedies are legitimately offered, while restoration is not denied to the contrite, and those who have been long barren can at length be fruitful, the verdict on which justice has determined may be forestalled and the picture of GOD's coming to judge the world never depart from the mind's eye. For the LORD will come in His glorious Majesty, as He Himself has foretold, and there will be with Him an innumerable host of angel-legions radiant in their splendour. Before the throne of His power will all the nations of the world be gathered; and all the men that in all ages and on all the face of the earth have been born, shall stand in the Judge's sight. Then shall be separated the just from the unjust, the guiltless from the

4 1 Pet. i. 13.

5 1 Thess. ii. 20.

6 The Ballerinii in an excellent note have shown that the series of six Sermons *de Collectis* were delivered in connexion with the annual Collections then in vogue at Rome for the sick and poor of the seven city regions. These collections seem to have been continued for several consecutive days (cf. Serm. VI. *primus collectarum dies*, and Serm. X. chap. 4), and probably began on the 6th of July (the octave of SS. Peter and Paul), the day on which in pagan times the *Ludi Apollinares* had also begun: this date being designedly chosen, as Leo himself says (Serm. VIII.), *ad destruendas antiqui hostis insidias in die quo impii sub idolorum suorum nomine diabolo serviebant*: cf. what he says also in the first and third chapters of this Sermon (IX.).

7 S. John viii. 44.

guilty; and when the sons of piety, their works of mercy reviewed, have received the Kingdom prepared for them, the unjust shall be upbraided for their utter barrenness, and those on the left having naught in common with those on the right, shall by the condemnation of the Almighty Judge be cast into the fire prepared for the torture of the devil and his angels, with him to share the punishment, whose will they choose to do. Who then would not tremble at this doom of eternal torment? Who would not dread evils which are never to be ended? But since this severity is only denounced in order that we may seek for mercy, we too in this present life must show such open-handed mercy that after perilous neglect returning to works of piety it may be possible for us to be set free from this doom. For this is the purpose of the Judge's might and of the Saviour's graciousness, that the unrighteous may forsake his ways and the sinner give up his wicked habits. Let those who wish Christ to spare them, have mercy on the poor; let them give freely to feed the wretched, who desire to attain to the society of the blessed. Let no man consider his fellow vile, nor despise in any one that nature which the Creator of the world made His own. For who that labours can deny that Christ claims that labour as done unto Himself? Your fellow-slave is helped thereby, but it is the LORD who will repay. The feeding of the needy is the purchase money of the heavenly kingdom and the free dispenser of things temporal is made the heir of things eternal. But how has such small expenditure deserved to be valued so highly except because our works are weighed in the balance of love, and when a man loves what GOD loves, he is deservedly raised into His kingdom, whose attribute of love has in part become his?

III. *We minister to Christ Himself in the person of His poor.*

To this pious duty of good works, therefore, dearly beloved, the day of Apostolic institution[8] invites us, on which the first collection of our holy offerings has been prudently and profitably ordained by the Fathers; in order that, because at this season formerly the Gentiles used superstitiously to serve demons, we might celebrate the most holy offering of our alms in protest against the unholy victims of the wicked. And because this has been most profitable to the growth of the Church, it has been resolved to make it perpetual. We exhort you, therefore, holy brethren throughout the churches of your several regions[9] on Wednesday next[1] to contribute of your goods, according to your means and willingness, to purposes of charity, that ye may be able to win that blessedness in which he shall rejoice without end, who "considereth the needy and poor[2]." And if we are to "consider" him, dearly beloved, we must use loving care and watchfulness, in order that we may find him whom modesty conceals and shamefastness keeps back. For there are those who blush openly to ask for what they want and prefer to suffer privation without speaking rather than to be put to shame by a public appeal. These are they whom we ought to "consider" and relieve from their hidden straits in order that they may the more rejoice from the very fact that their modesty as well as poverty has been consulted. And rightly in the needy and poor do we recognize the person of Jesus Christ our LORD Himself, "Who though He was rich," as says the blessed Apostle, "became poor, that He might enrich us by His poverty[3]." And that His presence might never seem to be wanting to us, He so effected the mystic union of His humility and His glory that while we adore Him as King and LORD in the Majesty of the Father, we might also feed Him in His poor, for which we shall be set free in an evil day from perpetual damnation, and for our considerate care of the poor shall be joined with the whole company of heaven.

IV. *To complete their acceptance by GOD, they must not neglect to lay all information against the Manichees who are in the city.*

But in order that your devotion, dearly beloved, may in all things be pleasing to GOD, we exhort you also to show due zeal in informing your presbyters of Manichees where-

8 *Dies apostolicæ institutionis*: this was, as note 6 explains, the octave of SS. Peter and Paul, but how far Leo actually attributes its institution to the Apostles themselves, is a little doubtful. In the next clause here he speaks of the Collection as *a patribus ordinata* (so too in Serm. VII. *dies saluberime a sanctis patribus institutus*, and Serm. XI. chap. 2: cf. Serm. X. chap. 1, *auctoritatem patrum*); whereas in Sermon VIII. the day is said to be *apostolicis traditionibus institutus*, and in Serm. XI. chap. 1, *apostolicis didicimus institutis*, and strongest of all the opening words of Serm. X. chap. 1, *apostolicæ traditionis instituta servantes ut diem quem illi ab impiorum consuetudine purgatum misericordiæ operibus consecrarunt celebremus*. *Patres* however often includes *apostoli*, e.g. Serm. LXXIII. chap. 1, *gratias agamus . . . . sanctorum patrum necessariæ tarditati*, where *patrum = apostoli aliique discipuli*. The fact is, as Bright points out upon a similar matter (the origin of Lent), Leo "would be prone to make that claim for any institute of his own church (see Bingham xxi. 1, 8.)" (n. 103.) On Serm. LXXIX. 1 the Ball. appropriately quote a dictum of S. Augustine's that what the universal Church has always held is correctly credited with the authority of the Apostles.

9 *Regionum*, viz. the seven regions into which Rome was then divided: see n. 6, above.

1 The Ball. wish to alter this to Thursday (against MSS.) to suit their calculations, by which as the detection of Manichæism at Rome, mentioned in chap. iv., occurred after the 6th of July, 443, this sermon must have been delivered in 444.

2 Ps. xli. 1.

3 2 Cor. viii. 9.

ever they be hidden[4]. For it is naught but piety to disclose the hiding-places of the wicked, and in them to overthrow the devil, whom they serve. For against them, dearly beloved, it becomes indeed the whole world and the whole Church everywhere to put on the armour of Faith: but your devotion ought to be foremost in this work, who in your progenitors learnt the Gospel of the Cross of Christ from the very mouth of the most blessed Apostles Peter and Paul. Men must not be allowed to lie hid who do not believe that the law given through Moses, in which God is shown to be the Creator of the Universe, ought to be received: who speak against the Prophets and the Holy Ghost, dare in their damnable profanity to reject the Psalms of David which are sung through the universal Church with all reverence, deny the birth of the Lord Christ, according to the flesh, say that His Passion and Resurrection was fictitious, not true, and deprive the baptism of regeneration of all its power as a means of grace. Nothing with them is holy, nothing entire, nothing true. They are to be shunned, lest they harm any one: they are to be given up, lest they should settle in any part of our city. Yours, dearly beloved, will be the gain before the Lord's judgment-seat of what we bid, of what we ask. For it is but right that the triumph of this deed also should be joined to the oblation of our alms, the Lord Jesus Christ in all things aiding us, Who lives and reigns for ever and ever. Amen.

SERMON X.

On the Collections, V.

I. *Our goods are given us not as our own possessions but for use in God's service.*

Observing the institutions of the Apostles' tradition, dearly beloved, we exhort you, as watchful shepherds, to celebrate with the devotion of religious practice that day which they[5] purged from wicked superstitions and consecrated to deeds of mercy, thus showing that the authority of the Fathers still lives among us, and that we obediently abide by their teaching. Inasmuch as the sacred usefulness of such a practice affects not only time past but also our own age, so that what aided them in the destruction of vanities, might contribute with us to the increase of virtues. And what so suitable to faith, what so much in harmony with godliness as to assist the poverty of the needy, to undertake the care of the weak, to succour the needs of the brethren, and to remember one's own condition in the toils of others[6]. In which work He only who knows what He has given to each, discerns aright how much a man can and how much he cannot do. For not only are spiritual riches and heavenly gifts received from God, but earthly and material possessions also proceed from His bounty, that He may be justified in requiring an account of those things which He has not so much put in our possession as committed to our stewardship. God's gifts, therefore, we must use properly and wisely, lest the material for good work should become an occasion of sin. For wealth, after its kind and regarded as a means, is good and is of the greatest advantage to human society, when it is in the hands of the benevolent and open-handed, and when the luxurious man does not squander nor the miser hoard it; for whether ill-stored or unwisely spent it is equally lost.

II. *The liberal use of riches is worse than vain, if it be for selfish ends alone.*

And, however praiseworthy it be to flee from intemperance, and to avoid the waste of base pleasures, and though many in their magnificence disdain to conceal their wealth, and in the abundance of their goods think scorn of mean and sordid parsimony, yet such men's liberality is not happy, nor their thriftiness to be commended, if their riches are of benefit to themselves alone; if no poor folks are helped by their goods, no sick persons nourished; if out of the abundance of their great possessions the captive gets not ransom, nor the stranger comfort, nor the exile relief. Rich men of this kind are needier than all the needy. For they lose those returns which they might have for ever, and while they gloat over the brief and not always free enjoyment of what they possess, they are not fed upon the bread of justice nor the sweets of mercy: outwardly splendid, they have no light within: of things temporal they have abundance, but utter lack of things eternal: for they inflict starvation on their own souls, and bring them to shame and nakedness by spending upon heavenly treasures none of these things which they put into their earthly storehouses.

III. *The duty of mercy outweighs all other virtues.*

But, perhaps there are some rich people, who, although they are not wont to help the Church's poor by bounteous gifts, yet keep other commands of God, and among their

[4] Cf. Lett. VII. and VIII.
[5] See Serm. IX. n. 6, and chap. iii. n. 8.
[6] i.e. apparently to do as you would be done by.

many meritorious acts of faith and uprightness think they will be pardoned for the lack of this one virtue. But this is so important that, though the rest exist without it, they can be of no avail. For although a man be full of faith, and chaste, and sober, and adorned with other still greater decorations, yet if he is not merciful, he cannot deserve mercy: for the LORD says, "blessed are the merciful, for GOD shall have mercy upon them[7]." And when the Son of Man comes in His Majesty and is seated on His glorious throne, and all nations being gathered together, division is made between the good and the bad, for what shall they be praised who stand upon the right except for works of benevolence and deeds of love which Jesus Christ shall reckon as done to Himself? For He who has made man's nature His own, has separated Himself in nothing from man's humility. And what objection shall be made to those on the left, except for their neglect of love, their inhuman harshness, their refusal of mercy to the poor? as if those on the right had no other virtues, those on the left no other faults. But at the great and final day of judgment large-hearted liberality and ungodly meanness will be counted of such importance as to outweigh all other virtues and all other shortcomings, so that for the one men shall gain entrance into the Kingdom, for the other they shall be sent into eternal fire.

IV. *And its efficacy, as Scripture proves, is incalculable.*

Let no one therefore, dearly beloved, flatter himself on any merits of a good life, if works of charity be wanting in him, and let him not trust in the purity of his body, if he be not cleansed by the purification of almsgiving. For "almsgiving wipes out sin[8]," kills death, and extinguishes the punishment of perpetual fire. But he who has not been fruitful therein, shall have no indulgence from the great Recompenser, as Solomon says, "He that closeth his ears lest he should hear the weak, shall himself call upon the LORD, and there shall be none to hear him[9]." And hence Tobias also, while instructing his son in the precepts of godliness, says, "Give alms of thy substance, and turn not thy face from any poor man: so shall it come to pass that the face of GOD shall not be turned from thee[1]." This virtue makes all virtues profitable; for by its presence it gives life to that very faith, by which "the just lives[2]," and which is said to be "dead without works[3]:" because as the reason for works consists in faith, so the strength of faith consists in works. "While we have time therefore," as the Apostle says, "let us do that which is good to all men, and especially to them that are of the household of faith[4]." "But let us not be weary in doing good; for in His own time we shall reap[4]." And so the present life is the time for sowing, and the day of retribution is the time of harvest, when every one shall reap the fruit of his seed according to the amount of his sowing. And no one shall be disappointed in the produce of that harvesting, because it is the heart's intentions rather than the sums expended that will be reckoned up. And little sums from little means shall produce as much as great sums from great means. And therefore, dearly beloved, let us carry out this Apostolic institution. And as the first collection will be next Sunday, let all prepare themselves to give willingly, that every one according to his ability may join in this most sacred offering. Your very alms and those who shall be aided by your gifts shall intercede for you, that you may be always ready for every good work in Christ Jesus our LORD, Who lives and reigns for ages without end. Amen.

SERMON XII.

ON THE FAST OF THE TENTH MONTH, I.[5]

I. *Restoration to the Divine image in which we were made is only possible by our imitation of GOD'S will.*

If, dearly beloved, we comprehend faithfully and wisely the beginning of our creation, we shall find that man was made in GOD'S image, to the end that he might imitate his Creator, and that our race attains its highest natural dignity, by the form of the Divine goodness being reflected in us, as in a mirror. And assuredly to this form the Saviour's grace is daily restoring us, so long as that which, in the

---

7 S. Matt. v. 7.

8 Ecclus. iii. 30. The purifying power of almsgiving is a favourite thought with Leo: cf. for instance Serm. XII. chap. 4, and XVIII. chap. 3, where he says, *castigatio corporis et instantia orationis tunc veram obtinent puritatem cum eleemosynarum sanctificatione nituntur.* In several places he compares its cleansing effect to the waters of baptism: e.g. Serm. XX. chap. 3, *in eleemosynis virtus quædam est instituta baptismatis, quia sicut aqua extinguit ignem, si eleemosyna peccatum—ut nemo diffidat regenerationis sibi nitorem etiam post multa peccata restitui, qui eleemosynarum studuerit purificatione mundari*: and again in Serm. VII. he says, *unusquisque—in usus atque alimoniam pauperum de vestris facultatibus conferatis scientes præter illud regenerationis lavacrum, in quo universorum ablutæ sunt maculæ peccatorum, hoc remedium infirmitati humanæ divinitus esse donatum ut si quid culparum in hac terrena habitatione contrahitur, eleemosynis deleatur.*

9 Prov. xxi. 13.

1 Tob. iv. 7 (one of the offertory sentences it will be remembered in the English Prayer-book).

2 Habb. ii. 4. 3 James ii. 26. 4 Gal. ii. 10 and 9.

5 That is the December or, as we should now call it, the Advent Embertide. Cf. Serm. XIX. chap. 2, where the four seasons, as arranged in Leo's day, are clearly set forth.

first Adam fell, is raised up again in the second. And the cause of our restoration is naught else but the mercy of GOD, Whom we should not have loved, unless He had first loved us, and dispelled the darkness of our ignorance by the light of His truth. And the LORD foretelling this by the holy Isaiah says, "I will bring the blind into a way that they knew not, and will make them walk in paths which they were ignorant of. I will turn darkness into light for them, and the crooked into the straight. These words will I do for them, and not forsake them[6]." And again he says, "I was found by them that sought Me not, and openly appeared to them that asked not for Me[6]. And the Apostle John teaches us how this has been fulfilled, when he says, "We know that the Son of GOD is come, and has given us an understandlng, that we may know Him that is true, and may be in Him that is true, even His Son[7]," and again, "let us therefore love GOD, because He first loved us[7]." Thus it is that GOD, by loving us, restores us to His image, and, in order that He may find in us the form of His goodness, He gives us that whereby we ourselves too may do the work that He does, kindling that is the lamps of our minds, and inflaming us with the fire of His love, that we may love not only Himself, but also whatever He loves. For if between men that is the lasting friendship which is based upon similarity of character, notwithstanding that such identity of wills is often directed to wicked ends, how ought we to yearn and strive to differ in nothing from what is pleasing to GOD. Of which the prophet speaks, "for wrath is in His indignation, and life in His pleasure[8]," because we shall not otherwise attain the dignity of the Divine Majesty, unless we imitate His will.

II. *We must love both God and our neighbour, and "our neighbour" must be interpreted in its widest sense.*

And so, when the LORD says, "Thou shalt love the LORD thy GOD, from all thy heart and from all thy mind: and thou shalt love thy neighbour as thyself[9]," let the faithful soul put on the unfading love of its Author and Ruler, and subject itself also entirely to His will in Whose works and judgments true justice and tender-hearted compassion never fail. For although a man be wearied out with labours and many misfortunes, there is good reason for him to endure all in the knowledge that adversity will either prove him good or make him better. But this godly love cannot be perfect unless a man love his neighbour also. Under which name must be included not only those who are connected with us by friendship or neighbourhood, but absolutely all men, with whom we have a common nature, whether they be foes or allies, slaves or free. For the One Maker fashioned us, the One Creator breathed life into us; we all enjoy the same sky and air, the same days and nights, and, though some be good, others bad, some righteous, others unrighteous, yet GOD is bountiful to all, kind to all, as Paul and Barnabas said to the Lycaonians concerning GOD's Providence, "who in generations gone by suffered all the nations to walk in their own ways. And yet He left Himself not without witness, doing them good, giving rain from heaven and fruitful seasons, and filling our hearts with food and gladness[1]." But the wide extent of Christian grace has given us yet greater reasons for loving our neighbour, which, reaching to all parts of the whole world, looks down on[2] no one, and teaches that no one is to be neglected. And full rightly does He command us to love our enemies, and to pray to Him for our persecutors, who, daily grafting shoots of the wild olive from among all nations upon the holy branches of His own olive, makes men reconciled instead of enemies, adopted sons instead of strangers, just instead of ungodly, "that every knee may bow of things in heaven, of things on earth, and of things under the earth, and every tongue confess that the LORD Jesus Christ is in the glory of GOD the Father[3]."

III. *We must be thankful, and show our thankfulness for what we have received, whether much or little.*

Accordingly, as GOD wishes us to be good, because He is good, none of His judgments ought to displease us. For not to give Him thanks in all things, what else is it but to blame Him in some degree. Man's folly too often dares to murmur against his Creator, not only in time of want, but also in time of plenty, so that, when something is not supplied, he complains, and when certain things are in abundance he is ungrateful. The lord of rich harvests thought scorn of his well-filled garners, and groaned over his abundant grape-gathering: he did not give thanks for the size of the crop, but complained of its poorness[3a]. And if the ground has been less prolific than its wont in the seed it has reared, and the vines

6 Is. xlii. 16, and lxv. 1.
7 1 John v 20, and iv. 19 (the latter loosely).
8 Ps. xxx. 5 (LXX.).
9 S. Matt. xxii. 37, 39.

1 Acts xiv. 16, 17. For gladness (*lætitia*) others read righteousness (*iustitia*).
2 *Despectat:* others *desperat* (despairs of).
3 Phil. ii. 10, 11
3a Viz. in S. Luke xii. 16—20.

and the olives have failed in their supply of fruit, the year is accused, the elements blamed, neither the air nor the sky is spared, whereas nothing better befits and reassures the faithful and godly disciples of Truth than the persistent and unwearied lifting of praise to GOD, as says the Apostle, "Rejoice alway, pray without ceasing: in all things give thanks. For this is the will of GOD in Christ Jesus in all things for you[4]." But how shall we be partakers of this devotion, unless vicissitudes of fortune train our minds in constancy, so that the love directed towards GOD may not be puffed up in prosperity nor faint in adversity. Let that which pleases GOD, please us too. Let us rejoice in whatever measure of gifts He gives. Let him who has used great possessions well, use small ones also well. Plenty and scarcity may be equally for our good, and even in spiritual progress we shall not be cast down at the smallness of the results, if our minds become not dry and barren. Let that spring from the soil of our heart, which the earth gave not. To him that fails not in good will, means to give are ever supplied. Therefore, dearly beloved, in all works of godliness let us use what each year gives us, and let not seasons of difficulty hinder our Christian benevolence. The LORD knows how to replenish the widow's vessels, which her pious deed of hospitality has emptied: He knows how to turn water into wine: He knows how to satisfy 5,000 hungry persons with a few loaves. And He who is fed in His poor, can multiply when He takes what He increased when He gave.

IV. *Prayer, fasting and almsgiving are the three comprehensive duties of a Christian.*

But there are three things which most belong to religious actions, namely prayer, fasting, and almsgiving, in the exercising of which while every time is accepted, yet that ought to be more zealously observed, which we have received as hallowed by tradition from the Apostles: even as this tenth month brings round again to us the opportunity when according to the ancient practice we may give more diligent heed to those three things of which I have spoken. For by prayer we seek to propitiate GOD, by fasting we extinguish the lusts of the flesh, by alms we redeem our sins: and at the same time GOD's image is throughout renewed in us, if we are always ready to praise Him, unfailingly intent on our purification and unceasingly active in cherishing our neighbour. This threefold round of duty, dearly beloved, brings all other virtues into action: it attains to GOD's image and likeness and unites us inseparably with the Holy Spirit. Because in prayer faith remains stedfast, in fastings life remains innocent, in almsgiving the mind remains kind. On Wednesday and Friday therefore let us fast: and on Saturday let us keep vigil with the most blessed Apostle Peter, who will deign to aid our supplications and fast and alms with his own prayers through our LORD Jesus Christ, who with the Father and the Holy Ghost lives and reigns for ever and ever. Amen.

SERMON XVI.

ON THE FAST OF THE TENTH MONTH.

I. *The prosperous must show forth their thankfulness to GOD, by liberality to the poor and needy.*

The transcendant power of GOD's grace, dearly beloved, is indeed daily effecting in Christian hearts the transference of our every desire from earthly to heavenly things. But this present life also is passed through the Creator's aid and sustained by His providence, because He who promises things eternal is also the the Supplier of things temporal. As therefore we ought to give GOD thanks for the hope of future happiness towards which we run by faith, because He raises us up to a perception of the happiness in store for us, so for those things also which we receive in the course of every year, GOD should be honoured and praised, who having from the beginning given fertility to the earth and laid down laws of bearing fruit for every germ and seed, will never forsake his own decrees but will as Creator ever continue His kind administration of the things that He has made. Whatever therefore the cornfields, the vineyards and the olive groves have borne for man's purposes, all this God in His bounteous goodness has produced: for under the varying condition of the elements He has mercifully aided the uncertain toils of the husbandmen so that wind, and rain, cold and heat, day and night might serve our needs. For men's methods would not have sufficed to give effect to their works, had not GOD given the increase to their wonted plantings and waterings. And hence it is but godly and just that we too should help others with that which the Heavenly Father has mercifully bestowed on us. For there are full many, who have no fields, no vineyards, no olive-groves, whose wants we must provide out of the store which GOD has given, that they too with us may bless GOD for the richness of the earth and rejoice at its possessors having received things which they have shared also with the poor and the stranger. That garner

[4] 1 Thess. v. 16.

is blessed and most worthy that all fruits should increase manifold in it, from which the hunger of the needy and the weak is satisfied, from which the wants of the stranger are relieved, from which the desire of the sick is gratified. For these men GOD has in His justice permitted to be afflicted with divers troubles, that He might both crown the wretched for their patience and the merciful for their loving-kindness.

II. *Almsgiving and fasting are the most essential aids to prayer.*

And while all seasons are opportune for this duty, beloved, yet this present season is specially suitable and appropriate, at which our holy fathers, being Divinely inspired, sanctioned the Fast of the tenth month, that when all the ingathering of the crops was complete, we might dedicate to GOD our reasonable service of abstinence, and each might remember so to use his abundance as to be more abstinent in himself and more open-handed towards the poor. For forgiveness of sins is most efficaciously prayed for with almsgiving and fasting, and supplications that are winged by such aids mount swiftly to GOD's ears: since as it is written, "the merciful man doeth good to his own soul [5]," and nothing is so much a man's own as that which he spends on his neighbour. For that part of his material possessions with which he ministers to the needy, is transformed into eternal riches, and such wealth is begotten of this bountifulness as can never be diminished or in any way destroyed, for "blessed are the merciful, for GOD shall have mercy on them [6]," and He Himself shall be their chief Reward, who is the Model of His own command.

III. *Christians' pious activity has so enraged Satan that he has multiplied heresies to wreak them harm.*

But at all these acts of godliness, dearly-beloved, which commend us more and more to GOD, there is no doubt that our enemy, who is so eager and so skilled in harming us, is aroused with keener stings of hatred, that under a false profession of the Christian name he may corrupt those whom he is not allowed to attack with open and bloody persecutions, and for this work he has heretics in his service whom he has led astray from the catholic Faith, subjected to himself, and forced under divers errors to serve in his camp. And as for the deception of primitive man he used the services of a serpent, so to mislead the minds of the upright he has armed these men's tongues with the poison of his falsehoods. But these treacherous designs, dearly beloved, with a shepherd's care, and so far as the LORD vouchsafes His aid, we will defeat. And taking heed lest any of the holy flock should perish, we admonish you with fatherly warnings to keep aloof from the "lying lips" and the "deceitful tongue" from which the prophet asks that his soul should be delivered [7]; because "their words," as says the blessed Apostle, "do creep as doth a gangrene [8]." They creep in humbly, they arrest softly, they bind gently, they slay secretly. For they "come," as the Saviour foretold, "in sheeps' clothing, but inwardly they are ravening wolves [9];" because they could not deceive the true and simple sheep, unless they covered their bestial rage with the name of Christ. But in them all he is at work who, though he is really the enemy of enlightenment, "transforms himself into an angel of light [1]." His is the craft which inspires Basilides; his the ingenuity which worked in Marcion; he is the leader under whom Sabellius acted; he the author of Photinus' headlong fall, his the authority and his the spirit which Arius and Eunomius served: in fine under his command and authority the whole herd of such wild beasts has separated from the unity of the Church and severed connexion with the Truth.

IV. *Of all heresies Manicheism is the worst and foullest.*

But while he retains this ever-varying supremacy over all the heresies, yet he has built his citadel upon the madness of the Manichees, and found in them the most spacious court in which to strut and boast himself: for there he possesses not one form of misbelief only, but a general compound of all errors and ungodlinesses. For all that is idolatrous in the heathen, all that is blind in carnal Jews, all that is unlawful in the secrets of the magic art, all finally that is profane and blasphemous in all the heresies is gathered together with all manner of filth in these men as if in a cesspool [2]. And hence it is too long a matter to describe all their ungodlinesses: for the number of the charges against them exceeds my supply of words. It will be sufficient to indicate a few instances, that you may, from what you hear, conjecture what from modesty we omit. In the matter of their rites, however, which are as indecent morally as they are religiously, we cannot keep

5 Prov. xi. 17. 6 S. Matt. v. 7.

7 Ps. cxx. 2. 8 2 Tim. ii. 17. 9 S. Matt. vii. 15.

1 2 Cor. xi. 14.

2 Strong as this language undoubtedly is, it is perhaps almost justifiable, if the story which he proceeds to indicate is not only true but characteristic of the sect.

silence about that which the LORD has been pleased to reveal to our inquiries, lest any one should think we have trusted in this thing to vague rumours and uncertain opinions. And so with bishops and presbyters sitting beside me, and Christian nobles assembled in the same place, we ordered their elect men and women to be brought before us. And when they had made many disclosures concerning their perverse tenets and their mode of conducting festivals, they revealed this story of utter depravity also, which I blush to describe, but which has been so carefully investigated that no grounds for doubt are left for the incredulous or for cavillers. For there were present all the persons by which the unutterable crime had been perpetrated, to wit a girl at most ten years old, and two women who had nursed her and prepared her for this outrage. There was also present the stripling who had outraged her, and the bishop, who had arranged their horrible crime. All these made one and the same confession, and a tale of such foul orgies[3] was disclosed as our ears could scarcely bear. And lest by plainer speaking we offend chaste ears, the account of the proceedings shall suffice, in which it is most fully shown that in that sect no modesty, no sense of honour, no chastity whatever is found: for their law is falsehood, their religion the devil, their sacrifice immorality.

V. *Every one should abjure such men, and give all the information they possess about them to the authorities.*

And so, dearly beloved, renounce all friendship with these men who are utterly abominable and pestilential, and whom disturbances in other districts have brought in great numbers to the city[4]: and you women especially refrain from acquaintance and intercourse with such men, lest while your ears are charmed unawares by their fabulous stories, you fall into the devil's noose, who, knowing that he seduced the first man by the woman's mouth, and drove all men from the bliss of paradise through feminine credulity, still lies in watch for your sex with more confident craft that he may rob both of their faith and of their modesty those whom he has been able to ensnare by the servants of his falseness. This, too, dearly beloved, I entreat and admonish you loyally to inform us[5], if any of you know where they dwell, where they teach, whose houses they frequent, and in whose company they take rest: because it is of little avail to any one that through the Holy Ghost's protection he is not caught by them himself, if he takes no action when he knows that others are being caught. Against common enemies for the common safety all alike should exercise the same vigilance lest from one member's wound other members also be injured, and they that think such men should not be given up, in Christ's judgment be found guilty for their silence even though they are not contaminated by their approval.

VI. *Zeal in rooting out heresy will make other pious duties more acceptable.*

Display then a holy zeal of religious vigilance, and let all the faithful rise in one body against these savage enemies of their souls. For the merciful GOD has delivered a certain portion of our noxious foes into our hands in order that by revelation of the danger the utmost caution might be aroused. Let not what has been done suffice, but let us persevere in searching them out: and by GOD's aid the result will be not only the continuance in safety of those who still stand, but also the recovery from error of many who have been deceived by the devil's seduction. And the prayers, and alms, and fasts that you offer to the merciful GOD shall be the holier for this very devotion, when this deed of faith also is added to all your other godly duties. On Wednesday and Friday, therefore, let us fast, and on Saturday let us keep vigil in the presence of the most blessed Apostle Peter; who, as we experience and know, watches unceasingly like a shepherd over the sheep entrusted to him by the LORD, and who will prevail in his entreaties that the Church of GOD, which was founded by his preaching, may be free from all error, through Christ our LORD. Amen.

SERMON XVII.

ON THE FAST OF THE TENTH MONTH, VI.

I. *The duty of fasting is based on both the Old and New Testaments, and is closely connected with the duties of prayer and almsgiving.*

The teaching of the Law, dearly beloved, imparts great authority to the precepts of the Gospel, seeing that certain things are transferred from the old ordinances to the new, and by the very devotions of the Church it is shown that the LORD Jesus Christ "came not

3 *Exsecramentum*, cf. Serm. LXXV. chap. 7, *ad illa non sacra sed exsecramenta perveniunt, quæ propter communem verecundiam non sunt nostro sermone promenda.*

4 The Ball. quote Aug. (Conf. v. chap. 10) to show that Rome had long ago been infested with Manichees. They identify the disturbances Leo here speaks of with Genseric's invasion of Africa and occupation of Carthage in 438.

5 For a like injunction, cf. Serm. X., chap 4, where the presbyters are to be told

to destroy but to fulfil the Law[6]." For since the cessation of the signs by which our Saviour's coming was announced, and the abolition of the types in the presence of the Very Truth, those things which our religion instituted, whether for the regulation of customs or for the simple worship of GOD, continue with us in the same form in which they were at the beginning, and what was in harmony with both Testaments has been modified by no change. Among these is also the solemn fast of the tenth month, which is now to be kept by us according to yearly custom, because it is altogether just and godly to give thanks to the Divine bounty for the crops which the earth has produced for the use of men under the guiding hand of supreme Providence. And to show that we do this with ready mind, we must exercise not only the self-restraint of fasting, but also diligence in almsgiving, that from the ground of our heart also may spring the germ of righteousness and the fruit of love, and that we may deserve GOD's mercy by showing mercy to His poor. For the supplication, which is supported by works of piety, is most efficacious in prevailing with GOD, since he who turns not his heart away from the poor soon turns himself to hear the LORD, as the LORD says: "be ye merciful as your Father also is merciful . . . . release and ye shall be released[7]." What is kinder than this justice? what more merciful than this retribution, where the judge's sentence rests in the power of him that is to be judged? "Give," he says, "and it shall be given to you[7]." How soon do the misgivings of distrust and the puttings off of avarice fall to the ground, when humanity[8] may fearlessly spend what the Truth pledges Himself to repay.

II. *He that lends to the LORD makes a better bargain than he that lends to man.*

Be stedfast, Christian giver: give what you may receive, sow what you may reap, scatter what you may gather. Fear not to spend, sigh not over the doubtfulness of the gain. Your substance grows when it is wisely dispensed. Set your heart on the profits due to mercy, and traffic in eternal gains. Your Recompenser wishes you to be munificent, and He who gives that you may have, commands you to spend, saying, "Give, and it shall be given to you." You must thankfully embrace the conditions of this promise. For although you have nothing that you did not receive, yet you cannot fail to have what you give. He therefore that loves money, and wishes to multiply his wealth by immoderate profits, should rather practise this holy usury and grow rich by such money-lending, in order not to catch men hampered with difficulties, and by treacherous assistance entangle them in debts which they can never pay, but to be His creditor and His money-lender, who says, "Give, and it shall be given to you," and "with what measure ye measure, it shall be measured again to you[9]." But he is unfaithful and unfair even to himself, who does not wish to have for ever what he esteems desirable. Let him amass what he may, let him hoard and store what he may, he will leave this world empty and needy, as David the prophet says, "for when he dieth he shall take nothing away, nor shall his glory descend with him[1]." Whereas if he were considerate of his own soul, he would trust his good to Him, who is both the proper Surety[2] for the poor and the generous Repayer of loans. But unrighteous and shameless avarice, which promises to do some kind act but eludes it, trusts not GOD, whose promises never fail, and trusts man, who makes such hasty bargains; and while he reckons the present more certain than the future, often deservedly finds that his greed for unjust gain is the cause of by no means unjust loss.

III. *Money-lending at high interest is in all respects iniquitous.*

And hence, whatever result follow, the money-lender's trade is always bad, for it is sin either to lessen or increase the sum, in that if he lose what he lent he is wretched, and if he takes more than he lent he is more wretched still. The iniquity of money-lending must absolutely be abjured, and the gain which lacks all humanity must be shunned. A man's possessions are indeed multiplied by these unrighteous and sorry means, but the mind's wealth decays because usury of money is the death of the soul[3]. For what GOD thinks of such men the most holy Prophet David makes clear, for when he asks, "LORD, who shall dwell in thy tabernacle, or who shall rest upon thy holy hill[4]?" he receives the Divine utterance in reply, from which he learns that that man attains to eternal rest who among other rules of holy living "hath not given his money upon usury[4]:" and thus he who gets deceitful gain from lending his money on usury is shown to be both an alien from GOD's tabernacle and

6 S. Matt. v. 17.

7 S. Luke vi. 36, 37, 38.

8 *Humanitas:* one MS. reads *humilitas* (man's humility), but *humanitas* occurs again in chap. iii. *lucrum quod omni caret humanitate.*

9 S. Luke vi. 38.

1 Ps. xlix. 17.

2 *Fide iussor* one of Leo's legal terms.

3 *Fœnus pecuniæ funus est animæ*, the epigrammatic play on words will not escape notice.

4 Ps. xv. 1 and 5.

an exile from His holy hill, and in seeking to enrich himself by other's losses, he deserves to be punished with eternal neediness.

IV. *Let us avoid avarice, and share* GOD'S *benefits with others.*

And so, dearly beloved, do ye who with the whole heart have put your trust in the LORD'S promises, flee from this unclean leprosy of avarice, and use GOD'S gift piously and wisely. And since you rejoice in His bounty, take heed that you have those who may share in your joys. For many lack what you have in plenty, and some men's needs afford you opportunity for imitating the Divine goodness, so that through you the Divine benefits may be transferred to others also, and that by being wise stewards of your temporal goods, you may acquire eternal riches. On Wednesday and Friday next, therefore, let us fast, and on Saturday keep vigil with the most blessed Apostle Peter, by whose prayers we may in all things obtain the Divine protection through Christ our LORD. Amen.

SERMON XIX.

ON THE FAST OF THE TENTH MONTH, VIII.

I. *Self-restraint leads to higher enjoyments.*

When the Saviour would instruct His disciples about the Advent of GOD'S Kingdom and the end of the world's times, and teach His whole Church, in the person of the Apostles, He said, "Take heed lest haply your hearts be overcharged with surfeiting and drunkenness, and care of this life[5]." And assuredly, dearly beloved, we acknowledge that this precept applies more especially to us, to whom undoubtedly the day denounced is near, even though hidden. For the advent of which it behoves every man to prepare himself, lest it find him given over to gluttony, or entangled in cares of this life. For by daily experience, beloved, it is proved that the mind's edge is blunted by over-indulgence of the flesh, and the heart's vigour is dulled by excess of food, so that the delights of eating are even opposed to the health of the body, unless reasonable moderation withstand the temptation and the consideration of future discomfort keep us from the pleasure. For although the flesh desires nothing without the soul, and receives its sensations from the same source as it receives its motions also, yet it is the function of the same soul to deny certain things to the body which is subject to it, and by its inner judgment to restrain the outer parts from things unseasonable, in order that it may be the oftener free from bodily lusts, and have leisure for Divine wisdom in the palace of the mind, where, away from all the noise of earthly cares, it may in silence enjoy holy meditations and eternal delights. And, although this is difficult to maintain in this life, yet the attempt can frequently be renewed, in order that we may the oftener and longer be occupied with spiritual rather than fleshly cares; and by our spending ever greater portions of our time on higher cares, even our temporal actions may end in gaining the incorruptible riches.

II. *The teaching of the four yearly fasts is that spiritual self-restraint is as necessary as corporeal.*

This profitable observance, dearly beloved, is especially laid down for the fasts of the Church, which, in accordance with the Holy Spirit's teaching, are so distributed over the whole year that the law of abstinence may be kept before us at all times. Accordingly we keep the spring fast in Lent, the summer fast at Whitsuntide, the autumn fast in the seventh month, and the winter fast in this which is the tenth month, knowing that there is nothing unconnected with the Divine commands, and that all the elements serve the Word of GOD to our instruction, so that from the very hinges on which the world turns, as if by four gospels we learn unceasingly what to preach and what to do. For, when the prophet says, "The heavens declare the glory of GOD, and the firmament showeth His handiwork: day unto day uttereth speech, and night showeth knowledge[6]," what is there by which the Truth does not speak to us? By day and by night His voices are heard, and the beauty of the things made by the workmanship of the One GOD ceases not to instil the teachings of Reason into our hearts' ears, so that "the invisible things of GOD may be perceived and seen through the things which are made," and men may serve the Creator of all, not His creatures[7]. Since therefore all vices are destroyed by self-restraint, and whatever avarice thirsts for, pride strives for, luxury lusts after, is overcome by the solid force of this virtue, who can fail to understand the aid which is given us by fastings? for therein we are bidden to restrain ourselves, not only in food, but also in all carnal desires. Otherwise it is lost labour to endure hunger and yet not put away wrong wishes; to afflict oneself by curtailing food, and yet not to flee from sinful thoughts. That is a carnal, not a spiritual fast, where the body only is stinted, and those things persisted in,

5 S. Luke xxi. 34.

6 Ps. xix. 1, 2.

7 Cf. Rom. i. 20 and 25.

which are more harmful than all delights. What profit is it to the soul to act outwardly as mistress and inwardly to be a captive and a slave, to issue orders to the limbs and to lose the right to her own liberty? That soul for the most part (and deservedly) meets with rebellion in her servant, which does not pay to GOD the service that is due. When the body therefore fasts from food, let the mind fast from vices, and pass judgment upon all earthly cares and desires according to the law of its King

III. *Thus fasting in mind as well as body, and giving alms freely, we shall win GOD'S highest favour.*

Let us remember that we owe love first to GOD, secondly to our neighbour, and that all our affections must be so regulated as not to draw us away from the worship of GOD, or the benefiting our fellow slave. But how shall we worship GOD unless that which is pleasing to Him is also pleasing to us? For, if our will is His will, our weakness will receive strength from Him, from Whom the very will came; "for it is GOD," as the Apostle says, "who worketh in us both to will and to do for (His) good pleasure[8]." And so a man will not be puffed up with pride, nor crushed with despair, if he uses the gifts which GOD gave to His glory, and withholds his inclinations from those things, which he knows will harm him. For in abstaining from malicious envy, from luxurious and dissolute living, from the perturbations of anger, from the lust after vengeance, he will be made pure and holy by true fasting, and will be fed upon the pleasures of incorruptible delights, and so he will know how, by the spiritual use of his earthly riches, to transform them into heavenly treasures, not by hoarding up for himself what he has received, but by gaining a hundred-fold on what he gives. And hence we warn you, beloved, in fatherly affection, to make this winter fast fruitful to yourselves by bounteous alms, rejoicing that by you the LORD feeds and clothes His poor, to whom assuredly He could have given the possessions which He has bestowed on you, had He not in His unspeakable mercy wished to justify them for their patient labour, and you for your works of love. Let us therefore fast on Wednesday and Friday, and on Saturday keep vigil with the most blessed Apostle Peter, and he will deign to assist with his own prayers our supplications and fastings and alms which our LORD Jesus Christ presents, Who with the Father and the Holy Ghost lives and reigns for ever and ever. Amen.

[8] Phil. ii. 13.

SERMON XXI.

ON THE FEAST OF THE NATIVITY, I.

I. *All share in the joy of Christmas.*

Our Saviour, dearly-beloved, was born today: let us be glad. For there is no proper place for sadness, when we keep the birthday of the Life, which destroys the fear of mortality and brings to us the joy of promised eternity. No one is kept from sharing in this happiness. There is for all one common measure of joy, because as our LORD the destroyer of sin and death finds none free from charge, so is He come to free us all. Let the saint exult in that he draws near to victory. Let the sinner be glad in that he is invited to pardon. Let the gentile take courage in that he is called to life. For the Son of GOD in the fulness of time which the inscrutable depth of the Divine counsel has determined, has taken on him the nature of man, thereby to reconcile it to its Author: in order that the inventor of death, the devil, might be conquered through that (nature) which he had conquered. And in this conflict undertaken for us, the fight was fought on great and wondrous principles of fairness; for the Almighty LORD enters the lists with His savage foe not in His own majesty but in our humility, opposing him with the same form and the same nature, which shares indeed our mortality, though it is free from all sin. Truly foreign to this nativity is that which we read of all others, "no one is clean from stain, not even the infant who has lived but one day upon earth[9]." Nothing therefore of the lust of the flesh has passed into that peerless nativity, nothing of the law of sin has entered. A royal Virgin of the stem of David is chosen, to be impregnated with the sacred seed and to conceive the Divinely-human offspring in mind first and then in body. And lest in ignorance of the heavenly counsel she should tremble at so strange a result[10], she learns from converse with the angel that what is to be wrought in her is of the Holy Ghost. Nor does she believe it loss of honour that she is soon to be the Mother of God[1]. For why should she be in despair over the novelty of such conception, to whom the power of the most High has promised to effect it. Her implicit faith is confirmed also by the attestation of a precursory miracle, and Elizabeth receives unexpected

[9] Job xix. 4.

[10] *Effectus*: the older editions read *affatus* (sc. the utterances of the angel).

[1] *Dei genetrix* (θεοτόκος): in opposing Eutyches, Leo is careful not to fall into Nestorianism. Bright's note 3 should be read on this passage, and esp. his quotation from Bp. Pearson (note 2 on Art. 3) *absit ut quisquam S. Mariam Divinæ gratiæ privilegiis et speciali gloria fraudare conetur.*

fertility: in order that there might be no doubt that He who had given conception to the barren, would give it even to a virgin.

II. *The mystery of the Incarnation is a fitting theme for joy both to angels and to men.*

Therefore the Word of GOD, Himself GOD, the Son of GOD who "in the beginning was with GOD," through whom "all things were made" and "without" whom "was nothing made[2]," with the purpose of delivering man from eternal death, became man: so bending Himself to take on Him our humility without decrease in His own majesty, that remaining what He was and assuming what He was not, He might unite the true form of a slave to that form in which He is equal to GOD the Father, and join both natures together by such a compact that the lower should not be swallowed up in its exaltation nor the higher impaired by its new associate. [3] Without detriment therefore to the properties of either substance which then came together in one person, majesty took on humility, strength weakness, eternity mortality: and for the paying off of the debt belonging to our condition, inviolable nature was united with passible nature, and true GOD and true man were combined to form one LORD, so that, as suited the needs of our case, one and the same Mediator between GOD and men, the Man Christ Jesus, could both die with the one and rise again with the other[3].

Rightly therefore did the birth of our Salvation impart no corruption to the Virgin's purity, because the bearing of the Truth was the keeping of honour. Such then beloved was the nativity which became the Power of GOD and the Wisdom of GOD even Christ, whereby He might be one with us in manhood and surpass us in Godhead. For unless He were true GOD, He would not bring us a remedy; unless He were true Man, He would not give us an example. Therefore the exulting angel's song when the LORD was born is this, "Glory to GOD in the Highest," and their message, "peace on earth to men of good will[4]." For they see that the heavenly Jerusalem is being built up out of all the nations of the world: and over that indescribable work of the Divine love how ought the humbleness of men to rejoice, when the joy of the lofty angels is so great?

III. *Christians then must live worthily of Christ their Head.*

Let us then, dearly beloved, give thanks to GOD the Father, through His Son, in the Holy Spirit[5], Who "for His great mercy, wherewith He has loved us," has had pity on us: and "when we were dead in sins, has quickened us together in Christ[6]," that we might be in Him a new creation and a new production. Let us put off then the old man with his deeds: and having obtained a share in the birth of Christ let us renounce the works of the flesh. Christian, acknowledge thy dignity, and becoming a partner in the Divine nature, refuse to return to the old baseness by degenerate conduct. Remember the Head and the Body of which thou art a member. Recollect that thou wert rescued from the power of darkness and brought out into GOD's light and kingdom. By the mystery of Baptism thou wert made the temple of the Holy Ghost: do not put such a denizen to flight from thee by base acts, and subject thyself once more to the devil's thraldom: because thy purchase money is the blood of Christ, because He shall judge thee in truth Who ransomed thee in mercy, who with the Father and the Holy Spirit reigns for ever and ever. Amen.

SERMON XXII.

ON THE FEAST OF THE NATIVITY, II.

I. *The mystery of the Incarnation demands our joy.*

Let us be glad in the LORD, dearly-beloved, and rejoice with spiritual joy that there has dawned for us the day of ever-new redemption, of ancient preparation[7], of eternal bliss. For as the year rolls round, there recurs for us the commemoration[8] of our salvation, which promised from the beginning, accomplished in the fulness of time will endure for ever; on which we are bound with hearts up-lifted[9] to adore the divine mystery: so that what is the effect of GOD's great gift may be celebrated by the Church's great rejoicings. For GOD the almighty and merciful, Whose nature is goodness, Whose will is power, Whose work is mercy: as soon as the devil's malignity killed us by the poison of his hatred, foretold at the very beginning of the world the remedy His piety had prepared for the restoration of us mortals: proclaiming to the serpent that the seed of the woman should come to crush the lifting of his baneful head by its power, signifying no doubt that Christ

2 S. John i. 1—3.

3 "Without—other" repeated in almost the same words in Letter XXVIII. chap. 3.

4 S. Luke ii. 14.

5 Bingham observes (b. xiv. c. 2, s. 1), that Leo here uses, though in a catholic sense, that form of doxology which had become associated with Arianism. He could well afford to do as S. Athanasius had done, who ascribes glory to the Father "through the Son" at the conclusion of four treatises. Bright.

6 Eph. ii. 4, 5.

7 *Præparationis* (viz. the day to which prophecies and types were leading up): another reading is *reparationis* (restoration), which is less apposite.

8 *Sacramentum.*

9 *Erectis sursum cordibus*, the phrase reminds us of the Eucharistic V. *sursum corda R. habemus ad Dominum.*

would come in the flesh, God and man, Who born of a Virgin should by His uncorrupt birth condemn the despoiler of the human stock. [1] Thus in the whole and perfect nature of true man was true God born, complete in what was His own, complete in what was ours. And "ours" we call what the Creator formed in us from the beginning and what He undertook to repair. For what the deceiver brought in and the deceived admitted had no trace in the Saviour Nor because He partook of man's weaknesses, did He therefore share our faults. He took the form of a slave without stain of sin, increasing the human and not diminishing the Divine: because that "emptying of Himself" whereby the Invisible made Himself visible and Creator and Lord of all things as He was, wished to be mortal, was the condescension of Pity not the failing of Power [1].

II. *The new character of the birth of Christ explained.*

Therefore, when the time came, dearly beloved, which had been fore-ordained for men's redemption [2], there enters these lower parts of the world, the Son of God, descending from His heavenly throne and yet not quitting His Father's glory, begotten in a new order, by a new nativity. In a new order, because being invisible in His own nature He became visible in ours, and He whom nothing could contain, was content to be contained: abiding before all time He began to be in time: the Lord of all things, He obscured His immeasurable majesty and took on Him the form of a servant: being God, that cannot suffer, He did not disdain to be man that can, and immortal as He is, to subject Himself to the laws of death [2]. And by a new nativity He was begotten, conceived by a Virgin, born of a Virgin, without paternal desire, without injury to the mother's chastity: because such a birth as knew no taint of human flesh, became One who was to be the Saviour of men, while it possessed in itself the nature of human substance. For when God was born in the flesh, God Himself was the Father, as the archangel witnessed to the Blessed Virgin Mary: "because the Holy Spirit shall come upon thee, and the power of the most High shall overshadow thee: and therefore, that which shall be born of thee shall be called holy, the Son of God [3]." The origin is different but the nature like: not by intercourse with man but by the power of God was it brought about: for a Virgin conceived, a Virgin bare, and a Virgin she remained. Consider here not the condition of her that bare but the will of Him that was born; for He was born Man as He willed and was able. If you inquire into the truth of His nature, you must acknowledge the matter to be human: if you search for the mode of His birth, you must confess the power to be of God. For the Lord Jesus Christ came to do away with not to endure our pollutions: not to succumb to our faults but to heal them [4]. He came that He might cure every weakness of our corruptness and all the sores of our defiled souls: for which reason it behoved Him to be born by a new order, who brought to men's bodies the new gift of unsullied purity. For the uncorrupt nature of Him that was born had to guard the primal virginity of the Mother, and the infused power of the Divine Spirit had to preserve in spotlessness and holiness that sanctuary which He had chosen for Himself: that Spirit (I say) who had determined to raise the fallen, to restore the broken, and by overcoming the allurements of the flesh to bestow on us in abundant measure the power of chastity: in order that the virginity which in others cannot be retained in child-bearing, might be attained by them at their second birth.

III. *Justice required that Satan should be vanquished by God made man.*

And, dearly beloved, this very fact that Christ chose to be born of a Virgin does it not appear to be part of the deepest design? I mean, that the devil should not be aware that Salvation had been born for the human race, and through the obscurity of that spiritual conception, when he saw Him no different to others, should believe Him born in no different way to others. For when he observed that His nature was like that of all others, he thought that He had the same origin as all had: and did not understand that He was free from the bonds of transgression because he did not find Him a stranger to the weakness of mortality. For though the true [5] mercy of God had infinitely many schemes to hand for the restoration of mankind, it chose that particular design which put in force for destroying the devil's work, not the efficacy of might but the dictates of justice. For the pride of the ancient foe not undeservedly

[1] From "Thus" to the end of the chapter is repeated in Lett. XXVIII. (Tome), chap. 3.

[2] From "there enters" to "death" is repeated in Lett. XXVIII. (Tome), chap 4.

[3] S. Luke i. 35.

[4] For the impeccability of Christ involved in this statement, cf. Serm. LXIV. chap. 2, and Lett. XXVIII. (Tome) chap. 3, and especially Bright s note 15 (to Sermon XXIII. chap. 2).

[5] *Verax*, literally truth speaking, and so genuine, sincere, &c.

made good its despotic rights over all men, and with no unwarrantable supremacy tyrannized over those who had been of their own accord lured away from God's commands to be the slaves of his will. And so there would be no justice in his losing the immemorial slavery of the human race, were he not conquered by that which he had subjugated. And to this end, without male seed Christ was conceived of a Virgin, who was fecundated not by human intercourse but by the Holy Spirit. And whereas in all mothers conception does not take place without stain of sin, this one received purification from the Source of her conception. For no taint of sin penetrated, where no intercourse occurred. Her unsullied virginity knew no lust when it ministered the substance. The Lord took from His mother our nature, not our fault [6]. The slave's form is created without the slave's estate, because the New Man is so commingled with the old, as both to assume the reality of our race and to remove its ancient flaw.

IV. *The Incarnation deceived the Devil and caused him to break the bond under which he held men.*

When, therefore, the merciful and almighty Saviour so arranged the commencement of His human course as to hide the power of His Godhead which was inseparable from His manhood under the veil of our weakness, the crafty foe was taken off his guard and he thought that the nativity of the Child, Who was born for the salvation of mankind, was as much subject to himself as all others are at their birth. For he saw Him crying and weeping, he saw Him wrapped in swaddling clothes, subjected to circumcision, offering the sacrifice which the law required. And then he perceived in Him the usual growth of boyhood, and could have had no doubt of His reaching man's estate by natural steps. Meanwhile, he inflicted insults, multiplied injuries, made use of curses, affronts, blasphemies, abuse, in a word, poured upon Him all the force of his fury and exhausted all the varieties of trial: and knowing how he had poisoned man's nature, had no conception that He had no share in the first transgression Whose mortality he had ascertained by so many proofs. The unscrupulous thief and greedy robber persisted in assaulting Him Who had nothing of His own, and in carrying out the general sentence on original sin, went beyond the bond on which he rested [7], and required the punishment of iniquity from Him in Whom he found no fault. And thus the malevolent terms of the deadly compact are annulled, and through the injustice of an overcharge the whole debt is cancelled. The strong one is bound by his own chains, and every device of the evil one recoils on his own head. When the prince of the world is bound, all that he held in captivity is released [8]. Our nature cleansed from its old contagion regains its honourable estate, death is destroyed by death, nativity is restored by nativity: since at one and the same time redemption does away with slavery, regeneration changes our origin, and faith justifies the sinner.

V. *The Christian is exhorted to share in the blessings of the Incarnation.*

Whoever then thou art that devoutly and faithfully boastest of the Christian name, estimate this atonement at its right worth. For to thee who wast a castaway, banished from the realms of paradise, dying of thy weary exile, reduced to dust and ashes, without further hope of living, by the Incarnation of the Word was given the power to return from afar to thy Maker, to recognize thy parentage, to become free after slavery, to be promoted from being an outcast to sonship: so that, thou who wast born of corruptible flesh, mayest be reborn by the Spirit of God, and obtain through grace what thou hadst not by nature, and, if thou acknowledge thyself the son of God by the spirit of adoption, dare to call God Father. Freed from the accusings of a bad conscience, aspire to the kingdom of heaven, do God's will supported by the Divine help, imitate the angels upon earth, feed on the strength of immortal sustenance, fight fearlessly on the side of piety against hostile temptations, and if thou keep thy allegiance [8a] in the heavenly warfare, doubt not that thou wilt be crowned for thy victory in the triumphant camp of the Eternal King, when the resurrection that is prepared for the faithful has raised thee to participate in the heavenly Kingdom.

VI. *The festival has nothing to do with Sun-worship, as some maintain.*

Having therefore so confident a hope, dearly beloved, abide firm in the Faith in which you are built: lest that same tempter whose

6 This sentence is found also in Lett XXVIII. (Tome), chap. 3; but here instead of *de matre Domini, natura* there is a variant reading, *de matre, hominis natura*.

7 *Dum vitiatæ originis præiudicium generale persequitur, chirographum quo nitebatur excedit.* Cf. Col. ii. 14, and Lett. CXXIV. 7.

8 *Captivitatis vasa rapiuntur:* the passage in the writer's mind is S. Luke xi. 21, 22, q.v.

8a *Si cælestis militiæ sacramenta servaveris:* here we have a return to the earlier classical meaning of *sacramentum*.

tyranny over you Christ has already destroyed, win you back again with any of his wiles, and mar even the joys of the present festival by his deceitful art, misleading simpler souls with the pestilential notion of some to whom this our solemn feast day seems to derive its honour, not so much from the nativity of Christ as, according to them, from the rising of the new sun[9]. Such men's hearts are wrapped in total darkness, and have no growing perception of the true Light: for they are still drawn away by the foolish errors of heathendom, and because they cannot lift the eyes of their mind above that which their carnal sight beholds, they pay divine honour to the luminaries that minister to the world. Let not Christian souls entertain any such wicked superstition and portentous lie. Beyond all measure are things temporal removed from the Eternal, things corporeal from the Incorporeal, things governed from the Governor. For though they possess a wondrous beauty, yet they have no Godhead to be worshipped. That power then, that wisdom, that majesty is to be adored which created the universe out of nothing, and framed by His almighty methods the substance of the earth and sky into what forms and dimensions He willed. Sun, moon, and stars may be most useful to us, most fair to look upon; but only if we render thanks to their Maker for them and worship God who made them, not the creation which does Him service. Then praise God, dearly beloved, in all His works and judgments. Cherish an undoubting belief in the Virgin's pure conception. Honour the sacred and Divine mystery of man's restoration with holy and sincere service. Embrace Christ born in our flesh, that you may deserve to see Him also as the God of glory reigning in His majesty, who with the Father and the Holy Spirit remains in the unity of the Godhead for ever and ever. Amen.

SERMON XXIII.

On the Feast of the Nativity, III.

I. *The truths of the Incarnation never suffer from being repeated.*

The things which are connected with the mystery[1] of to-day's solemn feast are well known to you, dearly-beloved, and have frequently been heard: but as yonder visible light affords pleasure to eyes that are unimpaired, so to sound hearts does the Saviour's nativity give eternal joy; and we must not keep silent about it, though we cannot treat of it as we ought. For we believe that what Isaiah says, "who shall declare his generation[2]?" applies not only to that mystery, whereby the Son of God is co-eternal with the Father, but also to this birth whereby "the Word became flesh." And so God, the Son of God, equal and of the same nature from the Father and with the Father, Creator and Lord of the Universe, Who is completely present everywhere, and completely exceeds all things, in the due course of time, which runs by His own disposal, chose for Himself this day on which to be born of the blessed virgin Mary for the salvation of the world, without loss of the mother's honour. For her virginity was violated neither at the conception nor at the birth: "that it might be fulfilled," as the Evangelist says, "which was spoken by the Lord through Isaiah the prophet, saying, behold the virgin shall conceive in the womb, and shall bear a son, and they shall call his name Emmanuel, which is interpreted, God with us[3]." For this wondrous child-bearing of the holy Virgin produced in her offspring one person which was truly human and truly Divine[4], because neither substance so retained their properties that there could be any division of persons in them; nor was the creature taken into partnership with its Creator in such a way that the One was the in-dweller, and the other the dwelling; but so that the one nature was blended[5] with the other. And although the nature which is taken is one, and that which takes is another, yet these two diverse natures come together into such close union that it is one and the same Son who says both that, as true Man, "He is less than the Father," and that, as true God, "He is equal with the Father."

II. *The Arians could not comprehend the union of God and man.*

This union, dearly beloved, whereby the Creator is joined to the creature, Arian blindness could not see with the eyes of intelligence, but, not believing that the Only-begotten of God was of the same glory and substance with the Father, spoke of the Son's Godhead as inferior, drawing its arguments from those

---

9 Such an idea is no doubt to be referred to the Manichæans.

1 *Sacramentum* (as usual). I would venture to urge that Bright is hardly justified in interpreting this as "sacred observance" here, unless I have misunderstood his note 8. Surely Leo means, the facts and details and consequences arising from the mystery of the Incarnation are well known to you. This agrees better with the context and is in accordance with his common use of the word.

2 Isaiah liii. 8.

3 S. Matt. i. 22, 23.

4 *Vere humanam vereque divinam unam edidit prole personam.*

5 *Misceretur*: Quesnel truly remarks that the fathers "*securius locuti sunt nondum litigantibus Eutychianis post cuius hæresis ortum cautim—locutus est Leo.* That no "fusion" of the natures is really implied Bright (note 11) clearly shows.

words which are to be referred to the "form of a slave," in respect of which, in order to show that it belongs to no other or different person in Himself, the same Son of GOD with the same form, says, "The Father is greater than I[6]," just as He says with the same form, "I and my Father are one[7]." For in "the form of a slave," which He took at the end of the ages for our restoration, He is inferior to the Father: but in the form of GOD, in which He was before the ages, He is equal to the Father. In His human humiliation He was "made of a woman, made under the Law[8]:" in His Divine majesty He abides the Word of GOD, "through whom all things were made[9]." [1]Accordingly, He Who in the form of GOD made man, in the form of a slave was made man. For both natures retain their own proper character without loss: and as the form of GOD did not do away with the form of a slave, so the form of a slave did not impair the form of GOD[1]. And so the mystery of power united to weakness, in respect of the same human nature, allows the Son to be called inferior to the Father: but the Godhead, which is One in the Trinity of the Father, Son, and Holy Ghost, excludes all notion of inequality. For the eternity of the Trinity has nothing temporal, nothing dissimilar in nature: Its will is one, Its substance identical, Its power equal, and yet there are not three GODS, but one GOD[2]; because it is a true and inseparable unity, where there can be no diversity[3]. Thus in the whole and perfect nature of true man was true GOD born, complete in what was His own, complete in what was ours. And by "ours" we mean what the Creator formed in us from the beginning, and what He undertook to repair. For what the deceiver brought in, and man deceived committed, had no trace in the Saviour; nor because He partook of man's weaknesses, did He therefore share our faults. He took the form of a slave without stain of sin, increasing the human and not diminishing the divine: for that "emptying of Himself," whereby the Invisible made Himself visible, was the bending down of pity, not the failing of power.

III. *The Incarnation was necessary to the taking away of sin.*

In order therefore that we might be called to eternal bliss from our original bond and from earthly errors, He came down Himself to us to Whom we could not ascend, because, although there was in many the love of truth, yet the variety of our shifting opinions was deceived by the craft of misleading demons, and man's ignorance was dragged into diverse and conflicting notions by a falsely-called science. But to remove this mockery, whereby men's minds were taken captive to serve the arrogant devil, the teaching of the Law was not sufficient, nor could our nature be restored merely by the Prophets' exhortations; but the reality of redemption had to be added to moral injunctions, and our fundamentally corrupt origin had to be re-born afresh. A Victim had to be offered for our atonement Who should be both a partner of our race and free from our contamination, so that this design of GOD whereby it pleased Him to take away the sin of the world in the Nativity and Passion of Jesus Christ, might reach to all generations[4]: and that we should not be disturbed but rather strengthened by these mysteries, which vary with the character of the times, since the Faith, whereby we live, has at no time suffered variation.

IV. *The blessings of the Incarnation stretch backwards as well as reach forward.*

Accordingly let those men cease their complaints who with disloyal murmurs speak against the dispensations of GOD, and babble about the lateness of the LORD's Nativity as if that, which was fulfilled in the last age of the world, had no bearing upon the times that are past. For the Incarnation of the Word did but contribute to the doing of that which was done[5]: and the mystery of man's salvation was never in the remotest age at a standstill. What the apostles foretold, that the prophets announced: nor was that fulfilled too late which has always been believed. But the Wisdom and Goodness of GOD made us more receptive of His call by thus delaying the work which brought salvation: so that what through so many ages had been foretold by many signs, many utterances, and many mysteries, might not be doubtful in these days of the Gospel: and that the Saviour's nativity, which was to exceed all wonders and all the measure of human knowledge, might engender in us a Faith so much the firmer, as the foretelling of it had been

6 S. John xiv. 28. 7 Ib. x. 30. 8 Gal. iv. 4.

9 S. John. i. 3.

1 From "accordingly" to "form of GOD" occurs again in Lett. XXVIII. (Tome) chap. 3.

2 Several times in this chapter and elsewhere in Leo the language reminds us forcibly of the Quicunque "which," says Bright (note 14), "whatever be its date, was clearly compiled by some one accustomed to the theological terminology of the Latin church of the fifth century."

3 From here to end of chapter occurs again in Lett. XXVIII. (Tome) chap. 3.

4 From what he goes on to say in the next chapter, it is clear that Leo meant that both *past* and *future* generations of mankind shared in the benefits of the Incarnation: cf. Bright's note 16.

5 *Hoc contulit faciendum quod factum*, i.e. the Incarnation was but a part (though an essential part) in the Divine scheme of redemption, and, as he goes on to show, could not have occurred sooner than it did occur: for it would have marred the sequence of the whole design: cf. Bright's note 17: also S. John viii. 56.

ancient and oft-repeated. And so it was no new counsel, no tardy pity whereby GOD took thought for men: but from the constitution of the world He ordained one and the same Cause of Salvation for all. For the grace of GOD, by which the whole body of the saints is ever justified, was augmented, not begun, when Christ was born: and this mystery of GOD's great love, wherewith the whole world is now filled, was so effectively presignified that those who believed that promise obtained no less than they, who were the actual recipients.

V. *The coming of Christ in our flesh corresponds with our becoming members of His body.*

Wherefore since the loving-kindness is manifest, dearly beloved, wherewith all the riches of Divine goodness are showered on us, whose call to eternal life has been assisted not only by the profitable examples of those who went before, but also by the visible and bodily appearing of the Truth Itself, we are bound to keep the day of the LORD's Nativity with no slothful nor carnal joy. And we shall each keep it worthily and thoroughly, if we remember of what Body we are members, and to what a Head we are joined, lest any one as an ill-fitting joint cohere not with the rest of the sacred building. Consider, dearly beloved, and by the illumination of the Holy Spirit thoughtfully bear in mind Who it was that received us into Himself, and that we have received in us: since, as the LORD Jesus became our flesh by being born, so we also became His body by being re-born. Therefore are we both members of Christ, and the temple of the Holy Ghost: and for this reason the blessed Apostle says, "Glorify and carry GOD in your body[6]:" for while suggesting to us the standard of His own gentleness and humility, He fills us with that power whereby He redeemed us, as the LORD Himself promises: "come unto Me all ye who labour and are heavy-laden, and I will refresh you. Take My yoke upon you and learn of Me, for I am meek and lowly of heart, and ye shall find rest to your souls[7]." Let us then take the yoke, that is not heavy nor irksome, of the Truth that rules us, and let us imitate His humility, to Whose glory we wish to be conformed: He Himself helping us and leading us to His promises, Who, according to His great mercy, is powerful to blot out our sins, and to perfect His gifts in us, Jesus Christ our LORD, Who lives and reigns for ever and ever. Amen.

SERMON XXIV.

ON THE FEAST OF THE NATIVITY, IV.

I. *The Incarnation fulfils all its types and promises.*

The Divine goodness, dearly beloved, has indeed always taken thought for mankind in divers manners, and in many portions, and of His mercy has imparted many gifts of His providence to the ages of old; but in these last times has exceeded all the abundance of His usual kindness, when in Christ the very Mercy has descended to sinners, the very Truth to those that are astray, the very Life to those that are dead: so that that Word, which is co-eternal and co-equal with the Father, might take our humble nature into union with His Godhead, and, being born GOD of GOD, might also be born Man of man. This was indeed promised from the foundation of the world, and had always been prophesied by many intimations of facts and words[8]: but how small a portion of mankind would these types and fore-shadowed mysteries have saved, had not the coming of Christ fulfilled those long and secret promises: and had not that which then benefited but a few believers in the prospect, now benefited myriads of the faithful in its accomplishment. Now no longer then are we led to believe by signs and types, but being confirmed by the gospel story we worship that which we believe to have been done; the prophetic lore[9] assisting our knowledge, so that we have no manner of doubt about that which we know to have been predicted by such sure oracles. For hence it is that the LORD says to Abraham: "In thy seed shall all nations be blessed[1]:" hence David, in the spirit of prophecy, sings, saying: "The LORD swore truth to David, and He shall not frustrate it: of the fruit of thy loins will I set upon thy seat[2];" hence the LORD again says through Isaiah: "behold a virgin shall conceive in her womb, and shall bear a Son, and His Name shall be called Emmanuel, which is interpreted, GOD with us[3]," and again, "a rod shall come forth from the root of Jesse, and a flower shall arise from his root[4]." In which rod, no doubt the blessed Virgin Mary is predicted, who sprung from the stock of Jesse and David and fecundated by the Holy Ghost, brought forth a new

[6] 1 Cor. vi. 20. *Glorificate et portate Deum in corpore vestro*, quoted again in this form in Sermon LIII. 3. Observe (1) that "*et portate* is doubtless a very old 'Western' gloss" (Bright, note 18), and (2) that the words "and in your spirit, which are GOD's" (A.V.) find no place in the Latin Versions, and are now omitted in R.V.

[7] S. Matt. xi. 28.

[8] Cf. Serm. XXIII., chap. 4.

[9] *Instrumentis* (lit. materials, stock-in-trade).

[1] Gen. xxii. 18. [2] Ps. xxxi. 14. [3] Is. vii. 14.

[4] Is. xi. 1; in the interpretation that follows there is apparently a play on the rod (*virga*) and the virgin (*virgo*).

flower of human flesh, becoming a virgin-mother.

II. *The Incarnation was the only effective remedy to the Fall.*

Let the righteous then rejoice in the LORD, and let the hearts of believers turn to GOD's praise, and the sons of men confess His wondrous acts; since in this work of GOD especially our humble estate realizes how highly its Maker values it: in that, after His great gift to mankind in making us after His image, He contributed far more largely to our restoration when the LORD Himself took on Him "the form of a slave." For though all that the Creator expends upon His creature is part of one and the same Fatherly love, yet it is less wonderful than man should advance to divine things than that GOD should descend to humanity. But unless the Almighty GOD did deign to do this, no kind of righteousness, no form of wisdom could rescue any one from the devil's bondage and from the depths of eternal death. For the condemnation that passes with sin from one upon all would remain, and our nature, corroded by its deadly wound, would discover no remedy, because it could not alter its state in its own strength. For the first man received the substance of flesh from the earth, and was quickened with a rational spirit by the in-breathing of his Creator[5], so that living after the image and likeness of his Maker, he might preserve the form of GOD's goodness and righteousness as in a bright mirror. And, if he had perseveringly maintained this high dignity of his nature by observing the Law that was given him, his uncorrupt mind would have raised the character even of his earthly body to heavenly glory. But because in unhappy rashness he trusted the envious deceiver, and agreeing to his presumptuous counsels, preferred to forestall rather than to win the increase of honour that was in store for him, not only did that one man, but in him all that came after him also hear the verdict: "earth thou art, and unto earth shalt thou go[6];" "as in the earthy," therefore, "such are they also that are earthy[7]," and no one is immortal, because no one is heavenly.

III. *We all become partakers in the Birth of Christ, by the re-birth of baptism.*

And so to undo this chain of sin and death, the Almighty Son of GOD, that fills all things and contains all things, altogether equal to the Father and co-eternal in one essence from Him and with Him, took on Him man's nature, and the Creator and LORD of all things deigned to be a mortal: choosing for His mother one whom He had made, one who, without loss of her maiden honour, supplied so much of bodily substance, that without the pollution of human seed the New Man might be possessed of purity and truth. In Christ, therefore, born of the Virgin's womb, the nature does not differ from ours, because His nativity is wonderful. For He Who is true GOD, is also true man: and there is no lie in either nature. "The Word became flesh" by exaltation of the flesh, not by failure of the Godhead: which so tempered its power and goodness as to exalt our nature by taking it, and not to lose His own by imparting it. In this nativity of Christ, according to the prophecy of David, "truth sprang out of the earth, and righteousness looked down from heaven[8]." In this nativity also, Isaiah's saying is fulfilled, "let the earth produce and bring forth salvation, and let righteousness spring up together[9]." For the earth of human flesh, which in the first transgressor, was cursed, in this Offspring of the Blessed Virgin only produced a seed that was blessed and free from the fault of its stock. And each one is a partaker of this spiritual origin in regeneration; and to every one when he is re-born, the water of baptism is like the Virgin's womb; for the same Holy Spirit fills the font, Who filled the Virgin, that the sin, which that sacred conception overthrew, may be taken away by this mystical washing.

IV. *The Manichæans, by rejecting the Incarnation, have fallen into terrible iniquities.*

In this mystery, dear beloved, the mad error of the Manichæans has no part, nor have they any partnership in the regeneration of Christ, who say that He was corporeally born of the Virgin Mary: so that, as they do not believe in His real nativity, they do not accept His real passion either; and, not acknowledging Him really buried, they reject His genuine resurrection. For, having entered on the perilous path of their abominable dogma, where all is dark and slippery, they rush into the abyss of death over the precipice of falsehood, and find no sure ground on which to rest; because, besides all their other diabolical enormities, on the very chief feast of Christ's worship, as their latest confession has made manifest[1], they revel in bodily as well as mental pollution, losing their own modesty as well as the purity of their Faith; so that they

5 Cf. 1 Cor. xv. 45, and Gen. ii. 7. 6 Gen. iii. 19. 7 1 Cor. xv. 48.

8 Ps. lxxxiv. 12. 9 Is. xlv. 8.

1 See Introd. p. vi., and for details of their iniquity, Serm. XVI. chaps. 4 and 5: the words *proxima confessione* fix the date of this sermon probably in 444 or 445.

are found to be as filthy in their rites as they are blasphemers in their doctrines.

V. *Other heresies contain some portion of truth, but the Manichæans contain none whatever.*

Other heresies, dearly beloved, although they are all rightly to be condemned in their variety, yet have each in some part of them that which is true. Arius, in laying down that the Son of God is less than the Father and a creature, and in thinking that the Holy Spirit was like all else made by the same (Father), has lost himself in great blasphemy; but he has not denied the eternal and unchangeable Godhead in the essence of the Father, though he could not see it in the Unity of the Trinity. Macedonius was devoid of the light of the Truth when he did not receive the Godhead of the Holy Spirit, but he did acknowledge one power and the same nature in the Father and the Son. Sabellius was plunged into inextricable error by holding the unity of substance to be inseparable in the Father, Son and Holy Spirit, but granted to a singleness of nature what he should have attributed to an equality of nature[2], and because he could not understand a true Trinity, he believed in one and the same person under a threefold appellation. Photinus, misled by his mental blindness, acknowledged in Christ true man of our substance, but did not believe Him born God of God before all ages, and so losing the entirety of the Faith, believed the Son of God to have taken on Him the true nature of human flesh in such a way as to assert that there was no soul in it, because the Godhead Itself took its place[3]. Thus, if all the errors which the catholic Faith has anathematized are recanted, something is found in one after another which can be separated from its damnable setting. But in the detestable dogma of the Manicheans there is absolutely nothing which can be adjudged tolerable in any degree.

VI. *Christians must cling to the one Faith and not be led astray.*

But you, dearly beloved, whom I address in no less earnest terms than those of the blessed Apostle Peter, "a chosen race, a royal priesthood, a holy nation, a people for God's own possession[4]," built upon the impregnable rock, Christ, and joined to the Lord our Saviour by His true assumption of our flesh, remain firm in that Faith, which you have professed before many witnesses, and in which you were reborn through water and the Holy Ghost, and received the anointing of salvation, and the seal of eternal life[5]. But "if any one preach to you any thing beside that which you have learnt, let him be anathema[6]:" refuse to put wicked fables before the clearest truth, and what you may happen to read or hear contrary to the rule of the catholic and Apostolic creed, judge it altogether deadly and diabolical. Be not carried away by their deceitful keepings of sham and pretended fasts which tend not to the cleansing, but to the destroying of men's souls. They put on indeed a cloke of piety and chastity, but under this deceit they conceal the filthiness of their acts, and from the recesses of their ungodly heart hurl shafts to wound the simple; that, as the prophet says, "they may shoot in darkness at the upright in heart[7]." A mighty bulwark is a sound faith, a true faith, to which nothing has to be added or taken away: because unless it is one, it is no faith, as the Apostle says, "one Lord, one faith, one baptism, one God and Father of all, who is above all, and through all, and in us all[8]." Cling to this unity, dearly beloved, with minds unshaken, and in it "follow after" all "holiness[9]," in it carry out the Lord's commands, because "without faith it is impossible to please God[1]," and without it nothing is holy, nothing is pure, nothing alive: "for the just lives by faith[2]," and he who by the devil's deception loses it, is dead though living, because as righteousness is gained by faith, so too by a true faith is eternal life gained, as says our Lord and Saviour. And this is life eternal, that they may know Thee, the only true God, and Jesus Christ, whom Thou hast sent[3]. May He make you to advance and persevere to the end, Who lives and reigns with the Father and the Holy Spirit, for ever and ever. Amen.

SERMON XXVI.

On the Feast of the Nativity, VI.

I. *Christmas morning is the most appropriate time for thoughts on the Nativity.*

On all days and at all times, dearly beloved, does the birth of our Lord and Saviour from the Virgin-mother occur to the thoughts of the

[2] *Quod æqualitati tribuere deberet, singularitati dedit*, cf. Lett. XV. chap. 2, where the Priscillianists' notion (of a *singularis unitas in tribus vocabulis sed non in tribus accipienda personis*), is said to be taken from Sabellianism.

[3] Cf. Ruff. *de Symb.* chap. 39, and Schaff, Ch. Hist., *in loco*, where the relation of Photinus to Marcellus is explained.

[4] 1 Pet. ii 9.

[5] *Chrisma* (*charisma*, gift. Quesnel) *salutis et signaculum vitæ æternæ*, the anointing and the sign of the cross are, as is well-known, two of the oldest baptismal ceremonies; see Bingham, Antiq. Bk. xi. chap. 9.

[6] Gal. i. 9.

[7] Ps. xi. 2.

[8] Eph. iv. 5, 6.

[9] Heb. xii. 14.

[1] Ib. xi. 6.

[2] Habbakuk ii. 4.

[3] S. John xvii. 3.

faithful, who meditate on divine things, that the mind may be aroused to the acknowledgment of its Maker, and whether it be occupied in the groans of supplication, or in the shouting of praise, or in the offering of sacrifice, may employ its spiritual insight on nothing more frequently and more trustingly than on the fact that GOD the Son of GOD, begotten of the co-eternal Father, was also born by a human birth. But this Nativity which is to be adored in heaven and on earth is suggested to us by no day more than this when, with the early light still shedding its rays on nature [4], there is borne in upon our senses the brightness of this wondrous mystery. For the angel Gabriel's converse with the astonished Mary and her conception by the Holy Ghost as wondrously promised as believed, seem to recur not only to the memory but to the very eyes. For to day the Maker of the world was born of a Virgin's womb, and He, who made all natures, became Son of her, whom He created. To-day the Word of GOD appeared clothed in flesh, and That which had never been visible to human eyes began to be tangible to our hands as well. To-day the shepherds learnt from angels' voices that the Saviour was born in the substance of our flesh and soul; and to-day the form of the Gospel message was pre-arranged by the leaders of the LORD's flocks [5], so that we too may say with the army of the heavenly host: "Glory in the highest to GOD, and on earth peace to men of good will."

II. *Christians are essentially participators in the nativity of Christ.*

Although, therefore, that infancy, which the majesty of GOD's Son did not disdain, reached mature manhood by the growth of years and, when the triumph of His passion and resurrection was completed, all the actions of humility which were undertaken for us ceased, yet to-day's festival renews for us the holy childhood of Jesus born of the Virgin Mary: and in adoring the birth of our Saviour, we find we are celebrating the commencement of our own life. For the birth of Christ is the source of life for Christian folk, and the birthday of the Head is the birthday of the body. Although every individual that is called has his own order, and all the sons of the Church are separated from one another by intervals of time, yet as the entire body of the faithful being born in the font of baptism is crucified with Christ in His passion, raised again in His resurrection, and placed at the Father's right hand in His ascension, so with Him are they born in this nativity. For any believer in whatever part of the world that is re-born in Christ, quits the old paths of his original nature [6] and passes into a new man by being re-born; and no longer is he reckoned of his earthly father's stock but among the seed of the Saviour, Who became the Son of man in order that we might have the power to be the sons of GOD. For unless He came down to us in this humiliation, no one would reach His presence by any merits of his own. Let not earthly wisdom shroud in darkness the hearts of the called on this point, and let not the frailty of earthly thoughts raise itself against the loftiness of GOD's grace, for it will soon return to the lowest dust. At the end of the ages is fulfilled that which was ordained from all eternity: and in the presence of realities, when signs and types have ceased, the Law and prophecy have become Truth: and so Abraham is found the father of all nations, and the promised blessing is given to the world in his seed: nor are they only Israelites whom blood and flesh [7] begot, but the whole body of the adopted enter into possession of the heritage prepared for the sons of Faith. Be not disturbed by the cavils of silly questionings, and let not the effects of the Divine word be dissipated by human calculation; we with Abraham believe in GOD and "waver not through unbelief [8]," but "know most assuredly that what the LORD promised, He is able to perform."

III. *Peace with GOD is His best gift to man.*

The Saviour then, dearly beloved, is born not of fleshly seed but of the Holy Spirit, in such wise that the condemnation of the first transgression did not touch Him. And hence the very greatness of the boon conferred demands of us reverence worthy of its splendour. For, as the blessed Apostle teaches, "we have received not the spirit of this world but the Spirit which is of GOD, that we may know the things which are given us by GOD [9]:" and that Spirit can in no other way be rightly worshipped, except by offering Him that which we received from Him. But in the

[4] *Nova etiam in elementis luce radiante*, the phrase seems to point to an early service as the time of delivering this sermon (possibly the *missa in gallicantu*).

[5] *Apud Dominicorum præsules gregum hodie evangelizandi forma præcondita est.* This clause has been taken to be an allusion to the reciting of the angelic hymn *Gloria in Excelsis*, at the Holy Eucharist, but as Bright (note 20, all of which should be read) says, "the words do not necessarily mean more than that the original Angelic Hymn (S. Luke ii. 14) was recited in the Christmas Day Service.

[6] *Interciso originalis tramite vetustatis.*

[7] *Sanguis et caro:* it is noticeable that the same order is observed in Heb. ii. 14.

[8] Rom. iv. 20, 21.

[9] 1 Cor. ii. 12.

treasures of the LORD's bounty what can we find so suitable to the honour of the present feast as the peace, which at the LORD's nativity was first proclaimed by the angel-choir? For that it is which brings forth the sons of GOD, the nurse of love and the mother of unity: the rest of the blessed and our eternal home; whose proper work and special office it is to join to GOD those whom it removes from the world. Whence the Apostle incites us to this good end, in saying, "being justified therefore by faith let us have peace towards GOD [1]." In which brief sentence are summed up nearly all the commandments; for where true peace is, there can be no lack of virtue. But what is it, dearly beloved, to have peace towards GOD, except to wish what He bids, and not to wish what He forbids? For if human friendships seek out equality of soul and similarity of desires, and difference of habits can never attain to full harmony, how will he be partaker of divine peace, who is pleased with what displeases GOD and desires to get delight from what he knows to be offensive to GOD? That is not the spirit of the sons of GOD; such wisdom is not acceptable to the noble family of the adopted. That chosen and royal race must live up to the dignity of its regeneration, must love what the Father loves, and in nought disagree with its Maker, lest the LORD should again say: "I have begotten and raised up sons, but they have scorned Me: the ox knoweth his owner and the ass his master's crib: but Israel hath not known Me and My people hath not acknowledged Me [2]."

IV. *We must be worthy of our calling as sons and friends of GOD.*

The mystery of this boon is great, dearly beloved, and this gift exceeds all gifts that GOD should call man son, and man should name GOD Father: for by these terms we perceive and learn the love which reached so great a height. For if in natural progeny and earthly families those who are born of noble parents are lowered by the faults of evil intercourse, and unworthy offspring are put to shame by the very brilliance of their ancestry; to what end will they come who through love of the world do not fear to be outcast from the family of Christ? But if it gains the praise of men that the father's glory should shine again in their descendants, how much more glorious is it for those who are born of GOD to regain the brightness of their Maker's likeness and display in themselves Him Who begat them, as saith the LORD: "Let your light so shine before men that they may see your good works and glorify your Father which is in heaven [3]?" We know indeed, as the Apostle John says that "the whole world lieth in the evil one [4]," and that by the stratagems of the Devil and his angels numberless attempts are made either to frighten man in his struggle upwards by adversity or to spoil him by prosperity, but "greater is He that is in us, than he that is against us [5]," and they who have peace with GOD and are always saying to the Father with their whole hearts "thy will be done [6]" can be overcome in no battles, can be hurt by no assaults. For accusing ourselves in our confessions and refusing the spirit's consent to our fleshly lusts, we stir up against us the enmity of him who is the author of sin, but secure a peace with GOD that nothing can destroy, by accepting His gracious service, in order that we may not only surrender ourselves in obedience to our King but also be united to Him by our free-will. For if we are like-minded, if we wish what He wishes, and disapprove what He disapproves, He will finish all our wars for us, He Who gave the will, will also give the power: so that we may be fellow-workers in His works, and with the exultation of Faith may utter that prophetic song: "the LORD is my light and my salvation: whom shall I fear? the LORD is the defender of my life: of whom shall I be afraid [7]?"

V. *The birth of Christ is the birth of peace to the Church.*

They then who "are born not of blood nor of the will of the flesh nor of the will of man but of GOD [8]," must offer to the Father the unanimity of peace-loving sons, and all the members of adoption must meet in the First-begotten of the new creation, Who came to do not His own Will but His that sent Him; inasmuch as the Father in His gracious favour has adopted as His heirs not those that are discordant nor those that are unlike Him, but those that are in feeling and affection one. They that are re-modelled after one pattern must have a spirit like the model. The birthday of the LORD is the birthday of peace: for thus says the Apostle, "He is our peace, who made both one [9];" since whether we be Jew or Gentile, "through Him we have access in one Spirit to the Father [9]." And it was this in particular that He taught His disciples before the day of His passion which He had of His own free-will fore-ordained, saying, "My peace I give unto you, My peace I leave for you [1];"

[1] Rom. v. 1. [2] Is. i. 2, 3.

[3] S. Matt. v. 16. [4] 1 S. John v. 19. [5] Cf. 1 John iv. 4, and 2 Kings vi. 16. [6] S. Matt. vi. 10. [7] Ps. xxvii. 1. [8] S. John i. 13. [9] Eph. ii. 14, 18. [1] S. John xiv. 27.

and lest under the general term the character of His peace should escape notice, He added, "not as the world give I unto you[1]." The world, He says, has its friendships, and brings many that are apart into loving harmony. There are also minds which are equal in vices, and similarity of desires produces equality of affection. And if any are perchance to be found who are not pleased with what is mean and dishonourable, and who exclude from the terms of their connexion unlawful compacts, yet even such if they be either Jews, heretics or heathens[2], belong not to GOD's friendship but to this world's peace. But the peace of the spiritual and of catholics coming down from above and leading upwards refuses to hold communion with the lovers of the world, resists all obstacles and flies from pernicious pleasures to true joys, as the LORD says: "Where thy treasure is, there will thy heart be also[3]:" that is, if what you love is below, you will descend to the lowest depth: if what you love is above, you will reach the topmost height: thither may the Spirit of peace lead and bring us, whose wishes and feeling are at one, and who are of one mind in faith and hope and in charity: since "as many as are led by the Spirit of GOD these are sons of GOD[4]" Who reigneth with the Son and Holy Spirit for ever and ever. Amen.

SERMON XXVII.

ON THE FEAST OF THE NATIVITY, VII.

I. *It is equally dangerous to deny the Godhead or the Manhood in Christ.*

He is a true and devout worshipper, dearly-beloved, of to-day's festival who thinks nothing that is either false about the LORD's Incarnation or unworthy about His Godhead. For it is an equally dangerous evil to deny in Him the reality of our nature and the equality with the Father in glory. When, therefore, we attempt to understand the mystery of Christ's nativity, wherein He was born of the Virgin-mother, let all the clouds of earthly reasonings be driven far away and the smoke of worldly wisdom be purged from the eyes of illuminated faith: for the authority on which we trust is divine, the teaching which we follow is divine. Inasmuch as whether it be the testimony of the Law, or the oracles of the prophets, or the trumpet of the gospel to which we apply our inward ear, that is true which the blessed John full of the Holy Spirit uttered with his voice of thunder[5]: "in the beginning was the Word: and the Word was with GOD, and the Word was GOD. The same was in the beginning with GOD. All things were made through Him, and without Him was nothing made[6]." And similarly is it true what the same preacher added: "the Word became flesh and dwelt in us: and we beheld His glory, the glory as of the only-begotten of the Father[6]." Therefore in both natures it is the same Son of GOD taking what is ours and not losing what is His own; renewing man in His manhood, but enduring unchangeable in Himself. For the Godhead which is His in common with the Father underwent no loss of omnipotence, nor did the "form of a slave" do despite to the "form of GOD," because the supreme and eternal Essence, which lowered Itself for the salvation of mankind, transferred us into Its glory, but did not cease to be what It was. And hence when the Only-begotten of GOD confesses Himself less than the Father[7], and yet calls Himself equal with Him[7], He demonstrates the reality of both forms in Himself: so that the inequality proves the human nature, and the equality the Divine.

II. *The Incarnation has changed all the possibilities of man's existence.*

The bodily Nativity therefore of the Son of GOD took nothing from and added nothing to His Majesty because His unchangeable substance could be neither diminished nor increased. For that "the Word became flesh" does not signify that the nature of GOD was changed into flesh, but that the Word took the flesh into the unity of His Person: and therein undoubtedly the whole man was received, with which within the Virgin's womb fecundated by the Holy Spirit, whose virginity was destined never to be lost[8], the Son of GOD was so inseparably united that He who was born without time of the Father's essence was Himself in time born of the Virgin's womb. For we could not otherwise be released from the chains of eternal death but by Him becoming humble in our nature, Who remained Almighty in His own. And so our LORD Jesus Christ, being at birth true man though He never ceased to be true GOD, made in Himself the beginning of a new creation,

---

[1] Ib.
[2] *Pagani* (lit. villagers or rustics): the later meaning arose from the fact that idolatry and superstition tends to linger longer in out-of-the-way rural districts, than in the more civilized towns: cf. "heath" and "heathen." See Bright's note 24, and the references quoted by him. Hooker, v. 80. 2; Trench, "on Study of Words," p. 69, &c [3] S. Matt. vi. 21.
[4] Rom. viii. 14.
[5] *Intonuit*, no doubt a reference to the name of Boanerges (sons of thunder) which he shared with his brother James (S. Mark iii. 17). [6] S John i. 1—3, 14. [7] S. John xiv. 28, and x. 30.
[8] *Et nunquam virginitate caritura*, cf. Letter XXVIII. (Tome) chap. 2, *beatam Mariam semper virginem*: these two passages seem to me much stronger than others quoted by Bright, n. 9, to prove Leo's belief in the perpetual virginity of the blessed Mary.

and in the "form" of His birth started the spiritual life of mankind afresh, that to abolish the taint of our birth according to the flesh there might be a possibility of regeneration without our sinful seed for those of whom it is said, "Who were born not of blood, nor of the will of the flesh, nor of the will of man, but of God [9]." What mind can grasp this mystery, what tongue can express this gracious act? Sinfulness returns to guiltlessness and the old nature becomes new; strangers receive adoption and outsiders enter upon an inheritance. The ungodly begin to be righteous, the miserly benevolent, the incontinent chaste, the earthly heavenly. And whence comes this change, save by the right hand of the Most High? For the Son of God came to "destroy the works of the devil [1]," and has so united Himself with us and us with Him that the descent of God to man's estate became the exaltation of man to God's.

III. *The Devil knows exactly what temptations to offer to each several person.*

But in this mercifulness of God, dearly beloved, the greatness of which towards us we cannot explain, Christians must be extremely careful lest they be caught again in the devil's wiles and once more entangled in the errors which they have renounced. For the old enemy does not cease to "transform himself into an angel of light [2]," and spread everywhere the snares of his deceptions, and make every effort to corrupt the faith of believers. He knows whom to ply with the zest of greed, whom to assail with the allurements of the belly, before whom to set the attractions of self-indulgence, in whom to instil the poison of jealousy: he knows whom to overwhelm with grief, whom to cheat with joy, whom to surprise with fear, whom to bewilder with wonderment: there is no one whose habits he does not sift, whose cares he does not winnow, whose affections he does not pry into: and wherever he sees a man most absorbed in occupation, there he seeks opportunity to injure him. Moreover he has many whom he has bound still more tightly because they are suited for his designs, that he may use their abilities and tongues to deceive others. Through them are guaranteed the healing of sicknesses, the prognosticating of future events, the appeasing of demons and the driving away of apparitions [3]. They also are to be added [4] who falsely allege that the entire condition of human life depends on the influences of the stars, and that that which is really either the divine will or ours rests with the unchangeable fates. And yet, in order to do still greater harm, they promise that they can be changed if supplication is made to those constellations which are adverse. And thus their ungodly fabrications destroy themselves; for if their predictions are not reliable, the fates are not to be feared: if they are, the stars are not to be venerated.

IV. *The foolish practice of some who turn to the sun and bow to it is reprehensible.*

From such a system of teaching proceeds also the ungodly practice of certain foolish folk who worship the sun as it rises at the beginning of daylight from elevated positions: even some Christians think it is so proper to do this that, before entering the blessed Apostle Peter's basilica, which is dedicated to the One Living and true God, when they have mounted the steps which lead to the raised platform [5], they turn round and bow themselves towards the rising sun and with bent neck do homage to its brilliant orb. We are full of grief and vexation that this should happen, which is partly due to the fault of ignorance and partly to the spirit of heathenism: because although some of them do perhaps worship the Creator of that fair light rather than the Light itself, which is His creature, yet we must abstain even from the appearance of this observance: for if one who has abandoned the worship of gods, finds it in our own worship, will he not hark back again to this fragment of his old superstition, as if it were allowable, when he sees it to be common both to Christians and to infidels?

V. *The sun and moon were created for use, not for worship.*

This objectionable practice must be given up therefore by the faithful, and the honour due to God alone must not be mixed up with those men's rites who serve their fellow-creatures. For the divine Scripture says: "Thou shalt worship the Lord thy God, and Him only shalt thou serve [6]." And the blessed Job, "a man without complaint," as the Lord

---

9 S. John i. 13.

1 1 S. John iii. 8.

2 2 Cor. xi. 14.

3 *Umbrarum.*

4 Cf. Lett. XV. chaps. 12—14, where such opinions are put down to the Spanish Priscillianists, though doubtless Leo is thinking here rather of the Manichæans, from whom they derived so many of their false views.

5 *Suggestum areæ superioris*: the older reading was *aræ*: some of the MSS. again read *arcæ* which is no doubt midway between the two. A learned dissertation on this passage by Ciampini quoted by Quesnel (Migne's Patrol. i. pp 529—534), established the true reading: he says also that this was the staircase up which the faithful climbed on bended knee in approaching the Vatican *basilica*. S. Leo has alluded to this curious practice already in Serm. XXII. chap. 6, *supra*. It is perhaps hardly necessary to add that this superstition has little, if any, connexion with the Christian habit of turning to the East, which is probably rather to the Altar as the centre of worship; for at all events in Western Christendom churches do not by any means universally 'orientate' (i.e. lie due east and west).

6 S. Matt. iv. 10.

says, "and one that eschews every evil[7]," said, "Have I seen the sun when it shone or the moon walking brightly, and my heart hath rejoiced in secret, and I have kissed my hand: what is my great iniquity and denial against the most High God[8]?" But what is the sun or what is the moon but elements of visible creation and material light: one of which is of greater brightness and the other of lesser light? For as it is now day time and now night time, so the Creator has constituted divers kinds of luminaries, although even before they were made there had been days without the sun and nights without the moon[9]. But these were fashioned to serve in making man, that he who is an animal endowed with reason might be sure of the distinction of the months, the recurrence of the year, and the variety of the seasons, since through the unequal length of the various periods, and the clear indications given by the changes in its risings, the sun closes the year and the moon renews the months. For on the fourth day, as we read, God said: "Let there be lights in the firmament of the heaven, and let them shine upon the earth, and let them divide between day and night, and let them be for signs and for seasons, and for days and years, and let them be in the firmament of heaven that they may shine upon earth."

VI. *Let us awake to the proper use of all our parts and faculties.*

Awake, O man, and recognize the dignity of thy nature. Recollect thou wast made in the image of God, which although it was corrupted in Adam, was yet re-fashioned in Christ. Use visible creatures as they should be used, as thou usest earth, sea, sky, air, springs, and rivers: and whatever in them is fair and wondrous, ascribe to the praise and glory of the Maker. Be not subject to that light wherein birds and serpents, beasts and cattle, flies and worms delight. Confine the material light to your bodily senses, and with all your mental powers embrace that "true light which lighteth every man that cometh into this world[1]," and of which the prophet says, "Come unto Him and be enlightened, and your faces shall not blush[2]." For if we "are a temple of God, and the Spirit of God dwelleth in[2a]" us, what every one of the faithful has in his own heart is more than what he wonders at in heaven. And so, dearly beloved, we do not bid or advise you to despise God's works or to think there is anything opposed to your Faith in what the good God has made good, but to use every kind of creature and the whole furniture of this world reasonably and moderately: for as the Apostle says, "the things which are seen are temporal: but the things which are not seen are eternal[3]." Hence because we are born for the present and reborn for the future, let us not give ourselves up to temporal goods, but to eternal: and in order that we may behold our hope nearer, let us think on what the Divine Grace has bestowed on our nature on the very occasion when we celebrate the mystery of the Lord's birthday. Let us hear the Apostle, saying: "for ye are dead, and your life is hid with Christ in God. But when Christ, who is your life, shall appear, then shall ye also appear with Him in glory[4]:" who lives and reigns with the Father and the Holy Ghost for ever and ever. Amen.

SERMON XXVIII.

On the Festival of the Nativity, VIII.

I. *The Incarnation an unceasing source of joy.*

Though all the divine utterances exhort us, dearly beloved, to "rejoice in the Lord always[5]," yet to-day we are no doubt incited to a full spiritual joy, when the mystery of the Lord's nativity is shining brightly upon us[6], so that we may have recourse to that unutterable condescension of the Divine Mercy, whereby the Creator of men deigned to become man, and be found ourselves in His nature whom we worship in ours. For God the Son of God, the only-begotten of the eternal and not-begotten Father, remaining eternal "in the form of God," and unchangeably and without time[7] possessing the property of being no way different to the Father He received "the form of a slave" without loss of His own majesty, that He might advance us to His state and not lower Himself to ours. Hence both natures abiding in possession of their own properties such unity is the result of the union that whatever of Godhead is there is inseparable from the manhood: and whatever of manhood, is indivisible from the Godhead.

II. *The Virgin's conception explained.*

In celebrating therefore the birthday of our Lord and Saviour, dearly beloved, let us

---

7 Job i. 8. 8 Ib. xxxi. 26—28.

9 He is of course following the Mosaic order of creation, where the creation of the day and night is ascribed to the first day and that of the Sun and Moon to the fourth day (Gen. i. 5, 1—19).

1 S. John i. 9. 2 Ps. xxxiv. 5. 2a 1 Cor. iii. 16.

3 2 Cor. iv. 18. 4 Col. iii. 3, 4. 5 Phil. iv. 4.

6 *Nativitatis Dominicæ sacramento nobis clarius coruscante*: cf. XXVI. chap. 1, note 1. I have no doubt that *sacramentum* here is almost equivalent to "the festival with its sacred observances" (cf. Bright's n. 8), but I have preferred to translate it as uniformly as possible by the same word "mystery." Cf. Sermon XXXI. chap. 1.

7 In contradiction of the Arian's position ἦν ποτε ὅτε οὐκ ἦν: cf. Lett. XXVIII. (Tome), chap. 2, *de æterno natus est coæternus: non posterior tempore.*

entertain pure thoughts of the blessed Virgin's child-bearing, so as to believe that at no moment of time was the power of the Word wanting to the flesh and soul which she conceived, and that the temple of Christ's body did not previously receive its form and soul that its Inhabitant might come and take possession but through Himself and in Himself was the beginning given to the New Man, so that in the one Son of GOD and Man there might be Godhead without a mother, and Manhood without a Father. For her virginity fecundated by the Holy Spirit at one and the same time brought forth without trace of corruption both the offspring and the Maker of her race. Hence also the same LORD, as the Evangelist relates, asked of the Jews whose son they had learnt Christ to be on the authority of the Scriptures, and when they replied that the tradition was He would come of David's seed, "How," saith He, "doth David in the Spirit call Him LORD, saying, the LORD said to my LORD: sit thou on My right hand till I place thy enemies as the footstool of thy feet[8]?" And the Jews could not solve the question put, because they did not understand that in the one Christ both the stock of David and the Divine nature were there prophesied.

III. *In redeeming man, justice as well as mercy had to be considered.*

But the majesty of the Son of GOD in which He is equal with the Father in its garb of a slave's humility feared no diminution, required no augmentation: and the very effect of His mercy which He expended on the restitution of man, He was able to bring about solely by the power of His Godhead; so as to rescue the creature that was made in the image of GOD from the yoke of his cruel oppressor. But because the devil had not shown himself so violent in his attack on the first man as to bring him over to his side without the consent of His free will, man's voluntary sin and hostile desires had to be destroyed in such wise that the standard of justice should not stand in the way of the gift of Grace. And therefore in the general ruin of the entire human race there was but one remedy in the secret of the Divine plan which could succour the fallen, and that was that one of the sons of Adam should be born free and innocent of original transgression, to prevail for the rest both by His example and His merits. Still further, because this was not permitted by natural generation, and because there could be no offspring from our faulty stock without seed, of which the Scripture saith, "Who can make a clean thing conceived of an unclean seed? is it not Thou who art alone[9]?" David's LORD was made David's Son, and from the fruit of the promised branch[1] sprang One without fault, the twofold nature coming together into one Person, that by one and the same conception and birth might spring our LORD Jesus Christ, in Whom was present both true Godhead for the performance of mighty works and true Manhood for the endurance of sufferings.

IV. *All heresies proceed from failure to believe the twofold nature of Christ.*

The catholic Faith then, dearly beloved, may scorn the errors of the heretics that bark against it, who, deceived by the vanity of worldly wisdom, have forsaken the Gospel of Truth, and being unable to understand the Incarnation of the Word, have constructed for themselves out of the source of enlightenment occasion of blindness. For after investigating almost all false believers' opinions, even those which presume to deny the Holy Spirit, we come to the conclusion that hardly any one has gone astray, unless he has refused to believe the reality of the two natures in Christ under the confession of one Person. For some have ascribed to the LORD only manhood[2], others only Deity[3]. Some have said that, though there was in Him true Godhead, His flesh was unreal[4]. Others have acknowledged that He took true flesh but say that He had not the nature of GOD the Father; and by assigning to His Godhead what belonged to His human substance, have made for themselves a greater and a lesser GOD, although there can be in true Godhead no grades: seeing that whatever is less than GOD, is not GOD[5]. Others recognizing that there is no difference between Father and Son, because they could not understand unity of Godhead except in unity of Person, have maintained that the Father is the same as the Son[6]: so that to be born and nursed, to suffer and die, to be buried and rise again, belonged to the same Father who sustained throughout the Person of both

8 S. Matt. xxii. 43, 44, quoted from Psalm cx. 1.

9 Job xiv. 4.

1 *Germinis* preferred to the older reading *generis* by the Ballerinii as agreeing better with Is. xl. 1 and Jer. xxiii. 5.

2 These were called 'Psilanthropists' (upholders of the mere manhood): of whom Cerinthus (the opponent of S. John) was the earliest propounder.

3 These are heretics like Sabellius the founder of the Patripassian impiety.

4 These are 'Docetists,' to whom Leo in Sermon LXV., chap. 4, compares the Eutychians *isti phantasmatici Christiani*. Simon Magus was the earliest exponent of this view.

5 These are Arians who, as Bright (n. 29) points out, in wishing to pacify the catholics by exalting the character of Christ without acknowledging His equality with the Father, fell into the error of setting up two Gods (an Uncreate and a Created).

6 This is the heresy alluded to in note 3 above.

Man and the Word. Certain have thought that our LORD Jesus Christ had a body not of our substance but assumed from higher and subtler elements [7]: whereas certain others have considered that in the flesh of Christ there was no human soul, but that the Godhead of the Word Itself fulfilled the part of soul [8]. But their unwise assertion passes into this form that, though they acknowledge the existence of a soul in the LORD, yet they say it was devoid of mind, because the Godhead of Itself was sufficient for all purposes of reason to the Man as well as to the GOD in Christ. Lastly the same people have dared to assert that a certain portion of the Word was turned into Flesh, so that in the manifold varieties of this one dogma, not only the nature of the flesh and of the soul but also the essence of the Word Itself is dissolved.

V. *Nestorianism and Eutychianism are particularly to be avoided at the present time.*

There are many other astounding falsehoods also which we must not weary your ears, beloved, with enumerating. But after all these various impieties, which are closely connected by the relationship that exists between one form of blasphemy and another, we call your devout attention to the avoiding of these two errors in particular: one of which, with Nestorius for its author, some time ago attempted to gain ground, but ineffectually; the other, which is equally damnable, has more recently sprung up with Eutyches as its propounder. The former dared to maintain that the blessed Virgin Mary was the mother of Christ's manhood only, so that in her conception and child-bearing no union might be believed to have taken place of the Word and the Flesh: because the Son of GOD did not Himself become Son of Man, but of His mere condescension linked Himself with created man. This can in no wise be tolerated by catholic ears, which are so imbued with the gospel of Truth that they know of a surety there is no hope of salvation for mankind unless He were Himself the Son of the Virgin who was His mother's Creator. On the other hand this blasphemous propounder of more recent profanity has confessed the union of the two Natures in Christ, but has maintained that the effect of this very union is that of the two one remained while the substance of the other no longer existed, which of course could not have been brought to an end except by either destruction or separation [9]. But this is so opposed to sound faith that it cannot be entertained without loss of one's Christian name. For if the Incarnation of the Word is the uniting of the Divine and human natures, but by the very fact of their coming together that which was twofold became single, it was only the Godhead that was born of the Virgin's womb, and went through the deceptive appearance of receiving nourishment and bodily growth: and to pass over all the changes of the human state, it was only the Godhead that was crucified, dead, and buried: so that according to those who thus think, there is no reason to hope for the resurrection, and Christ is not "the first-begotten from the dead [1];" because He was not One who ought to have been raised again, if He had not been One who could be slain.

VI. *The Deity and the Manhood were present in Christ from the very first.*

Keep far from your hearts, dearly beloved, the poisonous lies of the devil's inspirations, and knowing that the eternal Godhead of the Son underwent no growth while with the Father, be wise and consider that to the same nature to which it was said in Adam, "Thou art earth, and unto earth shalt thou go [2]," it is said in Christ, "sit Thou on My right hand [3]." According to that Nature, whereby Christ is equal to the Father, the Only-begotten was never inferior to the sublimity of the Father; nor was the glory which He had with the Father a temporal possession; for He is on the very right hand of the Father, of which it is said in Exodus, "Thy right hand, O LORD, is glorified in power [4];" and in Isaiah, "LORD, who hath believed our report? and the arm of the LORD, to whom is it revealed [5]?" The man, therefore, assumed into the Son of GOD, was in such wise received into the unity of Christ's Person from His very commencement in the body, that without the Godhead He was not conceived, without the Godhead He was not brought forth, without the Godhead He was not nursed. It was the same Person in the wondrous acts, and in the endurance of insults; through His human weakness crucified, dead and buried: through His Divine power, being

7 *Ab elementis superioribus et subtilioribus sumptum*, cf. Serm. XXX. chap. 2, *de sublimioris generis prodiisse materia*. This is the modification of "Docetism" adopted by the Gnostic Valentinus (see Bright's note 31).

8 This is the view of Apollinaris.

9 It is doubtful whether Eutyches did ever actually say this, but it was the logical inference from his position: as Gore (p. 57), says, "Eutyches never formulated a heresy: he was no philosopher; but he refused to say that the human nature remained in Christ after the Incarnation. He shrank from calling Christ 'of one substance' with us men: in some sort of way he left us to suppose that the human nature was absorbed into and lost in the Divinity.

1 Col. i. 18

2 Gen. iii. 19.

3 Ps. cix. 1.

4 Exod. xvi. 6.

5 Is. liii. 1.

raised the third day, He ascended to the heavens, sat down at the right hand of the Father, and in His nature as man received from the Father that which in His nature as God He Himself also gave[6].

VII. *The fulness of the Godhead is imparted to the Body* (*the Church*) *through the Head,* (*Christ*).

Meditate, dearly beloved, on these things with devout hearts, and be always mindful of the apostle's injunction, who admonishes all men, saying, "See lest any one deceive you through philosophy and vain deceit according to the tradition of men, and not according to Christ; for in Him dwelleth all the fulness of the Godhead bodily, and ye have been filled in Him[7]." He said not "spiritually" but "bodily," that we may understand the substance of flesh to be real, where there is the dwelling in the body of the fulness of the Godhead: wherewith, of course, the whole Church is also filled, which, clinging to the Head, is the body of Christ; who liveth and reigneth with the Father and the Holy Ghost, God for ever and ever. Amen.

SERMON XXXI.

On the Feast of the Epiphany, I.

I. *The Epiphany a necessary sequel to the Nativity.*

After celebrating but lately the day on which immaculate virginity brought forth the Saviour of mankind, the venerable feast of the Epiphany, dearly beloved, gives us continuance of joy, that the force of our exultation and the fervour of our faith may not grow cool, in the midst of neighbouring and kindred mysteries[8]. For it concerns all men's salvation, that the infancy of the Mediator between God and men was already manifested to the whole world, while He was still detained in the tiny town. For although He had chosen the Israelitish nation, and one family out of that nation, from whom to assume the nature of all mankind, yet He was unwilling that the early days of His birth should be concealed within the narrow limits of His mother's home: but desired to be soon recognized by all, seeing that He deigned to be born for all. To three[9] wise men, therefore, appeared a star of new splendour in the region of the East, which, being brighter and fairer than the other stars, might easily attract the eyes and minds of those that looked on it, so that at once that might be observed not to be meaningless, which had so unusual an appearance. He therefore who gave the sign, gave to the beholders understanding of it, and caused inquiry to be made about that, of which He had thus caused understanding, and after inquiry made, offered Himself to be found.

II. *Herod's evil designs were fruitless. The Wise men's gifts were consciously symbolical.*

These three men follow the leading of the light above, and with stedfast gaze obeying the indications of the guiding splendour, are led to the recognition of the Truth by the brilliance of Grace, for they supposed that a king's birth was notified in a human sense[1], and that it must be sought in a royal city. Yet He who had taken a slave's form, and had come not to judge, but to be judged, chose Bethlehem for His nativity, Jerusalem for His passion. But Herod, hearing that a prince of the Jews was born, suspected a successor, and was in great terror: and to compass the death of the Author of Salvation, pledged himself to a false homage. How happy had he been, if he had imitated the wise men's faith, and turned to a pious use what he designed for deceit. What blind wickedness of foolish jealousy, to think thou canst overthrow the Divine plan by thy frenzy. The Lord of the world, who offers an eternal Kingdom, seeks not a temporal. Why dost thou attempt to change the unchangeable order of things ordained, and to forestall others in their crime? The death of Christ belongs not to thy time. The Gospel must be first set on foot, the Kingdom of God first preached, healings first given to the sick, wondrous acts first performed. Why dost thou wish thyself to have the blame of what will belong to another's work, and why without being able to effect thy wicked design, dost thou bring on thyself alone the charge of wishing the evil? Thou gainest nothing and carriest out nothing by this intriguing. He that was born voluntarily shall die of His own free will. The Wise men, therefore, fulfil their desire, and come to the child, the Lord Jesus Christ, the same star going before them. They adore the Word in flesh, the Wisdom in infancy, the Power in weakness, the Lord of majesty in the reality of man: and by their gifts make

6 Cf. Lett. XXVIII. (Tome), chap. 6.

7 Col. ii. 8—10.

8 *Inter cognatarum solemnitatum vicina sacramenta*, cf. Serm. XXVIII. chap. 1, note 2.

9 The number "three" has no further scriptural support than the possible inference from their threefold offerings. It will be noticed that S. Leo knows nothing of their being kings, though that tradition is apparently as old as Tertullian (adv. Marc. iii. 13), see Bright's n. 38.

1 *Humano sensu significatum sibi regis ortum*, "by their natural thoughts' in Bright's translation: but I doubt whether the words could bear that meaning, and whether they suit the context: cf. Serm. XXXIV. chap. 2.

open acknowledgment of what they believe in their hearts, that they may show forth the mystery of their faith and understanding[2]. The incense they offer to God, the myrrh to Man, the gold to the King, consciously paying honour to the Divine and human Nature in union: because while each substance had its own properties, there was no difference in the power[3] of either.

III. *The massacre of the Innocents is in harmony with the Virgin's conception, which again teaches us purity of life.*

And when the wise men had returned to their own land, and Jesus had been carried into Egypt at the Divine suggestion, Herod's madness blazes out into fruitless schemes. He orders all the little ones in Bethlehem to be slain, and since he knows not which infant to fear, extends a general sentence against the age he suspects. But that which the wicked king removes from the world, Christ admits to heaven: and on those for whom He had not yet spent His redeeming blood, He already bestows the dignity of martyrdom. Lift your faithful hearts then, dearly-beloved, to the gracious blaze of eternal light, and in adoration of the mysteries dispensed for man's salvation[4] give your diligent heed to the things which have been wrought on your behalf. Love the purity of a chaste life, because Christ is the Son of a virgin. "Abstain from fleshly lusts which war against the soul[5]," as the blessed Apostle, present in his words as we read, exhorts us, "In malice be ye children[6]," because the Lord of glory conformed Himself to the infancy of mortals. Follow after humility which the Son of God deigned to teach His disciples. Put on the power of patience, in which ye may be able to gain[7] your souls; seeing that He who is the Redemption of all, is also the Strength of all. "Set your minds on the things which are above, not on the things which are on the earth[8]." Walk firmly along the path of truth and life: let not earthly things hinder you for whom are prepared heavenly things through our Lord Jesus Christ, who with the Father and the Holy Ghost liveth and reigneth for ever and ever. Amen.

[2] *Sacramentum fidei suæ intelligentiæque:* here *sacramentum* seems to come nearer to the older and more general use of the word among the Fathers, viz. symbol or sign.

[3] "He means, Christ had a king's power, both as God and as Man," Bright, n. 42.

[4] *Impensa humanæ saluti sacramenta.*

[5] 1 Peter ii. 11. [6] 1 Cor. xiv. 20.

[7] *Acquirere*, S. Luke xxi. 19. It is not clear from this whether in Leo's time the reading was future, "ye shall win" (R.V.), or imperative, "possess ye" (A.V.). The Vulgate now reads *possidebitis.*

[8] Col. iii. 2.

SERMON XXXIII.

On the Feast of the Epiphany, III.

I. *When we were yet sinners, Christ came to save.*

Although I know, dearly-beloved, that you are fully aware of the purpose of to-day's festival, and that the words of the Gospel[9] have according to use unfolded it to you, yet that nothing may be omitted on our part, I shall venture to say on the subject what the Lord has put in my mouth: so that in our common joy the devotion of our hearts may be so much the more sincere as the reason of our keeping the feast is better understood. The providential Mercy of God, having determined to succour the perishing world in these latter times, fore-ordained the salvation of all nations in the Person of Christ; in order that, because all nations had long been turned aside from the worship of the true God by wicked error, and even God's peculiar people Israel had well-nigh entirely fallen away from the enactments of the Law, now that all were shut up under sin[1], He might have mercy upon all.

For as justice was everywhere failing and the whole world was given over to vanity and wickedness, if the Divine Power had not deferred its judgment, the whole of mankind would have received the sentence of damnation. But wrath was changed to forgiveness, and, that the greatness of the Grace to be displayed might be the more conspicuous, it pleased God, to apply the mystery of remission to the abolishing of men's sins at a time when no one could boast of his own merits.

II. *The wise men from the East are typical fulfilments of God's promise to Abraham.*

Now the manifestation of this unspeakable mercy, dearly-beloved, came to pass when Herod held the royal power in Judæa, where the legitimate succession of Kings having failed and the power of the High-priests having been overthrown, an alien-born had gained the sovereignty: that the rising of the true King might be attested by the voice of prophecy, which had said: "a prince shall not fail from Juda, nor a leader from his loins, until He come for whom it is reserved[2], and He shall

[9] *Secundum consuetudinem evangelicus sermo reseraverit.* The Roman Gospel for the day was apparently then, as now with us, S. Matt. ii. 1—12: but the manifestation of Christ to the wise men was not universally so prominent a feature of the Festival as other manifestations of Him, e.g. His birth (Jan. 6 having been in the East the original Christmas Day), His baptism, &c.

[1] Gal. iii. 22, cf. Rom. xi. 32.

[2] Gen. xlix. 10, *donec veniat cui repositum est* (ᾧ ἀπόκειται), cf. Ezek. xxi. 27: the reading of A. and R. VV. is "until Shiloh

be the expectation of the nations." Concerning which an innumerable succession was once promised to the most blessed patriarch Abraham to be begotten not by fleshly seed but by fertile faith; and therefore it was compared to the stars in multitude that as father of all the nations he might hope not for an earthly but for a heavenly progeny. And therefore, for the creating of the promised posterity, the heirs designated under the figure of the stars are awakened by the rising of a new star, that the ministrations of the heaven might do service in that wherein the witness of the heaven had been adduced. A star more brilliant than the other stars arouses wise men that dwell in the far East, and from the brightness of the wondrous light these men, not unskilled in observing such things, appreciate the importance of the sign: this doubtless being brought about in their hearts by Divine inspiration, in order that the mystery of so great a sight might not be hid from them, and, what was an unusual appearance to their eyes, might not be obscure to their minds. In a word they scrupulously set about their duty and provide themselves with such gifts that in worshipping the One they may at the same time show their belief in His threefold function: with gold they honour the Person of a King, with myrrh that of Man, with incense that of GOD[3].

III. *The chosen race is no longer the Jews, but believers of every nation.*

And so they enter the chief city of the Kingdom of Judæa, and in the royal city ask that He should be shown them Whom they had learnt was begotten to be King. Herod is perturbed: he fears for his safety, he trembles for his power, he asks of the priests and teachers of the Law what the Scripture has predicted about the birth of Christ, he ascertains what had been prophesied: truth enlightens the wise men, unbelief blinds the experts: carnal Israel understands not what it reads, sees not what it points out; refers to the pages, whose utterances it does not believe. Where is thy boasting, O Jew? where thy noble birth drawn from the stem of Abraham? is not thy circumcision become uncircumcision[4]? Behold thou, the greater servest the less[5], and by the reading of that covenant[6] which thou keepest in the letter only, thou becomest the slave of strangers born, who enter into the lot of thy heritage. Let the fulness of the nations enter into the family of the patriarchs, yea let it enter, and let the sons of promise receive in Abraham's seed the blessing which his sons, according to the flesh, renounce their claim to. In the three Magi[7] let all people worship the Author of the universe: and let GOD be known not in Judæa alone, but in all the world, so that everywhere "His name" may be "great in Israel[8]." For while the dignity of the chosen race is proved to be degenerate by unbelief in its descendants, it is made common to all alike by our belief.

IV. *The massacre of the Innocents through the consequent flight of Christ, brings the truth into Egypt.*

Now when the wise men had worshipped the LORD and finished all their devotions, according to the warning of a dream, they return not by the same route by which they had come. For it behoved them now that they believed in Christ not to walk in the paths of their old line of life, but having entered on a new way to keep away from the errors they had left: and it was also to baffle Herod's design, who, under the cloke of homage, was planning a wicked plot against the Infant Jesus. Hence when his crafty hopes were overthrown, the king's wrath rose to a greater fury. For reckoning up the time which the wise men had indicated, he poured out his cruel rage on all the men-children of Bethlehem, and in a general massacre of the whole of that city[9] slew the infants, who thus passed to their eternal glory, thinking that, if every single babe was slain there, Christ too would be slain. But He Who was postponing the shedding of His blood for the world's redemption till another time, was carried and brought into Egypt by his parents' aid, and thus sought the ancient cradle of the Hebrew race, and in the power of a greater providence dispensing the princely office of the true Joseph, in that He, the Bread of Life and the Food of reason that came down from heaven, removed that worse than all famines under which the Egyptians' minds were labouring, the lack of truth[1], nor without

come;" the LXX. read ἕως ἂν ἔλθῃ τὰ ἀποκείμενα αὐτῷ, and the Vulgate, *donec veniat qui mittendus erat*. Origen paraphrases thus: "He should come for Whom the things were reserved, that is, the Christ of GOD, the Prince of the Divine promises. He alone could be called the expectation of the nations, for men of all nations believed in GOD through Him, according to the words of Isaiah, 'In His name shall the Gentiles trust.'" *Hom. in Genesin* xvii. § 6.

3 Cf. Serm. XXXI. chap. 2, above.

4 Rom. ii. 25.

5 Gen. xxv. 23.

6 Or "will" (*testamenti*, διαθήκης).

7 Cf. Sermon XXXI. chaps. i. and ii.

8 Ps. lxxvi. 1.

9 *Cæde generali universæ civitatis illius*; as the context shows, this phrase is rhetorically exaggerated.

1 Cf. Sermon XXXII. chap. 1, *Tunc autem Ægypto Salvator illatus est, ut gens antiquis erroribus dedita, iam ad vicinam salutem per occultam gratiam vocaretur; et quæ nondum eje cerat ab animo superstitionem, iam reciperet veritatem.*

that sojourn would the symbolism of that One Victim have been complete; for there first by the slaying of the lamb was fore-shadowed the health-bringing sign of the Cross and the LORD's Passover.

V. *We must keep this festival as thankful sons of light.*

Taught then, dearly-beloved, by these mysteries of Divine grace, let us with reasonable joy celebrate the day of our first-fruits and the commencement of the nations' calling: "giving thanks to" the merciful GOD "who made us worthy," as the Apostle says, "to be partakers of the lot of the saints in light: who delivered us from the power of darkness and translated us into the kingdom of the Son of His love[2]:" since as Isaiah prophesied, "the people of the nations that sat in darkness, have seen a great light, and they that dwelt in the land of the shadow of death, upon them hath the light shined[3]." Of whom he also said to the LORD, "nations which knew not thee, shall call on thee: and peoples which were ignorant of thee, shall run together unto thee[4]." This day "Abraham saw and was glad[5]," when he understood that the sons of his faith would be blessed in his seed that is in Christ, and foresaw that by believing he should be the father of all nations, "giving glory to GOD and being fully assured that What He had promised, He was able also to perform[6]." This day David sang of in the psalms saying: "all nations that thou hast made shall come and worship before Thee, O LORD: and they shall glorify Thy name[7];" and again: "The LORD hath made known His salvation: His righteousness hath He openly showed in the sight of the nations[8]." This in good truth we know to have taken place ever since the three wise men aroused in their far-off land were led by a star to recognize and worship the King of heaven and earth, [which to those who gaze aright ceases not daily to appear. And if it could make Christ known when concealed in infancy, how much more able was it to reveal Him when reigning in majesty][9]. And surely their worship of Him exhorts us to imitation; that, as far as we can, we should serve our gracious GOD who invites us all to Christ. For whosoever lives religiously and chastely in the Church and "sets his mind on the things which are above, not on the things that are upon the earth[1]," is in some measure like the heavenly light: and whilst he himself keeps the brightness of a holy life, he points out to many the way to the LORD like a star. In which regard, dearly-beloved, ye ought all to help one another in turn, that in the kingdom of GOD, which is reached by right faith and good works, ye may shine as the sons of light: through our LORD Jesus Christ, Who with GOD the Father and the Holy Spirit lives and reigns for ever and ever. Amen.

[2] Col. i. 12, 13. [3] Is. ix. 2. [4] Ib. lv. 5.
[5] S. John viii. 56.
[6] Rom. iv. 21. [7] Ps. lxxxvi. 9. [8] Ps. xcviii. 2.
[9] Both Quesnel and the Ballerinii condemn this passage inclosed in brackets as spurious. The former thinks it has crept into the text *ex annotatione marginali alicuius astrologiæ plus æquo dediti*. It is wanting in all the MSS. *melioris notæ*.
[1] Col. iii. 2.

SERMON XXXIV.

ON THE FEAST OF THE EPIPHANY, IV.

I. *The yearly observance of the Epiphany is profitable to Christians.*

It is the right and reasonable duty of true piety, dearly-beloved, on the days which bear witness to the works of Divine mercy, to rejoice with the whole heart and to celebrate with all honour the things which have been wrought for our salvation: for the very law of recurring seasons calls us to such devout observance, and has now brought before us the feast of the Epiphany, consecrated by the LORD's appearance soon after the day on which the Son of GOD co-eternal with the Father was born of a Virgin. And herein the providence of GOD has established a great safeguard to our faith, so that, whilst the worship of the Saviour's earliest infancy is repeated year by year, the production of true man's nature in Him might be proved by the original verifications themselves. For this it is that justifies the ungodly, this it is that makes sinners saints, to wit the belief in the true Godhead and the true Manhood of the one Jesus Christ, our LORD: the Godhead, whereby being before all ages "in the form of GOD" He is equal with the Father: the Manhood whereby in the last days He is united to Man in the "form of a slave." For the confirmation therefore of this Faith which was to be fore-armed against all errors, it was a wondrous loving provision of the Divine plan that a nation which dwelt in the far-off country of the East and was cunning in the art of reading the stars, should receive the sign of the infant's birth who was to reign over all Israel. For the unwonted splendour of a bright new star appeared to the wise men and filled their mind with such wonder, as they gazed upon its brilliance, that they could not think they ought to neglect what was announced to them with such distinctness. And, as the event showed, the grace of GOD was the disposing cause of this wondrous thing: who when the whole of Bethlehem itself was still unaware of Christ's birth, brought it to the knowledge of the nations who would believe, and declared that which human words could not yet explain, through the preaching of the heavens.

II. *Both Herod and the wise men originally had an earthly conception of the kingdom signified; but the latter learnt the truth, the former did not.*

But although it was the office of the Divine condescension to make the Saviour's Nativity recognizable to the nations, yet for the understanding of the wondrous sign the wise men could have had intimation even from the ancient prophecies of Balaam, knowing that it was predicted of old and by constant repetition spread abroad: "A star shall rise out of Jacob, and a man shall rise out of Israel, and shall rule the nations[2]." And so the three men aroused by God through the shining of a strange star, follow the guidance of its twinkling light, thinking they will find the babe designated at Jerusalem in the royal city. But finding themselves mistaken in this opinion, through the scribes and teachers of the Jews they learnt what the Holy Scripture had foretold of the birth of Christ; so that confirmed by a twofold witness, they sought with still more eager faith Him whom both the brightness of the star and the sure word of prophecy revealed. And when the Divine oracle was proclaimed through the chief priests' answers and the Spirit's voice declared, which says: "And thou, Bethlehem, the land of Judah, art not least among the princes of Judah; for out of thee shall come a leader to rule My people Israel[3]," how easy and how natural it was that the leading men among the Hebrews should believe what they taught! But it appears that they held material notions with Herod, and reckoned Christ's kingdom as on the same level as the powers of this world: so that they hoped for a temporal leader while he dreaded an earthly rival. The fear that racks thee, Herod, is wasted; in vain dost thou try to vent thy rage on the infant thou suspectest. Thy realm cannot hold Christ; the Lord of the world is not satisfied with the narrow limits of thy sway. He, whom thou dost not wish to reign in Judæa, reigns everywhere: and thou wouldst rule more happily thyself, if thou wert to submit to His command. Why dost thou not do with sincerity what in treacherous falseness thou dost promise? Come with the wise men, and in suppliant adoration worship the true King. But thou, from too great fondness for Jewish blindness, wilt not imitate the nations' faith, and directest thy stubborn heart to cruel wiles, though thou art doomed neither to stay Him whom thou fearest nor to harm them whom thou slayest.

III. *The perseverance of the Magi has led to the most important results.*

Led then, dearly beloved, into Bethlehem by obeying the guidance of the star, the wise men "rejoiced with very great joy," as the evangelist has told us: "and entering the house, found the child with Mary, His mother; and falling down they worshipped Him; and opening their treasures they presented to Him gifts, gold, frankincense and myrrh[4]." What wondrous faith of perfect knowledge, which was taught them not by earthly wisdom, but by the instruction of the Holy Spirit! Whence came it that these men, who had quitted their country without having seen Jesus, and had not noticed anything in His looks to enforce such systematic adoration, observed this method in offering their gifts? unless it were that besides the appearance of the star, which attracted their bodily eyes, the more refulgent rays of truth taught their hearts that before they started on their toilsome road, they must understand that He was signified to Whom was owed in gold royal honour, in incense Divine adoration, in myrrh the acknowledgment of mortality. Such a belief and understanding no doubt, as far as the enlightenment of their faith went, might have been sufficient in themselves and have prevented their using their bodily eyes in inquiring into that which they had beheld with their mind's fullest gaze. But their sagacious diligence, persevering till they found the child, did good service for future peoples and for the men of our own time: so that, as it profited us all that the apostle Thomas, after the Lord's resurrection, handled the traces of the wounds in His flesh, so it was of advantage to us that His infancy should be attested by the visit of the wise men. And so the wise men saw and adored the Child of the tribe of Judah, "of the seed of David according to the flesh[5]," "made from a woman, made under the law[6]," which He had come "not to destroy but to fulfil[7]." They saw and adored the Child, small in size, powerless to help others[8], incapable of speech, and in nought different to the generality of human children. Because, as the testimonies were trustworthy which asserted in Him the majesty of invisible Godhead, so it ought to be impossible to doubt that "the Word became flesh," and the eter-

[2] Numb. xxiv. 17: cf. Serm. XXXI. chap 2, above.
[3] Micah v. 2.

[4] S. Matt. ii. 10, 11.
[5] Rom. i. 3.
[6] Gal. iv.
[7] S. Matt. v. 17.
[8] *Alienæ opis indignum.*

nal essence of the Son of God took man's true nature: lest either the inexpressible marvels of his acts which were to follow or the infliction of sufferings which He had to bear should overthrow the mystery of our Faith by their inconsistency: seeing that no one at all can be justified save those who believe the Lord Jesus to be both true God and true Man.

IV. *The Manichæan heresy corrupts the Scriptures in order to disprove the truth.*

This peerless Faith, dearly-beloved, this Truth proclaimed throughout all ages, is opposed by the devilish blasphemies of the Manichæans: who to murder the souls of the deceived have woven a deadly tissue of wicked doctrine out of impious and forged lies, and over the ruins of their mad opinions men have fallen headlong to such depths as to imagine a Christ with a fictitious body, who presented nothing solid, nothing real to the eyes and touch of men[9], but displayed an empty shape of fancy-flesh. For they wish it to be thought unworthy of belief that God the Son of God placed Himself within a woman's body and subjected His majesty to such a degradation as to be joined to our fleshly nature and be born in the true body of human substance: although this is entirely the outcome of His power, not of His ill-treatment, and it is His glorious condescension, not His being polluted that should be believed in. For if yonder visible light is not marred by any of the uncleannesses with which it is encompassed, and the brightness of the sun's rays, which is doubtless a material creature, is not contaminated by any of the dirty or muddy places to which it penetrates, is there anything whatever its quality which could pollute the essence of that eternal and immaterial Light? seeing that by allying Himself to that creature which He had made after His own image He furnished it with purification and received no stain, and healed the wounds of its weakness without suffering loss of power. And because this great and unspeakable mystery of divine godliness was announced by all the testimonies of the Holy Scriptures, those opponents of the Truth of which we speak have rejected the law that was given through Moses and the divinely inspired utterances[1] of the prophets, and have tampered with the very pages of the gospels and apostles, by removing or inserting certain things: forging for themselves under the Apostles' names and under the words of the Saviour Himself many volumes of falsehood, whereby to fortify their lying errors and instil deadly poison into the minds of those to be deceived. For they saw that everything contradicted and made against them and that not only by the New but also by the Old Testament their blasphemous and treacherous folly was confuted. And yet persisting in their mad lies they cease not to disturb the Church of God with their deceits, persuading those miserable creatures whom they can ensnare to deny that man's nature was truly taken by the Lord Jesus Christ; to deny that He was truly crucified for the world's salvation: to deny that from His side wounded by the spear flowed the blood of Redemption and the water of baptism[2]: to deny that He was buried and raised again the third day: to deny that in sight of the disciples He was lifted above all the heights of the skies to take His seat on the right hand of the Father; and in order that when all the truth of the Apostles' Creed was destroyed, there may be nothing to frighten the wicked or inspire the saints with hope, to deny that the living and the dead must be judged by Christ; so that those whom they have robbed of the power of these great mysteries may learn to worship Christ in the sun and moon, and under the name of the Holy Spirit to adore Manichæus himself, the inventor of all these blasphemies.

V. *Avoid all dealings with the heretics, but intercede with God for them.*

To confirm your hearts therefore, dearly-beloved, in the Faith and Truth, let to-day's festival help you all, and let the catholic confession be fortified by the testimony of the manifestation of the Saviour's infancy, while we anathematize the blasphemy of those who deny the flesh of our nature in Christ: about which the blessed Apostle John has forewarned us in no doubtful utterance, saying, "every spirit which confesses Christ Jesus to have come in the flesh is of God: and every spirit which destroys Jesus is not of God, and this is Antichrist[3]." Consequently let no Christian have aught in common with men of this kind, let him have no alliance or intercourse with such. Let it advantage the whole Church that many of them in the mercy of God have been discovered, and that their

9 Whatever may be the correct reading here, *actionibus* with the better MSS. or *tactibus*, the conjecture of Quesnel from the reading of some MSS. *actibus*, the meaning must be such as is given in the translation.

1 *Oracula* representing the λόγια of the New Testament (viz. Acts vii. 38, Rom. iii. 2, &c.).

2 Cf. Ep. xxviii. (Tome) 5, *aperto per militis lanceam latere crucifixi intelligat unde sanguis et aqua fluxerit ut ecclesia Dei et lavacro rigaretur et poculo*, and almost immediately afterwards, where he interprets the spirit, water and blood of 1 S. John v. 8, as *spiritus sanctificationis et sanguis redemptionis et aqua baptismatis*.

3 1 John iv. 2, 3: see Letter XXVIII. (Tome) 5, n. 7, on the various reading.

own confession has disclosed how sacrilegious their lives were. Let no one be deceived by their discriminations between food and food, by their soiled raiment, by their pale faces. Fasts are not holy which proceed not on the principle of abstinence but with deceitful design. Let this be the end of their harming the unwary, and deluding the ignorant; henceforth no one's fall shall be excusable: no longer must he be held simple but extremely worthless and perverse who hereafter shall be found entangled in detestable error. A practice countenanced by the Church and Divinely instituted, not only do we not forbid, we even incite you to, that you should supplicate the LORD even for such: since we also with tears and mourning feel pity for the ruins of cheated souls, carrying out the Apostles' example of loving-kindness [4], so as to be weak with those that are weak and to "weep with those that weep [5]." For we hope that GOD's mercy can be won by the many tears and due amendment of the fallen: because so long as life remains in the body no man's restoration must be despaired of, but the reform of all desired with the LORD's help, "who raiseth up them that are crushed, looseth them that are chained, giveth light to the blind [6]:" to whom is honour and glory for ever and ever. Amen.

SERMON XXXVI.

ON THE FEAST OF THE EPIPHANY, VI.

I. *The story of the magi not only a byegone fact in history, but of everyday application to ourselves.*

The day, dearly-beloved, on which Christ the Saviour of the world first appeared to the nations must be venerated by us with holy worship: and to-day those joys must be entertained in our hearts which existed in the breasts of the three magi, when, aroused by the sign and leading of a new star, which they believed to have been promised, they fell down in presence of the King of heaven and earth. For that day has not so passed away that the mighty work, which was then revealed, has passed away with it, and that nothing but the report of the thing has come down to us for faith to receive and memory to celebrate; seeing that, by the oft-repeated gift of GOD, our times daily enjoy the fruit of what the first age possessed. And therefore, although the narrative which is read to us from the Gospel [7] properly records those days on which the three men, who had neither been taught by the prophets' predictions nor instructed by the testimony of the law, came to acknowledge GOD from the furthest parts of the East, yet we behold this same thing more clearly and abundantly carried on now in the enlightenment of all those who are called, since the prophecy of Isaiah is fulfilled when he says, "the LORD has laid bare His holy arm in the sight of all the nations, and all the nations upon earth have seen the salvation which is from the LORD our GOD;" and again, "and those to whom it has not been announced about Him shall see, and they who have not heard, shall understand [8]." Hence when we see men devoted to worldly wisdom and far from belief in Jesus Christ brought out of the depth of their error and called to an acknowledgment of the true Light, it is undoubtedly the brightness of the Divine grace that is at work: and whatever of new light illumines the darkness of their hearts, comes from the rays of the same star: so that it should both move with wonder, and going before lead to the adoration of GOD the minds which it visited with its splendour. But if with careful thought we wish to see how their threefold kind of gift is also offered by all who come to Christ with the foot of faith, is not the same offering repeated in the hearts of true believers? For he that acknowledges Christ the King of the universe brings gold from the treasure of his heart: he that believes the Only-begotten of GOD to have united man's true nature to Himself, offers myrrh; and he that confesses Him in no wise inferior to the Father's majesty, worships Him in a manner with incense.

II. *Satan still carries on the wiles of Herod, and, as it were, personates him in his opposition to Christ.*

These comparisons, dearly-beloved, being thoughtfully considered, we find Herod's character also not to be wanting, of which the devil himself is now an unwearied imitator, just as he was then a secret instigator. For he is tortured at the calling of all the nations, and racked at the daily destruction of his power, grieving at his being everywhere deserted, and the true King adored in all places. He prepares devices, he hatches plots, he bursts out into murders, and that he may make use of the remnants of those whom he still deceives, is consumed with envy in the persons of the Jews, lies treacherously in wait in the persons of heretics, blazes out into cruelty in the persons of the heathen. For he sees that

4 *Exsequentes apostolicæ pietatis exemplum.*

5 2 Cor. xi. 29; Rom. xii. 15.

6 Ps. cxlvi. 7, 8.

7 *Narratio evangelicæ lectionis.* This, according to Bright's n. 46 (q v.) "refers to the reading of passages of Scripture by the Lector as a part of the church service."

8 Is. lii. 10, 15.

the power of the eternal King is invincible, Whose death has extinguished the power of death itself; and therefore he has armed himself with all his skill of injury against those who serve the true King; hardening some by the pride that knowledge of the law engenders, debasing others by the lies of false belief, and inciting others to the madness of persecution. Yet the madness of this "Herod" is vanquished, and brought to nought by Him who has crowned even infants with the glory of martyrdom, and has endued His faithful ones with so unconquerable a love that in the Apostle's words they dare to say, "who shall separate us from the love of Christ? shall tribulation, or want, or persecution, or hunger, or nakedness, or peril, or the sword? as it is written, For thy sake are we killed all the day long, we are counted as sheep for the slaughter. But in all these things we overcome on account of Him who loved us[9]."

III. *The cessation of active persecution does not do away with the need of continued vigilance: Satan has only changed his tactics.*

Such courage as this, dearly-beloved, we do not believe to have been needful only at those times in which the kings of the world and all the powers of the age were raging against God's people in an outburst of wickedness, thinking it to redound to their greatest glory if they removed the Christian name from the earth, but not knowing that God's Church grows through the frenzy of their cruelty, since in the tortures and deaths of the martyrs, those whose number was reckoned to be diminished were augmented through the force of example[1]. In fine, so much strength has our Faith gained by the attacks of persecutors that royal princedoms have no greater ornament than that the lords of the world are members of Christ; and their boast is not so much that they were born in the purple as that they have been re-born in baptism. But because the stress of former blasts has lulled, and with a cessation of fightings a measure of tranquillity has long seemed to smile upon us, those divergences are carefully to be guarded against which arise from the very reign of peace. For the adversary having been proved ineffective in open persecutions now exercises a hidden skill in doing cruel hurt, in order to overthrow by the stumbling-block of pleasure those whom he could not strike with the blow of affliction. And so seeing the faith of princes opposed to him and the indivisible Trinity of the one Godhead as devoutly worshipped in palaces as in churches, he grieves at the shedding of Christian blood being forbidden, and attacks the mode of life of those whose death he cannot compass. The terror of confiscations he changes into the fire of avarice, and corrupts with covetousness those whose spirit he could not break by losses. For the malicious naughtiness which long use has ingrained into his very nature has not laid aside its hatred, but changed its character in order to subjugate the minds of the faithful by blandishments. He inflames those with covetous desires whom he cannot distress with tortures: he sows strifes, kindles passions, sets tongues a-wagging, and, lest more cautious hearts should draw back from his lawless wiles, facilitates opportunities for accomplishing crimes: because this is the only fruit of all his devices that he who is not worshipped with the sacrifice of cattle and goats, and the burning of incense, should be paid the homage of divers wicked deeds[2].

IV. *Timely repentance gains God's merciful consideration.*

Our state of peace[3], therefore, dearly-beloved, has its dangers, and it is vain for those who do not withstand vicious desires to feel secure of the liberty which is the privilege of their Faith. Men's hearts are shown by the character of their works, and the fashion of their minds is betrayed by the nature of their actions. For there are some, as the Apostle says, "who profess that they know God, but deny Him by their deeds[4]." For the charge of denial is truly incurred when the good which is heard in the sound of the voice is not present in the conscience. Indeed, the frailty of man's nature easily glides into faults: and because no sin is without its attractiveness, deceptive pleasure is quickly acquiesced in. But we should run for spiritual succour from the desires of the flesh: and the mind that has knowledge of its God should turn away from the evil suggestion of the enemy. Avail thyself of the long-suffering of God, and persist not in cherishing thy sin, because its punishment is put off. The sinner must not feel secure of his impunity, because if he loses

9 Rom. viii. 35.

1 Cf. Tertullian's famous boast in his *Apologeticus* (chap. I., § 176), *semen est Christianorum sanguis*, and Leo's own words again, Serm. LXXXII. 6, *non minuitur persecutionibus ecclesia sed augetur.*

2 The warning of this chapter is insisted on not only by Leo himself often elsewhere (see references in Bright's note 51), but, among others doubtless, by Cyprian in more than one passage, esp. in *De Lapsis*, where he accuses even the clergy of worldliness in the strongest terms.

3 Cf. Cypr. *de lapsis* v. *traditam nobis divinitus disciplinam pax longa corruperat.*

4 Titus i. 16.

the time for repentance he will find no place for mercy, as the prophet says, "in death no one remembers thee; and in the realms below who will confess to thee[5]?" But let him who experiences the difficulty of self-amendment and restoration betake himself to the mercy of a befriending God, and ask that the chains of evil habit may be broken off by Him "who lifts up those that fall and raises all the crushed[6]." The prayer of one that confesses will not be in vain since the merciful God "will grant the desire of those that fear Him[6]," and will give what is asked, as He gave the Source from Which to ask. Through our Lord Jesus Christ, Who liveth and reigneth with the Father and the Holy Ghost for ever and ever. Amen.

SERMON XXXIX.

On Lent, I.

I. *The benefits of abstinence shown by the example of the Hebrews.*

In former days, when the people of the Hebrews and all the tribes of Israel were oppressed for their scandalous sins by the grievous tyranny of the Philistines, in order that they might be able to overcome their enemies, as the sacred story declares, they restored their powers of mind and body by the injunction of a fast. For they understood that they had deserved that hard and wretched subjection for their neglect of God's commands, and evil ways, and that it was in vain for them to strive with arms unless they had first withstood their sin. Therefore abstaining from food and drink, they applied the discipline of strict correction to themselves, and in order to conquer their foes, first conquered the allurements of the palate in themselves. And thus it came about that their fierce enemies and cruel taskmasters yielded to them when fasting, whom they had held in subjection when full. And so we too, dearly-beloved, who are set in the midst of many oppositions and conflicts, may be cured by a little carefulness, if only we will use the same means. For our case is almost the same as theirs, seeing that, as they were attacked by foes in the flesh so are we chiefly by spiritual enemies. And if we can conquer them by God's grace enabling us to correct our ways, the strength of our bodily enemies also will give way before us, and by our self-amendment we shall weaken those who were rendered formidable to us, not by their own merits but by our shortcomings.

II. *Use Lent to vanquish the enemy, and be thus preparing for Eastertide.*

Accordingly, dearly-beloved, that we may be able to overcome all our enemies, let us seek Divine aid by the observance of the heavenly bidding, knowing that we cannot otherwise prevail against our adversaries, unless we prevail against our own selves. For we have many encounters with our own selves: the flesh desires one thing against the spirit, and the spirit another thing against the flesh[6a]. And in this disagreement, if the desires of the body be stronger, the mind will disgracefully lose its proper dignity, and it will be most disastrous for that to serve which ought to have ruled. But if the mind, being subject to its Ruler, and delighting in gifts from above, shall have trampled under foot the allurements of earthly pleasure, and shall not have allowed sin to reign in its mortal body[6a], reason will maintain a well-ordered supremacy, and its strongholds no strategy of spiritual wickednesses will cast down: because man has then only true peace and true freedom when the flesh is ruled by the judgment of the mind, and the mind is directed by the will of God. And although this state of preparedness, dearly-beloved, should always be maintained that our ever-watchful foes may be overcome by unceasing diligence, yet now it must be the more anxiously sought for and the more zealously cultivated when the designs of our subtle foes themselves are conducted with keener craft than ever. For knowing that the most hallowed days of Lent are now at hand, in the keeping of which all past slothfulnesses are chastised, all negligences atoned for, they direct all the force of their spite on this one thing, that they who intend to celebrate the Lord's holy Passover may be found unclean in some matter, and that cause of offence may arise where propitiation ought to have been obtained.

III. *Fights are necessary to prove our Faith.*

As we approach then, dearly-beloved, the beginning of Lent, which is a time for the more careful serving of the Lord, because we are, as it were, entering on a kind of contest in good works, let us prepare our souls for fighting with temptations, and understand that the more zealous we are for our salvation, the more determined must be the assaults of our opponents. But "stronger is He that is in us than He that is against us[7]," and through Him are we powerful in whose strength we rely: because it was for this that the Lord

5 Ps. vi. 6.

6 Ib. cxlv. 14, 19.

6a Cf. Gal. v. 17: and below, Rom. vi. 12.

7 1 S. John iv. 4.

allowed Himself to be tempted by the tempter, that we might be taught by His example as well as fortified by His aid. For He conquered the adversary, as ye have heard[8], by quotations from the law, not by actual strength, that by this very thing He might do greater honour to man, and inflict a greater punishment on the adversary by conquering the enemy of the human race not now as God but as Man. He fought then, therefore, that we too might fight thereafter: He conquered that we too might likewise conquer. For there are no works of power, dearly-beloved, without the trials of temptations, there is no faith without proof, no contest without a foe, no victory without conflict. This life of ours is in the midst of snares, in the midst of battles; if we do not wish to be deceived, we must watch: if we want to overcome, we must fight. And therefore the most wise Solomon says, "My son in approaching the service of God prepare thy soul for temptation [8a]." For He being a man full of the wisdom of God, and knowing that the pursuit of religion involves laborious struggles, foreseeing too the danger of the fight, forewarned the intending combatant; lest haply, if the tempter came upon him in his ignorance, he might find him unready and wound him unawares.

IV. *The Christian's armour is both for defence and for attack.*

So, dearly-beloved, let us who instructed in Divine learning come wittingly to the present contest and strife, hear the Apostle when he says, "for our struggle is not against flesh and blood, but against principalities and powers, against the rulers of this dark world, against spiritual wickedness in heavenly things[9]," and let us not forget that these our enemies feel it is against them all is done that we strive to do for our salvation, and that by the very fact of our seeking after some good thing we are challenging our foes. For this is an old-standing quarrel between us and them fostered by the devil's ill-will, so that they are tortured by our being justified, because they have fallen from those good things to which we, God helping us, are advancing. If, therefore, we are raised, they are prostrated: if we are strengthened, they are weakened. Our cures are their blows, because they are wounded by our wounds' cure. "Stand, therefore," dearly-beloved, as the Apostle says, "having the loins of your mind girt in truth, and your feet shod in the preparation of the gospel of peace, in all things taking the shield of faith in which ye may be able to extinguish all the fiery darts of the evil one, and put on the helmet of salvation and the sword of the Spirit, which is the Word of God [1]." See, dearly-beloved, with what mighty weapons, with what impregnable defences we are armed by our Leader, who is famous for His many triumphs, the unconquered Master of the Christian warfare. He has girt our loins with the belt of chastity, He has shod our feet with the bonds of peace: because the unbelted soldier is quickly vanquished by the suggester of immodesty, and he that is unshod is easily bitten by the serpent. He has given the shield of faith for the protection of our whole body; on our head has He set the helmet of salvation; our right hand has He furnished with a sword, that is with the word of Truth: that the spiritual warrior may not only be safe from wounds, but also may have strength to wound his assailant.

V. *Abstinence not only from food but from other evil desires, especially from wrath, is required in Lent.*

Relying, therefore, dearly-beloved, on these arms, let us enter actively and fearlessly on the contest set before us: so that in this fasting struggle we may not rest satisfied with only this end, that we should think abstinence from food alone desirable. For it is not enough that the substance of our flesh should be reduced, if the strength of the soul be not also developed. When the outer man is somewhat subdued, let the inner man be somewhat refreshed; and when bodily excess is denied to our flesh, let our mind be invigorated by spiritual delights. Let every Christian scrutinise himself, and search severely into his inmost heart: let him see that no discord cling there, no wrong desire be harboured. Let chasteness drive incontinence far away; let the light of truth dispel the shades of deception; let the swellings of pride subside; let wrath yield to reason; let the darts of ill-treatment be shattered, and the chidings of the tongue be bridled; let thoughts of revenge fall through, and injuries be given over to oblivion. In fine, let "every plant which the heavenly Father hath not planted be removed by the roots [2]." For then only are the seeds of virtue well nourished in us, when every foreign germ is uprooted from the field of wheat. If any one, therefore, has been fired by the desire for vengeance against another, so that he has given him up to prison or bound him with chains, let him make haste

[8] *Ut audistis*, viz. in the Gospel for Quadragesima, or the First Sunday in Lent then apparently as now S. Matt. iv. 1—11: cf. Serm. XL. 3. [8a] Ecclus. ii. 1. [9] Eph. vi. 12.

[1] Eph. vi. 14—17. [2] S. Matt. xv. 13.

to forgive not only the innocent, but also one who seems worthy of punishment, that he may with confidence make use of the clause in the LORD's prayer and say, "Forgive us our debts, as we also forgive our debtors[3]." Which petition the LORD marks with peculiar emphasis, as if the efficacy of the whole rested on this condition, by saying, "For if ye forgive men their sins, your Father which is in heaven also will forgive you: but if ye forgive not men, neither will your Father forgive you your sins[3]."

VI. *The right use of Lent will lead to a happy participation in Easter.*

Accordingly, dearly-beloved, being mindful of our weakness, because we easily fall into all kinds of faults, let us by no means neglect this special remedy and most effectual healing of our wounds. Let us remit, that we may have remission: let us grant the pardon which we crave: let us not be eager to be revenged when we pray to be forgiven. Let us not pass over the groans of the poor with deaf ear, but with prompt kindness bestow our mercy on the needy, that we may deserve to find mercy in the judgment. And he that, aided by GOD's grace, shall strain every nerve after this perfection, will keep this holy fast faithfully; free from the leaven of the old wickedness, in the unleavened bread of sincerity and truth[4], he will reach the blessed Passover, and by newness of life will worthily rejoice in the mystery of man's reformation through Christ our LORD, Who with the Father and the Holy Spirit lives and reigns for ever and ever. Amen.

SERMON XL.

ON LENT, II.

I. *Progress and improvement always possible.*

Although, dearly-beloved, as the Easter festival approaches, the very recurrence of the season points out to us the Lenten fast, yet our words also must add their exhortations which, the LORD helping us, may be not useless to the active nor irksome to the devout. For since the idea of these days demands the increase of all our religious performances, there is no one, I am sure, that does not feel glad at being incited to good works. For though our nature which, so long as we are mortal, will be changeable, is advancing to the highest pursuits of virtue, yet always has the possibility of falling back, so has it always the possibility of advancing. And this is the true justness of the perfect, that they should never assume themselves to be perfect, lest flagging in the purpose of their yet unfinished journey, they should fall into the danger of failure, through giving up the desire for progress.

And, therefore, because none of us, dearly-beloved, is so perfect and holy as not to be able to be more perfect and more holy, let us all together, without difference of rank, without distinction of desert, with pious eagerness pursue our race from what we have attained to what we yet aspire to, and make some needful additions to our regular devotions. For he that is not more attentive than usual to religion in these days, is shown at other times to be not attentive enough.

II. *Satan seeks to supply his numerous losses by fresh gains.*

Hence the reading of the Apostle's proclamation has sounded opportunely in our ears, saying, "Behold now is the accepted time, behold now is the day of salvation[5]." For what is more accepted than this time, what more suitable to salvation than these days, in which war is proclaimed against vices and progress is made in all virtues? Thou hadst indeed always to keep watch, O Christian soul, against the enemy of thy salvation, lest any spot should be exposed to the tempter's snares: but now greater wariness and keener prudence must be employed by thee when that same foe of thine rages with fiercer hatred. For now in all the world the power of his ancient sway is taken from him, and the countless vessels of captivity are rescued from his grasp. The people of all nations and of all tongues are breaking away from their cruel plunderer, and now no race of men is found that does not struggle against the tyrant's laws, while through all the borders of the earth many thousands of thousands are being prepared to be reborn in Christ[6]: and as the birth of a new creature draws near, spiritual wickedness is being driven out by those who were possessed by it. The blasphemous fury of the despoiled foe frets, therefore, and seeks new gains because it has lost its ancient right. Unwearied and ever-wakeful, he snatches at any sheep he finds straying carelessly from the sacred folds, intent on leading them over the steeps of pleasure and down the slopes of luxury into the abodes of death. And so he inflames their wrath, feeds their hatreds, whets their desires, mocks at their continence, arouses their gluttony.

3 S. Matt. vi. 12, 14, 15.

4 Cf. 1 Cor. v. 8.

5 2 Cor. vi. 2 from the Epistle for the First Sunday in Lent: cf. Serm. XXXVI. 1, n. 7.

6 Viz. by Baptism at the Easter festival.

III. *The twofold nature of Christ shown at the Temptation.*

For whom would he not dare to try, who did not keep from his treacherous attempts even on our LORD Jesus Christ? For, as the story of the Gospel has disclosed[7], when our Saviour, Who was true GOD, that He might show Himself true Man also, and banish all wicked and erroneous opinions, after the fast of 40 days and nights, had experienced the hunger of human weakness, the devil, rejoicing at having found in Him a sign of passible and mortal nature, in order to test the power which he feared, said, "If Thou art the Son of GOD, command that these stones become bread[8]." Doubtless the Almighty could do this, and it was easy that at the Creator's command a creature of any kind should change into the form that it was commanded: just as when He willed it, in the marriage feast, He changed the water into wine: but here it better agreed with His purposes of salvation that His haughty foe's cunning should be vanquished by the LORD, not in the power of His Godhead, but by the mystery of His humiliation. At length, when the devil had been put to flight and the tempter baffled in all his arts, angels came to the LORD and ministered to Him, that He being true Man and true GOD, His Manhood might be unsullied by those crafty questions, and His Godhead displayed by those holy ministrations. And so let the sons and disciples of the devil be confounded, who, being filled with the poison of vipers, deceive the simple, denying in Christ the presence of both true natures, whilst they rob either His Godhead of Manhood, or His Manhood of Godhead, although both falsehoods are destroyed by a twofold and simultaneous proof: for by His bodily hunger His perfect Manhood was shown, and by the attendant angels His perfect Godhead.

IV. *The fast should not end with abstinence from food, but lead to good deeds.*

Therefore, dearly-beloved, seeing that, as we are taught by our Redeemer's precept, "man lives not in bread alone, but in every word of GOD[9]," and it is right that Christian people, whatever the amount of their abstinence, should rather desire to satisfy themselves with the "Word of GOD" than with bodily food, let us with ready devotion and eager faith enter upon the celebration of the solemn fast, not with barren abstinence from food, which is often imposed on us by weakliness of body, or the disease of avarice, but in bountiful benevolence: that in truth we may be of those of whom the very Truth speaks, "blessed are they which hunger and thirst after righteousness, for they shall be filled[1]." Let works of piety, therefore, be our delight, and let us be filled with those kinds of food which feed us for eternity. Let us rejoice in the replenishment of the poor, whom our bounty has satisfied. Let us delight in the clothing of those whose nakedness we have covered with needful raiment. Let our humaneness be felt by the sick in their illnesses, by the weakly in their infirmities, by the exiles in their hardships, by the orphans in their destitution, and by solitary widows in their sadness: in the helping of whom there is no one that cannot carry out some amount of benevolence. For no one's income is small, whose heart is big: and the measure of one's mercy and goodness does not depend on the size of one's means. Wealth of goodwill is never rightly lacking, even in a slender purse. Doubtless the expenditure of the rich is greater, and that of the poor smaller, but there is no difference in the fruit of their works, where the purpose of the workers is the same.

V. *And still further it should lead to personal amendment and domestic harmony.*

But, beloved, in this opportunity for the virtues' exercise there are also other notable crowns, to be won by no dispersing abroad of granaries, by no disbursement of money, if wantonness is repelled, if drunkenness is abandoned, and the lusts of the flesh tamed by the laws of chastity: if hatreds pass into affection, if enmities be turned into peace, if meekness extinguishes wrath, if gentleness forgives wrongs, if in fine the conduct of master and of slaves is so well ordered that the rule of the one is milder, and the discipline of the other is more complete. It is by such observances then, dearly-beloved, that GOD's mercy will be gained, the charge of sin wiped out, and the adorable Easter festival devoutly kept. And this the pious Emperors of the Roman world have long guarded with holy observance; for in honour of the LORD's Passion and Resurrection they bend their lofty power, and relaxing the severity of their decrees set free many of their prisoners: so that on the days when the world is saved by the Divine mercy, their clemency, which is modelled on the Heavenly goodness, may be zealously followed by us. Let Christian peoples then imitate their princes, and be

7 *Ut evangelica patefecit historia*, cf. Serm. XXXIX. 3, n. 8.
8 S. Matt. iv. 3.
9 Ib. iv. 4, quoted from Deut. viii. 3.

1 S. Matt. v. 6.

incited to forbearance in their homes by these royal examples. For it is not right that private laws should be severer than public. Let faults be forgiven, let bonds be loosed, offences wiped out, designs of vengeance fall through, that the holy festival through the Divine and human grace may find all happy, all innocent: through our LORD Jesus Christ, Who with the Father and the Holy Spirit liveth and reigneth GOD for endless ages of ages. Amen.

SERMON XLII.

ON LENT, IV.

I. *The Lenten fast an opportunity for restoring our purity.*

In proposing to preach this most holy and important fast to you, dearly beloved, how shall I begin more fitly than by quoting the words of the Apostle, in whom Christ Himself was speaking, and by reminding you of what we have read[2]: "behold, now is the acceptable time, behold now is the day of salvation." For though there are no seasons which are not full of Divine blessings, and though access is ever open to us to GOD's mercy through His grace, yet now all men's minds should be moved with greater zeal to spiritual progress, and animated by larger confidence, when the return of the day, on which we were redeemed, invites us to all the duties of godliness: that we may keep the super-excellent mystery of the LORD's passion with bodies and hearts purified. These great mysteries do indeed require from us such unflagging devotion and unwearied reverence that we should remain in GOD's sight always the same, as we ought to be found on the Easter feast itself. But because few have this constancy, and, because so long as the stricter observance is relaxed in consideration of the frailty of the flesh, and so long as one's interests extend over all the various actions of this life, even pious hearts must get some soils from the dust of the world, the Divine Providence has with great beneficence taken care that the discipline of the forty days should heal us and restore the purity of our minds, during which the faults of other times might be redeemed by pious acts and removed by chaste fasting.

II. *Lent must be used for removing all our defilements, and of good works there must be no stint.*

As we are therefore, dearly-beloved, about to enter on those mystic days which are dedicated to the benefits of fasting, let us take care to obey the Apostle's precepts, cleansing "ourselves from every defilement of flesh and spirit[3]:" that by controlling the struggles that go on between our two natures, the spirit which, if it is under the guidance of GOD, should be the governor of the body, may uphold the dignity of its rule: so that we may give no offence to any, nor be subject to the chidings of reprovers. For we shall be rightly attacked with rebukes, and through our fault ungodly tongues will arm themselves to do harm to religion, if the conduct of those that fast is at variance with the standard of perfect purity. For our fast does not consist chiefly of mere abstinence from food, nor are dainties withdrawn from our bodily appetites with profit, unless the mind is recalled from wrong-doing and the tongue restrained from slandering. This is a time of gentleness and long-suffering, of peace and tranquillity: when all the pollutions of vice are to be eradicated and continuance of virtue is to be attained by us. Now let godly minds boldly accustom themselves to forgive faults, to pass over insults, and to forget wrongs. Now let the faithful spirit train himself with the armour of righteousness on the right hand and on the left, that through honour and dishonour, through ill repute and good repute, the conscience may be undisturbed in unwavering uprightness, not puffed up by praise and not wearied out by revilings. The self-restraint of the religious should not be gloomy, but sincere; no murmurs of complaint should be heard from those who are never without the consolation of holy joys. The decrease of worldly means should not be feared in the practice of works of mercy. Christian poverty is always rich, because what it has is more than what it has not. Nor does the poor man fear to labour in this world, to whom it is given to possess all things in the LORD of all things. Therefore those who do the things which are good must have no manner of fear lest the power of doing should fail them; since in the gospel the widow's devotion is extolled in the case of her two mites, and voluntary bounty gets its reward for a cup of cold water[4]. For the measure of our charitableness is fixed by the sincerity of our feelings, and he that shows mercy on others will never want for mercy himself. The holy widow of Sarepta discovered this, who offered the blessed Elias in the time of famine one day's food, which was all she had, and putting the prophet's hunger before her own needs, ungrudgingly gave up a handful of corn and a little oil[5]. But she did not lose

[2] Cf. Serm. XL. chap. ii. n. 5.

[3] 2 Cor. vii. 1.

[4] The reffs. are obviously to S. Luke xxi. 2—4, and S. Matt. x. 42 (q.v.).

[5] Cf. 1 Kings xvii. 11 and foll.

what she gave in all faith, and in the vessels emptied by her godly bounty a source of new plenty arose, that the fulness of her substance might not be diminished by the holy purpose to which she had put it, because she had never dreaded being brought to want.

III. *As with the Saviour, so with us, the devil tries to make our very piety its own snare.*

But, dearly-beloved, doubt not that the devil, who is the opponent of all virtues, is jealous of these good desires, to which we are confident you are prompted of your own selves, and that to this end he is arming the force of his malice in order to make your very piety its own snare, and endeavouring to overcome by boastfulness those whom he could not defeat by distrustfulness. For the vice of pride is a near neighbour to good deeds, and arrogance ever lies in wait hard by virtue: because it is hard for him that lives praiseworthily not to be caught by man's praise unless, as it is written, "he that glorieth, glorieth in the LORD[6]." Whose intentions would that most naughty enemy not dare to attack? whose fasting would he not seek to break down? seeing that, as has been shown in the reading of the Gospel[6a], he did not restrain his wiles even against the Saviour of the world Himself. For being exceedingly afraid of His fast, which lasted 40 days and nights, he wished most cunningly to discover whether this power of abstinence was given Him or His very own: for he need not fear the defeat of all his treacherous designs, if Christ were throughout subject to the same conditions as He is in body[7]. And so he first craftily examined whether He were Himself the Creator of all things, such that He could change the natures of material things as He pleased: secondly, whether under the form of human flesh the Godhead lay concealed, to Whom it was easy to make the air His chariot, and convey His earthly limbs through space. But when the LORD preferred to resist him by the uprightness of His true Manhood, than to display the power of His Godhead, to this he turns the craftiness of his third design, that he might tempt by the lust of empire Him in Whom the signs of Divine power had failed, and entice Him to the worship of himself by promising the kingdoms of the world. But the devil's cleverness was rendered foolish by GOD's wisdom, so that the proud foe was bound by that which he had formerly bound, and did not fear to assail Him Whom it behoved to be slain for the world.

[6] 1 Cor. x. 17. [6a] Cf. Serm. XXXVI. chap. i., note 7.
[7] *Si Christus eius esset conditionis cuius est corporis*, an obscurely expressed but intrinsically clear statement.

IV. *The perverse turn even their fasting into sin.*

This adversary's wiles then let us beware of, not only in the enticements of the palate, but also in our purpose of abstinence. For he who knew how to bring death upon mankind by means of food, knows also how to harm us through our very fasting, and using the Manichæans as his tools, as he once drove men to take what was forbidden, so in the opposite direction he prompts them to avoid what is allowed. It is indeed a helpful observance, which accustoms one to scanty diet, and checks the appetite for dainties: but woe to the dogmatizing of those whose very fasting is turned to sin. For they condemn the creature's nature to the Creator's injury, and maintain that they are defiled by eating those things of which they contend the devil, not GOD, is the author: although absolutely nothing that exists is evil, nor is anything in nature included in the actually bad. For the good Creator made all things good and the Maker of the universe is one, "Who made the heaven and the earth, the sea and all that is in them[8]." Of which whatever is granted to man for food and drink, is holy and clean after its kind. But if it is taken with immoderate greed, it is the excess that disgraces the eaters and drinkers, not the nature of the food or drink that defiles them. "For all things," as the Apostle says, "are clean to the clean. But to the defiled and unbelieving nothing is clean, but their mind and conscience is defiled[9]."

V. *Be reasonable and seasonable in your fasting.*

But ye, dearly-beloved, the holy offspring of the catholic Mother, who have been taught in the school of Truth by GOD's Spirit, moderate your liberty with due reasonableness, knowing that it is good to abstain even from things lawful, and at seasons of greater strictness to distinguish one food from another with a view to giving up the use of some kinds, not to condemning their nature. And so be not infected with the error of those who are corrupted merely by their own ordinances, "serving the creature rather than the Creator[1]," and offering a foolish abstinence to the service of the lights of heaven: seeing that they have chosen to fast on the first and second days of the week in honour of the sun and moon, proving themselves in this one instance of their perverseness twice disloyal to GOD, twice blasphemous, by setting up their

[8] Ps. cxlvi. 6. [9] Titus i. 15. [1] Rom. ix. 26.

fast not only in worship of the stars but also in contempt of the LORD's Resurrection. For they reject the mystery of man's salvation and refuse to believe that Christ our Lord in the true flesh of our nature was truly born, truly suffered, was truly buried and was truly raised. And in consequence, condemn the day of our rejoicing by the gloom of their fasting. And since to conceal their infidelity they dare to be present at our meetings, at the Communion of the Mysteries[2] they bring themselves sometimes, in order to ensure their concealment, to receive Christ's Body with unworthy lips, though they altogether refuse to drink the Blood of our Redemption. And this we make known to you, holy brethren, that men of this sort may be detected by you by these signs, and that they whose impious pretences have been discovered may be driven from the society of the saints by priestly authority. For of such the blessed Apostle Paul in his foresight warns GOD's Church, saying: "but we beseech you, brethren, that ye observe those who make discussions and offences contrary to the doctrine which ye learnt and turn away from them. For such persons serve not Christ the LORD but their own belly, and by sweet words and fair speeches beguile the hearts of the innocent[3]."

VI. *Make your fasting a reality by amendment in your lives.*

Being therefore, dearly-beloved, fully instructed by these admonitions of ours, which we have often repeated in your ears in protest against abominable error, enter upon the holy days of Lent with godly devoutness, and prepare yourselves to win GOD's mercy by your own works of mercy. Quench your anger, wipe out enmities, cherish unity, and vie with one another in the offices of true humility. Rule your slaves and those who are put under you with fairness, let none of them be tortured by imprisonment or chains. Forego vengeance, forgive offences: exchange severity for gentleness, indignation for meekness, discord for peace. Let all men find us self-restrained, peaceable, kind: that our fastings may be acceptable to GOD. For in a word to Him we offer the sacrifice of true abstinence and true godliness, when we keep ourselves from all evil: the Almighty GOD helping us through all, to Whom with the Son and Holy Spirit belongs one Godhead and one Majesty, for ever and ever. Amen.

[2] *In sacramentorum communione.*

[3] Rom. xvi. 17, 18.

SERMON XLVI.

ON LENT, VIII.

I. *Lent must be kept not only by avoiding bodily impurity but also by avoiding errors of thought and faith.*

We know indeed, dearly-beloved, your devotion to be so warm that in the fasting, which is the forerunner of the LORD's Easter, many of you will have forestalled our exhortations. But because the right practice of abstinence is needful not only to the mortification of the flesh but also to the purification of the mind, we desire your observance to be so complete that, as you cut down the pleasures that belong to the lusts of the flesh, so you should banish the errors that proceed from the imaginations of the heart. For he whose heart is polluted with no misbelief prepares himself with true and reasonable purification for the Paschal Feast, in which all the mysteries of our religion meet together. For, as the Apostle says, that "all that is not of faith is sin[4]," the fasting of those will be unprofitable and vain, whom the father of lying deceives with his delusions, and who are not fed by Christ's true flesh. As then we must with the whole heart obey the Divine commands and sound doctrine, so we must use all foresight in abstaining from wicked imaginations. For the mind then only keeps holy and spiritual fast when it rejects the food of error and the poison of falsehood, which our crafty and wily foe plies us with more treacherously now, when by the very return of the venerable Festival, the whole church generally is admonished to understand the mysteries of its salvation. For he is the true confessor and worshipper of Christ's resurrection, who is not confused about His passion, nor deceived about His bodily nativity. For some are so ashamed of the Gospel of the Cross of Christ, as to impudently nullify the punishment which He underwent for the world's redemption, and have denied the very nature of true flesh in the LORD, not understanding how the impassible and unchangeable Deity of GOD's Word could have so far condescended for man's salvation, as by His power not to lose His own properties, and in His mercy to take on Him ours. And so in Christ, there is a twofold form but one person, and the Son of GOD, who is at the same time Son of Man, is one LORD, accepting the condition of a slave by the design of loving-kindness, not by the law of necessity, because by His power He became humble, by His power passible, by

[4] Rom. xiv. 23.

His power mortal; that for the destruction of the tyranny of sin and death, the weak nature in Him might be capable of punishment, and the strong nature not lose aught of its glory.

II. *All the actions of Christ reveal the presence of the twofold nature.*

And so, dearly-beloved, when in reading or hearing the Gospel you find certain things in our LORD Jesus Christ subjected to injuries and certain things illumined by miracles, in such a way that in the same Person now the Humanity appears, and now the Divinity shines out, do not put down any of these things to a delusion, as if in Christ there is either Manhood alone or Godhead alone, but believe both faithfully, worship both right humbly; so that in the union of the Word and the Flesh there may be no separation, and the bodily proofs may not seem delusive, because the divine signs were evident in Jesus. The attestations to both natures in Him are true and abundant, and by the depth of the Divine purpose all concur to this end, that the inviolable Word not being separated from the passible flesh, the Godhead may be understood as in all things partaker with the flesh and the flesh with the Godhead. And, therefore, must the Christian mind that would eschew lies and be the disciple of truth, use the Gospel-story confidently, and, as if still in company with the Apostles themselves, distinguish what is visibly done by the LORD, now by the spiritual understanding and now by the bodily organs of sight. Assign to the man that He is born a boy of a woman: assign to GOD that His mother's virginity is not harmed, either by conception or by bearing. Recognize "the form of a slave" enwrapped in swaddling clothes, lying in a manger, but acknowledge that it was the LORD's form that was announced by angels, "proclaimed by the elements [5]," adored by the wise men. Understand it of His humanity that he did not avoid the marriage feast: confess it Divine that he turned water into wine. Let your own feelings explain to you why He shed tears over a dead friend: let His Divine power be realized, when that same friend, after mouldering in the grave four days, is brought to life and raised only by the command of His voice. To make clay with spittle and earth was a work of the body: but to anoint therewith and enlighten the eyes of the blind is an undoubted mark of that power which had reserved for the revelation of its glory that which it had not allowed to the early part of His natural life. It is truly human to relieve bodily fatigue with rest in sleep: but it is truly Divine to quell the violence of raging storms by a rebuking command. To set food before the hungry denotes human kindness and a philanthropic spirit: but with five loaves and two fishes to satisfy 5,000 men, besides women and children, who would dare deny that to be the work of Deity? a Deity which, by the co-operation of the functions of true flesh, showed not only itself in Manhood, but also Manhood in itself; for the old, original wounds in man's nature could not be healed, except by the Word of GOD taking to Himself flesh from the Virgin's womb, whereby in one and the same Person flesh and the Word co-existed.

III. *Hold fast to the statements of the Creed.*

This belief in the LORD's Incarnation, dearly-beloved, through which the whole Church is Christ's body [6], hold firm with heart unshaken and abstain from all the lies of heretics, and remember that your works of mercy will only then profit you, and your strict continence only then bear fruit, when your minds are unsoiled by any defilement from wrong opinions. Cast away the arguments of this world's wisdom, for GOD hates them, and none can arrive by them at the knowledge of the Truth, and keep fixed in your mind that which you say in the Creed. Believe [7] the Son of GOD to be co-eternal with the Father by Whom all things were made and without Whom nothing was made, born also according to the flesh at the end of the times. Believe Him to have been in the body crucified, dead, raised up, and lifted above the heights of heavenly powers, set on the Father's right hand, about to come in the same flesh in which He ascended, to judge the living and the dead. For this is what the Apostle proclaims to all the faithful, saying: "if ye be risen with Christ seek the things which are above, where Christ is sitting on the right hand of GOD. Set your mind on the things that are above, not on the things that are upon the earth. For ye are dead, and your life is hid with Christ in GOD. For when Christ, our life, shall appear, then shall ye also appear with Him in glory [8]."

IV. *Use Lent for general improvement in the whole round of Christian duties.*

Relying, therefore, dearly-beloved, on so great a promise, be heavenly not only in hope,

5 *Declaratam ab elementis*, viz. by the star in the East.

6 *Per quam tota Ecclesia corpus est Christi.* This is a great saying, by which the centrality of the doctrine of the Incarnation is fearlessly asserted.

7 Notice that both here and in the next sentence the construction is *credite Filium—credite Hunc* not *credite* in *Filium—* in *Hunc*, the exact language of the creed being the latter (I believe *in*, &c.).

8 Col. iii. 1—4.

but also in conduct. And though our minds must at all times be set on holiness of mind and body, yet now during these 40 days of fasting bestir yourselves[9] to yet more active works of piety, not only in the distribution of alms, which are very effectual in attesting reform, but also in forgiving offences, and in being merciful to those accused of wrong-doing, that the condition which GOD has laid down between Himself and us may not be against us when we pray. For when we say, in accordance with the LORD's teaching, "Forgive us our debts, as we also forgive our debtors[1]," we ought with the whole heart to carry out what we say. For then only will what we ask in the next clause come to pass, that we be not led into temptation and freed from all evils[2]: through our LORD Jesus Christ, Who with the Father and the Holy Spirit lives and reigns for ever and ever. Amen.

SERMON XLIX.

ON LENT, XI.

I. *The Lenten fast is incumbent on all alike.*

On all days and seasons, indeed, dearly-beloved, some marks of the Divine goodness are set, and no part of the year is destitute of sacred mysteries, in order that, so long as proofs of our salvation meet us on all sides, we may the more eagerly accept the never-ceasing calls of GOD's mercy. But all that is bestowed on the restoration of human souls in the divers works and gifts of grace is put before us more clearly and abundantly now, when no isolated portions of the Faith are to be celebrated, but the whole together. For as the Easter festival approaches, the greatest and most binding of fasts is kept, and its observance is imposed on all the faithful without exception; because no one is so holy that he ought not to be holier, nor so devout that he might not be devouter. For who, that is set in the uncertainty of this life, can be found either exempt from temptation, or free from fault? Who is there who would not wish for additions to his virtue, or removal of his vice? seeing that adversity does us harm, and prosperity spoils us, and it is equally dangerous not to have what we want at all, and to have it in the fullest measure. There is a trap in the fulness of riches, a trap in the straits of poverty. The one lifts us up in pride, the other incites us to complaint. Health tries us, sickness tries us, so long as the one fosters carelessness and the other sadness. There is a snare in security, a snare in fear; and it matters not whether the mind which is given over to earthly thoughts, is taken up with pleasures or with cares; for it is equally unhealthy to languish under empty delights, or to labour under racking anxiety.

II. *The broad road is crowded, the narrow way of salvation nearly empty.*

And thus is perfectly fulfilled that assurance of the Truth, by which we learn that "narrow and steep is the way that leads to life[3];" and whilst the breadth of the way that leads to death is crowded with a large company, the steps are few of those that tread the path of safety. And wherefore is the left road more thronged than the right, save that the multitude is prone to wordly joys and carnal goods? And although that which it desires is short-lived and uncertain, yet men endure toil more willingly for the lust of pleasure than for love of virtue. Thus while those who crave things visible are unnumbered, those who prefer the eternal to the temporal are hardly to be found. And, therefore, seeing that the blessed Apostle Paul says, "the things which are seen are temporal, but the things which are not seen are eternal[4]," the path of virtue lies hid and in concealment, to a certain extent, since "by hope we were saved[5]," and true faith loves that above all things, which it attains to without any intervention of the flesh. A great work and toil it is then to keep our wayward heart from all sin, and, with the numberless allurements of pleasure to ensnare it on all sides, not to let the vigour of the mind give way to any attack. Who "toucheth pitch, and is not defiled thereby[6]?" who is not weakened by the flesh? who is not begrimed by the dust? who, lastly, is of such purity as not to be polluted by those things without which one cannot live? For the Divine teaching commands by the Apostle's mouth that "they who have wives" should "be as though they had none: and those that weep as though they wept not; and those that rejoice as though they rejoiced not; and those that buy as though they possessed not; and those that use this world as though they used it not; for the fashion of this world passeth away[7]." Blessed, therefore, is the mind that passes the time of its pilgrimage in chaste sobriety, and loiters not

9 Lit. "polish yourselves up" (*expolite vos*).
1 S. Matt. vi. 12.
2 *A malis omnibus liberemus.* The free turn given to this passage is interesting: ἀπὸ τοῦ πονηροῦ (Vulg. *a malo*) being now considered personal "from the evil one" (R.V.).

3 S. Matt. vii. 14.
4 2 Cor. iv. 18.
5 Rom. viii. 24.
6 Ecclus. xiii. 1.
7 1 Cor. vii. 29—31. In the last clause but one, the Lat. runs, *qui utuntur hoc mundo tanquam non* utantur (as also the Vulg. and the margin of R.V., "(as not) using to the full," though the text reads. "as not abusing it").

in the things through which it has to walk, so that, as a stranger rather than the possessor of its earthly abode, it may not be wanting in human affections, and yet rest on the Divine promises.

III. *Satan is incited to fresh efforts at this season of the year.*

And, dearly-beloved, no season requires and bestows this fortitude more than the present, when by the observance of a special strictness a habit is acquired which must be persevered in. For it is well known to you that this is the time when throughout the world the devil waxes furious, and the Christian army has to combat him, and any that have grown lukewarm and slothful, or that are absorbed in worldly cares, must now be furnished with spiritual armour and their ardour kindled for the fray by the heavenly trumpet, inasmuch as he, through whose envy death came into the world[8], is now consumed with the strongest jealousy and now tortured with the greatest vexation. For he sees[9] whole tribes of the human race brought in afresh to the adoption of GOD's sons and the offspring of the New Birth multiplied through the virgin fertility of the Church. He sees himself robbed of all his tyrannic power, and driven from the hearts of those he once possessed, while from either sex thousands of the old, the young, the middle-aged are snatched away from him, and no one is debarred by sin either of his own or original, where justification is not paid for deserts, but simply given as a free gift. He sees, too, those that have lapsed, and have been deceived by his treacherous snares, washed in the tears of penitence and, by the Apostle's key unlocking the gates of mercy, admitted to the benefit of reconciliation[1]. He feels, moreover, that the day of the LORD's Passion is at hand, and that he is crushed by the power of that cross which in Christ, Who was free from all debt of sin, was the world's ransom and not the penalty of sin.

IV. *Self-examination by the standard of GOD'S commands the right occupation in Lent.*

And so, tha the malice of the fretting foe may effect nothing by its rage, a keener devotion must be awaked to the performance of the Divine commands, in order that we may enter on the season, when all the mysteries of the Divine mercy meet together, with preparedness both of mind and body, invoking the guidance and help of GOD, that we may be strong to fulfil all things through Him, without Whom we can do nothing. For the injunction is laid on us, in order that we may seek the aid of Him Who lays it. Nor must any one excuse himself by reason of his weakness, since He Who has granted the will, also gives the power, as the blessed Apostle James says, "If any of you lack wisdom, let him ask of GOD, Who giveth to all liberally and upbraideth not, and it shall be given him[2]." Which of the faithful does not know what virtues he ought to cultivate, and what vices to fight against? Who is so partial or so unskilled a judge of his own conscience as not to know what ought to be removed, and what ought to be developed? Surely no one is so devoid of reason as not to understand the character of his mode of life, or not to know the secrets of his heart. Let him not then please himself in everything, nor judge himself according to the delights of the flesh, but place his every habit in the scale of the Divine commands, where, some things being ordered to be done and others forbidden, he can examine himself in a true balance by weighing the actions of his life according to this standard. For the designing mercy of GOD[3] has set up the brightest mirror in His commandments, wherein a man may see his mind's face and realize its conformity or dissimilarity to GOD's image: with the specific purpose that, at least, during the days of our Redemption and Restoration, we may throw off awhile our carnal cares and restless occupations, and betake ourselves from earthly matters to heavenly.

V. *Forgiveness of our own sins requires that we should forgive others.*

But because, as it is written, "in many things we all stumble[4]," let the feeling of mercy be first aroused and the faults of others against us be forgotten; that we may not violate by any love of revenge that most holy compact, to which we bind ourselves in the LORD's prayer, and when we say "forgive us our debts as we also forgive our debtors," let us not be hard in forgiving, because we must be possessed either with the desire for revenge, or with the leniency of gentleness, and for man, who is ever exposed to the dangers of temptations, it is more to be desired that his own faults should not need punishment[5] than that he should get the faults of others punished. And

8 Wisdom ii. 24.

9 The allusion is of course to the large numbers of persons baptized every year at Easter.

1 *Portas misericordiæ Apostolica clave reserante ad remedia reconciliationis admitti:* no doubt confession and priestly absolution is meant with a reference to S. Matt. xvi. 19.

2 S. James i. 5.

3 *Artifex misericordia Dei.*

4 S. James iii. 2.

5 *Ut suas culpas habeat impunitas* (some through a misunderstanding of the argument read *punitas* here) *quam ut plectat alienas.*

what is more suitable to the Christian faith than that not only in the Church, but also in all men's homes, there should be forgiveness of sins? Let threats be laid aside; let bonds be loosed, for he who will not loose them will bind himself with them much more disastrously. For whatsoever one man resolves upon against another, he decrees against himself by his own terms. Whereas "blessed are the merciful, for God shall have mercy on them[6]:" and He is just and kind in His judgments, allowing some to be in the power of others to this end, that under fair government may be preserved both the profitableness of discipline and the kindliness of clemency, and that no one should dare to refuse that pardon to another's shortcomings, which he wishes to receive for his own.

VI. *Reconciliation between enemies and almsgiving are also Lenten duties.*

Furthermore, as the Lord says, that "the peacemakers are blessed, because they shall be called sons of God[7]," let all discords and enmities be laid aside, and let no one think to have a share in the Paschal feast that has neglected to restore brotherly peace. For with the Father on high, he that is not in charity with the brethren, will not be reckoned in the number of His sons. Furthermore, in the distribution of alms and care of the poor, let our Christian fast-times be fat and abound; and let each bestow on the weak and destitute those dainties which he denies himself. Let pains be taken that all may bless God with one mouth, and let him that gives some portion of his substance understand that he is a minister of the Divine mercy; for God has placed the cause of the poor in the hand of the liberal man; that the sins which are washed away either by the waters of baptism, or the tears of repentance, may be also blotted out by almsgiving; for the Scripture says, "As water extinguisheth fire, so alms extinguisheth sin[8]." Through our Lord Jesus Christ, &c.

SERMON LI.

A homily delivered on the Saturday before the Second Sunday in Lent—on the Transfiguration, *S. Matt.* xvii. 1—13.

I. *S. Peter's confession shown to lead up to the Transfiguration.*

The Gospel lesson, dearly-beloved, which has reached the inner hearing of our minds through our bodily ears, calls us to the understanding of a great mystery, to which we shall by the help of God's grace the better attain, if we turn our attention to what is narrated just before.

The Saviour of mankind, Jesus Christ, in founding that faith, which recalls the wicked to righteousness and the dead to life, used to instruct His disciples by admonitory teaching and by miraculous acts to the end that He, the Christ, might be believed to be at once the Only-begotten of God and the Son of Man. For the one without the other was of no avail to salvation, and it was equally dangerous to have believed the Lord Jesus Christ to be either only God without manhood, or only man without Godhead[9], since both had equally to be confessed, because just as true manhood existed in His Godhead, so true Godhead existed in His Manhood. To strengthen, therefore, their most wholesome knowledge of this belief, the Lord had asked His disciples, among the various opinions of others, what they themselves believed, or thought about Him: whereat the Apostle Peter, by the revelation of the most High Father passing beyond things corporeal and surmounting things human by the eyes of his mind, saw Him to be Son of the living God, and acknowledged the glory of the Godhead, because he looked not at the substance of His flesh and blood alone; and with this lofty faith Christ was so well pleased that he received the fulness of blessing, and was endued with the holy firmness of the inviolable Rock on which the Church should be built and conquer the gates of hell and the laws of death, so that, in loosing or binding the petitions of any whatsoever, only that should be ratified in heaven which had been settled by the judgment of Peter.

II. *The same continued.*

But this exalted and highly-praised understanding, dearly-beloved, had also to be instructed on the mystery of Christ's lower substance, lest the Apostle's faith, being raised to the glory of confessing the Deity in Christ, should deem the reception of our weakness unworthy of the impassible God, and incongruous, and should believe the human nature to be so glorified in Him as to be incapable of suffering punishment, or being dissolved in death. And, therefore, when the Lord said that He must go to Jerusalem, and suffer many things from the elders and scribes and chief of the priests, and the third day rise

[6] S. Matt. v. 7, quoted in the same form in Serm. XCV. chap. 7, q.v.
[7] S. Matt. v. 9.
[8] Ecclus. iii. 30.
[9] The same words are used in Lett. XXVIII. (Tome), chap. 5.

again, the blessed Peter who, being illumined with light from above, was burning with the heat of his confession, rejected their mocking insults and the disgrace of the most cruel death, with, as he thought, a loyal and outspoken contempt, but was checked by a kindly rebuke from Jesus and animated with the desire to share His suffering. For the Saviour's exhortation that followed, instilled and taught this, that they who wished to follow Him should deny themselves, and count the loss of temporal things as light in the hope of things eternal; because he alone could save his soul that did not fear to lose it for Christ. In order, therefore, that the Apostles might entertain this happy, constant courage with their whole heart, and have no tremblings about the harshness of taking up the cross, and that they might not be ashamed of the punishment of Christ, nor think what He endured disgraceful for themselves (for the bitterness of suffering was to be displayed without despite to His glorious power), Jesus took Peter and James and his brother John, and ascending a very high[1] mountain with them apart, showed them the brightness of His glory; because, although they had recognised the majesty of GOD in Him, yet the power of His body, wherein His Deity was contained, they did not know. And, therefore, rightly and significantly, had He promised that certain of the disciples standing by should not taste death till they saw "the Son of Man coming in His Kingdom[2]," that is, in the kingly brilliance which, as specially belonging to the nature of His assumed Manhood, He wished to be conspicuous to these three men. For the unspeakable and unapproachable vision of the Godhead Itself, which is reserved till eternal life for the pure in heart, they could in no wise look upon and see while still surrounded with mortal flesh. The LORD displays His glory, therefore, before chosen witnesses, and invests that bodily shape which He shared with others with such splendour, that His face was like the sun's brightness and His garments equalled the whiteness of snow.

III. *The object and the meaning of the Transfiguration.*

And in this Transfiguration the foremost object was to remove the offence of the cross from the disciple's heart, and to prevent their faith being disturbed by the humiliation of His voluntary Passion by revealing to them the excellence of His hidden dignity. But with no less foresight, the foundation was laid of the Holy Church's hope, that the whole body of Christ might realize the character of the change which it would have to receive, and that the members might promise themselves a share in that honour which had already shone forth in their Head. About which the LORD had Himself said, when He spoke of the majesty of His coming, "Then shall the righteous shine as the sun in their Father's Kingdom[3]," whilst the blessed Apostle Paul bears witness to the self-same thing, and says: "for I reckon that the sufferings of this time are not worthy to be compared with the future glory which shall be revealed in us[4]:" and again, "for ye are dead, and your life is hid with Christ in GOD. For when Christ our life shall appear, then shall ye also appear with Him in glory[5]." But to confirm the Apostles and assist them to all knowledge, still further instruction was conveyed by that miracle.

IV. *The significance of the appearance of Moses and Elias.*

For Moses and Elias, that is the Law and the Prophets, appeared talking with the LORD; that in the presence of those five men might most truly be fulfilled what was said: "In two or three witnesses stands every word[6]." What more stable, what more steadfast than this word, in the proclamation of which the trumpet of the Old and of the New Testament joins, and the documentary evidence of the ancient witnesses[7] combine with the teaching of the Gospel? For the pages of both covenants[8] corroborate each other, and He Whom under the veil of mysteries the types that went before had promised, is displayed clearly and conspicuously by the splendour of the present glory. Because, as says the blessed John, "the law was given through Moses: but grace and truth came through Jesus Christ[9]," in Whom is fulfilled both the promise of prophetic figures and the purpose of the legal ordinances: for He both teaches the truth of prophecy by His presence, and renders the commands possible through grace.

V. *S. Peter's suggestion contrary to the Divine order.*

The Apostle Peter, therefore, being excited by the revelation of these mysteries, despising

[1] *Præcelso* (Vulg. *excelso*): possibly the form of the adjective supports *Codex Bezæ* (D) in adding λίαν after ὑψηλόν.

[2] S. Matt. xvi. 28. Leo's application of the prophecy is almost too fanciful to be the true one, though he stands by no means alone among commentators (ancient and modern) in so applying it.

[3] S. Matt. xiii. 43.

[4] Rom. viii. 18.

[5] Col. iii. 3.

[6] Deut. xix. 15.

[7] *Antiquarum protestationum instrumenta.*

[8] *Utriusque* fœderis *paginæ* (instead of the more usual *Testamenti*).

[9] S. John i. 17.

things mundane and scorning things earthly, was seized with a sort of frenzied craving for the things eternal, and being filled with rapture at the whole vision, desired to make his abode with Jesus in the place where he had been blessed with the manifestation of His glory. Whence also he says, "Lord, it is good for us to be here: if thou wilt let us make three tabernacles[1], one for Thee, one for Moses, and one for Elias." But to this proposal the LORD made no answer, signifying that what he wanted was not indeed wicked, but contrary to the Divine order: since the world could not be saved, except by Christ's death, and by the LORD's example the faithful were called upon to believe that, although there ought not to be any doubt about the promises of happiness, yet we should understand that amidst the trials of this life we must ask for the power of endurance rather than the glory, because the joyousness of reigning cannot precede the times of suffering.

VI. *The import of the Father's voice from the cloud.*

And so "while He was yet speaking, behold a bright cloud overshadowed them, and behold a voice out of the cloud, saying, "This is My beloved Son, in whom I am well pleased; hear ye Him." The Father was indeed present in the Son, and in the LORD's brightness, which He had tempered to the disciples' sight, the Father's Essence was not separated from the Only-begotten: but, in order to emphasize the two-fold personality, as the effulgence of the Son's body displayed the Son to their sight, so the Father's voice from out the cloud announced the Father to their hearing. And when this voice was heard, "the disciples fell upon their faces, and were sore afraid," trembling at the majesty, not only of the Father, but also of the Son: for they now had a deeper insight into the undivided Deity of Both: and in their fear they did not separate the One from the Other, because they doubted not in their faith[2]. That was a wide and manifold testimony, therefore, and contained a fuller meaning than struck the ear. For when the Father said, "This is My beloved Son, in Whom, &c.," was it not clearly meant, "This is My Son," Whose it is to be eternally from Me and with Me? because the Begetter is not anterior to the Begotten, nor the Begotten posterior to the Begetter. "This is My Son," Who is separated from Me, neither by Godhead, nor by power, nor by eternity. "This is My Son," not adopted, but true-born, not created from another source, but begotten of Me: nor yet made like Me from another nature, but born equal to Me of My nature. "This is My Son," "through Whom all things were made, and without Whom was nothing made[2a]," because all things that I do He doth in like manner: and whatever I perform, He performs with Me inseparably and without difference: for the Son is in the Father and the Father in the Son[2a], and Our Unity is never divided: and though I am One Who begat, and He the Other Whom I begat, yet is it wrong for you to think anything of Him which is not possible of Me. "This is My Son," Who sought not by grasping, and seized not in greediness[2a], that equality with Me which He has, but remaining in the form of My glory, that He might carry out Our common plan for the restoration of mankind, He lowered the unchangeable Godhead even to the form of a slave.

VII. *Who it is we have to hear.*

"Here ye Him," therefore, unhesitatingly, in Whom I am throughout well pleased, and by Whose preaching I am manifested, by Whose humiliation I am glorified; because He is "the Truth and the Life[2b]," He is My "Power and Wisdom[2b]." "Hear ye Him," Whom the mysteries of the Law have foretold, Whom the mouths of prophets have sung. "Hear ye Him," Who redeems the world by His blood, Who binds the devil, and carries off his chattels, Who destroys the bond of sin, and the compact of the transgression. Hear ye Him, Who opens the way to heaven, and by the punishment of the cross prepares for you the steps of ascent to the Kingdom? Why tremble ye at being redeemed? why fear ye to be healed of your wounds? Let that happen which Christ wills and I will. Cast away all fleshly fear, and arm yourselves with faithful constancy; for it is unworthy that ye should fear in the Saviour's Passion what by His good gift ye shall not have to fear even at your own end.

VIII. *The Father's words have a universal application to the whole Church.*

These things, dearly-beloved, were said not for their profit only, who heard them with their own ears, but in these three Apostles the whole Church has learnt all that their eyes saw and their ears heard. Let all men's faith then be established, according to the preaching of the most holy Gospel, and let no one

[1] Sc. booths or tents.
[2] *Quia in fide non fuit hæsitatio, non fuit in timore discretio.*

[2a] S. John i. 3: and below, cf. x. 38: and again Phil. ii. 6.
[2b] S. John xiv. 6; 1 Cor. i. 24.

be ashamed of Christ's cross, through which the world was redeemed. And let not any one fear to suffer for righteousness' sake, or doubt of the fulfilment of the promises, for this reason, that through toil we pass to rest and through death to life; since all the weakness of our humility was assumed by Him, in Whom, if we abide in the acknowledgment and love of Him, we conquer as He conquered, and receive what he promised, because, whether to the performance of His commands or to the endurance of adversities, the Father's fore-announcing voice should always be sounding in our ears, saying, "This is My beloved Son, in Whom I am well pleased; hear ye Him:" Who liveth and reigneth, with the Father and the Holy Ghost, for ever and ever. Amen.

SERMON LIV.

On the Passion, III.; delivered on the Sunday before Easter.

I. *The two-fold Nature of Christ set forth.*

Among all the works of God's mercy, dearly-beloved, which from the beginning have been bestowed upon men's salvation, none is more wondrous, and none more sublime, than that Christ was crucified for the world. For to this mystery all the mysteries of the ages preceding led up, and every variation which the will of God ordained in sacrifices, in prophetic signs, and in the observances of the Law, foretold that this was fixed, and promised its fulfilment: so that now types and figures are at an end, and we find our profit in believing that accomplished which before we found our profit in looking forward to. In all things, therefore, dearly-beloved, which pertain to the Passion of our Lord Jesus Christ, the Catholic Faith maintains and demands that we acknowledge the two Natures to have met in our Redeemer, and while their properties remained, such a union of both Natures to have been effected that, from the time when, as the cause of mankind required, in the blessed Virgin's womb, "the Word became flesh," we may not think of Him as God without that which is man, nor as man without that which is God. Each Nature does indeed express its real existence by actions that distinguish it, but neither separates itself from connexion with the other. Nothing is wanting there on either side; in the majesty the humility is complete, in the humility the majesty is complete: and the unity does not introduce confusion, nor does the distinctiveness destroy the unity. The one is passible, the other inviolable; and yet the degradation belongs to the same Person, as does the glory. He is present at once in weakness and in power; at once capable of death and the vanquisher of it. Therefore, God took on Him whole Manhood, and so blended the two Natures together by means of His mercy and power, that each Nature was present in the other, and neither passed out of its own properties into the other.

II. *The two Natures acted conjointly, and the human sufferings were not compulsory, but in accordance with the Divine will.*

But because the design of that mystery which was ordained for our restoration before the eternal ages, was not to be carried out without human weakness and without Divine power[3], both "form" does that which is proper to it in common with the other, the Word, that is, performing that which is the Word's and the flesh that which is of the flesh. One of them gleams bright with miracles, the other succumbs to injuries. The one departs not from equality with the Father's glory, the other leaves not the nature of our race. But nevertheless even His very endurance of sufferings does not so far expose Him to a participation in our humility as to separate Him from the power of the Godhead. All the mockery and insults, all the persecution and pain which the madness of the wicked inflicted on the Lord, was not endured of necessity, but undertaken of free-will: "for the Son of Man came to seek and to save that which had perished[4]:" and He used the wickedness of His persecutors for the redemption of all men in such a way that in the mystery of His Death and Resurrection even His murderers could have been saved, if they had believed.

III. *Judas' infamy has never been exceeded.*

And hence, Judas, thou art proved more criminal and unhappier than all; for when repentance should have called thee back to the Lord, despair dragged thee to the halter. Thou shouldest have awaited the completion of thy crime, and have put off thy ghastly death by hanging, until Christ's Blood was shed for all sinners. And among the many miracles and gifts of the Lord's which might have aroused thy conscience, those holy mysteries, at least, might have rescued thee from thy headlong fall, which at the Paschal supper thou hadst received, being even then detected in thy treachery by the sign of Divine knowledge. Why dost thou

3 This passage from "both form" down to "race" is repeated almost word for word in Lett. XXVIII. (The Tome), chap. 4.

4 S. Luke xix. 10.

distrust the goodness of Him, Who did not repel thee from the communion of His body and blood, Who did not deny thee the kiss of peace when thou camest with crowds and a band of armed men to seize Him. But O man that nothing could convert, O "spirit going and not returning[5]," thou didst follow thy heart's rage, and, the devil standing at thy right hand, didst turn the wickedness, which thou hadst prepared against the life of all the saints, to thine own destruction, so that, because thy crime had exceeded all measure of punishment, thy wickedness might make thee thine own judge, thy punishment allow thee to be thine own hangman.

IV. *Christ voluntarily bartered His glory for our weakness.*

When, therefore, "God was in Christ reconciling the world to Himself[6]," and the Creator Himself was wearing the creature which was to be restored to the image of its Creator; and after the Divinely-miraculous works had been performed, the performance of which the spirit of prophecy had once predicted, "then shall the eyes of the blind be opened and the ears of the deaf shall hear; then shall the lame man leap as a hart, and the tongue of the dumb shall be plain[7];" Jesus knowing that the time was now come for the fulfilment of His glorious Passion, said, "My soul is sorrowful even unto death[8];" and again, "Father, if it be possible, let this cup pass from Me[8]." And these words, expressing a certain fear, show His desire to heal the affection of our weakness by sharing them, and to check our fear of enduring pain by undergoing it. In our Nature, therefore, the Lord trembled with our fear, that He might fully clothe our weakness and our frailty with the completeness of His own strength. For He had come into this world a rich and merciful Merchant from the skies, and by a wondrous exchange had entered into a bargain of salvation with us, receiving ours and giving His, honour for insults, salvation for pain, life for death: and He Whom more than 12,000 of the angel-hosts might have served[9] for the annihilation of His persecutors, preferred to entertain our fears, rather than employ His own power.

V. *S. Peter was the first to benefit by his Master's humiliation.*

And how much this humiliation conferred upon all the faithful, the most blessed Apostle Peter was the first to prove, who, after the fierce blast of threatening cruelty had dismayed him, quickly changed, and was restored to vigour, finding remedy from the great Pattern, so that the suddenly-shaken member returned to the firmness of the Head. For the bond-servant could not be "greater than the lord, nor the disciple greater than the master[9a]," and he could not have vanquished the trembling of human frailty had not the Vanquisher of Death first feared. The Lord, therefore, "looked back upon Peter[9a]," and amid the calumnies of priests, the falsehoods of witnesses, the injuries of those that scourged and spat upon Him, met His dismayed disciple with those eyes wherewith He had foreseen his dismay: and the gaze of the Truth entered into him, on whose heart correction must be wrought, as if the Lord's voice were making itself heard there, and saying, Whither goest thou, Peter? why retirest thou upon thyself? turn thou to Me, put thy trust in Me, follow Me: this is the time of My Passion, the hour of thy suffering is not yet come. Why dost thou fear what thou, too, shalt overcome? Let not the weakness, in which I share, confound thee. I was fearful for thee; do thou be confident of Me.

VI. *The mad counsel of the Jews was turned to their own destruction.*

"And when morning was come all the chief priests and elders of the people took counsel against Jesus to put him to death[1]." This morning, O ye Jews, was for you not the rising, but the setting of the sun, nor did the wonted daylight visit your eyes, but a night of blackest darkness brooded on your naughty hearts. This morning overthrew for you the temple and its altars, did away with the Law and the Prophets, destroyed the Kingdom and the priesthood, turned all your feasts into eternal mourning. For ye resolved on a mad and bloody counsel, ye "fat bulls," ye "many oxen," ye "roaring" wild beasts, ye rabid "dogs[1a]," to give up to death the Author of life and the Lord of glory; and, as if the enormity of your fury could be palliated by employing the verdict of him, who ruled your province, you lead Jesus bound to Pilate's judgment, that the terror-stricken judge being overcome by your persistent shouts, you might choose a man that was a murderer for pardon, and demand the crucifixion of the Saviour of the world. After this condemnation of Christ, brought about more by the cowardice than the power of Pilate, who with

5 Ps. lxxviii. 39. 6 2 Cor. v. 19.
7 Is. xxxv. 5, 6. 8 S. Matt. xxvi. 38, 39.
9 Cf. S. Matt. xxvi. 53. The whole of this is a wonderfully powerful passage.

9a Cf. S. Matt. x. 24 and below, S. Luke xxii. 61.
1 S. Matt. xxvii. 1. 1a Cf. Ps. xxii. 12, 13, 16.

washed hands but polluted mouth sent Jesus to the cross with the very lips that had pronounced Him innocent, the licence of the people, obedient to the looks of the priests, heaped many insults on the LORD, and the frenzied mob wreaked its rage on Him, Who meekly and voluntarily endured it all. But because, dearly-beloved, the whole story is too long to go through to-day, let us put off the rest till Wednesday, when the reading of the LORD's Passion will be repeated[2]. For the LORD will grant to your prayers, that of His own free gift we may fulfil our promise: through our LORD Jesus Christ, Who liveth and reigneth for ever and ever. Amen.

SERMON LV.

ON THE LORD'S PASSION IV., DELIVERED ON WEDNESDAY IN HOLY WEEK.

I. *The difference between the penitence and blasphemy of the two robbers is a type of the human race.*

That which we owe to your expectations, dearly-beloved, must be paid through the LORD's bountiful answer to your prayers that He Who has made you eager in the demanding would make us fit for the performing.

In speaking but lately of the LORD's Passion, we reached the point in the Gospel story, where Pilate is said to have yielded to the Jews' wicked shouts that Jesus should be crucified. And so when all things had been accomplished, which the Godhead veiled in frail flesh[3] permitted, Jesus Christ the Son of GOD was fixed to the cross which He had also been carrying, two robbers being similarly crucified, one on His right hand, and the other on the left: so that even in the incidents of the cross might be displayed that difference which in His judgment must be made in the case of all men; for the believing robber's faith was a type of those who are to be saved, and the blasphemer's wickedness prefigured those who are to be damned. Christ's Passion, therefore, contains the mystery of our salvation, and of the instrument which the iniquity of the Jews prepared for His punishment, the Redeemer's power has made for us the stepping-stone to glory[4]: and that Passion the LORD Jesus so underwent for the salvation of all men that, while hanging there nailed to the wood, He entreated the Father's mercy for His murderers, and said, "Father, forgive them, for they know not what they do[5]."

II. *The chief priests showed utter ignorance of Scripture in their taunts.*

But the chief priests, for whom the Saviour sought forgiveness, rendered the torture of the cross yet worse by the barbs of railery; and at Him, on Whom they could vent no more fury with their hands, they hurled the weapons of their tongues, saying, "He saved others; Himself he cannot save. If He is the King of Israel, let Him now come down from the cross, and we believe Him[6]." From what spring of error, from what pool of hatred, O ye Jews, do ye drink such poisonous blasphemies? What master informed you, what teaching convinced you that you ought to believe Him to be King of Israel and Son of GOD, who should either not allow Himself to be crucified, or should shake Himself free from the binding nails. The mysteries of the Law, the sacred observances of the Passover, the mouths of the Prophets never told you this: whereas you did find truly and oft-times written that which applies to your abominable wicked-doing and to the LORD's voluntary suffering. For He Himself says by Isaiah, "I gave My back to the scourges, My cheeks to the palms of the hand, I turned not My face from the shame of spitting[7]." He Himself says by David, "They gave Me gall for My food, and in My thirst they supplied Me with vinegar[8];" and again, "Many dogs came about Me, the council of evil-doers beset Me. They pierced My hands and My feet, they counted all My bones. But they themselves watched and gazed on Me, they parted My raiment among them, and for My robe they cast lots[8]." And lest the course of your own evil doings should seem to have been foretold, and no power in the Crucified predicted, ye read not, indeed, that the LORD descended from the cross, but ye did read, "The LORD reigned on the tree[9]."

III. *The triumph of the Cross is immediate and effective.*

The Cross of Christ, therefore, symbolizes[1] the true altar of prophecy, on which the oblation of man's nature should be celebrated by

[2] Leo seems here to speak as if the story of the Passion from the Gospels in his time was read only on the Sunday and Wednesday in Holy Week: various uses prevailed, for which cf. Bingham's Antiq. Bk. xiv. chap. iii. § 3.

[3] *Divinitas carnis velamine temperata.* It is not easy to render the exact force of this phrase in English without a danger of being misunderstood.

[4] *Gradum nobis fecit ad gloriam.* Quesnel's reading *gaudium*, though well supported by the MSS., is, I think with the Ball., unsatisfactory, cf. Serm. LI. chap. 7, *per crucis supplicium gradus vobis ascensionis parat ad regnum.*

[5] S. Luke xxiii. 34.

[6] S. Matt. xxvii. 42.

[7] Is. l. 6. [8] Ps. lxix. 21; xxii. 16, 17.

[9] Ps. xcvi. 10. "An ancient gloss, but without authority from existing MSS. or ancient versions, viz., ἀπὸ τοῦ ξύλου, was received by S. Justin Martyr and others as a genuine portion of the text." Speaker's Commentary *in loco*. Compare also the old Latin hymn ("The Royal Banners," H.A.M. 96, verse 3).

[1] *Sacramentum habet.*

means of a salvation-bringing Victim. There the blood of the spotless Lamb blotted out the consequences of the ancient trespass: there the whole tyranny of the devil's hatred was crushed, and humiliation triumphed gloriously over the lifting up of pride: for so swift was the effect of Faith that of the robbers crucified with Christ, the one who believed in Christ as the Son of GOD entered paradise justified. Who can unfold the mystery of so great a boon? who can state the power of so wondrous a change? In a moment of time the guilt of long evil-doing is done away; clinging to the cross, amid the cruel tortures of his struggling soul, he passes over to Christ; and to him, on whom his own wickedness had brought punishment, Christ's grace now gives a crown.

IV. *When the last act in the tragedy was over how must the Jews have felt?*

And then, having now tasted the vinegar, the produce of that vineyard which had degenerated in spite of its Divine Planter, and had turned to the sourness of a foreign vine [1a], the LORD says, "it is finished;" that is, the Scriptures are fulfilled: there is no more for Me to abide from the fury of the raging people: I have endured all that I foretold I should suffer. The mysteries of weakness are completed, let the proofs of power be produced. And so He bowed the head and yielded up His Spirit and gave that Body, Which should be raised again on the third day, the rest of peaceful slumber. And when the Author of Life was undergoing this mysterious phase, and at so great a condescension of GOD's Majesty, the foundations of the whole world were shaken, when all creation condemned their wicked crime by its upheaval, and the very elements of the world delivered a plain verdict against the criminals, what thoughts, what heart-searchings had ye, O Jews, when the judgment of the universe went against you, and your wickedness could not be recalled, the crime having been done? what confusion covered you? what torment seized your hearts?

V. *Chastity and charity are the two things most needful in preparing for Easter Communion.*

Seeing therefore, dearly-beloved, that GOD's Mercy is so great, that He has deigned to justify by faith many even from among such a nation, and had adopted into the company of the patriarchs and into the number of the chosen people us who were once perishing in the deep darkness of our old ignorance, let us mount to the summit of our hopes not sluggishly nor in sloth; but prudently and faithfully reflecting from what captivity and from how miserable a bondage, with what ransom we were purchased, by how strong an arm led out, let us glorify GOD in our body: that we may show Him dwelling in us, even by the uprightness of our manner of life. And because no virtues are worthier or more excellent than merciful loving-kindness and unblemished chastity, let us more especially equip ourselves with these weapons, so that, raised from the earth, as it were, on the two wings of active charity and shining purity, we may win a place in heaven. And whosoever, aided by GOD's grace, is filled with this desire and glories not in himself, but in the LORD, over his progress, pays due honour to the Easter mystery. His threshold the angel of destruction does not cross, for it is marked with the Lamb's blood and the sign of the cross [1b]. He fears not the plagues of Egypt, and leaves his foes overwhelmed by the same waters by which he himself was saved. And so, dearly-beloved, with minds and bodies purified let us embrace the wondrous mystery of our salvation, and, cleansed from all "the leaven of our old wickedness, let us keep [1b]" the LORD's Passover with due observance: so that, the Holy Spirit guiding us, we may be "separated" by no temptations "from the love of Christ [1b]," Who bringing peace by His blood to all things, has returned to the loftiness of the Father's glory, and yet not forsaken the lowliness of those who serve Him to Whom is the honour and the glory for ever and ever. Amen.

SERMON LVIII.

(ON THE PASSION, VII.)

I. *The reason of Christ suffering at the Paschal Feast.*

I know indeed, dearly-beloved, that the Easter festival partakes of so sublime a mystery as to surpass not only the slender perceptions of my humility, but even the powers of great intellects. But I must not consider the greatness of the Divine work in such a way as to distrust or to feel ashamed of the service which I owe; for we may not hold our peace upon the mystery of man's salvation, even if it cannot be explained. But, your prayers aiding us, we believe GOD's Grace will be granted, to sprinkle the barrenness of our heart with the dew of His inspira-

1a The reference is perhaps to Is. v. 1—5.

1b Cf. Exod. xii. 23; and below, 1 Cor. v. 8, and Rom. vii 35.

tion: that by the pastor's mouth things may be proclaimed which are useful to the ears of his holy flock. For when the LORD, the Giver of all good things, says: "open thy mouth, and I will fill it [2]," we dare likewise to reply in the prophet's words: "LORD, Thou shalt open my lips, and my mouth shall shew forth Thy praise [3]." Therefore beginning, dearly-beloved, to handle once more the Gospel-story of the LORD's Passion, we understand it was part of the Divine plan that the profane chiefs of the Jews and the unholy priests, who had often sought occasion of venting their rage on Christ, should receive the power of exercising their fury at no other time than the Paschal festival. For the things which had long been promised under mysterious figures had to be fulfilled in all clearness; for instance, the True Sheep had to supersede the sheep which was its antitype, and the One Sacrifice to bring to an end the multitude of different sacrifices. For all those things which had been divinely ordained through Moses about the sacrifice of the lamb had prophesied of Christ and truly announced the slaying of Christ. In order, therefore, that the shadows should yield to the substance and types cease in the presence of the Reality, the ancient observance is removed by a new Sacrament, victim passes into Victim, blood is wiped away by Blood, and the law-ordained Feast is fulfilled by being changed.

II. *The leading Jews broke their own Law, as well as failed to apprehend the new dispensation in destroying Christ.*

And hence, when the chief priests gathered the scribes and elders of the people together to their council, and the minds of all the priests were occupied with the purpose of doing wrong to Jesus, the teachers of the law put themselves without the law, and by their own voluntary failure in duty abolished their ancestral ceremonies. For when the Paschal feast began, those who ought to have adorned the temple, cleansed the vessels, provided the victims, and employed a holier zeal in the purifications that the law enjoined, seized with the fury of traitorous hate, give themselves up to one work, and with uniform cruelty conspire for one crime, though they were doomed to gain nothing by the punishment of innocence and the condemnation of righteousness, except the failure to apprehend the new mysteries and the violation of the old. The chiefs, therefore, in providing against a tumult arising on a holy day [4], showed zeal not for the festival, but for a heinous crime; and their anxiety served not the cause of religion, but their own incrimination. For these careful pontiffs and anxious priests feared the occurrence of seditious riots on the principal feast-day, not lest the people should do wrong, but lest Christ should escape.

III. *Jesus instituting the Blessed Sacrament showed mercy to the Traitor Judas to the last.*

But Jesus, sure of His purpose and undaunted in carrying out His Father's will, fulfilled the New Testament and founded a new Passover. For while the disciples were lying down with Him at the mystic Supper, and when discussion was proceeding in the hall of Caiaphas how Christ might be put to death, He, ordaining the Sacrament of His Body and Blood, was teaching them what kind of Victim must be offered up to GOD, and not even from this mystery was the betrayer kept away, in order to show that he was exasperated by no personal wrong, but had determined beforehand of his own free-will upon his treachery. For he was his own source of ruin and cause of perfidy, following the guidance of the devil and refusing to have Christ as director. And so when the LORD said, "Verily I say to you that one of you is about to betray Me," He showed that His betrayer's conscience was well known to Him, not confounding the traitor by harsh or open rebukes, but meeting him with mild and silent warnings that he who had never been sent astray by rejection, might the easier be set right by repentance. Why, unhappy Judas, dost thou not make use of so great long-suffering? Behold, the LORD spares thy wicked attempts; Christ betrays thee to none save thyself. Neither thy name nor thy person is discovered, but only the secrets of thy heart are touched by the word of truth and mercy. The honour of the apostolic rank is not denied thee, nor yet a share in the Sacraments. Return to thy right mind; lay aside thy madness and be wise. Mercy invites thee, Salvation knocks at the door, Life recalls thee to life. Lo, thy stainless and guiltless fellow-disciples shudder at the hint of thy crime, and all tremble for themselves till the author of the treachery is declared. For they are saddened not by the accusations of conscience, but by the uncertainty of man's changeableness; fearing lest what each knew against himself be less true than what the Truth Himself foresaw. But thou abusest the LORD's patience in this panic of the saints, and believest that thy bold front hides thee. Thou addest impudence to guilt, and art not frightened by so clear a test. And when the others refrain from

[2] Ps. lxxxi. 10. [3] Ps. li. 15. [4] Cf. S. Matt. xxvi. 5.

the food in which the LORD had set His judgment, thou dost not withdraw thy hand from the dish, because thy mind is not turned aside from the crime.

IV. *Various incidents of the Passion further explained and the reality of Christ's sufferings asserted.*

And thus it followed, dearly-beloved, that as John the Evangelist has narrated, when the LORD offered the bread which He had dipped to His betrayer, more clearly to point him out, the devil entirely seized Judas, and now, by his veritable act of wickedness, took possession of one whom he had already bound down by his evil designs. . For only in body was he lying there with those at meat: in mind he was arming the hatred of the priests, the falseness of the witnesses, and the fury of the ignorant mob. At last the LORD, seeing on what a gross crime Judas was bent, says, "What thou doest, do quickly[5]." This is the voice not of command but of permission, and not of fear but of readiness: He, that has power over all times, shows that He puts no hindrance in the way of the traitor, and carries out the Father's will for the redemption of the world in such a way as neither to promote nor to fear the crime which His persecutors were preparing. When Judas, therefore, at the devil's persuasion, departed from Christ, and cut himself off from the unity of the Apostolic body, the LORD, without being disturbed by any fear, but anxious only for the salvation of those He came to redeem, spent all the time that was free from His persecutors' attack on mystic conversation and holy teaching, as is declared in St. John's gospel: raising His eyes to heaven and beseeching the Father for the whole Church that all whom the Father had and would give the Son might become one and remain undivided to the Redeemer's glory, and adding lastly that prayer in which He says, "Father, if it be possible, let this cup pass from Me[6]." Wherein it is not to be thought that the LORD Jesus wished to escape the Passion and the Death, the sacraments of which He had already committed to His disciples' keeping, seeing that He Himself forbids Peter, when he was burning with devoted faith and love, to use the sword, saying, "The cup which the Father hath given Me, shall I not drink it[7]?" and seeing that that is certain which the LORD also says, according to John's Gospel, "For GOD so loved the world that He gave His only begotten Son, that everyone who believes in Him may not perish, but have eternal life[8];" as also what the Apostle Paul says, "Christ loved us and gave Himself for us, a victim to GOD for a sweet-smelling savour[9]." For the saving of all through the Cross of Christ was the common will and the common plan of the Father and the Son; nor could that by any means be disturbed which before eternal ages had been mercifully determined and unchangeably foreordained. Therefore in assuming true and entire manhood He took the true sensations of the body and the true feelings of the mind. And it does not follow because everything in Him was full of sacraments, full of miracles, that therefore He either shed false tears or took food from pretended hunger or feigned slumber. It was in our humility that He was despised, with our grief that He was saddened, with our pain that He was racked on the cross. For His compassion underwent the sufferings of our mortality with the purpose of healing them, and His power encountered them with the purpose of conquering them. And this Isaiah has most plainly prophesied, saying, "He carries our sins and is pained for us, and we thought Him to be in pain and in stripes and in vexation. But He was wounded for our sins, and was stricken for our offences, and with His bruises we are healed[1]."

V. *The resignation of Christ is an undying lesson to the Church*

And so, dearly-beloved, when the Son of GOD says, "Father, if it be possible, let this cup pass from Me[2]," He uses the outcry of our nature, and pleads the cause of human frailty and trembling: that our patience may be strengthened and our fears driven away in the things which we have to bear. At length, ceasing even to ask this now that He had in a measure palliated our weak fears, though it is not expedient for us to retain them, He passes into another mood, and says, "Nevertheless, not as I will but as Thou;" and again, "If this cup can not pass from Me, except I drink it, Thy will be done[2]." These words of the Head are the salvation of the whole Body: these words have instructed all the faithful, kindled the zeal of all the confessors, crowned all the martyrs. For who could overcome the world's hatred, the blasts of temptations, the terr cisf persecutors, had not Christ, in the name of all and for all, said to the Father, "Thy will be done?" Then let the words be learnt by all the Church's sons who have been purchased at so great a price, so freely justified: and when the

[5] S. John xiii. 27.
[6] S. Matt. xxvi. 39.
[7] S. John xviii. 11.
[8] Ib. iii. 16.
[9] Eph. v. 2.
[1] Is. liii. 45. Leo's version is a very literal translation of the LXX., which varies a good deal from the Vulgate and the A.V.; he omits, however, the clause, "the chastisement of our peace," &c., which is common to all three.
[2] S. Matt. xxvi. 39 and 42.

shock of some violent temptation has fallen on them, let them use the aid of this potent prayer, that they may conquer their fear and trembling, and learn to suffer patiently. From this point, dearly-beloved, our sermon must pass to the consideration of the details of the LORD's Passion, and lest we should burden you with prolixity, we will divide our common task, and put off the rest[3] till the fourth day of the week. GOD's grace will be vouchsafed to you if you pray Him to give me the power of carrying out my duty: through our LORD Jesus Christ, &c.

SERMON LIX.

(ON THE PASSION, VIII.: ON WEDNESDAY IN HOLY WEEK.)

I. *Christ's arrest fulfils His own eternal purpose.*

Having discoursed, dearly beloved, in our last sermon, on the events which preceded the LORD's arrest, it now remains, by the help of GOD's grace, to discuss, as we promised, the details of the Passion itself. When the LORD had made it clear by the words of His sacred prayer that the Divine and the Human Nature was most truly and fully present in Him, showing that the unwillingness to suffer proceeded from the one, and from the other the determination to suffer by the expulsion of all frail fears and the strengthening of His lofty power, then did He return to His eternal purpose, and "in the form of a" sinless "slave" encounter the devil who was savagely attacking Him by the hands of the Jews: that He in Whom alone was all men's nature without fault, might undertake the cause of all. The sins of darkness, therefore, assailed the true Light, and, for all their torches and lanterns[4], could not escape the night of their own unbelief, because they did not recognize the Fount of Light. They arrest Him, and He is ready to be seized; they lead Him away, and He is willing to be led; for though, if He had willed to resist, their wicked hands could have done Him no harm, yet thereby the world's redemption would have been impeded, and He, who was to die for all men's salvation, would have saved none at all.

II. *How great was Pilate's crime in allowing himself to be led astray by the Jews.*

Accordingly, permitting the infliction on Himself of all that the people's fury inflamed by the priests dared do, He is brought to Annas, father-in-law to Caiaphas, and thence Annas passes Him on to Caiaphas: and after the calumniators' mad accusations, after the lying falsehoods of suborned witnesses, He is transferred to Pilate's hearing by the delegation of the two high-priests, who in neglecting the Divine law, and exclaiming that they had "no king but Cæsar," as if they were devoted to the Roman laws, and had left the whole judgment in the hands of the governor, really sought for an accomplisher of their cruelty rather than an umpire of the case. For they gave up Jesus, bound in hard bonds, bruised by many buffets and blows, spat upon, already condemned by their shouts: so that amidst so many signs of their own verdict Pilate might not dare to acquit One Whom all desired to perish. In fact, the very inquiry shows both that he found in the Accused no fault, and that in his judgment he did not adhere to his purpose: for as judge he condemns One Whom he pronounces guiltless, invoking on the unrighteous people the blood of the Righteous Man with Whom he felt by his own conviction, and knew from his wife's dream[4a], he must have nothing to do. That stained soul is not cleansed by the washing of hands, there is no expiation in water-besprinkled fingers for the crime abetted by that wicked mind. Pilate's fault is, indeed, less than the Jews' crime; for it was they that terrified him with Cæsar's name, chode him with hateful words, and drove him to perpetrate his wickedness. But he also did not escape incrimination for playing into the hands of those that made the uproar, for abandoning his own judgment, and for acquiescing in the charges of others.

III. *Yet the Jews' guilt was infinitely greater.*

In bowing, therefore, dearly-beloved, to the madness of the implacable people, in permitting Jesus to be dishonoured by much mocking, and harassed with excessive insults, and in displaying Him to the eyes of His persecutors lacerated with scourges, crowned with thorns, and clothed in a robe of scorn, Pilate doubtless thought to appease the enemies' minds, so that, when they had glutted their cruel hate, they might cease further to persecute One Whom they beheld subjected to such a variety of afflictions. But their wrath was still in full blaze, and they cried out to him to release Barabbas and let Jesus bear the penalty of the cross, and thus, when with consenting murmur the crowd said, "His blood be on us and on our sons[4a]," those wicked folk gained, to their own damnation, what they had persistently demanded, "whose teeth," as the prophet bore witness, "were arms and arrows, and their tongue a sharp sword[5]." For in vain did they keep their

[3] This is Sermon LIX. which follows *in extenso*. See Serm. LIV., chap. vi. n. 2.

[4] The allusion doubtless is to the "lanterns and torches" mentioned by S. John xviii. 3.

[4a] Cf. S. Matt. xxvii. 19 and 25.

[5] Ps vii. 4.

own hands from crucifying the LORD of glory when they had hurled at Him the tongue's deadly darts and the poisoned weapons of words. On you, on you, false Jews and unholy leaders of the people, falls the full weight of that crime: and although the enormity of the guilt involves the governor and the soldiers also, yet you are the primary and chief offenders. And in Christ's condemnation, whatsoever wrong was done either by Pilate's judgment or by the cohorts carrying out of his commands, makes you only the more deserving of the hatred of mankind, because the impulse of your fury would not let even those be free from guilt who were displeased at your unrighteous acts.

IV. *Christ bearing His own cross is an eternal lesson to the Church.*

And so the LORD was handed over to their savage wishes, and in mockery of His kingly state, ordered to be the bearer of His own instrument of death, that what Isaiah the prophet foresaw might be fulfilled, saying, "Behold a Child is born, and a Son is given to us whose government is upon His shoulders[6]." When, therefore, the LORD carried the wood of the cross which should turn for Him into the sceptre of power, it was indeed in the eyes of the wicked a mighty mockery, but to the faithful a mighty mystery was set forth, seeing that He, the glorious vanquisher of the Devil, and the strong defeater of the powers that were against Him, was carrying in noble sort the trophy of His triumph, and on the shoulders of His unconquered patience bore into all realms the adorable sign of salvation: as if even then to confirm all His followers by this mere symbol of His work, and say, "He that taketh not his cross and followeth Me, is not worthy of Me[6a]."

V. *The transference of the cross from the* LORD *to Simon of Cyrene signifies the participation of the Gentiles in His sufferings.*

But as the multitudes went with Jesus to the place of punishment, a certain Simon of Cyrene was found on whom to lay the wood of the cross instead of the LORD; that even by this act might be pre-signified the Gentiles' faith, to whom the cross of Christ was to be not shame but glory. It was not accidental, therefore, but symbolical and mystical, that while the Jews were raging against Christ, a foreigner was found to share His sufferings, as the Apostle says, "if we suffer with Him, we shall also reign with Him[7]"; so that no Hebrew nor Israelite, but a stranger, was substituted for the Saviour in His most holy degradation. For by this transference the propitiation of the spotless Lamb and the fulfilment of all mysteries passed from the circumcision to the uncircumcision, from the sons according to the flesh to the sons according to the spirit: since as the Apostle says, "Christ our Passover is sacrificed for us[8]," Who offering Himself to the Father a new and true sacrifice of reconciliation, was crucified not in the temple, whose worship was now at an end, and not within the confines of the city which for its sin was doomed to be destroyed, but outside, "without the camp[9]," that, on the cessation of the old symbolic victims, a new Victim might be placed on a new altar, and the cross of Christ might be the altar not of the temple but of the world.

VI. *We are to see not only the cross but the meaning of it.*

Accordingly, dearly-beloved, Christ being lifted up upon the cross, let the eyes of your mind not dwell only on that sight which those wicked sinners saw, to whom it was said by the mouth of Moses, "And thy life shall be hanging before thine eyes, and thou shalt fear day and night, and shalt not be assured of thy life[1]." For in the crucified LORD they could think of nothing but their wicked deed, having not the fear, by which true faith is justified, but that by which an evil conscience is racked. But let our understandings, illumined by the Spirit of Truth, foster with pure and free heart the glory of the cross which irradiates heaven and earth, and see with the inner sight what the LORD meant when He spoke of His coming Passion: "The hour is come that the Son of man may be glorified[2]:" and below He says, "Now is My spirit troubled. And what shall I say? Father, save Me from this hour, but for this cause came I unto this hour. Father, glorify Thy Son." And when the Father's voice came from heaven, saying, "I have both glorified it and will glorify it again," Jesus in reply said to those that stood by, "This voice came not for Me but for you. Now is the world's judgment, now shall the prince of this world be cast out. And I, if I be lifted up from the earth, will draw all things unto Me[2]."

VII. *The power of the cross is universally attractive.*

O wondrous power of the Cross! O in-

[6] Is. ix. 6. The interpretation is fanciful, but not without some support from the parallel phrase in Is. xxii. 22

[6a] S. Matt. x. 38.

[7] 2 Tim. ii. 12.

[8] 1 Cor. v. 7.

[9] Heb. xiii. 12.

[1] Deut. xxviii. 66.

[2] S. John xii. 23; Ibid. 27, 28, 30—32. The reading *omni* (all things) will not escape notice in v. 32.

effable glory of the Passion, in which is contained the LORD's tribunal, the world's judgment, and the power of the Crucified! For thou didst draw all things unto Thee, LORD, and when Thou hadst stretched out Thy hands all the day long to an unbelieving people that gainsaid Thee [2a], the whole world at last was brought to confess Thy majesty. Thou didst draw all things unto Thee, LORD, when all the elements combined to pronounce judgment in execration of the Jews' crime, when the lights of heaven were darkened, and the day turned into night, and the earth also was shaken with unwonted shocks, and all creation refused to serve those wicked men. Thou didst draw all things unto Thee, LORD. for the veil of the temple was rent, and the Holy of Holies existed no more for those unworthy high-priests: so that type was turned into Truth, prophecy into Revelation, law into Gospel. Thou didst draw all things unto Thee, LORD, so that what before was done in the one temple of the Jews in dark signs, was now to be celebrated everywhere by the piety of all the nations in full and open rite. For now there is a nobler rank of Levites, there are elders of greater dignity and priests of holier anointing: because Thy cross is the fount of all blessings, the source of all graces, and through it the believers receive strength for weakness, glory for shame, life for death. Now, too, the variety of fleshly sacrifices has ceased, and the one offering of Thy Body and Blood fulfils all those different victims: for Thou art the true "Lamb of GOD, that takest away the sins of the world [3]," and in Thyself so accomplishest all mysteries, that as there is but one sacrifice instead of many victims, so there is but one kingdom instead of many nations.

VIII. *We must live not for ourselves but for Christ, who died for us.*

Let us, then, dearly-beloved, confess what the blessed teacher of the nations, the Apostle Paul, confessed, saying, "Faithful is the saying, and worthy of all acceptation, that Christ Jesus came into the world to save sinners [4]." For GOD's mercy towards us is the more wonderful that Christ died not for the righteous nor for the holy, but for the unrighteous and wicked; and though the nature of the Godhead could not sustain the sting of death, yet at His birth He took from us that which He might offer for us. For of old He threatened our death with the power of His death, saying, by the mouth of Hosea the prophet, "O death, I will be thy death, and I will be thy destruction, O hell [5]." For by dying He underwent the laws of hell, but by rising again He broke them, and so destroyed the continuity of death as to make it temporal instead of eternal. "For as in Adam all die, even so in Christ shall all be made alive [6]." And so, dearly-beloved, let that come to pass of which S. Paul speaks, "that they that live, should henceforth not live to themselves but to Him who died for all and rose again [7]." And because the old things have passed away and all things are become new, let none remain in his old carnal life, but let us all be renewed by daily progress and growth in piety. For however much a man be justified, yet so long as he remains in this life, he can always be more approved and better. And he that is not advancing is going back, and he that is gaining nothing is losing something. Let us run, then, with the steps of faith, by the works of mercy, in the love of righteousness, that keeping the day of our redemption spiritually, "not in the old leaven of malice and wickedness, but in the unleavened bread of sincerity and truth [8]," we may deserve to be partakers of Christ's resurrection, Who with the Father and the Holy Ghost liveth and reigneth for ever and ever. Amen.

SERMON LXII.

(ON THE PASSION, XI.)

I. *The mystery of the Passion passes man's comprehension.*

The Feast of the Lord's Passion [9] that we have longed for and that the whole world may well desire, has come, and suffers us not to keep silence in the tumult of our spiritual joys: because though it is difficult to speak often on the same thing worthily and appropriately, yet the priest is not free to withhold from the people's ears instruction by sermon on this great mystery of GOD's mercy, inasmuch as the subject itself, being unspeakable, gives him ease of utterance, and what is said cannot altogether fail where what is said can never be enough. Let human frailty, then, succumb to GOD's glory, and ever acknowledge itself unequal to the unfolding of His works of mercy. Let us toil in thought, fail in insight, falter in utterance: it is good that even our right thoughts about the LORD's Majesty should be insufficient. For, remembering what the prophet says, "Seek ye the LORD and be strengthened: seek His face always [1]," no one must assume that he has found all he seeks, lest he fail of coming near,

2a Cf. Is. lxv. 2.

3 S. John i. 29.

4 1 Tim. i. 15.

5 Hos. xiii. 14.

6 1 Cor. xv. 22.

7 2 Cor. v. 15.

8 1 Cor. v. 8.

9 *Festivitas dominicæ passionis* is at first sight a strange phrase, but in reality most suggestive.

1 Ps. cv. 4.

if he cease his endeavours. And amidst all the works of GOD which weary out man's wondering contemplation, what so delights and so baffles our mind's gaze as the Saviour's Passion? Ponder as we may upon His omnipotence, which is of one and equal substance with the Father, the humility in GOD is more stupendous than the power, and it is harder to grasp the complete emptying of the Divine Majesty than the infinite uplifting of the "slave's form" in Him. But we are much aided in our understanding of it by the remembrance that though the Creator and the creature, the Inviolable GOD and the passible flesh, are absolutely different, yet the properties of both substances meet together in Christ's one Person in such a way that alike in His acts of weakness and of power the degradation belongs to the same Person as the glory.

II. *The Creed takes up S. Peter's confession as the fundamental doctrine of the Church.*

In that rule of Faith, dearly-beloved, which we have received in the very beginning of the Creed, on the authority of apostolic teaching, we acknowledge our LORD Jesus Christ, whom we call the only Son of GOD the Father Almighty, to be also born of the Virgin Mary by the Holy Ghost. Nor do we reject His Majesty when we express our belief in His crucifixion, death, and resurrection on the third day. For all that is GOD's and all that is Man's are simultaneously fulfilled by His Manhood and His Godhead, so that in virtue of the union of the Passible with the Impassible, His power cannot be affected by His weakness, nor His weakness overcome by His power. And rightly was the blessed Apostle Peter praised for confessing this union, who when the LORD was inquiring what the disciples knew of Him, quickly anticipated the rest and said, "Thou art Christ, the Son of the living GOD [2]." And this assuredly he saw, not by the revelation of flesh or blood, which might have hindered his inner sight, but by the very Spirit of the Father working in his believing heart, that in preparation for ruling the whole Church he might first learn what he would have to teach, and for the solidification of the Faith, which he was destined to preach, might receive the assurance, "Thou art Peter, and upon this rock I will build My Church, and the gates of hell shall not prevail against it [2]." The strength, therefore, of the Christian Faith, which, built upon an impregnable rock, fears not the gates of death, acknowledges the one LORD Jesus Christ to be both true GOD and true Man, believing Him likewise to be the Virgin's Son, Who is His Mother's Creator: born also at the end of the ages, though He is the Creator of time: LORD of all power, and yet one of mortal stock: ignorant of sin, and yet sacrificed for sinners after the likeness of sinful flesh.

III. *The devil's devices were turned against himself.*

And in order that He might set the human race free from the bonds of deadly transgression, He hid the power of His majesty from the raging devil, and opposed him with our frail and humble nature. For if the cruel and proud foe could have known the counsel of GOD's mercy, he would have aimed at soothing the Jews' minds into gentleness rather than at firing them with unrighteous hatred, lest he should lose the thraldom of all his captives in assailing the liberty of One Who owed him nought. Thus he was foiled by his malice: he inflicted a punishment on the Son of GOD, which was turned to the healing of all the sons of men. He shed righteous Blood, which became the ransom and the drink for the world's atonement. The LORD undertook that which He chose according to the purpose of His own will. He permitted madmen to lay their wicked hands upon Him: hands which, in ministering to their own doom, were of service to the Redeemer's work. And yet so great was His loving compassion for even His murderers, that He prayed to the Father on the cross, and begged not for His own vengeance but for their forgiveness, saying, "Father, forgive them, for they know not what they do [3]." And such was the power of that prayer, that the hearts of many of those who had said, "His blood be on us and on our sons [3a]," were turned to penitence by the Apostle Peter's preaching, and on one day there were baptized about 3,000 Jews: and they all were "of one heart and of one soul [4]," being ready now to die for Him, Whose crucifixion they had demanded.

IV. *Why Judas could not obtain forgiveness through Christ.*

To this forgiveness the traitor Judas could not attain: for he, the son of perdition, at whose right the devil stood [5], gave himself up to despair before Christ accomplished the mystery of universal redemption. For in that the LORD died for sinners, perchance even he might have found salvation if he had not hastened to hang himself. But that evil heart, which was now given up to thievish frauds, and now busied with treacherous designs, had

[2] S. Matt. xvi. 16, 18.

[3] S. Luke xxiii. 34.
[3a] S. Matt. xxvii. 25.
[4] Acts iv. 32.
[5] Cf. Ps. cix. 6.

never entertained aught of the proofs of the Saviour's mercy. Those wicked ears had heard the LORD's words, when He said, "I same not to call the righteous but sinners[6]," and "The Son of man came to seek and to save that which was lost[7]," but they conveyed not to his understanding the clemency of Christ, which not only healed bodily infirmities, but also cured the wounds of sick souls, saying to the paralytic man, "Son, be of good cheer, thy sins are forgiven thee[8];" saying also to the adulteress that was brought to Him, "neither will I condemn thee; go and sin no more[9]," to show in all His works that He had come as the Saviour, not the Judge of the world. But the wicked traitor refused to understand this, and took measures against himself, not in the self-condemnation of repentance, but in the madness of perdition, and thus he who had sold the Author of life to His murderers, even in dying increased the amount of sin which condemned him.

V. *The cruelty of Christ's crucifixion is lost in its wondrous power.*

Accordingly that which false witnesses, cruel leaders of the people, wicked priests did against the LORD Jesus Christ, through the agency of a coward governor and an ignorant band of soldiers, has been at once the abhorrence and the rejoicing of all ages. For though the LORD's cross was part of the cruel purpose of the Jews, yet is it of wondrous power through Him they crucified. The people's fury was directed against One, and the mercy of Christ is for all mankind. That which their cruelty inflicts He voluntarily undergoes, in order that the work of His eternal will may be carried out through their unhindered crime. And hence the whole order of events which is most fully narrated in the Gospels must be received by the faithful in such a way that by implicit belief in the occurrences which happened at the time of the LORD's Passion, we should understand that not only was the remission of sins accomplished by Christ, but also the standard of justice satisfied. But that this may be more thoroughly discussed by the LORD's help, let us reserve this portion of the subject till the fourth day of the week[9a]. GOD's grace, we hope, will be vouchsafed at your entreaties to help us to fulfil our promise: through Jesus Christ our Lord, &c. Amen.

[6] S. Matt. ix. 13. [7] S. Luke xix. 10. [8] S. Matt. ix. 3.
[9] S. John viii. 11; this famous section therefore is recognized by S. Leo: see Bright's note 69.
[9a] See Serm. LIV. chap. vi. n. 8.

SERMON LXIII.

(ON THE PASSION, XII.: PREACHED ON WEDNESDAY.)

I. *GOD chose to save man by strength made perfect in weakness.*

The glory, dearly-beloved, of the LORD's Passion, on which we promised to speak again to-day, is chiefly wonderful for its mystery of humility, which has both ransomed and instructed us all, that He, Who paid the price, might also impart His righteousness to us. For the Omnipotence of the Son of GOD, whereby He is by the same Essence equal to the Father, might have rescued mankind from the dominion of the devil by the mere exercise of Its will, had it not better suited the Divine working to conquer the opposition of the foe's wickedness by that which had been conquered, and to restore our nature's liberty by that very nature by which bondage had come upon the whole race. But, when the evangelist says, "The Word became flesh and dwelt in us[1]," and the Apostle, "GOD was in Christ reconciling the world to Himself[2]," it was shown that the Only-begotten of the Most High Father entered on such a union with human humility, that, when He took the substance of our flesh and soul, He remained one and the same Son of GOD by exalting our properties, not His own: because it was the weakness, not the power that had to be reinforced, so that upon the union of the creature with the Creator there should be nothing wanting of the Divine to the assumed, nor of the human to the Assuming.

II. *GOD's plan was always partially understood, and is now of universal application.*

This plan of GOD's mercy and justice, though in the ages past it was in a measure enshrouded in darkness, was yet not so completely hidden that the saints, who have most merited praise from the beginning till the coming of the LORD, were precluded from understanding it: seeing that the salvation, which was to come through Christ, was promised both by the words of prophecy and by the significance of events, and this salvation not only they attained who foretold it, but all they also who believed their predictions. For the one Faith justifies the saints of all ages, and to the self-same hope of the faithful pertains all that by Jesus Christ, the Mediator between GOD and man, we acknowledge done, or our fathers reverently accepted as to be done. And between Jew and Gentile there is no distinction, since, as the Apostle says, "Circumcision is

[1] S. John i. 14 [2] Cor. v. 19.

nothing, and uncircumcision is nothing, but the keeping of GOD's commands[3]," and if they be kept in entirety of faith, they make Christians the true sons of Abraham, that is perfect, for the same Apostle says, "For whosoever of you were baptized in Christ Jesus, have put on Christ. There is neither Jew nor Greek: there is neither slave nor free: there is neither male nor female. For ye are all one in Christ. But if ye are Christ's, then are ye Abraham's seed, heirs according to promise[4]."

III. *The union of the Divine Head with Its members inseparable.*

There is no doubt therefore, dearly-beloved, that man's nature has been received by the Son of GOD into such a union that not only in that Man Who is the first-begotten of all creatures, but also in all His saints there is one and the self-same Christ, and as the Head cannot be separated from the members, so the members cannot be separated from the Head. For although it is not in this life, but in eternity that GOD is to be "all in all[4a]," yet even now He is the inseparable Inhabitant of His temple, which is the Church, according as He Himself promised, saying, "Lo! I am with you all the days till the end of the age[5]." And agreeably therewith the Apostle says, "He is the head of the body, the Church, which is the beginning, the first-begotten from the dead, that in all things He may have the pre-eminence, because in Him it was pleasing that all fulness (of the Godhead) should dwell, and that through Him all things should be reconciled in Himself[6]."

IV. *Christ's passion provided a saving mystery and an example for us to follow.*

And what is suggested to our hearts by these and many other references, save that we should in all things be renewed in His image Who, remaining "in the form of GOD[6a]," deigned to "take the form" of sinful flesh? For all our weaknesses, which come from sin, He took on Him without sharing in sin, so that He felt the sensation of hunger and thirst and sleep and fatigue, and grief and weeping, and suffered the fiercest pangs up to the extremity of death, because no one could be loosed from the snares of death, unless He in Whom alone all men's nature was guileless allowed Himself to be slain by the hands of wicked men. And hence our Saviour the Son of GOD provided for all that believe in Him both a mystery and an example[7], that they might apprehend the one by being born again, and follow the other by imitation. For the blessed Apostle Peter teaches this, saying, "Christ suffered for us, leaving you an example that ye should follow His steps. Who did no sin, neither was guile found in His mouth. Who when He was reviled, reviled not: when He suffered, threatened not, but gave Himself up to His unjust judge. Who Himself bare our sins in His body on the tree, that being dead to sins, we may live to righteousness[8]."

V. *Christ has not destroyed, but fulfilled and elevated the Law.*

As therefore there is no believer, dearly-beloved, to whom the gifts of grace are denied, so there is no one who is not a debtor in the matter of Christian discipline; because, although the severity of the mystic Law is done away, yet the benefits of its voluntary observance have increased, as the evangelist John says, "Because the Law was given through Moses, but grace and truth came through Jesus Christ[9]." For all things that, according to the Law, went before, whether in the circumcision of the flesh, or in the multitude of victims, or in the keeping of the Sabbath, testified of Christ, and foretold the grace of Christ. And He is "the end of the Law[1]," not by annulling, but by fulfilling its meanings. For although He is at once the Author of the old and of the new, yet He changed the symbolic rites connected with the promises, because He accomplished the promises and put an end to the announcement by the coming of the Announced. But in the matter of moral precepts, no decrees of the earlier Testament are rejected, but many of them are amplified by the Gospel teaching: so that the things which give salvation are more perfect and clearer than those which promise a Saviour.

VI. *The present effect of Christ's Passion is daily realized by Christians, especially in Holy Baptism.*

All therefore that the Son of GOD did and taught for the world's reconciliation, we not only know as a matter of past history, but appreciate in the power of its present effect. It is He Who, born of the Virgin Mother by the Holy Ghost, fertilizes His unpolluted Church with the same blessed Spirit, that by

---

3 1 Cor. vii. 19.

4 Gal. iii. 27—29.

4a 1 Cor. xv. 28.

5 S. Matt. xxviii. 20.

6 Col. i. 18–20: the word *Divinitatis* (of the Godhead) is omitted by some of the MSS. here.

6a Cf. Phil. ii. 6, 7.

7 *Sacramentum* (with its saving efficacy) *et exemplum* (with its spur to exertion), see Bright's n. 74.

8 1 Pet. ii. 21—24: notice the reading of the Vulgate *indicanti se iniuste* for the correct τῷ κρίνοντι δικαίως (namely GOD).

9 S. John i. 17.

1 Rom. x. 4.

the birth of Baptism an innumerable multitude of sons may be born to GOD, of Whom it is said, "who were born not of blood, nor of the will of the flesh, nor of the will of man, but of GOD[2]." It is He, in Whom the seed of Abraham is blessed by the adoption of the whole world[2a], and the patriarch becomes the father of nations by the birth, through faith not flesh, of the sons of promise. It is He Who, without excluding any nation, makes one flock of holy sheep from every nation under heaven, and daily fulfils what He promised, saying, "Other sheep also I have which are not of this fold; them also I must bring, and they shall hear My voice, and there shall be one flock and one shepherd[3]." For though to the blessed Peter first and foremost He says, "Feed My sheep[4];" yet the one LORD directs the charge of all the shepherds, and feeds those that come to the rock with such glad and well-watered pastures, that countless sheep are nourished by the richness of His love, and hesitate not to perish for the Shepherd's sake, even as the good Shepherd Himself was content to lay down His life for His sheep. It is He whose sufferings are shared not only by the martyrs' glorious courage, but also in the very act of regeneration by the faith of all the new-born. For the renunciation of the devil and belief in GOD[5], the passing from the old state into newness of life, the casting off of the earthly image, and the putting on of the heavenly form—all this is a sort of dying and rising again, whereby he that is received by Christ and receives Christ is not the same after as he was before he came to the font, for the body of the regenerate becomes the flesh of the Crucified[6].

VII. *The good works of Christians are only part of Christ's good works.*

This change, dearly-beloved, is the handiwork of the Most High[7], Who "worketh all things in all," so that by the good manner of life observed in each one of the faithful, we know Him to be the Author of all just works, and give thanks to GOD's mercy, Who so adorns the whole body of the Church with countless gracious gifts, that through the many rays of the one Light the same brightness is everywhere diffused, and that which is well done by any Christian whatsoever cannot but be part of the glory of Christ. This is that true Light which justifies and enlightens every man. This it is that rescues from the power of darkness and transfers us into the Kingdom of the Son of GOD. This it is that by newness of life exalts the desires of the mind and quenches the lusts of the flesh. This it is whereby the LORD's Passover is duly kept "with the unleavened bread of sincerity and truth" by the casting away of "the old leaven of wickedness[7a]" and the inebriating and feeding of the new creature with the very LORD. For naught else is brought about by the partaking of the Body and Blood of Christ than that we pass into that which we then take[8], and both in spirit and in body carry everywhere Him, in and with Whom we were dead, buried, and rose again, as the Apostle says, "For ye are dead, and your life is hid with Christ in GOD. For when Christ, your life, shall appear, then shall ye also appear with Him in glory[9]." Who with the Father, &c.

SERMON LXVII.

(ON THE PASSION, XVI.: DELIVERED ON THE SUNDAY.)

I. *The contemplation of the prophecies of Christ's sufferings are a great source of pious delight.*

The minds of the faithful, beloved, ought indeed always to be occupied with wonder at GOD's works and their reasoning faculties devoted particularly to those reflexions by which they may gain increase of faith. For so long as the pious heart's attention is directed either to the benefits which all enjoy, or to special gifts of His grace, it keeps aloof from many vanities and retires from bodily cares into a spiritual seclusion. But this must be the more eagerly and thoroughly done at the season of the LORD's Passion, that what is then read in the sacred lections may surely be received with the ears of understanding, and that the themes which are great in word may be seen to be yet greater from the mysterious realities which underlie them. For the first reason for our lifting up our hearts[1] is that the voices of the prophets have sung of the things which the truth of the Gospel has also narrated, not as destined to happen, but as having happened, and that what man's ears had not yet learnt was to be

---

2 S. John i. 13. 2a Cf. Gen. xxii. 18.
3 S. John x. 16. 4 Ib. xxi. 17.
5 The renouncing of the Devil and all his works and the professing of faith in GOD have always preceded the rite of Baptism: see Bright's notes 78 and 142.
6 *Corpus regenerati fiat caro crucifixi* an almost unduly strong assertion of the union between Christ, the Head and the members of His body, the Church effected by Holy Baptism: see Hooker, *Eccl. Pol.* v. 60. 2, quoted by Bright, n. 79.
7 Cf. Ps. lxxvii. 10 (LXX.) and 1 Cor. xvii. 6.

7a 1 Cor. v. 8.
8 *ut in id, quod sumimus, transeamus.* He uses the same strong expression in Letter LIX. 2, *ut accipientes virtutem cœlestis cibi, in carnem ipsius qui caro nostra factus est, transeamus.* 9 Col. iii. 3, 4.
1 *Erigendi sursum nostri cordis* the liturgical allusion is the same as that noticed in Sermon LXXIV. 5, n. 6.

accomplished, was already being proclaimed as fulfilled by the (Holy[2]) Spirit. For King David, whose seed according to the flesh is Christ, completed his life-time more than 1,100[2a] years before the day of the LORD's crucifixion, and endured none of those punishments which he relates as inflicted upon himself. But because by his mouth One spoke Who was to take suffering flesh of his stock, the story of the cross is rightly anticipated in the person of him who was the bodily ancestor of the Saviour. For David truly suffered in Christ, because Jesus was truly crucified in the flesh which He had from David.

II. *The Divine foreknowledge does not account for the Jews' wickedness so as to excuse them.*

Since then all things which Jewish ungodliness committed against the LORD of Majesty were foretold so long before[3], and the language of the prophets is concerned not so much with things to come as with things past, what else is thereby revealed to us but the unchangeable order of GOD's eternal decrees, with Whom the things which are to be decided are already determined, and what will be is already accomplished? For since both the character of our actions and the fulfilment of all our wishes are fore-known to GOD, how much better known to Him are His own works? And He was rightly pleased that things should be recorded as if done which nothing could hinder from being done. And hence when the Apostles also, being full of the Holy Ghost, suffered the threats and cruelty of Christ's enemies, they said to GOD with one consent, "For truly in this city against Thy holy Servant Jesus, Whom Thou hast anointed, Herod and Pontius Pilate, with the Gentiles and the peoples of Israel, were gathered together to do what Thy hand and Thy counsel ordained to come to pass[4]." Did then the wickedness of Christ's persecutors spring from GOD's plan, and was that unsurpassable crime prepared and set in motion by the hand of GOD? Clearly we must not think this of the highest Justice: that which was fore-known in respect of the Jews' malice is far different, indeed quite contrary to what was ordained in respect of Christ's Passion. Their desire to slay Him did not proceed from the same source as His to die: nor were their atrocious crime and the Redeemer's endurance the offspring of One Spirit. The LORD did not incite but permit those madmen's naughty hands: nor in His foreknowledge of what must be accomplished did He compel its accomplishment, even though it was in order to its accomplishment that He had taken flesh.

III. *Christ was in no sense the Author of His murderers' guilt.*

In fact, the case of the Crucified is so different from that of His crucifiers that what Christ undertook could not be reversed, while what they did could be wiped out. For He Who came to save sinners did not refuse mercy even to His murderers, but changed the evil of the wicked into the goodness of the believing, that GOD's grace might be the more wonderful, being mercifully put in force, not according to men's merits, but according to the multitude of the riches of GOD's wisdom and knowledge, seeing that they also who had shed the Saviour's blood were received into the baptismal flood. For, as says the Scripture, which contains the Apostles' acts when the preaching of the blessed Apostle Peter pierced the hearts of the Jews, and they acknowledged the iniquity of their crime, saying, "what shall we do, brethren?" the same Apostle said, "Repent and be baptized, each one of you, in the name of Jesus Christ for the remission of your sins, and ye shall receive the gift of the Holy Ghost. For to you is the promise, and to your sons, and to all that are afar off, whomsoever our LORD GOD has called," and soon after the Scripture goes on to say: "they therefore that received his word were baptized, and there were added on that day about 3,000 souls[5]." And so, in being willing to suffer their furious rage, the LORD Jesus Christ was in no way the Author of their crimes; nor did He force them to desire this, but permitted them to be able, and used the madness of the blinded people just as He did also the treachery of His betrayer, whom by kindly acts and words He vouchsafed to recall from the awful crime he had conceived, by taking him for a disciple, by promoting him to be an apostle, by warning him with signs, by admitting him to the revelation of holy mysteries[6], that one who had lacked no degree of kindness to correct him, might have no pretext for his crime at all.

[2] The epithet *sanctus* is of doubtful genuineness here.

[2a] This calculation is based apparently on that of Prosper's *Chronicon*, which again follows that of Eusebius.

[3] There is another reading here, *ut* (for *et*) *non tam de futuris quam de præsentibus* (for *præteritis*), &c., which the Ballerinii probably do right to reject. Trans. "foretold so long before *that* the language of the prophets is concerned not so much with the future as *with the present*."

[4] Acts iv. 27, 28; it is perhaps worth noticing that Leo does not strictly follow the Biblical account in saying that the Apostles were "full of the Holy Ghost" *at the time* of uttering this prayer: v. 31 says they were so filled *afterwards*.

[5] Acts ii. 37—41.

[6] *Consecrando mysteriis* I think he has, as so often, the institution of the Holy Eucharist especially in his mind together, of course, with other sacramental ordinances (such as Holy Baptism and matrimony) which our Saviour blessed with His sanction and made the means of holiness to His disciples.

IV. *The enormity of Judas' crime is set forth.*

But O ungodliest of men, "thou seed of Chanaan and not of Juda [7]," and no longer "a vessel of election," but "a son of perdition" and death, thou didst think the devil's instigations would profit thee better, so that, inflamed with the torch of greed, thou wert ablaze to gain 30 pieces of silver and sawest not what riches thou wouldst lose. For even if thou didst not think the LORD's promises were to be believed, what reason was there for preferring so small a sum of money to what thou hadst already received? Thou wast wont to command the evil spirits, to heal the sick, to receive honour with the rest of the apostles, and that thou mightest satisfy thy thirst for gain, it was open to thee to steal from the box that was in thy charge [8]. But thy mind, which lusted after forbidden things, was more strongly stimulated by that which was less allowed: and the amount of the price pleased thee not so much as the enormity of the sin. Wherefore thy wicked bargain is not so detestable merely because thou countedst the LORD so cheap, but because thou didst sell Him Who was the Redeemer, yea, even thine, and hadst no pity on thyself [9]. And justly was thy punishment put into thine own hands, because none could be found more cruelly bent on thy destruction than thyself.

V. *Christ's Passion was for our Redemption by mystery and example.*

The fact, therefore, that at the time appointed, according to the purpose of His will, Jesus Christ was crucified, dead, and buried was not the doom necessary to His own condition, but the method of redeeming us from captivity. For "the Word became flesh" in order that from the Virgin's womb He might take our suffering nature, and that what could not be inflicted on the Son of GOD might be inflicted on the Son of Man. For although at His very birth the signs of Godhead shone forth in Him, and the whole course of His bodily growth was full of wonders, yet had He truly assumed our weaknesses, and without share in sin had spared Himself no human frailty, that He might impart what was His to us and heal what was ours in Himself. For He, the Almighty Physician, had prepared a two-fold remedy for us in our misery, of which the one part consists of mystery and the other of example [1], that by the one Divine powers may be bestowed, by the other human weaknesses driven out [2]. Because as GOD is the Author of our justification, so man is a debtor to pay Him devotion.

VI. *We can only attain to Christ's perfection by following in His steps.*

Therefore, dearly-beloved, by this unspeakable restoration of our health no place is left us for pride or for idleness: because we have nothing which we did not receive [2a], and we are expressly warned not to treat the gifts of GOD's grace with negligence [2a]. For He that comes so timely to our aid justly urges us with precept, and He that leads us to glory mercifully incites us to obedience. Wherefore the LORD Himself is rightly made our way, because save through Christ there is no coming to Christ. But through Him and to Him does he take his way who treads the path of His endurance and humiliation, and on that road you may be sure there are not wanting the heats of toil, the clouds of sadness, the storms of fear. The snares of the wicked, the persecutions of the unbelieving, the threats of the powerful, the insults of the proud are there; and all these things the LORD of hosts and King of glory passed through in the form of our weakness and in the likeness of sinful flesh, to the end that amid the danger of this present life we might desire not so much to avoid and escape them as to endure and overcome them.

VII. *Christ's cry of "Forsaken" on the cross was to teach us the insufficiency of the human nature without the Divine.*

Hence it is that the LORD Jesus Christ, our Head, representing all the members of His body in Himself, and speaking for those whom He was redeeming in the punishment of the cross, uttered that cry which He had once uttered in the psalm, "O GOD, My GOD, look upon Me: why hast Thou forsaken Me [3]?" That cry, dearly-beloved, is a lesson, not a complaint. For since in Christ there is one person of GOD and man, and He could not have been forsaken by Him, from Whom He could not be separated, it is on behalf of us, trembling and weak ones, that He asks why the flesh that is afraid to suffer has not been heard. For when the Passion was beginning, to cure and correct our weak fear He had said,

7 Apocrypha, Hist. of Susanna, v. 56: said by Daniel to one of the two elders; cf. also Acts ix. 15, and S. John xvii. 12.

8 This last privilege which Leo, with curious sarcasm, coordinates with the other three is spoken of twice by S. John, viz. xii. 6, and xiii. 29.

9 *Redemptorem etiam tuum ne tibi parceres, vendidisti.* It seems to me that Leo's preaching power is nowhere better shown than in the passages where he draws out the heinousness of Judas' guilt: cf Sermon LVIII. chaps. 3 and 4, and Sermon LXII. chap. 4.

1 *Aliud est in sacramento, aliud in exemplo,* cf. Serm. LXIII. chap. 4, n. 7.

2 *Exigantur:* another reading perhaps more in keeping with the context and Leo's usual language is *erigantur* (raised): cf. Lett. XXVIII. (Tome), chap. 3, *humana augens, divina non minuens, &c.*

2a Cf. 1 Cor. iv. 7, and 1 Tim. iv. 14.

3 Ps. xxii. 1.

"Father, if it be possible, let this cup pass from Me: nevertheless not as I will but as Thou;" and again, "Father, if this cup cannot pass except I drink it, Thy will be done[4]." As therefore He had conquered the tremblings of the flesh, and had now accepted the Father's will, and trampling all dread of death under foot, was then carrying out the work of His design, why at the very time of His triumph over such a victory does He seek the cause and reason of His being forsaken, that is, not heard, save to show that the feeling which He entertained in excuse of His human fears is quite different from the deliberate choice which, in accordance with the Father's eternal decree, He had made for the reconciliation of the world? And thus the very cry of "Unheard" is the exposition of a mighty Mystery, because the Redeemer's power would have conferred nothing on mankind if our weakness in Him had obtained what it sought. Let these words, dearly-beloved, suffice to-day, lest we burden you by the length of our discourse: let us put off the rest till Wednesday. The LORD shall hear you if you pray that we may keep our promise through the bounty of Him Who lives and reigns for ever and ever. Amen.

SERMON LXVIII.

(ON THE PASSION, XVII.: DELIVERED ON THE WEDNESDAY.)

I. *Christ's Godhead never forsook Him in His Passion.*

The last discourse, dearly-beloved, of which we desire now to give the promised portion, had reached that point in the argument where we were speaking of that cry which the crucified LORD uttered to the Father: we bade the simple and unthinking hearer not take the words "My GOD, &c.," in a sense as if, when Jesus was fixed upon the wood of the cross, the Omnipotence of the Father's Deity had gone away from Him; seeing that GOD's and Man's Nature were so completely joined in Him that the union could not be destroyed by punishment nor by death. For while each substance retained its own properties, GOD neither held aloof from the suffering of His body nor was made passible by the flesh, because the Godhead which was in the Sufferer did not actually suffer. And hence, in accordance with the Nature of the Word made Man, He Who was made in the midst of all is the same as He through Whom all things were made. He Who is arrested by the hands of wicked men is the same as He Who is bound by no limits. He Who is pierced with nails is the same as He Whom no wound can affect. Finally, He Who underwent death is the same as He Who never ceased to be eternal, so that both facts are established by indubitable signs, namely, the truth of the humiliation in Christ and the truth of the majesty; because Divine power joined itself to human frailty to this end, that GOD, while making what was ours His, might at the same time make what was His ours. The Son, therefore, was not separated from the Father, nor the Father from the Son; and the unchangeable Godhead and the inseparable Trinity did not admit of any division. For although the task of undergoing Incarnation belonged peculiarly to the Only-begotten Son of GOD, yet the Father was not separated from the Son any more than the flesh was separated from the Word[5].

II. *Christ's death was voluntary on His part, and yet in saving others He could not save Himself.*

Jesus, therefore, cried with a loud voice, saying, "Why hast Thou forsaken Me?" in order to notify to all how it behoved Him not to be rescued, not to be defended, but to be given up into the hands of cruel men, that is to become the Saviour of the world and the Redeemer of all men, not by misery but by mercy; and not by the failure of succour but by the determination to die. But what must we feel to be the intercessory power of His life Who died and rose again by His own inherent power[6] For the blessed Apostle says that the Father "spared not His own Son, but gave Him up for us all[7];" and again, he says, "For Christ loved the Church, and gave Himself up for her, that He might sanctify it[8]." And hence the giving up of the LORD to His Passion was as much of the Father's as of His own will, so that not only did the Father "forsake" Him, but He also abandoned Himself in a certain sense, not in hasty flight, but in voluntary withdrawal. For the might of the Crucified restrained itself from those wicked men, and in order to avail Himself of a secret design, He refused to avail Himself of His open power. For how would He who had come to destroy death and the author of death by His Passion have saved sinners, if he had resisted His persecutors? This, then, had been the Jews' belief, that Jesus had been forsaken by GOD, against Whom they had been

4 S Matt. xxvi. 39, 42.

5 For the doctrine here stated, cf. Serm. LI., chap. vi.

6 *Quæ vero illic vitæ intercessio sentienda est, ubi anima et potestate est emissa et potestate revocata?* If we adopt Quesnel's conjecture *intercisio* for *intercessio* the meaning is I suppose, "What cutting off of the thread of life is conceivable in His case Who &c.?"

7 Rom. viii. 32.

8 Eph. v 2, and 25. 20

able to commit such unholy cruelty; for not understanding the mystery of His wondrous endurance, they said in blasphemous mockery: "He saved others, Himself He cannot save. If He be the King of Israel, let Him now come down from the cross, and we believe Him[9]." Not at your blind will, O foolish scribes and wicked priests, was the Saviour's power to be displayed, nor in obedience to blasphemers' evil tongues was the Redemption of mankind to be delayed; for if you had wished to recognize the Godhead of the Son of God, you would have observed His numberless works, and they must have confirmed you in that faith, which you so deceitfully promise. But if, as you yourselves acknowledge, it is true that He saved others, why have those many, great miracles, which have been done under the public gaze, done nothing to soften the hardness of your hearts, unless it be because you have always so resisted the Holy Ghost as to turn all God's benefits towards you into your destruction? For even though Christ should descend from the cross, you would yet remain in your crime.

III. *A transition was then being effected from the Old to the New Dispensation.*

Therefore the insults of empty exultation were scorned, and the Lord's mercy in restoring the lost and the fallen was not turned from the path of its purpose by contumely or reviling. For a peerless victim was being offered to God for the world's salvation, and the slaying of Christ the true Lamb, predicted through so many ages, was transferring the sons of promise into the liberty of the Faith. The New Testament also was being ratified, and in the blood of Christ the heirs of the eternal Kingdom were being enrolled; the High Pontiff was entering the Holy of Holies, and to intercede with God the spotless Priest was passing in through the veil of His flesh[9a]. In fine, so evident a transition was being effected from the Law to the Gospel, from the synagogue to the Church, from many sacrifices to the One Victim[1], that, when the Lord gave up the ghost, that mystic veil which hung before and shut out the inner part of the Temple and its holy recess was by sudden force torn from top to bottom[9a], for the reason that Truth was displacing figures, and forerunners were needless in the presence of Him they announced. To this was added a terrible confusion of all the elements, and nature herself withdrew her support from Christ's crucifiers. And although the centurion in charge of the crucifixion, in fright at what he had seen, said "truly this man was the Son of God[9a]," yet the wicked hearts of the Jews, which were harder than all tombs and rocks, is not reported to have been pierced by any compunction: so that it seems the Roman soldiers were then readier to recognize the Son of God than the priests of Israel.

IV. *Let us profit by fasting and good works at this sacred season of the year.*

Because, then, the Jews, deprived of all the sanctification imparted by these mysteries, turned their light into darkness and their "feasts into mourning[1a]," let us, dearly-beloved, prostrate our bodies and our souls and worship God's Grace, which has been poured out upon all nations, beseeching the merciful Father and the rich Redeemer from day to day to give us His aid and enable us to escape all the dangers of this life. For the crafty tempter is present everywhere, and leaves nothing free from his snares. Whom, God's mercy helping us, which is stretched out to us amid all dangers, we must ever with stedfast faith resist[1a], so that, though he never ceases to asail, he may never succeed in carrying the assault. Let all, dearly-beloved, religiously keep and profit by the fast, and let no excesses mar the benefits of such self-restraint as we have proved convenient both for soul and body. For the things which pertain to sobriety and temperance must be the more diligently observed at this season, that a lasting habit may be contracted from a brief zeal; and whether in works of mercy or in strict self-denial, no hours may be left idle by the faithful, seeing that, as years increase and time glides by, we are bound to increase our store of works, and not squander our opportunities. And to devout wills and religious souls God's Mercy will be granted, that He may enable us to obtain that which He enabled us to desire, Who liveth and reigneth with our Lord Jesus Christ His Son, and with the Holy Ghost, for ever and ever. Amen.

SERMON LXXI.

(On the Lord's Resurrection, I.; delivered on Holy Saturday in the Vigil of Easter[2].)

I. *We must all be partakers in Christ's Resurrection life.*

In my last sermon[3], dearly-beloved, not in-

9 S. Matt. xxvii. 42.
9a Cf. Heb. x. 20: and below, S. Matt. xxvii. 51 and 54.
1 The older editions here add *quæ Deus est* (which is God), which however both Quesnel and the Ball. reject as a marginal gloss.

1a Cf. Amos viii. 10: and below, 1 Pet. v. 9.
2 The time of delivery of this and the next Sermons was first identified by Quesnel with Easter Eve: for a most instructive note on the ceremonies of that day in early times, see Bright's n. 102.
3 Viz. Serm. LXX. in which (chap 6) he had promised to

appropriately, as I think, we explained to you our participation in the cross of Christ, whereby the life of believers contains in itself the mystery of Easter, and thus what is honoured at the feast is celebrated by our practice. And how useful this is you yourselves have proved, and by your devotion have learnt, how greatly benefited souls and bodies are by longer fasts, more frequent prayers, and more liberal alms. For there can be hardly any one who has not profited by this exercise, and who has not stored up in the recesses of his conscience something over which he may rightly rejoice. But these advantages must be retained with persistent care, lest our efforts fall away into idleness, and the devil's malice steal what GOD's grace gave. Since, therefore, by our forty days' observance [4] we have wished to bring about this effect, that we should feel something of the Cross at the time of the LORD's Passion, we must strive to be found partakers also of Christ's Resurrection, and "pass from death unto life [4a]," while we are in this body. For when a man is changed by some process from one thing into another, not to be what he was is to him an ending, and to be what he was not is a beginning. But the question is, to what a man either dies or lives: because there is a death, which is the cause of living, and there is a life, which is the cause of dying. And nowhere else but in this transitory world are both sought after, so that upon the character of our temporal actions depend the differences of the eternal retributions. We must die, therefore, to the devil and live to GOD: we must perish to iniquity that we may rise to righteousness. Let the old sink, that the new may rise; and since, as says the Truth, "no one can serve two masters [5]," let not him be lord who has caused the overthrow of those that stood, but Him Who has raised the fallen to victory.

II. *GOD did not leave His soul in hell, nor suffer His flesh to see corruption.*

Accordingly, since the Apostle says, "the first man is of the earth earthy, the second man is from heaven heavenly. As is the earthy, such also are they that are earthy; and as is the heavenly, such also are they that are heavenly. As we have borne the image of the earthy, so let us also bear the image of Him Who is from heaven [6]," we must greatly rejoice over this change, whereby we are translated from earthly degradation to heavenly dignity through His unspeakable mercy, Who descended into our estate that He might promote us to His, by assuming not only the substance but also the conditions of sinful nature, and by allowing the impassibility of Godhead to be affected by all the miseries which are the lot of mortal manhood. And hence that the disturbed minds of the disciples might not be racked by prolonged grief, He with such wondrous speed shortened the three days' delay which He had announced, that by joining the last part of the first and the first part of the third day to the whole of the second, He cut off a considerable portion of the period, and yet did not lessen the number of days. The Saviour's Resurrection therefore did not long keep His soul in Hades, nor His flesh in the tomb; and so speedy was the quickening of His uncorrupted flesh that it bore a closer resemblance to slumber than to death, seeing that the Godhead, Which quitted not either part of the Human Nature which He had assumed, reunited by Its power that which Its power had separated [7].

III. *Christ's manifestations after the Resurrection showed that His Person was essentially the same as before.*

And then there followed many proofs, whereon the authority of the Faith to be preached through the whole world might be based. And although the rolling away of the stone, the empty tomb, the arrangement of the linen cloths, and the angels who narrated the whole deed by themselves fully built up the truth of the LORD's Resurrection, yet did He often appear plainly to the eyes both of the women and of the Apostles [8], not only talking with them, but also remaining and eating with them, and allowing Himself to be handled by the eager and curious hands of those whom doubt assailed. For to this end He entered when the doors were closed upon the disciples, and gave them the Holy Spirit by breathing on them, and after giving them the light of understanding opened the secrets

---

continue the subject (*superest ut de obtinendo resurrectionis consortio disseramus: quod ne continuato sermone et mihi et vobis fiat onerosum, in diem sabbati promissa differemus*).

4 Acc. to Bright (n. 103), "As to the duration of Lent, there was anciently much diversity . . . . Although it was not until the time of Gregory II. (715—731) that it became strictly a forty *days'* fast, there is no doubt that in the fourth century if not earlier a period was generally observed which might be called 'forty days.'"

4a Cf. 1 S. John iii. 14.

5 S. Matt. vi. 24.

6 1 Cor. xv. 47—49. Leo's text agrees with the Vulgate in inserting 'heavenly' after 'from heaven,' and in translating φορέσωμεν (let us bear) not φορέσομεν (we shall bear), but is peculiar in its paraphrase at the end of the quotation ("the image of Him, &c.").

7 Cf. Serm. LXX. chap. 3, *nisi enim Verbum caro fieret, et tam solida consisteret unitas in utraque natura, ut a suscipiente susceptam nec ipsum breve mortis tempus abiungeret, nunquam valeret ad æternitatem redire mortalitas.* Bright (n. 96) quotes authorities ancient and more recent to show that this has always been the Christian's belief.

8 From this point to the end of the chapter the language is almost identical with a passage in Letter XXVIII. (Tome), chap. 5.

of the Holy Scriptures, and again Himself showed them the wound in the side, the prints of the nails, and all the marks of His most recent Passion, whereby it might be acknowledged that in Him the properties of the Divine and Human Nature remained undivided, and we might in such sort know that the Word was not what the flesh is, as to confess God's only Son to be both Word and Flesh.

IV. *But though it is the same, it is also glorified.*

The Apostle of the Gentiles, Paul, dearly-beloved, does not disagree with this belief, when he says, "even though we have known Christ after the flesh, yet now we know Him so no more[9]." For the Lord's Resurrection was not the ending, but the changing of the flesh, and His substance was not destroyed by His increase of power. The quality altered, but the nature did not cease to exist: the body was made impassible, which it had been possible to crucify: it was made incorruptible, though it had been possible to wound it. And properly is Christ's flesh said not to be known in that state in which it had been known, because nothing remained passible in it, nothing weak, so that it was both the same in essence and not the same in glory. But what wonder if S. Paul maintains this about Christ's body, when he says of all spiritual Christians, "wherefore henceforth we know no one after the flesh." Henceforth, he says, we begin to experience the resurrection in Christ, since the time when in Him, Who died for all, all our hopes were guaranteed to us. We do not hesitate in diffidence, we are not under the suspense of uncertainty, but having received an earnest of the promise, we now with the eye of faith see the things which will be, and rejoicing in the uplifting of our nature, we already possess what we believe.

V. *Being saved by hope, we must not fulfil the lusts of the flesh.*

Let us not then be taken up with the appearances of temporal matters, neither let our contemplations be diverted from heavenly to earthly things. Things which as yet have for the most part not come to pass must be reckoned as accomplished: and the mind intent on what is permanent must fix its desires there, where what is offered is eternal. For although "by hope we were saved[1]," and still bear about with us a flesh that is corruptible and mortal, yet we are rightly said not to be in the flesh, if the fleshly affections do not dominate us, and are justified in ceasing to be named after that, the will of which we do not follow. And so, when the Apostle says, "make not provision for the flesh in the lusts thereof[2]," we understand that those things are not forbidden us, which conduce to health and which human weakness demands, but because we may not satisfy all our desires nor indulge in all that the flesh lusts after, we recognize that we are warned to exercise such self-restraint as not to permit what is excessive nor refuse what is necessary to the flesh, which is placed under the mind's control[3]. And hence the same Apostle says in another place, "For no one ever hated his own flesh, but nourisheth and cherisheth it[4];" in so far, of course, as it must be nourished and cherished not in vices and luxury, but with a view to its proper functions, so that nature may recover herself and maintain due order, the lower parts not prevailing wrongfully and debasingly over the higher, nor the higher yielding to the lower, lest if vices overpower the mind, slavery ensues where there should be supremacy.

VI. *Our godly resolutions must continue all the year round, not be confined to Easter only.*

Let God's people then recognize that they are a new creation in Christ, and with all vigilance understand by Whom they have been adopted and Whom they have adopted[5]. Let not the things, which have been made new, return to their ancient instability; and let not him who has "put his hand to the plough[6]" forsake his work, but rather attend to that which he sows than look back to that which he has left behind. Let no one fall back into that from which he has risen, but, even though from bodily weakness he still languishes under certain maladies, let him urgently desire to be healed and raised up. For this is the path of health through imitation of the Resurrection begun in Christ, whereby, notwithstanding the many accidents and falls to which in this slippery life the traveller is liable, his feet may be guided from the quagmire on to solid ground, for, as it is written, "the steps of a man are directed by the Lord, and He will delight in his way. When the just man falls he shall not be overthrown, because the Lord will stretch out His

9 2 Cor. v. 16. It must be borne in mind that the application of the phrase after the flesh (κατὰ σάρκα) is mistaken: S. Paul means 'according to the ordinary view of man," as in Rom. viii. 1, and 2 Cor. x. 2. See Bright's note 107.

1 Rom. viii. 24.

2 Rom. xiii. 14.

3 Cf. Serm. XIX. chap. 1.

4 Eph. v. 29.

5 *Quo suscepta sit (sc. nova creatura) quemve susceperit*, i.e. Christ has taken on Him human nature, and we by virtue thereof are partakers of the Divine.

6 S. Luke ix. 62.

hand [7]." These thoughts, dearly-beloved, must be kept in mind not only for the Easter festival, but also for the sanctification of the whole life, and to this our present exercise ought to be directed, that what has delighted the souls of the faithful by the experience of a short observance may pass into a habit and remain unalterably, and if any fault creep in, it may be destroyed by speedy repentance. And because the cure of old-standing diseases is slow and difficult, remedies should be applied early, when the wounds are fresh, so that rising ever anew from all downfalls, we may deserve to attain to the incorruptible Resurrection of our glorified flesh in Christ Jesus our LORD, Who lives and reigns with the Father and the Holy Ghost for ever and ever. Amen.

SERMON LXXII.

(ON THE LORD'S RESURRECTION, II.)

I. *The Cross is not only the mystery of salvation, but an example to follow.*

The whole of the Easter mystery, dearly-beloved, has been brought before us in the Gospel narrative, and the ears of the mind have been so reached through the ear of flesh that none of you can fail to have a picture of the events: for the text of the Divinely-inspired story has clearly shown the treachery of the LORD Jesus Christ's betrayal, the judgment by which He was condemned, the barbarity of His crucifixion, and glory of His resurrection. But a sermon is still required of us, that the priests' exhortation may be added to the solemn reading of Holy Writ, as I am sure you are with pious expectation demanding of us as your accustomed due. Because therefore there is no place for ignorance in faithful ears, the seed of the Word, which consists of the preaching of the Gospel, ought to grow in the soil of your heart, so that, when choking thorns and thistles have been removed, the plants of holy thoughts and the buds of right desires may spring up freely into fruit. For the cross of Christ, which was set up for the salvation of mortals, is both a mystery and an example [8]: a sacrament where by the Divine power takes effect, an example whereby man's devotion is excited: for to those who are rescued from the prisoner's yoke Redemption further procures the power of following the way of the cross by imitation. For if the world's wisdom so prides itself in its error that every one follows the opinions and habits and whole manner of life of him whom he has chosen as his leader, how shall we share in the name of Christ, save by being inseparably united to Him, Who is, as He Himself asserted, "the Way, the Truth, and the Life [9]?" the Way that is of holy living, the Truth of Divine doctrine, and the Life of eternal happiness.

II. *Christ took our nature upon Him for our salvation.*

For when the whole body of mankind had fallen in our first parents, the merciful GOD purposed so to succour, through His only-begotten Jesus Christ, His creatures made after His image, that the restoration of our nature should not be effected apart from it, and that our new estate should be an advance upon our original position. Happy, if we had not fallen from that which GOD made us; but happier, if we remain that which He has re-made us. It was much to have received form from Christ; it is more to have a substance in Christ [1]. For we were taken up into its own proper self by that Nature (which condescended to those limitations which loving-kindness dictated and which yet incurred no sort of change. We were taken up by that Nature [2]), which destroyed not what was His in what was ours, nor what was ours in what was His; which made the person of the Godhead and of the Manhood so one in Itself that by co-ordination of weakness and power, the flesh could not be rendered inviolable through the Godhead, nor the Godhead passible through the flesh. We were taken up by that Nature, which did not break off the Branch from the common stock of our race, and yet excluded all taint of the sin which has passed upon all men. That is to say, weakness and mortality, which were not sin, but the penalty of sin, were undergone by the Redeemer of the World in the way of punishment, that they might be reckoned as the price of redemption. What therefore in all of us is the heritage of condemnation, is in Christ "the mystery of godliness [3]." For being free from debt, He gave Himself up to that most cruel creditor, and suffered the hands of Jews to be the devil's agents in torturing His spotless flesh. Which flesh He willed to be subject to death, even up to His (speedy) [4] resurrection, to this end, that believers in Him might find neither perse-

7 Ps. xxxvii. 23, 24.

8 Cf. Serm. LXIII. 4, above: *Salvator noster—et sacramentum condidit et exemplum: ut unum apprehenderent renascendo, alterum sequerentur imitando.*

9 S. John xiv. 6.

1 i.e. that both of the two natures in Christ should be ours, as he goes on to show.

2 The words in brackets are of doubtful genuineness, and seem in themselves a mediæval imitation of Leo's style.

3 *Sacramentum pietatis*, the regular Latin version of 1 Tim. iii. 16.

4 *Celerrimam.* The epithet spoils the argument, and is probably an interpolation. Cf. however Serm. LXXI. chap. 2, above.

cution intolerable, nor death terrible, by the remembrance that there was no more doubt about their sharing His glory than there was about His sharing their nature.

III. *The presence of the risen and ascended Lord is still with us.*

And so, dearly-beloved, if we unhesitatingly believe with the heart what we profess with the mouth, in Christ we are crucified, we are dead, we are buried; on the very third day, too, we are raised. Hence the Apostle says, "If ye have risen with Christ, seek those things which are above, where Christ is, sitting on God's right hand: set your affections on things above, not on things on the earth. For ye are dead, and your life is hid with Christ in God. For when Christ, your life, shall have appeared, then shall ye also appear with Him in glory [5]." But that the hearts of the faithful may know that they have that whereby to spurn the lusts of the world and be lifted to the wisdom that is above, the Lord promises us His presence, saying, "Lo! I am with you all the days, even till the end of the age [6]." For not in vain had the Holy Ghost said by Isaiah: "Behold! a virgin shall conceive and shall bear a Son, and they shall call His name Emmanuel, which is, being interpreted, God with us [7]." Jesus, therefore, fulfils the proper meaning of His name, and in ascending into the heavens does not forsake His adopted brethren, though "He sitteth at the right hand of the Father," yet dwells in the whole body, and Himself from above strengthens them for patient waiting while He summons them upwards to His glory.

IV. *We must have the same mind as was in Christ Jesus.*

We must not, therefore, indulge in folly amid vain pursuits, nor give way to fear in the midst of adversities. On the one side, no doubt, we are flattered by deceits, and on the other weighed down by troubles; but because "the earth is full of the mercy of the Lord [8]," Christ's victory is assuredly ours, that what He says may be fulfilled, "Fear not, for I have overcome the world [9]." Whether, then, we fight against the ambition of the world, or against the lusts of the flesh, or against the darts of heresy, let us arm ourselves always with the Lord's cross. For our Paschal feast will never end, if we abstain from the leaven of the old wickedness (in the sincerity of truth [1]). For amid all the changes of this life, which is full of various afflictions, we ought to remember the Apostle's exhortation, whereby he instructs us, saying, "Let this mind be in you which was also in Christ Jesus: Who being in the form of God counted it not robbery to be equal with God, but emptied Himself, taking the form of a bondservant, being made in the likeness of men and found in fashion as a man. Wherefore God also exalted Him, and gave Him a name which is above every name, that in the name of Jesus every knee should bow of things in heaven, of things on earth, and of things below, and that every tongue should confess that the Lord Jesus Christ is in the glory of God the Father [2]." If, he says, you understand "the mystery of great godliness," and remember what the Only-begotten Son of God did for the salvation of mankind, "have that mind in you which was also in Christ Jesus," Whose humility is not to be scorned by any of the rich, not to be thought shame of by any of the high-born. For no human happiness whatever can reach so great a height as to reckon it a source of shame to himself that God, abiding in the form of God, thought it not unworthy of Himself to take the form of a slave.

V. *Only he who holds the truth on the Incarnation can keep Easter properly.*

Imitate what He wrought: love what He loved, and finding in you the Grace of God, love in Him your nature in return, since as He was not dispossessed of riches in poverty, lessened not glory in humility, lost not eternity in death, so do ye, too, treading in His footsteps, despise earthly things that ye may gain heavenly: for the taking up of the cross means the slaying of lusts, the killing of vices, the turning away from vanity, and the renunciation of all error. For, though the Lord's Passover can be kept by no immodest, self-indulgent, proud, or miserly person, yet none are held so far aloof from this festival as heretics, and especially those who have wrong views on the Incarnation of the Word, either disparaging what belongs to the Godhead or treating what is of the flesh as unreal. For the Son of God is true God, having from the Father all that the Father is, with no beginning in time, subject to no sort of change, undivided from the One God, not different from the Almighty, the eternal Only-begotten of the eternal Father; so that the faithful intellect believing in the Father and the Son and the Holy Ghost in the same essence of the one Godhead, neither divides the Unity by suggesting degrees of dignity, nor confounds the Trinity by merging the Persons in one. But it is not enough to know the Son of God in the Father's natur

5 Col. iii. 1—4. 6 S. Matt. xxviii. 20. 7 Is. vii. 14; S. Matt. i. 23. 8 Ps. xxxiii. 5. 9 S. John xvi. 33.

1 Cf. 1 Cor. v. 8: the words in brackets are of doubtful authority.

2 Phil. ii. 5—11.

only, unless we acknowledge Him in what is ours without withdrawal of what is His own. For that self-emptying, which He underwent for man's restoration, was the dispensation of compassion, not the loss of power[3]. For, though by the eternal purpose of God there was "no other name under heaven given to men whereby they must be saved[4]," the Invisible made His substance visible, the Intemporal temporal, the Impassible passible: not that power might sink into weakness, but that weakness might pass into indestructible power.

VI. *A mystical application of the term "Passover" is given.*

For which reason the very feast which by us is named *Pascha*, among the Hebrews is called *Phase*, that is Pass-over[5], as the evangelist attests, saying, "Before the feast of Pascha, Jesus knowing that His hour was come that He should pass out of this world unto the Father[6]." But what was the nature in which He thus passed out unless it was ours, since the Father was in the Son and the Son in the Father inseparably? But because the Word and the Flesh is one Person, the Assumed is not separated from the Assuming nature, and the honour of being promoted is spoken of as accruing to Him that promotes, as the Apostle says in a passage we have already quoted, "Wherefore also God exalted Him and gave Him a name which is above every name." Where the exaltation of His assumed Manhood is no doubt spoken of, so that He in Whose sufferings the Godhead remains indivisible is likewise coeternal in the glory of the Godhead. And to share in this unspeakable gift the Lord Himself was preparing a blessed "passing over" for His faithful ones, when on the very threshhold of His Passion he interceded not only for His Apostles and disciples but also for the whole Church, saying, "But not for these only I pray, but for those also who shall believe on Me through their word, that they all may be one, as Thou also, Father, art in Me, and I in Thee, that they also may be one in us[7]."

VII. *Only true believers can keep the Easter Festival*

In this union they can have no share who deny that in the Son of God, Himself true God, man's nature abides, assailing the health-giving mystery and shutting themselves out from the Easter festival. For, as they dissent from the Gospel and gainsay the creed, they cannot keep it with us, because although they dare to take to themselves the Christian name, yet they are repelled by every creature who has Christ for his Head: for you rightly exult and devoutly rejoice in this sacred season as those who, admitting no falsehood into the Truth, have no doubt about Christ's Birth according to the flesh, His Passion and Death, and the Resurrection of His body: inasmuch as without any separation of the Godhead you acknowledge a Christ, Who was truly born of a Virgin's womb, truly hung on the wood of the cross, truly laid in an earthly tomb, truly raised in glory, truly set on the right hand of the Father's majesty; "whence also," as the Apostle says, "we look for a Saviour our Lord Jesus Christ. Who shall refashion the body of our humility to become conformed to the body of His glory[8]." Who liveth and reigneth, &c.

SERMON LXXIII.

(On the Lord's Ascension, I.)

I. *The events recorded as happening after the Resurrection were intended to convince us of its truth.*

Since the blessed and glorious Resurrection of our Lord Jesus Christ, whereby the Divine power in three days raised the true Temple of God, which the wickedness of the Jews had overthrown, the sacred forty days, dearly-beloved, are to-day ended, which by most holy appointment were devoted to our most profitable instruction, so that, during the period that the Lord thus protracted the lingering of His bodily presence, our faith in the Resurrection might be fortified by needful proofs. For Christ's Death had much disturbed the disciples' hearts, and a kind of torpor of distrust had crept over their grief-laden minds at His torture on the cross, at His giving up the ghost, at His lifeless body's burial. For, when the holy women, as the Gospel-story has revealed, brought word of the stone rolled away from the tomb, the sepulchre emptied of the body, and the angels bearing witness to the living Lord, their words seemed like ravings to the Apostles and other disciples. Which doubtfulness, the result of human weakness, the Spirit of Truth would most assuredly not have permitted to exist in His own preacher's breasts, had not their trembling anxiety and careful hesitation laid the foundations of our faith. It was our

---

3 Much the same language is used in Lett. XXVIII. (Tome) 3 and Serm. XXIII. 2.

4 Acts iv. 12.

5 *Phase id est transitus dicitur*, cf. the Vulgate, Exod. xii. 11, *est enim Phase* (*id est transitus*) *Domini*. The form of the word is due to defective transliteration, the correct Hebrew form being *Pesach*, which "is derived from a root which means to step over or to overleap, and thus points back to the historical origin of the festival (Exod. xii.)."—*Edersheim's Temple*, p. 179.

6 S. John xiii. 1; the word for "pass" here in the Gk. is μεταβῇ, in the Lat. *transeat*.

7 S. John xvii. 20, 21.

8 Phil. iii. 20, 21.

perplexities and our dangers that were provided for in the Apostles: it was ourselves who in these men were taught how to meet the cavillings of the ungodly and the arguments of earthly wisdom. *We* are instructed by their lookings, *we* are taught by their hearings, *we* are convinced by their handlings. Let us give thanks to the Divine management and the holy Fathers' necessary slowness of belief. Others doubted, that we might not doubt.

II. *And therefore they are in the highest degree instructive.*

Those days, therefore, dearly-beloved, which intervened between the LORD's Resurrection and Ascension did not pass by in uneventful leisure, but great mysteries[9] were ratified in them, deep truths[9] revealed. In them the fear of awful death was removed, and the immortality not only of the soul but also of the flesh established. In them, through the LORD's breathing upon them, the Holy Ghost is poured upon all the Apostles, and to the blessed Apostle Peter beyond the rest the care of the LORD's flock is entrusted, in addition to the keys of the kingdom. Then it was that the LORD joined the two disciples as a companion on the way, and, to the sweeping away of all the clouds of our uncertainty, upbraided them with the slowness of their timorous hearts. Their enlightened hearts catch the flame of faith, and lukewarm as they have been, are made to burn while the LORD unfolds the Scriptures. In the breaking of bread also their eyes are opened as they eat with Him: how far more blessed is the opening of their eyes, to whom the glorification of their nature is revealed than that of our first parents, on whom fell the disastrous consequences of their transgression.

III. *They prove the Resurrection of the flesh.*

And in the course of these and other miracles, when the disciples were harassed by bewildering thoughts, and the LORD had appeared in their midst and said, "Peace be unto you[1]," that what was passing through their hearts might not be their fixed opinion (for they thought they saw a spirit not flesh), He refutes their thoughts so discordant with the Truth, offers to the doubters' eyes the marks of the cross that remained in His hands and feet, and invites them to handle Him with careful scrutiny, because the traces of the nails and spear had been retained to heal the wounds of unbelieving hearts, so that not with wavering faith, but with most stedfast knowledge they might comprehend that the Nature which had been lain in the sepulchre was to sit on GOD the Father's throne.

IV. *Christ's Ascension has given us greater privileges and joys than the devil had taken from us.*

Accordingly, dearly-beloved, throughout this time which elapsed between the LORD's Resurrection and Ascension, GOD's Providence had this in view, to teach and impress upon both the eyes and hearts of His own people that the LORD Jesus Christ might be acknowledged to have as truly risen, as He was truly born, suffered, and died. And hence the most blessed Apostles and all the disciples, who had been both bewildered at His death on the cross and backward in believing His Resurrection, were so strengthened by the clearness of the truth that when the LORD entered the heights of heaven, not only were they affected with no sadness, but were even filled with great joy. And truly great and unspeakable was their cause for joy, when in the sight of the holy multitude, above the dignity of all heavenly creatures, the Nature of mankind went up, to pass above the angels' ranks and to rise beyond the archangels' heights, and to have Its uplifting limited by no elevation until, received to sit with the Eternal Father, It should be associated on the throne with His glory, to Whose Nature It was united in the Son. Since then Christ's Ascension is our uplifting, and the hope of the Body is raised, whither the glory of the Head has gone before, let us exult, dearly-beloved, with worthy joy and delight in the loyal paying of thanks. For to-day not only are we confirmed as possessors of paradise, but have also in Christ penetrated the heights of heaven, and have gained still greater things through Christ's unspeakable grace than we had lost through the devil's malice. For us, whom our virulent enemy had driven out from the bliss of our first abode, the Son of GOD has made members of Himself and placed at the right hand of the Father, with Whom He lives and reigns in the unity of the Holy Spirit, GOD for ever and ever. Amen.

SERMON LXXIV.

(ON THE LORD'S ASCENSION, II.)

I. *The Ascension completes our faith in Him, Who was GOD as well as man.*

The mystery of our salvation, dearly-beloved, which the Creator of the universe valued at the price of His blood, has now been carried out under conditions of humiliation from the day of His bodily birth to the end of His

[9] *Sacramenta—mysteria.*
[1] S. Luke xxiv. 36: S. John xx. 19.

Passion. And although even in "the form of a slave" many signs of Divinity have beamed out, yet the events of all that period served particularly to show the reality of His assumed Manhood. But after the Passion, when the chains of death were broken, which had exposed its own strength by attacking Him, Who was ignorant of sin, weakness was turned into power, mortality into eternity, contumely into glory, which the LORD Jesus Christ showed by many clear proofs in the sight of many, until He carried even into heaven the triumphant victory which He had won over the dead. As therefore at the Easter commemoration, the LORD's Resurrection was the cause of our rejoicing; so the subject of our present gladness is His Ascension, as we commemorate and duly venerate that day on which the Nature of our humility in Christ was raised above all the host of heaven, over all the ranks of angels, beyond the height of all powers, to sit with GOD the Father. On which Providential order of events we are founded and built up, that GOD's Grace might become more wondrous, when, notwithstanding the removal from men's sight of what was rightly felt to command their awe, faith did not fail, hope did not waver, love did not grow cold. For it is the strength of great minds and the light of firmly-faithful souls, unhesitatingly to believe what is not seen with the bodily sight, and there to fix one's affections whither you cannot direct your gaze. And whence should this godliness spring up in our hearts, or how should a man be justified by faith, if our salvation rested on those things only which lie beneath our eyes? Hence our LORD said to him who seemed to doubt of Christ's Resurrection, until he had tested by sight and touch the traces of His Passion in His very Flesh, "because thou hast seen Me, thou hast believed: blessed are they who have not seen and yet have believed [2]."

II. *The Ascension renders our faith more excellent and stronger.*

In order, therefore, dearly-beloved, that we may be capable of this blessedness, when all things were fulfilled which concerned the Gospel preaching and the mysteries of the New Testament, our LORD Jesus Christ, on the fortieth day after the Resurrection in the presence of the disciples, was raised into heaven, and terminated His presence with us in the body, to abide on the Father's right hand until the times Divinely fore-ordained for multiplying the sons of the Church are accomplished, and He comes to judge the living and the dead in the same flesh in which He ascended. And so that which till then was visible of our Redeemer was changed into a sacramental presence [3], and that faith might be more excellent and stronger, sight gave way to doctrine, the authority of which was to be accepted by believing hearts enlightened with rays from above.

III. *The marvellous effects of this Faith on all.*

This Faith, increased by the LORD's Ascension and established by the gift of the Holy Ghost, was not terrified by bonds, imprisonments, banishments, hunger, fire, attacks by wild beasts, refined torments of cruel persecutors. For this Faith throughout the world not only men, but even women, not only beardless boys, but even tender maids, fought to the shedding of their blood. This Faith cast out spirits, drove off sicknesses, raised the dead: and through it the blessed Apostles themselves also, who after being confirmed by so many miracles and instructed by so many discourses, had yet been panic-stricken by the horrors of the LORD's Passion and had not accepted the truth of His resurrection without hesitation, made such progress after the LORD's Ascension that everything which had previously filled them with fear was turned into joy. For they had lifted the whole contemplation of their mind to the Godhead of Him that sat at the Father's right hand, and were no longer hindered by the barrier of corporeal sight from directing their minds' gaze to That Which had never quitted the Father's side in descending to earth, and had not forsaken the disciples in ascending to heaven.

IV. *His Ascension refines our Faith: the ministering of angels to Him shows the extent of His authority.*

The Son of Man and Son of GOD, therefore, dearly-beloved, then attained a more excellent and holier fame, when He betook Himself back to the glory of the Father's Majesty, and in an ineffable manner began to be nearer to the Father in respect of His Godhead, after having become farther away in respect of His manhood. A better instructed faith then began to draw closer to a conception of the Son's equality with the Father without the necessity of handling the corporeal substance in Christ, whereby He is less than the Father, since, while the Nature of the glorified Body still remained the faith of believers was called upon

[2] S. John xx. 29.

[3] *In sacramenta transivit*, i.e. Christ's presence is now vouchsafed us only after a spiritual manner in His sacraments and means of grace.

to touch not with the hand of flesh, but with the spiritual understanding the Only-begotten, Who was equal with the Father. Hence comes that which the LORD said after His Resurrection, when Mary Magdalene, representing the Church, hastened to approach and touch Him: "Touch Me not, for I have not yet ascended to My Father[4]:" that is, I would not have you come to Me as to a human body, nor yet recognize Me by fleshly perceptions: I put thee off for higher things, I prepare greater things for thee: when I have ascended to My Father, then thou shalt handle Me more perfectly and truly, for thou shalt grasp what thou canst not touch and believe what thou canst not see. But when the disciples' eyes followed the ascending LORD to heaven with upward gaze of earnest wonder, two angels stood by them in raiment shining with wondrous brightness, who also said, "Ye men of Galilee, why stand ye gazing into heaven? This Jesus Who was taken up from you into heaven shall so come as ye saw Him going into heaven[5]." By which words all the sons of the Church were taught to believe that Jesus Christ will come visibly in the same Flesh wherewith He ascended, and not to doubt that all things are subjected to Him on Whom the ministry of angels had waited from the first beginning of His Birth. For, as an angel announced to the blessed Virgin that Christ should be conceived by the Holy Ghost, so the voice of heavenly beings sang of His being born of the Virgin also to the shepherds. As messengers from above were the first to attest His having risen from the dead, so the service of angels was employed to foretell His coming in very Flesh to judge the world, that we might understand what great powers will come with Him as Judge, when such great ones ministered to Him even in being judged.

V. *We must despise earthly things and rise to things above, especially by active works of mercy and love.*

And so, dearly-beloved, let us rejoice with spiritual joy, and let us with gladness pay GOD worthy thanks and raise our hearts' eyes unimpeded to those heights where Christ is. Minds that have heard the call to be uplifted must not be pressed down by earthly affections[6], they that are fore-ordained to things eternal must not be taken up with the things that perish; they that have entered on the way of Truth must not be entangled in treacherous snares, and the faithful must so take their course through these temporal things as to remember that they are sojourning in the vale of this world, in which, even though they meet with some attractions, they must not sinfully embrace them, but bravely pass through them. For to this devotion the blessed Apostle Peter arouses us, and entreating us with that loving eagerness which he conceived for feeding Christ's sheep by the threefold profession of love for the LORD, says, "dearly-beloved, I beseech you, as strangers and pilgrims, abstain from fleshly lusts which war against the soul[7]." But for whom do fleshly pleasures wage war, if not for the devil, whose delight it is to fetter souls that strive after things above, with the enticements of corruptible good things, and to draw them away from those abodes from which he himself has been banished? Against his plots every believer must keep careful watch that he may crush his foe on the side whence the attack is made. And there is no more powerful weapon, dearly-beloved, against the devil's wiles than kindly mercy and bounteous charity, by which every sin is either escaped or vanquished. But this lofty power is not attained until that which is opposed to it be overthrown. And what so hostile to mercy and works of charity as avarice from the root of which spring all evils[7a]? And unless it be destroyed by lack of nourishment, there must needs grow in the ground of that heart in which this evil weed has taken root, the thorns and briars of vices rather than any seed of true goodness. Let us then, dearly-beloved, resist this pestilential evil and "follow after charity[7a]," without which no virtue can flourish, that by this path of love whereby Christ came down to us, we too may mount up to Him, to Whom with GOD the Father and the Holy Spirit is honour and glory for ever and ever. Amen.

SERMON LXXV.

(ON WHITSUNTIDE, I.)

I. *The giving of the Law by Moses prepared the way for the outpouring of the Holy Ghost.*

The hearts of all catholics, beloved, realize that to-day's solemnity is to be honoured as one of the chief feasts, nor is there any doubt that great respect is due to this day, which the Holy Spirit has hallowed by the miracle of His most excellent gift. For from the day on which the LORD ascended up above all heavenly heights to sit down at GOD the

4 S. John xx. 17.
5 Acts i. 11.
6 *Sursum vocatos animos.* The allusion no doubt is to the V. *Sursum corda.* R. *habemus ad Dominum*, with which the Church Liturgy has always ushered us into the most solemn part of the Eucharistic worship (Col. iii. 1, 2). Cf. Bright's n. 122, and Serm. LXVII. chap. i.

7 1 Pet. ii. 11.
7a Cf. 1 Tim. vi. 10; and below, 1 Cor. xiv. 1.

Father's right hand, this is the tenth which has shone, and the fiftieth from His Resurrection, being the very day on which it began[8], and containing in itself great revelations of mysteries both new and old, by which it is most manifestly revealed that Grace was fore-announced through the Law and the Law fulfilled through Grace. For as of old, when the Hebrew nation were released from the Egyptians, on the fiftieth day after the sacrificing of the lamb the Law was given on Mount Sinai, so after the suffering of Christ, wherein the true Lamb of God was slain on the fiftieth day from His Resurrection, the Holy Ghost came down upon the Apostles and the multitude of believers, so that the earnest Christian may easily perceive that the beginnings of the Old Testament were preparatory to the beginnings of the Gospel, and that the second covenant was founded by the same Spirit that had instituted the first.

II. *How marvellous was the gift of "divers tongues."*

For as the Apostles' story testifies: "while the days of Pentecost were fulfilled and all the disciples were together in the same place, there occurred suddenly from heaven a sound as of a violent wind coming, and filled the whole house where they were sitting. And there appeared to them divided tongues as of fire, and it sat upon each of them. And they were all filled with the Holy Spirit, and began to speak with other tongues, as the Holy Spirit gave them utterance[9]." Oh! how swift are the words of wisdom, and where God is the Master, how quickly is what is taught, learnt. No interpretation is required for understanding, no practice for using, no time for studying, but the Spirit of Truth blowing where He wills[9a], the languages peculiar to each nation become common property in the mouth of the Church. And therefore from that day the trumpet of the Gospel-preaching has sounded loud: from that day the showers of gracious gifts, the rivers of blessings, have watered every desert and all the dry land, since to renew the face of the earth the Spirit of God "moved over the waters[9a]," and to drive away the old darkness flashes of new light shone forth, when by the blaze of those busy tongues was kindled the Lord's bright Word and fervent eloquence, in which to arouse the understanding, and to consume sin there lay both a capacity of enlightenment and a power of burning.

III. *The three Persons in the Trinity are perfectly equal in all things.*

But although, dearly-beloved, the actual form of the thing done was exceeding wonderful, and undoubtedly in that exultant chorus of all human languages the Majesty of the Holy Spirit was present, yet no one must think that His Divine substance appeared in what was seen with bodily eyes. For His Nature, which is invisible and shared in common with the Father and the Son, showed the character of His gift and work by the outward sign that pleased Him, but kept His essential property within His own Godhead: because human sight can no more perceive the Holy Ghost than it can the Father or the Son. For in the Divine Trinity nothing is unlike or unequal, and all that can be thought concerning Its substance admits of no diversity either in power or glory or eternity. And while in the property of each Person the Father is one, the Son is another, and the Holy Ghost is another, yet the Godhead is not distinct and different; for whilst the Son is the Only begotten of the Father, the Holy Spirit is the Spirit of the Father and the Son, not in the way that every creature is the creature of the Father and the Son, but as living and having power with Both, and eternally subsisting of That Which is the Father and the Son[1]. And hence when the Lord before the day of His Passion promised the coming of the Holy Spirit to His disciples, He said, "I have yet many things to say to you, but ye cannot bear them now. But when He, the Spirit of Truth shall have come, He shall guide you into all the Truth. For He shall not speak from Himself, but whatsoever He shall have heard, He shall speak and shall announce things to come unto you. All things that the Father hath are Mine: therefore said I that He shall take of Mine, and shall announce it to you[2]." Accordingly, there are not some things that are the Father's, and other the Son's, and other the Holy Spirit's: but all things whatsoever the Father has, the Son also has, and the Holy Spirit also has: nor was there ever a time when this communion did not exist, because with Them to have all things is to always exist. In them let no times, no grades, no differences be imagined[3], and, if no one can explain that which is true concerning God, let no one dare to assert what is not true. For it is more excusable not to make a full

8 *In eo* (Sc. *die*) *a quo cœpit* (Sc. *festum*), apparently an obscure way of saying that the first Whitsunday was the same day of the week (viz. the first) as the first Easter-day.

9 Acts ii. 1—4.

9a Cf. S. John iii. 8; and below, Gen. i. 2.

1 For this statement of the doctrine of the Trinity, esp. in regard to the Twofold Procession of the Holy Ghost, cf. Lett. XV. chap. 2. Bright quotes Swete's *History of the Doctrine*, p. 157.

2 S. John xvi. 12—15.

3 Cf. Serm. XXVIII. chap. 4, *cum gradus in vera Divinitate esse non possit*, and Serm. LXXII. chap. 5, *nec Unitatem gradibus dividat*, and Bright's notes 29 and 116 on the subject.

statement concerning His ineffable Nature than to frame an actually wrong definition. And so whatever loyal hearts can conceive of the Father's eternal and unchangeable Glory, let them at the same time understand it of the Son and of the Holy Ghost without any separation or difference. For we confess this blessed Trinity to be One God for this reason, because in these three Persons there is no diversity either of substance, or of power, or of will, or of operation.

IV. *The Macedonian heresy is as blasphemous as the Arian.*

As therefore we abhor the Arians, who maintain a difference between the Father and the Son, so also we abhor the Macedonians[4], who, although they ascribe equality to the Father and the Son, yet think the Holy Ghost to be of a lower nature, not considering that they thus fall into that blasphemy, which is not to be forgiven either in the present age or in the judgment to come, as the Lord says: "whosoever shall have spoken a word against the Son of Man, it shall be forgiven him, but he that shall have spoken against the Holy Ghost, it shall not be forgiven him either in this age or in the age to come[5]." And so to persist in this impiety is unpardonable, because it cuts him off from Him, by Whom he could confess: nor will he ever attain to healing pardon, who has no Advocate to plead for him. For from Him comes the invocation of the Father, from Him come the tears of penitents, from Him come the groans of suppliants, and "no one can call Jesus the Lord save in the Holy Ghost[6]," Whose Omnipotence as equal and Whose Godhead as one, with the Father and the Son, the Apostle most clearly proclaims, saying, "there are divisions of graces but the same Spirit; and the divisions of ministrations but the same Lord; and there are divisions of operations but the same God, Who worketh all things in all[6]."

V. *The Spirit's work is still continued in the Church.*

By these and other numberless proofs, dearly-beloved, with which the authority of the Divine utterances is ablaze, let us with one mind be incited to pay reverence to Whitsuntide, exulting in honour of the Holy Ghost, through Whom the whole catholic Church is sanctified, and every rational soul quickened; Who is the Inspirer of the Faith, the Teacher of Knowledge, the Fount of Love, the Seal of Chastity, and the Cause of all Power. Let the minds of the faithful rejoice, that throughout the world One God, Father, Son, and Holy Ghost, is praised by the confession of all tongues, and that that sign of His Presence, which appeared in the likeness of fire, is still perpetuated in His work and gift. For the Spirit of Truth Himself makes the house of His glory shine with the brightness of His light, and will have nothing dark nor lukewarm in His temple. And it is through His aid and teaching also that the purification of fasts and alms has been established among us. For this venerable day is followed by a most wholesome practice, which all the saints have ever found most profitable to them, and to the diligent observance of which we exhort you with a shepherd's care, to the end that if any blemish has been contracted in the days just passed through heedless negligence, it may be atoned for by the discipline of fasting and corrected by pious devotion. On Wednesday and Friday, therefore, let us fast, and on Saturday for this very purpose keep vigil with accustomed devotion, through Jesus Christ our Lord, Who with the Father and the Holy Ghost lives and reigns for ever and ever. Amen.

SERMON LXXVII.

(On Whitsuntide, III.)

I. *The Holy Ghost's work did not begin at Pentecost, but was continued because the Holy Trinity is One in action and in will.*

To-day's festival, dearly-beloved, which is held in reverence by the whole world, has been hallowed by that advent of the Holy Ghost, which on the fiftieth day after the Lord's Resurrection, descended on the Apostles and the multitude of believers[7], even as it was hoped. And there was this hope, because the Lord Jesus had promised that He should come, not then first to be the Indweller of the saints, but to kindle to a greater heat, and to fill with larger abundance the hearts that were dedicated to Him, increasing, not commencing His gifts, not fresh in operation because richer in bounty. For the Majesty of the Holy Ghost is never separate from the Omnipotence of the Father and the Son, and whatever the Divine government accomplishes in the ordering of

---

4 "Arianism had spoken both of the Son and the Holy Spirit as creatures. The Macedonians, rising up out of Semi-arianism, gradually reached the Church's belief as to the uncreated Majesty of the Son, even if they retained their objection to the Homoousion. But having, in their previously Semi-arian position, refused to extend their own Homoi-ousion to the Holy Spirit, they afterwards persisted in regarding Him 'as external to the one indivisible Godhead.' Newman's *Arians*, p. 226." Bright's n. 129. Macedonius, from whom the sect was named, was bp. of Constantinople alternately with his rival, the orthodox Paul, between 342 and 351, and from that date he held the See in full possession till 360, when he was finally deposed.

5 S. Matt. xii. 32.

6 1 Cor. xii. 3—6.

7 Bright (n. 133) quotes Aug (in Joan. Evan. Tr. 92, c. 1 and Serm. 267, 1) for the opinion, which Leo here seems to follow, that the "all" of Acts ii. 1 includes the 120 (cf. A i. 20) as well as the Twelve.

all things, proceeds from the Providence of the whole Trinity. Therein exists unity of mercy and loving-kindness, unity of judgment and justice: nor is there any division in action where there is no divergence of will. What, therefore, the Father enlightens, the Son enlightens, and the Holy Ghost enlightens: and while there is one Person of the Sent, another of the Sender, and another of the Promiser, both the Unity and the Trinity are at the same time revealed to us, so that the Essence which possesses equality and does not admit of solitariness is understood to belong to the same Substance but not the same Person.

II. *Each Person in the Trinity took part in our Redemption.*

The fact, therefore, that, with the co-operation of the inseparable Godhead still perfect, certain things are performed by the Father, certain by the Son, and certain by the Holy Spirit, in particular belongs to the ordering of our Redemption and the method of our salvation. For if man, made after the image and likeness of God, had retained the dignity of his own nature, and had not been deceived by the devil's wiles into transgressing through lust the law laid down for him, the Creator of the world would not have become a Creature, the Eternal would not have entered the sphere of time, nor God the Son, Who is equal with God the Father, have assumed the form of a slave and the likeness of sinful flesh. But because "by the devil's malice death entered into the world[8]," and captive humanity could not otherwise be set free without His undertaking our cause, Who without loss of His majesty should both become true Man, and alone have no taint of sin, the mercy of the Trinity divided for Itself the work of our restoration in such a way that the Father should be propitiated, the Son should propitiate[9], and the Holy Ghost enkindle. For it was necessary that those who are to be saved should also do something on their part, and by the turning of their hearts to the Redeemer should quit the dominion of the enemy, even as the Apostle says, "God sent the Spirit of His Son into our hearts, crying Abba, Father[1]," "And where the Spirit of the Lord is, there is liberty[2]," and "no one can call Jesus Lord except in the Holy Spirit[3]."

III. *But this apportionment of functions does not mar the Unity of the Trinity.*

If, therefore, under guiding grace, dearly-beloved, we faithfully and wisely understand what is the particular work of the Father, of the Son, and of the Holy Ghost, and what is common to the Three in our restoration, we shall without doubt so accept what has been wrought for us by humiliation and in the body as to think nothing unworthy about the One and Selfsame Glory of the Trinity. For although no mind is competent to think, no tongue to speak about God, yet whatever that is which the human intellect apprehends about the essence of the Father's Godhead, unless one and the selfsame truth is held concerning His Only-begotten or the Holy Spirit, our meditations are disloyal, and beclouded by the intrusions of the flesh, and even that is lost, which seemed a right conclusion concerning the Father, because the whole Trinity is forsaken, if the Unity therein is not maintained; and That Which is different by any inequality can in no true sense be One.

IV. *In thinking upon God, we must put aside all material notions.*

When, therefore, we fix our minds on confessing the Father and the Son and the Holy Ghost, let us keep far from our thoughts the forms of things visible, the ages of beings born in time, and all material bodies and places. Let that which is extended in space, that which is enclosed by limit, and whatever is not always everywhere and entire be banished from the heart. The conception of the Triune Godhead must put aside the idea of interval or of grade[4], and if a man has attained any worthy thought of God, let him not dare to withhold it from any Person therein, as if to ascribe with more honour to the Father that which he does not ascribe to the Son and Spirit. It is not true godliness to put the Father before the Only-begotten: insult to the Son is insult to the Father: what is detracted from the One is detracted from Both. For since Their Eternity and Godhead are alike common, the Father is not accounted either Almighty and Unchangeable, if He begat One less than Himself or gained by having One Whom before He had not[5].

V. *Christ as Man is less than the Father, as God co-equal.*

The Lord Jesus does, indeed, say to His disciples, as was read in the Gospel lection, "if ye loved Me, ye would assuredly rejoice, because I go to the Father, because the Father is greater than I[6];" but those ears,

---

8 Wisd. ii. 24.

9 "The Atonement is a reconciling not merely of man to God but of God to man," says Archbp. Trench, and that, as S. Thomas Aquinas explains, in regard to our sins not in regard to our nature, in which regard He always loves us (passages quoted by Bright, n. 54).

1 Gal. iv. 6. 2 2 Cor. iii. 17. 3 1 Cor. xii. 3.

4 See Serm. LXXV. chap. 3, n. 3.

5 See Serm. XXIII. chap. 2.

6 S. John xiv. 28; x. 30; xiv. 9. In the English Church, the Gospel for Whitsunday is still the same as it was in Leo's time at Rome.

which have often heard the words, "I and the Father are One[6]," and "He that sees Me, sees the Father also[6]," accept the saying without supposing a difference of Godhead or understanding it of that Essence which they know to be co-eternal and of the same nature with the Father. Man's uplifting, therefore, in the Incarnation of the Word, is commended to the holy Apostles also, and they, who were distressed at the announcement of the LORD's departure from them, are incited to eternal joy over the increase in their dignity; "If ye loved Me," He says, "ye would assuredly rejoice, because I go to the Father:" that is, if, with complete knowledge ye saw what glory is bestowed on you by the fact that, being begotten of GOD the Father, I have been born of a human mother also, that being invisible I have made Myself visible, that being eternal "in the form of GOD" I accepted the "form of a slave," "ye would rejoice because I go to the Father." For to you is offered this ascension, and your humility is in Me raised to a place above all heavens at the Father's right hand. But I, Who am with the Father that which the Father is, abide undivided with My Father, and in coming from Him to you I do not leave Him, even as in returning to Him from you I do not forsake you. Rejoice, therefore, "because I go to the Father, because the Father is greater than I." For I have united you with Myself, and am become Son of Man that you might have power to be sons of GOD. And hence, though I am One in both forms, yet in that whereby I am conformed to you I am less than the Father, whereas in that whereby I am not divided from the Father I am greater even than Myself. And so let the Nature, which is less than the Father, go[7] to the Father, that the Flesh may be where the Word always is, and that the one Faith of the catholic Church may believe that He Whom as Man it does not deny to be less, is equal as GOD with the Father.

VI. *And this equality which the Son has with the Father, the Holy Ghost also has.*

Accordingly, dearly-beloved, let us despise the vain and blind cunning of ungodly heretics, which flatters itself over its crooked interpretation of this sentence, and when the LORD says, "All things that the Father hath are Mine[8]," does not understand that it takes away from the Father whatever it dares to deny to the Son, and is so foolish in matters even which are human as to think, that what is His Father's has ceased to belong to His Only-begotten, because He has taken on Him what is ours. Mercy in the case of GOD does not lessen power, nor is the reconciliation of the creature whom He loves a falling off of Eternal glory. What the Father has the Son also has, and what the Father and the Son have, the Holy Ghost also has, because the whole Trinity together is One GOD. But this Faith is not the discovery of earthly wisdom nor the conviction of man's opinion: the Only-begotten Son has taught it Himself, and the Holy Ghost has established it Himself, concerning Whom no other conception must be formed than is formed concerning the Father and the Son. Because albeit He is not the Father nor the Son, yet He is not separable from the Father and the Son: and as He has His own personality in the Trinity, so has He One substance in Godhead with the Father and the Son, filling all things, containing all things, and with the Father and the Son controlling all things, to Whom is the honour and glory for ever and ever. Amen.

SERMON LXXVIII.

(ON THE WHITSUNTIDE FAST, I.)

I. *Since the Apostles' day till now self-restraint is the best defence against the devil's assaults.*

To-day's festival, dearly-beloved, hallowed by the descent of the Holy Ghost, is followed, as you know by a solemn fast, which being a salutary institution for the healing of soul and body, we must keep with devout observance. For when the Apostles had been filled with the promised power, and the Spirit of Truth had entered their hearts, we doubt not that among the other mysteries of heavenly doctrine this discipline of spiritual self-restraint was first thought of at the prompting of the Paraclete in order that minds sanctified by fasting might be fitter for the chrism to be bestowed on them[9]. The disciples of Christ had the protection of the Almighty aid, and the chiefs of the infant Church were guarded by the whole Godhead of the Father and the Son through the presence of the Holy Ghost. But against the threatened attacks of persecutors, against the terrifying shouts of the ungodly, they could not fight with bodily strength or pampered flesh, since that which delights the outer does most harm to the inner man, and the more one's fleshly substance is kept in subjection, the more purified is the reasoning soul.

---

6 Ibid.

7 *Vadat* (subj.); others read *vadit* (indic.) = goes, in which ase Christ is still imagined to be speaking. If we read *vadat*, His utterance ends with the last sentence.

8 S. John xvi. 15.

9 Cf. note 9 on Lett. CLVI. chap. 5.

II. *The tempter is foiled in attacks upon those who have learnt these tactics.*

And so those teachers, who have instructed all the Church's sons by their examples and their traditions, began the rudiments of the Christian warfare with holy fasts, that, having to fight against spiritual wickednesses, they might take the armour of abstinence, wherewith to slay the incentives to vice. For invisible foes and incorporeal enemies will have no strength against us, if we be not entangled in any lusts of the flesh. The desire to hurt us is indeed ever active in the tempter, but he will be disarmed and powerless, if he find no vantage ground within us from which to attack us. But who, encompassed with this frail flesh, and placed in this body of death, even one who has made much decided progress, can be so sure of his safety now, as to believe himself free from the peril of all allurements? Although Divine Grace gives daily victory to His saints[1], yet He does not remove the occasion for fighting, because this very fact is part of our Protector's Mercy, Who has always designed that something should remain for our ever-changing nature to win, lest it should boast itself on the ending of the battle.

III. *And so this fast comes very opportunely after the feast of Whitsuntide.*

Therefore, after the days of holy gladness, which we have devoted to the honour of the LORD rising from the dead and then ascending into heaven, and after receiving the gift of the Holy Ghost, a fast is ordained as a wholesome and needful practice, so that, if perchance through neglect or disorder even amid the joys of the festival any undue licence has broken out, it may be corrected by the remedy of strict abstinence, which must be the more scrupulously carried out in order that what was on this day Divinely bestowed on the Church may abide in us. For being made the Temple of the Holy Ghost, and watered with a greater supply than ever of the Divine Stream, we ought not to be conquered by any lusts nor held in possession by any vices in order that the habitation of Divine power may be stained with no pollution.

IV. *And by proper use of it we shall win GOD'S favour.*

And this assuredly it is possible for all to obtain, GOD helping and guiding us, if by the purification of fasting and by merciful liberality, we take pains to be set free from the filth of sins, and to be rich in the fruits of love. For whatever is spent in feeding the poor, in healing the sick, in ransoming prisoners, or in any other deeds of piety, is not lessened but increased, nor will that ever be lost in the sight of GOD which the loving-kindness of the faithful has expended, seeing that whatever a man gives in relief, he lays up for his own reward. For "blessed are the merciful, since GOD shall have mercy on them[2];" nor will shortcomings be remembered, where the presence of true religion has been attested. On Wednesday and Friday, therefore, let us fast, and on Saturday let us keep vigil in the presence of the most blessed Apostle, Peter, by whose prayers we surely trust to be set free both from spiritual foes and bodily enemies; through our LORD Jesus Christ, who with the Father and the Holy Ghost, lives and reigns for ever and ever. Amen.

SERMON LXXXII.

ON THE FEAST[3] OF THE APOSTLES PETER AND PAUL (JUNE 29).

I. *Rome owes its high position to these Apostles.*

The whole world, dearly-beloved, does indeed take part in all holy anniversaries, and loyalty to the one Faith demands that whatever is recorded as done for all men's salvation should be everywhere celebrated with common rejoicings. But, besides that reverence which to-day's festival has gained from all the world, it is to be honoured with special and peculiar exultation in our city, that there may be a predominance of gladness on the day of their martyrdom in the place where the chief of the Apostles met their glorious end[4]. For these are the men, through whom the light of Christ's gospel shone on thee, O Rome, and through whom thou, who wast the teacher of error, wast made the disciple of Truth. These are thy holy Fathers and true shepherds, who gave thee claims to be numbered among

---

[1] Cf. Serm. LXXXVIII. chap. 3, *licet quotidiano Dei munere a diversis contaminationibus emundemur, inhærent tamen incautis animis maculæ crassiores quas oporteat diligentiori cura ablui.*

[2] S. Matt. v. 7.

[3] *Natali*, lit. birthday; but the early Church gave this beautiful name to, and kept the memory of Saints on, the day of their death (cf. below, *in die martyrii eorum*) in all cases except that of S. John the Baptist (from the importance of his natural birthday in connexion with the LORD's Nativity). The Conversion of S. Paul is a later exception.

[4] It is of course well known that this is very debateable ground, and as such, it is wiser to leave it untouched in a work which is only intended as a means of rendering English-speaking people acquainted with Leo's views and statements. It will be noticed, however, that the historically verified connexion of S. Paul with Rome is as nothing in his eyes in comparison with the very apocryphal connexion of S. Peter: cf. below, *per sacram beati Petri sedem*, on which the Ballerinii very appropriately quote Prosper *de Ingratis:—*

Sedes Roma Petri, quæ pastoralis honore
facta caput mundo, quidquid non possidet armis
religione tenet.

The Roman Calendar still retains the double commemoration on June 29.

the heavenly kingdoms, and built thee under much better and happier auspices than they, by whose zeal the first foundations of thy walls were laid: and of whom the one that gave thee thy name defiled thee with his brother's blood [5]. These are they who promoted thee to such glory, that being made a holy nation, a chosen people, a priestly and royal state [5a], and the head of the world through the blessed Peter's holy See thou didst attain a wider sway by the worship of GOD than by earthly government. For although thou wert increased by many victories, and didst extend thy rule on land and sea, yet what thy toils in war subdued is less than what the peace of Christ has conquered.

II. *The extension of the Roman empire was part of the Divine scheme.*

For the good, just, and Almighty GOD, Who has never withheld His mercy from mankind, and has ever instructed all men alike in the knowledge of Himself by the most abundant benefits, has by a more secret counsel and a deeper love shown pity upon the wanderers' voluntary blindness and proclivities to evil, by sending His co-equal and co-eternal Word. Which becoming flesh so united the Divine Nature with the human that He by lowering His Nature to the uttermost has raised our nature to the highest. But that the result of this unspeakable Grace might be spread abroad throughout the world, GOD's Providence made ready the Roman empire, whose growth has reached such limits that the whole multitude of nations are brought into close connexion. For the Divinely-planned work particularly required that many kingdoms should be leagued together under one empire, so that the preaching of the world might quickly reach to all people, when they were held beneath the rule of one state. And yet that state, in ignorance of the Author of its aggrandisement though it rule almost all nations, was enthralled by the errors of them all, and seemed to itself to have fostered religion greatly, because it rejected no falsehood. And hence its emancipation through Christ was the more wondrous that it had been so fast bound by Satan.

III. *On the dispersing of the Twelve, St. Peter was sent to Rome.*

For when the twelve Apostles, after receiving through the Holy Ghost the power of speaking with all tongues, had distributed the world into parts among themselves, and undertaken to instruct it in the Gospel, the most blessed Peter, chief of the Apostolic band, was appointed to the citadel of the Roman empire, that the light of Truth which was being displayed for the salvation of all the nations, might spread itself more effectively throughout the body of the world from the head itself. What nation had not representatives then living in this city; or what peoples did not know what Rome had learnt? Here it was that the tenets of philosophy must be crushed, here that the follies of earthly wisdom must be dispelled, here that the cult of demons must be refuted, here that the blasphemy of all idolatries must be rooted out, here where the most persistent superstition had gathered together all the various errors which had anywhere been devised.

IV. *St. Peter's love conquered his fears in coming to Rome.*

To this city then, most blessed Apostle Peter, thou dost not fear to come, and when the Apostle Paul, the partner of thy glory, was still busied with regulating other churches, didst enter this forest of roaring beasts, this deep, stormy ocean with greater boldness than when thou didst walk upon the sea. And thou who hadst been frightened by the high priest's maid in the house of Caiaphas, hadst no fear of Rome the mistress of the world. Was there any less power in Claudius, any less cruelty in Nero than in the judgment of Pilate or the Jews' savage rage? So then it was the force of love that conquered the reasons for fear: and thou didst not think those to be feared whom thou hadst undertaken to love. But this feeling of fearless affection thou hadst even then surely conceived when the profession of thy love for the LORD was confirmed by the mystery of the thrice-repeated question. And nothing else was demanded of this thy earnest purpose than that thou shouldst bestow the food wherewith thou hadst thyself been enriched, on feeding His sheep whom thou didst love.

V. *S. Peter was providentially prepared for his great mission.*

Thy confidence also was increased by many miraculous signs, by many gifts of grace, by many proofs of power. Thou hadst already taught the people, who from the number of the circumcised had believed: thou hadst already founded the Church at Antioch, where first the dignity of the Christian name arose: thou hadst already instructed Pontus, Galatia, Cappadocia, Asia, and Bithynia, in the laws of the Gospel-message: and, without doubt as to the success of the work, with full knowledge of the short span of thy life didst carry

5 i.e. Romulus (the traditional founder of Rome) murdered his brother, Remus. 5a Cf. 1 S. Pet. ii. 9.

the trophy of Christ's cross into the citadel of Rome, whither by the Divine fore-ordaining there accompanied thee the honour of great power and the glory of much suffering.

VI. *Many noble martyrs have sprung from the blood of SS. Peter and Paul.*

Thither came also thy blessed brother-Apostle Paul, "the vessel of election [5b]," and the special teacher of the Gentiles, and was associated with thee at a time when all innocence, all modesty, all freedom was in jeopardy under Nero's rule. Whose fury, inflamed by excess of all vices, hurled him headlong into such a fiery furnace of madness that he was the first to assail the Christian name with a general persecution, as if GOD's Grace could be quenched by the death of saints, whose greatest gain it was to win eternal happiness by contempt of this fleeting life. "Precious," therefore, "in the eyes of the LORD is the death of His saints [6]:" nor can any degree of cruelty destroy the religion which is founded on the mystery of Christ's cross. Persecution does not diminish but increase the church, and the LORD's field is clothed with an ever richer crop, while the grains, which fall singly, spring up and are multiplied a hundred-fold [7]. Hence how large a progeny have sprung from these two Heaven-sown seeds is shown by the thousands of blessed martyrs, who, rivalling the Apostles' triumphs, have traversed the city far and wide in purple-clad and ruddy-gleaming throngs, and crowned it, as it were, with a single diadem of countless gems.

VII. *No distinction must be drawn between the merits of the two.*

And over this band, dearly-beloved, whom GOD has set forth for our example in patience and for our confirmation in the Faith, there must be rejoicing everywhere in the commemoration of all the saints, but of these two Fathers' excellence we must rightly make our boast in louder joy, for GOD's Grace has raised them to so high a place among the members of the Church, that He has set them like the twin light of the eyes in the body, whose Head is Christ. About their merits and virtues, which pass all power of speech, we must not make distinctions, because they were equal in their election [8], alike in their toils, undivided in their death. But as we have proved for ourselves, and our forefathers maintained, we believe, and are sure that, amid all the toils of this life, we must always be assisted in obtaining GOD's Mercy by the prayers of special interceders, that we may be raised by the Apostles' merits in proportion as we are weighed down by our own sins. Through our LORD Jesus Christ, &c.

SERMON LXXXIV [9].

CONCERNING THE NEGLECT OF THE COMMEMORATION.

I. *The Churchmen of Rome are in danger of forgetting past judgments and mercies, and becoming ungrateful to GOD.*

The fewness of those who were present has of itself shown, dearly-beloved, that the religious devotion wherewith, in commemoration of the day of our chastisement and release, the whole body of the faithful used to flock together in order to give GOD thanks, has on this last occasion been almost entirely neglected: and this has caused me much sadness of heart and great fear. For there is much danger of men becoming ungrateful to GOD, and through forgetfulness of His benefits not feeling sorrow for the chastisement, nor joy for the liberation. Accordingly I fear, dearly-beloved, lest that utterance of the Prophet be addressed in rebuke to such men, which says, "thou hast scourged them and they have not grieved: thou hast chastised them, and they have refused to receive correction [1]." For what amendment is shown by them in whom such aversion to GOD's service is found? One is ashamed to say it, but one must not keep silence: more is spent upon demons than upon the Apostles, and mad spectacles draw greater crowds than blessed martyrdoms [2]. Who was it that restored this city to safety? that rescued it from captivity? the games of the circus-goers or the care of the saints? surely it was by the saints' prayers that the sentence of Divine displeasure was

5b Acts ix. 15.

6 Ps. cxvi. 15.

7 This is a commonplace with the Fathers: S. Augustine is esp. fond of it; Hurter quotes from him *de catech. rud.* chap. xxiv. and four times on the Psalms. Cf. Serm. XXXVI. chap. iii. n. 1.

8 *Electio pares (fecit)* omitted by the oldest Vatican MS. but undoubtedly genuine, the allusion being obviously to S. Paul's claim to equal apostleship with the Twelve more than once advanced (e.g. 2 Cor. xi. 5, &c.). This then is an interesting passage when read side by side with Leo's Petrine claims, but does not really contradict them, though the language here used, esp. the figure of the two eyes, is strong.

9 There is some doubt as to the exact occasion of this sermon. It seems to have been connected with the yearly commemoration (not the first or second from the language Leo uses), of that 14 days' pillage of Rome by Genseric (in 455) and of the city's subsequent liberation, in which Leo took so important a part. But the date ascribed to the sermon's delivery (the octave of SS. Peter and Paul, i.e. July 6) does not tally well with its allusions to the *ludi Circenses* as counter-attractions to the recent Church functions. A reference to Serm. IX. n. 6, will remind the reader that it was the *ludi Apollinares* that, at least in the past, were associated with that date: perhaps Leo's phrase *ludus Circensium* is only a general description and would include the Apollinarian games as being still held *in Circo* as well as others. The *ludi Circenses* themselves were held Sept. 4—12.

1 Jer. v. 3.

2 *Martyria*, which the Ball. here consider means the churches built in honour (? on the scene) of the martyrdoms.

diverted, so that we who deserved wrath, were reserved for pardon.

II. *Let them avail themselves betimes of* GOD'S *long-suffering and return to Him.*

I entreat you, beloved, let those words of the Saviour touch your hearts, Who, when by the power of His mercy He had cleansed ten lepers, said that only one of them all had returned to give thanks [2a]: meaning without doubt that, though the ungrateful ones had gained soundness of body, yet their failure in this godly duty arose from ungodliness of heart. And therefore, dearly-beloved, that this brand of ingratitude may not be applied to you, return to the LORD, remembering the marvels which He has deigned to perform among us; and ascribing our release not, as the ungodly suppose, to the influences of the stars, but to the unspeakable mercy of Almighty GOD, Who has deigned to soften the hearts of raging barbarians, betake yourselves to the commemoration of so great a benefit with all the vigour of faith. Grave neglect must be atoned for by yet greater tokens of repentance. Let us use the Mercy of Him, Who has spared us, to our own amendment, that the blessed Peter and all the saints, who have always been near us in many afflictions, may deign to aid our entreaties for you to the merciful GOD, through Jesus Christ our LORD. Amen.

SERMON LXXXV.

ON THE FEAST OF S. LAURENCE THE MARTYR [3] (Aug. 10).

I. *The example of the martyrs is most valuable.*

Whilst the height of all virtues, dearly-beloved, and the fulness of all righteousness is born of that love, wherewith GOD and one's neighbour is loved, surely in none is this love found more conspicuous and brighter than in the blessed martyrs; who are as near to our LORD Jesus, Who died for all men, in the imitation of His love, as in the likeness of their suffering. For, although that Love, wherewith the LORD has redeemed us, cannot be equalled by any man's kindness, because it is one thing that a man who is doomed to die one day should die for a righteous man, and another that One Who is free from the debt of sin should lay down His life for the wicked [3a]: yet the martyrs also have done great service to all men, in that the LORD Who gave them boldness, has used it to show that the penalty of death and the pain of the cross need not be terrible to any of His followers, but might be imitated by many of them. If therefore no good man is good for himself alone, and no wise man's wisdom befriends himself only, and the nature of true virtue is such that it leads many away from the dark error on which its light is shed, no model is more useful in teaching GOD's people than that of the martyrs. Eloquence may make intercession easy, reasoning may effectually persuade; but yet examples are stronger than words, and there is more teaching in practice than in precept.

II. *The Saint's martyrdom described.*

And how gloriously strong in this most excellent manner of doctrine the blessed martyr Laurentius is, by whose sufferings to-day is marked, even his persecutors were able to feel, when they found that his wondrous courage, born principally of love for Christ, not only did not yield itself, but also strengthened others by the example of his endurance. For when the fury of the gentile potentates was raging against Christ's most chosen members, and attacked those especially who were of priestly rank, the wicked persecutor's wrath was vented on Laurentius the deacon, who was pre-eminent not only in the performance of the sacred rites, but also in the management of the church's property [4], promising himself double spoil from one man's capture: for if he forced him to surrender the sacred treasures, he would also drive him out of the pale of true religion. And so this man, so greedy of money and such a foe to the truth, arms himself with double weapon: with avarice to plunder the gold; with impiety to carry off Christ. He demands of the guileless guardian of the sanctuary that the church wealth on which his greedy mind was set should be brought to him. But the holy deacon showed him where he had them stored, by pointing to the many troops of poor saints, in the feeding and clothing of whom he had a store of riches which he could not lose, and which were the more entirely safe that the money had been spent on so holy a cause.

III. *The description of his sufferings continued.*

The baffled plunderer, therefore, frets, and blazing out into hatred of a religion, which had put riches to such a use, determines to

---

[2a] Cf. S. Luke xvii. 18.

[3] S. Laurence was the chief Deacon of the Church of Rome in the time of Sextus II., and was martyred in the persecution of Valerian, 258, in the way detailed by Leo in this Sermon. His was a very favourite festival in the Middle Ages both in the East and West.

[3a] Cf. Rom. v. 7, 8.

[4] It will be remembered that "the serving of tables" was from the first institution of the office one of the principal duties of the deacon (*levita*), see Acts vi. 1—6. This side of the office has latterly fallen into abeyance and is but slightly recognized in the English Ordinal.

pillage a still greater treasure by carrying off that sacred deposit[5], wherewith he was enriched, as he could find no solid hoard of money in his possession. He orders Laurentius to renounce Christ, and prepares to ply the deacon's stout courage with frightful tortures: and, when the first elicit nothing, fiercer follow. His limbs, torn and mangled by many cutting blows, are commanded to be broiled upon the fire in an iron framework[6], which was of itself already hot enough to burn him, and on which his limbs were turned from time to time, to make the torment fiercer, and the death more lingering.

IV. *Laurentius has conquered his persecutor.*

Thou gainest nothing, thou prevailest nothing, O savage cruelty. His mortal frame is released from thy devices, and, when Laurentius departs to heaven, thou art vanquished. The flame of Christ's love could not be overcome by thy flames, and the fire which burnt outside was less keen than that which blazed within. Thou didst but serve the martyr in thy rage, O persecutor: thou didst but swell the reward in adding to the pain. For what did thy cunning devise, which did not redound to the conqueror's glory, when even the instruments of torture were counted as part of the triumph? Let us rejoice, then, dearly-beloved, with spiritual joy, and make our boast over the happy end of this illustrious man in the LORD, Who is "wonderful in His saints[6a]," in whom He has given us a support and an example, and has so spread abroad his glory throughout the world, that, from the rising of the sun to its going down, the brightness of his deacon's light doth shine, and Rome is become as famous in Laurentius as Jerusalem was ennobled by Stephen. By his prayer and intercession[7] we trust at all times to be assisted; that, because all, as the Apostle says, "who wish to live holily in Christ, suffer persecution[8]," we may be strengthened with the spirit of love, and be fortified to overcome all temptations by the perseverance of stedfast faith. Through our LORD Jesus Christ, &c.

SERMON LXXXVIII.

ON THE FAST OF THE SEVENTH MONTH, III[9].

I. *The Fasts, which the ancient prophets proclaimed, are still necessary.*

Of what avail, dearly-beloved, are religious fasts in winning the mercy of GOD, and in renewing the fortunes of human frailty, we know from the statements of the holy Prophets, who proclaim that justice of GOD, Whose vengeance the people of Israel had again and again incurred through their iniquities, cannot be appeased save by fasting. Thus it is that the Prophet Joel warns them, saying, "thus saith the LORD your GOD, turn ye to Me with all your heart, with fasting and weeping and mourning, and rend your hearts and not your garments, and turn ye to the LORD your GOD, for He is merciful and patient, and of great kindness, and very merciful[1]," and again, "sanctify a fast, proclaim a healing, assemble the people, sanctify the church[1]." And this exhortation must in our days also be obeyed, because these healing remedies must of necessity be proclaimed by us too, in order that in the observance of the ancient sanctification Christian devotion may gain what Jewish transgression lost.

II. *Public services are of a higher character than private.*

But the respect that is paid to the Divine decrees always brings a special blessing, whatever may be the extent of our voluntary services, so that publicly proclaimed celebrations are of a higher character than those which rest on private institution[2]. For the exercise of self-restraint, which each individual imposes on himself at his own discretion, concerns the benefit of a certain portion only of the Church, but the fast which the whole Church undergoes leaves out no one from the general purification, and GOD's people then become strongest, when the hearts of all the faithful meet together in one common act of holy obedience, when in the camp of the Christian army there is on all sides the same making ready for the fight and for defence. Though the cruel enemy rage in restless fury, and spread all round his hidden snares, yet he will be able to catch no one and wound no one, if he find no one off his guard, no one given up to sloth, no one inactive in works of piety.

III. *The September fast calls us in this public way to self-amendment.*

To this unconquerable strength of unity, therefore, dearly-beloved, we are even now invited by the solemn Fast of the Seventh Month, that we may lift our souls to the LORD free from worldly cares and earthly concerns.

5 *Depositum*, viz. his faith, the παραθήκη of 1 Tim. vi. 20.

6 *Per cratem ferream* usually represented in pictures or statues of the saint as a gridiron.

6a Ps. lxviii. 35 (LXX.).

7 Cf. Sermon LXXXII. c. 7.

8 2 Tim iii. 12.

9 That is the September, or as we should now say, the Michaelmas Embertide.

1 Joel ii. 12, 13, and 15, 16.

2 He pursues the same thought in chap. 2 of Sermon LXXXIX. e.g. *tunc est efficacior sacratiorque devotio, quando in operibus pietatis totius Ecclesiæ unus animus et unus est census; publica enim præferenda sunt propriis et ibi intelligenda est præcipua ratio utilitatis, ubi vigilat cura communis.*

And because, always needful as this endeavour is, we cannot all adhere to it perpetually, and often through human frailty we fall back from higher things to the things of earth, let us at least on these days, which are most healthfully ordained for our correction, withdraw ourselves from worldly occupations, and steal a little time for promoting our eternal welfare. "For in many things," as it is written, "we all stumble[3]." And though by the daily gift of GOD[4] we be cleansed from divers pollutions, yet there cling to unwary souls for the most part darker stains, which need a greater care to wash them out, a stronger effort to destroy them. And the fullest abolition of sins is obtained when the whole Church offers up one prayer and one confession. For if the LORD has promised fulfilment of all they shall ask, to the holy and devout agreement of two or three, what shall be denied to many thousands of the people who unite in one act of worship, and with one breath make their common supplications[5]?

IV. *Community of goods and of actions is most precious in GOD'S sight.*

It is a great and very precious thing, beloved, in the LORD's sight, when Christ's whole people engage together in the same duties, and all ranks and degrees of either sex co-operate with the same intent: when one purpose animates all alike of declining from evil and doing good; when GOD is glorified in the works of His slaves, and the Author of all godliness[6] is blessed in unstinted giving of thanks. The hungry are nourished, the naked are clothed, the sick are visited, and men seek not their own but "that which is another's[7]," so long as in relieving the misery of others each one makes the most of his own means; and it is easy to find "a cheerful giver[7]," where a man's performances are only limited by the extent of his power. By this grace of GOD, "which worketh all in all[7]," the benefits and the deserts of the faithful are both enjoyed in common. For they, whose income is not like, can yet think alike, and when one rejoices over another's bounty his feelings put him on the same level with him whose powers of spending are on a different level. In such a community there is no disorder nor diversity, for all the members of the whole body agree in one strong purpose of godliness, and he who glories in the wealth of others is not put to shame at his own poverty. For the excellence of each portion is the glory of the whole body, and when we are all led by GOD's Spirit, not only are the things we do ourselves our own but those of others also over the doing of which we rejoice.

V. *Let us then make the best use possible of the opportunity.*

Let us then, dearly-beloved, lay hold upon this most sacred unity in all its blessed integrity and engage in the solemn fast with the concordant purpose of a good will. Nothing hard, nothing harsh is asked of anyone, nor is anything imposed beyond our strength, whether in the discipline of abstinence or in the amount of alms. Each knows what he can and what he cannot do: let every one pay his quota, assessing himself at a just and reasonable rate, that the sacrifice of mercy be not offered sadly nor reckoned among losses. Let so much be expended on pious work, as will justify the heart, wash the conscience, and in a word profit both giver and receiver. Happy indeed is that soul and truly to be admired which in its love of doing good fears not the failing of the means, and has no distrust that He will give him money still to spend, from Whom he had what he spent in the past. But because few possess this greatness of heart, and yet it is truly a pious thing for each one not to forsake the care of his own, we, without prejudice to the more perfect sort, lay down for you this general rule and exhort you to perform GOD's bidding according to the measure of your ability. For cheerfulness becomes the benevolent man, who should so manage his liberality that while the poor rejoice over the help supplied, home needs may not suffer. "And He that ministers seed to the sower, shall both provide bread to be eaten and multiply your seed and increase the fruits of your righteousness[8]." On Wednesday and Friday therefore let us fast; and on Saturday keep vigil all together[9] in the presence of the most blessed Apostle Peter, by whose merits and prayers we are sure GOD's mercy will be vouchsafed to us in all things through our LORD Jesus Christ, Who lives and reigns for ever and ever. Amen.

SERMON XC.

(ON THE FAST OF SEVENTH MONTH, V.)

I. *We must always be seeking pardon, because we are always liable to sin.*

We proclaim the holy Fast of the Seventh Month, dearly-beloved, for the exercise of

3 S. James iii. 2.
4 Cf. Serm. LXXVIII. 2. *donet licet sanctis suis quotidianam gratia Divina victoriam, non aufert tamen dimicandi materiam.*
5 Cf. S. Matt. xviii. 19, 20.
6 *Totius pietatis auctori*: cf. Collect for 23rd Sunday after Trinity, which is based on that in the Gregorian Sacramentary.
7 Cf. 1 Cor. x. 24; xii. 6: 2 Cor. ix. 7.
8 2 Cor. ix. 10.
9 *Pariter.* He thus keeps up the leading thought of this sermon to the end.

common devotions, confidently inciting you with fatherly exhortations to make Christian by your observance that which was formerly Jewish[1]. For it is at all times suitable and in agreement with both the New and Old Testament, that the Divine Mercy should be sought with chastisement both of mind and body, because nothing is more effectual in prevailing with GOD than that a man should judge himself and never cease from asking pardon, knowing that he is never without fault. For human nature has this flaw in itself, not planted there by the Creator but contracted by the transgressor[2], and transmitted to his posterity by the law of generation[3], so that from the corruptible body springs that which may corrupt the soul also. Hence although the inner man be now reborn in Christ and rescued from the bonds of captivity, it has unceasing conflicts with the flesh, and has to endure resistance in seeking to restrain vain desires. And in this strife such perfect victory is not easily obtained that even those habits which must be broken off do not still encumber us, and those vices which must be slain do not wound. However wisely and prudently the mind presides as judge over the outer senses, yet even amid the pains it takes to rule and the limits it imposes on the appetites of the flesh, the temptation is always too close at hand. For who so abstracts himself from pleasure or pain of body that his mind is not affected by that which delights or racks it from without? Joy and sorrow are inseparable from a man: no part of him is free from the kindlings of wrath, the over-powerings of delight, the castings down of affliction. And what turning away from sin can there be, where ruler and ruled alike are liable to the same passions? Rightly does the LORD exclaim that "the spirit indeed is willing but the flesh is weak[4]."

II. *Christ is Himself the Way, which He bids us tread.*

And lest we should be led by despair into sheer inaction, He promises that the Divine power shall make those things possible which are to man impossible from his own lack of power: "for narrow and strait is the way which leadeth unto life[5]," and no one could set foot on it, no one could advance one step, unless Christ by making Himself the Way unbarred the difficulties of approach: and thus the Ordainer of the journey becomes the Means whereby we are able to accomplish it, because not only does He impose the labour, but also brings us to the haven of rest. In Him therefore we find our Model of patience, in Whom we have our Hope of life eternal; for "if we suffer with Him, we shall also reign with Him[6]," since, as the Apostle says, "he that saith he abideth in Christ ought himself also to walk as He walked[7]." Otherwise we make a vain pretence and show, if we follow not His steps, Whose name we glory in, and assuredly they would not be irksome to us, but would free us from all dangers, if we loved nothing but what He commanded us to love.

III. *The love of GOD contrasted with the love of the world.*

For there are two loves from which proceed all wishes, as different in quality as they are different in their sources. For the reasonable soul, which cannot exist without love, is the lover either of GOD or the world. In the love of GOD there is no excess, but in the love of the world all is hurtful. And therefore we must cling inseparably to eternal treasures, but things temporal we must use like passers-by, that as we are sojourners hastening to return to our own land, all the good things of this world which meet us may be as aids on the way, not snares to detain us. Therefore the blessed Apostle makes this proclamation, "the time is short: it remains that those who have wives be as though they had none; and those who weep, as though they wept not; and those who rejoice, as though they rejoiced not; and those who buy, as though they possessed not; and those that use this world, as though they used it not. For the fashion of this world passes away[8]." But as the world attracts us with its appearance, and abundance and variety, it is not easy to turn away from it unless in the beauty of things visible the Creator rather than the creature is loved; for, when He says, "thou shalt love the LORD thy GOD from all thy heart, and from all thy mind, and from all thy strength[9]," He wishes us in nothing to loosen ourselves from the bonds of His love. And when He links the love of our neighbour also to this command, He enjoins on us the imitation of His own goodness, that we should love what He loves and do what He does. For although we be "GOD's husbandry and GOD's building," and "neither is he that planteth anything, nor he that watereth, but GOD that giveth the increase[1]," yet in all things He requires our

[1] The observances of the seventh month, especially of the Day of Atonement, will be found in Lev. xxiii. 26—44, and Numbers xxix.

[2] Sc. by Adam.

[3] *Generandi lege:* others read *generali lege*, by he universal law.

[4] S. Matt. xxvi. 41; for this passage, cf. Serm. XIX. chaps. 1 and 2, and LXXVIII. chap. 2.

[5] Matt. vii 14.

[6] 2 Tim. ii. 12.

[7] 1 S. John ii. 6.

[8] 1 Cor. vii. 29—31.

[9] S. Matt. xxii. 37.

[1] 1 Cor. iii. 9 and 7.

ministry and service, and wishes us to be the stewards of His gifts, that he who bears GOD's image may do GOD's will. For this reason, in the LORD's prayer we say most devoutly, "Thy Kingdom come, Thy will be done as in heaven, so also on earth." For what else do we ask for in these words but that GOD may subdue those whom He has not yet subdued, and as in heaven He makes the angels ministers of His will, so also on earth He may make men? And in seeking this we love GOD, we love also our neighbour: and the love within us has but one Object, since we desire the bond-servant to serve and the LORD to have rule.

IV. *The love of GOD is fostered by good works.*

This state of mind, therefore, beloved, from which earthly love is excluded, is strengthened by the habit of well-doing, because the conscience must needs be delighted at good deeds, and do willingly what it rejoices to have done. Thus it is that fasts are kept, alms freely given, justice maintained, frequent prayer resorted to, and the desires of individuals become the common wish of all. Labour fosters patience, gentleness extinguishes anger, loving-kindness treads down hatred, unclean desires are slain by holy aspirations, avarice is cast out by liberality, and burdensome wealth becomes the means of virtuous acts[2]. But because the snares of the devil are not at rest even in such a state of things, most rightly at certain seasons of the year the renewal of our vigour is provided for: and now in particular, when one who is greedy of present good might boast himself over the clemency of the weather and the fertility of the land, and having stored his crops in great barns, might say to his soul, "thou hast much goods, eat and drink," let him take heed to the rebuke of the Divine voice, and hear it saying, "Thou fool, this night they require thy soul of thee, and the things which thou hast prepared, whose shall they be[3]?" This should be the wise man's most anxious consideration, in order that, as the days of this life are short and its span uncertain, death may never come upon him unawares, and that knowing himself mortal he may meet his end fully prepared. And so, that this may avail both for the sanctification of our bodies and the renewal of our souls, on Wednesday and Friday let us fast, and on Saturday let us keep vigil with the most blessed Apostle Peter, whose prayers will help us to obtain fulfilment of our holy desires through Christ our LORD, Who with the Father and the Holy Ghost lives and reigns for ever and ever. Amen.

SERMON XCI.

ON THE FAST OF THE SEVENTH MONTH, VI.

I. *Abstinence must include discipline of the soul as well as of the body.*

There is nothing, dearly-beloved, in which the Divine Providence does not assist the devotions of the faithful. For the very elements of the world[4] also minister to the exercise of mind and body in holiness, seeing that the distinctly varied revolution of days and months opens for us the different pages of the commands, and thus the seasons also in some sense speak to us of that which the sacred institutions enjoin. And hence, since the year's course has brought back the seventh month to us, I feel certain that your minds are spiritually aroused to keep the solemn fast; since you have learnt by experience how well this preparation purifies both the outer and the inner parts of men, so that by abstaining from the lawful, resistance becomes easier to the unlawful. But do not limit your plan of abstinence, dearly-beloved, to the mortifying of the body, or to the lessening of food alone. For the greater advantages of this virtue belong to that chastity of the soul, which not only crushes the lusts of the flesh, but also despises the vanities of worldly wisdom, as the Apostle says, "take heed that no one deceive you through philosophy and empty deceit, according to the tradition of men[5]."

II. *And in particular we must abstain from heresy, and that of Eutyches as well as that of Nestorius.*

We must restrain ourselves, therefore, from food, but much more must we fast from errors that the mind, given up to no carnal pleasure, may be taken captive by no falsehood: because as in past days, so also in our own, there are not wanting enemies of the Truth, who dare to stir up civil wars within the catholic Church[6], in order that by leading the ignorant into agreement with their ungodly doctrines they may boast of increase in numbers through those whom they have been able

---

[2] From this point the oldest Vatican lectionary (3836) gives a very different ending to the Sermon, which the Ball. consider as genuine as the one given by the other MSS., and translated above: in which case they are probably right in inferring that Leo used the Sermon more than once, and wrote these two endings for two different occasions.

[3] S. Luke xii. 19, 20.

[4] Cf. Serm. XIX. 2, *per ipsius mundi cardines, quasi per quattuor evangelia, incessabiliter discimus quod et prædicemus et agamus.*

[5] Col. ii. 8.

[6] The occasion of this Sermon seems to have been either the same or a similar one to that of Serm. XCVI., in which we read that certain traders had come to Rome from Egypt after the murder of Proterius, supporting the heresy of Eutyches.

to sever from the Body of Christ. For what is so opposed to the Prophets, so repugnant to the Gospels, so at variance with the Apostles' teaching as to preach one single Nature in the LORD Jesus Christ born of Mary, and without respect to time co-eternal with the Eternal Father? If it is only man's nature which is to be acknowledged, where is the Godhead Which saves? if only GOD's, where is the humanity which is saved? But the catholic Faith, which withstands all errors, refutes these blasphemies also at the same time, condemning Nestorius, who divides the Divine from the human, and denouncing Eutyches, who nullifies the human in the Divine; seeing that the Son of True GOD, Himself True GOD, possessing unity and equality with the Father and with the Holy Ghost, has vouchsafed likewise to be true Man, and after the Virgin Mother's conception was not separated from her flesh and child-bearing, so uniting humanity to Himself as to remain immutably GOD; so imparting Godhead to man as not to destroy but enhance him by glorification. For He, Who became "the form of a slave," ceased not to be "the form of GOD," and He is not one joined with the other, but One in Both, so that ever since "the Word became Flesh" our faith is disturbed by no vicissitudes of circumstance, but whether in the miracles of power, or in the degradation of suffering, we believe Him to be both GOD, Who is Man, and Man, Who is GOD [7].

III. *The Truth of the Incarnation is proved both by the Eucharistic Feast and by the Divine institution of almsgiving.*

Dearly-beloved, utter this confession with all your heart and reject the wicked lies of heretics, that your fasting and almsgiving may not be polluted by any contagion with error: for then is our offering of the sacrifice clean and our gifts of mercy holy, when those who perform them understand that which they do. For when the LORD says, "unless ye have eaten the flesh of the Son of Man, and drunk His blood, ye will not have life in you [8]," you ought so to be partakers at the Holy Table, as to have no doubt whatever concerning the reality of Christ's Body and Blood. For that is taken in the mouth which is believed in Faith, and it is vain for them to respond Amen [9] who dispute that which is taken. But when the Prophet says, "Blessed is he, who considereth the poor and needy [1]," he is the praiseworthy distributor of clothes and food among the poor, who knows he is clothing and feeding Christ in the poor: for He Himself says, "as long as ye have done it to one of My brethren, ye have done it to Me [2]." And so Christ is One, True GOD and True Man, rich in what is His own, poor in what is ours, receiving gifts and distributing gifts, Partner with mortals, and the Quickener of the dead, so that in the "name of Jesus every knee should bow, of things in heaven, of things on earth, and of things under the earth, and that every tongue should confess that the LORD Jesus Christ is in the glory of GOD the Father [3]," living and reigning with the Holy Spirit for ever and ever. Amen.

SERMON XCV.

A HOMILY ON THE BEATITUDES, ST. MATT. V. 1—9.

I. *Introduction of the subject.*

When our LORD Jesus Christ, beloved, was preaching the gospel of the Kingdom, and was healing divers sicknesses through the whole of Galilee, the fame of His mighty works had spread into all Syria: large crowds too from all parts of Judæa were flocking to the heavenly Physician [4]. For as human ignorance is slow in believing what it does not see, and in hoping for what it does not know, those who were to be instructed in the divine lore [5], needed to be aroused by bodily benefits and visible miracles: so that they might have no doubt as to the wholesomeness of His teaching when they actually experienced His benignant power. And therefore that the LORD might use outward healings as an introduction to inward remedies, and after healing bodies might work cures in the soul, He separated Himself from the surrounding crowd, ascended into the retirement of a neighbouring mountain, and called His apostles to Him there, that from the height of that mystic seat He might instruct them in the loftier doctrines, signifying from the very nature of the place and act that He it was who had once honoured Moses by speaking to him: then indeed with a more terrifying justice, but now with a holier mercifulness, that what had been promised might be fulfilled when the Prophet Jeremiah says: "behold the days come when I will complete a new

---

7 For the whole of this chap. compare Lett. XXXI. chaps. 1 and 2.

8 S. John vi. 53.

9 This (acc. to the Ball.) is the Amen which the communicant said at the Reception of the Elements when the Priest said to Him, *Corpus Christi* and *sanguis Christi*: on the Eucharistic evidence against Eutyches, see Lett. LIX. chap. 2, and Serm. LXIII. chap. 7.

1 Ps. xli. 1.

2 S. Matt. xxv. 40.

3 Phil. ii. 10, 11.

4 Cf. S. Matt. iv. 23, 24.

5 *Divina eruditione firmandos* = τοὺς διδαχθησομένους, a common form of expression in Leo. Cf. Lett. XXVIII. the Tome, chap. 1, *quod voce omnium regenerandorum* (= τῶν ἀναγεννηθησομένων), *depromitur*.

covenant[6] for the house of Israel and for the house of Judah. After those days, saith the LORD, I will put My laws in their minds[7], and in their heart will I write them[8]." He therefore who had spoken to Moses, spoke also to the apostles, and the swift hand of the Word wrote and deposited the secrets of the new covenant[6] in the disciples' hearts: there were no thick clouds surrounding Him as of old, nor were the people frightened off from approaching the mountain by frightful sounds and lightning[9], but quietly and freely His discourse reached the ears of those who stood by: that the harshness of the law might give way before the gentleness of grace, and "the spirit of adoption" might dispel the terrors of bondage[1].

II. *The blessedness of humility discussed*

The nature then of Christ's teaching is attested by His own holy statements: that they who wish to arrive at eternal blessedness may understand the steps of ascent to that high happiness. "Blessed," He saith, "are the poor in spirit, for theirs is the kingdom of heaven[2]." It would perhaps be doubtful what poor He was speaking of, if in saying "blessed are the poor" He had added nothing which would explain the sort of poor: and then that poverty by itself would appear sufficient to win the kingdom of heaven which many suffer from hard and heavy necessity. But when He says "blessed are the poor *in spirit*," He shows that the kingdom of heaven must be assigned to those who are recommended by the humility of their spirits rather than by the smallness of their means. Yet it cannot be doubted that this possession of humility is more easily acquired by the poor than the rich: for submissiveness is the companion of those that want, while loftiness of mind dwells with riches[3]. Notwithstanding, even in many of the rich is found that spirit which uses its abundance not for the increasing of its pride but on works of kindness, and counts that for the greatest gain which it expends in the relief of others' hardships. It is given to every kind and rank of men to share in this virtue, because men may be equal in will, though unequal in fortune: and it does not matter how different they are in earthly means, who are found equal in spiritual possessions. Blessed, therefore, is poverty which is not possessed with a love of temporal things, and does not seek to be increased with the riches of the world, but is eager to amass heavenly possessions.

III. *Scriptural examples of humility.*

Of this high-souled humility the Apostles first[4], after the LORD, have given us example, who, leaving all that they had without difference at the voice of the heavenly Master, were turned by a ready change from the catching of fish to be fishers of men, and made many like themselves through the imitation of their faith, when with those first-begotten sons of the Church, "the heart of all was one, and the spirit one, of those that believed[5]:" for they, putting away the whole of their things and possessions, enriched themselves with eternal goods, through the most devoted poverty, and in accordance with the Apostles' preaching rejoiced to have nothing of the world and possess all things with Christ. Hence the blessed Apostle Peter, when he was going up into the temple, and was asked for alms by the lame man, said, "Silver and gold is not mine, but what I have that I give thee: in the Name of Jesus Christ of Nazareth, arise and walk[6]." What more sublime than this humility? what richer than this poverty? He hath not stores of money[7], but he hath gifts of nature. He whom his mother had brought forth lame from the womb, is made whole by Peter with a word; and he who gave not Cæsar's image in a coin, restored Christ's image on the man. And by the riches of this treasure not he only was aided whose power of walking was restored, but 5,000 men also, who then believed at the Apostle's exhortation on account of the wonder of this cure. And that poor man who had not what to give to the asker, bestowed so great a bounty of Divine Grace, that, as he had set one man straight on his feet, so he healed these many thousands of believers in their hearts, and made them "leap as an hart" in Christ whom he had found limping in Jewish unbelief.

IV. *The blessedness of mourning discussed.*

After the assertion of this most happy humility, the LORD hath added, saying, "Blessed are they which mourn, for they shall be comforted[8]." This mourning, beloved, to which eternal comforting is promised, is not the same as the affliction of this world: nor do those laments which are

6 Or testament (Lat. *testamentum*). 7 *In sensu ipsorum.*
8 Jer. xxxi. 31 and part of 33: the passage is quoted in full, Heb. viii. 8—12.
9 Cf. Heb. xii. 18 and foll.
1 S. Paul's language (Rom. viii. 15) is in his mind.
2 Matt. v. 3.
3 *Et illis in tenuitate amica est mansuetudo et istis divitiis familiaris elatio.*

4 The MSS. vary between *primum* and *primi.* The rendering above given practically represents either. If *primi*, however, is read, it may be questioned whether the true rendering is not "the first apostles after the LORD," which would be interesting as suggesting that S. Leo did not necessarily confine the title "apostle" to the Twelve. 5 Acts iv. 32.
6 Acts iii. 6. 7 *Præsidia pecuniæ.* 8 S. Matt. v. 4.

poured out in the sorrowings of the whole human race make any one blessed. The reason for holy groanings, the cause of blessed tears, is very different. Religious grief mourns sin either that of others' or one's own: nor does it mourn for that which is wrought by God's justice, but it laments over that which is committed by man's iniquity, where he that does wrong is more to be deplored than he who suffers it, because the unjust man's wrong-doing plunges him into punishment, but the just man's endurance leads him on to glory.

V. *The blessedness of the meek.*

Next the Lord says: "blessed are the meek, for they shall possess the earth by inheritance[9]." To the meek and gentle, to the humble and modest, and to those who are prepared to endure all injuries, the earth is promised for their possession. And this is not to be reckoned a small or cheap inheritance, as if it were distinct from our heavenly dwelling, since it is no other than these who are understood to enter the kingdom of heaven. The earth, then, which is promised to the meek, and is to be given to the gentle in possession, is the flesh of the saints, which in reward for their humility will be changed in a happy resurrection, and clothed with the glory of immortality, in nothing now to act contrary to the spirit, and to be in complete unity and agreement with the will of the soul[1]. For then the outer man will be the peaceful and unblemished possession of the inner man: then the mind, engrossed in beholding God, will be hampered by no obstacles of human weakness nor will it any more have to be said, "The body which is corrupted, weigheth upon the soul, and its earthly house presseth down the sense which thinketh many things[2]:" for the earth will not struggle against its tenant, and will not venture on any insubordination against the rule of its governor. For the meek shall possess it in perpetual peace, and nothing shall be taken from their rights, "when this corruptible shall have put on incorruption, and this mortal shall have put on immortality[3]:" that their danger may turn into reward, and what was a burden become an honour[4].

VI. *The blessedness of desiring righteousness.*

After this the Lord goes on to say: "blessed are they who hunger and thirst after righteousness, for they shall be satisfied[5]." It is nothing bodily, nothing earthly, that this hunger, this thirst seeks for: but it desires to be satiated with the good food of righteousness, and wants to be admitted to all the deepest mysteries, and be filled with the Lord Himself. Happy the mind that craves this food and is eager for such drink: which it certainly would not seek for if it had never tasted of its sweetness. But hearing the Prophet's spirit saying to him: "taste and see that the Lord is sweet[6];" it has received some portion of sweetness from on high, and blazed out into love of the purest pleasure, so that spurning all things temporal, it is seized with the utmost eagerness for eating and drinking righteousness, and grasps the truth of that first commandment which says: "Thou shalt love the Lord thy God out of all thy heart, and out of all thy mind, and out of all thy strength[7]:" since to love God is nothing else but to love righteousness[8]. In fine, as in that passage the care for one's neighbour is joined to the love of God, so, too, here the virtue of mercy is linked to the desire for righteousness, and it is said:

VII. *The blessedness of the merciful:*

"Blessed are the merciful, for God shall have mercy on them[9]." Recognize, Christian, the worth of thy wisdom, and understand to what rewards thou art called, and by what methods of discipline thou must attain thereto. Mercy wishes thee to be merciful, righteousness to be righteous, that the Creator may be seen in His creature, and the image of God may be reflected in the mirror of the human heart expressed by the lines of imitation. The faith of those who do good[1] is free from anxiety: thou shalt have all thy desires, and shalt obtain without end what thou lovest. And since through thine alms-giving all things are pure to thee, to that blessedness also thou shalt attain which is promised in consequence where the Lord says:

VIII. *The blessedness of a pure heart.*

"Blessed are the pure in heart, for they shall

---

9 S. Matt. v. 5. It will be observed that Leo's order for the 2nd and 3rd beatitudes is that of the English version, *not* that of the Vulgate.

1 *In nullo iam spiritui futura contraria et cum voluntate animi perfectæ unitatis habitura consensum*: compare S. Aug. *de Fide et Symbolo*, cap. 23, "*est autem animæ natura perfecta cum spiritui suo subditur et cum sequitur sequentem Deum—non est desperandum etiam corpus restitui naturæ propriæ—tempore opportuno in novissima tuba, cum mortui resurgent incorrupti et nos immutabimur.*" The interpretation of this beatitude in this way is fantastic, and very strange to modern notions.

2 Wisdom ix. 15.

3 1 Cor. xv. 53.

4 *Quod fuit oneri, sit honori*, the play on the words (which is quite classical) may perhaps be represented by the difference between *onerous* and *honorary*.

5 S. Matt. v. 6.

6 Ps. xxxiv. 8: *suavis*, A.V. and R.V. good, P.B.V. gracious, LXX. χρηστός.

7 Deut. vi. 5, quoted, it will be remembered, by our Lord as "the first and great commandment" in the law, S. Matt. xxii. 37: S. Mark xii. 30: S. Luke x. 27.

8 The two words for "love" here are different, and speak for themselves, *diligere* (ἀγαπᾶν) *Deum* and *amare* (ἐρᾶν) *iustitiam*.

9 S. Matt. v. 7.

1 *Operantium*: *operatio* is the regular patristic term for the doing of charitable actions; for this application of the beatitude and its promised reward, compare Ps. xli. 1—3.

see God[2]." Great is the happiness, beloved, of him for whom so great a reward is prepared. What, then, is it to have the heart pure, but to strive after those virtues which are mentioned above? And how great the blessedness of seeing God, what mind can conceive, what tongue declare? And yet this shall ensue when man's nature is transformed, so that no longer "in a mirror," nor "in a riddle," but "face to face[3]" it sees the very Godhead "as He is[4]," which no man could see[5]; and through the unspeakable joy of eternal contemplation obtains that "which eye has not seen, nor ear heard, neither has entered into the heart of man[5a]." Rightly is this blessedness promised to purity of heart. For the brightness of the true light will not be able to be seen by the unclean sight: and that which will be happiness to minds that are bright and clean, will be a punishment to those that are stained. Therefore, let the mists of earth's vanities be shunned. and your inward eyes purged from all the filth of wickedness, that the sight may be free to feed on this great manifestation of God. For to the attainment of this we understand what follows to lead.

IX. *The blessedness of peace-making.*

"Blessed are the peace-makers, for they shall be called the sons of God[6]." This blessedness, beloved, belongs not to any and every kind of agreement and harmony, but to that of which the Apostle speaks: "have peace towards God[7];" and of which the Prophet David speaks: "Much peace have they that love Thy law, and they have no cause of offence[8]." This peace even the closest ties of friendship and the exactest likeness of mind do not really gain, if they do not agree with God's will. Similarity of bad desires, leagues in crimes, associations of vice, cannot merit this peace. The love of the world does not consort with the love of God, nor doth he enter the alliance of the sons of God who will not separate himself from the children of this generation[9]. Whereas they who are in mind always with God, "giving diligence to keep the unity of the Spirit in the bond of peace[1]," never dissent from the eternal law, uttering that prayer of faith, "Thy will be done as in heaven so on earth[2]." These are "the peacemakers," these are thoroughly of one mind, and fully harmonious, and are to be called sons "of God and joint-heirs with Christ[3]," because this shall be the record of the love of God and the love of our neighbour, that we shall suffer no calamities, be in fear of no offence, but all the strife of trial ended, rest in God's most perfect peace, through our Lord, Who, with the Father and the Holy Spirit, liveth and reigneth for ever and ever. Amen.

2 S. Matt. v. 8. 3 1 Cor. xiii. 12. 4 1 S. John iii. 2.
5 Exod. xxxiii. 20; S. John. i. 18; 1 Tim. vi. 16.
5a Is. lxiv. 4; 1 Cor. ii. 9. 6 S. Matt. v. 9.

7 Rom. v. 1, where "we have" or "let us have" is the exact phrase.
8 Ps. cxix. 165. 9 *A carnali generatione.*
1 Eph. iv. 3. 2 S. Matt. vi. 10. 3 Rom. viii. 17.

LEO THE GREAT

INDEX OF BIBLICAL QUOTATIONS AND REFERENCES

The references are to the pages.

GENERAL INDEX

THE

BOOK OF PASTORAL RULE

AND

SELECTED EPISTLES

OF

GREGORY THE GREAT

BISHOP OF ROME

TRANSLATED, WITH INTRODUCTION, NOTES, AND INDICES

BY THE

REV. JAMES BARMBY, D.D.,

VICAR OF NORTHALLERTON, YORKSHIRE.

PREFATORY NOTE

The Text followed in these Translations is the Benedictine one, as given by Migne in *Patrologia, Vol. LXXVII., Sancti Gregorii Magni, Vol. III.* The same Text of the *Regula Pastoralis* has been published with an English Translation by the Rev. H. R. Bramley (James Parker and Co., 1874). The Translation now given is an original one, though the translator desires to express his obligations to his predecessor in the same task. The selection of Epistles translated has been made with the view of exhibiting Gregory's various activities, his various styles of correspondence, his views and character, as well as of illustrating the history of his time. Those which relate to certain important subjects—such as the Lombard invasion, the English Mission, the dispute about the title of 'Œcumenical Bishop,' correspondence with the Emperors and with the Potentates of Gaul—have been given in their entirety. Of such as relate to subjects of less moment specimens only have been selected, but sufficient, it is hoped, for presenting a picture of the writer under his various aspects, and in his various spheres of work. It is hoped also that the appended notes may serve to shew the connexion of the several Epistles with each other, and with the circumstances they refer to, as well as to explain obscure words or passages. For a better understanding of the correspondence relating to the Church in Gaul, a pedigree of the contemporary Merovingian Kings is appended.

CONTENTS OF THE PROLEGOMENA

PROLEGOMENA

State of the Empire.

For an understanding of Gregory's position, and of the purport of a great part of those of his epistles which are translated in this Series, a brief survey of the state of things, politically and ecclesiastically, at the time of his accession may in the first place be of service. There was now no separate Emperor of the West; what remained of the once great Western Empire being governed in the name of the Eastern Emperor, who had his court at Constantinople, by the Exarch of Italy, resident at Ravenna. The Kingdom of the Goths in Italy had ceased to be, the country having been recovered from them under Justinian about half a century before Gregory's accession, as well as the province of Africa from the Vandals.

The Lombards.

But the Emperor's hold on Italy was limited and precarious, a large portion of it being already occupied by the Lombards, whose first invasion, under Alboin, had been in 568: and accordingly Gregory, writing in the thirteenth Indiction (A.D. 594-5), speaks of their having been in Italy for twenty-seven years, and in the sixth Indiction (A.D. 602-3) of their having been there for thirty-five years [*Epp.*, *Lib.* V., *Ep.* 21, and *Lib.* XIII., *Ep.* 38]. Subsequently the Lombard King Autharis had advanced on Alboin's conquests, and is said to have proceeded to Rhegium, at the very toe of Italy, and there, riding up to a column on the shore through the tidal waves, to have touched it with the point of his spear and said, "So far shall extend the boundary of the Lombards" [Paul. Warnefr., *de gestis Longob.*, III. 33]. Autharis died in the first year of Gregory's popedom [*Epp.*, *Lib.* I., *Ep.* 17], and was succeeded by Agilulph, previously duke of Turin, whom Theodelinda, the widow of the deceased king, had selected as her consort. Under him, his royal seat being at Ticinum (*Pavia*), the Lombard dominion included the greater part of Northern Italy, reaching northward to the Alpine passes, the two great dukedoms of Spoletum and Beneventum in Southern Italy, with partial hold on Tuscia and elsewhere. The only parts that now distinctly acknowledged the sway of the Exarch were the Exarchate of Ravenna, on the eastern side of Italy, with Istria and Venetia further north, the duchies of Rome and Naples on the western side, portions of territory at the heel and toe of Italy, and the islands of Sicily, Sardinia, and Corsica. But beyond the limits of their actual occupation the Lombards kept the country in a continual state of disturbance and alarm; a great part of it appears to have been debatable ground, and no one could say definitely to whom it belonged.

No previous invaders seem to have been viewed by contemporaries with more horror, or painted in blacker colours, than the Lombards. Their Arian Christianity does not appear to have rendered them less odious than heathens would have been, or to have softened their alleged savagery. Gregory repeatedly in his letters speaks in the strongest possible terms of the misery of Italy "among the swords of the Lombards:" and it was doubtless the state of general distress thence arising, together with disorganization of the country from other causes, and the prevalence of calamity on whatever side he looked, that caused him continually to express his conviction that the signs of the times betokened the speedy approach of the Second Advent. It is in connexion with such a state of things that he stands out prominently as a political administrator of no common order. His position was one of peculiar difficulty. Though virtually, as bishop, the ruler of Rome, he was not a temporal potentate with power to act independently. He was but a subject of the Emperor, as he continually acknowledged, under the dominion of the Exarch of Ravenna, and possessed theoretically of spiritual jurisdiction only. And in his efforts to do good he was continually thwarted. He complains repeatedly in his letters of the insufficient aid afforded him by the distant Emperor, the counteraction of his own designs by the Exarch, and the corruption and iniquitous conduct of the imperial officers in Italy, which in more than one place he describes as even more trying than the oppressions of the Lombards. Still, in virtue of his high and influential position as bishop of old Rome, his commanding character, his indefatigable zeal, and his diplomatic talents, he did exert great political influence; and whatever success was attained in the defence of Italy against further aggression, or in effecting truces with the enemy, to him alone such success appears to have been due. Many of the letters translated in this volume shew his activity in this regard. A short summary of what may be gathered from them will be given below. All Europe, to the north of Italy, was now severed from the Western Empire. Britain had long been relinquished: the old provinces of Gaul were ruled and contended for by the descendants of Clovis of the Merovingian dynasty: Spain, with Narbonensian Gaul, was an independent Visigothic kingdom. The relations of these kingdoms to the Empire were at this time amicable; and it was in ecclesiastical, and not temporal, matters that Gregory had dealings with them, as will appear below.

Northern Europe.

His talents and activity in secular affairs were shewn also in his management of the possessions in various quarters with which the See of Rome had been endowed, known as "St. Peter's patrimony." In Sicily especially, and also in Campania, Calabria, Dalmatia and elsewhere, and to a small extent in Gaul, the Roman Church held lands so called, over all of which Gregory exercised personal superintendence by letters to his various agents, shewing a remarkable knowledge of the state of things in the several localities, and giving minute directions. While, on the one hand, he took care that the Church should not be defrauded of her just dues, on the other hand we find him repeatedly and strongly forbidding any unjust claims, or any oppression of the natives who cultivated the Church lands. The patrimony was commonly managed, under him, by agents on the spot, called *rectores patrimonii*, and often by deacons, or subdeacons, sent from Rome, to control the ordinary *rectores*, or act in the same capacity. We find bishops also in some cases acting as *rectores*. There was also a class of officials called *defensores ecclesiæ*, or Guardians of the Church, who were required to be authorized by letters from Rome under the Pope's hand (see V. 29; IX. 62; XI. 38). These letters of appointment, of which we have specimens in V. 29 and XI. 38, specified the protection of the poor as their primary duty. But their office had a much wider scope. We find them commissioned, not only to carry out various works of charity, but also to maintain the rights and property of churches, to rectify abuses in monasteries and hospitals (see e.g. I. 52; XIV. 2), to see to the canonical election of bishops (e.g. X. 77), and to the supply of episcopal ministrations during the suspension or incapacity of the holders of Sees (XIV. 2), to assist bishops in the exercise of discipline (X. 1), and even to rebuke and coerce bishops themselves when negligent of duty (III. 36; X. 10; XIII. 26, 27; XIV. 4). In some cases they were also themselves *rectores patrimonii* (IX. 18). Further, they constituted a *schola*, as did also the notaries and subdeacons; and in the first Indiction (A.D. 598) Gregory appointed that seven of their number should thenceforth be dignified with the name of *regionarii* (as was already the case with the notaries and subdeacons), which gave them rank, and entitled them to sit in assemblies of the clergy (VIII. 14). Though entrusted with such large powers in matters ecclesiastical, they do not seem to have been of necessity in sacred orders, and

The Patrimony.

might marry and have families (cf. III. 21; XII. 25). Some were subdeacons, as Anthemius, subdeacon and defensor of Campania (VII. 23). They might be apt, it seems, to take too much upon them: for we find Romanus, the defensor of Sicily, sharply rebuked for trenching on the prerogatives of a bishop (XI. 37). Though entitled, by special commission from the Roman See, to call even bishops to account, they were not to usurp their junctions. In some cases we find sworn *notarii* (otherwise called *chartularii*) attached to the patrimonies in addition to the *rectores*. Thus Adrian receives instructions as being *notarius Siciliæ*; and, on his being made *rector*, Pantaleo is appointed *notarius* (XIII. 18 and 34).

Notable among the subdeacons invested with authority for the number and particularity of the letters addressed to him is Peter, whom Gregory sent at once in the first year of his pontificate to Sicily, not only to look after the patrimony there and after the supply of corn sent annually thence to Rome, but also, for a time at least, to exercise delegated authority, in matters ecclesiastical, over the bishops of the island (see *Lib.* I., *Ep.* 1). From the letters to this Peter we learn a good deal about the way in which the lands of the patrimony, in Sicily at least, were cultivated, and how the revenues were derived from them. (See especially *Lib.* I., *Ep.* 44.) They were cultivated by native peasants, called by Gregory *rustici*, or *coloni*, who enjoyed the fruit of their labour, subject only to customary dues to the lords of the land; in this case to the Roman See. The principal dues we find referred to were, in the first place, a kind of land-tax, called *burdatio*, and further, the tithe of all the produce, which might be paid in kind, but seems to have been often commuted for a money payment. Among the prevalent abuses which Gregory peremptorily required to be corrected were excessive valuation of the tithe, irrespective of the current price of corn, when a money equivalent was paid, and in other cases the use of measures of too large capacity, and exactions in various ways of more than was fairly due. He orders schedules to be made and authorised, copies of which were to be given to the *rustici* in all the farms of the church, shewing what their legal payments were, so as to guard against their being wronged in future. There were other customary payments of smaller amounts, such as fees on the marriage of peasants, which, under limitations, he allows to be continued. It appears also from *Lib.* XII., *Ep.* 25, that these *rustici*, or *coloni*, were *ascripti glebæ*, so as not to be allowed to migrate from the estate (*massa*) to which they were attached, or to contract marriages beyond its limits. The several estates constituting the patrimony were called *massæ*, each of which might comprise several *fundi*; and it was customary to let these *massæ* to farmers (*conductores*), who were left to deal with the *rustici*, or *coloni*, being themselves responsible for a certain amount, whether in money or produce, to the officials of the Church. Gregory directed, among other things, that these *conductores*, should not be arbitrarily disturbed in their holdings, and that, on their death, members of their family should succeed them, guardians being appointed in case of their children being under age. Sicily was of great importance to Rome, as being a corn-growing country from which especially the Romans were supplied. Among Gregory's temporal responsibilities was that of seeing to a regular and adequate supply, a failure in which might be followed by famine in Rome: and we find him attentive to this duty, giving particular directions as to the procuring, storing, and shipping of the corn. (See e.g. *Lib.* I., *Ep.* 2, 44, 72.) In fact, provision generally for the welfare of the Roman citizens, and the general charge of the city, seems to have devolved upon the Pope. And it was doubtless his responsibilities in this regard, together with his more general political ones, in addition to his "care of all the churches," that caused him so continually to bemoan in his letters the billows of worldly business, incident to his office, which overwhelmed him, and hindered his advancement in the spiritual life. Remarkable, indeed, must have been his mental activity and his varied abilities, in that he was able, as appears from his epistles, to make himself accurately acquainted with, and personally attend to, so many matters, finding time also for theological composition and letters of spiritual counsel, and retaining his religious aspirations in the midst of all. And all this is the more striking when one considers the distressing state of health, especially from gout, of which he continually complains, and the fact also that, with his strong monastic predilections, matters of worldly business would be likely to be peculiarly distasteful to him. We get a further view of his multifarious engagements from what his biographer, John the Deacon, tells us of his having himself seen to the fourfold distribution—to the bishop, the clergy, the fabrics and services of the churches, and the poor —of the revenues of the See; his having himself caused to be sought out, and kept a list of, the recipients of charity; and himself taught the choristers in the *Orphanotrophium*, which he had himself founded in Rome. It appears to have been his principle and practice to rely on others for nothing which he could possibly do himself.

Ecclesiastical Affairs.

With regard to the state of things in the ecclesiastical sphere during Gregory's popedom, it may be observed first, that there was now a comparative cessation for a time of controversial warfare. The battle no longer raged over Arian, Nestorian, Monophysite, or Pelagian heresies; the Monothelitic controversy had not yet begun. Catholic orthodoxy, as defined by the first four Councils, was accepted generally, and enforced by the imperial power, with Gregory's full approval of coercive measures (see e.g. *Lib.* IX., *Ep.* 49; *Lib.* XI., *Ep.* 46)[1]; while outside the limits of the Empire it was professed and upheld by the Frankish rulers of Gaul, and at length at the commencement of Gregory's reign accepted in Spain by the Visigothic Reccared. The Lombards, indeed, with their king Agilulph, were still Arians; but his queen Theodelinda, with whom Gregory corresponded, was herself a devout Catholic. Hence he was not called on to come forward prominently in the field of controversy, for which indeed he does not appear to have been peculiarly fitted. For, though able to state clearly, and give the received reasons for, accepted dogmas, he nowhere evinces any great originality of conception, or depth of insight of his own. He is content to rest on authority; that especially of the four Councils, which he regards as the unassailable bulwarks of the true faith (see I. 25; III. 10; IV. 37), or of ancient fathers of the Church. Nor does he seem to have been well versed in the past history of controversy. An instance of his imperfect knowledge in this regard is found in the letters which he wrote after receiving from Cyriacus, the newly-appointed bishop of Constantinople, his confession of faith, in which Eudoxius, who had been prominent in the course of the Arian controversy, was condemned. Gregory had never heard of this noted heretic, though he had come across the name of a sect called Eudoxiani, and, not finding his name in the Latin books he was able to consult at Rome, he takes objection to his condemnation by Cyriacus (*Lib.* VII., *Ep.* 4); and it was not till he had consulted Eulogius of Alexandria, who was more learned than himself, that he was satisfied; and this simply on being informed that ancient fathers of repute had condemned this Eudoxius. "We know him (he writes) to be manifestly slain, against whom our heroes have cast so many darts" (VII. 34; VIII. 30). Again, in writing to the same Eulogius against the sect of *Agnoitæ*, who taught a certain limitation of our Lord's human knowledge, he appears to draw all his arguments from what he found in Augustine and other Latin Fathers, and he rejoices to hear that Eulogius had found the Greek Fathers (whom he himself, being wholly ignorant of Greek, was unable to consult) consentient (*Lib.* X., *Epp.* 35, 39).

1 "Prayer should ever be made for the life of our most pious and Christian lord the Emperor, and his most tranquil consort, &c., in whose times the mouths of heretics are silent, since, though their hearts seethe with the madness of perverse opinion, they presume not in the time of the catholic Emperor to utter the wrong things they think" (*Lib.* IX., *Ep.* 49).

But one subject of controversy there was, which especially troubled him; viz., that of "the three Chapters" (*tria capitula*), consequent upon the condemnation of the documents so-called, and of their deceased authors, at the instance of the Emperor Justinian, by the fifth General Council (A.D. 553). This condemnation had been in fact forced upon the Church by the Emperor in the said Council under his presidency at Constantinople, in spite of the protest of the great majority of the Western bishops, and of the then bishop of Rome, Vigilius. The grounds of objection to the condemnation were, that it was held to contravene the Council of Chalcedon, at which two of the writers whom it was proposed to condemn—Theodoret and Ibas—had been expressly acquitted of heresy; that to anathematize the dead, whatever their opinions might have been, was wrong; and further, that the condemnation was intended to conciliate the Monophysites, to whom the writers in question had been peculiarly obnoxious, and was in fact a concession to their heresy. Nor can it be doubted that a design to conciliate the Monophysite party, still strong and resolute in spite of its condemnation at Chalcedon, had been a main motive with Justinian in forcing a decree against the Three Chapters on the Church. Vigilius, however, had afterwards yielded to pressure, and assented, however inconsistently, to the condemnation of the Chapters; as did his successors in the See of Rome, including Gregory. Consequently several Churches of the West had renounced communion with Rome; and the schism thus arising—as in Liguria, which was under the metropolitan of Milan, and still more decidedly in Istria and Venetia under the metropolis of Aquileia—continued throughout the reign of Gregory. He in vain endeavoured, either by remonstrance or by trying to enlist the emperor's aid, to bring back the Istrian bishops to conformity; and it must have been distressing to him, that even the Lombard queen, Theodelinda, who was so orthodox a Catholic, and whom he esteemed so highly, and corresponded with so cordially, herself could not be induced to accept the fifth Council, so far as the condemnation of the Three Chapters was concerned. In his last extant letter to her, written in the year of his death, he regrets that severe illness prevented him from replying to certain arguments on the subject by an abbot, Secundus, which she had sent for his consideration, but transmits to her a copy of the Acts of the fifth council, and again repeats his constant protest that his acceptance of that Council by no means implied any disparagement of the previous councils, or of the Tome of pope Leo (*Lib.* XIV., *Ep.* 12). Further, the schism of the Donatists still lingered in the African provinces, though no longer powerful, and though a series of imperial edicts had been issued for their suppression. We find Gregory, in many letters, urging measures against them, and more rigid enforcement of the penal laws.

The Three Chapters.

The Donatists.

With regard to the spiritual authority over the Church at large, claimed in the time of Gregory, and by him asserted, and the extent to which such claims were then acknowledged, the following remarks may be made.

The spiritual authority of Rome.

Beyond the episcopal jurisdiction of the bishops of Rome over their own proper diocese, which comprised only the city of Rome, and their metropolitan jurisdiction over the seven suffragan bishops of the Roman territory—viz., those of Ostia, Portus, Silva Candida, Sabina, Præneste, Tusculum, and Albanum,—they had long exercised a more extended patriarchal jurisdiction, which (according to Rufinus towards the end of the fourth century) seems originally to have extended over the suburban provinces which were under the civil jurisdiction of the *vicarius urbis*, including the islands of Sicily, Sardinia, and Corsica. But, being the only patriarchs of the West, they had long exercised authority, more or less defined, over a much wider area, including Northern Italy, with its metropolis at Milan, Illyricum East and West, and Northern Africa. It is not necessary to attempt any review here of the growth, as years had gone on, of such extended jurisdiction, or of the degree and kind of authority over Churches that had been consequently claimed. Nor need we consider now the well-known instances of resistance to such authority, as notably in Africa by St. Cyprian in the third century, and at a later date in the same province when Zosimus was pope, in the case of Apiarius. For our present purpose it may be enough to say that the bishop of Rome was now generally acknowledged to be not only the sole Patriarch in the West, but also the highest in rank of all the bishops of Christendom. Still, even in some provinces where his authority was not openly disputed, there appears to have been, at any rate, jealousy of its exercise. For proofs of this in Africa, see II. 47, n. 1; IV. 34, n. 1; IX. 58, n. 1. For a notable instance in Western Illyricum, in the case of Maximus, bishop of Salona, see III. 47, and note there. At Ravenna also, the seat of the Exarch, there seems to have been jealousy of the claims of Rome, seeing that John, bishop of that See, in a letter to Gregory, though expressing himself as personally devoted to the Roman See, says that he had provoked no little ill-will of many enemies against himself for his defence of its authority (III. 57).

In Gaul, under the Merovingian princes, there are no signs of any dispute of the pope's spiritual jurisdiction, which was constantly asserted, over the Churches there: but the ancient Celtic Churches of the British islands still retained their independence. This last fact is apparent, not only from what Bede relates of the attitude of the British and Scottish Christians towards Augustine and the Roman mission, but also from the tone of the letter of the Irish Columbanus to Gregory, which will be found among the epistles (see *Lib.* IX., *Ep.* 127). With the Church in Spain, after its renunciation of Arianism under King Reccared at the beginning of Gregory's episcopate, he seems to have had little communication. He corresponded indeed with his friend Leander, of Seville, about the King's conversion, and wrote a letter to the latter (IX. 122), who had sent an offering to Rome. Further, he sent into Spain the abbot Cyriacus, who had been employed to bring about the assembling of a Council in Gaul, commending him in a somewhat adulatory epistle to one Claudius, who appears to have been a person of influence in the court of Reccared (IX. 120). But for what special purpose he was sent does not appear. There is, moreover, a long document, comprised under XIII. 45 in the Benedictine edition of the epistles, relating to two bishops who were said to have been uncanonically deposed, for the adjudication of whose case one John, a *defensor ecclesiæ*, is said to have been sent, and to have pronounced sentence. But this epistle is not found in all codices; nor does it appear from it, even if it were considered genuine, whether John's decision was accepted in Spain. On the whole, there is no sufficient evidence, but rather the contrary, of papal jurisdiction being recognized at that time in Spain as it certainly was in Gaul. It remains only to note the historical fact, that the whole Eastern branch of the Church Catholic never at any time submitted itself to the Roman See, notwithstanding occasional appeals to it by bishops or others when suffering under grievances.

With regard to Gregory's own view of the prerogatives of the Roman See beyond the limits of its proper metropolitan or patriarchal jurisdiction, he undoubtedly claimed for it a primacy not of rank only, but also of authority in the Church Universal; and this of divine right, as representing the See of the Prince of the apostles. Such claim had come, in his day, to be the tradition of the Roman Church, which he accepted as a matter of course, and handed on. In assertion of this claim he says in more than one place, "Petro totius ecclesiæ cura et principatus commissa est;" and again, "quis nesciat sanctam Ecclesiam in apostolorum principis soliditate firmatam. . . . Itaque, cum multi sint apostoli, pro ipso tamen principatu sola apostolorum principis sedes in auctoritate convaluit" (*Lib.* VII., *Ep.* 40); and he certainly regarded the like authority as residing still in what was called St. Peter's See.

But we nowhere find him asserting it in such a way as to merge the general episcopal commission in the Papacy, or to interfere with the canonical exercise of their independent jurisdiction by other patriarchs of ancient Apostolic Sees. He sent according to custom, after his accession, his confession of faith to the four Eastern patriarchs of Alexandria, Antioch, Jerusalem, and Constantinople, as to brethren: he never, even where his jurisdiction was acknowledged, interfered with the free election of bishops by their several Churches, except where he saw some canonical impediment, reserving only to himself the right of confirming the election (see e.g. *Lib.* II., *Ep.* 6; *Lib.* V., *Ep.* 17, &c.): and, lastly, his memorable emphatic protest against the assumption of the title of Universal Bishop by the patriarchs of Constantinople, with his total renunciation of any right of his own to assume such a title, has often been quoted as a standing protest against such papal supremacy as has subsequently been claimed and exercised. He seems to have regarded the See of St. Peter as everywhere supreme only in the sense of its being its prerogative to conserve inviolate the catholic faith and observance of the canons, wherever heresy or uncanonical proceedings called for protest and correction. He writes thus to John, bishop of Syracuse, "Si qua culpa in episcopis invenitur, nescio quis ei [*Sedi apostolicæ*] subjectus non sit: cum vero culpa non exigit, omnes secundum rationem humilitatis æquales sunt" (*Lib.* IX., *Ep.* 59). Again, to the *defensor* Romanus, "Si qua unicuique episcopo jurisdictio non servatur, quid aliud agitur, nisi ut per nos, per quos ecclesiasticus custodiri debuit ordo, confundatur?" (*Lib.* XI., *Ep.* 37). Again to Eulogius of Alexandria, protesting against being addressed as Universal Pope, and against the expression, *sicut jussistis*, "Quod verbum jussionis peto a meo auditu removere, quia scio qui sum, qui estis. Loco quim mihi fratres estis, moribus patres. Non ergo jussi, sed quæ utilia visa sunt indicare curavi. . . . Nec honorem esse deputo in quo fratres meos honorem suum perdere cognosco. Si enim universalem me Papam vestra sanctitas dicit, negat se hoc esse, quod me fatetur universum. Sed absit hoc." (*Lib.* VIII., *Ep.* 30). Further, there is the notable fact, that he distinctly accords to the patriarchs of Alexandria and Antioch equal shares with himself in the primacy of St. Peter's See;—to the former on the ground of his See having been founded by St. Mark, who had been sent by St. Peter; to the latter because (according to the Clementine tradition, which he takes for granted) St. Peter had been for seven years bishop of Antioch before he went to Rome. To Eulogius of Alexandria he writes, "Cum ergo unius atque una sit sedes, cui ex auctoritate divina tres nunc episcopi præsident, quicquid ergo de vobis boni audio, hoc mihi imputo. Si quid de me boni creditis, hoc vestris meritis imputate, quia in illo unum sumus qui ait, *Ut omnes unum sint, sicut et tu Pater in me, et ego in te, et ipsi in nobis unum sint*" (*Lib.* VII., *Ep.* 40. Cf. V. 39; X. 35; XIII. 41). He wrote thus in his anxiety to induce those two patriarchs to support him in his resistance to the assumptions of Constantinople; but his view of the principality of St. Peter's See not being vested exclusively in the See of Rome remains no less distinctly on record. The view to which he gives expression of the unity of the three Sees may perhaps have arisen thus. The tradition of the peculiarly Petrine origin of the Roman See, and hence its claim as of divine right to supremacy, having come by this time to be accepted in the West, the undoubted ancient jurisdiction, independently of Rome, of the great patriarchal sees of the East in their own regions, had to be accounted for in accordance with this theory: and hence they too were regarded as deriving their authority from St. Peter. Accordingly we do not find Gregory in any of his letters to the patriarchs of Alexandria and Antioch addressing them in a tone of command. It is true that in one letter to Eulogius of Alexandria he remonstrates with him urgently for allowing (as was alleged) simony in his diocese; but it is brotherly remonstrance only (*Lib.* XIII., *Ep.* 41).

[There is indeed a passage in one of Gregory's Epistles (II. 52) which has been taken to imply a claim to jurisdiction over them. (See note on passage in Migne's *Patrologia.*) Natalis, bishop of Salona, had disregarded the admonitions of two successive bishops of Rome; and Gregory writes to him, "Quod si quilibet ex quatuor patriarchis fecisset, sine gravissimo scandalo tanta contumacia transire nullo modo potuisset." But the intended meaning may be, not that such contumacy towards Rome would have been scandalous even in one of the great Eastern patriarchs, but that it could not have been passed over by them if shewn towards themselves in their own patriarchates. The words, it is true, suggest the former meaning, but the latter seems more likely to have been intended.]

The See of Constantinople.

On the other hand, towards the patriarch of Constantinople, when he considered him guilty of uncanonical procedure, he assumed a distinctly authoritative attitude. On his own authority he declared null and void (as his predecessor Pelagius II. had done) the synod at which the title of œcumenical bishop had been conferred on the Constantinopolitan patriarch (*Lib.* V., *Epp* 18, 21); he entertained the appeal to himself of the two presbyters John and Athanasius, reversed their condemnation by the patriarch of Constantinople, and ordered their restitution (*Lib.* VI., *Epp.* 14, 15, 16, 17, &c.); and in a letter to John of Syracuse he says, "Nam de Constantinopolitana ecclesia quod dicunt, quis eam dubitet sedi apostolicæ esse subjectam?" (*Lib.* IX., *Ep* 12.) For the See of Constantinople, though now patriarchal, was not even an ancient *sedes apostolica:* its bishop had indeed been assigned honorary rank (τὰ πρεσβεῖα τῆς τιμῆς) next after the bishop of Rome by the general Council of Constantinople (A.D. 381), but this only on the political ground of Constantinople being new Rome: patriarchal jurisdiction had indeed been confirmed to it over the Metropolitans of the Pontic, Arian, and Thracian dioceses by the 28th Canon of the Council of Chalcedon (A.D. 451); but this Canon had been repudiated at the time by Pope Leo of Rome. Hence the popes were ever peculiarly jealous of any new assumption, or uncanonical proceedings, on the part of the Constantinopolitan See, the ascendancy of which signified to them imperial domination rather than primitive ecclesiastical order or prerogative: and hence it is not to be wondered at that on the assumption of a title that seemed to imply universal supremacy Gregory was at once in arms, and asserted strongly all the authority that he believed to be inherent in his own Apostolic See. Such assertion, however, had no immediate effect in the absence of power to enforce it: it was disregarded at Constantinople: the Emperor Mauricius, who alone could have given practical effect to it, was appealed to by Gregory in vain; and, though Phocas, who succeeded him, is said to have issued a decree that "the Apostolic See of St. Peter, that is the Roman Church, should be the head of all Churches" (*Anastasius Bibliothec.*), yet it is an historical fact that neither Constantinople nor the Churches of the East generally, ever submitted to the claims of the Roman See.

Early life of Gregory.

There is no record of the year of Pope Gregory's birth. It was probably about A.D. 540, some ten years after Benedict of Nursia had founded the Benedictine order. He was well born, his father Gordianus being a wealthy Roman of senatorial rank, bearing the title of "Regionarius," which denoted some office of dignity. He received the education usual with young Romans of his rank in life, and is said to have been an apt scholar. The historian Gregory of Tours, who was his contemporary, states that in grammar, rhetoric, and logic he was considered second to none in Rome; and he also studied law. Such education, however, fell somewhat short of what we should now call a liberal one, leaving him, as it did, entirely unacquainted with any language but his own, and so a stranger to all Greek literature; with no apparent taste, that he anywhere displays in his writings, for art, poetry, or philosophy; and with scanty historical knowledge. He was, with regard to intellectual equipment, an educated Roman gentleman of his day, and no more; regarding the Roman nation as paramount in the world, and not aspiring beyond the studies thought sufficient for Roman citizens of rank, at a time when study of Greek literature and scientific culture had died out at Rome. In later life also, when he had time to devote himself to study and contemplation, he confined himself, with a purely devotional purpose, to Holy Scripture, in which (though of course only in the Latin version) he was thoroughly versed, or to the orthodox Latin Fathers, St. Augustine being his favourite. His condemnation of the study of classical heathen literature by Christians, appears strikingly in his letter to Desiderius (*Lib.* XI., *Ep.* 54). Still his early education, though thus limited, fitted him well for dealing with practical matters, for grasping the bearings of subjects that came before him, and for expressing himself clearly and often forcibly thereon; though his style is not free from the artificiality that was probably encouraged by the rhetorical training of his day. He was intended for, and at first pursued, secular occupations suitable to his rank in life; and at an unusually early age (certainly before 573, when he would be little more than 30 years of age) he was appointed by the Emperor Justin II. to the dignified office of *Prætor Urbanus*. In this early period he does not appear to have been distinguished by any peculiar saintliness of practice or demeanour. He dressed, at any rate, conformably to his rank: for Gregory of Tours speaks of the striking contrast of the monastic garb which he afterwards assumed with the silk attire, the sparkling gems, and the purple-striped trabea, with which he had formerly paced the streets of Rome. But, on the other hand, there is not the least reason to suppose that he had ever been loose or irreligious.

He had been religiously brought up. His father Gordianus is said to have been himself a religious man: his mother Silvia (who lived in ascetic seclusion after her husband's death), and the sisters of Gordianus, Tarsilla and Æmiliana (who lived in their own house as dedicated virgins), have obtained a place in the calendar of saints: and his biographer, John the Deacon, speaks of his early training having been that of a saint among saints. He never, in his own writings, alludes to any crisis in his early life at which he had become convinced of sin, saying rather (as in one of his letters) that, while living in the world, he had tried to live to God also, but had found it hard. But on the death of his father (the date of which is not known) his religious aspirations took a decided form; he kept but a small part of the patrimony that came to him, employing the rest in charitable uses, and especially in founding monasteries, of which he endowed six in Sicily, and one, dedicated to St. Andrew, on the site of his own house near the Church of St. John and St. Paul on the Cælian, "ad clivum Scauri" which he himself entered as a monk, and of which he was eventually elected abbot. The religious views of his age, in which he fully shared, would of necessity suggest to him the monastic life as the highest form of saintliness; and he may have been especially moved by the recent example of St. Benedict of Nursia, whom he greatly admired, and of whom he has left us in his Dialogues many interesting records. In the ardour of his devotion, his life in the monastery appears to have been ascetic to an extreme degree. He is said by his biographer to have been fed on raw vegetables (*crudo legumine*), supplied to him by his mother, who had become a recluse in a neighbouring cell; and his fasts made him continually ill, and endangered his life. He tells us himself in his Dialogues of one Holy Week towards the end of which he fainted from exhaustion, and was hardly kept alive: but before losing consciousness, being shocked at the idea of breaking his fast before Easter Day, he had requested the prayers of a very holy monk called Eleutherius; and the result was that, returning to consciousness, he remembered nothing of his previous pangs, felt no longer any craving for food, and could have continued his fast a day longer than was required. (*Dialog.*, *Lib.* iii. c. 33.) Such was the idea then entertained, and by him shared, of the way of attaining to the highest holiness. However he survived all, though the very weak health of which in his subsequent life he continually complains may have been due in part to such extreme self-discipline. Nor did he, it is said, relax his habits of study and prayer in consequence of the debility induced by his asceticism. It seems not to have precluded even energetic action of a practical kind. For it was at this period of his life that, according to John the Deacon his biographer, the well-known incident occurred of his seeing the English youths in the Roman slave-market, and obtaining the leave of pope Benedict I. to undertake a missionary enterprise for the conversion of the Angli, on an expedition for which purpose he had already set forth when the pope, moved by the remonstrances of the Roman people, recalled him to Rome.

Having thus become a devout monk, he remained one in heart throughout his life. His habits of life were, as far as they could be, still monastic while he sat upon the papal chair; and he never lost, and often gave expression to, his ardent longing for a return to monastic seclusion, as alone allowing closeness to God, as well as peace and happiness. See, for instance, what he says on this subject soon after his accession to the Emperor's sister Theoctista (*Epp.*, *Lib.* I., *Ep.* 5), or, after longer experience, to his old friend Leander of Seville (*Lib.* IX., *Ep.* 121).

But he was not allowed to enjoy for long the seclusion he so much desired; being summoned from his monastery by the pope to be ordained one of the seven deacons of Rome, and afterwards sent to Constantinople to be the pope's *apocrisiarius* (or *responsalis*) at the imperial court. There is some doubt as to which pope it was that thus ordained and commissioned him. From a combination of what is said by his biographers, Paul the Deacon and John the Deacon respectively, it seems most probable that it was Pope Benedict I. who summoned him from his monastery and ordained him, perhaps with the view of sending him to Constantinople, and that it was Pelagius II. (who succeeded Benedict A.D. 578) under whom he was actually sent. The office of *apocrisiarius* was usually filled by a deacon; and hence it is not unlikely that his employment in that office had been in view from the first, when he was called from his monastery and ordained. The popes at this time were in special need of an able representative at Constantinople for procuring, if possible, some effective aid against the Lombards, the Exarch at Ravenna having been appealed to in vain. Gregory remained at Constantinople for several years, probably from A.D. 578 to A.D. 585, first under the Emperor Tiberius, and then under Mauricius, who succeeded to the Empire A.D. 582. There is no extant record of instructions sent to him from Rome till A.D. 584, when Pope Pelagius wrote to him, representing the miserable state of Italy under the Lombards, the imminent danger of Rome, and the inaction of the Exarch, and directing him to press the Emperor for succour. He also desired him to send back to Rome the monk Maximianus, who, together with other monks of his monastery, had accompanied Gregory to Constantinople. This, his official residence in the imperial city, could not fail to be of advantage to him in the way of preparation for his subsequent position, as giving him a practical knowledge of the state of parties there, the ways of the court, and the conduct of political affairs. He also made friends of position and influence there, with whom he afterwards corresponded; among whom may be named Theoctista, the Emperor's sister, who had charge of the imperial children, Narses a patrician, Theodorus, physician to the Emperor, Gregoria, lady of the bedchamber to the Empress, and two patrician ladies, Clementina and Rusticiana. All these were religious persons, over whom he had gained influence, which he did not allow to die. He also formed at this time the intimate acquaintance of Leander, Bishop of Seville, who happened to be sojourning in Constantinople, and to whom he wrote afterwards very affectionate letters. It was at his instigation that he began, while at Constantinople, the *Magna Moralia*, or Exposition of the Book of Job, which he also dedicated to him in its completed form (*Moral. Libri.*, *Epist. Missoria*, c. 1; *Epp.*, *Lib.* V.

Ep. 49). For he found time from secular business for devotion and study with the monks who had followed him from Rome, including his particular friend Maximianus, as has been already mentioned.

"By their example (he writes in his Introduction to the *Magna Moralia*, above referred to) I was bound, as it were by the cable of an anchor, when tossing in the incessant buffeting of secular affairs, to the placid shore of prayer. For to their society, as to the bosom of a most safe harbour, I fled for escape from the rollings and the billows of earthly action; and, though that ministry had torn me from the monastery, and cut me off by the sword of its occupation from my former life of quiet, yet among them, through the converse of studious reading, the aspiration of daily compunction gave me life." He was engaged also at one time in a long dispute with Eutychius, the Constantinopolitan patriarch, who had written a treatise on the nature of the body after the resurrection, maintaining that it would be impalpable, and more subtle than air. Gregory maintained its palpability, alleging in proof that of the risen body of Christ. The Emperor Tiberius at length took cognizance of the dispute, and decided it in favour of Gregory, ordering the book of Eutychius to be burnt. The disputants are said to have been so exhausted by the long controversy that both had to take to their beds at its close (*Joan. Diac.*, *Lib.* I., c. 28, 29).

Gregory was at length (probably A.D. 585) allowed by Pelagius to return to Rome and re-enter his beloved monastery; and it was now probably that he was elected to be its abbot. But Pelagius appears still to have made use of him, a letter from that pope to Elias bishop of Aquileia on the subject of "The Three Chapters" being attributed by Paul the Deacon to the pen of Gregory (*De gestis Longobard.*, *Lib.* III.).

That period of peace, lasting some five years, Gregory constantly refers to, and doubtless with complete sincerity, as the happiest part of his life. It was interrupted by the death of Pelagius II., who fell a victim to an epidemic disease then raging on the 8th of February, A.D. 590, when we are informed that the whole clergy and people of Rome concurred in electing Gregory to the popedom, as the only man for the place at that time of peculiar trial. In addition to the general distress and alarm caused by the advancing Lombards, the Tiber had overflowed its banks, destroying property and stores of corn, famine was feared, and fatal disease prevailed. Men's hearts were failing them for fear, and for looking after those things that were coming on the earth. Gregory himself often speaks of the signs of the time as betokening the coming end of all things; and in one of his letters he compares Rome to an old and shattered ship, letting in the waves on all sides, tossed by a daily storm, its planks rotten and sounding of wreck. If any one could pilot the ship through the storm, there seems to have been a general feeling that the man was Gregory. He was most unwilling to undertake the task. When an embassy was sent to Constantinople for obtaining the Emperor's confirmation of the election, he sent at the same time a letter imploring him to withhold it. But the letter was intercepted by the prefect of the city, and another sent in its place, entreating confirmation. Meanwhile Gregory employed himself in preaching to the people, and calling them to repentance, in view of so many symptoms of the wrath of God. He instituted at this time the "Septiform Litany," to be chanted through the streets of the city by seven companies—of clergy, of laymen, of monks, of nuns, of married women, of widows, and of children and paupers—who, setting out from different churches, were to meet for common supplication. It was at the close of one such procession that the vision (not mentioned by any contemporaries, or by Bede) was afterwards said to have been seen, to which the name of the Castle of St. Angelo is attributed; the story being that, on approaching the basilica of St. Peter on the Vatican, Gregory saw above the monument of Hadrian an angel sheathing his sword in token that the plague was stayed. At length, the Emperor's confirmation of his election having arrived at Rome, he is said to have fled in disguise from the city, and hid himself in a forest cave, to have been pursued and discovered by means of a pillar of light that disclosed his hiding-place, to have been brought back to the city in triumph, conducted to the church of St. Peter, and there at once ordained, on the 3rd of September, A.D. 590 (*Paul. Diac.*, c. 13; *Joan. Diac.*, I. 44).

The four Eastern patriarchs at this time, to whom, according to custom, he sent letters immediately after his accession containing his confession of faith, were John (known as Jejunator, or the Faster) of Constantinople, Eulogius of Alexandria, Gregory of Antioch, and John of Jerusalem; to whom is added in the address at the head of the circular letter, "Anastasius, ex-patriarch of Antioch," who was indeed the true patriarch, having been deposed by the mere secular authority of the Emperor, Justin II. (*Evagr. H. E.*, V. 5). Consequently Gregory, though not venturing to ignore the patriarch in possession, addressed the deposed one also in his circular, and wrote him also separate letters, in which he recognized him as the rightful patriarch, and undertook to intercede with the Emperor Maurice in his behalf (I. 8, 25, 26). On the restoration of Anastasius to his See (A.D. 593) by the Emperor on the death of the interloper, Gregory wrote him a warm congratulatory letter (V. 39).

Of the other patriarchs John of Constantinople was succeeded during Gregory's pontificate (A.D. 596) by Cyriacus, and John of Jerusalem by Amos, and he (A.D. 600 or 601) by Isacius (see XI. 46). But the patriarchs of Jerusalem, though their position was recognized, were not at that time of any great influence or importance.

A brief summary may now suitably be given of some leading events of Gregory's pontificate in the order suggested by the successive Books of his Epistles, which correspond to the years of his reign. His biographer John the Deacon says of him that, having been pope for a little more than thirteen and a half years, he left in the archives (*in scrinio*) as many books of Epistles as he had reigned years, the last, or 14th, book being left incomplete because of his not having completed the 14th year of his reign (*Joan. Diac. Vit. S. Greg.*, IV. 71). Accordingly the Benedictine Editors of his works have arranged his extant epistles, according to what, to the best of their judgment, they conceived to have been the original order, in 14 books, answering to the successive years of his pontificate. Previous editions had given them in 12 books only, and many of them evidently placed wrongly in order of time. (*See Patrologiæ Tomus LXXV. Sancti Gregorii magni; Præfatio in Epistolas.*) Hence, supposing the Benedictine arrangement to be on the whole correct, we have in the successive books as now arranged reference to the historical events of the successive years to which the books are assigned. The dates given to the books are according to the Roman method of Indictions, one Indiction being a period of 15 years, and the successive years of each of such periods being called the 1st, 2nd, 3rd year of the Indiction, or the 1st, 2nd, 3rd Indiction, and so on to the 15th. Each Indiction year began with September; and Gregory, having been ordained on the 3rd of September, A.D. 590, which was the commencement of the 9th year of the then Indiction, the date of the first book of the epistles, corresponding to the first year of his reign, is given as Indiction IX.

Book I. Indiction IX. (A.D. 590-1.)

This first book introduces us at once to a view of the new pope's immediate vigilance and activity in affairs secular and sacred that demanded his attention.

Pontificate of Gregory.

(1.) We find him providing without delay for the efficient and just management of the patrimony of St. Peter, which has been spoken of above; and this especially in Sicily, whither (as has been also said above) he sent Peter the subdeacon as his agent with large powers. To him also he gave charge to keep him fully informed of all that was going on, and further committed to him ecclesiastical jurisdiction over the bishops of the island, directing him among other things to convene synods annually, and requiring the bishops to submit to his control (*Ep.* 1). This, however, seems to have been only a temporary arrangement, since in the following year he appointed Maximian, bishop of Syracuse, who had been a monk with himself and his peculiar friend in the Monastery of St. Andrew, to act as his vicar in the island. Such vicarial jurisdiction, however, was only conferred on Maximian personally, as was specified at the time (*Lib.* II., *Ep.* 7), and was not continued to his successor, though he also received the *pallium.* [It may be here observed that this decoration, in the time of Gregory, though usually conferred on Metropolitans, did not of necessity imply metropolitan jurisdiction. Cf. *Epp.*, *Lib.* IX., *Note to Ep.* 11.] At a later date we find Romanus the *Defensor*, who had been made *Rector patrimonii* in Sicily, charged apparently with an oversight of the churches similar to what had been entrusted to Peter (*Lib* IX., *Ep.* 18; *Lib.* XI., *Ep.* 37). (2) We find him also, through his commissioned subdeacons, at once careful to correct the irregularities of monks in Campania, Sicily, Corsica, and other smaller islands; such as their migrating from monastery to monastery, wandering about exempt from rule, and even taking to themselves wives, or having women resident in the same buildings with themselves (*Epp.* 41, 42, 50, 51, 52). (3.) Frequent directions are given for charitable donations to such as needed them (e.g. *Epp.* 18, 24, 39); and his *apocrisiarius* at Constantinople is charged to move the Emperors in behalf of the natives of Sardinia, who were said to be oppressed illegally by the duke of the island (*Ep.* 49). (4.) For the due election of bishops to vacant Sees, and the visitation of Sees during vacancy, in the case of Churches under his acknowledged jurisdiction, he gives careful orders, as e.g. in the case of Ariminum (*Epp.* 57, 58), of Menavia in Umbria (*Ep.* 81), and Saona in Corsica (*Ep.* 78). The canonical rule, which he was careful to observe, was to leave the people of the place (clergy, nobles, and commonalty) free to elect their own bishop; but still reserving to himself power to reject any unfit person. Thus, in one case, he rejects one Ocleatinus as a candidate for the See of Ariminum (*Epp.* 57, 58), and in another, in consequence of delay on the part of the electors, he departs from his usual practice by himself appointing a bishop of Saona (*Ep* 80). Over remiss or criminal bishops, as soon as he hears of their defaults—whereof, as of other things, he seems to have been speedily informed by his agents—he loses no time in bringing his authority to bear. It was in this, his first year, that he began a long continued correspondence with and with respect to Januarius, Bishop of Cagliari in Sardinia, who appears to have been a frivolous old man of very doubtful character (see *Ep.* 62, and *reff.*). Also with and with respect to Natalis, the convivial bishop of Salona in Western Illyricum, with reference both to his own habits and to his quarrel with the archdeacon Honoratus (see *Ep.* 19, and note with *reff.*). (5.) There will be found also in this first book letters of sympathy and friendship, such as he never ceased to write, some of which are to pious ladies of rank, including one to Theoctista, the Emperor's sister (*Ep.* 5), which is further interesting as containing a specimen of his usual way of interpreting Holy Scripture allegorically. Peculiarly charming as illustrative of his warm and abiding friendship is his long continued correspondence, begun in this year, with or with regard to Venantius, who had relinquished monastic for married life (see *Ep.* 34, and *note* with *reff.*). (6.) To be noted also in this Book, are his ineffectual attempts, though apparently supported by the Emperor, to bring the Istrian bishops to submission in the matter of the "Three Chapters" (see *Ep.* 16, and *notes*), and his invoking of the secular arm for suppression of what remained of the Donatist schism in Africa (see *Ep.* 74, and *notes*). (7.) Lastly, we find, in *Ep.* 43 to Leander of Seville, the first intimation of the important event of the conversion to Catholicity of Reccared, the Visigothic King of Spain.

Most, if not all, of the subjects above noted, or the like, recur frequently in subsequent years. It may suffice to have drawn attention to them here, noting only in connexion with the following books any new subjects that appear of special interest.

Book II. Indiction X. (A.D. 591-2.)

(1.) We meet in this book with the first allusion to the operations of the Lombards in Italy (*Ep.* 3); and hence this may be a suitable place for giving a brief sketch of Gregory's dealings with regard to them in the light thrown on the subject by his epistles. The Lombard King, Agilulf (as has been said above, p. vii.), had his headquarters at Ticinum (*Pavia*), the extensive dukedoms of Beneventum and Spoletum in Southern Italy being in the possession of his dukes. Early in the year before us (the 10th Indiction), it appears that Ariulf, duke of Spoletum, was believed to be marching either towards Ravenna or Rome. (See *Ep.* 3, which is dated in the *Collection* of Paul the Deacon and in *Cod. Colbert.* "die V. Kalend. Octob. Indict. 10," i.e. 27 Sept., A.D. 591.) Later in the same Indiction Gregory becomes aware of his approach, and addresses letters (*Epp.* 29, 30) to officers in command of the imperial forces with the purpose of urging them to meet the impending danger. Subsequently in the same year it appears from a letter to the Bishop of Ravenna (*Ep.* 46) that Ariulf was already besieging Rome. Gregory in this letter gives a sad account of the savagery of the besieger outside the walls, his own illness and depression, and the difficulties he had to contend with. He complains, in this as in other letters, of the conduct of Romanus Patricius, the Exarch at Ravenna, who would neither send aid nor sanction terms of peace. Further, troops had, he says, been withdrawn from Rome before the siege, so as to leave it insufficiently defended; and the soldiers of a legion that remained there, not receiving their pay, had refused to man the walls. In these straits Gregory appears at length to have come to terms with Ariulf on his own responsibility; for doing which he was afterwards blamed and reproached as having been duped by Ariulf. (See *Lib.* V., *Ep.* 40.) The peace, however, was not of long duration. The Exarch (probably soon afterwards, though the date is not clear) marched himself to Rome, and on his return seized certain cities—Satrium, Polimartium, Horta, Tudertua, Ameria, Perusia, Luceoli, and others—which had been ceded to the Lombards under treaty—perhaps that which Gregory himself had made. (Paul. Diac. *De gestis Longobard*, IV. 8. Cf *Epp.*, *Lib.* V., *Ep.* 40.) Agilulf, the Lombard King, incensed by this breach of faith, now came with an army from Ticinum, recaptured Perusia, and again besieged Rome. In a letter addressed some time afterwards to the Emperor (*Lib.* V., *Ep.* 40), Gregory gives a lamentable account of the misery that had ensued. Since the departure of Ariulf, he says, "troops had still further been withdrawn from the city for the fruitless defence of Perusia, the supply of corn had failed, while from the walls they saw Romans led away with ropes round their necks like dogs to be sold in France." He, with the præfect of the city, also called Gregory, and the military commander Castorius, had done all they could under extreme difficulty to guard the walls, for which he complains they afterwards got no thanks, but rather blame for neglect of duty in letting the corn run short. He himself, when the besiegers arrived, had been delivering his well-known course of homilies on Ezekiel, which he had been obliged to break off abruptly. The last ends thus:—"Let no one blame me if henceforth I cease my speaking, since, as you all see, our tribulations have increased; we are surrounded on all sides by swords; on all sides we are afraid for imminent danger of death. Some return to us with their hands cut off; others are reported to us as taken captive or slain. I am now forced to withhold my tongue from exposition, for my soul is weary of life." How long this siege lasted, or on what terms of agreement Agilulf at length departed, we are not told. Whatever arrangement was made, it was evidently due to Gregory alone. Paul the Deacon says only (*De gest. Longob.*, IV. 8), "that King Agilulf, matters being arranged, returned to Ticinum;" and adds, "and not long afterwards, at the suggestion especially of his wife Queen Theodelinda, as the blessed Gregory

The Lombards.

often admonished her in his letters, he concluded a most firm peace with the same most holy Pope Gregory, and with the Romans." But it is plain from epistles written subsequently that it was not till some years later that anything like a settled truce was concluded: for it was not till the second indiction, i.e. A.D. 598-9 (if the letters are rightly arranged, as they appear to be, by the Benedictine editors), that we find letters of thanks from Gregory to King Agilulf for peace at length concluded, and to Theodelinda for her good offices (*Lib.* IX., *Epp.* 42, 43). In the meantime, as appears from various letters, Gregory continued to urge the Emperor or the Exarch to arrange terms of peace, for which he asserts, though he was not believed, that Agilulf was prepared. He declares also that he could have himself made a separate peace with him so as to secure himself and Rome; but that he had been unwilling to do so, having the welfare of the whole republic at heart. He implies that the Exarch and his adherents were but serving their own ends in opposing terms of peace, their own exactions and oppressions during the continuance of hostilities being even more intolerable than the ravages of the Lombards (see *Lib.* V., *Epp.* 40, 42). In an urgent letter to the Empress Constantina he complains also of the cruel oppression of the natives of Sicily and Corsica under colour of raising funds for the war, and begs her to plead with the Emperor, for his own soul's sake as well as for real advantage to the republic, against the use of such iniquitous means (*Lib.* V., *Ep.* 41). These letters (if rightly placed) were written in the 13th Indiction (A.D. 394-5), and in the next we find a letter to one Secundus at Ravenna, in which negotiations with Agilulf with a view to peace are spoken of as still going on, which this Secundus is urged to further (*Lib.* VI., *Ep.* 30). But it was not, as has been already said, till the 2nd Indiction (A.D. 598—9) that any definite terms appear to have been agreed to (see *Lib.* IX., *Epp.* 4, 6, 42, 43, 98): and then, it seems, only for a limited time (see *Lib* X., *Ep.* 37;—"indicantes cum Langobardorum rege *usque ad mensem Martiam futuræ quartæ indictionis* de pace, propitiante Domino, convenisse"); and even so, Gregory does not appear to have felt secure: for in a letter written at this time to Januarius, bishop of Cagliari in Sardinia, alluding to the peace that had been made, he warns him to guard the island well in view still of possible danger from the Lombards (*Lib.* IX., *Ep.* 6. Cf. also *Lib.* X., *Ep.* 37). After the expiration of this truce (which, as has been seen, was from some time in the 2nd Indiction (588-9) to March in the 4th Indiction (A.D. 601), probably for two years), hostilities having again broken out, a second truce was concluded in September, A.D. 603, as appears from Paul the Deacon (*De gest. Longob.*, IV. 29), until April, A.D. 605: and that Gregory had been instrumental in procuring it through the influence of Queen Theodelinda on her husband, may be concluded from what he says in the last letter he addressed to her, not long before his death (*Lib.* XIV., *Ep.* 12).

We thus see how indefatigably active Gregory was in the political sphere of things. Lasting peace or security for Italy at that trying time it was beyond the power of man to bring about: but whatever was done towards mitigation of distress, and temporary cessation of hostilities, or approaches to better understanding with the Lombard King, appears plainly to have been due to Gregory. Nor should we leave out of sight his provision for the redemption of captives taken in war, whether out of ecclesiastical funds or others entrusted to him for the purpose, or by the sale, which he cordially sanctioned, of the sacred vessels of churches (IV. 17, 31; VII. 13, 26, 28, 38; IX. 17, &c.).

(2.) Attention may be directed to epistles 22, 23 in this book in connexion with the spiritual jurisdiction exercised by Rome over East as well as West Illyricum.

(3.) We may observe also the important import of epistle 41, with regard to the exemption of monasteries from episcopal control by Gregory. The constitutions, *De privelegiis monasteriorum*, therein contained were afterwards promulged by a council under him (called *Conciliæ Romanum III., sive Lateranense*) in April, A.D. 601, being signed by 20 bishops, 14 presbyters, and 3 or 4 deacons.

Book III. Indiction XI. (A.D. 592-3).

The following notable incidents are referred to in this Book:—

(1.) Two instances of the authority exercised (as above said) over the Illyrian Churches being, for a time at least, resisted or disregarded, and of the support of the Emperor being sought, and more or less obtained, in such resistance or disregard The first instance was in the case of Adrian, bishop of Thebæ Phthioticæ in Eastern Illyricum, as to which see note to *Ep.* 6. The second and more serious one (which has been already alluded to) was in the case of Maximus, elected and consecrated bishop of Salona in Western Illyricum, in defiance of Gregory's prohibition and excommunication. In this case the resistance was pertinacious and long continued, and it was not till after seven years that the matter was compromised and communion restored. A summary of the proceedings, with reference to all the epistles bearing on the case, will be found in a note to *Ep.* 47.

(2.) As illustrative of the relations between Rome and Constantinople, the case of John of Chalcedon and Athanasius of Isauria, whose appeal to the Roman See was entertained by Gregory. See note to *Lib.* III., *Ep.* 53.

(3.) The beginning of remonstrances, continued through two years, with the metropolitan bishops of Ravenna with regard to their assumption of dignity above that of other metropolitans, expressed especially by their use of the pallium on other occasions than during Mass. From the letters on this subject we may detect, as has been said above, some jealousy at the seat of the Exarch of the authoritative claims of the Roman See. See *Lib.* III., *Ep.* 56, with note and *reff.*

(4.) The conduct of Gregory, at once outspoken and submissive to imperial edicts, with respect to the recent prohibition by the Emperor of soldiers becoming monks. See *Ep.* 65, note and *reff.* The incident illustrates well Gregory's habitual deference to the authority of the state, except in matters purely spiritual.

(5.) His requirement of Jews not being allowed to obtain or keep possession of Christian slaves. There are other letters on this subject, viz. IV. 9, 21; VI. 32; VII. 24; IX. 36, 110. Even slaves already in the lawful possession of Jews, on declaring their desire to become Christians, were to be thenceforth free without any compensation to their owners; only that pagans bought by Jews simply with a view to sale might, on their declaring such desire, be sold by such Jews within three months after their purchase of them; but only to Christian masters. It may be here observed that, though such provisions seem hard upon Jewish owners, and though Jews were legally prohibited from proselytising or building new synagogues, yet we find Gregory in other respects very tender towards them, repeatedly forbidding their being at all molested in the synagogues they had, or being in any way persecuted into accepting baptism (I. 10, 35, 47; VIII. 25; IX. 6, 55; XIII. 12). Those on the estates of the Church might indeed be drawn towards Christianity by the prospect of reduced rents (II. 32, V. 8), but all compulsory conversion of them is denounced as wrong and unavailing (e.g. I. 47). On the other hand, with some apparent inconsistency, pagan peasants on the estates might be compelled to conform by intolerable exactions being laid upon them in case of their refusal (IV. 26), and idolaters or diviners were to be reclaimed, if freemen, by imprisonment, or, if slaves, by stripes and torments (IX. 65).

Book IV. Indiction XII. (A.D. 593-4).

In this book we may note:

(1.) The continued refusal of many at least of the bishops in Liguria, as well as in Istria and Venetia, to assent to the condemnation of the "Three Chapters" by the fifth Council, and with them of Theodelinda, the Catholic Lombard queen. See *Ep.* 2 and notes, with *Epp.* 3, 4, 38, 39.

(2.) The case of Paul, a bishop in Numidia, as indicating the continuance of disinclination to submit fully to the Roman See in the African provinces. See *Ep.* 34, with note. Cf. also *Ep.* 7, and IX. 58, 59.

(3.) The directions given by Gregory, and, as thereby shewn, the custom of the Church, with regard to the anointing of the baptized (*Ep.* 9, and *Ep.* 26, with note); and also his belief in the miraculous efficacy of the relics of saints, shewn in many other Epistles, but especially in *Ep.* 30 of this book.

Book V. Indiction XIII. (A.D. 594-5).

(1.) This year is memorable for the commencement of Gregory's earnest protest, continued through his subsequent life, against the title of Œcumenical, or Universal, Bishop (or Patriarch) assumed by the Patriarch of Constantinople. The title itself was not a new one. It appears to have been occasionally given during the fifth century as a title of honour to patriarchs generally, the first known instance being when Olympius Episc. Evazensis gave it to Dioscorus at Concil. Ephes. ii. (*Giesler's Eccles. Hist.* 2nd Period, 1st Division, Ch. iii., § 93, note 20; with *ref.* to Mansi, vi. 855). Justinian also had styled the patriarch of Constantinople "Œcumenical Patriarch" (Cod. i. 1, 7; Novell. iii., v., vi., vii., xvi., xiii.). The first known protest against it from Rome was on its assumption, A.D. 587[1], by John Jejunator at a synod at Constantinople, when Gregory's predecessor, Pelagius II., had disallowed the acts of the synod in consequence, and had withdrawn his apocrisiarius from communion with the patriarch (*Epp.* V. 18, 43; IX. 68). Gregory himself also had, as appears from the epistles above referred to, remonstrated through his representatives at Constantinople with the patriarch on the subject, and had received a letter from the emperor desiring him to let the matter rest (V. 19). But he was now provoked to resolute action by having received a communication from the patriarch in reference to the case of John the Presbyter, wherein the title of "Œcumenical Patriarch" was repeatedly assumed (*ib.*). The peculiar warmth of feeling and strength of language that mark his lengthened correspondence on the subject, are accounted for not only by the old jealousy felt at Rome (which has been noticed above) of any claim of Constantinople, in mere virtue of being the imperial city, to the prerogatives of an ancient Apostolic See, but also by the title being viewed as not being one of honour only, but as meaning really assumption of spiritual authority over the Church at large. Such assumption could only rest on the fact of Constantinople having come to be the imperial city: it had neither a shew of divine right, nor Apostolic tradition, nor canonical authority to go on. Rome, though for himself also Gregory earnestly disclaimed the title of Universal Bishop, was at any rate an ancient apostolic See, and viewed at that time generally as representing the authority of the Prince of the Apostles, to whom Christ himself had given the keys. But no such ancient prestige or apostolical commission could possibly be claimed for Constantinople: its ascendency over the whole Church would simply mean imperialism, and imperial domination over the whole Church would in fact have been likely to be its practical result: and thus, in his determined protest, Gregory might well feel himself to be contending for heavenly as against earthly jurisdiction, for Christ as against the world, for God as against Cæsar.

Title of Universal Bishop.

The following is a summary of the correspondence that ensued in this and following years:—

In this year Gregory despatched five letters to Sabinianus, his apocrisiarius at Con-

[1] That this was the date may be inferred from Gregory, in Epistle XLIII. of this fifth book, speaking of the synod having been held eight years ago.

stantinople :—1. A long one to be delivered to John Jejunator, the Patriarch (*Ep.* 18), dated Kal. Jan. Indict. 13 (i.e. Jany., A.D. 595), containing earnest remonstrances against pride in general, and against this display of it in particular, and expressing the hope that stronger measures may not be needed. 2. A private one to Sabinianus (*Ep.* 19), in a bitter tone against the patriarch, attributing the mildness of the letter now addressed to the latter to the Emperor's orders, but promising another by and by, such as would not be relished. 3. A long one to the Emperor Maurice (*Ep.* 20), earnestly desiring him to disallow the title, and, if necessary, coerce the patriarch to compliance. While acknowledging the Emperor's pious desire to promote peace among the Bishops, he contends that the only means to this end was to quell the assumption of the patriarch, the inconsistency of which with his ascetic habits, and his affectation of humility, are pointed out ironically. 4. Another to the Empress Constantina (*Ep.* 21), whose good disposition towards the Roman See he had heard of from Sabinianus. His object is to enlist her influence with the Emperor and his sons in the matter; and it is observable how, in addressing her, he speaks in a way he does not venture on to the Emperor, of the peril to her own soul if St. Peter should be dishonoured, to whom the power of binding and loosing had been given. 5. A long one to be transmitted through Sabinianus to the patriarchs of Alexandria and Antioch (*Ep.* 43), with the purpose of inducing them to join him in his protest. He represents the offensive title as an infringement on the rights and dignity of all patriarchs, not claiming in this letter any peculiar authority for the Roman patriarchate above the rest. He bids them not be afraid of the Emperor in the event, which he hopes will not ensue, of his continuing to support the Constantinopolitan patriarch, but to be ready to face all consequences.

In the following year (*Lib.* VI., *Indict.* XIV., i.e. A D. 595-6) we find an epistle, dated August (i.e. August, A.D. 596), to Eulogius, the patriarch of Alexandria only (*Ep.* 60), expressing surprise that the latter, in a letter received from him had not even alluded to the subject of the former epistle which had been addressed to the two patriarchs. It seems as if Eulogius had either been afraid to provoke the emperor's displeasure, or had attached less importance to the title than did Gregory himself, and so had maintained a discreet silence. In this epistle Gregory expresses the view, which has been alluded to above, of the sees of Rome and Alexandria being both in a sense St. Peter's, in virtue of the latter having been founded by St. Mark, whom St. Peter had sent. He had previously, in a letter to Anastasius of Antioch (V. 39), intimated a similar view of the See of Antioch being also in a certain sense St. Peter's; and in a subsequent letter to Eulogius (VII. 40) he sets forth more distinctly and at length his noteworthy position of all the three patriarchal Sees of Rome, Antioch, and Alexandria, having together the prerogatives of St. Peter's See.

In the following year (*Indict.* XV., A.D. 596-7) John Jejunator died, and was succeeded by Cyriacus, to whom Gregory wrote on receiving his synodical letter, addressing him in a friendly tone (*Ep.* 4), but urging in the course of his letter the rejection of the offensive title. He wrote again (*Ep.* 31) especially on the subject, still courteously, but pressing the matter strongly. To the emperor we find two letters; the first (*Ep.* 6) approving of the appointment of Cyriacus, but without any allusion to the burning question; the second (*Ep.* 33), after receiving one from the emperor, in which the desire had been expressed that the emissaries of the new patriarch should be honourably received at Rome. To this request Gregory replies that he has so received them, and admitted them to communion with him, hoping for the best; but that his own representatives at Constantinople would by no means be allowed to communicate with Cyriacus, unless the title were renounced. The emperor had said that the matter was a frivolous one. "Yes (says Gregory) the title is indeed frivolous, but its meaning and its consequences are serious;" and he repeats his continual assertion that whosoever assumes it is the precursor of Antichrist. In this year also he continued his efforts to induce the patriarchs Anastasius and Eulogius to join him in his protest. Anastasius, it seems, had not, like Eulogius, ignored the subject in his reply to the letter that had been addressed to both, but had said that in his opinion the matter was of little moment and not worth making a disturbance about; at the same time addressing Gregory in flattering terms. Gregory, in his reply (*Ep.* 27), which is somewhat ironical, insists again. To Eulogius also he writes again (*Ep.* 40), deprecating the too deferential manner in which he had been addressed by this patriarch, and setting forth his view of the oneness of the three sees. The offensive title itself is not in this letter specifically referred to. There is also a second letter to the two patriarchs jointly, explaining what had been done so far since the accession of Cyriacus, and reiterating his protest against allowance of the title. In the succeeding year (*Lib.* VIII., *Indict.* I., A.D. 597-8) there is again a letter (*Ep.* 30) to Eulogius, who appears to have written a third time to Gregory, at length alluding to the title so far as to say that he did not now use proud titles in addressing certain persons, but still apparently not prepared to take any action. As if to make up for for such inaction, he had seemingly been profuse in his compliments to Gregory, using the expression, "as thou hast commanded," and calling him "Universal Pope." Such language Gregory, in reply, earnestly protests against, disclaiming for himself, as much as for any other bishop, the name of Universal. In the following year (*Lib.* IX., *Indict.* II., A.D. 598-9) we find two letters; one of which is an encyclical one (*Ep.* 68), to Eusebius of Thessalonica and other Eastern bishops, in view of a synod about to be held at Constantinople, warning them against being cajoled there into assenting to the title, and threatening them with excommunication in case of their complying. From the second letter assigned to this year, which is again to Eulogius (*Ep.* 78), it would seem that the synod at Constantinople had been held, and that Eulogius himself had been there, though what had been done does not appear. The letter is in reply to one which had been received with reference to a different subject from Eulogius; and Gregory complains that the latter had still said nothing about the most important subject of all, namely the title. He supposes Eulogius to be waiting till he himself shall take decided action; and he accounts for his own apparent delay by saying that he had been unwilling to be himself the immediate author of schism. It seems as if he had felt at a loss what to do. His remonstrances with Cyriacus and the emperor had been entirely unavailing; he had failed to move the two great Eastern patriarchs, or the bishops of the East generally, to take up the question; and he shrank from so serious a step as breaking off communion with the whole Eastern Church. And so matters appear to have rested. We find no further epistle on the subject till four years later (*Lib.* XIII., *Indict.* VI., A.D. 602-3), when in a short letter (*Ep.* 40) to Cyriacus, with whom he appears to be still in communion, he urges him once more to give up the title. There are in the same year two letters, and one in the previous one (XII. 50), as well as two (X., 35, 39) in the third indiction, to Eulogius, in which the subject is not alluded to.

The Church in Gaul.

(2) We observe in this year the sending of the pallium to Virgilius, bishop of Arles in Gaul, and with it his delegation (*Epp.* 53, 54, 55) as the Pope's Vicar in the Kingdom of Childebert. As has been said above (see p. xii.), the spiritual authority of Rome over the Gallican Churches was not disputed; and Gregory exercised it vigilantly by means of letters to bishops, and to royal personages, labouring among other things to move them to put down simony, clerical immorality, and other prevalent abuses, and to assemble synods under authority from Rome for the correction of crying evils. But, though we find no resistance to his spiritual authority, neither do we find any evidence of his appeals to the consciences of the potentates of Gaul having had much practical effect in the directions indicated. Doubtless in a difficult field of action he did what he could; nor need we doubt that the

authoritative voice from Rome was at any rate some check on violence and disorder, though the results may not be very apparent in history.

The main divisions of Gaul at this time were Austrasia on the Eastern side, including part of what is now Germany, Burgundy to the West and South, and the smaller Neustria on the North-west. The limits as well as the possession of these territories were continually changing during the contests between the descendants of Clovis, some or other of whom ruled the whole of Gaul; all now professing Catholic Christianity. In the Indiction now before us (*Indict.* XIII., A.D. 594-5), as is pointed out in a note to *Ep.* 53, Childebert II., then aged about 25, ruled by far the greatest part of Gaul; and hence the jurisdiction intended to be conferred on Virgilius, when the pallium was sent him, may be taken as equally extensive. We find no instance of spiritual authority so claimed being disputed in Gaul.

BOOK VI. INDICTION XIV. (A.D. 595-6).

The English Mission.

(1) This year is memorable for the mission of Augustine to England, the progress of which, as indicated by the epistles, may be summarized as follows. The missionaries having left Rome, probably in the early spring of the year 596, and proceeded as far as the South coast of France, and having there turned faint-hearted, Augustine himself returned to Rome for leave to relinquish the enterprize. Gregory sent him back to his companions with the letter, addressed to them, numbered *Ep.* 51 in this sixth book. It is dated X. Kal. Aug. Indict. 14, *i.e.* 23 July, A.D. 596. For a view of the circumstances see note to vi. 51. He was now charged (as he does not appear to have been when first sent forth) with various letters of commendation, intended to speed him on his journey: viz. to the bishops of Marseilles, of *Turni* (al. *Turon:—Tours?*), of Arles, Vienne and Autun, to Arigius, designated as Patrician of Gaul, to Theodebert and Theoderic, the two boy-kings of Austrasia and of Burgundy, and to their powerful grandmother Brunehild, who at this time ruled Austrasia as the guardian of Theodebert. The course of the missionaries, after leaving Marseilles, would naturally be up the valley of the Rhone, and so northward as far as Autun, most at least of the letters above named being such as might be delivered on the way. Thence to their place of embarcation for the Isle of Thanet we find no intimation of their route, except that, in passing through Neustria, they were well received and aided by Clotaire II. (nephew of Charibert, the deceased father of Bertha), who at that time ruled the country, having his capital at Soissons. This appears, though there is no extant letter of commendation on this occasion to Clotaire, from a subsequent letter to him (XI. 61).

The landing of the missionaries on the Isle of Thanet was, according to Bede, in the following year, A.D. 597 (*H. E.*, I. 25, V. 24). It must have been early in the year, so as to allow time for the events, to be next noticed, which took place before its close. The next allusion to the mission found in the Epistles is Gregory's exulting announcement to Eulogius, bishop of Alexandria, of its remarkable success, and of the baptism of more than ten thousand Angli as early as the Christmas of the same year, 597 (VIII. 30). The date is definitely given in the letter to Eulogius;—"in the solemnity of the Lord's Nativity which was kept *in this first indiction;*"—The first indiction being from September, 597, to September, 598. In the meantime, as appears from the same letter, Augustine had already been consecrated bishop. The letter says vaguely "a Germanis Episcopis": but, according to John the Deacon (*Vit. S. Greg.* II. 36), and Bede (*H. E.*, I. 27), it was to Virgilius, bishop of Arles, that Augustine had gone, as directed by Gregory, for consecration.

The next batch of Epistles throwing light on the progress of the mission (after two others, IX. 11 and 108, wherein Queen Brunehild and Syagrius Bishop of Autun are thanked for their attention to the missionaries on their progress) is in Book XI, and thus assigned to Indiction 4, i.e. A.D. 600-1, some three years after the aforesaid letter to Eulogius. It comprises fourteen Epistles, some of which bear their own dates, and others are shewn by their contents to have been written at the same time. It is true that the dates of the dated epistles vary in different MSS. with regard to the time of year; but all the MSS agree in giving the same Indiction, viz. the fourth. The occasion of writing was when Augustine, according to Bede and John the Deacon, had sent the presbyter Laurentius and the monk Peter to Rome, to seek instructions on certain points, and to ask for more missionaries: whereupon, we are told, Gregory sent back the messengers accompanied by Mellitus, Justus, Paulinus, Rufinianus, and others, with replies to Augustine's questions, instructions for the constitution of the Church in Britain, the pallium for himself, and books, utensils and relics for the Churches (*Joann. Diac. in Vit. S. Greg.*, II. 36, 37; *Bede, H. E.*, I. 27, 29). We might have supposed from the narratives of John the Deacon and Bede that Augustine had sent Lawrence and Peter to Rome on his return to Britain after his own consecration by the bishop of Arles, and that the new band of missionaries had been sent out without delay. But the dates of the epistles shew, as has been seen above, that several years had intervened, at any rate, between Augustine's return and the sending out of the new missionaries. And indeed Bede himself intimates this in his recapitulation of events (*H. E.*, V. 24), though not in his narrative. For, having given A.D. 597 as the date of Augustine's first arrival in Britain, he gives A.D. 601 as that of the sending of the pallium with "more ministers, among whom was Paulinus."

The letters which these new missionaries carried with them were to the bishops Virgilius of Arles (*Ep.* 55), Desiderius of Vienne (*Ep.* 54), Aetherius of Lyons (*Ep.* 56), Arigius of Vapincum (*Ep.* 57), with a circular to various bishops of Gaul (*Ep.* 58); also to Queen Brunehild (*Ep.* 62), to kings Theodebert, Theoderic, and Clotaire (*Epp.* 59, 60, 61): to Augustine himself (*Ep.* 65), together with a long reply (*Ep.* 64) to his questions[1], to Ethelbert king of Kent (*Ep.* 66), and probably at the same time to Bertha his queen (*Ep.* 29)[2].

One more letter relating to the mission in Book XI. remains to be noticed; viz., *Ep.* 76, to Mellitus, which was sent after the rest, being intended to overtake the new band of missionaries on their journey through Gaul. Its main purpose seems to have been to modify what had been said in the letter to Ethelbert as to the destruction of heathen temples. See Note to *Ep.* 76. This is the last extant epistle referring to the English mission.

(2) To be noted also in this book is the first of the ten epistles addressed to the notorious queen Brunehild in Gaul (VI. 5). On her alleged character, and Gregory's mode of addressing her, see note to the epistle.

---

[1] Another letter to Augustine (*Ep.* 28), though placed in Book XI. by the Benedictine editors, may have been written in some previous year. It is one of congratulation on reported success, and of warning against elation. It seems to refer to the same news, received from Britain, that Gregory announced to Eulogius of Alexandria in his letter to him, A.D. 598, and resembles that letter in its exultant tone. Containing in itself no intimation of its own date, it seems more likely that it was written about the same time with the letter to Eulogius than that Gregory should have let several years elapse before finding an opportunity of congratulating Augustine on his success.

[2] The only reason for doubting whether the letter to Bertha was sent at the same time with that to Ethelbert, is that in the former the queen is exhorted to move her husband to follow her faith, whereas in the latter the king is addressed as already a Christian. The letter to Bertha is shewn by what is said in it to have been written after the arrival in Rome of Laurence and Peter, and that to Ethelbert, from its date, to have been sent by Mellitus and his companions when they left Rome for Britain. But there is nothing to shew that the letter to Bertha might not have been sent previously. It may be that the news of the king's conversion did not reach Rome till after the arrival there of Lawrence and Peter, and that Gregory had found an opportunity, before sending to Britain the new band of missionaries, of despatching a letter to the queen, urging her to bring it about. There would be time enough for his doing so, since the sending of Mellitus seems to have been delayed for a considerable time, owing, it may be, to Gregory's state of health at the time. See Preface to XI. 64. On the other hand, the language used in the letter to Bertha may possibly only mean that she ought to move her husband to greater zeal in propagating the faith, already embraced by himself, among his subjects. The exact date of Ethelbert's baptism is not known. Bede only says that he allowed the missionaries to preach freely before being himself converted, and that, after his conversion, he compelled no one to accept Christianity. It may, then, be only his reported lukewarmness in this regard that Gregory's exhortation to Bertha refers to.

Book VII. Indiction XV. (a.d. 596-7), and Book VIII. Indiction I. (a.d. 597-8).

Though no historical events of importance come for the first time before our notice in these books, attention may be drawn (1) to Gregory's policy of protecting monasteries from episcopal domination (VII. 12, 43; VIII. 15); (2) his sanction of the sale of church plate for charitable purposes (VII. 13, 38); (3) Specimens of his letters of spiritual counsel, especially to pious ladies of rank (VII. 25, 26, 30; VIII. 22).

Book IX. Indiction II. (a.d. 598-9).

Noticeable in this book are, (1) Gregory's renewed efforts, on Romanus Patricius being succeeded by Callinicus in the exarchate, to reclaim the Istrian bishops to communion with Rome (*Ep.* 9, 10, 93, &c.); (2) his interesting letter with reference to the ancient liturgical usages of the Roman Church (*Ep.* 12); (3) the correspondence between him and the Visigothic king Reccared in Spain, assigned to this year (*Epp.* 61, 121, 122); (4) his continued efforts to bring about the assembling of synods and correction of prevalent abuses in the Church of Gaul (*Ep.* 106, &c.); (5) the remarkable letter to him of the Irish saint Columbanus, illustrating the differences with regard to the computation of Easter between the Roman and Celtic Churches, and the attitude of the latter towards the Roman See (*Ep.* 127).

Book XI. Indiction IV. (a.d. 600-1).

Noticeable in this book are—

(1) The letter to Serenus, bishop of Marseilles, with regard to the use and abuse of pictures in Churches (*Ep.* 13).

(2) Two long letters to ladies of rank at Constantinople (*Epp.* 44, 45), the first of which is interesting, as in other ways, so for the account contained in it of supposed miracles at the monastery of St. Andrew in Rome, shewing, as many other epistles do, Gregory's firm belief in miraculous interventions; while the second is remarkable, not only for its spiritual counsels, but also for its expression of Gregory's views on the unlawfulness of married persons entering monasteries without mutual consent; on the efficacy of baptism; and on various points of doctrine.

(3) The letter to the bishops of Iberia, setting forth the various ways of reconciling various kinds of heretics to the Church, and containing a specimen of Gregory's controversial skill in his refutation of Nestorianism (*Ep.* 67).

(4) Evidence of Gregory's unremitted efforts to correct the immorality prevalent among the clergy in Gaul, shewn in his letter to queen Brunehild on the subject (*Ep.* 69).

(5) The letters relating to the English mission, notice of which has been forestalled under Book VI.

Book XIII. Indiction V. (a.d. 602-3).

In this Book we may note—

(1) Continued correspondence about the Church in Gaul, with references to a church, monastery, and hospital, founded by queen Brunehild at Autun, and to the synod for correction of abuses, long desired by Gregory, for the holding of which she had now requested a fit person to be sent from Rome (*Epp.* 6, 7, 8, 9, 10).

(2) The important event of the accession of Phocas to the empire (November, a.d. 602), with the letters of Gregory on the occasion to him and to his wife Leontia (*Epp.* 31, 38, 39).

Accession of Phocas.

The tone of high compliment—nay, of adulation—which marks these letters has been justly regarded as a blot, much to be regretted, on the lustre of Gregory's character. There is indeed no reason to conclude that he knew so far of the peculiar blackness of the usurper's character, as depicted by contemporary historians, and evinced by his disastrous and sanguinary reign. And, seeing that it appears from Epistle 38 that he had had no apocrisiarius resident at Constantinople towards the end of the reign of Mauricius, it may be that he had not been fully informed of the cruelties that accompanied the accession of Phocas to the imperial throne;—how, for instance, five sons of the former emperor had been murdered in succession before their father's eyes, and then the emperor himself, their bodies being thrown into the Tiber, and their heads exposed in Constantinople till putrefaction began. But, however this might be, Gregory's high-flown compliments addressed to the new potentates, and his excessive exultation on their accession, cannot but strike one as unseemly as well as premature. Nor is it pleasant to observe his exultant way of speaking of the fall of the late emperor, whose sad fate called for so much sympathy, and to whom he had himself once written in such terms as these:—"Since a sincere rectitude of faith shines in you, most Christian of princes, like a light sent from heaven, and since it is known to all that your Serenity embraces with all your heart the pure profession which wins the favour of God" (VI. 16). Again, "Amidst the cares of warfare, and innumerable anxieties which you sustain in your unwearied zeal for the government of the Christian republic, it is a great cause of joy to me, along with the whole world, that your Piety ever keeps guard over the faith whereby the empire of our lords is resplendent" (VI. 65). Again, about him, only some two years before his death, in a letter to the patriarch of Jerusalem, "Thanks should be given without cease to Almighty God, and prayer ever made for the life of our most pious and Christian lord the Emperor, and for his most tranquil spouse, and his most gentle offspring, in whose times the mouths of heretics are silent, &c." (XI. 46). Doubtless Maurice's inefficiency with regard to the Lombards had been exceedingly provoking, and perhaps still more so to Gregory himself, his support of the Patriarch of Constantinople in his assumption of the offensive title. And perhaps the gout from which Gregory appears to have been suffering intensely at the time may partly account for his having given vent as he did to feelings of irritation long suppressed. Then, with regard to his adulation of the new potentates, some excuse may be found in prevalent usage, or his own habitual deference to the powers that be, or his policy (apparent also in his letters to Brunehild) of enlisting their support by flattering addresses to the cause of religion and the Church. But still a painful impression remains; though, on the other hand, it may be observed with truth that few great historical characters of whom so much is known are stained by so few disfiguring blots as that of Gregory. It may be presumed that a prominent motive of his paying court to the rising suns was his hope of getting their support against the patriarch. He does not indeed refer distinctly to the title; but in his letter to Leontia (whom, rather than the emperor, with characteristic address, he warns about her spiritual prospects being dependent on the favour of St. Peter) we can hardly mistake the covert allusion. If so, his policy was not fruitless. For, though there is no sufficient foundation for the statement of Baronius, that Phocas formally conferred on pope Boniface III. the title of "Universal Bishop" which had been assumed by the patriarch, there seems to be no good reason for doubting that the new emperor took the pope's part against Cyriacus, who had offended him by his protection of Constantina and her daughters, and that, when Boniface, who had been Gregory's apocrisiarius at Constantinople, himself became pope, an imperial edict of some kind was issued in favour of the claims of Rome. The words of Anastasius, the biographer of the popes towards the end of the ninth century, with reference to it are these: "He (i.e. Boniface) obtained from the emperor Phocas that the Apostolic See of St. Peter, that is, the Roman Church, should be the head of all Churches, because the Church of Constantinople wrote itself the first of all Churches." The authority, however, of Anastasius, who lived in a time of hierarchical forgeries, cannot be relied on without reserve.

Book XIV. Indiction VII. (A.D. 603-4.)

In the course of this indiction (on the 12th of March, A.D. 604) Gregory died. The seventeen Epistles assigned to this last half-year of his life (one of which is dated December) shew no abatement of his care for all the Churches, or his activity in correspondence, notwithstanding his excessive affliction from gout, leaving him sometimes hardly able to speak, which he alludes to in his letter to Theodelinda, the Lombard queen (*Ep.* 12). This letter was probably written shortly before his death, since he speaks in it of the queen's messengers having left him between life and death, though he still contemplates the possibility of recovery. It is a peculiarly interesting one, not only for this reason, but also as being his last to her. He congratulates her in it on the recent baptism of her infant son Adulouvald in the catholic faith, sends for him a cross containing, as he alleges, wood from the true one, and also jewelled rings for his sister; he bids her thank her husband for peace concluded, and influence him, as she had ever done, to continue it; and he promises her an answer, in case of his recovery, to certain arguments against the condemnation of the Three Chapters by the fifth council, which she had sent for his consideration. It thus appears that to the end of his life he had failed to convince the Lombard queen on this subject, notwithstanding his influence over her, and the cordial relations ever subsisting between them.

Last year of Pontificate.

The view opened to us through this long series of letters into the mind and character of the great Gregory is of peculiar interest. The man himself stands out before us therein self-disclosed; his very faults and frailties, which a panegyrist would have veiled, giving life and reality to the picture. We may observe in the first place how conspicuous throughout is his unhesitating faith. No cloud of doubt seems to have cast its shadow on his certainty of the truth of Holy Writ and Christianity, and of the divine authority of the Catholic Church, speaking through Fathers and Councils as its exponents. Nor were either his temperament or his training such as to expose him to philosophic questionings. No less clear is the sincerity of his life as inspired and guided by his religious faith. Whatever inferior human motives may appear sometimes, there can be no doubt that his paramount aim was to devote himself to God's service. As was to be expected from the religious ideas of his age, his theory of the Christian life was ascetic in the extreme. Continual compunction, fear of judgment, fastings, tears, almsgiving, and heavenly contemplation, formed his ideal of holiness. Even lawful marriage he seems to tolerate, as a Zoar of escape from temptation, rather than to approve: and for a man to enjoy life as most people aim at doing—to sit, as it were, under his vine and under his fig-tree—appeared to him at any rate fraught with danger. Hence the more of both sexes that were able, and could be induced, to leave the active duties of life for monastic seclusion, the better he regarded it for them and for the world in whose behalf they might thus have leisure to pray. Still, on the other hand, such ascetic views were not found incompatible in his case with tender regard for others in their earthly joys and sorrows, and interest in their family life, as expressed in many kind and sympathetic letters to friends; and he was ever ready to meet their temporal as well as spiritual needs. His charitable donations in all directions were bounded only by his means; all oppression of the poor had in him a resolute opponent; nor can we but be struck by his keen sense of justice and regard for it in all his dealings. His gentle breeding, aided by Christian culture, induced a tone of courtesy, with delicate consideration for the feelings of others, in his letters generally; and he usually softens even rebuke with gentleness. Partly, it may be, to this habit may be traced the tone of flattery, which has been remarked on elsewhere, in his letters to potentates, or to others whom it was his purpose to conciliate; which was such indeed in some cases as to lay him open to a charge of insincerity. On the other hand, however, it is to be remembered

Gregory's character.

that, when strongly moved, he could write with very outspoken boldness, not without a vein of cutting irony, even to the Emperor. Witness his two letters (V. 40; VII. 33) to Mauricius on the two subjects that appear above all others to have distressed and irritated him. In such letters—and especially in some to various correspondents about the title of "Universal Bishop"—there are symptoms, no doubt, of much personal irritation, intensified perhaps by gout, under provoking circumstances. But, if his politic flattery in some cases, and his irritability in others, are to some minds disappointing in a saint, they are interesting to a student of human nature: and it is greatly to his credit that they nowhere indicate any merely selfish aims, but rather zeal—however alloyed by policy or by bitterness—for what he honestly believed to be the cause of God.

As a divine he merits his title of a Doctor of the Church. He was, indeed, neither original nor deeply learned; as a mystical interpreter of Scripture he was fanciful, and often, from our point of view, absurd; owing to his visionary turn and his uncritical credulity he may have fostered, and perhaps originated, some fond fables and superstitions, such as infected the general belief of Christians in the middle ages: but he grasped and set forth clearly the orthodox doctrines of the Church; in treating difficult theological questions he displays from time to time no small power of thought and argument; as a preacher of essential Christian morality he was ever sound and true; nor has any one more insisted on spiritual communion of the individual soul with God, or more strongly maintained the principle of justice, mercy and truth being of the essence of religion.

His diplomatic and practical talents, and his unwearied industry, have been already spoken of, and need no further notice in this brief final survey, the intention of which is to view him rather in his character as a saint and a divine.

PEDIGREE OF KINGS OF GAUL.

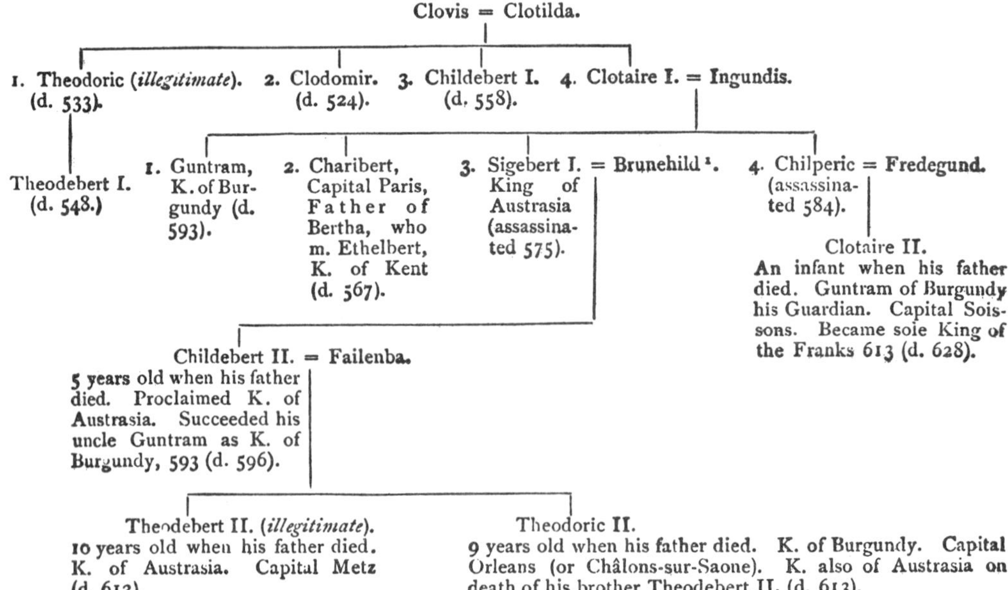

[1] Brunehild (or Brunehaut) was daughter of Athanagild, K. of the Visigoths in Spain. Septimania, and Narbonensian Gaul. She renounced Arianism for Catholicity on her marriage to Sigebert I. Made Guardian of Theodebert II. on the death of his father Childebert II. Expelled from Austrasia, 399, and received by Theodoric II. in Burgundy. Put to death under Clotaire II. 613.

THE BOOK OF PASTORAL RULE

PREFACE

THE title, *Liber Regulæ Pastoralis*, is the one adopted by the Benedictine Editors from several ancient MSS., being Gregory's own designation of his work when he sent it to his friend, Leander of Seville;—"Ut librum Regulæ Pastoralis, quem in episcopatus mei exordio scripsi . . . sanctitati tuæ transmitterem" (*Epp. Lib.* v., *Ep.* 49). The previously more usual one, *Liber Pastoralis Curæ*, may have been taken from the opening words of the book itself, "Pastoralis curæ me pondera fugere, etc." The book was issued (as appears from the passage above quoted in the Epistle to Leander) at the commencement of Gregory's episcopacy, and (as appears from its opening words) addressed to John, bishop of Ravenna, in reply to a letter received from him. But, though put into form for a special purpose on this occasion, it must have been the issue of long previous thought, as is further evident from the fact that in his *Magna Moralia*, or Commentary on the Book of Job, begun and in a great measure written during his residence in Constantinople, he had already sketched the plan of such a treatise, and expressed the hope of some day putting it into form. For we there find the prologue to the third book of the Regula already written, together with most of the headings contained in the first chapter of that book, followed by the words, "And indeed we ought to have denoted particularly what should be the order of admonition with respect to each of these points; but fear of prolixity deters us. Yet, with God's help, we hope to complete this task in another work, should some little time of this laborious life still remain to us" (*Moral. Lib.* xxx. c. 12 and 13).

The book appears to have been estimated as it deserved during the writer's life. It was sent by him, as we have seen, to Leander of Seville, apparently at the request of the latter, for the benefit of the Church in Spain; and there will be found among the Epistles one addressed to Gregory from Licinianus, a learned bishop of Carthagena in that country, in which it is highly praised, though a fear is expressed lest the standard required in it of fitness for the episcopal office might prove too high for ordinary attainment (*Epp. Lib.* II., *Ep.* 54). The Emperor Maurice, having requested and obtained a copy of it from Anatolius, Gregory's deacon at Constantinople, had it translated into Greek by Anastasius the patriarch of Antioch, who himself highly approved of it (*Epp. Lib.* XII., *Ep.* 24). It appears to have been taken to England by the Monk Augustine. This is asserted by Alfred the Great, who, nearly three hundred years afterwards, with the assistance of his divines, made a translation, or rather paraphrase, of it in the West Saxon tongue, intending, as he says, to send a copy to every bishop in his Kingdom [1].

Previously to this, there is evidence of the high repute in which the book was held in Gaul. In a series of councils held by command of Charlemagne, A.D. 813,—viz. at Mayence,

[1] Edited, with an English version, by Henry Sweet of Balliol College, and published for the Early English Text Society, 1871, Part I., p. 7.

Rheims, Tours, and Châlon-sur-Seine—the study of it was specially enjoined on all bishops, together with the New Testament Scriptures and the Canons of the Fathers[2]. Similarly at a Council held at Aix-la-Chapelle, A.D. 836[3]. Further, it appears from a letter of Hincmar[4], Archbishop of Rheims (A.D. 845—882), that a copy of it together with the Book of Canons was given into the hands of bishops before the altar at their consecration, and that they were admonished to frame their lives accordingly.

The work is well worthy of its old repute, being the best of its kind, and profitable for all ages. Two similar works had preceded it. First, that of Gregory Nazianzen (c. A.D. 362), known as his second oration, and called τοῦ αὐτοῦ ἀπολογητικός, which was written, like that of the later Gregory, to excuse the writer's reluctance to accept the episcopate, and to set forth the responsibilities of the office. It is obvious, from comparing the two treatises, that the earlier had suggested the later one; and indeed Pope Gregory acknowledges his indebtedness in his prologue to the second book of the *Regula*. The second somewhat similar treatise had been that of Chrysostom, 'De Sacerdotio,' in six books, c. A.D. 382. It also sets forth the awful responsibilities of the episcopal office; but there are no signs of pope Gregory having drawn from it.

It is to be observed that the subject of all these treatises is the office of episcopacy; not the pastoral or priestly office in its wider sense, as now commonly understood: and it is noteworthy how prominent in Gregory's view of it are the duties of preaching and spiritual guidance of souls. It is regarded, indeed, in the first place as an office of government—*locus regiminis, culmen regiminis*, denote it frequently—and hence the exercise of discipline comes prominently in; and the chief pastor is viewed also as an intercessor between his flock and God—See e.g. I. 10;—but it is especially as a teacher, and a physician of souls, that he is spoken of throughout the treatise; as one whose peculiar duty it is to be conversant with all forms of spiritual disease, and so be able to suit his treatment to all cases, to "preach the word, reprove, rebuke, exhort, with all long suffering and doctrine," and both by precept and example guide souls in the way of salvation. Gregory had not studied in vain the Pastoral Epistles of St. Paul. Remarkable indeed is his own discriminating insight, displayed throughout, into human characters and motives, and his perception of the temptations to which circumstances or temperament render various people—pastors as well as members of their flocks—peculiarly liable. No less striking, in this as in other works of his, is his intimate acquaintance with the whole of Holy Scripture. He knew it indeed through the Latin version only; his critical knowledge is frequently at fault; and far-fetched mystical interpretations, such as he delighted in, abound. But as a true expounder of its general moral and religious teaching he well deserves his name as one of the great Doctors of the Church. And, further, notwithstanding all his reverence for Councils and Fathers, as paramount authorities in matters of faith, it is to Scripture that he ever appeals as the final authority for conduct and belief.

---

[2] *Concil. Mogunt. Præfat.*;—*Concil. Rhemens. II.*, Canon x.;—*Concil. Turon. III.*, Canon iii.;—*Concil. Cabilon. II.*, Canon i.

[3] *Concil. Aquisgran.*, cap. i., *De Vita Episcoporum*, can. 7, 9, 10; cap. 2, *De doctrina episcoporum*.

[4] *Hincmar. Opp.* tom. ii. p. 389, *Ed. Paris*, 1645.

THE BOOK OF PASTORAL RULE

OF

SAINT GREGORY THE GREAT

ROMAN PONTIFF

TO JOHN, BISHOP OF THE CITY OF RAVENNA

PART I.

Gregory to his most reverend and most holy brother and fellow-bishop, John.

With kind and humble intent thou reprovest me, dearest brother, for having wished by hiding myself to fly from the burdens of pastoral care; as to which, lest to some they should appear light, I express with my pen in the book before you all my own estimate of their heaviness, in order both that he who is free from them may not unwarily seek them, and that he who has so sought them may tremble for having got them. This book is divided into four separate heads of argument, that it may approach the reader's mind by allegations arranged in order—by certain steps, as it were. For, as the necessity of things requires, we must especially consider after what manner every one should come to supreme rule; and, duly arriving at it, after what manner he should live; and, living well, after what manner he should teach; and, teaching aright, with how great consideration every day he should become aware of his own infirmity; lest either humility fly from the approach, or life be at variance with the arrival, or teaching be wanting to the life, or presumption unduly exalt the teaching. Wherefore, let fear temper the desire; but afterwards, authority being assumed by one who sought it not, let his life commend it. But then it is necessary that the good which is displayed in the life of the pastor should also be propagated by his speech. And at last it remains that, whatever works are brought to perfection, consideration of our own infirmity should depress us with regard to them, lest the swelling of elation extinguish even them before the eyes of hidden judgment. But inasmuch as there are many, like me in unskilfulness, who, while they know not how to measure themselves, are covetous of teaching what they have not learned; who estimate lightly the burden of authority in proportion as they are ignorant of the pressure of its greatness; let them be reproved from the very beginning of this book; so that, while, unlearned and precipitate, they desire to hold the citadel of teaching, they may be repelled at the very door of our discourse from the ventures of their precipitancy.

CHAPTER I.

That the unskilful venture not to approach an office of authority.

No one presumes to teach an art till he has first, with intent meditation, learnt it. What rashness is it, then, for the unskilful to assume pastoral authority, since the government of souls is the art of arts! For who can be ignorant that the sores of the thoughts of men are more occult than the sores of the bowels? And yet how often do men who have no knowledge whatever of spiritual precepts fearlessly profess themselves physicians of the heart, though those who are ignorant of the effect of drugs blush to appear as physicians of the flesh! But because, through the ordering of God, all the highest in rank of this present age are inclined to reverence religion, there are some who, through the outward show of rule within the holy Church, affect the glory of distinction. They desire to appear as teachers, they covet superiority to others, and, as the Truth attests, they seek the first salutations in the market-place, the first rooms at feasts, the first seats in assemblies (Matth. xxiii. 6, 7), being all the less able to administer worthily the office they have undertaken of pastoral care, as they have reached the magisterial position of humility out of elation only. For, indeed, in a magisterial position language itself is confounded when one thing is learnt and another taught[1]. Against such the Lord complains by the prophet, saying, *They have reigned, and not by Me; they have been set up as princes, and I knew it not* (Hos. viii. 4). For those reign of themselves, and not by the Will of the Supreme Ruler, who, supported by no virtues, and in no way divinely called, but inflamed by their own desire, seize rather than attain supreme rule. But them the Judge within both advances, and yet knows not; for whom by permission he tolerates, them surely by the judgment of reprobation he ignores. Whence to some who come to Him even after miracles He says, *Depart from Me, ye workers of iniquity, I know you not who ye are* (Luke xiii. 27). The unskilfulness of shepherds is rebuked by the voice of the Truth, when it is said through the prophet, *The shepherds themselves have not known understanding* (Isai. lvi. 11); whom again the Lord denounces, saying, *And they that handle the law knew Me not* (Jer. ii. 8). And therefore the Truth complains of not being known of them, and protests that He knows not the principality of those who know not Him; because in truth these who know not the things of the Lord are unknown of the Lord; as Paul attests, who says, *But if any man knoweth not, he shall not be known* (1 Cor. xiv. 38). Yet this unskilfulness of the shepherds doubtless suits often the deserts of those who are subject to them, because, though it is their own fault that they have not the light of knowledge, yet it is in the dealing of strict judgment that through their ignorance those also who follow them should stumble. Hence it is that, in the Gospel, the Truth in person says, *If the blind lead the blind, both fall into the ditch* (Matth. xv. 14). Hence the Psalmist (not expressing his own desire, but in his ministry as a prophet) denounces such, when he says, *Let their eyes be blinded that they see not, and ever bow thou down their back* (Ps. lxviii. 24[2]). For, indeed, those persons are eyes who, placed in the very face of the highest dignity, have undertaken the office of spying out the road; while those who are attached to them and follow them are denominated backs. And so, when the eyes are blinded, the back is bent, because, when those who go before lose the light of knowledge, those who follow are bowed down to carry the burden of their sins.

CHAPTER II.

That none should enter on a place of government who practise not in life what they have learnt by study.

There are some also who investigate spiritual precepts with cunning care, but what they penetrate with their understanding they trample on in their lives: all at once they teach the things which not by practice but by study they have learnt; and what in words they preach by their manners they impugn. Whence it comes to pass that when the shepherd walks through steep places, the flock follows to the precipice. Hence it is that the Lord through the prophet complains of the contemptible knowledge of shepherds, saying, *When ye yourselves had drunk most pure water, ye fouled the residue with your feet; and My sheep fed on that which had been trodden by your feet, and drank that which your feet had fouled* (Ezek. xxxiv. 18, 19). For indeed the shepherds drink most pure water, when with a right understanding they imbibe the streams of truth. But to foul the same water with their feet is to corrupt the studies of holy meditation by evil living. And verily the sheep drink the water fouled by their feet, when any of those subject to them follow not the words which they hear, but only imitate the bad examples which they see. Thirsting for the things said, but perverted by the works observed, they take in mud with their draughts, as from polluted fountains. Hence also it is written through the prophet, *A snare for the downfall of my people are evil priests* (Hos. v. 1; ix. 8). Hence again the Lord through the prophet says of the priests, *They are made to be for a stumbling-block of iniquity to the house of Israel.* For certainly no one does more harm in the Church than one who has the name and rank of sanctity, while he acts perversely. For him, when he transgresses, no one presumes to take to task; and the offence spreads forcibly for example, when out of reverence to his rank the sinner is honoured. But all who are unworthy would fly from the burden of so great guilt, if with the attentive ear of the heart they weighed the sentence of the Truth, *Whoso shall offend one of these little ones*

[1] In this passage the phrase *magisterium humilitatis* has reference to Matt. xx. 25, &c., or Luke xxii. 25, &c., and *ipsa lingua confunditur* to Gen. xi. 7. The meaning appears to be that, when men seek and attain in a spirit of pride the office which according to our Lord's teaching is one of humility, they are incapable of fulfilling its duties by speaking to others so to be understood and edify. They are as the arrogant builders of Babel, whose language the LORD confounded, that they might not understand one another's speech.

[2] In *Hebr.* and *Engl.* lxix. 24.

which believe in me, it were better for him that a millstone were hanged about his neck, and he were drowned in the depth of the sea (Matth. xviii. 6). By the millstone is expressed the round and labour of worldly life, and by the depth of the sea is denoted final damnation. Whosoever, then, having come to bear the outward show of sanctity, either by word or example destroys others, it had indeed been better for him that earthly deeds in open guise should press him down to death than that sacred offices should point him out to others as imitable in his wrong-doing; because, surely, if he fell alone, the pains of hell would torment him in more tolerable degree.

CHAPTER III.

Of the weight of government; and that all manner of adversity is to be despised, and prosperity feared.

So much, then, have we briefly said, to shew how great is the weight of government, lest whosoever is unequal to sacred offices of government should dare to profane them, and through lust of pre-eminence undertake a leadership of perdition. For hence it is that James affectionately deters us, saying, *Be not made many masters, my brethren* (James iii. 1). Hence the Mediator between God and man Himself—He who, transcending the knowledge and understanding even of supernal spirits, reigns in heaven from eternity—on earth fled from receiving a kingdom. For it is written, *When Jesus therefore perceived that they would come and take Him by force, to make Him a king, He departed again into the mountain Himself alone* (Joh. vi. 15). For who could so blamelessly have had principality over men as He who would in fact have reigned over those whom He had Himself created? But, because He had come in the flesh to this end, that He might not only redeem us by His passion but also teach us by His conversation, offering Himself as an example to His followers, He would not be made a king; but He went of His own accord to the gibbet of the cross. He fled from the offered glory of pre-eminence, but desired the pain of an ignominious death; that so His members might learn to fly from the favours of the world, to be afraid of no terrors, to love adversity for the truth's sake, and to shrink in fear from prosperity; because this often defiles the heart through vain glory, while that purges it through sorrow; in this the mind exalts itself, but in that, even though it had once exalted itself, it brings itself low; in this man forgets himself, but in that, even perforce and against his will, he is recalled to memory of what he is; in this even good things done aforetime often come to nothing, but in that faults even of long standing are wiped away. For commonly in the school of adversity the heart is subdued under discipline, while, on sudden attainment of supreme rule, it is forthwith changed and becomes elated through familiarity with glory. Thus Saul, who had before fled in consideration of his unworthiness, no sooner had assumed the government of the kingdom than he was puffed up (1 Kings x. 22; xv. 17, 30): for, desirous of being honoured before the people while unwilling to be publicly blamed, he cut off from himself even him who had anointed him to the kingdom. Thus David, who in the judgment of Him who chose him was well pleasing to Him in almost all his deeds, as soon as the weight of pressure was removed, broke out into a swelling sore (2 Kings xi. 3, *seq.*), and, having been as a laxly running one in his appetite for the woman, became as a cruelly hard one in the slaughter of the man; and he who had before known pitifully how to spare the bad learnt afterwards, without impediment of hesitation, to pant even for the death of the good (Ibid. 15). For, indeed, previously he had been unwilling to smite his captured persecutor; and afterwards, with loss to his wearied army, he destroyed even his devoted soldier. And in truth his crime would have snatched him farther away from the number of the elect, had not scourges called him back to pardon.

CHAPTER IV.

That for the most part the occupation of government dissipates the solidity of the mind.

Often the care of government, when undertaken, distracts the heart in divers directions; and one is found unequal to dealing with particular things, while with confused mind divided among many. Whence a certain wise man providently dissuades, saying, *My son, meddle not with many matters* (Ecclus. xi. 10); because, that is, the mind is by no means collected on the plan of any single work while parted among divers. And, when it is drawn abroad by unwonted care, it is emptied of the solidity of inward fear: it becomes anxious in the ordering of things that are without, and, ignorant of itself alone, knows how to think of many things, while itself it knows not. For, when it implicates itself more than is needful in things that are without, it is as though it were so occupied during a journey as to forget where it was going; so that, being estranged from the business of self-examination, it does not even consider the losses it is suffering, or know how great they are. For neither did

Hezekiah believe himself to be sinning (2 Kings xx. 13), when he shewed to the strangers who came to him his storehouses of spices; but he fell under the anger of the judge, to the condemnation of his future offspring, from what he supposed himself to be doing lawfully (Isai. xxxix. 4). Often, when means are abundant, and many things can be done for subordinates to admire, the mind exalts itself in thought, and fully provokes to itself the anger of the judge, though not breaking out in overt acts of iniquity. For he who judges is within; that which is judged is within. When, then, in heart we transgress, what we are doing within ourselves is hidden from men, but yet in the eyes of the judge we sin. For neither did the King of Babylon then first stand guilty of elation (Dan. iv. 16, *seq.*) when he came to utter words of elation, inasmuch as even before, when he had given no utterance to his elation, he heard the sentence of reprobation from the prophet's mouth For he had already wiped off the fault of the pride he had been guilty of, when he proclaimed to all the nations under him the omnipotent God whom he found himself to have offended.

But after this, elevated by the success of his dominion, and rejoicing in having done great things, he first preferred himself to all in thought, and afterwards, still vain-glorious, said, *Is not this great Babylon, that I have built for the house of the kingdom, and in the might of my power, and for the honour of my majesty?* (Dan. iv. 30.) Which utterance of his, as we see, fell openly under the vengeance of the wrath which his hidden elation kindled. For the strict judge first sees invisibly what he afterwards reproves by publicly smiting it. Hence him He turned even into an irrational animal, separated him from human society, changed his mind and joined him to the beasts of the field, that in obviously strict and just judgment he who had esteemed himself great beyond men should lose even his being as a man. Now in adducing these things we are not finding fault with dominion, but guarding the infirmity of the heart from coveting it, lest any that are imperfect should venture to snatch at supreme rule, or those who stumble on plain ground set foot on a precipice.

CHAPTER V.

Of those who are able to profit others by virtuous example in supreme rule, but fly from it in pursuit of their own ease.

For there are some who are eminently endowed with virtues, and for the training of others are exalted by great gifts, who are pure in zeal for chastity, strong in the might of abstinence, filled with the feasts of doctrine, humble in the long-suffering of patience, erect in the fortitude of authority, tender in the grace of loving-kindness, strict in the severity of justice. Truly such as these, if when called they refuse to undertake offices of supreme rule, for the most part deprive themselves of the very gifts which they received not for themselves alone, but for others also; and, while they meditate their own and not another's gain, they forfeit the very benefits which they desire to keep to themselves. For hence it was that the Truth said to His disciples, *A city that is set on an hill cannot be hid: neither do they light a candle and put it under a bushel, but on a candlestick, that it may give light to all that are in the house* (Matth v. 15). Hence He says to Peter, *Simon, Son of Jonas, lovest thou Me?* (Joh. xv. 16, 17); and he, when he had at once answered that he loved, was told, *If thou lovest Me, feed My sheep.* If, then, the care of feeding is the proof of loving, whosoever abounds in virtues, and yet refuses to feed the flock of God, is convicted of not loving the chief Shepherd. Hence Paul says, *If Christ died for all, then all died. And if He died for all, it remaineth that they which live should now no longer live unto themselves, but unto Him which died for them and rose again* (2 Cor. v. 15). Hence Moses says (Deut xxv. 5) that a surviving brother shall take to him the wife of a brother who has died without children, and beget children to the name of his brother; and that, if he haply refuse to take her, the woman shall spit in his face, and her kinsman shall loose the shoe from off one of his feet, and call his habitation the house of him that hath his shoe loosed. Now the deceased brother is He who, after the glory of the resurrection, said, *Go tell My brethren* (Matth. xxviii. 10). For He died as it were without children, in that He had not yet filled up the number of His elect. Then, it is ordered that the surviving brother shall have the wife assigned to him, because it is surely fit that the care of holy Church be imposed on him who is best able to rule it well. But, should he be unwilling, the woman spits in his face, because whosoever cares not to benefit others out of the gifts which he has received, the holy Church exprobrates even what he has of good, and, as it were, casts spittle on his face: and from one foot the shoe is taken away, inasmuch as it is written, *Your feet shod in preparation of the Gospel of Peace* (Ephes. vi. 15). If, then, we have the care of our neighbour as well as of ourselves upon us, we have each foot protected by a shoe. But he who, meditating his own advantage, neglects that of his neighbours, loses with disgrace one foot's shoe. And so there are some, as we have said, enriched with great gifts, who, while they are ardent for the studies of contemplation only, shrink from serving to their neighbour's benefit by preaching; they love a secret place of quiet, they long for a retreat for speculation. With respect to which conduct, they are, if strictly judged, undoubtedly guilty in proportion to the greatness of the gifts whereby they might have been publicly useful. For with what disposition of mind does one who might be conspicuous in profiting his neighbours prefer his own privacy to the advantage of others, when the Only-begotten of the supreme Father Himself came forth from the bosom of the Father into the midst of us all, that He might profit many?

CHAPTER VI.

That those who fly from the burden of rule through humility are then truly humble when they resist not the Divine decrees.

There are some also who fly by reason only of their humility, lest they should be preferred to others to whom they esteem themselves unequal. And theirs, indeed, if it be surrounded by other virtues, is then true humility before the eyes of God, when it is not pertinacious in rejecting what it is enjoined to undertake with profit. For neither is he truly humble, who understands how the good pleasure of the Supernal Will ought to bear sway, and yet contemns its sway. But, submitting himself to the divine disposals, and averse from the vice of obstinacy, if he be already prevented with gifts whereby he may profit others also, he ought, when enjoined to undertake supreme rule, in his heart to flee from it, but against his will to obey.

CHAPTER VII.

That sometimes some laudably desire the office of preaching, while others, as laudably, are drawn to it by compulsion.

Although sometimes some laudably desire the office of preaching, yet others are as laudably drawn to it by compulsion; as we plainly perceive, if we consider the conduct of two prophets, one of whom offered himself of his own accord to be sent to preach, yet the other in fear refused to go. For Isaiah, when the Lord asked whom He should send, offered himself of his own accord, saying, *Here I am; send me* (Isai. vi. 8). But Jeremiah is sent, yet humbly pleads that he should not be sent, saying, *Ah, Lord God! behold I cannot speak: for I am a child* (Jer. i. 6). Lo, from these two men different voices proceeded outwardly, but they flowed from the same fountain of love. For there are two precepts of charity; the love of God and of our neighbour. Wherefore Isaiah, eager to profit his neighbours through an active life, desires the office of preaching; but Jeremiah, longing to cleave sedulously to the love of his Creator through a contemplative life, remonstrates against being sent to preach. Thus what the one laudably desired the other laudably shrunk from; the latter, lest by speaking he should lose the gains of silent contemplation; the former, lest by keeping silence he should suffer loss for lack of diligent work. But this in both cases is to be nicely observed, that he who refused did not persist in his refusal, and he who wished to be sent saw himself previously cleansed by a coal of the altar; lest any one who has not been purged should dare to approach sacred ministries, or any whom supernal grace has chosen should proudly gainsay it under a show of humility. Wherefore, since it is very difficult for any one to be sure that he has been cleansed, it is safer to decline the office of preaching, though (as we have said) it should not be declined pertinaciously when the Supernal Will that it should be undertaken is recognized. Both requirements Moses marvellously fulfilled, who was unwilling to be set over so great a multitude, and yet obeyed. For peradventure he were proud, were he to undertake without trepidation the leadership of that innumerable people; and, again, proud he would plainly be were he to refuse to obey his Lord's command. Thus in both ways humble, in both ways submissive, he was unwilling, as measuring himself, to be set over the people; and yet, as presuming on the might of Him who commanded him, he consented. Hence, then, hence let all rash ones infer how great guilt is theirs, if they fear not to be preferred to others by their own seeking, when holy men, even when God commanded, feared to undertake the leadership of peoples. Moses trembles though God persuades him; and yet every weak one pants to assume the burden of dignity; and one who can hardly bear his own load without falling, gladly puts his shoulders under the pressure of others not his own: his own deeds are too heavy for him to carry, and he augments his burden.

CHAPTER VIII.

Of those who covet pre-eminence, and seize on the language of the Apostle to serve the purpose of their own cupidity.

But for the most part those who covet pre-eminence seize on the language of the Apostle to serve the purpose of their own cupidity, where he says, *If a man desire the office of a bishop, he desireth a good work* (1 Tim. iii. 1).

But, while praising the desire, he forthwith turns what he has praised to fear when at once he adds, *but a bishop must be blameless* (1 Tim. iii. 2). And, when he subsequently enumerates the necessary virtues, he makes manifest what this blamelessness consists in. And so, with regard to their desire, he approves them, but by his precept he alarms them; as if saying plainly, I praise what ye seek; but first learn what it is ye seek; lest, while ye neglect to measure yourselves, your blamefulness appear all the fouler for its haste to be seen by all in the highest place of honour. For the great master in the art of ruling impels by approval and checks by alarms; so that, by describing the height of blamelessness, he may restrain his hearers from pride, and, by praising the office which is sought, dispose them to the life required. Nevertheless it is to be noted that this was said at a time when whosoever was set over people was usually the first to be led to the torments of martyrdom. At that time, therefore, it was laudable to seek the office of a bishop, since through it there was no doubt that a man would come in the end to heavier pains. Hence even the office of a bishop itself is defined as a good work, when it is said, *If a man desire the office of a bishop, he desireth a good work* (1 Tim. iii. 1). Wherefore he that seeks, not this ministry of a good work, but the glory of distinction, is himself a witness against himself that he does not desire the office of a bishop; inasmuch as that man not only does not love at all the sacred office, but even knows not what it is, who, panting after supreme rule, is fed by the subjection of others in the hidden meditation of his thought, rejoices in his own praises, lifts up his heart to honour, exults in abundant affluence. Thus worldly gain is sought under colour of that honour by which worldly gains should have been destroyed: and, when the mind thinks to seize on the highest post of humility for its own elation, it inwardly changes what it outwardly desires.

CHAPTER IX.

That the mind of those who wish for pre-eminence for the most part flatters itself with a feigned promise of good works.

But for the most part those who covet pastoral authority mentally propose to themselves some good works besides, and, though desiring it with a motive of pride, still muse how they will effect great things: and so it comes to pass that the motive suppressed in the depths of the heart is one thing, another what the surface of thought presents to the muser's mind. For the mind itself lies to itself about itself, and feigns with respect to good work to love what it does not love, and with respect to the world's glory not to love what it does love. Eager for domination, it becomes timid with regard to it while in pursuit, audacious after attainment. For, while advancing towards it, it is in trepidation lest it should not attain it; but all at once, on having attained, thinks what it has attained to be its just due. And, when it has once begun to enjoy the office of its acquired dominion in a worldly way, it willingly forgets what it has cogitated in a religious way. Hence it is necessary that, when such cogitation is extended beyond wont, the mind's eye should be recalled to works already accomplished, and that every one should consider what he has done as a subordinate; and so may he at once discover whether as a prelate he will be able to do the good things he has proposed to do. For one can by no means learn humility in a high place who has not ceased to be proud while occupying a low one: one knows not how to fly from praise when it abounds, who has learnt to pant for it when it was wanting: one can by no means overcome avarice, when advanced to the sustentation of many, whom his own means could not suffice for himself alone. Wherefore from his past life let every one discover what he is, lest in his craving for eminence the phantom of his cogitation illude him. Nevertheless it is generally the case that the very practice of good deeds which was maintained in tranquillity is lost in the occupation of government; since even an unskilful person guides a ship along a straight course in a calm sea; but in one disturbed by the waves of tempest even the skilled sailor is confounded. For what is eminent dominion but a tempest of the mind, in which the ship of the heart is ever shaken by hurricanes of thought, is incessantly driven hither and thither, so as to be shattered by sudden excesses of word and deed, as if by opposing rocks? In the midst of all these dangers, then, what course is to be followed, what is to be held to, except that one who abounds in virtues should accede to government under compulsion, and that one who is void of virtues should not, even under compulsion, approach it? As to the former, let him beware lest, if he refuses altogether, he be as one who binds up in a napkin the money which he has received, and be judged for hiding it (Matth. xxv. 18). For, indeed, to bind up in a napkin is to hide gifts received under the listlessness of sluggish torpor. But, on the other hand, let the latter, when he craves government, take care lest, by his example of evil deeds, he become an obstacle to such as are journeying to the entrance of the kingdom, after the manner of the Pharisees, who, according to the Master's voice (Matth. xxiii. 13), neither go in themselves nor suffer others to go in. And he should also consider how, when an elected prelate undertakes the cause of the people, he goes, as it were, as a physician to one that is sick. If, then, ailments still live in his body, what presumption is his, to make haste to heal the smitten, while in his own face carrying a sore!

CHAPTER X.

What manner of man ought to come to rule.

That man, therefore, ought by all means to be drawn with cords to be an example of good living who already lives spiritually, dying to all passions of the flesh; who disregards worldly prosperity; who is afraid of no adversity; who desires only inward wealth; whose intention the body, in good accord with it, thwarts not at all by its frailness, nor the spirit greatly by its disdain: one who is not led to covet the things of others, but gives freely of his own; who through the bowels of compassion is quickly moved to pardon, yet is never bent down from the fortress of rectitude by pardoning more than is meet; who perpetrates no unlawful deeds, yet deplores those perpetrated by others as though they were his own; who out of affection of heart sympathizes with another's infirmity, and so rejoices in the good of his neighbour as though it were his own advantage; who so insinuates himself as an example to others in all he does that among them he has nothing, at any rate of his own past deeds, to blush for; who studies so to live that he may be able to water even dry hearts with the streams of doctrine; who has already learnt by the use and trial of prayer that he can obtain what he has requested from the Lord, having had already said to him, as it were, through the voice of experience, *While thou art yet speaking, I will say, Here am I* (Isai. lviii. 9). For if perchance any one should come to us asking us to intercede for him with some great man, who was incensed against him, but to us unknown, we should at once reply, We cannot go to intercede for you, since we have no familiar acquaintance with that man. If, then, a man blushes to become an intercessor with another man on whom he has no claim, with what idea can any one grasp the post of intercession with God for the people, who does not know himself to be in favour with Him through the merit of his own life? And how can he ask of Him pardon for others while ignorant whether towards himself He is appeased? And in this matter there is yet another thing to be more anxiously feared; namely, lest one who is supposed to be competent to appease wrath should himself provoke it on account of guilt of his own. For we all know well that, when one who is in disfavour is sent to intercede with an incensed person, the mind of the latter is provoked to greater severity. Wherefore let one who is still tied and bound with earthly desires beware lest by more grievously incensing the strict judge, while he delights himself in his place of honour, he become the cause of ruin to his subordinates.

CHAPTER XI.

What manner of man ought not to come to rule.

Wherefore let every one measure himself wisely, lest he venture to assume a place of rule, while in himself vice still reigns unto condemnation; lest one whom his own guilt depraves desire to become an intercessor for the faults of others. For on this account it is said to Moses by the supernal voice, *Speak unto Aaron; Whosoever he be of thy seed throughout their generations that hath a blemish, he shall not offer loaves of bread to the Lord his God* (Lev. xxi. 17). And it is also immediately subjoined; *If he be blind, if he be lame, if he have either a small or a large and crooked nose, if he be brokenfooted or brokenhanded, if he be hunchbacked, if he be bleareyed (lippus), if he have a white speck (albuginem) in his eye, if chronic scabies, if impetigo in his body, or if he be ruptured (ponderosus)* (Ibid. 18[2]). For that man is indeed blind who is unacquainted with the light of supernal contemplation, who, whelmed in the darkness of the present life, while he beholds not at all by loving it the light to come, knows not whither he is advancing the steps of his conduct. Hence by Hannah prophesying it is said, *He will keep the feet of his saints, and the wicked shall be silent in darkness* (1 Kings ii. 9). But that man is lame

[2] The designations here given of the bodily imperfections, enumerated in Levit. xxi. as disqualifying for priestly functions, are the same as those in the Tridentine edition of the Vulgate, except that instead of *herniosus* Gregory has *ponderosus*, which was a word used in the same sense, denoting one suffering from rupture (Cf. Augustine, *De Civitate Dei*, *Lib. ult.*, *cap.* viii.). The idea expressed by the latter word, and carried out in Gregory's application, was that of the weight (*pondus*), or downward pressure, of the intestines in a ruptured person. The Hebrew Bible (see A.V.), and also the rendering of the LXX. (μονόρχις), conveys a different idea of the ailment intended. The cutaneous diseases specified are denoted, here as in the Vulgate, by *jugis scabies* (ψώρα ἀγρία, LXX.; *scurvy*, A.V.) and *impetigo* (λειχὴν, LXX.; *scabbed*, A.V.). Whatever may be the exact meaning of the original Hebrew words, Gregory's conception of these diseases evidently was that the former was a chronic and painful eruption, proceeding from internal heat, and the latter a painless, but disfiguring, affection of the skin. The diseases of the eye, with regard to which the Hebrew (and consequently our A.V.) differs from the LXX. and Vulgate, are denoted by *lippus* (πτίλλος τοὺς οφθαλμούς, LXX.), and *albuginem habens* (ἔφηλος, LXX.); of which Gregory's conception was that the former was an affection, not properly of the eye, but of the eyelid, the flux from which impaired the power of vision; while the latter was an obscuration of the pupil itself, exhibiting a white colour.

who does indeed see in what direction he ought to go, but, through infirmity of purpose, is unable to keep perfectly the way of life which he sees, because, while unstable habit rises not to a settled state of virtue, the steps of conduct do not follow with effect the aim of desire. Hence it is that Paul says, *Lift up the hands which hang down, and the feeble knees, and make straight paths for your feet, lest that which is lame be turned out of the way; but let it rather be healed* (Heb. xii. 12, 13). But one with a small nose is he who is not adapted for keeping the measure of discernment. For with the nose we discern sweet odours and stenches: and so by the nose is properly expressed discernment, through which we choose virtues and eschew sins. Whence also it is said in praise of the bride, *Thy nose is as the tower which is in Lebanon* (Cant. vii. 4); because, to wit, Holy Church, by discernment, espies assaults issuing from this or that quarter, and detects from an eminence the coming wars of vices. But there are some who, not liking to be thought dull, busy themselves often more than needs in various investigations, and by reason of too great subtilty are deceived. Wherefore this also is added, *Or have a large and crooked nose.* For a large and crooked nose is excessive subtility of discernment, which, having become unduly excrescent, itself confuses the correctness of its own operation. But one with broken foot or hand is he who cannot walk in the way of God at all, and is utterly without part or lot in good deeds, to such degree that he does not, like the lame man, maintain them however weakly, but remains altogether apart from them. But the hunchbacked is he whom the weight of earthly care bows down, so that he never looks up to the things that are above, but is intent only on what is trodden on among the lowest. And he, should he ever hear anything of the good things of the heavenly country, is so pressed down by the weight of perverse custom, that he lifts not the face of his heart to it, being unable to erect the posture of his thought, which the habit of earthly care keeps downward bent. Of this kind of men the Psalmist says, *I am bent down and am brought low continually* (Ps. xxxviii 8). The fault of such as these the Truth in person reprobates, saying, *But the seed which fell among thorns are they which, when they have heard the word, go forth, and are choked with cares and riches and pleasures of life, and bear no fruit* (Luke viii. 14). But the blear eyed is he whose native wit flashes out for cognition of the truth, and yet carnal works obscure it. For in the blear-eyed the pupils are sound; but the eyelids, weakened by defluxion of humours, become gross; and even the brightness of the pupils is impaired, because they are worn continually by the flux upon them. The blear-eyed, then, is one whose sense nature has made keen, but whom a depraved habit of life confuses. To him it is well said through the angel, *Anoint thine eyes with eyesalve that thou mayest see* (Apoc. iii. 18). For we may be said to anoint our eyes with eyesalve that we may see, when we aid the eye of our understanding for perceiving the clearness of the true light with the medicament of good conduct. But that man has a white speck in his eye who is not permitted to see the light of truth, in that he is blinded by the arrogant assumption of wisdom or of righteousness. For the pupil of the eye, when black, sees; but, when it bears a white speck, sees nothing; by which we may understand that the perceiving sense of human thought, if a man understands himself to be a fool and a sinner, becomes cognizant of the clearness of inmost light; but, if it attributes to itself the whiteness of righteousness or wisdom, it excludes itself from the light of knowledge from above, and by so much the more fails entirely to penetrate the clearness of the true light, as it exalts itself within itself through arrogance; as of some it is said, *Professing themselves to be wise, they become fools* (Rom. i. 22). But that man has chronic *scabies* whom the wantonness of the flesh without cease overmasters. For in *scabies* the violent heat of the bowels is drawn to the skin; whereby lechery is rightly designated, since, if the heart's temptation shoots forth into action, it may be truly said that violent internal heat breaks out into *scabies* of the skin: and it now wounds the body outwardly, because, while sensuality is not repressed in thought, it gains the mastery also in action. For Paul had a care to cleanse away this itch of the skin, when he said, *Let no temptation take you but such as is human* (1 Cor. x. 13); as if to say plainly, It is human to suffer temptation in the heart; but it is devilish, in the struggle of temptation, to be also overcome in action. He also has *impetigo* in his body whosoever is ravaged in the mind by avarice; which, if not restrained in small things, does indeed dilate itself without measure.

For, as *impetigo* invades the body without pain, and, spreading with no annoyance to him whom it invades, disfigures the comeliness of the members, so avarice, too, exulcerates, while it pleases, the mind of one who is captive to it. As it offers to the thought one thing after another to be gained, it kindles the fire of enmities, and gives no pain with the wounds it causes, because it promises to the fevered mind abundance out of sin. But the comeliness of the members is destroyed, because the beauty of other virtues is also hereby marred: and it exulcerates as it were the whole body, in that it corrupts the mind with vices of all kinds; as Paul attests, saying, *The love of money is the root of all evils* (1 Tim. vi. 10). But the ruptured one is he who does not carry turpitude into action, but yet is immoderately weighed down by it in mind through continual cogitation; one who is indeed by no means carried away to the extent of nefarious conduct; but his mind still delights itself without prick of repugnance in the pleasure of lechery. For the disease of rupture is when *humor viscerum ad virilia labitur, quae profecto cum molestia dedecoris intumescunt.* He, then, may be said to be ruptured who, letting all his thoughts flow down to lasciviousness, bears in his heart a weight of turpitude; and, though not actually doing deeds of shame, nevertheless in mind is not withdrawn from them. Nor has he power to rise to the practice of good living before the eyes of men, because, hidden within him, the shameful weight presses him down. Whosoever, therefore, is subjected to any one of these diseases is forbidden to offer loaves of bread to the Lord, lest in sooth he should be of no avail for expiating the sins of others, being one who is still ravaged by his own.

And now, having briefly shewn after what manner one who is worthy should come to pastoral authority, and after what manner one who is unworthy should be greatly afraid, let us now demonstrate after what manner one who has attained to it worthily should live in it.

PART II.

Of the Life of the Pastor.

CHAPTER I.

How one who has in due order arrived at a place of rule ought to demean himself in it.

The conduct of a prelate ought so far to transcend the conduct of the people as the life of a shepherd is wont to exalt him above the flock. For one whose estimation is such that the people are called his flock is bound anxiously to consider what great necessity is laid upon him to maintain rectitude. It is necessary, then, that in thought he should be pure, in action chief; discreet in keeping silence, profitable in speech; a near neighbour to every one in sympathy, exalted above all in contemplation; a familiar friend of good livers through humility, unbending against the vices of evil-doers through zeal for righteousness; not relaxing in his care for what is inward from being occupied in outward things, nor neglecting to provide for outward things in his solicitude for what is inward. But the things which we have thus briefly touched on let us now unfold and discuss more at length.

CHAPTER II.

That the ruler should be pure in thought.

The ruler should always be pure in thought, inasmuch as no impurity ought to pollute him who has undertaken the office of wiping away the stains of pollution in the hearts of others also; for the hand that would cleanse from dirt must needs be clean, lest, being itself sordid with clinging mire, it soil whatever it touches all the more. For on this account it is said through the prophet, *Be ye clean that bear the vessels of the Lord* (Isai. lii. 11). For they bear the vessels of the Lord who undertake, on the surety of their own conversation, to conduct the souls of their neighbours to the eternal sanctuary. Let them therefore perceive within themselves how purified they ought to be who carry in the bosom of their own personal responsibility living vessels to the temple of eternity. Hence by the divine voice it is enjoined (Exod. xxviii. 15), that on the breast of Aaron the breastplate[1] of judgment should be closely pressed by binding fillets; seeing that lax cogitations should by no means possess the priestly heart, but reason alone constrain it; nor should he cogitate anything indiscreet or unprofitable, who, constituted as he is for example to others, ought to shew in the gravity of his life what store of reason he carries in his breast. And on this breastplate it is further carefully prescribed that the names of the twelve patriarchs should be engraved. For to carry always the fathers registered on the breast is to think without intermission on the lives of the ancients. For the priest then walks blamelessly when he pores continually on the examples of the fathers that went before him, when he considers without cease the footsteps of the Saints, and keeps down unlawful thoughts, lest he advance the

[1] For *breastplate* (A.V.) the LXX. has λογεῖον, and the Vulgate, from which St. Gregory quotes, *rationale*. On the significance of this word the application depends. Anciently an ornament called the *rationale* was attached to the vestments of bishops. "*Rationale* . . . Ornamenti genus quo ornantur casulæ aliaque vestes ecclesiasticæ" (Ducange). The vestment itself seems also to have been sometimes called the *rationale*. "Vestis episcopalis novæ legis, *le pallium*" (Ib.).

foot of his conduct beyond the limit of order. And it is also well called the breastplate of judgment, because the ruler ought ever with subtle scrutiny to discern between good and evil, and studiously consider what things are suitable for what, and when and how; nor should he seek anything for himself, but esteem his neighbours' good as his own advantage. Hence in the same place it is written, *But thou shalt put in the breastplate of Aaron doctrine and truth*[2], *which shall be upon Aaron's breast, when he goeth in before the Lord, and he shall bear the judgment of the children of Israel upon his breast in the sight of the Lord continually* (Ibid. 30). For the priest's bearing the judgment of the children of Israel on his breast before the face of the Lord means his examining the causes of his subjects with regard only to the mind of the judge within, so that no admixture of humanity cleave to him in what he dispenses as standing in God's stead, lest private vexation should exasperate the keenness of his censure. And, while he shews himself zealous against the vices of others, let him get rid of his own, lest either latent grudge vitiate the calmness of his judgment, or headlong anger disturb it. But when the terror of Him who presides over all things is considered (that is to say of the judge within), not without great fear may subjects be governed. And such fear indeed purges, while it humiliates, the mind of the ruler, guarding it against being either lifted up by presumption of spirit, or defiled by delight of the flesh, or obscured by importunity of dusty thought through lust for earthly things. These things, however, cannot but knock at the ruler's mind: but it is necessary to make haste to overcome them by resistance, lest the vice which tempts by suggestion should subdue by the softness of delight, and, this being tardily expelled from the mind, should slay with the sword of consent.

CHAPTER III.

That the ruler should be always chief in action.

The ruler should always be chief in action, that by his living he may point out the way of life to those that are put under him, and that the flock, which follows the voice and manners of the shepherd, may learn how to walk better through example than through words For he who is required by the necessity of his position to speak the highest things is compelled by the same necessity to exhibit the highest things. For that voice more readily penetrates the hearer's heart, which the speaker's life commends, since what he commands by speaking he helps the doing of by shewing. Hence it is said through the prophet, *Get thee up into the high mountain, thou that bringest good tidings to Sion* (Isai. xl. 9): which means that he who is engaged in heavenly preaching should already have forsaken the low level of earthly works, and appear as standing on the summit of things, and by so much the more easily should draw those who are under him to better things as by the merit of his life he cries aloud from heights above. Hence under the divine law the priest receives the shoulder for sacrifice, and this the right one and separate (Exod. xxix. 22); to signify that his action should be not only profitable, but even singular; and that he should not merely do what is right among bad men, but transcend even the well-doers among those that are under him in the virtue of his conduct, as he surpasses them in the dignity of his order. The breast also together with the shoulder is assigned to him for eating, that he may learn to immolate to the Giver of all that of himself which he is enjoined to take of the Sacrifice; that he may not only in his breast entertain right thoughts, but with the shoulder of work invite those who behold him to things on high; that he may covet no prosperity of the present life, and fear no adversity; that, having regard to the fear within him, he may despise the charm of the world, but considering the charm of inward sweetness, may despise its terrors. Wherefore by command of the supernal voice (Exod. xxix. 5) the priest is braced on each shoulder with the robe of the ephod, that he may be always guarded against prosperity and adversity by the ornament of virtues; so that walking, as S. Paul says (2 Cor. vi 7), *in the armour of righteousness on the right hand and on the left*, while he strives only after *those things which are before*, he may decline on neither side to low delight. Him let neither prosperity elate nor adversity perturb; let neither smooth things coax him to the surrender of his will, nor rough things press him down to despair; so that, while he humbles the bent of his mind to no passions, he may shew with how great beauty of the ephod he is covered on each shoulder. Which ephod is also rightly ordered to be made of gold, blue, purple, twice dyed scarlet, and fine twined linen (Exod. xxviii. 8), that it may be shewn by how great diversity of virtues the priest ought to be distinguished. Thus in the priest's robe before all things gold glitters, to shew that he should shine forth principally in the understanding of wisdom. And with it blue, which is resplendent with aerial colour, is

[2] For Urim and Thummim (as in A.V., retaining the Hebrew words), the LXX. has τὴν δήλωσιν καὶ τὴν αλήθειαν, and the Vulgate, quoted by St. Gregory, *Doctrinam et Veritatem*.

conjoined, to shew that through all that he penetrates with his understanding he should rise above earthly favours to the love of celestial things; lest, while caught unawares by his own praises, he be emptied of his very understanding of the truth. With gold and blue, purple also is mingled: which means, that the priest's heart, while hoping for the high things which he preaches, should repress in itself even the suggestions of vice, and as it were in virtue of a royal power, rebut them, in that he has regard ever to the nobility of inward regeneration, and by his manners guards his right to the robe of the heavenly kingdom. For it is of this nobility of the spirit that it is said through Peter, *Ye are a chosen generation, a royal priesthood* (1 Pet. ii. 9). With respect also to this power, whereby we subdue vices, we are fortified by the voice of John, who says, *As many as received Him, to them gave He power to become the sons of God* (John i. 12). This dignity of fortitude the Psalmist has in view when he says, *But with me greatly honoured have been Thy friends, O God; greatly strengthened has been their principality* (Ps. cxxxviii. 17). For truly the mind of saints is exalted to princely eminence while outwardly they are seen to suffer abasement. But with gold, blue, and purple, twice died scarlet is conjoined, to shew that all excellences of virtue should be adorned with charity in the eyes of the judge within; and that whatever glitters before men may be lighted up in sight of the hidden arbiter with the flame of inward love. And, further, this charity, since it consists in love at once of God and of our neighbour, has, as it were, the lustre of a double dye. He then who so pants after the beauty of his Maker as to neglect the care of his neighbours, or so attends to the care of his neighbours as to grow languid in divine love, whichever of these two things it may be that he neglects, knows not what it is to have twice dyed scarlet in the adornment of his ephod. But, while the mind is intent on the precepts of charity, it undoubtedly remains that the flesh be macerated through abstinence. Hence with twice dyed scarlet fine twined linen is conjoined. For fine linen (*byssus*) springs from the earth with glittering show: and what is designated by fine linen but bodily chastity shining white in the comeliness of purity? And it is also twisted for being interwoven into the beauty of the ephod, since the habit of chastity then attains to the perfect whiteness of purity when the flesh is worn by abstinence. And, since the merit of affliction of the flesh profits among the other virtues, fine twined linen shews white, as it were, in the diverse beauty of the ephod.

CHAPTER IV.

That the ruler should be discreet in keeping silence, profitable in speech.

The ruler should be discreet in keeping silence, profitable in speech; lest he either utter what ought to be suppressed or suppress what he ought to utter. For, as incautious speaking leads into error, so indiscreet silence leaves in error those who might have been instructed. For often improvident rulers, fearing to lose human favour, shrink timidly from speaking freely the things that are right; and, according to the voice of the Truth (Joh. x. 12), serve unto the custody of the flock by no means with the zeal of shepherds, but in the way of hirelings; since they fly when the wolf cometh if they hide themselves under silence. For hence it is that the Lord through the prophet upbraids them, saying, *Dumb dogs, that cannot bark* (Isai. lvi. 10). Hence again He complains, saying, *Ye have not gone up against the enemy, neither opposed a wall for the house of Israel, to stand in the battle in the day of the Lord* (Ezek. xiii. 5). Now to go up against the enemy is to go with free voice against the powers of this world for defence of the flock; and to stand in the battle in the day of the Lord is out of love of justice to resist bad men when they contend against us. For, for a shepherd to have feared to say what is right, what else is it but to have turned his back in keeping silence? But surely, if he puts himself in front for the flock, he opposes a wall against the enemy for the house of Israel. Hence again to the sinful people it is said, *Thy prophets have seen false and foolish things for thee: neither did they discover thine iniquity, to provoke thee to repentance* (Lam. ii. 14). For in sacred language teachers are sometimes called prophets, in that, by pointing out how fleeting are present things, they make manifest the things that are to come. And such the divine discourse convinces of seeing false things, because, while fearing to reprove faults, they vainly flatter evil doers by promising security: neither do they at all discover the iniquity of sinners, since they refrain their voice from chiding. For the language of reproof is the key of discovery, because by chiding it discloses the fault of which even he who has committed it is often himself unaware. Hence Paul says, *That he may be able by sound doctrine even to convince the gainsayers* (Tit. i. 9). Hence through Malachi it is said, *The priest's lips keep knowledge, and they shall seek the law at his mouth* (Malac. ii. 7). Hence through Isaiah the Lord admonishes, saying, *Cry aloud, spare not, lift up thy voice like a trumpet* (Isai. lviii. 1). For it is true that whosoever enters on the priesthood undertakes the office of a herald, so as to walk, himself crying aloud, before the coming of the judge who follows terribly. Wherefore, if the priest knows not how to preach, what voice of a loud cry shall the mute herald utter? For hence it is that the Holy Spirit sat upon the first pastors under the appearance of tongues (Acts ii. 3); because whomsoever He has filled, He himself at once makes eloquent. Hence it is enjoined on Moses that when the priest goes into the tabernacle he shall be encompassed with bells (Exod. xxviii. 33); that is, that he shall have about him the sounds of preaching, lest he provoke by his silence the judgment of Him Who beholds him from above. For it is written, *That his sound may be heard when he goeth in unto the holy place before the Lord, and when he cometh out, that he die not* (Exod. xxviii. 35). For the priest, when he goeth in or cometh out, dies if a sound is not heard from him, because he provokes the wrath of the hidden judge, if he goes without the sound of preaching. Aptly also are the bells described as inserted in his vestments. For what else ought we to take the vestments of the priest to be but righteous works; as the prophet attests when he says, *Let Thy priests be clothed with righteousness* (Ps. cxxxi. 9)? The bells, therefore, are inherent in his vestments to signify that the very works of the priest should also proclaim the way of life together with the sound of his tongue. But, when the ruler prepares himself for speaking, let him bear in mind with what studious caution he ought to speak, lest, if he be hurried inordinately into speaking, the hearts of hearers be smitten with the wound of error, and, while he perchance desires to seem wise, he unwisely sever the bond of unity. For on this account the Truth says, *Have salt in yourselves, and have peace one with another* (Mark ix. 49). Now by salt is denoted the word of wisdom. Let him, therefore, who strives to speak wisely fear greatly, lest by his eloquence the unity of his hearers be disturbed. Hence Paul says, *Not to be more wise than behoveth to be wise, but to be wise unto sobriety* (Rom. xii. 3). Hence in the priest's vestment, according to Divine precept, to bells are added pomegranates (Exod. xxviii. 34). For what is signified by pomegranates but the unity of the faith? For, as within a pomegranate many seeds are protected by one outer rind, so the unity of the faith comprehends the innumerable peoples of holy Church, whom a diversity of merits retains within her. Lest then a ruler should be unadvisedly hurried into speaking, the Truth in person proclaims to His disciples this which we have already cited, *Have salt in yourselves, and have peace one with another* (Mark ix. 49). It is as though He should say in a figure through the dress of the priest: Join ye pomegranates to bells, that in all ye say ye may with cautious watchfulness keep the unity of the faith. Rulers ought also to guard with anxious thought not only against saying in any way what is wrong, but against uttering even what is right overmuch and inordinately; since the good effect of things spoken is often lost, when enfeebled to the hearts of hearers by the incautious importunity of loquacity: and this same loquacity, which knows not how to serve for the profit of the hearers, also defiles the speaker. Hence it is well said through Moses, *The man that hath a flux of seed shall be unclean* (Levit. xv. 2). For the quality of the speech that is heard is the seed of the thought which follows, since, while speech is conceived through the ear, thought is engendered in the mind. Whence also by the wise of this world the excellent preacher was called a sower of words (*seminiverbius*) (Acts xvii. 18). Wherefore, he that suffers from a flux of seed is pronounced unclean, because, being addicted to much speaking, he defiles himself by that which, had it been orderly issued, might have produced the offspring of right thought in the hearts of hearers; and, while he incautiously spends himself in loquacity, he sheds his seed not so as to serve for generation, but unto uncleanness. Hence Paul also, in admonishing his disciple to be instant in preaching, when he says, *I charge thee before God and Christ Jesus, Who shall judge the quick and the dead by His appearing and His kingdom, preach the word, be instant opportunely, importunely*[3] (2 Tim. iv. 1), being about to say *importunely*, premises *opportunely*, because in truth importunity mars itself to the mind of the hearer by its own very cheapness, if it knows not how to observe opportunity.

CHAPTER V.

That the ruler should be a near neighbour to every one in compassion, and exalted above all in contemplation.

The ruler should be a near neighbour to every one in sympathy, and exalted above all in contemplation, so that through the bowels of loving-kindness he may transfer the infirmities of others to himself, and by loftiness

3 *Opportune, importune,* the second word being apparently understood in the sense of *importunately*.

of speculation transcend even himself in his aspiration after the invisible; lest either in seeking high things he despise the weak things of his neighbours, or in suiting himself to the weak things of his neighbours he relinquish his aspiration after high things. For hence it is that Paul is caught up into Paradise (2 Cor. xii. 3) and explores the secrets of the third heaven, and yet, though borne aloft in that contemplation of things invisible, recalls the vision of his mind to the bed of the carnal, and directs how they should have intercourse with each other in their hidden privacy, saying, *But on account of fornication let every man have his own wife, and let every woman have her own husband. Let the husband render unto the wife her due, and likewise the wife unto the husband* (1 Cor. vii. 2). And a little after (Ibid. v. 5), *Defraud ye not one the other, except it be with consent for a time, that ye may give yourselves to prayer, and come together again, that Satan tempt you not.* Lo, he is already initiated into heavenly secrets, and yet through the bowels of condescension he searches into the bed of the carnal; and the same eye of the heart which in his elevation he lifts to the invisible, he bends in his compassion upon the secrets of those who are subject to infirmity. In contemplation he transcends heaven, and yet in his anxious care deserts not the couch of the carnal; because, being joined at once to the highest and to the lowest by the bond of charity, though in himself mightily caught up in the power of the spirit into the heights above, yet among others, in his loving-kindness, he is content to become weak. Hence, therefore, he says, *Who is weak, and I am not weak? Who is offended, and I burn not?* (2 Cor. xi. 29). Hence again he says, *Unto the Jews I became as a Jew* (1 Cor. ix. 20). Now he exhibited this behaviour not by losing hold of his faith, but by extending his loving-kindness; so as, by transferring in a figure the person of unbelievers to himself, to learn from himself how they ought to have compassion shewn them; to the end that he might bestow on them what he would have rightly wished to have had bestowed upon himself, had he been as they. Hence again he says, *Whether we be beside ourselves, it is to God: or whether we be sober, it is for you* (2 Cor. v. 13). For he had known how both to transcend himself in contemplation, and to accommodate himself to his hearers in condescension. Hence Jacob, the Lord looking down from above, and oil being poured down on the stone, saw angels ascending and descending (Gen. xxviii. 12); to signify that true preachers not only aspire in contemplation to the holy head of the Church, that is to the Lord, above, but also descend in commiseration downward to His members. Hence Moses goes frequently in and out of the tabernacle, and he who is wrapped into contemplation within is busied outside with the affairs of those who are subject to infirmity. Within he considers the secret things of God; without he carries the burdens of the carnal. And also concerning doubtful matters he always recurs to the tabernacle, to consult the Lord before the ark of the covenant; affording without doubt an example to rulers; that, when in the outside world they are uncertain how to order things, they should return to their own soul as though to the tabernacle, and, as before the ark of the covenant, consult the Lord, if so, they may search within themselves the pages of sacred utterance concerning that whereof they doubt. Hence the Truth itself, manifested to us through susception of our humanity, continues in prayer on the mountain, but works miracles in the cities (Luke vi. 12), thus laying down the way to be followed by good rulers; that, though already in contemplation aspiring to the highest things, they should mingle in sympathy with the necessities of the infirm; since charity then rises wonderfully to high things when it is compassionately drawn to the low things of neighbours; and the more kindly it descends to the weak things of this world, the more vigorously it recurs to the things on high. But those who are over others should shew themselves to be such that their subjects may not blush to disclose even their secrets to them; that the little ones, vexed with the waves of temptation, may have recourse to their pastor's heart as to a mother's breast, and wash away the defilement they foresee to themselves from the filth of the sin that buffets them in the solace of his exhortation and in the tears of prayer. Hence also it is that before the doors of the temple the brazen sea for washing the hands of those who enter, that is the laver, is supported by twelve oxen (1 Kings vii. 23, *seq.*), whose faces indeed stand out to view, but whose hinder parts are hidden. For what is signified by the twelve oxen but the whole order of pastors, of whom the law says, as explained by Paul, *Thou shalt not muzzle the mouth of the ox that treadeth out the corn* (1 Cor. ix. 9; ex Deut. xxv. 4)? Their open works indeed we see; but what remains to them behind in the hidden retribution of the strict judge we know not. Yet, when they prepare the patience of their condescension for cleansing the sins of their neighbours in confession, they support, as it were, the laver before the doors of the temple; that whosoever is striving to enter the gate of eternity may shew his temptations to his pastor's heart, and, as it were, wash the hands of his thought and of his deed in the laver of the oxen. And for the most part it comes to pass that, while the ruler's mind becomes aware, through condescension, of the trials of others, it is itself also attacked by the temptations whereof it hears; since the same water of the laver in which a multitude of people is cleansed is undoubtedly itself defiled. For, in receiving the pollutions of those who wash, it loses, as it were, the calmness of its own purity. But of this the pastor ought by no means to be afraid, since, under God, who nicely balances all things, he is the more easily rescued from his own temptations as he is more compassionately distressed by those of others.

CHAPTER VI.

That the ruler should be, through humility, a companion of good livers, but, through the zeal of righteousness, rigid against the vices of evil-doers.

The ruler should be, through humility, a companion of good livers, and, through the zeal of righteousness, rigid against the vices of evil-doers; so that in nothing he prefer himself to the good, and yet, when the fault of the bad requires it, he be at once conscious of the power of his priority; to the end that, while among his subordinates who live well he waives his rank and accounts them as his equals, he may not fear to execute the laws of rectitude towards the perverse. For, as I remember to have said in my book on morals (*Lib.* xxi., *Moral*, *cap.* 10, *nunc. n.* 22), it is clear that nature produced all men equal; but, through variation in the order of their merits, guilt puts some below others. But the very diversity which has accrued from vice is ordered by divine judgment, so that, since all men cannot stand on an equal footing, one should be ruled by another. Hence all who are over others ought to consider in themselves not the authority of their rank, but the equality of their condition; and rejoice not to be over men, but to do them good. For indeed our ancient fathers are said to have been not kings of men, but shepherds of flocks. And, when the Lord said to Noe and his children, *Increase and multiply, and replenish the earth* (Gen. ix. 1), He at once added, *And let the fear of you and the dread of you be upon all the beasts of the earth.* Thus it appears that, whereas it is ordered that the fear and the dread should be upon the beasts of the earth, it is forbidden that it should be upon men. For man is by nature preferred to the brute beasts, but not to other men: and therefore it is said to him that he should be feared by the beasts, but not by men; since to wish to be feared by one's equal is to be proud against nature. And yet it is necessary that rulers should be feared by their subjects, when they find that God is not feared by them; so that those who have no dread of divine judgments may at any rate, through human dread, be afraid to sin. For superiors by no means shew themselves proud in seeking to inspire this fear, in which they seek not their own glory, but the righteousness of their subordinates. For in exacting fear of themselves from such as live perversely, they lord it, as it were, not over men, but over beasts, inasmuch as, so far as their subordinates are bestial, they ought also to lie subdued to dread.

But commonly a ruler, from the very fact of his being pre-eminent over others, is puffed up with elation of thought; and, while all things serve his need, while his commands are quickly executed after his desire, while all his subjects extol with praises what he has done well, but have no authority to speak against what he has done amiss, and while they commonly praise even what they ought to have reproved, his mind, seduced by what is offered in abundance from below, is lifted up above itself; and, while outwardly surrounded by unbounded favour, he loses his inward sense of truth; and, forgetful of himself, he scatters himself on the voices of other men, and believes himself to be such as outwardly he hears himself called rather than such as he ought inwardly to have judged himself to be. He looks down on those who are under him, nor does he acknowledge them as in the order of nature his equals; and those whom he has surpassed in the accident of power he believes himself to have transcended also in the merits of his life; he esteems himself wiser than all whom he sees himself to excel in power. For indeed he establishes himself in his own mind on a certain lofty eminence, and, though bound together in the same condition of nature with others, he disdains to regard others from the same level; and so he comes to be even like him of whom it is written, *He beholdeth all high things: he is a king over all the children of pride* (Job xli. 25). Nay, aspiring to a singular eminence, and despising the social life of the angels, he says, *I will place my seat in the north, and I will be like unto the Most High* (Isai. xiv. 13). Wherefore through a marvellous judgment he finds a pit of downfall within himself, while outwardly he exalts himself on the summit of power. For he is indeed made like unto the apostate angel, when, being a man, he disdains to be like unto men. Thus Saul, after merit of humility, became swollen with pride, when in the height of power: for his humility he was preferred, for his pride rejected; as the Lord attests, Who says, *When thou wast little in thine own sight, did I not make thee the head of the tribes of Israel* (1 Sam. xv. 17)? He had before seen himself little in his own eyes, but, when propped up by temporal power, he no longer saw himself little. For, preferring himself in comparison with others because he had more power than all, he esteemed himself great above all. Yet in a wonderful way, when he was little with himself, he was great with God; but, when he appeared great with himself, he was little with God. Thus commonly, while the mind is inflated from an affluence of subordinates, it becomes corrupted to a flux of pride, the very summit of power being pander to desire. And in truth he orders this power well who knows how both to maintain it and to combat it. He orders it well who knows how through it to tower above delinquencies, and knows how with it to match himself with others in equality. For the human mind commonly is exalted even when supported by no authority: how much more does it lift itself on high when authority lends itself to its support! Nevertheless he dispenses this authority aright, who knows how, with anxious care, both to take of it what is helpful, and also to reject what tempts, and with it to perceive himself to to be on a par with others, and yet to put himself above those that sin in his avenging zeal.

But we shall more fully understand this distinction, if we look at the examples given by the first pastor. For Peter, who had received from God the principality of Holy Church, from Cornelius, acting well and prostrating himself humbly before him, refused to accept immoderate veneration, saying, *Stand up; do it not; I myself also am a man* (Acts x. 26). But, when he discovers the guilt of Ananias and Sapphira, he soon shews with how great power he had been made eminent above all others. For by his word he smote their life, which he detected by the penetration of his spirit; and he recollected himself as chief within the Church against sins, though he did not acknowledge this, when honour was eagerly paid him, before his brethren who acted well. In one case holiness of conduct merited the communion of equality; in the other avenging zeal brought out to view the just claims of authority. Paul, too, knew not himself as preferred above his brethren who acted well, when he said, *Not for that we have dominion over your faith, but are helpers of your joy* (2 Cor. i. 23). And he straightway added, *For by faith ye stand:* as if to explain his declaration by saying, For this cause we have not dominion over your faith, because by faith ye stand; for we are your equals in that wherein we know you to stand. He knew not himself as preferred above his brethren, when he said, *We became babes in the midst of you* (1 Thess. ii. 7); and again, *But ourselves your servants through Christ* (2 Cor. iv. 5). But, when he found a fault that required to be corrected, straightway he recollected himself as a master, saying, *What will ye? Shall I come unto you with a rod* (1 Cor. iv. 21)?

Supreme rule, then, is ordered well, when he who presides lords it over vices, rather than over his brethren. But, when superiors correct their delinquent subordinates, it remains for them anxiously to take heed how far, while in right of their authority they smite faults with due discipline, they still, through custody of humility, acknowledge themselves to be on a par with the very brethren who are corrected; although for the most part it is becoming that in our silent thought we even prefer the brethren whom we correct to ourselves. For their vices are through us smitten with the vigour of discipline; but in those which we ourselves commit we are lacerated by not even a word of upbraiding. Wherefore we are by so much the more bounden before the Lord as among men we sin unpunished: but our discipline renders our subordinates by so much the freer from divine judgment, as it leaves not their faults without retribution here. Therefore, in the heart humility should be maintained, and in action discipline. And all the time there is need of sagacious insight, lest, through excessive custody of the virtue of humility, the just claims of government be relaxed, and lest, while any superior lowers himself more than is fit, he be unable to restrain the lives of his subordinates under the bond of discipline. Let rulers, then, maintain outwardly what they undertake for the benefit of others: let them retain inwardly what makes them fearful in their estimate of themselves. But still let even their subjects perceive, by certain signs coming out becomingly, that in themselves they are humble; so as both to see something to be afraid of in their authority, and to acknowledge something to imitate with respect to humility. Therefore let those who preside study without intermission that in proportion as their power is seen to be great externally it be kept down within themselves internally; that it vanquish not their thought; that the heart be not carried away to delight in it; lest the mind become unable to control that which in lust of domination it submits itself to. For, lest the heart of a ruler should be betrayed into elation by delight in personal power, it is rightly said by a certain wise man, *They have made thee a leader: lift not up thyself, but be among them as one of them* (Ecclus. xxxii. 1). Hence also Peter says, *Not as being lords over God's heritage, but being made ensamples to the flock* (1 Pet. v. 3). Hence the Truth in person, provoking us to higher virtuous desert, says, *Ye know that the princes of the Gentiles exercise dominion over them, and they that are greater exercise authority upon them. It shall not be so among you, but whosoever will be greater among you, let him be your minister; and whosoever will be chief among you, let him be your servant; even as the Son of Man came not to be ministered to, but to minister* (Matth. xx. 25). Hence also He indicates what punishments are in store for the servant who has been elated by his assumption of government, saying, *But and if that evil servant shall say in his heart, My lord delayeth his coming, and shall begin to smite his fellow-servants, and to eat and drink with the drunken, the lord of that servant shall come in a day when he looketh not for him, and in an hour that he is not aware of, and shall cut him asunder, and appoint him his portion with the hypocrites* (Matth. xxiv. 48, *seq.*). For he is rightly numbered among the hypocrites, who under pretence of discipline turns the ministry of government to the purpose of domination. And yet sometimes there is more grievous delinquency, if among perverse persons equality is kept up more than discipline. For Eli, because, overcome by false affection, he would not punish his delinquent sons, smote himself along with his sons before the strict judge with a cruel doom (1 Sam. iv. 17, 18). For on this account it is said to him by the divine voice, *Thou hast honoured thy sons more than Me* (Ibid. ii. 29). Hence, too, He upbraids the shepherds through the prophet, saying, *That which was broken ye have not bound up, and that which was cast away ye have not brought back* (Ezek. xxxiv. 4). For one who had been cast away is brought back, when any one who has fallen into sin is recalled to a state of righteousness by the vigour of pastoral solicitude. For ligature binds a fracture when discipline subdues a sin, lest the wound should bleed mortally for want of being compressed by the severity of constraint. But often a fracture is made worse, when it is bound together unwarily, so that the cut is more severely felt from being immoderately constrained by ligaments. Hence it is needful that when a wound of sin in subordinates is repressed by correction, even constraint should moderate itself with great carefulness, to the end that it may so exercise the rights of discipline against delinquents as to retain the bowels of loving-kindness. For care should be taken that a ruler shew himself to his subjects as a mother in loving-kindness, and as a father in discipline. And all the time it should be seen to with anxious circumspection, that neither discipline be rigid nor loving-kindness lax. For, as we have before now said in our book on Morals (*Lib.* xx., *Moral* n. 14, c. 8, *et ep.* 25, *lib.* 1), there is much wanting both to discipline and to compassion, if one be had without the other. But there ought to be in rulers towards their subjects both compassion justly considerate, and discipline affectionately severe. For hence it is that, as the Truth teaches (Luke x. 34), the man is brought by the care of the Samaritan half dead into the inn, and both wine and oil are applied to his wounds; the wine to make them smart, the oil to soothe them. For whosoever superintends the healing of wounds must needs administer in wine the smart of pain, and in oil the softness of loving-kindness, to the end that through wine what is festering may be purged, and through oil what is curable may be soothed. Gentleness, then, is to be mingled with severity; a sort of compound is to be made of both; so that subjects be neither exulcerated by too much asperity, nor relaxed by too great kindness. Which thing, according to the words of Paul (Heb. ix. 4), is well signified by that ark of the tabernacle, in which, together with the tables, there is a rod and manna; because, if with knowledge of sacred Scripture in the good ruler's breast there is the rod of constraint, there should be also the manna of sweetness. Hence David says, *Thy rod and thy staff, they have comforted me* (Ps. xxiii. 4). For with a rod we are smitten, with a staff we are supported. If, then, there is the constraint of the rod for striking, there should be also the comfort of the staff for supporting. Wherefore let there be love, but not enervating; let there be vigour, but not exasperating; let there be zeal, but not immoderately burning; let there be pity, but not sparing more than is expedient; that, while justice and mercy blend themselves together in supreme rule, he who is at the head may both soothe the hearts of his subjects in making them afraid, and yet in soothing them constrain them to reverential awe.

CHAPTER VII.

That the ruler relax not his care for the things that are within in his occupation among the things that are without, nor neglect to provide for the things that are without in his solicitude for the things that are within.

The ruler should not relax his care for the things that are within in his occupation among the things that are without, nor neglect to provide for the things that are without in his solicitude for the things that are within; lest either, given up to the things that are without, he fall away from his inmost concerns, or, occupied only with the things that are within, bestow not on his neighbours outside himself what he owes them. For it is often the case that some, as if forgetting that they have been put over their brethren for their souls' sake, devote themselves with the whole effort of their heart to secular concerns: these, when they are at hand, they exult in transacting, and, even when there is a lack of them, pant after them night and day with seethings of turbid thought; and when, haply for lack of opportunity, they have quiet from them, by their very quiet they are wearied all the more. For they count it pleasure to be tired by action: they esteem it labour not to labour in earthly businesses. And so it comes to pass that, while they delight in being hustled by worldly tumults, they are ignorant of the things that are within, which they ought to have taught to others. And from this cause, undoubtedly, the life also of their subjects is benumbed; because, while desirous of advancing spiritually, it meets a stumbling-block on the way in the example of him who is set over it. For when the head languishes, the members fail to thrive; and it is in vain for an army to follow swiftly in pursuit of enemies if the very leader of the march goes wrong. No exhortation sustains the minds of the subjects, and no reproof chastises their faults, because, while the office of an earthly judge is executed by the guardian of souls, the attention of the shepherd is diverted from custody of the flock; and the subjects are unable to apprehend the light of truth, because, while earthly pursuits occupy the pastor's mind, dust, driven by the wind of temptation, blinds the Church's eyes. To guard against this, the Redeemer of the human race, when He would restrain us from gluttony, saying, *Take heed to yourselves that your hearts be not overcharged with surfeiting and drunkenness* (Luke xxi. 34), forthwith added, *Or with cares of this life:* and in the same place also, with design to add fearfulness to the warning, He straightway said, *Lest perchance that day come upon you unawares* (Ibid.): and He even declares the manner of that coming, saying, *For as a snare shall it come on all them that dwell on the face of the whole earth* (Ibid. 35). Hence He says again, *No man can serve two masters* (Luke xvi. 13). Hence Paul withdraws the minds of the religious from consort with the world by summoning, nay rather enlisting them, when he says, *No man that warreth for God entangleth himself with the affairs of this life, that he may please him to whom he has approved himself* (2 Tim. ii. 4). Hence to the rulers of the Church he both commends the studies of leisure and points out the remedies of counsel, saying, *If then ye should have secular judgments, set them to judge who are contemptible in the church* (1 Cor. vi. 4); that is, that those very persons whom no spiritual gifts adorn should devote themselves to earthly charges. It is as if he had said more plainly, Since they are incapable of penetrating the inmost things, let them at any rate employ themselves externally in necessary things. Hence Moses, who speaks with God (Exod. xviii. 17, 18), is judged by the reproof of Jethro, who was of alien race, because with ill-advised labour he devotes himself to the people's earthly affairs: and counsel too is presently given him, that he should appoint others in his stead for settling earthly strifes, and he himself should be more free to learn spiritual secrets for the instruction of the people.

By the subjects, then, inferior matters are to be transacted, by the rulers the highest thought of; so that no annoyance of dust may darken the eye which is placed aloft for looking forward to the onward steps. For all who preside are the head of their subjects; and, that the feet may be able to take a straight course, the head ought undoubtedly to look forward to it from above, lest the feet linger on their onward journey, the body being bent from its uprightness and the head bowed down to the earth. But with what conscience can the overseer of souls avail himself among other men of his pastoral dignity, while engaged himself in the earthly cares which it was his duty to reprehend in others? And this indeed is what the Lord, in the wrath of just retribution, menaced through the prophet, saying, *And there shall be like people, like priest* (Hos. iv. 9). For the priest is as the people, when one who bears a spiritual office acts as do others who are still under judgment with regard to their carnal pursuits. And this indeed the prophet Jeremiah, in the great sorrow of his charity, deplores under the image of the destruction of the temple, saying, *How is the gold become dim! The most excellent colour is changed; the stones of the sanctuary are poured out in the top of all the streets* (Lam. iv. 1). For what is expressed by gold, which surpasses all other metals, but the excellency of holiness? What by the most excellent colour but the reverence that is about religion, to all men lovely? What are signified by the stones of the sanctuary but persons in sacred orders? What is figured under the name of streets but the latitude of this present life? For, because in Greek speech the word for latitude is πλάτος, streets (*plateæ*) have been so called from their breadth, or latitude. But the Truth in person says, *Broad and spacious is the way that leadeth to destruction* (Matth. vii. 13). Gold, therefore, becomes dim when a life of holiness is polluted by earthly doings; the most excellent colour is changed, when the previous reputation of persons who were believed to be living religiously is diminished. For, when any one after a habit of holiness mixes himself up with earthly doings, it is as though his colour were changed, and the reverence that surrounded him grew pale and disregarded before the eyes of men. The stones of the sanctuary also are poured out into the streets, when those who, for the ornament of the Church, should have been free to penetrate internal mysteries as it were in the secret places of the tabernacle seek out the broadways of secular causes outside. For indeed to this end they were made stones of the sanctuary, that they might appear in the vestment of the high-priest within the holy of holies. But, when ministers of religion exact not the Redeemer's honour from those that are under them by the merit of their life, they are not stones of the sanctuary in the ornament of the pontiff. And truly these stones of the sanctuary lie scattered through the streets, when persons in sacred orders, given up to the latitude of their own pleasures, cleave to earthly businesses. And it is to be observed that they are said to be scattered, not in the streets, but in the top of the streets; because, even when they are engaged in earthly matters, they desire to appear topmost; so as to occupy the broad ways in their enjoyment of delight, and yet to be at the top of the streets in the dignity of holiness.

Further, there is nothing to hinder us from taking the stones of the sanctuary to be those of which the sanctuary was itself constructed; which lie scattered in the top of the streets when men in sacred orders, in whose office the glory of holiness had previously seemed to stand, devote themselves out of preference to earthly doings. Secular employments, therefore, though they may sometimes be endured out of compassion, should never be sought after out of affection for the things themselves; lest, while they weigh down the mind of him who loves them, they sink it, overcome by its own burden, from heavenly places to the lowest. But, on the other hand, there are some who undertake the care of the flock, but desire to be so at leisure for their own spiritual concerns as to be in no wise occupied with external things. Such persons, in neglecting all care for what pertains to the body, by no means meet the needs of those who are put under them. And certainly their preaching is for the most part despised; because, while they find fault with the deeds of sinners, but nevertheless afford them not the necessaries of the present life, they are not at all willingly listened to. For the word of doctrine penetrates not the mind of one that is in need, if the hand of compassion commends it not to his heart. But the seed of the word readily germinates, when the loving-kindness of the preacher waters it in the hearer's breast. Whence, for a ruler to be able to infuse what may profit inwardly, it is necessary for him, with blameless consideration, to provide also for outward things. Let pastors, then, so glow with ardour in regard to the inward affections of those they have the charge of as not to relinquish provision also for their outward life. For, as we have said, the heart of the flock is, even as it were of right, set against preaching, if the care of external succour be neglected by the pastor. Whence also the first pastor anxiously admonishes, saying, *The elders which are among you I beseech, who am also an elder, and a witness of the sufferings of Christ, and also a partaker of the glory that shall be revealed, feed the flock of God which is among you* (1 Pet. v. 1): in which place he shewed whether it was the feeding of the heart or of the body that he was commending, when he forthwith added, *Providing for it, not by constraint, but willingly, according to God, not for filthy lucre, but of a ready mind.* In these words, indeed, pastors are kindly forewarned, lest, while they satisfy the want of those who are under them, they slay themselves with the sword of ambition; lest, while through them their neighbours are refreshed with succours of the flesh, they themselves remain fasting from the bread of righteousness. This solicitude of pastors Paul stirs up when he says, *If any provide not for his own, and especially for those of his own house, he hath denied the faith, and is worse than an infidel* (1 Tim. v. 8). In the midst of all this, then, they should fear, and watchfully take heed, lest, while occupied with outward care, they be whelmed away from inward intentness. For usually, as we have already said, the hearts of rulers, while unwarily devoting themselves to temporal solicitude, cool in inmost love; and, being carried hither and thither abroad, fear not to forget that they have undertaken the government of souls. It is necessary, then, that the solicitude expended on those who are put under us should be kept within a certain measure. Hence it is well said to Ezekiel, *The priests shall not shave their heads, nor suffer their locks to grow long, but polling let them poll their heads* (Ezek. xliv. 20). For they are rightly called priests who are set over the faithful for affording them sacred guidance. But the hairs outside the head are thoughts in the mind; which, as they spring up insensibly above the brain, denote the cares of the present life, which, owing to negligent perception, since they sometimes come forth unseasonably, advance, as it were, without our feeling them. Since, then, all who are over others ought indeed to have external anxieties, and yet should not be vehemently bent upon them, the priests are rightly forbidden either to shave their heads or to let their hair grow long; that so they may neither cut off from themselves entirely thoughts of the flesh for the life of those who are under them, nor again allow them to grow too much. Thus in this passage it is well said, *Polling let them poll their heads;* to wit, that the cares of temporal anxiety should both extend themselves as far as need requires, and yet be cut short soon, lest they grow to an immoderate extent. When, therefore, through provident care for bodies applied externally life is protected [*or*, through provident care applied externally the life of bodies is protected], and again, through moderate intentness of heart, is not impeded[1], the hairs on the priest's head are both preserved to cover the skin, and cut short so as not to veil the eyes.

CHAPTER VIII.

That the ruler should not set his heart on pleasing men, and yet should give heed to what ought to please them.

Meanwhile it is also necessary for the ruler to keep wary watch, lest the lust of pleasing men assail him; lest, when he studiously penetrates the things that are within, and providently supplies the things that are without, he seek to be beloved of those that are under him more than truth; lest, while, supported by his good deeds, he seems not to belong to the world, self-love estrange him from his Maker. For he is the Redeemer's enemy who through the good works which he does covets being loved by the Church instead of Him; since a servant whom the bridegroom has sent with gifts to the bride is guilty of treacherous thought if he desires to please the eyes of the bride. And in truth this self-love, when it has got possession of a ruler's mind, sometimes carries it away inordinately to softness, but sometimes to roughness. For from love of himself the ruler's mind is inclined to softness, because, when he observes those that are under him sinning, he does not presume to reprove them, lest their affection for himself should grow dull; nay sometimes he smooths down with flatteries the offence of his subordinates which he ought to have rebuked. Hence it is well said through the prophet, *Woe unto them that sew cushions under every elbow, and make pillows under the head of every stature to catch souls* (Ezek. xiii. 18); inasmuch as to put cushions under every elbow is to cherish with bland flatteries souls that are falling from their uprightness and reclining themselves in this world's enjoyment. For it is as though the elbow of a recumbent person rested on a cushion and his head on pillows, when the hardness of reproof is withdrawn from one who sins, and when the softness of favour is offered to him, that he may lie softly in error, while no roughness of contradiction troubles him. But so rulers who love themselves undoubtedly shew themselves to those by whom they fear they may be injured in their pursuit of temporal glory. Such indeed as they see to have no power against them they ever keep down with roughness of rigid censure, never admonish them gently, but, forgetful of pastoral kindness, terrify them with the rights of domination. Such the divine voice rightly upbraids through the prophet, saying, *But with austerity and power did ye rule them* (Ezek. xxiv. 4). For, loving themselves more than their Maker, they lift up themselves haughtily towards those that are under them, considering

[1] The wording of this passage is obscure, and may be corrupt. In a corresponding one in Gregory's Epistles (*Lib.* VII. *Ep.* 4), in other respects the same as this, we find, instead of "et rursus per moderatam cordis intentionem non impeditur," "et rursus per *immoderatam* cordis *intentio* non impeditur." Here, though *non* before *impeditur* is absent from many MSS., and consequently rejected by the Benedictine editors, it seems necessary for the sense. The whole passage is thus capable of being intelligibly rendered thus: "When, therefore, through provident care (*providentiam*) externally applied the life of bodies is protected, and again intentness of heart is not impeded through immoderate (*providentiam*)." In both passages the general drift is clear enough, as follows: When, through adequate taking thought on the part of the priest for people's bodily needs, their life is protected from harm, and yet his attention to such external matters is not so excessive as to hinder the devotion of his heart to spiritual things, then the meaning of Ezekiel's words is fulfilled. For the hairs of the head, denoting thoughts of the brain for temporal concerns, are allowed to advance so far as to afford needful protection, but not to such an immoderate extent as to obscure the sight of the eyes, i.e. spiritual vision.

not what they ought to do, but what they can do; they have no fear of future judgment; they glory insolently in temporal power; it pleases them to be free to do even unlawful things, and that no one among their subordinates should contradict them. He, then, who sets his mind on doing wrong things, and yet wishes all other men to hold their peace about them, is himself a witness to himself that he desires to be loved himself more than the truth, which he is unwilling should be defended against him. There is indeed no one who so lives as not to some extent to fail in duty. He, then, desires the truth to be loved more fully than himself, who wishes to be spared by no one against the truth. For hence Peter willingly accepted Paul's rebuke (Galat. ii. 11); hence David humbly listened to the reproof of his subject (2 Sam. xii. 7); because good rulers, being themselves unconscious of loving with partial affection, believe the word of free sincerity from subjects to be the homage of humility. But meanwhile it is necessary that the care of government be tempered with so great skill of management that the mind of subjects, when it has become able to feel rightly on some subjects, should so advance to liberty of speech that liberty still break not out into pride; lest, while liberty of the tongue is perchance conceded to them overmuch, the humility of their life be lost. It is to be borne in mind also, that it is right for good rulers to desire to please men; but this in order to draw their neighbours by the sweetness of their own character to affection for the truth; not that they should long to be themselves loved, but should make affection for themselves as a sort of road by which to lead the hearts of their hearers to the love of the Creator. For it is indeed difficult for a preacher who is not loved, however well he may preach, to be willingly listened to. He, then, who is over others ought to study to be loved to the end that he may be listened to, and still not seek love for its own sake, lest he be found in the hidden usurpation of his thought to rebel against Him whom in his office he appears to serve. Which thing Paul insinuates well, when, manifesting the secret of his affection for us, he says, *Even as I please all men in all things* (1 Cor. x. 33). And yet he says again, *If I yet pleased men, I should not be the servant of Christ* (Gal. i. 10). Thus Paul pleases, and pleases not; because in that he desires to please he seeks that not he himself should please men, but truth through him.

CHAPTER IX.

That the ruler ought to be careful to understand how commonly vices pass themselves off as virtues.

The ruler also ought to understand how commonly vices pass themselves off as virtues. For often niggardliness palliates itself under the name of frugality, and on the other hand prodigality hides itself under the appellation of liberality. Often inordinate laxity is believed to be loving-kindness, and unbridled wrath is accounted the virtue of spiritual zeal. Often precipitate action is taken for the efficacy of promptness, and tardiness for the deliberation of seriousness. Whence it is necessary for the ruler of souls to distinguish with vigilant care between virtues and vices, lest either niggardliness get possession of his heart while he exults in seeming frugal in expenditure; or, while anything is prodigally wasted, he glory in being as it were compassionately liberal; or in remitting what he ought to have smitten he draw on those that are under him to eternal punishment; or in mercilessly smiting an offence he himself offend more grievously; or by immaturely anticipating mar what might have been done properly and gravely; or by putting off the merit of a good action change it to something worse.

CHAPTER X.

What the ruler's discrimination should be between correction and connivance, between fervour and gentleness.

It should be known too that the vices of subjects ought sometimes to be prudently connived at, but indicated in that they are connived at; that things, even though openly known, ought sometimes to be seasonably tolerated, but sometimes, though hidden, be closely investigated; that they ought sometimes to be gently reproved, but sometimes vehemently censured. For, indeed, some things, as we have said, ought to be prudently connived at, but indicated in that they are connived at, so that, when the delinquent is aware that he is discovered and borne with, he may blush to augment those faults which he considers in himself are tolerated in silence, and may punish himself in his own judgment as being one whom the patience of his ruler in his own mind mercifully excuses. By such connivance the Lord well reproves Judah, when He says through the prophet, *Thou hast lied, and hast not remembered Me, nor laid it to thy heart, because I have held My peace and been as one that saw not* (Isai. lvii. 11). Thus He both connived at faults and made them known, since He both held His peace against the sinner, and nevertheless declared this very thing, that He had held His peace. But some things, even though openly known, ought to be seasonably tolerated; that is, when circumstances afford no suitable opportunity for openly correcting them. For sores by being unseasonably cut are the worse enflamed; and, if medicaments suit not the time, it is undoubtedly evident that they lose their medicinal function. But, while a fitting time for the correction of subordinates is being sought, the patience of the prelate is exercised under the very weight of their offences. Whence it is well said by the Psalmist, *Sinners have built upon my back* (Ps. cxxviii. 3). For on the back we support burdens; and therefore he complains that sinners had built upon his back, as if to say plainly, Those whom I am unable to correct I carry as a burden laid upon me.

Some hidden things, however, ought to be closely investigated, that, by the breaking out of certain symptoms, the ruler may discover all that lies closely hidden in the minds of his subordinates, and, by reproof intervening at the nick of time, from very small things become aware of greater ones. Whence it is rightly said to Ezekiel, *Son of man, dig in the wall* (Ezek. viii. 8); where the said prophet presently adds, *And when I had digged in the wall, there appeared one door. And he said unto me, Go in, and see the wicked abominations that they do here. So I went in and saw; and behold every similitude of creeping things, and abomination of beasts, and all the idols of the house of Israel, were pourtrayed upon the wall* (Ibid. 9, 10). Now by Ezekiel are personified men in authority; by the wall is signified the hardness of their subordinates. And what is digging in a wall but opening the hardness of the heart by sharp inquisitions? Which wall when he had dug into, there appeared a door, because when hardness of heart is pierced either by careful questionings or by seasonable reproofs, there is shewn as it were a kind of door, through which may appear the interior of the thoughts in him who is reproved. Whence also it follows well in that place, *Go in and see the wicked abominations that they do here* (Ibid.). He goes in, as it were, to see the abominations, who, by examination of certain symptoms outwardly appearing, so penetrates the hearts of his subordinates as to become cognizant of all their illicit thoughts. Whence also he added, *And I went in and saw; and behold every similitude of creeping things, and abomination of beasts* (Ibid.). By creeping things thoughts altogether earthly are signified; but by beasts such as are indeed a little lifted above the earth, but still crave the rewards of earthly recompense. For creeping things cleave to the earth with the whole body; but beasts are in a large part of the body lifted above the earth, yet are ever inclined to the earth by gulosity. Therefore there are creeping things within the wall, when thoughts are revolved in the mind which never rise above earthly cravings. There are also beasts within the wall, when, though some just and some honourable thoughts are entertained, they are still subservient to appetite for temporal gains and honour, and, though in themselves indeed lifted, as one may say, above the earth, still through desire to curry favour, as through the throat's craving, demean themselves to what is lowest. Whence also it is well added, *And all the idols of the house of Israel were pourtrayed upon the wall* (Ezek. viii. 10), inasmuch as it is written, *And covetousness, which is idolatry* (Colos. iii. 5). Rightly therefore after beasts idols are spoken of, because some, though lifting themselves as it were above the earth by honourable action, still lower themselves to the earth by dishonourable ambition. And it is well said, *Were pourtrayed;* since, when the shows of external things are drawn into one's inner self, whatever is meditated on under imagined images is, as it were, pourtrayed on the heart. It is to be observed, therefore, that first a hole in the wall, and afterwards a door, is perceived, and that then at length the hidden abomination is made apparent; because, in fact, of every single sin signs are first seen outwardly, and afterwards a door is pointed out for opening the iniquity to view; and then at length every evil that lies hidden within is disclosed.

Some things, however, ought to be gently reproved: for, when fault is committed, not of malice, but only from ignorance or infirmity, it is certainly necessary that the very censure of it be tempered with great moderation. For it is true that all of us, so long as we subsist in this mortal flesh, are subject to the infirmities of our corruption. Every one, therefore, ought to gather from himself how it behoves him to pity another's weakness, lest, if he be too fervently hurried to words of reprehension against a neighbour's infirmity, he should seem to be forgetful of his own. Whence Paul admonishes well, when he says, *If a man be overtaken in any fault, ye which are spiritual restore such an one in the spirit of meekness, considering thyself, lest thou also be tempted* (Galat. vi. 1); as if to say plainly, When what thou seest of the infirmity of another displeases thee, consider what thou art; that so the spirit may moderate itself in the zeal of reprehension, while for itself also it fears what it reprehends.

Some things, however, ought to be vehemently reproved, that, when a fault is not recognized by him who has committed it, he may be made sensible of its gravity from the mouth of the reprover; and that, when any one smooths over to himself the evil that he has perpetrated, he may be led by the asperity of his censurer to entertain grave fears of its effects against himself. For indeed it is the duty of a ruler to shew by the voice of preaching the glory of the supernal country, to disclose what great temptations of the old enemy are lurking in this life's journey, and to correct with great asperity of zeal such evils among those who are under his sway as ought not to be gently borne with; lest, in being too little incensed against faults, of all faults he be himself held guilty. Whence it is well said to Ezekiel, *Take unto thee a tile, and thou shalt lay it before thee, and pourtray upon it the city Jerusalem* (Ezek. iv. 1). And immediately it is subjoined, *And thou shalt lay siege against it, and build forts, and cast a mount, and set camps against it, and set battering rams against it round about.* And to him, for his own defence, it is forthwith subjoined, *And do thou take unto thee an iron frying-pan, and thou shalt set it for a wall of iron between thee and the city.* For of what does the prophet Ezekiel bear the semblance but of teachers, in that it is said to him, *Take unto thee a tile, and thou shalt lay it before thee, and pourtray upon it the city Jerusalem?*

For indeed holy teachers take unto themselves a tile, when they lay hold of the earthly heart of hearers in order to teach them: which tile in truth they lay before themselves, because they keep watch over it with the entire bent of their mind: on which tile also they are commanded to pourtray the city Jerusalem, because they are at the utmost pains to represent to earthy hearts by preaching a vision of supernal peace. But, because the glory of the heavenly country is perceived in vain, unless it be known also what great temptations of the crafty enemy assail us here, it is fitly subjoined, *And thou shalt lay siege against it, and build forts.* For indeed holy preachers lay siege about the tile on which the city Jerusalem is delineated, when to a mind that is earthy but already seeking after the supernal country they shew how great an opposition of vices in the time of this life is arrayed against it. For, when it is shewn how each several sin besets us in our onward course, it is as though a seige were laid round the city Jerusalem by the voice of the preacher. But, because preachers ought not only to make known how vices assail us, but also how well-guarded virtues strengthen us, it is rightly subjoined, *And thou shalt build forts.* For indeed the holy preacher builds forts, when he shews what virtues resist what vices. And because, as virtue increases, the wars of temptation are for the most part augmented, it is rightly further added, *And thou shalt cast a mount, and set camps against it, and set battering rams round about.* For, when any preacher sets forth the mass of increasing temptation, he casts a mount. And he sets camps against Jerusalem when to the right intention of his hearers he foretells the unsurveyed, and as it were incomprehensible, ambuscades of the cunning enemy. And he sets battering-rams round about, when he makes known the darts of temptation encompassing us on every side in this life, and piercing through our wall of virtues.

But although the ruler may nicely insinuate all these things, he procures not for himself lasting absolution, unless he glow with a spirit of jealousy against the delinquencies of all and each. Whence in that place it is further rightly subjoined, *And do thou take to thee an iron frying-pan, and thou shalt set it for a wall of iron between thee and the city.* For by the frying-pan is denoted a frying of the mind, and by iron the hardness of reproof.

But what more fiercely fries and excruciates the teacher's mind than zeal for God? Hence Paul was being burnt with the frying of this frying-pan when he said, *Who is made weak, and I am not made weak? Who is offended, and I burn not?* (2 Cor. xi. 29). And, because whosoever is inflamed with zeal for God is protected by a guard continually, lest he should deserve to be condemned for negligence, it is rightly said, *Thou shalt set it for a wall of iron between thee and the city.* For an iron frying-pan is set for a wall of iron between the prophet and the city, because, when rulers already exhibit strong zeal, they keep the same zeal as a strong defence afterwards between themselves and their hearers, lest they should be destitute then of the power to punish from having been previously remiss in reproving.

But meanwhile it is to be borne in mind that, while the mind of the teacher exasperates itself for rebuke, it is very difficult for him to avoid breaking out into saying something that he ought not to say. And for the most part it happens that, when the faults of subordinates are reprehended with severe invective, the tongue of the master is betrayed into excess of language. And, when rebuke is immoderately hot, the hearts of the delinquents are depressed to despair. Wherefore it is necessary for the exasperated ruler, when he considers that he has wounded more than he should have done the feelings of his subordinates, to have recourse in his own mind to penitence, so as by lamentations to obtain pardon in the sight of the Truth ; and even for this cause, that it is through the ardour of his zeal for it that he sins. This is what the Lord in a figure enjoins through Moses, saying, *If a man go in simplicity of heart with his friend into the wood to hew wood, and the wood of the axe fly from his hand, and the iron slip from the helve and smite his friend and slay him, he shall flee unto one of the aforesaid cities and live ; lest haply the next of kin to him whose blood has been shed, while his heart is hot, pursue him, and overtake him, and smite him mortally* (Deut. xix. 4, 5). For indeed we go with a friend into the wood as often as we betake ourselves to look into the delinquencies of subordinates. And we hew wood in simplicity of heart, when with pious intention we cut off the vices of delinquents. But the axe flies from the hand, when rebuke is drawn on to asperity more than need requires. And the iron leaps from the helve, when out of reproof issues speech too hard. And he smites and slays his friend, because overstrained contumely cuts him off from the spirit of love. For the mind of one who is reproved suddenly breaks out into hatred, if immoderate reproof charges it beyond its due. But he who smites wood incautiously and destroys his neighbour must needs fly to three cities, that in one of them he may live protected ; since if, betaking himself to the laments of penitence, he is hidden under hope and charity in sacramental unity, he is not held guilty of the perpetrated homicide. And him the next of kin to the slain man does not kill, even when he finds him ; because, when the strict judge comes, who has joined himself to us by sharing in our nature, without doubt He requires not the penalty of his fault from him whom faith hope and charity hide under the shelter of his pardon.

CHAPTER XI.

How intent the ruler ought to be on meditations in the Sacred Law.

But all this is duly executed by a ruler, if, inspired by the spirit of heavenly fear and love, he meditate daily on the precepts of Sacred Writ, that the words of Divine admonition may restore in him the power of solicitude and of provident circumspection with regard to the celestial life, which familiar intercourse with men continually destroys ; and that one who is drawn to oldness of life by secular society may by the aspiration of compunction be ever renewed to love of the spiritual country. For the heart runs greatly to waste in the midst of human talk ; and, since it is undoubtedly evident that, when driven by the tumults of external occupations, it loses its balance and falls, one ought incessantly to take care that through keen pursuit of instruction it may rise again. For hence it is that Paul admonishes his disciple who had been put over the flock, saying, *Till I come, give attendance to reading* (1 Tim. iv. 13). Hence David says, *How have I loved Thy Law, O Lord! It is my meditation all the day* (Ps. cix. 97). Hence the Lord commanded Moses concerning the carrying of the ark, saying, *Thou shalt make four rings of gold, which thou shalt put in the four corners of the ark, and thou shalt make staves of shittim-wood, and overlay them with gold, and shalt put them through the rings which are by the sides of the ark, that it may be borne with them, and they shall always be in the rings, nor shall they ever be drawn out from them* (Exod. xxv. 12, *seq.*). What but the holy Church is figured by the ark? To which four rings of gold in the four corners are ordered to be adjoined, because, in that it is thus extended towards the four quarters of the globe, it is declared undoubtedly to be equipped for journeying with the four books of the holy Gospel. And staves of shittim-wood are made, and are put through the same rings for carrying, because strong and persevering teachers, as incorruptible pieces of timber, are to be sought for, who by cleaving ever to instruction out of the sacred volumes may declare the unity of the holy Church, and, as it were, carry the ark by being let into its rings. For indeed to carry the ark by means of staves is through preaching to bring the holy Church before the rude minds of unbelievers by means of good teachers. And these are also ordered to be overlaid with gold, that, while they are resonant to others in discourse, they may also themselves glitter in the splendour of their lives. Of whom it is further fitly added, *They shall always be in the rings, nor shall they ever be drawn out from them* ; because it is surely necessary that those who attend upon the office of preaching should not recede from the study of sacred lore. For to this end it is that the staves are ordered to be always in the rings, that, when occasion requires the ark to be carried, no tardiness in carrying may arise from the staves having to be put in ; because, that is to say, when a pastor is enquired of by his subordinates on any spiritual matter, it is exceedingly ignominious, should he then go about to learn, when he ought to solve the question. But let the staves remain ever in the rings, that teachers, ever meditating in their own hearts the words of Sacred Writ, may lift without delay the ark of the covenant ; as will be the case if they teach at once whatever is required. Hence the first Pastor of the Church well admonishes all other pastors saying, *Be ready always to give an answer to every man that asketh you a reason of the hope that is in you* (1 Pet. iii. 15): as though he should say plainly, That no delay may hinder the carrying of the ark, let the staves never be withdrawn from the rings.

PART III.

HOW THE RULER, WHILE LIVING WELL, OUGHT TO TEACH AND ADMONISH THOSE THAT ARE PUT UNDER HIM.

PROLOGUE.

Since, then, we have shewn what manner of man the pastor ought to be, let us now set forth after what manner he should teach. For, as long before us Gregory Nazianzen of reverend memory has taught, one and the same exhortation does not suit all, inasmuch as neither are all bound together by similarity of character. For the things that profit some often hurt others; seeing that also for the most part herbs which nourish some animals are fatal to others; and the gentle hissing that quiets horses incites whelps; and the medicine which abates one disease aggravates another; and the bread which invigorates the life of the strong kills little children. Therefore according to the quality of the hearers ought the discourse of teachers to be fashioned, so as to suit all and each for their several needs, and yet never deviate from the art of common edification. For what are the intent minds of hearers but, so to speak, a kind of tight tensions of strings in a harp, which the skilful player, that he may produce a tune not at variance with itself, strikes variously? And for this reason the strings render back a consonant modulation, that they are struck indeed with one quill, but not with one kind of stroke. Whence every teacher also, that he may edify all in the one virtue of charity, ought to touch the hearts of his hearers out of one doctrine, but not with one and the same exhortation.

CHAPTER I.

What diversity there ought to be in the art of preaching.

Differently to be admonished are these that follow:—

Men and women.
The poor and the rich.
The joyful and the sad.
Prelates and subordinates.
Servants and masters.
The wise of this world and the dull.
The impudent and the bashful.
The forward and the fainthearted.
The impatient and the patient.
The kindly disposed and the envious.
The simple and the insincere.
The whole and the sick.
Those who fear scourges, and therefore live innocently; and those who have grown so hard in iniquity as not to be corrected even by scourges.
The too silent, and those who spend time in much speaking.
The slothful and the hasty.
The meek and the passionate.
The humble and the haughty.
The obstinate and the fickle.
The gluttonous and the abstinent.
Those who mercifully give of their own, and those who would fain seize what belongs to others.
Those who neither seize the things of others nor are bountiful with their own; and those who both give away the things they have, and yet cease not to seize the things of others.
Those that are at variance, and those that are at peace.
Lovers of strifes and peacemakers.
Those that understand not aright the words of sacred law; and those who understand them indeed aright, but speak them without humility.
Those who, though able to preach worthily, are afraid through excessive humility; and those whom imperfection or age debars from preaching, and yet rashness impels to it.
Those who prosper in what they desire in temporal matters; and those who covet indeed the things that are of the world, and yet are wearied with the toils of adversity.
Those who are bound by wedlock, and those who are free from the ties of wedlock.
Those who have had experience of carnal intercourse, and those who are ignorant of it.
Those who deplore sins of deed, and those who deplore sins of thought.
Those who bewail misdeeds, yet forsake them not; and those who forsake them, yet bewail them not.
Those who even praise the unlawful things they do; and those who censure what is wrong, yet avoid it not.
Those who are overcome by sudden passion, and those who are bound in guilt of set purpose.

Those who, though their unlawful deeds are trivial, yet do them frequently; and those who keep themselves from small sins, but are occasionally whelmed in graver ones.

Those who do not even begin what is good, and those who fail entirely to complete the good begun.

Those who do evil secretly and good publicly; and those who conceal the good they do, and yet in some things done publicly allow evil to be thought of them.

But of what profit is it for us to run through all these things collected together in a list, unless we also set forth, with all possible brevity, the modes of admonition for each?

(*Admonition* 1.) Differently, then, to be admonished are men and women; because on the former heavier injunctions, on the latter lighter are to be laid, that those may be exercised by great things, but these winningly converted by light ones.

(*Admonition* 2.) Differently to be admonished are young men and old; because for the most part severity of admonition directs the former to improvement, while kind remonstrance disposes the latter to better deeds. For it is written, *Rebuke not an elder, but entreat him as a father* (1 Tim. v. 1).

CHAPTER II.

How the poor and the rich should be admonished.

(*Admonition* 3.) Differently to be admonished are the poor and the rich: for to the former we ought to offer the solace of comfort against tribulation, but in the latter to induce fear as against elation. For to the poor one it is said by the Lord through the prophet, *Fear not, for thou shall not be confounded* (Isai. liv. 4). And not long after, soothing her, He says, *O thou poor little one, tossed with tempest* (Ibid. 11). And again He comforts her, saying, *I have chosen thee in the furnace of poverty* (Ibid. xlviii. 10). But, on the other hand, Paul says to his disciple concerning the rich, *Charge the rich of this world, that they be not high-minded nor trust in the uncertainty of their riches* (1 Tim. vi. 17); where it is to be particularly noted that the teacher of humility in making mention of the rich, says not *Entreat*, but *Charge;* because, though pity is to be bestowed on infirmity, yet to elation no honour is due. To such, therefore, the right thing that is said is the more rightly commanded, according as they are puffed up with loftiness of thought in transitory things. Of them the Lord says in the Gospel, *Woe unto you that are rich, which have your consolation* (Luke vi. 24). For, since they know not what eternal joys are, they are consoled out of the abundance of the present life. Therefore consolation is to be offered to those who are tried in the furnace of poverty; and fear is to be induced in those whom the consolation of temporal glory lifts up; that both those may learn that they possess riches which they see not, and these become aware that they can by no means keep the riches that they see. Yet for the most part the character of persons changes the order in which they stand; so that the rich man may be humble and the poor man proud. Hence the tongue of the preacher ought soon to be adapted to the life of the hearer, so as to smite elation in a poor man all the more sharply as not even the poverty that has come upon him brings it down, and to cheer all the more gently the humility of the rich as even the abundance which elevates them does not elate them.

Sometimes, however, even a proud rich man is to be propitiated by blandishment in exhortation, since hard sores also are usually softened by soothing fomentations, and the rage of the insane is often restored to health by the bland words of the physician, and, when they are pleasantly humoured, the disease of their insanity is mitigated. For neither is this to be lightly regarded, that, when an adverse spirit entered into Saul, David took his harp and assuaged his madness (1 Sam. xviii. 10). For what is intimated by Saul but the elation of men in power, and what by David but the humble life of the holy? When, then, Saul is seized by the unclean spirit, his madness is appeased by David's singing; since, when the senses of men in power are turned to frenzy by elation, it is meet that they should be recalled to a healthy state by the calmess of our speech, as by the sweetness of a harp. But sometimes, when the powerful of this world are taken to task, they are first to be searched by certain similitudes, as on a matter not concerning them; and, when they have pronounced a right sentence as against another man, then in fitting ways they are to be smitten with regard to their own guilt; so that the mind puffed up with temporal power may in no wise lift itself up against the reprover, having by its own judgment trodden on the neck of pride, and may not try to defend itself, being bound by the sentence of its own mouth. For hence it was that Nathan the prophet, having come to take the king to task, asked his judgment as if concerning the cause of a poor man against a rich one (2 Sam. xii. 4, 5, *seq.*), that the king might first pronounce sentence, and afterwards hear of his own guilt, to the end that he might by no means contradict the righteous doom that he had uttered against himself. Thus the holy man, considering both the sinner and the king, studied in a wonderful order first to bind the daring culprit by confession, and afterwards to cut him to the heart by rebuke. He concealed for a while whom he aimed at, but smote him suddenly when he had him. For the blow would perchance have fallen with less force had he purposed to smite the sin openly from the beginning of his discourse; but by first introducing the similitude he sharpened the rebuke which he concealed. He had come as a physician to a sick man; he saw that the sore must be cut; but he doubted of the sick man's patience. Therefore he hid the medicinal steel under his robe, which he suddenly drew out and plunged into the sore, that the patient might feel the cutting blade before he saw it, lest, seeing it first, he should refuse to feel it.

CHAPTER III.

How the joyful and the sad are to be admonished.

Admonition 4. Differently to be admonished are the joyful and the sad. That is, before the joyful are to be set the sad things that follow upon punishment; but before the sad the promised glad things of the kingdom. Let the joyful learn by the asperity of threatenings what to be afraid of: let the sad hear what joys of reward they may look forward to. For to the former it is said, *Woe unto you that laugh now! For ye shall weep* (Luke vi. 25); but the latter hear from the teaching of the same Master, *I will see you again, and your heart shall rejoice, and your joy no man shall take from you* (Joh. xvi. 22). But some are not made joyful or sad by circumstances, but are so by temperament. And to such it should be intimated that certain defects are connected with certain temperaments; that the joyful have lechery close at hand, and the sad wrath. Hence it is necessary for every one to consider not only what he suffers from his peculiar temperament, but also what worse thing presses on him in connection with it; lest, while he fights not at all against that which he has, he succumb also to that from which he supposes himself free.

CHAPTER IV.

How subjects and prelates are to be admonished.

(*Admonition* 5.) Differently to be admonished are subjects and prelates: the former that subjection crush them not, the latter that superior place elate them not: the former that they fail not to fulfil what is commanded them, the latter that they command not more to be fulfilled than is just: the former that they submit humbly, the latter that they preside temperately. For this, which may be understood also figuratively, is said to the former, *Children, obey your parents in the Lord:* but to the latter it is enjoined, *And ye, fathers, provoke not your children to wrath* (Coloss. iii. 20, 21). Let the former learn how to order their inward thoughts before the eyes of the hidden judge; the latter how also to those that are committed to them to afford outwardly examples of good living. For prelates ought to know that, if they ever perpetrate what is wrong, they are worthy of as many deaths as they transmit examples of perdition to their subjects. Wherefore it is necessary that they guard themselves so much the more cautiously from sin as by the bad things they do they die not alone, but are guilty of the souls of others, which by their bad example they have destroyed. Wherefore the former are to be admonished, lest they should be strictly punished, if merely on their own account they should be unable to stand acquitted; the latter, lest they should be judged for the errors of their subjects, even though on their own account they find themselves secure. Those are to be admonished that they live with all the more anxiety about themselves as they are not entangled by care for others; but these that they accomplish their charge of others in such wise as not to desist from charge of themselves, and so to be ardent in anxiety about themselves as not to grow sluggish in the custody of those committed to them. To the one, who is at leisure for his own concerns, it is said, *Go to the ant, thou sluggard, and consider her ways, and learn wisdom* (Prov. vi. 6): but the other is terribly admonished, when it is said, *My son, if thou be surety for thy friend, thou hast stricken thy hand with a stranger, and art snared with the words of thy mouth, and art taken with thine own speeches* (Ibid. 1). For to be surety for a friend is to take charge of the soul of another on the surety of one's own behaviour Whence also the hand is stricken with a stranger, because the mind is bound with the care of a responsibility which before was not. But he is snared with the words of his mouth, and taken with his own speeches, because, while he is compelled to speak good things to those who are committed to him, he must needs himself in the first place observe the things that he speaks. He is therefore snared with the words of his mouth, being constrained by the requirement of reason not to let his life be relaxed to what agrees not with his teaching. Hence before the strict judge he is compelled to accomplish as much in deed as it is plain he has enjoined on others with his voice. Thus in the passage above cited this exhortation is also presently added, *Do therefore what I say, my son, and deliver thyself, seeing thou hast fallen into the hands of thy neighbour: run up and down, hasten, arouse thy friend; give not sleep to thine eyes, nor let thine eyelids slumber* (Prov. vi. 3). For whosoever is put over others for an example of life is admonished not only to keep watch himself, but also to arouse his friend. For it is not enough for him to keep watch in living well, if he do not also sever him when he is set over from the torpor of sin. For it is well said, *Give not sleep to thine eyes, nor let thine eyelids slumber* (Ibid. 4). For indeed to give sleep to the eyes is to cease from earnestness, so as to neglect altogether the care of our subordinates. But the eyelids slumber when our thoughts, weighed down by sloth, connive at what they know ought to be reproved in subordinates. For to be fast asleep is neither to know nor to correct the deeds of those committed to us. But to know what things are to be blamed, and still through laziness of mind not to amend them by meet rebukes, is not to sleep, but to slumber. Yet the eye through slumbering passes into the deepest sleep; since for the most part, when one who is over others cuts not off the evil that he knows, he comes sooner or later, as his negligence deserves, not even to know what is done wrong by his subjects.

Wherefore those who are over others are to be admonished, that through earnestness of circumspection they have eyes watchful within and round about, and strive to become living creatures of heaven (Ezek. i. 18). For the living creatures of heaven are described as full of eyes round about and within (Revel. iv. 6). And so it is meet that those who are over others should have eyes within and round about, so as both in themselves to study to please the inward judge, and also, affording outwardly examples of life, to detect the things that should be corrected in others.

Subjects are to be admonished that they judge not rashly the lives of their superiors, if perchance they see them act blamably in anything, lest whence they rightly find fault with evil they thence be sunk by the impulse of elation to lower depths. They are to be admonished that, when they consider the faults of their superiors, they grow not too bold against them, but, if any of their deeds are exceedingly bad, so judge of them within themselves that, constrained by the fear of God, they still refuse not to bear the yoke of reverence under them. Which thing we shall shew the better if we bring forward what David did (1 Sam. xxiv. 4 *seq.*). For when Saul the persecutor had entered into a cave to ease himself, David, who had so long suffered under his persecution, was within it with his men. And, when his men incited him to smite Saul, he cut them short with the reply, that he ought not to put forth his hand against the Lord's anointed. And yet he rose unperceived, and cut off the border of his robe. For what is signified by Saul but bad rulers, and what by David but good subjects? Saul's easing himself, then, means rulers extending the wickedness conceived in their hearts to works of woful stench, and their shewing the noisome thoughts within them by carrying them out into deeds. Yet him David was afraid to strike, because the pious minds of subjects, witholding themselves from the whole plague of backbiting, smite the life of their superiors with no sword of the tongue, even when they blame them for imperfection. And when through infirmity they can scarce refrain from speaking, however humbly, of some extreme and obvious evils in their superiors, they cut as it were silently the border of their robe; because, to wit, when, even though harmlessly and secretly, they derogate from the dignity of superiors, they disfigure as it were the garment of the king who is set over them; yet still they return to themselves, and blame themselves most vehemently for even the slightest defamation in speech. Hence it is also well written in that place, *Afterward David's heart smote him, because he had cut off the border of Saul's robe* (Ibid. 6). For indeed the deeds of superiors are not to be smitten with the sword of the mouth, even when they are rightly judged to be worthy of blame. But if ever, even in the least, the tongue slips into censure of them, the heart must needs be depressed by the affliction of penitence, to the end that it may return to itself, and, when it has offended against the power set over it, may dread the judgment against itself of Him by whom it was set over it. For, when we offend against those who are set over us, we go against the ordinance of Him who set them over us. Whence also Moses, when he had become aware that the people complained against himself and Aaron, said, *For what are we? Not against us are your murmurings, but against the Lord* (Exod. xvi. 8).

CHAPTER V.

How servants and masters are to be admonished.

(*Admonition* 6). Differently to be admonished are servants and masters. Servants, to wit, that they ever keep in view the humility of their condition; but masters, that they lose not recollection of their nature, in which they are constituted on an equality with servants. Servants are to be admonished that they despise not their masters, lest they offend God, if by behaving themselves proudly they gainsay His ordinance: masters, too, are to be admonished, that they are proud against God with respect to His gift, if they acknowledge not those whom they hold in subjection by reason of their condition to be their equals by reason of their community of nature. The former are to be admonished to know themselves to be servants of masters; the latter are to be admonished to acknowledge themselves to be fellow-servants of servants. For to those it is said, *Servants, obey your masters according to the flesh* (Coloss. iii. 22); and again, *Let as many servants as are under the yoke count their masters worthy of all honour* (1 Tim. vi. 1); but to these it is said, *And ye, masters, do the same things unto them, forbearing threatening, knowing that both their and your Master is in heaven* (Ephes. vi. 9).

CHAPTER VI.

How the wise and the dull are to be admonished.

(*Admonition* 7). Differently to be admonished are the wise of this world and the dull. For the wise are to be admonished that they leave off knowing what they know: the dull also are to be admonished that they seek to know what they know not. In the former this thing first, that they think themselves wise, is to be thrown down; in the latter, whatsoever is already known of heavenly wisdom is to be built up; since, being in no wise proud, they have, as it were, prepared their hearts for supporting a building. With those we should labour that they become more wisely foolish, leave foolish wisdom, and learn the wise foolishness of God: to these we should preach that from what is accounted foolishness they should pass, as from a nearer neighbourhood, to true wisdom. For to the former it is said, *If any man among you seemeth to be wise in this world, let him become a fool, that he may be wise* (1 Cor. iii. 18): but to the latter it is said, *Not many wise men after the flesh* (Ibid. 26); and again, *God hath chosen the foolish things of the world to confound the wise* (Ibid. 27). The former are for the most part converted by arguments of reasoning; the latter sometimes better by examples. Those it doubtless profits to lie vanquished in their own allegations; but for these it is sometimes enough to get knowledge of the praiseworthy deeds of others. Whence also the excellent teacher, who was debtor to the wise and foolish (Rom. i. 14), when he was admonishing some of the Hebrews that were wise, but some also that were somewhat slow, speaking to them of the fulfilment of the Old Testament, overcame the wisdom of the former by argument, saying, *That which decayeth and waxeth old is ready to vanish away* (Heb. viii. 13). But, when he perceived that some were to be drawn by examples only, he added in the same epistle, *Saints had trial of mockings and scourgings, yea moreover of bonds and imprisonment; they were stoned, they were sawn asunder, were tempted, were slain with the sword* (Ibid. xi. 36, 37): and again, *Remember those who were set over you, who spoke to you the Word of God, whose faith follow, looking to the end of their conversation* (Ibid. xiii. 7); that so victorious reason might subdue the one sort, but the gentle force of example persuade the other to mount to greater things.

CHAPTER VII.

How the impudent and bashful are to be admonished.

(*Admonition* 8). Differently to be admonished are the impudent and the bashful. For those nothing but hard rebuke restrains from the vice of impudence; while these for the most part a modest exhortation disposes to amendment. Those do not know that they are in fault, unless they be rebuked even by many; to these it usually suffices for their conversion that the teacher at least gently reminds them of their evil deeds. For those one best corrects who reprehends them by direct invective; but to these greater profit ensues, if what is rebuked in them be touched, as it were, by a side stroke. Thus the Lord, openly upbraiding the impudent people of the Jews, saying, *There is come unto thee a whore's forehead; thou wouldest not blush* (Jerem. iii. 3). But again He revives them when ashamed, saying, *Thou shalt forget the confusion of thy youth, and shalt not remember the reproach of thy widowhood; for thy Maker will reign over thee* (Isai. liv. 4). Paul also openly upbraids the Galatians impudently sinning, when he says, *O foolish Galatians, who hath bewitched you* (Galat. iii. 1)? And again, *Are ye so foolish, that, having begun in the Spirit, ye are now made perfect in the flesh* (Ibid. 3)? But the faults of those who are ashamed he reprehends as though sympathizing with them, saying, *I rejoiced in the Lord greatly, that now at the last ye have flourished again to care for me, as indeed ye did care, for ye lacked oppor-*

tunity (Philipp. iv. 10); so that hard upbraiding might discover the faults of the former, and a softer address veil the negligence of the latter.

CHAPTER VIII.

How the forward and the faint-hearted are to be admonished.

(*Admonition* 9.) Differently to be admonished are the forward and the faint-hearted. For the former, presuming on themselves too much, disdain all others when reproved by them; but the latter, while too conscious of their own infirmity, for the most part fall into despondency. Those count all they do to be singularly eminent; these think what they do to be exceedingly despised, and so are broken down to despondency. Therefore the works of the forward are to be finely sifted by the reprover, that wherein they please themselves they may be shewn to displease God.

For we then best correct the forward, when what they believe themselves to have done well we shew to have been ill done; that whence glory is believed to have been gained, thence wholesome confusion may ensue. But sometimes, when they are not at all aware of being guilty of the vice of forwardness, they more speedily come to correction if they are confounded by the infamy of some other person's more manifest guilt, sought out from a side quarter; that from that which they cannot defend, they may be made conscious of wrongly holding to what they do defend. Whence, when Paul saw the Corinthians to be forwardly puffed up one against another, so that one said he was of Paul, another of Apollos, another of Cephas, and another of Christ (1 Cor. i. 12; iii. 4), he brought forward the crime of incest, which had not only been perpetrated among them, but also remained uncorrected, saying, *It is reported commonly that there is fornication among you, and such fornication as is not even among the Gentiles, that one should have his father's wife. And ye are puffed up, and have not rather mourned, that he that hath done this deed might be taken away from among you* (1 Cor. v. 1, 2). As if to say plainly, Why say ye in your forwardness that ye are of this one or of the other, while shewing in the dissoluteness of your negligence, that ye are of none of them?

But on the other hand we more fitly bring back the faint-hearted to the way of well-doing, if we search collaterally for some good points about them, so that, while some things in them we attack with our reproof, others we may embrace with our praise; to the end that the hearing of praise may nourish their tenderness, which the rebuking of their fault chastises. And for the most part we make more way with them for their profit, if we also make mention of their good deeds; and, in case of some wrong things having been done by them, if we find not fault with them as though they were already perpetrated, but, as it were, prohibit them as what ought not to be perpetrated; that so both the favour shewn may increase the things which we approve, and our modest exhortation avail more with the faint-hearted against the things which we blame. Whence the same Paul, when he came to know that the Thessalonians, who stood fast in the preaching which they had received, were troubled with a certain faint-heartedness as though the end of the world were nigh at hand, first praises that wherein he sees them to be strong, and afterwards, with cautious admonition, strengthens what was weak. For he says, *We are bound to thank God always for you, brethren, as it is meet, because that your faith groweth exceedingly, and the charity of every one of you all toward each other aboundeth; so that we ourselves too glory in you in the churches of God for your patience and faith* (2 Thess. i. 3, 4). But, having premised these flattering encomiums of their life, a little while after he subjoined, *Now we beseech you, brethren, by the coming of our Lord Jesus Christ, and our gathering together unto Him, that ye be not soon shaken in mind, or be troubled, neither by spirit, nor by word, nor by letter as sent by us, as that the day of the Lord is at hand* (Ibid. ii. 1). For the true teacher so proceeded that they should first hear, in being praised, what they might thankfully acknowledge, and afterwards, in being exhorted, what they should follow; to the end that the precedent praise should settle their mind, lest the subjoined admonition should shake it; and, though he knew that they had been disquieted by suspicion of the end being near, he did not yet reprove them as having been so, but, as if ignorant of the past, forbade them to be disquieted in future; so that, while they believed themselves to be unknown to their preacher with respect even to the levity of their disquietude, they might be as much afraid of being open to blame as they were of being known by him to be so.

CHAPTER IX.

How the impatient and the patient are to be admonished.

(*Admonition* 10.) Differently to be admonished are the impatient and the patient. For the impatient are to be told that, while they neglect to bridle their spirit, they are hurried through many steep places of iniquity which they seek not after, inasmuch as fury drives the mind whither desire draws it not, and, when perturbed, it does, not knowing, what it afterwards grieves for when it knows The impatient are also to be told that, when carried headlong by the impulse of emotion, they act in some ways as though beside themselves, and are hardly aware afterwards of the evil they have done; and, while they offer no resistance to their perturbation, they bring into confusion even things that may have been well done when the mind was calm, and overthrow under sudden impulse whatever they have haply long built up with provident toil. For the very virtue of charity, which is the mother and guardian of all virtues, is lost through the vice of impatience. For it is written, *Charity is patient* (1 Cor. xiii. 4). Wherefore where patience is not, charity is not. Through this vice of impatience, too, instruction, the nurse of virtues, is dissipated. For it is written, *The instruction of a man is known by his patience* (Prov. xix. 11). Every man, then, is shewn to be by so much less instructed as he is convicted of being less patient. For neither can he truly impart what is good through instruction, if in his life he knows not how to bear what is evil in others with equanimity.

Further, through this vice of impatience for the most part the sin of arrogance pierces the mind; since, when any one is impatient of being looked down upon in this world, he endeavours to shew off any hidden good that he may have, and so through impatience is drawn on to arrogance; and, while he cannot bear contempt, he glories ostentatiously in self-display. Whence it is written, *Better is the patient than the arrogant* (Eccles. vii. 9); because, in truth, one that is patient chooses to suffer any evils whatever rather than that his hidden good should come to be known through the vice of ostentation. But the arrogant, on the contrary, chooses that even pretended good should be vaunted of him, lest he should possibly suffer even the least evil. Since, then, when patience is relinquished, all other good things also that have been done are overthrown, it is rightly enjoined on Ezekiel that in the altar of God a trench be made; to wit, that in it the whole burnt-offerings laid on the altar might be preserved (Ezek. xliii. 13). For, if there were not a trench in the altar, the passing breeze would scatter every sacrifice that it might find there. But what do we take the altar of God to be but the soul of the righteous man, which lays upon itself before His eyes as many sacrifices as it has done good deeds? And what is the trench of the altar but the patience of good men, which, while it humbles the mind to endure adversities, shews it to be placed low down after the manner of a ditch? Wherefore let a trench be made in the altar, lest the breeze should scatter the sacrifice laid upon it: that is, let the mind of the elect keep patience, lest, stirred with the wind of impatience, it lose even that which it has wrought well. Well, too, this same trench is directed to be of one cubit, because, if patience fails not, the measure of unity is preserved. Whence also Paul says, *Bear ye one another's burdens, and so ye shall fulfil the law of Christ* (Galat. vi. 2). For the law of Christ is the charity of unity, which they alone fulfil who are guilty of no excess even when they are burdened. Let the impatient hear what is written, *Better is the patient than the mighty, and he that ruleth his spirit than he that taketh cities* (Prov. xvi. 32). For victory over cities is a less thing, because that which is subdued is without; but a far greater thing is that which is conquered by patience, since the mind itself is by itself overcome, and subjects itself to itself, when patience compels it to bridle itself within. Let the impatient hear what the Truth says to His elect; *In your patience ye shall possess your souls* (Luke xxi. 19). For we are so wonderfully made that reason possesses the soul, and the soul the body. But the soul is ousted from its right of possession of the body, if it is not first possessed by reason. Therefore the Lord pointed out patience as the guardian of our state, in that He taught us to possess ourselves in it. Thus we learn how great is the sin of impatience, through which we lose the very possession of what we are. Let the impatient hear what is said again through Solomon; *A fool uttereth all his mind, but a wise man putteth it off, and reserves it until afterwards* (Prov. xxix. 11). For one is so driven by the impulse of impatience as to utter forth the whole mind, which the perturbation within throws out the more quickly for this reason, that no discipline of wisdom fences it round. But the wise man puts it off, and reserves it till afterwards. For, when injured, he desires not to avenge himself at the present time, because in his tolerance he even wishes that men should be spared; but yet he is not ignorant that all things are righteously avenged at the last judgment.

On the other hand the patient are to be admonished that they grieve not inwardly for what they bear outwardly, lest they spoil with the infection of malice within a sacrifice of so great value which without they offer whole;

and lest the sin of their grieving, not perceived by men, but yet seen as sin under the divine scrutiny, be made so much the worse as it claims to itself the fair shew of virtue before men.

The patient therefore should be told to study to love those whom they must needs bear with; lest, if love follow not patience, the virtue exhibited be turned to a worse fault of hatred. Whence Paul, when he said, *Charity is patient*, forthwith added, *Is kind* (1 Cor. xiii. 4); shewing certainly that those whom in patience she bears with in kindness also she ceases not to love. Whence the same excellent teacher, when he was persuading his disciples to patience, saying, *Let all bitterness, and wrath, and indignation, and clamour, and evil speaking be put away from you* (Ephes. iv. 31), having as it were now set all outward things in good order, turns himself to those that are within, when he subjoins, *With all malice* (Ibid.); because, truly, in vain are indignation, clamour, and evil speaking put away from the things that are without, if in the things that are within malice, the mother of vices, bears sway; and to no purpose is wickedness cut off from the branches outside, if it is kept at the root within to spring up in more manifold ways. Whence also the Truth in person says, *Love your enemies, do good to them which hate you, and pray for them which persecute you and say evil of you falsely* (Luke vi. 27). It is virtue therefore before men to bear with adversaries; but it is virtue before God to love them; because the only sacrifice which God accepts is that which, before His eyes, on the altar of good work, the flame of charity kindles. Hence it is that to some who were patient, and yet did not love, He says, *And why seest thou the mote in thy brother's eye, and seest not the beam in thine own eye*? (Matth. vii. 3; Luke vi. 41). For indeed the perturbation of impatience is a mote; but malice in the heart is a beam in the eye. For that the breeze of temptation drives to and fro; but this confirmed iniquity carries almost immoveably. Rightly, however, it is there subjoined, *Thou hypocrite, first cast out the beam out of thine own eye, and then shalt thou see to cast out the mote out of thy brother's eye* (Ibid.); as if it were said to the wicked mind, inwardly grieving while shewing itself by patience outwardly as holy, First shake off from thee the weight of malice, and then blame others for the levity of impatience; lest, while thou takest no pains to conquer pretence, it be worse for thee to bear with the faultiness of others.

For it usually comes to pass with the patient that at the time, indeed, when they suffer hardships, or hear insults, they are smitten with no vexation, and so exhibit patience as to fail not to keep also innocence of heart; but, when after a while they recall to memory these very same things that they have endured, they inflame themselves with the fire of vexation, they seek reasons for vengeance, and, in retracting, turn into malice the meekness which they had in bearing. Such are the sooner succoured by the preacher, if the cause of this change be disclosed. For the cunning adversary wages war against two; that is, by inflaming one to be the first to offer insults, and provoking the other to return insults under a sense of injury. But for the most part, while he is already conqueror of him who has been persuaded to inflict the injury, he is conquered by him who bears the infliction with an equal mind. Wherefore, being victorious over the one whom he has subjugated by incensing him, he lifts himself with all his might against the other, and is grieved at his firmly resisting and conquering; and so, because he has been unable to move him in the very flinging of insults, he rests meanwhile from open contest, and provoking his thought by secret suggestion, seeks a fit time for deceiving him. For, having lost in public warfare, he burns to lay hidden snares. In a time of quiet he returns to the mind of the conqueror, brings back to his memory either temporal harms or darts of insults, and by exceedingly exaggerating all that has been inflicted on him represents it as intolerable; and with so great vexation does he perturb the mind that for the most part the patient one, led captive after victory, blushes for having borne such things calmly, and is sorry that he did not return insults, and seeks to pay back something worse, should opportunity be afforded. To whom, then, are these like but to those who by bravery are victorious in the field, but by negligence are afterwards taken within the gates of the city? To whom are they like but to those whom a violent attack of sickness removes not from life, but who die from a relapse of fever coming gently on? Therefore the patient are to be admonished, that they guard their heart after victory; that they be on the lookout for the enemy, overcome in open warfare, laying snares against the walls of their mind; that they be the more afraid of a sickness creeping on again; lest the cunning enemy, should he afterwards deceive them, rejoice with the greater exultation in that he treads on the necks of conquerors which had long been inflexible against him.

CHAPTER X.

How the kindly-disposed and the envious are to be admonished.

(*Admonition* 11.) Differently to be admonished are the kindly-disposed and the envious. For the kindly-disposed are to be admonished so to rejoice in what is good in others as to desire to have the like as their own; so to praise with affection the deeds of their neighbours as also to multiply them by imitation, lest in this stadium of the present life they assist at the contest of others as eager backers, but inert spectators, and remain without a prize after the contest, in that they toiled not in the contest, and should then regard with sorrow the palms of those in the midst of whose toils they stood idle. For indeed we sin greatly if we love not the good deeds of others: but we win no reward if we imitate not so far as we can the things which we love. Wherefore the kindly-disposed should be told that if they make no haste to imitate the good which they applaud, the holiness of virtue pleases them in like manner as the vanity of scenic exhibitions of skill pleases foolish spectators: for these extol with applauses the performances of charioteers and players, and yet do not long to be such as they see those whom they praise to be. They admire them for having done pleasing things, and yet they shun pleasing in like manner. The kindly-disposed are to be told that when they behold the deeds of their neighbours they should return to their own heart, and presume not on actions which are not their own, nor praise what is good while they refuse to do it. More heavily, indeed, must those be smitten by final vengeance who have been pleased by that which they would not imitate.

The envious are to be admonished how great is their blindness who fail by other men's advancement, and pine away at other men's rejoicing; how great is their unhappiness who are made worse by the bettering of their neighbour, and in beholding the increase of another's prosperity are uneasily vexed within themselves, and die of the plague of their own heart. What can be more unhappy than these, who, when touched by the sight of happiness, are made more wicked by the pain of seeing it? But, moreover, the good things of others which they cannot have they might, if they loved them, make their own. For indeed all are constituted together in faith as are many members in one body; which are indeed diverse as to their office, but in mutually agreeing with each other are made one. Whence it comes to pass that the foot sees by the eye, and the eyes walk by the feet; that the hearing of the ears serves the mouth, and the tongue of the mouth concurs with the ears for their benefit; that the belly supports the hands, and the hands work for the belly. In the very arrangement of the body, therefore, we learn what we should observe in our conduct. It is, then, too shameful not to act up to what we are. Those things, in fact, are ours which we love in others, even though we cannot follow them; and what things are loved in us become theirs that love them. Hence, then, let the envious consider of how great power is charity, which makes ours without labour works of labour not our own. The envious are therefore to be told that, when they fail to keep themselves from spite, they are being sunk into the old wickedness of the wily foe. For of him it is written, *But by envy of the devil death entered into the world* (Wisd. ii. 24). For, because he had himself lost heaven, he envied it to created man, and, being himself ruined, by ruining others he heaped up his own damnation. The envious are to be admonished, that they may learn to how great slips of ruin growing under them they are liable; since, while they cast not forth spite out of their heart, they are slipping down to open wickedness of deeds. For, unless Cain had envied the accepted sacrifice of his brother, he would never have come to taking away his life. Whence it is written, *And the Lord had respect unto Abel and to his offering, but unto Cain and to his offering He had not respect. And Cain was very wroth, and his countenance fell* (Gen. iv. 4). Thus spite on account of the sacrifice was the seed-plot of fratricide. For him whose being better than himself vexed him he cut off from being at all. The envious are to be told that, while they consume themselves with this inward plague, they destroy whatever good they seem to have within them. Whence it is written, *Soundness of heart is the life of the flesh, but envy the rottenness of the bones* (Prov. xiv. 30). For what is signified by the flesh but certain weak and tender actions, and what by the bones but brave ones? And for the most part it comes to pass that some, with innocence of heart, in some of their actions seem weak; but others, though performing some stout deeds before human eyes, still pine away inwardly with the pestilence of envy towards what is good in others. Wherefore it is well said, *Soundness of heart is the life of the flesh;* because, if innocence of mind is kept, even such things as are weak outwardly are in time strengthened. And rightly it is there added, *Envy is the rottenness of the bones;* because through the vice of spite what seems strong to human eyes perishes in the eyes of

God. For the rotting of the bones through envy means that certain even strong things utterly perish.

CHAPTER XI.

How the simple and the crafty are to be admonished.

(*Admonition* 12.) Differently to be admonished are the simple and the insincere. The simple are to be praised for studying never to say what is false, but to be admonished to know how sometimes to be silent about what is true. For, as falsehood has always harmed him that speaks it, so sometimes the hearing of truth has done harm to some. Wherefore the Lord before His disciples, tempering His speech with silence, says, *I have many things to say unto you, but ye cannot bear them now* (Joh. xvi. 12). The simple are therefore to be admonished that, as they always avoid deceit advantageously, so they should always utter truth advantageously. They are to be admonished to add prudence to the goodness of simplicity, to the end that they may so possess the security of simplicity as not to lose the circumspection of prudence. For hence it is said by the teacher of the Gentiles, *I would have you wise in that which is good, but simple concerning evil* (Rom xvi. 19) Hence the Truth in person admonishes His elect, saying, *Be ye wise as serpents, but simple as doves* (Matth. x. 16); because, to wit, in the hearts of the elect the wisdom of the serpent ought to sharpen the simplicity of the dove, and the simplicity of the dove temper the wisdom of the serpent, to the end that neither through prudence they be seduced into cunning, nor from simplicity grow torpid in the exercise of the understanding.

But, on the other hand, the insincere are to be admonished to learn how heavy is the labour of duplicity, which with guilt they endure. For, while they are afraid of being found out, they are ever seeking dishonest defences, they are agitated by fearful suspicions. But there is nothing safer for defence than sincerity, nothing easier to say than truth. For, when obliged to defend its deceit, the heart is wearied with hard labour. For hence it is written, *The labour of their own lips shall cover them* (Ps. cxxxix. 10). For what now fills them then covers them, since it then presses down with sharp retribution him whose soul it now elevates with a mild disquietude. Hence it is said through Jeremiah, *They have taught their tongue to speak lies, and weary themselves to commit iniquity* (Jerem. ix. 5): as if it were said plainly, They who might have been friends of truth without labour, labour to sin; and, while they refuse to live in simplicity, by labours require that they should die. For commonly, when taken in a fault, while they shrink from being known to be such as they are, they hide themselves under a veil of deceit, and endeavour to excuse their sin, which is already plainly perceived; so that often one who has a care to reprove their faults, led astray by the mists of the falsehood that surrounds them, finds himself to have almost lost what he just now held as certain concerning them. Hence it is rightly said through the prophet, under the similitude of Judah, to the soul that sins and excuses itself, *There the urchin had her nest* (Isai. xxxiv. 15). For by the name of urchin is denoted the duplicity of a mind that is insincere, and cunningly defends itself; because, to wit, when an urchin is caught, its head is perceived, and its feet appear, and its whole body is exposed to view; but no sooner has it been caught than it gathers itself into a ball, draws in its feet, hides its head, and all is lost together within the hands of him that holds it which before was all visible together. So assuredly, so insincere minds are, when they are seized hold of in their transgressions. For the head of the urchin is perceived, because it appears from what beginning the sinner has advanced to his crime; the feet of the urchin are seen, because it is discovered by what steps the iniquity has been perpetrated; and yet by suddenly adducing excuses the insincere mind gathers in its feet, in that it hides all traces of its iniquity; it draws in the head, because by strange defences it makes out that it has not even begun any evil; and it remains as it were a ball in the hand of one that holds it, because one that takes it to task, suddenly losing all that he had just now come to the knowledge of, holds the sinner rolled up within his own consciousness, and, though he had seen the whole of him when he was caught, yet, illuded by the tergiversation of dishonest defence, he is in like measure ignorant of the whole of him. Thus the urchin has her nest in the reprobate, because the duplicity of a crafty mind, gathering itself up within itself, hides itself in the darkness of its self-defence.

Let the insincere hear what is written, *He that walketh in simplicity walketh surely* (Prov. x. 9). For indeed simplicity of conduct is an assurance of great security. Let them hear what is said by the mouth of the wise man, *The holy spirit of discipline will flee deceit* (Wisd. i. 5). Let them hear what is again affirmed by the witness of Scripture, *His communing is with the simple* (Prov. iii. 32). For God's communing is His revealing of secrets to human minds by the illumination of His presence. He is therefore said to commune with the simple, because He illuminates with the ray of His visitation concerning supernal mysteries the minds of those whom no shade of duplicity obscures. But it is a special evil of the double-minded, that, while they deceive others by their crooked and double conduct, they glory as though they were surpassingly prudent beyond others; and, since they consider not the strictness of retribution, they exult, miserable men that they are, in their own losses. But let them hear how the prophet Zephaniah holds out over them the power of divine rebuke, saying, *Behold the day of the Lord cometh, great and horrible, the day of wrath, that day; a day of darkness and gloominess, a day of cloud and whirlwind, a day of trumpet and clangour, upon all fenced cities, and upon all lofty corners* (Zephan. i. 15, 16). For what is expressed by fenced cities but minds suspected, and surrounded ever with a fallacious defence; minds which, as often as their fault is attacked, suffer not the darts of truth to reach them? And what is signified by lofty corners (a wall being always double in corners) but insincere hearts; which, while they shun the simplicity of truth, are in a manner doubled back upon themselves in the crookedness of duplicity, and, what is worse, from their very fault of insincerity lift themselves in their thoughts with the pride of prudence? Therefore the day of the Lord comes full of vengeance and rebuke upon fenced cities and upon lofty corners, because the wrath of the last judgment both destroys human hearts that have been closed by defences against the truth, and unfolds such as have been folded up in duplicities. For then the fenced cities fall, because souls which God has not penetrated will be damned. Then the lofty corners tumble, because hearts which erect themselves in the prudence of insincerity are prostrated by the sentence of righteousness.

CHAPTER XII.

How the whole and the sick are to be admonished.

(*Admonition* 13.) Differently to be admonished are the whole and the sick. For the whole are to be admonished that they employ the health of the body to the health of the soul; lest, if they turn the grace of granted soundness to the use of iniquity, they be made worse by the gift, and afterwards merit the severer punishments, in that they fear not now to use amiss the more bountiful gifts of God. The whole are to be admonished that they despise not the opportunity of winning health for ever. For it is written, *Behold now is the acceptable time, behold now is the day of salvation* (2 Cor. vi. 2). They are to be admonished lest, if they will not please God when they may, they may be not able when, too late, they would. For hence it is that Wisdom afterward deserts those whom, too long refusing, she before called, saying, *I have called, and ye refused; I have stretched out my hand, and no man regarded; ye have set at naught all my counsel, and would none of my reproof: I will also laugh at your destruction, and will mock when what you feared cometh* (Prov. i. 24, *seq.*). And again, *Then shall they call upon me, and I will not hearken; they shall rise early, and shall not find me* (Ibid. 28). And so, when health of body, received for the purpose of doing good, is despised, it is felt, after it is lost, how precious was the gift: and at the last it is fruitlessly sought, having been enjoyed unprofitably when granted at the fit time. Whence it is well said through Solomon, *Give not thine honour unto aliens and thy years unto the cruel, lest haply strangers be filled with thy wealth, and thy labours be in the house of a stranger, and thou moan at the last, when thy flesh and thy body are consumed* (Ibid. v. 9, *seq.*). For who are aliens from us but malignant spirits, who are separated from the lot of the heavenly country? And what is our honour but that, though made in bodies of clay, we are yet created after the image and likeness of our Maker? Or who else is cruel but that apostate angel, who has both smitten himself with the pain of death through pride, and has not spared, though lost, to bring death upon the human race? He therefore gives his honour unto aliens who, being made after the image and likeness of God, devotes the seasons of his life to the pleasures of malignant spirits. He also surrenders his years to the cruel one who spends the space of life accorded him after the will of the ill-domineering adversary. And in the same place it is well added, *Lest haply strangers be filled with thy wealth, and thy labours be in the house of a stranger*. For whosoever, through the healthy estate of body received by him, or the wisdom of mind granted to him, labours not in the practice of virtues but in the perpetration of vices, he by no means fills his own house, but the habitations of strangers, with his wealth: that is, he multiplies the deeds of unclean spirits, and indeed so acts, in his luxuriousness or his pride, as even to increase the number of the lost by the addition of himself. Further, it is well added, *And thou moan at the last, when thy flesh and thy body are consumed*. For, for the most part, the health of the flesh which has been received is spent through vices: but, when it is suddenly withdrawn, when the flesh is worn with afflictions, when the soul is already urged to go forth, then lost health, long enjoyed for ill, is sought again as though for living well. And then men moan for that they would not serve God, when altogether unable to repair the losses of their negligence by serving Him. Whence it is said in another place, *When He slew them, then they sought Him* (Ps. lxxvii. 34).

But, on the other hand, the sick are to be admonished that they feel themselves to be sons of God in that the scourge of discipline chastises them. For, unless He purposed to give them an inheritance after correction, He would not have a care to educate them by afflictions. For hence the Lord says to John by the angel, *Whom I love I rebuke and chasten* (Rev. iii. 19; Prov. iii. 11). Hence again it is written, *My son despise not thou the discipline of the Lord, nor faint when thou art rebuked of Him. For whom the Lord loveth He chasteneth, and scourgeth every son whom He receiveth* (Heb. xii. 5, 6). Hence the Psalmist says, *Many are the tribulations of the righteous, and out of all these hath the Lord delivered them* (Ps. xxxiii. 20). Hence also the blessed Job, crying out in his sorrow, says, *If I be righteous, I will not lift up my head, being saturated with affliction and misery* (Job x. 15). The sick are to be told that, if they believe the heavenly country to be their own, they must needs endure labours in this as in a strange land. For hence it was that the stones were hammered outside, that they might be laid without sound of hammer in the building of the temple of the Lord; because, that is, we are now hammered with scourges without, that we may be afterwards set in our places within, without stroke of discipline, in the temple of God; to the end that strokes may now cut away whatever is superfluous in us, and then the concord of charity alone bind us together in the building. The sick are to be admonished to consider what severe scourges of discipline chastise our sons after the flesh for attaining earthly inheritances. What pain, then, of divine correction is hard upon us, by which both a never-to-be-lost inheritance is attained, and punishments which shall endure for ever are avoided? For hence Paul says, *We have had fathers of our flesh as our educators, and we gave them reverence: shall we not much more be in subjection unto the Father of spirits and live? And they indeed for a few days educated us after their own will; but He for our profit in the receiving of His sanctification* (Heb. xii. 9, 10).

The sick are to be admonished to consider how great health of the heart is in bodily affliction, which recalls the mind to knowledge of itself, and renews the memory of infirmity which health for the most part casts away, so that the spirit, which is carried out of itself into elation, may be reminded by the smitten flesh from which it suffers to what condition it is subject. Which thing is rightly signified to Balaam (had he but been willing to follow obediently the voice of God) in the very retardation of his journey (Num. xxii. 23, *seq.*). For Balaam is on his way to attain his purpose; but the animal which is under him thwarts his desire. The ass, stopped by the prohibition, sees an angel which the human mind sees not; because for the most part the flesh, slow through afflictions, indicates to the mind from the scourge which it endures the God whom the mind itself which has the flesh under it did not see, in such sort as to impede the eagerness of the spirit which desires to advance in this world as though proceeding on a journey, until it makes known to it the invisible one who stands in its way. Whence also it is well said through Peter, *He had the dumb beast of burden for a rebuke of his madness, which speaking with a man's voice forbade the foolishness of the prophet* (2 Pet. ii. 16). For indeed a man is rebuked as mad by a dumb beast of burden, when an elated mind is reminded by the afflicted flesh of the good of humility which it ought to retain. But Balaam did not obtain the benefit of this rebuke for this reason, that, going to curse, he changed his voice, but not his mind. The sick are to be admonished to consider how great a boon is bodily affliction, which both washes away committed sins and restrains those which might have been committed, which inflicts on the troubled mind wounds of penitence derived from outward stripes. Whence it is written, *The blueness of a wound cleanseth away evil, and stripes in the secret parts of the belly* (Prov. xx. 30). For the blueness of a wound cleanseth away evil, because the pain of scourges cleanses iniquities, whether meditated or perpetrated. But by the appellation of belly the mind is wont to be understood. For that the mind is called the belly is taught by that sentence in which it is written, *The spirit of man is the lamp of the Lord, which searcheth all the secret parts of the belly* (Ibid. 27). As if to say, The illumination of Divine inspiration, when it comes into a man's mind, shews it to itself by illuminating it, whereas before the coming of the Holy Spirit it both could entertain bad thoughts and knew not how to estimate them. Then, the blueness of a wound cleanses away evil, and stripes in the secret parts of the belly, because when we are smitten outwardly, we are recalled, silent and afflicted, to memory of our sins, and bring back before our eyes all our past evil deeds, and through what we suffer outwardly we grieve inwardly the more for what we have done. Whence it comes to pass that in the midst of open wounds of the body the secret stripe in the belly cleanses us more fully, because a hidden wound of sorrow heals the iniquities of evil-doing.

The sick are to be admonished, to the end that they may keep the virtue of patience, to consider incessantly how great evils our Redeemer endured from those whom He had created; that He bore so many vile insults of reproach; that, while daily snatching the souls of captives from the hand of the old enemy, He took blows on the face from insulting men; that, while washing us with the water of salvation, He hid not His face from the spittings of the faithless; that, while delivering us by His advocacy from eternal punishments, He bore scourges in silence; that, while giving to us everlasting honours among the choirs of angels, He endured buffets; that, while saving us from the prickings of our sins, He refused not to submit His head to thorns; that, while inebriating us with eternal sweetness, He accepted in His thirst the bitterness of gall; that He Who for us adored the Father though equal to Him in Godhead, when adored in mockery held His peace; that, while preparing life for the dead, He Who was Himself the life came even unto death. Why, then, is it thought hard that man should endure scourges from God for evil-doing, if God underwent so great evils for well-doing? Or who with sound understanding can be ungrateful for being himself smitten, when even He Who lived here without sin went not hence without a scourge?

CHAPTER XIII.

How those who fear scourges and those who contemn them are to be admonished.

(*Admonition* 14.) Differently to be admonished are those who fear scourges, and on that account live innocently, and those who have grown so hard in wickedness as not to be corrected even by scourges. For those who fear scourges are to be told by no means to desire temporal goods as being of great account, seeing that bad men also have them, and by no means to shun present evils as intolerable, seeing they are not ignorant how for the most part good men also are touched by them. They are to be admonished that, if they desire to be truly free from evils, they should dread eternal punishments; nor yet continue in this fear of punishments, but grow up by the nursing of charity to the grace of love. For it is written, *Perfect charity casteth out fear* (1 Joh. iv. 18). And again it is written, *Ye have not received the spirit of bondage again in fear, but the spirit of adoption of sons, wherein we cry, Abba, Father* (Rom. viii. 15). Whence the same teacher says again, *Where the Spirit of the Lord is, there is liberty* (2 Cor. iii. 17). If, then, the fear of punishment still restrains from evil-doing, truly no liberty of spirit possesses the soul of him that so fears. For, were he not afraid of the punishment, he would doubtless commit the sin. The mind, therefore, that is bound by the bondage of fear knows not the grace of liberty. For good should be loved for itself, not pursued because of the compulsion of penalties. For he that does what is good for this reason, that he is afraid of the evil of torments, wishes that what he fears were not, that so he might commit what is unlawful boldly. Whence it appears clearer than the light that innocence is thus lost before God, in whose eyes evil desire is sin.

But, on the other hand, those whom not even scourges restrain from iniquities are to be smitten with sharper rebuke in proportion as they have grown hard with greater insensibility. For generally they are to be disdained without disdain, and despaired of without despair, so, to wit, that the despair exhibited may strike them with dread, and admonition following may bring them back to hope. Sternly, therefore, against them should the Divine judgments be set forth, that they may be recalled by consideration of eternal retribution to knowledge of themselves. For let them hear that in them is fulfilled that which is written, *If thou shouldest bray a fool in a mortar, as if with a pestle pounding barley, his foolishness will not be taken away from him* (Prov. xxvii. 22). Against these the prophet complains to the Lord, saying, *Thou hast bruised them, and they have refused to receive discipline* (Jer. v. 3). Hence it is that the Lord says, *I have slain and destroyed this people, and yet they have not returned from their ways* (Isai. ix. 13). Hence He says again, *The people hath not returned to Him that smiteth them* (Jer. xv. 6). Hence the prophet complains by the voice of the scourgers, saying, *We have taken care for Babylon, and she is not healed* (Jer. li. 9). For Babylon is taken care for, yet still not restored to health, when the mind, confused in evil-doing, hears the words of rebuke, feels the scourges of rebuke, and yet scorns to return to the straight paths of salvation. Hence the Lord reproaches the children of Israel, captive, but yet not converted from their iniquity, saying, *The house of Israel is to Me become dross: all they are brass, and tin, and iron, and lead, in the midst of the furnace* (Ezek. xxii. 18); as if to say plainly, I would have purified them by the fire of tribulation, and I sought that they should become silver or gold; but they have been turned before me in the furnace into brass, tin, iron, and lead, because even in tribulation they have broken forth, not to virtue, but to vices. For indeed brass, when it is struck, returns a sound more than all other metals. He, therefore, who, when subjected to strokes, breaks out into a sound of murmuring is turned into brass in the midst of the furnace. But tin, when it is dressed with art, has a false show of silver. He, then, who is not free from the vice of pretence in the midst of tribulation becomes tin in the furnace. Moreover, he who plots against the life of his neighbour uses iron. Wherefore iron in the furnace is he who in tribulation loses not the malice that would do hurt. Lead, also, is the heaviest of metals. He, then, is found as lead in the furnace who, even when placed in the midst of tribulation, is not raised above earthly desires. Hence, again, it is written, *She hath wearied herself with much labour, and her exceeding rust went not out from her, not even by fire* (Ezek. xxiv. 12). For He brings upon us the fire of tribulation, that He may purge us from the rust of vices; but we lose not our rust even by fire, when even amid scourges we lack not vice. Hence the Prophet says again, *The founder hath melted in vain; their wickednesses are not consumed* (Jer. vi. 29).

It is, however, to be known that sometimes, when they remain uncorrected amid the hardness of scourges, they are to be soothed by sweet admonition. For those who are not corrected by torments are sometimes restrained from unrighteous deeds by gentle blandishments. For commonly the sick too, whom a strong potion of medicine has not availed to cure, have been restored to their former health by tepid water; and some sores which cannot be cured by incision are healed by fomentations of oil; and hard adamant admits not at all of incision by steel, but is softened by the mild blood of goats.

CHAPTER XIV.

How the silent and the talkative are to be admonished.

Admonition 15.) Differently to be admonished are the over-silent, and those who spend time in much speaking. For it ought to be insinuated to the over-silent that while they shun some vices unadvisedly, they are, without its being perceived, implicated in worse. For often from bridling the tongue overmuch they suffer from more grievous loquacity in the heart; so that thoughts seethe the more in the mind from being straitened by the violent guard of indiscreet silence. And for the most part they overflow all the more widely as they count themselves the more secure because of not being seen by fault-finders without. Whence sometimes a man's mind is exalted into pride, and he despises as weak those whom he hears speaking. And, when he shuts the mouth of his body, he is not aware to what extent through his pride he lays himself open to vices. For his tongue he represses, his mind he exalts; and, little considering his own wickedness, accuses all in his own mind by so much the more freely as he does it also the more secretly. The over-silent are therefore to be admonished that they study anxiously to know, not only what manner of men they ought to exhibit themselves outwardly, but also what manner of men they ought to shew themselves inwardly; that they fear more a hidden judgment in respect of their thoughts than the reproof of their neighbours in respect of their speeches. For it is written, *My son, attend unto my wisdom, and bow thine ear to my prudence, that thou mayest guard thy thoughts* (Prov. v. 1). For, indeed, nothing is more fugitive than the heart, which deserts us as often as it slips away through bad thoughts. For hence the Psalmist says, *My heart hath failed me* (Ps. xxxix. 13[1]). Hence, when he returns to himself, he says, *Thy servant hath found his heart to pray to Thee* (2 Sam. vii. 27). When, therefore, thought is kept under guard, the heart which was wont to fly away is found. Moreover, the over-silent for the most part, when they suffer some injustices, come to have a keener sense of pain from not speaking of what they endure. For, were the tongue to tell calmly the annoyances that have been caused, the pain would flow away from the consciousness. For closed sores torment the more; since, when the corruption that is hot within is cast out, the pain is opened out for healing. They, therefore, who are silent more than is expedient, ought to know this, lest, amid the annoyances which they endure while they hold their tongue, they aggravate the violence of their pain. For they are to be admonished that, if they love their neighbours as themselves, they should by no means keep from them the grounds on which they justly blame them. For from the medicine of the voice there is a concurrent effect for the health of both parties, while on the side of him who inflicts the injury his bad conduct is checked, and on the side of him who sustains it the violent heat of pain is allayed by opening out the sore. For those who take notice of what is evil in their neighbours, and yet refrain their tongue in silence, withdraw, as it were, the aid of

[1] In *English Bible*, xl. 12.

medicine from observed sores, and become the causers of death, in that they would not cure the venom which they could have cured. The tongue, therefore, should be discreetly curbed, not tied up fast. For it is written, *A wise man will hold his tongue until the time* (Eccles. xx. 7); in order, assuredly, that, when he considers it opportune, he may relinquish the censorship of silence, and apply himself to the service of utility by speaking such things as are fit. And again it is written, *A time to keep silence, and a time to speak* (Eccles. iii. 7). For, indeed, the times for changes should be discreetly weighed, lest either, when the tongue ought to be restrained, it run loose to no profit in words, or, when it might speak with profit, it slothfully restrain itself. Considering which thing well, the Psalmist says, *Set a watch, O Lord, on my mouth, and a door round about my lips* (Ps. cxl. 3[2]). For he seeks not that a wall should be set on his lips, but a door: that is, what is opened and shut. Whence we, too, ought to learn warily, to the end that the voice discreetly and at the fitting time may open the mouth, and at the fitting time silence close it.

But, on the other hand, those who spend time in much speaking are to be admonished that they vigilantly note from what a state of rectitude they fall away when they flow abroad in a multitude of words. For the human mind, after the manner of water, when closed in, is collected unto higher levels, in that it seeks again the height from which it descended; and, when let loose, it falls away in that it disperses itself unprofitably through the lowest places. For by as many superfluous words as it is dissipated from the censorship of its silence, by so many streams, as it were, is it drawn away out of itself. Whence also it is unable to return inwardly to knowledge of itself, because, being scattered by much speaking, it excludes itself from the secret place of inmost consideration. But it uncovers its whole self to the wounds of the enemy who lies in want, because it surrounds itself with no defence of watchfulness. Hence it is written, *As a city that lieth open and without environment of walls, so is a man that cannot keep in his spirit in speaking* (Prov. xxv. 28). For, because it has not the wall of silence, the city of the mind lies open to the darts of the foe; and, when by words it casts itself out of itself, it shews itself exposed to the adversary. And he overcomes it with so much the less labour as with the more labour the mind itself, which is conquered, fights against itself by much speaking.

Moreover, since the indolent mind for the most part lapses by degrees into downfall, while we neglect to guard against idle words we go on to hurtful ones; so that at first it pleases us to talk of other men's affairs; afterwards the tongue gnaws with detraction the lives of those of whom we talk; but at last breaks out even into open slanders. Hence are sown pricking thorns, quarrels arise, the torches of enmities are kindled, the peace of hearts is extinguished. Whence it is well said through Solomon, *He that letteth out water is a well-spring of strifes* (Prov. xvii. 14). For to let out water is to let loose the tongue to a flux of speech. Wherefore, on the other hand, in a good sense it is said again, *The words of a man's mouth are as deep water* (Ibid. xviii. 4). He therefore who letteth out water is the wellspring of strifes, because he who curbs not his tongue dissipates concord. Hence on the other hand it is written, *He that imposes silence on a fool allays enmities* (Ibid. xxvi. 10). Moreover, that any one who gives himself to much speaking cannot keep the straight way of righteousness is testified by the Prophet, who says, *A man full of words shall not be guided aright upon the earth* (Ps. cxxxix. 12[3]). Hence also Solomon says again, *In the multitude of words there shall not want sin* (Prov. x. 19). Hence Isaiah says, *The culture of righteousness is silence* (Isai. xxxii. 17), indicating, to wit, that the righteousness of the mind is desolated when there is no stint of immoderate speaking. Hence James says, *If any man thinketh himself to be religious, and bridleth not his tongue, but deceiveth his own heart, this man's religion is vain* (James i. 26). Hence again he says, *Let every man be swift to hear, but slow to speak* (Ibid. 19). Hence again, defining the power of the tongue, he adds, *An unruly evil, full of deadly poison* (Ibid. iii. 8). Hence the Truth in person admonishes us, saying, *Every idle word that men shall speak, they shall give account thereof in the day of judgment* (Matth. xii. 36). For indeed every word is idle that lacks either a reason of just necessity or an intention of pious usefulness. If then an account is required of idle discourse, let us weigh well what punishment awaits much speaking, in which there is also the sin of hurtful words.

CHAPTER XV

How the slothful and the hasty are to be admonished.

(*Admonition* 16.) Differently to be admonished are the slothful and the hasty. For the

[2] In *English Bible*, cxli. 3.

[3] In *English Bible*, cxli. 11.

former are to be persuaded not to lose, by putting it off, the good they have to do; but the latter are to be admonished lest, while they forestall the time of good deeds by inconsiderate haste, they change their meritorious character. To the slothful therefore it is to be intimated, that often, when we will not do at the right time what we can, before long, when we will, we cannot. For the very indolence of the mind, when it is not kindled with befitting fervour, gets cut off by a torpor that stealthily grows upon it from all desire of good things. Whence it is plainly said through Solomon, *Slothfulness casteth into a deep sleep* (Prov. xix. 15). For the slothful one is as it were awake in that he feels aright, though he grows torpid by doing nothing: but slothfulness is said to cast into a deep sleep, because by degrees even the wakefulness of right feeling is lost, when zeal for well-doing is discontinued. And in the same place it is rightly added, *And a dissolute soul shall suffer hunger* (Ibid.) For, because it braces not itself towards higher things, it lets itself run loose uncared for in lower desires; and, while not braced with the vigour of lofty aims, suffers the pangs of the hunger of low concupiscence, and, in that it neglects to bind itself up by discipline, it scatters itself the more abroad, hungry in its craving after pleasures. Hence it is written again by the same Solomon, *The idle man is wholly in desires* (Prov. xxi. 26). Hence in the preaching of the Truth Himself (Matth. xii. 44, 45) the house is said indeed to be clean when one spirit has gone out; but, when empty, it is taken possession of by his returning with many more. For the most part the slothful, while he neglects to do things that are necessary, sets before him some that are difficult, but is inconsiderately afraid of others; and so, as though finding something that he may reasonably fear, he satisfies himself that he has good reason for remaining torpid. To him it is rightly said through Solomon, *The sluggard would not plough by reason of the cold: therefore shall he beg in summer, and it shall not be given unto him* (Prov. xx. 4). For indeed the sluggard ploughs not by reason of the cold, when he finds an excuse for not doing the good things which he ought to do. The sluggard ploughs not by reason of the cold, when he is afraid of small evils that are against him, and leaves undone things of the greatest importance. Further it is well said, *He shall beg in summer, and it shall not be given unto him.* For whoso toils not now in good works will beg in summer and receive nothing, because, when the burning sun of judgment shall appear, he will then sue in vain for entrance into the kingdom. To him it is well said again through the same Solomon, *He that observeth the wind doth not sow: and he that regardeth the clouds never reapeth* (Eccles. xi. 4). For what is expressed by the wind but the temptation of malignant spirits? And what are denoted by the clouds which are moved of the wind but the oppositions of bad men? The clouds, that is to say, are driven by the winds, because bad men are excited by the blasts of unclean spirits. He, then, that observeth the wind soweth not, and he that regardeth the clouds reapeth not, because whosoever fears the temptation of malignant spirits, whosoever the persecution of bad men, and does not sow the seed of good work now, neither doth he then reap handfuls of holy recompense.

But on the other hand the hasty, while they forestall the time of good deeds, pervert their merit, and often fall into what is evil, while failing altogether to discern what is good. Such persons look not at all to see what things they are doing when they do them, but for the most part, when they are done, become aware that they ought not to have done them. To such, under the guise of a learner, it is well said in Solomon, *My son, do nothing without counsel, and after it is done thou shalt not repent* (Ecclus. xxxii. 24). And again, *Let thine eyelids go before thy steps* (Prov. iv. 25). For indeed our eyelids go before our steps, when right counsels prevent our doings. For he who neglects to look forward by consideration to what he is about to do advances his steps with his eyes closed; proceeds on and accomplishes his journey, but goes not in advance of himself by looking forward; and therefore the sooner falls, because he gives no heed through the eyelid of counsel to where he should set the foot of action.

CHAPTER XVI.

How the meek and the passionate are to be admonished.

(*Admonition* 17.) Differently to be admonished are the meek and the passionate. For sometimes the meek, when they are in authority, suffer from the torpor of sloth, which is a kindred disposition, and as it were placed hard by. And for the most part from the laxity of too great gentleness they soften the force of strictness beyond need. But on the other hand the passionate, in that they are swept on into frenzy of mind by the impulse of anger, break up the calm of quietness, and so throw into confusion the life of those that are put under them. For, when rage drives them headlong, they know not what they do in their anger, they know not what in their anger they suffer from themselves. But sometimes, what is more serious, they think the goad of their anger to be the zeal of righteousness. And, when vice is believed to be virtue, guilt is piled up without fear. Often, then, the meek grow torpid in the laziness of inactivity; often the passionate are deceived by the zeal of uprightness. Thus to the virtue of the former a vice is unawares adjoined, but to the latter their vice appears as though it were fervent virtue. Those, therefore, are to be admonished to fly what is close beside themselves, these to take heed to what is in themselves; those to discern what they have not, these what they have. Let the meek embrace solicitude; let the passionate ban perturbation. The meek are to be admonished that they study to have also the zeal of righteousness: the passionate are to be admonished that to the zeal which they think they have they add meekness. For on this account the Holy Spirit has been manifested to us in a dove and in fire; because, to wit, all whom He fills He causes to shew themselves as meek with the simplicity of the dove, and burning with the fire of zeal.

He then is in no wise full of the Holy Spirit, who either in the calm of meekness forsakes the fervour of zeal, or again in the ardour of zeal loses the virtue of meekness. Which thing we shall perhaps better shew, if we bring forward the authority of Paul, who to two who were his disciples, and endowed with a like charity, supplies nevertheless different aids for preaching. For in admonishing Timothy he says, *Reprove, entreat, rebuke, with all long-suffering and doctrine* (2 Tim. iv. 2). Titus also he admonishes, saying, *These things speak, and exhort, and rebuke with all authority* (Tit. ii. 15). What is the reason that he dispenses his teaching with so great art as, in exhibiting it, to recommend authority to the one, and long-suffering to the other, except that he saw Titus to be of a meeker spirit, and Timothy of one a little more fervid? The former he inflames with the earnestness of zeal; the latter he moderates by the gentleness of long-suffering. To the one he adds what is wanting, from the other he subtracts what is overabundant. The one he endeavours to push on with a spur, the other to keep back with a bridle. For the great husbandman who has the Church in charge waters some shoots that they may grow, but prunes others when he sees that they grow too much; lest either by not growing they should bear no fruit, or by growing over much they should lose the fruits they may put forth. But far different is the anger that creeps in under the guise of zeal from that which confounds the perturbed heart without pretext of righteousness. For the former is extended inordinately in that wherein it ought to be, but the latter is ever kindled in that wherein it ought not to be. It should indeed be known that in this the passionate differ from the impatient, that the latter bear not with things brought upon them by others, but the former themselves bring on things to be borne with. For the passionate often follow after those who shun them, stir up occasion of strife, rejoice in the toil of contention; and yet such we better correct, if in the midst of the commotion of their anger we do shun them. For, while they are perturbed, they do not know what we say to them; but, when brought back to themselves, they receive words of exhortation the more freely in proportion as they blush at having been the more calmly borne with. But to a mind that is drunk with fury every right thing that is said appears wrong. Whence to Nabal when he was drunk Abigail laudably kept silence about his fault, but, when he had digested his wine, as laudably told him of it (1 Sam. xxv. 37). For he could for this reason perceive the evil he had done, that he did not hear of it when drunk.

But when the passionate so attack others that they cannot be altogether shunned, they should be smitten, not with open rebuke, but sparingly with a certain respectful cautiousness. And this we shall shew better if we bring forward what was done by Abner. For, when Asahel attacked him with the violence of inconsiderate haste, it is written, *Abner spake unto Asahel, saying, Turn thee aside from following me, lest I be driven to smite thee to the ground. Howbeit he scorned to listen, and refused to turn aside. Whereupon Abner smote him with the hinder end of the spear in the groin, and thrust him through, and he died* (2 Sam. ii. 22, 23). For of whom did Asahel present a type but of those whom fury violently seizes and carries headlong? And such, in this same attack of fury, are to be shunned cautiously in proportion as they are madly hurried on. Whence also Abner, who in our speech is called the lantern of the father, fled; because when the tongue of teachers, which indicates the supernal light of God, sees the mind of any one borne along over the steeps of rage, and refrains from casting back darts of words against the angry person, it is as though it were unwilling to smite one that is pursuing. But, when the passionate will not pacify themselves by any consideration, and, like Asahel, cease not to pursue and to be mad, it is necessary that those who endeavour to repress these furious ones should by no means lift themselves up in fury, but exhibit all possible calmness; and yet adroitly bring something to bear whereby they may by a side thrust prick the heart of the furious one. Whence also Abner, when he made a stand against his pursuer, pierced him, not with a direct stroke, but with the hinder end of his spear. For to strike with the point is to oppose with an onset of open rebuke: but to smite the pursuer with the hinder end of the spear is calmly to touch the furious one with certain hits, and, as it were, by sparing him overcome him. Asahel moreover straightway fell, because agitated minds, when they feel themselves to be spared, and yet are touched inwardly by the answers given in calmness, fall at once from the elevation to which they had raised themselves. Those, then, who rebound from the onset of their heat under the stroke of gentleness die, as it were, without steel.

CHAPTER XVII.

How the humble and the haughty are to be admonished.

(*Admonition* 18.) Differently to be admonished are the humble and the haughty. To the former it is to be insinuated how true is that excellence which they hold in hoping for it; to the latter it is to be intimated how that temporal glory is as nothing which even when embracing it they hold not. Let the humble hear how eternal are the things that they long for, how transitory the things which they despise; let the haughty hear how transitory are the things they court, how eternal the things they lose. Let the humble hear from the authoritative voice of the Truth, *Every one that humbleth himself shall be exalted* (Luke xviii. 14). Let the haughty hear, *Every one that exalteth himself shall be humbled* (Ibid.). Let the humble hear, *Humility goeth before glory;* let the haughty hear, *The spirit is exalted before a fall* (Prov. xv. 33; xvi. 18). Let the humble hear, *Unto whom shall I have respect, but to him that is humble and quiet, and that trembleth at my words* (Isai. lxvi. 2)? Let the haughty hear, *Why is earth and ashes proud* (Ecclus. x. 9)? Let the humble hear, *God hath respect unto the things that are humble.* Let the haughty hear, *And lofty things He knoweth afar off* (Psal. cxxxvii. 6[4]). Let the humble hear, *That the Son of Man came not to be ministered unto, but to minister* (Matth. xx. 28); let the haughty hear, that *The beginning of all sin is pride* (Ecclus. x. 13). Let the humble hear, that *Our Redeemer humbled himself, being made obedient even unto death* (Philip ii. 8); let the haughty hear what is written concerning their head, *He is king over all the sons of pride* (Job xli. 25). The pride, therefore, of the devil became the occasion of our perdition, and the humility of God has been found the argument for our redemption. For our enemy, having been created among all things, desired to appear exalted above all things; but our Redeemer, remaining great above all things, deigned to become little among all things.

Let the humble, then, be told that, when they abase themselves, they ascend to the likeness of God; let the haughty be told that, when they exalt themselves, they fall into imitation of the apostate angel. What, then, is more debased than haughtiness, which, while it stretches itself above itself, is lengthened out beyond the stature of true loftiness? And what is more sublime than humility, which, while it depresses itself to the lowest, conjoins itself to its Maker who remains above the highest? There is, however, another thing in these cases that ought to be carefully considered; that some are often deceived by a false show of humility, while some are beguiled by ignorance of their own haughtiness. For commonly some who think themselves humble have an admixture of fear, such as is not due to men; while an assertion of free speech commonly goes with the haughty. And when any vices require to be rebuked, the former hold their peace out of fear, and yet esteem themselves as being silent out of humility; the latter speak in the impatience of haughtiness, and yet believe themselves to be speaking in the freedom of uprightness. Those the fault of timidity under a show of humility keeps back from rebuking what is wrong; these the unbridled impetuosity of pride, under the image of freedom, impels to rebuke things they ought not, or to rebuke them more than they ought. Whence both the haughty are to be admonished not to be free more than is becoming, and the humble are to be admonished not to be more submissive than is right; lest either the former turn the defence of righteousness into a display of pride, or the latter, while they study more than needs to submit themselves to men, be driven even to pay respect to their vices.

It is, however, to be considered that for the most part we more profitably reprove the haughty, if with our reproofs of them we mingle some balms of praise. For some other good things that are in them should be introduced into our reproofs, or at all events some that might have been, though they are not; and then at last the bad things that displease us

4 In *English Bible*, cxxxviii. 6.

should be cut away, when previous allowance of the good things that please us has made their minds favourably disposed to listen. For unbroken horses, too, we first touch with a gentle hand, that we may afterwards subdue them to us even with whips. And the sweetness of honey is added to the bitter cup of medicine, lest the bitterness which is to be of profit for health be felt harsh in the act of tasting; but, while the taste is deceived by sweetness, the deadly humour is expelled by bitterness. In the case, then, of the haughty the first beginnings of our rebuke should be tempered with an admixture of praise, that, while they admit the commendations which they love, they may accept also the reproofs which they hate.

Moreover, we shall in most cases better persuade the haughty to their profit, if we speak of their improvement as likely to profit us rather than them; if we request their amendment to be bestowed upon us more than on themselves. For haughtiness is easily bent to good, if its bending be believed to be of profit to others also. Whence Moses, who journeyed through the desert under the direction of God and the leading of the cloudy pillar, when he would draw Hobab his kinsman from converse with the Gentile world, and subdue him to the dominion of Almighty God, said, *We are journeying unto the place of which the Lord said, I will give it to you; Come with us, and we will do thee good; for the Lord hath spoken good concerning Israel. And when the other had replied to him, I will not go with thee, but will return to my own land in which I was born;* he straightway added, *Leave us not, I pray thee; for thou knowest in what places we should encamp in the wilderness, and thou shalt be our guide* (Num. x. 29, *seq.*). And yet Moses was not straitened in his own mind by ignorance of the way, seeing that acquaintance with Deity had opened out within him the knowledge of prophecy; and the pillar went before him outwardly, while inwardly familiar speech in his sedulous converse with God instructed him concerning all things. But, in truth, as a man of foresight, talking to a haughty hearer, he sought succour that he might give it; he requested a guide on the way, that he might be able to be his guide unto life. Thus he so acted that the proud hearer should become all the more attentive to the voice that persuaded him to better things from being supposed to be necessary, and, in that he believed himself to be his exhorter's guide, he should bow himself to the words of exhortation.

CHAPTER XVIII.

How the obstinate and the fickle are to be admonished.

(*Admonition* 19.) Differently to be admonished are the obstinate and the fickle. The former are to be told that they think more of themselves than they are, and therefore do not acquiesce in the counsels of others: but the latter are to be given to understand that they undervalue and disregard themselves too much, and so are turned aside from their own judgment in successive moments of time. Those are to be told that, unless they esteemed themselves better than the rest of men, they would by no means set less value on the counsels of all than on their own deliberation: these are to be told that, if they at all gave heed to what they are, the breeze of mutability would by no means turn them about through so many sides of variableness. To the former it is said through Paul, *Be not wise in your own conceits* (Rom. xii. 16): but the latter on the other hand should hear this; *Let us not be carried about with every wind of doctrine* (Ephes. iv. 14). Concerning the former it is said through Solomon, *They shall eat of the fruits of their own way, and be filled with their own devices* (Prov. i. 31); but concerning the latter it is written by him again, *The heart of the foolish will be unlike* (Ibid. xv. 7). For the heart of the wise is always like itself, because, while it rests in good persuasions, it directs itself constantly in good performance. But the heart of the foolish is unlike, because, while it shews itself various through mutability, it never remains what it was. And since some vices, as out of themselves they generate others, so themselves spring from others, it ought by all means to be understood that we then better wipe these away by our reproofs, when we dry them up from the very fountain of their bitterness. For obstinacy is engendered of pride, and fickleness of levity.

The obstinate are therefore to be admonished, that they acknowledge the haughtiness of their thoughts, and study to vanquish themselves; lest, while they scorn to be overcome by the right advice of others outside themselves, they be held captive within themselves to pride. They are to be admonished to observe wisely how the Son of Man, Whose will is always one with the Father's, that He may afford us an example of subduing our own will, says, *I seek not mine own will, but the will of the Father which hath sent me* (Joh. v. 30). And, still more to commend the grace of this virtue, He declared beforehand that He would retain the same in the last judgment, saying, *I can of myself do nothing, but as I hear I judge* (Ibid.). With what conscience, then, can a man disdain to acquiesce in the will of another, seeing that the Son of God and of Man, when He comes to shew forth the glory of his power, testifies that of his own self he does not judge?

But, on the other hand, the fickle are to be admonished to strengthen their mind with gravity. For they then dry up the germs of mutability in themselves when they first cut off from their heart the root of levity; since also a strong fabric is built up when a solid place is first provided whereon to lay the foundation. Unless, then, levity of mind be previously guarded against, inconstancy of the thoughts is by no means conquered. From this Paul declared himself to be free, when he said, *Did I use levity? or the things that I purpose do I purpose according to the flesh, that with me there should be yea and nay* (2 Cor. i. 17)? As if to say plainly, For this reason I am moved by no breeze of mutability, that I yield not to the vice of levity.

CHAPTER XIX.

How those who use food intemperately and those who use it sparingly are to be admonished.

(*Admonition* 20.) Differently to be admonished are the gluttonous and the abstinent. For superfluity of speech, levity of conduct, and lechery accompany the former; but the latter often the sin of impatience, and often that of pride. For were it not the case that immoderate loquacity carries away the gluttonous, that rich man who is said to have fared sumptuously every day would not burn more sorely than elsewhere in his tongue, saying, *Father Abraham, have mercy on me, and send Lazarus, that he may dip the tip of his finger in water, and cool my tongue; for I am tormented in this flame* (Luke xvi. 24). By these words it is surely shewn that in his daily feasting he had frequently sinned by his tongue, seeing that, while burning all over, he demanded to be cooled especially in his tongue. Again, that levity of conduct follows closely upon gluttony sacred authority testifies, when it says, *The people sat down to eat and drink, and rose up to play* (Exod. xxxii. 6). For the most part also edacity leads us even to lechery, because, when the belly is distended by repletion, the stings of lust are excited. Whence also to the cunning foe, who opened the sense of the first man by lust for the apple, but bound it in a noose of sin, it is said by the divine voice, *On breast and belly shalt thou creep* (Gen. iii. 14); as if it were plainly said to him, In thought and in maw thou shalt have dominion over human hearts. That lechery follows upon gluttony the prophet testifies, denouncing hidden things while he speaks of open ones, when he says, *The chief of the cooks broke down the walls of Jerusalem* (Jer. xxxix. 9; 2 Kings xxv. 10)[5]. For the chief of the cooks is the belly, to which the cooks pay observance with great care, that it may itself be delectably filled with viands. But the walls of Jerusalem are the virtues of the soul, elevated to a longing for supernal peace. The chief of the cooks, therefore, throws down the walls of Jerusalem, because, when the belly is distended with gluttony, the virtues of the soul are destroyed through lechery.

On the other hand, were it not that impatience commonly shakes the abstinent out of the bosom of tranquillity, Peter would by no means, when saying, *Supply in your faith virtue, and in your virtue knowledge, and in your knowledge abstinence* (2 Pet. i. 5), have straightway vigilantly added, *And in your abstinence patience.* For he foresaw that the patience which he admonished them to have would be wanting to the abstinent. Again, were it not that the sin of pride sometimes pierces through the cogitations of the abstinent, Paul would by no means have said, *Let not him that eateth not judge him that eateth* (Rom. xiv. 3). And again, speaking to others, while glancing at the maxims of such as gloried in the virtue of abstinence, he added, *Which things have indeed a show of wisdom in superstition and humility, and for not sparing of the body, not in any honour for the satisfying of the flesh* (Coloss. ii. 25). Here it is to be noted that the excellent preacher, in his argument, joins a show of humility to superstition, because, when the flesh is worn more than needs by abstinence, humility is displayed outwardly, but on account of this very humility there is grievous pride within. And unless the mind were sometimes puffed up by the virtue of abstinence, the arrogant Pharisee would by no means have studiously numbered this among his great merits, saying, *I fast twice in the week* (Luke xviii. 12).

Thus the gluttonous are to be admonished, that in giving themselves to the enjoyment of dainties they pierce not themselves through with the sword of lechery; and that they perceive how great loquacity, how great levity of mind, lie in wait for them through eating; lest, while they softly serve the belly, they become cruelly bound in the nooses of vice.

5 The designation (Rab-tabbachim) of Nabuzaradan, who acted for Nebuchadnezzar after the capture of Jerusalem, is rendered in the LXX. ἀρχιμάγειρος, i.e. Chief Cook.

For by so much the further do we go back from our second parent as by immoderate indulgence, when the hand is stretched out for food, we renew the fall of our first parent. But, on the other hand, the abstinent are to be admonished ever anxiously to look out, lest, while they fly the vice of gluttony, still worse vices be engendered as it were of virtue; lest, while they macerate the flesh, their spirit break out into impatience; and so there be no virtue in the vanquishing of the flesh, the spirit being overcome by anger. Sometimes, moreover, while the mind of the abstinent keeps anger down, it is corrupted, as it were, by a foreign joy coming in, and loses all the good of abstinence in that it fails to guard itself from spiritual vices. Hence it is rightly said through the prophet, *In the days of your fasts are found your wills* (Isai. lviii. 3, lxx.). And shortly after, *Ye fast for debates and strifes, and ye smite with the fists* (Ibid.). For the will pertains to delight, the fist to anger. In vain, then, is the body worn by abstinence, if the mind, abandoned to disorderly emotions, is dissipated by vices. And again, they are to be admonished that, while they keep up their abstinence without abatement, they suppose not this to be of eminent virtue before the hidden judge; lest, if it be perchance supposed to be of great merit, the heart be lifted up to haughtiness. For hence it is said through the prophet, *Is it such a fast that I have chosen? But break thy bread to the hungry, and bring the needy and the wanderers into thine house* (Ibid. 5).

In this matter it is to be considered how small the virtue of abstinence is accounted, seeing that it is not commended but for other virtues. Hence Joel says, *Sanctify a fast.* For indeed to sanctify a fast is to shew abstinence of the flesh to be worthy of God by other good things being added to it. The abstinent are to be admonished that they then offer to God an abstinence that pleases Him, when they bestow on the indigent the nourishment which they withhold from themselves. For we should wisely attend to what is blamed by the Lord through the prophet, saying, *When ye fasted and mourned in the fifth and seventh month for these seventy years, did ye at all fast a fast unto Me? And when ye did eat and drink, did ye not eat for yourselves, and drink for yourselves* (Zach. vii. 5 *seq.*)? For a man fasts not to God but to himself, if what he withholds from his belly for a time he gives not to the needy, but keeps to be offered afterwards to his belly.

Wherefore, lest either gluttonous appetite throw the one sort off their guard, or the afflicted flesh trip up the other by elation, let the former hear this from the mouth of the Truth, *And take heed to yourselves, lest at any time your hearts be overcharged in surfeiting and drunkenness and cares of this world* (Luke xxi. 34). And in the same place there is added a profitable fear; *And so that day come upon you unawares. For as a snare shall it come on all them that dwell on the face of the whole earth* (Ibid. 35). Let the latter hear, *Not that which goeth into the mouth defileth a man; but that which cometh out of the mouth, this defileth a man* (Matth. xv. 11). Let the former hear, *Meat for the belly, and the belly for meats; but God shall destroy both it and them* (1 Cor. vi. 13). And again, *Not in rioting and drunkenness* (Rom. xiii. 13). And again, *Meat commendeth us not to God* (1 Cor. viii. 8). Let the latter hear, *To the pure all things are pure: but unto them that are defiled and unbelieving is nothing pure* (Tit. i. 15). Let the former hear, *Whose God is their belly, and whose glory is in their own confusion* (Philip. iii. 19). Let the latter hear, *Some shall depart from the faith;* and a little after, *Forbidding to marry, and commanding to abstain from meats, which God hath created to be received with thanksgiving of them which believe and know the truth* (1 Tim. iv. 1, 3). Let those hear, *It is good neither to eat flesh nor to drink wine, nor anything whereby thy brother stumbleth* (Rom. xiv. 21). Let these hear, *Use a little wine for thy stomach's sake and thine often infirmities* (1 Tim. v. 23). Thus both the former may learn not to desire inordinately the food of the flesh, and the latter not dare to condemn the creature of God, which they lust not after.

CHAPTER XX.

How to be admonished are those who give away what is their own, and those who seize what belongs to others.

(*Admonition* 21.) Differently to be admonished are those who already give compassionately of their own, and those who still would fain seize even what belongs to others. For those who already give compassionately of their own are to be admonished not to lift themselves up in swelling thought above those to whom they impart earthly things; not to esteem themselves better than others because they see others to be supported by them. For the lord of an earthly household, in distributing the ranks and ministries of his servants, appoints some to rule, but some to be ruled by others. Those he orders to supply to the rest what is necessary, these to take what they receive from others. And yet it is for the most part those that rule who offend, while those that are ruled remain in favour with the good man of the house. Those who are dispensers incur wrath; those who subsist by the dispensation of others continue without offence. Those, then, who already give compassionately of the things which they possess are to be admonished to acknowledge themselves to be placed by the heavenly Lord as dispensers of temporal supplies, and to impart the same all the more humbly from their understanding that the things which they dispense are not their own. And, when they consider that they are appointed for the service of those to whom they impart what they have received, by no means let vain glory elate their minds, but let fear depress them. Whence also it is needful for them to take anxious thought lest they distribute what has been committed to them unworthily; lest they bestow something on those on whom they ought to have spent nothing, or nothing on those on whom they ought to have spent something, or much on those on whom they ought to have spent little, or little on those on whom they ought to have spent much; lest by precipitancy they scatter unprofitably what they give; lest by tardiness they mischievously torment petitioners; lest the thought of receiving a favour in return creep in; lest craving for transitory praise extinguish the light of giving; lest accompanying moroseness beset an offered gift; lest in case of a gift that has been well offered the mind be exhilarated more than is fit; lest, when they have fulfilled all aright, they give something to themselves, and so at once lose all after they have accomplished all. For, that they may not attribute to themselves the virtue of their liberality, let them hear what is written, *If any man administer, let him do it as of the ability which God administereth* (1 Pet. iv. 11). That they may not rejoice immoderately in benefits bestowed, let them hear what is written, *When ye shall have done all those things which are commanded you, say, We are unprofitable servants, we have done that which was our duty to do* (Luke xvii. 10). That moroseness may not spoil liberality, let them hear what is written, *God loveth a cheerful giver* (2 Cor. ix. 7). That they may not seek transitory praise for a gift bestowed, let them hear what is written, *Let not thy left hand know what thy right hand doeth* (Matth. vi. 3). That is, let not the glory of the present life mix itself with the largesses of piety, nor let desire of favour know anything of the work of rectitude. That they may not require a return for benefits bestowed, let them hear what is written, *When thou makest a dinner or a supper, call not thy friends, nor thy brethren, neither thy kinsmen, nor thy rich neighbours, lest they also bid thee again, and a recompense be made thee. but, when thou makest a feast, call the poor, the maimed, the lame, the blind: and thou shalt be blessed; for they have not whereof to recompense thee* (Luke xiv. 12 *seq.*). That they may not supply too late what should be supplied at once, let them hear what is written, *Say not unto thy friend, go and come again, and to-morrow I will give, when thou mightest give immediately* (Prov. iii. 28). Lest, under pretence of liberality, they should scatter what they possess unprofitably, let them hear what is written, *Let thine alms sweat in thine hand.* Lest, when much is necessary, little be given, let them hear what is written, *He that soweth sparingly shall reap also sparingly* (2 Cor. ix. 6). Lest, when they ought to give little, they give too much, and afterwards, badly enduring want themselves, break out into impatience, let them hear what is written, *Not that other men be eased, and ye burdened, but by an equality, that your abundance may supply their want, and that their abundance may be a supply to your want* (Ibid. viii. 13, 14). For, when the soul of the giver knows not how to endure want, then, in withdrawing much from himself, he seeks out against himself occasion of impatience. For the mind should first be prepared for patience, and then either much or all be bestowed in bounty, lest, the inroad of want being borne with but little equanimity, both the reward of previous bounty be lost, and subsequent murmuring bring worse ruin on the soul. Lest they should give nothing at all to those on whom they ought to bestow something, let them hear what is written, *Give to every man that asketh of thee* (Luke vi. 30). Lest they should give something, however little, to those on whom they ought to bestow nothing at all, let them hear what is written, *Give to the good man, and receive not a sinner: do well to him that is lowly, and give not to the ungodly* (Ecclus. xii. 4). And again, *Set out thy bread and wine on the burial of the just, but eat and drink not thereof with sinners* (Tobit iv. 17).

For he gives his bread and wine to sinners who gives assistance to the wicked for that they are wicked. For which cause also some of the rich of this world nourish players with profuse bounties, while the poor of Christ are tormented with hunger. He, however, who gives his bread to one that is indigent, though he be a sinner, not because he is a sinner, but because he is a man, does not in truth nourish a sinner, but a poor righteous man, because what he loves in him is not his sin, but his nature.

Those who already distribute compassionately what they possess are to be admonished also that they study to keep careful guard, lest, when they redeem by alms the sins they have committed, they commit others which will still require redemption; lest they suppose the righteousness of God to be saleable, thinking that if they take care to give money for their sins, they can sin with impunity. For, *The soul is more than meat, and the body than raiment* (Matth. vi. 25; Luke xii. 23). He, therefore, who bestows meat or raiment on the poor, and yet is polluted by iniquity of soul or body, has offered the lesser thing to righteousness, and the greater thing to sin; for he has given his possessions to God, and himself to the devil.

But, on the other hand, those who still would fain seize what belongs to others are to be admonished to give anxious heed to what the Lord says when He comes to judgment. For He says, *I was an hungered, and ye gave Me no meat: I was thirsty, and ye gave Me no drink: I was a stranger, and ye took Me not in: naked, and ye clothed Me not; sick, and in prison, and ye visited Me not* (Matth. xxv. 42, 43). And these he previously addresses, saying, *Depart from Me, ye cursed, into eternal fire, which is prepared for the devil and his angels* (Ibid. 41). Lo, they are in no wise told that they have committed robberies or any other acts of violence, and yet they are given over to the eternal fires of Gehenna. Hence, then, it is to be gathered with how great damnation those will be visited who seize what is not their own, if those who have indiscreetly kept their own are smitten with so great punishment. Let them consider in what guilt the seizing of goods must bind them, if not parting with them subjects to such a penalty. Let them consider what injustice inflicted must deserve, if kindness not bestowed is worthy of so great a chastisement.

When they are intent on seizing what is not their own, let them hear what is written, *Woe to him that increaseth that which is not his! How long doth he heap up against himself thick clay* (Hab. ii. 6)? For, indeed, for a covetous man to heap up against him thick clay is to pile up earthly gains into a load of sin. When they desire to enlarge greatly the spaces of their habitation, let them hear what is written, *Woe unto you that join house to house and lay field to field, even till there be no place left. What, will ye dwell alone in the midst of the earth* (Isai. v. 8)? As if to say plainly, How far do ye stretch yourselves, ye that cannot bear to have comrades in a common world? Those that are joined to you ye keep down, and ever find some against whom ye may have power to stretch yourselves. When they are intent on increasing money, let them hear what is written, *The covetous man is not filled with money; and he that loveth riches shall not reap fruit thereof* (Eccles. v. 9). For indeed he would reap fruit of them, were he minded, not loving them, to disperse them well. But whoso in his affection for them retains them, shall surely leave them behind him here without fruit. When they burn to be filled at once with all manner of wealth, let them hear what is written, *He that maketh haste to be rich shall not be innocent* (Prov. xxviii. 20): for certainly he who goes about to increase wealth is negligent in avoiding sin; and, being caught after the manner of birds, while looking greedily at the bait of earthly things, he is not aware in what a noose of sin he is being strangled. When they desire any gains of the present world, and are ignorant of the losses they will suffer in the world to come, let them hear what is written, *An inheritance to which haste is made in the beginning in the last end shall lack blessing* (Prov. xx. 21). For indeed we derive our beginning from this life, that we may come in the end to the lot of blessing. They, therefore, that make haste to an inheritance in the beginning cut off from themselves the lot of blessing in the end; since, while they crave to be increased in goods here through the iniquity of avarice, they become disinherited there of their eternal patrimony. When they either solicit very much, or succeed in obtaining all that they have solicited, let them hear what is written, *What is a man profited, if he should gain the whole world, but lose his own soul* (Matth. xvi. 26)? As if the Truth said plainly, What is a man profited, though he gather together all that is outside himself, if this very thing only which is himself he damns? But for the most part the covetousness of spoilers is the sooner corrected, if it be shewn by the words of such as admonish them how fleeting is the present life; if mention be made of those who have long endeavoured to grow rich in this world, and yet have been unable to remain long among their acquired riches; from whom hasty death has taken away suddenly and all at once whatever, neither all at once nor suddenly, they have gathered together; who have not only left here what they had seized, but have carried with them to the judgment arraignments for seizure. Let them, therefore, be told of examples of such as these, whom they would, doubtless, even themselves, in words condemn; so that, when after their words they come back to their own heart, they may blush at any rate to imitate those whom they judge.

CHAPTER XXI.

How those are to be admonished who desire not the things of others, but keep their own; and those who give of their own, yet seize on those of others

(*Admonition* 22.) Differently to be admonished are those who neither desire what belongs to others nor bestow what is their own, and those who give of what they have, and yet desist not from seizing on what belongs to others. Those who neither desire what belongs to others nor bestow what is their own are to be admonished to consider carefully that the earth out of which they are taken is common to all men, and therefore brings forth nourishment for all in common. Vainly, then, do those suppose themselves innocent, who claim to their own private use the common gift of God; those who, in not imparting what they have received, walk in the midst of the slaughter of their neighbours; since they almost daily slay so many persons as there are dying poor whose subsidies they keep close in their own possession. For, when we administer necessaries of any kind to the indigent, we do not bestow our own, but render them what is theirs; we rather pay a debt of justice than accomplish works of mercy. Whence also the Truth himself, when speaking of the caution required in shewing mercy, says, *Take heed that ye do not your justice before men* (Matth. vi. 1). The Psalmist also, in agreement with this sentence, says, *He hath dispersed, he hath given to the poor, his justice endureth for ever* (Ps. cxii. 9).

For, having first mentioned bounty bestowed upon the poor, he would not call this mercy, but rather justice: for it is surely just that whosoever receive what is given by a common lord should use it in common. Hence also Solomon says, *Whoso is just will give and will not spare* (Prov. xxi. 26). They are to be admonished also anxiously to take note how of the fig-tree that had no fruit the rigorous husbandman complains that it even cumbers the ground.

For a fig-tree without fruit cumbers the ground, when the soul of the niggardly keeps unprofitably what might have benefited many. A fig-tree without fruit cumbers the ground, when the fool keeps barren under the shade of sloth a place which another might have cultivated under the sun of good works.

But these are wont sometimes to say, We use what has been granted us; we do not seek what belongs to others; and, if we do nothing worthy of the reward of mercy, we still commit no wrong. So they think, because in truth they close the ear of their heart to the words which are from heaven. For the rich man in the Gospel who was clothed in purple and fine linen, and feasted sumptuously every day, is not said to have seized what belonged to others, but to have used what was his own unfruitfully; and avenging hell received him after this life, not because he did anything unlawful but because by immoderate indulgence he gave up his whole self to what was lawful.

The niggardly are to be admonished to take notice that they do God, in the first place, this wrong; that to Him Who gives them all they render in return no sacrifice of mercy. For hence the Psalmist says, *He will not give his propitiation to God, nor the price of the redemption of his soul* (Psal. xlviii. 9[6]). For to give the price of redemption is to return good deeds for preventing grace. Hence John cries aloud saying, *Now the axe is laid unto the root of the tree. Every tree which bringeth not forth good fruit shall be hewn down and cast into the fire* (Luke iii. 9). Let those, therefore, who esteem themselves guiltless because they do not seize on what belongs to others look forward to the stroke of the axe that is nigh at hand, and lay aside the torpor of improvident security, lest, while they neglect to bear the fruit of good deeds, they be cut off from the present life utterly, as it were from the greenness of the root.

But, on the other hand, those who both give what they have and desist not from seizing on what belongs to others are to be admonished not to desire to appear exceeding munificent, and so be made worse from the outward show of good. For these, giving what is their own without discretion, not only, as we have said above, fall into the murmuring of impatience, but, when want urges them, are swept along even to avarice. What, then, is more wretched than the mind of those in whom avarice is born of bountifulness, and a crop of sins is sown as it were from virtue? First, then, they are to be admonished to learn how to keep what is theirs reasonably, and then in the end not to go about getting what is another's. For, if the root of the fault is not burnt out in the profusion itself, the thorn of avarice, exuberant through the branches, is never dried up. So then, cause for seizing is withdrawn, if the right of possession be first adjusted well. But then, further, let those who are admonished be told how to give mercifully what they have, when they have learnt not to confound the good of mercy by throwing into it the wickedness of robbery. For they violently exact what

[6] In *English Bible*, xlix. 9.

they mercifully bestow. For it is one thing to shew mercy on account of our sins; another thing to sin on account of shewing mercy; which can no longer indeed be called mercy, since it cannot grow into sweet fruit, being embittered by the poison of its pestiferous root. For hence it is that the Lord through the prophet rejects even sacrifices themselves, saying, *I the Lord love judgment, and I hate robbery in a whole burnt offering* (Isai. lxi. 8). Hence again He has said, *The sacrifices of the ungodly are abominable, which are offered of wickedness* (Prov. xxi. 28). Such persons also often withdraw from the indigent what they give to God.

But the Lord shews with what strong censure he disowns them, saying through a certain wise man, *Whoso offereth a sacrifice of the substance of the poor doeth as one that killeth the son before the father's eyes* (Ecclus. xxxiv. 20). For what can be more intolerable than the death of a son before his father's eyes? Wherefore it is shewn with what great wrath this kind of sacrifice is beheld, in that it is compared to the grief of a bereaved father. And yet for the most part people weigh well how much they give; but how much they seize they neglect to consider. They count, as it were, their wage, but refuse to consider their defaults. Let them hear therefore what is written, *He that hath gathered wages hath put them into a bag with holes* (Hagg. i. 6). For indeed money put into a bag with holes is seen when it is put in, but when it is lost it is not seen. Those, then, who have an eye to how much they bestow, but consider not how much they seize, put their wages into a bag with holes, because in truth they look to them when they gather them together in hope of being secure, but lose them without looking.

CHAPTER XXII.

How those that are at variance and those that are at peace are to be admonished.

(*Admonition* 23.) Differently to be admonished are those that are at variance and those that are at peace. For those that are at variance are to be admonished to know most certainly that, in whatever virtues they may abound, they can by no means become spiritual if they neglect becoming united to their neighbours by concord. For it is written, *But the fruit of the Spirit is love, joy, peace* (Gal. v. 22). He then that has no care to keep peace refuses to bear the fruit of the Spirit. Hence Paul says, *Whereas there is among you envying and strife, are ye not carnal* (1 Cor. iii. 3)? Hence again he says also, *Follow peace with all men and holiness, without which no man shall see the Lord* (Heb. xii. 14). Hence again he admonishes, saying, *Endeavouring to keep the unity of the Spirit in the bond of peace: there is one body and one Spirit, even as ye are called in one hope of your calling* (Eph. iv. 3, 4). The one hope of our calling, therefore, is never reached, if we run not to it with a mind at one with our neighbours. But it is often the case that some, by being proud of some gifts that they especially partake of, lose the greater gift of concord; as it may be if one who subdues the flesh more than others by bridling of his appetite should scorn to be in concord with those whom he surpasses in abstinence. But whoso separates abstinence from concord, let him consider the admonition of the Psalmist, *Praise him with timbrel and chorus* (Ps. cl. 4). For in the timbrel a dry and beaten skin resounds, but in the chorus voices are associated in concord. Whosoever then afflicts his body, but forsakes concord, praises God indeed with timbrel, but praises Him not with chorus. Often, however, when superior knowledge lifts up some, it disjoins them from the society of other men; and it is as though the more wise they are, the less wise are they as to the virtue of concord. Let these therefore hear what the Truth in person says, *Have salt in yourselves, and have peace one with another* (Mark ix. 50). For indeed salt without peace is not a gift of virtue, but an argument for condemnation. For the better any man is in wisdom, the worse is his delinquency, and he will deserve punishment inexcusably for this very reason, that, if he had been so minded, he might in his prudence have avoided sin. To such it is rightly said through James, *But if ye have bitter envying and strife in your hearts, glory not, and lie not against the truth. This wisdom descendeth not from above, but is earthly, sensual, devilish. But the wisdom that is from above is first pure, then peaceable* (James iii. 14, 15, 17). Pure, that is to say, because its ideas are chaste; and also peaceable, because it in no wise through elation disjoins itself from the society of neighbours. Those who are at variance are to be admonished to take note that they offer to God no sacrifice of good work so long as they are not in charity with their neighbours. For it is written, *If thou bring thy gift to the altar, and there rememberest that thy brother hath ought against thee, leave there thy gift before the altar, and go thy way first to be reconciled to thy brother, and then thou shalt come and offer thy gift* (Matth. v. 23, 24). Now by this precept we are led to consider how intolerable the guilt of men is shewn to be when their sacrifice is rejected. For, whereas all evils are washed away when followed by what is good, let us consider how great must be the evils of discord, seeing that, unless they are utterly extinguished, they allow no good to follow. Those who are at variance are to be admonished that, if they incline not their ears to heavenly commands, they should open the eyes of the mind to consider the ways of creatures of the lowest order; how that often birds of one and the same kind desert not one another in their social flight, and that brute beasts feed in herds together. Thus, if we observe wisely, irrational nature shews by agreeing together how great evil rational nature commits by disagreement; when the latter has lost by the exercise of reason what the former by natural instinct keeps. But, on the other hand, those that are at peace are to be admonished to take heed lest, while they love more than they need do the peace which they enjoy, they have no longing to reach that which is perpetual. For commonly tranquil circumstances more sorely try the bent of minds, so that, in proportion as the things which occupy them are not troublesome, the things which invite them come to appear less lovely, and the more present things delight, eternal things are the less sought after. Whence also the Truth speaking in person, when He would distinguish earthly from supernal peace, and provoke His disciples from that which now is to that which is to come, said, *Peace I leave with you, My peace I give unto you* (Joh. xiv. 27). That is, I leave a transitory, I give a lasting peace. If then the heart is fixed on that which is left, that which is to be given is never reached. Present peace, therefore, is to be held as something to be both loved and thought little of, lest, if it is loved immoderately, the mind of him that loves be taken in a fault. Whence also those who are at peace should be admonished lest, while too desirous of human peace, they fail entirely to reprove men's evil ways, and, in consenting to the froward, disjoin themselves from the peace of their Maker; lest, while they dread human quarrels without, they be smitten by breach of their inward covenant. For what is transitory peace but a certain footprint of peace eternal? What, then, can be more mad than to love footprints impressed on dust, but not to love him by whom they have been impressed? Hence David, when he would bind himself entirely to the covenants of inward peace, testifies that he held no agreement with the wicked, saying, *Did not I hate them, O God, that hate thee, and waste away on account of thine enemies? I hated them with perfect hatred, they became enemies to me* (Ps. cxxxviii. 21, 22[7]). For to hate God's enemies with perfect hatred is both to love what they were made, and to chide what they do, to be severe on the manners of the wicked, and to profit their life. It is therefore to be well weighed, when there is rest from chiding, how culpably peace is kept with the worst of men, if so great a prophet offered this as a sacrifice to God, that he excited the enmities of the wicked against himself for the Lord. Hence it is that the tribe of Levi, when they took their swords and passed through the midst of the camp because they would not spare the sinners who were to be smitten, are said to have consecrated their hands to God (Exod. xxxii. 27 *seq.*). Hence Phinehas, spurning the favour of his fellow-countrymen when they sinned, smote those who came together with the Midianites, and in his wrath appeased the wrath of God (Num. xxv. 9). Hence in person the Truth says, *Think not that I am come to send peace on earth: I came not to send peace, but a sword* (Matth. x. 34). For, when we are unwarily joined in friendship with the wicked, we are bound in their sins. Whence Jehoshaphat, who is extolled by so many praises of his previous life, is rebuked for his friendship with King Ahab as though nigh unto destruction, when it is said to him through the prophet, *Thou givest help to the ungodly, and art joined in friendship with them that hate the Lord; and therefore thou didst deserve indeed the wrath of the Lord: nevertheless there are good works found in thee, in that thou hast taken away the groves out of the land of Judah* (2 Chron. xix. 2, 3). For our life is already at variance with Him who is supremely righteous by the very fact of agreement in the friendships of the froward. Those who are at peace are to be admonished not to be afraid of disturbing their temporal peace, if they break forth into words of rebuke. And again they are to be admonished to keep inwardly with undiminished love the same peace which in their external relations they disturb by their reproving voice. Both which things David declares that he had prudently observed, saying, *With them that hate peace I was peaceable; when I spake unto them, they fought against me without a cause* (Ps. cxix. 7[8]). Lo, when he spoke, he was fought against; and yet, when fought against, he was peaceable, because he neither ceased to reprove those that were mad against him, nor forgot to love those who were reproved. Hence also Paul says, *If it be possible, as much as lieth in you, have peace with all men* (Rom. xii. 18).

[7] In *English Bible*, Ps. cxxxiv.

[8] Ibid., Ps. cxx.

For, being about to exhort his disciples to have peace with all, he said first, *If it be possible*, and added, *As much as lieth in you.* For indeed it was difficult for them, if they rebuked evil deeds, to be able to have peace with all. But, when temporal peace is disturbed in the hearts of bad men through our rebuke, it is necessary that it should be kept inviolate in our own heart. Rightly, therefore, says he, *As much as lieth in you.* It is indeed as though he said, Since peace stands in the consent of two parties, if it is driven out by those who are reproved, let it nevertheless be retained undiminished in the mind of you who reprove. Whence the same apostle again admonishes his disciples, saying, *If any man obey not our word, note that man by this epistle; and have no company with him, that he may be confounded* (2 Thess. iii. 14). And straightway he added, *Yet count him not as an enemy, but reprove him as a brother* (Ibid. 15). As if to say, Break ye outward peace with him, but guard in your heart's core internal peace concerning him; that your discord with him may so smite the mind of the sinner that peace depart not from your hearts even though denied to him.

CHAPTER XXIII.

How sowers of strifes and peacemakers are to be admonished.

(*Admonition* 24.) Differently to be admonished are sowers of strifes and peacemakers. For sowers of strifes are to be admonished to perceive whose followers they are. For of the apostate angel it is written, when tares had been sown among the good crop, *An enemy hath done this* (Matth. xiii. 28). Of a member of him also it is said through Solomon, *An apostate person, an unprofitable man, walketh with a perverse mouth, he winketh with his eyes, he beateth with his foot, he speaketh with his finger, with froward heart he deviseth mischief continually, he soweth strifes* (Prov. vi. 12—14). Lo, him whom he would speak of as a sower of strifes he first named an apostate; since, unless after the manner of the proud angel he first fell away inwardly by the alienation of his mind from the face of his Maker, he would not afterwards come to sow strifes outwardly. He is rightly described too as winking with his eyes, speaking with his finger, beating with his foot. For it is inward watch that keeps the members outwardly in orderly control. He, then, who has lost stability of mind falls off outwardly into inconstancy of movement, and by his exterior mobility shews that he is stayed on no root within. Let sowers of strifes hear what is written, *Blessed are the peacemakers, for they shall be called the children of God* (Matth. v. 9). And on the other hand let them gather that, if they who make peace are called the children of God, without doubt those who confound it are the children of Satan. Moreover, all who are separated by discord from the greenness of loving-kindness are dried up: and, though they bring forth in their actions fruits of well-doing, yet there are in truth no fruits, because they spring not from the unity of charity. Hence, therefore, let sowers of strifes consider how manifoldly they sin; in that, while they perpetrate one iniquity, they eradicate at the same time all virtues from human hearts. For in one evil they work innumerable evils, since, in sowing discord, they extinguish charity, which is in truth the mother of all virtues. But, since nothing is more precious with God than the virtue of loving-kindness, nothing is more acceptable to the devil than the extinction of charity. Whosoever, then, by sowing of strifes destroy the loving-kindness of neighbours, serve God's enemy as his familiar friend; because by taking away from them this, by the loss of which he fell, they have cut off from them the road whereby to rise.

But, on the other hand, the peacemakers are to be admonished that they detract not from the efficacy of so great an undertaking through not knowing between whom they ought to establish peace. For, as there is much harm if unity be wanting to the good, so there is exceeding harm if it be not wanting to the bad. If, then, the iniquity of the perverse is united in peace, assuredly there is an accession of strength to their evil doings, since the more they agree among themselves in wickedness, by so much the more stoutly do they dash themselves against the good to afflict them. For hence it is that against the preachers of that vessel of damnation, to wit, Antichrist, is it said by the divine voice to the blessed Job, *The members of his flesh stick close to each other* (Job xli. 14 [9]). Hence, under the figure of scales, it is said of his satellites, *One is joined to another, and not even a breathing-hole cometh between them* (xli. 7 [9]). For, indeed, his followers, from being divided by no opposition of discord among themselves, are by so much the more strongly banded together in the slaughter of the good. He then who associates the iniquitous together in peace supplies strength to iniquity, since they

[9] So Vulgate. Gregory always takes Leviathan to signify the devil.

worse press down the good, whom they persecute unanimously. Whence the excellent preacher, being overtaken by violent persecution from Pharisees and Sadducees, endeavoured to divide among themselves those whom he saw to be violently united against himself, when he cried out, saying, *Men, brethren, I am a Pharisee, the son of Pharisees; of the hope and resurrection of the dead I am called in question* (Acts xxiii. 6). And, whereas the Sadducees denied the hope and resurrection of the dead, which the Pharisees in accordance with the precepts of Holy Writ believed, a dissension was caused in the unanimity of the persecutors; and Paul escaped unhurt from the divided crowd, which before, when united, had savagely assailed him. Those, therefore, who are occupied with the desire of making peace, are to be admonished that they ought first to infuse a love of internal peace into the minds of the froward, to the end that external peace may afterwards avail to do them good; so that, while their heart is hanging on cognition of the former, they be by no means hurried into wickedness from perception of the latter; and, while they see before them that which is supernal, they in no way turn that which is earthly to serve to their own detriment. But, if any perverse persons are such that they could not harm the good, even though they lusted to do so, between them, indeed, earthly peace ought to be established, even before they have risen to the knowledge of supernal peace; even so that they, whom the wickedness of their impiety exasperates against the lovingkindness of God, may at any rate be softened out of love of their neighbour, and, as it were from a neighbouring position, may pass to a better one, and so rise to what is as yet far from them, the peace of their Maker.

CHAPTER XXIV.

How the rude in sacred learning, and those who are learned but not humble, are to be admonished.

(*Admonition* 25.) Differently to be admonished are those who do not understand aright the words of the sacred Law, and those who understand them indeed aright, but speak them not humbly. For those who understand not aright the words of sacred Law are to be admonished to consider that they turn for themselves a most wholesome draught of wine into a cup of poison, and with a medicinal knife inflict on themselves a mortal wound, when they destroy in themselves what was sound by that whereby they ought, to their health, to have cut away what was diseased. They are to be admonished to consider that Holy Scripture is set as a kind of lantern for us in the night of the present life, the words whereof when they understand not aright, from light they get darkness. But in truth a perverse bent of mind would not hurry them to understand it wrong, did not pride first puff them up. For, while they think themselves wise beyond all others, they scorn to follow others to things better understood: and, in order to extort for themselves from the unskilful multitude a name for knowledge, they strive mightily both to upset the right views of others and to confirm their own perverse views. Hence it is well said by the prophet, *They have ripped up the women with child of Gilead, that they might enlarge their border* (Amos i. 13). For Gilead is by interpretation a heap of witness (Gen. xxxi. 47, 48). And, since the whole congregation of the Church together serves by its confession for a witness to the truth, not unfitly by Gilead is expressed the Church, which witnesses by the mouth of all the faithful whatever is true concerning God. Moreover, souls are called with child, when of divine love they conceive an understanding of the Word, so that, if they come to their full time, they may bring forth their conceived intelligence in the shewing forth of work. Further, to enlarge their border is to extend abroad the fame of their reputation. They have therefore ripped up the women with child of Gilead that they might enlarge their border, because heretics assuredly slay by their perverse preaching the souls of the faithful who had already conceived something of the understanding of the truth, and extend for themselves a name for knowledge. The hearts of little ones, already big with conception of the word, they cleave with the sword of error, and, as it were, make for themselves a reputation as teachers. When, therefore, we endeavour to instruct these not to think perversely, it is necessary that we first admonish them to shun vain glory. For, if the root of elation is cut off, the branches of wrong assertion are consequently dried up. They are also to be admonished to take heed, lest, by gendering errors and discords, they turn into a sacrifice to Satan the very same law of God which has been given for hindering sacrifices to Satan. Whence the Lord complains through the prophet, saying, *I gave them corn, wine, and oil, and I multiplied to them silver and gold, which they sacrificed to Baal* (Hos. ii. 8). For indeed we receive corn from the Lord, when, in the more obscure sayings, the husk of the letter being drawn off, we perceive in the marrow of the

Spirit the inward meaning of the Law. The Lord proffers us His wine, when He inebriates us with the lofty preaching of His Scripture. His oil also He gives us, when, by plainer precepts, He orders our life gently and smoothly. He multiplies silver, when He supplies to us eloquent utterances, full of the light of truth. With gold also He enriches us, when He irradiates our heart with an understanding of the supreme splendour. All which things heretics offer to Baal, because they pervert them in the hearts of their hearers by a corrupt understanding of them all. And of the corn of God, of His wine and oil, and likewise of His silver and gold, they offer a sacrifice to Satan, because they turn aside the words of peace to promote the error of discord. Wherefore they are to be admonished to consider that, when of their perverse mind they make discord out of the precepts of peace, they themselves, in the just judgment of God, die from the words of life.

But, on the other hand, those who understand indeed aright the words of the Law, but speak them not humbly, are to be admonished, that, in divine discourses, before they put them forth to others, they should examine themselves; lest, in following up the deeds of others, they leave themselves behind; and lest, while thinking rightly of all the rest of Holy Scripture, this only thing they attend not to, what is said in it against the proud. For he is indeed a poor and unskilful physician, who would fain heal another's disease while ignorant of that from which he himself is suffering. Those, then, who speak not the words of God humbly should certainly be admonished, that, when they apply medicines to the sick, they see to the poison of their own infection, lest in healing others they die themselves. They ought to be admonished to take heed, lest their manner of saying things be at variance with the excellence of what is said, and lest they preach one thing in their speaking and another in their outward bearing. Let them hear, therefore, what is written, *If any man speak let him speak as the oracles of God* (1 Pet. iv. 11). If then the words they utter are not of the things that are their own, why are they puffed up on account of them as though they were their own? Let them hear what is written, *As of God, in the sight of God, speak we in Christ* (2 Cor. ii. 17). For he speaks of God in the sight of God, who both understands that he has received the word of preaching from God, and also seeks through it to please God, not men. Let them hear what is written, *Every one that is proud in heart is an abomination to the Lord* (Prov. xvi. 5). For, surely, when in the Word of God he seeks his own glory, he invades the right of the giver; and he fears not at all to postpone to his own praise Him from whom he has received the very thing that is praised. Let them hear what is said to the preacher through Solomon, *Drink water out of thine own cistern, and running waters of thine own well. Let thy fountains be dispersed abroad, and divide thy waters in the streets. Have them to thyself alone, and let not strangers be partakers with thee* (Prov. v. 15—17). For indeed the preacher drinks out of his own cistern, when, returning to his own heart, he first listens himself to what he has to say. He drinks the running waters of his own well, if he is watered by his own word. And in the same place it is well added, *Let thy fountains be dispersed abroad, and divide thy waters in the streets.* For indeed it is right that he should himself drink first, and then flow upon others in preaching. For to disperse fountains abroad is to pour outwardly on others the power of preaching. Moreover, to divide waters in the streets is to dispense divine utterances among a great multitude of hearers according to the quality of each. And, because for the most part the desire of vain glory creeps in when the Word of God has free course unto the knowledge of many, after it has been said, *Divide thy waters in the streets*, it is rightly added, *Have them to thyself alone, and let not strangers be partakers with thee.* He here calls malignant spirits strangers, concerning whom it is said through the prophet in the words of one that is tempted, *Strangers are risen up against me, and strong ones have sought after my soul* (Ps. liii. 5[1]). He says therefore, *Both divide thy waters in the streets, and yet have them to thyself alone;* as if he had said more plainly, It is necessary for thee so to serve outwardly in preaching as not to join thyself through elation to unclean spirits, lest in the ministry of the divine word thou admit thine enemies to be partakers with thee. Thus we divide our waters in the streets, and yet alone possess them, when we both pour out preaching outwardly far and wide, and yet in no wise court human praises through it.

CHAPTER XXV.

How those are to be admonished who decline the office of preaching out of too great humility, and those who seize on it with precipitate haste.

(*Admonition* 26.) Differently to be admonished are those who, though able to

[1] In *English Bible*, liv. 3.

preach worthily, are afraid by reason of excessive humility, and those whom imperfection or age forbids to preach, and yet precipitancy impells. For those who, though able to preach with profit, still shrink back through excessive humility are to be admonished to gather from consideration of a lesser matter how faulty they are in a greater one. For, if they were to hide from their indigent neighbours money which they possessed themselves, they would undoubtedly shew themselves to be promoters of their calamity. Let them perceive, then, in what guilt those are implicated who, in with-holding the word of preaching from their sinning brethren, hide away the remedies of life from dying souls. Whence also a certain wise man says well, *Wisdom that is hid, and treasure that is unseen, what profit is in them both* (Ecclus. xx. 32)? Were a famine wasting the people, and they themselves kept hidden corn, undoubtedly they would be the authors of death. Let them consider therefore with what punishment they must be visited who, when souls are perishing from famine of the word, supply not the bread of grace which they have themselves received. Whence also it is well said through Solomon, *He that hideth corn shall be cursed among the people* (Prov. xi. 26). For to hide corn is to retain with one's self the words of sacred preaching. And every one that does so is cursed among the people, because through his fault of silence only he is condemned in the punishment of the many whom he might have corrected. If persons by no means ignorant of the medicinal art were to see a sore that required lancing, and yet refused to lance it, certainly by their mere inactivity they would be guilty of a brother's death. Let them see, then, in how great guilt they are involved who, knowing the sores of souls, neglect to cure them by the lancing of words. Whence also it is well said through the prophet, *Cursed is he who keepeth back his sword from blood* (Jer. xlviii. 10). For to keep back the sword from blood is to hold back the word of preaching from the slaying of the carnal life. Of which sword it is said again, *And my sword shall devour flesh* (Deut. xxxii. 42).

Let these, therefore, when they keep to themselves the word of preaching, hear with terror the divine sentences against them, to the end that fear may expel fear from their hearts. Let them hear how he that would not lay out his talent lost it, with a sentence of condemnation added (Matth. xxv. 24, &c.). Let them hear how Paul believed himself to be pure from the blood of his neighbours in this, that he spared not their vices which required to be smitten, saying, *I take you to record this day, that I am pure from the blood of all men: for I have not shunned to declare unto you all the counsel of God* (Acts xx. 26, 27). Let them hear how John is admonished by the angelic voice, when it is said, *Let him that heareth say, Come* (Rev. xxii. 17); in order doubtless that he into whose heart the internal voice has found its way may by crying aloud draw others whither he himself is carried; lest, even though called, he should find the doors shut, if he approaches Him that calls him empty. Let them hear how Esaias, because he had held his peace in the ministry of the word when illuminated by supernal light, blamed himself with a loud cry of penitence, saying *Woe unto me that I have held my peace* (Isai. vi. 5). Let them hear how through Solomon the knowledge of preaching is promised to be multiplied to him who is not held back by the vice of torpor in that whereto he has already attained. For he says, *The soul which blesseth shall be made fat; and he that inebriates shall be inebriated also himself* (Prov. xi. 25). For he that blesses outwardly by preaching receives the fatness of inward enlargement; and, while he ceases not to inebriate the minds of his hearers with the wine of eloquence, he becomes increasingly inebriated with the draught of a multiplied gift. Let them hear how David offered this in the way of gift to God, that he did not hide the grace of preaching which he had received, saying, *Lo I will not refrain my lips, O Lord, thou knowest: I have not hid thy righteousness within my heart: I have declared thy truth and thy salvation* (Ps. xxxix. 10, 11[a]). Let them hear what is said by the bridegroom in his colloquy with the bride; *Thou that dwellest in the gardens, thy friends hearken: make me to hear thy voice* (Cant. viii. 13). For the Church dwelleth in the gardens, in that she keeps in a state of inward greenness the cultivated nurseries of virtues. And that her friends hearken to her voice is, that all the elect desire the word of her preaching; which voice also the bridegroom desires to hear, because he pants for her preaching through the souls of his elect. Let them hear how Moses, when he saw that God was angry with His people, and commanded swords to be taken for executing vengeance, declared those to be on God's side who should smite the crimes of the offenders without delay, saying, *If any man is the Lord's, let him join himself to me: put every man his sword upon his thigh; go in and out from gate to gate through the midst of the camp, and slay every man his*

[a] In *English Bible* Ps. xl.

brother and friend and neighbour (Exod. xxxii. 27). For to put sword upon thigh is to set earnestness in preaching before the pleasures of the flesh; so that, when any one is earnest to speak holy words, he must needs have a care to subdue illicit suggestions. But to go from gate to gate is to run to and fro with rebuke from vice to vice, even to every one by which death enters in unto the soul. And to pass through the midst of the camp is to live with such impartiality within the Church that one who reproves the sins of offenders turns aside to shew favour to none. Whence also it is rightly added, *slay every man his brother and friend and neighbour.* He in truth slays brother and friend and neighbour who, when he finds what is worthy of punishment, spares not even those whom he loves on the score of relationship from the sword of his rebuke. If, then, he is said to be God's who is stirred up by the zeal of divine love to smite vices, he surely denies himself to be God's who refuses to rebuke the life of the carnal to the utmost of his power.

But, on the other hand, those whom imperfection or age debars from the office of preaching, and yet precipitancy impells to it, are to be admonished lest, while rashly arrogating to themselves the burden of so great an office, they cut off from themselves the way of subsequent improvement; and, while seizing out of season what they are not equal to, they lose even what they might at some time in due season have fulfilled; and be shewn to have justly forfeited their knowledge because of their attempt to display it improperly. They are to be admonished to consider that young birds, if they try to fly before their wings are fully formed, are plunged low down from the place whence they fain would have risen on high. They are to be admonished to consider that, if on new buildings not yet compacted a weight of timbers be laid, there is built not a habitation, but a ruin. They are to be admonished to consider that, if women bring forth their conceived offspring before it is fully formed, they by no means fill houses, but tombs. For hence it is that the Truth Himself, Who could all at once have strengthed whom He would, in order to give an example to His followers that they should not presume to preach while imperfect, after He had fully instructed His disciples concerning the power of preaching, forthwith added, *But tarry ye in the city until ye be endued with power from on high* (Luke xxiv. 49). For indeed we tarry together in the city, if we restrain ourselves within the enclosures of our souls from wandering abroad in speech; so that, when we are perfectly endued with divine power, we may then go out as it were from ourselves abroad, instructing others also. Hence through a certain wise man it is said, *Young man, speak scarcely in thy cause; and if thou hast been twice asked, let thy answer have a beginning* (Ecclus. xxxii. 10). Hence it is that the same our Redeemer, though in heaven the Creator, and even a teacher of angels in the manifestation of His power, would not become a master of men upon earth before His thirtieth year, in order, to wit, that He might infuse into the precipitate the force of a most wholesome fear, in that even He Himself, Who could not slip, did not preach the grace of a perfect life until He was of perfect age. For it is written, *When he was twelve years old, the child Jesus tarried behind in Jerusalem* (Luke ii. 42, 43). And a little afterwards it is further said of Him, when He was sought by His parents, *They found him in the temple, sitting in the midst of the doctors, hearing them, and asking them questions* (Ibid. v. 46). It is therefore to be weighed with vigilant consideration that, when Jesus at twelve years of age is spoken of as sitting in the midst of the doctors, He is found, not teaching, but asking questions. By which example it is plainly shewn that none who is weak should venture to teach, if that child was willing to be taught by asking questions, who by the power of His divinity supplied the word of knowledge to His teachers themselves. But, when it is said by Paul to his disciple, *These things command and teach: let no man despise thy adolescence* (1 Tim. iv. 11, 12), we must understand that in the language of Holy Writ youth is sometimes called adolescence[3]. Which thing is the sooner evident, if we adduce the words of Solomon, who says, *Rejoice O young man in thy adolescence* (Eccles. xi. 9). For unless he meant the same by both words, he would not call him a young man whom he was admonishing in his adolescence.

CHAPTER XXVI.

How those are to be admonished with whom everything succeeds according to their wish, and those with whom nothing does.

(*Admonition* 27.) Differently to be admonished are those who prosper in what they desire in temporal matters, and those who covet indeed the things that are of this world,

3 The word *adolescentia*, used in the Vulgate, implies properly the age of immaturity, while growth is still going on. "ADOLESCENTIA, prima hominis ætas post pueritiam, et ante juventutem.' *Facciolati.* St. Gregory's intention is to preclude the idea of Timothy having been called to "command and teach" at so immature an age as the word might seem to imply.

but yet are wearied with the labour of adversity. For those who prosper in what they desire in temporal matters are to be admonished, when all things answer to their wishes, lest, through fixing their heart on what is given, they neglect to seek the giver; lest they love their pilgrimage instead of their country; lest they turn the supplies for their journey into hindrances to their arrival at its end; lest, delighted with the light of the moon by night, they shrink from beholding the clearness of the sun. They are, therefore, to be admonished to regard whatever things they attain in this world as consolations in calamity, but not as the rewards of retribution; but, on the other hand, to lift their mind against the favours of the world, lest they succumb in the midst of them with entire delight of the heart. For whosoever in the judgment of his heart keeps not down the prosperity he enjoys by love of a better life, turns the favours of this transitory life into an occasion of everlasting death. For hence it is that under the figure of the Idumæans, who allowed themselves to be vanquished by their own prosperity, those who rejoice in the successes of this world are rebuked, when it is said, *They have given my land to themselves for an inheritance with joy, and with their whole heart and mind* (Ezek. xxxvi. 5). In which words it is to be observed, that they are smitten with severe rebuke, not merely because they rejoice, but because they rejoice with their whole heart and mind. Hence Solomon says, *The turning away of the simple shall slay them, and the prosperity of fools shall destroy them* (Prov. i. 32). Hence Paul admonishes, saying, *They that buy, as though they possessed not; and they that use this world, as though they used it not* (1 Cor. vii. 30). So may the things that are supplied to us be of service to us outwardly to such extent only as not to turn our minds away from desire of supernal delight; and thus the things that afford us succour in our state of exile may not abate the mourning of our soul's pilgrimage; and we, who see ourselves to be wretched in our severance from the things that are eternal, may not rejoice as though we were happy in the things that are transitory. For hence it is that the Church says by the voice of the elect, *His left hand is under my head, and his right hand shall embrace me* (Cant. ii. 6). The left hand of God, to wit prosperity in the present life, she has put under her head, in that she presses it down in the intentness of her highest love. But the right hand of God embraces her, because in her entire devotion she is encompassed with His eternal blessedness. Hence again, it is said through Solomon, *Length of days is in her right hand, but in her left hand riches and glory* (Prov. iii. 16). In speaking, then, of riches and glory being placed in her left hand, he shewed after what manner they are to be esteemed. Hence the Psalmist says, *Save me with thy right hand* (Ps. cvii. 7[4]). For he says not, *with thy hand*, but *with thy right hand;*' in order, that is, to indicate, in saying *right hand*, that it was eternal salvation that he sought. Hence again it is written, *Thy right hand, O Lord, hath dashed in pieces the enemies* (Exod. xv. 6). For the enemies of God, though they prosper in His left hand, are dashed to pieces with His right; since for the most part the present life elevates the bad, but the coming of eternal blessedness condemns them.

Those who prosper in this world are to be admonished to consider wisely how that prosperity in the present life is sometimes given to provoke people to a better life, but sometimes to condemn them more fully for ever. For hence it is that to the people of Israel the land of Canaan is promised, that they may be provoked at some time or other to hope for eternal things. For that rude nation would not have believed the promises of God afar off, had they not received also something nigh at hand from Him that promised. In order, therefore, that they may be the more surely strengthened unto faith in eternal things, they are drawn on, not only by hope to realities, but also by realities to hope. Which thing the Psalmist clearly testifies, saying, *He gave them the lands of the heathen, and they took the labours of the peoples in possession, that they might keep his statutes and seek after his law* (Ps. civ. 44[5]). But, when the human mind follows not God in His bountiful gifts with an answer of good deeds, it is the more justly condemned from being accounted to have been kindly nurtured. For hence it is said again by the Psalmist, *Thou castedst them down when they were lifted up* (Ps. lxxii. 18[6]). For in truth when the reprobate render not righteous deeds in return for divine gifts, when they here abandon themselves entirely and sink themselves in their abundant prosperity, then in that whereby they profit outwardly they fall from what is inmost. Hence it is that to the rich man tormented in hell it is said, *Thou in thy lifetime receivedst thy good things* (Luke xvi. 25). For on this account, though an evil man, he here received good things, that there he might receive evil things

---

[4] In *English Bible*, cviii. 6. [5] Ibid. cv. 44. [6] Ibid. lxxiii. 18.

more fully, because here even by good things he had not been converted.

But, on the other hand, those who covet indeed the things that are of the world, but yet are wearied by the labour of adversity, are to be admonished to consider anxiously with how great favour the Creator and Disposer of all things watches over those whom He gives not up to their own desires. For a sick man whom the physician despairs of he allows to take whatever he longs for: but one of whom it is thought that he can be cured is prohibited from many things that he desires; and we withdraw money from boys, for whom at the same time, as our heirs, we reserve our whole patrimony. Let, then, those whom temporal adversity humiliates take joy from hope of an eternal inheritance, since Divine Providence would not curb them in order to educate them under the rule of discipline, unless it designed them to be saved for ever. Those, therefore, who in respect of the temporal things which they covet, are wearied with the labour of adversity are to be admonished to consider carefully how for the most part even the righteous, when temporal power exalts them, are caught by sin as in a snare. For, as in the former part of this volume we have already said, David, beloved of God, was more upright when in servitude than when he came to the kingdom (1 Sam. xxiv. 18). For, when he was a servant, in his love of righteousness he feared to smite his adversary when taken; but, when he was a king, through the persuasion of lasciviousness, he put to death by a deceitful plan even a devoted soldier (2 Sam. xi. 17). Who then can without harm seek wealth, or power, or glory, if they proved harmful even to him who had them unsought? Who in the midst of these things shall be saved without the labour of a great contest, if he who had been prepared for them by the choice of God was disturbed among them by the intervention of sin? They are to be admonished to consider that Solomon, who after so great wisdom is described as having fallen even into idolatry, is not said to have had any adversity in this world before his fall; but the wisdom that had been granted him entirely left his heart, because not even the least discipline of tribulation had guarded it.

CHAPTER XXVII.

How the married and the single are to be admonished.

(*Admonition* 28.) Differently to be admonished are those who are bound in wedlock and those who are free from the ties of wedlock. For those who are bound in wedlock are to be admonished that, while they take thought for each other's good, they study, both of them, so to please their consorts as not to displease their Maker; that they so conduct the things that are of this world as still not to omit desiring the things that are of God; that they so rejoice in present good as still, with earnest solicitude, to fear eternal evil; that they so sorrow for temporal evils as still to fix their hope with entire comfort on everlasting good; to the end that, while they know what they are engaged in to be transitory, but what they desire to be permanent, neither the evils of the world may break their heart while it is strengthened by the hope of heavenly good, nor the good things of the present life deceive them, while they are saddened by the apprehended evils of the judgment to come. Wherefore the mind of married Christians is both weak and stedfast, in that it cannot fully despise all temporal things, and yet can join itself in desire to eternal things. Although it lies low meanwhile in the delights of the flesh, let it grow strong in the refreshment of supernal hope: and, if it has the things that are of the world for the service of its journey, let it hope for the things that are of God for the fruit of its journey's end: nor let it devote itself entirely to what it is engaged in now, lest it fall utterly from what it ought stedfastly to hope for. Which thing Paul well expresses briefly, saying, *They that have wives as though they had none, and they that weep as though they wept not, and they that rejoice as though they rejoiced not* (1 Cor. vii. 29, 30). For he has a wife as though he had none who so enjoys carnal consolation through her as still never to be turned by love of her to evil deeds from the rectitude of a better aim. He has a wife as though he had none who, seeing all things to be transitory, endures of necessity the care of the flesh, but looks forward with longing to the eternal joys of the spirit. Moreover, to weep as though we wept not is so to lament outward adversities as still to know how to rejoice in the consolation of eternal hope. And again, to rejoice as though we rejoiced not is so to take heart from things below as still never to cease from fear concerning the things above. In the same place also a little afterwards he aptly adds, *For the fashion of this world passeth away* (v. 31); as if he had said plainly, Love not the world abidingly, since the world which ye love cannot itself abide. In vain ye fix your affections on it as though it were continuing, while that which ye love itself is fleeting. Husbands and wives are to be admonished, that those things wherein they sometimes displease one another they bear with mutual patience, and by mutual exhortations remedy. For it is written, *Bear ye one another's burdens, and so ye shall fulfil the law of Christ* (Galat. vi. 2). For the law of Christ is Charity; since it has from Him bountifully bestowed on us its good things, and has patiently borne our evil things. We, therefore, then fulfil by imitation the law of Christ, when we both kindly bestow our good things, and piously endure the evil things of our friends. They are also to be admonished to give heed, each of them, not so much to what they have to bear from the other as to what the other has to bear from them. For, if one considers what is borne from one's self, one bears more lightly what one endures from another.

Husbands and wives are to be admonished to remember that they are joined together for the sake of producing offspring; and, when, giving themselves to immoderate intercourse, they transfer the occasion of procreation to the service of pleasure, to consider that, though they go not outside wedlock yet in wedlock itself they exceed the just dues of wedlock. Whence it is needful that by frequent supplications they do away their having fouled with the admixture of pleasure the fair form of conjugal union. For hence it is that the Apostle, skilled in heavenly medicine, did not so much lay down a course of life for the whole as point out remedies to the weak when he said, *It is good for a man not to touch a woman: but on account of fornication let every man have his own wife, and let every woman have her own husband* (1 Cor. vii. 1, 2). For in that he premised the fear of fornication, he surely did not give a precept to such as were standing, but pointed out the bed to such as were falling, lest haply they should tumble to the ground. Whence to such as were still weak he added, *Let the husband render unto the wife her due; and likewise also the wife unto the husband* (v. 3). And, while in the most honourable estate of matrimony allowing to them something of pleasure, he added, *But this I say by way of indulgence, not by way of command* (v. 6). Now where indulgence is spoken of, a fault is implied; but one that is the more readily remitted in that it consists, not in doing what is unlawful, but in not keeping what is lawful under control. Which thing Lot expresses well in his own person, when he flies from burning Sodom, and yet, finding Zoar, does not still ascend the mountain heights. For to fly from burning Sodom is to avoid the unlawful fires of the flesh. But the height of the mountains is the purity of the continent. Or, at any rate, they are as it were upon the mountain, who, though cleaving to carnal intercourse, still, beyond the due association for the production of offspring, are not loosely lost in pleasure of the flesh. For to stand on the mountain is to seek nothing in the flesh except the fruit of procreation. To stand on the mountain is not to cleave to the flesh in a fleshly way. But, since there are many who relinquish indeed the sins of the flesh, and yet, when placed in the state of wedlock, do not observe solely the claims of due intercourse, Lot went indeed out of Sodom, but yet did not at once reach the mountain heights; because a damnable life is already relinquished, but still the loftiness of conjugal continence is not thoroughly attained. But there is midway the city of Zoar, to save the weak fugitive; because, to wit, when the married have intercourse with each other even incontinently, they still avoid lapse into sin, and are still saved through mercy. For they find as it were a little city, wherein to be protected from the fire; since this married life is not indeed marvellous for virtue, but yet is secure from punishment. Whence the same Lot says to the angel, *This city is near to flee unto, and it is small, and I shall be saved therein. Is it not a little one, and my soul shall live in it* (Gen. xix. 20)? So then it is said to be near, and yet is spoken of as a refuge of safety, since married life is neither far separated from the world, nor yet alien from the joy of safety. But the married, in this course of conduct, then preserve their lives as it were in a small city, when they intercede for each other by continual supplications. Whence it is also rightly said by the Angel to the same Lot, *See I have accepted thy prayers concerning this thing also, that I will not overthrow the city for the which thou hast spoken* (v. 21). For in truth, when supplication is poured out to God, such married life is by no means condemned. Concerning which supplication Paul also admonishes, saying, *Defraud ye not one the other, except it be with consent for a time, that ye may give yourselves to prayer* (1 Cor. vii. 5).

But, on the other hand, those who are not bound by wedlock are to be admonished that they observe heavenly precepts all the more closely in that no yoke of carnal union bows them down to worldly cares; that, as they are free from the lawful burden of wedlock, the unlawful weight of earthly anxiety by no means press them down; that the last day find them all the more prepared, as it finds them less encumbered; lest from being free and able, and yet neglecting, to do better things, they therefore be found deserving of worse punishment. Let them hear how the

Apostle, when he would train certain persons for the grace of celibacy, did not contemn wedlock, but guarded against the worldly cares that are born of wedlock, saying, *This I say for your profit, not that I may cast a snare upon you, but for that which is comely, and that ye may attend upon the Lord without hindrance* (1 Cor. vii. 3, 5). For from wedlock proceed earthly anxieties; and therefore the teacher of the Gentiles persuaded his hearers to better things, lest they should be bound by earthly anxiety. The man, then, whom, being single, the hindrance of secular cares impedes, though he has not subjected himself to wedlock, has still not escaped the burdens of wedlock. The single are to be admonished not to think that they can have intercourse with disengaged women without incurring the judgment of condemnation. For, when Paul inserted the vice of fornication among so many execrable crimes, he indicated the guilt of it, saying, *Neither fornicators, nor idolaters, nor adulterers, nor effeminate, nor abusers of themselves with mankind, nor thieves, nor covetous, nor drunkards, nor revilers, nor extortioners, shall possess the kingdom of God* (1 Cor. vi. 9, 10). And again, *But fornicators and adulterers God will judge* (Heb. xiii. 4). They are therefore to be admonished that, if they suffer from the storms of temptation with risk to their safety, they should seek the port of wedlock. For it is written, *It is better to marry than to burn* (1 Cor. vii. 9). They come, in fact, to marriage without blame, if only they have not vowed better things. For whosoever has proposed to himself the attainment of a greater good has made unlawful the less good which before was lawful. For it is written, *No man, having put his hand to the plough, and looking back, is fit for the kingdom of God* (Luke ix. 62). He therefore who has been intent on a more resolute purpose is convicted of looking back, if, leaving the larger good, he reverts to the least.

CHAPTER XXVIII.

How those are to be admonished who have had experience of the sins of the flesh, and those who have not.

(*Admonition* 29.) Differently to be admonished are those who are conscious of sins of the flesh, and those who know them not. For those who have had experience of the sins of the flesh are to be admonished that, at any rate after shipwreck, they should fear the sea, and feel horror at their risk of perdition at least when it has become known to them; lest, having been mercifully preserved after evil deeds committed, by wickedly repeating the same they die. Whence to the soul that sins and never ceases from sin it is said, *There is come unto thee a whore's forehead; thou refuseth to be ashamed* (Jer. iii. 3). They are therefore to be admonished to take heed, to the end that, if they have refused to keep whole the good things of nature which they have received, they at least mend them after they have been rent asunder. And they are surely bound to consider, how many in so great a number of the faithful both keep themselves undefiled and also convert others from the error of their way. What, then, will they be able to say, if, while others are standing in integrity, they themselves, even after loss, come not to a better mind? What will they be able to say, if, when many bring others also with themselves to the kingdom, they bring not back even themselves to the Lord who is waiting for them? They are to be admonished to consider past transgressions, and to shun such as are impending. Whence, under the figure of Judæa, the Lord through the prophet recalls past sins to the memory of souls corrupted in this world, to the end that they may be ashamed to be polluted in sins to come, saying, *They committed whoredoms in Egypt; they committed whoredoms in their youth: then were their breasts pressed, and the teats of their virginity were bruised* (Ezek. xxiii. 3). For indeed breasts are pressed in Egypt, when the will of the human soul is prostituted to the base desire of this world. Teats of virginity are bruised in Egypt, when the natural senses, still whole in themselves, are vitiated by the corruption of assailing concupiscence.

Those who have had experience of the sins of the flesh are to be admonished to observe vigilantly with how great benevolence God opens the bosom of His pity to us, if after transgressions we return to Him, when He says through the prophet, *If a man put away his wife, and she go from him and become another man's, shall he return to her again? Shall not that woman be polluted and contaminated? But thou hast played the harlot with many lovers; yet return again to me, saith the Lord* (Jer. iii. 1). So, concerning the wife who has played the harlot and is deserted, the argument of justice is put forward: and yet to us returning after fall not justice, but pity is displayed. Whence we are surely meant to gather how great is our wickedness, if we return not, even after transgression, seeing that, when transgressing, we are spared with so great pity: or what pardon for the wicked there will be from Him who, after our sin, ceases not to call us. And indeed this mercifulness, in calling after transgression, is well expressed through the Prophet, when to man turned away from God it is said, *Thine eyes shall see thy teacher, and thine ears shall hear the word of one behind thy back admonishing thee* (Isai. xxx. 20, 21). For indeed the Lord admonished the human race to their face, when to man, created in Paradise, and standing in free will, He declared what He ought to do or not to do. But man turned his back on the face of God, when in his pride he despised His commands. Yet still God deserted him not in his pride, in that He gave the Law for the purpose of recalling man, and sent exhorting angels, and Himself appeared in the flesh of our mortality. Therefore, standing behind our back, He admonished us, in that, even though despised, He called us to the recovery of grace. What, therefore, could be said generally of all alike must needs be felt specially with regard to each. For every man hears the words of God's admonition set as it were before him, when, before he commits sin, he knows the precepts of His will. For still to stand before His face is not yet to despise Him by sinning. But, when a man forsakes the good of innocence, and of choice desires iniquity, he then turns his back on the face of God. But lo, even behind his back God follows and admonishes him, in that even after sin He persuades him to return to Himself. He recalls him that is turned away, He regards not past transgressions, He opens the bosom of pity to the returning one. We hearken, then, to the voice of one behind our back admonishing us, if at least after sins we return to the Lord inviting us. We ought therefore to feel ashamed for the pity of Him Who calls us, if we will not fear His justice: since there is the more grievous wickedness in despising Him in that, though despised, He disdains not to call us still.

But, on the other hand, those that are unacquainted with the sins of the flesh are to be admonished to fear headlong ruin the more anxiously, as they stand upon a higher eminence. They are to be admonished to be aware that the more prominent be the place they stand on, so much the more frequent are the arrows of the lier-in-wait by which they are assailed. For he is wont to rouse himself the more ardently, the more stoutly he sees himself to be vanquished: and so much the more he scorns and feels it intolerable to be vanquished, as he perceives the unbroken camp of weak flesh to be set in array against him. They are to be admonished to look up incessantly to the rewards, and then undoubtedly they will gladly tread under foot the labours of temptation which they endure. For, if attention be fixed on the attained felicity apart from the passage to it, the toil of the passage becomes light. Let them hear what is said through the Prophet; *Thus saith the Lord unto the eunuchs, Whoso shall have kept my sabbaths, and chosen the things that I would, and kept my covenant, I will give unto them in mine house and within my walls a place and a name better than of sons and of daughters* (Isai. lvi. 4, 5). For they indeed are eunuchs, who, suppressing the motions of the flesh, cut off within themselves affection for wrong-doing. Moreover, in what place they are held with the Father is shewn, forasmuch as in the Father's house, that is in His eternal mansion, they are preferred even before sons. Let them hear what is said through John; *These are they which have not been defiled with women; for they are virgins, and follow the Lamb whithersoever He goeth* (Rev. xiv. 4); and how they sing a song which no one can utter but those hundred and forty four thousand. For indeed to sing a song to the Lamb singularly is to rejoice with Him for ever beyond all the faithful, even for incorruption of the flesh. Yet the rest of the elect can hear this song, although they cannot utter it, because, through charity, they are joyful in the exaltation of those others, though they rise not to their rewards. Let those who are unacquainted with the sins of the flesh hear what the Truth in person says concerning this purity; *Not all receive this word* (Matth. xix. 11). Which thing He denoted as the highest, in that He spoke of it as not belonging to all: and, in foretelling that it would be difficult to receive it, He signifies to his hearers with what caution it should be kept when received.

Those who are unacquainted with the sins of the flesh are therefore to be admonished both to know that virginity surpasses wedlock, and yet not to exalt themselves above the wedded: to the end that, while they put virginity first, and themselves last, they may both keep to that which they esteem as best, and also keep guard over themselves in not vainly exalting themselves.

They are to be admonished to consider that commonly the life of the continent is put to shame by the action of secular persons, when the latter take on themselves works beyond their condition, and the former do not stir up their hearts to the mark of their own order. Whence it is well said through the Prophet, *Be thou ashamed, O Sidon, saith the sea* (Isai. xxiii. 4). For Sidon is as it were brought to shame by the voice of the sea, when the life of him who is fortified, and as it were stedfast, is reproved by comparison with the life of those who are secular and fluctuating in this world. For often there are some who, returning to the Lord after sins of the flesh, shew themselves the more ardent in good works as they see themselves the more liable to condemnation for bad ones: and often certain of those who persevere in purity of the flesh, seeing that they have less in the past to deplore, think that the innocency of their life is fully sufficient for them, and inflame themselves with no incitements of ardour to fervour of spirit. And for the most part a life burning with love after sin becomes more pleasing to God than innocence growing torpid in security. Whence also it is said by the voice of the Judge, *Her sins which are many are forgiven, for she loved much* (Luke vii. 47); and, *Joy shall be in heaven over one sinner that repenteth more than over ninety and nine just persons which need no repentance* (xv. 7). Which thing we the sooner gather from experience itself, if we weigh the judgments of our own mind. For we love the land which produces abundant fruit after thorns have been ploughed out of it more than that which has had no thorns, but which, when cultivated, yields a barren harvest. Those who know not the sins of the flesh are to be admonished not to prefer themselves to others for the loftiness of their superior order, while they know not how great things are done by their inferiors better than by themselves. For in the inquisition of the righteous judge the quality of actions changes the merits of orders. For who, considering the very outward appearance of things, can be ignorant that in the nature of gems the carbuncle is preferred to the jacinth? But still a jacinth of cerulean colour is preferred to a pale carbuncle; because to the former its show of beauty supplies what the order of nature denied it, and the latter, which natural order had preferred, is debased by the quality of its colour. Thus, then, in the human race both some in the better order are the worse, and some in the worse order are the better; since these by good living transcend the lot of their lower state, and those lessen the merit of their higher place by not coming up to it in their behaviour.

CHAPTER XXIX.

How they are to be admonished who lament sins of deed, and those who lament only sins of thought.

(*Admonition* 30.) Differently to be admonished are those who deplore sins of deed, and those who deplore sins of thought. For those who deplore sins of deed are to be admonished that perfected lamentations should wash out consummated evils, lest they be bound by a greater debt of perpetrated deed than they pay in tears of satisfaction for it. For it is written, *He hath given us drink in tears by measure* (Ps. lxxix. 6): which means that each person's soul should in its penitence drink the tears of compunction to such extent as it remembers itself to have been dried up from God through sins. They are to be admonished to bring back their past offences incessantly before their eyes, and so to live that these may not have to be viewed by the strict judge.

Hence David, when he prayed, saying, *Turn away thine eyes from my sins* (Ps. l. 11[7]), had said also a little before, *My fault is ever before me* (v. 5); as if to say, I beseech thee not to regard my sin, since I myself cease not to regard it. Whence also the Lord says through the prophet, *And I will not be mindful of thy sins, but be thou mindful of them* (Isai. xliii. 25, 26). They are to be admonished to consider singly all their past offences, and, in bewailing the defilements of their former wandering one by one, to cleanse at the same time even their whole selves with tears. Whence it is well said through Jeremiah, when the several transgressions of Judæa were being considered, *Mine eye hath shed divisions of waters* (Lam. iii. 48). For indeed we shed divided waters from our eyes, when to our several sins we give separate tears. For the mind does not sorrow at one and the same time alike for all things; but, while it is more sharply touched by memory now of this fault and now of that, being moved concerning all in each, it is purged at once from all.

They are to be admonished to build upon the mercy which they crave, lest they perish through the force of immoderate affliction. For the Lord would not set sins to be deplored before the eyes of offenders, were it His will to smite them with strict severity Himself. For it is evident that it has been His will to hide from His own judgment those whom in anticipation He has made judges of themselves. For hence it is written, *Let us come beforehand before the face of the Lord in confession* (Ps. xciv. 2[8]). Hence through Paul it is said, *If we would judge ourselves, we should not be judged* (1 Cor. xi. 31). And again, they are to be admonished so to be confident in hope as not to grow torpid in careless security. For commonly the crafty foe, when he sees the soul which he trips up by sin to be afflicted for its fall, seduces it by the blandishments of baneful security. Which thing is figuratively expressed in the history of Dinah. For it is written, *Dinah went*

[7] In *English Bible*, li. 3.

[8] Ibid. xcv. 2.

out to see the women of that land; and when Sichem, the son of Hemor the Hivite, prince of the country, saw her, he loved her, and seized her, and lay with her, and defiled her by force; and his soul clave unto her, and he soothed her with kind blandishments when she was sad (Gen. xxxiv. 1-3). For indeed Dinah goes out to see the women of a foreign land, when any soul, neglecting its own concerns, and giving heed to the actions of others, wanders forth out of its own proper condition and order. And Sichem, prince of the country, overpowers it; inasmuch as the devil corrupts it, when found occupied in external cares. *And his soul clave unto her*, because he regards it as united to himself through iniquity. And because, when the soul comes to a sense of its sin, it stands condemned, and would fain deplore its transgression, but the corrupter recalls before its eyes empty hopes and grounds of security to the end that he may withdraw from it the benefit of sorrow, therefore it is rightly added in the text, *And soothed her with blandishments when she was sad.* For he tells now of the heavier offences of others, now of what has been perpetrated being nothing, now of God being merciful; or again he promises time hereafter for repentance; so that the soul, seduced by these deceptions, may be suspended from its purpose of penitence, to the end that it may receive no good hereafter, being saddened by no evil now, and that it may then be more fully overwhelmed with punishment, in that now it even rejoices in its transgressions.

But, on the other hand, those who bewail sins of thought are to be admonished to consider anxiously within the recesses of their soul whether they have sinned in delight only, or also in consent. For commonly the heart is tempted, and in the sinfulness of the flesh experiences delight, and yet in its judgment resists this same sinfulness; so that in the secrets of thought it is both saddened by what pleases it and pleased by what saddens it. But sometimes the soul is so whelmed in a gulph of temptation as not to resist at all, but follows of set purpose that whereby it is assailed through delight; and, if outward opportunity be at hand, it soon consummates in effect its inward wishes. And certainly, if this is regarded according to the just animadversion of a strict judge, the sin is one, not of thought, but of deed; since, though the tardiness of circumstances has deferred the sin outwardly, the will has accomplished it inwardly by the act of consent.

Moreover, we have learnt in the case of our first parent that we perpetrate the iniquity of every sin in three ways; that is to say, in suggestion, delight, and consent. Thus the first is perpetrated through the enemy, the second through the flesh, the third through the spirit. For the lier-in-wait suggests wrong things; the flesh submits itself to delight; and at last the spirit, vanquished by delight, consents. Whence also that serpent suggested wrong things; then Eve, as though she had been the flesh, submitted herself to delight; but Adam, as the spirit, overcome by the suggestion and the delight, assented. Thus by suggestion we have knowledge of sin, by delight we are vanquished, by consent we are also bound. Those, therefore, who bewail iniquities of thought are to be admonished to consider anxiously in what measure they have fallen into sin, to the end that they may be lifted up by a measure of lamentation corresponding to the degree of the downfall of which they are inwardly conscious; lest, if meditated evils torment them too little, they lead them on even to the perpetration of deeds. But in all this they should be alarmed in such wise that they still be by no means broken down. For often merciful God absolves sins of the heart the more speedily in that He allows them not to issue in deeds; and meditated iniquity is the more speedily loosed from not being too tightly bound by effected deed. Whence it is rightly said by the Psalmist, *I said I will declare against myself my iniquities to the Lord, and thou forgavest the impiety of my heart* (Ps. xxxi. 5). For in that he added impiety of heart, he indicated that it was iniquities of thought that he would declare: and in saying, *I said I will declare*, and straightway subjoining, *And thou forgavest*, he shewed how easy in such a case pardon was. For, while but promising that he would ask, he obtained what he promised to ask for; so that, since his sin had not advanced to deed, neither should his penitence go so far as to be torment; and that meditated affliction should cleanse the soul which in truth no more than meditated iniquity had defiled.

CHAPTER XXX.

How those are to be admonished who abstain not from the sins which they bewail, and those who, abstaining from them, bewail them not.

(*Admonition* 31.) Differently to be admonished are those who lament their transgressions, and yet forsake them not, and those who forsake them, and yet lament them not. For those who lament their transgressions and yet forsake them not are to be admonished to learn to consider anxiously that they cleanse themselves in vain by their weeping, if they wickedly defile themselves in their living, seeing that the end for which they wash themselves in tears is that, when clean, they may return to filth. For hence it is written, *The dog is returned to his own vomit again, and the sow that was washed to her wallowing in the mire* (2 Pet. ii. 22). For the dog, when he vomits, certainly casts forth the food which weighed upon his stomach; but, when he returns to his vomit, he is again loaded with what he had been relieved from. And they who mourn their transgressions certainly cast forth by confession the wickedness with which they have been evilly satiated, and which oppressed the inmost parts of their soul; and yet, in recurring to it after confession, they take it in again. But the sow, by wallowing in the mire when washed, is made more filthy. And one who mourns past transgressions, yet forsakes them not, subjects himself to the penalty of more grievous sin, since he both despises the very pardon which he might have won by his weeping, and as it were rolls himself in miry water; because in withholding purity of life from his weeping he makes even his very tears filthy before the eyes of God. Hence again it is written, *Repeat not a word in thy prayer* (Ecclus. vii. 14). For to repeat a word in prayer is, after bewailing, to commit what again requires bewailing. Hence it is said through Isaiah, *Wash you, be ye clean* (Isai. i. 16). For he neglects being clean after washing, whosoever after tears keeps not innocency of life. And they therefore are washed, but are in no wise clean, who cease not to bewail the things they have committed, but commit again things to be bewailed. Hence through a certain wise man it is said, *He that is baptized from the touch of a dead body and toucheth it again, what availeth his washing* (Ecclus. xxxiv. 30[9])? For indeed he is baptized from the touch of a dead body who is cleansed from sin by weeping: but he touches a dead body after his baptism, who after tears repeats his sin.

Those who bewail transgressions, yet forsake them not, are to be admonished to acknowledge themselves to be before the eyes of the strict judge like those who, when they come before the face of certain men, fawn upon them with great submission, but, when they depart, atrociously bring upon them all the enmity and hurt they can. For what is weeping for sin but exhibiting the humility of one's devotion to God? And what is doing wickedly after weeping but putting in practice arrogant enmity against Him to whom entreaty has been made? This James attests, who says, *Whosoever will be a friend of this world becomes the enemy of God* (James iv. 4). Those who lament their transgressions, yet forsake them not, are to be admonished to consider anxiously that, for the most part, bad men are unprofitably drawn by compunction to righteousness, even as, for the most part, good men are without harm tempted to sin. Here indeed is found a wonderful measure of inward disposition in accordance with the requirements of desert, in that the bad, while doing something good, but still without perfecting it, are proudly confident in the midst of the very evil which even to the full they perpetrate; while the good, when tempted of evil to which they in no wise consent, plant the steps of their heart towards righteousness through humility all the more surely from their tottering through infirmity. Thus Balaam, looking on the tents of the righteous, said, *May my soul die the death of the righteous, and may my last end be like theirs* (Num. xxiii. 10). But, when the time of compunction had passed, he gave counsel against the life of those whom he had requested for himself to be like even in dying: and, when he found an occasion for the gratification of his avarice, he straightway forgot all that he had wished for himself of innocence. Hence it is that Paul, the teacher and preacher of the Gentiles, says, *I see another law in my members, warring against the law of my mind, and bringing me into captivity to the law of sin, which is in my members* (Rom. vii. 23). He is of a truth tempted for this very purpose, that he may be the more stedfastly confirmed in good from the knowledge of his own infirmity. Why is it, then, that the one is touched with compunction, and yet draws not near unto righteousness, while the other is tempted, and yet sin defiles him not, but for this evident reason, that neither do good things not perfected help the bad, nor bad things not consummated condemn the good?

But, on the other hand, those who forsake their transgressions, and yet mourn them not, are to be admonished not to suppose the sins to be already remitted which, though they multiply them not by action, they still cleanse away by no bewailings. For neither has a writer, when he has ceased from writing, obliterated what he had written by reason of his having added no more: neither has one who offers insults made satisfaction by merely holding his peace, it being certainly necessary for him to impugn his former words of pride by words of subsequent humility: nor is a debtor absolved by not increasing his debt, unless he also pays what he has incurred. Thus also, when we offend against God, we by no means make satisfaction by ceasing

[9] In *Engl. Bib.* xxxiv. 25.

from iniquity, unless we also follow up the pleasures which we have loved by lamentations set against them. For, if no sin of deed had polluted us in this life, our very innocence would by no means suffice for our security as long as we live here, since many unlawful things would still assail our heart. With what conscience, then, can he feel safe, who, having perpetrated iniquities, is himself witness to himself that he is not innocent?

For it is not as if God were fed by our torments: but He heals the diseases of our transgressions by medicines opposed to them; that we, who have departed from Him delighted by pleasures, may return to Him embittered by tears; and that, having fallen by running loose in unlawful things, we may rise by restraining ourselves even in lawful ones; and that the heart which mad joy had flooded may be burnt clean by wholesome sadness: and that what the elation of pride had wounded may be cured by the dejection of a humble life. For hence it is written, *I said unto the wicked, Deal not wickedly; and to the transgressors, lift not up the horn* (Ps. lxxiv. 5 [1]). For transgressors lift up the horn, if they in no wise humble themselves to penitence after knowledge of their iniquity. Hence again it is said, *A bruised and humbled heart God doth not despise* (Ps. l. 19 [2]). For whosoever mourns his sins yet forsakes them not bruises indeed his heart, but scorns to humble it. But he who forsakes his sins yet mourns them not does indeed already humble his heart, but refuses to bruise it. Hence Paul says, *And such indeed were ye; but ye are washed, but ye are sanctified* (1 Cor. vi. 11); because, in truth, amended life sanctifies those whom the ablution of the affliction of tears cleanses through penitence. Hence Peter, when he saw some affrighted by consideration of their evil deeds, admonished them, saying, *Repent, and be baptized every one of you* (Acts ii. 38). For, being about to speak of baptism, he spoke first of the lamentations of penitence; that they should first bathe themselves in the water of their own affliction, and afterwards wash themselves in the sacrament of baptism. With what conscience, then, can those who neglect to weep for their past misdeeds live secure of pardon, when the chief pastor of the Church himself believed that penitence must be added even to this Sacrament which chiefly extinguishes sins?

[1] In *English Bible*, lxxv. 4.

[2] Ibid. li. 17.

CHAPTER XXXI.

How those are to be admonished who praise the unlawful things of which they are conscious, and those who, while condemning them, in no wise guard against them.

(*Admonition* 32.) Differently to be admonished are they who even praise the unlawful things which they do, and those who censure what is wrong, and yet avoid it not. For they who even praise the unlawful things which they do are to be admonished to consider how for the most part they offend more by the mouth than by deeds. For by deeds they perpetrate wrong things in their own persons only; but with the mouth they bring out wickedness in the persons of as many as there are souls of hearers, to whom they teach wicked things by praising them. They are therefore to be admonished that, if they evade the eradication of evil, they at least be afraid to sow it. They are to be admonished to let their own individual perdition suffice them. And again they are to be admonished that, if they fear not to be bad, they at least blush to be seen to be what they are. For usually a sin, when it is concealed, is shunned; because, when a soul blushes to be seen to be what nevertheless it does not fear to be, it comes in time to blush to be what it shuns being seen to be. But, when any bad man shamelessly courts notice, then the more freely he perpetrates every wickedness, the more does he come even to think it lawful; and in what he imagines to be lawful he is without doubt sunk ever more and more. Hence it is written, *They have declared their sin as Sodom, neither have they hidden it* (Isai. iii. 9). For, had Sodom hidden her sin, she would still have sinned, but in fear. But she had utterly lost the curb of fear, in that she did not even seek darkness for her sin. Whence also again it is written, *The cry of Sodom and Gomorrah is multiplied* (Gen. xviii. 20). For sin with a voice is guilt in act; but sin with even a cry is guilt at liberty.

But, on the other hand, those who censure wrong things and yet avoid them not are to be admonished to weigh circumspectly what they can say in their own excuse before the strict judgment of God, seeing they are not excused from the guilt of their crimes, even themselves being judges. What, then, are these men but their own summoners? They give their voices against misdeeds, and deliver themselves up as guilty in their doings. They are to be admonished to perceive how it even now comes of the hidden retribution of judgment that their mind is enlightened to see the evil which it perpetrates, but strives not to overcome it; so that the better it sees the worse it may perish; because it both perceives the light of understanding, and also relinquishes not the darkness of wrong-doing. For, when they neglect the knowledge that has been given to help them, they turn it into a testimony against themselves; and from the light of understanding, which they had in truth received that they might be able to do away their sins, they augment their punishments. And, indeed, this their wickedness, doing the evil which it condemns, has already a taste here of the judgment to come; so that, while kept liable to eternal punishment, it shall not meanwhile be absolved here in its own test of itself; and that it may experience there the more grievous torments, in that here it forsakes not the evil which even itself condemns. For hence the Truth says, *That servant which knew his lord's will, and prepared not himself, neither did according to his will, shall be beaten with many stripes* (Luke xii. 47). Hence the Psalmist says, *Let them go down quick into hell* (Ps. liv. 16 [3]). For the quick know and feel what is being done about them; but the dead can feel nothing. For they would go down dead into hell if they committed what is evil without knowledge. But when they know what is evil, and yet do it, they go down quick, miserable, and feeling, into the hell of iniquity.

CHAPTER XXXII.

How those are to be admonished who sin from sudden impulse and those who sin deliberately.

(*Admonition* 33.). Differently to be admonished are those who are overcome by sudden passion and those who are bound in guilt of set purpose. For those whom sudden passion overcomes are to be admonished to regard themselves as daily set in the warfare of the present life, and to protect the heart, which cannot foresee wounds, with the shield of anxious fear; to dread the hidden darts of the ambushed foe, and, in so dark a contest, to guard with continual attention the inward camp of the soul. For, if the heart is left destitute of the solicitude of circumspection, it is laid open to wounds; since the crafty enemy strikes the breast the more freely as he catches it bare of the breastplate of forethought. Those who are overcome by sudden passion are to be admonished to cease caring too much for earthly things; since, while they entangle their attention immoderately in transitory things, they are not aware of the darts of sins which pierce them. Whence, also, the utterance of one that is stricken and yet sleeps is expressed by Solomon, who says, *They have beaten me, and I was not pained; they have dragged me, and I felt it not. When shall I awake and again find wine* (Prov. xxiii. 35)? For the soul that sleeps from the care of its solicitude is beaten and feels not pain, because, as it foresees not impending evils, so neither is it aware of those which it has perpetrated. It is dragged, and in no wise feels it, because it is led by the allurements of vices, and yet is not roused to keep guard over itself. But again it wishes to awake, that it may again find wine, because, although weighed down by the sleep of its torpor from keeping guard over itself, it still strives to be awake to the cares of the world, that it may be ever drunk with pleasures; and, while sleeping to that wherein it ought to have been wisely awake, it desires to be awake to something else, to which it might have laudably slept. Hence it is written previously, *And thou shalt be as one that sleepeth in the midst of the sea, and as a steersman that is lulled to rest, having let go the rudder* (Prov. xxiii. 35). For he sleeps in the midst of the sea who, placed among the temptations of this world, neglects to look out for the motions of vices that rush in upon him like impending heaps of waves. And the steersman, as it were, lets go the rudder when the mind loses the earnestness of solicitude for guiding the ship of the body. For, indeed, to let go the rudder in the sea is to leave off intentness of forethought among the storms of this life. For, if the steersman holds fast the rudder with anxious care, he now directs the ship among the billows right against them, now cleaves the assaults of the winds aslant. So, when the mind vigilantly guides the soul, it now surmounts some things and treads them down, now warily turns aside from others, so that it may both by hard exertion overcome present dangers, and by foresight gather strength against future struggles. Hence, again, of the strong warriors of the heavenly country it is said, *Every man hath his sword upon his thigh because of fears in the night* (Cant. iii. 8). For the sword is put upon the thigh when the evil suggestion of the flesh is subdued by the sharp edge of holy preaching. But by the night is expressed the blindness of our infirmity; since any opposition that is impending in the night is not seen. Every man's sword, therefore, is put upon his thigh because of fears in the night; that is, because holy men, while they fear things which they do not see, stand always prepared for the strain of a struggle. Hence, again, it is said to the bride, *Thy nose is as*

3 In *English Bible*, lv. 15.

the tower that is in Lebanon (Cant. vii. 4). For the thing which we perceive not with our eyes we usually anticipate by the smell. By the nose, also, we discern between odours and stenches. What, then, is signified by the nose of the Church but the foreseeing discernment of Saints? It is also said to be like to the tower that is in Lebanon, because their discerning foresight is so set on a height as to see the struggles of temptations even before they come, and to stand fortified against them when they do come. For things that are foreseen when future are of less force when they are present; because, when every one has become more prepared against the blow, the enemy, who supposed himself to be unexpected, is weakened by the very fact of having been anticipated.

But, on the other hand, those who of set purpose are bound in guilt, are to be admonished to perpend with wary consideration how that, when they do what is evil of their own judgment, they kindle stricter judgment against themselves; and that by so much the harder sentence will smite them as the chains of deliberation have bound them more tightly in guilt. Perhaps they might sooner wash away their transgressions by penitence, had they fallen into them through precipitancy alone. For the sin is less speedily loosened which of set purpose is firmly bound. For, unless the soul altogether despised eternal things, it would not perish in guilt advisedly. In this, then, those who perish of set purpose differ from those who fall through precipitancy; that the former, when they fall by sin from the state of righteousness, for the most part fall also into the snare of desperation. Hence it is that the Lord through the Prophet reproves not so much the wrong doings of precipitance as purposes of sin, saying, *Lest perchance my indignation come out as fire, and be inflamed, and there be none to quench it because of the wickedness of your purposes* (Jer. iv. 4). Hence, again, in wrath He says, *I will visit upon you according to the fruit of your purposes* (Ibid. xxiii. 2). Since, then, sins which are perpetrated of set purpose differ from other sins, the Lord censures purposes of wickedness rather than wicked deeds. For in deeds the sin is often of infirmity or of negligence, but in purposes it is always of malicious intent. Contrariwise, it is well said through the Prophet in describing a blessed man, *And he sitteth not in the chair of pestilence* (Ps. i. 1). For a chair is wont to be the seat of a judge or a president. And to sit in the chair of pestilence is to commit what is wrong judicially; to sit in the chair of pestilence is to discern with the reason what is evil, and yet deliberately to perpetrate it. He sits, as it were, in the chair of perverse counsel who is lifted up with so great elation of iniquity as to endeavour even by counsel to accomplish evil. And, as those who are supported by the dignity of the chair are set over the crowds that stand by, so sins that are purposely sought out transcend the transgressions of those who fall through precipitancy. Those, then, who even by counsel bind themselves in guilt are to be admonished hence to gather with what vengeance they must at some time be smitten, being now made, not companions, but princes, of evil-doers.

CHAPTER XXXIII.

How those are to be admonished who commit very small but frequent faults, and those who, while avoiding such as are very small, are sometimes plunged in such as are grievous.

(*Admonition* 34.) Differently to be admonished are those who, though the unlawful things they do are very small, yet do them frequently, and those who keep themselves from small sins, but are sometimes plunged in such as are grievous. Those who frequently transgress, though in very small things, are to be admonished by no means to consider the quality of the sins they commit, but the quantity. For, if they scorn being afraid when they weigh their deeds, they ought to be alarmed when they number them; seeing that deep gulphs of rivers are filled by small but innumerable drops of rain; and bilge-water, increasing secretly, has the same effect as a storm raging openly; and the sores that break out on the members in scab are minute; but, when a multitude of them gets possession in countless numbers, it destroys the life of the body as much as one grievous wound inflicted on the breast. Hence for certain it is written, *He that contemneth small things falleth by little and little* (Ecclus. xix. 1). For he that neglects to bewail and avoid the smallest sins falls from the state of righteousness, not indeed suddenly, but bit by bit entirely. Those who transgress frequently in very little things are to be admonished to consider anxiously how that sometimes there is worse sin in a small fault than in a greater one. For a greater fault, in that it is the sooner acknowledged to be one, is by so much the more speedily amended; but a smaller one, being reckoned as though it were none at all, is retained in use with worse effect as it is so with less concern. Whence for the most part it comes to pass that the mind, accustomed to light evils, has no horror even of heavy ones, and, being fed up by sins, comes at last to a sort of sanction of iniquity, and by so much the more scorns to be afraid in greater matters as it has learnt to sin in little ones without fear.

But, on the other hand, those who keep themselves from small sins, but are sometimes plunged in grievous ones, are to be admonished anxiously to apprehend the state they are in; how that, while their heart is lifted up for very small things guarded against, they are so swallowed up in the very gulph of their own elation as to perpetrate others that are more grievous, and, while they outwardly master little ills, but are puffed up inwardly with vain glory, they prostrate their soul, overcome within itself by the sickness of pride, amid greater ills even outwardly. Those, then, who keep themselves from little faults, but are sometimes plunged in such as are grievous, are to be admonished to take care lest they fall inwardly where they suppose themselves to be standing outwardly, and lest, according to the retribution of the strict judge, elation on account of lesser righteousness become a way to the pitfall of more grievous sin. For such as, vainly elated, attribute their keeping of the least good to their own strength, being justly left to themselves, are overwhelmed in greater sins; and by falling they learn that their standing was not of themselves, so that immeasurable ills may humble the heart that is exalted by the smallest good. They are to be admonished to consider that, while in their more grievous faults they bind themselves in deep guilt, they nevertheless for the most part sin worse in the little faults which they guard against; because, while in the former they do what is wicked, in the latter they hide from men that they are wicked. Whence it comes to pass that, when they perpetrate greater evils before God, it is a case of open iniquity; and when they are careful to observe small good things before men, it is a case of pretended holiness. For hence it is that it is said of the Pharisees, *Straining out a gnat, but swallowing a camel* (Matth. xxiii. 24). As if it were said plainly, The least evils ye discern; the greater ye devour. Hence it is that they are again reproved by the mouth of the Truth, when they are told, *Ye tithe mint and anise and cummin, and omit the weightier matters of the Law, judgment and mercy and truth* (Ibid. 23). For neither is it to be carelessly heard that, when He said that the least things were tithed, He chose indeed to mention the lowest of herbs, but yet such as are sweet-smelling; in order, surely, to shew that, when pretenders observe small things, they seek to extend for themselves the odour of a holy reputation; and, though they omit to fulfil the greatest things, they still observe such of the smallest as smell sweetly far and wide in human judgment.

CHAPTER XXXIV.

How those are to be admonished who do not even begin good things, and those who do not finish them when begun.

(*Admonition* 35.) Differently to be admonished are they who do not even begin good things, and those who in no wise complete such as they have begun. For as to those who do not even begin good things, for them the first need is, not to build up what they may wholesomely love, but to demolish that wherein they are wrongly occupied. For they will not follow the untried things they hear of, unless they first come to feel how pernicious are the things that they have tried; since neither does one desire to be lifted up who knows not the very fact that he has fallen; nor does one who feels not the pain of a wound seek any healing remedy. First, then, it is to be shewn to them how vain are the things that they love, and then at length to be carefully made known to them how profitable are the things that they let slip. Let them first see that what they love is to be shunned, and afterwards perceive without difficulty that what they shun is to be loved. For they sooner accept the things which they have not tried, if they recognize as true whatever discourse they may hear concerning the things that they have tried. So then they learn to seek true good with fulness of desire, when they have learnt with certainty of judgment how vainly they have held to what was false. Let them be told, therefore, both that present good things will soon pass away from enjoyment, and also that the account to be given of them will nevertheless endure, without passing away, for vengeance; since both what pleases them is withdrawn from them now against their will, and what pains them is reserved them, also against their will, for punishment. Thus may they be wholesomely filled with alarm by the same things in which they harmfully take delight; so that when the stricken soul, in sight of the deep ruin of its fall, perceives that it has reached a precipice, it may retrace its steps backward, and, fearing what it had loved, may learn to esteem highly what it once despised.

For hence it is that it is said to Jeremiah when sent to preach, *See, I have this day set thee over the nations and over the kingdoms, to pluck out, and to pull down, and to destroy, and to scatter, and to build, and to plant* (Jer. i. 10). Because, unless he first destroyed wrong things, he could not profitably build right things; unless he plucked out of the hearts of his hearers the thorns of vain love, he would certainly plant to no purpose the words of holy preaching. Hence it is that Peter first overthrows, that he may afterwards build up, when he in no wise admonished the Jews as to what they were now to do, but reproved them for what they had done, saying, *Jesus of Nazareth, a man approved of God among you by powers and wonders and signs, which God did by Him in the midst of you, as ye yourselves know; Him, being delivered by the determinate counsel and foreknowledge of God, ye have by the hands of wicked men crucified and slain; whom God hath raised up, having loosed the pains of hell* (Acts ii. 22—24); in order, to wit, that having been thrown down by a recognition of their cruelty, they might hear the building up of holy preaching by so much the more profitably as they anxiously sought it. Whence also they forthwith replied, *What then shall we do, men and brethren?* And it is presently said to them, *Repent and be baptized, every one of you* (Ibid. 37, 38). Which words of building up they would surely have despised, had they not first wholesomely become aware of the ruin of their throwing down. Hence it is that Saul, when the light from heaven shone upon him, did not hear immediately what he was to do aright, but what he had done wrong. For, when, fallen to the earth, he enquired. saying, *Who art Thou, Lord?* it was straightway replied, *I am Jesus of Nazareth, whom thou persecutest.* And when he forthwith replied, *Lord, what wilt Thou have me to do?* it is added at once, *Arise, and go into the city, and it shall be told thee there what thou must do* (Acts ix. 4, &c.; xxii. 8, &c.). Lo, the Lord, speaking from heaven, reproved the deeds of His persecutor, and yet did not at once shew him what he had to do. Lo, the whole fabric of his elation had already been thrown down, and then, humble after his downfall, he sought to be built up: and when pride was thrown down, the words of building up were still kept back; to wit, that the cruel persecutor might long lie overthrown, and rise afterwards the more firmly built in good as he had fallen utterly upset from his former error. Those, then, who have not as yet begun to do any good are first to be overthrown by the hand of correction from the stiffness of their iniquity, that they may afterwards be lifted up to the state of well-doing. For this cause also we cut down the lofty timber of the forest, that we may raise it up in the roof of a building: but yet it is not placed in the fabric suddenly; in order, that is, that its vicious greenness may first be dried out: for the more the moisture thereof is exuded in the lowest, by so much the more solidly is it elevated to the topmost places.

But, on the other hand, those who in no wise complete the good things they have begun are to be admonished to consider with cautious circumspection how that, when they accomplish not their purposes, they tear up with them even the things that had been begun. For, if that which is seen to be a thing to be done advances not through assiduous application, even that which had been well done falls back. For the human soul in this world is, as it were, in the condition of a ship ascending against the stream of a river: it is never suffered to stay in one place, since it will float back to the nethermost parts unless it strive for the uppermost. If then the strong hand of the worker carry not on to perfection the good things begun, the very slackness in working fights against what has been wrought. For hence it is that it is said through Solomon, *He that is feeble and slack in work is brother to him that wasteth his works* (Prov. xviii. 9). For in truth he who does not strenuously execute the good things he has begun imitates in the slackness of his negligence the hand of the destroyer. Hence it is said by the Angel to the Church of Sardis, *Be watchful, and strengthen the things which remain, that are ready to die; for I find not thy works complete before my God* (Rev. iii. 2). Thus, because the works had not been found complete before his God, he foretold that those which remained, even such as had been done, were about to die. For, if that which is dead in us be not kindled into life, that which is retained as though still alive is extinguished too. They are to be admonished that it might have been more tolerable for them not to have laid hold of the right way than, having laid hold of it, to turn their backs upon it. For unless they looked back, they would not grow weak with any torpor with regard to their undertaken purpose. Let them hear, then, what is written, *It had been better for them not to have known the way of righteousness than, after they have known it, to be turned backward* (2 Pet. ii. 21). Let them hear what is written; *I would thou wert cold or hot: but, because thou art lukewarm, and neither cold nor hot, I will begin to spue thee out of my mouth* (Rev. iii. 15, 16). For he is hot who both takes up and completes good purposes; but he is cold who does not even begin any to be completed. And as transition is made through lukewarmness from cold to heat, so through lukewarmness there is a return from heat to cold. Whosoever, then, has lost the cold of unbelief so as to live, but in no wise passes beyond lukewarmness so as to go on to burn, he doubtless, despairing of heat, while he lingers in pernicious lukewarmness, is in the way to become cold. But, as before lukewarmness there is hope in cold, so after cold there is despair in lukewarmness. For he who is yet in his sins loses not his trust in conversion: but he who after conversion has become lukewarm has withdrawn the hope that there might have been of the sinner. It is required, then, that every one be either hot or cold, lest, being lukewarm, he be spued out: that is, that either, being not yet converted, he still afford hope of his conversion, or, being already converted, he be fervent in virtues; lest he be spued out as lukewarm, in that he goes back in torpor from purposed heat to pernicious cold.

CHAPTER XXXV.

How those are to be admonished who do bad things secretly and good things openly, and those who do contrariwise.

(*Admonition* 36.) Differently to be admonished are those who do bad things in secret and good things publicly, and those who hide the good things they do, and yet in some things done publicly allow ill to be thought of them. For those who do bad things in secret and good things publicly are to be admonished to consider with what swiftness human judgments flee away, but with what immobility divine judgments endure. They are to be admonished to fix the eyes of their mind on the end of things; since, while the attestation of human praise passes away, the heavenly sentence, which penetrates even hidden things, grows strong unto lasting retribution. When, therefore, they set their hidden wrong things before the divine judgment, and their right things before human eyes, both without a witness is the good which they do publicly, and not without an eternal witness is their latent transgression. So by concealing their faults from men, and displaying their virtues, they both discover while they hide what they deserve to be punished for, and hide while they discover what they might have been rewarded for. Such persons the Truth calls whited sepulchres, beautiful outward, but full of dead men's bones (Matth. xxiii. 27); because they cover up the evil of vices within, but by the exhibition of certain works flatter human eyes with the mere outward colour of righteousness. They are therefore to be admonished not to despise the right things they do, but to believe them to be of better desert. For those greatly misjudge their own good things who think human favour sufficient for their reward. For, when transitory praise is sought in return for right doing, a thing worthy of eternal reward is sold for a mean price. As to which price being received, indeed, the Truth says, *Verily I say unto you, they have received their reward* (Matth. vi. 2, 5, 6). They are to be admonished to consider that, when they prove themselves bad in hidden things, but yet offer themselves as examples publicly in good works, they shew that what they shun is to be followed; they cry aloud that what they hate is to be loved: in fine, they live to others, and die to themselves.

But, on the other hand, those who do good things in secret, and yet in some things done publicly allow evil to be thought of them, are to be admonished that, while what is good in them quickens themselves in the virtue of well-doing, they themselves slay not others through the example of a bad repute; that they love not their neighbours less than themselves, nor, while themselves imbibing a wholesome draught of wine, pour out a pestiferous cup of poison to minds intent on observing them. These assuredly in one way little help the life of their neighbour, and in the other greatly burden it, while they both study to do what is right unseen, and also, in some things in which they set an example, sow from themselves the seeds of evil. For whosoever is already competent to tread under foot the lust of praise commits a fraud on edification, if he conceals the good things he does; and he steals away, as it were, the roots of germination after having cast the seed, who shews not forth the work that is to be imitated. For hence in the Gospel the Truth says, *That they may see your good works, and glorify your Father which is in heaven* (Matth. v. 16). But then there comes also this sentence, which has the appearance of enjoining something very different, namely, *Take heed that ye do not your righteousness before men, to be seen of them* (Matth. vi. 1).

What means then its being enjoined both that our work is so to be done as not to be seen, and yet that it should be seen, but that the things we do are to be hidden, lest we ourselves should be praised, and yet to be shewn, that we may increase the praise of our heavenly Father? For, when the Lord forbade us to do our righteousness before men, He straightway added, *To be seen of them.* And again, when He enjoined that our good works were to be seen of men, He forthwith subjoined, *That they may glorify your Father which is in heaven* (Matth. v. 16). In what manner, then, they are to be seen, and in what manner they are not to be seen, He shewed in the end of His injunctions, to the effect that the mind of the worker should not seek for his work to be seen on his own account, and yet that on account of the glory of the heavenly Father he should not conceal it. Whence it commonly comes to pass that a good work is both in secret when it is done publicly, and again in public when it is done secretly. For he that in a public good work seeks not his own, but the heavenly Father's glory, hides what he has done, in that he has had Him only for a witness whom he has desired to please And he who in his secret good work covets being observed and praised has done this before men, even though no one has seen what he has done; because he has adduced so many witnesses to his good work as he has sought human praises in his heart. But when bad repute, so far as it prevails without sin committed, is not obliterated from the minds of lookers on, the cup of guilt is offered, in the way of example, to all who think evil. Whence also it generally comes to pass, that those who carelessly allow evil to be thought of them do not indeed commit wickedness in their own persons, but still, through those who may have taken example from them, offend in a more manifold way. Hence it is that Paul says to those who ate certain unclean things without pollution, but in this their eating put a stumbling-block of temptation in the way of the imperfect, *Take heed, lest by any means this liberty of yours become a stumblingblock to them that are weak* (1 Cor. viii. 9); and again, *And by thy conscience shall the weak brother perish, for whom Christ died. But when ye so sin against the brethren, and wound their weak conscience, ye sin against Christ* (Ibid. ii. 12). Hence it is that Moses, when he said, *Thou shalt not curse the deaf*, at once added, *Nor put a stumblingblock before the blind* (Lev. xix. 14). For to curse the deaf is to disparage one who is absent and does not hear; but to put a stumbling-block before the blind is to act indeed with discernment, but yet to give cause of offence to him who has not the light of discernment.

CHAPTER XXXVI.

Concerning the exhortation to be addressed to many at once, that it may so aid the virtues of each among them that vices contrary to such virtues may not grow up through it.

These are the things that a Bishop of souls should observe in the diversity of his preaching, that he may solicitously oppose suitable medicines to the diseases of his several hearers. But, whereas it is a matter of great anxiety, in exhorting individuals, to be of service to them according to their individual needs, since it is a very difficult thing to instruct each person in what concerns himself, dealing out due consideration to each case, it is yet far more difficult to admonish innumerable hearers labouring under various passions at one and the same time with one common exhortation. For in this case the speech is to be tempered with such art that, the vices of the hearers being diverse, it may be found suitable to them severally, and yet be not diverse from itself; that it pass indeed with one stroke through the midst of passions, but, after the manner of a two-edged sword, cut the swellings of carnal thoughts on either side; so that humility be so preached to the proud that yet fear be not increased in the timid; that confidence be so infused into the timid that yet the unbridled licence of the proud grow not; that solicitude in well doing be so preached to the listless and torpid that yet licence of immoderate action be not increased in the unquiet; that bounds be so set on the unquiet that yet careless torpor be not produced in the listless; that wrath be so extinguished in the impatient that yet negligence grow not in the easy and soft-hearted; that the soft-hearted be so inflamed to zeal that yet fire be not added to the wrathful; that liberality in giving be so infused into the niggardly that yet the reins of profusion be in no wise loosened to the prodigal; that frugality be so preached to the prodigal that yet care to keep perishable things be not increased in the niggardly; that marriage be so praised to the incontinent that yet those who are already continent be not called back to voluptuousness; that virginity of body be so praised to the continent that yet fecundity of the flesh come not to be despised by the married. Good things are so to be preached that ill things be not assisted sideways. The highest good is so to be praised that the lowest be not despaired of. The lowest is so to be cherished that there be no cessation of striving for the highest from the lowest being thought sufficient.

CHAPTER XXXVII.

Of the exhortation to be applied to one person, who labours under contrary passions.

It is indeed a serious labour for the preacher to keep an eye in his public preaching to the hidden affections and motives of individuals, and, after the manner of the palæstra, to turn himself with skill to either side: yet he is worn with much severer labour, when he is compelled to preach to one person who is subject to contrary vices. For it is commonly the case that some one is of too joyous a constitution, and yet sadness suddenly arising immoderately depresses him. The preacher, therefore, must give heed that the temporary sadness be so removed that the constitutional joyousness be not increased; and that the constitutional joyousness be so curbed that the temporary sadness be not aggravated. This man is burdened by a habit of immoderate precipitancy, and yet sometimes the power of a suddenly-born fear impedes his doing what ought to be done in haste. That man is burdened by a habit of immoderate fear, and yet sometimes is impelled in what he desires by the rashness of immoderate precipitancy. In the one, therefore, let the fear that suddenly arises be so repressed that his long-nourished precipitancy do not further grow. In the other let the precipitancy that suddenly arises be so repressed that yet the fear stamped on him by constitution do not gather strength. And, indeed, what is there strange in the physicians of souls being on their guard in these things, when those who heal not hearts but bodies govern themselves with so great skill of discernment? For it is often the case that extreme faintness weighs down a weak body, which faintness ought to be met by strong remedies; but yet the weak body cannot bear a strong remedy. He, therefore, who treats the case gives heed so to draw off the supervening malady that the pre-existing weakness of the body be in no wise increased, lest perchance the faintness should pass away with the life. He compounds, then, his remedy with such discernment as at one and the same time to meet both the faintness and the weakness. If, then, medicine for the body administered without division can be of service in a divided way, why should not medicine for the soul, applied in one and the same preaching, be of power to meet moral diseases in diverse directions: which medicine is the more subtle in its operation in that invisible things are dealt with?

CHAPTER XXXVIII.

That sometimes lighter vices are to be left alone, that more grievous ones may be removed.

But since, when the sickness of two vices attacks a man, one presses upon him more lightly, and the other perchance more heavily, it is undoubtedly right to haste to the succour of that through which there is the more rapid tendency to death. And, if the one cannot be restrained from causing the death which is imminent unless the other which is contrary to it increase, the preacher must be content by skilful management in his exhortation to suffer one to increase, to the end that he may keep the other back from causing the death which is imminent. When he does this, he does not aggravate the disease, but preserves the life of his sufferer to whom he administers the medicine, that he may find a fitting time for searching out means of recovery. For there is often one who, while he puts no restraint on his gluttony in food, is presently pressed hard by the stings of lechery, which is on the point of overcoming him, and who, when, terrified by the fear of this struggle, he strives to restrain himself through abstinence, is harassed by the temptation of vain-glory: in which case certainly one vice is by no means extinguished unless the other be fostered. Which plague then should be the more ardently attacked but that which presses on the man the more dangerously? For it is to be tolerated that through the virtue of abstinence arrogance should meanwhile grow against one that is alive, lest through gluttony lechery should cut him off from life entirely. Hence it is that Paul, when he considered that his weak hearer would either continue to do evil or rejoice in the reward of human praise for well-doing, said, *Wilt thou not be afraid of the power? Do that which is good, and thou shalt have praise of the same* (Rom. xiii. 3). For it is not that good things should be done in order that no human power may be feared, or that the glory of transitory praise may be thereby won; but, considering that the weak soul could not rise to so great strength as to shun at the same time both wickedness and praise, the excellent preacher in his admonition offered something and took away something. For by conceding mild ailments he drew off keener ones; that, since the mind could not rise all at once to the relinquishing of all its vices, it might, while left in familiarity with some one of them, be taken off without difficulty from another.

CHAPTER XXXIX.

That deep things ought not to be preached at all to weak souls.

But the preacher should know how to avoid drawing the mind of his hearer beyond its strength, lest, so to speak, the string of the soul, when stretched more than it can bear, should be broken. For all deep things should be covered up before a multitude of hearers, and scarcely opened to a few. For hence the Truth in person says, *Who, thinkest thou, is the faithful and wise steward, whom his lord has appointed over his household, to give them their measure of wheat in due season?* (Luke xii. 42). Now by a measure of wheat is expressed a portion of the Word, lest, when anything is given to a narrow heart beyond its capacity, it be spilt. Hence Paul says, *I could not speak unto you as unto spiritual, but as unto carnal. As it were to babes in Christ, I have given you milk to drink, and not meat* (1 Cor. iii. 1, 2). Hence Moses, when he comes out from the sanctuary of God, veils his shining face before the people; because in truth He shews not to multitudes the secrets of inmost brightness (Exod. xxxiv. 33, 35). Hence it is enjoined on him by the Divine voice that, if any one should dig a cistern, and not cover it, and an ox or ass should fall into it, he should pay the price (Exod. xxi. 33, 34), because when one who has arrived at the deep streams of knowledge covers them not up before the brutish hearts of his hearers, he is adjudged as liable to penalty, if through his words a soul, whether clean or unclean, be caught on a stumbling-stone. Hence it is said to the blessed Job, *Who hath given understanding unto the cock?* (Job xxxviii. 36). For a holy preacher, crying aloud in time of darkness, is as the cock crowing in the night, when he says, *It is even now the hour for us to arise from sleep* (Rom. xiii. 11). And again, *Awake ye righteous, and sin not* (1 Cor. xv. 34). But the cock is wont to utter loud chants in the deeper hours of the night; but, when the time of morning is already at hand, he frames small and slender tones; because, in fact, he who preaches aright cries aloud plainly to hearts that are still in the dark, and shews them nothing of hidden mysteries, that they may then hear the more subtle teachings concerning heavenly things, when they draw nigh to the light of truth.

CHAPTER XL.

Of the work and the voice of preaching.

But in the midst of these things we are brought back by the earnest desire of charity to what we have already said above; that every preacher should give forth a sound more by his deeds than by his words, and rather by good living imprint footsteps for men to follow than by speaking shew them the way to walk in. For that cock, too, whom the Lord in his manner of speech takes to represent a good preacher, when he is now preparing to crow, first shakes his wings, and by smiting himself makes himself more awake; since it is surely necessary that those who give utterance to words of holy preaching should first be well awake in earnestness of good living, lest they rouse others with their voice while themselves torpid in performance; that they should first shake themselves up by lofty deeds, and then make others solicitous for good living; that they should first smite themselves with the wings of their thoughts; that whatsoever in themselves is unprofitably torpid they should discover by anxious investigation, and correct by strict animadversion, and then at length set in order the life of others by speaking; that they should take heed to punish their own faults by bewailings, and then denounce what calls for punishment in others; and that, before they give voice to words of exhortation, they should proclaim in their deeds all that they are about to speak.

PART IV.

HOW THE PREACHER, WHEN HE HAS ACCOMPLISHED ALL ARIGHT, SHOULD RETURN TO HIMSELF, LEST EITHER HIS LIFE OR HIS PREACHING LIFT HIM UP.

But since often, when preaching is abundantly poured forth in fitting ways, the mind of the speaker is elevated in itself by a hidden delight in self-display, great care is needed that he may gnaw himself with the laceration of fear, lest he who recalls the diseases of others to health by remedies should himself swell through neglect of his own health; lest in helping others he desert himself, lest in lifting up others he fall. For to some the greatness of their virtue has often been the occasion of their perdition; causing them, while inordinately secure in confidence of strength, to die unexpectedly through negligence. For virtue strives with vices; the mind flatters itself with a certain delight in it; and it comes to pass that the soul of a well-doer casts aside the fear of its circumspection, and rests secure in self-confidence; and to it, now torpid, the cunning seducer enumerates all things that it has done well, and exalts it in swelling thoughts as though superexcellent beyond all beside. Whence it is brought about, that before the eyes of the just judge the memory of virtue is a pitfall of the soul; because, in calling to mind what it has done well, while it lifts itself up in its own eyes, it falls before the author of humility. For hence it is said to the soul that is proud, *For that thou art more beautiful, go down, and sleep with the uncircumcised* (Ezek. xxxii. 19): as if it were plainly said, Because thou liftest thyself up for the comeliness of thy virtues, thou art driven by thy very beauty to fall. Hence under the figure of Jerusalem the soul that is proud in virtue is reproved, when it is said, *Thou wert perfect in my comeliness which I had put upon thee, saith the Lord, and having confidence in thy beauty thou hast committed fornication in thy renown* (Ibid. xvi. 14, 15). For the mind is lifted up by confidence in its beauty, when, glad for the merits of its virtues, it glories within itself in security. But through this same confidence it is led to fornication; because, when the soul is deceived by its own thoughts, malignant spirits, which take possession of it, defile it through the seduction of innumerable vices But it is to be noted that it is said, *Thou hast committed fornication in thy renown:* for when the soul leaves off regard for the supernal ruler, it forthwith seeks its own praise, and begins to arrogate to itself all the good which it has received for shewing forth the praise of the giver; it desires to spread abroad the glory of its own reputation, and busies itself to become known as one to be admired of all. In its renown, therefore, it commits fornication, in that, forsaking the wedlock of a lawful bed, it prostitutes itself to the defiling spirit in its lust of praise. Hence David says, *He delivered their virtue into captivity, and their beauty into the enemy's hands* (Ps. lxvii. 61 [4]). For virtue is delivered into captivity and beauty into the enemy's hands, when the old enemy gets dominion over the deceived soul because of elation in well doing. And yet this elation in virtue tempts somewhat, though it does not fully overcome, the mind even of the elect.

But it, when lifted up, is forsaken, and, being forsaken, it is recalled to fear. For hence David says again, *I said in mine abundance, I shall not be moved for ever* (Ps. xxix. 7 [5]). But he added a little later what he underwent for having been puffed up with confidence in his virtue, *Thou didst turn thy face from me, and I was troubled* (Ibid. v. 8). As if he would say plainly, I believed myself strong in the midst of virtues, but, being forsaken, I become aware how great was my infirmity. Hence he says again, *I have sworn and am stedfastly purposed to keep the judgments of thy righteousness* (Ps. cxviii. 106 [6]). But, because it was beyond his powers to continue the keeping which he sware, straightway, being troubled, he found his weakness. Whence also he all at once betook himself to the aid of prayer, saying, *I am humbled all together; quicken me, O Lord, according to Thy word* (Ibid. v. 107). But sometimes Divine government, before advancing a soul by gifts, recalls to it the memory of its infirmity, lest it be puffed up for the virtues it has received. Whence the Prophet Ezekiel, before being led to the contemplation of heavenly things, is first called a son of man; as though the Lord plainly admonished him, saying, Lest thou shouldest lift up thy heart in elation for these things which thou seest, perpend cautiously what thou art; that, when thou penetratest the highest things, thou mayest remember that thou art a man, to the end that, when rapt beyond thyself, thou mayest be recalled in anxiety to thyself by the curb of thine infirmity. Whence it is needful that, when abundance of virtues flatters us, the eye of the soul should return to its own weaknesses, and salubriously depress itself; that it should look, not at the right things that it has done, but those that it has left undone; so that, while the heart is bruised by recollection of infirmity, it may be the more strongly confirmed in virtue before the author of humility. For it is generally for this purpose that Almighty God, though perfecting in great part the minds of rulers, still in some small part leaves them imperfect; in order that, when they shine with wonderful virtues, they may pine with disgust at their own imperfection, and by no means lift themselves up for great things, while still labouring in their struggle against the least; but that, since they are not strong enough to overcome in what is last and lowest, they may not dare to glory in their chief performances.

See now, good man, how, compelled by the necessity laid upon me by thy reproof, being intent on shewing what a Pastor ought to be, I have been as an ill-favoured painter pourtraying a handsome man; and how I direct others to the shore of perfection, while myself still tossed among the waves of transgressions. But in the shipwreck of this present life sustain me, I beseech thee, by the plank of thy prayer, that, since my own weight sinks me down, the hand of thy merit may raise me up.

[4] In *English Bible*, lxviii. 61.
[5] Ibid. xxx. 6.
[6] Ibid. cxix. 106.

See *Pedigree of Kings of Gaul*, Prolegomena, p. xxx.

REGISTER OF THE EPISTLES OF SAINT GREGORY THE GREAT.

BOOK I.

THE MONTH OF SEPTEMBER, INDICTION IX., BEING THE FIRST YEAR OF HIS ORDINATION.

EPISTLE I.

To all the Bishops of Sicily.

Gregory, servant of the servants of God [1], to all the bishops constituted throughout Sicily.

We have plainly perceived it to be very necessary that, even as our predecessors thought fit to do, we should commit all things to one and the same person; and that, where we cannot be present ourselves, our authority should be represented through him to whom we send our instructions. Wherefore, with the help of God, we have appointed Peter, subdeacon of our See, our delegate in the province of Sicily. Nor can we doubt as to the conduct of him to whom, with the help of God, we are known to have committed the charge of the whole patrimony of our church.

This also we have plainly perceived to be a thing that ought to be done; that once in the year your whole fraternity should assemble, at Syracuse or Catana, receiving, as we have charged him, the honour due to you; to the end that, together with the aforesaid Peter, subdeacon of our See, you may settle with due discretion whatever things pertain to the advantage of the churches of the province, or to the relief of the necessities of the poor and oppressed, or to the admonition of all, and the correction of those whose transgressions may peradventure be proved. From which council far be animosities, which are the nutriment of crimes, and may inward grudges die away, and that discord of souls which is beyond measure execrable. Let concord well-pleasing to God, and charity, approve you as His priests. Conduct all things, therefore, with such deliberation and calmness that yours may most worthily be called an Episcopal Council.

EPISTLE II.

To Justinus, Prætor of Sicily.

Gregory to Justinus, Prætor of Sicily.

What my tongue speaks my conscience approves; since even before you had become engaged in the employments of any office of dignity, I have greatly loved and greatly respected you. For the very modesty of your deportment made certain incipient claims on affection even from one who had been loth. And, when I heard that you had come to administer the prætorship of Sicily, I greatly rejoiced. But, since I have discovered that a certain ill-feeling is creeping in between you and the ecclesiastics, I have been exceedingly distressed. But now that you are occupied with the charge of civil administration, and I with the care of this ecclesiastical government, we can properly love one another in particular so far as we do no harm to the general community. Wherefore I beseech you by Almighty God, before Whose tremendous judgment we must give account of our deeds, that your Glory have always the fear of Him before your eyes, and never allow anything to come in whereby even slight dissension may arise between us. Let no gains draw you aside to injustice; let not either the threats or the favours of any one cause you

---

1 "Sanctus Gregorius primus omnium se in principio epistolarum suarum servum servorum Dei satis humiliter definivit." (*Joan Diac. in Vit. S. Greg.* l. ii. c. 1). The designation, however, had been used by others before him, as by Pope Damasus (*Ep.* IV. *ad Stephanum et Africæ Episcopos*), and Augustine (*Ep. ad Vitalem*). Gregory may have been the first to use it habitually. It is true that in the *Registrum Epistolarum* we find it four times only, viz. in the headings of Epistles I. 1, I. 36, VI. 51, XIII. 1. But it may have been omitted in the copies of his letters preserved at Rome. This is probable from the fact that it occurs in the letters relating to the English Mission as given by Bede, though absent from the same letters in the *Registrum*.

to deviate from the path of rectitude. See now short life is: think, ye that exercise judicial authority, b fore what judge ye must at some time go. It is therefore to be diligently considered that we shall leave all gains behind us here, and that of harmful gains we shall carry with us to the judgment the pleas only that are against us for them. Those advantages, then, are to be sought by us which death may in no wise take away, but which the end of the present life may shew to be such as will endure for ever.

As to what you write concerning the corn, the magnificent Citonatus asserts very differently that no more has been transmitted than what was supplied for replenishing the public granary in satisfaction of what was due for the past indiction. Give attention to this matter, since, if what is transmitted be at all defective, it will be the death not of any one single person only, but of the whole people together[2].

Now for the management of the patrimony of Sicily I have sent, as I think under the guidance of God, such a man as you will be in entire accord with, if you are a lover of what is right, as I have found you to be. Moreover, as to your desire that I should remember you kindly, I confess the truth when I say that, unless any injustice should creep in from the snares of the ancient foe, I have learnt thy Glory's modesty to be such that I shall not blush to be thy friend.

EPISTLE III.

To Paul, Scholasticus.

Gregory to Paul, &c.

However strangers smile upon me on account of the dignity of my priestly office, this I take not much account of; but I do grieve not a little at your smiling upon me on this account, seeing that you know what I long for, and yet suppose me to have received advancement. For to me it would have been the highest advancement, if what I wished could have been fulfilled; if I could have accomplished my desire, which you have been long acquainted with, in the enjoyment of longed-for rest. Yet, since I am now detained in the city of Rome, tied by the chains of this dignity, I have something wherein I may even rejoice in addressing your Glory, seeing that, when the most eminent lord the ex-consul Leo comes, I suspect that you will not remain in Sicily; and when thou thyself also, tied by thine own dignity, shalt come to be detained in Rome, thou wilt come to know what sorrow and what bitterness I suffer. But when the magnificent lord Maurentius, the *Chartularius*, comes to you, I pray thee concur with him in regard to the present straits of the Roman city, since outside we are stabbed without cease by hostile swords. But we are still more heavily pressed by danger within through a sedition of the soldiers. Further, we commend to your Glory in all respects Peter our sub-deacon, whom we have sent to rule the patrimony of the Church.

EPISTLE IV.

To John, Bishop of Constantinople[3].

Gregory to John, Bishop of Constantinople.

If the virtue of charity consists in the love of one's neighbour, and we are commanded to love our neighbours as ourselves, how is it that your Blessedness does not love me even as yourself? For I know with what ardour, with what anxiety, you wished to fly from the burden of the episcopate; and yet you made no opposition to this same burden of the episcopate being imposed on me. It is evident, then, that you do not love me as yourself, seeing that you have wished me to take on myself that load which you were unwilling should be imposed on you. But since I, unwórthy and weak, have taken charge of an old and grievously shattered ship (for on all sides the waves enter, and the planks, battered by a daily and violent storm, sound of shipwreck), I beseech thee by Almighty God to stretch out the hand of thy prayer to me in this my danger, since thou canst pray the more strenuously as thou standest further removed from the confusion of the tribulations which we suffer in this land.

My synodical epistle I will transmit with all possible speed, having despatched Bacauda, our brother and fellow-bishop, immediately after my ordination, as the bearer of this letter, while pressed by many and serious engagements.

EPISTLE V.

To Theoctista, Sister of the Emperor.

Gregory to Theoctista, &c

With how great devotion my mind prostrates itself before your Venerableness I cannot fully express in words; nor yet do I labour to give utterance to it, since, even though I were silent, you read in your heart your own sense

[2] The population of Rome had long been greatly dependent on Sicily for the supply of corn, which it was the duty of the prætor to purchase and transmit to Rome. Famine might result from failure of this supply. Hence what is said further on the subject in this Epistle. Cf. "Neminem vestrum præterit, judices, omnem utilitatem opportunitatemque provinciæ Siciliæ quæ ad commoda populi Romani adjuncta sit consistere in re frumentaria maxime. Nam cæteris rebus adjuvamur ex illa provincia, hac vero alimur et sustinemur." (Cicero in Verrem, Act II. lib. 3, c. 5.)

[3] For notice of him, see III. 53, note.

of my devotion. I wonder, however, that you withdrew your countenance, till of late bestowed on me, from this my recent engagement in the pastoral office; wherein, under colour of episcopacy, I have been brought back to the world; in which I am involved in such great earthly cares as I do not at all remember having been subjected to even in a lay state of life. For I have lost the deep joys of my quiet, and seem to have risen outwardly while inwardly falling down. Whence I grieve to find myself banished far from the face of my Maker. For I used to strive daily to win my way outside the world, outside the flesh; to drive all phantasms of the body from the eyes of my soul, and to see incorporeally supernal joys; and not only with my voice but in the core of my heart I used to say, *My heart hath said unto Thee, I have sought Thy face, Thy face, Lord, will I seek* (Ps. xxvi. 8). Moreover desiring nothing, fearing nothing, in this world, I seemed to myself to stand on a certain summit of things, so that I almost believed to be fulfilled in me what I had learnt of the Lord's promise through the prophet, *I will lift thee up upon the high places of the earth* (Isai. lviii. 14). For he is lifted up upon the high places of the earth who treads under foot through looking down upon them in his mind even the very things of the present world which seem lofty and glorious. But, having been suddenly dashed from this summit of things by the whirlwind of this trial, I have fallen into fears and tremors, since, even though I have no fears for myself, I am greatly afraid for those who have been committed to me. On every side I am tossed by the waves of business, and sunk by storms, so that I may truly say, *I am come into the depth of the sea, and the storm hath overwhelmed me* (Ps. lxviii. 3[4]). After business I long to return to my heart; but, driven therefrom by vain tumults of thoughts, I am unable to return. From this cause, then, that which is within me is made to be far from me, so that I cannot obey the prophetic voice which says, *Return to your heart, transgressors* (Isai. xlvi. 8). But, pressed by foolish thoughts, I am impelled only to exclaim, *My heart hath failed me* (Ps. xxxix. 13[5]). I have loved the beauty of the contemplative life as a Rachel, barren, but keen of sight and fair (Gen. xxix.), who, though in her quietude she is less fertile, yet sees the light more keenly. But, by what judgment I know not, Leah has been coupled with me in the night, to wit, the active life; fruitful, but tender-eyed; seeing less, but bringing forth more. I have longed to sit at the feet of the Lord with Mary, to take in the words of His mouth; and lo, I am compelled to serve with Martha in external affairs, to be careful and troubled about many things (Luke x. 39, *seq.*). A legion of demons having been, as I believed, cast out of me, I wished to forget those whom I had known, and to rest at the feet of the Saviour; and lo it is said to me, so as to compel me against my will, *Return to thine house, and declare how great things the Lord hath done for thee* (Mark v. 19). But who in the midst of so many earthly cares may be able to preach the wondrous works of God, it being already difficult for me even to call them to mind? For, pressed as I am in this office of dignity by a crowd of secular occupations, I see myself to be of those of whom it is written, *While they were being raised up thou didst cast them down* (Ps. lxxii. 18[6]). For he said not, Thou didst cast them down after they had been raised up, but while they were being raised up; because all bad men fall inwardly, while through the support of temporal dignity they seem outwardly to rise. Wherefore their very raising up is their fall, because, while they rely on false glory, they are emptied of true glory. Hence, again, he says, *Consuming away as smoke shall they consume away* (Ps. xxxvi. 20[7]). For smoke in rising consumes away, and in extending itself vanishes. And so indeed it comes to pass when present felicity accompanies the life of a sinner, since whereby he is shewn to be exalted, thereby it is brought about that he should cease to be. Hence, again, it is written, *My God, make them like a wheel* (Ps. lxxxii. 14[8]). For a wheel is lifted up in its hinder parts, and in its fore parts falls. But to us the things that are behind are the goods of the present world, which we leave behind us; but the things that are before are those which are eternal and permanent, to which we are called, as Paul bears witness, saying, *Forgetting those things which are behind, and reaching forth to those things which are before* (Phil. iii. 13). The sinner, therefore, when he is advanced in the present life, is made to be as a wheel, since, while falling in the things which are before, he is lifted up in the things which are behind. For, when he enjoys in this life the glory which he must leave behind, he falls from that which comes after this life. There are indeed many who know how so to control their outward advancement as by no means to fall inwardly thereby. Whence it is written, *God casteth not away the mighty, seeing that He also Himself is mighty* (Job xxxvi. 5). And it is said through Solomon,

4 In *English Bible*, lxix. 2. 5 Ibid. xl. 12.

6 In *English Bible*, lxxiii. 18. 7 Ibid. xxxvii. 20. 8 Ibid. lxxxiii. 13.

A man of understanding shall possess governments (Prov. i. 5). But to me these things are difficult, since they are also exceedingly burdensome; and what the mind has not received willingly it does not control fitly. Lo, our most serene Lord the Emperor has ordered an ape to be made a lion. And, indeed, in virtue of his order it can be called a lion, but a lion it cannot be made. Wherefore his Piety must needs himself take the blame of all my faults and short-comings, having committed a ministry of power to a weak agent.

EPISTLE VI.

To Narses, Patrician [9].

Gregory to Narses, &c

In describing loftily the sweetness of contemplation, you have renewed the groans of my fallen state, since I hear what I have lost inwardly while mounting outwardly, though undeserving, to the topmost height of rule. Know then that I am stricken with so great sorrow that I can scarcely speak; for the dark shades of grief block up the eyes of my soul. Whatever is beheld is sad, whatever is thought delightful appears to my heart lamentable For I reflect to what a dejected height of external advancement I have mounted in falling from the lofty height of my rest. And, being sent for my faults into the exile of employment from the face of my Lord, I say with the prophet, in the words, as it were of destroyed Jerusalem, *He who should comfort me hath departed far from me* (Lam. i. 16). But when, in seeking a similitude to express my condition and title, you frame periods and declamations in your letter, certainly, dearest brother, you call an ape a lion. Herein we see that you do as we often do, when we call mangy whelps pards or tigers. For I, my good man, have, as it were, lost my children, since through earthly cares I have lost works of righteousness. Therefore *call me not Noemi. that is fair; but call me Mara, for I am full of bitterness* (Ruth i. 20). But as to your saying that I ought not to have written, "That you should plough with *bubali* [1] in the Lord's field," seeing that when in the sheet shewn to the blessed Peter both *bubali* and all wild beasts were presented to view; thou knowest thyself that it is subjoined, *Slay and eat* (Acts x. 13). Thou, then, who hadst not yet slain these beasts, why didst thou already wish to eat them through obedience? Or knowest thou not that the beast about which thou wrotest refused to be slain by the sword of thy mouth? Thou must needs, then, satisfy the hunger of thy desire with those whom thou hast been able to prick and slay (*Lit.*, to slay through compunction) [2].

Further, as to the case of our brethren, I think that, if God gives aid, it will be as thou hast written. It was not, however, by any means right for me to write about it at present to our most serene lords, since at the very outset one should not begin with complaints. But I have written to my well-beloved son, the deacon Honoratus [3], that he should mention the matter to them in a suitable manner at a seasonable time, and speedily inform me of their reply. I beg greetings to be given in my behalf to the lord Alexander, the lord Theodorus [4], my son Marinus, the lady Esicia, the lady Eudochia, and the lady Dominica.

EPISTLE VII.

To Anastasius, Patriarch of Antioch [5].

Gregory to Anastasius, &c.

I have found what your Blessedness has written to be as rest to the weary, as health to the sick, as a fountain to the thirsty, as shade to the oppressed with heat. For those words of yours did not seem even to be expressed by the tongue of the flesh, inasmuch as you so disclosed the spiritual love which you bear me as if your soul itself were speaking. But very hard was that which followed, in that your love enjoined me to bear earthly burdens, and that, having first loved me spiritually, you

---

9 There are other letters from Gregory to this Narses, viz. iv. 32, vi. 14, and perhaps vii. 30. He may have been the same as the Narses who was a famous general of the Emperor Maurice, and who was eventually burnt alive by Phocas. (Theoph., Sim. V.)

1 The animal called βούβαλος is described by Pliny (l. 8, c. 15) as "animal ferum in Africa, vitulo ac cervo simile." The reference in the text is to Amos vi. 12, where the Vulgate has, "Numquid currere queunt in petris equi, aut arari potest in bubalis?" The clause in the epistle, "ut in agro Dominico cum bubalis arares," appears to be a quotation from a previous letter of Gregory's, in which he may have announced his election to Narses.

2 The whole passage is rather obscure to us, not having before us the letter from Narses, which is replied to, or the previous one from Gregory, to which Narses had referred. The drift seems to be as follows. Gregory, in his former letter, had compared his being elected pope to a *bubalus* being set to plough in the Lord's field. Narses had replied to the effect that, even if he were a *bubalus*, he was not therefore unfit, since *bubali*, with other wild beasts, had been in St. Peter's sheet, and pronounced clean. To this Gregory now rejoins, "Yes; but those beasts were to be slain before they might be eaten; and so you must first slay me *per compunctionem*—i.e. by so pricking me with 'the sword of your mouth' as to induce me to comply—before you may eat me *per obedientiam*—i.e. make use of me in the way you wish through my obedience to your desire. Not being thus so far slain, I have a right to protest against being made pope against my will"

3 Honoratus was at this time Gregory's apocrisiarius at Constantinople. We find several letters addressed to him in this capacity, but none throwing light on the case here referred to.

4 Theodorus was the court physician at Constantinople, to whom Epistles III. 66, IV. 31, VII. 28, are addressed.

5 Anastasius had been threatened with deposition and exile (A.D. 563) by the Emperor Justinian, and the sentence had been carried into effect (A.D. 570) by Justinian's successor, Justin II. Notwithstanding this, Gregory after his own accession acknowledged him as the true patriarch of Antioch; and, probably owing to his intercession with the Emperor Maurice, Anastasius was restored to his patriarchal See on the death of Gregory, who had been intruded into it, A.D. 593. Other Epistles to, or concerning this Anastasius are I. 25, 26, 28; V. 39; VII. 27, 33; VIII. 2.

afterwards, loving me as I think in temporal wise, pressed me down to the ground with the burden you laid upon me; so that, losing utterly all uprightness of soul, and forfeiting the keen vision of contemplation, I may say, not in the spirit of prophecy, but from experience, *I am bowed down and brought low altogether* (Ps. cxviii. 107[6]). For indeed such great burdens of business press me down that my mind can in no wise lift itself up to heavenly things. I am tossed by the billows of a multitude of affairs, and, after the ease of my former quiet, am afflicted by the storms of a tumultuous life, so that I may truly say, *I am come into the depth of the sea, and the storm hath overwhelmed me* (Ps. lxviii. 3[7]). Stretch out, therefore, the hand of your prayer to me in my danger, you that stand on the shore of virtue. But as to your calling me the mouth and the lantern of the Lord, and alleging that I profit many, this also adds to the load of my iniquities, that, when my iniquity ought to have been chastised, I receive praises instead of chastisement. But with what a bustle of earthly business I am distracted in this place, I cannot express in words; yet you can gather it from the shortness of this letter, in which I say so little to him who I love above all others. Further, I apprize you that I have requested our most serene lords with all possible urgency to allow you to come to the threshold of Peter, the prince of the apostles, with your dignity restored to you, and to live here with me so long as it may please God; to the end that, as long as I am accounted worthy of seeing you, we may relieve the weariness of our pilgrimage by speaking to each other of the heavenly country

EPISTLE IX.

To Peter the Subdeacon.

Gregory to Peter, &c.

Gregory, a servant of God, presbyter and abbot of the monastery of Saint Theodore in the province of Sicily constituted in the territory of Panormus, has given us to understand that men of the farm of Fulloniacus, which belongs to the holy Roman Church, are endeavouring to encroach on the boundaries of the farm of Gerdinia, bordering on the said farm of the holy Roman Church, which they [*i.e. monks of St. Theodore*] have possessed without dispute for innumerable years. And for this cause we desire you to go to the city of Panormus, and investigate the question in such sort (with the view of the right of possession remaining with those who have had it heretofore) that, if you shall find that the aforesaid monastery of Saint Theodore has possessed the boundaries concerning which the dispute has arisen without disturbance for forty years, you shall not allow it to suffer any damage, even though it were to the advantage of the holy Roman Church, but provide in all ways for its undisturbed security. But, if the agents of the holy Roman Church should shew that the monastery has not been in possession without dispute of its right for forty years, but that any question has been raised within that time concerning the said boundaries, let it be set at rest peaceably and legally by arbitrators chosen for the purpose. For not only do we wish that questions of wrong-doing that have never yet been mooted should be raised, but also that such as have been raised by others than ourselves should be speedily set at rest. Let thy Experience, therefore, cause all to be so effectively adjusted, that no question relating to this matter may be hereafter referred to us again. Further, we desire that the testament of Bacauda, late *Xenodochus*, continue valid as when first made.

The month of November: ninth Indiction.

6 In *English Bible*, cxix. 107.

7 Ibid. lxix. 2.

EPISTLE X.

To Bacauda and Agnellus, Bishops.

Gregory to Bacauda, &c

The Hebrews dwelling in Terracina have petitioned us for licence to hold, under our authority, the site of their synagogue which they have held hitherto. But, inasmuch as we have been informed that the same site is so near to the church that even the sound of their psalmody reaches it, we have written to our brother and fellow-bishop Peter that, if it is the case that the voices from the said place are heard in the church, the Jews must cease to worship there. Therefore let your Fraternity, with our above-named brother and fellow-bishop, diligently inspect this place, and if you find that there has been any annoyance to the church, provide another place within the fortress, where the aforesaid Hebrews may assemble, so that they may be able to celebrate their ceremonies without impediment[8]. But let your Fraternity provide such a place, in case of their being deprived of this one, that there be no cause of complaint in future. But we forbid the aforesaid Hebrews to be oppressed or vexed unreasonably; but,

8 For the result of this order, see below, Ep. 35. For other instances of Gregory's tolerant attitude towards Jews, and his deprecation of force being used for their conversion, see that Epistle, and also I. 47; IX. 6. But he is strict in prohibiting their possession of slaves who were already, or might become, Christians, and will allow them no compensation for the loss of such (cf. iii. 38; IV. 9, 21; IX. 109, 110).

as they are permitted, in accordance with justice, to live under the protection of the Roman laws, let them keep their observances as they have learnt them, no one hindering them: yet let it not be allowed them to have Christian slaves.

EPISTLE XI.

To Clementina, Patrician[9].

Gregory to Clementina, &c.

Having received your Glory's letter speaking of the passing away of the late Eutherius of magnificent memory, we give you to understand that our mind no less than yours is disturbed by such a sorrow, in that we see how men of approved repute are by degrees removed from this world, whose ruin is already evidenced in the actual effects of the causes thereof. But it becomes us to withdraw ourselves from it by the wise precaution of conversion[1], lest it involve us too in its own ruin. And indeed our sorrow for the loss of friends ought to be the more tolerable as our condition of mortality requires from us that we should lose them. Nevertheless, for the loss of aid to our carnal life He Who granted permission for its removal is powerful to console, and to come Himself as a comforter into the vacant place.

That we are unable to accede to your request that the deacon Anatholius should be sent to you is due to the circumstances of the case, and not to any rigorous austerity. For we have appointed him our steward[2], having committed our episcopal residence to his management.

EPISTLE XII.

To John, Bishop of Urbs Vetus (*Orvieto*).

Gregory to John, &c.

Agapitus, abbot of the monastery of St. George, informs us that he endures many grievances from your Holiness; and not only in things that might be of service to the monastery in time of need, but that you even prohibit the celebration of masses in the said monastery, and also interdict burial of the dead there. Now, if this is so, we exhort you to desist from such inhumanity, and allow the dead to be buried, and masses to be celebrated there without any further opposition, lest the aforesaid venerable Agapitus should be compelled to complain anew concerning the matters referred to.

9 Another Epistle, X. 15, is addressed to the same lady.
1 The word *conversio* commonly denotes entering a monastery.
2 *Vicedominum.*

EPISTLE XVI.

To Severus, Bishop of Aquileia[3].

Gregory to Severus, &c.

As, when one who walks through devious ways takes anew the right path, the Lord embraces him with all eagerness, so afterwards, when one deserts the way of truth, He is more saddened with grief for him than He rejoiced over him with joy when he turned from error; since it is a less degree of sin not to know the truth than not to abide in it when known: and what is committed in error is one thing, but what is perpetrated knowingly is another. And we, from having formerly rejoiced in thy being incorporated in the unity of the Church, are now the more abundantly distressed for thy dissociation from the catholic society. Accordingly we desire thee, at the instance of the bearer of these presents, according to the command of the most Christian and most serene Emperor, to come with thy adherents to the threshold of the blessed Apostle Peter, that, a synod being assembled by the will of God, judgment may be passed concerning the doubt that is entertained among you.

EPISTLE XVII.

To all the Bishops of Italy.

Gregory to all, &c.

Inasmuch as the abominable Autharit[4] during this Easter solemnity which has been lately completed, forbade children of Lombards being baptized in the catholic faith, for which sin the Divine Majesty cut him off, so that he should not see the solemnity of another Easter, it becomes your Fraternity to warn all the Lombards in your districts, seeing that grievous mortality is everywhere

3 The bishops of Istria, of whom the bishop of Aquileia was Metropolitan, still refused to accept the decree of the fifth (Ecumenical Council, which had, under the dictation of the Emperor Justinian, condemned certain writings of three deceased prelates, Theodore of Mopsuesta, Theodoret, and Ibas, called "the three chapters" (*tria capitula*). Severus, the Metropolitan, summoned in this letter with his suffragans to Rome, disregarded the summons, going instead, at the instance of the Exarch Smaragdus, to Ravenna, where he remained a year. On his return to his See he still held out, though many of his bishops conformed. A schism hence ensued in Istria, which continued during the life of Gregory (Joan. Diac. *Vit. S. Greg.* iv. 37, 38). Other Epistles referring to the Istrian schism are II. 46, 51; V. 51; IX. 9, 10; XIII. 33.

4 Autharit (*al.* Autharith, called by Paul. Diac. *Authari*), who died at Pavia in this year (A.D. 591). had been king of the Lombards for six years, having effected extensive conquests in Italy. "Rex Authari apud Ticinum Nonas Septembris veneno, ut tradunt, accepto moritur, postquam sex regnaverat annos." (*Paul. Diac. de gestis Longob.* iii. 36). It is he who is said to have advanced to Rhegium at the toe of Italy. and there, riding up to a pillar in the sea, to have touched it with the point of his spear, and said, "As far as this shall the boundaries of the Lombards extend." (*Paul. Diac.* iii. 33.) He had been a determined Arian. He was succeeded by Agilulph, whom his widow Theodelinda, a Catholic Bavarian princess, selected as her consort. With her Gregory carried on a very friendly correspondence, and, probably through her influence, Agilulph himself, originally an Arian, is said to have been converted to Catholicity. Gregory's etters to Theodelinda are IV. 4, 38; IX. 43; XIV. 12.

imminent, that they should reconcile these their children who have been baptized in Arian heresy to the catholic faith, and so appease the wrath of the Almighty Lord which hangs over them. Warn, then, those whom you can; with all the power of persuasion you possess seize on them, and bring them to a right faith; preach to them eternal life without end; that, when you shall come into the sight of the strict judge, you may be able, in consequence of your solicitude, to shew in your own persons a shepherd's gains.

EPISTLE XVIII.

To Peter the Subdeacon.

Gregory to Peter, &c.

We have been informed that Marcellus of the Barutanian Church, who has had penance assigned him in the monastery of Saint Adrian in the same city of Panormus, not only is in want of food, but also suffers inconvenience from scarcity of clothing. Therefore we hold it necessary to enjoin your Activity by this present order to appoint for him as much as you may see to be needful in the way of food clothing and bedding for his own maintenance, and provision for his servant; so that his want and nakedness may be provided for with such timely care that what you assign to this same man may be reckoned afterwards to your own account. So act, therefore, that you may both fulfil our command, and also by ordering this very thing well you may be able yourself to partake of the profit of the same. Further, there is this other matter that we enjoin you to look to without regard to the old custom that has now grown up; namely, that if any cities in the province of Sicily, for their sins, are known to be without pastoral government through the lapses of their priests, you should see whether there be any worthy of the office of priesthood among the clergy of the churches themselves, or out of the monasteries, and, after first enquiring into the gravity of their behaviour, send them to us, that the flock of each place may not be found destitute for any length of time through the lapse of its pastor. But if you should discover any vacant place in which no one of the same church is found fitted for such a dignity, send us word after the like careful enquiry, that some one may be provided whom God may have judged worthy of such ordination. For it is not right that from the deviation of one the Lord's flock should be in danger of wandering abroad among precipices without a shepherd. For thus both the administration of places will go on, and there will remain no suspicion of the lapsed being restored to their former rank; and so may they repent the better.

EPISTLE XIX.

To Natalis, Bishop of Salona[5].

Gregory to Natalis, &c.

The acts of your synod which you have transmitted to us, in which the Archdeacon Honoratus is condemned, we perceive to be full of the seed of strifes, seeing that the same person is at one and the same time advanced to the dignity of the priesthood against his will, and removed from the office of the diaconate as though unworthy of it. And, as it is just that no one who is unwilling should be advanced by compulsion, so I think we must be of opinion that no one who is innocent should be deposed from the ministry of his order unjustly. Nevertheless, since discord hateful to God excuses thy part in the transaction, we admonish thee to restore his place and administration to the Archdeacon Honoratus, and agree to supply him with attendance sufficient for his divine ministry. If cause of offence is still fomented between you, let the aforesaid Archdeacon submit himself to our audience and enquiry, when admonished to do so, and let thy love send to us a person instructed in the case, that in the presence of both, the Lord assisting us, we may be able to decide what justice approves without respect of persons.

EPISTLE XX.

To Honoratus, Deacon of Salona.

Gregory to Honoratus, &c.

Having read the contradictory letters which thou and thy bishop have addressed to us against each other, we grieve that there is so little charity between you. Nevertheless we enjoin thee to continue in the administration of thy office, and, if the cause of offence between you can, under the power of grace, be settled on the spot, we believe it will be

5 Salona was the metropolis of the province of Dalmatia in Western Illyricum. The misdoings of its bishop, Natalis, gave rise to a lengthy correspondence. See, in addition to this letter, I. 20; II. 18, 19, 20, 52; III. 8, 32. He had, as appears from this letter and others, desired to get rid of his archdeacon Honoratus, having apparently some grudge against him, and with this view would have ordained him priest against his will, none but deacons being then capable of holding the office of archdeacon. He was accused also of addiction to unbecoming conviviality, and of neglecting his episcopal duties. Eventually, after continued contumacy, he appears to have satisfied Gregory in the matter of Honoratus, and also to have reformed his own habits of life, after writing what appears from Gregory's reply to it to have been a racy letter in defence of conviviality, which was taken in good part and replied to in a good-humoured vein (II. 52). Gregory subsequently said of him, "I was at one time much distressed concerning our brother and fellow bishop Natalis, having experienced proud behaviour from him. But since he has himself corrected his manners, he has overcome me, and comforted my sadness" (II. 46).

greatly to the advantage of your souls. But in case the discord between you has so set you in arms against each other that you have no will to allay the swelling of your offence, do thou without delay come to be heard before us, and let thy bishop send to us on his own behalf such person as he may choose, furnished with instructions; that, after minutely considering the whole case, we may settle what may appear fit between the parties. But we would have thee know that we shall make strict enquiry of thee on all points, as to whether the ornaments[6], either those of thine own church, or such as have been collected from various churches, are being now kept with all care and fidelity. For, if any of them shall be found to have been lost through negligence or through any person's dishonesty, thou wilt be involved in the guilt of this, being, in virtue of thy office of Archdeacon, peculiarly responsible for the custody of the said church.

EPISTLE XXI.

To Natalis, Bishop of Salona[7].

Gregory to Natalis, &c.

We have received at the hands of the deacon Stephen, whom you sent to us, the letters of thy Reverence, wherein you congratulate us on our promotion. And truly what has been offered in the kindness and earnestness of charity demands full credence, reason having prompted your pontifical order to rejoice with us. We therefore, being cheered by your greeting, declare in conscience that I undertook the burden of this dignity with a sick heart. But, seeing that I could not resist the divine decrees, I have recovered a more cheerful frame of mind. Wherefore we write to entreat your Reverence that both we and the Christian flock committed to our care may enjoy the succour of your prayers, to the end that in the security of that protection we may have power to overcome the hurricanes of these times.

The month of February, ninth indiction

EPISTLE XXV.

To John, Bishop of Constantinople, and the other Patriarchs.

Gregory, to John of Constantinople, Eulogius of Alexandria, Gregory of Antioch, John of Jerusalem, and Anastasias, Ex-Patriarch of Antioch. *A paribus*[8].

When I consider how, unworthy as I am, and resisting with my whole soul, I have been compelled to bear the burden of pastoral care, a darkness of sorrow comes over me, and my sad heart sees nothing else but the shadows which allow nothing to be seen. For to what end is a bishop chosen of the Lord but to be an intercessor for the offences of the people? With what confidence, then, can I come as an intercessor for the sins of others to Him before Whom I am not secure about my own? If perchance any one should ask me to become his intercessor with a great man who was incensed against him, and to myself unknown, I should at once reply, I cannot go to intercede for you, having no knowledge of that man from familiar acquaintance with him. If then, as man with man, I should properly blush to become an intercessor with one on whom I had no claim, how great is the audacity of my obtaining the place of intercessor for the people with God, whose friendship I am not assured of through the merit of my life! And in this matter I find a still more serious cause of alarm, since we all know well that, when one who is in disfavour is sent to intercede with an incensed person, the mind of the latter is provoked to still greater severity. And I am greatly afraid lest the community of believers, whose offences the Lord has so far indulgently borne with, should perish through the addition of my guilt to theirs. But, when in one way or another I suppress this fear, and with mind consoled give myself to the care of my pontifical office, I am deterred by consideration of the immensity of this very task.

"For indeed I consider with myself what watchful care is needed that a ruler may be pure in thought, chief in action, discreet in keeping silence, profitable in speech, a near neighbour to every one in sympathy, exalted above all in contemplation, a companion of good livers through humility, unbending against the vices of evil-doers through zeal for righteousness[9]." All which things when I try to search out with subtle investigation, the very wideness of the consideration cramps me in the particulars. For, as I have already said, there is need of the greatest care that "the ruler be pure in thought, &c." [A long passage, thus beginning, and ending with

6 *Cimelia*, from Gr. κειμήλια.

7 This appears to have been the formal answer to the official letter sent by the bishop of Salona to Gregory, congratulating him on his accession to the popedom, having no connexion with, and perhaps written before, the preceding Epistle XIX.

8 *A paribus* denotes that the Epistle is a copy of an identical one that has been sent to more than one person, *exemplis* being perhaps understood. Cf. I. 80; VI. 52, 54, 58; IX. 60, 106.

9 What is here printed between inverted commas, with much of what has come before, occurs also in *Regula Pastoralis*, II. 1. So also long passages afterwards, as will be seen.

"beyond the limit of order," is found also in *Regula Pastoralis*, Pt. II. ch. 2, which see.]

Again, when I betake myself to consider the works required of the pastor, I weigh within myself what intent care is to be taken that he be "chief in action, to the end that by his living, he may point out the way of life to them that are put under him, &c." [See *Reg. Past.*, Pt. II. ch. 3, to the end.]

Again, when I betake myself to consider the duty of the pastor as to speech and silence, I weigh within myself with trembling care how very necessary it is that he should be discreet in keeping silence and profitable in speech, "lest he either utter what ought to be suppressed or suppress what ought to be uttered, &c." [See *Reg. Past.*, III., 4, down to "keep the unity of the faith."]

Again, when I betake myself to consider what manner of man the ruler ought to be in sympathy, and what in contemplation, I weigh within myself that he "should be a near neighbour to every one in sympathy, and exalted above all in contemplation, to the end that through the bowels of loving-kindness, &c." [See *Reg. Past.*, Pt. II. ch. 5, to the end.]

Again, when I betake myself to consider what manner of man the ruler ought to be in humility, and what in strictness, I weigh within myself how necessary it is that he "should be, through humility, a companion to good livers, and, through the zeal of righteousness rigid against the vices of evil-doers, &c." [See *Regula Pastoralis*, Pt. II. ch. 6, down to "towards the perverse;" there being only a slight variation, not affecting the sense, in the wording of the concluding clause.] For hence it is that "Peter who had received from God, &c." [See *Reg. Past.*, Pt. II. ch. 6, down to "dominates over vices rather than over his brethren."] He orders well the authority he has received who has learnt both to maintain it and to keep it in check. He orders it well who knows how both through it to tower above sins, and with it to set himself on an equality with other men.

Moreover, the virtue of humility ought to be so maintained that the rights of government be not relaxed; lest, when any prelate has lowered himself more than is becoming, he be unable to restrain the life of his subordinates under the bond of discipline; and the severity of discipline is to be so maintained that gentleness be not wholly lost through the over-kindling of zeal. For often vices shew themselves off as virtues, so that niggardliness would fain appear as frugality, extravagance as liberality, cruelty as righteous zeal, laxity as loving-kindness. Wherefore both discipline and mercy are far from what they should be, if one be maintained without the other. But there ought to be kept up with great skill of discernment both mercy justly considerate, and discipline smiting kindly. "For hence it is that, as the Truth teaches (Luke x. 34), the man is brought by the care of the Samaritan, &c." [See *Reg. Past.*, Pt. II. ch. 6, down to "manna of sweetness."]

Thus, having undertaken the burden of pastoral care, when I consider all these things and many others of like kind, I seem to be what I cannot be, especially as in this place whosoever is called a Pastor is onerously occupied by external cares; so that it often becomes uncertain whether he exercises the function of a pastor or of an earthly noble. And indeed whosoever is set over his brethren to rule them cannot be entirely free from external cares; and yet there is need of exceeding care lest he be pressed down by them too much. "Whence it is rightly said to Ezekiel, The priests shall not shave their heads, &c." [See *Reg. Past.*, Pt. II., ch. 7, to the end.]

But in this place I see that no such discreet management is possible, since cases of such importance hang over me daily as to overwhelm the mind, while they kill the bodily life. Wherefore, most holy brother, I beseech thee by the Judge who is to come, by the assembly of many thousand angels, by the Church of the firstborn who are written in heaven, help me, who am growing weary under this burden of pastoral care, with the intercession of thy prayer, lest its weight oppress me beyond my strength. But, being mindful of what is written, *Pray for one another, that ye may be healed* (James v. 16), I give also what I ask for. But I shall receive what I give. For, while we are joined to you through the aid of prayer, we hold as it were each other by the hand while walking through slippery places, and it comes to pass, through a great provision of charity, that the foot of each is the more firmly planted in that one leans upon the other.

Besides, since with the heart man believeth unto righteousness, and with the mouth confession is made unto salvation, I confess that I receive and revere, as the four books of the Gospel so also the four Councils: to wit, the Nicene, in which the perverse doctrine of Arius is overthrown; the Constantinopolitan also, in which the error of Eunomius and Macedonius is refuted; further, the first Ephesine, in which the impiety of Nestorius is condemned; and the Chalcedonian, in which the pravity of Eutyches and Dioscorus is reprobated. These with full devotion I embrace, and adhere to with most entire approval; since on them, as on a four-square stone, rises the structure of the holy faith; and whosoever, of whatever life and behaviour he may be, holds not fast to their solidity, even though he is seen to be a stone, yet he lies outside the building. The fifth council also I equally venerate, in which the epistle which is called that of Ibas, full of error, is reprobated; Theodorus, who divides the Mediator between God and men into two subsistences, is convicted of having fallen into the perfidy of impiety; and the writings of Theodoritus, in which the faith of the blessed Cyril is impugned, are refuted as having been published with the daring of madness. But all persons whom the aforesaid venerable Councils repudiate I repudiate; those whom they venerate I embrace; since, they having been constituted by universal consent, he overthrows not them but himself, whosoever presumes either to loose those whom they bind, or to bind those whom they loose. Whosoever, therefore, thinks otherwise, let him be anathema. But whosoever holds the faith of the aforesaid synods, peace be to him from God the Father, through Jesus Christ His Son, Who lives and reigns consubstantially God with Him in the Unity of the Holy Spirit for ever and ever. Amen.

EPISTLE XXVI.

To Anastasius, Patriarch of Antioch.

[The beginning of this epistle is the same as that of Epistle VII. to the same Anastasius as far as the words "stand on the shore of virtue"; after which it is continued as follows.]

But, as to your calling me the mouth and lantern of the Lord, and alleging that I profit many by speaking, and am able to give light to many, I confess that you have brought me into a state of the greatest doubt in my estimate of myself. For I consider what I am, and detect in myself no sign of all this good. But I consider also what you are, and I do not think that you can lie. When, then, I would believe what you say, my infirmity contradicts me. When I would dispute what is said in my praise, your sanctity contradicts me. But I pray you, holy man, let us come to some agreement in this our contest, that, though it is not as you say, it may be so because you say it. Moreover, I have addressed my synodical epistle to you, as to the other patriarchs, your brethren[1]; inasmuch as with me you are always what it has been granted you to be by the gift of Almighty God, without regard to what you are accounted not to be by the will of men[2]. I have given some instructions to Boniface the guardian (*defensori*), who is the bearer of these presents, for him to communicate to your holiness in private. Moreover, I have sent you keys of the blessed apostle Peter, who loves you, which are wont to shine forth with many miracles when placed on the bodies of sick persons[3].

EPISTLE XXVII.

To Anastasius, Archbishop of Corinth.

Gregory to Anastasius, &c.

In proportion as the judgments of God are unsearchable ought they to be an object of fear to human apprehension; so that mortal reason, being unable to comprehend them, may of necessity bow under them the neck of a humble heart, to the end that it may follow with the mind's obedient steps where the will of the Ruler may lead. I, then, considering that my infirmity cannot reach to the height of the apostolic See, had rather have declined this burden, lest, having pastoral rule, I should succumb in action through inadequate administration. But, since it is not for us to go against the will of the Lord who disposes all, I obediently followed the way in which it pleased the merciful hand of the Ruler to deal with me. For it was necessary that your Fraternity should be informed, even though the present opportunity had not occurred, how the Lord had vouchsafed that I, however unworthy, should preside over the apostolic See. Since, then, reason required this to be done, and an opportunity having occurred through our sending to you the bearer of these presents, that is, Boniface the guardian (*defensorem*), we are careful not only to offer to your Fraternity by letter the good wishes of charity, but also to inform you of our ordination, as we believe you would wish us to do. Wherefore let your Charity, by a letter in reply, cause us to rejoice for the unity of the Church and the acceptable news of your own welfare; to the end that our bodily absence from each other, which distance of place causes us to endure, may become as presence through interchange of letters. We exhort you, also, since we have despatched the above-mentioned

[1] The Benedictine Editors adopt the reading *patribus* instead of *fratribus*. But the sense seems to require the latter.

[2] See Ep. 7, note 1.

[3] Keys of St. Peter's sepulchre, in which had been inserted filings from his alleged chains preserved at Rome, were often sent by Gregory to distinguished friends (cf. III. 48; VI. 6; VII. 26; VIII. 35; IX. 122; XI. 66), to be hung round the neck (VI. 6), or deposited (XI. 66), or used for healing. For an account of how the filings were obtained, see IV. 30. In one instance the key is described as being of gold (VII. 26). To Eulogius of Alexandria is sent a small cross containing filings from the chains, to be applied to his sore eyes.

bearer of these presents on certain necessary business to the feet of the most clement prince, and since the mutability of the time is wont to generate many hindrances on the way, that your priestly affection would bestow upon him whatever may be necessary either in provision for his journey by land or in procuring for him the means of navigation, that through God's mercy, he may be able the more quickly to accomplish his intended journey.

EPISTLE XXVIII.

To Sebastian, Bishop of Rhisinum [*in Dalmatia*].

Gregory to Sebastian, &c.

Although I deserved to receive no letters from your Blessedness, yet I also do not forget my own forgetfulness; I blame my negligence, I stir up my sluggishness with goads of love, that one who will not pay what he owes of his own accord, may learn even under blows to render it. Furthermore, I inform you that I have prepared a full representation, with urgent prayers to our most pious lords, to the effect that they ought to have sent the most blessed lord patriarch Anastasius, with the use of the pallium granted him, to the threshold of the blessed Peter, prince of the apostles, to celebrate with me the solemnities of Mass; to the end that, though he were not allowed to return to his See, he might at least live with me, retaining his dignity. But of the reason that has arisen for keeping back what I had thus written the bearer of these presents will inform you. Nevertheless, ascertain the mind of the said lord Anastasius, and inform me in your letters of whatever he may wish to be done in this business[4].

EPISTLE XXIX.

To Aristobulus, Ex-prefect and *Antigraphus*[5].

Gregory to Aristobulus, &c.

For fully expressing my affection I confess that my tongue suffices not: but your own affection will better tell you all that I feel towards you. I have heard that you are suffering from certain oppositions. But I am not greatly grieved for this, since it is often the case that a ship which might have reached the depths of the ocean had the breeze been favourable is driven back by an opposing wind at the very beginning of its voyage, but by being driven back is recalled into port. Furthermore, if you should by any chance receive for interpretation a lengthy letter of mine, translate it, I pray you, not word for word, but so as to give the sense; since usually, when close rendering of the words is attended to, the force of the ideas is lost.

[4] See Ep. 7, note 1.

[5] I.e. Secretary. "Scriptor idem est et cancellarius . . . quod rescribit literis missis ad dominum suum.' Du Cange.

EPISTLE XXXIII.

To Romanus, Patrician, and Exarch of Italy.

Gregory to Romanus, &c.

Even though there were no immediate cause for writing to your Excellency, yet we ought to shew solicitude for your health and safety, so as to learn through frequent intercommunication what we desire to hear about you. Besides, it has come to our knowledge that Blandus, bishop of the city of Hortanum[6], has been detained now for a long time by your Excellency in the city of Ravenna. And the result is that the Church decays, being without a ruler, and the people as being without a shepherd; and infants there, for their sins, die without baptism[7]. And again, since we do not believe that your Excellency has detained him except on the ground of some probable transgression, it is proper that a synod should be held to bring to light any crime that is charged against him. And, if such fault is found in him as to lead to his degradation from the priesthood, it is necessary that we should look out for another to be ordained, lest the Church of God should remain untended, and destitute in what the Christian religion does not allow it to be without. But, if your Excellency should perceive that the case is otherwise with him than it is said to be, allow him, I pray you, to return to his church, that he may fulfil his duty to the souls committed to his charge.

The month of March; the ninth Indiction.

[6] Al. Orta, in Tuscia.

[7] This alleged consequence of the bishop's absence from his See does not imply that he alone could administer baptism, but only that his authorization was required for its administration. See Bingham, Bk. II. ch. iii. Sect. 3, 4, and references there given: e.g. Ignat. *Ep. ad Smyrn.* n. viii., "It is not lawful either to baptize or celebrate the Eucharist without the bishop; but that which he allows is well-pleasing to God:" Hieron. *Dialog. c. Lucifer*, p. 139, "Thence it comes, that, without the order of the bishop neither presbyter nor deacon has the right of baptizing;" *Can. Apost.* c. xxxviii., "Let the presbyters and deacons execute no office without the knowledge of the bishop; for it is to him that the Lord's people are committed, and he must give an account of their souls." It was usual in episcopal cities to have only one baptistery, connected with the bishop's church; and there all would be baptized, if not by the bishop himself (who was accounted the chief minister of baptism), yet under his direction and superintendence. Cf. Bingham, Bk. VIII., ch. vii., Sect. 6: Bk. XI., ch. vii., Sect. 12, 13.

EPISTLE XXXIV.

To Venantius, ex-monk, Patrician of Syracuse [8].

Gregory to Venantius, &c.

Many foolish men have supposed that, if I were advanced to the rank of the episcopate, I should decline to address thee, or to keep up communication with thee by letter. But this is not so; since I am compelled by the very necessity of my position not to hold my peace. For it is written, *Cry aloud, spare not, lift up thy voice like a trumpet* (Isai. lviii. 1). And again it is written, *I have given thee for a watchman unto the house of Israel, thou shalt hear the word at my mouth, and declare it to them from me* (Ezek. iii. 17). And what follows to the watchman or to the hearer from such declaration being kept back or uttered is forthwith intimated; *If, when I say to the wicked, Thou shalt surely die, thou declare it not to him, nor speak to him, that he may turn from his wicked way and live, the wicked man himself shall die in his iniquity; but his blood will I require at thine hand. Yet if thou declare it to the wicked, and he turn not from his iniquity and from his wicked way, he himself indeed shall die in his iniquity, but thou hast delivered thy soul.* Hence also Paul says to the Ephesians, *My hands are pure this day from the blood of all of you. For I have not shunned to declare unto you all the counsel of God* (Acts xx. 26, 27). He would not, then, have been pure from the blood of all, had he refused to declare unto them the counsel of God. For when the pastor refuses to rebuke those that sin, there is no doubt that in holding his peace he slays them. Compelled, therefore, by this consideration, I will speak whether you will or no; for with all my powers I desire either thee to be saved or myself to be rescued from thy death. For thou rememberest in what state of life thou wast, and knowest to what thou hast fallen without regard to the animadversion of supernal strictness. Consider, then, thy fault while there is time; dread, while thou canst, the severity of the future judge; lest thou then find it bitter, having shed no tears to avoid it now. Consider what is written; *Pray that your flight be not in the winter, neither on the Sabbath day* (Matth. xxiv. 20). For the numbness of cold impedes walking in the winter, and, according to the ordinance of the law, it is not lawful to walk on the Sabbath day. He, then, attempts to fly in the winter or on the Sabbath day, who then wishes to fly from the wrath of the strict Judge when it is no longer allowed him to walk. Wherefore, while there is time, while it is allowed, fly thou from the animadversion which is of so great dreadfulness: consider what is written; *Whatsoever thine hand findeth to do, do it with thy might; for there is neither work, nor device, nor wisdom, in the grave whither thou hastenest* (Eccles. ix. 10). By the witness of the Gospel thou knowest that divine severity accuses us for idle talk, and demands a strict account of an unprofitable word (Matth. xii. 36). Consider, then, what it will do for perverse doing, if in its judgment it reprobates some for talking. Ananias had vowed money to God (Acts v. 2 *seq.*), which, afterwards, overcome by diabolical persuasion, he withheld. But by what death he was

---

8 The relations of Gregory to this Venantius are interesting; other letters throwing light on them being III. 60; VI. 43, 44; IX. 123; XI. 30, 35, 36, 78. Venantius was a patrician, resident in Sicily, who, having become a monk, had discovered that he had mistaken his vocation and returned to secular life. In the letter before us he is kindly, but very earnestly, written to, in the hope of inducing him to retrace a step which, from Gregory's point of view, was so dangerous to his friend's soul. But the remonstrance was in vain. Venantius appears, from an allusion in the letter, to have been associated with a literary set of friends who took a view of the purpose of life not in accordance with the monastic theory: and other motives may have disposed him to listen to their advice, since we find him afterwards married to a lady called Italica. She appears to have been, like Venantius, of patrician rank, and resident in Sicily, and to have possessed property there; for see III. 60, an epistle addressed to "Italica Patricia," remonstrating with her for her alleged harsh treatment of certain poor people, who were under the protection of the Church. It appears from this letter that Gregory had known her previously, and it is observable that he makes allusion to her personal charms (*pulchritudo in superficie corporis*). There being no allusion in this letter to any husband, it cannot be concluded that she was, at the time when it was written, married to Venantius: but we may reasonably suppose her to have been the same Italica who was subsequently addressed as his wife, for see IX. 123, "Domno Venantio patricio et Italicæ jugalibus." The marriage may possibly have taken place soon after Gregory's first letter to Venantius, which, if the date assigned be correct, was written in the 9th Indiction (A.D. 590-1). It cannot well have been much later, since in the 4th Indiction, i.e. A.D. 600-1 (still supposing the assigned dates correct) there were two girls, the issue of the marriage, who were also written to by Gregory after their father's death, and seem then to have been already old enough to be betrothed. See XI. 35, 36, 78. At some time subsequent to his marriage we find a letter of serious admonition addressed to Venantius (VI. 43), who had quarrelled with his bishop on some matters of business, and acted violently.

But, notwithstanding all such causes for displeasure, Gregory continued on terms of cordial friendship with the married couple, and took a warm interest in their children. Having heard of Venantius being dangerously ill, he wrote a letter of sympathy, addressed to him and his wife jointly, and at the end sent greetings to his "most sweet daughters, the lady Barbara and the lady Antonina" (IX. 123). Subsequently, when Venantius was suffering from gout, he addressed him earnestly, but kindly; and, when he was on his death-bed, and the inheritance of the daughters was in jeopardy owing to certain claims made by certain persons on their father's estate, he wrote a short kind letter to the little ladies, bidding them keep up their spirits so as to comfort their father, assuring them that he himself would protect them after their father's death, and speaking of the debt of gratitude he owed for the goodness to himself of both their parents. The mother not being written to, or alluded to as alive, may be supposed to have died previously. At the same time he wrote to John, bishop of Syracuse (the same bishop with whom Venantius had been once for a time at variance), urging him to do what he could to induce Venantius, even in his last moments, to resume the monastic habit for the safety of his soul, and no less urgently charging him to take up the cause of the orphan girls. Lastly (XI. 87), the girls are once more addressed by Gregory in a kind letter, from which it seems that, young as they must have been, marriage was already in contemplation for them, and in which he expresses his hope of seeing them at Rome. The correspondence thus summarised is peculiarly interesting, as shewing both Gregory's strong sense of the sin and danger to the soul of returning to the world from the monastic life, and also the continuance of his friendship and affection to one who had thus sinned, and the interest he could still take in his domestic happiness and the welfare of his family.

mulcted thou knowest. If then he was deserving of the penalty of death who withdrew the money which he had given to God, consider of how great penalty thou wilt be deserving in the divine judgment, who hast withdrawn, not money, but thyself, from Almighty God, to whom thou hadst devoted thyself in the monastic state of life. Wherefore, if thou wilt hear the words of my rebuke so as to follow them, thou wilt come to know in the end how kind and sweet they are. Lo, I confess it, I speak mourning, and constrained by sorrow for what thou hast done. I scarce can utter words; and yet thy mind, conscious of guilt, is hardly able to bear what it hears, blushes, is confounded, remonstrates. If, then, it cannot bear the words of dust, what will it do at the judgment of the Creator? And yet I acknowledge the exceeding mercy of heavenly grace, in that it beholds thee flying from life, and nevertheless still reserves thee for life; that it sees thee acting proudly, and still bears with thee; that through its unworthy servants it administers to thee words of rebuke and admonition. So great a thing is this that thou oughtest anxiously to ponder on what Paul says; *We exhort you, brethren, that ye receive not the grace of God in vain: for he saith, I have heard thee in a time accepted, and in the day of salvation have I succoured thee. Behold now is the acceptable time, behold now is the day of salvation* (2 Cor. vi. 1 *seq.*).

But I know that, when my letter is received, forthwith friends come about thee, thy literary clients are called in, and advice about the purpose of life is sought from the promoters of death; who, loving not thee, but what belongs to thee, tell thee nothing but what may please thee at the time. For such, as thou thyself rememberest, were those thy former counsellors, who drew thee on to the perpetration of so great a sin. To quote to thee something from a secular author[9], "All things should be considered with friends, but the friends themselves should be considered first." But, if in thy case thou seekest an adviser, take me, I pray thee, as thy adviser. For no one can be more to be relied on for advice than one who loves not what is thine, but thee. May Almighty God make known to thy heart with what love and with what charity my heart embraces thee, though so far only as not to offend against divine grace. For I so attack thy fault as to love thy person; I so love thy person as not to embrace the viciousness of thy fault. If, therefore, thou believest that I love thee, approach the threshold of the apostles, and use me as an adviser. But if perchance I am supposed to be too keen in the cause of God, and am suspected for the ardour of my zeal, I will call the whole Church together into counsel on this question, and whatever all are of opinion should be done for good, this I will in no wise contradict, but gladly fulfil and subscribe to what is decided in common. May Divine grace keep thee while accomplishing what I have warned thee to do.

9 Seneca, *Epist.* 3: "Tu omnia cum amico delibera. sed de ipso prius. Post amicitiam credendum est; ante amicitiam judicandum."

EPISTLE XXXV.

To Peter, Bishop of Terracina.

Gregory to Peter, &c.

Joseph, a Jew, the bearer of these presents, has informed us that, the Jews dwelling in the camp of Terracina having been accustomed to assemble in a certain place for celebrating their festivities, thy Fraternity had expelled them thence, and that they had migrated, and this with thy knowledge and consent, to another place for in like manner observing their festivities; and now they complain that they have been expelled anew from this same place. But, if it is so, we desire thy Fraternity to abstain from giving cause of complaint of this kind, and that they be allowed, as has been the custom, to assemble in the place which, as we have already said, they had obtained with thy knowledge for their place of meeting. For those who dissent from the Christian religion must needs be gathered together to unity of faith by gentleness, kindness, admonition, persuasion, lest those whom the sweetness of preaching and the anticipated terror of future judgment might have invited to believe should be repelled by threats and terrors. It is right, then, that they should come together kindly to hear the word of God from you rather than that they should become afraid of overstrained austerity.

EPISTLE XXXVI.

To Peter the Subdeacon.

Gregory, bishop, servant of the servants of God, to Peter the Subdeacon.

The code of instructions which I gave thee on thy going to Sicily must be diligently perused, so that the greatest care may be taken concerning bishops, lest they mix themselves up in secular causes, except so far as the necessity of defending the poor compels them. But what is inserted in the same code concerning monks or clerics ought, I think, in no respect to be varied from. But let thy

Experience observe these things with such great attention as may fulfil my desire in this regard. Further, it has come to my ears that from the times of Antoninus, the defensor, till now, during these last ten years, many persons have endured certain acts of violence from the Roman Church, so that some publicly complain of their boundaries having been violently invaded, their slaves abstracted, and their moveables carried off by force, and not by any judicial process. In all such cases I desire thy Experience to keep intent watch, and whatsoever during these last ten years may be found to have been taken away by violence, or retained unjustly in the name of the Church, to restore it by authority of this my order to him to whom it is found to belong; lest he who has suffered violence should be obliged to come to me, and undertake the labour of so long a journey, in which case it could not be ascertained here before me whether or not he spoke the truth. Having regard, then, to the majesty of the Judge who is to come, restore all things that have been sinfully taken away, knowing that thou bringest great gain to me, if thou gatherest [heavenly] reward rather than riches. But we have ascertained that what the greater part complain of is the loss of their slaves, saying that, if any man's bondman, peradventure running away from his master, has declared himself to belong to the Church, the rectors [1] of the Church have at once kept him as a bondman belonging to the Church, without any trial of the case, but supporting with a high hand the word of the bondman. This displeases me as much as it is abhorrent from the judgment of truth. Wherefore I desire thy Experience to correct without delay whatever may be found to have been so done: and it is also fit that any such slaves as are now kept in ecclesiastical possession, as they were taken away without trial, should be restored before trial; so that, if holy Church has any legitimate claim to them, their possessors may then be dispossessed by regular process of law. Correct all these things irretractably, since thou wilt be truly a soldier of the blessed apostle Peter if in his causes thou keep guard over the truth, even without his receiving anything. But, if thou seest anything that may justly be claimed as belonging to the Church, beware lest thou ever try to assert such claim by force; especially as I have established a decree under pain of anathema, that *tituli* may not ever be put by our Church on any urban or rural farm [2]; but whatever may in reason be claimed for the poor ought also to be defended by reason; lest, a good thing being done in a manner that is not good, we be convicted of injustice before Almighty God even in what we justly seek. Moreover, I pray thee, let noble laymen, and the glorious [Prætor] [3] love thee for thy humility, not dread thee for thy pride. And yet, if by any chance thou knowest them to be doing any injustice to the indigent, turn thy humility at once into exaltation, so as to be always submissive to them when they do well, and opposed to them when they do ill. But so behave that neither thy humility be remiss nor thy authority stiff, to the end that uprightness season humility, and humility render thy very uprightness gentle. Further, since it has been customary for bishops to assemble here for the anniversary [4] of the pontiff, forbid their coming for the day of my ordination, since foolish and vain superfluity delights me not. But if they must needs assemble, let them come for the anniversary [4] of Peter, the prince of the apostles, to render thanks to him by whose bounty they are pastors. Farewell. Given this XVII day of the Kalends of April, in the ninth year of the Emperor Mauricius.

EPISTLE XXXIX.

To Anthemius, Subdeacon [5].

Gregory to Anthemius, &c.

We charged thee on thy departure, and remember to have afterwards enjoined on thee by letter, to take care of the poor, and, if thou shouldest find any in those parts to be in want, to inform me by letter: and thou hast been at pains to do this with regard to very few. Now, I desire that, as soon as thou hast received this present order, thou offer to Pateria, my father's sister, forty *solidi* for shoe-money for her boys, and four hundred *modii* of wheat; to the lady Palatina, the widow of Urbicus, twenty *solidi* and three hundred *modii* of wheat; to the lady Viviana, widow of Felix, twenty *solidi* and three hundred *modii* of wheat. And let all these eighty *solidi* be charged together in thy accounts. But bring hither with speed the sum of thy receipts, and be here, with the Lord's help, by Easter Day.

[1] As to the *rectores patrimonii*, see *Proleg.* p. vii.

[2] *Titulum imponere* seems to have meant originally setting up a scroll or tablet on a property to assert a title to it; it might be in some cases with a view to sale, letting, or to confiscation.

[3] I.e. the Prætor of Sicily.

[4] *Natalem*, i.e. birthday; denoting usually, in the case of a dignitary, the day of his inauguration; and, in the case of a deceased saint, the day of his death.

[5] He was the subdeacon who had charge of the patrimony in Campania, as appears from other letters to him (see Index of Epistles).

EPISTLE XLI.

To Peter, Subdeacon.

Gregory to Peter, &c.

The venerable Paulinus bishop of the city of Taurum (*Taurianum in Brutia*), has told us that his monks have been scattered by reason of barbaric invasions, and that they are now wandering through the whole of Sicily, and that, being without a ruler, they neither have a care of their souls, nor pay attention to the discipline of their profession. On this account we enjoin thee to search out with all care and diligence, and collect together, these same monks, and to place them with the said bishop, their ruler, in the monastery of Saint Theodorus situate in the city of Messana, that both such as are there now, whom we find to be in need of a ruler, and those of his congregation whom you may have found and brought back, may be able, under his leadership, to serve the Almighty Lord together. Know also that we have signified this matter to the venerable Felix, bishop of the same city, lest anything ordained in the diocese committed to him should be disturbed without his knowledge.

EPISTLE XLII.

To Anthemius, Subdeacon[6].

Gregory to Anthemius, &c.

John, our brother and fellow-bishop, in a schedule sent to us by his cleric Justus, has among many other things intimated to us as follows: that some monks of the diocese of Surrentum[7] transmigrate from monastery to monastery as they please, and depart from the rule of their own abbot out of desire for a worldly life; nay even (what is known to be unlawful) that they aim severally at having property of their own. Wherefore we command thy Experience by this present order, that no monk be henceforth allowed to migrate from monastery to monastery, and that thou permit not any one of them to have anything of his own. But, if any one whatever should so presume, let him be sent back with adequate constraint to the monastery in which he lived at first, to be under the rule of his own abbot from which he had escaped; lest, if we allow so great an iniquity to take its course uncorrected, the souls of those that are lost be required from the souls of their superiors. Further, if any of the clergy should chance to become monks, let it not be lawful for them to return anew to the same church in which they had formerly served, or to any other; unless one should be a monk of such a life that the bishop under whom he had formerly served should think him worthy of the priesthood, so that he may be chosen by him, and by him ordained to such place as he may think fit. And since we have learnt that some among the monks have plunged into such great wickedness as publicly to take to themselves wives, do thou seek them out with all vigilance, and, when found, send them back with due constraint to the monasteries of which they had been monks. But neglect not to deal also with the clergy who profess monasticism, as we have said above. For so thou wilt be pleasing in the eyes of God, and be found partaker of a full reward.

EPISTLE XLIII.

To Leander Bishop of Hispalis (*Seville*)[8]

Gregory to Leander, &c.

I should have wished to reply to your letters with full application of mind, were I not so worn by the labour of my pastoral charge as to be more inclined to weep than to say anything. And this your Reverence will take care to understand and allow for in the very text of my letters, when I speak negligently to one whom I exceedingly love. For, indeed, I am in this place tossed by such billows of this world that I am in no wise able to steer into port the old and rotten ship of which, in the hidden dispensation of God, I have assumed the guidance. Now in front the billows rush in, now at the side heaps of foamy sea swell up, now from behind the storm follows on. And, disquieted in the midst of all this, I am compelled sometimes to steer in the very face of the opposing waters; sometimes, turning the ship aside, to avoid the threats of the billows slantwise. I groan, because I feel that through my negligence the bilgewater of vices increases, and, as the storm meets the vessel violently, the rotten planks already sound of shipwreck.

6 Rector patrimonii and defensor in Campania. See abov Ep. 39.

7 In Compania, *hodie Sorrento*.

8 Gregory had made the acquaintance of Leander, bishop of the Metropolitan See of Hispalis (*Seville*) in Spain, during his residence at Constantinople. It was at the instigation of Leander, together with the request of the monks who had followed him from his Roman Monastery to Constantinople, that he had begun, when there, to expound the book of Job. The earlier part of his "Moralium libri, sive Expositio in librum B. Job," had been delivered in oral discourses at Constantinople, but afterwards revised, arranged, and completed in thirty-five books. The whole, when finished, was addressed to Leander. All this appears from the "Epistola Missoria" prefixed to the completed treatise. Gregory evidently had a peculiar affection for Leander. Other epistles addressed to him are V. 49, and IX. 121. He is spoken of also in the Dialogues of Gregory, Lib. III. cap. 31, being there referred to as "dudum mihi in amicitiis familiariter iunctus."

With tears I remember how I have lost the placid shore of my rest, and with sighs I behold the land which still, with the winds of affairs blowing against me, I cannot reach. If, then, thou lovest me, dearest brother, stretch out to me in the midst of these billows the hand of thy prayer; that from helping me in my labours thou mayest, in very return for the benefit, be the stronger in thine own.

I cannot, however, at all fully express in words my joy on having learnt that our common son, the most glorious King Rechared, has been converted with most entire devotion to the Catholic faith[9]. In describing his character to me in thy letters thou hast made me love him, though I know him not. But, since you know the wiles of the ancient foe, how against conquerors he prepares all the fiercer war, let your Holiness keep watch the more warily over him, that he may accomplish what he has well begun, nor lift himself up for good works accomplished; that he may keep the faith which he has come to know by the merits also of his life, and shew by his works that he is a citizen of the eternal kingdom, to the end that after a course of many years he may pass from kingdom to kingdom.

But with respect to trine immersion in baptism, no truer answer can be given than what you have yourself felt to be right; namely that, where there is one faith, a diversity of usage does no harm to holy Church. Now we, in immersing thrice, signify the sacraments of the three days' sepulture; so that, when the infant is a third time lifted out of the water, the resurrection after a space of three days may be expressed. Or, if any one should perhaps think that this is done out of veneration for the supreme Trinity, neither so is there any objection to immersing the person to be baptized in the water once, since, there being one substance in three subsistences, it cannot be in any way reprehensible to immerse the infant in baptism either thrice or once, seeing that by three immersions the Trinity of persons, and in one the singleness of the Divinity may be denoted. But, inasmuch as up to this time it has been the custom of heretics to immerse infants in baptism thrice, I am of opinion that this ought not to be done among you; lest, while they number the immersions, they should divide the Divinity, and while they continue to do as they have been used to do, they should boast of having got the better of our custom.

Moreover, I send to your to me most sweet Fraternity the volumes of which I have appended a notice below. What I had spoken in exposition of the blessed Job, which you express in your letter your wish to have sent to you, being weak both in sense and language as I had delivered it in homilies, I have tried as I could to change into the form of a treatise, which is in course of being written out by scribes. And, were I not crippled by the haste of the bearer of these presents, I should have wished to transmit to you the whole without diminution; especially as I have written this same work for your Reverence, that I may be seen to have sweated in my labours for him whom I love above all others. Besides, if you find time allowed you from ecclesiastical engagements, you already know how it is with me: even though absent in the body, I behold thee always present with me; for I carry the image of thy countenance stamped within the bowels of my heart. Given in the month of May.

9 Reccared, the Visigoth King in Spain, had declared himself a Catholic A.D. 587 and formally renounced Arianism and adopted the Catholic Creed at the Council of Toledo, A.D. 589. The date of the letter before us, if rightly placed, is A.D. 591.

EPISTLE XLIV.

To Peter, Subdeacon of Sicily.

Gregory to Peter, &c.

With regard to our having so long delayed sending off thy messenger, we have been so occupied with the engagements of the Paschal festival that we have been unable to let him go sooner. But, with regard to the questions on which thou hast desired instruction, thou wilt learn below how, after fully considering them all, we have determined them.

We have ascertained that the peasants[1] of the Church are exceedingly aggrieved in respect of the prices of corn, in that the sum appointed them to pay is not kept in due proportion in times of plenty. And it is our will that in all times, whether the crops of corn be more or less abundant, the measure of proportion be according to the market price[2]. It is our will also that corn which is

1 *Rusticos ecclesiæ*; i.e. the native cultivaters of the land, called elsewhere *coloni*, and by Cicero (*In Verrem*), *aratores*. See *Proleg.*

2 It appears from Cicero, that, when the Romans annexed Sicily, they found the greater part of the land subject by ancient custom to a tithe of the corn and other produce, and that such tithe continued to be exacted by the Roman government, which derived thence its main revenue from the island: further, that the custom had grown up of allowing a pecuniary composition for the tithe, and that this custom, intended originally for the accommodation of the tithe payers, had been abused to their detriment by over valuation in years when corn was cheap. One of the charges against Verres was, that this had been done under him as Prætor. When wheat was selling in Sicily for two or at the most three sesterces per *modius*, the peasants had been made to compound for their tithes at the rate of three *denarii*, i.e. twelve sesterces (*Cic. in Verr. Divin.* 10; *Act* II. *Lib.* iii. 6, 18). The Roman Church having succeeded the Roman Government in the lordship of the "Patrimony of St. Peter," it appears that the Church officials had not been guiltless of similar unfair exactions. Hence the direction here in this Epistle that the valuations of the tithe in successive years should follow the market price.

lost by shipwreck be fully accounted for; but on condition that there be no neglect on thy part in transmitting it; lest, the proper time for transmitting it being allowed to pass by, loss should ensue from your fault[3]. Moreover, we have seen it to be exceedingly wrong and unjust that anything should be received from the peasants of the Church in the way of *sextariatics*[4], or that they should be compelled to give a larger *modius* than is used in the granaries of the Church. Wherefore we enjoin by this present warning that corn may never be received from the peasants of the Church in *modii* of more than eighteen *sextarii;* unless perchance there be anything that the sailors are accustomed to receive over and above, the consumption of which on board ship they themselves attest.

We have also ascertained that on some estates[5] of the Church a most unjust exaction is practised, in that three and a half [*modii*] in seventy are demanded by the farmers[6];—a thing shameful to be spoken of. And yet even this is not enough; but something besides is said to be exacted according to a custom of many years. This practice we altogether detest, and desire it to be utterly extirpated from the patrimony. But, whether in this or in other minute imposts, let thy Experience consider what is paid too much per pound, and what is in any way unfairly received from the peasants; and reduce all to a fixed payment, and, so far as the powers of the peasants go, let them make a payment in gross amounting to seventy-two[7]: and let neither grains[8] beyond the pound, nor an excessive pound, nor any further imposts beyond the pound, be exacted; but, through thy valuation, according as there is ability to pay, let the payment be made up to a certain sum, that so there may be in no wise any shameful exaction. But, lest after my death these very imposts, which we have disallowed as extras but allowed in augmentation of the regular payments, should again in any way be put on additionally, and so the sum of the payment should be found to be increased and the peasants be compelled to pay additional charges over and above what is due, we desire thee to draw up charters of security, to be signed by thee, declaring that each person is to pay such an amount, to the exclusion of grains (*siliquæ*), imposts, or granary dues. Moreover, whatever out of these several items used to accrue to the rector [sc. *patrimonii*], we will that by virtue of this present order it shall accrue to thee out of the total sum paid.

Before all things we desire thee carefully to attend to this; that no unjust weights be used in exacting payments. If thou shouldest find any, break them and cause true ones to be made. For my son the servant of God, Diaconus, has already found such as displeased him; but he had not liberty to change them. We will, then, that, saving excepted *cibaria* of small value[9], nothing else beyond the just weights be exacted from the husbandmen[1] of the Church.

Further, we have ascertained that the first charge of *burdatio*[2] exceedingly cripples our peasants, in that before they can sell the produce of their labour they are compelled to pay taxes; and, not having of their own to pay with, they borrow from public pawnbrokers[3], and pay a heavy consideration for the accommodation; whence it results that they are crippled by heavy expenses. Wherefore we enjoin by this present admonition that thy

3 This refers to the corn which was sent annually in large quantities to Rome, and on which the Romans were in a great measure dependent for their supply. Those in Sicily who furnished it were, it seems, responsible for its delivery, taking the risk of loss by sea. But it rested with the Church officials to provide for its being shipped; and, if any loss on the voyage ensued from their delay, the parties otherwise responsible were to be indemnified.

4 *Ex sextariaticis.* This appears to have been a technical term, denoting unjust exaction of the following kind. The peasants (*rustici*) on an estate had to supply, let us say, so many *modii* of corn to be shipped for Rome. But the *modius* varied in capacity. It is said originally to have contained sixteen *sextarii,* a sextarius being between a pint and a quart. But it appears below that one of eighteen *sextarii* was in use in the time of Gregory, and by him allowed. This limit, however, seems to have been sometimes exceeded, and herein consisted the abuse complained of. In a subsequent epistle (XIII. 34) a *modius* of even twenty-five *sextarii* is spoken of as having been in one case used:—"We understand that the *modius* by which the husbandmen (*coloni*) were compelled to give their corn was one of twenty-five *sextarii.*"

5 *Massis.* These *massæ* might include several farms (*fundi,* or *prædia*), and were let or leased to farmers (*conductores*), who made their profit out of them. Cf. xiv. 14, "Massam quæ Aquas Salvias nuncupatur cum omnibus fundis suis;" also v. 31, "Conductoribus massarum per Galliam."

6 *Conductores.* See last note.

7 *Pensantem ad septuagena bina.* It would seem that, in addition to the abuse of using *modii* of too large capacity, there was the additional one of exacting more *modii* than were legally due, three and a half being added to every seventy; i. e. one to every twenty. Cf. *Cicero in Verrem,* "Ab Siculis aratoribus, præter decumam, ternæ quinquagesimæ (i.e. three for every fifty) exigebantur." If the reading *septuagena bina* be correct, it would seem that Gregory allowed two to be added to every seventy perhaps on the ground of long-established custom. The readings, however, vary; and what was meant is uncertain.

8 *Siliquæ.* In Roman weights the *uncia* contained 144 *siliquæ,* and the *as* or *libra* 12 *unciæ.* The reference seems to be to cases in which the grain or other produce was rendered by weight. The just pound was not to be exceeded.

9 *Præter excepta et vilia cibaria.* Cibaria bears the general sense of victuals or provender; and specifically, "Cibarium, teste, Plin. I. 18, c. 9, ubi de siligine agit, dicitur farina quæ post pollinem seu florem excussum restat, postquam nihil aliud remanet nisi furfures: *the second sort of flour.* Eadem dicitur secundarium. Ex ea qui conficitur vocatur panis cibarius, quia solet esse communis vulgi cibus." Facciolati. The adjective *cibarius* is applied to provisions generally, wine, oil, bread, &c., of a common and inferior kind, and consumed by the common people. The reference in the text may be to refuse and inferior grain or other breadstuff, of which an excessive weight might be exacted to make up for its inferior quality.

1 *Colonis,* meaning the same as *rustici.* See note 1.

2 *Burdationis.* This appears to have been a kind of land tax, payable in the first instance, before the peasants had been able to convert their produce into money. "Burdatio est pensio quæ a rusticis præstatur prædii nomine, quod Burdam vocant, nostri Borde." Alteserra.

3 *Auctionariis.* "Mercator qui res suas auget; et proprie dicitur ille qui hic vel illic res parvas et veteres et tritas eruit, ut postea carius vendat." Du Cange.

Experience advance to them from the public fund all that they might have borrowed from strangers, and that it be repaid by the peasants of the Church by degrees as they may have wherewith to pay, lest, while for a time in narrow circumstances, they should sell at too cheap a rate what might afterwards have sufficed for the payment of the due, and even so not have enough.

It has come to our knowledge also that immoderate fees[4] are received on the marriages of peasants: concerning which we order that no marriage fees shall exceed the sum of one *solidus*. If any are poor, they should give even less; but if any are rich, let them by no means exceed the aforesaid sum of a *solidus*. And we desire no part of these marriage fees to be credited to our account, but that they should go to the benefit of the farmer (*conductorem*).

We have also ascertained that when some farmers die their relatives are not allowed to succeed them, but that their goods are withdrawn to the uses of the Church: with regard to which thing we decree that the relatives of the deceased who live on the property of the Church shall succeed them as their heirs, and that nothing shall be withdrawn from the substance of the deceased. But, if any one should leave young children, let discreet persons be chosen to take charge of their parents' goods, till they come to such an age as to be able to manage their own property.

We have ascertained also that, if any one of a family has committed a fault, he is required to make amends, not in his own person, but in his substance: concerning which practice we order that, whosoever has committed a fault, he shall be punished in his own person as he deserves[5]. Moreover, let no present (*commodum*) be received from him, unless perchance it be some trifle which may go to the profit of the officer who may have been sent to him. We have ascertained also that, as often as a farmer has taken away anything unjustly from his husbandman, it is indeed required from the farmer, but not restored to him from whom it was taken: concerning which thing we order that whatever may have been taken away by violence from any one of a family be restored to him from whom it was taken away, and not accrue to our profit, lest we ourselves should seem to be abettors of violence. Furthermore, we will that, if thy Experience should at any time despatch those who are under thy command in causes that arise beyond the limits of the patrimony, they may indeed receive small gratuities from those to whom they are sent; yet so that they themselves may have the advantage of them: for we would not have the treasury of the Church defiled by base gains. We also command thy Experience to see to this: that farmers never be appointed on the estates of the Church for a consideration (*commodum*); lest, a consideration being looked for, the farmers should be frequently changed; of which changing what else is the result but that the Church farms are never cultivated? But lest also the leases [i.e. by the Church to the farmers] be adjusted according to the sum of the payments due. We desire thee to receive no more from the estates of the Church on account of the store-houses and stores beyond what is customary; but let thine own stores which we have ordered to be procured be procured from strangers.

It has come to our ears that three pounds of gold have been unjustly taken away from Peter the farmer of Subpatriana; concerning which matter examine closely Fantinus the guardian (*defensorem*[6]); and, if they have manifestly been unjustly and improperly taken, restore them without any delay. We have also ascertained that the peasants have paid a second time the *burdation*[7] which Theodosius had exacted from them but had failed to pay over, so that they have been taxed twice. This was done because his substance was not sufficient for meeting his debt to the Church. But, since we are informed through our son, the servant of God Diaconus, that this deficiency can be made good out of his effects, we will that fifty-seven *solidi* be repaid to the peasants without any abatement, lest they should be found to have been taxed twice over. Moreover, if it is the case that forty *solidi* of his effects remain over and above what will indemnify the peasants (which sum thou art said also to have in thy hands), we will that they be given to his daughter, to enable her to recover her effects which she had pawned. We desire also her father's goblet (*batiolam*) to be restored to her.

The glorious *magister militum* Campanianus had left twelve *solidi* a year out of the Varronian estate to his notary John; and this we order thee to pay every year without any hesitation to the granddaughter of Euplus the farmer, although she may have received all the

4 *Commoda*. The word *commodum* denotes properly a bounty (as to soldiers over and above their pay), a gratuity, a voluntary offering, though used also for a stipend, or payment generally. The peasants (*rustici*) might not marry without permission. Cf. xii. 25, "ut eum districte debeas commonere ne filios suos quolibet ingenio vel excusatione foris alicubi in conjugio, sociare præsumat, sed in ea massa cui lege et conditione ligati sunt socientur." For such permission they were, it seems, accustomed to pay a fee, in theory perhaps voluntary, but virtually exacted as a due.

5 Because a fine would have to be paid out of the common substance of the family, and so all would be punished for the offence of one.

6 On the office of *defensores*, see *Proleg.*

7 See note 2.

chattels of the said Euplus, except perhaps his cash; and we desire thee also to give her out of his cash five-and-twenty *solidi.* A silver saucer[8] is said to have been pawned for one *solidus*, and a cup for six *solidi.* After interrogating Dominicus the secretary, or others who may know, redeem the pledge, and restore the aforesaid little vessels.

We thank thy Solicitude for that, after I had enjoined thee, in the business of my brother, to send him back his money, thou hast so consigned the matter to oblivion as if something had been said to thee by the last of thy slaves But now let even thy Negligence—I cannot say thy Experience—study to get this done; and whatever of his thou mayest find to be in the hands of Antoninus send back to him with all speed.

In the matter of Salpingus the Jew a letter has been found which we have caused to be forwarded to thee, in order that, after reading it and becoming fully acquainted with his case, and that of a certain widow who is said to be implicated in the same business, thou mayest make answer as may appear to thee just concerning the fifty-one *solidi* which are known to be returnable, so that the creditors may in no way be defrauded unjustly of the debts due to them.

A moiety of his legacy has been given to Antoninus; a moiety will be redeemed: which moiety we desire to be made up to him out of the common substance; and not to him only, but also to the guardians (*defensoribus*) and strangers (*pergrinis*) to whom he [the testator] has left anything under the title of a legacy. To the family (*familiæ*) also we desire the legacy to be paid; which, however, is our concern. Having, then, made up the account for our part, that is for three-quarters, make the payment[9].

We desire thee to give something out of the money of the Church of Canusium to the clergy of the same Church, to the end that they who now suffer from want may have some sustenance; and that, if it should please God that a bishop should be ordained, he may have a maintenance.

As to lapsed[1] priests, or any others of the clergy, we desire thee in dealing with their property to keep free from any contamination. But seek out the poorest regular monasteries which know how to live according to God, and consign the lapsed to penance in these monasteries; and let the property of the lapsed go to the benefit of the place in which they are consigned to penance, to the end that those who have the care of their correction may have aid themselves from their means. But, if they have relations, let their property be given to their legitimate relations; yet so that an allowance for those to whom they have been consigned for penance be sufficiently provided. But, if any of an ecclesiastical community, whether priests, levites, or monks, or clerics, or any others, shall have lapsed, we will that they be consigned to penance, but that the Church shall retain its claim to their property. Yet let them receive for their own use enough to maintain them during their penance, lest, if left destitute, they should be burdensome to the places whereto they have been consigned. If any have relations on the ecclesiastical domain, let their property be delivered to them, that it may be preserved in their hands subject to the Church's claim.

Three years ago the subdeacons of all the churches in Sicily, in accordance with the custom of the Roman Church, were forbidden all conjugal intercourse with their wives. But it appears to me hard and improper that one who has not been accustomed to such continency, and has not previously promised chastity, should be compelled to separate himself from his wife, and thereby (which God forbid) fall into what is worse. Hence it seems good to me that from the present day all bishops should be told not to presume to make any one a subdeacon who does not promise to live chastely; that so what was not of set purpose desired in the past may not be forcibly required, but that cautious provision may be made for the future. But those who since the prohibition of three years ago have lived continently with their wives are to be praised and rewarded, and exhorted to continue in their good way. But, as for those who since the prohibition have been unwilling to abstain from intercourse with their wives, we desire them not to be advanced to a sacred order; since no one ought to approach the ministry of the altar but one who has been of approved chastity before undertaking the ministry.

For Liberatus the tradesman, who has commended himself to the Church, dwelling on the Cincian estate, we desire thee to make an annual provision; which provision do thou estimate thyself as to what it ought to be, that it may be reported to me and charged in thy accounts. With regard to the present indiction I have already got information from our son the servant of God Diaconus.

---

8 *Suppositorium.* The word itself might denote anything put under another, or supporting another. Here its being associated with a cup (*calix*), and both being called small vessels (*vascula*), suggests the translation in the text.

9 The meaning of these directions is obscure owing to our ignorance of the circumstances.

1 The word *lapsi* was the regular one for denoting clergy, or others, who had fallen into sin rendering them liable to excommunication.

One John, a monk, has died and left Fantinus the guardian (*defensorem*) his heir to the extent of one half. Hand over to the latter what has been left him, but charge him not to presume to do the like again. But appoint what he should receive for his work, so that it be not fruitless to him; and let him remember that one who lives on the pay of the Church should not pant after private gains. But, if anything should accrue to the Church, without sin and without the lust of concupiscence, through those who transact the business of the Church, it is right that these should not be without fruit of their labour. Still let it be reserved for our judgment how they should be remunerated[2].

As to the money of Rusticianus, look thoroughly into the case, and carry out what appears to thee to be just. Admonish the magnificent Alexander[3] to conclude the cause between himself and holy Church; which if he peradventure shall neglect to do, do thou, in the fear of God and with honour preserved, bring this same cause to an issue as thou art able We desire thee also to expend something in this business; and, if it can be done, let him be spared the cost of what has to be given to others, provided he terminates the cause which he has with us.

Restore without any delay the donation of the handmaiden of God[4] who has lapsed and been sent into a monastery, to the end that (as I have said above) the same place that bears the toil of attending to her may have provision for her from what she has. But recover also whatever of hers is in the hands of others, and hand it over to the aforesaid monastery

Send to us the payments of Xenodochius of Via Nova to the amount thou hast told us of, since thou hast them by thee. But give something, according to thy discretion, to the agent whom thou hast deputed in the same patrimony.

Concerning the handmaiden of God who was with Theodosius, by name Extranea, it seems to me that thou shouldest give her an allowance, if thou thinkest it advantageous, or at any rate return to her the donation which she made. The house of the monastery which Antoninus had taken from the monastery, giving thirty *solidi* for it, restore thou without the least delay, the money being repaid. After thoroughly investigating the truth restore the onyx phials[5], which I send back to thee by the bearer of these presents.

If Saturninus is at liberty and not employed with thee, send him to us. Felix, a farmer under the lady Campana, whom she had left free and ordered to be exempt from examination, said that seventy-two *solidi* had been taken from him by Maximus the sub-deacon, for paying which he asserted that he sold or pledged all the property that he had in Sicily. But the lawyers said that he could not be exempt from examination concerning acts of fraud. However, when he was returning to us from Campania, he perished in a storm. We desire thee to seek out his wife and children, to redeem whatever he had pledged, repay the price of what he had sold, and moreover provide them with some maintenance; seeing that Maximus had sent the man into Sicily and there taken from him what he alleged. Ascertain, therefore, what has been taken from him, and restore it without any delay to his wife and children. Read all these things over carefully, and put aside all that familiar negligence of thine. My writings which I have sent to the peasants cause thou to be read over throughout all the estates, that they may know in what points to defend themselves, under our authority, against acts of wrong; and let either the originals or copies be given them. See that thou observe everything without abatement: for, with regard to what I have written to thee for the observance of justice, I am absolved; and, if thou art negligent, thou art guilty. Consider the terrible Judge who is coming: and let thy conscience now anticipate His advent with fear and trembling, lest it should then fear [not?] without cause, when heaven and earth shall tremble before Him. Thou hast heard what I wish to be done: see that thou do it.

[2] It was against monastic rule for monks or nuns to retain property of their own after profession, or the power of disposing of it by will. It became the common property of the monastery. Cf. *Justinian*, *Novell.* V. c. 38. See also what was said above about the goods of lapsed members of religious communities. In a subsequent Epistle (IX. 7), Gregory annulls a will that had been made by an abbess Sirica. The case of one Probus, an abbot (Appendix, *Ep.* IX.), who was allowed to make a will, is no real exception to the rule. For Gregory gave him special permission to do so on his own petition, on the equitable ground that at the time of his hasty ordination as abbot, not having been a monk previously, he had neglected to make provision for his son by will, as he had intended to do, and as he had then a right to do. In the case before us Gregory acts with lenient consideration. Though condemning the bequest of the monk John to the guardian Fantinus, he allows the latter to take it on the ground that he deserved, but had not so far received, a proper remuneration for his services.

[3] *Magnificum virum.* Who this Alexander was is not known. His designation implies a position of rank. An Alexander appears afterwards as Prætor of Sicily (VI. 8): but the Prætor of this year was Justinus (see above, Ep. II.), who was apparently succeeded by Libertinus (III. 38).

[4] *Ancillæ Dei.* So were called, not professed nuns only, but also others who devoted themselves to virginity and religious lives Gregory's own aunts, Tarsilla and Æmiliana, who lived as dedicated virgins in their own home. were instances. See *Proleg.* p. xiv.

[5] *Amulas.* "Amula, minor ama. vas vinarium, in quo sacra oblatio continetur." Du Cange.

EPISTLE XLVI.

To Peter the Subdeacon.

Gregory to Peter, &c.

The divine precepts admonish us to love our neighbours as ourselves; and, seeing that we are enjoined to love them with this charity, how much more ought we to succour them by supplies to their carnal needs, that we may relieve their distress, if not in all respects, yet at least with some support. Inasmuch, then, as we have found that the son of the most worthy Godiscalchus is in distress, not only from loss of sight, but also from want of food, we hold it necessary to provide for him as far as possible. Wherefore we enjoin thy Experience by this present order to supply to him for sustaining life twenty-four *modii* of wheat every year, and also twelve *modii* of beans and twenty *decimates*[6] of wine; which may afterwards be debited in thy accounts. So act, therefore, that the bearer of these presents may have to complain of no delay in receiving the gifts of the Lord, and that thou mayest be found partaker in the well administered benefit.

EPISTLE XLVII.

To Virgilius, Bishop of Arelate *(Arles)* and Theodorus, Bishop of Massilia *(Marseilles)*.

Gregory to Virgilius, Bishop of Arelate, and Theodorus, Bishop of Massilia, in Gaul.

Though the opportunity of a suitable time and suitable persons has failed me so far for writing to your Fraternity and duly returning your salutation, the result has been that I can now at one and the same time acquit myself of what is due to love and fraternal relationship, and also touch on the complaint of certain persons which has reached us, with respect to the way in which the souls of the erring should be saved. Very many, though indeed of the Jewish religion, resident in this province, and from time to time travelling for various matters of business to the regions of Massilia, have apprized us, that many of the Jews settled in those parts have been brought to the font of baptism more by force than by preaching. Now, I consider the intention in such cases to be worthy of praise, and allow that it proceeds from the love of our Lord. But I fear lest this same intention, unless adequate enforcement from Holy Scripture accompany it, should either have no profitable result, or even (which God forbid) the loss of the souls which we wish to save should further ensue. For, when any one is brought to the font of baptism, not by the sweetness of preaching, but by compulsion, he returns to his former superstition, and dies the worse from having been born again. Let, therefore, your Fraternity stir up such men by frequent preaching, to the end that through the sweetness of their teacher they may desire the more to change their old life. For so our purpose is rightly accomplished, and the mind of the convert returns not again to his former vomit. Wherefore discourse must be addressed to them, such as may burn up the thorns of error in them, and illuminate what is dark in them by preaching, so that your Fraternity may through your frequent admonition receive a reward for them, and lead them, so far as God may grant it, to the regeneration of a new life.

6 "*Decimatas* vini duas pensantes per unamquamque decimatam libras 60 (Ap. Anastasium in Hadriano) . . . mensuræ vinariæ species videtur." Du Cange.

EPISTLE XLVIII.

To Theodorus, Duke of Sardinia.

Gregory to Theodorus, &c.

The justice which you bear in your mind you ought to shew in the light of your deeds. Now Juliana, abbess of the monastery of Saint Vitus which Vitula of venerable memory had once built, has intimated to us that possession of the aforesaid monastery is claimed by Donatus, your official; who, seeing himself to be fortified by your patronage, scorns to have resort to a judicial examination of the case. But now let your Glory enjoin this same official, with the aforesaid hand-maiden of God, to submit the matter to arbitration to the end that whatever may be decided as to the question in dispute by the judgment of the arbitrators may be carried into effeet; so that, whatever he may find he has to lose or keep, what he does may not be done as a deed of virtue, but set down to the justice of the law.

Further, Pompeiana, a religious lady, who is known to have established a monastery in her own house, has complained that the mother of her deceased son-in-law wishes to annul his will, to the end that her son's last disposition of his property may be made of none effect. On this account we hold it necessary with paternal charity to exhort your Glory to lend yourself willingly, with due regard to justice, to pious causes, and kindly order that whatever these persons have a rightful claim to be secured to them. Now, we beseech the Lord to direct the way of your life propitiously, and grant you a prosperous administration of your dignified office.

EPISTLE XLIX.

To Honoratus, Deacon[7].

Gregory to Honoratus, &c.

Since we have undertaken, however undeserving, a place of government, it is our duty to succour our brethren in need, so far as our power extends. Januarius, then, our brother and fellow-bishop of the metropolitan city of Caralis (*Cagliari*), has been here in the city of Rome, and informed us that the glorious *magister militum*, Theodorus, who is known to have received the dukedom of the island of Sardinia, is doing many things there contrary to the commands of our most pious lords, whereby with fitting clemency and gentleness they removed many hardships of proprietors, or of citizens of their empire. Wherefore we desire you at a suitable time to represent the case to our most pious lords in accordance with what the provincials of the aforesaid island justly and reasonably demand; seeing that on a previous occasion also their sacred imperial letters were sent to the glorious *Magister militum* Edancius, who was in the seventh indiction duke of Sardinia, in which they ordered all these present grievances to be redressed, to the end that their commands, proceeding from the bountifulness of their piety, might be observed unshaken by dukes who might come in course of time to be in power, and that the benefit thereof might not be squandered away by administrators; that so a quiet life might be led under the clement empire of our lords, and for the ordinance which with tranquil mind they grant to their subjects they might receive multiplied compensation at the coming of the eternal judge.

EPISTLE L.

To Anthemius the Subdeacon[8].

Gregory to Anthemius, &c.

Even as, through the ordering of God as it hath pleased Him, we have received the place of government, so ought we to be solicitous for the souls committed to us. Now we find that in the Eumorphian island[9], in which, as is well known, there is an oratory of the blessed Peter, Prince of the Apostles, a large number of men with their wives from various patrimonies have fled to it for refuge, through stress of barbarian ferocity[1] This we consider inexpedient: for, there being other places of refuge near at hand, why should women have their abode there with monks? Wherefore we enjoin thy Experience by this present order from this time forward to allow no woman, whether she be under ecclesiastical jurisdiction or any other, to take up her abode or tarry there; but let them provide for themselves a place of refuge (there being, as has been said above, so many in the neighbourhood) wherever they may choose; so that all intercourse with women may henceforth be put an end to; lest, if we should desist from taking all the care we can, and guarding against the snares of the enemy, we henceforth (which God forbid) should be culpable in case of anything wrong taking place. Delay not, therefore, to give to the abbot Felix, the bearer of these presents, one thousand five hundred pounds of lead, which he is known to be in want of in the same island, which may be charged afterwards in thy accounts, when the whole quantity shall be known. So proceed, then, that thou mayest provide thyself with some, if any can be profitably used for the buildings of the same island. Moreover, since congregations of monks in the islands are exposed to hardship, we forbid boys under eighteen years of age to be received into these monasteries. Or, if there are any now there, let thy Experience remove them, and send them to the city of Rome. We desire thee in all respects to observe this in Palmaria also and the other islands.

EPISTLE LII.

To Symmachus the Defensor[2].

Gregory to Symmachus, &c.

My son Boniface the deacon has told me that thy Experience had written to say that a monastery built by Labina, a religious lady, is now ready for monks to be settled in it. And indeed I praised thy solicitude; but we wish that some other place than that which has been assigned for the purpose should be provided; but with the condition, in view of the insecurity of the time, that one above the sea be looked out for, which is either fortified by its position, or at all events can be fortified without much labour. So may we send monks thither, to the end that the island itself, hitherto without a monastery, may be improved by having this way of life upon it.

For carrying out and providing for this business we have given directions to Horosius, the bearer of this present order, with whom thy Experience must go round the

---

7 Honoratus was Gregory's *apocrisiarius* at Constantinople.

8 Anthemius was *Denfensor ecclesiæ* in Campania.

9 An island, as well as Palmaria mentioned afterwards, near the Campanian coast, and hence under the care of Anthemius.

1 Alluding to the Lombards, who at this time were ravaging Italy.

2 I.e. of the Church in Corsica, as appears from the letter.

shores of Corsica, and if any more suitable place in the possession of any private person should be found, we are prepared to give a suitable price, that we may be able to make some secure arrangement. We have enjoined the aforesaid Horosius to proceed to the island Gorgonia; and let thy Experience accompany him, and do you so avenge the evils that we have ascertained to have found entrance there that through the punishment you shall inflict the aforesaid island may remain corrected for the future also. Let the same abbot Horosius set in order the monasteries of this island, and so hasten to return to us. Let, then, thy Experience so act that in both these matters, that is, both in providing for monasteries in Corsica, and in correcting the monks of Gorgonia, thou mayest make haste to obey, not our will, but that of Almighty God.

Moreover we desire that the priests who abide in Corsica shall be forbidden to have any intercourse with women, except it may be a mother, or a sister, or a wife, towards whom chastity should be observed[3]. But to the three persons about whom thy Experience has written to my son the aforesaid deacon Boniface, give whatsoever thou deemest sufficient for them, since they are in grievous need; and this we will allow thee afterwards in thy accounts. Given in the month of July.

EPISTLE LVI.

To Peter, Subdeacon.

Gregory to Peter, &c.

Being exceedingly desirous of observing the festivals of saints, we have thought it needful to address this our letter of direction to thy Experience, informing thee that we have arranged for the dedication with all solemnity, with the help of the Lord, in the month of August, of the Oratory of the Blessed Mary lately built in the cell of brethren where the abbot Marinianus is known to preside, to the end that what we have begun may through the Lord's operation be completed. But, inasmuch as the poverty of that cell requires that we should assist in that day of festival, we therefore desire thee to give for celebrating the dedication, to be distributed to the poor, ten *solidi* in gold, thirty *amphoræ* of wine, two hundred lambs, two *orcæ* of oil, twelve wethers, and a hundred hens, which may be afterwards charged in thy accounts. Provide therefore for this being done at once without any delay, that our desires, God granting it, may take speedy effect.

EPISTLE LVII.

To Severus, Bishop.

Gregory to Severus, &c.

We learn from thy Fraternity's epistle that, with regard to the choice of a bishop, some are agreed in favour of Ocleatinus, with whom, since we disallow him, they need not further concern themselves[4]. But give notice to the inhabitants of that city that, if they should find any one in their own Church fit for that work, they all transfer their choice to him. Otherwise the bearer of these presents will point out a person, of whom I have told him, in favour of whom the notification of the election should be made. Do you, moreover, be prudent and careful with regard to your visitation of the same Church, that its property may be preserved inviolate, and its interests attended to after the accustomed manner under your management.

EPISTLE LVIII.

To Arsicinus Duke, the Clergy, Nobility, and Common People (*ordini et plebi*) of the City of Ariminum.

Gregory to Arsicinus, &c.

How ready is the devotion of your love in expectation of a pontiff the text of the report which you have addressed to us shews. But, since the ordainer ought in such cases to be exceedingly careful, we are watching over this case with due deliberation. And so we warn your Charity by this present writing that no

3 The clergy who had been married before ordination were not required to put away their wives. Can. Apostol. V. expressly forbids their doing so under pain of excommunication. The 3rd Nicene Canon, which forbids any bishop, presbyter, or any of the clergy, to have a woman dwelling with him except a mother, or sister, or aunt, or such persons only as are above suspicion, does not touch the case of wives, being directed against the custom of the clergy having females who were neither wives nor of their own kindred, to live with them, who were called *synesactæ*, or *agapetæ*. Accordingly a law of Honorius and the younger Theodosius, made in pursuance of the Nicene Canon, adds to the above injunction, "That those who were married before their husbands were ordained should not be relinquished upon pretence of chastity, it being reasonable that those should be joined to the clergy who by their conversation had made their husbands worthy of the priesthood" (*Cod. Theodor. lib.* xvi. *tit.* ii. *de Episc.* l. xliv. Also *Cod. Just. lib.* i. *tit.* iii. *leg.* xix. See Bingham, Bk. vi. ch. ii. sect. 13). But in the West it was now the established rule that neither bishops, priests, nor deacons should have conjugal intercourse with their wives after ordination: and it has been seen under Ep. XLIV. how this rule had been extended to subdeacons. Gregory tells us in his Dialogues (*Lib.* iv. cap. 11) of a holy presbyter in the province of Nursia, who at the time of his ordination had a wife (*presbyteram suam*), whom he thenceforth loved as a sister, but avoided as an enemy, never suffering her to come near him for fear of temptation: and he adds, "For this is the way of holy men, that in order to keep far away from what is unlawful they cut themselves off even from what is lawful." Cf. IX. 60. "Hoc tantummodo adjecto ut hi, sicut canonica decrevit auctoritas, uxores quas caste debent regere non relinquant."

4 The vacant See referred to was that of Ariminum. See following epistle. Severus, who had been commissioned to act as visitor during the vacancy, was bishop of Ficulum, or Ficocle in the same province. See V. 25.

one need trouble himself to apply to us in favour of Ocleatinus: but, if any one is found in your own city to undertake this work with profit, so that he cannot be objected to by us, let your choice concur in his favour. But, if no one should be found fit for it, we have mentioned to the bearers of these presents one to whom you may no less accord your consent. But do you with one accord pray faithfully, that, whosoever may be ordained, he may be able both to be profitable to you and to display priestly service worthy of our God.

EPISTLE LXI.

To Gennadius, Patrician and Exarch of Africa.

Gregory to Gennadius, &c.

That you have unceasingly the fear of God before your eyes, and pursue justice, the subdued necks of enemies testify; but, that the grace of Christ may keep your Glory in the same prosperity, restrain, as you have been wont, with speedy prohibition whatever things you discover to be committed wrongfully, so that, fortified with the arms of justice, you may overcome hostile attacks with the power of faith, which is the top of all virtue. Now Marinianus, our brother and fellow-bishop of the city of Turris[5] has tearfully represented to us that the poor of his city are being vexed everywhere, and afflicted by expenses in the way of gifts or payments[6]; and further that the religious[7] of his church endure serious molestation from the men of Theodorus the *magister militum*, and suffer bodily injuries; and that this thing is breaking out to such a pitch that (shocking to say) they are thrust into prison, and that he himself also is seriously hindered by the aforesaid glorious person in causes pertaining to his Church. How opposed such things are, if indeed they are true, to the discipline of the republic you yourselves know. And, since it befits your Excellency to amend all these things, greeting your Eminence I demand of you that you suffer them to be done no more; but straitly order him to abstain from harming the Church, and that none be aggrieved by burdens laid upon them, or payments[8], beyond what reason allows, and that, if there should be any suits, they be determined not by the terror of power, but by order of law. I pray you, then, so correct all these things, the Lord inspiring you, by the menace of your injunction that the glorious Theodorus and his men may abstain from such things, if not out of regard to rectitude, yet at any rate out of fear inspired by your command; that so, to the advancement of your credit and reward, justice with liberty may flourish in the parts committed to your charge.

EPISTLE LXII.

To Januarius, Archbishop of Caralis (Cagliari) in Sardinia.

Gregory to Januarius, &c.

If our Lord Himself by the testimony of Holy Scripture declares Himself to be the husband of widows and father of orphans, we also, the members of His body, ought with the soul's supreme affection to set ourselves to imitate the head, and saving justice, to stand by orphans and widows if need be. And, having been given to understand that Catella, a religious woman who has a son serving here in the holy Roman Church over which under God we preside, is being troubled by the exactions and molestations of certain persons, we think it needful to exhort your Fraternity by this letter not to refuse (saving justice) to afford your protection to this same woman, knowing that by things of this kind you both make the Lord your debtor and bind us to you the more in the bonds of charity. For we wish the causes of the aforesaid woman, whether now or in future, to be terminated by your judgment, that she may be relieved from the annoyance of legal proceedings, and yet be by no means excused from submitting to a just judgment. Now I pray the Lord to direct your life in a prosperous course towards Himself, and Himself to bring you in His mercy to the kingdom of glory which is to come.

EPISTLE LXIII.

To Januarius, Bishop of Caralis (*Cagliari*) in Sardinia[9].

Gregory to Januarius, &c.

Though your Fraternity in the zeal of right-

---

5 *Turritana civitas*, a city in Sardinia, called by Pliny (lib. iii. c. 7) *Turris Lybissonis*, and by Ptolemy (lib. iii. c. 5) *Turris Byssonis*.

6 *Commodalibus dispendiis*. The word *commodum* is used not only for a stipend, or a present or gratuity, but also for exacted payments, "Pro quavis pensitatione vel etiam exactione usurpat Gregor. M." Du Cange.

7 *Religiosos ecclesiae*. By the terms *religiosi* and *religiosæ* were denoted not only monks, nuns, dedicated virgins, and clergy, but also other persons devoted to piety and good works in connection with the Church. Cf. xi. 54, "laico religioso." See *reff.* in Index under *Religiosus*.

8 *Angariis seu commodis*. *Angarium*, or *angaria*, denotes any forced service imposed on people, either rendered in person or in money payment. See also V. 8, note 4.

9 Other letters addressed to or relating to this bishop, who was an old man of very unsatisfactory character, are I. 63; II. 49; III. 36; IV. 8, 9, 15, 26, 27, 29; V. 2; IX. 1, 2, 3, 6, 7, 8, 25, 65; XIV. 2.

eousness gives fitting attention to the protection of divers persons, yet we believe that you will be the more prone to succour those whom a letter from us may commend to you. Know then that Pompeiana, a religious woman, has represented to us through one of her people that she endures many grievances continually and unreasonably from certain men, and on this account has petitioned us to commend her in our letters to you. Wherefore, greeting your Fraternity with the affection of charity that is due to you, we have felt that we must needs commend the aforesaid woman to you, that, with due regard to justice, thy Fraternity may not allow her to be aggrieved in any way contrary to equity, or to be subjected to any expense unadvisedly. But if it should happen that she has any suits, let the matter of dispute be debated before chosen arbitrators, and whatsoever shall be decided, let it be so carried into effect quietly through your assistance that both reward may accrue to you for such a work, and she who has been commended by our letters may rejoice in having found justice.

EPISTLE LXVI.

To Felix, Bishop of Messana (*Messene*).

Gregory to Felix, &c.

Customs which are found to bring a burden upon churches it becomes us in our consideration to discontinue, lest any should be forced to contribute to quarters from which they ought rather to look for contributions. Accordingly, it is thy duty to preserve intact the custom of the clergy and others, and to transmit to them every year what has been accustomed: but for the future we forbid thee to transmit anything to us. And, since we take no delight in presents (*xeniis*)[1], we have received with thanks the *Palmatianæ*[2] which thy Fraternity has sent us, but have caused them to be sold for an adequate price, which we have transmitted separately to thy Fraternity, for fear lest thou shouldest have felt the expense. Further, since we have learnt that thy Charity is desirous of coming to us, we admonish thee by the present letter not to take the trouble of coming: but pray for us, that the more we are separated by length of way, the more we may be joined one to another in mind, with the help of Christ, by charity; to the end that, aiding each other by mutual supplication, we may resign our office unimpaired to the Judge that is to come.

EPISTLE LXVII.

To Peter, Subdeacon.

Gregory to Peter, &c.

If with kind disposition we meet the needs of our neighbours by shewing compassion, we shall undoubtedly find the Lord mercifully inclined to our petitions. Now we have learnt that Pastor, who labours under exceeding weakness of sight, having a wife and two slaves, who also had formerly been with the glorious lady Jonatha, is suffering from great need. Wherefore, we admonish thy Experience, by the writing of this present order, not to delay giving him for his sustenance three hundred *modii* of wheat, and also as many *modii* of beans, which may afterwards be charged in thy accounts. So act, then, as both thyself to obtain the benefit of reward for thy good service, and to carry our orders into effect. In the month of August.

EPISTLE LXXII.

To Peter, Subdeacon.

Gregory to Peter, &c.

Thou hast learnt from a former letter[3] that we have desired our brethren and fellow-bishops dwelling in the island of Sicily to assemble here for the anniversary of the blessed Peter the apostle. But, seeing that their suit with the magnificent Justin the ex-praetor[4] has meanwhile hindered them, and that there is not now sufficient time for coming and returning, we do not wish them to be troubled before winter. But Gregory of Agrigentum, Leo of Catana, and Victor of Panormus, we by all means desire to come to us before winter[5]. Further, get together from strangers[6] corn of this year's growth to the value of fifty pounds of gold, and lay it up in Sicily in places where it will not rot, that we may send thither in the month of February as many ships as we can to convey this corn to us. But, in case of our delaying to send ships, do thou thyself provide some, and, with the help of the Lord, transmit this same corn to us in February, with the exception, however, of the

[1] See II. 23, note 8.

[2] Probably *vestes palmatæ*, i.e. robes interwoven or embroidered with palm leaves.

[3] See Ep. XXXVI.

[4] See Ep. II. If this Epistle is rightly assigned to the ninth Indiction, the title *ex-prætor* may possibly be an error in the text, since Justin is still addressed as *prætor* in the following Indiction (II. 33). Libertinus appears to have succeeded him as Prætor of Sicily in the eleventh Indiction. See III. 38.

[5] Two of these bishops, Gregory and Leo, are referred to afterwards as having been at Rome to answer to certain charges. See II. 33, and III. 12.

[6] *Extraneis*, i.e. growers or vendors of corn outside the patrimony of the Church.

corn which we expect to have sent to us now, according to custom, in the months of September or October. Let thy Experience, then, so proceed that, without annoyance to any husbandman (*colonus*) of the Church[7], the corn may be collected, since there has been here such a scanty crop that, unless by God's help corn be collected from Sicily, there is a serious prospect of famine. But keep guard in all ways over the ships that have always been assigned to the use of Holy Church, as the letters also addressed to thee by the glorious ex-consul Leo concur in directing thee to do. Moreover, many come hither desiring sundry lands or islands belonging to our Church to be leased to them; and some, indeed, we refuse, but to others we have already granted their request. But let thy Experience see to the advantage of Holy Church, remembering that thou hast before the most sacred body of the blessed apostle Peter received power over his patrimony. And, though letters should reach you from hence, allow nothing to be done in any way to the disadvantage of the patrimony, since we neither remember to have given, nor are disposed to give away, any thing without good reason.

EPISTLE LXXIV.

To Gennadius, Patrician and Exarch of Africa.

Gregory to Gennadius, &c.

As the Lord hath made your Excellency to shine with the light of victories in the military wars of this life, so ought you to oppose the enemies of the Church with all activity of mind and body, to the end that from both kinds of triumph your reputation may shine forth more and more, when in forensic wars, too, you firmly resist the adversaries of the Catholic Church in behalf of the Christian people, and bravely fight ecclesiastical battles as warriors of the Lord. For it is known that men heretical in religion, if they have liberty allowed them to do harm (which God forbid), rise strenuously against the catholic faith, to the end that they may transfuse, if they can, the poison of their heresy to the corrupting of the members of the Christian body. For we have learnt that they are lifting up their necks against the Catholic Church, the Lord being opposed to them, and desire to pervert the faith of the Christian profession. But let your Eminence suppress their attempts, and subdue their proud necks to the yoke of rectitude[8]. Moreover, order the council of catholic bishops to be admonished not to appoint their primate on the ground of his standing, without regard to the merits of his life, since before God it is not the more distinguished rank, but the action of a better life, that is approved[9]. But let the primate himself live, not, as is customary, here and there in the country, but in one city according to their selection, to the end that he may be better able to bring to bear the influence of the dignity that has fallen to him in resisting the Donatists. Moreover, if any from the Council of Numidia should desire to come to the Apostolic See, permit them to do so; and stop any who may be disposed to bring charges against their character. Great increase of glory will accrue to your Excellency with the Creator, if through you the union of the divided churches could be restored. For when He beholds the gifts granted by Him given back to His glory, He bestows gifts so much the more abundantly as He sees the dignity of His religion to be thereby enlarged. Furthermore, bestowing on you, as is due, the affection of our paternal charity, we beseech the Lord to make your arm strong for subduing your enemies, and to sharpen your soul with zeal for the faith like the edge of a quivering sword.

EPISTLE LXXV.

To Gennadius, Patrician, and Exarch throughout Africa.

Gregory to Gennadius, Patrician, &c.

Had not such great success of the military exploits of your Excellency arisen from the merit of your faith and from the grace of the Christian religion, it would not have been so greatly to be wondered at, since we know that the like has been granted to military leaders of old time. But when, God granting it, you forestall future victories, not by carnal provision, but rather by prayers, it becomes a matter of astonishment how your glory comes down upon you,

---

7 See I. 44, note 1.

8 The heretics (so called, though they were really rather schismatics than heretics) were the Donatists, who still lingered in Africa in spite of imperial edicts for their suppression. What Gregory here urges the Exarch to do is to put in force the existing laws against them. A series of imperial laws against the Donatists will be found in *Cod. Theod.* Bk. xvi. *tit.* 5, that of Honorius, A.D. 414, being especially severe.

9 It was the immemorial custom in the provinces of Africa generally for the senior bishop of the province according to the date of his consecration to be appointed primate, instead of the bishop of the civil metropolis being such in virtue of his See, as was the rule elsewhere. (The province of Africa proper, or Africa Proconsularis, was however an exception; for in it the bishop of Carthage was always the primate). Hence in Africa the designation Metropolitan was not used, but that of Primate or Senior (*Senex*). Gregory here, though allowing the old custom of movable primacies, forbids the necessary election of the senior bishop: and this in order to guard against the appointment of unfit persons. His main motive, as appears from Epistle LXXVI., addressed to the bishops of the province of Numidia, was to preclude the elevation to the primacy of any bishop who had once been a Donatist. For in it he allows the retention of the old African custom in all respects, save only that no bishop who had been a Donatist was ever to be appointed primate.

not from counsels of this world, but from God, who bestows it from above. For where is not the renown of your deserts in people's mouths? And report goes that it is not from a desire of shedding blood that you constantly court these wars, but for the sake of extending the republic in which we see that God is worshipped, to the end that the name of Christ may be spread abroad through subject nations by preaching of the faith. For, as your outward deeds of valour make you eminent in this life, so also the inward adornment of your character, proceeding from a clean heart, glorifies you in making you partaker of celestial joys to come. For we have learnt that your Excellency has done very many things of advantage for feeding the sheep of the blessed Peter, Prince of the apostles, so as to have restored to him no small portions of his patrimony, which had been denuded of their proper cultivators, by supplying them with Datitian settlers. Whatever, then, with Christian disposition you confer on him, you receive retribution for through hope in the judgment to come. Wherefore we have thought fit to commend to your Eminence Hilarus[1], who is also the bearer of these presents, that you may bestow on him (though ever with regard to justice) your accustomed affection in matters wherein he may intimate his need of your help. Now, addressing to you the greeting of our paternal charity, we beseech our God and Saviour mercifully to protect your Eminence for the consolation of the holy republic, and to fortify you with the strength of His arm for spreading His name more and more through the neighbouring nations.

EPISTLE LXXVII.

To all the Bishops of Numidia.

Gregory to all the Bishops of Numidia.

If ever, most dear brethren in Christ, a troublesome mixture of tares intrudes itself among green corn, it is necessary for the hand of the husbandman to root it up entirely, lest the future fruit of the fertile corn should be obstructed. Wherefore let us too, who, however unworthy, have undertaken the cultivation of the field of the Lord, hasten to render the corn pure from all offence of tares, that the field of the Lord may fructify with more abundant increase. Now you requested through Hilarus our chartulary[2] from our predecessor of blessed memory that you might retain all the customs of past time, which, from the beginnings of the ordinances of the blessed Peter, Prince of the apostles, long antiquity has so far retained. And we, indeed, according to the tenour of your representation, allow your custom (so long as it clearly makes no claim to the prejudice of the catholic faith) to remain undisturbed, whether as to constituting primates or as to other points; save that with respect to those who attain to the episcopate from among the Donatists, we by all means forbid them to be advanced to the dignity of primacy, even though their standing should denote them for that position[3]. But let it suffice them to take care of the people committed to them, without aiming at the topmost place of the primacy in preference to those prelates whom the Catholic faith hath both taught and engendered in the bosom of the Church. Do you, therefore, most dear brethren, anticipate our admonitions in the zeal of the charity of the Lord, knowing that the strict Judge will bring into examination all we do, and will approve every one of us with regard not to the prerogative of a higher rank, but to the merits of our works. I beseech you, therefore, love ye one another mutually, having peace among yourselves in Christ, and with one purpose of heart oppose ye heretics and enemies of the Church. Be ye solicitous for the souls of your neighbours: persuade all ye can to faith by the preaching of charity, holding before them also the terror of the future judgment; inasmuch as ye are appointed to be shepherds, and the Lord of the flocks expects from the shepherds to whom He has committed them the fruit of a multiplied flock. And if He should foresee an augmentation of His own flock through your bestowal of more diligent care upon it, He will assuredly adorn you with manifold gifts of the heavenly kingdom. Furthermore, addressing to you the greeting of fraternal love, I pray the Lord that He would make you, whom He has chosen to be shepherds of souls, worthy in His sight, and Himself so order our deeds here that He may accept them as they deserve in the future life.

EPISTLE LXXVIII.

To Leo, Bishop in Corsica.

Gregory to Leo, &c.

Our pastoral charge constrains us to come with anxious consideration to the succour of a church that is destitute of the control of a priest[4]. And, inasmuch as we have learnt

[1] See I. 77, note 2.

[2] "Chartularius. Qui chartas tractant, qui chartis deserviunt. . . . Dignitas ecclesiastica etiam fuit." Du Cange. This Hilary is commended to Gennadius the Exarch of Africa, I. 75, and again mentioned as Gregory's Chartulary in Africa, II. 48; X. 37; XII. 28, 29.

[3] See I. 74, note 9.

[4] *Sacerdotis.* The term includes bishops as well as presbyters, and is used in this and the two following Epistles, as usually

that the church of Saona for many years, since the death of its pontiff, has been thus entirely destitute, we have thought it needful to enjoin on thy Fraternity the work of visiting it, to the end that through thy ordering its welfare may be promoted. In this church also and in its parishes we grant thee licence to ordain deacons and presbyters; concerning whom, however, let it be thy care to make diligent enquiry, that they be not personally in any respect such as are rejected by the sacred canons. But whomsoever thy Fraternity has perceived to be worthy of so great a ministry, having ascertained that their manners and actions fit them for ordination, them, by permission of our authority, thou mayest freely promote to the aforesaid office. We desire thee, therefore, to make use of all the property of the above named church as though thou wert its proper pontiff, until we write to thee again. Be, then, so diligent and careful in all these matters that through thy ordering all things may, with the help of God, be salubriously arranged to the Church's profit.

EPISTLE LXXIX.

To Martinus, Bishop in Corsica.

Gregory to Martinus, &c.

To those who ask for what is just it behoves us to lend a kindly ear, to the end both that the petitioners may find the remedies they hope for, and that the anxious care of a shepherd be not wanting to the Church. And inasmuch as the church of Tanates, in which thy Fraternity was formerly adorned with sacerdotal dignity, has for its sins been so taken possession of and ruined by hostile savagery that no further hope remains of thy returning thither, we appoint thee, by authority of these presents, undisputed cardinal priest [5] in the Church of Saona, which has now been long deprived of the aid of a pontiff. Do thou therefore so arrange and order all things according to the injunctions of the canons with vigilant care in the love of God, that both thy Fraternity may rejoice in having attained thy desires, and the Church of God may be filled with answering joy for having received thee as Cardinal pontiff.

elsewhere by Gregory, to denote the former in distinction from the latter. The occasion of this and the two following Epistles will be seen to be as follows. The See of Saona in Corsica had been for some time vacant. It rested with the clergy and nobles of the island (see above, Ep. LXXX.), to elect a new bishop; but they had failed to do so; and consequently Gregory remedied their neglect by himself filling up the vacancy. His right to do so would not be questioned there, Corsica as well as Sicily being among the Suburbicarian provinces which were under the acknowledged patriarchal jurisdiction of the See of Rome. Meanwhile he also commissioned Leo, the bishop of a neighbouring See (to whom this letter is addressed), to make a visitation of the Church of Saona, and exercise episcopal authority there, till the new bishop should take possession. There are several other Epistles, not included in this translation, appointing visitors of various churches.

EPISTLE LXXX.

To the Clergy and Nobles of Corsica.

Gregory to the Clergy, &c. . . . *A paribus* [6].

Although for a long time it has caused you no sorrow that the Church of God should be without a pontiff, yet as for us, we are both compelled by the charge of the office we bear and bound especially by the charity of our love for you, to take thought for its government, knowing that in its supervision lies at the same time advantage to your souls. For, if the care of a shepherd be wanting to a flock, it easily falls into the snares of the lier in wait. Accordingly, inasmuch as the church of Saona has long been deprived of the aid of a priest, we have held it necessary to constitute Martinus, our brother and fellow-bishop, cardinal priest of the same [7], but to enjoin on Leo our brother and fellow-bishop the work of its visitation. To the latter we have also granted licence to ordain presbyters and deacons in it and in its parishes, and have permitted him to make use of its property so long as he shall be there, as though he were its proper pontiff. And so we admonish you by these present writings that your Charity receive the aforesaid visitor with all devotion, and shew him obedience in whatever is reasonable, as becomes sons of the Church, to the end that, supported by your devotion, he may be able to accomplish all that is found to conduce to the advantage of the above-named church.

5 Cardinal bishops, presbyters, or deacons, meant formerly such as were regularly instituted and attached to some particular see, parish, or church, which constituted their title (*titulas*). They were then said to be *incardinati*, the act of so instituting them being called *incardinatio*. Cf. II. 37; XIV. 7.

6 See I, 25, note 8.

7 See note under Ep. LXXIX.

BOOK II

EPISTLE III.

To Velox, *Magister militum.*

Gregory to Velox, &c.

We informed your Glory some time ago that soldiers had been prepared to come to your parts; but, inasmuch as your letter had signified to us that the enemy were collected and were marching hitherward, we for this reason have detained them here. But now it appears to be advantageous that a certain number of soldiers should be sent to you, whom let thy Glory be careful to admonish and exhort to be prepared for toil. And, when you find an opportunity, confer with our glorious sons Maurilius and Vitalianus, and do whatever, with the help of God, they may appoint you to do for the advantage of the republic. And, should you ascertain that the unspeakable Ariulph [1] is making an incursion hitherward or to the parts about Ravenna, do you labour in his rear, as becomes brave men, to the end that your renown may by God's help advance still more in the republic from the quality of your labour. This, however, before all, we admonish you to do: to release without any delay or excuse the family of Maloin and Adobin, Vigild and Grussing [2], who are known to be with the glorious *Magister militum* Maurilius, to the end that the men of the aforesaid Maurilius, when they come to your parts, may without any impediment march along with them.

[In *Colbert.* and *Paul. diac.*, Die. V. Kal. Oct. Indict. 10.]

EPISTLE VI.

To the Neapolitans.

Gregory to the clergy, nobles, gentry, and commonalty [3] dwelling at Naples.

Although the sincere devotion of spiritual sons in behalf of their mother Church needs no exhortation, nevertheless, it ought to be stirred up by letter, lest it should suppose itself slighted. On this account I approach your love with an admonition of paternal charity, that with many tears and with one accord we may render thanks to our Redeemer, who has not suffered you to walk along pathless ways under so perverse a teacher, but has made publicly known the crimes of your unworthy pastor. For Demetrius, to wit, who even before had not deserved to be called a bishop, has been found to be involved in transactions to such an extent and of such a kind that, if he had received judgment without mercy according to the character of his deeds, he would undoubtedly have been condemned to a most hard death by both divine and human laws. But since, being reserved for penance, he has been deprived of the dignity of the priesthood, we cannot suffer the Church of God to remain long without a teacher, since it is laid down by canonical rules that, on the death or removal of a pastor, the church should not be long deprived of the priesthood [4]. Wherefore, I have thought it necessary to admonish your Charity by this present writing that neither delay nor the discord which has been wont to generate scandals ensue to hinder your election of a pontiff. But seek you out with all care such a person as all by common consent may rejoice in, and as is in no respect rejected by the sacred canons; to the end that the office which the most wicked of men had polluted by his evil administration may be worthily filled and administered by him, whoever he may be, who, by the grace of Christ, and with His approval, shall be ordained.

---

[1] Ariulph was the Lombard Duke of Spoletum, one of the principal cities in Italy occupied by the Lombards. For further reference to him cf. II. 29, 30, 46; IX. 98. He was at this time preparing, and suspected by Gregory of such intention, for an attack on Rome. Cf. *Prologom.* Velox (to whom this letter is addressed), and Maurilius and Vitalian (alluded to in it, and addressed in *Epp.* 29, 30), were Roman Generals (*magistri militum*) in command of imperial forces: but where they were is not apparent. From an allusion to Suana (or *Soana*) as within reach of the last two they may be supposed to have been somewhere in Tuscia.

[2] Apparently a *familia* of slaves belonging to Velox, but at this time with Maurilius.

[3] *Clero, nobilibus, ordini et plebi.* *Ordo* seems to denote persons of official or other rank, above the commonalty, but below the nobility. In some cases the corresponding address is to *clero, ordini et plebi* (as in I. 81; V. 26); in others to *clero et nobilibus* only. All such expressions shew that the election of bishops rested with the members, laity as well as clergy, of each church, though the bishop of Rome, wherever his jurisdiction extended reserved to himself the power of approving or disallowing the election. In the election at Naples, referred to in this Epistle, there appears to have been a difficulty in arriving at an unanimous choice. Other Epistles referring to the case are II. 9, 10, 15, 26; III. 35. From the last of these it appears how it was eventually settled. See especially note 6 under II. 9.

[4] *Sacerdotii;* meaning here episcopacy. See I. 78, note 2.

EPISTLE VII.

To Maximianus, Bishop of Syracuse[5].

Gregory to Maximianus, &c.

We execute more efficiently our heavenly commission, if we share our burdens with our brethren. For this cause we appoint thee, our most reverend brother and fellow-bishop, to have administration over all the churches of Sicily in the name of the Apostolical See, so that whosoever there is reckoned as being in a condition of religion may by our authority be subject to thy Fraternity, to the end that it may not hereafter be necessary for them to make such long sea-voyages in resorting to us for slight causes. But if by any chance there are matters of difficulty which can by no means be settled by the judgment of thy Fraternity, in these only let our judgment be solicited, that so we may occupy ourselves more efficaciously in greater causes, being relieved from the least. And be it understood that we give this delegation of authority, not to thy place, but to thy person, because we have learnt from thy past life what we may presume of thee in thy future conduct.

The month of December, the tenth Indiction.

EPISTLE IX.

To the Neapolitans.

Gregory to the gentry and commonalty (*ordini et plebi*) residing at Naples.

The communication you have addressed to us has made manifest what your opinion is of our brother and fellow-bishop Paulus[6]: and we congratulate you in that your experience of him for a few days has been such that you desire to have him as your cardinal bishop[7]. But, since in matters of supreme importance there ought to be no hasty decision, so we, Christ helping us, will arrange after mature deliberation what is to be done hereafter, his character meanwhile, in course of time, having become better known to you.

Wherefore, most beloved sons, obey ye the aforesaid man, if you truly love him, and with devoted minds meet his wishes in peaceful concurrence, to the end that the affection of your mutual charity may so bind you to each other, that the enemy who flies about you raging may find no way through any of you for creeping in to break up your unanimity. Further, when we shall have perceived the aforesaid bishop offering to God the fruit of souls which we long for, God Himself also approving, we will do afterwards whatever divine inspiration may suggest to our heart, with regard to his person and to your desire.

EPISTLE X.

To Paulus, Bishop of Naples[8].

Gregory to Paulus, &c.

If we administer safely the priestly office which we have received, without doubt both Divine assistance and the affection of our spiritual sons will not be wanting to us. Wherefore let thy Fraternity take care to shew thyself in all things such that the testimony which the clergy, the nobility, and all the people together, of the city of Naples bears to thee may be strengthened by the increase of thy goodness. Thou oughtest, then, so to bind thyself to continual employment in exhorting the aforesaid people that the Divine husbandman may store in his garners the fruit of thy word, which thou shalt have gathered from them by thy labours. But till such time as we shall be able, God revealing to us His will, to deliberate concerning the things which our aforesaid sons request us should be done, we grant leave for clerics to be ordained from the ranks of the laity, and also for manumissions to be solemnly celebrated before thee in the same church. Moreover we desire thee to observe without hesitation the customs of the clerical order and of the pres-

5 Maximianus had been a monk, and for a time abbot, in Gregory's monastery of St. Andrew at Rome, had accompanied him to Constantinople, and been recommended by him, soon after his own accession, and elected Bishop of Syracuse (*Joan. Diac. Vit. S. Greg.* ii. 11, 12). He was highly esteemed by Gregory, and mentioned in his Dialogues as having been miraculously delivered from shipwreck on his return from Constantinople to Rome (*Dialog.* iii. 36. Cf. *Hom.* 34 *in Evang.*). His appointment now as delegate of the Roman See in Sicily would relieve Peter the subdeacon of his temporary jurisdiction over the ecclesiastics there. Maximianus died in November, A.D. 594. See V. 17, 22. It is to be observed that the general authority now given to Maximianus was granted to him personally, and not permanently to the See of Syracuse.

6 He was bishop of Nepe, which, as well as Naples, was in the urbicarian province of Rome. The filling up of the See of Naples appears to have been a cause of great anxiety to Gregory, probably because of the party feeling prevailing in the city. In his first letter to the Neapolitans (*supra*, Ep. 6), he had contemplated the speedy election of a new bishop in the usual way; but it appears from this Epistle that he had seen reason to defer such election, sending meanwhile Paulus of Nepe to administer the See. Some at least in Naples appear to have wished this Paulus to be elected soon after his arrival among them; but this Gregory would not allow till he could see better how things were going. Such provisional arrangement continued, it seems, for more than a year, another bishop having been commissioned to supply Paul's place in his own Church of Nepe against the Easter festival (II. 26). That Gregory's fear of opposition to Paul were justified appears from the subsequent mention of a violent attack made on him by a party opposed to him at Naples (III. 1). He meanwhile, not liking his position, had already been anxious to return to his own See (II. 15), but had not been allowed. When he went at last, it seems that an election had taken place, but had proved futile from the person chosen having refused to be ordained (III. 15). Eventually the election had taken place, by Gregory's direction, not at Naples, but at Rome (III. 35), one Fortunatus being chosen (III. 61). The whole history of the case illustrates the troubles incident to popular election of bishops at that time, especially in great cities.

7 See I. 79, note 5.

8 Though called here Episcopus Neapolitanus, it is apparent from this and other Epistles that he was as yet only the episcopa visitor, not the regular, or cardinal, bishop of Naples.

byters of the above-named church: and do thou also keep such diligent watch in the instruction of the same, that, abstaining from all that is unsuitable or unlawful, they may stand fast, under thy exhortations, ministering with due obedience, in the service of our God. The month of January, the tenth Indiction.

EPISTLE XII.

To Castorius, Bishop of Ariminum.

Gregory to Castorius, &c.

The illustrious lady Timothea has intimated to us by a petitionary notification, as is set forth below, that she has founded an oratory within the city of Ariminum in a place belonging to her, which she desires to have consecrated in honour of the holy cross. And, accordingly, dearest brother, if the said construction is in the jurisdiction of thy city, and if it is known that no body has been buried there, then, after reception in the first place of a legitimate endowment, that is, of two-thirds of her whole property (excepting slaves), of her movables and fixtures and live stock, the usufract being reserved to her for her life, and such endowment having been secured by municipal deeds, thou wilt solemnly consecrate the aforesaid oratory without any public mass, on the condition that no baptistery shall be constructed in the same place in future times, and that thou appoint not a cardinal presbyter[9]. And if perchance she should prefer having masses said there, let her know that she must ask thy Love for a presbyter, to the end that nothing else may be presumed by any other priest whatever. Further, thou wilt reverently deposit the holy things[1] she has provided.

EPISTLE XV.

To Paul, Bishop.

Gregory to Paul, &c.

I appointed thy Fraternity to preside for the present over the church of Naples, to the end that thou mightest convert all thou canst to God by persuasive preaching. And, while thou oughtest to be giving thy whole mind to this work, thou art in haste to return before bringing forth this fruit to the Lord, and requestest me to settle the affairs of this same church speedily, my mind being meanwhile by no means unoccupied in this matter. But, being desirous of fortifying securely the well-being of this Church, I hold it needful to consider the matter with long continued deliberation, so as to be able to arrange its affairs by the ordination of a worthy person, whom Christ may reveal to us. Wherefore let thy Fraternity meanwhile study to watch for the good of souls, so that the opinion I have of thee may be strengthened by the effect of thy working. All thou hast written concerning the deacon Peter has now been made known to us by the ex-consul Theodorus. And so, now that I know that he is constant to thee, and, according to thy testimony, studies the advantage of the Church, he ought to be afraid of no one's opposition or enmity, but persevere in benefiting the Church and serving God all the more watchfully as he feels that others have a grudge against him; that so they may have no power at all to injure him. Moreover, thy Fraternity ought not hereafter to be suspected with regard to him; since no surreptitious proceedings will have effect on me[2].

EPISTLE XVIII.

To Natalis, Bishop of Salona[3].

Gregory to Natalis, &c.

I have learnt, dearest brother, from many who have come from thy city that, neglecting thy pastoral charge, thou occupiest thyself wholly in feastings: which report I should not have believed had not my own experience of thy conduct confirmed it. For that thou in no wise art intent on reading, in no wise givest attention to exhortation, but art even ignorant of the very use and purpose of ecclesiastical order, there is this in evidence, that thou knowest not how to observe reverence to those who are put over thee. For, when thou hadst been forbidden in writing by our predecessor of holy memory to retain in thy heart the soreness of thy long displeasure against Honoratus thy archdeacon, and when this had been positively interdicted thee by myself also, thou, disregarding the commands of God, and setting at naught our letters, didst attempt by a cunning device to degrade the aforesaid Honoratus thy archdeacon under colour of promoting him to a higher dignity. Thus it was contrived that, he being removed from the post of archdeacon, thou mightest call in another who would have fallen in with thy manner of life, the aforesaid man having, as I think, displeased thee for no other cause but that he prevented thee from giving sacred vessels and vestments to thy relations. Which case both I now, and my predecessor of holy memory formerly, have wished to subject to an accurate investigation; but thou, being conscious of what thou hadst done,

9 See I. 79, note 5.

1 *Sanctuaria*, meaning apparently relics, the deposition of which usually accompanied the consecration of holy places.

2 For the occasion of this letter, see II. 9, note 6.

3 Salona was the metropolis of the province of Dalmatia in the diocese of Illyricum Occidentale, and Natalis, in virtue of his occupancy of the See, the Ecclesiastical Metropolitan of the province. For Gregory's subsequent dealings with this bishop, see II. 19, 20, 52; III. 8, 32. For the occasion of this Epistle, see I. 19, note 5.

hast put off sending hither a representative instructed for trial of the case. Wherefore let thy Fraternity, even after admonition so often repeated, repent of the error of thy wrongdoing, and restore the aforesaid Honoratus to his post immediately on the receipt of my letter. Which if thou shouldest defer doing, know that the use of the pallium, granted thee by this See, is taken from thee. But if, even when thou hast lost the pallium, thou still persistest in thy contumacy, know that thou art deprived of participation of the body and blood of the Lord. And after this it will be needful for us to enquire more fully into the charges against thee, and to consider with the utmost care and investigation whether thou shouldest retain even thy episcopate. Him also who, against the rule of justice, has consented to be promoted to the place of another we depose from the dignity of the said archdeaconry. And, should he presume any longer to minister in this same office, let him know that he is deprived of participation in holy communion. Do thou, therefore, dearest brother, in no wise provoke us further, lest, having set us at naught when in an attitude of charity towards thee, thou shouldest find us very hard in our severity. Having, therefore, restored the archdeacon Honoratus to his place, send to us with speed a person instructed in the case, who may be able to shew to me by his allegations how the matter should be equitably proceeded with For we have commanded the said archdeacon to come to us, that, having heard the assertions of the parties, we may come to whatever decision may be just and well-pleasing to Almighty God. For we defend no one on the ground of personal love, but, God helping us, keep the rule of justice, putting aside respect to any man's person.

EPISTLE XIX.

To all the Bishops of Dalmatia.

Gregory to all the bishops constituted throughout Dalmatia.

Though desiring to visit your Fraternity frequently through the intercourse of letters, yet, when some special case demands our attention, we wish to take the opportunity of fulfilling two duties at once, so as both to refresh our brotherly souls in the way of visitation and to explain accurately matters that come up for notice, lest ignorance of them should leave the mind confused. Now when our brother Natalis, bishop of the city of Salona, wished to advance the archdeacon Honoratus to the order of the priesthood, who thereupon declined being advanced to a higher order, the latter demanded my predecessor of holy memory, in a petition that he sent, that he should not be so advanced against his will. For he alleged that the thing was attempted, not for the sake of promoting him, but in consequence of displeasure against him. Thereupon our predecessor of holy memory addressed letters to Natalis, our brother and fellow-bishop, interdicting him from promoting the archdeacon Honoratus against his will, or retaining in his heart the soreness of the displeasure which he had conceived against him. And when we too had laid the same interdiction on the said Natalis, he, not only disregarding the commands of God, but also setting at naught our letters, attempted, it is said, craftily to degrade the aforesaid archdeacon, in a way contrary to custom, under colour of promoting him to a higher dignity. Thus it was contrived that, having removed him from the archdeaconry, he might call in another person to minister in the place of the deposed archdeacon. Now we think that this Honoratus may have fallen under the displeasure of his bishop on account of having prevented him from giving sacred vessels to his relations: and both my predecessor of holy memory formerly and I now have wished to investigate the case accurately; but he, conscious of what he had done, has put off sending a representative with a view to its trial, lest the truth with respect to his doings might appear. We therefore, now that he has been already so often admonished by letter, and has so far been pertinaciously obstinate. have taken order for his being admonished once more in letters sent to him through the bearer of these presents, to the end that he may, immediately on the arrival of the bearer of these presents, receive the archdeacon Honoratus into his former place. And if, with heart still hardened, he should contumaciously defer restoring him to the said position, we order that for his contumacy so many times exhibited he be deprived of the use of the pallium granted to him by this See. But if, even after loss of the pallium, he should persevere in the same pertinacity, we order him to be debarred from participation in the body and blood of the Lord. For it is right that he should find those severe in justice whom he set at naught when they approached him in charity. Wherefore neither do we now deviate from the path of justice, which the aforesaid bishop has despised; but, when he whose guilt has by no means been made apparent to us has been restored to his place, we enjoin the bishop Natalis to send to us a person with instructions, who may be able by his allegations to prove to us the right intentions of the said bishop. For we have caused also the said archdeacon to come to us, that, having heard the assertions of both parties, we may decide whatever may be just, whatever may be well pleasing to Almighty God. For we defend no one on the ground of personal love, but, God helping us, keep the rule of justice without respect to any man's person.

EPISTLE XX.

To Antoninus, Subdeacon[4].

Gregory to Antoninus, &c.

Honoratus, archdeacon of the Church of Salona, had demanded from my predecessor of holy memory, in a petition that he sent, that he should by no means be forced by his bishop to be advanced against his will, in a way contrary to custom, to a higher order.

[*Here follows an account of the subsequent proceedings, almost word for word the same as that given in Epistle XIX.*]

Wherefore we have thought it right to support thy Experience by the authority of this present order, that thou mayest resort to Salona, and at least try by exhortation to induce Natalis, our brother and fellow-bishop, who has been admonished by so many letters, to restore the above-mentioned Honoratus to his place immediately. But if, as has been his wont, he should contumaciously delay doing this, forbid him by authority of the Apostolic See the use of the pallium which has been granted him by this See. But if, even after loss of the pallium, thou shouldest find him persevering in the same pertinacity, thou shalt deprive the said bishop of participation in holy communion. Moreover, him who, against the rule of justice, has consented to be promoted to another man's place we order to be deposed from the dignity of the same archdeaconry. And, if he should presume to minister further in the same place, we deprive him of participation in holy communion. For it is right that he should find those severe in justice whom he sets at naught when approaching him in charity. Wherefore, when the archdeacon Honoratus has been restored to his place, let the aforesaid bishop, at thy instigation, send to us a person with instructions, who may be able by his allegations to prove to us that the bishop's intention is or has been just.

[*What follows corresponds exactly with the conclusion of Epistle XIX.*]

As to our brother and fellow-bishop Malchus[5], thou wilt take care to make him find a surety, that he may come to us as soon as possible, to the end that, without any delay or loitering, he may render us an account of his proceedings, and so be able to return to his own with security.

EPISTLE XXII.

To all the Bishops of Illyricum[6].

Gregory to all the bishops, &c.

It both affords us joy for your carefulness, and makes your Fraternity safe in your own ordination, if the order of ancient custom is maintained. Since, then, we have learnt from the letters which you have sent to us through the presbyter Maximianus and the deacon Andreas that the consent of all of you and the will of the most serene Prince have concurred in the person of our brother and fellow-bishop John, we feel great exultation that, under God's direction, such a one has been advanced to the office of priesthood[7] as the judgment of all has approved as worthy. Wherefore, in accordance with your request, we confirm our aforesaid brother and fellow-bishop by the authority of our assent in the order of priesthood wherein he has been constituted, and declare our ratification of his consecration by sending him the pallium. And since, according to custom, we have committed to him vicariate jurisdiction in our stead, we must of necessity take the precaution of exhorting your Fraternity that you in no wise hesitate to obey him in matters pertaining to ecclesiastical order and the right course of discipline, or in other things not precluded by canonical decrees; that the soundness of your judgment in electing him may be declared by the obedience which you shew.

---

[4] This Antoninus was *rector patrimonii* in Dalmatia (see III. 22), and, though but a subdeacon, appears to have had had the same kind of jurisdiction over the clergy given him in the pope's name even in ecclesiastical matters as had been committed Peter the subdeacon in Sicily. (See I. 1.)

[5] This Malchus was a bishop in Dalmatia (cf. Lib. I. Ep. 38, 'Ad Malchum episcopum Dalmatiæ,") and appears to have been in charge of some part of the patrimony there, for his administration of which he had been called to account, and was therefore summoned to Rome to clear himself. He died there suddenly after his case had been heard, and judgment had been given against him, Gregory being calumniously accused of having caused his death. His case is referred to II. 20. 46; III. 22, 47; IV. 47.

[6] This Epistle, as appears from the following one, was on the occasion of the election of John to the See of Justiniana Prima in Eastern Illyricum, which, though annexed by the Emperor Gratian (379) to the Eastern Empire, had remained under the spiritual control of the Roman See. Accordingly Pope Damasus had assigned to the bishop of Thessalonica vicariate jurisdiction under Rome over the new præfecture: and this arrangement had continued to the time of Pope Vigilius, when the Emperor Justinian assigned to Achrida, called by him Justiniana Prima, Metropolitan jurisdiction over the five provinces of the Dacian civil diocese with the two Pannonias in the diocese of Illyricum Occidentale (*Justin. Novell.* cxxxi. c. iii.). Hence Justiniana Prima became the seat thenceforth of the ecclesiastical Vicariate also. The election to the See, being a metropolitan one, appears to have been made in this instance by the suffragan bishops with the concurrence of the Emperor; after which the Bishop of Rome was applied to for confirmation. In the case before us it was readily given, the pallium sent, and the vicariate jurisdiction renewed. A case will appear below in which such confirmation was refused, but dispensed with by the Emperor, who supported the elected bishop against the Pope. See III. 47, note 1.

[7] *Sacerdotii*, meaning here episcopacy. See I. 78, note 1.

EPISTLE XXIII.

To John, Bishop.

Gregory to John, Bishop of Prima Justiniana in Illyricum.

It is clearly a manifest evidence of goodness that the consent of all should concur in the election of one person. Since, then, the account which we have received from our brethren and fellow-bishops declared that you are summoned to the position of priesthood by the unanimous consent of the whole council and the will of the most serene Prince, we have rendered thanks with great exultation to Almighty God our Creator, who has made your life and actions so commendable in the past as to bring about (what is exceedingly to your credit) your approving yourself to the judgment of all. With them we also fully agree with regard to the person of your Fraternity. And we implore Almighty God that, as His Grace has chosen your Charity, so He would keep you in all respects under His protection. We have sent you the pallium according to custom, and, renewing our commission, we appoint you to act as vicar of the Apostolic See, admonishing you that you so shew yourself gentle to your subjects that they may be provoked to love you rather than to fear you. And, if perchance any fault of theirs should require notice, you will be careful so to correct their transgressions as by no means to discard paternal affection from your mind Be watchful and assiduous in the care of the flock committed to you, and strict in the zeal of discipline, so that the wolf lying in wait may not prevail to disturb the Lord's sheepfold, or have opportunity for deceit, so as to hurt the sheep. Make haste with full purpose of heart to win souls to our God; and know that we have received the name of shepherd not for repose, but for labour. Let us, then, shew forth in our work what our name denotes. If we weigh with right consideration the prerogative of the priesthood, it will be to those who are diligent and do their duty well for honour, but to those who are negligent assuredly for a burden. For, as this name, in the sight of God, conducts those who labour and are assiduous for the salvation of souls to eternal glory, so in the case of the idle and sluggish it tends to punishment. Through our tongue let the people committed to us learn that there is another life. Let the teaching of your Fraternity be to them an acceptable spur to urge them on, and your life an example for imitation. For your Fraternity's preaching should disclose to them what to love and what to fear, and your efficiency in this way should reap the fruit of eternal retribution. But let your deliberate care especially constrain you never to attempt to make any unlawful ordinations; but, whenever any are promoted to the clerical order, or, it may be, to some higher rank, let them be ordained, not for bribes or entreaties, but for merit. In no ordination let any consideration, in any way whatever, surreptitiously reach your Fraternity, lest you should be entangled (which God forbid) in the snares of simoniacal heresy. *For what shall it profit a man*, as the Truth says, *if he shall gain the whole world, and lose his own soul* (Mark viii. 36)? Hence it is necessary for us to look to God in all we do, to despise temporal and perishable things, and to direct the desire of our heart to the good things of eternity. Your Holiness's present[8] I was altogether unwilling to accept, since it were very unseemly for us to seem to have received gifts from our plundered and afflicted brethren. But your messengers got the better of me by another argument, proffering it to one from whom your Fraternity's offerings may not be withheld[9]. For this you ought before all things to study: how you may provide imperishable gifts to be offered to the coming judge of souls, to the end that He may have respect both to you for your profitable labour, and to us likewise for our exhortation.

EPISTLE XXVI.

To John, Bishop.

Gregory to John, &c.

Inasmuch as we have enjoined on our brother and fellow-bishop Paulus the work of the visitation of the Neapolitan church, therefore let not thy Fraternity shrink from assuming the visitation of the Nepesine Church, to the end that, according to the requirements of the Paschal festivity, whatever the solemnity of divine service demands may, through thy operation, be in all respects fulfilled. Until, then, we may be able to consider what should be done with regard to our aforesaid brother and fellow-bishop, let thy Fraternity strive to shew thyself so skilful and vigilant in all things that the absence of the bishop aforesaid may not at all be felt[1].

The month of April, the tenth Indiction.

---

8 *Xenia*. The term denotes, among other kinds of presents, such as were voluntarily offered to superiors, as by the people of a province to proconsuls. Those here referred to were such as it was the custom for bishops to send to the Pope after their ordination or from time to time. We find other instances of Gregory deprecating such presents. "The temporal *Xenia* which you have sent us, though we are in no need of such, we have nevertheless accepted with due charity." (VI. 64, *Ad Dominicam episcopum Carthaginensem*.) Cf. also I. 66. The word is used also for presents of all kinds. Cf. e.g. the letter to Ethelbert (XI. 66).

9 Meaning St. Peter.

1 See II. 9, note 6.

EPISTLE XXVII.

To Rusticiana, Patrician[2].

Gregory to Rusticiana, &c.

On receiving the epistle of your Excellency I was relieved by the welcome news of your welfare, hoping that the Lord in His mercy may protect and direct your life and doings. But I wondered much why you have turned from your intention and vow to accomplish a good work in respect of your meditated journey to the holy places[3], seeing that, when anything good is by the gift of the Creator conceived in the heart, it is needful that it be carried out with quick devotion, lest, while the cunning plotter strives to ensnare the soul, he should afterwards suggest impediments, whereby the mind, weakened by occupations, may fail to carry its desires into effect. Whence it is necessary that your Excellency should anticipate all impediments that come in the way of pious designs, and gasp after the fruit of good work with all the efforts of your heart, that so you may succeed in living tranquilly in the present world and gaining possession of a heavenly kingdom in the future. But as to what you have written to us of Passivus having attempted to spread some calumnies against you, consider, on the other hand, that the most pious emperors have not only been unwilling to listen to them, but have also received the author of them roughly; and turn the whole hope of your soul to Him Who powerfully prevents men in this world from doing as much harm as they long to do, that so He may beat back the wicked intentions of men by the opposition of His arm, and Himself mercifully shatter their attempts, as He has been wont to do. I entreat that the glorious lord Appio and the lady Eusebia, the Lord Eudoxius and the lady Gregoria, be greeted in my name through you.

EPISTLE XXIX.

To Maurilius and Vitalianus[4].

Gregory to Maurilius and Vitalianus, *magistris militum.*

On receiving your Glory's letters we gave thanks to God that we were assured of your safety; and we greatly rejoiced at your careful provision; and what you wrote about was at once prepared. But the magnificent Aldio wrote to us after the arrival of your men that Ariulph was already near at hand, and we feared that the soldiers sent to you might fall into his hands. Yet here also, so far as God may give aid, our son the glorious *magister militum* has prepared himself against him. But, if the enemy himself should advance hither, let your Glory also, as you have been accustomed to do, accomplish what you can in his rear. For we hope in the power of Almighty God, and that of the blessed Peter himself, the Prince of the apostles, on whose anniversary he desires to shed blood, that he may find him also without delay opposed to him.

EPISTLE XXX.

To Maurilius and Vitalianus.

Gregory to Maurilius and Vitalianus, *magistris militum*[5].

We have entreated your Glory through our son Vitalianus both by word and letter, charging you to communicate with him. But on the eleventh day of the month of January[6] Ariulph sent us this letter which we forward to you. Wherefore, when you have read it, see if the people of Suana[7] have stood fast in the fidelity they promised to the republic, and take adequate hostages from them, such as you can rely on; and moreover bind them anew by oaths, restoring to them what you took from them in the way of a pledge, and bringing them to a right mind by your discourses. But, should you quite distinctly ascertain that they have treated with Ariulph about their surrender to him, or at any rate have given him hostages, as the letter of Ariulph which we have forwarded to you leads us to suspect, then (after wholesome deliberation, lest your souls or mine be burdened with respect to our oaths), do ye whatever ye may judge to be of advantage to the republic. But let your Glory so act that neither anything be done for which we could be blamed by our adversaries, nor (which may the Lord avert) anything neglected which the advantage of the republic requires. Furthermore, my glorious sons, take anxious heed, since the enemy, so far as I have ascertained, has an army collected, and is said to be stationed at Narina[8]; and if, God being

---

2 Other letters addressed to this patrician lady are IV. 46: VIII. 22: XI. 44: XIII. 22. She appears to have been a widow, no husband being alluded to, who had migrated with her family from Rome to Constantinople (cf. VIII. 22, and XIII. 22). She is spoken of in subsequent letters as a person of slender frame and weak health, and subject to gout. Her family, to whom greetings are always sent, being her children either by birth or marriage, were Appio and Eusebia, Eudoxius and Gregoria, the former, and perhaps the latter also, being a married couple. Strategius also, a son of Appio and Eusebia, apparently a child, has afterwards greetings sent to him. They had daughters also, whose names are not given.

3 Two years later (see IV. 46, Indict. XII. i.e. A.D. 593-4) she appears to have made a pilgrimage to Mount Sinai.

4 Cf. II. 3.

5 "Abest hæc Epist. a plerisque MSS." (*Benedict Ed.*)

6 In Collect. Pauli Diac., *Junii.* (*Ibid.*)

7 Or Soana, a town in Tuscia.

8 Perhaps Narnia, in Umbria.

angry with him, he should resolve to bend his course hitherward, do you plunder his positions so far as the Lord may aid you, or certainly let those whom you send carefully require night-watches[9], lest news of any sad event should reach us[1].

EPISTLE XXXII.

To Peter, Subdeacon of Sicily.

Gregory to Peter, &c.

By information received from Romanus the guardian (*defensore*) I have learnt that the monastery of handmaidens of God which is on the farm of Monotheus has suffered wrong from our church of Villa Nova with respect to a farm belonging to the latter, which is said to have been leased to the said monastery. If this is so, let thy Experience restore to them the farm, and also the payments from the same farm for the two indictions during which thou hast exacted them. Moreover, since many of the Jews dwell on the estates of the Church, I desire that, if any of them should be willing to become Christians, some little of their dues be remitted to them, to the end that others also, incited by this benefit, may be moved to a like desire.

Cows which are now barren from age, or bulls which appear to be quite useless, ought to be sold, so that at least some profit may accrue from their price. But as to the herds of mares which we keep very unprofitably, I wish them all to be dispersed, and four hundred only of the younger kept for breeding; which four hundred ought to be presented to the farmers[2]—so many to each, to the end that they may make some return to us from them in successive years: for it is very hard for us to spend sixty *solidi* on the herdsmen, and not get sixty pence from these same herds. Let then thy Experience so proceed that some may be divided among all the farmers, and others dispersed and converted into money. But so arrange with the herdsmen themselves throughout our possessions that they may be able to make some profit by cultivation of the ground. All the implements which, either at Syracuse or at Panormus, can be claimed by the Church must be sold before they perish entirely from age.

On the arrival of the servant of God, brother Cyriacus, at Rome I questioned him closely as to whether he had communicated with thee about the receiving of a bribe in the cause of a certain woman. And the same brother says that he had learnt the state of the case from thy telling him, for that he had been commissioned by thee to ascertain who was the person commissioned to pay the bribe. This I believed, and immediately received him familiarly into favour, introduced him to the people and clergy, increased his stipend[3], placed him in a superior rank among the guardians, praising his fidelity before all, in that he had acquitted himself so faithfully in thy service; and I have consequently sent him back to thee. But, inasmuch as thou art in great haste, and I, though sick, am desirous of seeing thee, do thou leave some one whom thou hast fully proved to take thy place in the Syracusan district, and thyself make haste to come to me, that, if it should please Almighty God, we may consult together as to whether thou thyself oughtest to return thither or another person should be appointed in thy place. At the same time I have sent Benenatus the notary to occupy thy place in the patrimony in the district of Panormus till such time as Almighty God may ordain what pleases Him.

I have strongly rebuked Romanus for his levity, because in the Guest-house (*xenodochium*) which he kept, as I have now discovered, he has been taken up more with his own profits than with [heavenly] rewards. Him, therefore, if it should haply seem good to thee, leave in thy place. See how thou mayest best fortify him, by alarming and admonishing him, that he may act kindly and carefully towards the peasants (*rusticos*[4]); and shew himself towards strangers and townspeople changed and active. In saying this, however, I am not selecting any person, but leave this to thy judgment. It is enough for me to have selected an occupier of thy place in the district of Panormus; and I wish thee to see thyself to providing one for the Syracusan district. When thou comest, bring with thee the moneys and ornaments (*ornamenta*) on the part, or of the substance of Antoninus. Bring also the payments of the ninth and tenth indictions which thou hast exacted, and with them all thy accounts. Take care, if it should please God, to cross the sea for this city before the anniversary of Saint Cyprian, lest any danger should ensue (which

9 *Sculcas*. SCULCÆ, excubiæ; pro exculcæ, vocabulo truncato, ut *cubiæ* pro *excubiæ*. Du Cange.

1 In *Colbert. Vet.* the date is added, "Die 14 Kal. Jan. Indict. 10." The dates are evidently uncertain.

2 *Conductores*. See I. 44, note 6.

3 *Presbyterium*. The term, as here used, means apparently a pecuniary allowance to presbyters. Cf. V. 33, *Ad Gaudentiam Episcopum*; "Fraternitatem tuam præsentibus hortamur affatibus ut clericis Capuanæ Ecclesiæ quartam in *presbyterium* eorum de hoc quod ante dictæ ecclesiæ singulis annis accesserit juxta antiquam consuetudinem distribuere secundum personarum studeat qualitatem, quatenus aliquod stipendiorum habentes solatium, ministerium officiumque suum circa eamdem ecclesiam devotiore mente provocentur impendere."

4 See I. 44, note 1.

God forbid) from the constellation which always threatens the sea at that season.

Furthermore, I would have thee know that I have no slight compunctions of mind for having been grievously set against the servant of God Pretiosus for no grievous fault of his, and driven him from me, sad and embittered. And I wrote to the lord bishop[5] requesting him to send the man to me, if willing to do so; but he was altogether unwilling. Now him I ought not to distress, nor can I do so; since, occupied as he is in the causes of God, he ought to be supported by comfort, not depressed by bitterness. But the said Pretiosus, as I hear, is altogether distressed because he cannot return to me. I, however, as I have said, cannot distress the lord bishop, who is not willing to send him, and I am doubtful between the two. Do thou then, if in thy little diminutive body thou hast the greater wisdom, manage the matter so that I may have my will, and the lord bishop be not distressed. Yet, if thou see him to be at all distressed, say no more about it. I have, however, taken it amiss that he has excommunicated the lord Eusebius[6], a man of so great age and in such bad health. Wherefore it is needful for thee to speak privately to the said lord bishop, that he be not hasty in pronouncing sentences, since cases which are to be decided by sentences must needs be weighed beforehand with careful and very frequent consideration.

When the recruiting officers[7] come, who, as I hear, are already raising recruits in Sicily, charge thy substitute to offer them some little present[8], so as to render them well-disposed towards him. But, before thou comest away, give also something, according to ancient custom, to the prætor's officials; but do it by the hands of him thou leavest in thy place, so as to conciliate their favour towards him. Also, lest we should seem to them to be at all uncivil, direct thy substitutes to carry out in all respects the orders we have given to thy Experience as to what is to be given to any individuals or monasteries. But when thou comest, we will, with the help of God consider together how these things should be arranged. The three hundred *solidi* which I sent to be given through thee to the poor I do not think ought to be committed to their discretion. Let them carry out, then, those directions I have spoken of with reference to particular places and persons.

Now I remember having written before now to say that the legacies, which, according to the representation of Antoninus the guardian (*defensoris*), are due from us to monasteries or others, were to be paid as had been appointed. And I know not why thy Experience has delayed to accomplish this. Wherefore we desire thee to pay in full our portion of these legacies from the moneys of the church, that when thou comest to me, thou mayest not leave there the groans of the poor against thee. Bring also with thee at the same time the securities which have been found relating to the substance of the same Antoninus.

I have learnt on the information of Romanus that the wife of Redemptus, when dying, directed by word of mouth one silver shell to be sold, and the proceeds given to her freedmen, and also left a silver platter to a certain monastery; in respect of both of which bequests we desire her wishes to be fully carried out, lest from the least things we be betrayed into greater sins.

Further, I have learnt on the information of the Abbot Marinianus that the building in the Prætorian Monastery is not yet even half completed: which being the case, what can we praise for it but thy Experience's fervour[9]? But even now let this admonition rouse thee; and, as far as thou canst, assert thyself in the construction of this same monastery. I said that nothing was to be given them for the cost; but I did not prohibit their building the monastery. But so proceed as to enjoin in all ways on him whom thou mayest depute in thy place at Panormus that he construct this same monastery at the charge of the ecclesiastical revenue, and that I may have no more private complaints from the abbot.

Moreover, I have learnt that thou knowest certain things on the farms, even in considerable numbers, to belong to others; but, owing to the entreaty of certain persons or to timidity, thou art afraid to restore them to their owners. But, if thou wert truly a Christian, thou wouldest be afraid of the judgment of God more than of the voices of men. Take notice that I unceasingly admonish thee on this matter; which if thou neglect to set right, thou wilt have also my voice for witness against thee. If thou shouldest find any of the laity fearing God who might receive the tonsure and become agents under the rector[1], I give my full con-

5 Maximianus (as appears from Epistle 34), whom Gregory had himself appointed bishop of Syracuse. Cf. II. 7, and note.

6 This Eusebius was an abbot in Sicily. Letters follow about him to Maximianus (*Ep.* 34), and to him (*Ep.* 36).

7 *Scribonibus.* The term denoted officers sent from the imperial court into the provinces for executing certain duties; in this case for raising recruits for the imperial army. Cf. V. 30, note 8.

8 *Parum aliquid xenii.* On *xenia*, see II. 23, note 8.

9 We note here the sarcastic vein in which Gregory from time to time pleasantly stimulates Peter to activity.

1 I.e. the *rector patrimonii.* The purport of this direction

sent. It will be necessary that letters also be sent to them.

Concerning the case of the son of Commissus the *scholasticus* [2], thou hast taken advice; and it appears that what he claims is not just in law. We are unwilling to burden the poor to their disadvantage; but, inasmuch as he has given himself trouble in this matter, we desire thee to give him fifty *solidi*, which must certainly be charged in thy accounts. As to the expense thou hast incurred on the business of the Church in the case of Prochisus, either reimburse thyself there out of his revenues, or, should his revenues be clearly insufficient for the repayment, thou must needs receive what is due to thee here from the deacon. But presume not to say anything about Gelasius the subdeacon, since his crime calls for the severest penance even to the end of his life.

Furthermore, thou has sent me one sorry nag and five good asses. That nag I cannot ride, he is such a sorry one; and those good asses I cannot ride, because they are asses. But we beg that, if you are disposed to content us, you will let us have something suitable. We desire thee to give to the abbot Eusebius a hundred *solidi* of gold, which must certainly be charged in thy accounts. We have learnt that Sisinnius, who was a judge at Samnium, is suffering from grievous want in Sicily, to whom we desire thee to supply twenty *decimates* [3] of wine and four *solidi* yearly. Anastasius, a religious person (*religiosus* [4]), is said to be living near the city of Panormus in the oratory of Saint Agna, to whom we desire six *solidi* of gold to be given. We desire also six *solidi*, to be charged in thy accounts, to be given to the mother of Urbicus the Prior [5]. As to the case of the handmaiden of God, Honorata, what seems good to me is this: that thou shouldest bring with thee when thou comest all her substance which evidently existed before the time of the episcopate of John, bishop of Laurinum [6]. But let the same handmaiden of God come with her son, that we may speak with her, and do whatever may please God. The volume of the Heptateuch [7] out of the goods of Antoninus we desire to be given to the Prætorian monastery, and the rest of his books to be brought hither by thee.

EPISTLE XXXIII.

To Justinus, Prætor [8].

Gregory to Justinus, &c.

The spite of the ancient foe has this way of its own, that in the case of those whom, through God resisting him, he cannot delude into the perpetration of evil deeds, he maims their reputation for a time by false reports. Seeing, then, that a sinister rumour about our brother and fellow-bishop Leo [9] had disseminated certain things inconsistent with his priestly profession, we caused strict and lengthened enquiry to be made as to whether they were true, and we have found no fault in him touching the things that had been said. But, that nothing might seem to be omitted, and that no possible doubt might remain in our heart, we caused him over and above to take a strict oath before the most sacred body of the blessed Peter. And, when he had done this, we rejoiced with great exultation that from a proof of this kind his innocence evidently shone forth. Wherefore let your Glory receive the aforesaid man with all charity, and shew him reverence such as is becoming towards a priest; nor let any doubtfulness remain in your heart touching the charges from which he has now been purged. But it lies upon you so to cleave in all respects to the above-named bishop, that you may be seen fittingly and becomingly in his person to honour God, whose minister he is.

EPISTLE XXXIV.

To Maximianus, Bishop of Syracuse.

Gregory to Maximianus, &c.

I remember to have often admonished you to be by no means hasty in passing sentence. And lo, I have now learnt that your Fraternity in a fit of anger has excommunicated the most reverend abbot Eusebius. Now I am much

seems to be that agents from the laity might be appointed with advantage to assist the *rector patrimonii*; and these must first be made *clerici* by receiving the tonsure, so as to be qualified to act for the Church. The rectors themselves were usually at least subdeacons.

2 *Scholastici*. The designation appears to have been applied generally to scholarly and learned persons. Cf. Hieron. *in Catal Scriptor. Eccles.*, "Serapion ob elegantiam ingenii cognomen scholastici meruit." In Gregory's Epistles it seems to denote usually men learned in the law, who might advise on legal points or sit as assessors. In I. 44 (to Peter the subdeacon) *scholastici* are spoken of as having given a legal opinion; Epistle 36 in Bk. IX. is addressed "Severo scholastico exarchi," and he is spoken of as one of those "qui assistant judicibus." Cf. also IX. 58, 59, for the employment of "Martinus Scholasticus, vir eloquentissimus," in a case of disputed jurisdiction over the primate of the African province of Bizacia. Such *scholastici* were evidently persons of importance. Gregory addresses them by the title of "Gloria vestra" (IV. 40), and of "Magnitudo tua" (IX. 58). In IX. 12 he speaks of the form of prayer which followed the words of Institution in the Canon of the Mass as having been composed by a *scholasticus* (*precem quam scholasticus composuerat*), perhaps using the term in the general sense of a scholar.

3 See I. 46, note. 4 See I. 61, note 7.

5 *Præposit*. The word, though used also in a more general sense, usually denotes the Prior of a monastery, appointed as the Abbot's vice-gerent.

6 *Episcopi Laurinensis*. If the reading is correct, the See intended is unknown. Holstein (*Annot. in Geograph. Sacra*, p. 21) suggests *Carinensem*, denoting the Sicilian See of Carine, or Camarina.

7 I.e. the first seven books of the Bible.

8 Now Prætor of Sicily. Cf. I. 2.

9 Bishop of Catana in Sicily. Cf. I. 72.

astonished that neither his former conversation, nor his advanced age, nor his long-continued sickness, could turn your mind from wrath. For, whatever his transgression may have been, the very affliction of sickness ought to have sufficed as a scourge for him. For to one crushed by divine discipline it was superfluous to add human scourges. But perhaps thou hast been allowed to exceed in the case of such a person, in order that thou mightest become more cautious in the case of others of less account, and ponder long when thou art disposed to smite any one through a sentence. Yet still comfort this same man with a sweetness proportionate to the fury with which thou hast exasperated him, since it is very unjust that the very persons who have loved thee most should find thee without cause most bitter against themselves.

EPISTLE XXXVI.

To the Abbot Eusebius.

Gregory to Eusebius, &c.

Let thy Charity believe me that I have been greatly saddened for thy sadness, as though I had myself suffered wrong in thee. But, when I afterwards learnt that, even after the most reverend Maximianus, our brother and fellow-bishop, had restored thee to his favour and communion, thy Love would not accept communion from him, I then knew that what had been done before was just. The humility of God's servants ought to appear in a time of affliction: but those who lift themselves up against their superiors shew that they scorn to be God's servants. And, indeed, what he once did ought not to have been done; but still it ought to have been taken by thee with all humility: and again, when he restored to thee his favour, he ought to have been met with thanks. And because it was not so done by thee, I feel that to us in every way there is cause for tears. For it is no great thing for us to be humble to those by whom we are honoured; for even any worldly man would do this: but we ought especially to be humble to those at whose hands we suffer. For the Psalmist says, *See my humility before mine enemies* (Psal. ix. 14). What life are we leading, if we will not be humble even to our fathers? Wherefore, most beloved son, I beseech thee that all bitterness pass away from thy heart, lest perchance the end should be near, and the ancient foe should, through the iniquity of discord, bar against us the way to the eternal kingdom. Further, we have caused a hundred *solidi* to be given to thy Love through Peter the subdeacon, which I beg thee to accept without offence.

EPISTLE XXXVII.

To John, Bishop of Squillacium (*Squillace, in Calabria*).

Gregory to John, &c.

The care of our pastoral office warns us to appoint for bereaved churches bishops of their own, who may govern the Lord's flock with pastoral solicitude. Accordingly we have held it necessary to appoint thee, John, bishop of the *civitas Lissitana (Lissus*, hodie *Alessio ?)*, which has been captured by the enemy, to be cardinal [1] in the Church of Squillacium, that thou mayest carry on the cure of souls once undertaken by thee, having regard to future retribution. And although, being driven from thine own Church by the invading enemy, thou must govern another Church which is now without a shepherd, yet it must be on condition that, in case of the former city being set free from the enemy, and under the protection of God restored to its former state, thou return to the Church in which thou wast first ordained. If, however, the aforesaid city continues to suffer under the calamity of captivity, thou must remain in this Church wherein thou art by us incardinated [2]. Moreover, we enjoin thee never to make unlawful ordinations, or allow any bigamist, or one who has taken a wife who was not a virgin, or one ignorant of letters, or one maimed in any part of his body, or a penitent, or one liable to any condition of service, to attain to sacred orders. And, shouldest thou find any of this kind, thou must not dare to advance them. Africans generally, and unknown strangers, applying for ecclesiastical orders, on no account accept, seeing that some Africans are Manichæans, and some have been rebaptized; while many strangers, though being in minor orders, are proved to have pretended to a higher dignity. We also admonish thy Fraternity to watch wisely over the souls committed to thee, and to be more intent on winning souls than on the profits of the present life. Be diligent in keeping and disposing of the goods of the Church, that the coming Judge, when He comes to judge, may approve thee as having in all respects worthily executed the office of shepherd which thou hast taken upon thee.

EPISTLE XLI.

To Castorius, Bishop.

Gregory to Castorius, Bishop of Ariminum (*Rimini*).

What lamentable supplications have been poured out to us by Luminosus, abbot of the

[1] See I. 79, note 5.

[2] See as above.

monastery of St. Andrew and St. Thomas, in the city of Ariminum, appears from the text of the subjoined petition. With regard to this matter we exhort thy Fraternity that, on the death of the abbot of this same monastery, thy church shall under no pretext interfere in scheduling or taking charge of the property of the said monastery, acquired or to be acquired. And we desire thee to ordain as abbot of the same monastery none other but him whom the whole congregation may by common consent demand as being worthy in character and apt for monastic discipline. Moreover, we entirely forbid public masses to be celebrated there by the bishop, lest occasion be given for popular assemblies in the retreats of God's servants, and also lest too frequent an entrance of women be a cause of scandal (which God forbid), especially to the simpler souls. Further, we ordain that this paper by us written shall be carefully held to, and kept in force and unadulterated in all future time by thee and the bishops that shall be ordained after thee; that so, with the help of God, both thy church may be content with its own rights and no more, and also the said monastery, being subject henceforth to none but general or canonical jurisdiction, and free from all annoyances and vexations, may accomplish its divine work with the utmost devotion of heart.

[*In place of the epistle as above given the following, with the appended paper on the privileges of monasteries, is found in some Codices.*]

Gregory to Castorius, Bishop of Ariminum.

What lamentable supplications Luminosus, abbot of the monastery of Saints Andrew and Thomas, in the city of Ariminum, has poured out to us, appears from the text of the subjoined petition. For from his account we learn that in very many monasteries the monks have suffered many prejudices and annoyances from prelates. It is therefore the duty of thy Fraternity to make provision for their future quiet by a wholesome arrangement, to the end that those who have their conversation therein in God's service may, His grace assisting them, persevere with minds free from disturbance. But, lest from a custom which ought to be rather amended than continued, any one should presume to cause any kind of annoyance to monks, it is necessary that the things which we have caused to be enumerated below should be so carefully observed by the fraternity of bishops that no possible occasion of introducing disquiet may be found hereafter.

Of the privileges of Monasteries.

We therefore interdict in the name of our Lord Jesus Christ, and forbid by the authority of the blessed Peter, Prince of the apostles, in whose stead we preside over this Roman Church, that any bishop or secular person hereafter presume in any way to devise occasions of interfering with regard to the revenues, property, or writings of monasteries, or of the cells or vills thereto appertaining, or have recourse to any tricks or exactions: but, if any case should by chance arise as to land disputed between their churches and any monasteries, and it cannot be arranged amicably, let it be terminated without intentional delay before selected abbots and other fathers who fear God, sworn upon the most holy Gospels. Also on the death of the abbot of any congregation, let no stranger be ordained, or any but one of the same congregation whom the society of the brethren shall of its own accord have elected unanimously, and who shall have been elected without fraud or venality. But, if they cannot find a suitable person among themselves, let them in like manner elect some one from some other monastery to be ordained. Nor, when an abbot has been constituted, let any person whatever on any pretext be put over him, unless perchance (which God forbid) crimes be apparent which are shewn to be punishable by the sacred canons. Likewise the rule is to be observed, that monks must not, without the consent of the abbot, be removed from monasteries for constituting other monasteries, or for sacred orders, or for any clerical office. We also disallow ecclesiastical schedules of the property of a monastery to be made by bishops. But if, circumstances requiring it, the abbot of a place should have questions with other abbots concerning property that has come into possession, let the matter be terminated also by their counsel or judgment. On the death also of an abbot let not the bishop on any pretext intermeddle in the scheduling or taking charge of the property of the monastery, acquired, or given, or to be acquired. We also entirely forbid public masses to be celebrated by him in a convent, lest in the retreats of the servants of God and their places of refuge any opportunity for a popular concourse be afforded, or an unwonted entrance of women should ensue, which would be by no means of advantage to their souls. Nor let him dare to place his episcopal chair there, or have any power whatever of command, or of holding any ordination, even the most ordinary, unless he should be requested to do so by the abbot of the place; that so the monks may always remain under the power of their abbots: and let no bishop detain a monk in any church without a testimonial and permission from his abbot, or promote one without such permission to any dignity. We ordain, then, that this paper by us written be kept to for all future time, in force and unadulterated, by all bishops; that both they may be content with the rights of their own churches and no more, and that the monasteries be subject to no ecclesiastical conditions, or compelled services, or obedience of any kind to secular authorities (saving only canonical jurisdiction[3]), but, freed from all vexations and annoyances, may accomplish their divine work with the utmost devotion of heart.

EPISTLE XLII.

To Luminosus, Abbot.

Gregory to Luminosus, abbot of the monastery of Saint Thomas of Ariminum.

We were glad to receive thine own and thy congregation's petition, and accede to thy requests in accordance with the statutes of the Fathers and with form of law. For to our brother and fellow-bishop Castorius a letter has been sent by our order, whereby we have taken away entirely from him and his successors all power to harm thy monastery; so that neither may he any longer come among you to be a burden to you, nor schedules be made of the property of the monastery, nor any public procession[4] take place there; this only jurisdiction being still left to him, that he must ordain in the place of a deceased abbot another whom the common consent of the congregation may have chosen as worthy. But now, these things being thus accomplished, be you diligent in the work of God, and assiduously devote yourselves to prayer, lest you should seem not so much to have sought security of mind for prayer, as to have wished to escape strict episcopal control over you while living amiss.

EPISTLE XLVI.

To John, Bishop.

Gregory to John, Bishop of Ravenna[5].

That I have not replied to the many letters of your Blessedness attribute not to sluggishness on my part, but to weakness, seeing that, on account of my sins, when Ariulph, coming to the Roman city, killed some and mutilated others, I was affected with such great sadness as to fall into a colic sickness. But I wondered much why it was that that well-known care of your Holiness for me was of no advantage to this city and to my needs. When, however, your letters reached me, I became aware that you are indeed taking pains to act, but yet have no one on whom you can bring your action to bear. I therefore attribute it to my sins that this man[6] with whom we are now concerned both evades fighting against our enemies and also forbids our making peace; though indeed at present, even if he wished us to make it, we are utterly unable, since Ariulph, having the army of Authar and Nordulf, desires their subsidies[7] to be given him ere he will deign to speak to us at all about peace.

But, as to the case of the bishops of Istria[8], I have learnt the truth of all you had told me in your letters from the commands which have come to me from the most pious princes, bidding me abstain for the present from compelling them. I indeed feel with you, and rejoice greatly in your zeal and ardour, with regard to what you have written, and acknowledge myself to have become in many ways your debtor. Know nevertheless that I shall not cease to write with the greatest zeal and freedom on this same matter to the most serene lords. Moreover the animosity of the aforesaid most excellent Romanus Patricius ought not to move you, since, as we are above him in place and rank, we ought so much the more to tolerate with forbearance and dignity any light conduct on his part.

If, however, there is any opportunity of prevailing with him, let your Fraternity work upon him, so that we may make peace with Ariulph, if to some small extent we may, since the soldiery have been removed from the city of Rome, as he himself knows. But the Theodosiacs[9], who have remained here, not having received their pay, are with difficulty induced to guard the walls; and how shall the city subsist, left destitute as it is by all, if it has not peace?

3 The text here ("nullis canonicis juris deserviant") appears to be corrupt, being unintelligible. The sense of the corresponding clause in the shorter Epistle has been given in the translation.

4 *Processio* usually denotes the celebration of Mass.

5 For elucidation of the circumstances of this Epistle see above, Epistles 3, 29, 30.

6 Viz. Romanus Patricius, mentioned below, the Exarch of Ravenna, and as such representing the Emperor in Italy. See I. 33, "Ad Romanum Patricium et Exarchum Italiæ."

7 *Precaria*; apparently subsidies demanded for the support of the invading army. *Precarium* (or *Precarim*), which has various applications, appears to be capable of this sense. See *Du Cange*.

8 The Istrian bishops still held out in refusing to accept the condemnation of "The Three Chapters" passed in the fifth Œcumenical Council at the instance of the Emperor Justinian. Gregory, soon after his accession, had summoned Severus, Bishop of Aquileia and Metropolitan, with his suffragans, to Rome; and this, as he alleges, by command of the Emperor, though the latter had now, it appears, forbidden further proceedings. See I. 16, and note.

9 I.e. the soldiers of the Theodosian Legion.

Furthermore, as to the girl redeemed from captivity, about whom you have written to us asking us to enquire into her origin, we would have your Holiness know that an unknown person cannot easily be traced. But as to what you say about one who has been ordained being ordained again, it is exceedingly ridiculous, and outside the consideration of one disposed as you are, unless perchance some precedent is adduced which ought to be taken into account in judging him who is alleged to have done any such thing. But far be it from your Fraternity to entertain such a view. For, as one who has been once baptized ought not to be baptized again, so one who has been once consecrated cannot be consecrated again to the same order. But in case of any one's attainment of the priesthood having been accompanied by slight misdemeanour, he ought to be adjudged to penance for the misdemeanour, and yet retain his orders.

With regard to the city of Naples [1], in view of the urgent insistance of the most excellent Exarch, we give you to understand that Arigis [2], as we have ascertained, has associated himself with Ariulph, and is breaking his faith to the republic, and plotting much against this same city; to which unless a duke be speedily sent, it may already be reckoned among the lost.

As to what you say to the effect that alms should be sent to the city of the schismatic Severus which has been burnt [3], your Fraternity is of this opinion as being ignorant of the bribes that he sends to the Court in opposition to us. And, even though these were not sent, we should have to consider that compassion is to be shewn first to the faithful, and afterwards to the enemies of the Church. For indeed there is near at hand the city Fanum, in which many have been taken captive, and to which I have already in the past year desired to send alms, but did not venture to do so through the midst of the enemy. It therefore seems to me that you should send the Abbot Claudius thither with a certain amount of money, in order to redeem the freemen whom he may find there detained in slavery for ransom, or any who are still in captivity. But, as to the sum of money to be thus sent, be assured that whatever you determine will please me. If, moreover, you are treating with the most excellent Romanus Patricius for allowing us to make peace with Ariulph, I am prepared to send another person to you, with whom questions of ransom may be better arranged.

Concerning our brother and fellow-bishop Natalis [4] I was at one time greatly distressed, in that I had found him acting haughtily in certain matters; but, since he has himself amended his manners, he has overcome me and consoled my distress. In connexion with this matter admonish our brother and fellow-bishop Malchus [5] that before he comes to us he render his accounts, and then depart elsewhere if it is necessary. And if we find his conduct good, it will perhaps be necessary for us to restore to him the patrimony which he had charge of.

EPISTLE XLVII.

To Dominicus, Bishop.

Gregory to Dominicus, Bishop of Carthage [6].

We have received with the utmost gratification the letters of your Fraternity, which have reached us somewhat late by the hands of Donatus and Quodvultdeus, our most reverend brethren and fellow-bishops, and also Victor the deacon with Agilegius the notary. And though we thought that we had suffered loss from the tardiness of their coming, yet we find gain from their more abundant charity; seeing that from this delay in point of time there appears no interruption, but rather increase of the love which, by the mercy of God, through your contemplation of the priestly office, your practice of reading, and your maturity of age, we know to be already firmly planted in you. For it would not flow so largely from you, had it not very many most abundant veins in your heart. Let us, therefore, most holy brother, hold fast with unshaken firmness this mother and guard of virtues. Let not the tongues of the deceitful

1 With respect to Rome Gregory has already complained that the Exarch would neither send forces for its defence nor allow peace to be made with Ariulph. So also with regard to Naples, which Gregory understands to be now threatened by the Lombards. The Exarch, it appears, had been urgent in insisting that it should hold out against the enemy ("excellentissimo exarcho instanter imminente"), but without giving any help for the purpose. What Gregory here says is that without aid from the Exarch its defence was hopeless.

2 Arigis was the Lombard duke of Beneventum.

3 Viz. Aquileia, of which Severus was bishop and Metropolitan, called here *schismaticus* because of his holding out against Rome in the matter of the Three Chapters. The bribes he is said below to have sent to Constantinople would be for inducing the mperor to take his part against Gregory.

4 See above, Ep. 20, in this Book, and I. 19, note 5, where references to other Epistles are given.

5 See II. 20, note 5.

6 The bishop of Carthage was primate of the province of Africa Proconsularis in virtue of his See. For the custom with regard to primacy in other African provinces, see I. 74, note 2. The fact, apparent from this letter, that Dominicus had delayed sending to Gregory on his accession the congratulatory letter that had been expected, and Gregory's carefulness to assure him, in the course of the studiously courteous letter, of his desire to respect the ancient privileges of Churches, may be among the symptoms, otherwise apparent, of the authoritative claims of the Roman See being still viewed with some jealousy in the African Church. Cf. in Book VIII. Epistle 33, to the same Dominicus, in which Gregory, in praising his reverence for the Apostolic See. attributes such reverence to his knowledge of the origin of the African episcopacy, refraining from asserting in this case any prerogative of divine right belonging to the See of S. Peter Other letters to Dominicus are V. 5; VII. 35; XII. 1.

diminish it in us, or any snares of the ancient enemy corrupt it. For this joins what is divided, and keeps together what is joined. This lifts up what is lowly without tumour; this brings down what is lifted up without dejection. Through this the unity of the universal Church, which is the knitting together of the Body of Christ, rejoices in its several parts through the mind's equalization of them, though having in it dissimilarity from the diversity of its members. Through this these members both exult in the joy of others, though in themselves afflicted, and also droop for the sorrows of others, though in themselves joyful. For seeing that, as the teacher of the Gentiles testifies, if one member suffers anything, the other members suffer with it, and if one member glories, all the members rejoice with it, I doubt not that you groan for our perturbation, as it is quite certain that we rejoice for your peace.

Now as to your Fraternity rejoicing with us on our ordination, it displays to me the affection of most sincere charity. But I confess that a force of sorrow strikes through my soul from contemplation of this order of ministry. For heavy is the weight of priesthood; seeing that it is necessary for a priest, first to live so as to be an example to others, and then to be on his guard not to lift up his heart because of the example which he shews. He should ever be thinking of the ministry of preaching, considering with most intense fear how that the Lord, when about to depart to receive for Himself a kingdom, and giving talents to His servants, says, *Trade ye till I come* (Luke xix. 13). Which trading surely we carry on only if by our living and our speaking we win the souls of our neighbours; if by preaching the joys of the heavenly kingdom we strengthen all that are weak in divine love; if by terribly sounding forth the punishments of hell we bend the froward and the timid; if we spare no one against the truth; if, given to heavenly friendships, we fear not human enmities. And indeed it was in thus shewing himself that the Psalmist knew that he had offered a kind of Sacrifice to God, when he said, *Did I not hate them, O God, that hated thee, and was I not grieved with thine enemies! Yea I hated them with a perfect hatred, and they became enemies unto me* (Ps. cxxxviii. 21[7]). But in view of this burden I tremble for my infirmity, and look to the returning of the Master of the house, after receiving His kingdom, to take account of us. But with what heart shall I bear His coming, if from the trading I undertook I render Him no gain, or almost none? Do thou, therefore, most dear brother, help me with thy prayers; and what thou seest me to fear for myself, consider daily on thine own account with anxious dread. For through the bond of charity both what I say of myself is thy concern, and what I desire thee to do is mine.

Further, as to what your Fraternity writes about ecclesiastical privileges, keep to this without any hesitation, since, as we defend our own rights, so we observe those of all several churches. Nor do I through partiality grant to any Church whatever more than it deserves, nor do I under the instigation of ambition derogate from any what belongs to it by right; but I desire to honour my brethren in all ways, and study accordingly that each may be advanced in honour, so long as there can be no opposition to it of right on the part of one against the other. Further, I greatly rejoice with you in the manners of your messengers, in whom it has been shewn me how much you love me, in that you have sent to me elect brethren and sons.

Given the tenth of the Kalends of August, tenth indiction.

EPISTLE XLVIII.

To Columbus, Bishop[8].

Gregory to Columbus, &c.

It is known, most dear brother in Christ, that the ancient enemy, who by cunning persuasion deposed the first man from the delights of Paradise to this life of care, and in him even then inflicted the penalty of mortality on the human race, does now with the same cunning, so as more easily to seize the flock, endeavour to infect the shepherds of the Lord's sheep with infused poisons, and already to claim them as his own by right. But we, who, though unworthy, have undertaken the government of the Apostolic See in the stead of Peter the prince of the apostles, are compelled by the very office of our pontificate to resist the general enemy by all the efforts in our power. Now the bearers of these presents, Constantius and Mustellus, have in a petition presented to us given us to understand, and the deacons of the Church of Pudentiana constituted in the province of Numidia assert, that Maximianus, prelate of the same Church, corrupted by a bribe from the Donatists, has by a new licence allowed a bishop to be made in the place where he lives; which thing, though previous usage allowed it,

7 In *English Bible*, cxxxix. 21.

8 This Columbus was one of the bishops in Numidia, who seems to have enjoyed the peculiar confidence of Gregory, being written to on various questions concerning the Church there, and charged with seeing to the exercise of discipline over other bishops, though not himself the primate. He is addressed (III. 68; VIII. 13) as being himself especially devoted to the Roman See. Other letters addressed to him are III. 48; IV. 35; VI. 37; VII. 2; VIII. 28; XII. 8; XII. 28.

is prohibited from remaining and continuing by the catholic faith[9]. On this account, then, we have deemed it necessary to exhort thy Fraternity by these present writings that, when Hilarus our *chartularius* comes to thee, this same case be subjected to a thorough and wise investigation in an united general council of bishops, having the terror of the coming judge before their eyes. And if this charge should be proved with sufficient evidences by the bearers of these presents against the aforesaid bishop, let him by all means be degraded from the dignity and office which he enjoys, that both he may return to the gains of penitence through acknowledgment of his fault, and others may not presume to attempt such things.

For it is right that one who has sold our Lord Jesus Christ to a heretic for money received, as is said to have been done, should be removed from handling the mysteries of His most holy body and blood. Further, if, apart from this accusation, there is any contest afoot among them, as is contained in the petition of the deacons themselves, with respect to certain wrongs or private transactions, this let thy Fraternity with our aforesaid *chartularius* fully enquire into with evidence adduced, and decide it according to justice between all the parties.

But, further, we have learnt through the information given us by the bearers of these presents that the heresy of the Donatists is for our sins spreading daily, and that very many, leave being given them through venality, are being baptized a second time by the Donatists. How serious a matter this is, brother, it behoves us with the whole bent of our minds to consider. Lo, the wolf tears the Lord's flock, no longer stealthily in the night, but in the open light; and we see him advance in the slaughter of the sheep, and with no solicitude, with no darts of words, do we oppose him. What fruits, then, of a multiplied flock shall we shew to the Lord, if even that of which we have undertaken the feeding we see with easy mind mangled by the wild beast? Let us therefore study to inflame our hearts by imitation of earthly shepherds, who often keep watch through winter nights, pinched with showers and frost, lest even one sheep, and perchance not a profitable one, should perish. And, if the prowler should have bitten it with greedy mouth, how do they busy themselves, with what palpitations of heart do they pant, with what cries do they leap forward to rescue the captured sheep, stimulated by the pressing need, lest anything lost through their carelessness should be required of them by the lord of the flock! Let us then watch, lest anything should perish: and, if anything should by chance have been seized, let us bring it back to the Lord's flock by the cries of divine discourses, that He who is the Shepherd of shepherds may mercifully vouchsafe to approve us in His judgment as having kept watch over His sheepfold. This also it is needful for you to attend to wisely; that, if there should be any proper petition on the part of the same bishop against the bearers of these presents, it should be thoroughly enquired into; and, if haply they themselves also should rightly deserve to be smitten for their own fault, we pronounce that they should by no means be spared on the ground of their having had the toil of resorting to us.

In the month of August, tenth indiction.

EPISTLE XLIX.

To Januarius, Archbishop.

Gregory to Januarius, archbishop of Caralis (*Cagliari*).

If with integrity of heart we consider the priestly office which we administer, the concord of personal charity ought so to unite us with our sons that, as we are fathers in name, so we should be proved by our affection to be so in deed. While, then, we ought to be such as has been said above, we wonder why such a mass of complaints has arisen against thy Fraternity. We still indeed hesitate to believe it: but, that we may be able to ascertain the truth, we have sent to your parts John the notary of our See, supported by our injunction, who may compel all parties to abide the judgment of chosen arbitrators, and by his own execution carry their judgments into effect. Wherefore we exhort thy Fraternity by this present writing to consider well with thyself beforehand the merits of the cases; and, if you find that you have taken or hold anything unjustly, in consideration of your priesthood to restore it before trial.

Now, among numerous complaints, the most distinguished Isidore has complained of having been excommunicated and anathematised by thy Fraternity for invalid reasons. And, when we had wished to learn from one of thy clergy who was here for what cause this had been done, he gave us to understand that it had been done for no other cause than that the man had done thee an injury. This distresses us exceedingly; since, if it is so, thou shewest that thou dost not think of heavenly things, but givest signs of having thy conversation among things of earth, having brought to bear

[9] The Donatists had formerly been allowed their own bishops, tolerated along with the Catholic ones. This liberty was now disallowed, probably in accordance with imperial edicts. See I 74, note 8.

the malediction of anathema to avenge a private wrong; which is a thing forbidden by the sacred rules. Wherefore for the future be thoroughly circumspect and careful, and presume not to inflict any such penalty again for vindication of thine own wrongs. For, shouldest thou do anything of the kind, know that it will afterwards be avenged on thyself.

EPISTLE LI.

To all Bishops.

Gregory to all bishops in the matter of the Three Chapters[1].

I have received your letters with the utmost gratification: but I shall have far abundant joy, if it should be my lot to rejoice in your return from error. Now the forefront of your Epistle notifies that you suffer severe persecution. But persecution, if endured irrationally, is of no profit at all unto salvation. For it is impious in any one to expect a recompense of reward for sin. For you ought to know, as the blessed Cyprian says, that it is not the suffering that makes the martyr, but the cause for which he suffers. This being so, it is exceedingly incongruous for you to glory in the persecution whereof you speak, seeing that you are not thereby at all advanced towards eternal rewards. Let, then, purity of faith bring your Charity back to your mother church who bare you; let no bent of your mind dissociate you from the unity of concord; let no persuasion deter you from seeking again the right way. For in the synod which dealt with the three chapters it is distinctly evident that nothing pertaining to faith was subverted, or in the least degree changed; but, as you know, the proceedings had reference only to certain individuals; one of whom, whose writings evidently deviated from the rectitude of the Catholic Faith, was not unjustly condemned[2].

Moreover, as to what you write about Italy among other provinces having been especially scourged since that time, you ought not to twist this into a reproach, since it is written, *Whom the Lord loveth he chasteneth, and scourgeth every son whom he receiveth* (Hebr. xii. 6). If, then, it is as you say, Italy has been since that time the more loved by God, and in all ways approved, having been counted worthy of enduring the scourge of the Lord. But, since it is not as ye try to make out by way of insulting over her, attend ye to reason.

After the Pope Vigilius of illustrious memory, having been appointed in the royal city[3], promulgated a sentence of condemnation against Theodora, then empress, or against the Acephali[4], the city of Rome was then attacked and captured by enemies. Does it follow from this that the Acephali had a good case, or that they were unjustly condemned, because such things happened after their condemnation? Away with the thought! For it is not fit that either any one of you, or any others who have been instituted in the mysteries of the Catholic Faith, should say or in any way acknowledge this. This then being recognized, retire ye even now at length from the determination you have come to. Wherefore, that full satisfaction may be infused into your minds, and all doubt removed, with respect to the three chapters, I have judged it of advantage to send you the book which my predecessor of holy memory, Pope Pelagius, had written on this subject[5]. Which book if you should be willing to read again and again, putting aside the spirit of wilful self-defence, I have confidence that you will follow it in all respects, and, notwithstanding all, return to union with us. But if henceforth, after perusal of this book, you should decide to persist in your present determination, you will doubtless shew that you gave yourselves up not to reason but to obstinacy. Wherefore once more, in a spirit of compassion, I admonish your Charity, that, inasmuch as under God the

1 This letter, being in reply to one from the bishops addressed who are spoken of as being at the time schismatics, cannot have been meant for the universal episcopate. They were probably those of Istria or elsewhere, who were out of communion with Rome because of their refusal to accept the condemnation of the "Three Chapters" by the fifth Council. See I. 16, note 3: IV. 1, 2, 3, 4, 38. 39.

2 I.e. Theodorus of Mopsuestia, whose person, and not his writings only, was anathematized in the fifth Council. The sentence was; "Prædicta tria capitula anathematizamus, id est, Theodorum Mopsuestenum cum nefandis ejus scriptis, et quæ impie Theodoritus conscripsit, et impiam epistolam quæ dicitur Ibæ, et defensores eorum."

3 Vigilius, having gone to Constantinople with pope Agapetus, who died there, was selected by the Empress Theodora as his successor, and sent back to Italy with an order from her to Belisarius to bring about his election (Liberatus, *Breviar.* c. 22). Gregory seems to have been unaware of the fact stated by Liberatus, namely that Vigilius had come to a secret understanding with the Empress that he would support the Monophysite party and disallow the Council of Chalcedon, as there is good evidence that he did after his accession. It is true that he afterwards declared for orthodoxy, and condemned all abettors of the Eutychian heresy. But this appears to have been not till A.D. 540, in reply to a letter received from the Emperor Justinian, and therefore subsequent to the occupation of Rome by the Gothic King Theodatus, which was in 536, and to its siege by Vitiges, who retired in 538. Thus what Gregory goes on to say about Rome having been attacked and captured by enemies after the condemnation of heresy by Vigilius must be due to serious ignorance of the facts of the case. Nor does he appear to have known—at any rate he does not intimate—that the condemnation of the Three Chapters, pressed upon the fifth Council by the Emperor Justinian, had been in spite of the opposition of Vigilius, though it is true that this sorry pope did afterwards assent to it.

4 The Monophysites—or some of them—had come to be so called, as being without a head, after their leader, Peter Mongus, had accepted the See of Alexandria on the doctrinal basis of Zeno's *Henoticon*.

5 Pelagius I., who succeeded Vigilius, though he had formerly with him opposed the condemnation of the Three Chapters, upheld it after his accession to the popedom. The "book" sent by Gregory to the bishops may have been the Epistle given as Ep. VII., among those attributed to Pelagius, addressed to Helias and the bishops of Istria.

purity of our faith has remained inviolate in the matter of the Three Chapters, ye put away from you all swelling of mind, and return to your mother the Church, who expects and invites her sons; and this all the more speedily as you know that she expects you daily.

EPISTLE LII.

To Natalis, Bishop[6].

Gregory to Natalis, Bishop of Salona.

As though forgetting the tenour of former letters, I had determined to say nothing to your Blessedness but what should savour of sweetness: but, now that in your epistle you have recurred in the way of argumentation to preceding letters, I am once more compelled to say perhaps some things that I had rather not have said.

For in defence of feasts your Fraternity mentions the feast of Abraham, in which by the testimony of Holy Scripture he is said to have entertained three angels (Gen. xviii.). In view of this example, neither will we blame your Blessedness for feasting, if we come to know that you entertain angels. Again you say that Isaac gave a blessing to his son when satiated (Gen. xxvii. 27). Now as to both these things in the Old Testament—since they were so done in the way of history as still to have a meaning in the way of allegory—would that we could so read through the accounts of the things done as to perceive and take thought for the things to be done. For indeed the one, in saluting one only of the three angels, declared the Persons of the Trinity to be of one Substance; the other blessed his son when satiated, because one who is filled with divine banquets has his senses extended into the power of prophecy. But the words of Holy Writ are divine banquets. If, then, you read diligently—if, drawing example from what is outward, you penetrate what is inward—you will be satiated, as it were, from hunting in the field, and fill the stomach of the soul, so as to be able to announce things to come to your son placed before you, to wit to the people you have taken in charge. But one who prophesies anything of God is already in the dark as to this world; for it is assuredly right and fit that he whose senses are bright inwardly through intelligence should see less through concupiscence here below.

Take, therefore, these things to yourselves; and, if you know yourselves to be such as I have said, you need not at all doubt of our esteem. I also find your Blessedness rejoicing if you bear the name of "a gluttonous man" along with the world's Creator. As to this I briefly comment thus; that, if you are called so falsely, you do truly bear this name along with the world's Creator; but, if it is true of you, who can doubt that it was false of Him? A like name does not avail to acquit you, if the cause for it is unlike. For even the thief who was condemned to die endured the cross with Him; but a like crucifixion did not acquit him whom his own guilt bound. But now I beseech God with all the prayers I can offer that not the name only, but the cause for it, may join your most holy Fraternity to our Creator.

Further, your Holiness in your letters rightly praises feasts which are made with the intention of bestowing charity. But yet you should know that they then truly proceed from charity, when at them the lives of the absent are not backbitten, no one is censured in derision, and no idle tales about secular affairs, but the words of sacred reading, are heard; when the body is not pampered more than is needful, but only its weakness refreshed, that it may be kept in health for the practice of virtue. If, then, you thus conduct yourselves in your feasts, I own that you are masters of abstinence.

As to your alleging to me the testimony of the apostle Paul, where he says, *Let not him that eateth not judge him that eateth* (Rom. xiv. 3), I think that this was altogether out of place, seeing both that I am not one that eateth not, and also that Paul did not here mean to say that the members of Christ, who are mutually bound to each other in His body, that is to say in his Church, with the bond of charity, should have no care whatever for each other. If, indeed, I had nothing to do with thee, nor thou with me, I should rightly be compelled to hold my peace, lest I should blame one whom I could not mend. This precept, then, was given only with reference to persons who go about to judge those who have not been committed to their care. But now that we, by the ordering of God, are one, we should be much in fault were we to pass over in silence what calls for our correction. Lo, thy Fraternity has taken it amiss to have been blamed by me about feasts, while I, who surpass thee in my position, though not in my life, am ready to be found fault with by all, and by all to be amended. And him only do I esteem to be a friend to me, through whose tongue I wipe off the stains of my soul before the appearance of the strict judge.

But as to what you say, most sweet brother, about your being unable to read because of the pressure of tribulations upon you, I think this avails little for your excuse, since Paul

[6] See I. 19, note 5, with reff.

says, *Whatsoever things are written are written for our instruction, that we through patience and comfort of the Scriptures might have hope* (Rom. xv. 4). If, then, holy Scripture has been prepared for our comfort, we ought by so much the more to read it as we find ourselves the more wearied under the burden of tribulations. But if we are to rely only on that sentence which you quote in your letter, wherein the Lord says, *When they deliver you up, take no thought how or what ye shall speak, for it shall be given you in that hour what ye shall speak; for it is not ye that speak, but the Spirit of your Father that speaketh in you* (Matth. x. 19), I say that Holy Scriptures have been given us in vain, if, being filled with the Spirit, we have no need of external words. But, dearest brother, trusting in God without doubt, when we are straightened in a time of persecution, is one thing; what we ought to do when the Church is at peace is another. For it is our duty, through this same Spirit, to learn by reading now what we may be able to shew forth also in suffering, should cause arise.

Now, I rejoice exceedingly that you declare in your letter that you are giving attention to exhortation. For thus I know that you are wisely fulfilling the duties of your position, if you take pains to draw others also to your Maker. But your saying in the same sentence that you are not like me saddens me at once, after I had begun to rejoice, since I think that it is in derision that you give me praises which in truth I do not recognize as due. However, I give thanks to Almighty God that through you heretics are being recalled to holy Church. But it is needful for you to have a care that those also who are contained in the bosom of holy Church live so that they be not her adversaries through their evil lives. For, if they give themselves not to heavenly desires, but to earthly lusts and pleasures, sons of strangers are being nourished in her bosom.

Now as to your declaring that you cannot possibly be ignorant of the degrees of ecclesiastical rank, I too fully know them with regard to you; and I am therefore much distressed that, if you knew the order of things, you have failed, to your greater blame, in knowing it with regard to me. For, after letters had been addressed to your Blessedness by my predecessor and myself in the cause of the archdeacon Honoratus, then, the sentence of both of us being set at nought, the said Honoratus was deprived of the rank belonging to him. Which thing if any one of the four patriarchs had done, such great contumacy could by no means have been allowed to pass without the most grievous offence. Nevertheless, now that your Fraternity has returned to your proper position, I do not bear in mind the wrong done either to myself or to my predecessor.

But as to your saying that what has been handed down and guarded by my predecessors ought to be observed in our times also, far be it from me to infringe in any church the statutes of our ancestors with regard to my fellow priests, since I do myself an injury if I disturb the rights of my brethren. But when your accredited messengers arrive, I shall know the rights of the case between you and the aforesaid archdeacon Honoratus; and my own personal examination of it will shew you that, if you have the support of justice on your side, you will sustain no injury from me; as indeed you never have done. But in case justice supports the plea of the often-before-named Honoratus, I will shew by my acquittal of him that in judgment I have no knowledge even of persons whom I knew.

Concerning the article of excommunication which, if I may say so, was of necessity added to our letters (though even the second and the third time with a condition interposed), your Blessedness complains unreasonably, since the apostle Paul says, *Having in a readiness to revenge all disobedience* (2 Cor. x. 6). But let these things pass: let us return to what concerns us now. For, if the lord Natalis acts as he should do, I cannot but be friends with him, knowing how much I am a debtor to his affection.

EPISTLE LIV.

Here follows the Epistle of Saint Licinianus, bishop, concerning the Book of Rules, addressed to Saint Gregory, pope of the city of Rome[7].

To the most blessed lord pope Gregory, Licinianus, bishop.

The Book of Rules issued by Thy Holiness, and by the aid of divine grace conveyed to us, we have read with all the more pleasure for the spiritual rules which we find contained in it. Who can fail to read that with pleasure wherein by constant meditation he may find medicine for his soul; wherein, despising the fleeting things of this world which vary in their mutability, he may open the eyes of his soul to the settled estate of eternal life? This

7 Licinianus was bishop of Carthagena in Spain, a Latin ecclesiastical writer. Isidore (*Lib. de illustribus Ecclesiæ scriptoribus*, c. 29) says of him, "In scripturis doctus, cujus quidem nonnullas epistolas legimus. De sacramento denique baptismatis unam, et ad Eutropium abbatem postea Valentiæ episcopum plurimas; reliqua vero industriæ et laboris ejus ad nostram notitiam minime pervenerunt. Claruit temporibus Mauricii Augusti; occubuit Constantinopoli veneno ut ferunt, extinctus ab æmulis Sed, ut scriptum est, *Justus quacunque morte præoccupatus fuerit, anima ejus in refrigerio est.*" The "Book of Rules' which he had received, was Gregory's *Regula Pastoralis*.

book of thine is a palace of all virtues. In it prudence fixes the boundary line between good and evil; justice gives each one his own, while it subjects the soul to God, and the body to the soul. In it fortitude also is found ever the same in adversity and in prosperity, being neither broken by opposition nor lifted up by success. In it temperance subdues the rage of lust, and discriminately imposes a limit upon pleasures. In it thou comprehendest all things that pertain to the partaking of eternal life; and not only for pastors layest down a rule of life, but also to those who have no office of government thou suppliest a rule of life. For pastors may learn in thy fourfold division what they should be in coming to this office; what life they should lead after coming to it; how and what they should teach, and what they should do to avoid being lifted up in so high a position as that of priesthood. This excellent teaching of thine is attested by the holy ancient fathers, doctors, and defenders of the Church; Hilary, Ambrose, Augustin, Gregory Nazianzen: these all bear testimony to thee as did the prophets to the apostles. Saint Hilary says, in expounding the words of the Apostle who was the teacher of the Gentiles, "For so he signifies that the things belonging to discipline and morals serve to the good desert of the priesthood, if those things also which are necessary for the science of teaching and guarding the faith shall not be wanting among the rest; since it does not all at once constitute a good and useful priest only to act innocently, or only to preach knowingly, seeing that, though a man be innocent, he profits himself only unless he be learned, and that he that is learned is without the authority of a teacher unless he be innocent[8]." Saint Ambrose gives attestation to this book of thine in the books which he wrote about Duties (*de officiis*). Saint Augustin gives attestation, saying, "In action dignity should not be loved in this life, neither power; since all things under the sun are vain. But the work itself which is done by means of this dignity or power, if it is rightly and profitably done, this is what avails for that weal of subjects which is according to God. Wherefore the Apostle says, 'He that desireth the office of a bishop desireth a good work.' He wished to explain what *episcopus* means; that it is a title denoting work, not dignity. For it is a Greek word derived hence;—that he who is put over others overlooks those whom he is put over, to wit, as taking care of them; for episcopacy is overlooking. Therefore, if we choose, we may say in Latin that to exercise the office of a bishop is to overlook; so that one who delights to be over others and not to profit them may understand that he is no bishop. For so it is that no one is prohibited from longing to become acquainted with truth, for which purpose leisure is to be commended; but as to a position of superiority, without which the people cannot be governed, though it may be held and administered becomingly, it is unbecoming to covet it. Wherefore charity seeks holy leisure, so as to have time for perceiving and defending the truth. But if [the burden of government] be imposed, it is to be undertaken on account of the obligation of charity. But not even so should delight in the truth be altogether forsaken, lest the former sweetness should be withdrawn, and the present obligation be oppressive' (*Lib.* viii. de *Trinit.*, *num.* 1).

Saint Gregory attests, whose style thou followest, and after whose example thou didst desire to hide thyself in order to avoid the weight of priesthood; which weight, of what sort it is, is clearly declared in the whole of thy book: and yet thou bearest what thou wast afraid of. For thy burden is borne upwards, not downwards; not so as to sink thee to the depths, but to lift thee to the stars; whilst by the grace of God, and the merit of obedience, and the efficiency of good work, that is made sweet which seemed to have heaviness through human weakness. For thou sayest the things that are in agreement with the apostles and with apostolic men. For, being fair, thou hast said things fair, and in them hast shewn thyself fair. I would not have thee liken thyself to an ill-favoured painter painting fair things, seeing that spiritual teaching issues from a spiritual soul. The human painter is by most men esteemed more highly than the inanimate picture. But put not this down to flattery or adulation, but to truth: for it neither becomes me to lie, nor thee to commend what is false. I then, though plainly sincere, have seen thee and all that is thine to be fair, and have seen myself as ill-favoured enough in comparison with thee. Wherefore I pray thee by the grace of God which abounds in thee that thou reject not my prayer, but willingly teach me what I confess myself ignorant of. For we are compelled of necessity to do what thou teachest.

For, when there is no skilled person found for the sacerdotal office, what is to be done but that an unskilled one such as I am, should be ordained? Thou orderest that no unskilled one should be ordained. But let thy prudence

[8] This and the succeeding quotations from the works of Fathers are inaccurately given, and in places hardly intelligible. Where this is so, the original passages have been followed in the translations.

consider whether it may not suffice him for skill to know Jesus Christ and Him crucified: for, if this does not suffice, there will, according to this book, be no one who can be called skilled: and so no one will be a priest, if none, unless he be skilled, should be one. For with open front we resist bigamists, lest the sacrament should be thus corrupted. What if the husband of one wife should have touched a woman before his wife? What if he should not have had a wife, and yet should not have been without touch of a woman? Comfort us with thy pen, that we may not be punished either for our own sin or that of others. For we are exceedingly afraid lest we should be forced to do what we ought not to do. Lo, obedience must be paid to thy precepts, that such a one may be made a priest as apostolical authority approves; and such a one as is sought is not found. Thus faith will cease, which cometh of hearing; baptism will cease, if there should be no one to baptize; those most holy mysteries will cease which are effected through priests and ministers. In either case danger remains: either such a one must be ordained as ought not to be, or there must be no one to celebrate or administer sacred mysteries.

A few years ago Leander, Bishop of Hispalis, on his return from the royal city, saw us in passing, and told us that he had some homilies issued by your Blessedness on the Book of Job. And, as he passed by in haste, he did not shew them to us as we requested. But thou wrotest afterwards to him about trine immersion, and saidest in thy letter, as I am told, that thou wast dissatisfied with that work, and hadst determined on maturer consideration to change those homilies into the form of a treatise [9].

We have indeed six books of Saint Hilary, Bishop of Pictavia, which he turned into Latin from the Greek of Origen: but he has not expounded the whole of the book of holy Job in order. And I am not a little surprised that a man so very learned and so holy should translate the silly tales of Origen about the stars. I, most holy father, can in no wise be persuaded to believe that the heavenly luminaries are rational spirits, Holy Scripture not declaring them to have been made either along with angels or along with men. Let then your Blessedness deign to transmit to my littleness not only this work, but also the other books on morals which in this Book of Rules thou speakest of having composed. For we are thine, and are delighted to read what is thine. For to me it is a desirable and glorious thing, as thy Gregory says, to learn even to extreme old age. May God the Holy Trinity vouchsafe to preserve your crown unharmed for instructing His Church, as we hope, most blessed father.

---

9 See I. 43.

BOOK III

EPISTLE I.

To Peter, Subdeacon.

Gregory to Peter, Subdeacon of Campania.

What a crime has been committed in the Lucullan fort against our brother and fellow-bishop Paul[1] the account which has been sent to us has made manifest. And, inasmuch as the magnificent Scholasticus, judge of Campania, happens at the present time to be with us here, we have especially enjoined on him the duty of visiting the madness of so great perversity with strict correction. But, since the bearer of the aforesaid account has requested us to send some one to represent ourselves, we therefore send the subdeacon Epiphanius, who, together with the aforesaid judge, may be able to investigate and ascertain by whom the sedition was raised or instigated, and to visit it with suitable punishment. Let thy Experience then make haste to give aid in this case with all thy power, to the end both that the truth may be ascertained, and that vengeance may proceed against the guilty parties. Wherefore, since the slaves of the glorious Clementina are said to have had to do with this same crime, and to have used language calculated to stir up the sedition, do thou subject them strictly to immediate punishment, nor let your severity be relaxed in consideration of her person, since they ought to be smitten all the more as they have transgressed out of mere pride as being the servants of a noble lady. But you ought also to make thorough enquiry whether the said lady was privy to so atrocious a crime, and whether it was perpetrated with her knowledge, that from our visitation of it all may learn how dangerous it is not only to lay hands on a priest, but even to transgress in words against one. For, if anything should be done remissly or omitted in this case, know that thou especially wilt have to bear the blame and the risk; nor wilt thou find any plea for excuse with us. For in proportion as this business will commend thee to us if it be most strictly investigated and corrected, know that our indignation will become sharp against thee, if it be smoothed over.

Moreover, for the rest, if any slaves from the city should have taken refuge in the monastery of Saint Severinus, or in any other church of this same fort, as soon as this has come to thy knowledge, by no means allow them to remain there, but let them be brought to the church within the city; and, if they should have just cause of complaint against their masters, they must needs leave the church with suitable arrangements made for them. But, if they should have committed any venial fault, let them be restored without delay to their masters, the latter having taken oath to pardon them.

EPISTLE II.

To Paulus, Bishop[2].

Gregory to Paulus, &c.

Although it has distressed us in no slight degree to hear of the injury that thou hast suffered, yet we have matter of consolation in learning that the affair is to thy credit, in that, so far as the account sent to us has disclosed the facts, thou hast suffered in the cause of uprightness and equity. Wherefore, that it may redound to the greater glory of thy Fraternity, this occurrence ought neither to shake thy constancy nor turn thee aside from the way of truth. For it is to the greater reward of priests if they continue in the path of truth even after injuries. But, lest the madness of such great impiety should remain unpunished, and pernicious insubordination break out to a worse degree, we have enjoined the magnificent Scholasticus, judge of Campania, who is at present here, that he should avenge what has been done with the repression it deserves. But, inasmuch as thy men have requested us to commission some one to represent ourselves, know that we have for this reason sent to Naples the subdeacon Epiphanius, who may

[1] The *Castellum*, or *Castrum*, *Lucullanum* was a small island adjoining Naples. Respecting Paul, bishop of Nepe, who had been sent as visitor to the See of Naples during a vacancy, and his difficulties there, cf. II. 9, 10, 15; III. 35.

[2] See preceding Epistle.

be able, with the judge above named, to investigate and ascertain the truth, to the end that by his instancy he may cause worthy vengeance to be executed on those who may be shewn to have instigated or perpetrated so great a crime.

EPISTLE III.

To John, Abbot[3].

Gregory to John, &c.

Thy Love has requested me that brother Boniface might be ordained Prior (*præpositus*)[4] in thy monastery; as to which request I wonder much why it has not been done before. For since the time when I caused him to be given to thee thou oughtest already to have ordained him.

With regard to the tunic of Saint John[5], I have been altogether gratified by thy anxiety to tell me of it. But let thy Love endeavour to send me this tunic, or (better still) this same bishop who has it, with his clergy and with the tunic itself, to the end that we may enjoy the blessing thereof, and be able to derive benefit from this bishop and his clergy. I have been desirous of putting an end to the cause that is pending with Florianus, and have already advanced to him as much as eighty *solidi*, which I believe he proposes should be given him in compensation for the monastery's debt; and I am altogether desirous that this cause should be settled, inasmuch as Stephen the *chartularius* is said to be urgent that the aforesaid Florianus should transfer it to public cognizance, and it is distasteful to us to be engaged in a public lawsuit. Wherefore we must needs make some concession, so as to be able to bring this same cause to a composition. When this shall have been done, we will inform your Love of it.

But do thou give thy whole attention to the souls of the brethren. Let it be now enough that the reputation of the monastery has been stained through your negligence. Do not often go abroad. Appoint an agent for these causes, and do thou leave thyself time for reading and prayer.

Be attentive to hospitality; as far as thou art able, give to the poor; yet so as to keep what ought to be restored to Florianus.

Moreover, among the brethren of thy monastery whom I see I do not find addiction to reading. Wherefore you must needs consider how great a sin it is, that God should have sent you alimony from the offerings of others, and you should neglect learning the commandments of God.

Further, with regard to the six twelfths, unless we see the original deed, or a copy of it, we can do nothing. But I have sent an order to the servant of God, Florentinus, that, if the truth should be made apparent to him, he restore to you the six twelfths; after the restoration of which we will either grant the remaining six twelfths on lease or commute the revenue.

EPISTLE V.

To Peter, Subdeacon.

Gregory to Peter, Subdeacon of Campania.

As we have no wish to disturb the privileges of laymen in their judgments, so, when they judge wrongfully, we desire thee to resist them with moderate authority. For to restrain violent laymen is not to act against the laws, but to support law. Since then Deusdedit, the son-in-law of Felix of Orticellum, is said to have done violent wrong to the bearer of these presents, and still unlawfully to detain her property, in such sort that the dejection of her widowhood is found not to move his compassion, but to confirm his malice, we charge thy Experience that against the aforesaid man, as well as in other cases wherein the aforesaid woman asserts that she suffers prejudice, thou afford her the succour of thy protection, and not allow her to be oppressed by any one whatever, lest either thou be found to neglect what without prejudice to equity is commanded thee, or widows and other poor persons, finding no help where they are, be put to expense by the length of the journey hither.

EPISTLE VI.

To John, Bishop.

Gregory to John, bishop of Prima Justiniana[6].

[3] Probably John, abbot of the monastery of St. Lucia in Syracuse, referred to as engaged in a dispute about property in VII. 39.

[4] See II. 32, note 5.

[5] This tunic is referred to by John the Deacon (*Vit. S. Greg.* iii. 57, 59), and supposed by him to have been that of St. John the Evangelist, and identical with one of the vestments afterwards preserved under the altar of St. John in the *Basilica Constantiniana* at Rome, fragments of which he says were given away as relics, and possessed of miraculous virtue.

[6] As to the See of Prima Justiniana, the Metropolitan jurisdiction assigned to it by the Emperor Justinian, and the vicariate jurisdiction that had been transferred to it from Thessalonica by the popes, see note on *Lib.* II., *Ep.* 22. The circumstances referred to in this and the following letter are interesting as shewing, among other things, the relations of the See of Rome to the Church in Illyricum, and the action of the Emperors with regard to it. They may be epitomized as follows. Thebæ Phthioticæ was a See in the province of Thessalia, of which Larissa was the Metropolis. But, as appears from what Gregory says in Epistle VII., Thebæ had been for some reason exempted from the metropolitan jurisdiction of the bishop of Larissa by pope Pelagius II. John and Cosmas, two deposed deacons of the Church of Thebæ, had sent a representation to the Emperor.

After the long afflictions which Adrian, bishop of the city of Thebæ, has endured from his fellow-priests, as though they had been his enemies, he has fled for refuge to the Roman city. And though his first representation had been against John, bishop of Larissa, to wit that in pecuniary causes he had given judgment without regard to the laws, yet after this he complained most grievously rather against the person of thy Fraternity, accusing thee of having deposed him unjustly from the degree of priesthood. But we, giving no credence to petitions that have not been enquired into, perused the acts of the proceedings, whether before our brother and fellow-bishop John, or before thy Fraternity. And indeed concerning the judgment of the above-named John, bishop of Larissa, which was suspended on appeal, both the most pious emperors, in their orders sent to the bishop of Corinth, have sufficiently decreed, and we have decreed also, Christ helping us, in our letters directed through the bearers of these presents to the aforesaid John of Larissa. But having ventilated the conflicting judgments, the examination of which the imperial commands had committed to thee, and inspected the series of proceedings held before the bishop John concerning the incriminated persons, we find that thou hast investigated almost nothing pertaining to the questions named and assigned to thee for decision, but by certain machinations hast produced witnesses against the deacon Demetrius, who were to allege with a view to the condemnation of this same bishop, that they had heard this Demetrius bearing testimony concerning the said bishop;—a thing not even lawful to be heard of. And when Demetrius in person denied having done so, it appears that, contrary to the custom of the priesthood and canonical discipline, thou gavest him into the hands of the prætor of the province as a deacon deposed from his dignity[7]. And when, mangled by many stripes, he might perchance have said some things falsely against his bishop under the pressure of torment, we find that to the very end of the business he confessed absolutely nothing of the things about which he was interrogated. Neither do we find anything else in the proceedings themselves, whether in the depositions of witnesses or in the declaration of Adrian, to his disadvantage. But it is only that thy Fraternity, I know not with what motive, in contempt of law, human and divine, has pronounced an abrupt sentence against him; which, even though it had not been suspended on appeal, being pronounced in contravention of the laws and canons, could not rightly in itself have stood. Further, after, as is abundantly evident, the appeal had been handed to thee, we wonder why thou hast not sent thy people to us to render an account of thy judgment according to the undertaking delivered to our deacon Honoratus by the representatives of thy church. This omission convicts thee either of contumacy or of trepidation of conscience. If, then, these things which have been brought before us have the rampart of truth, inasmuch as we consider that, taking advantage of your vicariate jurisdiction under us, you are presuming unjustly, we will, with the help of Christ, decree further concerning these things, according to the result of our deliberations.

But as regards the present, by the authority of the blessed Peter, Prince of the apostles, we decree that, the decrees of thy judgment being first annulled and made of none effect, thou be deprived of holy communion for the space of thirty days, so as to implore pardon of our God for so great transgression with the utmost penitence and tears. But, if we should come to know that thou hast been remiss in carrying out this our sentence, know thou that not the injustice only, but also the

---

accusing their bishop, Adrian, of defalcations in money matters, and also of certain misdemeanours; the latter being that he had retained in office one of his deacons, Stephen, whose shameful life was notorious, and that he had ordered baptism to be refused to certain infants, who had consequently died unbaptized. The Emperor (Mauricius) referred the matter to John, bishop of Larissa, as Metropolitan of Thessalia, who, notwithstanding the exemption of Thebæ from his jurisdiction by pope Pelagius II., took it up, and decided against Adrian, at any rate with respect to his alleged pecuniary defalcations. Adrian appealed against this decision to the Emperor, who thereupon deputed certain persons (not bishops) to enquire and report, and, on receiving their report, exempted Adrian from further proceedings, sending an order to that effect to the Bishop of Corinth, who was Metropolitan of the adjoining province of Achaia. Meanwhile John of Larissa had imprisoned Adrian, and elicited from him (under compulsion, it was said) an ambiguous confession of his guilt, and also obtained from the Emperor a second order committing the reinvestigation and final adjudication of the case to John, bishop of Prima Justiniana, who confirmed the sentence of John of Larissa, and deposed Adrian from his See. Adrian now at last appealed to the pope, and went himself to Rome to seek aid from Gregory, who took up the case at once and strenuously declared the past proceedings unfair, uncanonical, and void, ordered the immediate restoration of Adrian to his See, excommunicated John of Prima Justiniana, and forbade John of Larissa, under pain of excommunication, to assume hereafter any metropolitan jurisdiction over the church of Thebæ. Now it is plain that, till Adrian's final appeal, no recourse was had by any of the parties concerned to the See of Rome, and that the Emperor, who alone was at first appealed to, took the matter up on his own authority without reference to Rome: nor was it till he had failed of redress from Constantinople that Adrian himself appealed to Gregory. But it is equally evident that Gregory, when appealed to, asserted his own plenary jurisdiction as a matter of course and without hesitation: nor is there any evidence to shew that his assertion of authority was resisted either by the Illyrican prelates or the Emperor. It was probably a case in which the Emperor himself took little interest; and he might be glad that the pope should take it out of his hands and settle it. It was otherwise, however, in a subsequent case (though occurring not in Eastern, but in Western Illyricum), in which Gregory was at issue with the Emperor with respect to the appointment of a bishop to the See of Salona, as will be seen hereafter. See III. 47, note 2.

7 Otherwise he could not have been examined by scourging, as it appears he was. For clerics were by law exempt from the question.

contumacy, of thy Fraternity will have to be more severely punished. But, as to our aforesaid brother and fellow-bishop Adrian, condemned by thy sentence, which, as we have said, was consistent with neither canons nor laws, we order that he be restored, Christ being with him, to his place and rank; so that neither may he be injured by the sentence of thy Fraternity pronounced in deviation from the path of justice, nor may thy Charity remain uncorrected; that so we may appease the indignation of the future judge.

EPISTLE VII.

To John, Bishop.

Gregory to John, bishop of Larissa.

Our brother Adrian, bishop of the city of Thebæ, has come to Rome, bitterly complaining of having been condemned, neither lawfully nor canonically, on certain charges by thy Fraternity, and also by John, bishop of Prima Justiniana. And, when for a long time we saw no representative of the opposite party arrive here who might have replied to his objections, we delivered for perusal [8], with a view to the necessary ascertainment of the truth, the proceedings which had taken place before you. From these we ascertained that John and Cosmas, deacons who had been deposed from their office, one for frailty of the body and the other for fraudulent dealing with ecclesiastical property, had sent a representation to our most pious emperors against him, with respect to pecuniary matters and also criminal charges.

They, in their commands sent to thee, desired thee (that is with strict observance of law and canons) to take cognizance of the matter, so as to pass a sentence firm in law as to the pecuniary questions, but, as to the criminal charges, to report to their Clemency after a searching examination. Now if thy Fraternity had received in a right frame of mind these such right commands, you would never have accepted for a general accusation of their bishop men removed from their own office for their transgressions, and already hostilely disposed; especially as by their representation addressed to our most pious lords their untruthfulness is detected, in that they declared that they made it with the consent of all the clergy.

Yet after this, to touch briefly and summarily on some of the proceedings before thee, the first head of accusation was concerning the Theban deacon Stephen, whom the bishop Adrian had failed to deprive of the dignity of his order, though supposed to have been aware of his most shameful life As to this head, no witnesses were produced to shew that bishop Adrian had any knowledge of the matter, except that Stephen alone, a man of shameful life and on his own confession to be condemned, is alleged to have said so. The second charge made against him appears to have been concerning infants having been debarred by his order from receiving holy baptism, and so having died with the filth of sin unwashed away. But none of the witnesses brought forward against him declared their knowledge of anything of the kind having come under the notice of bishop Adrian, but said that they had learnt it from the mothers of the infants, whose husbands, it is said, had been removed from the church for their crimes. But even so they did not declare that the hour of death had overtaken those infants while unbaptized, as was contained in the invidious representation of the accusers, it being evident that they had been baptized in the city of Demetrias. So much then for the criminal charges.

But, as to the pecuniary matters, after what manner they were adjudged by thee is attested by the enquiry of the men deputed by the prince in pursuance of the most pious order of the most serene princes [9]. For, when the oft-named Adrian had appealed against thy sentence, then, so far as we have ascertained from the depositions of four witnesses which were laid before John, bishop of Prima Justiniana, he was thrust into most close confinement, and forced by thy Fraternity to produce a document in which he confessed the charges brought against him. And it is true that in the document so produced by him he is found to have assented to thy sentence as to pecuniary matters. But the criminal charges he touched on in an indefinite and dubious sort of way, so that both thy purpose might be frustrated by the raising of certain clouds, and he might afterwards the better escape from his confession in the obscurity of a perplexed mode of speech. And when the appeal handed in by his people, and the rest of the proceedings under thy cognizance, had been reported to the most pious princes, and Honoratus, deacon of our See, with the glorious *antigraphus* [1] Sebastian having been deputed, as we have said, he was exempted by the most serene lords from all further orders. But, by

[8] "Relegenda tradidimus," not "relegimus;" presumably because, the Acts being drawn up in Greek, Gregory was unable to read them himself.

[9] The Emperor Mauricius had associated his son Theodosius, being four years of age, with himself in the empire. Hence "principibus."

[1] See I. 39, note.

what sought out contrivances I know not, another imperial order was again elicited, requiring John, bishop of Prima Justiniana, to enquire closely and pass judgment concerning all the aforesaid charges. In which trial all bishop Adrian's clergy, and Demetrius the deacon, the latter in the midst of torments, declared that all this calumny against bishop Adrian had been got up by the contrivance of thy Fraternity. Nor were any of the criminal charges that had been made in thy audience against the bishop Adrian proved. But there came up, contrary to canons and laws, another cruel and crafty enquiry directed against his deacon Demetrius and other persons, in the course of which nothing was discovered for which the oft-mentioned Adrian could have been lawfully condemned, but rather ground for his acquittal. But with respect to John, prelate of the city of Prima Justiniana, and his most iniquitous and abominable judgment, we shall take further measures. As to bishop Adrian, we find both that he has laboured under thy enmity in a way ill-befitting thy priestly character, and that he has been condemned in pecuniary matters for no just cause by the sentence of thy Fraternity.

Since then, having been deposed also by the above-said John bishop of Prima Justiniana in contravention of law and canons, he could not be left deprived of his rank and honour, we have decreed that he be reinstated in his church, and recalled to the order of his proper dignity. And, though thou oughtest to have been deprived of the communion of the Lord's body, for that, setting at naught the admonition of my predecessor of holy memory, whereby he exempted him and his church from the jurisdiction of thy authority, thou hast again presumed to retain some jurisdiction over them, yet we, decreeing more humanely, and still allowing thee the sacrament of communion, decree that thy Fraternity shall abstain from all exercise of the jurisdiction formerly held by thee over him and his church; but that, according to the written instructions of our predecessor, if any case should possibly arise, whether touching the faith, or criminal, or pecuniary, against the aforesaid Adrian our fellow-priest, it be either taken cognizance of, if the question be a slight one, by those who are or may be our representatives in the royal city, or, if it be an arduous one, it be brought hither to the Apostolic See, to the end that it may be heard and decided before ourselves. But, if thou shouldest attempt at any time, on any pretext or by any surreptitious device, to contravene these our ordinances, know that we decree thee to be deprived of holy communion, and not to partake of it except at the close of thy life, unless upon leave granted by the Roman pontiff. For this we lay down as a rule, agreeably to the teaching of the holy fathers, that whosoever knows not how to obey the holy canons, neither is he worthy to minister or receive the communion at the holy altars. Moreover let thy Fraternity restore to him without any delay the sacred property, or any other, movable or immovable, which thou art said to retain so far; a specification whereof, that has been handed to us, we append to this letter. Concerning which if any question arises between you, we desire it to be considered by our representative in the royal city.

EPISTLE VIII.

To Natalis, Archbishop.

Gregory to Natalis, archbishop of Salona[2].

Whilst every kind of business demands[3] anxious investigation of the truth, what pertains to deposition from sacerdotal rank should be considered with especial strictness, since here the matter in hand is not concerning persons constituted in a humble position, but, as it were, concerning reversal of divine benediction. This consideration has also moved us to exhort your Fraternity with respect to the person of Florentius, bishop of the city of Epidaurus. For indeed we have been told that he had been accused on certain criminal charges, and that, without any canonical proof being sought, and without previous sentence of any sacerdotal council, he has been deposed from his office of dignity, not by law, but by authority. Inasmuch, then, as no man can be removed from the rank of episcopacy except for just causes by the concordant sentence of priests, we exhort your Fraternity to cause the aforesaid man to be recalled from the banishment into which he has been driven, and his case enquired into in a consultation of bishops. And, should he be convicted by canonical proof of the charges brought against him, without doubt he must be visited with canonical punishment. But, should the facts be found by the synodical inquisition to be otherwise than had been supposed, it is necessary both that his accusers should dread the rigour of justice, and that the incriminated person should have the approbation of his innocence preserved inviolate. But we have committed by our order the execution of the above-mentioned business to Antoninus, our subdeacon, to the end that decisions may be come to in accordance with the laws and

[2] Natalis was Metropolitan of the province of Dalmatia. See II. 18, note 3.

[3] I.e. episcopal rank. Here, as below in this Epistle and elsewhere, by *sacerdotes* are meant bishops.

canons, and, with the help of the Lord, be carried into effect.

EPISTLE IX.

To Antoninus, Subdeacon[4].

Gregory to Antoninus, &c.

It has come to our ears that Florentius, bishop of the city of Epidaurus, his property having first been seized, has been condemned, for certain crimes not proved, without a sacerdotal council. And, inasmuch as he ought not to suffer canonical punishment, no canonical sentence having been pronounced for his condemnation, we enjoin thy Experience to urge upon our brother and fellow-bishop Natalis that he should cause the aforesaid man to be recalled from the banishment into which he is said to have been driven. And a council of bishops having been assembled, if the charges brought against him should be canonically proved, we will that the sentence of our aforesaid brother and fellow-bishop Natalis shall take effect against him. But, should he be absolved by a general judgment, thou must not permit him to be subject to prejudice on the part of any one, and must carefully and rigorously insist on his aforesaid property being restored to him. It is therefore needful that the heavier thou feelest the burden of such negotiations to be, with the maturer and more vigilant execution thou take pains to fulfil them.

EPISTLE X.

To Savinus, Subdeacon[5].

Gregory to Savinus, &c.

Bad men have gone forth and disturbed your minds, understanding neither what they say nor whereof they affirm, pretending that in the times of Justinian of pious memory something was detracted from the faith of the holy synod of Chalcedon, which with all faith and all devotion we venerate. And in like manner all the four synods of the holy universal Church we receive as we do the four books of the holy Gospel. But concerning the persons with respect to whom something had been done after the close of the synod, there was something ventilated in the times of Justinian of pious memory: yet so that neither was the faith in any respect violated, nor anything else done with regard to these same persons but what had been determined at the same holy synod of Chalcedon. Moreover, we anathematize any one who presumes to detract anything from the definition of the faith which was promulged in the said synod, or, as though by amending it, to change its meaning: but, as it was there promulged, so in all respects we guard it. Thee, therefore, most dear son, it becomes to return to the unity of Holy Church, that thou mayest end thy days in peace; lest the malignant spirit, who cannot prevail against thee through thy other works, may from this cause find a way at the day of thy departure of barring thy entrance into the heavenly Kingdom.

EPISTLE XII.

To Maximianus, Bishop.

Gregory to Maximianus, bishop of Syracuse

I wrote some time ago to your Fraternity desiring you to send to the Roman city those who had alleged anything against Gregory, bishop of the city of Agrigentum[6]. And we exhort you by this present epistle that this should be immediately done. Wherefore hasten to send with speed the persons themselves, and the rest of the documents, that is the reports of proceedings and the petitions that have been given in. Nor do we allow any delay or excuse to be sought; to the end that, when thay have been sent, as we have said, with speed to the Roman city, we may know how, with the help of God, we may most advantageously deal with him

EPISTLE XV.

To Scholasticus, Judge.

Gregory to Scholasticus, judge of Campania.

While we were greatly distressed in our care for the city of Naples, bereaved of the solace of a priest[7], the arrival of the bearers of these presents with the decree for the election of our subdeacon Florentius, had afforded us some relief under so great a burden of thought. But, when it appeared that our said subdeacon, flying from the very city, had deprecated his ordination with tears, know ye that our sadness

4 I.e. of Dalmatia. The case referred to in this and the preceding letter is interesting as illustrating canonical procedure against incriminated bishops. Natalis, as Metropolitan, had entertained a charge against one of his suffragans and pronounced judgment against him on his own authority. Gregory insists that he had no right to do so except in a synod of bishops. It appears that Natalis (as to whose character and relations to Gregory, see II. 18, and *reff.* in note), paid no regard in this instance to the pope's remonstrances, and the latter found no means of enforcing his orders. For, in a letter written five years later (A.D. 597), long after the death of Natalis, we find Gregory writing, "The inhabitants of the city of Epidaurus have most urgently demanded that Florentius, who they say is their bishop, should be restored to them by us, asserting that he had been driven into exile invalidly by the mere will of the bishop Natalis." (*Lib.* viii. *Indict.* i. *Ep.* 11).

5 It does not appear who this Savinus was. The Epistle refers to the condemnation of the *Three Chapters* by the fifth General Council. See *Proleg.* p. xi.

6 Cf. I. 72.

7 For an account of the circumstances of the vacancy at Naples after the deposition of Demetrius, cf. II. 6, note 3; II. 9, note 6

increased, as if from some heavier dispensation. Wherefore, greeting you well, we exhort your Greatness to assemble the chief men or the people of the city, so as to take thought for the election of another, who may be worthy to be promoted to the priesthood with the consolation of Christ. Then, the decree having been solemnly passed, and transmitted to this city, let the ordination proceed, with the help of Christ, among yourselves. But, should you not find a suitable person on whom you can agree, at any rate choose ye three upright and wise men, to be sent to this city as representing the community, and to whose judgment the whole population may assent. Perhaps, when they come hither, they will find such a one as may be ordained as your bishop without reproach, to the end that your bereaved city may neither within itself want an inspector of its deeds, nor, when the care of a priest is supplied to it, afford entrance to hostile snares from without.

EPISTLE XXII.

To Antoninus, Subdeacon.

Gregory to Antoninus, Subdeacon, Rector of the patrimony in Dalmatia.

It is commonly reported in these parts that our brother and fellow-bishop, Natalis of the Church of Salona, is dead. If this is true, let thy Experience with all speed and all care hasten to admonish the clergy and people of that city that with one consent they elect a priest for ordination; and, when the nomination of the person who may be elected has been made, thou wilt take care to transmit it to us, that he may be ordained with our consent, as has been the case from ancient times. And this above all things thou must look to, that in this election neither any bribery in any way whatever come in, nor the patronage of any persons whatever prevail. For if one is elected through the patronage of certain persons, he is obliged out of deference to them to comply with their wishes after his ordination, and so it comes to pass that the possessions of that church are lessened, and ecclesiastical order is not maintained. They must, therefore, under thy superintendence, elect such a person as will not be unsuitably subservient to the will of any one, but one who in the adornment of his life and conversation may be found worthy of such a high degree. But of the possessions or ornaments of the same church cause an inventory to be faithfully written out in thy presence. And, lest any of the possessions themselves should be lost, admonish Respectus the deacon and Stephanus the chief notary (*primicerium notariarum*) to take sole charge of these possessions, warning them that they will have to make good out of their own substance any diminution of them that may have arisen from their negligence.

Moreover, strictly charge Malchus [8], our brother and fellow-bishop, that he refrain entirely from intermeddling in this matter. For, should we learn that anything has been done or attempted by him against our will, let him know that he will incur no slight guilt and danger. But of this also take care to warn him, that he must be careful to set down and complete the accounts of our patrimony which he has had in charge; for doing which let him make haste, laying aside all excuses, to come to us from the Sicilian parts. Let him, then, in no wise presume to meddle with the affairs of the Church of Salona, lest he should be under further liability to it, and possibly found culpable. For he is said to have many things belonging to the aforesaid church; and report goes that he was well-nigh the prime mover in the sale of its possessions, and in other unlawful doings. And, should this be found in manifest truth to be as it is said to be, he may be certain that it will by no means remain unavenged.

Let any necessary expenses be defrayed by the steward who was in office at the time of the aforesaid bishop's death, that so he may explain his accounts to the future bishop as he knows them to be. All the things that we have enjoined on thee to be done it is certainly necessary that thou shouldest do with the advice of our son, the magnificent and most eloquent Marcellus [9], to the end that thou mayest be able to carry out carefully and effectively all that is contained in this paper of directions, and that no blame for negligence may belong to thee.

EPISTLE XXIX.

To the Presbyters and Clergy of Mediolanum (*Milan*) [1].

Gregory to the presbyters, deacons, and clergy of the church of Mediolanum.

8 For an account of this Malchus and his doings, see II. 20, note 5.

9 Proconsul of Dalmatia: see IX. 5. For subsequent proceedings in connexion with the election of a successor to Natalis at Salona, see III. 47. It appears that the co-operation of the proconsul Marcellus, anticipated in this Epistle, was not in fact obtained, but that he acted independently, and in opposition to Gregory. Cf. IX. 5.

1 As to the great Metropolitan See of Milan having been anciently independent of the See of Rome, cf. Bingham, Bk. IX., Ch. I., Sect. 10, 11. As to Pope Gregory's attitude with regard to it, as shewn in this and the two following Epistles, we may remark as follows. (1) The electors addressed (*Ep.* 29) are the clergy only, not (as is usual in other cases) including the laity of the Church. This may be due to the ancient custom of that Church. (2) The electors, having already made their choice, seem to have sent messengers to announce it to the pope

We have received your Love's epistle, which, though it bore no subscription, was accredited by the persons of the bearers, the presbyter Magnus and the cleric Hippolytus. Having read it, we find that you are all agreed in favour of our son Constantius, deacon of your church, who has been well known to me for long. And, when I represented the Apostolical See in the royal city, he stuck close to me for a long time; but I never found anything in him that could at all be found fault with. Nevertheless, since it has been for long my deliberate determination to interfere in no man's favour with a view to his undertaking the burden of pastoral care, I can but follow up your election with my prayers that Almighty God, who is ever prescient of our future doings, may supply you with a pastor such that in his tongue and manners you may be able to find pastures of divine exhortation; one in whose disposition humility may shine forth together with rectitude, and severity with loving-kindness; one who may be able to shew you the way of life not in his speaking only but also in his living; that so from his example your love may learn to sigh with longing for the eternal country. Wherefore, most dear sons, we, warned by our sense of the censorship of our office, urge you in this matter of getting yourselves a bishop that none of you look to your own gain without regard to the common advantage, lest, if any one is eager after his own individual interest, he should be deceived by a frivolous estimate: for the mind that is bound by cupidity does not examine with a free judgment a person's claims to preference. Considering, therefore, what things are profitable for all, pay ye ever in all things most complete obedience to him whom Divine grace may put over you. For, when once put over you, he must not be further judged by you; though now he ought to be the more thoroughly judged as he may not be judged hereafter. But, when with God's leave a pastor has been consecrated for you, commit ye yourselves to him with all your heart, and in him serve the Lord the Almighty, who has put him over you.

But, inasmuch as supernal judgment is wont to provide pastors for peoples according to their deservings, do you seek spiritual things, love heavenly things, despise things temporal and fugitive; and hold it for most certain that you will have a pastor who shall please God, if you in your own doings please God. Lo, all the things of this world, which we used to hear from the sacred page were doomed to perish, we see already ruined. Cities are overthrown, camps uprooted, churches destroyed; and no tiller of the ground inhabits our land. Among ourselves who are left, very few in number, the sword of man incessantly rages along with calamities wherewith we are smitten from above. Thus we see before our eyes the evils which we long ago heard should come upon the world, and the very regions of the earth have become as pages of books to us. In the passing away, then, of all things, we ought to take thought how that all that we have loved was nothing. View, therefore, with anxious heart the approaching day of the eternal judge, and by repenting anticipate its terrors. Wash away with tears the stains of all your transgressions. Allay by temporal lamentation the wrath that hangs over you eternally. For our loving Creator, when He shall come for judgment, will comfort us with all the greater favour as He sees now that we are punishing ourselves for our own transgressions.

We are now sending to you, by the favour of God, John our subdeacon, the bearer of these presents, to this end;—that, with the help of Almighty God, he may see to your bishop-elect being consecrated after the manner of his predecessor. For, as we demand our rights from others, so we conserve their several rights to all.

EPISTLE XXX.

To John, Subdeacon.

Gregory to John, &c

Inasmuch as it is manifest that the Apostolic See is, by the ordering of God, set over all Churches, there is, among our manifold cares, especial demand for our attention, when our decision is awaited with a view to the consecration of a bishop. Now on the death of Laurentius, bishop of the church of Mediolanum, the clergy reported to us that they had unanimously agreed in the election of our son Constantius, their deacon. But, their report not having been subscribed, it becomes necessary, that we may omit nothing in the way of caution, for thee to proceed to Genua (*Genoa*), supported by the authority of this order[2]. And, inasmuch as there are many Milanese at

(*Ep.* 29). (3) Gregory disclaims all desire of interfering either in the election or in the consecration of the new Metropolitan, according to ancient custom by his own suffragans, or in any way infringing the prescriptive rights of the Church of Milan. But he sends his own subdeacon, both to assure himself of the unanimity of the election and to see to the consecration being effected according to precedent. He also intimates (*Epp.* 30, 31) the ecessity of his own assent to the consecration.

2 The reason of John the subdeacon being directed to go to Genoa rather than to Milan may have been danger from the Lombards in approaching the latter place, as well as the fact of many of the Milanese having, for the same reason, taken refuge in Genoa

present there under stress of barbarian ferocity, thou must call them together, and enquire into their wishes in common. And, if no diversity of opinion separates them from the unanimity of the election—that is to say, if thou ascertainest that the desire and consent of all continues in favour of our aforesaid son, Constantius,—then thou art to cause him to be consecrated by his own bishops, as ancient usage requires, with the assent of our authority, and the help of the Lord; to the end that through the observance of such custom both the Apostolic See may retain the power belonging to it, and at the same time may not diminish the rights which it has conceded to others.

EPISTLE XXXI.

To Romanus, Patrician.

Gregory to Romanus, Patrician, and Exarch of Italy.

We believe that your Excellency is already aware of the death of Laurentius, bishop of the church of Mediolanum. And since, so far as we have learnt from the report of the clergy, all have agreed in the election of our son Constantius, deacon of the same church, it was necessary for us, for keeping up old usage, to send a soldier of our church, to cause him in whose favour he finds the will and consent of all to concur unanimously to be consecrated by his own bishops, as ancient usage requires, though still with our assent. Wherefore, greeting you with fatherly affection as in duty bound, we request your Excellency to vouchsafe your support, justice approving, to the aforesaid Constantius, whether elected or not, whenever need may arise; to the end that this service may both exalt you here before your enemies, and commend you beforehand in the future life before God. For he is one of mine, and was once associated with me on very intimate terms. And you ought to hold as yours, and to love peculiarly, those whom you know to be ours.

EPISTLE XXXII.

To Honoratus, Archdeacon.

Gregory to Honoratus, Archdeacon of Salona[3].

The mandates of ourselves and of our predecessor had reached thy Love not long ago, in which thou wert acquitted of the charges calumniously brought against thee; and we ordered thee to be reinstated without any dispute in the order of thy rank. But, inasmuch as again after no great lapse of time, thou camest to the city of Rome complaining of some improper proceedings among you concerning the alienation of sacred vessels, and as, while we had persons with us here who might have replied to thy objections, Natalis, thy bishop, departed this life, we have judged it necessary to confirm further by this present letter those same mandates, both our predecessor's and our own, which (as has been said) we sent not long ago for thy acquittal. Wherefore, acquitting thee fully of all the charges brought against thee, we will that thou continue without any dispute in the rank of thy order, so that the question raised by the aforesaid man may not on any pretext prejudice thee in the least degree. Moreover, as to the heads of thy complaint, we have straitly charged Antoninus, subdeacon and rector in your parts of the patrimony of holy Church over which, by God's providence, we preside, that, if he should find ecclesiastical persons implicated in them, he decide these cases with the utmost strictness and authority. But, in case of the business being with such persons as the vigour of ecclesiastical jurisdiction cannot reach, he is to deposit the proofs under each particular head among the public acts, and transmit them to us without any delay, that, being accurately informed, we may know how, with the help of Christ, to dispose of the matter.

EPISTLE XXXIII.

To Dynamius, Patrician.

Gregory to Dynamius, Patrician of Gaul.

He who administers faithfully what is another's shews how well he dispenses what is his own. And this your Glory makes manifest to us in that, intent on your annual offering, you have rendered the blessed Peter, Prince of the apostles, the fruits of his revenues. In paying him what is his faithfully, you have made these gifts to him your own. For indeed it becomes the glorious people of this earth who think of eternal glory so to act that in virtue of their excelling in temporal power, they may procure for themselves a reward that is not temporal. Accordingly, addressing to you the greeting which we owe, we implore Almighty God both to replenish your life with present good, and to extend it to the lofty joys of eternity. For we have received through our son Hilarus (*al* Hilarius) of the aforesaid revenues of our Church four hundred Gallican *solidi*[4]. We now send you as the benediction of the blessed apostle Peter a small cross, wherein are inserted benefits from his chains[5], which for a time bound his neck: but may

[3] See I. 19, note 5.

[4] As to Gallic money, cf. VI. 7, and note.

[5] Cf. I. 26, note 3.

they loose yours from sins for ever. Moreover in its four parts round about are contained benefits from the gridiron of the blessed Laurence, whereon he was burnt, that it, whereon his body was consumed by fire for the truth's sake, may inflame your soul to the love of the Lord.

EPISTLE XXXV.

To Peter, Subdeacon.

Gregory to Peter, subdeacon of Campania [6].

Our brother and fellow-bishop Paul has often requested us to allow him to return to his own church. And, having perceived this to be reasonable, we have thought it needful to accede to his petition. Consequently let thy Experience convene the clergy of the Neapolitan church, to the end that they may choose two or three of their number, and not omit to send them hither for the election of a bishop. But let them also intimate, in their communication to us, that those whom they send represent them all in this election, so that their church may have its own bishop validly ordained. For we cannot allow it to be any longer without a ruler of its own. Should they perchance try in any way to set aside thy admonition, bring to bear on them the vigour of ecclesiastical discipline. For he will be giving proof of his own perverseness, whosoever does not of his own accord assent to this proceeding. Moreover, cause to be given to the aforesaid Paul, our brother and fellow-bishop, one hundred *solidi*, and one little orphan boy, to be selected by himself, for his labour in behalf of the same church. Further, admonish those who are to come hither as representing all for the election of a bishop, to remember that they must bring with them all the episcopal vestments, and also as much money as they may foresee to be necessary for him who may be elected bishop to have to his own use. But lose no time in despatching those of the clergy who are selected as we have said, that, seeing that there are present here divers nobles of the city of Naples, we may treat with them concerning the election of a bishop, and take counsel together with the help of the Lord.

EPISTLE XXXVI.

To Sabinus, Guardian (*Defensorem*).

Gregory to Sabinus, Guardian of Sardinia.

Certain serious matters having come to our ears which require canonical correction, we therefore charge thy Experience not to neglect to cause Januarius, our brother and fellow-bishop, together with John the notary, to appear before us with all speed, all excuses being laid aside, that in his presence what has been reported to us may be subjected to a thorough investigation. Further, if the religious women Pompeiana and Theodosia, according to their request, should wish to come hither, afford them your succour in all ways, that they may be able, through your assistance, to accomplish their desires: but especially be careful by all means to bring with you the most eloquent Isidore, as he has requested, that, the merits of his case which he is known to have against the Church of Caralis having been fully gone into, he may be able to have it legally terminated.

Furthermore, some personal misdemeanours having been reported to us of the presbyter Epiphanius, it is necessary for you to investigate everything diligently, and to make haste to bring at the same time with you the women with whom he is said to have sinned, or others whom you suppose to know anything about the matter; that so the truth may be clearly laid open to the rigour of ecclesiastical discipline.

Now you will take care to accomplish all these things so efficiently as to lay yourself open to no blame for negligence, knowing that it will be entirely at your peril if this our order should in any way be slackly executed.

EPISTLE XXXVIII.

To Libertinus, Præfect [7].

Gregory to Libertinus, Præfect of Sicily.

From the very beginning of your administration God has willed you to go forth to vindicate His cause, and of His mercy has reserved for you this reward, with praise attending it. For it is reported that one Nasas, a most wicked Jew, has with a temerity that calls for punishment erected an altar under the name of the blessed Elias, and by sacrilegious seduction has enticed many Christians to worship there; nay, has also, it is said, acquired Christian slaves, and devoted them to his own service and profit. Whilst, then, he ought to have been most severely punished for such great crimes, the glorious Justinus [8], soothed (as has been written to us) by the charm of avarice, put off avenging the injury done to God. But let your Glory institute a strict examination into all these things, and, if it should be found manifest that such things have been done, make haste to visit

[6] See II. 6, note 3.

[7] In some MSS. *prætori*, in others *exprætori*. It seems probable from the contents of this letter that Libertinus had succeeded Justinus (see I. 2) as prætor of Sicily.

[8] See I. 2.

them most strictly and corporally on this wicked Jew, in such sort that you may thereby both conciliate the favour of God to yourself, and shew yourself by this example, to your own reward, a model to posterity. Moreover, set at liberty, without any equivocation, according to the injunctions of the laws[9], whatever Christian slaves it shall appear that he has acquired; lest (which God forbid) the Christian religion should be polluted by being subjected to Jews. Do you therefore with all speed correct these things most strictly, that not only may we give thanks to you for this discipline, but also bear testimony to your goodness in case of need.

EPISTLE XLV.

To Andrew, Bishop.

Gregory to Andrew, Bishop of Tarentum [*Taranto, in Calabria*].

A man may look without alarm to the tribunal of the eternal Judge, if only, conscious of his own guilt, he strives to pacify Him by befitting penitence. Now that thou hadst a concubine we find to be manifestly true, with regard to whom also an adverse suspicion has arisen in the minds of some. But, since in doubtful cases judgment ought not to be absolute, we have chosen to leave the matter to thine own conscience. If, then, after being constituted in sacred orders thou rememberest having been defiled by carnal intercourse, thou must resign the dignity of priesthood, nor presume by any means to approach its ministration, knowing that thou wilt administer it to the peril of thy soul, and without doubt have to render an account to our God, if, being conscious of this crime, thou shouldest desire to continue in the order wherein thou art, concealing the truth. Wherefore we again exhort thee that, if thou knowest thyself to have been deceived by the craft of the ancient foe, thou hasten to overcome him, while thou mayest, by adequate penitence, lest, as we hope may not be, thou be reckoned as partner with him in the day of judgment. If, however, thou art not conscious of this guilt, thou must needs continue in the order wherein thou art.

Furthermore, since, against due order, thou didst doom a woman on the Church-roll[1] to be cruelly beaten with cudgels, although we do not think that she died eight months afterwards, yet, because thou hast had no regard to thy order, we therefore sentence thee to abstain for two months from the administration of mass. Meanwhile, being suspended from thy office, it will become thee to weep for what thou hast done. For it is very right that, now that the examples of praiseworthy priests do not provoke thee to the tranquil rectitude befitting thy position, at any rate the medicine of correction should compel thee.

EPISTLE XLVI.

To John, Bishop.

Gregory to John, Bishop of Calliopolis [*Gallipoli, in Calabria*].

From the reports sent to us by thy Fraternity it appears that Andrew, our brother and fellow-bishop, undoubtedly had a concubine. But, since it is uncertain whether he has touched her while constituted in sacred orders, it is necessary that thou shouldest warn him with earnest exhortation that, if he knows himself to have had intercourse with her while in sacred orders, he should retire from the office which he holds, and minister no longer. And if, though conscious of having done this thing, he should conceal his sin and presume to minister, let him know that peril hangs over his soul in the divine judgment.

As to the woman on the Church-roll, whom he caused to be chastised with cudgels, though we do not believe that she died eight months afterwards, yet, since he caused her to be thus punished inconsistently with his sacred calling, do thou suspend him for two months from the solemnization of mass, that at any rate this disgrace may teach him how to behave himself in future.

Moreover, the clergy of the aforesaid bishop, in a petition presented to us, which is subjoined below, allege that they endure much ill-treatment from him. Wherefore let thy Fraternity take care to ascertain all these things accurately, and so to correct and arrange them in a reasonable way that they may be under no necessity hereafter of resorting hither on account of this matter. In the month of July, indiction 11.

EPISTLE XLVII.

To the Clergy of the Church of Salona[2].

Gregory to the clergy, &c.

Having read your letter, beloved, we learn

---

9 In Cod. *lib.* 1, *tit.* 10; "Judæus servum Christianum nec comparare debebit, nec largitatis aut alioquocunque titulo consequetur. Quod si aliquis Judæorum . . ., non solum mancipii damno multetur, verum etiam capitali sententia puniatur." Eusebius also (*De Vita Constantini, lib.* iv. c. 27) speaks of a law passed by Constantine forbidding Jews to have Christian slaves, and ordering any that might be found to be set at liberty, and the Jew to be fined. Cf. II. 21.

1 *Mulierem de matriculis. Matricula* was probably a list or roll of names of widows and others who were supported by the Church.

2 For notice of the Metropolitan See of Salona, and Gregory's dealings with its former bishop Natalis, see II. 18, note 3. The appointment of a successor to Natalis engaged Gregory in a long

that you have made choice of Honoratus your archdeacon; and know ye that it is altogether pleasing to us that you have chosen for the order of episcopacy a man tried of old and of grave manner of life. We too join with you in approbation of his personal character, inasmuch as it is already known to us; and it has been our own wish also that he should be ordained as your priest according to your desire. For which cause we exhort you to persist in his election without any ambiguity. Nor ought any circumstances to disincline you from his person, since, as this laudable choice is now approved, so it will impose both a burden on your souls and a stain of unfaithfulness on your reputation, if any one should seduce you (which God forbid) to turn aside your love from him. But as to those who are not at one with you in this desired election, we have caused them to be admonished by Antoninus our subdeacon, that they may be able to agree with you. To him also we have already given our injunctions as to what ought to be done with respect to the person of our brother and fellow-bishop Malchus[3]. But, inasmuch as we have ourselves also written to him, we believe that he will without delay keep himself quiet from disquieting you. If by any chance he should in any way whatever neglect to obey, his contumacy will in every way be mulcted with the utmost rigour of canonical punishment.

struggle for maintenance of his authority over the Illyrican churches, which on this occasion seems to have been, for some time at least, slightly regarded. What took place, as gathered from his extant letters, may be thus summarised. Immediately on hearing of the death of Natalis he wrote to Antoninus, the *rector patrimonii* in Dalmatia, charging him to see to the canonical election of a successor, and to its notification, when made, to himself, that it might be approved, as was customary, by the See of Rome (III. 22). This was in the 11th Indiction, i.e. between Sept. A.D. 592 and Sept. A.D. 593. Subsequently, having been informed that the clergy of Salona had elected their archdeacon Honoratus, he wrote to them in the letter before us, approving their choice, and exhorting them to stick to it, being evidently aware of a party opposed to it. This Honoratus was the man whom he had previously supported against Bishop Natalis, who had attempted to deprive him of his archdeaconry. See II. 18, 19, 20; III. 32. Hence it was not improbable that the election of Honoratus would be opposed by the partizans of the late bishop, who, as appears from his correspondence with Gregory, had been a convivial man, with a pleasant vein of wit, and thus likely to be popular with many. But, whatever the cause, Gregory before long received the startling intelligence that not only had the election of Honoratus, confirmed by himself, been set aside, but that another candidate, one Maximus, had been actually ordained under the alleged authority of an order from the Emperor. This defiance of his authority was the more offensive as he had already, having apparently got wind of the candidature of Maximus, prohibited his ordination under pain of excommunication of both him and his ordainers (IV. 10). He accordingly wrote a strongly-worded letter (IV. 20), dated May, A.D. 594, prohibiting Maximus from undertaking any episcopal functions, and from officiating at the altar, till it should be ascertained whether the emperor had really ordered his consecration. But Maximus treated this prohibition with contempt, and appealed against the Pope to the Emperor, who thereupon wrote to Gregory, requesting him to condone the fact of the ordination having taken place without his assent, and bidding him receive Maximus with honour if he should resort to Rome, as he was apparently desired to do. This was at the time when John Jejunator, the patriarch of Constantinople, had recently incensed Gregory by his assumption of the title of Universal Bishop, and when the latter was urging the Emperor to disallow the title. Writing on this subject to the Empress Constantina, he alludes also to the case of Maximus, hoping through her, whose religious reverence for St. Peter he appeals to, to move the Emperor. In his letter to her (V. 72), written in the 13th Indiction (594-5), he consents, in deference to the Emperor's wish, to look over the fact of Maximus having been ordained without his leave; but he insists on his appearing at Rome to answer to other charges, including especially that of simony, and his having disregarded the excommunication pronounced against him. He also protests strongly against his bishops being allowed to appeal to the secular power in ecclesiastical causes. But he did not thus move the Emperor, who appears from one of Gregory's letters to Maximus (VI. 25) to have directed any charges against the latter to be entertained in his own locality rather than at Rome. Meanwhile Maximus continued to disregard Gregory's repeated letters summoning him to Rome, being apparently supported by a majority of his own people and of his suffragan bishops. For in a letter to the Salonitans (VI. 26), written in the 14th Indiction (395-6), Gregory expresses his surprise that Honoratus alone among the clergy of Salona, and one only of the suffragan bishops, had refused to communicate with Maximus, notwithstanding his excommunication. However, as time went on, Gregory's persistence seems to have had some effect. In the 15th Indiction (596-7) one of the suffragan bishops, Sabinianus of Jadera, who had previously communicated with Maximus, deserts him, and is invited by Gregory to come to Rome to be absolved, and to bring with him any others whom he could persuade to come (VII. 15). Sabinianus did not go, but retired for a time to a monastery by way of expressing penitence, after which Gregory in the following year granted him full absolution (VIII. 10, 24). Perhaps about a year later, in the 2nd Indiction (IX. 5), we find Gregory writing to Marcellus, the proconsul of Dalmatia, in reply to a letter from him in which he had expressed his regret for being apparently out of favour with the pope, and his wish to be reconciled. This Marcellus had been, according to what Gregory says in his reply, the prime and original abettor of Maximus; and it would seem that he had now become desirous of coming to terms with the pope. In the same year we find a letter to one Julianus, described as *Scribo*, at Salona, who had addressed Gregory with a view to peace, asserting that Maximus enjoyed both the affection of his people and the favour of the court (IX. 41).

In replying to both these correspondents Gregory shews no signs of giving way: but in the same Indiction (588-9) he did give way to an extent that seems at first sight surprising, considering the resolute tone of his previous correspondence. He may have been partly moved to make some concession by such letters as those from Marcellus and Julianus, testifying to the character of Maximus and to the support he continued to receive; but the intercessor who really prevailed with him at last appears evidently to have been Callinicus, Exarch of Italy, resident at Ravenna, to whom Maximus had applied after failing to induce the Emperor himself to interfere. In one of his letters (IX. 67), Gregory says that Maximus, having failed to influence "the greater powers of the world" in his behalf, had betaken himself to the lesser ones, and implies that it was to their intercession that the concession he was prepared to make was due. It may be supposed that by "the greater powers" are meant the imperial family, and that among "the lesser" Callinicus was at any rate the most influential: for in writing to the latter (IX. 9) he says, "In the cause of Maximus we can no longer resist the importunity of thy Sweetness;" and again to Marinianus, bishop of Ravenna, "I have received repeated and pressing letters from my most excellent son the lord exarch Callinicus in behalf of Maximus. Overcome by his importunity, &c." (IX. 10). Nor is the reason far to seek why the intercession of Callinicus should at that particular time prevail. For Gregory was in correspondence with him, and most anxious to secure his co-operation, in the reconciliation to the Roman Church of the Istrian bishops, who had so far been out of communion with Rome in the matter of "the Three Chapters," and was therefore likely to wish to oblige him. However induced, he now consented that Maximus should appear, not before himself at Rome, as he had before so resolutely insisted, but before Marinianus, bishop of Ravenna, and promised to accede to whatever the latter might determine (IX. 10). Nay, he even accepted the proposal of Marinianus that the charges against Maximus should not be investigated at all, but that a declaration on oath by the accused of his own innocence should be accepted as a sufficient purgation; requiring only that he should do such penance as the bishop of Ravenna might impose for having disregarded the excommunication pronounced at Rome (IX. 79, 80). He wrote also to Constantius, bishop of Milan, requesting him to proceed to Ravenna in order to act in concert with Marinianus in case of Maximus not having confidence in the latter (IX. 67). But the bishop of Ravenna appears to have acted alone: and the result was that Maximus was acquitted of simony and all other charges, and, after doing the penance assigned by Marinianus at Ravenna, was, seven years after his ordination, cordially received by Gregory into communion, and had the pallium sent him (IX. 81, 82, 125). The epistles to be consulted for a view of the whole proceedings are III. 22, 47; IV. 10, 20, 47; V. 21; VI. 3, 25, 26, 27; VII. 17; VIII. 10, 24; IX. 5, 10, 41, 67, 79, 80, 81, 82, 125.

[3] See III. 22.

EPISTLE XLVIII.

To Columbus, Bishop[4].

Gregory to Columbus, &c.

Even before receiving thy Fraternity's letter, I knew thee from the report of thy deserved reputation to be a good servant of God. And now that I have received it, I understand more fully that what fame had already spread abroad was well founded; and I greatly rejoice in thy deserts, in that thou exhibitest manners and deeds that testify to a praiseworthy life. Since, then, I feel that these things are conferred on thee by the Supernal Majesty, I congratulate thee; and I bless God our Creator, who denies not the gifts of His mercy to His humble servants. On this account I declare it to be true that thy Fraternity so kindles me with the flame of charity to love thee, and my spirit is so united to thee, that I both desire to see thee and am also with thee in heart, though absent. Thou perceivest in thine own thoughts that this is so. For in truth unity of minds in charity has power to unite more than bodily presence can. Furthermore, that with thy whole mind, thy whole heart, thy whole soul, thou cleavest and art devoted to the Apostolic See I am now assured, as, indeed, before thy letter had borne testimony to the fact, I plainly knew. Wherefore, first addressing thee with the greeting of charity which is due, I exhort thee not to cease to be mindful of what thou hast promised to the blessed Peter, Prince of the apostles.

Wherefore be thou urgent with the primate of thy synod[5], that boys be in no wise admitted to sacred orders, lest they fall by so much the more dangerously as they hasten more speedily to mount to higher places. Let there be no venality in ordination: let not the influence or entreaty of any persons obtain anything in contravention of these our prohibitions. For without doubt God is offended if any one is promoted to sacred orders, not for merit, but by favour (which God forbid) or venality.

If, then, thou art aware of these things being done, keep not silence, but oppose them urgently; since, if perchance thou shouldest neglect them, or conceal them when known of, the chain of sin will bind not those alone who do such things, but no light guilt before God will touch thee also in the matter. If, then, anything of the kind is committed, it ought to be restrained by canonical punishment, lest so great a wickedness, with sin in others, acquire strength from connivance.

I have, therefore, the sooner given leave of departure to the bearer of these presents, Victorinus, thy Fraternity's deacon, whom I think to be thy imitator, and whom I have received with charity; and by him I have transmitted to thee for a blessing keys of the blessed Peter, in which something from his chains is included.

Lastly, with regard to the unity and peace of the council which, under God, you are taking measures to assemble, let thy Charity rejoice my mind by informing me of everything particularly.

EPISTLE XLIX.

To Adeodatus, Bishop.

Gregory to Adeodatus, Primate bishop of the province of Numidia.

After what manner the charity of affection has bound your Fraternity to usward the tenour of your letters has evidently shewn; and they have afforded us great matter of rejoicing, in that we have found them to be composed in a spirit of loving-kindness, and to glow with affection well-pleasing to God. As, then, we have briefly said, the epistle which you have addressed to us has so laid open your mind that its author might be supposed not to be absent from us at all. For, indeed, persons are not to be accounted absent whose feelings are not at variance with mutual charity. And though, as you say in your letter, neither your strength nor your age allow you to come to us, that we might be gratified by the bodily presence of your Fraternity, yet, seeing that we are one with you and you with us in feeling, we are entirely present one to the other, while we see each other in a mind made one through love. Furthermore, greeting your Fraternity with the suitable affection of charity, we exhort you that you study with all your heart so to acquit yourself wisely in the office of primacy which under God you hold, that it may both profit your soul to have attained to this rank, and that you may stand out as a good example for imitation to others in the future.

Be, then, especially careful with regard to ordination; and by no means admit any to aspire to sacred orders but such as are somewhat advanced in age and pure in deeds, lest perchance they cease for ever to be what they immaturely haste to be. For you must first examine the life and manners of those who are to be placed in any sacred order; and, that you may be able to admit such as are worthy to this office, let not the influence or the entreaty of any persons whatever inveigle

---

[4] See II. 48, note 8.

[5] With regard to Primates in Africa, see I. 74, note 9. The primate of Numidia at this time was Adeodatus. See below, *Ep.* 49.

you. But before all things it behoves you to be cautious that no venality may have place in ordination, lest (which God forbid) the greater danger hang over both the ordained and the ordainers. If ever, then, there is need for such things to be taken in hand, call grave and experienced men into your counsels, and consider the matter in common deliberation with them. And before all others it is fit that you should in all cases call in Columbus our brother and fellow-bishop. For we believe that, if you shall have done what is to be done with his advice, no one will find anything in any way to find fault with in you; and know ye that it will be as acceptable to us as if it had been done with our advice; inasmuch as his life and manners have in all respects so approved themselves to us that it is clearly apparent to all that what is done with his consent will be darkened by no blot of faultiness. But the bearer of these presents, Victorinus, deacon of our fellow-bishop abovenamed, has been such a herald of your merits as exceedingly to refresh our spirits with regard to your behaviour. And we pray the Almighty Lord to cause the good that has been reported of you to shine forth more fully in operation as well-pleasing to Him.

When, therefore, the council which you are taking measures to assemble has, with the succour of God, been brought to a conclusion, rejoice us by telling of its unity and concord, and give us information on all points.

EPISTLE LI.

To Maximianus, Bishop.

Gregory to Maximinianus, Bishop of Syracuse[6].

My brethren who live with me familiarly urge me by all means to write something briefly about the miracles of the Fathers done in Italy, which we have heard of. With this view I am in great need of the assistance of your Charity, to mention to me shortly what comes back to your memory, and what you happen to have known. For I remember your telling me something, which I have now forgotten, about the lord[7] Abbot Nonnosus, who was with the lord[7] Anastasius of Pentomi[8]. And therefore this, or anything else, I beg thee to communicate to me by letter without delay, if indeed thou art not intending to come to me thyself shortly.

6 See II. 7, note 5.

7 *Domno.*, "Abbas autem, quia vices Christi agere creditur, Domnus et Abbas vocetur." *Regula S. Benedicti*, c. 63.

8 The miracles attributed to Nonnosus, which are here referred to, are told in *Dialog.* I. 7, as having been communicated to Gregory by Maximianus and an old monk called Laurio. Nonnosus, at the time when they were wrought, had been Prior under Anastasius of a monastery on the summit of Mount Soracte.

EPISTLE LIII.

To John, Bishop.

Gregory to John, Bishop of Constantinople[9].

Though consideration of the case moves me, yet charity also impels me to write, since I have written once and again to my most holy brother the lord John, but have received no letter from him. For some one else, a secular person, addressed me under his name; seeing that, if those were really his letters, I have not been vigilant, having believed of him something far different from what I have found. For I had written about the case of the most reverend presbyter John, and about the questions of the monks of Isauria, one of whom, being in priest's orders,

9 John Jejunator (or the Faster), so called from his ascetic habits. Gregory had known and esteemed him during his residence at Constantinople. See above, III. 4. The occasion of the letter before us was as follows. Two presbyters, John of Chalcedon and Athanasius of Isauria (the latter being also a monk in the monastery of St. Mile in Isauria), had been accused of heresy at Constantinople, found guilty, and one of them beaten with cudgels in the church. They had gone to Rome to lay their grievances before the pope, who had written to John Jejunator the Patriarch more than once to protest against so uncanonical a punishment. The Patriarch seems to have replied that he knew nothing about the matter: whereupon Gregory sent him this stinging letter. In the following year (593-4), it appears from a letter to Narses, a patrician at Constantinople, that the case was still pending. Narses had reported the Patriarch as wishing to act canonically; and Gregory, doubtfully hoping so, threatens strong measures if it should be otherwise (IV. 32). Afterwards (A.D. 594-5) it seems as if the Patriarch had written on the subject pleasantly: for at the end of a long letter to him protesting against his assumption of the title of "Œcumenical Bishop," Gregory alludes to his "scripta dulcissima atque suavissima" in the matter of John and Athanasius, promising a reply (V. 18). In the following year (A.D. 595-6) we find that the charges of heresy against the two presbyters had been entertained before Gregory in a Roman synod; and this apparently with the assent of the Patriarch, who had transmitted a statement of the case. John of Chalcedon had been fully acquitted of heresy; but some doubt still remained as to the orthodoxy of Athanasius. Accordingly John was at once sent back to Constantinople with a letter from Gregory to the Patriarch, reversing the sentence against him which had been passed at Constantinople and demanding that he should be received with favour and reinstated. As though doubtful of the Patriarch's compliance, Gregory addressed also the Emperor, and Theoctistus, a relation of the Emperor's, requesting them to protect the acquitted appellant (VI. 14, 15, 16, 17). In the same year Athanasius, who had explained or retracted what had been objected to in his writings, was also declared orthodox, and sent back to Constantinople as acquitted. But this was after the death of John Jejunator; and accordingly the letter demanding the reinstatement of Athanasius was addressed to his successor Cyriacus (VI. 66; VII. 5). How John Jejunator would have acted at this stage of the proceedings, had he lived, we have no means of knowing; nor is there record of the action of Cyriacus. The only further reference to the subject in the epistles is in one to the two Patriarchs of Alexandria and Antioch (VII. 34), in writing to whom Gregory sets forth at some length the doctrinal questions that had been treated in the trial of Athanasius, as though desirous of having the assent of those apostolical and patriarchal sees, which (as we have seen) he elsewhere acknowledges as sharing with his own the authority of St. Peter, to the decision come to at Rome. The whole history of the case, which, as has been seen, was protracted through several years, is of some importance as illustrating Gregory's claim to entertain appeals from Constantinople, and to reverse at Rome what had been decided there; though it is not equally clear, from what is before us in this particular case, how such claims were viewed at Constantinople. On the one hand we find no sign of the appeal of the two presbyters to Rome having been objected to; while, on the other, Gregory evidently had his doubts as to whether the Roman decision would be acted on at Constantinople; and whether it was so or not we do not know. The letters about it, above referred to, are III. 53; IV. 32; V. 18; VI. 14, 15, 16, 17, 66; VII. 5, 34.

has been beaten with clubs in your church; and thy most holy Fraternity (as appears from the signature of the letter) has written back to me professing ignorance of what I wrote about. At this reply I was exceedingly astonished, revolving within myself in silence, if he speaks the truth, what can be worse than that such things should be done against the servants of God, and even he who was close at hand should not know? For what excuse can a shepherd have if the wolf devours the sheep and the shepherd knows it not? But, if your Holiness knew both what I referred to in my letter and what had been done, whether against John the presbyter or against Athanasius, monk of Isauria and presbyter, and wrote to me, I know not; what can I reply to this, since the Truth says through His Scripture, *The mouth that lieth slayeth the soul* (Wisd. i. 11)? I demand of thee, most holy brother; has that so great abstinence of thine come to this, that by denial thou wouldest hide from thy brother what thou knewest to have been done? Had it not been better that flesh should go into that mouth for food, than that falsehood should come out of it for deceiving a neighbour; especially when the Truth says, *Not that which goeth into the mouth defileth a man; but that which cometh out of the mouth, this defileth a man* (Matth. xv. 11)? But far be it from me to believe anything of the kind of your most holy heart. Those letters were headed with your name, but I do not think they were yours. I had written to the most blessed lord John; but I believe that that familiar of yours has replied,—that youngster, who as yet has learnt nothing about God; who knows not the bowels of charity; who in his wicked doings is accused by all; who daily lays snares against the deaths of divers people by means of concealed wills; who neither fears God nor regards men. Believe me, most holy brother, you must first correct this man, that from the example of those who are near to you those who are not near may be better amended. Do not give ear to his tongue: he ought to be directed after the counsel of your holiness; not your holiness swayed by his words. For, if you listen to him, I know that you cannot have peace with your brethren. For I, as my conscience bears me witness, wish to quarrel with no man; and with all my power I avoid it. And, though I desire exceedingly to be at peace with all mankind, it is especially so with you, whom I exceedingly love, if only you are yourself the person whom I knew. For, if you do not observe the canons, and wish to tear to pieces the statutes of the Fathers, I know not who you are. So act, then, most holy and most dear brother, that we may mutually recognize each other, lest, if the ancient foe should move us two to take offence, he slay many through his most atrocious victory. As for me, to shew that I seek to do nothing in a haughty spirit, if that youngster of whom I have before spoken did not hold the topmost place of evil doing with thy Fraternity, I could meanwhile have passed over in silence what is ready to my hand from the canons, and have sent back to thee with confidence the persons who came to me at the first, knowing that your Holiness would receive them with charity. But even now I say; Either receive these same persons, restoring them to their orders, and leaving them in quiet; or, if perchance thou art unwilling to do this, observe in their case the statutes of the Fathers and the definitions of the canons, putting aside all altercation with me. But, if thou shouldest do neither, we indeed are unwilling to bring on a quarrel, but still do not shun one if it comes from your side. Moreover your Fraternity knows well what the canons say about bishops who desire to inspire fear by blows. For we have been made shepherds, not persecutors. And the excellent preacher says, *Argue, beseech, rebuke, with all longsuffering and doctrine* (2 Tim. iv. 2). But new and unheard of is this preaching, which exacts faith by blows. But I need not speak at length by letter about these things, since I have sent my most beloved son, the deacon Sabinianus, as my representative in ecclesiastical matters, to the threshold of our lords; and he will speak with you about everything more particularly. Unless you are disposed to wrangle with us, you will find him prepared for all that is just. Him I commend to your Blessedness, that he at least may find that lord John whom I knew in the royal city.

EPISTLE LVI.

To John, Bishop.

Gregory to John, Bishop of Ravenna[1].

It is not long since certain things had been

[1] This John, and apparently previous bishops of Ravenna, appear to have assumed a dignity not conceded to other metropolitans; perhaps on the ground of Ravenna being the seat of the Exarch, and having been once the imperial residence. The pallium usually granted to Metropolitans was allowed to be used by them only during the celebration of the Eucharist; and we find Gregory, in several epistles, restricting them to such use of it, when he sent it to them. John was reported to have worn it while receiving the laity in the sacristy before celebration; and he owned to having worn it in solemn processions through the city, alleging custom and peculiar privilege. Further, his clergy, when accompanying him in processions, had been accustomed to carry napkins (*mappulæ*), which appear to have been signs of dignity. It is for these assumptions that Gregory now remonstrates with him; but apparently in vain with regard to the use of the pallium in processions through the city: for Marinianus, the successor of John, continued the custom, though whether he finally persisted in it does not appear. Other letters referring to the subject are V. 15; VI. 34, 61.

told us about thy Fraternity concerning which we remember having declared ourselves in full, when Castorius, notary of the holy church over which we preside, went into your parts. For it had come to our ears that some things were being done in your church contrary to custom and to the way of humility, which alone, as you well know, exalts the priestly office. Now, if your Wisdom had received our admonitions kindly or with episcopal seriousness, you ought not to have been incensed by them, but have corrected these same things with thanks to us. For it is contrary to ecclesiastical use, if even unjust correction (the which be far from us) is not most patiently borne.

But your Fraternity has been too much moved; and when, in the swelling of thy heart, as if to justify thyself, thou wrotest that thou didst not use the pallium except after the sons of the Church had been dismissed from the sacristy [2], and at the time of mass, and in solemn litanies, thou madest acknowledgment in words with most manifest truth of having usurped something contrary to the usage of the Church in general. For how can it be that at a time of ashes and sackcloth, through the streets among the noises of the people thou couldest do lawfully what thou hast disclaimed the doing of as being unlawful in the assembly of the poor and nobles, and in the sacristy of the Church? Yet this, dearest brother, is not, we think, unknown to thee; that it has hardly ever been heard of any metropolitan in any parts of the world that he has claimed to himself the use of the pallium except at the time of mass. And that you knew well this custom of the Church in general you have shewn most plainly by your epistles, in which you have sent to us appended the precept of our predecessor John of blessed memory, to the effect that all the customs conceded in the way of privilege to you and your church by our predecessors should be retained. You acknowledge, then, that the custom of the Church in general is different, seeing that you claim the right of doing what you do on the score of privilege. Thus, as we think, we can have no remaining doubtfulness in this matter. For either the usage of all metropolitans should be observed also by thy Fraternity, or, if thou sayest that something has been specially conceded to thy church, it is for your side to shew the precept of former pontiffs of the Roman City wherein these things have been conceded to the Church of Ravenna. But, if this is not shewn, it remains, seeing that you establish your claim to do such things on the score neither of general custom nor of privilege, that you prove yourself to have usurped in what you have done. And what shall we say to the future judge, most beloved brother, if we defend the use of that heavy yoke and chain on our neck with a view, I do not say to ecclesiastical, but to a certain secular dignity; judging ourselves to be lowered if we are without so great a weight even for a short space of time? We desire to be adorned with the pallium, being, it may be, unadorned in character; whereas nothing shines more splendidly on a bishop's neck than humility.

It is therefore the duty of thy Fraternity, if thou art firmly determined to defend thy honours with any kind of arguments, either to follow the use of the generality without written authority, or to defend thyself under privileges shewn in writing. Or, if lastly thou doest neither, we will not have thee set an example of presumption of this sort to other metropolitans. But, lest thou shouldest perchance think that we, in thus writing to you, have neglected what belongs to fraternal charity, know ye that careful search has been made in our archives for the privileges of thy Church. And indeed some things have been found, sufficient to obviate entirely the aims of thy Fraternity, but nothing to support the contentions of your Church on the points in question. For even concerning the very custom of thy Church which thou allegest against us, which custom we wrote before should be proved on your side, we would have you know that we have already taken thought sufficiently, having questioned our sons, Peter the deacon and Gaudiosus the *primicerius* [3], and also Michael the guardian (*defensorem*) of our see, or others who on various commissions have been sent by our predecessors to Ravenna; and they have most positively denied that thou hast done these things in their presence. It is therefore apparent that what was done in secret must have been an unlawful usurpation. Hence what has been latently introduced can have no firm ground to justify its continuance. What things, then, thou or thy predecessors have presumed to do superfluously do thou, having regard to charity, and with brotherly kindness, study to correct. To no degree attempt—I do not say of thine own

2 *Secretarium*, viz. the chamber adjoining the church in which the vestments and sacred utensils were kept, and the clergy vested for service; and in which also, as appears from this and the following epistle, the bishop was accustomed to receive the laity before mass. From the custom of holding synods in the apartments so called, the sessions of synods were also themselves sometimes called *secretaria*.

3 The term *primicerius* is variously applied, denoting the chiefs of departments. In *Ep.* 22, *supra*, we find *primicerium notariorum*. In VII. 32, we find also the designation *Secundicerius*.

accord, but after the fashion set by others, even thy predecessors,—to deviate from the rule of humility. For, to sum up shortly what I have said above, I admonish thee to this effect; that unless thou canst shew that this has been allowed thee by my predecessors in the way of privilege, thou presume not any more to use the pallium in the streets, lest thou come not to have even for mass what thou audaciously usurpest even in the streets. But as to thy sitting in the sacristy, and receiving the sons of the Church with the pallium on (which thing thy Fraternity has both done and disclaimed), we now for the present make no complaint; since, following the decision of synods, we refuse to punish minor faults, which are denied. Yet we know this to have been done once and again, and we prohibit its being done any more. But let thy Fraternity take careful heed, lest presumption which in its commencement is pardoned be more severely visited if it proceeds further.

Furthermore, you have complained that certain of the sacerdotal order in the city of Ravenna are involved in serious criminal charges. Their case we desire thee either to examine on the spot, or to send them hither (unless, indeed, difficulty of proof owing to the distance of the places stands in the way of this), that the case may be examined here. But if, relying on the patronage of great people, which we do not believe, they should scorn to submit to thy judgment or to come to us, and should refuse contumaciously to answer to the charges made against them, we desire that after thy second and third admonition, thou interdict them from the ministry of the sacred office, and report to us in writing of their contumacy, that we may deliberate how thou oughtest to make a thorough enquiry into their doings, and correct them according to canonical definitions. Let, therefore, thy Fraternity know that we are most fully absolved from responsibility in this case, seeing that we have committed to you a thorough investigation of the matter; and that, if all their sins should pass unpunished, the whole weight of this enquiry redounds to the peril of thy soul. And know, beloved, that thou wilt have no excuse at the future judgment, if thou dost not correct the excesses of thy clergy with the utmost severity of canonical strictness, and if thou allowest any against whom such excesses shall have been proved to profane sacred orders any longer.

Further, what you have written in defence of the use of napkins by your clergy is strenuously opposed by our own clergy, who say that this has never been granted to any other Church whatever, and that neither have the clergy of Ravenna, either there or in the Roman city, presumed, to their knowledge, in any such way, nor, if it has been attempted in the way of furtive usurpation, does it form a precedent. But, even though there had been such presumption in any church whatever, they assert that it ought to be corrected, not being by grant of the Roman pontiff, but merely a surreptitious presumption. But we, to save the honour of thy Fraternity, though against the wish of our aforesaid clergy, still allow the use of napkins to your first deacons (whose former use of them has been testified to us by some), but only when in attendance upon thee. The use of them, at any other time, or by any other persons, we most strictly prohibit.

EPISTLE LVII.

From John, Bishop of Ravenna to Pope Gregory[4].

My most reverend fellow-servant Castorius, notary of your Apostolical See, has delivered to me my lord's epistle, compounded of honey and of venom; which has yet so infixed its stings as still to leave place for healing appliances. For my lord, while he reproves pride and speaks of divine judgment following it, in a certain way professes himself with reason to be mild and placid.

You have alleged, then, that I, ambitious of novelty, have usurped the use of the pallium beyond what had been indulged to my predecessors. This let not the conscience of my own lord, which is governed by the divine right hand, in any way allow itself to believe; nor let him open his most sacred ears to the uncertainty of common report. First, because I, though a sinner, still know how grave a thing it is to transgress the limits assigned to us by the Fathers, and that all elation leads to nothing but a fall. For, if our ancestors did not tolerate pride in kings, how much more is it not to be endured in priests! Then, I remember how I was nourished in the lap and in the bosom of your most holy Roman Church, and therein by the aid of God advanced. And how should I be so daring as to presume to oppose that most holy see, which transmits its laws to the universal Church, for maintaining whose authority, as God knows, I have seriously excited the ill-will of many enemies

4 See *Ep.* 56. John of Ravenna, notwithstanding his obsequious language in this letter, appears to have been by no means disposed to give way. For see Gregory's subsequent letter to him (V. 15), in which he is sharply accused of duplicity. And not only he, but his successor in the see also, appear to have continued the practice of wearing the pallium in public processions. What he says in the letter before us of his having incurred odium by his defence of the authority of the Roman See may be noted as significant of some jealousy of such authority at Ravenna.

against myself? But let not my most blessed lord suppose that I have attempted anything contrary to ancient custom, as is attested by many and nearly all the citizens of this city, and as the above-written most reverend notary, even though he had taken no part in the proceedings, might have testified, inasmuch as it was not till the sons of the Church were descending from the sacristy [5], and the deacons were coming in for proceeding immediately [to the altar] that the first deacon has been accustomed to invest the bishop of the Church of Ravenna with the pallium, which he has also been accustomed in like manner to use in solemn litanies.

Wherefore let no one endeavour to insinuate anything against me to my lord, since, if any one wishes to do so, he cannot prove that any novelty has been introduced by me. For in what manner I have obeyed your commands and served your interests when cause required, may Almighty God make manifest to your most sincere heart: and I attribute it to my sins that after so many labours and difficulties which I endure within and without I should deserve to experience such a change. But again this among other things consoles me, that most holy fathers sometimes chastise their sons for the purpose only of advancing them the more, and that, after this devotion and satisfaction, you will not only conserve to the holy Church of Ravenna her ancient privileges, but even confer greater ones in your own times.

For with respect to the napkins, the use of which by my presbyters and deacons your Apostleship alleges to be a presumption, I confess in truth that it irks me to say anything on the subject, since the truth by itself, which alone prevails with my lord, is sufficient. For, this being allowed to the smaller churches constituted around the city, the apostleship of my lord will also be able in all ways to find, if he deigns to enquire of the venerable clergy of his own first Apostolical See, that as often as priests or levites of the Church of Ravenna have come to Rome for the ordination of bishops or for business, they all have *proceeded* [6] with napkins before the eyes of your most holy predecessors without any blame. Wherefore also at the time when I, sinner as I am, was ordained there by your predecessor, all my presbyters and deacons used them while *proceeding* [6] in attendance on the lord pope. And since our God in His providence has placed all things in your hand and most pure conscience, I adjure you by the very Apostolical See, which you formerly adorned by your character, and now govern with due dignity, that you in no respect diminish on account of my deservings the privileges of the Church of Ravenna, which is intimately yours; but, even according to the voice of prophecy, let it be laid upon me and upon my father's house, according to its deserving. I have, therefore, for your greater satisfaction, subjoined all the privileges which have been indulged by your predecessors to the holy Church of Ravenna, though none the less finding assurance in your venerable archives in reference to the times of the consecration of my predecessors. But now whatever, after ascertaining the truth, you may command to be done, is in God's power and yours; since I, desiring to obey the commands of my lord's Apostleship, have taken care, notwithstanding ancient custom, to abstain till I receive further orders.

EPISTLE LIX.

To Secundinus, Bishop.

Gregory to Secundinus, Bishop of Tauromenium. [*In Sicily.*]

Some time ago we ordered that the baptistery [7] should be removed from the monastery of Saint Andrew, which is above Mascalæ, because of inconvenience to the monks, and that an altar should be erected in the place where the fonts now are. But the carrying out of this order has been put off so far. We therefore admonish thy Fraternity that thou interpose no further delay after receiving this our letter, but that the fonts themselves be filled up [8], and an altar at once erected there for celebration of the sacred mysteries; to the end that the aforesaid monks may be at liberty to celebrate more securely the work of God, and that our mind be not provoked against thy Fraternity for negligence.

EPISTLE LX.

To Italica, Patrician [9].

Gregory to Italica, &c.

We have received your letter, which is full

5 *Ut mox procedatur.* The word *procedere* is used here, and elsewhere, for approaching the altar for celebration. Cf. below, and VII. 34.

6 *Procedebant.* See last note.

7 Baptisteries (*baptisteria*) were anciently separate buildings adjoining churches (cf. VI. 22), the *fontes* being the pools of water (called also *piscinæ* and κολυμβήθρα) therein contained. (See Bingham, B. VIII. C. VII. *Sect.* 1, 4.) The inconvenience to the monks of having a baptistery at their monastery would be from the concourse of people resorting to it, which would interfere with monastic seclusion. For a similar reason Gregory more than once forbids public masses in monasteries. Cf. e.g. II. 41; VI. 46.

8 Fonts were anciently sunken pools. "In medio habet fontem in terra excavatam ad quinque ulnas . . . tribus gradibus in id descensus est." *Onuphrius, de baptisterio Lateran.*

9 Possibly the same lady whom the ex-monk Venantius married. See I. 34, note 8, and IX. 123. The correspondence that took place at this time between her and Gregory seems to have arisen from some question of legal right, in which she appeared to

of sweetness, and rejoice to hear that your Excellency is well. Such is the sincerity of our own mind with regard to it that paternal affection does not allow us to suspect any latent ill-feeling concealed under its calmness. But may Almighty God bring it to pass, that, as we think what is good of you, so your mind may respond with good towards us, and that you may exhibit in your deeds the sweetness which you express in words. For the most glorious health and beauty on the surface of the body profit nothing if there is a hidden sore within. And that discord is the more to be guarded against to which exterior peace affords a body-guard. But as to what your Excellency in your aforesaid epistle takes pains to recall to our recollection, remember that you have been told in writing that we would not settle anything with you concerning the causes of the poor so as to cause offence, or with public clamour. We remember writing to you to this effect, and also know, God helping us. how to restrain ourselves with ecclesiastical moderation from the wrangling of suits at law, and, according to that apostolical sentence, to endure joyfully the spoiling of our goods. But this we suppose you to know; that our silence and patience will not be to the prejudice of future pontiffs after me in the affairs of the poor. Wherefore we, in fulfilment of our aforesaid promise, have already determined to keep silence on these questions; nor do we desire to mix ourselves personally in these transactions, wherein we feel that too little kindness is being shewn. But, lest you should hence imagine, glorious daughter, that we still altogether renounce what pertains to concord, we have given directions to our son, Cyprianus the deacon, who is going to Sicily, that, if you arrange about these matters in a salutary way, and without sin to your soul, he should settle them with you by our authority, and that we should be no further vexed by the business, which may thus be brought to a conclusion amicably. Now may Almighty God, who well knows how to turn to possibility things altogether impossible, may He inspire you both to arrange your affairs with a view to peace, and, for the good of your soul, to consult the benefit of the poor of this Church in matters which concern them.

the latter to be dealing harshly with some poor persons, perhaps peasants (*rustici*) on an estate of the Church (*hujus Ecclesiæ pauperibus*). The passing tribute paid in this letter to the lady's personal charms is characteristic of Gregory's complimentary style, and (supposing her to have been the same Italica who became the bride of Venantius) suggests one attraction which may have drawn the latter away from his intended monastic life. Further, on the same supposition, we may perhaps read with interest between the lines of this letter something of the feeling subsisting at the time of writing between the correspondents. She, being a well-bred patrician lady, had evidently written to him with gentle courtesy. But he detected, or thought he detected, something wanting in the tone of her letter. Nor was she likely to feel warmly towards him who now called her to account, if it were he whom she knew to have done all he could to alienate Venantius from her. He, on the other hand, while addressing her in return with all the courtesy due to her rank and character, and evidently anxious to avoid unpleasantness, shews signs of not being entirely satisfied as to her feelings towards himself, or her readiness to follow his admonitions. It is interesting to observe that, judging from the tone of subsequent Epistles, we may conclude very friendly relations to have been afterwards maintained between Gregory and the wedded pair.

EPISTLE LXV.

To Mauricius Augustus[1].

Gregory to Mauricius, &c.

He is guilty before Almighty God who is not pure of offence towards our most serene lords in all he does and says. I, however, unworthy servant of your Piety, speak in this my representation neither as a bishop, nor as your servant in right of the republic, but as of private right, since, most serene lord, you have been mine since the time when you were not yet lord of all.

On the arrival here of the most illustrious Longinus, the equerry (*stratore*), I received the law of my lords, to which, being at the time worn out by bodily sickness, I was unable to make any reply. In it the piety of my lords has ordained that it shall not be lawful for any one who is engaged in any public administration to enter on an ecclesiastical office. And this I greatly commended, knowing by most evident proof that one who is in haste to desert a secular condition and enter on an ecclesiastical office is not wishing to relinquish secular affairs, but to change them. But, at its being said in the same law that it should not be lawful for him to become a monk, I was altogether surprised, seeing that his accounts can be rendered through a monastery, and it can be arranged for his debts also to be recovered from the place into which he is received. For with whatever devout intention a person may have wished to become a monk, he should first restore what he has wrongly gotten, and take thought for his soul all the more truly as he is the more disencumbered. It is added in the same law that no one who has been marked on the hand[2] may become a monk. This ordinance, I confess to my lords, has alarmed me greatly, since by

[1] This letter is supposed to have been written in the third Indiction (A.D. 592-3); the law complained of having been issued in the previous year. The epistle, which follows, to the Emperor's physician on the same subject, shews how much Gregory had it at heart. Some five years later it appears from a letter to divers metropolitans, dated December, A.D. 597 (VIII. 5), that an amicable agreement had meanwhile been come to, both the Emperor and the Pope having made some concessions. Cf. also the end of *Ep.* 24 in Book X.

[2] Cf. below, "in terrena militia signatus." It appears that not slaves only, but soldiers also, were sometimes marked on the hand. Cf. Cyprian, *Ad Donatum*, "Te quem jam spiritualibus castris militia signavit."

it the way to heaven is closed against many, and what has been lawful until now is made unlawful. For there are many who are able to live a religious life even in a secular condition: but there are very many who cannot in any wise be saved with God unless they give up all things. But what am I, in speaking thus to my lords, but dust and a worm? Yet still, feeling that this ordinance makes against God, who is the Author of all, I cannot keep silence to my lords. For power over all men has been given from heaven to the piety of my lords to this end, that they who aspire to what is good may be helped, and that the way to heaven may be more widely open, so that an earthly kingdom may wait upon the heavenly kingdom. And lo, it is said in plain words that one who has once been marked to serve as an earthly soldier may not, unless he has either completed his service or been rejected for weakness of body, serve as the soldier of our Lord Jesus Christ.

To this, behold, Christ through me the last of His servants and of yours will answer, saying; From a notary I made thee a Count of the body-guard; from Count of the body-guard I made thee a Cæsar; from a Cæsar I made thee Emperor; and not only so, but also a father of emperors. I have committed my priests into thy hand; and dost thou withdraw thy soldiers from my service? Answer thy servant, most pious lord, I beseech thee; what wilt thou answer to thy Lord when He comes and thus speaks?

But peradventure it is believed that no one among them turns monk with a pure motive. I, your unworthy servant, know how many soldiers who have become monks in my own days have done miracles, have wrought signs and mighty deeds. But by this law it is forbidden that even one of such as these should become a monk.

Let my lord enquire, I beg, what former emperor ever enacted such a law, and consider more thoroughly whether it ought to have been enacted. And indeed it is a very serious consideration, that now at this time any are forbidden to leave the world; a time when the end of the world is drawing nigh. For lo! there will be no delay: the heavens on fire, the earth on fire, the elements blazing, with angels and archangels, thrones and dominions, principalities and powers, the tremendous Judge will appear. Should He remit all sins, and say only that this law has been promulged against Himself, what excuse, pray, will there be? Wherefore by the same tremendous Judge I beseech you, that all those tears, all those prayers, all those fasts, all those alms of my lord, may not on any ground lose their lustre before the eyes of Almighty God: but let your Piety, either by interpretation or alteration, modify the force of this law, since the army of my lords against their enemies increases the more when the army of God has been increased for prayer.

I indeed, being subject to your command, have caused this law to be transmitted through various parts of the world; and, inasmuch as the law itself is by no means agreeable to Almighty God, lo, I have by this my representation declared this to my most serene lords. On both sides, then, I have discharged my duty, having both yielded obedience to the Emperor, and not kept silence as to what I feel in behalf of God.

EPISTLE LXVI.

To Theodorus, Physician.

Gregory to Theodorus, &c.

What benefits I enjoy from Almighty God and my most serene lord the Emperor my tongue cannot fully express. For these benefits what return is it in me to make, but to love their footsteps sincerely? But, on account of my sins, by whose suggestion or counsel I know not, in the past year he has promulged such a law in his republic that whoso loves him sincerely must lament exceedingly. I could not reply to this law at the time, being sick. But I have just now offered some suggestions to my lord. For he enjoins that it shall be lawful for no one to become a monk who has been engaged in any public employment, for no one who is a paymaster [3], or who has been marked in the hand, or enrolled among the soldiers, unless perchance his military service has been completed. This law, as those say who are acquainted with old laws, Julian was the first to promulge, of whom we all know how opposed he was to God. Now if our most serene lord has done this thing because perhaps many soldiers were becoming monks, and the army was decreasing, was it by the valour of soldiers that Almighty God subjugated to him the empire of the Persians? Was it not only that his tears were heard, and that God, by an order which he knew not of, subdued to his empire the empire of the Persians?

Now it seems to me exceedingly hard that he should debar his soldiers from the service of Him who both gave him all and granted to him to rule not only over soldiers but even over priests. If his purpose is to save pro-

3 *Nullus qui optio.*—"*Optiones:* Militaris annonæ eragatores: distribiteurs des vivres aux soldats" (Cod. Th.) D'Arnis Lexicon Manuale.

perty from being lost, why might not those same monasteries into which soldiers have been received pay their debts, retaining the men only for monastic profession? Since these things grieve me much, I have represented the matter to my lord. But let your Glory take a favourable opportunity of offering him my representation privately. For I am unwilling that it should be given publicly by my representative (*responsalis*), seeing that you who serve him familiarly can speak more freely and openly of what is for the good of his soul, since he is occupied with many things, and it is not easy to find his mind free from greater cares. Do thou, then, glorious son, speak for Christ. If thou art heard, it will be to the profit of the soul of thy aforesaid lord and of thine own. But if thou art not heard, thou hast profited thine own soul only.

EPISTLE LXVII.

To Domitian, Metropolitan[4].

Gregory to Domitian, &c.

On receiving the letters of your most sweet Blessedness I greatly rejoiced, since they spoke much to me of sacred Scripture. And, finding in them the dainties that I love, I greedily devoured them. Therein also were many things intermingled about external and necessary affairs. And you have acted as though preparing a banquet for the mind, so that the offered dainties might please the more from their diversity. And if indeed external affairs, like inferior and ordinary kinds of food, are less savoury, yet they have been treated by you so skilfully as to be taken gladly, since even contemptible kinds of food are usually made sweet by the sauce of one who cooks well. Now, while the truth of the History is kept to, what I had said some time ago about its divine meaning ought not to be rejected. For, although, since you will have it so, its meaning may not suit my case, yet, from its very context, what was said as being drawn from it may be held without hesitation. For her violator (*i.e. Dinah's*) is called the prince of the country (Genes. xxxiv. 2), by whom the devil is plainly denoted, seeing that our Redeemer says, *Now shall the prince of this world be cast out* (John xii. 31). And he also seeks her for his wife, because the evil spirit hastens to possess lawfully the soul which he has first corrupted by hidden seduction. Wherefore the sons of Jacob, being very wroth, take their swords against the whole house of Sichem and his country (Genes. xxxiv. 25), because by all who have zeal those also are to be attacked who become abettors of the evil spirit. And they first enjoin on them circumcision, and afterwards, while they are sore, slay them. For severe teachers, if they know not how to moderate their zeal, though cutting off the bias of corruption by preaching, nevertheless, when delinquents already mourn for the evil they had done, are frequently still savage in roughness of discipline, and harder than they should be. For those who had already cut off their foreskins ought not to have died, since such as lament the sin of lechery, and turn the pleasure of the flesh into sorrow, ought not to experience from their teachers roughness of discipline, lest the Redeemer of the human race be Himself loved less, if in His behalf the soul is afflicted more than it should be. Hence also to these his sons Jacob says, *Ye have troubled me, and made me odious to the Canaanites* (Ibid. v. 30). For, when teachers still cruelly attack what the delinquents already mourn for, the weak mind's very love for its Redeemer grows cold, because it feels itself to be afflicted in that wherein of itself it does not spare itself.

So much therefore I would say in order to shew that the sense which I set forth is not improbable in connexion with the context. But what has been inferred from the same passage by your Holiness for my comfort I gladly accept, since in the understanding of sacred Scripture whatever is not opposed to a sound faith ought not to be rejected. For, even as from the same gold some make necklaces, some rings, and some bracelets, for ornament, so from the same knowledge of sacred Scripture different expositors, through innumerable ways of understanding it, compose as it were various ornaments, which

[4] This Domitian, Bishop of Melitene and Metropolitan of Roman Armenia, was a kinsman of the Emperor Maurice, and had lately been successfully employed by him in coming to terms with the Persian king, Chosroes II., as is related in the histories of Evagrius and Theophylact. The latter describes him as "holy in life, sweet in speech, ready in action, most prudent in council" (*Hist.* iv. 14). He also gives at length an eloquent sermon of his, delivered after the cession, through his mediation, of the city Martyropolis in Mesopotamia to the Roman Emperor (IV. 16). Chosroes II., who is said to have had a strong regard for Domitian, appears to have had some leanings towards Christianity. We are told that, when flying from his enemies in Persia, and in doubt whether to seek refuge with the Romans or the Turks, he had let his horse take its own course, calling on the God of the Christians for guidance, and thus found his way to Circesium, where he was received by Probus the Governor (*Theophyl.* IV. 10; *Evagr. H.E.* VI. 16). Further, it is related that, on one occasion, when Probus, bishop of Chalcedon, had been sent to him as ambassador by the Emperor, he requested to be shewn a portrait of the Blessed Virgin, which he adored when he saw it, saying that he had seen the original in a vision (*Theophyl.* V. 15); and also that he attributed his own success in arms, and the pregnancy of his favourite wife Syra (Shirin), who was herself a Christian, to the intercession of S. Sergius, whom he had invoked, and that he sent a cross of pure gold, adorned with jewels, which he had vowed, with other presents, to the shrine of the saint, together with a letter of acknowledgment addressed to him (*Theophyl.* V. 13, 14; *Evagr. H E.* VI. 20). But he certainly never became a Christian, though it appears from the letter before us that Domitian had done his best to convert him. The earlier part of this epistle refers evidently to some allegorical interpretation of Scripture by Gregory after his usual manner, to which Domitian had taken objection.

nevertheless all serve for the adornment of the heavenly bride. Further, I rejoice exceedingly that your most sweet Blessedness, even though occupied with secular affairs, still brings back its genius vigilantly to the understanding of Holy Writ. For so indeed it is needful that, if the former cannot be altogether avoided, the latter should not be altogether put aside. But I beseech you by Almighty God, stretch out the hand of prayer to me who am labouring in so great billows of tribulation, that by your intercession I may be lifted up to the heights, who am pressed down to the depths by the weight of my sins. Moreover, though I grieve that the Emperor of the Persians has not been converted, yet I altogether rejoice for that you have preached to him the Christian faith; since, though he has not been counted worthy to come to the light, yet your Holiness will have the reward of your preaching. For the Ethiopian, too, goes black into the bath, and comes out black; but still the keeper of the bath receives his pay.

Further, of Mauricius you say well, that from the shadow I may know the statue; that is, that in small things I may perpend greater things. In this matter, however, we trust him, since oaths and hostages bind his soul to us.

BOOK IV

EPISTLE I.

To Constantius, Bishop.

Gregory to Constantius, Bishop of Mediolanum (*Milan*).

On receiving the letters of your Fraternity I returned great thanks to Almighty God, that I was counted worthy to be refreshed by the celebration of your ordination. Truly that all, by the gift of God, with one accord concurred in your election, is a fact which thy Fraternity ought with the utmost consideration to estimate, since, after God, you are greatly indebted to those who with so submissive a disposition desired you to be preferred before themselves.

It becomes you, therefore, with priestly benignity to respond to their behaviour, and with kind sympathy to attend to their needs. If perchance there are any faults in any of them, rebuke these with well-considered reproofs, so that your very priestly indignation be mingled with a savour of sweetness, and that so you may be loved by your subjects even when you are greatly feared. Such conduct will also induce great reverence for your person in their judgment; since, as hasty and habitual rage is despised, so discriminate indignation against faults for the most part becomes the more formidable in proportion as it has been slow.

Further, John our subdeacon, who has returned, has reported many good things of you; as to which we beseech Almighty God Himself to fulfil what He has begun; to the end that He may shew thee to have advanced in good inwardly and outwardly both now among men and hereafter among the angels.

Moreover, we have sent thee, according to custom, a pallium to be used in the sacred solemnities of mass. But I beg you, when you receive it, to vindicate its dignity and its meaning by humility.

EPISTLE II.

To Constantius, Bishop.

Gregory to Constantius, Bishop of Mediolanum.

My most beloved son, the deacon Boniface, has conveyed to me certain private information through thy Fraternity's letter; namely that three bishops, having sought out rather than found an occasion, have separated themselves from the pious communion of your Fraternity, saying that you have assented to the condemnation of the Three Chapters [1], and have given a security [2]. And, indeed, whether there has been any mention made of the Three Chapters in any word or writing whatever thy Fraternity remembers well; although thy Fraternity's predecessor, Laurentius, did send forth a most strict security to the Apostolic See, to which most noble men in legitimate number subscribed; among whom I also, at that time holding the prætorship of the city, likewise subscribed; since after such a schism had taken place about nothing, it was right that the Apostolic See should take heed, with the view of guarding in all respects the unity of the Universal Church in the minds of priests. But as to its being said that our daughter, Queen Theodelinda, after hearing this news, has withdrawn herself from thy communion, it is for all reasons evident that, though she has been seduced to some little extent by the words of bad men, yet, on the arrival of Hippolytus the notary, and John the abbot, she will seek in all ways the communion of your Fraternity [3]. To her also I have addressed a letter [4], which I beg your Fraternity to trans-

---

[1] As to the schism from Rome in the province of Istria consequent on the condemnation of "The Three Chapters" by the fifth General Council, see I. 16, note 3. It appears that in the adjacent province of Liguria, of which Mediolanum (*Milan*) was the metropolis, there was a like rejection of the fifth council on the part at least of some bishops, who had consequently declined communion with their newly-appointed Metropolitan Constantius, who was believed to have agreed formally to the condemnation of The Three Chapters.

[2] *Cautionem fecisse*: i.e. had pledged himself to the pope by a formal document to uphold the fifth council in its condemnation of the said Chapters.

[3] Theodelinda, the Lombard queen, was a catholic Christian, though her husband Agilulph was still an Arian. Ticinum (or Pavia), which was the residence of the Lombard Kings, was under the Metropolitan jurisdiction of Milan; and it appears that, under the influence of the dissentient bishops of the province, she too had refused to communicate with the new Metropolitan. Gregory's anticipation, expressed in what follows, that she would easily be brought round, was premature: for ten years later (A.D. 603-4) we find Gregory still taking pains to overcome her scruples with regard to the fifth council. See XIV. 12.

[4] Viz. Epistle 4 below. This letter, however, was not delivered to the queen by the bishop Constantius, to whom it had been sent, because of the allusion contained in it to the fifth council, which she appears to have been resolute in rejecting. The new bishop thought she would be more likely to accept him as orthodox, if it were only said that he adhered in all respects to the faith of the four previous councils, including that of Chalcedon. See below, *Ep.* 39. Accordingly another letter (*Ep.* 38), in which

mit to her without delay. Further, with regard to the bishops who appear to have separated themselves, I have written another letter, which when you have caused to be shewn to them, I doubt not that they will repent of the superstition of their pride before thy Fraternity.

Furthermore, you have accurately and briefly informed me of what has been done, whether by King Ago [5] or by the Kings of the Franks. I beg your Fraternity to make known to me in all ways what you have so far ascertained. But, if you should see that Ago, King of the Lombards, is doing nothing with the Patrician [6], promise him on our part that I am prepared to give attention to his case, if he should be willing to arrange anything with the republic advantageously.

EPISTLE III.

To Constantius, Bishop.

Gregory to Constantius, Bishop of Mediolanum.

It has come to my knowledge that certain bishops of your diocese, seeking out rather than finding an occasion, have attempted to sever themselves from the unity of your Fraternity, saying that thou hadst given a security [7] at the Roman city for thy condemnation of the three Chapters. And the fact is that they say this because they do not know how I am accustomed to trust thy Fraternity even without security. For if there had been need for anything of the kind, your mere word of mouth could have been trusted. I, however, do not recollect any mention between us of the three Chapters either in word or in writing. But as for them, if they soon return from their error, they should be spared, because, according to the saying of the Apostle Paul, *They understand neither what they say nor whereof they affirm* (1 *Tim.* i. 7). For we, truth guiding us and our conscience bearing witness, declare that we keep the faith of the holy synod of Chalcedon in all respects inviolate, and venture not to add anything to, or to subtract anything from, its definition [8]. But, if any one would fain take upon himself to think anything, either more or less, contrary to it, and to the faith of this same synod, we anathematize him without any hesitation, and decree him to be alien from the bosom of Mother Church. Any one, therefore, whom this my confession does not bring to a right mind, no longer loves the synod of Chalcedon, but hates the bosom of Mother Church. If then those who appear to have been thus daring have presumed thus to speak in zeal of soul, it remains for them, having received this satisfaction, to return to the unity of thy Fraternity, and not divide themselves from the body of Christ, which is the holy universal Church.

EPISTLE IV.

To Queen Theodelinda.

Gregory to Theodelinda, Queen of the Lombards [9].

It has come to our knowledge by the report of certain persons that your Glory has been led on by some bishops even to such an offence against holy Church as to withdraw yourself from the communion of Catholic unanimity. Now the more we sincerely love you, the more seriously are we distressed about you, that you believe unskilled and foolish men, who not only do not know what they talk about, but can hardly understand what they have heard.

For they say that in the times of Justinian of pious memory, some things were ordained contrary to the council of Chalcedon; and, while they neither read themselves nor believe those who do, they remain in the same error which they themselves feigned to themselves concerning us. For we, our conscience bearing witness, declare that nothing was altered, nothing violated, with respect to the faith of this same holy council of Chalcedon; but that whatever was done in the times of the aforesaid Justinian was so done that the faith of the council of Chalcedon should in no respect be disturbed. Further, if any one presumes to speak or think anything contrary to the faith of the said synod, we detest his

allusion to the fifth council was omitted, was prepared and sent in accordance with the advice of Constantius. See further, note 8, under Epistle 3.

5 I.e. Agilulph the Lombard King. The time (Indict. XII., i.e. A.D. 593-4) was after he had invested Rome and returned to Pavia, and when Gregory had in vain urged Romanus Patricius, the Exarch at Ravenna, to come to terms with him. Gregory appears prepared to approach him now with a view to a separate peace with himself, which he says afterwards (see V. 36, 40) he could have made if he had been so minded. Letters bearing on the subject are V. 36, 40, 41, 42; VI. 30; IX. 4, 6, 42, 43, 98. See also *Proleg*. p. xxi.

6 I.e. Romanus Patricius, the Exarch.

7 *Cautionem fecisse*. See *Ep*. 2, note 2.

8 The contention of those who disapproved of the condemnation of "The Three Chapters" by the fifth council was not only that the condemnation of deceased persons was wrong as well as useless, but also that it impugned the faith of the Council of Chalcedon. For that Council had not condemned the writers who were now condemned; and two of them, Theodoret of Cyrus and Ibas of Edessa, had even appeared before it, and been accepted as orthodox. Further, the condemnation was regarded as a concession to the Monophysites who had been condemned at Chalcedon, the writers in question having been peculiarly obnoxious to the Monophysite party. And it does appear to be the case that a main motive of the Emperor Justinian in forcing the condemnation of The Three Chapters on the Church had been to conciliate the Monophysites, and to induce them to conform. Hence Gregory's anxiety to shew that what had been done at the fifth did not touch the faith as previously defined.

9 This letter was not delivered to Theodelinda, Epistle XXXVIII. having been afterwards substituted for it. See note 4 under *Ep*. 2.

opinion, with interposition of anathema. Since then you know the integrity of our faith under the attestation of our conscience, it remains that you should never separate yourself from the communion of the Catholic Church, lest all those tears of yours, and all those good works should come to nothing, if they are found alien from the true faith. It therefore becomes your Glory to send a communication with all speed to my most reverend brother and fellow-bishop Constantius, of whose faith, as well as his life, I have long been well assured, and to signify by your letters addressed to him how kindly you have accepted his ordination, and that you are in no way separated from the communion of his Church; although I think that what I say on this subject is superfluous: for, though there has been some degree of doubtfulness in your mind, I think that it has been removed from your heart on the arrival of my son John the abbot, and Hippolytus the notary.

EPISTLE V.

To Boniface, Bishop.

Gregory to Boniface, Bishop of Regium (*Reii*).

It is a shame for priests to be admonished about matters of divine worship. For they are then to their disgrace required to do what they ought themselves to require to be done. Yet lest, as I do not suppose, thy Fraternity should neglect in any respect the things that pertain to the work of God, we have thought fit to exhort thee specially on this very head. We therefore admonish thee that the clergy of the city of Regium be to no extent released by the indulgence of thy Fraternity in duties demanded by their office. But in the things that pertain to God let them be most instantly and most earnestly compelled. We desire thee also to study the reputation of the aforesaid clergy, that nothing bad, nothing that at all contravenes ecclesiastical discipline, be heard of them; seeing that it is to its adornment, not to foulness of deeds, that their office appertains. Further, we decree that what we determined in the case of the Sicilians be observed by thy subdeacons [1]; nor mayest thou suffer this our decision to be infringed by the contumacy or temerity of any one whatever; that so, as we believe will be the case, all that has been said above being most strictly kept in force by thee, thou mayest neither prove a transgressor of our admonition, nor be accused as guilty of remissness in the order of pastoral rule which has been committed to thee.

[1] See I. 44, p. 91; also below, *Ep.* 36.

EPISTLE VI.

To Cyprian, Deacon.

Gregory to Cyprian, Deacon and Rector of Sicily.

It has been reported to us that a native of the province of Lucania, Petronilla by name, was converted [2] through the exhortation of the bishop Agnellus, and that all her property, though she had it in her own power, she nevertheless bestowed on the monastery which she entered even by a special deed of gift: also that the aforesaid bishop died leaving half of his substance to one Agnellus, his son, who is said to be a notary of our Church, and half to the said monastery. But, when they had fled for refuge to Sicily because of the calamity impending on Italy, the above-named Agnellus is said to have corrupted her morals and defiled her, and, finding her with child, to have seduced her from the monastery, and to have taken away with her all her belongings, both those that had been her own and such as she might have had given her by his own father, and that, after perpetrating such and so great a crime, he claims these things as his own. We therefore exhort thy Love to cause the aforesaid man, and the above-named woman, to be summarily brought before thee, and to institute a most thorough enquiry into the case. And, if thou shouldest find it to be as reported to us, determine an affair defiled by so many iniquities with the utmost severity of expurgation; to the end that both strict retribution may overtake the above-named man, who has regarded neither his own nor her condition, and that, she having been first punished and consigned to a monastery under penance, all the property that had been taken away from the oft above-named place, with all its fruits and accessions, may be restored.

EPISTLE VII.

To Gennadius, Patrician.

Gregory to Gennadius, Patrician and Exarch of Africa.

We are well assured that the mind of your religious Excellency is inflamed with zeal of divine love against those things especially which are done in unseemly wise in the churches. We therefore the more gladly impose on you the correction of faults in ecclesiastical cases as we have confidence in the bent of your pious disposition. Be it known, then, to your Excellence that it has been reported to us by some who have come to us

[2] *Conversam*, with the usual sense of monastic profession.

from the African parts that many things are being committed in the council of Numidia contrary to the way of the Fathers and the ordinances of the canons. And, being unable to bear any longer the frequent complaints that have reached us about such things, we committed them to be enquired into to our brother and fellow-bishop Columbus [3], of whose gravity his very reputation, which is spread abroad, now allows us not to doubt. Wherefore, greeting you with fatherly affection, we exhort your Excellence that in all things pertaining to ecclesiastical discipline you should lend him the support of your assistance, lest, if what is done amiss should not be enquired into and visited, it should grow with greater license into future excesses through precedent of long continuance. Know moreover, most excellent son, that if you seek victories, and are dealing for the security of the province committed to you, nothing will avail you more for this end than being zealous in restraining as far as possible the lives of priests and the intestine wars of Churches.

EPISTLE VIII.

To Januarius, Bishop.

Gregory to Januarius, Bishop of Caralis (*Cagliari*).

We think indeed that thy position may in itself be enough to compel thee to be instant in the fulfilment of pious duties. But, lest remissness of any kind should intervene to abate thy zeal, we have thought it right to exhort thee especially with regard to them. Now it has come to our knowledge that your Stephen, when departing this life, by his last will and testament directed a monastery to be founded. But it is said that his desire is so far unaccomplished owing to the delay of the honourable lady Theodosia, his heiress. Wherefore we exhort thy Fraternity to pay the utmost attention to this matter, and admonish the above-named lady, to the end that within a year's space she may establish a monastery as has been directed, and construct everything without dispute according to the will of the departed. But if she should put off the completion of the design out of negligence or artfulness (as, for instance, if she is unable to found it in the place that had been appointed, and it is thought fit that it be placed elsewhere, and the matter is neglected through the intervening delay), then we desire that it be built by the diligence of thy Fraternity, and that, all things being set in order, the effects and revenues that have been left be appropriated by thee to this venerable place. For so thou wilt both escape condemnation for remissness before the awful Judge, and, in accordance with our most religious laws, wilt be accomplishing with episcopal zeal the pious wishes of the departed, which had been disregarded [4].

EPISTLE IX.

To Januarius, Bishop.

Gregory to Januarius, Bishop of Caralis (*Cagliari*).

Pastoral zeal ought indeed in itself to have sufficiently instigated thee, even without our aid, to protect profitably and providently the flock of which thou hast taken charge, and to preserve it with diligent circumspection from the cunning devices of enemies. But, since we have found that thy Charity needs also the written word of our authority for the augmentation of thy firmness, it is necessary for us, by the exhortation of brotherly love, to strengthen thy faltering disposition towards the earnestness of religious activity.

Now it has come to our knowledge that thou art remiss in thy guardianship of the monasteries of the handmaidens of God situated in Sardinia; and, though it had been prudently arranged by thy predecessors that certain approved men of the clergy should have the charge of attending to their needs, this has now been so entirely neglected that women specially dedicated to God are compelled to go in person among public functionaries about tributes and other liabilities, and are under the necessity of running to and fro through villages and farms for making up their taxes, and of mixing themselves unsuitably in business which belongs to men. This evil let thy Fraternity remove by an easy correction; that is, by carefully deputing one man of approved life and manners, and o such age and position as to give rise to no evil suspicion of him, who may, with the fear of God, so assist the inmates of these monasteries that they may no longer be allowed to wander, against rule, for any cause whatever, private or public, beyond their venerable precincts; but that whatever has to be done in their behalf may be transacted reasonably by him whom you shall depute. But let the nuns themselves, rendering praises to God and confining themselves to their monasteries, no longer suggest any evil suspicion to the minds of the faithful. But if any one of them, either through former license, or through an evil custom of impunity, has

3 See II. 48, note 1.

4 For subsequent proceedings with regard to this intended monastery, see IV. 15; V. 2.

been seduced, or should in future be led, into the gulph of adulterous lapse, we will that, after enduring the severity of adequate punishment, she be consigned for penance to some other stricter monastery of virgins, that she may there give herself to prayers and fastings, and profit herself by penitence, and afford an example of the more rigorous kind of discipline, such as may inspire fear in others. Further, let any one who may be detected in any iniquity with women of this class be deprived of communion, if he be a layman; but, if he be a cleric, let him also be removed from his office, and thrust into a monastery for his ever to be deplored excesses.

We also desire thee to hold councils of bishops twice in the year, as is said to have been the custom of thy province, as well as being ordered by the authority of the sacred canons; that, if any among them be of moral character inconsistent with his profession, he may be convicted by the friendly rebuke of his brethren, and also that measures may be taken with paternal circumspection for the security of the flock committed to him, and for the well-being of souls. It has come to our knowledge also that male and female slaves of Jews, who have fled for refuge to the Church on account of their faith, are either restored to their unbelieving masters, or paid for according to their value in lieu of being restored. We exhort therefore that thou by no means allow so bad a custom to continue; but that whosoever, being a slave to Jews, shall have fled for refuge to venerable places, thou suffer him not in any degree to sustain prejudice. But, whether he had been a Christian before, or been baptized now, let him be supported in his claim for freedom, without any loss to the poor, by the patronage of ecclesiastical compassion.

Let not bishops presume to sign baptized infants a second time on the forehead with chrism; but let the presbyters anoint those who are to be baptized on the breast, that the bishops may afterwards anoint them on the forehead[5].

With regard also to founding monasteries, which divers persons have ordered to be built, if thou perceivest that any persons to whom the charge has been assigned put it off on unjust pretexts, we desire thee to insist sagaciously according to what the laws enjoin, lest (as God forbid should be the case) the pious intentions of the departed should be frustrated through thy neglect. Further, as to the monastery which Peter is said to have formerly ordered to be constructed in his house, we have seen fit that thy Fraternity should make accurate enquiry into the amount of the revenues there. And in case of there being a suitable provision, when all diminutions of the property and what is said to have been dispersed have been recovered, let the monastery with all diligence and without any delay be founded. But, if the means are insufficient or detrimental[6], we desire thee, after closely investigating everything as has been commanded, to send a report to us, that we may know how to deliberate with the Lord's help with regard to its construction. Let, then, thy Fraternity give wise attention to all the points above referred to, so as neither to be found to have transgressed the tenour of our admonitions nor to stand liable to divine judgment for too little zeal in thy pastoral office.

EPISTLE X.

To all the Bishops of Dalmatia.

Gregory to all the bishops through Dalmatia[7].

It behoved your Fraternity, having the eyes of the flesh closed out of regard to Divine judgment, to have omitted nothing that appertains to God and to a right inclination of mind, nor to have preferred the countenance of any man whatever to the uprightness of justice. But now that your manners have been so perverted by secular concerns, that, forgetting the whole path of the sacerdotal dignity that is yours, and all sense of heavenly fear, you study to accomplish what may please yourselves and not God, we have held it necessary to send you these specially strict written orders, whereby, with the authority of the blessed Peter, Prince of the apostles, we enjoin that you presume not to lay hands on any one whatever in the city of Salona, so far as regards ordination to episcopacy, without our consent and permission; nor to ordain any one in the same city otherwise than as we have said.

But if, either of your own accord, or under compulsion from any one whatever, you should presume or attempt to do anything contrary to this injunction, we shall decree you to be deprived of participation of the Lord's body and blood, that so your very handling of the business, or your very inclination to transgress our order, may cut you off from the sacred mysteries, and no one may be accounted a bishop whom you may ordain. For we wish

[5] For the meaning of this order, and its subsequent modification, see note to IV. 26.

[6] The word is *damnosa*, meaning perhaps injuriously excessive.

[7] On the occasion of this Epistle, see III. 47, note 2.

no one to be rashly ordained whose life can be found fault with. And so, if the deacon Honoratus is shewn to be unworthy, we desire that a report may be sent us of the life and manners of him who may be elected, that whatever is to be done in this matter we may allow to be carried out salubriously with our consent.

For we trust in Almighty God that, as far as in us lies, we may never suffer to be done what may damage our soul; never what may damage your Church. But, if the voluntary consent of all should so fix on one person that by the favour of God he may be proved worthy, and there should be no one to dissent from his being ordained, we wish him to be consecrated by you in this same church of Salona under the license granted in this present epistle; excepting notwithstanding the person of Maximus, about whom many evil reports have reached us: and, unless he desists from coveting the higher order, it remains, as I think, that after full enquiry, he should be deprived also of the very office which he now holds.

EPISTLE XI.

To Maximianus, Bishop.

Gregory to Maximianus, Bishop of Syracuse.

It had indeed been committed to thy Fraternity long ago by our authority to correct in our stead any excesses or unseemly proceedings that there might be in the Church and other venerable places of Sicily[8]. But, seeing that a complaint has reached us of some things having been so far neglected, we have thought it fit that thy Fraternity should again be specially stirred up to correct them.

For we learn that in the case of revenues of Churches that have been newly acquired the canonical disposition of their fourth parts does not prevail[9], but that the bishops of the several places distribute a fourth part of the ancient revenues only, retaining for their own use those that have been recently acquired. Wherefore let thy Fraternity make haste actively to correct this evil custom that has crept in, so that, whether in the case of former revenues or of such as have accrued now or may accrue, the fourth parts may be dispensed according to the canonical distribution of them. For it is unseemly that one and the same substance of the Church should be rated, as it were, under two different laws, namely, that of usurpation and that of the canons.

Permit not presbyters, deacons, and other clerks of whatever order, who serve churches, to be abbots of monasteries; but let them either, giving up clerical duties, be advanced to the monastic order, or, if they should decide to remain in the position of abbot, let them by no means be allowed to have clerical employment. For it is very unsuitable that, if one cannot fulfil the duties of either of these positions with diligence proportional to its importance, any one should be judged fit for both, and that so the ecclesiastical order should impede the monastic life, and in turn the rule of monasticism impede ecclesiastical utility. Of this thing also we have taken thought to warn thy Charity; that, if any one of the bishops should depart this life, or (which God forbid) should be removed for his transgressions, the hierarchs and all the chief of the clergy being assembled, and in thy presence making an inventory of the property of the Church, all that is found should be accurately described, and nothing should be taken away in kind, or in any other way whatever, from the property of the Church, as is said to have been done formerly, as though in return for the trouble of making the inventories. For we desire all that pertains to the protection of what belongs to the poor to be so executed that in their affairs no opportunity may be left for the venality of self-interested men.

Let visitors of churches, and their clerks who with them are at trouble in parishes that are not of their own city, receive according to thy appointment some subsidy for their labour. For it is just that they should get payment in the places where they are found to lend their services.

We most strongly forbid young women to be made abbesses. Let thy Fraternity, therefore, permit no bishop to veil any but a sexagenarian virgin, whose age and character may demand this being done; that so, this as well as the above-named points being set right with the Lord's help by the urgency of thy strict requirement, thou mayest hasten to bind up again with canonical ties the long loosened state of venerable things, and also that divine affairs may be arranged, not by the incongruous wills of men, but with adequate strictness. The month of October, Indiction 12.

EPISTLE XV.

To Januarius, Bishop.

Gregory to Januarius, Bishop of Caralis (*Cagliari*).

Theodosia, a religious lady, being desirous of carrying out the intention of her late hus-

8 See II. 7.

9 For the canonical rule as to the fourfold division of Church funds, cf. Gregory's letter to Augustine, XI. 64, *Responsio prima*.

band Stephen by the building of a monastery[1], has begged us to transmit our letters to your Fraternity, whereby, through our commendation, she may the more readily be counted worthy of your aid. She asserts that her husband had given directions for the monastery to be constructed on the farm called Piscenas, which has come into the possession of the guest-house (*Xenodochii*) of the late bishop Thomas. Now, though the possessor of the property would allow her to found it on land that is not her own, yet seeing that the lord with reason objects[2], we have thought it right to agree to her petition; which is that she should, with the Lord's help, construct a monastery for handmaidens of God in a house belonging to herself, which she asserts that she has at Caralis. But, since she says that the aforesaid house is burdened by guests and visitors, we exhort thy Fraternity to take pains to assist her in all ways, and lend the aid of thy protection to her devotion, so that thy assistance and assiduity may make thee partaker of the reward of her departed husband's earnestness and her own. As to the relics which she requests may be placed there, we desire that they be deposited with due reverence by thy Fraternity.

EPISTLE XVIII.

To Maurus, Abbot.

Gregory to Maurus, &c.

The care of churches which is evidently inherent in the priestly office compels us to be so solicitous that no fault of neglect may appear with regard to them. Since, however, we have learnt that the church of Saint Pancratius, which had been committed to presbyters, has been frequently neglected, so that people coming there on the Lord's day to celebrate the solemnities of mass have returned murmuring on finding no presbyter, we therefore, after mature deliberation, have determined to remove those presbyters, and with the favour of God constitute for the same church a congregation of monks in a monastery, to the end that the abbot who shall preside there may give care and attention in all respects to the aforesaid church. And we have also thought fit to put thee, Maurus, over this monastery as abbot, ordaining that the lands of the aforesaid church, and whatever may have come into its possession, or accrued from its revenues, be applied to this thy monastery, and belong to it without any diminution; but on condition whatever needs to be effected or repaired in the church above written may be so effected and repaired by thee without fail.

But lest, after the removal of the presbyters to whom this church had previously been committed, it should seem to be without provision for divine service, we therefore enjoin thee by the tenour of this authority to supply it with a *peregrine*[3] presbyter to celebrate the sacred solemnities of mass, who, nevertheless, must needs both live in thy monastery, and have from it provision for his maintenance.

But let this also above all be thy care, that there over the most sacred body of the blessed Pancratius the work of God be executed daily without fail. These things, then, which by the tenour of this precept we depute thee to do, we will that not only thou perform, but that they be also so observed and fulfilled for ever by those who shall succeed thee in thy office and place, that there may be no possibility henceforth of neglect being found in the aforesaid church.

EPISTLE XX.

To Maximus, Pretender (*Præsumptorem*)[4].

Gregory to Maximus, Pretender in Salona.

Though the merits of any one's life were in other respects such as to offer no impediment to his ordination to priestly offices, yet the crime of canvassing in itself is condemned by the severest strictness of the canons. Now we have been informed that thou, having either obtained surreptitiously, or pretended, an order from the most pious princes, hast forced thy way to the order of priesthood[5], which is of all men to be venerated, while being in thy life unworthy. And this without any hesitation we believed, inasmuch as thy life and age are not unknown to us, and further, because we are not ignorant of the mind of our most serene lord the Emperor, in that he is not accustomed to mix himself up

[1] See also IV. 8, and V. 2.

[2] The farm Piscenas appears to have been held by the tenure called *Emphyteusis*, according to which the *possessor* of the land (called also *Emphyteuta*) was not its real owner, though on condition of his cultivating it properly and paying certain fixed dues to the owner (*dominus*), he had a perpetual right of possession (*jus in re*), which passed to his heirs, and could be sold by him to others. In the latter case, however, the *dominus* had the option of himself buying up the possessor's right at the price offered by the proposed purchaser, and he could object to the transference of *possessio* to persons unable to maintain the property in good condition. In all cases of transference, other than devolution to heirs, a fiftieth part of the purchase money, or of the value of the property, was also payable to the *dominus*. (Article on *Emphyteusis* in Smith's Dictionary of Greek and Roman Antiquities.) In the case before us the lord of the property seems to have refused his consent to any part of it being alienated in Mortmain to a monastery. It may be supposed that the possession of the farm Piscenas had been in Stephen the testator himself when he directed a monastery to be founded on it, and that it had passed after his death into other hands.

3 *Peregrinum presbyterum;* meaning apparently one not belonging to the house as a member of it, though living and maintained there.

4 See III. 47, note 2.

5 *Sacerdotii ordinem*, meaning here, as elsewhere, the order of episcopacy.

in the causes of priests, lest he should in any way be burdened by our sins. An unheard-of wickedness is also spoken of; that, even after our interdiction, which was pronounced under pain of excommunication of thee and those who should ordain thee, it is said that thou wast brought forward by a military force, and that presbyters, deacons, and other clergy were beaten. Which proceeding we can in no wise call a consecration, since it was celebrated by excommunicated men. Since, therefore, without any precedent, thou hast violated such and so great a dignity, namely that of the priesthood, we enjoin that, until I shall have ascertained from the letters of our lords or of our *responsalis*, that thou wast ordained under a true and not a surreptitious order, thou and thy ordainers by no means presume to handle anything connected with the priestly office, and that you approach not the service of the holy altar till you have heard from us again. But, if you should presume to act in contravention of this order, be ye anathema from God and from the blessed Peter, Prince of the apostles, that your punishment may afford an example to other catholic churches also, through their contemplation of the judgment upon you. The month of May, Indiction 12.

EPISTLE XXI.

To Venantius, Bishop.

Gregory to Venantius, Bishop of Luna (*in Etruria*).

It has reached us by the report of many that Christian slaves are detained in servitude by Jews living in the city of Luna[6]; which thing has seemed to us by so much the more offensive as the sufferance of it by thy Fraternity annoys us. For it was thy duty, in respect of thy place, and in thy regard for the Christian religion, to leave no occasion for simple souls to serve Jewish superstition not through persuasion, but, in a manner, by right of authority. Wherefore we exhort thy Fraternity that, according to the course laid down by the most pious laws, no Jew be allowed to retain a Christian slave in his possession. But, if any are found in their power, let liberty be secured to them by protection under the sanction of law. But as to any that are on the property of Jews, though they be themselves free from legal obligation, yet, since they have long been attached to the cultivation of their lands as bound by the condition of their tenure, let them continue to cultivate the farms they have been accustomed to do, rendering their payments to the aforesaid persons, and performing all things that the laws require of husbandmen or natives, except that no further burden be imposed on them. But, whether any one of these should wish to remain in his servitude, or any to migrate to another place, let the latter consider with himself that he will have lost his rights as a husbandman by his own rashness, though he has got rid of his servitude by force of law. In all these things, then, we desire thee to exert thyself so wisely that neither mayest thou be a guilty pastor of a dismembered flock, nor may thy too little zeal render thee reprehensible before us.

EPISTLE XXIII.

To Hospito, Duke of the Barbaricini[7].

Gregory to Hospito, &c.

Since no one of thy race is a Christian, I hereby know that thou art better than all thy race, in that thou in it art found to be a Christian. For, while all the Barbaricini live as senseless animals, know not the true God, but adore stocks and stones, in the very fact that thou worshippest the true God thou shewest how much thou excellest them all. But carry thou out the faith which thou hast received in good deeds and words, and offer what is in thy power to Christ in whom thou believest, so as to bring to Him as many as thou canst, and cause them to be baptized, and admonish them to set their affection on eternal life. And if perchance thou canst not do this thyself, being otherwise occupied, I beg thee, with my greeting, to succour in all ways our men whom we have sent to your parts, to wit my fellow-bishop Felix, and my son, the servant of God, Cyriacus[8], so that in aiding their labours thou mayest shew thy devotion to Almighty God, and that He whose servants thou succourest in their good work may be a helper to thee in all good deeds. We have sent you through them a blessing[9] of St. Peter the apostle, which I beg you to receive, as you ought to do, kindly. The month of June, Indiction 12.

---

6 On the holding of Christian slaves by Jews, and the treatment of Jews generally, cf. *Proleg*. p. xxi.

7 The Barbaricini appear to have been a native tribe in Sardinia, having its own duke, Zabardas (see *Ep*. 24) being the duke of the island.

8 These two ecclesiastics had been sent into Sardinia to promote the conversion of the natives, which seems to have been remissly attended to, not only by the Christian lay proprietors, but also by the bishops of the island. See below, *Epp*. 25, 26. The bishop Felix was not commissioned to supersede the ordinary episcopal jurisdiction, but to act as a missionary bishop in aid. Cf. V. 41.

9 *Benedictio*, here as elsewhere, means a present;—in this case, being said to be from St. Peter, containing doubtless something that had acquired sanctity from him; probably, as in other cases, filings from his chains. Cf. I. 26, note 3.

EPISTLE XXIV.

To Zabardas, Duke of Sardinia.

Gregory to Zabardas, &c.

From the letters of my brother and fellow-bishop Felix, and of the servant of God, Cyriacus, we have learnt your Glory's good qualities. And we give great thanks to Almighty God, that Sardinia has got such a duke; one who so knows how to do his duty to the republic in earthly matters as to know also how to exhibit to Almighty God dutiful regard for the heavenly country. For they have written to me that you are arranging terms of peace with the Barbaricini on such conditions as to bring these same Barbaricini to the service of Christ. On this account I rejoice exceedingly, and, should it please Almighty God, will speedily notify your gifts to our most serene princes. Do you, therefore, accomplish what you have begun, shew the devotion of your heart to Almighty God, and help to the utmost of your power those whom we have sent to your parts for the conversion of the Barbaricini[1]; knowing that such works may avail much to aid you both before our earthly princes and in the eyes of the heavenly king.

EPISTLE XXV.

To the Nobles and Proprietors in Sardinia.

Gregory to the Nobles, &c.

I have learnt from the report of my brother and fellow-bishop Felix, and my son the servant of God, Cyriacus[2], that nearly all of you have peasants (*rusticos*[3]) on your estates given to idolatry. And this has made me very sorry, since I know that the guilt of subjects weighs down the life of their superiors, and that, when sin in a subject is not corrected, sentence is flung back on those who are over them. Wherefore, magnificent sons, I exhort that with all care and all solicitude ye be zealous for your souls, and see what account you will render to Almighty God for your subjects. For indeed they have been committed to you for this end, that both they may serve for your advantage in earthly things, and you, through your care for them, may provide for their souls in the things that are eternal. If, then, they pay what they owe you, why pay you not them what you owe them? That is to say, your Greatness should assiduously admonish them, and restrain them from the error of idolatry, to the end that by their being drawn to the faith you may make Almighty God propitious to yourselves. For, lo, you observe how the end of this world is close at hand; you see that now a human, now a divine, sword rages against us: and yet you, the worshippers of the true God, behold stones adored by those who are committed to you, and are silent[4]. What, I pray you, will you say in the tremendous judgment, when you have received God's enemies into your power, and yet disdain to subdue them to God and recall them to Him? Wherefore, addressing you with due greeting, I beg that your Greatness would be earnestly on the watch to give yourselves to zeal for God, and hasten to inform me in your letters which of you has brought how many to Christ. If, then, haply from any cause you are unable to do this, enjoin it on our aforesaid brother and fellow-bishop Felix, or my son Cyriacus, and afford them succour for the work of God, that so in the retribution to come you may be in a state to partake of life by so much the more as you now afford succour to a good work.

[1] See preceding Epistle.
[2] See above, *Ep.* 23.
[3] As to *rustici*, or *coloni*, see I. 44, note 1.

EPISTLE XXVI.

To Januarius, Bishop.

Gregory to Januarius, Bishop of Caralis (*Cagliari*).

We have ascertained from the report of our fellow-bishop Felix and the abbot Cyriacus that in the island of Sardinia priests are oppressed by lay judges, and that thy ministers despise thy Fraternity; and that, so far as appears, while you aim only at simplicity, discipline is neglected. Wherefore I exhort thee that, putting aside all excuses, thou take pains to rule the Church of which thou hast received the charge, to keep up discipline among the clergy, and fear no one's words. But, as I hear, thou hast forbidden thy Archdeacon to live with women, and up to this time art set at naught with regard to this thy prohibition. Unless he obey thy command, our will is that he be deprived of his sacred order.

There is another thing also which is much to be deplored; namely, that the negligence of your Fraternity has allowed the peasants (*rusticos*) belonging to thy Church to remain up to the present time in infidelity. And what is the use of my admonishing you to bring such as do not belong to you to God, if you neglect to recover your own from infidelity? Hence you must needs be in all ways vigilant for their conversion. For, should I succeed in finding a pagan peasant belonging to any

[4] Cf. IV. 23, note 8.

bishop whatever in the island of Sardinia, I will visit it severely on that bishop.

But now, if any peasant should be found so perfidious and obstinate as to refuse to come to the Lord God, he must be weighted with so great a burden of payment as to be compelled by the very pain of the exaction to hasten to the right way[5].

It has also come to our knowledge that some in sacred orders who have lapsed, either after doing penance or before, are recalled to the office of their ministry; which is a thing that we have altogether forbidden; and the most sacred canons also declare against it. Whoso, then, after having received any sacred order, shall have lapsed into sin of the flesh, let him so forfeit his sacred order as not to approach any more the ministry of the altar. But, lest those who have been ordained should ever perish, previous care should be taken as to what kind of people are ordained, so that it be first seen to whether they have been continent in life for many years, and whether they have had a care for reading and a love of almsgiving. It should be enquired also whether a man has perchance been twice married. It should also be seen to that he be not illiterate, or under liability to the state, so as to be compelled after assuming a sacred order to return to public employment. All these things therefore let your Fraternity diligently enquire into, that, every one having been ordained after diligent examination, none may be easily liable to be deposed after ordination. These things which we have written to your Fraternity do you make known to all the bishops under you, since I myself have been unwilling to write to them, lest I might seem to lessen your dignity.

It has also come to our ears that some have been offended by our having forbidden presbyters to touch with chrism those who are to be baptized. And we indeed acted according to the ancient use of our Church: but, if any are in fact hereby distressed, we allow that, where there is a lack of bishops, presbyters may touch with chrism, even on their foreheads, those who are to be baptized[6].

EPISTLE XXVII.

To Januarius, Bishop.

Gregory to Januarius, Bishop of Caralis (*Cagliari*).

Thy Fraternity ought indeed to have been so attentive to pious duties as to be in no need at all of our admonitions to induce thee to fulfil them: yet, as certain particulars that require correction have come to our knowledge, there is nothing incongruous in your having besides a letter addressed to you bearing our authority.

Wherefore we apprize you that we have been given to understand that it has been the custom for the Guest-houses (*Xenodochia*) constituted in the parts about Caralis to submit their accounts in detail from time to time to the bishop of the city; that is, so as to be governed under his guardianship and care.

5 The *rustici*, or *coloni*, who cultivated the land, made their living out of it, having to pay dues in money or in kind (see I. 44). Gregory's suggestion is that such dues should be made so heavy in the case of natives who refused to be converted as to starve hem into compliance. Elsewhere we find him deprecating compulsion, or any kind of persecution, for the conversion of Jews and heretics, on the ground that forced conversions were unreal. But he appears to have had no such conpunctions in the case of these illiterate pagans. This is not the only instance of religious zeal betraying him into a certain human inconsistency. Cf, IX. 65.

6 See above, IV. 9. There is some doubt as to what the practice was which Gregory had forbidden in his former epistle, but now allows. In Ep IX. he had said, "Episcopi baptizatos infantes signare bis in fronte chrismate non præsumant; sed presbyteri baptizandos ungant in pectore, ut episcopi postmodum ungere debeant in fronte." There is obvious reference here to the two unctions, before and after baptism. The first, in preparation for baptism, was with simple oil, on the breast and other parts of the body, and was administered by presbyters both in the East and West: the second, for confirmation after baptism, was with chrism (a mixture of oil and balsam), on the forehead, and in the Eastern Churches might be, as it still is, administered immediately after baptism by the baptizing presbyter, but in the West was usually reserved for the bishop in person. It would seem that in Sardinia the Eastern usage had been followed with regard to the presbyter signing the baptized child on the forehead with chrism immediately after baptism, but that it had been also customary for the bishop afterwards to repeat the rite ("signare bis in fronte chrismate"). Such repetition Gregory, in Ep. IX., appears to forbid in cases where the presbyter had already administered the rite; but, in the second clause of the sentence, he directs that the Western usage should thenceforth be observed: the presbyter who baptized was to anoint on the breast before the baptism; but the bishop, and he alone, on the forehead with chrism afterwards. Such being the most obvious meaning of what is said in Ep. IX. the equally obvious meaning of the concession in Ep. XXVI. would be allowance for presbyters, in the absence of bishops, to confirm with chrism after baptism, according to the Eastern usage, but for the fact that the expression now used is not *baptizatos*, but *baptizandos*. Hence one opinion is that all that is here allowed to presbyters is the anointing of the forehead with chrism, as well as the breast with oil, *previously* to baptism; in which case of course it would not be confirmation. But it seems more likely that the intention was to allow presbyters to administer confirmation in the absence of bishops, the term *baptizandos* being used loosely to denote candidates for baptism. The fact that it is only where bishops could not be had (*ubi desunt episcopi*) that the practice is allowed adds probability to this view; and also his saying that in his previous prohibition he had been following the ancient custom of the Roman Church, which was to reserve the signing the forehead with chrism after baptism, i.e. confirmation, to the bishop. Innocent I. (*Ep.* i. *ad Decent.* c. iii.) lays down the rule thus; "Presbyteris, qui, seu extra episcopum seu præsente episcopo, baptizant, chrismate baptizatos ungere licet, sed quod ab episcopo fuerit consecratum; non tamen frontem ex eodem oleo signare, quod solis debetur episcopis, quum tradunt Spiritum Sanctum Paracletum." Here, we observe, the usage of the Roman Church allows the baptizing presbyter to anoint with chrism after baptism, only not therewith to sign the forehead for actual confirmation; and this is still the Roman usage. It should be observed further that in all cases, in the East as well in the West, confirmation was regarded as belonging peculiarly to the Bishop's office, the chrism used having always been consecrated by him, though it might be applied by presbyters: and thus Gregory, in allowing presbyters to administer the rite in Sardinia would not regard any essential principle of Church order as being infringed. He only shews the same wise liberality as we find evidence of in other cases, allowing varieties of usage in various churches, where no important principle seemed to be involved. Thus he approves of single instead of triune immersion in baptism being practised in Spain (I. 43), and bids Augustine in England adopt according to his discretion the customs of other Churches (XI. 64). With regard to the essential *form* of confirmation recognized in the time of Gregory, it appears evidently from these epistles to have been *unction*, and not mere imposition of hands. It is also evident that it was administered, as in the East now, to infants; cf. XIII. 18, where the phrase is "ad consignandos infantes."

Now, as thy Charity is said to have so far neglected this, we exhort, as has been said, that the inmates who are or have been established in these Guest-houses submit their accounts in detail from time to time. And let such persons be ordained to preside over them as may be found most worthy in life, manners and industry, and at any rate *religiosi*[7], whom judges may have no power of annoying, lest, if they should be such as could be summoned to the courts, occasion might be given for wasting the feeble resources which they have: concerning which resources we wish thee to take the greatest care, so that they be given away to no one without thy knowledge, lest the carelessness of thy Fraternity should go so far as to let them be plundered.

Moreover, thou knowest that the bearer of these presents, Epiphanius the presbyter, was criminally accused in the letters of certain Sardinians. We, then, having investigated his case as it was our will to do, and finding no proof of what was charged against him, have absolved him, so that he might be restored to his place. We therefore desire thee to search out the authors of the charge against him: and, unless he who sent those same letters be prepared to support his charges by canonical and most strict proofs, let him on no account approach the mystery of holy communion.

Further, as to Paul the cleric, who is said to have been often detected in malpractices, and who had fled into Africa, having returned to a lay state of life in despite of his cloth, if it is so, we have seen to his being given up to penance after previous corporal punishment, to the end that, according to the apostolic sentence, by means of affliction of the flesh the spirit may be saved, and also that he may be able to wash away with continual tears the earthly filth of sin, which he is said to have contracted by wicked works.

Moreover, in accordance with the injunctions of the canons, let no religious person (*religiosus*) associate with those who have been suspended from ecclesiastical communion.

Further, for ordinations or marriages of clerics, or from virgins who are veiled, let no one presume to receive any fee, unless they should prefer to offer something of their own accord.

As to what should be done in the case of women who have left monasteries for a lay life, and have taken husbands, we have conversed at length with thy Fraternity's aforesaid presbyter, from whose report your Holiness may be more fully informed.

Further, let religious clerics (*religiosi clerici*)[7a] avoid resort to or the patronage of laymen; but let them be in all respects subject to thy jurisdiction according to the canons, lest through the remissness of thy Fraternity the discipline of the Church over which thou presidest should be dissolved.

Lastly, as to the men who have sinned with the aforesaid women who had left their monasteries, and are said to be now suspended from communion, if thy Fraternity should observe them to have repented worthily for such a wickedness, we will that thou restore them to holy communion.

EPISTLE XXIX.

To Januarius, Bishop.

Gregory to Januarius, Bishop of Caralis (*Cagliari*).

It has come to our knowledge that in the place within the province of Sardinia called Phausiana it is said to have been once the custom to ordain a bishop; but that, through stress of circumstances, the custom has for long fallen into disuse. But, as we are aware that now, owing to scarcity of priests, certain pagans remain there, living like wild beasts, and entirely ignorant of the worship of God, we exhort thy Fraternity to make haste to ordain a bishop there according to the ancient way; such a one, that is, as may be suitable for this work, and may take pains to bring wanderers into the Lord's flock with pastoral zeal; that so, while he devotes himself there to the saving of souls, neither may you be found to have required what was superfluous, nor may we repent of having re-established in vain what had been once discontinued.

EPISTLE XXX.

To Constantina Augusta.

Gregory to Constantina, &c.

The Serenity of your Piety, conspicuous for religious zeal and love of holiness, has charged me with your commands to send to you the head of Saint Paul, or some other part of his body, for the church which is being built in honour of the same Saint Paul in the palace. And, being desirous of receiving commands from you, by exhibiting the most ready obedience to which I might the more provoke your favour towards me, I am all the more distressed that I neither can nor dare do what you enjoin. For the bodies of the apostles

[7] For what was meant by *religiosi* and *religiosæ*, see I. 61, note 7. It appears from what is said here that persons recognized as such were ordinarily exempt from certain claims upon them by the state to which others might be liable.

[7a] For the meaning of *religiosi*, see I. 61, n. 7. They were not of necessity *clerici*. In X. 54, we find *religioso laico*.

Saint Peter and Saint Paul glitter with so great miracles and terrors in their churches that one cannot even go to pray there without great fear. In short, when my predecessor, of blessed memory, was desirous of changing the silver which was over the most sacred body of the blessed apostle Peter, though at a distance of almost fifteen feet from the same body, a sign of no small dreadfulness appeared to him. Nay, I too wished in like manner to amend something not far from the most sacred body of Saint Paul the apostle; and, it being necessary to dig to some depth near his sepulchre, the superintendent of that place found some bones, which were not indeed connected with the same sepulchre; but, inasmuch as he presumed to lift them and transfer them to another place, certain awful signs appeared, and he died suddenly.

Besides all this, when my predecessor, of holy memory, was desiring in like manner to make some improvements not far from the body of Saint Laurence the martyr, it not being known where the venerable body was laid, diggings were made in the course of search, and suddenly his sepulchre was unawares disclosed; and those who were present and working, monks and *mansionarii*[8], who saw the body of the same martyr, which they did not indeed presume to touch, all died within ten days, so that none might survive who had seen the holy body of that righteous man.

Moreover, let my most tranquil lady know that it is not the custom of the Romans, when they give relics of saints, to presume to touch any part of the body; but only a cloth (*brandeum*) is put into a box (*pyxide*), and placed near the most sacred bodies of the saints: and when it is taken up it is deposited with due reverence in the Church that is to be dedicated, and such powerful effects are thereby produced there as might have been if their bodies had been brought to that special place. Whence it came to pass in the times of Pope Leo, of blessed memory, as has been handed down from our forefathers, that, certain Greeks being in doubt about such relics, the aforesaid pontiff took scissors and cut this same cloth (*brandeum*), and from the very incision blood flowed. For in the Roman and all the Western parts it is unendurable and sacrilegious for any one by any chance to desire to touch the bodies of saints: and, if one should presume to do this, it is certain that this temerity will by no means remain unpunished. For this reason we greatly wonder at the custom of the Greeks, who say that they take up the bones of saints; and we scarcely believe it. For certain Greek monks who came here more than two years ago dug up in the silence of night near the church of Saint Paul, bodies of dead men lying in the open field, and laid up their bones to be kept in their own possession till their departure. And, when they were taken and diligently examined as to why they did this, they confessed that they were going to carry those bones to Greece to pass for relics of saints. From this instance, as has been already said, the greater doubt has been engendered in us whether it be true that they really take up the bones of saints, as they are said to do.

But what shall I say of the bodies of the blessed apostles, when it is well known that, at the time when they suffered, believers came from the East to recover their bodies as being those of their own countrymen? And, having been taken as far as the second milestone from the city, they were deposited in the place which is called Catacumbas. But, when the whole multitude came together and endeavoured to remove them thence, such violence of thunder and lightning terrified and dispersed them that they on no account presumed to attempt such a thing again. And then the Romans, who of the Lord's loving-kindness were counted worthy to do this, went out and took up their bodies, and laid them in the places where they are now deposited.

Who then, most serene lady, can there be so venturesome as, knowing these things, to presume, I do not say to touch their bodies, but even at all to look at them? Such orders therefore having been given me by you, which I could by no means have obeyed, it has not, so far as I find, been of your own motion; but certain men have wished to stir up your Piety against me, so as to withdraw from me (which God forbid) the favour of your good will, and have therefore sought out a point in which I might be found as if disobedient to you. But I trust in Almighty God that your most kind good will is in no way being stolen away from me, and that you will always have with you the power of the holy apostles, whom with all your heart and mind you love, not from their bodily presence, but from their protection.

Moreover, the napkin, which you have likewise ordered to be sent you, is with his body, and so cannot be touched, as his body cannot be approached. But since so religious a desire of my most serene lady ought not to be wholly unsatisfied, I will make haste to transmit to you some portion of the chains which Saint

8 "*Mansionarius*. Sacristain d'une église, chargé de la garder, de sonner les cloches pour l'office divin, de préparer les reliquaires, etc." – D'Arnis.

Peter the apostle himself bore on his neck and his hands, from which many miracles are displayed among the people; if at least I should succeed in removing it by filing. For, while many come frequently to seek a blessing from these same chains, in the hope of receiving a little part of the filings, a priest attends with a file, and in the case of some seekers a portion comes off so quickly from these chains that there is no delay: but in the case of other seekers the file is drawn for long over the chains, and yet nothing can be got from them.

In the month of June, Indiction 12.

EPISTLE XXXI.

To Theodorus, Physician.

Gregory to Theodorus, Physician to the Emperor.

I myself give thanks to Almighty God, that distance does not separate the hearts of those who truly love each other mutually. For lo, most sweet and glorious son, we are far apart in body, and yet are present with each other in charity. This your works, this your letters testify, this I experienced in you when present, this I recognize in your Glory when absent. May this make you both beloved of men and worthy for ever before Almighty God. For, charity being the mother of virtues, you bring forth the fruits of good works for this reason, that you keep in your soul the very root of those fruits. Now what you have sent me, God inspiring you, for the redemption of captives, I confess that I have received both with joy and with sorrow. With joy, that is, for you, whom I thus perceive to be preparing a mansion in the heavenly country; but with exceeding sorrow for myself, who, over and above my care of the property of the holy apostle Peter, must now also give an account of the property of my most sweet son, the lord Theodorus, and be held responsible for having spent it carefully or negligently. But may Almighty God, who has poured into your mind the bowels of His own mercy, who has granted to you to take anxious thought for what is said of our Saviour by the excellent preacher—*That, though he was rich, yet for us he became poor* (2 Cor. viii. 9)—may He, at the coming of the same Saviour, shew you to be rich in virtues, cause you to stand free from all fault, and grant to you heavenly for earthly joys, abiding joys for transitory.

As to what you say you desire to be done for you near the most sacred body of the holy apostle Peter, be assured that, though your tongue were silent, your charity bids the doing of it. Would indeed that we were worthy to pray for you: but that I am not worthy I have no doubt. Still, however, there are here many worthy folk, who are being redeemed from the enemy by your offering, and serve our Creator faithfully, with regard to whom you have done what is written; *Lay up alms in the bosom of the poor, and it shall pray for thee* (Ecclus. xxix. 15).

But, since he loves the more who presumes the more, I have some complaint against the most sweet disposition of my most glorious son the lord Theodorus; namely that he has received from the holy Trinity the gift of genius, the gift of wealth, the gift of mercy and charity, and yet is unceasingly bound up in secular causes, is occupied in continual processions, and neglects to read daily the words of his Redeemer. For what is sacred Scripture but a kind of epistle of Almighty God to His creature? And surely, if your Glory were resident in any other place, and were to receive letters from an earthly emperor, you would not loiter, you would not rest, you would not give sleep to your eyes, till you had learnt what the earthly emperor had written.

The Emperor of Heaven, the Lord of men and angels, has sent thee his epistles for thy life's behoof; and yet, glorious son, thou neglectest to read these epistles ardently. Study then, I beseech thee, and daily meditate on the words of thy Creator. Learn the heart of God in the words of God, that thou mayest sigh more ardently for the things that are eternal, that your soul may be kindled with greater longings for heavenly joys. For a man will have the greater rest here in proportion as he has now no rest in the love of his Maker. But, that you may act thus, may Almighty God pour into you the Spirit the Comforter: may He fill your soul with His presence, and in filling it, compose it.

As to me, know ye that I suffer here many and innumerable bitternesses. But I give thanks to Almighty God that I suffer far less than I deserve.

I commend to your Glory my son, your patient, the lord Narses. I know indeed that you hold him as in all respects commended to you; but I beg you to do what you are doing, that, in asking for what I see is being done, I may by my asking have a share in your reward. Furthermore, I have received the blessing[9] of your Excellency with the charity wherewith it was sent to me. And I have presumed to send you, in acknowledgment of your love, a duck with two small ducklings, that, as often as your eye is led to look at it, the memory also of me may be

9 *Benedictionem* in the sense of *a present*, as elsewhere in the epistles. Cf. Gen. xxxiii. 11; 2 Kings v. 15.

recalled to you among the occupations and tumults of business.

EPISTLE XXXII.

To Narses the Patrician.

Gregory to Narses, &c.

Your most sweet Charity has said much to me in your letters in praise of my good deeds, to all which I briefly reply, *Call me not Noemi, that is beautiful; but call me Mara, that is bitter; for I am full of bitterness* (Ruth i. 20).

But as to the cause of the presbyters [1], which is pending with my brother and fellow-bishop, the most reverend Patriarch John, we have, as I think, for our adversary the very man whom you assert to be desirous of observing the canons. Further, I declare to thy Charity that I am prepared, with the help of Almighty God, to prosecute this same cause with all my power and influence. And, should I see that in it the canons of the Apostolic See are not observed, Almighty God will give unto me what I may do against the contemners of the same.

As to what your Charity has written to me, asking me to give thanks for you to my son the chief physician and ex-præfect Theodorus, I have done so, and have by no means ceased to commend you as much as I could. Further, I beg you to pardon me for replying to your letters with brevity; for I am pressed by such great tribulations that it is not allowed me either to read or to speak much by letter. This only I say to thee, *For the voice of my groaning I have forgotten to eat my bread* (Ps. ci. 5 [2]). All that are with you I beg you to salute in my name. Give my salutations to the lady Dominica, whose letter I have not answered, because, though she is Latin, she wrote to me in Greek.

EPISTLE XXXIII.

To Anthemius, Subdeacon.

Gregory to Anthemius, &c.

Those whom our Redeemer vouchsafes to convert to himself from Judaical perdition we ought, with reasonable moderation, to assist; lest (as God forbid should be the case) they should suffer from lack of food. Accordingly we charge thee, under the authority of this order, not to neglect to give money every year to the children of Justa, who is of the Hebrews; that is to Julianus, Redemptus, and Fortuna, beginning from the coming thirteenth Indiction; and know that the payment is by all means to be charged in thy accounts.

[1] Probably Athanasius and John. See III. 53.

[2] In *English Bible*, cii. 4.

EPISTLE XXXIV.

To Pantaleo, Præfect

Gregory to Pantaleo, Præfect of Africa.

How the law urgently prosecutes the most abominable pravity of heretics is not unknown to your Excellency [3]. It is therefore no light sin if these, whom both the integrity of our faith and the strictness of the laws condemn, should find licence to creep up again in your times. Now in those parts, so far as we have learnt, the audacity of the Donatists has so increased that not only do they with pestiferous assumption of authority cast out of their churches priests of the catholic faith, but fear not even to rebaptize those whom the water of regeneration had cleansed on a true confession. And we are much surprised, if indeed it is so, that, while you are placed in those parts, bad men should be allowed thus to exceed. Consider only in the first place what kind of judgment you will leave to be passed upon you by men, if these, who in the times of others were with just reason put down, find under your administration a way for their excesses. In the next place know that our God will require at your hand the souls of the lost, if you neglect to amend, so far as possibility requires it of you, so great an abomination. Let not your Excellency take amiss my thus speaking. For it is because we love you as our own children that we point out to you what we doubt not will be to your advantage. But send to us with all speed our brother and fellow-bishop Paul [4],

3 As to imperial edicts against the African Donatists, see I. 74, note 8. It would seem from this and the following letter that enforcement of the laws for their repression had been relaxed of late. It will be observed from this and other instances that Gregory, though often in general terms deprecating the use of force in matters of faith, did not scruple, when occasion arose, to call in the aid of the secular arm; and in this case with some heat and acrimony. Cf. IV. 35, below.

4 This Paul was one of the bishops of Numidia, against whom some charges of misconduct, not specified, had been brought. His case has some significance as shewing that, though the spiritual authority of the bishop of Rome over the Church in Africa had now come to be acknowledged in a way that it had not been in the age of Cyprian, yet there seems to have been still some resistance to its exercise. This appears also from the fact that it was not the primate of Numidia, but Columbus, a bishop notable for his devotion to the Roman See, that Gregory mainly and most confidentially corresponded with in relation to ecclesiastical affairs (see II. 48, note 1), and that this Columbus complained of being in disfavour with many on the ground of the frequent communications he received from Rome (VII. 2). In the case before us Gregory's desire (urgently expressed in this letter to Pantaleo, and in that which follows to the primate and Columbus jointly), that Paul should at once be sent to Rome for trial was not complied with. For two years later (VI. 63), Gregory complains of this, and also expresses surprize that the accused bishop should have been excommunicated by the African authorities, and no news sent thereof to himself by the primate. Then, in the following year (VII. 2), writing to Columbus, he finds himself unable to refuse his assent to Paul's resorting to Constantinople to lay his case before the Emperor. However in the year after this it appears that he did go at length to Rome, but not so as to have his case decided there: for Gregory sends

lest opportunity should be given to any one under any excuse for hindering his coming; in order that, on ascertaining the truth more fully, we may be able, with God's help, to settle by a reasonable treatment of the case how the punishment of so great a crime ought to be proceeded with.

EPISTLE XXXV.

To Victor and Columbus, Bishops[5].

Gregory to Victor and Columbus, Bishops of Africa.

After what manner a disease, if neglected in its beginning, acquires strength we have proved from our own necessities, whosoever of us have had our lot in this life. If, then, it were met by the foresight of skilful physicians at its birth, we know that it would cease before doing very much harm from being attended to too late. On this consideration, then, reason ought to impel us, when diseases of souls are beginning, to make haste to resist them by all the means in our power, lest, while we neglect applying wholesome medicines, they steal away from us the lives of many whom we are striving to win for our God. Wherefore it behoves us so with watchful carefulness to guard the folds of sheep which we see ourselves to be put over as keepers that the prowling wolf may find everywhere shepherds to resist him, and may have no way of entrance thereinto.

For indeed we find that the stings of the Donatists have in your parts so disturbed the Lord's flock, as though it were guided by no shepherd's control. And there has been reported to us what we cannot speak of without heavy sorrow, seeing that very many have already been torn by their poisoned teeth. Lastly, in order with most wicked audacity to drive catholic priests from their churches, they are said, in their most atrocious wickedness, even to have slain many besides, on whom the water of regeneration had conferred salvation, by rebaptizing them. All this saddens our mind exceedingly, for that, while you are placed there, it has been allowed to damned presumption to perpetrate such wickedness.

In this matter we exhort your Fraternity by this present writing, that, after discussion held and a council assembled, you should eagerly and with all your power so oppose this still nascent disease that neither may it acquire strength from neglect nor scatter the woes of pestilence in the flock committed to your charge. For, if in any way whatever (as we do not believe will be the case) you neglect to resist iniquity in its beginning, they will wound very many with the sword of their error. And it is in truth a most serious thing to allow to be ensnared in the noose of diabolical fraud those whom we are able to rescue beforehand from being entangled. Moreover it is better to prevent any one from being wounded than to search out how one that is wounded may be healed. Considering this, therefore, hasten ye by sedulous prayer and all the means in your power, to quell sacrilegious wickedness, so that subsequent news, through the aid of the grace of Christ, may cause us more joy for the punishment of those men than sadness for their excesses.

Furthermore, take all possible pains to send to us with all speed our brother and fellow-bishop Paul[6], to the end that, on learning more particularly from him the causes of so great a crime, we may be able by the succour of our Creator to apply the medicine of fitting rebuke to this most atrocious wickedness.

EPISTLE XXXVI.

To Leo, Bishop.

Gregory to Leo, Bishop of Catana[7].

We have found from the report of many that a custom has of old obtained among you, for subdeacons to be allowed to have intercourse with their wives. That any one should any more presume to do this was prohibited by the servant of God, the deacon of our see, under the authority of our predecessor[8], in this way; that those who at that time had been coupled to wives should choose one of two things, that is, either to abstain from their wives, or on no account whatever presume to exercise their ministry. And, according to report, Speciosus, then a subdeacon, did for this reason suspend himself from the office of administration, and up to the time of his death bore indeed the office of a notary, but ceased from the ministry which a subdeacon should have exercised. After his death we have learnt that his widow, Honorata, has been relegated to a monastery by thy Fraternity for having associated herself with a husband. And so if, as is said, her husband

him back to Africa to have his case enquired into, only enjoining Columbus, to whom he writes, to do his utmost to see justice done, he himself believing the accused to be innocent, and attributing the charges against him to odium incurred by his measures against the Donatists. The final issue does not appear. See also XII. 8.

5 Victor was now primate of Numidia, having succeeded Adeodatus (see III. 49). As to the African custom with respect to primates, see I. 74, note 9. For notice of Columbus, see II. 48, note 7.

6 See last Epistle, note 4.

7 Catana was one of the sees in Sicily.

8 This order had been given by pope Pelagius II. A.D. 588. In I. 44 Gregory had seen fit to relax the stringency of this order in the case of existing subdeacons who had not on their ordination pledged themselves to chastity.

suspended himself from ministration, it ought not to be to the prejudice of the aforesaid woman that she has contracted a second marriage, especially if she had not been joined to the subdeacon with the intention of abstaining from the pleasures of the flesh.

If, then, you find the truth to be as we have been informed, it is right for you to release altogether the aforesaid woman from the monastery, that she may be at liberty to return without any fear to her husband.

But for the future let thy Fraternity be exceedingly careful, in the case of any who may be promoted to this office, to look to this with the utmost diligence, that, if they have wives, they shall enjoy no licence to have intercourse with them: but you must still strictly order them to observe all things after the pattern of the Apostolic See.

EPISTLE XXXVIII.

To Queen Theodelinda.

Gregory to Theodelina, Queen of the Lombards[9].

It has come to our knowledge from the report of certain persons that your Glory has been led on by some bishops even to the offence against holy Church of suspending yourself from the communion of Catholic unanimity. Now the more we sincerely love you, the more seriously are we distressed about you, that you believe unskilled and foolish men, who not only do not know what they talk about, but can hardly understand what they have heard; who, while they neither read themselves, nor believe those who do, remain in the same error which they have themselves feigned to themselves concerning us. For we venerate the four holy synods; the Nicene, in which Arius, the Constantinopolitan, in which Macedonius, the first Ephesine, in which Nestorius, and the Chalcedonians, in which Eutyches and Dioscorus, were condemned; declaring that whosoever thinks otherwise than these four synods did is alien from the true faith. We also condemn whomsoever they condemn, and absolve whomsoever they absolve, smiting, with interposition of anathema, any one who presumes to add to or take away from the faith of the same four synods, and especially that of Chalcedon, with respect to which doubt and occasion of superstition has arisen in the minds of certain unskilled men.

Seeing, then, that you know the integrity of our faith from my plain utterance and profession, it is right that you should have no further scruple of doubt with respect to the Church of the blessed Peter, Prince of the apostles: but persist ye in the true faith, and make your life firm on the rock of the Church; that is on the confession of the blessed Peter, Prince of the apostles, lest all those tears of yours and all those good works should come to nothing, if they are found alien from the true faith. For as branches dry up without the virtue of the root, so works, to whatsoever degree they may seem good, are nothing, if they are disjoined from the solidity of the faith.

It therefore becomes your Glory to send a communication with all speed to our most reverend brother and fellow-bishop Constantius, of whose faith and life I have long been well assured, and to signify by your letters addressed to him how kindly you accept his ordination, and that you are in no wise separated from the communion of his Church, so that we may truly rejoice with a common exultation, as for a good and faithful daughter. Know also that you and your works will please God, if, before his assize comes, they be approved by the judgment of his priests.

[9] This letter was substituted for Ep. IV., which had been previously written, but not delivered. See note 4 under Epistle II. above.

EPISTLE XXXIX.

To Constantius, Bishop.

Gregory to Constantius, Bishop of Mediolanum (*Milan*).

Having read the letter of your Holiness, we find that you are in a state of serious distress, principally on account of the bishops and citizens of Briscia (*Brescia*), who bid you send them a letter in which you are asked to swear that you have not condemned the Three Chapters[1]. Now, if your Fraternity's predecessor Laurentius did not do this, it ought not to be required of you. But, if he did it, he was not with the universal Church, and contradicted what he had sworn to in his security[2]. But, inasmuch as we believe him to have kept his oath, and to have continued in the unity of the Catholic Church, there is no doubt that he did not swear to any of his bishops that he had not condemned the Three Chapters. Hence your Holiness may conclude that you ought not to be forced to do what was in no

[1] See above, Epistle II., note 1.

[2] *Cautionis suæ*, as to the meaning of which expression, see above, Epistle II., note 2. It appears certain from what Gregory says, here and in Epistle II., that Laurentius, the predecessor of Constantius, had pledged himself by oath to the Bishop of Rome to uphold the condemnation of "The Three Chapters." But it seems that some of his suffragans now asserted that he had sworn to them that he had not assented to such condemnation, and that on this understanding they had remained in his communion. Gregory does not seem certain how the matter stood: but he goes on the supposition that he could not have perjured himself as the bishops alleged.

wise done by your predecessor. But, lest those who have thus written to you should be offended, send them a letter declaring under interposition of anathema that you neither take away anything from the faith of the synod of Chalcedon nor received those who do, and that you condemn whomsoever it condemned, and absolve whomsoever it absolved. And thus I believe that they may be very soon satisfied[3]

Further, as to what you write about many of them being offended because you name our brother and fellow-bishop John of the Church of Ravenna during the solemnities of mass, you should enquire into the ancient custom; and, if it has been the custom, it ought not now to be found fault with by foolish men. But, if it has not been the custom, a thing ought not to be done at which some may possibly take offence. Yet I have been at pains to make careful enquiry whether the same John our brother and fellow-bishop names you at the altar; and they say that this is not done. And, if he does not make mention of your name, I know not what necessity obliges you to make mention of his. If indeed it can be done without any one taking offence, your doing anything of this kind is very laudable, since you shew the charity you have towards your brethren.

Further, as to what you write of your having been unwilling to transmit my letter to Queen Theodelinda on the ground that the fifth synod was named in it, if you believed that she might thereby be offended, you did right in not transmitting it. We are therefore doing now as you recommend, namely, that we should only express approval of the four synods. Yet, as to the synod which was afterwards held in Constantinople, called by many the fifth, I would have you know that it neither ordained nor held anything in opposition to the four most holy synods, seeing that nothing was done in it with respect to the faith, but only with respect to persons; and persons, too, about whom nothing is contained in the acts of the Council of Chalcedon[4]; but, after the canons had been promulged, discussion arose, and final action was ventilated concerning persons. Yet still we have done as you desired, making no mention of this synod. But we have also written to our daughter the queen what you wrote to us about the bishops. Ursicinus, who wrote something to you against our brother and fellow-bishop John, you ought by your letters addressed to him, with sweetness and reason, to restrain from his intention. Further, concerning Fortunatus[5], we desire your Fraternity to be careful, lest you be in any way surreptitiously influenced by bad men. For I hear that he ate at the table of the Church with your predecessor Laurentius for many years until now, that he sat among the nobles, and subscribed, and that with our brother's knowledge he served in the army. And now, after so many years, your Fraternity thinks that he should be driven from the position which he now occupies. This seems to me altogether incongruous. And so I have given you this order through him, but privately. Still, if there is anything reasonable that can be alleged against him, it ought to be submitted to our judgment. But, if it please Almighty God, we will send letters through your man to our son the lord Dynamius.

EPISTLE XLVI.

To Rusticiana, Patrician.

Gregory to Rusticiana, &c.

On receiving your Excellency's letters I was glad to hear that you had reached Mount Sinai. But believe me, I too should have liked to go with you, but by no means to return with you. And yet I find it very difficult to believe that you have been at the holy places and seen many Fathers. For I believe that, if you had seen them, you would by no means have been able to return so speedily to the city of Constantinople. But now that the love of such a city has in no wise departed from your heart, I suspect that your Excellency did not from the heart devote yourself to the holy things which you saw with the bodily eye. But may Almighty God illuminate your mind by the grace of His loving-kindness and give unto you to be wise, and to consider how fugitive are all temporal things, since, while we are thus speaking, both time runs on and the Judge approaches, and lo the moment is even now near when against our will we must give up the world which of our own accord we will not. I beg that the

3 See above, Ep. II., note 4.

4 Here Gregory is in error, for in the eighth, ninth, and tenth sessions of the council of Chalcedon Theodoret and Ibas, whose writings were anathematized in that fifth council, were heard in their own defence, and definitely acquitted of heresy. It is true that there is no mention of them in the Definition of faith, agreed upon in the fifth session of Chalcedon, or in the Canons, which were perhaps all that Gregory had before him. It is true also that there was no reference at Chalcedon to Theodore of Mopsuestia, who was especially and personally anathematized at the fifth council, he having died many years before the council of Chalcedon was held. But the cases of Theodoret and Ibas had been prominently before the synod; and this not, as Gregory here goes on to intimate, in a supplementary sort of way at the end of the main proceedings: for the eighth, ninth, and tenth sessions had been occupied with them, after which there had been other sessions. For similar inaccuracy on Gregory's part in referring to past events, see II. 51, note 2; and for an instance of his imperfect acquaintance with the history of past controversies, see VII. 4.

5 Concerning this Fortunatus, see also V. 4.

lord Apio and the lady Eusebia, and their daughters, be greeted in my behalf. As to that lady my nurse, whom you commend to me by letter, I have the greatest regard for her, and desire that she should be in no way incommoded. But we are pressed by such great straits that we cannot excuse even ourselves from exactions (*angariis*)[6] and burdens at this present time.

EPISTLE XLVII.

To Sabinianus, Deacon[7].

Gregory to Sabinianus, &c.

Thou knowest what has been done in the case of the prevaricator Maximus[8]. For after the most serene lord the Emperor had sent orders that he should not be ordained[9], then he broke out into a higher pitch of pride. For the men of the glorious patrician Romanus[1] received bribes from him, and caused him to be ordained in such a manner that they would have killed Antoninus, the subdeacon and rector of the patrimony, if he had not fled. But I despatched letters to him, after I had learnt that he had been ordained against reason and custom, telling him not to presume to celebrate the solemnities of mass unless I should first ascertain from our most serene lords what they had ordered with regard to him. And these my letters, having been publicly promulged or posted in the city, he caused to be publicly torn, and thus bounced forth more openly into contempt of the Apostolic See. How I was likely to endure this thou knowest, seeing that I was before prepared rather to die than that the Church of the blessed apostle Peter should degenerate in my days. Moreover thou art well acquainted with my ways, that I bear long; but if once I have determined not to bear, I go gladly in the face of all dangers. Whence it is necessary with the help of God to meet danger, lest he be driven to sin to excess. Look to what I say, and consider what great grief inspires it.

But it has come to my ears that he has sent [to Constantinople] a cleric, I know not whom, to say that the bishop Malchus[2] was put to death in prison for money. Now as to this there is one thing that thou mayest shortly suggest to our most serene lords;—that, if I their servant had been willing to have anything to do with the death of Lombards, the nation of the Lombards at this day would have had neither king nor dukes nor counts, and would have been divided in the utmost confusion. But, since I fear God, I shrink from having anything to do with the death of any one. Now the bishop Malchus was neither in prison nor in any distress; but on the day when he pleaded his cause and was sentenced he was taken without my knowledge by Boniface the notary to his house, where a dinner was prepared for him, and there he dined, and was treated with honour by the said Boniface, and in the night suddenly died, as I think you have already been informed. Moreover I had intended to send our Exhilaratus to you in connection with that business; but, as I considered that the case was now done with, I consequently abstained from doing so.

6 The word *angaria*, which is of frequent occurrence, denotes exactions and forced services of various kinds.

7 He was the pope's *apocrisiarius* at Constantinople.

8 See III. 47, note 2.

9 In his letter to Maximus (IV. 20), Gregory had only expressed a suspicion that the alleged order of the Emperor for his consecration had been fictitious. He now seems to have satisfied himself that it was so. For a review of the whole case, see III. 47, note 2.

1 Romanus Patricius was the Exarch of Italy. See I. 33; II. 46; III. 31; V. 24.

2 See II. 20, note 5.

BOOK V

EPISTLE II.

To **Felix**, Bishop, and Cyriacus, Abbot[1].

Gregory to Felix, &c.

The tenor of the report submitted to you sufficiently explains the complaint of the religious lady Theodosia, in which we have found on reading it many heads of accusation, not befitting priestly gentleness, against our brother and fellow-bishop Januarius; so much so that, after the foundation by her of a monastery for servants of God, all that pertains to avarice, turbulence, and wrong is said to have been exhibited at the time of the very dedication of the oratory. Wherefore, if the case is as we find in her aforesaid representation, and if you are aware that anything at all unbecoming has been committed besides, we exhort you that, all wrongs having first been redressed, you press upon Musicus, the abbot of the monastery of Agilitanus[2], that he lose no time in giving the greatest attention to his monks whom he had begun to settle there, to the end that, this venerable place being with the Lord's help set in order by you in a decent and regular manner, neither may we be disturbed by the frequent complaints of the aforesaid religious lady that her good desires are not fulfilled, nor may it be to the detriment of your soul that so pious a design should languish, as we do not believe it will, through any neglect of yours.

EPISTLE IV.

To Constantius, Bishop.

Gregory to Constantius, Bishop of Mediolanum (*Milan*).

If licence to be restored to their rank be granted to the lapsed, the force of ecclesiastical discipline is undoubtedly broken, while in the hope of restoration each person fears not to give way to his evil inclinations. Your Fraternity, for instance, has consulted us as to whether Amandinus, ex-presbyter and ex-abbot, who was deposed by your predecessor for fault requiring it, should be called back to his rank; which thing is not allowable; and we decree that it cannot on any account be done. Yet, if it should be the case that his manner of life deserves it, seeing that he has been deprived altogether of his sacred office, assign him a place in a monastery, as you may see fit, before other monks. Above all things, then, take care that no one's supplication persuade you in any way to restore the lapsed to their sacred orders, lest such punishment should be supposed not to be definitely ordained for them, but only a temporary expedient.

As to Vitalianus the ex-presbyter, about whom you write that he should be strictly guarded, we will cause him to be sent into Sicily, that, being deprived of all hope of departure thence, he may then at least constrain himself to penitential bewailing. Jobinus also, of Portus Veneris, once deacon and abbot, we have decreed to be deprived of his office, and written that another should be ordained in his place In like manner also we decree that the three subdeacons, whom your Fraternity has notified to us as having lapsed, shall ever cease from and stand deprived of their office, and that nothing beyond lay communion be allowed them. Further, we have adjudged the ex-presbyter Saturninus to give security that he will not ever presume to approach the ministry of his sacred order. And we desire him to remain, with deprivation of his sacred order, in the same island in which he was, permitting him to have and exercise care and solicitude with respect to monasteries; for we believe that, his lapse having made him more wary, he will now the more carefully keep guard over those who are committed to him.

Further, concerning John, notary of your church, the charity wherewith we love you and have long loved you warns us to write, lest you should order anything with regard

---

[1] They had been sent by Gregory into Sardinia with the special purpose of promoting the conversion of the natives, which had been neglected by the bishops and clergy of the island. See V. 41, and IV. 23, note 8.

[2] Apparently the designation of the monastery which had been now at length founded by Theodosia in execution of her late husband's will. See above, IV. 8, 15. In IV. 15, Gregory had acceded to her desire, in view of certain difficulties in carrying out her husband's intention, to found a nunnery in a house of her own at Cagliari. But it seems that a monastery of monks had in the end been founded.

to him while you are still provoked by his fault. Guarding, then, against this, enquire fully by all means in your power into the possessions of your church; by which means neither may you offend God, nor may he be able to find a ground for accusing you before men. For we write, not as defending John or commending him personally without reason, but lest your soul should be in any way burdened with sin under the incitement of anger. Whence it is needful, as we have before said, that you should by no means neglect to enquire, in the fear of God, with a full investigation into the possessions of your church.

Furthermore, the epistle of your most dear Fraternity has caused us to wonder much with respect to the person of Fortunatus[3]. But either that letter was not dictated by you, or certainly, if it is yours, we by no means recognize in it our brother the lord Constantius. For you ought to have paid, and still ought to pay, attention to the fact that it is in behalf of your reputation that we write. For, when he asserts that he suffers wrong among you, and has been unable to procure the guardian's (*defensoris*) aid, what else does he intimate but ill-will on your part? Wherefore, that neither this affair may dim your reputation in some quarters nor damage possibly ensue in any way with good cause to your church, you ought to send hither a person instructed by you, that the nature of the case may be examined, and the matter terminated, without ill-will on your part. And for this reason especially, that if, after his complaint, sentence should be pronounced among yourselves in your favour, he will be believed to have been defeated, not reasonably, but by power alone. But we, out of the charity wherewith we are bound to you, desist not from admonishing you to do what will be for your good repute, knowing that, though this exhortation saddens you for the time, it will afterwards cause you joy, when the animosity of contention has passed away. In the month of September, Indiction 13. (In Vatic. *The month of December, Indict.* 13.)

EPISTLE V.

To Dominicus, Bishop.

Gregory to Dominicus, Bishop of Carthage.

Prosper your delegate (*responsalis*), the bearer of these presents, has been with us, and after other expressions of your charity handed us your second letters with an allegation of the imperial commands, and a paper giving an account of the synod that has been held among you[4]. Having read all, we rejoiced for your pastoral zeal, and that our most pious lords had given no ear to the calumnies of venal persons brought against you on the plea of religion; but especially that your Fraternity has so taken pains to preserve the African province as in no wise to neglect to restrain with priestly fervour the devious sects of heretics; concerning the quieting of whom we remember having laid down the law so fully, even before consulting the letters of your Charity, that we do not believe that anything needs to be said again in reply to you about them. Although, however, this is so, and though we desire all heretics to be repressed always with vigour and reason by catholic priests, yet, on looking thoroughly into what has been done among you, we are in fact apprehensive lest offence should thereby be caused (which thing may the Lord avert) to the primates of other councils. For at the conclusion of your acts you have promulged a sentence, in which, while ordering the searching out of those heretics, you have brought in that those who neglect the duty are to be punished by forfeiture of their possessions and dignities. It is therefore best, most dear brother, that, in dealing with matters outside ourselves that require correction, charity among ourselves should first be preserved, and that we should be subject in mind (as I judge to be peculiarly proper to your Gravity) even to persons below us in dignity. For you will then more advantageously meet the errors of heretics with your whole united powers when, as befits your priesthood, you study to keep ecclesiastical concord among yourselves.

EPISTLE VIII.

To Cyprian, Deacon.

Gregory to Cyprian, deacon and rector of the patrimony of Sicily.

Concerning the Manicheans who are on our possessions I have frequently admonished thy Love to press them with the utmost diligence, and recall them to the Catholic faith. If, then, the time requires it, make enquiries in person, or, if other business does not allow this, through others. Further, it has come to my ears that there are Hebrews on our possessions

3 See IV. 39.

4 This had been a synod held at Carthage for the suppression of the Donatists. Cf. I. 74, note 8. Gregory, while fully approving, as he shews elsewhere, of strict enforcement of the imperial laws against them, expresses fear in this epistle lest the council lately held might have gone too far, so as to endanger the unity of the African Church, in exceeding the decrees of synods that had been held elsewhere, and especially in ordering severe measures against bishops or others who might be remiss in the work of suppressing heresy.

who will not by any means be converted to God. But it seems to me that thou shouldest send letters through all our possessions on which these Hebrews are known to be, promising them particularly from me that whosoever of them shall have been converted to our true Lord God Jesus Christ shall have the burdens of his holding lightened. And this I wish to have done in such sort that, if one has a payment to make of one *solidus*, a third should be remitted him; if of three or four, that one *solidus* should be remitted; if of any more, the remission should still be made in the same proportion, or at any rate according as thy Love sees fit, so that one who is converted may have some relief of his burden, and the Church may not be put to heavy expense. Nor shall we do this unprofitably, if by lightening the burdens of their payments we bring them to the grace of Christ, since, though they themselves came with little faith, yet those who may be born of them will now be baptized with more faith: thus we gain either them or their children. And whatever amount of payment we let them off for the sake of Christ is nothing serious. Furthermore, some time ago, when John the deacon came, thy Love wrote something to me, the whole of which I read at the time, but let many days intervene before replying; and then, after such delay, replied to all particulars as I recollected them. But now I think that one point escaped my memory, and suspect that I gave no reply about it. For thou hadst written that loans were being advanced to peasants (*rusticis*) through certain undertakers for their debt [5], lest in borrowing from others they should be burdened either by exactions or by the prices of things [6]. This particular was to me most acceptable; and, if indeed I have already written about it, observe what I wrote. But if, as I suspect, I gave in my reply no definite direction on the subject, thou must not hesitate to advance money for the advantage of the peasants, since the ecclesiastical property will not thus be wasted, and out of it the peasants will derive advantage. And, if there are other things which thou considerest to be advantageous, thou must carry them out without any hesitation.

[5] *Per manus quorundam debiti conductorum.* If the word *debiti* (absent from some MSS.) is read here, the meaning may be that certain persons, called *debiti conductores*, undertook the recovery of the arrears of the *rustici*, and that through them easy loans were advanced to such as were unable to pay at the proper time. Cf. I. 44, p. 89. For the ordinary meaning of *conductores* (without *debiti*), in connexion with the Church estates, see I. 44, p, 89, note 5.

[6] *Aut in angariis aut in rerum pretio.* The word *angaria* is applicable to any kind of vexatious exaction, either in the way of forced labour or in other ways. "Per angarias intelliguntur vexationes et injuriæ quælibet." Du Cange. It may be used here for exorbitant interest on loans obtained from usurers. As to *rerum pretio*, cf. I. 44, p. 89, about *burdatio*, and note 2.

EPISTLE XI.

To John, Bishop.

Gregory to John, Bishop of Ravenna.

I find that your Fraternity is greatly distressed on account of being forbidden by the censure of reason to wear the pallium in litanies. But through the most excellent Patrician, and through the most eminent Prefect, and through other noble men of your city, you have urgently requested to have this allowed you. Now we, having made careful enquiry of Adeodatus, some time thy Fraternity's deacon, have ascertained that it was never the custom of thy predecessors to use the pallium during litanies, except at the solemnities of the blessed John the Baptist, the blessed Apostle Peter, and the blessed martyr Apollinaris. But we were by no means bound to believe him, since many of our delegates have often been at your Fraternity's city, who declare that they never saw anything of the kind. And in this matter credence is rather to be given to many than to one, who is attesting something in behalf of his own Church. But, since we do not wish your Fraternity to be distressed, or the petition of our sons to be of no avail with us, we concede the use of the pallium, until we shall gain some more accurate knowledge, on the days of the Nativity of the Blessed John the Baptist, of the blessed Apostle Peter, and the blessed martyr Apollinaris, and on the day of the celebration of your ordination. But in the sacristy, according to former custom, after the sons of the Church have been received and dismissed, your Fraternity may put on the pallium, and so proceed to the solemnization of mass, arrogating to yourself nothing more in the daring of rash presumption; lest, while something is snatched at out of order in exterior habiliment, what might have been done in due order be neglected. Given in the month of October; Indiction 13.

EPISTLE XV.

To John, Bishop.

Gregory to John, Bishop of Ravenna.

In the first place this makes me sad; that thy Fraternity writes to me with a double heart, exhibiting one sort of blandishment in letters, but another sort with the tongue in secular intercourse. In the next place, it grieves me that my brother John even to this day retains on his tongue those gibes which notaries while still boys are wont to indulge in. He speaks bitingly, and seems to delight in such pleasantry. He flatters his friends in their presence, and maligns them in their absence. Thirdly, it is to me grievous and altogether execrable, that he imputes shameful crimes to his servants[7], whatever the hour may be, calling them "effeminate;" and, what is still more grievous, this is done openly. Then there is this in addition, that there is no discipline for keeping guard over the life of the clergy, but that he exhibits himself only as their lord. The last thing, but first in importance as evidence of elation, is about his use of the pallium outside the church, which is a thing he never presumed to do in the times of my predecessors, and what none of his predecessors ever presumed to do, as our delegates testify (except it might be when relics were deposited, though with regard to relics one person only could be found to say that it was so); yet this in my days, in contempt of me, with extreme audacity, he not only did, but even made a habit of doing.

From all these things I find that the dignity of the Episcopacy is with him all in outside show, not in his mind. And indeed I return thanks to Almighty God that at the time when this came to my knowledge, which had never reached the ears of my predecessors, the Lombards were posted between me and the city of Ravenna. For perchance I had it in my mind to shew to men how severe I can be[8].

Lest, however, thou shouldest suppose that I wish thy church to be depressed or lessened in dignity, remember where the deacon of Ravenna used to stand in solemnization of mass at Rome, and enquire where he stands now; and thou wilt recognize the fact that I desire to honour the church of Ravenna. But that any one whatever should snatch at anything out of pride, this I cannot tolerate.

Nevertheless I have already written on this matter to our deacon at Constantinople, that he should enquire of all who have under them even thirty or forty bishops. And if there is anywhere this custom of their walking in litanies wearing the pallium, God forbid that through me the dignity of the church of Ravenna should seem to be in any way lessened.

Reflect, therefore, dearest brother, on all that I have said above: think of the day of thy call: consider what account thou wilt render of the burden of epi copacy. Amend those manners of a notary. See what becomes a bishop in tongue and in deed. Be entirely sincere to thy brethren. Do not speak one thing, and have another in thy heart. Do not desire to seem more than thou art, that so thou mayest be able to be more than thou seemest. Believe me, when I came to my present position, I had such consideration and charity towards thee that, if thou hadst wished to keep hold of this my charity, thou still wouldest not have ever found such a brother as myself, or one so sincerely loving thee, or so concurring with thee in all devotion: but when I came to know of thy words and thy manners, I confess I started back. I beseech thee, then, by Almighty God, amend all that I have spoken of, and especially the vice of duplicity. Allow me to love thee; and for the present and the future life it may be of advantage to thee to be loved of thy brethren. Reply, however, to all this, not by words, but by behaviour.

EPISTLE XVII.

To Cyprian, Deacon[1].

Gregory to Cyprian, &c.

I received your letters of most bitter import about the death of the lord Maximianus[2] in the month of November. And he indeed has reached the rewards he longed for, but the unhappy people of the city of Syracuse is to be commiserated as not having been counted worthy to have such a pastor long. Accordingly let thy Love take anxious heed that such a one may be chosen for ordination in the same church as may not seem to obtain undeservedly the same place of rule after the lord Maximianus. And indeed I believe that the majority would choose the presbyter Trajan, who, as is said, is of a good disposition, but, as I suspect, not fit for ruling in that place. Yet, if a better cannot be found, and if there are no charges against him, he may be condescended to under stress of very great necessity. But, if my wishes are asked with regard to this election, I inform thee privately of what I do wish: for no one in this same church appears to me so worthy after the lord Maximianus as John the archdeacon of the church of Catana. And, if his election can be brought about, I believe that he will be found an exceedingly fit person. But he too must first be enquired about by thee privately as to any charges against him that may stand in the way. If he should be found free from any, he may be rightly chosen. Should this be done, our brother and fellow-bishop Leo[3] will also have to give him leave to go, that he may be found

7 "Servis tuis turpia crimina imponis,"—apparently meaning that at all hours he was accustomed to call them by opprobrious names.

8 The meaning may be, "I am thankful now that the fact of communication between Rome and Ravenna being blocked by the Lombards when the matter first reached my ears prevented my acting so peremptorily as I might then have been disposed to do."

1 The deacon Cyprian had succeeded the sub-deacon Peter as *rector patrimonii* in Sicily, and Gregory's general agent there, through whom he acted in ecclesiastical as well as temporal matters, at any rate now, after the death of Maximianus of Syracuse.

2 See II. 7, note 5.

3 Bishop of Catana where this John was archdeacon.

free to be ordained. These things, then, I have taken care to intimate to thy Love; and it will now be thy concern to look round thee on all sides carefully, and arrange what is pleasing to God.

EPISTLE XVIII.

To John, Bishop.

Gregory to John, Bishop of Constantinople[4].

At the time when your Fraternity was advanced to Sacerdotal dignity, you remember what peace and concord of the churches you found. But, with what daring or with what swelling of pride I know not, you have attempted to seize upon a new name, whereby the hearts of all your brethren might have come to take offence. I wonder exceedingly at this, since I remember how thou wouldest fain have fled from the episcopal office rather than attain it. And yet, now that thou hast got it, thou desirest so to exercise it as if thou hadst run to it with ambitious intent. For, having confessed thyself unworthy to be called a bishop, thou hast at length been brought to such a pass as, despising thy brethren, to covet to be named the only bishop. And indeed with regard to this matter, weighty letters were addressed to your Holiness by my predecessor Pelagius of holy memory; in which he annulled the acts of the synod, which had been assembled among you in the case of our once brother and fellow-bishop Gregory, because of that execrable title of pride, and forbade the archdeacon, whom he had sent according to custom to the threshold of our lord, to celebrate the solemnities of mass with you. But after his death, when I, unworthy, succeeded to the government of the Church, both through my other representatives and also through our common son the deacon Sabinianus, I have taken care to address your Fraternity, not indeed in writing, but by word of mouth, desiring you to restrain yourself from such presumption. And, in case of your refusing to amend, I forbade his celebrating the solemnities of mass with you; that so I might first appeal to your Holiness through a certain sense of shame, to the end that, if the execrable and profane assumption could not be corrected through shame, strict canonical measures might be then resorted to. And, since sores that are to be cut away should first be stroked with a gentle hand, I beg you, I beseech you, and with all the sweetness in my power demand of you, that your Fraternity gainsay all who flatter you and offer you this name of error, nor foolishly consent to be called by the proud title. For truly I say it weeping, and out of inmost sorrow of heart attribute it to my sins, that this my brother, who has been constituted in the grade of episcopacy for the very end of bringing back the souls of others to humility, has up to the present time been incapable of being brought back to humility; that he who teaches truth to others has not consented to teach himself, even when I implore him.

Consider, I pray thee, that in this rash presumption the peace of the whole Church is disturbed, and that it is in contradiction to the grace that is poured out on all in common; in which grace doubtless thou thyself wilt have power to grow so far as thou determinest with thyself to do so. And thou wilt become by so much the greater as thou restrainest thyself from the usurpation of a proud and foolish title: and thou wilt make advance in proportion as thou art not bent on arrogation by derogation of thy brethren. Wherefore, dearest brother, with all thy heart love humility, through which the concord of all the brethren and the unity of the holy universal Church may be preserved. Certainly the apostle Paul, when he heard some say, *I am of Paul, I of Apollos, but I of Christ* (1 Cor. i. 13), regarded with the utmost horror such dilaceration of the Lord's body, whereby they were joining themselves, as it were, to other heads, and exclaimed, saying, *Was Paul crucified for you? or were ye baptized in the name of Paul* (ib.)? If then he shunned the subjecting of the members of Christ partially to certain heads, as if beside Christ, though this were to the apostles themselves, what wilt thou say to Christ, who is the Head of the universal Church, in the scrutiny of the last judgment, having attempted to put all his members under thyself by the appellation of Universal? Who, I ask, is proposed for imitation in this wrongful title but he who, despising the legions of angels constituted socially with himself, attempted to start up to an eminence of singularity, that he might seem to be under none and to be alone above all? Who even said, *I will ascend into heaven, I will exalt my throne above the stars of heaven: I will sit upon the mount of the testament, in the sides of the North: I will ascend above the heights of the clouds; I will be like the most High* (Isai. xiv. 13).

For what are all thy brethren, the bishops of the universal Church, but stars of heaven, whose life and discourse shine together amid the sins and errors of men, as if amid the shades of night? And when thou desirest to put thyself above them by this proud title, and to tread down their name in comparison with thine, what else dost thou say but *I will*

[4] On the occasion of this letter and subsequent correspondence on the same subject, see Prolegomena, pp. xiv., xxii.

ascend into heaven; I will exalt my throne above the stars of heaven? Are not all the bishops together clouds, who both rain in the words of preaching, and glitter in the light of good works? And when your Fraternity despises them, and you would fain press them down under yourself, what else say you but what is said by the ancient foe, *I will ascend above the heights of the clouds?* All these things when I behold with tears, and tremble at the hidden judgments of God, my fears are increased, and my heart cannot contain its groans, for that this most holy man the lord John, of so great abstinence and humility, has, through the seduction of familiar tongues, broken out into such a pitch of pride as to attempt, in his coveting of that wrongful name, to be like him who, while proudly wishing to be like God, lost even the grace of the likeness granted him, and because he sought false glory, thereby forfeited true blessedness. Certainly Peter, the first of the apostles, himself a member of the holy and universal Church, Paul, Andrew, John,—what were they but heads of particular communities? And yet all were members under one Head. And (to bind all together in a short girth of speech) the saints before the law, the saints under the law, the saints under grace, all these making up the Lord's Body, were constituted as members of the Church, and not one of them has wished himself to be called universal. Now let your Holiness acknowledge to what extent you swell within yourself in desiring to be called by that name by which no one presumed to be called who was truly holy.

Was it not the case, as your Fraternity knows, that the prelates of this Apostolic See, which by the providence of God I serve, had the honour offered them of being called universal by the venerable Council of Chalcedon[5]. But yet not one of them has ever wished to be called by such a title, or seized upon this ill-advised name, lest if, in virtue of the rank of the pontificate, he took to himself the glory of singularity, he might seem to have denied it to all his brethren.

But I know that all arises from those who serve your Holiness on terms of deceitful familiarity; against whom I beseech your Fraternity to be prudently on your guard, and not to lay yourself open to be deceived by their words. For they are to be accounted the greater enemies the more they flatter you with praises. Forsake such; and, if they must needs deceive, let them at any rate deceive the hearts of worldly men, and not of priests. *Let the dead bury their dead* (Luke ix. 60). But say ye with the prophet, *Let them be turned back and put to shame that say unto me, Aha, Aha* (Ps. lxix. 4). And again, *But let not the oil of the sinner lard my head* (Ps. cxl. 5).

Whence also the wise man admonishes well, *Be in peace with many: but have but one counsellor of a thousand* (Ecclus. vi. 6). For *Evil communications corrupt good manners* (1 Cor. xv. 33). For the ancient foe, when unable to break into strong hearts, looks out for weak persons who are associated with them, and, as it were, scales lofty walls by ladders set against them. So he deceived Adam through the woman who was associated with him. So, when he slew the sons of the blessed Job, he left the weak woman, that, being unable of himself to penetrate his heart, he might at any rate be able to do so through the woman's words. Whatever weak and secular persons, then, are near you, let them be shattered in their own persuasive words and flattery, since they procure to themselves the eternal enmity of God from their very frowardness in being seeming lovers.

Of a truth it was proclaimed of old through the Apostle John, *Little children, it is the last hour* (1 John ii. 18), according as the Truth foretold. And now pestilence and sword rage through the world, nations rise against nations, the globe of the earth is shaken, the gaping earth with its inhabitants is dissolved. For all that was foretold is come to pass. The king of pride is near, and (awful to be said!) there is an army of priests in course of preparation for him, inasmuch as they who had been appointed to be leaders in humility enlist themselves under the neck of pride. But in this matter, even though our tongue protested not at all, the power of Him who in His own person peculiarly opposes the vice of pride is lifted up for vengeance against elation. For hence it is written, *God resisteth the proud, but giveth grace unto the humble* (Jam. iv. 6). Hence, again, it is said, *Whoso exalteth his heart is unclean before God* (Prov. xvi. 5). Hence, against the man that is proud it is written, *Why is earth and ashes proud* (Ecclus. x. 9)? Hence the Truth in person says, *Whosoever*

5 As to this assertion (repeated in V. 20, 43, and in VIII. 30), Giesler says, "Gregory was mistaken in believing that at the Council of Chalcedon the name *Universalis Episcopus* was given to the bishop of Rome. He is styled οἰκουμενικὸς ἀρχιεπίσκοπος (Mansi VI. 1006, 1012), as other patriarchs also. But in another place the title was surreptitiously introduced into the Latin acts by the Romish legates. In the sentence passed on Dioscurus, actio iii (Mansi VI. 1048), the Council say, ὁ ἁγιώτατος καὶ μακαριώτατος ἀρχιεπίσκοπος τῆς μεγάλης καὶ πρεσβυτέρας Ῥώμης Λέων: on the contrary, in the Latin acts which Leo sent to the Gallic bishops (Leonis, Ep. 103, al. 82), we read; 'Sanctus ac beatissimus Papa, caput universalis Ecclesiæ, Leo.' In the older editions the beginning of Leo's Epist. 97 (ap. Quesn. 134, Baller. 165), runs thus: 'Leo Romæ et universalis catholicæque Ecclesiæ Episcopus Leoni semper Augusto salutem.' Quesnel and the Ballerini, however, found in all the Codices only, 'Leo Episcopus Leoni Augusto.'" (Giesler's Eccl. Hist., 2nd Period, 1st Division, ch. iii. § 94, note 72).

exalteth himself shall be abased (Luke xiv. 11). And, that he might bring us back to the way of life through humility, He deigned to exhibit in Himself what He teaches us, saying, *Learn of me; for I am meek and lowly in heart* (Matth. xi. 29). For to this end the only begotten Son of God took upon Himself the form of our weakness; to this end the Invisible appeared not only as visible but even as despised; to this end He endured the mocks of contumely, the reproaches of derision, the torments of suffering; that God in His humility might teach man not to be proud. How great, then, is the virtue of humility for the sake of teaching which alone He who is great beyond compare became little even unto the suffering of death! For, since the pride of the devil was the origin of our perdition, the humility of God has been found the means of our redemption. That is to say, our enemy, having been created among all things, desired to appear exalted above all things; but our Redeemer remaining great above all things, deigned to become little among all things.

What, then, can we bishops say for ourselves, who have received a place of honour from the humility of our Redeemer, and yet imitate the pride of the enemy himself? Lo, we know our Creator to have descended from the summit of His loftiness that He might give glory to the human race, and we, created of the lowest, glory in the lessening of our brethren. God humbled Himself even to our dust; and human dust sets his face as high as heaven, and with his tongue passes above the earth, and blushes not, neither is afraid to be lifted up: even man who is rottenness, and the son of man that is a worm.

Let us recall to mind, most dear brother, this which is said by the most wise Solomon, *Before thunder shall go lightning, and before ruin shall the heart be exalted* (Ecclus. xxxii. 10); where, on the other hand it is subjoined, *Before glory it shall be humbled.* Let us then be humbled in mind, if we are striving to attain to real loftiness. By no means let the eyes of our heart be darkened by the smoke of elation, which the more it rises the more rapidly vanishes away. Let us consider how we are admonished by the precepts of our Redeemer, who says, *Blessed are the poor in spirit; for theirs is the kingdom of heaven* (Matth. v. 3). Hence, also, he says by the prophet, *On whom shall my Spirit rest, but on him that is humble, and quiet, and that trembleth at my words* (Isai. lxvi. 2)? Of a truth, when the Lord would bring back the hearts of His disciples, still beset with infirmity, to the way of humility, He said, *Whosoever will be chief among you shall be least of all* (Matth. xx. 27). Whereby it is plainly seen how he is truly exalted on high who in his thoughts is humbled. Let us, therefore, fear to be numbered among those who seek the first seats in the synagogues, and greetings in the market, and to be called of men Rabbi. For, contrariwise, the Lord says to His disciples, *But be not ye called Rabbi: for one is your master; and all ye are brethren. And call no man your Father upon the earth, for one is your Father* (Matth. xxiii. 7, 8).

What then, dearest brother, wilt thou say in that terrible scrutiny of the coming judgment, if thou covetest to be called in the world not only father, but even general father? Let, then, the bad suggestion of evil men be guarded against; let all instigation to offence be fled from. *It must needs be* (*indeed*) *that offences come; nevertheless, woe to that man by whom the offence cometh* (Matth. xviii. 7). Lo, by reason of this execrable title of pride the Church is rent asunder, the hearts of all the brethren are provoked to offence. What! Has it escaped your memory how the Truth says, *Whoso shall offend one of these little ones which believe in me, it were better for him that a mill stone were hanged about his neck, and that he were drowned in the depth of the sea* (Ib. v. 6)? But it is written, *Charity seeketh not her own* (1 Cor. xiii. 4). Lo, your Fraternity arrogates to itself even what is not its own. Again it is written, *In honour preferring one another* (Rom. xii. 10). And thou attemptest to take the honour away from all which thou desirest unlawfully to usurp to thyself singularly. Where, dearest brother, is that which is written, *Have peace with all men, and holiness, without which no man shall see the Lord* (Heb. xii. 14)? Where is that which is written, *Blessed are the peacemakers; for they shall be called the children of God* (Matth. v. 9)?

It becomes you to consider, lest any root of bitterness springing up trouble you, and thereby many be defiled. But still, though we neglect to consider, supernal judgment will be on the watch against the swelling of so great elation. And we indeed, against whom such and so great a fault is committed by this nefarious attempt,—we, I say, are observing what the Truth enjoins when it says, *If thy brother shall sin against thee, go and tell him his fault between thee and him alone. If he shall hear thee, thou hast gained thy brother. But if he will not hear thee, take with thee one or two more, that in the mouth of one or two witnesses every word may be established. But if he will not hear them, tell it unto the Church. But if he will not hear the Church, let him be to thee as an heathen man and a publican* (Matth. xviii. 15). I therefore have once and again through my representatives taken care to reprove in humble words this sin against the whole Church; and now I write myself. Whatever it was my duty to do in the way of humility I have not omitted. But, if I am despised in my reproof, it remains that I must have recourse to the Church.

Wherefore may Almighty God show your Fraternity how great love for you constrains me when I thus speak, and how much I grieve in this case, not against you, but for you. But the case is such that in it I must prefer the precepts of the Gospel, the ordinances of the Canons, and the welfare of the brethren, to the person even of him whom I greatly love.

I have received the most sweet and pleasant letter of your Holiness with respect to the case of the presbyters John and Athanasius [6], about which, the Lord helping me, I will reply to you in another letter; for, being surrounded by the swords of barbarians, I am now oppressed by such great tribulations that it is not allowed me, I will not say to treat of many things, but hardly even to breathe. Given in the Kalends of January; Indiction 13.

EPISTLE XIX.

To Sabinianus, Deacon [7].

Gregory to Sabinianus, &c.

In the cause of our brother the most reverend John, bishop of Constantinople, I have been unwilling to write two letters. But one I have drawn up briefly, which may seem to combine both requisites; that is to say, both honesty and kindness.

Let therefore thy Love take care to give him this letter which I have now addressed to him in compliance with the wish of the Emperor. For in the sequel another will be sent him such as his pride will not rejoice in. For he has come even to this; that, taking occasion of the case of John the presbyter, he transmitted hither the acts, wherein almost in every line he called himself οἰκουμενικὸν (*œcumenical*) patriarch. But I hope in Almighty God that the Supernal Majesty will confound his hypocrisy. But I wonder how he could so deceive thy Love as that thou shouldest allow the Lord Emperor to be persuaded to write to me himself concerning this matter, admonishing me to have peace with him. For, if the Lord Emperor wishes to observe justice, he ought to have admonished him to refrain from the proud title, and then at once there would be peace between us. I suspect, however, that thou hast not all considered with what cunningness this has been done by our aforesaid brother John. For it is for this purpose that he has done it; that the Lord Emperor might be obeyed, and so he himself might seem to be confirmed in his vanity, or that I might not obey him, and so his mind might be irritated against me. But we will keep to the right way, fearing nothing in this cause except the Almighty Lord. Wherefore let thy Love be in nothing afraid. All things that you see to be lofty in this world against the truth in behalf of the truth despise; trust in the grace of Almighty God, and the help of the blessed Apostle Peter. Remember the voice of the Truth, which says, *Greater is he that is in you than he that is in the world* (1 John iv. 4); and in this cause whatever has to be done, do it with the utmost authority. For now that we can in no wise be protected from the swords of our enemies, now that for love of the republic we have lost silver, gold, slaves and clothing, it is too ignominious that through those men we should lose even the faith. For to assent to that atrocious title is nothing else than to lose the faith. Wherefore, as I have written to thee already in former letters, never do thou presume to *proceed* with him [8].

EPISTLE XX.

To Mauricius Augustus.

Gregory to Mauricius, &c.

Our most pious and God-appointed lord, among his other august cares and burdens, watches also in the uprightness of spiritual zeal over the preservation of peace among the priesthood, inasmuch as he piously and truly considers that no one can govern earthly things aright unless he knows how to deal with divine things, and that the peace of the republic hangs on the peace of the universal Church. For, most serene lord, what human power, and what strength of fleshly arm would presume to lift irreligious hands against the lofty height of your most Christian Empire, if the concordant hearts of priests were studious to implore their Redeemer for you with the tongue, and also, as they ought to do, by their deservings? Or what sword of a most savage race would advance with so great cruelty to the slaughter of the faithful, unless the life

6 Cf. III. 53, and *reff.*

7 Sabinianus was at this time the pope's *apocrisiarius*, or *responsalis*, at Constantinople.

8 *Cum eo procedere*, i.e. in effect, to communicate with him. *Procedere* means to approach the altar for celebration. Cf. III 57, "ingredientibus diaconibus ut mox procedatur."

of us, who are called priests but are not, were weighed down by works most wicked. But, while we neglect the things that concern us, and think of those that concern us not, we associate our sins with the barbaric forces, and our fault, which weighs down the forces of the republic, sharpens the swords of the enemy. But what shall we say for ourselves, who press down the people of God which we are unworthily set over with the loads of our sins; who destroy by example what we preach with the tongue; who by our works teach unrighteous things, and with our voice only set forth the things that are righteous? Our bones are worn down by fasts, and in our mind we swell. Our body is covered with vile raiment, and in elation of heart we surpass the purple. We lie in ashes, and look down upon loftiness. Teachers of humility, we are chiefs of pride; behind the faces of sheep we hide the teeth of wolves[9]. But what is the end of these things except that we persuade men, but are manifest to God? Wherefore most providently for restraining warlike movements does the most pious Lord seek the peace of the Church, and, for compacting it, deigns to bring back the hearts of its priests to concord. And this indeed is what I wish; and, as far as I am concerned, I render obedience to his most serene commands. But since it is not my cause, but God's, since the pious laws, since the venerable synods, since the very commands of our Lord Jesus Christ are disturbed by the invention of a certain proud and pompous phrase, let the most pious Lord cut the place of the sore, and bind the resisting patient in the chains of august authority. For in binding up these things tightly you relieve the republic; and, while you cut off such things, you provide for the lengthening of your reign.

For to all who know the Gospel it is apparent that by the Lord's voice the care of the whole Church was committed to the holy Apostle and Prince of all the Apostles, Peter. For to him it is said, *Peter, lovest thou Me? Feed My sheep* (John xxi. 17). To him it is said, *Behold Satan hath desired to sift you as wheat; and I have prayed for thee, Peter, that thy faith fail not. And thou, when thou art converted, strengthen thy brethren* (Luke xxii. 31). To him it is said, *Thou art Peter, and upon this rock I will build My Church, and the gates of hell shall not prevail against it. And I will give unto thee the keys of the kingdom of heaven; and whatsoever thou shalt bind on earth shall be bound also in heaven; and whatsoever thou shalt loose on earth shall be loosed also in heaven* (Matth. xvi. 18).

Lo, he received the keys of the heavenly kingdom, and power to bind and loose is given him, the care and principality of the whole Church is committed to him, and yet he is not called the universal apostle; while the most holy man, my fellow-priest John, attempts to be called universal bishop. I am compelled to cry out and say, *O tempora, O mores!*

Lo, all things in the regions of Europe are given up into the power of barbarians, cities are destroyed, camps overthrown, provinces depopulated, no cultivator inhabits the land, worshippers of idols rage and dominate daily for the slaughter of the faithful, and yet priests, who ought to lie weeping on the ground and in ashes, seek for themselves names of vanity, and glory in new and profane titles.

Do I in this matter, most pious Lord, defend my own cause? Do I resent my own special wrong? Nay, the cause of Almighty God, the cause of the Universal Church.

Who is this that, against the evangelical ordinances, against the decrees of canons, presumes to usurp to himself a new name? Would indeed that one by himself he were, if he could be without any lessening of others,—he that covets to be universal.

And certainly we know that many priests of the Constantinopolitan Church have fallen into the whirlpool of heresy, and have become not only heretics, but even heresiarchs. For thence came Nestorius, who, thinking Jesus Christ, the Mediator of God and men, to be two persons, because he did not believe that God could be made man, broke out even into Jewish perfidy. Thence came Macedonius, who denied that God the Holy Spirit was consubstantial with the Father and the Son. If then any one in that Church takes to himself that name, whereby he makes himself the head of all the good, it follows that the Universal Church falls from its standing (which God forbid), when he who is called Universal falls. But far from Christian hearts be that name of blasphemy, in which the honour of all priests is taken away, while it is madly arrogated to himself by one.

Certainly, in honour of Peter, Prince of the apostles, it was offered by the venerable synod of Chalcedon to the Roman pontiff[1]. But none of them has ever consented to use this name of singularity, lest, by something being given peculiarly to one, priests in general should be deprived of the honour due to them. How is it then that we do not seek the glory of this title even when offered, and another

[9] The ironical allusion here to John the Faster is evident.

[1] Cf. V. 18, and note 5.

presumes to seize it for himself though not offered?

He, then, is rather to be bent by the mandate of our most pious Lords, who scorns to render obedience to canonical injunctions. He is to be coerced, who does wrong to the holy Universal Church, who swells in heart, who covets rejoicing in a name of singularity, who also puts himself above the dignity of your Empire through a title peculiar to himself.

Behold, we all suffer offence for this thing. Let then the author of the offence be brought back to a right way of life; and all quarrels of priests will cease. For I for my part am the servant of all priests, so long as they live as becomes priests. For whosoever, through the swelling of vain glory, lifts up his neck against Almighty God and against the statutes of the Fathers, I trust in Almighty God that he will not bend my neck to himself, not even with swords.

Moreover what has been done in this city on our hearing of this title, I have indicated in full to my deacon and *responsalis* Sabinianus. Let then the piety of my Lords think of me as their own, whom they have always cherished and countenanced beyond others, and who desire to render obedience to you, and yet fear to be found guilty in the heavenly and tremendous judgment, and, according to the petition of the aforesaid deacon Sabinianus, let my most pious Lord either deign to judge this business, or to move the often before mentioned man to desist at length from this attempt. If then through the most just judgment of your Piety he should comply with your orders, even though they be mild ones, we shall return thanks to Almighty God, and rejoice for the peace granted through you to all the Church. But should he persist any longer in his present contention, we hold this sentence of the Truth to be already made good; *Every one that exalteth himself shall be humbled* (Luke xiv. 11; xviii. 14). And again it is written, *Before a fall the heart is lifted up* (Prov. xvi. 18). I however, rendering obedience to the commands of my Lords, have both written sweetly to my aforesaid fellow-priest, and humbly admonished him to amend himself of this coveting of empty glory. If therefore he be willing to hear me, he has a devoted brother. But, if he persists in pride, I already see what will follow:—that he will find Him as his adversary of whom it is written, *God resisteth the proud, but giveth grace unto the humble* (Jam. iv. 6).

EPISTLE XXI.

To Constantina Augusta[2].

Gregory to Constantina, &c.

Almighty God, who holds in His right hand the heart of your Piety, both protects us through you and prepares for you rewards of eternal remuneration for temporal deeds. For I have learnt from the letters of the deacon Sabinianus my *responsalis* with what justice your Serenity is interested in the cause of the blessed Prince of the apostles Peter against certain persons who are proudly humble and feignedly kind. And I trust in the bounty of our Redeemer that for these your good offices with the most serene Lord and his most pious sons you will receive retribution also in the heavenly country. Nor is there any doubt that you will receive eternal benefits, being loosed from the chains of your sins, if in the cause of his Church you have made him your debtor to whom the power of binding and of loosing has been given. Wherefore I still beg you to allow no man's hypocrisy to prevail against the truth, since there are some who, according to the saying of the excellent preacher, by sweet words and fair speeches seduce the hearts of the innocent,—men who are vile in raiment, but puffed up in heart. And they affect to despise all things in this world, and yet seek to acquire for themselves all the things that are of this world. They confess themselves unworthy before all men, but cannot be content with private titles, since they covet that whereby they may seem to be more worthy than all. Let therefore your Piety, whom Almighty God has appointed with our most serene Lord to be over the whole world, through your favouring of justice render service to Him from whom you have received your right to so great a dominion, that you may rule over the world that is committed to you so much the more securely as you more truly serve the Author of all things in the execution of truth.

Furthermore, I inform you that I have received a letter from the most pious Lord desiring me to be pacific towards my brother and fellow-priest John. And indeed so it became the religious Lord to give injunctions to priests. But, when this my brother with new presumption and pride calls himself universal bishop, having caused himself in the time of our predecessor of holy memory to be designated in synod by this so proud a title, though all the acts of that synod were abrogated,

[2] The main purport of this letter to the Empress is to induce her to move the Emperor to disallow the title of Universal Bishop assumed by the patriarch of Constantinople; but at the end of the letter he takes occasion to solicit her good offices also in the case of Maximus, bishop of Salona, for an account of which, with references to other letters on the subject, cf. III. 47, note 2.

being disallowed by the Apostolic See,—the most serene Lord gives me a somewhat distressing intimation, in that he has not rebuked him who is acting proudly, but endeavours to bend me from my purpose, who in this cause of defending the truth of the Gospels and Canons, of humility and rectitude; whereas my aforesaid brother and fellow-priest is acting against evangelical principles and also against the blessed Apostle Peter, and against all the churches, and against the ordinances of the Canons. But the Lord, in whose hands are all things, is almighty; of Him it is written, *There is no wisdom nor prudence nor counsel against the Lord* (Prov. xxi. 30). And indeed my often before mentioned most holy brother endeavours to persuade my most serene Lord of many things: but well I know that all those prayers of his and all those tears will not allow my Lord to be in any thing cajoled by any one against reason or his own soul.

Still it is very distressing, and hard to be borne with patience, that my aforesaid brother and fellow-bishop, despising all others, should attempt to be called sole bishop. But in this pride of his what else is denoted than that the times of Antichrist are already near at hand? For in truth he is imitating him who, scorning social joy with the legions of angels, attempted to start up to a summit of singular eminence, saying, *I will exalt my throne above the stars of heaven, I will sit upon the mount of the testament, in the sides of the North, and will ascend above the heights of the clouds, and I will be like the most High* (Isai. xiv. 13). Wherefore I beseech you by Almighty God not to allow the times of your Piety to be polluted by the elation of one man, nor in any way to give any assent to so perverse a title, and that in this case your Piety may by no means despise me; since, though the sins of Gregory are so great that he ought to suffer such things, yet there are no sins of the Apostle Peter that he should deserve in your times to suffer thus. Wherefore again and again I beseech you by Almighty God that, as the princes your ancestors have sought the favour of the holy Apostle Peter, so you also take heed both to seek it for yourselves and to keep it, and that his honour among you be in no degree lessened on account of our sins who unworthily serve him, seeing that he is able both to be your helper now in all things and hereafter to remit your sins.

Moreover, it is now even seven years that we have been living in this city among the swords of the Lombards. How much is expended on them daily by this Church, that we may be able to live among them, is not to be told. But I briefly indicate that, as in the regions of Ravenna the Piety of my Lords has for the first army of Italy a treasurer (*sacellarium*) to defray the daily expenses for recurring needs, so I also in this city am their treasurer for such purposes And yet this Church, which at one and the same time unceasingly expends so much on clergy, monasteries, the poor, the people, and in addition on the Lombards, lo it is still pressed down by the affliction of all the Churches, which groan much for this pride of one man, though they do not presume to say anything.

Further, a bishop of the city of Salona has been ordained without the knowledge of me and my *responsalis*, and a thing has been done which never happened under any former princes. When I heard of this, I at once sent word to that prevaricator, who had been irregularly ordained, that he must not presume by any means to celebrate the solemnities of mass, unless we should have first ascertained from our most serene Lords that they had ordered this to be done; and this I commanded him under pain of excommunication. And yet, scorning and despising me, supported by the audacity of certain secular persons, to whom he is said to give many bribes so as to impoverish his Church, he presumes up to this time to celebrate mass, and has refused to come to me according to the order of my Lords. Now I, obeying the injunction of their Piety, have from my heart forgiven this same Maximus, who had been ordained without my knowledge, his presumption in passing over me and my *responsalis* in his ordination, even as though he had been ordained with my authority. But his other wrong doings—to wit his bodily transgressions, which I have heard of, and his having been elected through bribery, and his having presumed to celebrate mass while excommunicated—these things, for the sake of God, I cannot pass over without enquiry. But I hope, and implore the Lord, that no fault may be found in him with respect to these things that are reported, and that his case may be terminated without peril to my soul. Nevertheless, before this has been ascertained, my most serene Lord, in the order that has been despatched, has enjoined me to receive him with honour when he comes. And it is a very serious thing that a man of whom so many things of such a nature are reported should be honoured before such things have been enquired into and sifted, as they ought in the first place to be. And, if the causes of the bishops who are committed to me are settled before my most pious Lords under the patronage of others, what shall I do, unhappy that I am, in this Church? But that my bishops despise me, and have recourse to secular judges against me, I give thanks to

Almighty God that I attribute it to my sins. This however I briefly intimate, because I am waiting for a little while; and, if he should long delay coming to me, I shall in no wise hesitate to exercise strict canonical discipline in his case. But I trust in Almighty God, that He will give long life to our most pious Lords, and order things for us under your hand, not according to our sins, but according to the gifts of His grace. These things, then, I suggest to my most tranquil lady, since I am not ignorant with how great zeal for rectitude the most pure conscience of her Serenity is moved.

EPISTLE XXIII.

To Castorius, Notary.

Gregory to Castorius, &c.

Our hearing of the death of our brother and fellow-bishop John[3] has greatly saddened us, especially as that city at this time has lost the solace of pastoral care. Wherefore, since very many advantages to the Church itself demand that, under the guidance of Christ, a priest should be ordained without delay, we accordingly charge thy Experience to exhort the clergy and people with all urgency that they delay not to elect for themselves a priest to be consecrated. This however, and before all things, we desire thee to press upon them, that in the general cause they regard not their own private interests. Let there be no venality, then, in this election, lest, while they covet rewards, they lose their discrimination of choice, and think that man worthy for this office who may have pleased them, not by his merits, but by his gifts. For let them especially and absolutely know this, that he is not only unworthy of the priesthood, but will also certainly become further culpable, whosoever may presume to make merchandise of the gift of God by thinking to purchase it for a price. Wherefore let not him that is liberal in bribes, but him that is worthy for his merits, be chosen. For the penalty will affect both the elected and the electors, if they attempt with sacrilegious mind to violate the purity of the priesthood. Moreover, whether one or two may have been elected, by all means warn five of the senior presbyters and five of the leading people[4] to come to us together. But with respect to the clergy, if, besides those who determine to come, you are of opinion that the presence of any others is necessary, send them to us without delay, that there may be no plea of excuse, nor any delay ensue, in setting the Church in order.

3 Viz. John, bishop of Ravenna, as to whom see III. 56, 57; V. 11, 15. Marinianus was elected in his place. See VI. 34, 61.

4 *De præcedentibus.* Al. *de præcedentibus diaconibus.*

EPISTLE XXV.

To Severus, Bishop.

Gregory to Severus, Bishop of Ficulum.

The report that has been sent to us has informed us of the death of the bishop John[5]. Wherefore we solemnly delegate to thy Fraternity the work of the visitation of the bereaved Church: which work it becomes thee so to execute that no one may presume to interfere with respect to the promotions of the clergy, the revenues, ornaments, ministrations, or whatever else belongs to the patrimony of the same Church. *According to custom.*

EPISTLE XXVI.

To the people of Ravenna.

Gregory to the clergy, gentry, and common people of Ravenna[6].

Having been informed of the death of your bishop, we have taken care to delegate to our brother and fellow-bishop Severus of Ficulum the visitation of the bereaved Church, to whom we have given in charge to allow nothing with respect to the promotions of the clergy, the revenues, ornaments, and ministrations, to be usurped by any one. It is for you to render obedience to his assiduous exhortations. *According to custom.*

EPISTLE XXIX.

To Vincomalus, Guardian (*Defensorem*)[7].

Gregory to Vincomalus, &c.

With a view to the advantage of the Church it is our will and pleasure, that, if thou art held bound by no condition of, or liability to, bodily service, and hast not been a cleric of any other city, and if there is no canonical objection to thee, thou take the office of guardian of the Church, that thou mayest execute incorruptly and with alacrity whatever may be enjoined thee by us for the benefit of the poor, using this privilege which after deliberation we have conferred upon thee, so as to do thy diligence faithfully in accomplishing all that may be enjoined on thee by us, as having to render an account of thy doings under the judgment of our God. This epistle we have dictated, to be committed to writing, to Paterius, notary of our Church; In the month of March, Indiction 13.

5 Viz. John, bishop of Ravenna. See Ep. 23.

6 Cf. II. 6, note 3.

7 We have in this epistle the form of appointment to the office of *Defensor Ecclesiæ*. Cf. XI. 38. From IX. 62 it appears that the functions of the office had in some cases been usurped by persons not duly authorized, as it is there ordered that none should be recognized but such as possessed letters of appointment. The only duties of the office specified in this form of appointment have reference to the poor—"pro pauperum commodis;" but it is evident from the many epistles addressed to *defensores*, that they had a much wider scope. See *Prolegomena*, p. vii.

EPISTLE XXX.

To Mauricius Augustus.

Gregory to Mauricius, &c.

The Piety of my Lords, which has been wont mercifully to sustain your servants, has shone forth here in so kind a supply that the need of all the feeble has been relieved by the succour of your bounty. On this account we all with prayers and tears beseech Almighty God, who has moved the heart of your Clemency to do this thing, that He would preserve the empire of our Lords safe in His unfailing love, and by the aid of His own majesty extend their victories in all nations. The thirty pounds of gold which my fellow-servant Busa brought, Scribo [8] has distributed faithfully to priests, persons in need, and others. And, since certain females devoted to a religious life (*sanctimoniales fœminæ*) have come to this city from divers provinces, having fled hither after captivity, of whom some, so far as there was room for them, have been placed in monasteries, but others, who could not be taken in, lead a life of singular destitution, it has been thought good that what could be spared from the relief of the blind, maimed and feeble should be distributed to them, so that not only needy natives, but also strangers who arrive here, might receive of the compassion of our Lords. Hence it has been brought about that all alike with one accord pray for the life of our lords, that so Almighty God may give you a long and quiet life, and grant to the most happy offspring of your Piety to flourish long in the Roman republic. The pay also of the soldiers has been so distributed by my aforesaid fellow-servant Scribo [8], in the presence also of the glorious Castus, *magister militum*, that all received with thanks the gifts of our lords under due discipline, and abstained from all murmuring such as was formerly wont to prevail among them.

EPISTLE XXXVI.

To Severus, *Scholasticus*.

Gregory to Severus, *Scholasticus* to the Exarch [9].

Those who assist judges and are bound to them by sincere attachment ought to advise them and suggest to them what may both save their souls and not derogate from their reputation. This being so, since we know with what sincere loyalty you love the most excellent Exarch, we have been careful to inform your Greatness of the things that have been done, that, being aware of them, you may move him to assent to them reasonably.

Know then that Agilulph, King of the Lombards, is not unwilling to conclude a general peace, if only the lord Patricius will consent to an arbitration. For he complains that many acts of violence were committed in his regions during the time of peace. And since, if reasonable grounds for arbitration should be found, he desires to have satisfaction made to himself, he also himself promises to make satisfaction in all ways, if it should appear that any wrong was committed on his side during the peace. Since then it is no doubt reasonable to agree to what he asks, there ought to be an arbitration, that, if any wrongs have been done on either side, they may be adjusted; so that it may be possible, with the protection of God, to establish a general peace; for how necessary for us all this is you well know. Act therefore wisely as you have been wont to do, that the most excellent Exarch may consent to this without delay, lest peace should appear to be refused by him, as should not be. For, should he be unwilling to consent, he indeed [Agilulph] again promises to conclude a special peace with us; but we know that divers islands and other places would undoubtedly in that case be ruined. However, let him [the Exarch] consider these things, and hasten to make peace, to the end that at any rate during this cessation of hostilities we may have some degree of quiet, and the forces of the republic may with the help of God be the better repaired for resistance.

EPISTLE XXXIX.

To Anastasius, Bishop [1].

Gregory to Anastasius, Bishop of Antioch.

Glory to God in the highest and on earth peace to men of good will (Luke ii. 14), because that great river which once had left the rocks of Antioch dry has returned at length to its proper channel, and waters the subject valleys that are near, so as also to bring forth fruit, some thirty-fold, some sixty-fold, and some an hundred-fold. For now there is no doubt that many flowers of souls are growing up in its valleys, and that they will come even to ripe fruit through the streams of your tongue. Wherefore with voice of heart and mouth from our inmost soul we render due

---

8 Or *Scribo* may be the official designation of the officer commissioned to distribute the imperial bounty. Cf. II. 32, note 7.

9 "Scholasticus—Quivis eloquens, disertus, oratoriæ facultatis et politiaris literaturæ studiis eruditus.—Advocatus, patronus, qui causam in foro agit; sed proprie peritus, eloquens, disertus patronus (*Cod. Theod*)." [D'Arnis' Lexicon Manuale.] Severus may be concluded to have been the Exarch's legal adviser.

1 See I. 7, note 5. Anastasius had now been recently restored to his patriarchal see.

praise to Almighty God, and rejoice in your Blessedness, not with you only, but with all who are subject to you. I have received the letters of your Holiness, to me most sweet and pleasant, while we ourselves, if I may so speak, are sweating under the same toil with you. And indeed I know how heavy must be to thee the burden of external cares after those heights of rest, wherein with the hand of the heart thou wert touching heavenly secrets. But remember that thou rulest an Apostolic See, and assuagest sorrow the more readily from being made all things to all men. In the Books of Kings, as your accomplished Holiness knows, a certain man is described who used either hand for the right hand (1 Chron. xii. 2). And, with regard to this, I am not doubtful about the lord Anastasius, of old my most sweet and most holy patron, that, while he draws earthly works to heavenly profit, he turns the left hand to the right hand's use; so that his heavenly intentness may accomplish its work, so to speak, with the right hand, and also, when he is led in his care of temporal things towards the interests of justice, the left hand may acquire the strength of the right.

And indeed these things cannot be without heavy labour and trouble. But let us remember the labours of those who went before us; and what we endure will not be hard. For *We must through many tribulations enter into the kingdom of God* (Acts xiv. 22). And, *We were pressed out of measure, yea and above strength, insomuch that we were weary even of life. But we ourselves, too, had the answer of death in ourselves, that we should not trust in ourselves* (2 Cor. i. 8, 9). And yet *The sufferings of this present time are not worthy to be compared with the supervening glory which shall be revealed in us* (Rom. viii. 18). How then can we that are weak sheep pass without labour through the heat of this world wherein we know that even rams have suffered under heavy toil?

Further, what tribulations I suffer in this land from the swords of the Lombards, from the iniquities of judges, from the press of business, from the care of subjects, and also from bodily affliction, I am unable to express either by pen or tongue. Concerning which things even though I might say something briefly, I hesitate, lest to your most holy Charity, while afflicted by your own tribulations, I should add mine also. But may Almighty God both in the abundance of His loving-kindness fill the mind of your most holy Blessedness with all comfort, and grant at some time, on account of your intercession, to unworthy me to rest from these evils which I suffer. Amen. Grace. These words, as you see, taken from what you had written, I insert in my epistles, that your Blessedness may perceive with regard to Saint Ignatius that he is not only yours, but also ours[2]. For, as we have his master, the Prince of the apostles in common, so also no one of us ought to have to himself alone the disciple of this same Prince[3]. Moreover, we have received your blessing[4], which is of sweet smell and of a good savour, with the feelings that were due to it. And we give thanks to Almighty God that what you do, what you say, and what you give, is fragrant and savoury. For your life therefore let us say together, let us say all, *Glory to God in the highest, and on earth peace to men of good will.*

EPISTLE XL.

To Mauricius Augustus.

Gregory to Mauricius, &c.

The Piety of my Lords in their most serene commands, while set on refuting me on certain matters, in sparing me has by no means spared me. For by the use therein of the term simplicity they politely call me silly. It is true indeed that in Holy Scripture, when simplicity is spoken of in a good sense, it is often carefully associated with prudence and uprightness. Hence it is written of the blessed Job, *The man was simple and upright* (Job i. 1). And the blessed Apostle Paul admonishes saying, *Be ye simple in evil and prudent in good* Rom. xvi. 19). And the Truth in person) admonishes saying, *Be ye prudent as serpents, and simple as doves* (Matth. x. 16); thus shewing it to be very unprofitable if either prudence should be wanting to simplicity, or simplicity to prudence. In order, then, to make His servants instructed for all things He desired them to be both simple as doves, and prudent as serpents, that so both the cunning of the serpent might sharpen in them the simplicity of the dove, and the simplicity of the dove temper the cunning of the serpent.

I therefore, who am denounced in the most serene commands of my Lords as simple without the addition of prudence, as having been deceived by the cunning of Ariulph, am plainly and undoubtedly called silly; which I also myself acknowledge to be the case. For, though your Piety were silent, the facts

[2] The expression is found in the spurious, but not in what are held to be the genuine, epistles of St. Ignatius.

[3] For Gregory's view of Antioch having been St. Peter's see previously to his presiding over that of Rome, and of the sees of Rome, Alexandria, and Antioch jointly representing the see of the Prince of the Apostles, see especially VII. 40. Cf. also VI. 60; VIII. 2; X. 35.

[4] *Benedictio*, meaning *a present*. See IV. 31, note 9.

cry out. For, if I had not been silly, I should by no means have come to endure what I suffer in this place among the swords of the Lombards. Moreover, in what I stated about Ariulph, that he was prepared with all his heart to come to terms with the republic, seeing that I am not believed, I am reproved also as having lied. But, although I am not a priest[5], I know it to be a grave injury to a priest that, being a servant of the truth, he should be believed to be deceitful. And I have been for some time aware that Nordulph is believed before me, and Leo before me, and that now easy credence is given to those who seem to be in your confidence more than to my assertions.

And indeed if the captivity of my land were not increasing day by day, I would gladly pass over in silence contempt and ridicule of myself. But this does afflict me exceedingly, that from my bearing the charge of falsehood it ensues also that Italy is daily led captive under the yoke of the Lombards. And, while my representations are in no wise believed, the strength of the enemy is increasing hugely. This however I suggest to my most pious Lord, that he would think anything that is bad of me, but, with regard to the advantage of the republic and the cause of the rescue of Italy, not easily lend his pious ears to any one, but believe facts rather than words. Moreover, let not our Lord, in virtue of his earthly power, too hastily disdain priests, but with excellent consideration, on account of Him whose servants they are, so rule over them as also to pay the reverence that is due to them. For in Holy Writ priests are sometimes called gods, and sometimes angels. For even through Moses it is said of him who is to be put upon his oath, *Bring him unto the gods* (Exod. xxii. 8); that is unto the priests. And again it is written, *Thou shalt not revile the gods* (Ib. 28), to wit, the priests. And the prophet says, *The priest's lips shall keep knowledge, and they shall seek the law at his mouth; for he is the angel of the Lord of hosts* (Malach. ii. 7), Why, then, should it be strange if your Piety were to condescend to honour those to whom even God Himself in His word gives honour, calling them angels or gods?

Ecclesiastical history also testifies that, when accusations in writing against bishops had been offered to the Prince Constantine of pious memory, he received indeed the bills of accusation, but, calling together the bishops who had been accused, he burnt before their eyes the bills which he had received, saying, *Ye are gods, constituted by the true God. Go, and settle your causes among you, for it is not fit that we should judge gods.* Yet in this sentence, my pious Lord, he conferred more on himself by his humility than on them by the reverence paid to them. For before him there were pagan princes in the republic, who knew not the true God, but worshipped gods of wood and stone; and yet they paid the greatest honour to their priests. What wonder then if a Christian emperor should condescend to honour the priests of the true God, when pagan princes, as we have already said, knew how to bestow honour on priests who served gods of wood and stone?

These things, then, I suggest to the piety of my Lords, not in my own behalf, but in behalf of all priests. For I am a man that is a sinner. And, since I offend against Almighty God incessantly every day, I surmise that it will be some amends for this at the tremendous judgment, that I am smitten incessantly every day by blows. And I believe that you appease the same Almighty God all the more as you more severely afflict me who serve Him badly. For I had already received many blows, and when the commands of my Lords came in addition, I found consolations that I was not hoping for. For, if I can, I will briefly enumerate these blows.

First, that the peace which without any cost to the republic I had made with the Lombards who were in Tuscany was withdrawn from me. Then, the peace having been broken, the soldiers were removed from the Roman city. And some indeed were slain by the enemy, but others were placed at Narnii and Perusium (*Perugia*); and Rome was left, that Perusium might be held. After this a still heavier blow was the arrival of Agilulph, so that I saw with my own eyes Romans tied by the neck with ropes like dogs, to be taken to France for sale. And, because we who were within the city under the protection of God escaped his hands, a ground was thence sought for making us appear culpable; to wit, because corn ran short, which cannot by any means be kept in large quantities for long in this city; as I have shewn more fully in another representation. On my own account indeed I was in no wise disturbed, since I declare, my conscience bearing me witness, that I was prepared to suffer any adversity whatever, so long as I came out of all these things with the safety of my soul. But for the glorious men, Gregory the præfect, and Castorius the military commander (*magistro militum*), I have been distressed in no small degree, seeing that they in no way neglected to do all that could be done, and endured most severe toil in watching

5 This may be an ironical allusion to something the Empero had said in his letter to Gregory.

and guarding the city during the siege, and, after all this, were smitten by the heavy indignation of my Lords. As to them, I clearly understand that it is not their conduct, but my person, that goes against them. For, having with me alike laboured in trouble, they are alike troubled after labour.

Now as to the Piety of my Lords holding out over me the formidable and terrible judgment of Almighty God, I beseech you by the same Almighty God to do this no more. For as yet we know not how any of us will stand there. And Paul, the excellent preacher, says, *Judge nothing before the time, until the Lord come, who both will bring to light the hidden things of darkness, and will make manifest the counsels of the hearts* (1 Cor. iv. 5). Yet this I briefly say, that, unworthy sinner as I am, I rely more on the mercy of Jesus when He comes than on the justice of your Piety. And there are many things that men are ignorant of with regard to this judgment; for perhaps He will blame what you praise, and praise what you blame. Wherefore among all these uncertainties I return to tears only, praying that the same Almighty God may both direct our most pious Lord with His hand and in that terrible judgment find him free from all defaults. And may He make me so to please men, if need be, as not to offend against His eternal grace[6].

EPISTLE XLI.

To Constantina Augusta.

Gregory to Constantina, &c.

Knowing how my most serene Lady thinks about the heavenly country and the life of her soul, I consider that I should be greatly in fault were I to keep silence on matters that ought to be represented to her for the fear of God.

Having ascertained that there are many of the natives in the island of Sardinia who still, after the evil custom of their race, practise sacrifices to idols, and that the priests of the same island are sluggish in preaching our Redeemer, I sent thither one of the bishops of Italy, who with the co-operation of the Lord has brought many of the natives to the faith. But he has reported to me a sacrilegious proceeding, namely, that those in the island who sacrifice to idols pay a bribe to the judge for license to do this. And, when some of them had been baptized and had ceased sacrificing to idols, the same payment had been exacted by this same judge of the island, even after their baptism, which they had been previously accustomed to make for leave to sacrifice to idols. And, when the aforesaid bishop found fault with him, he replied that he had promised so large a *suffragium*[7] that he could not make it up except by aid from cases of this kind. But the island of Corsica is oppressed by such an excessive number of exactors and such a burden of exactions, that those who are in it are hardly able to make up what is exacted except by selling their children. Hence it ensues that the proprietors of this island, deserting the pious republic, are forced to take refuge with that most wicked nation of the Lombards. For what can they suffer from barbarians harder or more cruel than being so straitened and squeezed as to be compelled to sell their children? Moreover, in the island of Sicily one Stephen, *chartularius* of the maritime parts, is said to practise such illegalities and such oppressions, invading places that belong to various persons, and without any legal process putting up titles[8] on properties and houses, that, if I wished to tell every one of his doings that have come to my ears, I could not accomplish the task in a large volume.

Let my most serene Lady look to all these things wisely, and assuage the groans of the oppressed. For I suspect that these things have not come to your most pious ears. For if they could have reached them, they would by no means have continued until now. But they should be represented now at a suitable time to our most pious Lord, that he may remove such and so great a burden of sin from his own soul, from the empire, and from his sons. I know he will say that whatever is collected from the aforesaid islands is transmitted to us for the expenses of Italy. But in reply to this I suggest that, even though less expenditure were bestowed on Italy, he should still rid his empire of the tears of the oppressed. For perhaps, too, such great expenditure in this land profits less than it might do because the money for it is collected with some admixture of sin. Let therefore our most serene Lords give orders that nothing be collected with sin. And I know that, though less is given for the advantage of the republic, the republic is thereby much aided. And though perhaps it may be less aided by a less expenditure, yet it is better that we should not live temporally, than that you should find any hindrance in the way of eternal life. For consider what must be the

6 For the circumstances referred to in this epistle, see *Proleg.*, p. xix. It shews how outspoken Gregory could be, when greatly moved, in addressing the Emperor, notwithstanding his accustomed deference.

7 i.e. the payment to the imperial government required from judges or other functionaries in consideration of their appointment. "Suffragium. Pecuniæ quæ suffragii titulo ab Imperatoribus accipiebantur cum honores deferebant, quæ δεσποτικὰ vocantur in formula jurisjurandi.—Novellæ Justiniani 8, cujus titulus est, *ut judices sine suffragio fiant*." Du Cange.

8 *Titulos*, i.e. notices put upon properties, asserting claim, or announcing sale, &c.

feelings, what the state of heart of parents, when they part with their children lest they should be tormented. But how one ought to feel for the children of others is well known to those who have children of their own. Let it then suffice for me to have briefly represented these things, lest, if your Piety were not to know what is being done in these parts, I should suffer for the guilt of my silence before the strict judge.

EPISTLE XLII.

To Sebastian, Bishop.

Gregory to Sebastian, Bishop of Sirmium.

I have received the most sweet and pleasant letter of thy Fraternity, which, though you are never absent from my heart, has nevertheless made your Holiness as it were present with me bodily. But I beseech Almighty God to protect you with His right hand, and to grant you a tranquil life here, and, when it shall please Him, eternal rewards. But I beg you, if you love me with that love wherewith you always loved me when we were together, to pray for me more earnestly, that so Almighty God may loose me from the bands of my sins, and make me to stand free in His sight, released from the burden of this corruption. For, however inestimable be the sweetness of the heavenly country for drawing one towards it, yet there are many sorrows in this life to impel us daily to the love of heavenly things. And these only please me exceedingly from the very fact that they do not allow anything to please me in this world.

For we can by no means describe, most holy brother, what we suffer in this land at the hands of your friend, the lord Romanus[9]. Yet I may briefly say that his malice towards us has surpassed the swords of the Lombards; so that the enemies who kill us seem kinder than the judges of the republic, who by their malice, rapines, and deceits wear us out with anxiety. And to bear at the same time the charge of bishops and clergy, and also of monasteries and people, and to watch anxiously against the plots of the enemy, and to be ever suspicious of the deceitfulness and malice of the dukes; what labours and what sorrows all this involves, your Fraternity may the more truly estimate as you more purely love me who suffer these things

Furthermore, while addressing you with the greeting that I owe you, I inform you that it has come to my knowledge from the report of Boniface the *defensor*, that our brother the most holy lord Anastasius the patriarch[1] has wished to commit to you the government of the Church in one of his cities, and that you have refused your assent. This your feeling and your wisdom I most gladly approve of, and strongly commend; and I account you happy, and myself unhappy in having consented at such a time as this to undertake the government of the Church. If, however, by any chance, in condescension to your brethren, and as being intent on works of mercy, you should ever decide to consent to such a proposal, I beg you by no means to prefer any one else's love to mine. For there are in the island of Sicily Churches without bishops, and, if by the guidance of God you are pleased to take the government of a Church, you will be able to do this better near the threshold of the blessed apostle Peter, with his aid. But if you are not so pleased, remain happily as you are, that this resolution may continue in you; and pray for us unhappy ones. Now may Almighty God keep you under His protection, in whatever place it be His will that you should be, and bring you to heavenly rewards.

EPISTLE XLIII.

To Eulogius and Anastasius, Bishops.

Gregory to Eulogius, Bishop of Alexandria, and Anastasius, Bishop of Antioch.

When the excellent preacher says, *As long as I am the apostle of the Gentiles I will honour my ministry* (Rom. xi. 13); saying again in another place, *We became as babes among you* (1 Thess. ii. 7), he undoubtedly shews an example to us who come after him, that we should retain humility in our minds, and yet keep in honour the dignity of our order, so that neither should our humility be timid nor our elevation proud. Now eight years ago, in the time of my predecessor of holy memory Pelagius, our brother and fellow-bishop John in the city of Constantinople, seeking occasion from another cause, held a synod in which he attempted to call himself Universal Bishop. Which as soon as my said predecessor knew, he despatched letters annulling by the authority of the holy apostle Peter the acts of the said synod; of which letters I have taken care to send copies to your Holiness. Moreover he forbade the deacon who attended us the most pious Lords for the business of the Church to celebrate the solemnities of mass with our aforesaid fellow-priest. I also, being of the same mind with him, have sent similar letters to our aforesaid fellow-priest, copies of which I have thought it right to send to your Blessedness, with this especial purpose, that we may first assail with moderate force the mind of our before-named brother con-

[9] Romanus Patricius, the Exarch.

[1] Viz. of Antioch.

cerning this matter, wherein by a new act of pride, all the bowels of the Universal Church are disturbed. But, if he should altogether refuse to be bent from the stiffness of his elation, then, with the succour of Almighty God, we may consider more particularly what ought to be done.

For, as your venerable Holiness knows, this name of Universality was offered by the holy synod of Chalcedon to the pontiff of the Apostolic See which by the providence of God I serve [2]. But no one of my predecessors has ever consented to use this so profane a title; since, forsooth, if one Patriarch is called Universal, the name of Patriarch in the case of the rest is derogated. But far be this, far be it from the mind of a Christian, that any one should wish to seize for himself that whereby he might seem in the least degree to lessen the honour of his brethren. While, then, we are unwilling to receive this honour when offered to us, think how disgraceful it is for any one to have wished to usurp it to himself perforce.

Wherefore let not your Holiness in your epistles ever call any one Universal, lest you detract from the honour due to yourself in offering to another what is not due. Nor let any sinister suspicion make your mind uneasy with regard to our most serene lords, inasmuch as he fears Almighty God, and will in no way consent to do anything against the evangelical ordinances, against the most sacred canons. As for me, though separated from you by long spaces of land and sea, I am nevertheless entirely conjoined with you in heart. And I trust that it is so in all respects with your Blessedness towards me; since, when you love me in return, you are not far from me. Hence we give thanks the more to that grain of mustard seed (Matth. xiii. 31, 32), for that from what appeared a small and despicable seed it has been so spread abroad everywhere by branches rising and extending themselves from the same root that all the birds of heaven may make their nests in them. And thanks be to that leaven which, in three measures of meal, has leavened in unity the mass of the whole human race (Matth. xiii. 33); and to the little stone, which, cut out of the mountain without hands, has occupied the whole face of the earth (Dan. ii. 35), and which to this end everywhere distends itself, that from the human race reduced to unity the body of the whole Church might be perfected, and so this distinction between the several members might serve for the benefit of the compacted whole.

Hence also we are not far from you, since in Him who is everywhere we are one. Let us then give thanks to Him who, having abolished enmities, has caused that in His flesh there should be in the whole world one flock, and one sheepfold under Himself the one shepherd; and let us be ever mindful how the preacher of truth admonishes us, saying, *Be careful to keep the unity of the spirit in the bond of peace* (Ephes. iv. 3), and, *Follow peace with all men, and holiness, without which no man shall see God* (Hebr. xii. 14). And he says also to other disciples, *If it be possible, as much as lieth in you, having peace with all men* (Rom. xii. 18) For he sees that the good cannot have peace with the bad; and therefore, as ye know, he premised, *If it be possible.*

But, because peace cannot be established except on two sides, when the bad fly from it, the good ought to keep it in their inmost hearts. Whence also it is admirably said, *As much as lieth in you;* meaning that it should remain in us even when it is repelled from the hearts of evil men. And such peace we truly keep, when we treat the faults of the proud at once with charity and with persistent justice, when we love them and hate their vices. For man is the work of God; but vice is the work of man. Let us then distinguish between what God and what man has made, and neither hate the man on account of his error nor love the error on account of the man.

Let us then with united mind attack the evil of pride in the man, that from his enemy, that is to say his error, the man himself may first be freed. Our Almighty Redeemer will supply strength to charity and justice; He will supply to us, though placed far from each other, the unity of His Spirit; even He by whose workmanship the Church, having been constructed as it were after the manner of the ark with the four sides of the world, and bound together with the compacture of incorruptible planks and the pitch of charity, is disturbed by no opposing winds, by the swelling of no billow coming from without.

But inasmuch as, with His grace steering us, we ought to seek that no wave coming upon us from without may throw us into confusion, so ought we to pray with all our hearts, dearest brethren, that the right hand of His providence may draw out the accumulation of internal bilgewater within us. For indeed our adversary the devil, who, in his rage against the humble, as a roaring lion walketh about seeking whom he may devour (1 Pet. v. 8), no longer, as we perceive, walks about the folds but so resolutely fixes his teeth in certain necessary members of the Church that, unless with the favour of the Lord, the heedful crowd

[2] Cf. V. 18, and note.

of shepherds unanimously run to the rescue, no one can doubt that he will soon tear all the sheepfold; which God forbid. Consider, dearest brethren, who it is that follows close at hand, of whose approach such perverse beginnings are breaking out even in priests. For it is because he is near of whom it is written, *He is king over all the sons of pride* (Job xli. 25)—not without sore grief I am compelled to say it—that our brother and fellow-bishop John, despising the Lord's commands, apostolical precepts, and rules of Fathers, attempts through elation to be his forerunner in name.

But may Almighty God make known to your Blessedness with what sore groaning I am tormentèd by this consideration; that he, the once to me most modest man, he who was beloved of all, he who seemed to be occupied in alms, deeds, prayers, and fastings, out of the ashes he sat in, out of the humility he preached, has grown so boastful as to attempt to claim all to himself, and through the elation of a pompous expression to aim at subjugating to himself all the members of Christ, which cohere to one Head only, that is to Christ. Nor is it surprising that the same tempter who knows pride to be the beginning of all sin, who used it formerly before all else in the case of the first man, should now also put it before some men at the end of virtues, so as to lay it as a snare for those who to some extent seemed to be escaping his most cruel hands by the good aims of their life, at the very goal of good work, and as it were in the very conclusion of perfection.

Wherefore we ought to pray earnestly, and implore Almighty God with continual supplications, that He would avert this error from that man's soul, and remove this mischief of pride and confusion from the unity and humility of the Church. And with the favour of the Lord we ought to concur, and make provision with all our powers, lest in the poison of one expression the living members in the body of Christ should die. For, if this expression is suffered to be allowably used, the honour of all patriarchs is denied: and while he that is called Universal perishes perchance in his error, no bishop will be found to have remained in a state of truth.

It is for you then, firmly and without prejudice, to keep the Churches as you have received them, and not to let this attempt at a diabolical usurpation have any countenance from you. Stand firm; stand secure; presume not ever to issue or to receive writings with the falsity of the name Universal in them. Bid all the bishops subject to your care abstain from the defilement of this elation, that the Universal Church may acknowledge you as Patriarchs not only in good works but also in the authority of truth. But, if perchance adversity is the consequence, we ought to persist unanimously, and shew even by dying that in case of harm to the generality we do not love anything of our own especially. Let us say with Paul, *To me to live is Christ, and to die is gain* (Philip. i. 21). Let us hear what the first of all pastors says; *If ye suffer anything for righteousness' sake, happy are ye* (1 Pet. iii. 14). For believe me that the dignity which we have received for the preaching of the truth we shall more safely relinquish than retain in behalf of the same truth, should case of necessity require it. Finally, pray for me, as becomes your most dear Blessedness, that I may shew forth in works what I am thus bold to say to you.

EPISTLE XLVIII.

To Andrew, Scholasticus[3].

Gregory to Andrew, &c.

We have been desirous of carrying out the wish of the most excellent the lord Patrician as to the person of Donatus, the archdeacon; but, seeing that it is very dangerous to the soul to lay hands on any one rashly, we took care to examine by a thorough investigation into his life and deeds. And, since many things have been discovered, as we have written to the said lord Patrician, which remove him far from the episcopate, we, fearing the judgment of God, have not thought fit to consent to his ordination. But neither have we presumed to ordain John, the presbyter, who is ignorant of the psalms, since this circumstance certainly shewed him to be too little in earnest about himself. These, then, being excluded, when we had urged the parties to choose some one from among their own people[4], and they declared that they had no one fit for this office, and when we together with them were the more distressed, they at length, with one common voice and consent, repeatedly solicited our venerable brother the presbyter Marinianus, who they learnt had been associated with me for a long time in a monastery. He, shrinking from the office, was at last, by various means, with difficulty persuaded to give assent to their petition. And, since we were well acquainted with his life, and knew him to be solicitous in winning souls, we did not delay his ordination. Let, therefore, your Glory receive him as is

3 On the term "Scholasticus," see V. 36, note 9. It appears from this and other epistles that persons thus designated were addressed as "Gloria vestra." The "Patrician" mentioned in this letter as having recommended the Archdeacon Donatus to succeed John as Archbishop of Ravenna, was Romanus Patricius, Exarch of Italy, who died A.D. 598. He is often addressed or referred to in the Epistles. See Index.

4 See above, V. 23.

becoming, and extend to his newness the aid of your succour. For to all, as you know, newness in any office whatever is very trying. But I have great confidence that Almighty God, who has vouchsafed to put him over His flock, will both stimulate him to give heed to what is inward, and comfort him with the loving-kindness of His grace for administering what is outward. But, inasmuch as, after his long enjoyment of quiet, his newness, as we have before said, will without doubt expose him to perturbation, I beg that, when he shall come to you flying from the whirlwinds of secular storms, he may always find in your heart a haven of rest, and be cheered by the boon of your charity. But you will soon learn how much you will find yourselves able to agree; for he comes unwillingly to the episcopate [5].

EPISTLE XLIX.

To Leander, Bishop.

Gregory to Leander, Bishop of Hispalis (*Seville*).

With what ardour I am athirst to see thee thou readest in the tables of thine own heart, since thou lovest me exceedingly. But since I cannot see thee, separated as thou art from me by long tracts of country, I have done what charity towards thee dictated, namely to transmit to thy Holiness, on the arrival here of our common son Probinus the presbyter, the book of Pastoral Rule, which I wrote at the commencement of my episcopate, and the books which thou knewest I had already composed on the exposition of the blessed Job. Some sheets indeed of the third and fourth parts of that work I have not sent to thy Charity, having already given those sheets only of the said parts to monasteries. These, then, which I send let thy Holiness earnestly peruse, and more earnestly deplore my sins, lest it be to my more serious blame that I am seen as it were to know what I omit to do. But with how great tumults of business I am oppressed in this Church the very brevity of my epistle will signify to thy Charity, seeing that I say so little to him whom more than all I love.

EPISTLE LII.

To John, Archbishop.

Gregory to John, Archbishop of the Corinthians.

The equity and solicitude of Secundinus our brother and fellow-bishop, which had been well known to us of old, is shewn also by the tenor of your letters. In this matter he has greatly pleased us, and made us glad, in that in the cause of Anastasius [6], once bishop, which we charged him to enquire into, he has both exercised his vigilance diligently and judged the crimes that were discovered as justice required, and as was right. But in all these things we return thanks to Almighty God for that, when certain accusers held back, He brought the truth to his knowledge, lest the originator of such great crimes should escape detection. But seeing that, in the sentence wherein it is evident that the above-named Anastasius has been justly condemned and deposed, our above-named brother and fellow-bishop has visited the offence of certain persons in such a manner as to reserve them for our judgment, we therefore have seen fit to signify by this present epistle what is to be held to and observed concerning them.

As to Paul the deacon then, the bearer of these presents, although his fault is exceedingly to his shame and discredit—namely, that deluded by promises, he held back from accusation of his late bishop who has been lately deposed, and that, in the eagerness of cupidity, he consented, against his own soul, to keep silence rather than declare the truth—yet, since it befits us to be more kind than strict, we pardon him this fault, and decide that he is to be received again into his rank and position. For we believe that the affliction which he has endured since the time of the sentence being pronounced may suffice for the punishment of this fault. But as to Euphemius and Thomas, who received sacred orders for relinquishing their accusation, it is our will that they be deprived of these sacred orders, and, having been deposed from them, so continue; and we decree that they shall never, under any pretext or excuse, be restored to sacred orders. For it is in the highest degree improper, and contrary to the rule of ecclesiastical discipline, that they should enjoy the dignity which they have received, not for their merits, but as the reward of wickedness. Yet, inasmuch as it is fit for us to incline to mercy more than to strict justice, it is our will that the same Euphemius and Thomas be restored to the rank and position, but to that only, from which they had been promoted to sacred orders, and receive during all the days of their life the stipends of these positions, as they had been before accustomed. Further, as to Clematius the reader, I appoint, from a like motive of benignity, that he is to be restored

[5] For subsequent notices of Marinianus, see Index.

[6] Anastasius, bishop of the Metropolitan See of Corinth, had been deposed for some serious crime, the nature of which is not mentioned, Secundinus, bishop of some other see, having apparently been commissioned by Gregory to investigate the charges against him. John, to whom this letter is addressed had now succeeded him. See also Epp. LVII., LVIII.

to his rank and position. To all these also, that is, to Paul the deacon, to Euphemius, Thomas, and Clematius, let your Fraternity take care to supply their emoluments, according to the rank and position in which each of them is, as each has been accustomed to receive them, from this present thirteenth indiction without any diminution. Inasmuch, therefore, as the above-named Paul the deacon asserts that he expended much for the advantage of your Church, and desires to be aided by the succour of your Fraternity for recovery of the same, we exhort that, if this is so, you should concur with him in all possible ways, and support him with your aid, for recovering what he has given, since no reason allows that he should unjustly suffer loss in what he has expended for the advantage of the generality. Furthermore, let your Fraternity restore without delay the three pounds of gold which, at the instance of our above-named brother and fellow-bishop Secundinus, it appears that the said Paul the deacon gave for the benefit of your Church, lest (which God forbid) you should seem to burden him, not reasonably, but out of mere caprice.

EPISTLE LIII.

To Virgilius, Bishop.

Gregory to Virgilius, Bishop of Arelate (*Arles*).

O how good is charity, which through an image in the mind exhibits what is absent as present to ourselves, through love unites what is divided, settles what is confused, associates things that are unequal, completes things that are imperfect! Rightly does the excellent preacher call it the bond of perfectness; since, though the other virtues indeed produce perfectness, yet still charity binds them together so that they can no longer be loosened from the heart of one who loves. Of this virtue, then, most dear brother, I find thee to be full, as both those who came from the Gallican parts and the words also of thy letter addressed to me testify to me of thee.

Now as to thy having asked therein, according to ancient custom, for the use of the pallium and the vicariate of the Apostolic See, far be it from me to suspect that thou hast sought eminence of transitory power, or the adornment of external worship, in our vicariate and in the pallium. But, since it is well known to all whence the holy faith proceeded in the regions of Gaul, when your Fraternity asks for a repetition of the old custom of the Apostolic See, what is it but that a good offspring reverts to the bosom of its mother?[7] With willing mind therefore we grant what has been asked for, lest we should seem either to withdraw from you anything of the honour due to you, or to have despised the petition of our most excellent son king Childebert. But the present state of things requires the greater earnestness, that with increase of dignity solicitude also may advance, and watchfulness in the custody of others may grow, and the merits of your life may serve as an example to your subjects, and that your Fraternity may never seek your own through the dignity accorded you, but the gains of the heavenly country. For you know what the blessed apostle says, groaning, *For all seek their own, not the things which are Jesus Christ's* (Philip. ii. 21).

For I have learnt from information given me by certain persons that in the parts of Gaul and Germany no one attains to holy orders except for a consideration given. If this is so, I say it with tears, I declare it with groans, that, when the priestly order has fallen inwardly, neither will it be able to stand outwardly for long. For we know from the Gospel what our Redeemer in person did; how He went into the temple, and overthrew the seats of them that sold doves (Matth. xxi. 12). For to sell doves is to receive a temporal consideration for the Holy Spirit, whom, being consubstantial with Himself, God Almighty gives to men through the imposition of hands. From which evil what follows is already intimated. For of those who presumed to sell doves in the temple of God the seats fell by God's judgment.

And in truth this transgression is propagated with increase among subordinates. For he who is promoted to any sacred order for a price, being already corrupted in the very root of his advancement, is the more ready to sell to others what he has bought. And where is that which is written, *Freely ye have received, freely give* (Matth. x. 8)?

And, seeing that the simoniacal heresy was

7 Gregory here asserts the view of his day, which after his manner he takes for granted, that Gaul had derived its Christianity from Rome. Similarly, long before him, pope Zosimus (417—418), writing to the bishops of Gaul in support of the jurisdiction over them of Patroclus of Arles, speaks of such jurisdiction being of ancient right, derived from Trophimus having been sent from Rome as first bishop of Arles, and all Gaul having received the stream of faith from that fountain. Gregory of Tours (*Hist. Franc.* i. 28), referring to *Passio S. Saturnini Episc. Solos.*, speaks of seven missionary bishops having been sent from Rome to Gaul "Decio et Grato consulibus," i.e. A.D. 250, including Trophimus, who is said to have founded the see of Arles. But the see of Arles must have existed before the date assigned, since it appears from Cyprian (Ep. VI. 7), that in 254 Marcian had long been its bishop. And generally, the well-known differences of the Gallican liturgy and usages from the Roman, to which pope Gregory himself alludes in his letter to Augustine (XI. 64), as well as Irenæus of Lyons, in the second century, being said to have been a disciple of Polycarp, points to an Asiatic rather than Roman origin of the Church in Gaul.

the first to arise against the holy Church, why is it not considered, why is it not seen, that whoso ordains any one for money, causes him, in advancing him, to become a heretic?

Another very detestable thing has also been reported to us; that some persons, being laymen, through desire of temporal glory, are tonsured on the death of bishops, and all at once are made priests. In such cases it is already known what manner of man he is who attains to priesthood, passing suddenly from a lay estate to sacred leadership. And one who has never served as a soldier fears not to become a leader of the religious[8]. How is that man to preach who has perhaps never heard any one else preach? Or how shall he correct the ills of others who has never yet bewailed his own? And, where Paul the apostle prohibits a neophyte from coming to sacred orders, we are to understand that, as one was then called a neophyte who had been newly planted in the faith, so we now reckon among neophytes one who is still new in holy conversation.

Moreover, we know that walls after being built, are not made to carry a weight of timber till they are dried of the moisture of their newness, lest, if a weight be put on them before they are settled, it bear down the whole fabric together to the ground. And, when we cut trees for a building, we wait for the moisture of their greenness to be first dried out, lest, if the weight of the fabric is imposed on them while still fresh, they be bent from their very newness, and be the sooner broken and fall down from having been elevated prematurely. Why, then, is not this scrupulously seen to among men, which is so carefully considered even in the case of timber and stones?

On this account your Fraternity must needs take care to admonish our most excellent son king Childebert that he remove entirely the stain of this sin from his kingdom, to the end that Almighty God may give him the greater recompense with Himself as He sees him both love what He loves and shun what He hates.

And so we commit to your Fraternity, according to ancient custom, under God, our vicariate in the Churches which are under the dominion of our most excellent son Childebert[9], with the understanding that their proper dignity, according to primitive usage, be preserved to the several metropolitans. We have also sent a pallium for thy Fraternity to use within the Church for the solemnization of mass only. Further, if any one of the bishops should by any chance wish to travel to any considerable distance, let it not be lawful for him to remove to other places without the authority of thy Holiness. If any question of faith, or it may be relating to other matters, should have arisen among the bishops, which cannot easily be settled, let it be ventilated and decided in an assembly of twelve bishops. But, if it cannot be decided after the truth has been investigated, let it be referred to our judgment.

Now may Almighty God keep you under His protection, and grant unto you to preserve by your behaviour the dignity that you have received. Given the 12th day of August, Indiction 13.

EPISTLE LIV.

To all the Bishops of the Kingdom of Childebert.

Gregory to all the Bishops of Gaul who are under the kingdom of Childebert[1].

To this end has the provision of the divine dispensation appointed that there should be diverse degrees and distinct orders, that, while the inferiors shew reverence to the more powerful and the more powerful bestow love on the inferiors, one contexture of concord may ensue of diversity, and the administration of all several offices may be properly borne. Nor indeed could the whole otherwise subsist; unless, that is, a great order of differences of this kind kept it together. Further, that creation cannot be governed, or live, in a state of absolute equality we are taught by the example of the heavenly hosts, since, there being angels and also archangels, it is manifest that they are not equal; but in power and rank, as you know, one differs from another. If then among these who are without sin there is evidently this distinction, who of men can refuse to submit himself willingly to this order of things which he knows that even angels obey? For hence peace and charity embrace each other mutually, and the sincerity of concord remains firm in the reciprocal love which is well pleasing to God.

Since, then each single duty is then salubriously fulfilled when there is one president who may be referred to, we have therefore perceived it to be opportune, in the Churches that are under the dominion of our most excel-

8 *Religiosorum*. The appellation is applied to persons generally who gave themselves to a religious life, including monks, nuns, dedicated virgins, and the like. It must be here taken to include the clergy.

9 Childebert II., the son of Sigebert I. and Brunehild, was at this time the ruler of nearly all the dominions of the Franks in Gaul. Having been proclaimed by the Australasian nobles king of Austrasia on the death of his father, A.D. 575, he acquired also Burgundy on the death of his uncle Guntramn in 593. These kingdoms at this time comprised by far the greatest part of Gaul, the kingdom of what was called Neustria under Clotaire II. including only a small territory on the north-west coast.

1 See preceding Epistle, note 9.

lent son king Childebert, to give our vicariate jurisdiction, according to ancient custom, to our brother Virgilius, bishop of the city of Arelate, to the end that the integrity of the catholic faith, that is of the four holy synods, may be preserved under the protection of God with attentive devotion, and that, if any contention should by chance arise among our brethren and fellow-priests, he may allay it by the vigour of his authority with discreet moderation, as representing the Apostolic See. We have also charged him that, if such a dispute should arise in any cases as to require the presence of others, he should assemble our brethren and fellow-bishops in competent number, and discuss the matter salubriously with due regard to equity, and decide it with canonical integrity. But if a contention (which may the Divine power avert) should happen to arise on matters of faith, or any business come up about which there may peichance be serious doubt, and he should be in need of the judgment of the Apostolic See in place of his own greatness, we have directed him that, having diligently enquired into the truth, he should take care to bring the question under our cognizance by a report from himself, to the end that it may be terminated by a suitable sentence so as to remove all doubt.

And, since it is necessary that the bishops should assemble at suitable times for conference before him to whom we have granted our vicariate jurisdiction as often as he may think it, we exhort that none of you presume to be disobedient to his orders, or defer attending the general conclave, unless perchance bodily infirmity should prevent any one, or a just excuse in any case should allow his absence. Yet let such as are unavoidably prevented from attending the synod send a presbyter or a deacon in their stead, to the end that the things that, with the help of God, may be decided by our vicar, may come to the knowledge of him who is absent by a faithful report through the person whom he had sent, and be observed with unshaken steadfastness, and that there be no occasion of excuse for daring to violate them.

About this also we take the precaution of warning you, that none of you may attempt in any way to depart to places at any great distance without the authority of our aforesaid brother and fellow-bishop Virgilius, knowing that the orders of our predecessors, who granted vicariate jurisdiction to his predecessors, undoubtedly lay this down.

Furthermore, we exhort that each one of you give careful attention to his own office, so that he who desires to receive the reward promised for feeding the sheep may guard the flock committed to him with carefulness and prayer, lest the prowling wolf should invade and tear the sheep entrusted to him, and there should be in the retribution punishment instead of reward. We hope, therefore, most dear brethren, and we entreat Almighty God with all our prayers, that He would make you to be fervent more and more in the constancy of His love, and grant you especially to be retained in the peace of the Church, and in agreement together.

It has been reported to us that some are promoted to sacred orders through simoniacal heresy; and we have ordered our above-written brother and fellow-bishop Virgilius that this must be altogether prohibited; and, that your Fraternity may know and studiously observe this, our letter to him is to be read in your presence. Given the 12th day of August, Indiction 13.

EPISTLE LV.

TO KING CHILDEBERT.

Gregory to Childebert, king of the Franks[a].

The letter of your Excellency has made us exceedingly glad, testifying as it does that you are careful, with pious affection, of the honour and reverence due to priests. For you thus shew to all that you are faithful worshippers of God, while you love His priests with the acceptable veneration that is due to them, and hasten with Christian devotion to do whatever may advance their position. Whence also we have received with pleasure what you have written, and grant what you desire with willing mind; and accordingly we have committed, with the favour of God, our vicariate jurisdiction to our brother Virgilius, bishop of the city of Arelate, according to ancient custom and your Excellency's desire; and have also granted him the use of the pallium, as has been the custom of old.

But, inasmuch as some things have been reported to us which greatly offend Almighty God, and confound the honour and reverence due to the priesthood, we beg that they may be in every way amended with the support of the censure of your power, lest, while headstrong and perverse doings run counter to your devotion, your kingdom, or your soul (which God forbid) be burdened by the guilt of others.

Further, it has come to our knowledge that on the death of bishops some persons from being laymen are tonsured, and mount to the episcopate by a sudden leap. And thus one

[a] See Ep. LIII., note 9.

who has not been a disciple is in his inconsiderate ambition made a master. And, since he has not learned what to teach, he bears the office of priesthood only in name; for he continues to be a layman in speech and action as before. How, then, is he to intercede for the sins of others, not having in the first place bewailed his own? For such a shepherd does not defend, but deceives, the flock; since, while he cannot for very shame try to persuade others to do what he does not do himself, what else is it but that the Lord's people remains a prey to robbers, and catches destruction from the source whence it ought to have had a great support of wholesome protection? How bad and how perverse a proceeding this is let your Excellency's Highness consider even from your own administration of things. For it is certain that you do not put a leader over an army unless his work and his fidelity have first been apparent; unless the virtue and industry of his previous life have shewn him to be a fit person. But, if the command of an army is not committed to any but men of this kind, it is easily gathered from this comparison of what sort a leader of souls ought to be. But it is a reproach to us, and we are ashamed to say it, that priests snatch at leadership who have not seen the very beginning of religious warfare.

But this also, a thing most execrable, has been reported to us as well: that sacred orders are conferred through simoniacal heresy, that is for bribes received. And, seeing that it is exceedingly pestiferous, and contrary to the Universal Church, that one be promoted to any sacred order not for merit but for a price, we exhort your Excellency to order so detestable a wickedness to be banished from your kingdom. For that man shews himself to be thoroughly unworthy of this office, who fears not to buy the gift of God with money, and presumes to try to get by payment what he deserves not to have through grace.

These things, then, most excellent son, I admonish you about for this reason, that I desire your soul to be saved. And I should have written about them before now, had not innumerable occupations stood in the way of my will. But now that a suitable time for answering your letter has offered itself, I have not omitted what it was my duty to do. Wherefore, greeting your Excellency with the affection of paternal charity, we beg that all things which we have enjoined on our above-named brother and fellow-bishop to be done and observed, may be carried out under the protection of your favour, and that you allow them not to be in any way upset by the elation or pride of any one. But, as they were observed by his predecessor under the reign of your glorious father, so let them be observed now also, by your aid, with zealous devotion. It is right, then, that we should thus have a return made to us; and that, as we have not deferred fulfilling your will, so you too, for the sake of God and the blessed Peter, Prince of the apostles, should cause our ordinances to be observed in all respects; that so your Excellency's reputation, praiseworthy and well-pleasing to God, may extend itself all around. Given the 12th day of August, Indiction 13.

EPISTLE LVI.

To Marinianus, Bishop.

Gregory to Marinianus, Bishop of Ravenna.

Moved by the benevolence of the Apostolical See and the order of ancient custom, we have thought fit to grant the use of the pallium to thy Fraternity, who art known to have undertaken the office of government in the Church of Ravenna[3]. And remember thou to use it in no other way but in the proper Church of thy city, when the sons (i.e. *laity*) have been already dismissed, as thou art proceeding from the audience chamber[4] to celebrate the sacred solemnities of mass; but, when mass is finished, thou wilt take care to lay it by again in the audience chamber. But outside the Church, we do not allow thee to use it any more, except four times in the year, in the litanies which we named to thy predecessor John; giving thee at the same time this admonition; that, as through the Lord's bounty thou hast obtained from us the use of an adornment of this kind to the honour of the priestly office, so thou strive to adorn also the office undertaken by thee to the glory of Christ with probity of manners and of deeds. For thus wilt thou be conspicuous for two adornments answering to each other, if with such a vesture of the body as this the good qualities also of thy soul agree. For all privileges also which appear evidently to have been formerly granted to thy Church we confirm by our authority, and decree that they continue inviolate.

EPISTLE LVII.

To John, Bishop.

Gregory to John, Bishop of the Corinthians

Now that our God, from whom nothing is hidden, having cast out an atrocious plague of pollution from the government of His Church[5],

---

3 With regard to the use of the pallium claimed by, and allowed to, John, the preceding bishop of Ravenna, see III. 56, 57; V. 11, 15. For further contentions with Marinianus on the subject, see VI. 34, 61.

4 *Salutatario*: called in previous letters to Archbishop John, *secretarium*. See III. 56, note 2.

5 See above, V. 52, and Ep. LVIII., below.

has been pleased to advance you to the rule thereof, there is need of anxious precaution on your part that the Lord's flock, after the wounds and various evils inflicted by its former shepherd, may find consolation and wholesome medicine in your Fraternity. Thus, then, let the hand of your action wipe away the stain of the previous contagion, so as to suffer no traces even to remain of that execrable wickedness.

Let, therefore, your solicitude towards your subjects be worthy of praise. Let discipline be exhibited with gentleness. Let rebuke be with discernment. Let kindness mitigate wrath; let zeal sharpen kindness: and let one be so seasoned with the other that neither immoderate punishment afflict more than it ought, nor again laxity impair the rectitude of discipline. Let the conduct of your Fraternity be a lesson to the people committed to you. Let them see in you what to love, and perceive what to make haste to imitate. Let them be taught how to live by your example. Let them not deviate from the straight course through your leading; let them find their way to God by following you; that so thou mayest receive as many rewards from the Saviour of the human race as thou shalt have won souls for Him. Labour therefore, most dear brother, and so direct the whole activity of thy heart and soul, that thou mayest hereafter be counted worthy to hear, *Well done, thou good and faithful servant: enter thou into the joy of thy Lord* (Matth. xxv. 21).

As you requested in your letter which we received through our brother and fellow-bishop Andrew, we have sent you the pallium, which it is necessary that you should so use as your predecessors, by the allowance of our predecessors, are proved to have used it.

Furthermore, it has come to our ears that in those parts no one attains to any sacred order without the giving of a consideration. If this is so, I say with tears, I declare with groans, that, when the priestly order has fallen inwardly, neither will it stand long outwardly. For we know from the Gospel what our Redeemer in person did; how He went into the temple, and overthrew the seats of them that sold doves (Matth. xxi. 12). For to sell doves is to receive a temporal consideration for the Holy Spirit, whom, being consubstantial with Himself, Almighty God gives to men through imposition of hands. And what follows from this evil, as I have said before, is intimated; for the seats of those who presumed to sell doves in the temple of God fell by the judgment of God. And in truth this transgression is propagated with increase among subordinates. For one who attains to a sacred dignity tainted in the very root of his promotion is himself the more prepared to sell to others what he has bought. And where then is that which is written, *Freely ye have received; freely give* (Matth. x. 8)? And, since the simoniacal heresy was the first to arise against holy Church, why is it not considered, why is it not seen, that whosoever ordains any one for a price in promoting him causes him to become a heretic? Seeing, then, that the holy universal Church utterly condemns this most atrocious wickedness, we exhort your Fraternity in all ways to repress, with all the urgency of your solicitude, this so detestable and so huge a sin in all places that are under you. For, if we shall perceive anything of the kind to be done henceforth, we will correct it, not with words, but with canonical punishment; and we shall begin to have a different opinion of you; which ought not so to be.

Further, your Fraternity knows that formerly the pallium was not given except for a consideration received. But, since this was incongruous, we held a council before the body of the blessed Peter, Prince of the apostles, and forbade under a strict interdiction the receiving of anything, as well for this as for ordinations.

It is your duty then, that neither for a consideration, nor for favour or the solicitation of certain persons, you consent to any persons being advanced to sacred orders. For it is a grave sin, as we have said, and we cannot suffer it to continue without reproof.

I delayed receiving the above named Andrew, our brother and fellow-bishop, because by the report of our brother and fellow-bishop Secundinus we learnt that he had forged letters, as to himself from us, in the proceedings against John of Larissa[6]. And, unless your goodness had induced us, we would on no account have received him. Given the 15th day of the month of August, Indiction 13.

EPISTLE LVIII.

To all the Bishops throughout Helladia[7].

Gregory to all bishops constituted in the province of Helladia.

I return thanks with you, dearest brethren, to Almighty God, who has caused the hidden sore which the ancient enemy had introduced to come to the knowledge of all, and has cut it away by a wholesome incision from the body of His Church. Herein we have cause both to rejoice and to mourn; to rejoice, that is, for

[6] See III. 6, 7.

[7] Meaning, we may suppose, the province of Achaia, of which Corinth was the metropolis.

the correction of a crime, but to mourn for the fall of a brother. But, since for the most part the fall of one is wont to be the safeguard of another, whosoever fears to fall, let him give heed to this, that he afford no way of approach to the enemy, nor think that deeds done lie hidden. For the Truth proclaims, *There is nothing hidden that shall not be revealed* (Matth. x. 26). For this voice is already the herald of our doings, and He himself, being witness, brings in all ways to public view what is done in secret. And who may strive to hide his deeds before Him Who is both their witness and their judge? But, since sometimes, when one thing is attended to, another is not guarded against, it behoves every one to be watchful against all the snares of the enemy, lest, while he conquers in one point he be vanquished in another. For an earthly enemy too, when he desires to invade fortified places, thus employs the art of warfare. For indeed he lays ambushes latently; but shews himself as though entirely bent on the storming of one place, so that, while there is a running together for defence of that place where the danger is imminent, other places about which there is no suspicion may be taken. And the result is, that he who, when perceived, was repulsed by the valour of his opponent, obtains by stealth what he could not obtain by fighting. But, since in all these things there is need of the aid of divine protection, let every one of us cry to the Lord with the voice of the heart, saying, *Lord, remove not Thy help far from me; look Thou to my defence* (Ps. xxi. 20)[8]. For it is manifest that, unless He Himself should help, and defend those who cry to Him, our enemy cannot be vanquished.

Furthermore, know ye that, having received the letter of your Charity through Andrew our brother and fellow-bishop, we have transmitted the pallium to John our brother, the bishop of the Corinthians; whom it is by all means fitting that you should obey, especially as the order of ancient custom claims this, and his good qualities, to which you yourselves bear testimony, invite it. For from the account given me by certain persons I have learnt that in those parts no one attains to any sacred order without the giving of a consideration. If this is so, I say with tears, I declare with groans, that, when the priestly order has fallen inwardly, neither will it be able to stand long outwardly. For we know from the Gospel what our Redeemer did in person; how He went into the temple, and overthrew the seats of them that sold doves. For in truth to sell doves is to receive a temporal consideration for the Holy Spirit, whom, being consubstantial with Himself, Almighty God gives to men through imposition of hands. And, as I have said before, what follows from this evil is intimated; for the seats of them that presumed to sell doves in the temple of God fell by God's judgment. And in truth this transgression is propagated with increase among subordinates. For he who is advanced to a sacred order already tainted in the very root of his promotion is himself more prepared to sell to others what he has bought. And where is that which is written, *Freely ye have received; freely give* (Matth. x. 8)? And, since the simoniacal heresy was the first to arise against the holy Church, why is it not considered, why is it not seen, that whosoever ordains any one for a price in promoting him causes him to become a heretic? And so we exhort that none of you suffer this to be done any more; or dare to promote any to sacred orders for the favour or supplication of any person, except such a one as the character of his life and actions has shewn to be worthy. For, if we should perceive the contrary in future, know ye that it will be repressed with strict and canonical punishment. Given on the 15th day of the month of August, Indiction 13.

[8] In *English Bible*, xxii.

BOOK VI

EPISTLE I.

To Marinianus, Bishop.

Gregory to Marinianus, Bishop of Ravenna.

As unjust demands should not be conceded, so the petition of such as desire what is lawful ought not to be set aside. Now your Fraternity's presbyters, deacons and clergy have presented to us a petition complaining that the late John, your predecessor, made a will burdening his Church with various bequests. And they have petitioned that these, which are to the detriment of his Church, should under no excuse be paid, as being prohibited by law. And although, heredity and succession having been by him renounced, no reason binds thee to satisfy any such claims, nevertheless we hereby exhort thee over and above that with regard to such bequests as he has made, contrary to the ordinances of the laws, of property belonging to his Church, or acquired by him in his episcopate, your Fraternity neither lend your authority nor on any account consent to them. But, if he has wished or directed anything to be done with regard to his private property which he had before his episcopate, and which he had not previously bestowed upon his Church, it is necessary that this disposition should be held valid in all respects, and that no one of the ecclesiastics should attempt against reason on any pretext to set it aside.

But, inasmuch as during his life he often begged of us that we should confirm by our authority what he had conferred on the monastery which he had himself constructed near the church of Saint Apollinaris, and we promised to do this, we hold it needful to exhort your Fraternity to suffer nothing of what he has there conferred and constituted to be diminished, but to see to all being preserved and firmly established. Since, then, he is known to have made mention of this monastery, and of the property conferred on it, in the will which he made, you must know that we have not confirmed this part of it by reason of our following his last wishes, but because, as we have said, we promised it to him when he was alive. Let your Fraternity, therefore, make haste so carefully to accomplish all these things that both what was by him constituted and by us confirmed in the above-named monastery may be maintained, and what he has by will directed to be given or done to the detriment of his Church may have no validity, seeing that the law forbids it.

EPISTLE II.

To the Clergy and People of Ravenna.

Gregory to the clergy and people of the Church of Ravenna.

We have been informed that certain men, instigated by the malignant spirit, have wished to corrupt your minds by false speech with regard to the reputation of our brother and fellow-bishop Marinianus[1]; saying that this our brother venerates the holy synod of Chalcedon less than becomes him[2]. On this head both he himself in person will satisfy you all of the integrity of his faith, and we fully testify that, having been nursed from his cradle in the bosom of the holy Universal Church, he has held the right preaching of the faith with the attestation of his life. For he venerates the holy Nicene synod in which Arius, the Constantinopolitan, in which Macedonius, the first Ephesine, in which Nestorius, and the holy Chalcedonian, in which Dioscorus and Eutyches were condemned. And if any one presumes ever to speak anything against the faith of these four synods and against the tome and definition of pope Leo of holy memory, let him be anathema. Accordingly, receiving the fullest satisfaction, love ye your pastor in entire charity with a pure heart, that the intercession of the same your pastor, poured out purely before God, may avail to your profit.

---

[1] See above, V. 48, note 3.

[2] The ground of this charge against Marinianus was doubtless his acceptance of the condemnation of the "Three Chapters" by the fifth council, which condemnation, notwithstanding Rome's approval of it, was still objected to in many quarters as contravening the council of Chalcedon. See I. 16, note 3; IV. 2, note 1; IV. 38, 39; XIV. 12.

EPISTLE III.

To Maximus of Salona.

Gregory to Maximus, pretender to the Church of Salona [3].

As often as anything is said to have been done contrary to ecclesiastical discipline, we dare not leave it unexamined, lest we should be guilty before God for connivance. Now it has come to our ears that thou wast ordained by means of simoniacal heresy. Nay and many other things have been said of thee here, whereof there was one especially on account of which we held it needful to prohibit thee urgently by letter from celebrating the solemnities of mass until we might ascertain the state of the case more certainly. Wherefore, lest the children of the Church should be too long without a shepherd, and lest, in case of these things which are said remaining unexamined, vice of this nature should extend itself to many, we exhort thee to make haste to come to us, laying aside all excuses, to the end that with due regard to justice we may be able to gain knowledge of these things, and terminate them according to the canonical institutes, Christ shewing us the way. But do thou so act that there be no more of these successive delays of thy coming, lest thy very absence point thee out as the more obnoxious to these charges against thee, and lest we should be thus compelled to pass in council a harder sentence on thee, not only for thy alleged crimes from which thou evadest purging thyself, but also for the fault of disobedience, to wit as one that is contumacious.

EPISTLE V.

To Queen Brunichild.

Gregory to Brunichild, Queen of the Franks [4].

The laudable and God-pleasing goodness of your Excellence is manifested both by your government of your kingdom and by your education of your son [5]. To him you have not only with provident solicitude conserved intact the glory of temporal things, but have also seen to the rewards of eternal life, having planted his mind in the root of the true faith with maternal, as became you, and laudable care of his education. Whence not undeservedly it ensues that he should surpass all the kingdoms of the nations [6], in that he both worships purely and confesses truly the Creator of these nations. But that faith may shine forth in him the more laudably in his works, let the words of your exhortation kindle him, to the end that, as royal power shews him lofty among men, so goodness of conduct may make him great before God.

Now inasmuch as past experience in many instances gives us confidence in the Christianity of your Excellence, we beg of you, for the love of Peter, Prince of the apostles, whom we know that you love with your whole heart, that you would cherish with the aid of your patronage our most beloved son the presbyter Candidus [7], who is the bearer of these presents, together with the little patrimony for the government of which we have sent him, to the end that, strengthened by the favour of your support, he may be able both to manage profitably this little patrimony, which is evidently beneficial towards the expenses of the poor, and also to recover into the possession of this little patrimony anything that may have been taken away from it. For it is not without increase of your praise that after so long a time a man belonging to Church has been sent for the management of this patrimony. Let your Excellency, then, deign so willingly to give your attention to what we request of you that the blessed Peter, Prince of the apostles, to whom the power of binding and loosing has been given by the Lord Jesus Christ, may both grant to your Excellence to rejoice here in your offspring, and after courses of many years

3 Cf. III. 47, note 2. As is there stated, Maximus does not seem to have paid the slightest attention to this letter.

4 This is the first of the ten letters of Gregory to the notorious Brunechild. A daughter of Athanagild, king of the Visigoths in Spain, she had married Sigebert I., one of the grandsons of Clovis, who reigned over that part of the dominion of the Franks which was called Austrasia, having on her marriage renounced Arianism for Catholicity. Sigebert having been assassinated A.D. 575, his son Childebert II., then only five years old, was proclaimed King of Austrasia; whereupon Brunechild herself became the virtual ruler of the kingdom. So she was again after the death of Childebert, A.D. 596, as guardian of Theodebert II., his illegitimate son, who succeeded him at the age of ten years. See *Pedigree of Kings of Gaul*, p. xxx.

The praises lavished on her by Gregory in this and his other epistles to her appear strangely inconsistent with the character given her by the historians of the time. It has been suggested in explanation; 1. That the historians may have maligned her, attributing to her crimes that were not her own; 2. That, whatever her misdemeanours, Gregory might not have heard of them, knowing of her only as a faithful Catholic, and a supporter of the Church; 3. That no such misdemeanours had become notorious when Gregory wrote to her in such flattering terms, the worst doings imputed to her having in fact been after his death. She survived him some nine years. Still, when we consider Gregory's diplomatic turn, together with his habitual deference to potentates apparent elsewhere, we cannot think it unlikely that he might ignore purposely in his addresses to them even their known moral delinquencies, so long as he could enlist their support of religion and orthodoxy, or their loyalty to the see of Rome. And, after all, Brunechild may not have been much worse than some other Frank royalties, all of whom he would be naturally and properly desirous of conciliating, and making the best of them he could. A less defensible instance of apparently politic flattery is found in his letters to the Emperor Phocas and his Empress Leontia after the deposition and murder of Mauricius. See XIII. 31, 38, 39, and *Proleg.*, p. xxvii.

5 Childebert II. (see last note), who had been a minor when he came to the throne. He would now, if the epistle was written, as supposed, in the 14th Indiction (595-6), be about 25 years old.

6 Since the death of his uncle Guntramn, A.D. 593, he had become King of Burgundy as well as of Austrasia.

7 It was the sending Candidus, a presbyter from Rome, to take charge of the patrimony in Gaul in place of Dynamius, a patrician, who had previously managed it (see *Ep.* 6), that offered occasion for this and the following letter.

cause you to be found, absolved from all ills, before the face of the eternal Judge.

EPISTLE VI.

To King Childebert.

Gregory to Childebert, King of the Franks [8].

As much as royal dignity is above that of other men, so much in truth does the high position of your kingdom excel that of the kingdoms of other nations. And yet to be a king is not extraordinary, there being others also; but to be a Catholic, which others are not counted worthy to be, this is enough. For as the splendour of a great lamp shines by the clearness of its light in the darkness of earth's night, so the clear light of your faith glitters and flashes amid the dark perfidy of other nations. Whatever the other kings glory in having you have. But they are in this regard exceedingly surpassed, because they have not the chief good thing which you have. In order, then, that they may be overcome in action as well as in faith, let your Excellence always shew yourself kind to your subjects. And, if there are any things such as to offend your mind, punish them not without enquiry. For then you will the more please the King of kings, that is the Almighty Lord, if, restraining your power, you feel that you may not do all that you can.

Now that you keep purity of faith both in mind and deed, the love that is in you of the blessed Peter, Prince of the apostles, evidently shews, whose property has been so far well governed and preserved under the sway of your supremacy. But since Dynamius the Patrician, who on our recommendation looked after this property, is not able, as we have learnt, to govern it now, lest the little patrimony which is in your parts should be ruined from neglect, we have therefore sent the bearer of these presents, our most beloved son the presbyter Candidus [9] to govern it, whom we commend in all respects to your Excellency, greeting you in the first place with paternal charity, with the request that, if by any chance any wrong has been done there, or if the property of the same little patrimony is detained by any one, the matter may be set right, and what has been alienated may be restored to its original ownership; that so your equity, as well as your faith, may shine forth to all nations, which will be something very glorious and laudable.

Moreover we have sent to your Excellency Saint Peter's keys, containing a portion of his chains, to protect you from all evils, when hung on your neck [1].

[8] Cf. last Epistle, notes 5, 6, 7

[9] See last Epistle note 8.

EPISTLE VII.

To Candidus, Presbyter.

Gregory to Candidus, Presbyter, going to the patrimony of Gaul.

Now that thou art proceeding, with the help of our Lord God Jesus Christ, to the government of the patrimony that is in Gaul, we desire thy Love to procure with the money thou mayest receive clothing for the poor, or English boys of about seventeen or eighteen years of age, who may profit by being given to God in monasteries, that so the money of Gaul, which cannot be spent in our country [2], may be expended profitably in its own locality. Further, if you should succeed in getting anything from the moneys accruing to revenue which are called *ablatae* [3], from this too we desire thee to procure clothing for the poor, or, as we have before said, boys who may profit in the service of Almighty God. But, since such as can be found there are pagans, I desire that a presbyter be sent hither with them to provide against the case of any sickness occurring on the way, that he may baptize those whom he sees to be about to die. Wherefore let your Love so proceed as to lose no time in accomplishing these things diligently.

EPISTLE VIII.

To the Bishops of Epirus.

Gregory to Theodorus, Demetrius, Philip, Zeno, and Alcissonus, Bishops of Epirus.

The notification of your letters, most dear brethren, has made known to us that our brother Andrew has, by the favour of God, been solemnly ordained bishop of the city of Nicopolis. And, since you signify that his consecration has taken place with the assent of the clergy and provincials, we rejoice; and we pray that the good which you testify of him may remain in him, and by the co-operation of God's grace receive increase, since the goodness of prelates is the safety of their subordinates. It is your duty then to make haste studiously to imitate what you shew by your praises to be pleasing to you in his person. For it is faulty before men and penal

[1] See IV. 30.

[2] Probably because of the inferior value in Italy of Gallic gold. "Nullus solidum integri ponderis calumniosæ approbationis obtentu recuset exactor, excepto eo Gallico cujus aurum minore æstimatione taxatur." *Novella Majoriani.*

[3] Some kind of due, so-called. See Du Cange under Ablata: —"Ablatio, Exactio, Tolta. . . 'Liberos deinceps esse constituimus ab omni tallia, ablatione et exactione, et questu.' (A. 1173)."

before God for any one to be unwilling to imitate the good that pleases him. Wherefore let your obedience supply credit to your testimony. Let no one gainsay him in what, with preservation of integrity, he may enjoin for the common profit of the Church. Let each one of you willingly exhibit his devotion; that, while there is among you priestly concord pleasing to God and constant, no ill feeling may avail to loose you from the bond of mutual charity, or difference disturb you. For neither will there be access to your hearts for the crafty foe, since he knows that he can in no degree be admitted or received, where sincere charity finds place.

Moreover be ye attentive, most dear brethren, and bestow on the flock committed to you the vigilance which ye have taken upon yourselves, and which ye owe; meet the frauds of the enemy by attention and prayer. Surrender with uncontaminated faith to our God the people over which ye are, that your priestly office may avail you not for a penalty but for a crown before the sight of the eternal Judge.

Know ye then that we have sent a pallium to the above-written Andrew our brother and fellow-bishop, and have granted him all the privileges which our predecessors conferred on his predecessors.

Furthermore, it has come to our ears that sacred orders in your parts are conferred for a consideration given. And, if this is so, I say it with tears, I declare it with groans, &c. [See Lib. V. Ep. 53, to "become a heretic"][4]. On this account I admonish and conjure you to be altogether attentive to this, that no giving of a consideration, no favour, no supplication of any persons whatsoever, put in any claim in regard to sacred orders, but that one be promoted to this office whom gravity of manners and behaviour commends. For if, as we do not believe will be the case, we should perceive anything of the kind to be done, we will correct it, as is fit, with canonical severity. Now may Almighty God, who orders all things wonderfully by the power of His wisdom, and guards what He has ordered, grant unto you both to will and to do what He commands.

EPISTLE IX.

To Donus, Bishop.

Gregory to Donus, Bishop of Messana (*Messene*).

Moved by the benevolence of the Apostolic See, and by the order of ancient custom, we have thought fit to grant to thee, who art known to have undertaken the office of government in the Church of Messana, the use of the pallium; to wit, at such times and in such manner as we dispute not that thy predecessor used it; at the same time warning thee that, as thou rejoicest in having received from us a decoration of this kind to the honour of thy priestly office, so also thou strive, by probity of manners and deeds, to adorn, to the glory of Christ, the office which thou hast undertaken under our authority. For so wilt thou be conspicuous for decorations mutually answering to each other, if with such an habiliment of the body as this all good qualities of thy soul also agree. For all the privileges which are known to have been granted of old to thy Church we confirm by our authority, and decree that they shall continue inviolate.

EPISTLE XII.

To Montana and Thomas.

Gregory to Montana, &c.

Since our Redeemer, the Maker of every creature, vouchsafed to assume human flesh for this end, that, the chain of slavery wherewith we were held being broken by the grace of His Divinity, He might restore us to pristine liberty, it is a salutary deed if men whom nature originally produced free, and whom the law of nations has subjected to the yoke of slavery, be restored by the benefit of manumission to the liberty in which they were born. And so, moved by loving-kindness and by consideration of this case, we make you, Montana and Thomas, servants of the holy Roman Church which with the help of God we serve, free from this day, and Roman citizens, and we release to you all your private property.

And, inasmuch as thou, Montana, declarest that thou hast applied thy mind to monastic profession, we therefore this day give and grant to thee two *unciæ*, which the presbyter Gaudiosus by the disposition of his last will is known to have left to thee in the way of institution [5], provided that all go in all respects to the advantage of the monastery of Saint Laurence, over which the abbess Constantina presides, and in which by the mercy of God thou art about to make profession. But, if it should appear that thou hast in any way concealed any part of the property left by the above-written Gaudiosus, the whole of this must undoubtedly be transferred to the possession of our Church.

[4] This form of protest against simony is found, in the same words, in several other letters.

[5] *Institutionis*; a legal term, denoting apparently the constituting of a person as an inheritor.

Moreover to thee, Thomas above-written, whom for enhancement of thy freedom we desire also to serve among the notaries, we in like manner this day give and grant by this writ of manumission the five *unciæ* which the aforesaid presbyter Gaudiosus by his last will left to thee under the title of inheritance, together with the dowry which he had bestowed upon thy mother; to wit with this annexed law and condition, that, in case of thy dying without legitimate children, that is children born in lawful wedlock, all that we have granted thee shall revert without any diminution to the possession of the holy Roman Church. But, if thou shouldest have children born in wedlock, as we have said, and recognized by the law, and shouldest leave them surviving thee, then we appoint thee to remain master of this same property without any condition, and give thee full power to make a will with respect to it. These things, then, which we have appointed and granted by this charter of manumission, know ye that we and our successors will observe without any demur. For the rule of justice and reason suggests that one who desires his own orders to be observed by his successors should undoubtedly keep to the will and ordinances of his predecessor. This writ of manumission we have dictated to the notary Paterius to be put in writing, and for the fullest security have subscribed it with our own hand, together with three chief presbyters and three deacons, and have delivered it to you.

Done in the city of Rome.

EPISTLE XIV.

To the Count Narses[6].

Gregory to Narses, &c.

Your Charity, being anxious to learn our opinion, has been at the pains of writing to us to ask what we think of the book against the presbyter Athanasius which was sent to us. Having thoroughly perused some parts of it, we find that he has fallen into the dogma of Manichæus. But he who has noted some places as heretical by a mark set against them slips also himself into Pelagian heresy; for he has marked certain places as heretical which are catholicly expressed and entirely orthodox. For when this is written; that when Adam sinned his soul died, the writer shews afterwards how it is said to have died, namely that it lost the blessedness of its condition. Whosoever denies this is not a Catholic. For God had said, *In the hour ye eat thereof, in death ye shall die* (Gen. ii. 17). When, therefore, Adam ate of the forbidden tree, we know that he did not die in the body, seeing that after this he begat children and lived many years. If, then, he did not die in the soul, the impious conclusion follows that He himself lied who foretold that in the day that he sinned he should die. But it is to be understood that death takes place in two ways; either from ceasing to live, or with respect to the mode of living. When, then, man's soul is said to have died in the eating of the forbidden thing, it is meant, not in the sense of ceasing to live, but with regard to the mode of living;—that he should live afterwards in pain who had been created to live happily in joy[7]. He, then, who has marked this passage in the book sent to me by my brother the bishop John as heretical is a Pelagian; for his view is evidently that of Pelagius, which the apostle Paul plainly confutes in his epistles. The particular passages in his epistle I need not quote, as I write to one who knows. But Pelagius, who was condemned in the Ephesine synod, maintained this view with the intention of shewing that we were redeemed by Christ unreally. For, if we did not through Adam die in the soul, we were redeemed unreally, which it were impious to say. Further, having examined the acts of the synod of Ephesus, we find nothing at all about Adelphius and Sava, and the others who are said to have been condemned there, and we think that, as the synod of Chalcedon was in one place falsified by the Constantinopolitan Church[8], so something of the kind has been done with regard to the synod of Ephesus. Wherefore let your Charity make a thorough search for old copies of the acts of this synod, and thus see whether anything of the kind is found there, and send such copy as you may find to me, which I will return as soon as I have read it. For recent copies are not entirely to be trusted; and it is for this reason that I have been in doubt, and have not wished as yet to reply in this case to my aforesaid brother the bishop John. Further, the Roman copies are much more correct than the Greek

[6] On the case of John of Chalcedon and Athanasius of Isauria, referred to in this and the three following letters, see III. 53, note 9.

[7] Cf. VII. 34 and IX. 49, where the same argument, in nearly the same words, is set forth.

[8] The reference may be to Canon xxviii. of the Council of Chalcedon, assigning rank and jurisdiction to the patriarchs of Constantinople, which was protested against by the Roman legates at the Council. and afterwards disallowed by Pope Leo. It is omitted in the Latin version of the canons published by Dionysius Exiguus about the beginning of the sixth century, though it had been in the *Prisca Versio* which he amended. It appears as if Gregory, not finding it in the Latin version before him, supposed it to have been interpolated at Constantinople; the fact being that it had been purposely omitted at Rome, as not having the Pope's sanction. If such is the allusion, it may seem strange that Gregory did not know the circumstances better. But this is not the only instance of his imperfect knowledge of past events, even in ecclesiastical matters. Cf. II. 51, note 2.

ones, since, as we have not your cleverness, so neither have we any impostures.

Now concerning the presbyter John, know that his case has been decided in synod, whereby I have clearly ascertained that his adversaries have wished and long endeavoured to make him out a heretic, but have entirely failed.

Salute in my name your friends, who are ours: ours also, who are yours, salute you heartily through me. May Almighty God protect thee with His hand in the midst of so many thorns, that thou mayest, unhurt, gather those flowers which the Lord hath chosen.

EPISTLE XV.

To John, Bishop.

Gregory to John, Bishop of Constantinople.

As the pravity of heretics is to be repressed by the zeal of a right faith, so the integrity of a true confession is to be embraced. For, if one who declares himself sound in the faith is scorned, the faith of all is brought into doubt, and fatal errors are generated from inconsiderate strictness. And hence not only are wandering sheep not recalled to their lord's folds, but even those that are within them are exposed to be cruelly torn by the teeth of wild beasts. Let us then fully consider this, most dear brother, and not suffer any one who truly professes the catholic faith to be distressed under pretext of heresy, nor (which God forbid) allow heresy to grow the more under shew of correcting it.

But we have wondered much why those who were deputed by you as judges in a matter of faith against John, presbyter of the church of Chalcedon, believed report, disregarding truth, and would not believe him when he distinctly professed his faith; especially as his accusers, when asked what was the heresy of the Marcionists which they spoke of, and on the ground of which they endeavoured to make him out guilty, replied by a plain confession that they did not know. From which circumstance it evidently comes out that, without regard to God, not justly, but against their own souls, they were desirous only of injuring him personally of their own mere will. We therefore, after Council held (as the tenor of the proceedings before us shews), having thoroughly examined and considered all that was necessary, inasmuch as we have been unable to find the aforesaid presbyter in any respect guilty, and especially as the plea which he delivered to the judges delegated by you is in entire accordance with the integrity of a right faith, we I say on this account, disapproving the sentence of the said judges, through the revealing grace of Christ our God and Redeemer, pronounce him by our definite sentence catholic and free from all charge of heresy. Seeing, then, that we have sent him back to your Holiness, it is for you to receive him with the kindness which you shew to all, and bestow on him your priestly charity, and defend him from all molestation, nor allow any one to busy himself in causing him trouble: but, as you defend others from oppression, so from him ought you not to withold your succour.

EPISTLE XVI.

To Mauricius, Augustus.

Gregory to Mauricius, &c.

Seeing that in you, most Christian of princes, uncorrupt soundness of faith shines as a beam sent down from heaven, and that it is known to all that your Serenity embraces fervently and loves with entire devotion of heart the pure profession in which by God's favour you are powerful, we have perceived it to be very necessary to make request for those whom one and the same faith enlightens, to the end that the Piety of our lords may protect them with its favour, and defend them from all molestation. When certain men scorn the confession of faith of such persons they are shewn to contradict the true faith. For, since the Apostle declares that confession of the mouth is made unto salvation, he who will not consent to believe a right profession accuses himself in rejecting others (Rom. x. 10).

Now all the proceedings against John, presbyter of the church of Chalcedon, having been read in council and considered in order, we have found that he has suffered the greater injustice in that, when he declared and shewed himself to be a Catholic, it was not his guilt, but an uncertain accusation of long standing, that crushed him; and this to such an extent that his accusers declared in their open reply that they did not know the heresy of the Marcionists which they referred to. And, whereas they ought therefore to have been rejected from the very beginning of the trial, they were allowed, vague as they were, to remain in court for his accusation. But, lest at any rate alleged report might injure him, he produced a written confession of his faith with the purpose of shewing evidently that he was a professor and follower of the right faith. But this the judges deputed by the most holy John, our brother and fellow-bishop, unjustly and unreasonably disregarded; and so, in doing all they could to put him down, shewed themselves more to blame than he. For no one doubts that it is unfaithfulness not to have faith in the faithful. Seeing then that, everything having been thoroughly enquired into and considered, the decision of the holy Council with me, by the revealing grace of Divine power, has declared the above-written John the presbyter to be a Catholic, and that no spot of heretical pravity has been found in him, I entreat that the pious protection of your Serenity may order him to be kept unharmed from all annoyance, nor allow a professor of the catholic faith to suffer any molestation. For not to believe one who professes truly is not to purge heresy, but to make it. If this should be allowed, occasion of infidelity will arise, and people will themselves incur the guilt which they would correct unwarily.

These things therefore let the most Serene Lord with pious precaution consider, and, as I have already requested, with profuse entreaties I again implore, that he allow not an innocent man to be afflicted anew as though he were guilty; to the end that Almighty God, who sees your Clemency love and defend the purity of catholic rectitude, may cause you both to rule over a pacified republic with your foes subdued, and to reign with His saints in life eternal.

EPISTLE XVII.

To Theotistus.

Gregory to Theotistus, kinsman of the Emperor.

We know that the Christianity of your Excellency is always intent on good works; and therefore we provide for you occasions for reaping reward, which you are certain to be glad of, so that we by so providing may have a share in your merits.

We therefore inform you that John the presbyter, the bearer of these presents, has come out free from those by whom he had been accused. For having, according to his request held a council, and subjected his faith to a subtle scrutiny, we found him guiltless of any wrong confession. And, inasmuch as he appeared to be, by the mercy of God, a professor and follower of the right faith, we absolved him by our definite sentence; especially as his accusers professed that they did not know what the heresy of the Marcionists, which they spoke of, was. On this account, saluting you with paternal affection, we request you to protect him with the grace of your favour. And, lest any one hereafter should be disposed to afflict him to no purpose, or in any way to cause him annoyance in this matter, let the advocacy of your Excellency so protest and defend him—and this the more instantly in consideration of your own reward—that no unjust affliction may any more consume him, and that the Creator and Redeemer of the human race, whom you worship with a sincere confession, may recompense your action in this behalf among your many good works. The month of October. Indiction 14.

EPISTLE XVIII.

To John, Bishop.

Gregory to John, Bishop of Syracuse.

Moved by the benevolence of the Apostolic See and by the order of ancient custom, we have thought fit to grant to thy Fraternity, who art known to have received the office of government in the Church of Syracuse, the use of the pallium; that is, at such times and in such manner as thou knowest without doubt that it was used by thy predecessor; nevertheless admonishing thee that, as thou rejoicest in having received from us the use of this decoration for the honour of thy priestly office, so also by probity of manners and deeds thou strive to adorn the office thou hast received unto our glory in Christ. For thus wilt thou be conspicuous for decorations mutually answering to each other, if with this habit for the body the excellence also of thy mind agrees.

For all privileges which are known to have been granted formerly to thy Church we confirm by our authority, and decree that they shall remain inviolate.

EPISTLE XXII.

To Peter, Bishop.

Gregory to Peter, Bishop of Aleria in Corsica.

Inasmuch as in the isle of Corsica, at the place Nigeunum, in the possession which is called Cellas Cupias belonging to the holy Roman Church, which by the providence of God we serve, we have ordered to be founded a basilica, with a baptistery[9], to the honour of the blessed Peter, Prince of the apostles, and of Laurentius the martyr, we therefore hereby exhort thy Fraternity to proceed at once to the aforesaid place, and with observance of the venerable solemnities of dedication to consecrate solemnly the aforesaid church and baptistery. Deposit also reverently the holy relics (*sanctuaria*) which you have received.

EPISTLE XXIV.

To Marinianus, Bishop.

Gregory to Marinianus, Bishop of Ravenna.

We have received by the deacon Virgilius

9 Baptisteries were anciently buildings contiguous to but apart from the churches. Cf. III. 59, note 7.

the letter of your Fraternity, in which you inform us that certain of the clergy and people have cried out that it is contrary to the laws and canons that the cause between your Church and the abbot Claudius should be examined and decided here. But, had they paid attention to ecclesiastical order and to the persons between whom the case is pending, they would by all means have abstained from needless complaint; especially as the cause could not be pleaded there, where the aforesaid abbot has complained of having endured injustice from your predecessor and of still suffering from it. For the objection might perhaps have been made if he had not appealed to a superior authority, and sought to have the rights of his case determined before it. Nay, but dost thou not thyself know that the case which arose on the part of the presbyter John against John of Constantinople, our brother and fellow-bishop, came before the Apostolic See, and was decided by our sentence?[1] If, then, a cause was brought under our cognizance from that city where the prince is, how much more should an affair between you have the truth about it ascertained and be terminated here? But as for you, let not the words of foolish men there move you, and believe not that through us any detriment to your Church is caused. For, if you will enquire of the servant of God Secundinus your deacon and of Castorius our notary, you will learn from them how your predecessor had already desired to arrange this case. But your Fraternity has done wisely in sending persons hither for this business, and in not listening to vain words. Now we trust in Almighty God that this cause may be terminated in a way well-pleasing to God, so that no room may be left for renewed complaint, and that neither party may be aggrieved unjustly. The sword[2] which our most beloved son Peter, then deacon and guardian (*defensor*) in your parts, had left for us with your predecessor, please to send to us by the servant of God Secundinus, and Castorius the notary, the bearers of these presents.

EPISTLE XXV.

To Maximus of Salona.

Gregory to Maximus, intruder in the Church of Salona[3].

While, seeking this or that excuse, thou deferrest obedience to our letters, while thou puttest off coming to us for ascertainment of the truth after being so often admonished, thou lendest credibility all the more to what is alleged against thee; and, even though there had been nothing else to go against thee and do thee harm, thy delay alone would render thee culpable and accuse thee. Humble thyself at length, and submit thyself to obedience, and make haste to come to us without any excuses, that, the truth being investigated and ascertained, in the fear of God, whatever may be fair and canonical may be decided. For be assured that we will observe towards thee justice and the ordinances of the canons, and, by the revelation of God, who is the Author of truth, will terminate thy cause agreeably to justice. For, as to thy demand that we should send some one to your city, in whose presence there might be proof of the things alleged, this would be in some degree excusable, if reason ever imposed on the accused the necessity of proof. But, inasmuch as this burden lies not on thee but on thine accusers, do not thou hesitate to come to us, as we have before said, putting it off no longer; and either thine accuser will be present without delay to support with suitable proof what has been alleged as to simoniacal heresy or other things; or certainly, as far as regards a sound settlement of this business, a just dealing with it will, through the intervention of Peter, Prince of the apostles, ensue; that so no guiltiness may confound us before God for any connivance, now that these things have come to our knowledge. But, as to thy allegation that our most serene lords have ordered cognizance of the matter to be taken in your city, we indeed have received no other commands of theirs on the subject except that thou wert to come to us. But, even if by chance, occupied as they are by many thoughts and anxieties for the good of their republic which by the divine bounty has been granted to them, this has been suggested to them, and a command has been surreptitiously elicited from them, yet, inasmuch as it is known to us and to all how our most pious lords love discipline, observe degrees, venerate the canons, and refrain from mixing themselves up in the causes of priests, we will still execute with instancy what is for the good both of their souls and of the republic, and what we are driven to by regard to the terrible and tremendous judgment.

Cease then from all excuses, and delay not to appear here, that, fortified by investigation of the truth, we may at length bring thy cause to a termination. But, whereas we have been informed that thou art greatly afraid and altogether in trepidation lest we should avenge on

1 See III. 53, note 9, and *reff.* there. It seems from what Gregory here says, that it was not in the East only, but also in Italy, at Ravenna, that the authority of the Roman See met with opposition; perhaps mainly on the ground of Ravenna having been an Imperial city, and being still the seat of the Exarch of Italy. Cf. III. 57, note 4.

2 *Spatam.* Cf. VI. 61, note 8.

3 See III. 47, note 2.

thee the known fact of thy having forced thy way irregularly into the order of priesthood without our consent, this was indeed an intolerable misdemeanour: but, in accordance with the commands of our most serene lord the Emperor, we forgive thee this, provided that thou in no wise persist any longer in the error of thy contumacy; and we are by no means moved against thee on this account. But other things that have been reported to us we cannot suffer to pass without enquiry.

Now inasmuch as we long ago sent thee a letter warning thee by no means to dare to celebrate the solemnities of mass till we should ascertain the will of the said our most serene lord, and as thou hast cunningly contrived that this letter should not come into thy hands, though thou nevertheless knewest in one way or another what its purport was, but hast refused to comply with it;—we therefore confirm what was before sent thee in writing, that thou must not dare to celebrate the solemnities of mass until all that has been alleged against thee has been thorougly enquired into and sifted. And, if, with perverse daring, thou shouldest presume to celebrate, know that thou art not free from the former threat of interdiction from communion. For, even though there were no other transgressions, we deprive thee of the communion of the body and blood of the Lord for this sin of pride alone. Wherefore, shewing the obedience that becomes thee, make haste, as we have said, with all diligence to come to us; but so as to have a space of thirty days for preparing for thy journey; and so, laying aside all excuses, defer not thy appearance here.

Moreover, if any occasion of hindering thy journey has arisen from the judges, or the military force, or the people, we acknowledge the skilfulness with which things are done. Do thou thyself, then, see what account of this obligation thou canst render either to men here or to Almighty God in the future judgment, having by thy contempt provoked a strict sentence against thee.

Furthermore, it has come to my knowledge that my brother and fellow-bishop Paulinus, and Honoratus, archdeacon of the Church of Salona [4], for having refused to give assent to thy presumption are suffering grievous molestation at thy hands, so as to have been constrained to give sureties to the end that may not be at liberty to leave the city or their own houses. If this is so, do thou on receipt of this present writing, returning at last, though late, to a sound mind, desist from molesting either of them, that they may have free license either to come to me if they wish, or to go anywhere else for their advantage.

EPISTLE XXVI.

To the Salonitans.

Gregory to his most beloved sons, the clergy and nobles dwelling at Salona [5].

It has come to my ears, that certain men of perverse disposition, in order to poison your minds, beloved, have tried to insinuate to you that I am moved by some grudge against Maximus, and that I am desiring to carry out not so much what is canonical as what anger dictates. But far, far be it from the priestly mind to be moved in any cause by private feeling. It is on the contrary as taking thought for you, beloved, and as fearing the judgment of Almighty God on my own soul, that I desire the case of this same Maximus to be thoroughly investigated, as to whether he is burdened by no such crimes as are a bar to ordination, and makes no attempt to attain to the priestly office through simoniacal heresy; that is by giving bribes to some of his electors. He will then be a free intercessor for you before the Lord, if he shall come to the place of intercession bound by no sins of his own.

And yet his sin of pride is already manifestly shewn, in that, having been summoned to come to us, he resists under various excuses, shuns coming, is afraid to come. What then is he afraid of, if his conscience does not accuse him with respect to the things he is charged with? Lo, beloved, ye have now been long without a pastor, and may Almighty God make known to you how earnestly and from the bottom of my heart I sympathize with you in your destitution. For I hear what ravages are being made in the Lord's flock. But, when there is no shepherd, who may watch against the wolves? Wherefore urge ye the aforesaid Maximus to come hither to us, to the end that we may confirm him if we are able to find him innocent; but, if the things that are said of him should turn out to be true, that you, beloved, may be no longer left destitute through the interposition of his person.

For as to me, be assured that I am not moved against him by any grudge or any animosity of private feeling; but whatever may be canonical and just with the help of God I will determine.

4 In the letter to the Salonitans, which follows, it appears that Honoratus only among the clergy of Salona (having been the rival candidate for the bishopric and supported by the Pope), and Paulinus only among the suffragan bishops, had refused to communicate with Maximus.

5 See III. 47, note 2.

But I have been greatly astonished that among so many clergy and people of the Church of Salona hardly two in sacred orders have been found—to wit our brother and fellow-bishop Paulinus and my most beloved son Honoratus, archdeacon of the same Church—who refused to communicate with Maximus when he seized the priesthood, and who remembered that they were Christians.

For you ought, most dear sons, to have considered your own orders, and recognized as rejected him whom the Apostolical See rejected, that he might first be purged, if he could be, from the charges brought against him, and that then your Love might communicate with him without being partakers in his liability. We however are bound to your Charity in the bowels of loving-kindness; and, since we have learnt that some of you were pressed by force to accept him and communicate with him, we implore Almighty God to absolve you from all guilt of your own sins and from all implication in the liability of others, and to give you the grace of His protection in the present life, and grant to us to rejoice for you in the eternal country.

EPISTLE XXVII.

To the Clergy and People of Jadera[6].

Gregory to the presbyters, deacons, and clergy, nobles and people, dwelling at Jadera, and who have communicated with the prevaricator Maximus.

It has come to my knowledge that some of you, deceived by ignorance or under compulsion, have communicated with those who, their fault as you know requiring it, have been deprived of communion by the Apostolic See, but that others, with wholesome discretion, have under the Lord's protection abstained; and as much as I rejoice in those that have been constant so much do I groan for those who have gone astray, since they have partaken of the mysteries of holy communion, which have been granted to us by Divine loving-kindness for absolution, rather to the detriment of their souls. And because (as I pray Almighty God to make known to you) I earnestly and from the bottom of my heart sympathize with your Charity, I adjure and entreat you with fatherly affection, that every one of you abstain from unlawful communion, and altogether shun those whom the Apostolic See does not receive into the fellowship of its communion, lest any one should stand guilty in the sight of the eternal Judge from that whereby he might have been saved.

Moreover I have discovered that certain men of perverse mind in your parts have tried to insinuate that I am moved against Maximus by some grudge, and that I desire to carry out not what is canonical, but what anger dictates. But far, far be this from the priestly mind, that it should be moved in any cause by private animosity. But as for me, it is as taking thought for the people dwelling in those parts and for my own soul, and as fearing the judgment of Almighty God, that I wish to have the cause of this Maximus enquired into, and, God shewing me the way, to decide canonically. Now, inasmuch as I have written to him frequently that he was not to celebrate the sacred solemnities of mass until I had been able to obtain knowledge of his case, he would in any case be deprived of communion; and now his sin of pride is openly shewn from this,—that, having (as I have said) been often admonished to come to us, under various excuses he refuses, he shuns, he fears coming. What then is he afraid of, if his conscience does not accuse him with regard to the things that have been said? Since then you know these things, now that you can make no excuse on the plea of ignorance, I beseech, I exhort, I warn you, that you altogether refrain from fellowship with forbidden communion, and that not one of you presume, against his own soul, to communicate with any priest who communicates with the above written Maximus.

Since however I hear, as I have said before, that some of you fell in ignorance, and that some were even driven by force to communicate, I implore the Almighty Lord, that He would keep with His perpetual protection, and answer with His wished for bounty, those who have given no assent to this iniquity; and as to those whom either party spirit, or ignorance, or any other cause soever, has drawn into a fault, that He would absolve them from all guilt of their sins, and from all implication in the liability of others, and both give them all the grace of His protection in the present life, and grant to me to rejoice for them in the eternal country. Wherefore, that this intercession may avail for you with God our Saviour, do ye shew obedience to our exhortations for the weal of your souls, and receive the holy communion from those whom ye know to have abstained, and to abstain still, from communion with the aforesaid Maximus.

6 See III. 47, note 2. Jadera was one of the sees in the province of Dalmatia of which Salona was the Metropolis. The bishop of Jadera, Sabinianus, had communicated with Maximus, and probably assisted in ordaining him, but afterwards repented. See below, VII. 17; VIII. 10, 24. It may have been because Gregory had heard that there was already a party in Jadera prepared to renounce Maximus that he wrote this letter to strengthen it.

EPISTLE XXIX.

To Marinianus, Bishop.

Gregory to Marinianus, Bishop of Ravenna[7].

We wonder why the discernment of thy Fraternity should have been so changed in a short time that it does not consider what it asks for. On this account we grieve, since thou affordest manifest proof that the words of evil counsellors have availed with thee more than the study of divine lore has profited thee. And, when thou oughtest to be protecting monasteries, and with all thy power congregating the religious therein so as to make gain from the gathering together of souls, thou art on the contrary desiring to exercise thyself in oppressing them, as thy letters testify; and, what is worse, art trying to make us partakers in thy fault; to wit, in wishing, with our consent, to oppress the monastery which thy predecessor founded under the name of looking after its property and business affairs.

For thou oughtest to call to mind that, in thy presence, and in the presence also of sundry of thy presbyters, deacons, and clerics, we granted, as they requested, a precept contrary to the testament of thy predecessor. Yet, though the disposition he had made with regard to the monastery itself was still therein confirmed, thou now dissemblest this, and demandest of us that we should order the contrary. And indeed we know that this device is not thine own; but, when thou refusest not to listen to those who say incongruous things, thou injurest not only thine own reputation, but also souls. Since, then, I love thee much, I urgently admonish thee—consider this attentively—that thou care not more for money than for souls. The former should be regarded collaterally; but the latter should be regarded with the whole bent of the mind, and vehemently striven after. On this spend vigilantly thy labour and solicitude, since our Redeemer seeks from the priest's office not gold, but souls.

Further, it has reached our ears that monasteries which are constituted under thy Fraternity are oppressed by importunities and various annoyances from the clergy. That this may no longer be so, restrain it by strict prohibition, to the end that the monks who live therein may be able to exult freely in the praises of our God.

With regard to the clerics Romanus and Dominicus, who presumed with rash daring to depart from this city without our blessing, though they were to have been stricken with heavier punishment, nevertheless such relaxation ought to be made in a spirit of kindness that they be urged to come back to their duty. The month of April, Indict. 14.

7 Cf. above, VI. 1.

EPISTLE XXX.

To Secundus.

Gregory to Secundus, servant of God at Ravenna[8].

Now that Castorius[9] has returned and made known to us all that has been done between you and King Agilulph, we have taken care to send him back to you with all speed, lest any one should find an excuse against us on the ground of delay. Having learnt then from him all that is to be done, give the matter your earnest attention, and press in all ways for this peace to be arranged, since, as report goes, there are some who are trying to hinder it. On this account make haste to act strenuously, that your labour may not remain without effect. For both these parts and various islands are already placed in great danger.

Stir up with such words as thou canst use our brother the bishop Marinianus[1]: for I suspect that he has fallen asleep. For certain persons have come to me, among whom were some aged mendicants, who were questioned by me as to what they had received and from whom they had received it; and they told me particularly how much had been given them on their journey, and by whom it had been given. But, when I enquired of them what my aforesaid brother had given them, they replied that they had asked him, but had received nothing at all from him; so that they did not get even bread on the way, though it has always been the familiar usage of that Church to give to all. For they said, He answered saying, I have nothing that I can give you. And I am surprised, if he who has clothes, money, and storehouses, has nothing to give to the poor.

Tell him, then, that with his place he should change his disposition too. Let him not believe reading and prayer alone to be enough for him, so that he should think to sit apart, and nowise fructify with his hand; but let him have a liberal hand; let him succour those who suffer need; let him believe the wants of others to be his own; since, if he has not these things, he bears but a bishop's empty name. I did indeed give him some admonitions about his soul in my letter; but he

8 Gregory appears to have communicated with this Secundus, rather than with the bishop of Ravenna, for reasons which appear below, and to have employed him in negotiations with the Exarch for peace with the Lombards.

9 A Castorius is mentioned in Gregory's letter to the Emperor as having been the *magister militum* in command at Rome during its siege by Agilulph. This may be the same person.

1 For his appointment to the see of Ravenna, cf. V. 48.

has sent me no reply whatever; whence I suppose that he has not even deigned to read them. For this reason it is needless now for me to admonish him at all in my letter to him; and so I have written only what I was able to dictate as his adviser in wordly matters. For it is not incumbent on me to tire myself by dictation for a man who does not read what is said to him. Let, then, thy Love speak to him about all these things privately, and admonish him how he ought to demean himself, lest through present negligence he lose the advantage of his former life, which God forbid.

EPISTLE XXXII.

To Fortunatus, Bishop.

Gregory to Fortunatus, Bishop of Neapolis (*Naples*).

We have written before now to your Fraternity that, if any [slaves] by the inspiration of God, desire to come from Jewish superstition to the Christian faith, their masters have no liberty to sell them, but that from the time of their declaring their wish they have a full claim to freedom. But since, so far as we have learnt, they [i.e. Jewish masters], weighing with nice discrimination neither our wish nor the ordinances of the law, think that they are not bound by this condition in the case of pagan slaves, your Fraternity ought to attend to such cases, and, if any one of their slaves, whether he be a Jew or a pagan, should wish to become a Christian, after his wish has been openly declared, let not any one of the Jews, under cover of any device or argument whatever, have power to sell him; but let him who desires to be converted to the Christian faith be in all ways supported by you in his claim to freedom. Lest, however, those who have to lose slaves of this kind should consider that their interests are unreasonably prejudiced, it is fitting that with careful consideration you should observe this rule;—that if pagans when they have been brought out of foreign parts for the sake of traffic should chance to flee to the Church, and say that they wish to become Christians, or even outside the Church should announce this wish, then, till the end of three months during which a buyer to sell them to may be sought for, they [the Jewish owners] may receive their price; that is to say, from a Christian buyer. But if after the aforesaid three months any one of such slaves should declare his wish and desire to become a Christian, let not either any one afterwards dare to buy him, or his master, under colour of any occasion whatever, dare to sell him; but let him unreservedly attain to the benefit of freedom; since he (i.e. the master) is in such case understood to have acquired him not for sale but for his own service. Let, then, your Fraternity so vigilantly observe all these things that neither the supplication of any nor respect of persons may avail to inveigle you[2].

EPISTLE XXXIV.

To Castorius, Notary.

Gregory to Castorius, our notary at Ravenna.

When Florentinus, deacon of the Church of Ravenna, treated with us in behalf of our most reverend brother and fellow-bishop Marinianus concerning the use of the pallium, on our asking him what was the ancient custom, he replied that the bishop of the Church of Ravenna used the pallium in all litanies[3]. But that this was not so we both learnt from others, and it appeared evidently from the letters of the former bishop John, which we shewed to him. But he said what he had been ordered to say. For, at the time when this same John was inhibited by thee from presuming to use the pallium out of order and unadvisedly, he wrote to us that the ancient custom had been this; that the bishop of that city should use the pallium in solemn litanies. We send thee, for thy information, copies of his letters. But when Adeodatus, deacon of the aforesaid Church, at the time when he was here, in like manner pressed us strongly concerning this use of the pallium, we, desiring to ascertain the truth, in like manner had him questioned as to what the custom was: and he, that he might persuade us to believe him, and succeed in obtaining from us what he sought, testified under oath that it had been the ancient custom for the bishop of his city to use the pallium in four or five solemn litanies. Let therefore thy Experience look to the matter diligently, and enquire with all carefulness how many solemn litanies there have been from ancient times. Take care also to make enquiry by calling them, not the solemn, but the greater litanies; that when, through what the aforesaid deacon Adeodatus testified to us and what the letter of the aforesaid bishop John acknowledges, it shall appear how many of these solemn litanies there were, we, knowing how often the pallium used to be worn in litanies, may most willingly grant the privilege. But do not make this enquiry of those who are put forward by the ecclesiastics,

---

2 As to ownership by Jews of converted slaves, see *Prolegom.*, p. xxi., and other Epistles there referred to.

3 Marinianus had succeeded John as bishop of Ravenna For Gregory's dispute with John concerning the use of the pallium, see above, III. 56, 57; V. 11, 15, and below, VI. 61.

but of others whom you know to be impartial; and whatever after careful investigation you discover communicate to us with accuracy, that having ascertained the truth, as we have said, we may relieve the mind of our brother and fellow-bishop, the most reverend Marinianus.

EPISTLE XXXV.

To Anthemius, Subdeacon.

Gregory to Anthemius, our Neapolitan Subdeacon[4].

How great is our grief, and how great the affliction of our heart, from what has taken place in the regions of Campania we cannot express; but thou mayest thyself gather it from the greatness of the calamity. With regard to this state of things, we send thy Experience by the magnificent Stephen, bearer of these presents, money for the succour of the captives who have been taken, admonishing thee that thou give thy whole attention to the business, and carry it out strenuously; and, in the case of freemen whom thou knowest to have no sufficient means for their own redemption, that thou make haste to redeem them. But, should there be any slaves, and thou findest that their masters are so poor that they cannot come forward to redeem them, hesitate not to recover them also. In like manner also thou wilt take care to redeem the slaves of the Church who have been lost by thy neglect. Further, whomsoever thou shalt have redeemed, thou wilt by all means be at pains to make out a list, containing their names, and a statement of where each is staying, and what he is doing, and where he came from; which list thou mayest bring with thee when thou comest. Moreover, hasten to shew thyself so diligent in this business that those who are to be redeemed may incur no risk through thy negligence, or thou come afterwards to be highly culpable before us. But work especially for this also; that, if possible, thou mayest be able to recover those captives at a moderate price. But set down in writing, with all clearness and nicety, the whole sum expended, and transmit to us this thy written account with speed. The month of May, Indiction 14.

EPISTLE XXXVII.

To Columbus, Bishop.

Gregory to Columbus, Bishop of Numidia[5]

The letters of your Fraternity, full of priestly sweetness, we have received at the hands of Rogatianus the deacon, the bearer of these presents. And their kind expressions rejoiced us much, especially as we were informed through them of what we long to hear of, your welfare. But the devotion of your Holiness we have both known of old; and as you now write, so we hold it to be. For of what kind the sincerity of your Fraternity towards us is we need nothing to satisfy us, since we know it from the love of our own heart which encircles you. We have given to the above-named bearer, whom you commended to us by letter, writings addressed to the Rector of the patrimony of Sicily, bidding him urge the opposite party to do what is just, to the end that, idle excuses being put aside, the whole case in dispute may be speedily brought to an end.

We now inform your Holiness that a certain man has come to us, Peter by name, who asserted that he was a bishop, and requested from us a remedy of his complaint. And at first indeed he related things that might have been deserving of pity; but on enquiry we found things to be very different from what he told us, and his behaviour has exceedingly distressed us. But, inasmuch as, separated as we are by so great a distance, we could by no means learn thoroughly the gist of his ca e, we have been unable to determine it, being in doubt. But now, seeing that the aforesaid deacon, who is returning to you, has asked that this person should be allowed to go with him, and he himself has requested to be sent to you, both of them knowing that your Holiness has, as becomes you, zeal for the faith and a love of justice, the proposal has been acceptable to us, and we have granted what they asked. Since, then, you being on the spot can ascertain the merits of the case more thoroughly, we exhort you so to observe what is just and canonical towards the same Peter that both the requirements of rectitude may be fulfilled by you in all respects, and his case may be seen to have been judged after the fear of God and the rules of the Church. But, if any one is said to have been privy to, or a partaker in, the things which the aforesaid Peter is accused of, accurate enquiry must be made, and, when the truth is known, judgment in like manner pronounced canonically.

Furthermore, a thing altogether hard to be borne, and hostile to the right faith, has come to our ears; namely that catholics (which is awful to be told) and religious persons[6] (which is worse) consent to their children and their slaves, or others whom they have in their

---

4 The occasion of this letter seems to have been some recent aggression of the Lombards in the Neapolitan district, resulting in the capture of many prisoners of war.

5 See II. 48, note 7.

6 *Religiosi*. See I. 61, note 7.

power, being baptized in the heresy of the Donatists. And so, if this is true, let your Fraternity study with all your power to correct it, to the end that the purity of the faith may through your solicitude stand inviolate, and innocent souls who might be saved by catholic baptism perish not from the infection of heretics. Whosoever, then, of the persons above mentioned has suffered any one belonging to him to be baptized among the Donatists, study with all your power, and with all urgency, to recall such to the catholic faith. But, if any one of such persons should under any pretext endure the doing of this thing in the case of such as are his in future, let him be cut off entirely from the communion of the clergy.

EPISTLE XLIII.

To Venantius, Patrician.

Gregory to Venantius, Patrician, and Ex-monk[7].

Your communication to us has found us much distressed from having become aware that offence has arisen between you and John our brother and fellow-bishop, in whose agreement with you we were desirous of rejoicing. For, whatever the cause may have been, rage ought not to have broken out to such a pitch that your armed men, as we have heard, should have burst into the episcopal palace, and committed divers evil deeds in a hostile manner, and that this affair should meanwhile separate you from his paternal charity. Could not the dispute, whatever it may have been, have been quietly arranged, so that neither party might suffer disadvantage, nor good feeling be disturbed? Now it is not unknown to us of what gravity, of what holiness, of what gentleness, our above-named brother is. Whence we gather that, unless excessive force of vexation had compelled him, his Fraternity would by no means have resorted to the measure by which you say that you are aggrieved. We however, on hearing of it by letter from him, at once wrote to him, admonishing him to receive your offerings as before, and not only to allow masses to be celebrated in your house, but, if you wish it, even to officiate himself, and that he ought to have prosecuted his cause without breach of charity. And, inasmuch as we wish none to come or continue to be at variance, we have taken care to renew this same admonition. Hence it is necessary, dearest son, that you, as becomes sons, should shew him the reverence due to a priest, and not provoke his spirit to anger. For with whom will you have assured goodwill, it (which God forbid) you are at variance with your priest? Wherefore, putting away swelling of spirit, try ye so to transact the causes that ye have one with another that both charity may remain inviolate, and what is to your mutual advantage may be peaceably attained.

[7] Cf. I. 34, note 8.

EPISTLE XLIV.

To John, Bishop.

Gregory to John, Bishop of Syracuse[8].

Although there may have been cause to provoke the spirit of your Fraternity not unreasonably to anger, so that you would neither receive the offerings of the lord Venantius nor allow the sacred solemnities of mass to be celebrated in his house, yet, inasmuch as our earthly interests should be prosecuted in such a manner that no quarrel may avail to sever us from the bond of charity, we therefore exhort your Holiness, as we have already written, that you should both receive the offerings of the aforesaid man with all sweetness and God-pleasing sincerity, and allow the mysteries of the mass to be performed in his house; and that, as we have written, you should, if perchance he should wish it, go there in person, and by celebrating mass with him renew your former friendly feeling. For it is your duty to bestow priestly affection on sons, though still, in causes that may arise, by no means to pretermit, as reason approves, the jurisdiction of your Church. Wherefore, considering this, it is necessary that your Fraternity should try so to demean yourself with discreet moderation with respect to these matters as both to transact advantageously what the nature of the business requires, and not to recede from the grace of paternal charity.

EPISTLE XLVI.

To Felix, Bishop of Pisaurum (*Pesaro*).

Gregory to Felix, Bishop, &c.

We wonder at your Fraternity, that, disregarding the tenor of the precept given you by our predecessor of holy memory, you should consecrate the monastery constructed by John, the bearer of these presents, otherwise than as ancient use demands. For, while it is ordered among other things in the said precept that you should dedicate the place itself without a public mass, still, as we have heard, your chair has been placed there, and the sacred solemnities of mass are there publicly celebrated. If this is true, we hereby exhort you that, putting aside all excuse, you cause your

[8] Cf. preceding Epistle. John, previously archdeacon of Catana, had been elected in the previous year (594) with Gregory's approval as the successor of Maximianus of Syracuse (V. 17), and had recently had the pallium sent him (V.I. 18.).

chair to be altogether removed thence, and that henceforth you perform no public masses there. But, as both custom and the tenor of the precept direct, if they should wish mass to be celebrated for them there, let a presbyter be appointed by thee for the purpose [9].

Further, we desire that with the favour of God there shall always remain a congregation of servants of God in the same monastery, as the aforesaid John has requested, and as is now the case. As to the cup also which he informs me has been taken away by your Fraternity, if it be so, make haste to restore it. These things, then, let your Holiness so study to fulfil that the aforesaid bearer may have no need to resort to us again on the same account.

EPISTLE XLVIII.

To Urbicus, Abbot.

Gregory to Urbicus, Abbot of Saint Hermes, which is situated in Panormus.

Whosoever, incited by divine inspiration, hastens to leave the employments of this world and to be converted to God should so be received with charity, and refreshed in all ways with kind consolations, that, by the help of God, he may delight in all ways to persevere in the state of life which he has chosen. Since, then, Agatho, the bearer of these presents, desires to be converted [1] in thy Love's monastery, we exhort thee to receive him with all sweetness and love, and by assiduous exhortation kindle his longing for eternal life, and study to be diligently solicitous for his soul's salvation; to the end that, while by thy admonition he shall persist with devoted mind in the service of our God, it may both profit him to have left the world, and his conversion may be to the increase of thine own reward. Know, however, that he is to be so received only if his wife also should wish to be similarly converted. For, when the bodies of both have been made one by the tie of wedlock, it is unseemly that part should be converted and part remain in the world [2].

EPISTLE XLIX.

To Palladius, Bishop.

Gregory to Palladius, Bishop of Santones in Gaul (*Saintes*).

Leuparic your presbyter, the bearer of these presents, when he came to us informed us that your Fraternity has built a church in honour of the blessed apostles Peter and Paul, and also of the martyrs Laurentius and Pancratius, and placed there thirteen altars, of which we learn that four have remained not yet dedicated because of your desiring to deposit there relics of the above-named saints. And, seeing that we have reverently supplied you with relics of the Saints Peter and Paul, and also of the martyrs Laurentius and Pancratius, we exhort you to receive them with reverence, and deposit them with the help of the Lord, providing before all things that supplies for the maintenance of those who serve there be not wanting.

EPISTLE L.

To Queen Brunichild.

Gregory to Brunichild, Queen of the Franks.

The tenor of your letters, which evinces a religious spirit and the earnestness of a pious mind, causes us not only to commend the purpose of your request, but also to grant willingly what you demand. For indeed it would ill become us to refuse what Christian devotion and the desire of an upright heart solicits, especially as we know that you demand, and embrace with your whole heart, what may both protect the faith of believers, and work no less the salvation of souls. Accordingly, greeting your Excellency with befitting honour, we inform you that to Leuparic, the bearer of these presents, through whom we received your communication, and whom you described as a presbyter, we have handed over, according to your Excellency's request, with the reverence due to them, certain relics of the blessed apostles Peter and Paul. But, that laudable and religious devotion may be more and more conspicuous among you, you must see that these benefits of the saints be deposited with reverence and due honour, and that those who serve in attendance on them be vexed with no burdens or molestations, lest perchance, under the pressure of outward necessity, they be rendered unprofitable and slow in the service of God, and (which God forbid) the benefits of the saints that have been bestowed sustain injury and neglect. Let, then, your Excellency see to their quiet, to the end that, while they are guarded by your bounty from all disquietude, they may render praises to our God with minds undisturbed, and that reward may also accrue to you in the life eternal.

EPISTLE LI.

To the Brethren going to England (*Angliam*) [3].

Gregory, servant of the servants of God, to the servants of our Lord Jesus Christ.

---

9 Cf. II. 41.

1 *Conversion* has its usual sense of embracing monastic life.

2 See also on this subject, XI. 45, XI. 50.

3 This, with the eight following letters (51-59), were committed to Augustine, who is spoken of in several of them as the bearer, when he was sent back from Rome to rejoin his com

Since it had been better not to have begun what is good than to return back from it when begun, you must, most beloved sons, fulfil the good work which with the help of the Lord you have begun. Let, then, neither the toil of the journey nor the tongues of evil-speaking men deter you; but with all instancy and all fervour go on with what under God's guidance you have commenced, knowing that great toil is followed by the glory of an eternal reward. Obey in all things humbly Augustine your provost (*præposito*), who is returning to you, whom we also appoint your abbot, knowing that whatever may be fulfilled in you through his admonition will in all ways profit your souls. May Almighty God protect you with His grace, and grant to me to see the fruit of your labour in the eternal country; that so, even though I cannot labour with you, I may be found together with you in the joy of the reward; for in truth I desire to labour. God keep you safe, most beloved sons. Given the tenth day of the Kalends of August, the fourteenth year of the Emperor our lord Mauricius Tiberius, the most pious Augustus, the thirteenth year of the consulship of our said lord, Indiction 14.

EPISTLE LII.

To Pelagius and Serenus, Bishops.

Gregory to Pelagius of Turni[4] and Serenus of Masilia (*Marseilles*) Bishops of Gaul. *A paribus*[5].

Although with priests who have the charity that is well pleasing to God religious men need no commendation, yet, since an apt time for writing has offered itself, we have thought well to send a letter to your Fraternity, mentioning that we have sent into your parts, with the help of the Lord, for the benefit of souls, the servant of God Augustine, of whose earnestness we are assured, with other servants of God. Him your Holiness must needs assist with priestly earnestness, and hasten to afford him your succour. We have also enjoined him, that so you may be the more ready to support him, to make you fully acquainted with the matter he has in hand, knowing that, when it is known to you, you will lend yourselves with entire devotion for God's sake to succour him as the case requires.

Moreover, we commend in all ways to your charity our common son the presbyter Candidus, whom we have sent for the government of the patrimony of our Church. Given on the tenth day of the Kalends of August, Indiction 14.

EPISTLE LIII.

To Virgilius, Bishop.

Gregory to Virgilius, Bishop of Arelate (*Arles*), Metropolitan.

Although we are confident that your Fraternity is intent on good works, and that you come forward of your own accord in causes well-pleasing to God, we nevertheless deem it advantageous to address you with fraternal charity, that, being provoked also by our letters, you may increase the solace which it becomes you voluntarily to bestow. And accordingly we inform your Holiness that we have sent Augustine, the servant of God, the bearer of these presents, with other servants of God, for the winning of souls in the parts whither he is going, as he will be able himself to inform you face to face. In these circumstances you must needs aid him with prayer and assistance, and, where need may require, afford him the support of your succour, and refresh him, as is fit, with fatherly and priestly consolation, to the end that, when he shall have obtained the succour of your Holiness, if he should succeed in winning any gain for God, as we hope he may, you too may be able to gain a reward along with him, having devoutly administered to his good works the abundance of your support. Moreover, as to Candidus the presbyter, our common son, and the little patrimony of our Church, let your Fraternity, as being of one mind with us, study to hold both as commended to you; that so, with the help of your Holiness, something may thence accrue for the sustenance of the poor. Inasmuch, then, as your predecessor held this patrimony for many years, and

---

panions. Bede (*H.E.* I. 23), and John the deacon (*Vit. S. Greg.* II. 33), say that the missionaries—"cum aliquantulum itineris confecissent" (Bede)—"post dies aliquot" (John Diac.)—were deterred by what they had heard of the difficulties of their undertaking, and sent Augustine to Rome to request leave to give it up, and that Gregory sent him back to them with letters of admonition and of commendation. No commendatory letters seem to have been given them when they first set out. Those now sent are addressed to the bishops of Turni (*al. Turon.*), Marseilles, Arles, Vienne, Autun, and Aix in Provenee, to the abbot of Lerins, to Arigius, Patrician of Gaul, to Theodoric and Theodebert, the two boy-kings of Burgundy and Austrasia, and to queen Brunechild their grandmother, who at this time ruled Austrasia as Theodebert's guardian. See *Pedigree of Kings of Gaul*, p. xxx. The letters which come first in order, 51 and 52, being dated 22 July A.D. 596, we may conclude that the missionaries had been originally despatched in the spring of the same year. They appear to have got as far as the Southern coast of Provence, since the letters to the bishop of Aix and the Abbot of Lerins shew that Augustine had already visited them, though not, apparently, any others to whom letters are now addressed. The mission was accompanied by Candidus, sent out as *Rector* of the patrimony in Gaul (cf. Ep. VII.), who is also commended in the letters. The patrimony appears to have been attended to previously in a way not satisfactory to Gregory by the bishops of Arles (see below, Epp. LIII., LV.). This letter is not found in the *Registrum Epistolorum*; but given by Bede (I. 23), and by John the Deacon (*Vit. S. Greg.* lib. ii. c. 34).

4 *De Turnis*; in Colbert. *Turonis*. The latter name in itself would seem to denote *Tours*. But it is not easy to see why a common letter should have been addressed to the Bishops of Tours and Marseilles. And, further, would Tours on the Loire be likely to lie on the route which the missionaries would take to Britain?

5 See I. 25, note 8.

kept in his own hands the collected payments, let your Fraternity consider whose the moneys are, and to whom they should be paid, and restore them to us, handing them to the above-written presbyter Candidus, our son. For it is very execrable that what has been preserved by the kings of the nations should be said to be taken away by bishops.

EPISTLE LIV.

To Desiderius and Syagrius, Bishops.

Gregory to Desiderius of Vienna (*Vienne*), and Syagrius of Augustodunum (*Autun*), Bishops of Gaul. *A paribus*[6].

Having regard to your sincere charity we are well assured that out of love for Peter, the Prince of the apostles, you will devotedly afford your succour to our men; especially since the nature of the case requires you to give assistance even of your own accord, and the more when you see them labour. Wherefore we inform your Holiness that, the Lord so ordering it, we have despatched Augustine, the servant of God, the bearer of these presents, whose zeal and earnestness are well known to us, with other servants of God, in behalf of souls in those parts; from whose account of things when you have fully learnt what is enjoined on him, let your Fraternity bestow your succour on him in all ways which the case may require, that you may be able, as is becoming and fit, to be helpers of a good work. Let, then, your Fraternity study to shew yourself so devoted in this matter that your action may prove to us the truth of the good report that we have heard of you. We commend to you in all respects our most beloved common son, Candidus the presbyter, to whom we have committed the patrimony of our Church situated in those parts.

EPISTLE LV.

To Protasius, Bishop.

Gregory to Protasius, Bishop of Aquae in Gaul (*Aix*).

How great love of the blessed Peter, Prince of the apostles, distinguishes you is evident, not only from the prerogative of your office, but also from the devotion you bestow on what is to the advantage of his Church. And having learnt that this is the case from the relation of Augustine, servant of God, the bearer of these presents, we rejoice exceedingly for the affection and zeal for truth that is in you; and we give thanks that, though absent in the body, you still shew that you are with us in heart and mind, seeing that you exhibit brotherly charity towards us, as is fit. In order then that actual fact may confirm the good report of you, tell our brother and fellow-bishop Virgilius to hand over to us the payments which his predecessor received for many years and retained in his own hands: for it is the property of the poor. And if perchance, as we do not believe will be the case, he should desire in any way to excuse himself, do you, who know the real truth more exactly, inasmuch as you acted as steward (*vicedominus*) at that time, explain to him how the matter stands, and urge him not to retain in his hands the property of Saint Peter and of his poor. But, though perhaps our men may not need this, do not refuse your testimony in the case; that so, with regard to the truth as well as to the devotion of your good will, the blessed apostle Peter, for whose love you do this, may respond to you by his intercession both here and in the life to come. We heartily commend to your Holiness the presbyter Candidus, our common son, to whom we have committed the charge of this patrimony.

EPISTLE LVI.

To Stephen, Abbot[7].

Gregory to Stephen, &c.

The account given us by Augustine, servant of God, the bearer of these presents, has made us joyful, in that he has told us that your Love is vigilant as you ought to be; and he further affirms that the presbyters and deacons and the whole congregation live in unanimity and concord. And, since the goodness of presidents is the salutary rule of their subjects, we implore Almighty God to enkindle thee always in good works by the grace of His loving-kindness, and to keep those who are committed to thee from all temptation of diabolical deceit, and grant to them to live with thee in charity and in the manner of life that pleases Him.

But, since the enemy of the human race never rests from plotting against our doings, so as to deceive in some part souls that are serving God, therefore, most beloved son, we exhort thee to exercise vigilantly thy anxious care, and so to keep those who are committed to thee by prayer and heedfulness that the prowling wolf may find no opportunity for tearing the flock: to the end that, when thou shalt have rendered to our God unharmed those of whom thou hast undertaken the charge, He may both of His grace repay thee with rewards for thy labour and multiply in thee longings for eternal life.

6 See I. 25, note 8.

7 In *Cod. Colbert.* Stephen is described as "abbati de monasterio quod est Lirino;" i e. the famous monastery on the island of that name (*Lerins*) now known as *L'ile de St. Honorat*. This was probably Stephen's monastery.

We have received the spoons and plates which thou hast sent us, and we thank thy Charity, because thou hast shewn how thou lovest the poor in having sent for their use such things as they need.

EPISTLE LVII.

To Arigius, Patrician[8].

Gregory to Arigius, Patrician of Gaul.

We have learnt from the servant of God, Augustine, the bearer of these presents, how great goodness, how great gentleness, with the charity that is well-pleasing to Christ, is in you resplendent; and we give thanks to Almighty God, who has granted you these gifts of His loving-kindness, through which you may have it in your power to be highly esteemed among men, and—what is truly profitable—glorious in His sight. We therefore pray Almighty God, that He would multiply in you these gifts which He has granted, and keep you with all yours under His protection, and so dispose the doings of your Glory in this world that they may be to your benefit both here, and—what is more to be wished—in the life to come. Saluting, then, your Glory with paternal sweetness, we beg of you that the bearer of these presents, and the servants of God who are with him, may obtain your succour in what is needful, to the end that, while they experience your favour, they may the better fulfil what has been enjoined on them to do.

Furthermore, we commend to you in all respects our son the presbyter Candidus, whom we have sent for the government of the patrimony of our Church which is in your parts; trusting that your Glory will receive a reward in return from our God, if with devout mind you lend your succour to the concerns of the poor.

EPISTLE LVIII.

To Theodoric and Theodebert[1].

Gregory to Theodoric and Theodebert, brethren, Kings of the Franks. *A paribus*[2].

Since Almighty God has adorned your kingdom with rectitude of faith, and has made it conspicuous among other nations by the purity of its Christian religion, we have conceived great expectations of you, that you will by all means desire that your subjects should be converted to that faith in virtue of which you are their kings and lords. This being so, it has come to our knowledge that the nation of the Angli is desirous, through the mercy of God, of being converted to the Christian faith, but that the priests in their neighbourhood neglect them, and are remiss in kindling their desires by their own exhortations. On this account therefore we have taken thought to send to them the servant of God Augustine, the bearer of these presents, whose zeal and earnestness are well known to us, with other servants of God. And we have also charged them to take with them some priests from the neighbouring parts, with whom they may be able to ascertain the disposition of the Angli, and, as far as God may grant it to them, to aid their wishes by their admonition. Now, that they may have it in their power to shew themselves efficient and capable in this business, we beseech your Excellency, greeting you with paternal charity, that these whom we have sent may be counted worthy to find the grace of your favour. And, since it is a matter of souls, let your power protect and aid them; that Almighty God, who knows that with devout mind and with all your heart you take an interest in His cause, may propitiously direct your causes, and after earthly dominion bring you to heavenly kingdoms.

Futhermore, we request your Excellency to hold as commended to you our most beloved son, Candidus, a presbyter, and the *rector* of the patrimony of our Church, to the end that the blessed Peter, Prince of the apostles, may answer you by his intercession, while, looking to the reward, you afford your protection in the concerns of his poor.

EPISTLE LIX.

To Brunichild, Queen of the Franks.

Gregory to Brunichild, &c.

The Christianity of your Excellence has been so truly known to us of old that we do not in the least doubt of your goodness, but rather hold it to be in all ways certain that you will devoutly and zealously concur with us in the cause of faith, and supply most abundantly the succour of your religious sincerity. Being for this reason well assured, and greeting you with paternal charity, we inform you that it has come to our knowledge how that the nation of the Angli, by God's permission, is

8 The term *Patricius* was used to designate governors of provinces under the Frank kings. Cf. III. 33, "Dynamio patricio Galliarum," and *Greg. Turon.* (IV. 24), "Guntramnus rex, amoto Agricola patricio, Celsum patriciatus honore donavit. There were at this time two Burgundian *Patricii*, one, called the *Patricius* absolutely, residing at Arles, the other at Marseilles (*Greg. Turon*).

1 Childebert II. son of Sigebert I. and Brunechild, who had reigned over nearly all the dominions of the Franks in Gaul (see VI. 5, note 5), died in this year. A.D. 596, and was succeeded by his illegitimate son Theodebert II. as king of Austrasia, and by his second son Theoderic II. as king of Burgundy. These two kings were only ten and seven years of age respectively when their father died, and their grandmother Brunechild was appointed guardian of the former. Hence Gregory, writing now after the death of Childebert, addresses formal letters in identical terms to the two minors, but another (Ep. LIX.) to Brunechild. See *Pedigree of Kings of Gaul*, p. xxx.

2 See I. 25, note 8.

desirous of becoming Christian, but that the priests who are in their neighbourhood have no pastoral solicitude with regard to them. And lest their souls should haply perish in eternal damnation, it has been our care to send to them the bearer of these presents, Augustine the servant of God, whose zeal and earnestness are well known to us, with other servants of God; that through them we might be able to learn their wishes, and, as far as is possible, you also striving with us, to take thought for their conversion. We have also charged them that for carrying out this design they should take with them presbyters from the neighbouring regions. Let, then, your Excellency, habitually prone to good works, on account as well of our request as of regard to the fear of God, deign to hold him as in all ways commended to you, and earnestly bestow on him the favour of your protection, and lend the aid of your patronage to his labour; and, that he may have the fullest fruit thereof, provide for his going secure under your protection to the above-written nation of the Angli, to the end that our God, who has adorned you in this world with good qualities well-pleasing to Him, may cause you to give thanks here and in eternal rest with His saints.

Furthermore, commending to your Christianity our beloved son Candidus, presbyter and *rector* of the patrimony of our Church which is situated in your parts, we beg that he may in all things obtain the favour of your protection.

EPISTLE LX.

To Eulogius, Bishop.

Gregory to Eulogius, Bishop of Alexandria.

Charity, the mother and guardian of all that is good, which binds together in union the hearts of many, regards not as absent him whom it has present in the mind's eye. Since then, dearest brother, we are held together by the root of charity, neither will bodily absence nor distance of places have power to assert any claim over us, inasmuch as we who are one are surely not far from each other. Now we wish to have always this common charity with the rest of our brethren. Yet there is something that binds us in a certain peculiar way to the Church of Alexandria, and compels us, as it were by a special law, to be the more prone to love it. For, as it is known to all that the blessed evangelist Mark was sent by Saint Peter the apostle, his master, to Alexandria, so we are bound together in the unity of this master and his disciple, so that I seem to preside over the see of the disciple because of the master, and you over the see of the master because of the disciple.

Moreover to this unity of hearts we are bound also by the merits of your Holiness, since we know that you follow profitably the ordinances of your founder, and feel how you betake yourself with entire devotion to the bosom of your master, whence sprung the preaching of salvation in your parts. And so, when we received the letters of your Holiness, as much as our heart rejoiced in your brotherly visitation, so much is it oppressed with sadness for the untold burdens which you refer to, and we groan with you in brotherly sympathy for your grief. But, since a shaking of various kinds is extending itself everywhere, in the midst of a common need one should grieve less for one's own, but study rather, by patiently enduring, to overcome what we cannot altogether avoid.

But what we ourselves are suffering from the swords of the Lombards in the daily plundering and mangling and slaying of our citizens, we refuse to tell, lest, while speaking of our own sorrows, we should increase yours from the sympathy which you bestow upon us.

Furthermore, a little time ago we sent to Sabinianus, who represents our Church in the royal city, a letter from ourselves, which he should have sent on to your Fraternity[3]. If you have received it, we wonder why you have sent us no reply to it. And accordingly, since caution must be taken lest the pride of any one whatever introduce offence in the Churches, it is needful that you should carefully peruse it, and with all diligence and full bent of mind maintain what pertains to your dignity and to the peace of the Church.

Now may Almighty God, who by the grace of His loving-kindness has conferred on you the disposition and charity that becomes a priest, protect you in His service, and keep you within and without from all adversity, and mercifully grant that the souls of wanderers may be converted to Himself by your preaching.

We have received with the charity that was due to the bearer of these presents, our common son the deacon Isidore, who brought to us the benediction[4] of Saint Mark the evangelist. And you indeed, being resplendent in the merit of a good life, have sent to us the sweetly smelling word, which is nigh unto Paradise. But we, to wit because we are sinners, send you wood from the West, which,

3 See V. 43, which is probably the letter here referred to, being one sent to the two patriarchs of Alexandria and Antioch, urging them to join in resisting the assumption of the title of universal Bishop by the patriarch of Constantinople.

4 *Benedictionem*, with reference to the present of sweet wood that had been sent. Cf. 2 Kings v. 15, "Take a *blessing* of thy servant."

being suitable for the building of ships, signifies the tumult of our mind, as being ever tossed in the sea-waves; and we wished indeed to send larger pieces, but the ship was not large enough to hold them[5]. In the month of August, Indiction 14.

EPISTLE LXI.

To Castorius, Notary[6].

Gregory to Castorius, &c.

The magnificent lord Andreas presses me continually about restoring the use of the pallium in the Church of Ravenna according to ancient custom. And thou knowest that the bishop John wrote to me that it had been the custom for the bishops of the said Church to use the pallium in solemn litanies[7]. Adeodatus, deacon of that church, when he besought me earnestly on the same subject, satisfied me by oath that the bishops of the said place were accustomed to use the pallium in litanies four times in the year. But the aforesaid lord Andreas says in his letters that the bishop of Ravenna was in the habit of using the pallium in litanies at all times except in Lent. And these litanies, which he does not blush to say were daily, he asserts to be solemn ones. Whence I have been altogether astonished. But let thy Experience regard no man's person, no man's words; keep the fear of God and rectitude only before thine eyes, and enquire of senior persons, and of the Archdebon of that same Church, who would not, I think, perjure himself for the honour of another, and of others of older standing who had been in sacred orders before the times of bishop John, or if there are any others of riper age not in holy orders; and let them come before the body of Saint Apollinaris, and touching his sepulchre swear what had been the custom before the times of bishop John; since, as thou knowest, he was a man who presumed greatly and endeavoured in his pride to arrogate many things to himself. And whatever may be sworn to by faithful and grave men, according to the subjoined form, we desire to be retained in the same Church. But see that thou act not negligently, and that no one corrupt thy faithfulness and devotion in this matter; for thy zeal I know. Act assiduously, yet so that the aforesaid Church be not lowered in a way contrary to justice, but that it retain the usage that existed before the times of bishop John. Moreover, for satisfying thyself, do not enquire of two or three persons, but of as many as thou canst find of old standing and grave character, that so we may neither deny to that Church what has been of ancient custom, nor concede to it what has been coveted and attempted newly. But do all kindly and sweetly, so that both thy action may be strict and thy tongue gentle. The sword[8] which has been left at Ravenna, as we have already written, bring hither with thee; and carefully attend to what our son Boniface the deacon and the magnificent Maurentius the *chartularius* have written to thee about.

I swear by the Father, Son, and Holy Spirit, the inseparable Trinity of Divine Power, and by this body of the blessed martyr Apollinaris, that out of favour to no person, and without any advantage to myself intervening, I give my testimony. But this I know, and am personally cognizant of, that, before the times of the late bishop John, the Bishop of Ravenna, in the presence of this or that *apocrisiarius* of the Apostolic See, on such and such days, had the custom of using the pallium, and I am not aware that he had herein usurped latently, or in the absence of the *apocrisiarius*.

EPISTLE LXIII.

To Gennadius, Patrician[9].

Gregory to Gennadius, Patrician of Africa.

We doubt not that your Excellency remembers how two years ago we wrote in behalf of Paul our brother and fellow-bishop, asking you to afford him the support of your Dignity in his desire to come to us on account of the trouble he was said to be undergoing from persecution on the part of the Donatists, to the end that, since it had been reported to us that he could get no aid against them there, we might, after ascertaining the truth, give him advice with fraternal sympathy, and treat with him as to what should be done in the way of a wholesome arrangement against the madness of pestiferous presumption. And, so far as our aforesaid brother gave us to understand, he not only failed to get succour from any one, but was prevented by various hindrances from being able to come with safety to the Roman city. Yet, when we had caused your epistle to be read to him, he replied that he is not suffering from the ill-will of certain persons because he repressed the Donatists, but rather says that he is in disfavour with many for his defence of the Catholic faith; and he told me many things besides, which, since this is not a fit time for mentioning them, we have thought best to keep to ourselves.

---

5 Cf. VII. 40; IX. 78.

6 On the subject of this Epistle, cf. above, Ep. XXXIV., with references in note.

7 Cf. V. 11; VI. 34.

8 *Spatam*, a word usually signifying a kind of sword. Cf. VI. 24, where this same *spata* is referred to.

9 On the subject of this letter, see IV. 34, 35.

Since, then, the question before us is not one of earthly affairs, but of the health of souls, and your assertion and his are different, we have been unable to say anything particularly in reply, not having investigated the truth, seeing that, when we received the letters of your Excellency, we were confined by bodily sickness. But when Almighty God, if it should please Him, shall have restored us to our former health, we will sift the truth as we can by diligent enquiry. And according to what we may be able to learn we will so settle the case through the mercy of God that not only the health of souls in the cure whereof you deign to take an interest, lost now by them that err, may be restored, but also that which the maintainers of the true faith still possess may, through the protecting grace of our Redeemer, be preserved.

But with regard to the above-named bishop, whom you assert to be deprived of communion, we greatly wonder how it is that a letter from your Excellency, and not from his primate, has announced this to us.

EPISTLE LXV.

To Mauricius, Emperor.

Gregory to Mauricius Augustus.

Amidst the cares of warfare and innumerable anxieties which you sustain in your unwearied zeal for the government of the Christian republic, it is a great cause of joy to me along with the whole world that your Piety ever watches over custody of the faith whereby the empire of our lords is resplendent. Whence I fully trust that, as you guard the causes of God with the love of a religious mind, so God guards and aids yours with the grace of His Majesty. Now after what manner the serenity of your Piety, out of regard to righteousness and zeal for the purest religion, has been moved against the most flagitious pravity of the Donatists, the tenor of the commands which you have sent most clearly shews. But the most reverend bishops who have come from the African province assert that these have been so disregarded through ill-advised connivance that neither is the judgment of God held in fear there, nor are the imperial commands so far carried into effect; adding also this: that in the aforesaid province, through the bribes of the Donatists prevailing, the Catholic faith is publicly let to sale. But on the other hand the glorius Gennadius[1] has likewise complained of one of those who made such complaints: and two others also have borne like testimony with him on the subject. But, inasmuch as in this case a secular judge was concerned, I have thought it right to send these bishops to the footsteps of your Piety, that they may represent in person to your most serene ears what they declare themselves to have endured for the catholic faith.

For these reasons I beseech the Christianity of my lords, for the weal of their souls and the life of their most pious offspring, to give orders by a strict mandate for the punishment of such as you find to be such as have been described, and to arrest with the hand of rescue the ruin of those who are perishing, and to apply the medicine of correction to insane minds, and cure them of the poisonous bite of error; that so, the darkness of pestiferous pravity having been driven away by the remedy of your provision, and the true faith having shed abroad in those parts the rays of its serenity, heavenly triumph may await you before the eyes of our Redeemer, because whomsoever you defend outwardly from the enemy, them you also set free inwardly from the poison of diabolical fraud; which is a still more glorious thing.

[1] Gennadius was the Exarch of Africa.

EPISTLE LXVI.

To Athanasius, Presbyter.

Gregory to Athanasius, Presbyter of Isauria.

As we are afflicted and mourn for those whom the error of heretical pravity has cut off from the unity of the Church, so we rejoice with those whom their profession of the catholic faith retains within her bosom. And, as it is our duty to oppose the impiety of the former with pastoral solicitude, so it is fitting for us to bestow favour on the pious professions of the latter, and to declare their views to be sound. And accordingly, a suspicion of unsoundness in the faith having arisen against thee, Athanasius, presbyter of the monastery of Saint Mile, called Tamnacus, which is established in the province of Lycaonia, thou, in order that the integrity of the profession of faith might appear, didst elect to have recourse to the Apostolical See over which we preside, asserting also that, having been corporally chastised, thou hadst done some things unjustly and impetuously. And, although things done under compulsion by no means fall under the censure of the canons, and they are rightly accounted to be of no weight (since he himself invalidates them who compels what is unjust to be confessed and done), and though that confession is rather to be received and embraced which is shewn to proceed from the spontaneous will, as is known to be the case in that which thou madest before us;—yet still, to avoid the possibility of uncertainty, we took the precaution of writing about thee to our brother and fellow-bishop, the prelate of the city of Constantinople, that he might inform us by letter of what had been done. He, after being often admonished by us, wrote in reply to the effect that a volume had been found in thy possession, which contained many heretical statements, and that on this account he had been incensed against thee. He having lent this to us in his desire to satisfy us, we read the earlier portions of it attentively: and inasmuch as we found in it manifest poison of heretical pravity, we forbade its being read any more. But, since thou hast assured us that thou hadst read it in simplicity, and, in order to cut off all ground for uncertain suspicion, hast handed to us a paper in thine own handwriting in which, expounding thy faith, thou hast most plainly condemned all heresies in general, or whatever is opposed to the integrity of the Catholic faith or profession, and hast declared that thou hadst always received and didst still receive all that the four holy Ecumenical synods receive, and hadst condemned and didst still condemn what they condemn, and hast promised also to accept and hold to that synod which was held in the times of the emperor Justinian concerning the Three Chapters, and, being forbidden by us to read that same volume in which the poison of pestiferous error is interwoven, rejecting also and condemning all that in it is said or latently implied against the integrity of the Catholic faith, thou hast promised that thou wilt not read it again;—we, moved by these reasons (thy faith also having clearly appeared to us from the paper under thine own hand, God guarding thee, to be catholic), decree thee to be, according to thy profession, free from all stain of heretical perversity, and catholic; and we pronounce that thou hast proved thyself, by the grace of Christ Jesus our Saviour to be in all things a professor and follower of the unadulterated faith: and we give thee free licence, notwithstanding all, to return to thy monastery, resuming thy place and rank.

We wish to write also on this matter to our most beloved brother, the prelate of the city of Constantinople, who has been ordained in the place of the aforesaid holy John [2]. But, since it is the custom that we should not write before his synodical epistle has reached us, we have therefore delayed. But, after it has reached us, we will inform him of these things when we find a convenient opportunity.

---

[2] Cyriacus (A.D. 595) succeeded John the Faster as patriarch of Constantinople. For the letter afterwards written to him with reference to Athanasius, cf. VII. 5.

BOOK VII

EPISTLE II.

To Columbus, Bishop.

Gregory to Columbus, Bishop of Numidia [1].

We received at the hands of the bearer, your deacon, the epistle of your Fraternity, in which you informed us of what had been done among you with regard to the person of the bishop Paul. This has been done so late that he could not now have appeared here in person. For his Excellency also, our son Gennadius the Patrician, sent his chancellor to us with reference to the same case. But when we had caused enquiry to be made whether he was willing to plead against him [i.e. against the bishop Paul] before us, he replied that he had been by no means sent with this intent, but had only brought hither certain three persons from his Church who would allege many things against him. While, then, we neither found him prepared to commence an action, nor were moved by the quality of those persons to regard them as fit accusers of a bishop, we could not gainsay or offer hindrance to the often before-mentioned bishop Paul, who petitioned us in the hope of having leave given him to resort to the royal city; but we presently allowed him according to his petition, with two others whom he should take with him, to set forth. If, then, there have been any things that could be reasonably said against him, the proper course would have been for him to come here at once, and for your Fraternity to inform us of all particulars, as you have now done. For, as to your having signified to us that you suffer from the enmities of many on account of our frequently visiting you by our letters, there is no doubt, most reverend brother, that the good suffer from the grudges of the bad, and that those who are intent on divine works are harassed by the oppositions of the perverse. But, in proportion as these bad things are around you, ought you to be more instantly occupied with the care of the government committed to you, and to watch for the custody of the flock of Christ; and in proportion as the contrariety of unrighteous men presses upon you, ought the care of pastoral solicitude to inflame you to be more active, and very certain of the promised reward, to the end that you may be able to offer to the chief Shepherd gain from the work given you to do.

[1] On the subject of this letter, see IV. 34, 35: also VI. 63.

EPISTLE IV.

To Cyriacus, Bishop.

Gregory to Cyriacus, Bishop of Constantinople.

We have received with becoming charity our common sons, George the presbyter and Theodore your deacon; and we rejoice that you have passed from the care of ecclesiastical business to the government of souls, since, according to the voice of the Truth, *He that is faithful in a little will be faithful also in much* (Luke xvi. 10). And to the servant who administers well it is said, *Because thou hast been faithful over a few things, I will make thee ruler over many things* (Matth. xxv. 23); to whom also it is presently said further with respect to eternal retribution, *Enter thou into the joy of thy Lord.* Now you say in your letter that you had exceedingly wished for rest. But in this you shew that you have fitly assumed pastoral responsibility, since, as a place of rule should be denied to those who covet it, so it should be offered to those who fly from it. *And no man taketh this honour unto himself, but he that is called of God, as was Aaron* (Hebr. v. 4). And again the same excellent preacher says, *If one died for all, then all died; and Christ died for all. It remaineth that they which live should not henceforth live unto themselves, but unto him which died for them, and rose again* (2 Cor. v. 14, 15). And to the shepherd of holy Church it is said, *Simon, son of Jonas, lovest thou me? Feed My sheep* (John xxi. 17). From which words it appears that, if one who is able refuses to feed the sheep of Almighty God, he shews that he does not love the chief Shepherd. For if the Only-begotten of the Father, for accomplishing the good of all, came forth from the secrecy of the Father into the midst of us, what shall we say, if we prefer our secrecy to the good of our neighbours? Thus rest is to be desired by us with all our heart; and yet for the advantage of many it should sometimes be laid aside. For, as we ought with full desire to fly from occupation, so, if there should be a want of some one to preach, we must needs put a willing shoulder under the burden of occupation. And this we are taught by the conduct of two prophets[a], one of whom attempted to shun the office of preaching, while the other desired it. For to the Lord who sent him Jeremias replied saying, *Ah, Lord God, I cannot speak; for I am a child* (Jer. i. 6). And when Almighty God sought for some one to preach, saying, *Whom shall I send, and who will go for us?* Isaias offered himself of his own accord, saying, *Here am I, send me* (Isai. vi. 8). Lo, different voices proceeded outwardly from the two, but they flowed from the same fountain of love.

For indeed there are two precepts of charity; to wit, the love of God and of one's neighbour. Wherefore Isaias, wishing to profit his neighbours by an active life, desires the office of preaching; but Jeremias, longing to cling assiduously to the love of his Maker by a contemplative life, protests against being sent to preach. What, then, one laudably desired the other laudably shrunk from: the latter, lest by speaking he should lose the gains of silent contemplation; the former lest by keeping silence he should feel the loss of diligent work. But this is nicely to be observed in both, that he who refused did not resist finally, and he who wished to be sent saw himself previously purged by a coal from the altar; that so no one who has not been purged should dare to approach sacred ministries, nor any one whom heavenly grace chooses refuse proudly under a show of humility.

Moreover I find you in your epistles seeking with great longing after serenity of mind, and panting for tranquillity of thought apart from perturbation. But I know not in what manner your Fraternity can attain to this. For one who has undertaken the pilotage of a ship must needs watch all the more as he further recedes from shore, so as sometimes to foresee from signs the coming storms; sometimes, when they come, either, if they are small, to ride over them in a straight course, or, if they swell violently, to avoid them as they rush on by steering sideways; and often to watch alone when all who are without charge of the ship are at rest. How, moreover, having undertaken the burden of pastoral charge, can you have serenity of thought, seeing that it is written, *Behold giants groan under the waters* (Job xxvi. 5)? For, according to the words of John, *The waters are peoples* (Rev. xvii. 15). And the groaning of giants under the waters means that whoso in this world has increased in degree of power, as though in a sort of massive size of body, feels the load of greater tribulation by so much the more as he has taken on himself the care of ruling peoples. But, if the power of the Holy Spirit breathes upon the afflicted mind, forthwith what was done bodily for the people of Israel takes place with us spiritually. For it is written, *But the children of Israel walked upon dry land in the midst of the sea* (Exod. xiv. 29). And through the prophet the Lord promises saying, *When thou passest through the waters, I will be with thee, and the rivers shall not overflow thee* (Isai. xliii. 2). For the rivers overflow those whom the active business of this world confounds with perturbation of mind. But he who is sustained in mind by the grace of the Holy Spirit passes through the waters, and yet is not overflowed by the rivers, because in the midst of crowds of peoples he so proceeds along his way as not to sink the head of his mind beneath the active business of the world.

I also, who, unworthy as I am, have come to a place of rule, had sometimes determined to seek some place of retirement: but, seeing the Divine counsels to be opposed to me, I submitted the neck of my heart to my Maker's yoke; especially reflecting on this, that no hidden places whatever can save the soul without the grace of God; and this we observe sometimes, when even saints go astray. For Lot was righteous in the depraved city itself, and sinned on the mountain (Gen. xix.). But why speak of these instances, when we know of greater ones? For what is pleasanter than Paradise? What safer than Heaven? And yet man out of Paradise, and the angel from heaven, by sinning fell. His power, then, should be sought, His grace implored, without whom we are nowhere without fault, with whom we are nowhere without righteousness. We should, then, take care that perturbation of thought get not the better of our minds; for it can by no means be entirely got rid of. For whosoever is in a place of rule must needs have to think sometimes even of earthly things, and to have a care also of external things, that the flock committed to him may be able to subsist for accomplishing what it has to do. But it should be most carefully seen to, that this same care pass not due measure, and that, when lawfully admitted into the heart, it be not allowed to become excessive. Whence

[a] What follows about Isaiah and Jeremiah occurs also in the *Pastoralis Cura*, I. 7.

it is rightly said through Ezekiel[3], *Let not the priests shave their heads, nor suffer their locks to grow long; but polling let them poll their heads* (Ezek. xliv. 20). For what are hairs in the head by signification but thoughts in the mind? For, rising above the brain insensibly, they denote cares of the present life, which from negligent perception, since they come on sometimes importunely, advance as it were without our feeling them. Since, then, all who are over others ought indeed to have outward anxieties, and yet not to devote themselves to them exceedingly, the priests are rightly forbidden either to shave the head or to let their locks grow long, so that they may neither entirely cut off from themselves carnal thoughts for the life of their subjects, nor again allow them to grow too much. And it is also there well said, *Polling let them poll their heads*; meaning that the anxieties of a temporal charge should both proceed as far as is needful, and yet should be soon cut short, lest they grow to an immoderate length. While therefore both, through external provision administered, the life of bodies is protected, and again intentness of heart is not hindered through the same being immoderate, the hairs on the head of the priest are kept to cover the skin, and cut short so as not to veil the eyes.

Furthermore, we have received in full faith your letters addressed to us, and give thanks to Almighty God, who, by the mutual confession of the faithful, guards the coat that is without seam woven from the top throughout, that is to say His Church, in the unity of grace, from all rent of error; and against the deluge (so to speak) of so many sins of the perishing world constructs an ark of many planks in which the elect of Almighty God may be preserved unto life. For, when we in our turn send the confession of our faith to you, and you shew your charity towards us, what are we doing in holy Church but smearing the ark with pitch; lest any wave of error enter, and kill all the spiritual as being men, and the carnal as being beasts.

But, when you have wisely professed a right faith, it remains doubtless that you should keep the more warily the peace of hearts, because of what the Truth says, *Have salt in yourselves, and have peace one with another* (Mark ix. 50). And Paul the apostle admonishes, saying, *Endeavouring to keep the unity of the Spirit in the bond of peace* (Ephes. iv. 3). And again he says, *Follow peace with all men, and holiness, without which no man shall see God* (Hebr. xii. 14). Which peace indeed you will then truly have with us, if you turn away from the pride of a profane name, according to what the same teacher of the Gentiles says, *O Timothy, keep that which is committed to thy trust, avoiding profane novelties of words* (1 Tim. vi. 20). For indeed it is too bad, if these who have been made preachers of humility should glory in the elation of a vain name, when the true preacher says, *But God forbid that I should glory, save in the cross of our Lord Jesus Christ* (Gal. vi. 14). He then is truly glorious who glories not in temporal power, but, for the name of Christ, glories in His passion. Herein therefore we embrace you from the bottom of our heart, herein we recognize you as priests, if, rejecting the vanity of words, you occupy the place of holiness with holy humility. For behold, we have been scandalized by this impious appellation, and retain in our mind and express in words by no means slight complaints. But your Fraternity knows how the Truth says, *If thou offerest thy gift before the altar, and there rememberest that thy brother hath ought against thee, leave there thy gift, and go thy way to be first reconciled to thy brother, and then thou shalt come and offer thy gift* (Matth. v. 23, 24). Herein is to be considered, that, while every fault is done away by the offering of sacrifice, so great is the evil of offence engendered in another's heart that from one who has so sinned the Lord accepts not the sacrifice itself which is wont to do away sin. Take heed then with speed to wipe off cause of offence from your heart, that Almighty God may be able to regard as acceptable the sacrifice of your offering.

Furthermore, while you have truly and accurately professed the right faith, we find that among those whom you have held to be condemned by the most holy general synods you have condemned a certain Eudoxius; whose name we have not found mentioned in the Latin language either in synods or in the books of the bishops of blessed memory, Epiphanius, Augustin, or Philaster, whom we know to have been the chief disputants against heretics[4]. Now if any one of the catholic

---

3 The following fanciful interpretation of Ezekiel's direction to priests is found also, almost word for word, in the *Pastoralis Cura*, II. 7. See note there.

4 It is a sign of Gregory's scanty knowledge of the history of controversies that so far he seems never to have heard of so noted an Arian leader as Eudoxius, whose followers, under the name of Eudoxians, had been specifically condemned in the 1st Canon of the first general Council of Constantinople. But it appears from a subsequent letter (VII. 34), that there was no copy at Rome of the canons of that Council, which had not in fact been accepted there, probably because of the 3rd Canon, which assigned a primacy of honour after Rome to the See of Constantinople, as being new Rome. When he wrote this subsequent letter, he had become aware that the Eudoxians had been so condemned, but still had no idea who Eudoxius had been. The fact was that he was not well versed in past ecclesiastical history, and, being totally ignorant of Greek, could only consult such Latin writings as were within his reach; and in these he had

Fathers really condemns him, we undoubtedly follow their opinion. If, however, in your synodical epistle you have wished to condemn by name those also who, apart from the holy synods, are condemned in the writings of the Fathers, your Fraternity has mentioned too few by many; but if those whom the general synods reject, then too many by this one. But in the midst of all these things it is to be remembered, that in order that we may be free to profess the true faith and to order whatever has to be done in peace and concord, we ought to pray incessantly for the life of our most serene lords and of their offspring, that Almighty God would subdue barbarous nations under their feet, and grant them long and happy lives, to the end that through a Christian empire the faith which is in Christ may reign.

EPISTLE V.

To Cyriacus, Bishop.

Gregory to Cyriacus, Bishop of Constantinople.

When in time past I represented the Apostolic See in the royal city, I became acquainted with the good qualities of your Holiness. And I greatly rejoice that the care of souls has been committed to you. And though unworthy, I beseech Almighty God with all the prayers in my power that He would even increase His grace in you, and cause you to gather gain of souls for the eternal country. But, whereas you say that you are weak for this work that has been put upon you, we know that the first virtue is acknowledgment of infirmity; and from this we gather that you can fulfil well the ministry you have undertaken, that we see how, out of humility, you acknowledge your own infirmity For we are all infirm; but he is more infirm who has not strength to consider his infirmity. But you, most blessed brethren, are for this reason strong, that, distrusting your own strength, you trust in the power of Almighty God.

I cannot, however, express by the words of a letter how much my heart is bound to your Charity. But I pray that Almighty God may by the gift of His grace multiply the same charity that is between us, and may take away all occasion of offence, lest the holy Church, united by the profession of the true faith, and compacted by conjunction of the hearts of the faithful, should suffer any damage from priests disputing with each other, which God forbid. I at any rate, in all that I speak, in all that I say, against the proud conduct of certain persons, still, through the bounty of Almighty God, never relinquish custody of inward charity; but so execute outwardly what belongs to justice as by no means to disregard inwardly what belongs to love and kindness. And do you also ever return my love, and guard what belongs to peace and kindness; that, remaining of one mind, so as to allow no dissension to come in between us, we may be better able from the very unity of our hearts to obtain what we seek from the Lord.

Furthermore, I commend to your Holiness John, presbyter of Chalcedon, and Athanasius of Isauria, that no one may set you against them by underhand misrepresentations; for I have thoroughly examined their faith, and have found them sound in their confessions, which have also been given in writing.

Now may the Holy Trinity protect you with His hand, and render you always vigilant and careful in the custody of souls, to the end that in the eternal retribution you may be counted worthy to be crowned, not only for your own work, but also for the amelioration of your subjects.

EPISTLE VI.

To Mauricius Augustus.

Gregory to Mauricius Augustus.

Almighty God, who has made your Piety to be the guardian of ecclesiastical peace, preserves you by the same faith which, through unity among priests, you preserve; and when you submit your heart humbly to the yoke of heavenly loving-kindness, it is brought to pass by heavenly grace that you tread your enemies under the foot of valour. For it cannot be of small advantage that, when John of holy memory had departed this life, your Piety long hesitated, and somewhat deferred the time, while seeking counsel in the fear of Almighty God, in order, to wit, that the cause of God might be ordered, as it should be, with great fear[5]. Whence also I think that my brother and fellow-priest Cyriacus is proved to be exceedingly fit for pastoral rule, in that the long deliberation of your Piety has raised him to this degree. And we all know how diligent and how practised he has long been in the administration of ecclesiastical affairs. Whence also I doubt not that it has been brought about by Divine ordering that one who had admin-

failed to find Eudoxius mentioned. He applied, however, to the patriarchs of Alexandria and Antioch for further information on the subject (see VII. 34, and VIII. 30), and was at length satisfied that Eudoxius had been a veritable heretic, having been condemned by many Greek Fathers of repute, and concluded that he was "manifestly slain, against whom our heroes have cast so many darts" (VIII. 30).

5 What is said here shews that the appointment of the Patriarchs of Constantinople rested in fact entirely with the Emperor.

istered the least things well should fitly undertake the greater, and should pass from the charge of affairs to the government of souls. Wherefore in all our prayers we beseech Almighty God to repay this good work to the Serenity of our lords and to their pious offspring both in the present world and also with a perpetual recompense, and to grant to my aforesaid brother and fellow-priest, who has been put over the Lord's flock, to shew himself fully solicitous in the care of souls; that he may be able irreprovably both to correct what is wrong in his subjects and to foster what is right unto further increase; to the end that the judgment of your Piety concerning him may be approved, not only before men, but also before the eyes of the Supernal Majesty.

The venerable men, George the presbyter and Theodore the deacon, in consideration of the command of my lords and the imminence of the winter season, I have not allowed to be delayed in this city

EPISTLE VII.

To Peter, Domitian, and Elpidius.

Gregory to Peter, Domitian, and Elpidius, Bishops[6].

I rejoice exceedingly that you welcomed with great joy the ordination of the most holy Cyriacus, my brother and fellow-priest. And since we have learnt from the preaching of Paul the apostle that *If one member rejoice, all the members rejoice with it* (1 Cor. xii. 26), you must needs consider with how great exultation I rejoice with you in this thing, wherein not one member, but many members of Christ have rejoiced. Nevertheless, so far as I have been able to consider your Fraternity's letters on a cursory perusal, great joy has carried you away into immoderate praise of this my brother. For you say that he has appeared in the Church like the sun, so that you all cried out, *This is the day which the Lord hath made; let us rejoice and be glad in it* (Ps. cxvii. 24)[7]. Yet surely this is a promise of the life to come, seeing that it is said, *The righteous shall shine forth as the sun* (Matth. xiii. 43; Wisd. iii. 7). For, in whatsoever virtue any one may excel, how can he shine forth as the sun while still in the present life, wherein *The corruptible body presseth down the soul, and the earthly tabernacle weigheth down the mind that museth upon many things* (Wisd. ix. 15); wherein *We see another law in our members warring against the law of our mind, and bringing us into captivity by the law of sin which is in our members* (Rom. vii. 23); wherein *Even in ourselves we have the answer of death, that we should not trust in ourselves* (2 Cor. i. 9); wherein also the Prophet cries aloud, *Fear and trembling are come upon me, and darkness hath covered me* (Ps. liv. 6)[8]? For it is written also, *A wise man abideth as the sun; a fool changeth as the moon* (Ecclus. xxvii. 12); where the comparison of the sun is not applied to the splendour of his brightness, but to perseverance in well-doing. But the good beginning of his ordination could not as yet be praised by you with regard to perseverance. And as to your saying that you cried out, *This is the day which the Lord hath made*, you ought to have considered of whom this is said. For what comes before is this; *The stone which the builders refused, the same is made the head-stone of the corner. This is the Lord's doing, and it is marvellous in our eyes* (Ps. cxvii. 22)[9]. And with regard to this same stone it is forthwith added, *This is the day which the Lord hath made*. For He who for strength of building is said to be a stone, for the grace of illumination is called the Day, being also made, because He became incarnate. In Him we are enjoined to rejoice and be glad, because He has overcome in us the darkness of our error by the light of His excellence. In praise of a creature, then, that expression ought not to have been used which is suitable to the Creator alone.

But why should I find fault with these things, knowing as I do how joy carries away the mind? For your charity engendered in you great gladness, which gladness of heart the tongue applauding followed. This being so, the praise which charity found to hand cannot now be called a fault. But to me concerning my most holy brother there should have been briefly said what I might accept with satisfaction, seeing that I knew him to be one who has long given to me especially this proof of his greatness; that, having been occupied in so many affairs of ecclesiastical administration, he has kept a tranquil heart in the midst of turbulent throngs, and always restrained himself with a gentle bearing. And this indeed is no small commendation of a great and unshaken mind, not to have been perturbed among the perturbations of business.

6 Who these bishops were, who had assisted at the ordination of Cyriacus and sent a report of it to Geegory, does not appear. In the objection taken by the latter to the language of lauuation with which the new patriarch had been hailed at Constantinople we may perhaps detect something of his habitual jealousy of the assumptions of the Constantinopolitan See. Of Cyriacus himself he appears to have had a high opinion, and to have welcomed his accession, hoping at first that he would renounce the offensive title of œcumenical bishop which had been assumed by John Jejunator. In this, however, he was disappointed, and afterwards inveighed against the new patriarch for proud presumption no less than against the old one.

7 cxviii. 24.

8 lv. 5.

9 cxviii. 22.

Furthermore, your Fraternity should be instant in continual prayers, that Almighty God may guard in our aforesaid brother and fellow-priest what has been well begun, and ever lead him on to what is better still. This should ever be the prayer of you, most holy ones, and of the people subject to him. For the deserts of rulers and peoples are so connected with each other that often the lives of subjects are made worse from the fault of those who are over them, and often the lives of pastors fall off from the ill desert of peoples. For that the evil doings of one who is over others does very great harm to those who are under him the Pharisees are evidence, of whom it is written, *Ye shut up the kingdom of heaven against men. For ye neither go in yourselves, neither suffer ye them that are entering to go in* (Matth. xxiii. 13). And that the fault of peoples does much harm to the life of pastors we perceive in what David did (2 Kings ii. 24). For he, praised by the testimony of God, he, conscious of heavenly mysteries, being inflated by the tumour of hidden elation, sinned in numbering the people; and yet the punishment fell upon the people for David's sin. Why was this? Because in truth according to the desert of subject peoples are the hearts of rulers disposed. Now the righteous Judge rebuked the fault of the sinner by visitation on those on account of whom he sinned. But, because he himself, waxing proud of his own will, was not free from fault, he himself also received punishment of his fault. For the fierce wrath, which smote the people bodily, prostrated also the ruler of the people with inmost sorrow of heart. Consider therefore these things mutually; and, even as he who is put over you and over the people should intercede for all, so should all of you pray for his conversation and manners, that before Almighty God both you may profit by imitation of him, and he may be aided by your deserts. Further, let us all with one accord pray continually with great weeping to the utmost of our powers for our most serene lords and their pious offspring, that protecting heavenly grace may guard their lives, and subdue the necks of the nations to the Christian empire.

EPISTLE XI.

To Rufinus, Bishop of Ephesus.

Gregory to Rufinus, &c.

The charity of your acts of friendship in the past has moved us to visit your Fraternity with the present letter. For we have been refreshed with great joy by learning from reports given us of your health that all is well with you. But, while this is so, we implore Almighty God, that as in the present life, which is as it were a shadow of the future one, He has granted you to rejoice in the transitory welfare of your body, so in that heavenly country wherein is true life He may cause us to give thanks and rejoice with a common exultation for the perfected salvation of your soul. Now the bearer of this, desiring to be commended to you by a letter from us, having been asked by us whether he had learnt letters as becomes a clerk, replied that he was ignorant of them. What further commendation, then, with regard to him I should give to your Fraternity I know not; except that you should be solicitous about his soul, and watch over him with pastoral zeal, so that, as he cannot read, your tongue may be a book to him, and that in the goodness of your preaching and work he may see what to follow. For the living voice usually draws the heart more closely than perfunctory reading. But, while, as his master, you supply him inwardly with this spiritual teaching, let not outward care for him also be wanting, that by its aid he come to long for spiritual things, and lest, if such aid is slighted, you should no longer have one to preach to.

EPISTLE XII.

To Respecta, Abbess.

Gregory to Respecta, Abbess of Massilia (*Marseilles*) in Gaul.

The demand of a pious wish ought to be accomplished by a consequent result, that so the benefit demanded may be validly attained, and sincerity of devotion may laudably shine forth. Accordingly to the monastery consecrated to the honour of Saint Cassian wherein you are selected to preside—in accordance with the petition of our children Dynamius and Aureliana, who are shewn, in their religious devotion, to have united it to the house in their possession by connecting the buildings—we have seen fit to allow these privileges:—We appoint that on the death of the abbess of the aforesaid monastery, not a stranger, but one whom the congregation may choose for itself from among its own members, shall be ordained; whom (provided however that she be judged worthy of this ministry) the bishops of the same place shall ordain. Further, with regard to the property and management of the same monastery, we decree that neither bishop nor any ecclesiastic shall have any power; but appoint that these things shall in all respects pertain to the charge of thy Solicitude, or of her who may be abbess in the same place after thee. If on the day of the Saint's anniversary, or of the dedication, of the aforesaid monastery the bishop should resort thither for celebrating the sacred solemnities of mass, still his office must be so executed that his chair be not placed there, except on the aforesaid days while he is celebrating there the solemnities of mass. And when he departs, let his chair be at the same time removed from the same oratory. But on all other days let the offices of mass be performed by the presbyter whom the same bishop may appoint.

Furthermore, with regard to the life and deeds of the handmaidens of God, or of the abbess who may be constituted in the above-written monastery, we enjoin on the bishop, in the fear of God, to devote careful attention to them; so that, if any of those who dwell there, her fault demanding it, ought to be subjected to punishment, he may himself visit the offence according to the vigour of the sacred canons. These things, then, being by us ordained and granted, do thou, in the ordering of thy congregation, study to shew thyself so earnestly attentive in all respects that the malice of the malignant foe may find nothing there that can be contaminated. All these things, therefore, embraced in this paper of injunctions, we ordain to be observed, under Christ's protection, in all respects and by all persons for ever in thy monastery, to the end that the benefits of the privileges allowed may always continue firm and inviolate. The month of November, Indict. 15.

EPISTLE XIII.

To Fortunatus, Bishop.

Gregory to Fortunatus, Bishop of Fanum[1].

As it is reprehensible and deserving of punishment for any one to sell consecrated vessels except in cases sanctioned by law and the sacred canons, so it is not a matter for reproach or penalty if they should be disposed of with a compassionate purpose for the redemption of captives. Since, then, we find from the information given us by your Fraternity that you have borrowed money for the redemption of captives, and have not the means of repaying it, and on this account desire, with our authority, to dispose of some consecrated vessels,—in this case, seeing that the decrees of both the laws and the canons approve, we have thought fit to lend our approval, and grant you leave to dispose of the consecrated vessels. But, lest their sale should possibly lead to any ill-feeling against yourself, they ought to be disposed of, up to the amount of the debt, in the presence of John our *defensor*, and their price should be paid to the creditors, to the end that, the business being completed with observance of this kind, neither may the creditors feel loss from having lent the money, nor your Fraternity sustain ill-will now or at any future time.

[1] Fanum Fortunæ in Picenum (*Fano*).

EPISTLE XV.

To George, Presbyter.

Gregory to George, Presbyter, and to Theodore, deacon, of the Church of Constantinople.

Mindful of your goodness and charity, I greatly blame myself, that I gave you leave to return so soon: but, since I saw you pressing me importunately once and again for leave to go, I considered that it might be a serious matter for your Love to tarry with us longer. But, after I had learnt that you had lingered so long on your journey owing to the winter season, I confess that I was sorry that you had been sent away so soon. For, if your Love was unable to accomplish your intended journey, it had been better that you had lingered with me than away from me.

Moreover, after your departure I learnt from information given me by my most beloved sons the deacons that your Love had said that our Almighty Lord and Saviour Jesus Christ, when He descended into hell, saved all who there acknowledged Him as God, and delivered them from the pains due to them. With regard to this subject I desire that your Charity should think very differently. For, when He descended into hell, He delivered through His grace those only who both believed that He should come and observed His precepts in their lives. For it is evident that after the incarnation of the Lord no one can be saved, even of those who hold His faith, who have not the life of faith; since it is written, *They acknowledge that they know God, but in deeds they deny Him* (Tit. i. 16). And John says, *He that saith that he knows Him, and keepeth not His commandments, is a liar* (1 John ii. 4). James also, the brother of the Lord, writes saying, *Faith without works is dead* (Jam. ii. 20). If, then, believers now are not saved without good works, while the unbelieving and reprobate without good action were saved by our Lord descending into hell, then the lot of those who never saw the incarnation of the Lord was better than that of these who have been born after the mystery of His incarnation. But what fatuity it argues to say or think this the Lord Himself testifies to His disciples, when He says, *Many kings and prophets have desired to see the things which ye see, and have not seen them* (Matth. xiii. 17; Luke x. 24). But, that I may not detain your Love with argument of my own, learn what Philaster, in the book which he wrote about heresies, says about this heresy. His words are these; "They are heretics who say that the Lord descended into hell, and announced himself after death to all who were already there, so that in acknowledging Him there they might be saved; seeing that this is contrary to the prophet David where he says, *But in hell who shall acknowledge thee* (Ps. vi. 6)? And to the Apostle; *As many as have sinned without law shall perish without law* (Rom. ii. 12)." And with his words the blessed Augustine also agrees in the book which he wrote about heresies.

Considering, therefore, all these things, hold ye nothing but what the true faith teaches through the Catholic Church: namely, that the Lord in descending into hell rescued from infernal durance those only whom while living in the flesh He preserved through His grace in faith and good conduct. For in that which He says in the Gospel, *When I shall be lifted up from the earth, I will draw all to myself* (John xii. 32), He means all that are elect. For one could not be drawn to God after death who had separated himself from God by evil living. May Almighty God keep you under His protection, that, wherever ye are, ye may feel in soul and body the aid of His grace.

EPISTLE XVII.

To Sabinianus, Bishop.

Gregory to Sabinianus, Bishop of Jadera [2].

If thou hadst been at pains to weigh with careful consideration the rule of ecclesiastical administration and the order of ancient custom, neither would any fault of unlawful presumption have crept in upon thee, nor would others have incurred danger by occasion of thy sin. Now there is no doubt that thou wast aware how that, certain things having come to our ears about Maximus which were no slight bar to his advancement to the priesthood, we had not given our assent to it, and that it was our will that he should not attain to what he strove after till there had been adequate satisfaction concerning the things that were said. But, when thou oughtest by all means to have observed this, it came rather to pass that he, snatching at the episcopate with the greediness of a blind mind, inclined thee unwarily to favour him in spite of our prohibition. But, lest even then the things that had been reported to us should remain unexamined, he was summoned to come hither by letters from us. And, when he was so perversely inclined as to defer doing so, we took care to admonish him in repeated letters, under pain of interdiction from communion, to make haste to come to us for his purification, putting aside all excuses: but he chose rather to submit to excommunication than to evince obedience. Whence the result is (awful to be said), that the pravity of his perverse disposition involves others in his own perdition. Now however, inasmuch as we have learnt that thou dissentest from his wickedness, we exhort thee by the present writing (that so it may profit thy soul to have severed thyself, even though late, from him) that thou henceforth neither communicate with him nor make mention of his name in the sacred solemnities of mass; and also that thou defer not coming to us without delay, yea and bring others with thee too, such as thou canst, whether bishops or other religious persons, so that (the cause being thoroughly examined), both your absolution, should the case require it, may fittingly and decently ensue, and that those who have fallen into the sin of the like temerity may be recalled to the way of salvation, with the help of the blessed Peter, Prince of the apostles, by an arrangement well-pleasing to Christ. Moreover, let any bishop or religious person that may come to us know that he will sustain no prejudice or injustice, but that all will be arranged so as to please our Redeemer after full ascertainment of the truth; to the end that even from our way of ordering the matter, with the Lord's approval, it may appear to all that we are not moved by private grudge against any man, but by zeal for God and for the adjustment of ecclesiastical order.

EPISTLE XIX

To Marinianus, Archbishop.

Gregory to Marinianus, Archbishop of Ravenna [3].

Your Fraternity has been long aware after what manner the Church of Ariminum has been hitherto deprived of pastoral government by reason of the known bodily affliction of the priest who was ordained by us [4]. Now we, moved by the prayers of the inhabitants of that place, having frequently exhorted him to return with the help of the Lord to his Church, if he should feel himself relieved from this affliction of the head whereby he was kept away, he has been expected now for four years since the leave of absence given him. And, when at the instance of clergy and citizens who have come from thence and urged us with

[2] See VI. 27, note 6.

[3] Concerning the election of Marinianus, see V. 48.

[4] Viz. Castorius. See II. 41.

entreaties, we urgently exhorted him to return with them, the Lord helping him, if able to do so, he begged of us by a supplication in writing[5], that, inasmuch as by reason of this affliction wherewith he is held he can in no wise rise to the government of the same Church, or to the office undertaken by him, we should ordain a bishop to this same Church. Hence, seeing that the charge laid upon us of caring for all the Churches constrains us to see that pastoral guardianship be no longer wanting to the flock of the faithful, and being compelled by their entreaties, and by his renunciation on the ground of his own inability, we have resolved that a bishop should be ordained to this same Church of Ariminum: and, having issued our precept according to custom, we have not failed to admonish the clergy and people of the same Church, to the end that they may concur with concordant provision to choose for themselves a prelate[6]. We therefore exhort your Fraternity that him whom all with one consent shall choose (as they themselves also have requested leave to do) you cause to be summoned before you; and test him by cautious enquiry on all sides. And if, by favour of the Lord, none of the things that are punished with death in the text of the Heptateuch are found in him, and if, on the report of trustworthy persons, his life should approve itself to you, send him to us with the certification of his election, adding your own letter of testification, to the end that a prelate of this same Church may, under the ordering of the Lord, be by us consecrated.

EPISTLE XX.

To the Clergy and People of Ariminum[7].

Gregory to the Clergy, &c.

Our pastoral charge constrains us to succour with anxious consideration any Churches that are deprived of the government of a priest. Accordingly, inasmuch as your Church has long been deprived of pastoral rule from the malady, as you know, of its own priest, we, moved by your entreaties, have not failed to admonish the said bishop, that, if he should feel himself recovered from that malady, he should resume the ministry of the priesthood undertaken by him. And he, having been again and again warned by us, has now under the pressure of the same malady intimated by a supplication addressed to us in writing that by reason of this malady he can by no means rise to the government of the said Church or to the office undertaken by him. We therefore, compelled by the hopeless condition of this same person, have held it necessary to take thought for the setting in order of your Church. We exhort, then, that all of you, with one consent, without noise or disturbance, choose with the help of the Lord such a priest to preside over you as may not be disapproved by the venerable canons, and also be found worthy of so great a ministry. And let him, when required, come to us to be ordained, with the solemnity of a decree attested by the subscriptions of all and followed up by the written approval of the visitor[8], to the end that your Church, by the Lord's ordering, may have its own priest.

We desire also that him whom your unanimity may have chosen you take without delay to our brother and fellow-bishop Marinianus at Ravenna[9], that, having been thoroughly examined and tested by him, he may be supported by his testimony also when he comes to us.

EPISTLE XXIII.

To Fortunatus and Anthemius[9a].

Gregory to Fortunatus, bishop, and Anthemius, guardian (*defensori*).

Catellus, the bearer of these presents, has informed us that his sister, who had been betrothed to one Stephen, has, through divine mercy moving her, been converted[1] in a monastery at Naples, and that the same Stephen improperly detains a house and some other things belonging to her. And, inasmuch as legal decrees (*Caus.* 17, q. 2, c. 28) have appointed that a betrothed woman, should she wish to be converted, shall suffer no loss whatever, let thy Fraternity, together with Anthemius the subdeacon, endeavour by diligent enquiry to investigate the truth. And if, as we have been informed, you find that the Stephen abovenamed is keeping a house or anything else unjustly, let him be urgently warned by your exhortation to restore without any delay or altercation what he unduly detains, and not to defer under any kind of excuse the restitution of what is not his own. And if perchance you find him neglect your exhortation, notify this to us, giving also an accurate account of the

[5] Cf. XI. 47 as to the supersession of a bishop incapacitated by illness, except at his own written request, being uncanonical.

[6] See Ep. XX., which follows.

[7] See preceding Epistle.

[8] Viz. a bishop Sebastian, who had been commissioned, as was usual in such cases, to visit the church of Ariminum during the incapacity of its proper bishop. The Epistle which follows this (Ep. XXI., which, as not throwing further light on the proceedings, has not been translated) is addressed to him, directing him to see to the due election, &c., of a successor to Castorius.

[9] As Metropolitan. See preceding Epistle.

[9a] Fortunatus was bishop of Naples, and Anthemius a subdeacon, and *Defensor* of Campania.

[1] *Conversam fuisse;* the usual phrase for taking to monastic life.

facts of the case, to the end that, when the merits of the case are known, he may be forced by other means, in accordance with equity, to make the restitution which he scorns to make of his own accord out of regard to honesty. Commending the bearer of these presents to thy Fraternity, we exhort thee to allow him no longer to suffer from delay on this account.

EPISTLE XXV.

To Gregoria.

Gregory to Gregoria, Lady of the Bedchamber (*cubiculariæ*) to Augusta.

I have received the longed for letters of your Sweetness, in which you have been at pains all through to accuse yourself of a multitude of sins: but I know that you fervently love the Almighty Lord, and I trust in His mercy that the sentence which was pronounced with regard to a certain holy woman proceeds from the mouth of the Truth with regard to you: *Her sins, which are many, are forgiven her, for she loved much* (Luke vii. 47). And how they were forgiven is shewn also by what follows afterwards; that she sat at the Lord's feet, and heard the word from His mouth (Luke x. 39)[2]. For, being rapt in the contemplative, she had transcended the active life, which Martha her sister still pursued (Ib. 40). She also sought earnestly her buried Lord, and, stooping over the sepulchre, found not His body. But, even when the disciples went away, she remained standing before the door of the sepulchre, and whom she sought as dead, Him she was counted worthy to see alive, and announced to the disciples that He had risen again. And this was by the wonderful dispensation of the loving-kindness of God, that life should be announced by a woman's mouth, because by a woman's mouth had been the first taste of death in Paradise. And at another time also, with another Mary, she saw the Lord after His resurrection, and held His feet. Bring before your eyes, I pray you, what hands held whose feet. That woman who had been a sinner in the city, those hands which had been polluted with iniquity, touched the feet of Him who sits at the right hand of the Father above all the angels. Let us estimate, if we can, what those bowels of heavenly loving-kindness are, that a woman who had been plunged through sin into the whirlpool's depth should be thus lifted high on the wing of love through grace. It is fulfilled, sweet daughter, it is fulfilled, what was promised to us by the prophetic voice concerning this time of the holy Church: *And in that day the house of David shall be an open fountain for ablution of the sinner and of her that is unclean* (Zach. xiii. 1). For the house of David is an open fountain for ablution to us sinners, because we are washed from the filth of our iniquities by mercy now disclosed through the son of David our Saviour.

But as to what thy Sweetness has added in thy letters, namely that thou wilt continue to be urgent with me till I write that it has been revealed to me that thy sins are forgiven, thou hast demanded a difficult, nay even an unprofitable thing; difficult indeed, because I am unworthy of having a revelation made to me; but unprofitable, because thou oughtest not to become secure about thy sins, except when in the last day of thy life thou shalt be able no longer to bewail them. But, until that day comes, thou oughtest, ever suspicious and ever fearful, to be afraid of faults, and wash them with daily tears. Assuredly the apostle Paul had already ascended into the third heaven, had also been caught up into Paradise, and heard secret words which it was not lawful for a man to speak (2 Cor. xii. 2, &c.), and yet, still fearful, he said, *I keep under my body, and bring it into subjection, lest that by any means, while preaching to others, I myself should become a castaway* (1 Cor. ix. 27). One who is caught up into heaven still fears; and shall one whose conversation is still on earth desire already not to fear? Consider, most sweet daughter, that security is wont to be the mother of carelessness. Thou oughtest not, then, in this life to have security, whereby thou mayest be rendered careless. For it is written, *Happy is the man that is always afraid* (Prov. xxviii. 14). And again it is written, *Serve the Lord in fear, and rejoice unto him with trembling* (Ps. ii. 11). In short, then, it must needs be that in the time of this life trembling possess your soul, to the end that it may hereafter rejoice without end through the joy of security. May Almighty God fill your soul with the grace of His Holy Spirit, and, after the tears which you daily shed in prayer, bring you to eternal joys.

EPISTLE XXVI.

To Theoctista, Patrician[3].

Gregory to Theoctista, &c.

That your Excellency, though placed in so

[2] It will be observed that Gregory identifies the woman who had been a sinner in the city with the sister of Martha, and also with the Magdalene.

[3] This patrician lady was sister of the Emperor Mauricius (see I. 5), and appears from what is said in this letter to have been governess of the imperial children, and in close attendance on the Empress Constantina. The letter is in many respects interesting and characteristic. In it may be noted Gregory's way of retaining influence over devout ladies in high circles, and through them hoping to influence others; his favourite method of allegorizing the Old Testament Scriptures; his ten-

great a tumult of affairs, is full of the fruitfulness of the sacred word, and incessantly pants after eternal joys, for this I give great thanks to Almighty God, in that in you I see fulfilled what is written of the elect fathers, *But the children of Israel walked on dry land through the midst of the sea* (Exod. xv. 19). But on the other hand, *I am come into the depth of the sea, and the storm hath overwhelmed me* (Ps. lxviii. 3)[4]. But you, as I see, walk with dry feet through the waves of secular affairs to the country of promise. Let us give thanks, then, to that Spirit who lifts up the hearts which He fills; who amid the tumults of men makes a solitude in the soul; and in whose presence there is no place, wherein a soul moved by compunction can be, which is not a secret one. For you inhale the odour of eternal sweetness, and so ardently love the bridegroom of your soul as to be able to say with the heavenly bride, *Draw me after thee; we run in the odour of thine ointments* (Cant. i. 3). But in the letters of your Excellency I find this deficiency; that you have been unwilling to tell me about your most serene mistress, how studiously she reads, or how she is moved by compunction in her reading. For your presence ought to be of great advantage to her, that amid the billows of affairs under which she continually suffers, and by which, whether she will or no, she is drawn abroad, she may be recalled inwardly to the love of the heavenly country. And this also you ought to investigate, as often as tears are given her for her soul, whether her compunction arises still from fear, or whether now from love[5].

For there are two kinds of compunction, as you know: one that is afraid of eternal pains, the other that sighs for heavenly rewards; since the soul that is athirst for God is first moved to compunction by fear, and afterwards by love. For in the first place it is affected to tears because, while recollecting its evil doings, it fears to suffer for them eternal punishments. But, when fear has died away in the anxiety of a long sorrow, a certain security has birth from a sense of pardon; and the mind is enflamed with love of heavenly joys. And one who previously wept for fear of punishment begins afterwards to weep most bitterly for being kept back from the kingdom. For the soul contemplates what are those choirs of angels, what is the very society of blessed spirits, what the vision of the inward brightness of God; and laments more for the lack of unending good than it wept before when it feared eternal evil; and thus it comes to pass that the compunction of fear, when perfected, draws the mind to the compunction of love. All this is well described in the sacred and true history, understood figuratively, which says, *Axa the daughter of Caleph sighed sitting on an ass. And her father said to her, What wouldest thou? Who answered, Give me a blessing, Thou hast given me a South and dry land; give me also a watered land. And her father gave her the upper springs, and the nether springs* (Josh. xv. 18)[6]. For indeed Axa sits on an ass, when the soul presides over the irrational motions of the flesh. And sighing she seeks a watered land from her father, because the grace of tears is to be sought with great longing from our Creator. For there are some who have already freely received the gift of speaking in behalf of justice, of protecting the oppressed, of giving of their own to the needy, of having ardour of faith, but have not yet the grace of tears. These, that is to say, have a South and dry land, but still need springs of water; because, while they are occupied in good works, wherein they are great and fervent, they have still sore need (either from fear of punishment, or from love of the heavenly kingdom) to lament the sins which they cannot be without while they live. But since, as I have said, there are two kinds of compunction, her father gave her the upper springs and the nether springs. For the soul receives the upper springs, when she afflicts herself in tears for desire of the heavenly kingdom; but she receives the nether springs, when she shudders with weeping at the punishments of hell. And indeed the nether springs are given first, and the upper springs afterwards. But, because the compunction of love is far above the other indignity, there was need for the upper springs to be mentioned first, and the nether springs afterwards. You then, who through the operation of the Almighty Lord know by experience both kinds of compunction, ought anxiously to try to discover day by day how much you are profiting your most serene mistress by your words.

Further, I beg you to take especial care to instruct in good morals the little lords whom you are bringing up, and to admonish the glorious eunuchs who are appointed to attend them that they should speak to them such things as may move their minds to mutual

dency to regard remarkable incidents as miraculous; and his allusion to the very large number of females at that time leading a monastic life in Rome. Cf. XI. 45, addressed to the same lady.

4 Ps. lxix. 2.

5 The whole passage which follows about two kinds of compunction, with the allegorical interpretation of the story of Achsah, is found, word for word, in the Dialogues, Lib. III. cap. 34.

6 In Joshua xv. 18, instead of "and she lighted off her ass," as in the English Version, the Vulgate has "suspiravitque ut sedebat in asino."

charity between themselves and to gentleness towards subjects; lest, if they should conceive now any grudge against each other, it should break out openly hereafter. For in truth the words of those who bring up children will be either milk, if they are good, or poison if they are evil. Let them therefore so speak now to the little ones that the latter may shew hereafter what good words they had sucked from the mouths of those who nursed them.

Furthermore, my beloved son, Sabinianus the deacon, has brought thirty pounds of gold, sent by your Excellency to be given for the redemption of captives and for distribution to the poor; with regard to which I rejoice, but tremble for myself, seeing that I shall have to render an account before the tremendous Judge, not only of the substance of Saint Peter, Prince of the apostles, but also of your possessions. But to you may Almighty God return heavenly things for earthly, and eternal for temporal. I have now to inform you that from the city of Crotona, which, lying on the Adriatic Sea in the land of Italy, was taken last year by the Lombards, many noble men and many noble women were led away captive, and children were parted from their parents, parents from their children, husbands from their wives, and wives from their husbands; of whom some have already been redeemed. But, because of the heavy prices put upon them, many have remained so far in the hands of those most abominable Lombards. But I sent at once for their redemption a moiety of the money sent by you. Out of the other moiety I have arranged for the purchase of bed-clothes for the handmaidens of God whom you in Greek language call *monastriae;* seeing that they suffer from grievous bareness in their beds during the very severe cold of this winter; there being many of them in this city. For, according to the official list of them, they are found to be three thousand in number. They do indeed receive fourscore pounds a year from the possessions of Saint Peter, Prince of the apostles. But what is this for so great a multitude, especially in this city, where everything is so dear? Their life, moreover, is such, and strict to such a degree in tears and abstinence, that we believe that, but for them, not one of us could have subsisted for so many years in this place among the swords of the Lombards.

Furthermore, I send you, as a blessing from Saint Peter the apostle, a key from his most sacred body; with respect to which key the miracle has been wrought which I now relate. A certain Lombard, having found it on his entrance into a city in the parts beyond the Po, and, paying no regard to it as Saint Peter's key, but wishing to make something of it for himself in that he saw it to be of gold, took out a knife to cut it. But presently seized by a spirit, he plunged the knife wherewith he had thought to cut it into his own throat, and in the same hour fell down dead. And when Autharith, king of the Lombards[7], and many others belonging to him came to the place, and he who had stabbed himself was lying apart in one place dead, and this key on the ground in another, exceeding fear came upon all, so that no one ventured to lift this same key from the ground. Then a certain Lombard who was a Catholic, and known to be given to prayer and almsgiving, Minulf by name, was called, and himself lifted it from the ground. But Autharith, in consideration of this miracle, made another golden key, and sent it along with this to my predecessor of holy memory, declaring what kind of miracle had through it occurred. I have taken thought, then, to send your Excellence this key, through which Almighty God cut off a proud and faithless man, that through it you who fear and love Him may be enabled to have both present and eternal welfare.

EPISTLE XXVII.

To Anastasius, Bishop.

Gregory to Anastasius, Bishop of Antioch.

I have received through the hands of our common son the deacon Sabinianus the longed for letter of your most sweet Holiness, in which the words have flowed not from your tongue but from your soul. And it is not surprising that one speaks well who lives perfectly. And, since you have learnt, through the Spirit teaching you in the school of the heart, the precepts of life—to despise all earthly things and to speed to the heavenly country,—in proportion as you have advanced in good you think what is good of others. But, when I heard many things said in the letters of your Blessedness in praise of me, I understood your intention; how that you wished to describe not what I am, but what I ought to be. But as to your saying that I ought to remember my manner of life, and on no account give place to the malignant spirit who seeks to sift souls, I indeed recollect myself to have been always of bad manner of life, and hasten to overcome and put an end to this my manner of life, if I can. If however, as you believe, I have had anything good in me, I trust in the help of Almighty God that I have not forgotten it. But your Holiness, as I see, by the words of sweetness at the beginning and

7 See I. 17, note 4.

the words that follow, has wished your letter to be like a bee, which carries both honey and a sting, satiating me with the honey and piercing me with the sting. But meanwhile I return to meditation on the words of Solomon, *That better are the wounds of one that loves than the kisses of a flattering foe* (Prov. xxvii. 6). Thus, as to your saying that we ought not to give occasion of offence for no cause at all, this is what your son, our most pious lord (for whose life we ought continually to pray) has already written repeatedly; and what he says out of power I know that you say out of love. Nor do I wonder that you have made use of imperial language in your letters, since there is a very close relationship between love and power. For both presume in a princely way; both ever speak with authority.

And indeed on the receipt of the synodical epistle of our brother and fellow-bishop Cyriacus it was not worth my while to make a difficulty on account of the profane title at the risk of disturbing the unity of holy Church: but nevertheless I took care to admonish him with respect to this same superstitious and proud title, saying that he could not have peace with us unless he corrected the elation of the aforesaid expression, which the first apostate invented. You, however, ought not to say that this is a matter of no consequence, since, if we bear it with equanimity, we are corrupting the faith of the Universal Church; for you know how many not only heretics but heresiarchs have issued from the Constantinopolitan Church. And, not to speak of the injury done to your dignity, if one bishop is called Universal, the Universal Church comes to ruin, if the one who is universal falls. But far, far be this levity from my ears. Yet I trust in Almighty God that what He has promised He will soon fulfil; *Whosoever exalteth himself shall be humbled* (Luke xiv. 11).

So much, in the midst of many occupations. I have briefly replied to what you have said in your letters: for what I ought not just now to express in writing remains imprinted on my mind. I beg your Blessedness always to recall me to your memory in your holy prayers, that so your intercessions may rescue me from temporal and eternal ills. Pray moreover zealously and fervently for the most serene lord the Emperor; for his life is very necessary for the world. I refrain from saying more, for I doubt not that you know.

EPISTLE XXVIII.

To Theodore, Physician.

Gregory to Theodore, Physician at Constantinople.

My most beloved son the deacon Sabinianus[8], on his return to me, brought me no letter from your Glory; but he conveyed hither what had been sent for the poor and captives; whence I understood the reason. It was that you would not speak by letters to a man, having by a good deed made your address to Almighty God. For this same deed of yours has a voice of its own, which calls to the secret ears of God, as it is written, *Hide thy alms in the bosom of the poor, and it shall entreat for thee* (Eccles. xxix. 15). And indeed to me, I confess, it is sad to expend what is not my own, and to add to the accounts which I keep of the substance of the Church those also of the property of my most sweet son the lord Theodore. And yet I rejoice with your benignity that you carefully attend to and observe what the Truth says; *Give alms, and behold, all things are clean unto you* (Luke xi 41); and this which is written, *Even as water quencheth fire, so alms quench sin* (Ecclus. iii. 33). Paul the apostle also says, *Let your abundance supply their want, that their abundance also may be a supply to your want* (2 Cor. viii. 14). Tobias admonishes his son, saying, *If thou hast much, give abundantly: but if thou hast little, of that little impart willingly* (Tob. iv. 9). You therefore observe all these precepts: but we beg you to pray for us, lest we should dispense the fruits of your labours indiscreetly, and not as need requires; lest from that whereby you diminish sins we should heap up sins. Now may Almighty God keep you under His protection, and so grant you human favour in an earthly court as to bring you after a long life to the eternal joys of a heavenly court.

We send you as the benediction of Saint Peter, Prince of the apostles, whom you greatly love, a key from his most sacred body, in which is enclosed iron from his chains, that what bound his neck for martyrdom, may loose yours from all sins.

EPISTLE XXX.

To Narses, the religious (*Narsae religioso*)[9].

Gregory to Narses, &c.

When I was sending Romanus the guardian (*defensorem*) to the royal city, he sought long for your letters, but they could not be found:

8 Gregory's *apocrisiarius* at Constantinople, and eventually his successor in the See of Rome. See III. 53.

9 On the designation *Religiosus*, cf. I. 61, note 7. The Narses here addressed as "Religiosus" was probably the same as the "Narses Comes" of I. 6, and VI. 14, and the "Narses Patricius" of IV. 32 (see note to I. 6). For it is evident from the letters that he was of high rank at Constantinople, and greetings are sent through him to the same persons as in the other letters. He had now, we may suppose, devoted himself to the service of the Church in some capacity.

but afterwards they were found among many letters from other persons, your Sweetness therein telling me of your afflictions and tribulations of spirit, and making known the oppositions to you of bad men. But, I pray you, in all this recall to your mind what I believe too that you never forget, *That all who will live godly in Christ suffer persecution.* (2 Tim. iii. 12). And with regard to this I confidently say that you would live less godly if you suffered persecution less. For let us hear what else the same teacher of the Gentiles says to his disciples; *Yourselves know, brethren, our entrance in unto you, that it was not in vain; for we had before suffered and been shamefully entreated* (1 Thess. ii. 1). Lo, most sweet son, the holy preacher declared that his entrance would have been of no effect, if he had not been shamefully entreated; and thy Charity wishes to say good things, but refuses to endure evil things. Wherefore thou must needs gird thyself up more tightly in the midst of adverse circumstances, that adversity itself may the more increase thy desire for the love of God and thy earnestness in good works. So the seeds of harvests germinate the more fruitfully for being covered over with frost; so fire is kept down by a blast, that it may grow greater. I know indeed that from the perverse speeches of so many evil tongues thou endurest a violent storm, and bearest in thy soul billows of contradictions. But remember what the Lord says by the Psalmist, *I heard thee in the secret place of storm; I proved thee at the waters of contradiction* (Psal. lxxx. 8)[9a]. For, if in the midst of them that contradict thou doest the things that are of God, then thou art proved a true worker.

Further, your most sweet Charity has written to me that I should write something in the way of admonition to the monasteries which, through your prayers and influence, have been instituted by our son the lord Paul. But, if they are vessels of God, I know that they have through the grace of compunction a fountain of wisdom within, and ought not to take in the little drops of my dryness. Further, your perfect wisdom recollects that in Paradise there was no rain, but a fountain ascended from the midst of Paradise to water the face of the ground. Those souls, then, that through the grace of compunction have a fountain in themselves have no need of rain from another's tongue.

Further, you inform me in your letter of the passing away of the lady Esychia[1]; and I rejoiced with great exultation that that good soul, which laboured in a foreign country, has arrived happily at its own. Further, greet in my behalf my glorious daughters, the lady Dominica and the lady Eudochia. But, inasmuch as I hear that it is now a long time since the aforesaid lady Dominica was made a prioress, let your Charity watch over her in this regard; that, as she is no longer compelled to serve in the toil of an earthy court, she may fly perfectly from all noises of this world, devote herself entirely to God, and leave no part of herself outside herself; but that she also gather together as many souls as she can to the service of her Creator, that their minds through her word may receive the grace of compunction, and that she herself may so much the more speedily be absolved from all her sins as, through her life and her tongue, the souls of others also shall have broken loose from the bands of sins. Moreover, since no one among men in this world is without sin (and what else is sinning but flying from God?), I say confidently that this my daughter also has some sins. Wherefore, that she may perfectly satisfy her mistress, that is eternal Wisdom, let her, who fled alone, return with many. For the guilt of turning away will be imputed to no one who in returning brings back gain.

Further, I beg you to greet in my behalf the lord Alexander and the lord Theodorus. But with respect to your saying in your letter that I ought to write to my most excellent daughter the lady Gurdia, and her most holy daughter the lady Theoctista[2], and their magnificent husbands, the lord Marinus and the lord Christidorus, and to give them some admonition about their souls, your most sweet Greatness well knows that there are none at present in the city of Constantinople who can translate well into Greek what has been dictated in Latin. For keeping to the words, but attending little to the sense, they both fail to make the words understood and also mangle the sense. On this account I have written shortly to my aforesaid daughter the lady Gurdia; but have not addressed the others. Further, I have sent you two *camisiae* and four *oraria*, which I beg may be humbly

[9a] Ps. lxxxi. 7.

[1] Cf. I. 6, where greetings were sent to this lady, there also designated as *Domna*.

[2] The Emperor Maurice is said to have had a sister called Gordia, who may have been the lady here referred to. Her daughter Theoctista may be concluded from the epithet "sanctissima" to have been piously disposed; and it may have been a fear lest her piety should suffer through the temptations of fashionable life that had led Narses, who was himself religious, to suggest to Gregory that he should write letters of admonition to the husbands of these ladies, as well as to themselves. Gregory's reluctance to do so may have arisen from a fear of giving offence to such distinguished people from the purport of what he could only write in Latin being misunderstood. Elsewhere apparent are his caution and delicacy in dealing with great people.

offered, with the blessing of St. Peter, to the aforesaid men. Besides, a certain person on his death has left me by will a little boy; taking thought for whose soul, I have sent him to your Sweetness, that he may live in this world in the service of one through whom he may be able to attain to the liberty of heaven. Further, I beg your most sweet Charity to visit frequently my most beloved son, the deacon Anatolius, whom I have sent to represent the Church in the royal city, that after the toils which he endures in secular causes he may find rest with you in the word of God, and wipe away the sweat of this his earthly toil as it were with a kind of white napkin. Commend him to all who are known to you, though I am sure that, if he is perfectly known, he needs no commendation. Yet do you shew with regard to him how much you love the holy apostle Peter, and me. Now may Almighty God guard your Charity, to me most sweet, from enemies within and without, and, when it shall please Him, bring you to heavenly kingdoms.

EPISTLE XXXI.

To Cyriacus, Bishop.

Gregory to Cyriacus, Bishop of Constantinople.

We have received the letters of your Blessedness, which speak to us in words not of the tongue but of the soul. For they open to me your mind, which, however, was not closed to me, since of myself I retain experience of the same sweetness. Wherefore I return thanks continually to Almighty God, since, if charity the mother of virtues abides in your heart towards us, you will never lose the branches of good works, seeing that you retain the very root of goodness. You ought, then, to shew the beauty of this charity to me and to all your brethren by this good work in the first place,—your hastening to discard that word of pride whereby grave offence is engendered in the Churches, thus fulfilling in all ways what is written, *Endeavouring to keep the unity of the Spirit in the bond of peace* (Ephes. iv. 3): and again, *Give none occasion to the adversary to speak reproachfully* (1 Tim. v. 14). For then will true charity be displayed, if there is no schism among us through an example of pride. For, as for me, I call Jesus to witness in my soul, that to no one among men from the highest to the lowest do I wish to give occasion of offence. I desire that all should be great and honourable, yet so that their honour detract not from the honour of Almighty God. For whoso covets to be honoured against God to me is not honourable. But, that you may learn what good will I have towards your Blessedness, I have sent my son the deacon Anatolius to the feet of our most pious lords, for satisfying their Piety and your Fraternity that I desire to injure no man in this matter, but to keep the humility that is pleasing to God, and the concord of holy Church. And because Antichrist, the enemy of God, is near at hand, I studiously desire that he may not find anything belonging to himself, not only in the manners, but even in the titles of priests. Let then what has been introduced after a new fashion be removed in like manner as it was brought in, and peace in the Lord will remain with us inviolate. For what pleasantness, what charity, will there be amongst us, if we cheer ourselves up with words, while we are galled by facts? Let then your Holiness so act that we may feel in our inmost hearts the good things you speak of, to the end that, the hearts of priests being in unanimity, when we supplicate for the life of our most pious lords, we may be counted worthy to be heard all the more as peace illuminates your prayers before the eyes of God, and no stain of discord darkens them.

EPISTLE XXXII.

To Anastasius, Presbyter[3].

Gregory to Anastasius, &c.

That a good man out of the good treasure of his heart bringeth forth good things (Matth. xii. 35; Luke vi. 45), this thy Charity has shewn, both in thy habitual life and lately also in thy epistle; wherein I find two persons at issue with regard to virtues; that is to say, thyself contending for charity, and another for fear and humility. And, though occupied with many things, though ignorant of the Greek language, I have nevertheless sat as judge of your contention. But, in very truth, thou hast, in my judgment, thyself conquered thy opponent by the apostolical sentence, which I proffered to you during your contention, *That there is no fear in charity, but perfect charity casteth out fear; because fear hath torment. He that feareth is not made perfect in charity.* I know then how much thy Fraternity is made perfect in charity. And, since thou lovest Almighty God much, thou oughtest to presume on thy neighbour much. For it is not places or ranks that make us neighbours to our Creator; but either our good deserts join us to Him, or our bad deserts separate us from

3 This epistle appears to have been in reply to one from a presbyter. Anastasius (*al.* Athanasius), of Jerusalem announcing his promotion to the abbacy of a monastery there. There had been, it seems, a standing feud between the abbots of this monastery and the bishops of Jerusalem, the continuance of which Gregory gracefully deprecates in the course of his letter.

Him. Since, then, it is still uncertain what any one is inwardly, how was it that thou wast afraid to write, ignorant as thou art as to which of us two is the superior? And indeed that thou livest well I know, but I am conscious myself of being burdened by many sins. And, though thou art thyself a sinner, still thou art much better than I, since thou bearest thine own sins only, but I those also of the persons committed to me. In this, then, I look upon thee as lofty, in this I look upon thee as great, that in a great place and lofty before human eyes thou hast not felt thyself advanced at all. For therein, while honour is paid thee by men outwardly, thy mind is sunk into depths, because burdened by distracting cares. But to thee Almighty God has done as it is written; *He hath laid down ascents in the heart, in the valley of tears* (Ps. lxxxiii. 6). To me, however, thou mightest have appeared far loftier, far more sublime, hadst thou never undertaken the leadership of the monastery which is called Neas, seeing that in that monastery, as I hear, there is indeed an appearance of monks kept up, but many secular things are done under the garb of sanctity. But even to this I shall think that heavenly grace has brought thee, if what in that place displeases Almighty God should be corrected under thy guidance.

But, since there have been wont to be quarrels between the father of this same monastery and the pastor of the Church of Jerusalem, I believe that Almighty God has willed that thy Love and my most holy brother and fellow-priest Amos should be at the same time at Jerusalem for this end, that the quarrels which I have spoken of should be put an end to. Shew, then, now how much you loved before. For I know that both of you are abstinent, both learned, both humble; whence the glory of our Saviour must needs be praised, according to the language of the Psalm, in timbrel and chorus (Ps. cl. 4). For in a timbrel the sound from the skin is dry, but in a chorus there is a concord of voices. What therefore is denoted by a timbrel but abstinence, and what by a chorus but unanimity? Since then by abstinence ye praise the Lord in timbrel, I beg that by unanimity ye praise Him in chorus. The Truth also in person says, *Have salt in yourselves, and have peace one with another* (Mark ix. 50). What is denoted by salt but wisdom, as Paul attests, who says, *Let your speech be alway in grace, seasoned with salt* (Col. iv. 6)? Since, then, we know that you have salt through the teaching of the heavenly word, it remains that through the grace of charity you keep with all your hearts peace between yourselves. All this I say, dearest brother, because I love you both exceedingly, and am much afraid lest the sacrifices of your prayers should be stained by any dissension between you.

The blessing which you sent, first by Exhilaratus the *Secundicerius* [4], and afterwards by Sabinianus the deacon, I received with thanksgiving, since from a holy place it became you to send holy things, and to shew by your very gift whom you serve continually. May Almighty God protect you with His right hand, and preserve you scatheless from all evils.

EPISTLE XXXIII.

To Mauricius Augustus.

Gregory to Mauricius Augustus.

The provident piety of my lords, lest perchance any scandal might be engendered in the unity of Holy Church by the dissension of priests, has once and again deigned to admonish me to receive kindly the representatives of my brother and fellow-priest Cyriacus, and to give them liberty to return soon. And although, most pious lord, all your injunctions are suitable and provident, yet I find that by such an admonition I am reproved as being in your judgment indiscreet. But, even though my mind has been wounded in no slight degree by a proud and profane title, could I possibly be guilty of so great indiscretion as not to know what I owed to the unity of the faith and to ecclesiastical concord, and to refuse to receive the representatives and the synodical letter of my brother on account of bitterness from whatever cause intervening? Far be this from me. Such wisdom had been unwisdom. For what is due from us for conserving unity of faith is one thing; what is due for restraining elation is another. Times therefore were to be distinguished, lest the newness of my aforesaid brother might in any point be disturbed [5]. Whence also I received his representatives with great affection. Whatever charity I owed to them I displayed, and honoured them more than it had been the ancient custom to do, and caused them to celebrate the sacred solemnities of mass with me; since, even as my deacon ought not to serve, for exhibition of the sacred mysteries, him who has either committed the sin of elation or corrects it not himself when committed by others, so it was right that his ministers should attend, in the celebration of mass, on me, who, under

4 See III. 56, note 3.

5 So literally;—"Ne prædicti fratri mei ex quolibet articulo novitas turbaretur." The meaning seems to be, Lest Cyriacus should be troubled immediately on his accession. He was to be remonstrated with in due time; but rejection at once of his synodical letter and of his emissaries would have been premature.

the keeping of God, have not fallen into the error of pride.

I have however taken care to admonish earnestly the same my brother and fellow-bishop that, if he desires to have peace and concord with all, he must refrain from the appellation of a foolish title. As to this, the piety of my lords has charged me in their orders, saying that offence ought not to be engendered among us for the appellation of a frivolous name. But I beseech your imperial Piety to consider that some frivolous things are very harmless, and others exceedingly harmful. Is it not the case that, when Antichrist comes and calls himself God, it will be very frivolous, and yet exceedingly pernicious? If we regard the quantity of the language used, there are but a few syllables; but if the weight of the wrong, there is universal disaster. Now I confidently say that whosoever calls himself, or desires to be called, Universal Priest, is in his elation the precursor of Antichrist, because he proudly puts himself above all others. Nor is it by dissimilar pride that he is led into error; for, as that perverse one wishes to appear as God above all men, so whosoever this one is who covets being called sole priest, he extols himself above all other priests. But, since the Truth says, *Every one that exalteth himself shall be humbled* (Luke xiv. 11; xviii. 14), I know that every kind of elation is the sooner burst as it is the more inflated. Let then your Piety charge those who have fallen into an example of pride not to generate any offence by the appellation of a frivolous name. For I, a sinner, who by the help of God retain humility, need not to be admonished to humility. Now may Almighty God long guard the life of our most serene lord for the peace of holy Church and the advantage of the Roman republic. For we are sure, that, if you live who fear the Lord of heaven, you will allow no proud doings to prevail against the truth.

EPISTLE XXXIV.

To Eulogius, Bishop.

Gregory to Eulogius, Bishop of Alexandria, and Anastasius, Bishop of Antioch[6].

The charity wherewith I am greatly bound to you allows me by no means to keep silence, that your Holiness may know all that is going on among us, and, deceived by no false rumours, may keep more perfectly the way of your justice and rectitude, as you have perfectly begun to do. Now the representatives (*responsales*) of our brother and fellow-bishop Cyriacus came to me, bringing me his synodical epistle. And indeed between us and him there is, as your Blessedness knows, serious difference on account of the appellation of a profane name; but I thought that his representatives sent in the cause of the faith ought to be received, lest the sin of elation which has arisen in the Constantinopolitan Church almost against all priests, might cause a shaking of the faith and a breach in ecclesiastical unity. I also caused the same representatives, inasmuch as they very humbly requested it, to celebrate with me the solemnities of mass, because, as I have taken care to intimate to the most serene lord the Emperor, it was right that the representatives of our brother and fellow priest Cyriacus should communicate with me, since by God's help I have not fallen into the error of elation. But my deacon ought not to celebrate the solemnities of mass with our aforesaid brother Cyriacus, since, through a profane title, he has either committed or accedes to the sin of pride; lest if he (my deacon) proceeds[7] with one who is in such a position of elation, we might seem (which God forbid) to confirm the vanity of that foolish name. But I have taken care to admonish our said brother to correct himself of such elation, since, if he does not correct it, he will in no way have peace with us.

Furthermore, our said brother in his synodical letters has by the grace of God expressed himself in all respects as a Catholic. But he has condemned a certain Eudoxius, whom we find neither condemned in synods, nor repudiated by his predecessors in their synodical letters[8]. It is true that the canons of the council of Constantinople condemn the Eudoxians; but they say nothing as to who their author Eudoxius was. But the Roman Church does not possess so far these same canons, or the acts of that council, nor has it accepted them, though it has accepted this same synod with regard to what was defined by it against Macedonius. It does certainly repudiate the other heresies therein spoken of, which had already been condemned by other Fathers: but so far it knows nothing about the Eudoxians. Some things are indeed told in Sozomen's history about a certain Eudoxius, who is said to have usurped the episcopate of the Church of Constantinople. But this history itself the Apostolic See refuses to accept, since it contains many false state-

[6] As to the first subject of this epistle, with references to others on the same subject, see *Prolegom.*, p. xxii.

[7] *Procedit*, the usual term for proceeding to the Holy Table for celebration. See III. 57, note 5.

[8] Cf. VII. 4.

ments, and praises Theodore of Mopsuestia too much, and says that he was a great doctor of the Church even to the day of his death. It remains then that, if any one receives that history, he contradicts the synod held in the times of Justinian of pious memory concerning the three chapters. But one who cannot contradict this synod must needs reject that history. Moreover in the Latin language we have so far found nothing about this Eudoxius, either in Philaster or in the blessed Augustine, who wrote much about heresies. Let therefore your Charity inform me in your letters if any one of the approved Fathers among the Greeks has made mention of him.

Furthermore three years ago, with reference to the case of the monks of Isauria, who were accused as being heretics[9], my brother and fellow-bishop the lord John once sent me letters for my satisfaction, in which he attempted to shew that they had contradicted the definitions of the synod of Ephesus; and he forwarded to me certain chapters, purporting to be those of the same synod, which they were said to oppose[1]. Now among other things it was in these chapters asserted concerning the soul of Adam, that by sin it did not die, in that the devil does not enter into the heart of man; and that whoso said it was so was anathema. When this was read to me I was much grieved. For if the soul of Adam, who was the first to sin, did not die by sin, how was it said to him concerning the forbidden tree, *In the day that ye eat thereof ye shall surely die* (Gen. ii. 17)? And certainly Adam and Eve ate of the forbidden tree, and yet in their flesh they lived afterwards more than nine hundred years. It is therefore evident that in his flesh he did not die. If then he did not die in his soul, the impious conclusion follows that God pronounced a false sentence concerning him, when He said that in the day that he ate he should die. But far be this error, far be it from the true faith. For what we say is, that the first man died in soul in the day that he sinned, and that through him the whole human race is condemned in this penalty of death and corruption. But through the second man we trust that we can be freed, both now from the death of the soul, and hereafter from all corruption of the flesh in the eternal resurrection:—as moreover we said to the aforesaid representatives; 'We say that the soul of Adam died by sin, not from the substance of living, but from the quality of living. For, inasmuch as substance is one thing, and quality another, his soul did not so die as not to be, but so died as not to be blessed. Yet this same Adam returned afterwards to life through penitence.'

But that the devil enters into the heart of man cannot be denied, if the Gospel is believed. For it is there written, *And after the sop Satan entered into him* (John xiii. 27). And again it is therein also said, *When the devil had now put himself into the heart of Judas, that Judas should betray Him* (Ibid. 2). He that denies this falls into Pelagian heresy. Seeing then that, having examined the Ephesine synod, we found nothing of the kind to be contained therein, we caused to be brought to us also a very old Codex of the same synod from the Church of Ravenna, and we found it to agree with the report of the synod which we have so as to differ in no respect, and to contain nothing else in its decree of anathema and rejection, except that they reject the twelve chapters of Cyril of blessed memory. But this whole argument we set forth much more fully and particularly to his representatives when they were with us, and most fully satisfied them. Wherefore lest either these or any like things should creep in yonder, so as to cause offence to holy Church, it is necessary for us to indicate these things to your Holiness. And, although we know our brother and fellow-bishop Cyriacus to be orthodox, yet on account of others we ought to be cautious, that the seeds of error may be trampled down before they spring up to public view.

I received the letters of your Holiness on the arrival here of our common son the deacon Sabinianus; but, as their bearer is already prepared for departure and cannot be detained, I will reply when the deacon, my *responsalis*, comes.

EPISTLE XXXV.

To Dominicus, Bishop.

Gregory to Dominicus, Bishop of Carthage.

Though we believe that thy Fraternity gives attention with pastoral vigilance to the care of monasteries, yet we think it necessary to inform you of what we have learnt about a monastery in the African province. Now the abbot Cumquodeus, the bearer of these presents, complains that, if at any time he wishes to restrain under regular discipline the monks over whom he presides, they at once leave the monastery, and are allowed to wander wherever they will. Seeing, then, that this is both altogether pernicious to themselves and also sets an example of perdition to others, we exhort your Fraternity that, if it

9 See III. 53, note 9.

1 Cf. VI. 14, where the same doctrinal questions are similarly discussed in the same connexion.

is so, you should bring ecclesiastical censure to bear upon them, and withhold them by suitable punishment from such undoubted presumption; and that you should so bring them to obedience by salubrious provision, subduing their proud minds to the yoke of discipline, that correction may recall from guilt others whom their example might have provoked to similar transgression, and teach them to obey their superiors, as is fit. But, since he tells us that stray monks are defended by some bishops, let your Fraternity give careful attention to this, and restrain them by your menaces in all ways from such defence. The month of July, Indiction 15.

EPISTLE XXXVIII.

To Donus, Bishop.

Gregory to Donus, Bishop of Messana (*Messene*).

The ordinances both of the sacred canons and of the laws allow the utensils of the Church to be sold for the redemption of captives. And so, seeing that Faustinus, the bearer of these presents, is proved to have contracted a debt of three hundred and thirty *solidi* for the purpose of redeeming his daughters from the yoke of captivity, and that, thirty thereof having been repaid, it is certain that he has not sufficient means for the repayment of the remaining sum, we exhort thy Fraternity by this communication that thou by all means give him fifteen pounds, taking his receipt for the same, out of the silver in thy hands belonging to the Meriensian Church, of which he is known to be a soldier; so that, it being sold, and the debt paid, he may be freed from the bond of his obligation. But of this also your Fraternity should be careful, that in case of the aforesaid Church having so much current coin, he should receive from it the amount above-written; but otherwise you must needs supply him for the purpose in view with the sum we have stated from the consecrated vessels. For, as it is a very serious thing to sell idly ecclesiastical utensils, so on the other hand it is wrong, under pressing necessity of this kind, for an exceedingly desolated Church to prefer its property to its captives, or to loiter in redeeming them.

EPISTLE XXXIX.

To John, Bishop.

Gregory to John, Bishop of Syracuse.

Lest attention to secular affairs should disjoin the hearts of religious men (which God forbid) from mutual charity, very earnest endeavour should be made to bring any matter that has come into dispute to the easiest possible termination. Since, then, from the information of Cæsarius, abbot of St. Peter's monastery, constituted in a place called Baias, we find that between him and John, abbot of St. Lucia's monastery, constituted in the city of Syracuse, there has arisen a serious question about certain boundaries, we, lest this contention should be prolonged between them, have taken thought for their dispute being terminated by the determination of a land-measurer. And accordingly we have written to the *defensor* Fantinus, bidding him direct John the land-measurer, who has gone from Rome to Panormus, to resort to your Fraternity.

We exhort, therefore, that you go with him to the places about which there is contention, and, both parties having been brought together, cause the places in dispute to have their boundaries defined in your presence, though still with a claim of prescription for forty years preserved to either party. But, whatever may be determined, let it be your Fraternity's anxious and studious care to have it so observed that no strife may henceforth be stirred up anew, nor any further complaint reach us.

We believe that it is not unknown to your Fraternity that the venerable abbot Cæsarius was formerly our friend; and therefore, saving equity, we commend him to you in all respects. And, seeing that he is entirely inexperienced in secular causes, it is needful for him to be aided by your solicitude; yet so that, in this as in all cases, you observe, as is fit, reason and justice.

EPISTLE XL.

To Eulogius, Bishop.

Gregory to Eulogius, Bishop of Alexandria.

Your most sweet Holiness has spoken much in your letter to me about the chair of Saint Peter, Prince of the apostles, saying that he himself now sits on it in the persons of his successors. And indeed I acknowledge myself to be unworthy, not only in the dignity of such as preside, but even in the number of such as stand. But I gladly accepted all that has been said, in that he has spoken to me about Peter's chair who occupies Peter's chair. And, though special honour to myself in no wise delights me, yet I greatly rejoiced because you, most holy ones, have given to yourselves what you have bestowed upon me. For who can be ignorant that holy Church has been made firm in the solidity of the Prince of the apostles, who derived his name from the firmness of his mind, so as to be called Petrus from *petra*. And to him it is said by the voice of the Truth, *To thee I will give the keys of the kingdom of heaven* (Matth. xvi. 19). And again it is said to him, *And when thou art converted, strengthen thy brethren* (xxii. 32). And once more, *Simon, son of Jonas, lovest thou Me? Feed My sheep* (Joh. xxi. 17). Wherefore, though there are many apostles, yet with regard to the principality itself the See of the Prince of the apostles alone has grown strong in authority, which in three places is the See of one[2]. For he himself exalted the See in which he deigned even to rest and end the present life. He himself adorned the See to which he sent his disciple as evangelist. He himself stablished the See in which, though he was to leave it, he sat for seven years. Since then it is the See of one, and one See, over which by Divine authority three bishops now preside, whatever good I hear of you, this I impute to myself. If you believe anything good of me, impute this to your merits, since we are one in Him Who says, *That they all may be one, as Thou, Father, art in me, and I in thee, that they also may be one in us* (Joh. xvii. 21). Moreover, in paying you the debt of salutation which is due to you, I declare to you that I exult with great joy from knowing that you labour assiduously against the barkings of heretics; and I implore Almighty God that He would aid your Blessedness with His protection, so as through your tongue to uproot every root of bitterness from the bosom of holy Church, lest it should germinate again to the hindrance of many, and through it many should be defiled. For having received your talent you think on the injunction, *Trade till I come* (Luke xix. 13). I therefore, though unable to trade at all, nevertheless rejoice with you in the gains of your trade, inasmuch as I know this, that if operation does not make me partaker, yet charity does make me a partaker in your labour. For I reckon that the good of a neighbour is common to one that stands idle, if he knows how to rejoice in common in the doings of the other.

Furthermore, I have wished to send you some timber: but your Blessedness has not indicated whether you are in need of it: and we can send some of much larger size, but no ship is sent hither capable of containing it: and I think shame to send the smaller sort. Nevertheless let your Blessedness inform me by letter what I should do.

I have however sent you, as a small blessing from the Church of Saint Peter who loves you, six of the smaller sort of Aquitanian cloaks (*pallia*), and two napkins (*oraria*); for, my affection being great, I presume on the acceptableness of even little things. For affection itself has its own worth, and it is quite certain that there will be no offence in what out of love one has presumed to do.

Moreover I have received the blessing of the holy Evangelist Mark, according to the note appended to your letter. But, since I do not drink *colatum*[3] and *viritheum*[4] with pleasure, I venture to ask for *cognidium*[5], which last year, after a long interval, your Holiness caused to be known in this city. For we here get from the traders the name of *cognidium*, but not the thing itself. Now I beg that the prayers of your Holiness may support me against all the bitternesses which I suffer in this life, and defend me from them by your intercessions with Almighty God.

EPISTLE XLII.

To Marinianus, Bishop.

Gregory to Marinianus, Bishop of Ravenna.

We find from the information given in your Fraternity's letter that the sons of the Church of Cornelium are continually supplicating you to consecrate a bishop for them in place of their former bishop who has lapsed, and that you are in doubt as to what should be done in the matter, and await our plain command. Inasmuch, then, as no sort of reason allows any one who has departed criminally to be recalled to the place from which he has lapsed, and as the ordinances of the sacred canons allow not a Church to be without a bishop beyond three months, lest (which God forbid) the ancient foe should lie in wait to tear the Lord's flock, your Fraternity ought to comply with their entreaty, and ordain a bishop in the place of the lapsed one. For, seeing that you ought to have admonished them to this thing by your exhortations before they asked you, you can have no excuse for refusing them when they demand it of you, since a Church of God ought not to remain long widowed of a bishop of its own.

EPISTLE XLIII.

To Marinianus, Bishop.

Gregory to Marinianus, Bishop of Ravenna.

It has for some time reached us from the

[2] As to the view here expressed of the unity of the three Sees of Rome, Antioch, and Alexandria, see *Prolegom.*, p. xii.

[3] "Colaticus. Lapides quoque medicinalium, mortariarum, et pigmentariarum usibus apti (*Isid. Lib.* 16. *Orig. cap.* 4)." Du Cange. But *colatum* here appears to have been some drink.

[4] *Genus potionis*, Papiæ, Ægyptios vel Alexandrinos—Illud forte de quo S. Hieronymus de Vita Clericorum cum *palmarum fructus exprimuntur in liquorem, coctisque frugibus aqua pinguior coloratur.*" Du Cange.

[5] "Potionis species apud Ægyptianos, vel saltem Alexandrinos." Du Cange.

report of many that the monasteries constituted in the district of Ravenna are everywhere aggrieved by the domination of your clergy; so that—grievous to be said—under the pretext of government they take possession of them as if they were their own. Condoling in no small degree with these monasteries, we sent letters to your predecessor bidding him correct this evil. But, seeing that he was soon overtaken by the close of life, we remember having written in like manner to your Fraternity, lest this burden on the monasteries should continue. And because, as we have discovered, there has been loitering so far in the correction of this thing, we have thought fit to address you a second time by this letter. We exhort you, then, that, putting aside all delay and all excuses, you so study to relieve these monasteries from this kind of grievance that clerics, or such as are in sacred orders, may henceforth have no leave of access to them on any other ground except only for the purpose of praying, or if perchance they should be invited for solemnizing the sacred mysteries of mass. But, lest haply the monasteries should sustain a burden through the promotion of any monk or abbot, you must take care that, if any of the abbots or monks of any monastery should accede to any clerical office or sacred order, he shall have, as we have said, no power there any longer, lest under cover of this occasion the monasteries should be compelled to sustain the burdens which we prohibit. Let not your Holiness, then, after this second admonition, delay correcting all this with vigilant care, lest, if we should after this perceive you to be negligent (as we do not believe will be the case), we be compelled to provide otherwise for the quiet of the monasteries. For be it known to you that we will no longer suffer the congregations of the servants of God to be subjected to such requirements. Lest, however, any excuse should be put forward with regard to the monks, let your Fraternity without fail send hither such person as you may see to be serviceable, and we will depute monks to go with him to you, to provide for whom you must place them in monasteries, if indeed there are among you places such as may afford them a maintenance.

BOOK VIII

EPISTLE I.

To Peter, Bishop.

Gregory to Peter, Bishop of Corsica[1].

On receiving the letters of your Fraternity we returned great thanks to Almighty God, that you had been so good as to refresh us with the news of the gathering in of many souls. And accordingly let your Fraternity strive anxiously to bring to perfection, with the help of the Lord, the work which you have begun. And with regard to those who have once been faithful, but from negligence or under constraint have returned to the worship of idols, make haste to bring them back to the faith, imposing on them a penance of a few days, that they may bewail their guilt, and keep to that to which they return, God helping them, the more firmly as they shall have perfectly deplored that from which they now depart; and with regard to those who have not yet been baptized, let thy Fraternity make haste, by admonishing, by beseeching, by alarming them about the coming judgment, and also by giving reasons why they should not worship stocks and stones, to gather them in to Almighty God; that so, at His advent, when the strict day of judgment comes, thy Holiness may be found in the number of the Saints. For what more profitable work or more lofty canst thou be engaged in than taking thought for the quickening and gathering together of souls and bringing in immortal gain to thy Lord, Who has given to thee the post of preaching?

Further, we send thy Fraternity fifty *solidi* for procuring vestments for those who are to be baptized; and we have also caused to be given to the presbyter of the Church situated in Mount Negeugnus[2] the possession which thy Fraternity has asked for, so that its value may be deducted from the money that he had been accustomed to receive.

Further, your Fraternity has asked to be allowed to make for yourself an episcopal residence in the church that is not far from the same mountain; which proposal I most gladly accede to, since the nearer you are, the more will you be able to do good to the souls that are there.

In consideration of your Holiness's intercessions for him we have made the bearer of these presents an acolyte, and have sent him back to attend upon you, in order that, if he should be of still more service in winning souls, he may be in a position to be still further advanced.

EPISTLE II.

To Anastasius, Bishop of Antioch.

Gregory to Anastasius, Patriarch of Antioch.

I have received the letters of your most sweet Blessedness, which flowed with tears for words. For I saw in them a cloud flying aloft as clouds do; but, though it carried with it a darkness of sorrow, I could not easily discover at its commencement whence it came or whither it was going, since by reason of the darkness I speak of I did not fully understand its origin. Yet it becomes you, most holy ones, ever to recall to mind what the preacher to the Gentiles says; *In the last times perilous times shall be at hand, and there shall be men loving themselves, covetous, lifted up* (1 Tim. iv. 1); and what follows, which it would be a trouble for me to speak, and which is not necessary for you to hear. Lo, in your holy old age, your Blessedness labours under many tribulations; but consider in whose seat you sit[3]. Is it not in his to whom it was said by the voice of the truth, *When thou shalt be old, another shall gird thee and carry thee whither thou wouldest not* (Joh. xxi. 18)? But in saying this I recollect that your Holiness even from your youth has toiled under many adversities. Say then with the good king, *I will think again over all my years in the bitterness of my soul* (Isai. xxxviii. 15). For there are many who, as you say in your letter, make to themselves pastime over our wounds: but we know who said, *Ye shall lament and weep, but the world shall rejoice; and ye shall be sorrowful* (Joh. xvi. 20): where also he forthwith adds, *But your sorrow shall*

---

1 Bishop of *Aleria* in Corsica. Cf. VI. 22.

2 A basilica, with a baptistery attached, had been built on this Mount Negeugnus (or *Nigeunus*), on land belonging to the Roman See, for the purpose of "winning souls." Cf. VI. 22.

3 Cf. V. 39, note 3.

be turned into joy, But, since we already suffer what was foretold, it remains that we should also hope for what was promised. For as to these of whom you say that they themselves lay on the burdens which they ought to have lightened, I know that they are those who come in sheep's clothing, and inwardly are ravening wolves (Matth. vii.). But they are so much the more to be endured as they persecute us not only with a malicious mind, but also in religious guise. And in that they desire to have to themselves above others what it were not fit that they should have even with their brethren, we are in no wise disturbed at this, since we trust in Almighty God that those who desire what belongs to others will be the sooner deprived even of what is their own. For we know who said, *That every one that exalteth himself shall be abased* (Luke xiv. 11). And again it is written, *Before a fall the heart is exalted* (Prov. xvi. 18).

But in these days, as I find, new wars of heretics are arising, about whom I have before now written to your Blessedness, in such sort that they attempt to invalidate the prophets, the Gospels, and all the sayings of the Fathers. But, while the life of your Holiness endures, we trust in the favour of our Protector that their mouths which have been opened against the solidity of the truth may be the sooner stopped, inasmuch as, however sharp may be the swords that are employed, they recoil broken when they strike the rock. Moreover there is this by the great favour of Almighty God; that among those who are divided from the doctrine of Holy Church there is no unity, since every kingdom divided against itself shall not stand (Luke xi.). And holy Church is always more thoroughly equipped in her teaching when assaulted by the questionings of heretics; so that what was said by the Psalmist concerning God against heretics is fulfilled, *They are divided from the wrath of his countenance, and his heart hath drawn nigh* (Ps. liv. 22[4]). For while they are divided in their wicked error, God brings His heart near to us, because, being taught by contradictions, we more thoroughly learn to understand Him.

Further, what ills we suffer from the swords of barbarians, and what from the perversity of judges, I shrink from relating to your Blessedness, lest I should increase your groaning, which I ought to diminish by consolation. But in all these things the precepts of our Master comfort me, who says, *These things have I spoken unto you, that in me ye might have peace. In the world ye shall have tribulation* (John xvi. 33). For I consider to whom it was said, *This is your hour, and the power of darkness* (Luke xxii. 53). If, then, the hour of light will be afterwards, since it is said to the elect, *Ye are the light of the world* (Matth. v. 14), and as it is written, *The righteous shall have dominion over them in the morning* (Ps. xlviii. 15)[5], whatever we suffer in the hour of the power of darkness is not to be deplored.

Moreover your most sweet Holiness tells me that you would have wished, if it could have been so, to converse with me without paper and pen, and grieves that a distance almost as far as the East is from the West lies between us. But this which I feel I declare is true; that on paper your soul speaks to me without paper, since in the words of your Holiness charity alone sounds, and we are not divided by distance of place who, of the gift of Almighty God, are joined together in the bond of love. Why then seek you to have given you the wings of a dove covered with silver, when you already have them? For indeed these wings are love of God and of our neighbour. For by these holy Church flies aloft, and by these transcends all that is earthly; which if your Holiness had not, you would not have come to me by letter with so great charity.

Further, I beg you to pray earnestly in behalf of the weakness of my heart, to the end that Almighty God may through your intercession defend my soul from all evils, and the sooner snatch me away from the hurricanes of this time, which are so many, and bring me to the shores of eternal rest.

I have received all the very rich blessings[6], directed to me, which thou, as a man of God poor in spirit, hast sent me, saying of them, For what can a poor man give but what is poor? But had you not been poor through a spirit of humility, your blessings would not have been rich. May Almighty God guard you by His protection from all evils; and, since your life is very necessary for all good men, bring you after many years yet to come to the joys of the heavenly country.

EPISTLE III.

To Donus, Bishop of Messana (*in Sicily*).

Gregory to Donus, &c.

The most eloquent man, our son Faustinus, has come to us and complained that his late father Peltrasius left some things which were not his own to your Church for his burial. And indeed he knows himself, and we have

---

[4] In *English Bible*, lv. 21 (differently rendered from the Hebrew).

[5] In *English Bible*, xlix. 14.

[6] See IV. 31, note 9

heard, what the secular law is in such a case; namely, that the heir is bound to pay if his father has bequeathed what was not his own. But, as we know that your Fraternity lives by the law of God and not of the world, it seems to me very unjust that an amber cup, and a boy who is said to be of a certain church situate on his property in the diocese of Consentia, should be detained by thy Fraternity. For, when the most reverend Palumbus, now bishop, but then archdeacon, had testified that things were as I have said, you certainly ought to have taken his word, and restored what was not your own. Further, you ought in my opinion to have considered the golden brooch, which would be his whole substance were there anything for the sustenance of those he had left behind him, and accepted it at that time for his burial. Nevertheless, you know our ordinance, how that we have entirely forbidden the old custom in our Church, nor give our assent to any one being allowed to acquire burial-places for a human body for a price. For, if the men of Sichem, who were as we suppose Gentiles, offered without charge to Abraham sepulture for the dead Sara to be buried in a place of her own, and were hardly prevailed upon by his great importunity to receive a price for her place of burial, ought we, who are called bishops, to make any charge for burying the bodies of the faithful? This, then, we commit to the judgment of your Fraternity[7].

The aforesaid most eloquent man complains also of this; that Sisinnius, the guardian (*defensor*) of thy Church, unreasonably detains slaves in his possession: concerning whom also he asserts that it had been decided by the judgment of bishop Maximianus of holy memory that the detainer of them should give them up, but that he has so far wilfully put off their restitution. We therefore exhort thy Fraternity that, if the case has manifestly been adjudged, what was ordained be carried out. Otherwise, some one being deputed to act in the case, cause him to resort to the parts of our brother and fellow-bishop Secundinus for judgment, that, when it shall have been declared by his sentence to whom the slaves in question belong, neither the one party may appear to suffer prejudice nor the other bear a grudge.

EPISTLE V.

To various Metropolitans and Bishops[8].

Gregory to Eusebius of Thessalonica, Urbitius of Dyracchium, Constantius of Mediolanum (*Milan*), Andrew of Nicopolis, John of Corinth, John of Prima Justiniana, John *Cretensi Scoritano*, John of Larissa, Marinianus of Ravenna, Januarius of Caralis (*Cagliari*) in Sardinia, and all the bishops of Sicily.

I have taken care to transmit to your Fraternity the law which the most pious Emperor has issued, to the effect that such as are bound by engagements of military service or public liabilities, may not in any case, in order to escape risk of being called to account, assume the condition of ecclesiastics, or become monks: and this I especially press upon you, that such as are involved in secular engagements are not to be received hastily among the clergy of the Church, since, while they live in an ecclesiastical condition no otherwise than they had lived before, they are by no means trying to escape secular affairs, but to change them. But, if any such should even seek a monastery, they are by no means to be received unless they have first been absolved from their public liabilities. Further, if any from the military order are in haste to become monks, they are not to be received rashly, or until their life has been fully enquired into. And, according to the regular rule, they ought to undergo a probation of three years, and then, God granting it, assume the monastic habit. And if they have thus been proved and accepted, and are anxious, for the good of their souls, to do penance for the sins they have committed, then, with a view to their heavenly life and gain, monastic profession should not be denied them. With respect to this matter also, believe me, the most serene and most Christian Emperor is in every way pacified, and willingly allows the monastic profession of those whom he knows not to be implicated in public liabilities. The Month of December, first Indiction.

EPISTLE VI.

To Amos, Patriarch of Jerusalem.

Gregory to Amos, Bishop of Jerusalem.

Being confident that your Fraternity pays regard to the ordinances of the canons and the vigour of discipline, lest the falseness of one of your clerics should succeed in imposing on you so as to escape the strictness of ecclesiastical order, we have thought it right to inform you of his fault, that through your solicitude he may be subjected to the discipline from which he has fled. We understand, then, that Peter, an acolyte, whom we had caused to serve under our son the deacon Sabinianus, our ecclesiastical representative in the royal city, has fled, and resorted to your Church. If this is true, let your Fraternity be at pains to secure him, and send him back hither when

[7] For similar disapproval of burial fees, cf. IX. 3.
[8] On the subject of this Epistle, see III. 65, 66.

an opportunity occurs. But if by chance, fearing this, he shall have departed from your Church, and be lurking in various places to escape detection, order him to be diligently sought for in all your parishes, and, when found, send him back to us, as we have before said. And we desire also to notify through you that he is deprived of communion: nor let him dare to receive the mysteries of the Lord's body and blood until he shall return to us, unless by chance he should be in imminent peril of death.

EPISTLE X.

To Sabinianus, Bishop of Jadera[9].

Gregory to Sabinianus, &c.

As to one who perseveres in a fault punishment is rightly due, so pardon should be granted to those who return to a better mind. For, as in the former case anger against the culprit is deservedly provoked, so in the latter good-will displayed is wont to promote concord. And so, inasmuch as a recollection of the gravity of the priestly office has now withdrawn thy Fraternity from fellowship and communion with Maximus, into which thoughtlessness had before betrayed thee; and this to such an extent that thou couldest by no means allow thyself to be content with mere separation from him without also bewailing thy past transgression by betaking thyself to the retirement of a monastery, therefore doubt not that thou art received again into our favour and communion: for, as much as thy fault had before offended us, so much has thy penitence appeased us. We exhort thee, therefore, most beloved brother, that thou be instant in bestowing pastoral solicitude on the Lord's flock, and be diligently on the watch to make profit of the sheep committed to thy charge; that so the retribution of a copious reward may abound to thee in proportion as thou shalt offer multiplied fruits of thy labour at the coming of the eternal Judge. Strive then to rescue those who have fallen into sin; strive to shew the way of retracing their steps to those that go astray; strive to recall salubriously to the grace of communion those who have been deprived of communion. Let the coming back of your Charity lay on you the duty of rescuing others, and be an example of salvation; to the end that, while your anxious care shall direct the wandering steps of sheep to the folds of the chief shepherd, both they themselves may not be left exposed to the teeth of wolves, and (what is above all things to be desired) that the compensation of condign retribution may await thee in the life eternal.

9 See VII. 17, and note on VI. 27.

As to the cause about which you wrote to us, requesting us to guard against any clandestine proceedings against you in the royal city, let not this matter disturb your mind. For we have with all possible care given orders to our *responsalis* to shew himself solicitous and on his guard. And we trust in the power of our God that things are being so conducted that the opposition of no one shall avail against reason, so as in any way to trouble you or to bear hard upon you.

Furthermore, the inhabitants of the city of Epidaurus have most urgently requested us to restore to them Florentius, whom they allege to be their bishop, asserting that he was driven into exile invalidly by the mere will of the bishop Natalis[1]. And so, if your Fraternity has any knowledge of his case, please to inform us accurately by letter. But, if so far you have no knowledge of it, make enquiry, and report to us, that we may be able, with the Lord's help, to deliberate with full knowledge before us as to what should be determined concerning him. In the month of February, first Indiction.

EPISTLE XIII.

To Columbus.

Gregory to Columbus, Bishop of Numidia[2].

How we may presume on your Charity we gather from the disposition of our own mind with regard to you. Nor do we think that you love the Apostolic See otherwise than as it loves you. Whence it must needs be that we should more peculiarly commend those whom we know to be, as they should be, devoted in the Church of the blessed Peter, Prince of the apostles, to you whose life the action as well as the dignity of a priest adorns, and of whose sincerity we already hold proof from past experience.

As to our brother, therefore, and fellow-bishop Paul[3], the bearer of these presents, with what billows and adversities he is tossed in your parts he tells us is not unknown to your Holiness. And seeing that he asserts that the complaints against him which you have told us have come to your ears are not true, but raised against him at the instigation of his adversaries, and that he trusts to be able by the help of the Lord to surmount them all, with the truth to support him and with you to take cognizance, we exhort you, most beloved brother, that, in whatever points considerations of justice are clearly on his side, you afford him becomingly the hand of succour, and aid him with priestly sympathy. Let, then, no circum-

1 See III. 8, and III. 9, note 2.
2 See II. 48, note 8.
3 See IV. 34, note 4.

stance, no influence of any persons, deflect you from studious regard to equity. But, leaning on the Lord's precepts, set at naught whatever is opposed to rectitude. In defending one party or the other insist constantly on justice. Shrink not from incurring ill-will, if such there be, in behalf of truth; that thou mayest find in the advent of our Redeemer by so much the greater fruit of reward as, not neglecting His commands, thou shalt have devoted thyself to the countenance and defence of justice. In the month of March, first Indiction.

EPISTLE XIV.

To Boniface, First Guardian (*Defensorem*).

Gregory to Boniface concerning the privileges of Guardians[4].

Those who labour faithfully in the interests of the Church should receive the benefit of suitable remuneration, so that both we may be seen to have made a worthy return for their services, and they may shew themselves the more useful for the favour of the solace granted them. Seeing, then, that those who hold the office of Guardians are known to labour in the causes of the Church and in the service of the pontiffs, we have thought fit that they should enjoy the following prerogatives, granted to them for recompense;—appointing that, as in the school (*schola*) of notaries and subdeacons, through the indulgence of pontiffs long agó, there have been constituted *regionarii*, so also among the Guardians seven who may have commended themselves by proved utility shall be distinguished by the dignity of *regionarii*. And we appoint that these, in the absence of the pontiff, shall have leave to sit anywhere in any assembly of clergy, and enjoy in all respects the privileges of their dignity. Furthermore, if any one, attaining to this position of priority, should by any chance live in another province for his own advantage, he must needs still occupy in all respects his place of priority, so that he may be the chief of all the guardians, as being one who, even before he obtained his position of priority, had not ceased by assiduous personal attention to devote himself to the interests of the Church and the service of the pontiff. These decrees, then, by us constituted, which have been ordained for the privileges and constitution of Guardians, we appoint to be kept in perpetual force and irrefragably;—whether such things as we have decreed in writing, or such as are seen to have been ordained in our presence: and we decree also that they shall not be upset or changed in whole or in part on any occasion whatever by any of the pontiffs. For it is a very harsh proceeding, and especially contrary to good conduct in priests, that any one should endeavour, under any manner of excuse, to rescind what has been well ordained, and also by his example to teach others to dissolve his own constitutions after his own time. The month of April, first Indiction.

4 See *Prolegom.*, p. vii.

EPISTLE XV.

To Marinianus, Bishop of Ravenna.

Gregory to Marinianus, &c.

How necessary it is to provide for the quiet of monasteries[5], and to take measures for their perpetual security, you are aware from the office you formerly filled in government of a monastery. And so, seeing that we have learnt how the monastery of the blessed John and Stephen in the city of Classis, over which our common son, the abbot Claudius, is known to preside, has suffered many prejudices and grievances from your predecessors, it is right that the provision of your Fraternity should make salutary arrangements for the quiet of its inmates in future; to the end that living there in the service of God, His grace also assisting them, they may persevere with free mind. But lest, owing to the custom which ought rather to be amended, any one at any time should presume to cause any annoyance there, it is necessary that the points which we have taken care to enumerate below be so guarded by the careful attention of your Fraternity that no occasion of causing them disquiet may possibly be found in future. Let no one, then, any more dare, by any kind of inquisition whatever, to diminish anything from the revenues or charters of the aforesaid monastery, or of any place that in any manner whatever pertains to it, or to attempt any kind of usurpations or stratagems. But if perchance any matter of dispute should arise between the Church of Ravenna and the aforesaid monastery, and it cannot be settled amicably, let it be concluded without voluntary delay before men who fear God chosen by the parties, oath being made upon the most holy Gospels. Further, on the death of an abbot, let not a stranger be ordained, but one whom the congregation may choose of its own free will for itself from the same congregation, and who shall have been chosen without any fraud or venality. But, if they should be unable to find a suitable person among themselves, let them

5 For other Epistles in which bishops are forbidden to interfere, except in case of need, with monasteries, see Index under *Monasteries*. Also *Prolegom.*, p. xx.

in like manner wisely choose for themselves for ordination one from some other monastery. And, when an abbot comes, let no person whatever on any occasion whatever be put over him in his own monastery, unless perchance in the case (which God forbid) of crimes which are shewn to be punishable by the sacred canons. This rule also must be no less carefully observed; that against the will of the abbot of such monastery monks be not removed thence for furnishing other monasteries, or for sacred orders, or for any clerical office. But in cases of there being monks in abundance, sufficient for celebrating praises to God and for satisfying the requirements of monasteries, let the abbot offer with devotion, of those who are to spare, such as he may be able to find worthy in the sight of God. But if, while having a sufficient number he should refuse to give any, then let the bishop of Ravenna take of such as are to spare for furnishing other monasteries. Nevertheless, let no one be taken out thence for an ecclesiastical office, except such as the abbot of the place, on having notice given him, may offer of his own accord. Whosoever also from the aforesaid monastery shall have attained to any ecclesiastical order, let him thenceforth have neither any power there nor leave to dwell there [6].

It is to be observed also that no schedule of the property and charters of this monastery must be made by ecclesiastics, if ever circumstances require one: but let the abbot of the place with other abbots make an inventory of the property.

Further, as often as the abbot may perchance wish to go or send to the Roman pontiff in the interest of his monastery, let him have entire liberty to do so.

Furthermore, though the visits of bishops should be looked for with desire by monasteries, yet, seeing that it has been reported to us that the aforesaid monastery in the times of your predecessor was burdened by occasion of entertainment, it is right that your Holiness should regulate this in a becoming manner, so that the prelate of the city may have access to the monastery as often as he pleases for the sake of visiting and exhorting. But let the bishop so fulfil the office of charity there that the monastery incur not any burden. Now the aforesaid abbot not only does not fear your Fraternity's frequent access to the monastery, but even longingly desires it, knowing that it is quite impossible that the substance of the monastery should be burdened through you. Given in the month of April, first Indiction.

EPISTLE XVII.

To Maurentius.

Gregory to Maurentius, *magister militum* [7].

My most beloved son, Cyprian the deacon, had pleased me much by his return to me, if his whole self had returned to me. But now that your Glory has stayed in Sicily, I know most certainly that he has returned indeed in body, but in mind has remained in Sicily. Yet, in saying this, I rejoice with you for your quiet as much as I groan for my own occupations. And to this I earnestly exhort you, that, if the pleasant savour of inward sweetness has touched the palate of your heart, your mind be so rapt within itself that all which sounds without, all that delights without, may be distasteful. Moreover I commend you for avoiding concourses of men, seeing that a mind which desires to be renewed in God through the grace of compunction often relapses into its old state through evil conversation and words. I have sought for some to join you in a society for sacred reading, but have found no one, and I exceedingly lament the scarcity of what is good. And though I, a sinner, am very much occupied, yet, if you should wish to come to the threshold of the blessed apostle Peter, you will be able to have me as a close associate in the study of Holy Writ. May Almighty God keep you under His heavenly protection, and grant you to remain defended against the snares of the ancient foe.

EPISTLE XVIII.

To Agnellus, Bishop of Terracina.

Gregory to Agnellus, &c.

It has come to our ears—a thing shocking to be told—that some in your parts worship trees, and perpetrate many other unlawful things contrary to the Christian faith. And we wonder why your Fraternity has delayed correcting this by strict punishment. On this account we exhort you by this present writing to cause these persons to be sought out by diligent enquiry, and such vengeance to be executed on them that both God may be pacified and their punishment may be an example of rebuke to others.

We have written also to Maurus the Viscount that he should afford aid to your Fraternity in this matter, that so you may be unable to find

[6] This is among the many evidences found in Gregory's Epistles that monks in his day were essentially laymen. The active duties incumbent on the clergy were held to be inconsistent with monastic life.

[7] This letter is interesting as one of those which shew Gregory's carefulness to retain influence over pious lay friends of position, and his uniform tone of courtesy in addressing them. Maurentius appears to have been a military officer of studious habits in Sicily.

any excuse for nor apprehending them. Further, as we find that many excuse themselves from keeping watch over the walls, let your Fraternity be careful to suffer no man, either under the name of our or your Church, or under any other pretext, to be exempted from keeping watch: but let all generally be compelled, to the end that, while all keep watch, the custody of the city may, by the help of the Lord, be the better provided for.

EPISTLE XX.

To Marinianus, Bishop of Ravenna.

Gregory to Marinianus, &c.

John, the bearer of these presents, complains that his wife, flying from the molestations of one George, has long been residing within venerable precincts[8], and has so far met with no assistance. Since she asserts that there is a dispute about her condition[9], and has asked that it should be commended to your Fraternity, we hereby exhort you that you afford your protection to this woman, and permit her not to be in any way aggrieved by any one unreasonably. But if the question about her station still continues, let it be your care that, without any oppression, and in a legal manner, it may be submitted for judgment; so that when, after ascertainment of the truth, what is agreeable to the order of law has been determined, neither party may complain of having suffered wrong. The month of May, first Indiction.

EPISTLE XXI.

To John, Bishop of Syracuse.

Gregory to John, &c.

Felix, the bearer of these presents, has complained to us that, being born of Christian parents, he was given (i.e. *as a slave*) by a certain Christian to a Samaræan[1], which is an atrocious thing to be said. And, though neither order of law nor reverence for religion allow men of such like superstition in any way whatever to possess Christian slaves, yet he asserts that he remained for eighteen years in that man's service. But he says that, when your predecessor Maximianus of holy memory became aware of the fact, he was freed by him, moved, as was becoming, by priestly zeal, from the service of that Samaræan. But, inasmuch as the son of the said Samaræan is said after five years to have become a Christian, and certain persons are trying to reclaim the aforesaid Felix, according to his own account, to his service, let your Holiness enquire diligently into the facts that we have been informed of, and, if they should be found true, study to protect him, and allow him on no pretext whatever to be aggrieved by any one, seeing that, while the laws plainly forbid slaves of that superstitious sect who are before their masters in coming to the faith being reclaimed to their service, how much more ought not this man—born of Christian parents, and a Christian from his childhood—to be subjected in any wise to this contention; especially as neither could be the slave of that other man's father, who it is clear was rather liable to punishment by law for his wicked presumption? And so, as we have said, let the defence of your Holiness so protect him reasonably that no one may be at liberty, under any pretence whatever, in any degree to afflict him.

EPISTLE XXII.

To Rusticiana, Patrician[2].

Gregory to Rusticiana, &c.

I remember having before now written to your Excellency, and repeatedly urged you to lose no time in revisiting the thresholds of the blessed Peter, Prince of the apostles. And what means your so great delight in the city of Constantinople, and your oblivion of the city of Rome, I know not. I have not so far been thought worthy of getting any information from you on this head. For how far it might be of advantage to your soul for reaping the rewards of eternal life, and how far it would suit also in all respects your glorious daughter, the lady Eusebia, this we fully give our attention to, and you may no less fully consider. But, if you enquire of my son Peter, your servant, whom I have found to be wise beyond his age and to be studying to attain ripeness, you will find how great is the love towards your Excellency of all who dwell here, and how great their desire to be thought worthy of seeing you again. And if, the Lord teaching us, we are admonished in Holy Writ that we should love even our enemies, we ought to consider how wrong it is to shew no love even to those who

8 The woman had fled to the precincts of some church for protection from one George, who apparently claimed her as his slave. The right of temporary asylum in sacred precincts, from which refugees could not be taken without the bishop's assent, rested on imperial edicts. "Vide lib. I. Cod., tit. 12, cap. 3, ubi imperatores Theodosius et Valentianus plurima de septis ecclesiasticis statuunt. . . . Vocantur etiam *claustra dominica*, et continent atria et porticus ecclesiæ, domum episcopi, xxx vel xl passus in circuitu, et domus quæ in eis fuerint. Tandem cessavit ista immunitas ob abusus." (Note to I. 37 in Migne's *Patrilogia*). Cf. X. 37, where directions are given to Januarius, bishop of Cagliari, for his course of action in such cases.

9 I.e. as to whether she was a free-woman or a slave.

1 *Samaræo*, meaning apparently a Samaritan, and as such incapable, as Jews were, of holding Christian slaves. See *Prolegom.*, p. xxi., and references there. In the case before us here the Samaritan claimant had himself become a Christian; and an attempt had been made on this plea to recover for him the Christian slave who had been emancipated from his father. But this Gregory will by no means allow.

2 See II. 27, note 2.

love us. But, if haply we are said to be loved, we know most certainly that no one can have affection for those whom he does not wish to see. If, however, you are afraid of the swords and wars of Italy, you should attentively observe how great is the protection of the blessed Peter, Prince of the apostles, in this city, wherein, without a large force of people, and without military aid, we are preserved under God for so many years among swords. This we say, because we love. But may Almighty God grant whatever He sees to be of advantage to your soul for ever, and to the renown of your house at the present time.

The ten pounds of gold which your Excellency has sent for the redemption of captives I have received at the hands of my aforesaid son. But I pray that the heavenly grace which granted to you that you should give them for your soul's reward may also grant to me to dispense them without any contagion of sin; lest we should be stained by that whereby you wipe away sins. May Almighty God, who looks upon the weakness of your body and your pilgrimage, comfort you ever by His grace, and by the life and health of my most sweet son the lord Strategius[3]; that so He may nurture him both for you through many years and for Himself through eternity, and may both replenish you and all your house with present good and grant you to have grace from above. We further beg that the glorious lord Eudoxius may be greeted in our behalf.

EPISTLE XXIII.

To Fantinus, Guardian (*Defensorem*).

Gregory to Fantinus, &c.

From the information of the lady abbess of the monastery of Saint Stephen in the territory of Agrigentum we find that many of the Jews, divine grace inspiring them, wish to be converted to the Christian faith; but that it is necessary for some one to go thither by our command. Accordingly we enjoin thee, in virtue of the authority hereby given thee, that, putting aside every excuse, thou make haste to go to the aforesaid place, and with the favour of God aid their desire by thy exhortations. If, however, it seems long and dreary for them to look forward to the Paschal solemnity, and thou findest them anxious for baptism now, then, lest long delay should possibly change their minds (which God forbid), speak thou with our brother the bishop of that place, that, penitence and abstinence having been prescribed them for forty days, he may baptize them under the protection of the mercy of Almighty God on a Lord's day, or on any very noted festival that may chance to occur; since the character of the present time too, on account of impending calamity, impels us not to defer the fulfilment of their desires by any procrastination. Further, whomsoever of them thou ascertainest to be poor and without sufficient means for buying vestments for themselves, we desire thee to supply with vestments for their baptism; and know that the price that thou mayest give for them is to be charged in thy accounts. But, if they should choose to wait for the holy season of Easter, speak again with the bishop, that they may for the present become catechumens, and that he may go to them frequently, and pay careful attention to them, and kindle their minds by the admonition of his exhortations, so that the more distant the expected festival is, the more may they prepare themselves and with fervent desire look forward to it.

Furthermore, let it be thy care to enquire with all zeal and diligence whether the abovenamed monastery over which the aforesaid lady presides has sufficient means, or whether it suffers any need. And whatever thou mayest truly ascertain, as well as what is done with respect to those who desire to be baptized, make haste to inform us in full. The Month of June, first Indiction.

EPISTLE XXIV.

To Sabinianus, Bishop of Jadera[4].

Gregory to Sabinianus, &c.

I am well delighted in thy sincerity, dearest brother, knowing how, with the discrimination of a careful judgment, it both obeys where obedience is due and resists where resistance is due with priestly zeal. For with what alacrity of devotion thou hast submitted to what we enjoined for the fault of thy past transgression is disclosed to us by the contents of the letters which thou hast sent to us by the bearer of these presents. For indeed my beloved brother could not take it otherwise than as it was enjoined by one who loves him. Hence I trust in the compassion of Almighty God that His grace so protects thee that, having been thus absolved also from other sins, thou mayest rejoice in having wholesomely obeyed. But as to what thy Charity has signified about being distressed by the jealousy of the excommunicated prevaricator Maximus, thou oughtest not to be disturbed; but it becomes thee by patiently enduring to bear up against the billows that swell vainly to some small degree, and by the virtue of perseverence to subdue

3 A grandchild of Rusticiana. See as above.

4 See VI. 27, VII. 17, VIII. 10, and III. 47, note 2.

the foaming of the waves. For patience knows how to smooth what is rough, and constancy to overcome fierceness. Let not, then, adversity deject your spirits, but inflame them. Let priestly vigour shew thee in all things the more bold. For this is a true evidence of truth, for one to exhibit himself as all the readier in hard circumstances, and all the braver in such as are adverse. Wherefore, that no blow may avail to upset the firmness of thy rectitude from its good determination, plant, as thou hast begun to do, the steps of thy soul on the solidity of that rock on which thou knowest that our Redeemer has founded the Church throughout the world, that so the right footsteps of a sincere heart may not stumble on a devious way.

As to the things about which thou hast written, or which the bearer of these presents has explained in our presence, do not suppose that we are neglecting them: we are very carefully considering them.

Further, we have already, both before and now, given accurate information about everything to our most beloved son the deacon Anatolius[5]; exhorting him to lose no time, with the aid of our Creator, in acting strictly and zealously in whatever pertains to the advantage and quiet of your Charity and of your sons. And so let not sorrow affect your Fraternity, nor the enmity of any one whatever afflict you. For, with the assistance of Divine Grace, we trust that it will not be long before the presumption of the aforesaid excommunicated prevaricator will be more strictly repressed, and your quiet, as you desire, arrive. We have also by no means omitted to write about his perverseness to our most excellent son the Exarch[6], who is anxious to commend him to us.

As to the presbyter about whom thy Fraternity has consulted us through the representation of the bearer of these presents, know that after his lapse he cannot by any means remain in, or be restored to, his sacred order. Still he ought to be somewhat mildly dealt with, inasmuch as he is said to have readily confessed his fault.

Furthermore, this same bearer spoke at the same time of certain privileges of your Church granted by our predecessors.

About the writings thus referred to by your Charity we wish to be more accurately informed. Or, if any of them are lying in the registry of your Church, it is necessary that copies of them be transmitted hither; that we may be able with willing mind to renew whatever concerns reverence for your dignity or the genius of the aforesaid Church.

If our common son, the glorious lord Marcellus[7], should be minded to come hither, urgently persuade him to do so; for on all accounts I desire to see him. But, if he should choose to remain where he is, do you so exhibit yourselves to him in beseeming charity that you may be able to respond, as becomes you, to the affection which he has towards you. May Almighty God keep and protect you with the gift of His grace, and enflame your heart to do the things that are well pleasing to Him.

EPISTLE XXIX.

To Eulogius, Bishop of Alexandria.

Gregory to Eulogius, &c.

An address from a learned man is always profitable, because the hearer either learns what he had known himself to be ignorant of, or, what is more, comes to know what he did not know he had been ignorant of. A hearer of the latter kind I have now become, your most holy Blessedness having been minded to write to me, asking me to send you the acts of all the martyrs, which were collected in the times of Constantine, of pious memory, by Eusebius of Cæsarea. But before receiving the letter of your Blessedness I did not know of these acts, whether they had been collected, or whether not. I therefore give thanks that, instructed by your most holy teaching, I have begun to know what I was ignorant of. For beside what is contained about the acts of the holy martyrs in the books of the same Eusebius, I am not aware of any collections in the archives of this our Church, or in the libraries of the city of Rome, unless it be some few things collected in one single volume. We have indeed the names of almost all the martyrs, with their passions assigned to particular days, collected in one volume; and we celebrate the solemnities of mass on such days in commemoration of them. Yet it is not indicated in this volume who each was, and how he suffered; but only his name, the place, and day, of his passion are put down. Hence it results that many of divers countries and provinces are known to have been crowned with martyrdom, as I have said, through their several days. But these we believe you have. That, however, which you wish to have sent to you we have sought for, but have not found; but, though we have not found it, we will still search, and, if it can be found, will send it.

5 At this time Gregory's *apocrisiarius* at Constantinople. Cf. VII. 31, IX. 82.

6 Callinicus, who was at this time Exarch of Italy at Ravenna. See IX. 9, with note, and III. 47, note 2.

7 Proconsul of Dalmatia. Cf. IX. 5, and III. 47, note 2.

With regard to what you write about the timber being short in length, the cause was in the kind of ship by which it was sent; for, if a larger ship had come, we could have sent larger pieces of timber. But as to your saying that, if we send larger pieces, you will pay for them, we thank you indeed for your liberality, but we are precluded from accepting a price, since the Gospel forbids it. For we do not buy the timber which we send; and how can we accept a price, when it is written, *Freely ye have received, freely give* (Matth. x. 8)? We have therefore sent now through the ship-master timber of short length in accordance with the size of the ship, whereof a notice is subjoined. Next year, however, should it please Almighty God, we will prepare larger pieces.

We have received with the kindliness wherewith it was sent the blessing of Saint Mark the Evangelist, nay, it may be said more truly, of Saint Peter the Apostle[8]; and, greeting you well, we beg your Blessedness to deign to pray for us, that so we may be counted worthy to be soon delivered from present evils, and not to be excluded from future joys.

EPISTLE XXX.

To Eulogius, Bishop of Alexandria.

Gregory to Eulogius, &c.

Our common son, the bearer of these presents, when he brought the letters of your Holiness found me sick, and has left me sick; whence it has ensued that the scanty water of my brief epistle has been hardly able to exude to the large fountain of your Blessedness. But it was a heavenly boon that, while in a state of bodily pain, I received the letter of your Holiness to lift me up with joy for the instruction of the heretics of the city of Alexandria, and the concord of the faithful, to such an extent that the very joy of my mind moderated the severity of my suffering. And indeed we rejoice with new exultation to hear of your good doings, though at the same time we by no means suppose that it is a new thing for you to act thus perfectly. For that the people of holy Church increases, that spiritual crops of corn for the heavenly garner are multiplied, we never doubted that this was from the grace of Almighty God which flowed largely to you, most blessed ones. We therefore render thanks to Almighty God, that we see fulfilled in you what is written, *Where there is much increase, there the strength of the oxen is manifest* (Prov. xiv. 4). For, if a strong ox had not drawn the plough of the tongue over the ground of the hearts of hearers, so great an increase of the faithful would by no means have sprung up.

But, since in the good things you do I know that you also rejoice with others, I make you a return for your favour, and announce things not unlike yours; for while the nation of the Angli, placed in a corner of the world, remained up to this time misbelieving in the worship of stocks and stones, I determined, through the aid of your prayers for me, to send to it, God granting it, a monk of my monastery for the purpose of preaching. And he, having with my leave been made bishop by the bishops of Germany, proceeded, with their aid also, to the end of the world to the aforesaid nation; and already letters have reached us telling us of his safety and his work; to the effect that he and those that have been sent with him are resplendent with such great miracles in the said nation that they seem to imitate the powers of the apostles in the signs which they display. Moreover, at the solemnity of the Lord's Nativity which occurred in this first indiction, more than ten thousand Angli are reported to have been baptized by the same our brother and fellow-bishop. This have I told you, that you may know what you are effecting among the people of Alexandria by speaking, and what in the ends of the world by praying. For your prayers are in the place where you are not, while your holy operations are shewn in the place where you are.

In the next place, as to the person of Eudoxius the heretic[9], about whose error I have discovered nothing in the Latin language, I rejoice that I have been most abundantly satisfied by your Blessedness. For you have adduced the testimonies of the strong men, Basil, Gregory, and Epiphanius; and we acknowledge him to be manifestly slain, at whom our heroes have cast so many darts. But with regard to these errors which are proved to have arisen in the Church of Constantinople, you have replied on all heads most learnedly, and as it became you to utter the judgment of so great a see. Whence we give thanks to Almighty God, that the tables of the covenant are still in the ark of God. For what is the priestly heart but the ark of the covenant? And since spiritual doctrine retains its vigour therein, without doubt the tables of the law are lying in it.

Your Blessedness has also been careful to declare that you do not now make use of proud titles, which have sprung from a root of vanity, in writing to certain persons, and

[8] Cf. VII. 40, for Gregory's view of the sees of Rome, Alexandria, and Antioch, jointly representing the see of St. Peter.

[9] Cf. VII. 4, and 34.

you address me saying, *As you have commanded.* This word, *command*, I beg you to remove from my hearing, since I know who I am, and who you are. For in position you are my brethren, in character my fathers. I did not, then, command, but was desirous of indicating what seemed to be profitable. Yet I do not find that your Blessedness has been willing to remember perfectly this very thing that I brought to your recollection. For I said that neither to me nor to any one else ought you to write anything of the kind; and lo, in the preface of the epistle which you have addressed to myself who forbade it, you have thought fit to make use of a proud appellation, calling me Universal Pope. But I beg your most sweet Holiness to do this no more, since what is given to another beyond what reason demands is subtracted from yourself. For as for me, I do not seek to be prospered by words but by my conduct. Nor do I regard that as an honour whereby I know that my brethren lose their honour. For my honour is the honour of the universal Church: my honour is the solid vigour of my brethren. Then am I truly honoured when the honour due to all and each is not denied them. For if your Holiness calls me Universal Pope, you deny that you are yourself what you call me universally. But far be this from us. Away with words that inflate vanity and wound charity.

And, indeed, in the synod of Chalcedon, and afterwards by subsequent Fathers, your Holiness knows that this was offered to my predecessors[1]. And yet not one of them would ever use this title, that, while regarding the honour of all priests in this world, they might keep their own before Almighty God. Lastly, while addressing to you the greeting which is due, I beg you to deign to remember me in your holy prayers, to the end that the Lord for your intercessions may absolve me from the bands of my sins, since my own merits may not avail me.

EPISTLE XXXIII.

To Dominicus.

Gregory to Dominicus, Bishop of Carthage.

The letter of your Holiness, which we received at the hands of the bearer of these presents, so expressed priestly moderation as to soothe us, in a manner, with the bodily presence of its author. Nor indeed does infrequency of communication cause any harm where the affection of love remains uninterrupted in one's mind. Great, moreover, is the power of charity, beloved brother, which binds hearts one to another in mutual affection with the chain of its sincerity, and suffers them not to be loosened from the cohesion of grace, which conjoins things disjoined, keeps together things united, and causes persons who are unknown by sight to be known through love. Whosoever therefore fixes his heart on the hinge of charity, him no impulse of any adversity whatever tears from the habitation of the heavenly country, since, in whatever direction he may turn himself, he parts not from the threshold of the commandments. Hence also it is said by the excellent preacher in praise of this same charity, *Which is the bond of perfectness* (Coloss. iii. 14). We see, then, what great praise is due to that which not only engenders perfectness in the soul, but also binds it.

Wherefore, since the language of thy letters shews thee to be inflamed with the fire of this virtue, I rejoice in the Lord with abundant exultation, and hope that it may shine forth in thee more and more, seeing that the flame of the shepherd is the light of the flock. For it becomes the Lord's priest[2] to shine in manners and life, to the end that the people committed to him may be able, as it were in the mirror of his life, both to choose what to follow, and to see what to correct.

Knowing, furthermore, whence priestly ordination took its beginning in the African parts, you act laudably in recurring with wise recollection, in your love of the Apostolic See, to the origin of your office, and in continuing with commendable constancy in your affection towards it[3]. For indeed it is certain that whatever reverence and devotion in priestly wise you shew to it, this you add to your own honour; seeing that you hereby invite it to be bound with answering love to you.

It remains, most dear brother, that we beseech Almighty God with continual prayer that He would direct the steps of our hearts into the pathway of His truth, and bring us to the heavenly kingdoms, granting us by the grace of His protection to exhibit in our works the office which we bear in name. The Month of August, first Indiction[4].

EPISTLE XXXIV.

To John, Bishop of Scyllacium[5].

Gregory to John, &c.

It is evidently a very serious thing, and contrary to what a priest should aim at, to

[1] Cf. V. 18, note 5.

[2] "Dominicam sacerdotam," perhaps with allusion to the name of Dominicus.

[3] See II, 47, note 6.

[4] The date varies in some few MSS.

[5] The address in the text is "Episcopo Scillitano." Tha

wish to disturb privileges formerly granted to any monastery, and to endeavour to bring to naught what has been arranged for quiet. Now the monks of the Castilliensian monastery in your Fraternity's city have complained to us that you are taking steps to impose upon the said monastery certain things contrary to what had been allowed by your predecessors and sanctioned by long custom, and to disturb ancient arrangements by a certain injurious novelty. Wherefore we hereby exhort your Fraternity that, if this is so, you refrain from troubling this monastery under any excuse, and that you try not, through any opportunity of usurpation, to upset what has been long secured to it, but that you study, without any gainsaying, to preserve all its privileges inviolate, and know that no more is lawful to you with regard to the said monastery than was lawful to your predecessors.

Further, inasmuch as they have likewise complained that thy Fraternity has taken certain things from the monastery under the guise of their being, as it were, an offering[6], it is necessary that, if thou recollectest having received anything unbecomingly, thou restore it without delay, lest the sin of avarice seriously convict thee, whom priestly munificence ought to have shewn liberal towards monasteries. Therefore, while thou preservest all things which, as we have said, have been allowed and preserved by thy predecessors, let it be thy care to keep careful watch over the acts and lives of the monks residing there, and, if thou shouldest find any one living amiss, or (which God forbid) guilty of any sin of uncleanness, to correct such by strict and regular emendation. For, as we desire your Fraternity to abstain from incongruous usurpations, so we admonish you to be in all ways solicitous in what pertains to rectitude of discipline and the guardianship of souls.

The monks of the aforesaid monastery have also informed us that the camp which is called Scillacium is built on ground belonging to their monastery, and that on this account those who live there pledged themselves in writing[7] to pay a *solatium*[8] every year; but that they afterwards thought scorn of it, and idly withheld their stipulated payment. Let then your Fraternity take care to learn the truth accurately; and, if you should find it so, urgently see to their not delaying to give what they promised, and what also reason requires; that so both they may possess quietly what they hold, and the rights of the monastery may incur no damage.

Furthermore, the monks of the aforesaid monastery have complained to us that their abbot has granted to thy Fraternity by title of gift land within the camp of Scillacium, to the extent of six hundred feet, under pretext of building a church: and accordingly it is our will that as much land as the walls of the church, when built, can surround shall be claimed as belonging to the church. But let whatever may be outside the walls of the said church revert without dispute to the possession of the monastery. For the ordinances neither of worldly laws nor of the sacred canons permit the property of a monastery to be segregated by any title from its ownership. On this account restore thou this gift of land which has been granted against reason.

the see was that of Scyllacium in Brutia appears from the contents of the epistle. Scyllacium itself appears to have been a *Castrum*, which had been erected on land belonging to a monastery. The epistle is illustrative of Gregory's anxiety to protect the property and privileges of monasteries against bishops. See *Prolegom.*, p. xx., and references in Index under *Monasteries*.

[6] *Sub xenii quasi specie.* For the meaning of the word *xenium*, see II. 23, note 8.

[7] *Libellis factis*; meaning apparently that there had been written memoranda of agreement.

[8] The word *solatium* is variously used; sometimes for any kind of aid or succour; sometimes for remuneration for services done, or grants in aid; here apparently for payment in the way of rent for the land occupied.

EPISTLE XXXV.

To Leontius, Ex-Consul.

Gregory to Leontius, &c.

Since in a great house there are not only vessels of gold and of silver, but also of wood and of earth, and some indeed to honour but some to dishonour (2 Tim. ii. 20), who can be ignorant that in the bosom of the Universal Church some as vessels of dishonour are deputed to the lowest uses, but others, as vessels of honour, are fitted for clean uses. And yet it commonly comes to pass that the citizens of Babylon serve in task-work for Jerusalem, while the citizens of Jerusalem, that is of the heavenly country, are deputed to the task-work of Babylon. For when the elect of God, endowed with moral excellence, distinguished for moderation, seeking not their own gain, are deputed to earthly business, what else is it but that the citizens of holy Jerusalem serve in the work of Babylon? And when some, unbridled in immorality, hold places of holy dignity, and in the very things which they seem to do well seek praise to themselves, what else is it but that the citizens of Babylon execute the task-work of the heavenly Jerusalem? For so Judas, mixed with the apostles, long preached the Redeemer of the human race, and did signs with the rest; but, because he had been a citizen of Babylon, he executed his work as task-work for the heavenly Jerusalem. But on the other hand Joseph, being carried into Egypt, served an earthly court, bore the charge of administration in temporal things, exhibited whatever was justly due to a transitory kingdom; but, because he was still a citizen of holy Jerusalem, he administered the service of Babylon, as has been seen above, in the way of task-work only. A follower of him, good man, I believe thee to be, knowing thee, though involved in earthly action, to act with a gentle spirit, to keep in all respects the citadel of humility, and to give to every one what is just. For such good things are reported by many of your Glory that I would fain not hear of such things, but see them: yet still I am fed by the good renown of him whom I am not allowed to see. But the woman who poured from the alabaster box, exhibiting a type of the Holy Church, that is of all the elect, filled the house with the ointment (Luke vii.). And we, as often as we hear anything of good people, draw in as it were through our nostrils a breath of sweetness. And when Paul the Apostle said, *We are a good odour of Christ unto God* (2 Cor. ii. 15), it is plainly given to be understood that he exhibited himself as a savour indeed to the present, but as an odour to the absent. We therefore, while we cannot be nourished by the savour of your presence, are so by the odour of your absence.

For this also we greatly rejoice, that the gifts which you sent us were not unlike your character. For indeed we received oil of the holy cross[9], and wood of aloes; one to bless by the touch, the other to give a sweet smell when kindled. For it was becoming that a good man should send us things that might appease the wrath of God against us.

Many other things also you have sent for our store-houses, since, as we subsist both in soul and in flesh, it was needful that we should be sustained in both. And yet in transmitting these things your most sweet soul declares that it blushes much for shame, and holds out the shield of charity before this same shamefacedness. But I altogether rejoice in these words, since from this attestation of the soul I know that he can never take away what is another's who blushes even in bestowing what is his own. Your gifts however, which you call small, are great: but I think that your Glory's very humility enhances them yet the more. And you beg me to receive them kindly. But meanwhile recall to your memory the two mites of a certain widow (Luke xxvii.). For, if she pleased God who offered a little with a good will, why should not he please men who with a humble mind has given much? Furthermore we send you, as a blessing from Saint Peter, Prince of the apostles, a key of his most sacred sepulchre, in which is inserted a blessing from his chains[1], that what bound his neck for martyrdom may loose yours from all sins.

---

9 "Oil of the cross" is spoken of not infrequently from the 6th century downward as efficient for healing. In the *Itinerarium* attributed to Antoninus of Placentia in that century mention is made of *ampullæ* of onyx stone containing oil being brought into contact with the wood of the true cross which was supposed to be preserved in Constantine's Church on Golgotha, and the oil thereupon at once boiling over. It may have been oil which was believed to have thus acquired healing virtue that was originally meant by "oil of the cross." But in the following century we find notice of a belief that oil flowed miraculously from the wood of the cross itself. For Adamnan, in his book *De locis sanctis* (which is mentioned by Bede, *H.E.* V. 15, as presented by him to King Aldfrid of Northumbria, and published by Mabillon, *de S. Adamn. Act. Benedict. sæc.* iii. part ii. p. 456), speaks of his informant, Arcuulf, a Gallic bishop, having seen at Constantinople, a piece of the true cross which had been sent thither by Helena, from the knots of which an odorous liquid with healing virtues flowed.

1 Filings from the supposed chains of St. Peter, preserved at Rome, were inserted in keys for his sepulchre (cf. IV. 30), and these keys were sent by Gregory to various persons as valuable charms. Cf. I. 26, note 3.

ST. GREGORY THE GREAT

INDEX OF TEXTS

INDEX OF SUBJECTS